8 B-4	(a) Estimated uncollectible accounts $5,570
8 B-5	(a) May 1, cash collected from note, $31,350
8 B-6	(c) Total current assets, $72,440
8 B-7	(c) One-year interest charge originally included in face amount of note, $6,240
Case 8-1	No key figure

9 A-1	(a) Gross profit percentage, 1992, 39%
9 A-2	(a) (1) Inventory, FIFO, $126,540
9 A-3	(a) (1) Inventory, FIFO, $125,200; (b) Gross profit, LIFO, $177,000
9 A-4	No key figure
9 A-5	(b) Cost percentage, 75%
9 A-6	(b) Inventory, Jan. 7, $80,500
9 A-7	(b) Cost of goods sold, $6,250
9 B-1	(a) Gross profit percentage, 1992, 29%
9 B-2	(a) (1) Inventory, FIFO, $135,340
9 B-3	(a) (1) Inventory, FIFO, $74,980
9 B-4	No key figure
9 B-5	(a) Cost percentage, 68%
9 B-6	(b) Inventory, Jan. 7, $20,400
9 B-7	(b) Cost of goods sold $1,385
Case 9-1	(b) Gross profit, $9,800

10 A-1	(c) Total cost of equuipment, $94,560
10 A-2	Depreciation for Year 2, (b) $27,000; (c) $25,000
10 A-3	Depreciation for Year 2, (b) $96,800; (c) $96,000
10 A-4	No key figure
10 A-5	New truck, book value Aug. 15, $16,000
10 A-6	(c) Accumulated depletion, $3,069,000
10 A-7	No key figure
10 B-1	(a) Total cost of equipment, $220,714
10 B-2	Depreciation for Year 2, (b) $48,800; (c) $48,000
10 B-3	Depreciation for Year 2, (b) $80,100; (c) $75,000
10 B-4	No key figure
10 B-5	New computation of book value, Sept. 20, $95,000
10 B-6	(c) Accumulated depletion, $5,300,400
10 B-7	No key figure
Case 10-1	No key figure
Case 10-2	(b) Adjusted net income, $15,600

Part 3	(a) Total assets: Alpine, $499,900; Nordic, $486,300; (b) revised cumulative net income: Alpine, $195,000; Nordic, $219,000

11 A-1	No key figure
11 A-2	(b) Oct. 31, interest expense on Midwest Bank note, $3,200
11 A-3	(b) June 30, interest expense on First Bank note, $4,666.67
11 A-4	(b) Amortization of discount on First State Bank note, $1,700
11 A-5	No key figure
11 A-6	(b) Payroll taxes expense, $3,836
11 A-7	(b) Payroll taxes deducted from employees' earnings, $9,141.68
11 B-1	No key figure
11 B-2	April 20, face amount of note, $51,840
11 B-3	Oct. 31, interest expense on Sun National Bank note, $4,704
11 B-4	(b) Amortization of discount on Stylecraft note, $1,344

11 B-5	No key figure
11 B-6	(b) Payroll taxes expense, $1,644
11 B-7	(b) Payroll taxes deducted from employees' earnings, $9,595.20
Case 11-1	No key figure
Case 11-2	No key figure

12 A-1	(b) Total assets, $309,800
12 A-2	(a) Net income, $69,500; (c) total assets, $194,500
12 A-3	(a) (2) Share to Lewis, $31,000
12 A-4	(a) Share to Axle, $214,600
12 A-5	(d) Bonus to Hale, $30,000
12 A-6	(d) Debit to Swartz, Capital, $26,250
12 A-7	(b) Cash payment by Hand, $12,000
12 B-1	(b) Total assets, $196,800
12 B-2	(a) Net income, $64,000; (c) total assets, $227,720
12 B-3	(a) (2) Share to Dyer, $32,800
12 B-4	(a) Share to Trump, $129,200
12 B-5	(c) Bonus to existing partners, $90,000
12 B-6	(c) Bonus to Kim, $30,000
12 B-7	(a) Cash to Peat, $15,200
Case 12-1	(b) Second year, share to Ramirez, $57,000
Case 12-2	(a) Brad's share, Capital account, $75,000

13 A-1	No key figure
13 A-2	No key figure
13 A-3	(a) Profit under percentage-of-completion, 1991, $4,000,000
13 A-4	No key figure
13 A-5	No key figure
13 B-1	No key figure
13 B-2	No key figure
13 B-3	(a) Gross profit using percentage-of-completion, $184,000
13 B-4	No key figure
13 B-5	No key figure
Case 13-1	No key figure

14 A-1	No key figure
14 A-2	(a) Total stockholders' equity, $2,585,000
12 A-3	Total stockholders' equity, $1,984,000
14 A-4	(b) Total stockholders' equity, $1,147,500
14 A-5	(b) Total assets, $1,509,200
14 A-6	(e) Total paid-in capital, $12,500,000
14 B-1	No key figure
14 B-2	(a) Total stockholders' equity, $8,360,000
14 B-3	Total stockholders' equity, $2,063,000
14 B-4	(d) Stockholders' equity, $887,600
14 B-5	(b) Total assets, $1,089,800
14 B-6	(g) Total paid-in capital, $9,660,000
Case 14-1	No key figure
Case 14-2	No key figure

15 A-1	No key figure
15 A-2	(a) Income before extraordinary items, $610,000
15 A-3	(a) Net income, $1,980,000
15 A-4	(a) Net income, $265,000
15 A-5	Retained earnings, Dec. 31, $346,600

(continued over)

15 A-6   (b) Total stockholders' equity, $7,487,500

15 A-7   (a) Total paid-in capital, $3,228,000;
          (b) Retained earnings, $469,800

15 B-1   No key figure

15 B-2   (a) Income before extraordinary items, $11,350,000

15 B-3   (a) Net income, $1,070,000

15 B-4   (a) Net income, $280,000

15 B-5   Retained earnings, Dec. 31, $874,000

15 B-6   (b) Total stockholders' equity, $5,667,500

15 B-7   (a) Total paid-in capital, $2,495,000
          (b) Retained earnings, $437,000

Case 15-1   No key figure

Case 15-2   No key figure

16 A-1   (c) Bond Interest Expense, $450,000

16 A-2   (b) Net bond liability, bonds issued at 96,
             $57,640,000

16 A-3   (a) Bond Interest Expense (Nov. 1), $624,000

16 A-4   (a) Carrying value of bonds, June 30, 1992,
             $9,393,750

16 A-5   (a) Carrying value of bonds, June 30, 1992,
             $6,204,450

16 A-6   (c) No key figure

16 B-1   (c) Bond Interest Expense, $1,000,000

16 B-2   (b) Net bond liability, bonds issued at 98,
             $29,420,000

16 B-3   (b) Bond Interest Expense, (Sept. 1), $159,000

16 B-4   (a) Carrying value of bonds, Dec. 31, 1991,
             $5,650,200

16 B-5   (a) Carrying value of bonds, Dec. 31, 1992,
             $8,272,600

16 B-6   No key figure

Case 16-1   (b) Loss on retirement, $600,000

Case 16-2   (b) (1) Loss on Retirement of Bonds, $3,250,000

Case 16-3   No key figure

Appendix A

1   (c) Present value, $17,511

2   (b) Amortization of discount, Dec. 31, $15,710

3   (c) Net liability, Dec. 31, $23,197

4   (a) Present value of payments, five-year lease,
      $8,154,000

5   (b) (2) Discount on Notes Receivable, $86,640

6   (d) Lease payment obligation, Dec. 31, $40,184

17 A-1   (b) (2) Loss on Sale, $350

17 A-2   Unrealized Loss, Dec. 31, $4,500

17 A-3   (b) Market value, Dec. 31, $64,000

17 A-4   (c) Consolidated total assets, $10,540,000

17 A-5   Consolidated total assets, $3,880,000

17 A-6   Consolidated total assets, $1,121,000

17 B-1   (b) (2) Gain on Sale, $350

17 B-2   Gain on Sale, Dec. 31, $8,600

17 B-3   (b) Market value at Dec. 31, $92,500

17 B-4   (c) Consolidated total assets, $6,920,000

17 B-5   Consolidated total assets, $3,928,000

17 B-6   Consolidated total assets, $602,000

Case 17-1   No key figure

Appendix B

1   No key figure

2   (b) Exchange rate, $0.61 per deutsche mark

3   (b) Loss on Fluctuations of Foreign Exchange
      Rates, $16,000

4   (c) Sales price per unit, $1,275

18 A-1   (c) Taxable income, $53,750

18 A-2   Adjusted gross income, (a) $47,900; (b) $55,800

18 A-3   (a) Taxable income, $54,500

18 A-4   (b) Total income tax, $26,462

18 A-5   (a) Income taxes expense, $137,700

18 B-1   (c) Taxable income, $35,000

18 B-2   Adjusted gross income, (a) $86,400; (b) $57,344

18 B-3   Taxable income, $59,750

18 B-4   (a) Revised taxable income, $193,750

18 B-5   (a) Income taxes expense, $204,000

Case 18-1   (c) Net income if stock issued, $126,550

Case 18-2   Disposable income, sole proprietorship, $59,291

19 A-1   No key figure

19 A-2   Net cash used by investing activities, $(11,000)

19 A-3   Net cash flow from operating activities, $254,000

19 A-4   Net cash flow from operating activities, $475,000

19 A-5   Net cash flow from operating activities, $175,000

19 B-1   No key figure

19 B-2   Net cash used by investing activities, $(15,000)

19 B-3   Net cash flow from operating activities, $316,000

19 B-4   Net cash flow from operating activities, $80,000

19 B-5   Net cash flow from operating activities, $1,060,000

Case 19-1   No key figure

Case 19-2   No key figure

Appendix C

1   Net cash flow from operating activities, $614,000

2   No key figure

3   No key figure

20 A-1   (a) Net income, ProTech, Inc., 7%

20 A-2   (d) Net income, 1991, $157,500

20 A-3   (f) Operating income, $192,000

20 A-4   (a) (6) Operating cycle, Hill Corporation, 192 days

20 A-5   (b) (3) Working capital, $864,000

20 A-6   No key figure

20 A-7   Total current assets, $1,500; net sales, $3,840

20 B-1   Net income, Harvest King, 6%

20 B-2   (c) Operating cycle, 114.1 days

20 B-3   (d) Net Income, 1991, $48,000

20 B-4   (a) (6) Operating cycle, Another World, 102 days

20 B-5   (f) Operating income, $75,000

20 B-6   Total current assets, $1,410,000

20 B-7   (c) Price-earnings ratio, American Van Lines,
      13 to 1

Case 20-1   No key figure

Case 20-2   No key figure

Appendix D

1   No key figure

2   No key figure

3   No key figure

4   (b) Restated 19 X 2 year-end stock price, $81

5   Net income (loss), constant dollar, $(9,000);
     current cost, $14,000

(continued on back cover)

Accounting:
The Basis for
Business Decisions

Eighth Edition

Accounting: The Basis for Business Decisions

Robert F. Meigs
San Diego State University

Walter B. Meigs
University of Southern California

McGRAW-HILL PUBLISHING COMPANY

New York | St. Louis | San Francisco | Auckland | Bogotá | Caracas | Hamburg
Lisbon | London | Madrid | Mexico | Milan | Montreal | New Delhi | Oklahoma City
Paris | San Juan | São Paulo | Singapore | Sydney | Tokyo | Toronto

Accounting:
The Basis for
Business Decisions

3 4 5 6 7 8 9   DOC DOC   9 4 3 2 1.

ISBN 0-07-041689-3

This book was set in Century Schoolbook by York Graphic Services, Inc.
The editors were Robert D. Lynch, David A. Damstra, and Edwin Hanson;
the designer was Nicholas Krenitsky;
the production supervisor was Diane Renda.
New drawings were done by Fine Line Illustrations, Inc.
R. R. Donnelley & Sons Company was printer and binder.

Library of Congress Cataloging-in-Publication Data

Meigs, Robert F.
    Accounting, the basis for business decisions/Robert F. Meigs,
Walter B. Meigs.—8th ed.
        p.   cm.
    Authors' names in reverse order in earlier editions.
    ISBN 0-07-041689-3
    1. Accounting.   I. Meigs, Walter B.   II. Title.
HF5635.M4887   1990
657—dc20   89-37383

Contents

Preface xxiii

Part 1

The Accounting Cycle

CHAPTER 1
ACCOUNTING: The Language of Business 3

WHAT IS ACCOUNTING? 4
The purpose and nature of accounting. The functions of an accounting system. Communicating accounting information—who uses accounting reports? The distinction between accounting and bookkeeping. Careers in accounting. The public accounting profession—the CPA. **Case in Point.** Private accounting. Governmental accounting. Accounting education: careers as faculty members. Accounting—a stepping stone to top management. Generally accepted accounting principles (GAAP). Development of generally accepted accounting principles—the FASB. Accounting as the basis for business decisions. Internal control.

FINANCIAL STATEMENTS:
The Starting Point in the Study of Accounting 14
The balance sheet. The concept of the business entity. Assets. Liabilities. Owner's equity. The accounting equation. Effects of business transactions upon the balance sheet. Effect of business transactions upon the accounting equation. Forms of business organization.

USES OF FINANCIAL STATEMENTS
BY OUTSIDERS 25
Bankers and other creditors. Owners. Wide distribution of financial statements.

END-OF-CHAPTER REVIEW 27
Concepts introduced or emphasized in Chapter 1.

Key terms introduced or emphasized in Chapter 1.   Demonstration problem for your review.   Solution to demonstration problem. Self-test questions.

ASSIGNMENT MATERIAL   30
Review questions.   Exercises.   Problems.   Business decision case.   Answers to the self-test questions.

CHAPTER 2
RECORDING CHANGES IN FINANCIAL POSITION   41
The role of accounting records.

THE LEDGER   42
The use of ledger accounts.   Debit and credit entries.   Double-entry accounting—the equality of debits and credits.   Recording transactions in ledger accounts: illustration.   Running balance form of accounts.

THE JOURNAL   50
Why use a journal?   The general journal: illustration of entries. Posting.

THE TRIAL BALANCE   57
Uses and limitations of the trial balance.   Locating errors.   Some tips on record-keeping procedures.

THE ACCOUNTING CYCLE:
An Introduction   59
Manual and computer-based systems: a comparison.

END-OF-CHAPTER REVIEW   61
Concepts introduced or emphasized in Chapter 2.   Key terms introduced or emphasized in Chapter 2.   Demonstration problem for your review.   Solution to demonstration problem.   Self-test questions.

ASSIGNMENT MATERIAL   68
Review questions.   Exercises.   Problems.   Business decision cases.   Answers to the self-test questions.

CHAPTER 3
MEASURING BUSINESS INCOME   81
What is net income?   The income statement: a preview   **Case in Point.   Case in Point.**   Revenue.   Expenses.   Debit and credit rules for revenue and expense.   Ledger accounts for revenue and expenses.   Investments and withdrawals by the owner. Recording revenue and expense transactions: an illustration.   The ledger.   The trial balance.

ADJUSTING ENTRIES:
The Next Step in the Accounting Cycle   94
The adjusted trial balance.

FINANCIAL STATEMENTS   97
The income statement.   The statement of owner's equity.   The
balance sheet.   Relationships among the financial statements.

CLOSING THE TEMPORARY ACCOUNTS   100
Closing entries for expense accounts.   Closing the Income Summary
account.   Closing the owner's drawing account.   Summary of the
closing process.   After-closing trial balance.   Sequence of
procedures in the accounting cycle.   Accounting procedures in a
computer-based system.   Accrual basis of accounting versus cash
basis of accounting.

END-OF-CHAPTER REVIEW   107
Concepts introduced or emphasized in Chapter 3.   Key terms
introduced or emphasized in Chapter 3.   Demonstration problem for
your review.   Self-test questions.

ASSIGNMENT MATERIAL   112
Review questions.   Exercises.   Problems.   Business decision
cases.   Answers to the self-test questions.

CHAPTER 4
COMPLETION OF THE ACCOUNTING CYCLE   127

Accounting periods and financial statements.   Transactions affecting
more than one accounting period.

ADJUSTING ENTRIES:
A Closer Look   128
Types of adjusting entries.   Characteristics of adjusting entries.
Apportioning recorded costs.   Apportioning unearned revenue.
Case in Point.   Recording unrecorded expenses.   Recording
unrecorded revenue.   Adjusting entries and the accrual basis of
accounting.

THE WORK SHEET   138
Preparing the work sheet.   Uses for the work sheet.   The
accounting cycle.   Preparing monthly financial statements without
closing the accounts.   Reversing entries.

END-OF-CHAPTER REVIEW   155
Concepts introduced or emphasized in Chapter 4.   Key terms
introduced or emphasized in Chapter 4.   Demonstration problem for
your review.   Self-test questions.

ASSIGNMENT MATERIAL   160
Review questions.   Exercises.   Problems.   Business decision
cases.   Answers to the self-test questions.

COMPREHENSIVE PROBLEM FOR PART 1:
Friend with a Truck   176

Part 2

Merchandising Concerns, Internal Control, and Accounting Systems

CHAPTER 5
ACCOUNTING FOR PURCHASES AND SALES OF MERCHANDISE — 181

MERCHANDISING COMPANIES — 182
Revenue from sales.   Sales returns and allowances.   Credit terms.
Sales discounts.   Costs of goods sold.   The periodic inventory
system.   Beginning inventory and ending inventory.   Purchases of
merchandise.   Shoplifting and inventory "shrinkage" losses.
Income statement for a merchandising company.   Analyzing the
income statement.   Work sheet for a merchandising business.
Financial statements.   Closing entries.   Summary of
merchandising transactions and related accounting entries.   Sales
taxes.   Perpetual inventory systems.   **Case in Point.**
Classified financial statements.   The purpose of balance sheet
classification.   Classification and format of income statements.

END-OF-CHAPTER REVIEW — 203
Concepts introduced or emphasized in Chapter 5.   Key terms
introduced or emphasized in Chapter 5.   Demonstration problem for
your review.   Solution to demonstration problem.   Self-test
questions.

ASSIGNMENT MATERIAL — 208
Review questions.   Exercises.   Problems.   Business decision
cases.   Answers to the self-test questions.

CHAPTER 6
INTERNAL CONTROL AND ACCOUNTING SYSTEMS — 220

THE SYSTEM OF INTERNAL CONTROL — 221
Accounting controls and administrative controls.   Relationship
between the accounting system and the system of internal control.
Guidelines to achieving strong internal control.   The role of business
documents.   Recording purchase invoices at net price.   Limitations
and cost of internal control.

**TAILORING AN ACCOUNTING SYSTEM
TO THE NEEDS OF A LARGER BUSINESS** — 229
Special journals.   Sales journal.   Controlling accounts and
subsidiary ledgers.   Purchases journal.   Cash receipts journal.
Cash payments journal.   The general journal.   Showing the source
of postings in ledger accounts.   Reconciling subsidiary ledgers with
controlling accounts.   Variations in special journals.

COMPUTER-BASED ACCOUNTING SYSTEMS — 245
Recording retail sales—computers reduce the work.   Advantages of
computer-based systems.   **Case in Point.**

END-OF-CHAPTER REVIEW   247
Concepts introduced or emphasized in Chapter 6.   Key terms
introduced or emphasized in Chapter 6.   Self-test questions.

ASSIGNMENT MATERIAL   249
Review questions.   Exercises.   Problems.   Business decision
cases.   Answers to the self-test questions.

COMPREHENSIVE PROBLEM FOR PART 2:
Crestline Lumber Co.   264

Part 3

Accounting for Assets

CHAPTER 7
THE CONTROL OF CASH TRANSACTIONS   269
Reporting cash in the balance sheet.   The statement of cash flows.
Management responsibilities relating to cash.   Basic requirements for
internal control over cash.   Cash receipts.   **Case in Point.**
Cash disbursements.   **Case in Point.**   The voucher system.
Recording approved vouchers.   Petty cash.   Bank checking
accounts.   Making deposits.   Control features of bank checking
accounts.   Bank statements.   Reconciling the bank balance.

END-OF-CHAPTER REVIEW   288
Concepts introduced or emphasized in Chapter 7.   Key terms
introduced or emphasized in Chapter 7.   Demonstration problem for
your review.   Solution to demonstration problem.   Self-test
questions.

ASSIGNMENT MATERIAL   292
Review questions.   Exercises.   Problems.   Business decision
cases.   Answers to the self-test questions.

CHAPTER 8
RECEIVABLES   304
Case in Point.

ACCOUNTS RECEIVABLE   305
Uncollectible accounts.   The allowance for doubtful accounts.
Writing off an uncollectible account receivable.   Recovery of an
account receivable previously written off.   Monthly estimates of credit
losses.   Direct charge-off method.   Credit card sales.   Internal
controls for receivables.

NOTES RECEIVABLE   315
Nature of interest.   Accounting for notes receivable.   **Case in
Point.**   Discounting notes receivable.   Evaluating the quality of
notes and accounts receivable.   Notes receivable with interest

included in the face amount.   Comparison of the two forms of notes receivable.   The concept of present value.   An illustration of notes recorded at present value.   Installment receivables.

END-OF-CHAPTER REVIEW   328
Concepts introduced or emphasized in Chapter 8.   Key terms introduced or emphasized in Chapter 8.   Self-test questions.

ASSIGNMENT MATERIAL   331
Review questions.   Exercises.   Problems.   Business decision cases.   Answers to the self-test questions.

CHAPTER 9
INVENTORIES   343
Inventory defined.   Periodic inventory system versus perpetual inventory system.   The matching principle as applied to inventories. Inventory valuation and the measurement of income.   Importance of an accurate valuation of inventory.   Taking a physical inventory. The year-end cutoff of transactions.   Pricing the inventory.   Cost basis of inventory valuation.   Inventory valuation methods. Evaluation of the methods.   Consistency in the valuation of inventory. The environment of inflation.   The lower-of-cost-or-market rule (LCM). **Case in Point.**   Estimating ending inventory and cost of goods sold. The gross profit method of estimating ending inventory.   The retail method of estimating ending inventory.   Internal control of inventories.   **Case in Point.**   Perpetual inventory system. Internal control and perpetual inventory systems.   **Case in Point.** Perpetual inventory records.   Need for an annual physical inventory.

END-OF-CHAPTER REVIEW   367
Concepts introduced or emphasized in Chapter 9.   Key terms introduced or emphasized in Chapter 9.   Demonstration problem for your review.   Solution to demonstration problem.   Self-test questions.

ASSIGNMENT MATERIAL   371
Review questions.   Exercises.   Problems.   Business decision case.   Answers to the self-test questions.

CHAPTER 10
PLANT AND EQUIPMENT, DEPRECIATION,
AND INTANGIBLE ASSETS   383
PLANT AND EQUIPMENT   384
Plant and equipment—a stream of services.   Major categories of plant and equipment.   Determining the cost of plant and equipment. Capital expenditures and revenue expenditures.

DEPRECIATION   388
Allocating the cost of plant and equipment over the years of use. Causes of depreciation.   Methods of computing depreciation.

Management's responsibility for depreciation methods and related estimates.   Depreciation and income taxes.   Inflation and depreciation.   Historical cost versus replacement cost.

DISPOSAL OF PLANT AND EQUIPMENT   397

Gains and losses on disposal of plant and equipment.   Gains and losses for income tax purposes.   Trading in used assets on new.
Case in Point.

INTANGIBLE ASSETS   401

Characteristics.   Operating expenses versus intangible assets. Amortization.   Goodwill.   Patents.   Trademarks and trade names.   Franchises.   Copyrights.   Other intangibles and deferred charges.   Research and development (R&D) costs.

NATURAL RESOURCES   406

Accounting for natural resources.   Depreciation, amortization, and depletion—a common goal.

END-OF-CHAPTER REVIEW   407

Concepts introduced in Chapter 10.   Key terms introduced or emphasized in Chapter 10.   Self-test questions.

ASSIGNMENT MATERIAL   410

Review questions.   Exercises.   Problems.   Business decision cases.   Answers to the self-test questions.

COMPREHENSIVE PROBLEM FOR PART 3:
Alpine Village and Nordic Sports   **421**

Part 4

Current Liabilities, Partnerships, and Accounting Principles

CHAPTER 11
CURRENT LIABILITIES AND PAYROLL ACCOUNTING   **425**

The nature of liabilities.   Timely recognition of liabilities.   **Case in Point.**   Current liabilities.   Accounts payable.

NOTES PAYABLE   428

Notes payable issued to banks.   Notes payable with interest charges included in the face amount.   Comparison of the two forms of notes payable.   Loss contingencies.   **Case in Point.**

PAYROLL ACCOUNTING   434

Internal control over payrolls.   **Case in Point.**   Deductions from earnings of employees.   Social security taxes (FICA).   **Case in Point.**   Federal income taxes.   Other deductions from employees' earnings.   Employer's responsibility for amounts withheld.   Payroll records and procedures.   Payroll taxes on the employer. Distinction between employees and independent contractors.

END-OF-CHAPTER REVIEW 441

Concepts introduced or emphasized in Chapter 11.   Key terms introduced or emphasized in Chapter 11.   Demonstration problem for your review.   Solution to demonstration problem.   Self-test questions.

ASSIGNMENT MATERIAL 444

Review questions.   Exercises.   Problems.   Business decision cases.   Answers to the self-test questions.

CHAPTER 12
PARTNERSHIPS 454

Significant features of a partnership.   **Case in Point.**   Advantages and disadvantages of a partnership.   Limited partnerships.   The partnership contract.   Partnership accounting.   **Case in Point.** Opening the accounts of a new partnership.   Additional investments. Drawing accounts.   Loans from partners.   Closing the accounts of a partnership at year-end.   Partnership profits and income taxes. The nature of partnership profits.   Dividing partnership net income among the partners.   Admission of a new partner.   Withdrawal of a partner.   Death of a partner.   Liquidation of a partnership.

END-OF-CHAPTER REVIEW 476

Concepts introduced or emphasized in Chapter 12.   Key terms introduced or emphasized in Chapter 12.   Self-test questions.

ASSIGNMENT MATERIAL 478

Review questions.   Exercises.   Problems.   Business decision cases.   Answers to the self-test questions.

CHAPTER 13
ACCOUNTING PRINCIPLES AND CONCEPTS 490

The need for recognized accounting standards.   Generally accepted accounting principles (GAAP).   Authoritative support for accounting principles.   The accounting entity concept.   The going-concern assumption.   The time period principle.   The stable-dollar assumption.   The objectivity principle.   Asset valuation: the cost principle.   Revenue recognition: the realization principle.   Expense recognition: the matching principle.   **Case in Point.**   The consistency principle.   The disclosure principle.   Materiality. Conservatism as a guide in resolving uncertainties.   Audited financial statements.   Setting new accounting standards.   The conceptual framework project.   Professional judgment: an essential element in financial reporting.

END-OF-CHAPTER REVIEW 506

Concepts introduced or emphasized in Chapter 13.   Key terms introduced or emphasized in Chapter 13.   Self-test questions.

ASSIGNMENT MATERIAL   508
Review questions.   Exercises.   Problems.   Business decision
case.   Answers to the self-test questions.

Part 5

Corporations

CHAPTER 14
CORPORATIONS: Organization and Stockholders' Equity   **521**

What is a corporation?   Advantages of the corporate form of
organization.   Disadvantages of the corporate form of organization.
Income taxes in corporate financial statements.   Formation of a
corporation.   Stockholders' equity.   Cash dividends.   What is
capital stock?   Authorization and issuance of capital stock.
Preferred stock and common stock.   Characteristics of preferred
stock.   **Case in Point.**   Market price of preferred stock.   **Case
In Point.**   Market price of common stock.   **Case in Point.**   The
role of an underwriter.   Stock issued for assets other than cash.
Subscriptions to capital stock.   Donated capital.   Stockholder
records in a corporation.   Book value per share of common stock.
Balance sheet for a corporation illustrated.

END-OF-CHAPTER REVIEW   541
Concepts introduced or emphasized in Chapter 14.   Key terms
introduced or emphasized in Chapter 14.   Demonstration problem for
your review.   Solution to demonstration problem.   Self-test
questions.

ASSIGNMENT MATERIAL   545
Review questions.   Exercises.   Problems.   Business decision
cases.   Answers to the self-test questions.

CHAPTER 15
CORPORATIONS:
Operations, Earnings per Share, and Dividends   **556**

REPORTING THE RESULTS OF OPERATIONS   557
Developing predictive information.   Reporting unusual items—an
illustration.   Continuing operations.   Discontinued operations.
Case in Point.   Extraordinary items.   Changes in accounting
principle.   Earnings per share (EPS).   Primary and fully diluted
earnings per share.

OTHER STOCKHOLDERS' EQUITY TRANSACTIONS   564
Cash dividends.   Dividend dates.   Liquidating dividends.   Stock
dividends.   Stock splits.   **Case in Point.**   Statement of retained
earnings.   Prior period adjustments.   Treasury stock.

Recording purchases of treasury stock.   Reissuance of treasury stock.   Statement of stockholders' equity.   Illustration of stockholders' equity section.

END-OF-CHAPTER REVIEW   575
Concepts introduced or emphasized in Chapter 15.   Key terms introduced or emphasized in Chapter 15.   Demonstration problem for your review.   Solution to demonstration problem.   Self-test questions.

ASSIGNMENT MATERIAL   579
Review questions.   Exercises.   Problems.   Business decision cases.   Answers to the self-test questions.

CHAPTER 16
BONDS PAYABLE, LEASES, AND OTHER LIABILITIES   591

BONDS PAYABLE   592
What is a bond issue?   Tax advantage of bond financing.   The issuance of bonds payable.   Bonds issued between interest dates. The concept of present value.   The present value concept and bond prices.   Bonds issued at a discount.   Bonds issued at a premium. Year-end adjustments for bond interest expense.   Straight-line amortization: a theoretical shortcoming. Effective interest method of amortization.   Retirement of bonds payable.   Bond sinking fund. Market prices of bonds.   **Case in Point.**   **Case in Point.** Convertible bonds payable.   Conversion of bonds from the investor's viewpoint.   **Case in Point.**

LEASES   611
Operating leases.   Capital leases.

OTHER LONG-TERM LIABILITIES   613
Mortgage notes payable.   Liabilities for pension plans.

END-OF-CHAPTER REVIEW   614
Concepts introduced or emphasized in Chapter 16.   Key terms introduced or emphasized in Chapter 16.   Self-test questions.

ASSIGNMENT MATERIAL   617
Review questions.   Exercises.   Problems.   Business decision cases.   Answers to the self-test questions.

APPENDIX A:
Applications of Present Value   626

THE CONCEPT OF PRESENT VALUE   626
Present value tables.   Selecting an appropriate discount rate. Discounting annual cash flows.   Discount periods of less than one year.

ACCOUNTING APPLICATIONS
OF THE PRESENT VALUE CONCEPT   630
Valuation of long-term notes receivable and payable (Chapters 8 and

11).   Estimating the value of goodwill (Chapter 10).   Market prices
of bonds (Chapter 16).   Capital lease (Chapter 16).   Problems.

CHAPTER 17
INVESTMENTS IN CORPORATE SECURITIES   636

INVESTMENTS IN MARKETABLE SECURITIES   637
Accounting for marketable securities.   Marketable debt securities
(bonds).   Marketable equity securities (stocks).   Gains and losses
from sales of investments.   Balance sheet valuation of marketable
securities.   **Case in Point.**   Applying the lower-of-cost-or-market
rule: an illustration.   Presentation of marketable securities in financial
statements.

INVESTMENTS FOR PURPOSES
OF INFLUENCE OR CONTROL   644
The equity method.   Parent and subsidiary companies.   Growth
through the acquisition of subsidiaries.   **Case in Point.**   Financial
statements for a consolidated economic entity.

CONSOLIDATED FINANCIAL STATEMENTS:
Concepts and Mechanics   648
Methods of consolidation.   Consolidation at the date of acquisition.
Intercompany eliminations.   Acquisition of subsidiary's stock at a
price above book value.   Less than 100% ownership in subsidiary.
Consolidated income statement.   Accounting for investments in
corporate securities: a summary.

END-OF-CHAPTER REVIEW   656
Concepts introduced in Chapter 17.   Key terms introduced or
emphasized in Chapter 17.   Self-test questions.

ASSIGNMENT MATERIAL   658
Review questions.   Exercises.   Problems.   Business decision
cases.   Answers to the self-test questions.

APPENDIX B:
International Accounting and Foreign Currency Transactions   670
What is international accounting?   Foreign currencies and exchange
rates.   Accounting for transactions with foreign companies.
Currency fluctuations—who wins and who loses?   Consolidated
financial statements that include foreign subsidiaries.

ASSIGNMENT MATERIAL   679
Review questions.   Problems.

Part 6

Special Reports and Uses of Accounting
Information

CHAPTER 18
INCOME TAXES AND BUSINESS DECISIONS
685

Tax Reform Act of 1986.   Tax planning versus tax evasion.   The critical importance of income taxes.   The federal income tax: history and objectives.   Classes of taxpayers.

INCOME TAXES; INDIVIDUALS
689

Cash basis of accounting for income tax returns.   Tax rates. Income tax formula for individuals.   Total income and gross income. Deductions to arrive at adjusted gross income.   Deductions from adjusted gross income.   Personal exemptions.   Taxable income— individuals.   Capital gains and losses.   Computing the tax liability. Quarterly payments of estimated tax.   Tax returns, tax refunds, and payment of the tax.   Computation of individual income tax illustrated. Alternative Minimum Tax.   Partnerships.

INCOME TAXES; CORPORATIONS
702

Taxation of corporations.   Corporation tax rates.   Taxable income of corporations.   Illustrative tax computation for corporation. Accounting income versus taxable income.   Alternative accounting methods offering possible tax advantages.   Interperiod income tax allocation.

TAX PLANNING
708

Form of business organization.   Tax planning in the choice of financial structure.   **Case in Point.**   Tax shelters.

END-OF-CHAPTER REVIEW
711

Concepts introduced or emphasized in Chapter 18.   Key terms introduced or emphasized in Chapter 18.   Demonstration problem for your review.   Solution to demonstration problem.   Self-test questions.

ASSIGNMENT MATERIAL
716

Review questions.   Exercises.   Problems.   Business decision cases.   Answers to the self-test questions.

CHAPTER 19
MEASURING CASH FLOWS
728

STATEMENT OF CASH FLOWS
729

Purpose of the statement.   Example of a statement of cash flows. Classification of cash flows.   Critical importance of cash flow from operating activities.   Approaches to preparing a statement of cash flows.

PREPARING A STATEMENT OF CASH FLOWS:
An Illustration
734

Cash flows from operating activities.   Cash payments for merchandise and for expenses.   Differences between net income and net cash flow from operating activities.   Reporting operating cash flow: the direct and indirect methods.   Cash flows from investing activities.   Cash flows from financing activities.   Relationship between the statement of cash flows and the balance sheet.   The statement of cash flows: a second look.

END-OF-CHAPTER REVIEW   746
Concepts introduced or emphasized in Chapter 19.   Key terms introduced or emphasized in Chapter 19.   Demonstration problem for your review.   Solution to demonstration problem.   Self-test questions.

ASSIGNMENT MATERIAL   751
Review questions.   Exercises.   Problems.   Business decision cases.   Answers to the self-test questions.

APPENDIX C:
The Indirect Method   765
Illustration of the direct and indirect methods.   Comparison of the direct and indirect methods.   Differences between net income and net cash flow from operating activities.   Reconciling net income with net cash flow.   1 Adjustments for "noncash" expenses. 2 Adjusting for timing differences.   3 Adjusting for "nonoperating" gains and losses.   The indirect method: a summary.   Indirect method may be required in a supplementary schedule.

ASSIGNMENT MATERIAL   770
Problems.

CHAPTER 20
ANALYSIS AND INTERPRETATION
OF FINANCIAL STATEMENTS   772
What is your opinion of the level of corporate profits?   **Case in Point.**   Some specific examples of corporate earnings . . . and losses.   Sources of financial information.   Comparative financial statements.   Tools of analysis.   Dollar and percentage changes. **Case in Point.**   Trend percentages.   Component percentages. Ratios.   Comparative data in annual reports of major corporations. Standards of comparison.   Quality of earnings.   Quality of assets and the relative amount of debt.   Impact of inflation.   Illustrative analysis for Seacliff Company.   Analysis by common stockholders. Return on investment (ROI).   Leverage.   Analysis by long-term creditors.   Analysis by preferred stockholders.   Analysis by short-term creditors.   Summary of analytical measurements.

END-OF-CHAPTER REVIEW   795
Concepts introduced in Chapter 20.   Key terms introduced or emphasized in Chapter 20.   Demonstration problem for your review. Solution to demonstration problem.   Self-test questions.

ASSIGNMENT MATERIAL   799
Review questions.   Exercises.   Problems.   Business decision cases.   Answers to the self-test questions.

APPENDIX D:
Accounting for the Effects of Inflation   815
What is inflation?   Profits—fact or illusion?   **Case in Point.**
Two approaches to "inflation accounting."   Disclosing the effects of
inflation in financial statements.
"Inflation Accounting"—an Illustration
Net income measured in constant dollars.   Interpreting the constant
dollar income statement.   Gains and losses in purchasing power.
Interpreting the net gain or loss in purchasing power.   Net income on
a current cost basis.   Interpreting a current cost income statement.
Expressing comparative data in dollars of constant purchasing power.
Interpreting comparative data stated in constant dollars.

ASSIGNMENT MATERIAL   826
Review questions.   Exercises.   Problems.

COMPREHENSIVE PROBLEMS FOR PART 6:
Bristol-Myers Company   831

Part 7

Managerial Accounting: Cost Accounting Systems

CHAPTER 21
INTRODUCTION TO MANAGERIAL ACCOUNTING:
ACCOUNTING FOR MANUFACTURING OPERATIONS   850
INTRODUCTION TO MANAGERIAL ACCOUNTING   852
Interdisciplinary nature of managerial accounting.   Our approach to
managerial accounting.   Overlap of managerial and financial
accounting.

ACCOUNTING FOR MANUFACTURING OPERATIONS   854
Comparison of a merchandising company with a manufacturer.
Types of manufacturing costs.   Product costs and period costs.
Inventories of a manufacturing business.   Flow of costs parallels the
physical flow of goods.   Accounting for manufacturing costs: an
illustration.   Materials inventory.   Direct labor.   Manufacturing
overhead.   Direct and indirect manufacturing costs.   Overhead
application rate.   Overhead "cost drivers."   **Case in Point.**
Work in process inventory, finished goods inventory, and the cost of
goods sold.   Schedule of cost of finished goods manufactured.
Financial statements of a manufacturing company.

END-OF-CHAPTER REVIEW   869
Concepts introduced in Chapter 21.   Key terms introduced or
emphasized in Chapter 21.   Demonstration problem for your review.
Solution to demonstration problem.   Self-test questions.

ASSIGNMENT MATERIAL   873
Review questions.   Exercises.   Problems.   Business decision
cases.   Answers to the self-test questions.

**CHAPTER 22
COST ACCOUNTING SYSTEMS** 886

What is a cost accounting system? **Case in Point.** Two basic types of cost accounting systems.

JOB ORDER COST SYSTEMS 888
The job cost sheet. Flow of costs in a job cost system: an illustration. Accounting for direct materials. Accounting for direct labor costs. Accounting for overhead costs. Accounting for completed jobs. Job order cost systems in service industries.

PROCESS COST SYSTEMS 895
Characteristics of a process cost system. Flow of costs in a process cost system. Equivalent full units—the key to determining unit cost. Determining unit costs. Process cost summary for the mixing department. Process cost summary for the packaging department. Process cost systems: actual overhead or applied overhead? Just-in-time systems and other special situations. **Case in Point.**

END-OF-CHAPTER REVIEW 909
Concepts introduced or emphasized in Chapter 22. Key terms introduced or emphasized in Chapter 22. Demonstration problem for your review. Solution to demonstration problem. Self-test questions.

ASSIGNMENT MATERIAL 913
Review questions. Exercises. Problems. Business decision cases.

**COMPREHENSIVE PROBLEM FOR PART 7:
Apex Computer, Inc.** 925

Part 8

Managerial Accounting: Planning and Control

**CHAPTER 23
COST-VOLUME-PROFIT ANALYSIS** 931

Cost-volume relationships. Behavior of unit costs. **Case in Point.** Cost behavior in business. Analysis of semivariable costs: determining the fixed and variable elements. Cost-volume-profit relationships. Cost-volume-profit analysis: an illustration. **Case in Point.** Using cost-volume-profit relationships. Importance of sales mix in cost-volume-profit analysis. Contribution margin per unit of scarce resource. Assumptions underlying cost-volume-profit analysis. Summary of basic cost-volume-profit relationships.

END-OF-CHAPTER REVIEW 950
Concepts introduced or emphasized in Chapter 23. Key terms introduced or emphasized in Chapter 23. Demonstration problem for your review. Solution to demonstration problem. Self-test questions.

ASSIGNMENT MATERIAL   954
Review questions.   Exercises.   Problems.   Business decision
cases.   Answers to the self-test questions.

CHAPTER 24
MEASURING AND EVALUATING SEGMENT PERFORMANCE   963

SEGMENTS OF A BUSINESS   964
The need for information about segment performance.   Profit centers,
investment centers, and cost centers.

RESPONSIBILITY ACCOUNTING SYSTEMS   966
Responsibility accounting: an illustration.   Assigning revenue and
costs to segments of a business.   **Case in Point.**   Variable costs.
Contribution margin.   Fixed costs.   Traceable fixed cost.
Common fixed costs.   Segment margin.   When is a segment
"unprofitable"?   Evaluating segment managers.   Arguments
against allocating common fixed costs to segments.   Nonfinancial
objectives and information.   **Case in Point.**

VARIABLE COSTING   975
Full costing: the traditional view of product costs.   Variable costing: a
different view of product costs.   Illustration of variable costing.
Fluctuations in the level of production.

END-OF-CHAPTER REVIEW   983
Concepts introduced or emphasized in Chapter 24.   Key terms
introduced or emphasized in Chapter 24.   Demonstration problem for
your review.   Solution to demonstration problem.   Self-test
questions.

ASSIGNMENT MATERIAL   988
Review questions.   Exercises.   Problems.   Business decision
case.   Answers to the self-test questions.

CHAPTER 25
BUDGETING AND STANDARD COSTS   999

BUDGETING:
The Basis for Planning and Control   1000
Benefits derived from budgeting.   Establishing budgeted amounts.
The budget period.   The master budget: a "package" of related
budgets.   Steps in preparing a master budget.   Preparing the
master budget: an illustration.   Using budgets effectively.   Flexible
budgeting.

STANDARD COSTS: FOCUSING ATTENTION
ON COST VARIANCES   1015
Establishing and revising standards.   Cost variances.   Illustration
of standard costs.   Materials price and materials quantity variances.
Labor rate and labor efficiency variances.   Manufacturing overhead
variances.   Valuation of finished goods.   Evaluation of cost
variances.   Summary of cost variances.

END-OF-CHAPTER REVIEW   1025
Concepts introduced or emphasized in Chapter 25.   Key terms
introduced or emphasized in Chapter 25.   Self-test questions.

ASSIGNMENT MATERIAL   1028
Review questions.   Exercises.   Problems.   Business decision
case.   Answers to the self-test questions.

CHAPTER 26
RELEVANT INFORMATION, INCREMENTAL ANALYSIS,
AND CAPITAL BUDGETING   1040

THE CONCEPT OF RELEVANT INFORMATION   1041
Accepting special orders.   Make or buy decisions.   Opportunity
costs.   Sunk costs versus out-of-pocket costs.   Scrap or rebuild
defective units.   Whether to discontinue an unprofitable product line.

CAPITAL BUDGETING   1048
Payback period.   Return on average investment.   Discounting
future cash flows.   Replacement of old equipment.   Concluding
comments.

END-OF-CHAPTER REVIEW   1055
Concepts introduced or emphasized in Chapter 26.   Key terms
introduced or emphasized in Chapter 26.   · Self-test questions.

ASSIGNMENT MATERIAL   1057
Review questions.   Exercises.   Problems.   Business decision
case.   Answers to the self-test questions.

Index   1069

Preface

A new edition provides authors with an opportunity to add new material, to condense the coverage of topics that have declined in relative importance, to reorganize portions of the book to improve instructional efficiency, and to refine and polish the treatment of basic subject matter. We have tried to do all these things in this edition.

The environment of accounting is changing fast, and the shift toward computers, the increasing public interest in income tax policies, and the growing importance of international business activity affect the goals and content of an introductory text in accounting. In order to function intelligently as a citizen as well as in the business community, every individual needs more than ever before an understanding of basic accounting concepts. Our goal is to present accounting as an essential part of the decision-making process for the voter, the taxpayer, the government official, the business manager, and the investor.

This edition, like the preceding one, is designed for use in the first college-level course in accounting. In this course, instructors often recognize three groups of students: those who stand at the threshold of preparation for a career in accounting, students of business administration who need a thorough understanding of accounting as an important element of the total business information system, and students from a variety of other disciplines who will find the ability to use and interpret accounting information a valuable accomplishment. During the process of revision, we have tried to keep in mind the needs and interests of all three groups.

NEW FEATURES IN THIS EDITION

In the Text:

1 Five *Comprehensive Problems* designed to review the major concepts introduced in a group of related chapters. We consider these *Comprehensive Problems* to be one of the most useful new learning aids in this eighth edition. The first of these problems, which follows Chapter 4, is a short "practice set" covering the entire accounting cycle. Another *Comprehensive Problem* offers students an opportunity to analyze and evaluate the financial statements of a well-known corporation.

2 Well over 100 entirely new exercises and problems. In addition, the vast majority of exercises, problems, and cases carried forward from the prior edition have been revised.

3 Numerous real-world exercises and problems, based upon recent events involving well-known corporations.

4 Most chapters contain several problems designed for solution using one of our spreadsheet packages, such as *Lotus Connection.* These problems are identified by the computer terminal symbol shown in the left margin. Our supplemental package includes spreadsheet templates for these problems in IBM (5½ and 3½ in) and Macintosh formats.

5 *Self-test questions* included at the end of each chapter, along with answers to provide students with immediate feedback. (***Note to students:*** These questions are intended as a self-study device for quickly reviewing the most important concepts of an entire chapter. Because of their comprehensive nature, they tend to be more difficult than the average multiple choice question likely to appear on an examination.)

6 A new format for our chapter summaries, now including a section explaining how each chapter "fits in" to the overall study of accounting.

7 An extensive revision of the managerial accounting chapters. This revision involves changes in topical coverage, emphasis, sequence of presentation, terminology, and, in some cases, our positions on controversial issues. A number of new topics are covered in these chapters, including "just-in-time" manufacturing operations and overhead "cost drivers" in highly automated factories. Among the other features of the managerial revisions are:

a A virtually new chapter on accounting for manufacturing operations, now emphasizing the flow of costs in a perpetual inventory system.

b An all new chapter on measuring and evaluating the performance of segments of a business enterprise.

8 Increased emphasis throughout the text upon accounting theory and generally accepted accounting principles.

9 Increased emphasis upon the use of accounting information for decision making purposes.

10 A new appendix explaining and illustrating the "indirect method" of measuring and reporting the net cash flow from operating activities.

New Features in the Supplemental Package:

In this eighth edition, we have attempted to enhance virtually every element of our supplemental package of learning and teaching aids, as well as to provide a variety of new and innovative supplements. These efforts include:

1 *Instructional Videotapes,* by Lloyd Brandt. A chapter-by-chapter video presentation of the entire accounting principles course.

2 A financial statement analysis case, *Premium Foods Corporation,* by Christie W. Johnson. This application simulates the analysis and evaluation of the information contained in an annual report. The entire solution may be prepared manually, but the case also lends itself to the optional use of spreadsheet software in performing many of the analytical steps.

3 Many new *Accounting Applications.* A variety of new and realistic accounting simulations, covering the basic accounting cycle, corporate reporting, financial statement analysis, and managerial accounting topics. All applications are available in a manual format. In addition, many applications are available in "tutorial" computer-based formats, or in a format using one of our general ledger software packages. In many cases, we offer several versions of an application, enabling instructors to vary the assignment from one semester to the next.

4 A greatly expanded *Test Bank.* We have more than tripled the size of our test bank. For each chapter, we now provide 20 true-false questions, more than 50 multiple choice questions, and more than 10 exercises. Also included are four 10-Minute Quizzes for each chapter.

Our *Achievement Test* package also has been expanded, now including two sets of tests covering two chapters each, as well as two sets covering four chapters per test.

5 An enhanced *Study Guide,* now providing explanations of the reasoning behind the correct answer to each true-false and multiple choice question.

6 Two new computer-based self-study aids. The *Computerized Tutorial System* enables students to test themselves using objective questions and exercises, and to receive immediate feedback, with explanations of the correct answers (available for IBM (in 3½ and 5¼ in formats). *The Accounting Lab,* by Peter L. McMickle, utilizes the unique capabilities of Apple Computer's *HyperCard* to provide students with instructional material, examples, and self-test questions (available for Macintosh).

FEATURES CARRIED FORWARD
FROM PRIOR EDITIONS

Special qualities that are carried forward from prior editions include:

1 Depth of coverage. Topics are covered in a depth that will qualify the student for subsequent course work in accounting.

2 Accuracy in all problem material and solutions. All problems, solutions, and examination materials have been developed and tested first-hand by the authors in their own classes for introductory accounting students. This personal attention to accuracy is supplemented by independent testing by other accounting faculty.

3 Perspective—careful effort throughout the text and problems to utilize current and realistic prices, interest rates, and profit levels.

4 People-oriented problems which depict the complex decisions that must be made by men and women acting as managers, investors, and in other roles.

5 Abundant problem material, including review questions, exercises, two sets of problems, Business Decision Cases, and Comprehensive Problems. In addition, each chapter includes self-test questions, a glossary of key terms, and most chapters include a demonstration problem to assist students in developing skill in analyzing and solving accounting problems.

6 Checklist of key figures for problems, Business Decision Cases, and Comprehensive Problems included at the front and back of the textbook.

7 Coverage of computer-based accounting systems integrated into the early "accounting cycle" chapters.

8 Frequent use of real business examples—termed *Cases in Point*—to illustrate key accounting concepts.

9 The most thorough coverage of income taxes found in any principles of accounting textbook. Our coverage of income taxes emphasizes basic concepts likely to remain relevant for many years to come.

10 An appendix featuring an introductory level discussion of international accounting and foreign currency translation, complete with problem material.

11 Careful integration into the text and problem material of recent pronouncements of the Financial Accounting Standards Board.

12 The most comprehensive package of supplementary materials available for any accounting textbook.

NEW AND EXTENSIVELY REVISED CHAPTERS

In terms of chapter content, this eighth edition represents our most extensive revision to date. Two chapters are entirely new, and many have been extensively revised. New topics have been added to most chapters; and we have shifted a number of topics among our chapters and appendixes to improve the sequence of presentation.

In Chapter 1, our discussion of careers in accounting has been expanded to include opportunities in accounting education, and the use of a background in accounting as a "stepping stone" to positions in top management. Each of the first five chapters has been revised to place more emphasis upon the theoretical concepts that underlie accounting practices, particularly the accounting principles of realization and matching.

Chapters 5 and 6 have been extensively rewritten, with a considerable shifting of material between these chapters. Chapter 5, "Accounting for Purchases and Sales of Merchandise," now shorter than in the preceding edition, focuses upon merchandising transactions and classified financial statements. In the revised Chapter 6, we combine our discussions of the related topics of internal control and accounting systems. The new format is shorter and, we believe, more effective.

Chapter 8, "Receivables," has been revised to reflect the growing popularity of the "balance sheet method" of estimating uncollectible accounts now that so many computer programs automatically "age" accounts receivable. We also explain the new income tax rules relating to uncollectible accounts expense.

Our discussion of accounting for the effects of inflation, formerly included in Chapter 13, has been moved to an appendix following Chapter 20. As a result, we have been able to expand substantially our discussion of accounting principles in Chapter 13. Among the topics given additional emphasis are the nature and sources of accounting principles, the FASB's standard setting process, the potential usefulness of the conceptual framework project, and the crucial role of professional judgment in accounting practice.

Chapter 19, "Measuring Cash Flows," is now followed by a new appendix illustrating and explaining the "indirect method" of reporting net cash flows from operating activities.

Our six "managerial accounting" chapters (21 through 26) represent the area of greatest change. Chapter 21 is all new, beginning our discussion of managerial accounting topics with product costing, rather than with responsibility accounting systems. In addition, this chapter now assumes the use of a perpetual inventory system. Chapter 21 also explores the problem of identifying the overhead "cost drivers" in the modern factory.

Chapter 22, "Cost Accounting Systems," has been completely revised to illustrate more clearly the basic operations of both job order and process cost systems. The implications of "just-in-time" systems also are discussed in this chapter.

Chapter 23, "Cost-Volume-Profit Analysis," has been moved to precede the discussion of segment performance. This move provides students with the background needed to distinguish between variable costs and fixed costs—a concept essential in evaluating managerial performance. Also new to Chapter 23 is the "high low" method of distinguishing between fixed and variable costs.

Chapter 24, "Measuring and Evaluating Segment Performance," is all new to this eighth edition.

Our Chapter 25 deals with two major topics: budgeting and standard costs. Our discussion of budgeting has been revised to focus upon the sequence of steps in the budgeting process. The sections of Chapter 25 dealing with standard costs have been entirely rewritten, reflecting a new approach to this topic.

SUPPLEMENTARY MATERIALS

A distinguishing feature of this textbook is the wide variety of supplementary learning and teaching aids for students and instructors. A graphic illustration of these supplements appears at the end of this preface.

For Students:

1 *A self-study guide* The **Study Guide** enables students to measure their progress by immediate feedback. This self-study guide includes a summary of the highlights of each chapter and an abundance of objective questions and short exercises. Answers to all questions and exercises are provided immediately following each chapter. As an additional study aid, the reasoning behind the answer to each multiple choice question is explained in detail. This guide provides a useful review for students before classroom discussion and examinations.

2 *Working papers* Partially completed working papers are available for all Group A and Group B problems, for all Business Decisions Cases, and for all

Comprehensive Problems. These working papers save time, because much of the data "given" in a problem has already been entered on the working paper. In addition, the working papers often provide guidance in organizing the solutions.

The working papers are available in a variety of packages, so that students may purchase only those working papers relating to their course assignments. The following sets of accounting work sheets are available:

Group A Problems, Chapters 1 through 15
Group A Problems, Chapters 14 through 26
Group B Problems, Chapters 1 through 15
Group B Problems, Chapters 14 through 26
Group A and Group B Problems, Chapters 1 through 15
Group A and Group B Problems, Chapters 14 through 26
Blank Accounting Forms, all chapters

All packages include working papers for the Business Decision Cases and any appendixes relating to the chapters.

For instructors who prefer to have students develop solutions "from scratch," the package of **Blank Accounting Forms** provides enough of each type of columnar paper for the typical two-semester course.

3 *Computer Tutorial* Using objective questions and exercises from our Study Guide, this computer-based supplement allows students to test themselves on any chapter. For objective questions, the tutorial provides immediate on-screen explanations of why incorrect answers are wrong, along with page references to discussions in the textbook. To assist in solving exercises, the tutorial includes a built-in calculator and numerous "help screens" (IBM, $3\frac{1}{2}$ and $5\frac{1}{4}$ formats).

4 *The Accounting Lab,* by Peter L. McMickle. This software package uses the unique capabilities of Apple Computer's **HyperCard** to provide students with tutorial material, examples, and self-test questions. This self-study aid is designed for use on a Macintosh personal computer.

5 *Accounting Applications* Accounting applications are simulations of various accounting activities. This eighth edition offers a wide variety of these applications in both manual and computer-based formats. A brief description of our many accounting applications follows:

Accounting Cycle Applications—Manual Format

Traditional practice sets, intended to "pull together" for students the steps in the accounting cycle. We offer several variations of these accounting cycle sets, many of which are also available in computer-based formats.

Our unique "two-week" sets enable students to step into the accounting cycle in the middle of the month. Thus, the transactions recorded during the first two weeks appear in the journals to serve as examples. This minimizes the routine work, but allows students to perform all of the end of period procedures. Applications available in the "two-week" format include **Authenticity, Color Copy Co., Remington Restaurant Supply,** and **Big Screen Systems.** Each of these sets require from 6 to 8 hours to complete.

Two applications are available in "full-month" versions, in which the students enter the accounting cycle at the beginning of the month. These sets, **Another Century** and **Facts-by-Fax** require 8 to 10 hours to complete.

We also offer two accounting cycle applications that utilize realistic business documents in lieu of a narrative of transactions. These sets, *Acme Parts* and *Echo Paint Co.,* are authored by Richard A. Wright.

Accounting Cycle Applications—Computer-Based

Computer-based accounting cycle applications are available in either a "tutorial" format, or utilizing "real-world" general ledger software.

Both *Remington Restaurant Supply* (narrative) and *Echo Paint Co.* (business forms) are available in a "tutorial" computer-based format. The computer program simulates general ledger software, but identifies any input errors made by the students and provides guidance in making corrections (IBM).

We also offer two *CYMA* packages. *CYMA* is a widely used general ledger software system. In each of our *CYMA* packages, we provide the input for two separate accounting cycle applications. Also, this software may be used to work most accounting cycle problems, and to maintain personal accounting records or those for a small business (available in IBM 3½ and 5¼ in formats).

Other Accounting Applications

We also offer accounting applications suitable for use at other points in the principles course. These include:

Shadow Mountain Hotel   An application emphasizing financial reporting by a corporate entity. Suitable for use after Chapter 17.

Premium Foods Corporation, by Christie W. Johnson. A financial statement analysis case, based upon a realistic simulation of an annual report. Suitable for use after Chapter 20.

Executive Woodcraft Company, by Ronald W. Hilton. A managerial accounting application emphasizing product costing. Includes optional modules on cost-volume-profit analysis, budgeting, and special order analysis. Suitable for use after Chapter 22.

6 *Spreadsheet Software,* by E. James Meddaugh. These packages provide spreadsheet templates enabling students to use a personal computer in working problems designated by the computer terminal symbol illustrated in the left margin. *Lotus Connection* suits students with access to Lotus 1-2-3, *Macintosh Connection* is intended for use with Excel, and *Spreadsheet Connection* includes a student version of VP Planner, an IBM-compatible spreadsheet software.

7 *The Use of Spreadsheets in Accounting,* by Enzo V. Allegretti. A self-study manual for students to assist in the creation of spreadsheets to solve the exercises and problems.

Supplements for Instructors

1 *Solutions manual*   A comprehensive manual containing answers to all review questions, exercises, Group A and Group B problems, and Business Decision cases contained in the text.

In the development of problem material for this book, special attention has been given to the inclusion of problems of varying length and difficulty. By referring to the time estimates, difficulty ratings, and problem descriptions in the *Solutions Manual,* instructors can choose problems that best fit the level, scope, and emphasis of the course they are offering.

2 *Solutions to accounting applications* A separate manual containing complete solutions to all nine of our manual and computer-based accounting applications. Separating these solutions from the solutions to problem material accommodates those instructors who want to make the regular *Solutions Manual* available to students in a laboratory or in the reserve section of the library.

3 *An instructor's guide* This separate manual includes the following three sections for each chapter of the textbook:

a A brief topical outline of the chapter listing in logical sequence the topics the authors like to discuss in class.

b An assignment guide correlating specific exercises and problems with various topics covered in the chapter.

c Comments and observations.

The "Comments and observations" sections indicate the authors' personal views as to relative importance of topics and identify topics with which some students have difficulty. Specific exercises and problems are recommended to demonstrate certain points. Many of these sections include "Asides," introducing real-world situations (not included in the text) that are useful in classroom discussions.

Also included in the Instructor's Guide are sample assignment schedules, ideas for using each element of the supplemental package, and solutions to the sets of Achievement Tests and Comprehensive Examinations.

4 Four separate sets of *achievement tests* and *comprehensive examinations.* Sets A and B both consist of twelve 50-minute achievement tests, each covering two chapters, and two comprehensive examinations covering the first and second halves of the textbook. The A and B sets are parallel, differing only in the sequence of questions and in quantitative problem data. The two sets of parallel tests may be used in the same classroom to ensure that no student sits next to someone taking an identical examination, or may be alternated from one semester to the next.

Sets C and D each include six 50-minute achievement tests, each covering *four* chapters, and two 1 hour and 40 minute comprehensive examinations. The C and D sets parallel one another, differing only in the sequence of questions and in quantitative problem data.

5 *A new and enlarged test bank* With an abundance of true-false questions, multiple-choice questions, and short exercises organized on a chapter-by-chapter basis, this supplement is a valuable resource for instructors who prepare their own examinations. In its new format, this is one of the largest test banks ever to accompany any accounting textbook. Also included in the new *Test Bank* are four *10-Minute Quizzes* relating to each chapter.

6 *Transparencies of solutions to exercises, problems, and cases* This visual aid enables instructors to display by overhead projector the complete solution to every numerical exercise, problem, Business Decision Case, and Comprehensive Problem in the text. The transparencies now use a bold typeface for greater clarity.

7 *Teaching transparencies* A large number of transparencies have been produced for use in the classroom to illustrate various accounting concepts and procedures. These transparencies all differ from the illustrations appearing in the textbook and are enhanced by the use of color.

8 *Instructional videotapes* A series of instructional videotapes prepared especially for this edition by Lloyd Brandt. They are an excellent back up to live instruction, suitable for use in an accounting lab or on closed circuit TV.

Contributions by Others

The eighth edition has benefited from a number of perceptive reviews. We wish to express our sincere thanks to these reviewers, who are listed at the conclusion of this Preface.

We owe a special debt to Wai P. Lam, University of Windsor. Professor Lam, the coauthor of the Canadian edition of this book, prepared an unusually comprehensive review of the entire text as well as a thorough check of all exercises and problems.

Our special thanks go also to Virginia Bakay, University of Nevada-Las Vegas, and Audrie M. Beck, American University, for assisting us in the proof stages of this edition with detailed reviews of text examples and end-of-chapter problem material.

We want to thank Enzo Allegretti, Mary Ferrara, Ronald Hilton, Christie Johnson, Peter McMickle, James Meddaugh, and Richard Wright, each of whom has authored elements of our supplements package. The contributions of these talented people have also enabled us to improve the text in many ways.

We are most appreciative of the expert attention given this book and its many supplements by the staff of McGraw-Hill, especially Bob Lynch, David Damstra, Ed Hanson, Larry Goldberg, Nick Krenitsky, Judy Motto, San Rao, and Diane Renda.

The assistance of Jennifer Allen, Susha Asaf, Patty Cavalline, Peggy DeJong, and Rosemary Savage was most helpful in preparation of the manuscript for both the text and supplements.

We are also grateful to the Financial Accounting Standards Board, which granted us permission to quote from FASB Statements, Discussion Memoranda, Interpretations, and Exposure Drafts. All quotations are copyrighted © by the Financial Accounting Standards Board, High Ridge Park, Stamford, Connecticut 06905, U.S.A. and are reprinted with permission. Copies of the complete documents are available from the FASB.

Robert F. Meigs
Walter B. Meigs

Acknowledgments

REVIEWERS OF THIS EDITION

- Sarah L. Adams, California State University-Chico
- Skinner Anderson, Sonoma State University, California
- Joseph D. Aubert, Bemidji State University, Minnesota
- Walter O. Baggett, Manhattan College, New York
- Virginia Bakay, University of Nevada-Las Vegas
- Audrie M. Beck, The American University, Washington, DC
- Brenda S. Birkett, Southern University, Louisiana
- Roy Broxterman, Hutchinson Community College, Kansas
- Barry S. Buchoff, Towson State University, Maryland
- Roberta Jacobs Cable, Pace University, New York
- Janet Cassagio, Nassau Community College, New York
- J. V. Colmie, Thomas Nelson Community College, Virginia
- Philip W. Conklin, Springfield College, Massachusetts
- Joseph P. Cunniff, Quincy Junior College, Massachusetts
- Jarvis Dean, Chattanooga State Technical Community College, Tennessee
- Carleton M. Donchess, Bridgewater State College, Massachusetts
- Joanne B. Edwards, Westbrook College, Maine
- Frances L. Engel, Niagara University, New York
- Carolyn Fitzmorris, Hutchinson Community College, Kansas
- Selwyn W. Glincher, Quincy Junior College, Massachusetts
- Dennis A. Gutting, Orange County Community College, New York
- G. Kent Harding, Thames Valley State Technical College, Connecticut
- William B. Herd, Springfield Technical Community College, Massachusetts
- Barry J. Hiney, Western New England College, Massachusetts

ACKNOWLEDGMENTS

- Cynthia Holloway, Tarrant County Junior College, Northeast, Texas
- Paul P. Hoppe, University of Connecticut at Stamford
- Linda J. Jones, Neosho County Community College, Kansas
- Edward G. Kelly, Delaware Technical and Community College
- Nancy L. Kelly, Middlesex Community College, Connecticut
- Richard F. Kusek, Loyola University of Chicago
- Wai P. Lam, University of Windsor, Canada
- Marcella Y. Lecky, The University of Southwestern Louisiana
- Robert F. Lilly, Clackamas Community College, Oregon
- William C. Lins, Rutgers University, New Jersey
- L. R. Loschen, Eastern New Mexico University
- William J. Mack, Purdue University, Indiana
- John A. Miller, Jr., St. Louis Community College at Florissant Valley
- Frank R. Molitor, Middlesex County College, New Jersey
- Lois Anne New, Sam Houston State University, Texas
- Leslie S. Oakes, Rutgers University, New Jersey
- Harris M. O'Brien, North Harris County College, Texas
- Mary J. Phelan, Southeastern Massachusetts University
- Patrick T. Reihing, Nassau Community College, New York
- Anne J. Rich, Quinnipiac College, Connecticut
- Lyle K. Rowe, San Diego Mesa College, California
- Fabiola Rubio, El Paso Community College, Texas
- Leo A. Ruggle, Mankato State University, Minnesota
- Scott Sandstrom, College of the Holy Cross, Massachusetts
- Clifford A. Sexton, Jr., Nebraska Wesleyan University
- Josephus Shepherd, University of California, Santa Cruz
- S. Murray Simons, Northeastern University, Massachusetts
- Beverly Ann Soriano, Framingham State College, Massachusetts
- Daniel J. Sullivan, Leeward Community College, Hawaii
- Norman A. Sunderman, Angelo State University, Texas
- Maurice F. Tassin, Louisiana Technical University
- Gwen Totterdale, San Diego State University, California
- James F. Ward, University of Notre Dame, Indiana
- Henry Weiman, Bronx Community College, New York

■ Charlotte J. Wright, Oklahoma State University

■ James G. S. Yang, Montclair State College, New Jersey

■ Charles P. Zlatkovich, University of Texas, El Paso

■ David J. Zwibel, Kingsborough Community College, New York

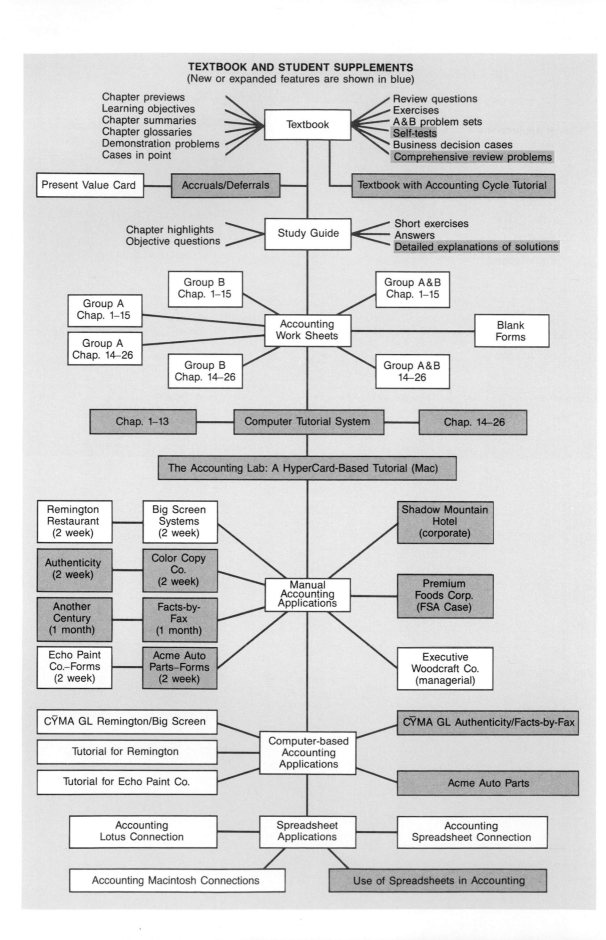

TEXTBOOK AND STUDENT SUPPLEMENTS
(New or expanded features are shown in blue)

Chapter previews
Learning objectives
Chapter summaries
Chapter glossaries
Demonstration problems
Cases in point

Textbook

Review questions
Exercises
A&B problem sets
Self-tests
Business decision cases
Comprehensive review problems

Present Value Card | Accruals/Deferrals | Textbook with Accounting Cycle Tutorial

Chapter highlights
Objective questions

Study Guide

Short exercises
Answers
Detailed explanations of solutions

Group B Chap. 1–15
Group A&B Chap. 1–15
Group A Chap. 1–15
Group A Chap. 14–26

Accounting Work Sheets

Blank Forms

Group B Chap. 14–26
Group A&B 14–26

Chap. 1–13 | **Computer Tutorial System** | Chap. 14–26

The Accounting Lab: A HyperCard-Based Tutorial (Mac)

Remington Restaurant (2 week)
Big Screen Systems (2 week)
Authenticity (2 week)
Color Copy Co. (2 week)
Another Century (1 month)
Facts-by-Fax (1 month)
Echo Paint Co.–Forms (2 week)
Acme Auto Parts–Forms (2 week)

Manual Accounting Applications

Shadow Mountain Hotel (corporate)
Premium Foods Corp. (FSA Case)
Executive Woodcraft Co. (managerial)

CYMA GL Remington/Big Screen
Tutorial for Remington
Tutorial for Echo Paint Co.

Computer-based Accounting Applications

CYMA GL Authenticity/Facts-by-Fax
Acme Auto Parts

Accounting Lotus Connection

Spreadsheet Applications

Accounting Spreadsheet Connection

Accounting Macintosh Connections | Use of Spreadsheets in Accounting

SUPPLEMENTS FOR INSTRUCTORS
(New or expanded supplements are shown in blue)

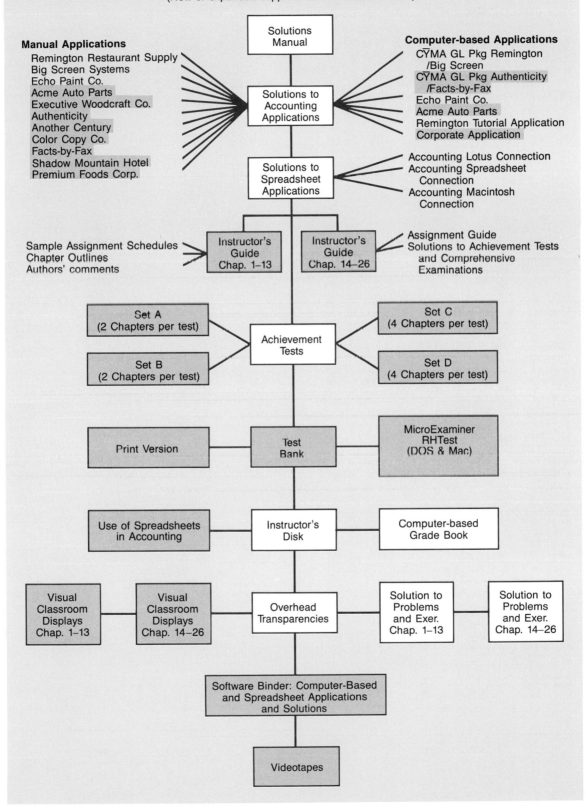

Solutions Manual

Manual Applications
- Remington Restaurant Supply
- Big Screen Systems
- Echo Paint Co.
- Acme Auto Parts
- Executive Woodcraft Co.
- Authenticity
- Another Century
- Color Copy Co.
- Facts-by-Fax
- Shadow Mountain Hotel
- Premium Foods Corp.

Computer-based Applications
- CYMA GL Pkg Remington /Big Screen
- CYMA GL Pkg Authenticity /Facts-by-Fax
- Echo Paint Co.
- Acme Auto Parts
- Remington Tutorial Application
- Corporate Application

Solutions to Accounting Applications

Solutions to Spreadsheet Applications
- Accounting Lotus Connection
- Accounting Spreadsheet Connection
- Accounting Macintosh Connection

- Sample Assignment Schedules
- Chapter Outlines
- Authors' comments

Instructor's Guide Chap. 1–13

Instructor's Guide Chap. 14–26

- Assignment Guide
- Solutions to Achievement Tests and Comprehensive Examinations

Set A (2 Chapters per test)

Set B (2 Chapters per test)

Achievement Tests

Set C (4 Chapters per test)

Set D (4 Chapters per test)

Print Version

Test Bank

MicroExaminer RHTest (DOS & Mac)

Use of Spreadsheets in Accounting

Instructor's Disk

Computer-based Grade Book

Visual Classroom Displays Chap. 1–13

Visual Classroom Displays Chap. 14–26

Overhead Transparencies

Solution to Problems and Exer. Chap. 1–13

Solution to Problems and Exer. Chap. 14–26

Software Binder: Computer-Based and Spreadsheet Applications and Solutions

Videotapes

PART 1

The Accounting Cycle

In these first four chapters, the continuing example of Roberts Real Estate Company is used to illustrate the concepts of double-entry accrual accounting for a small, service-type business. Accounting for a merchandising concern will be introduced in Part 2.

1 Accounting: The Language of Business

2 Recording Changes in Financial Position

3 Measuring Business Income

4 Completion of the Accounting Cycle

Accounting: The Language of Business

This introductory chapter explores the nature of accounting and the environment in which it is developed and used. We emphasize the challenging career opportunities open to accountants, the use of accounting reports, and the institutions which influence accounting practice. A basic financial statement—the balance sheet—is illustrated and discussed. We explain the nature of assets, liabilities, and owner's equity; and why a balance sheet always "balances." Attention is focused upon the set of standards called *generally accepted accounting principles.* Specific accounting principles introduced in Chapter 1 include the concept of the business entity, the cost principle, objectivity, the going-concern assumption, and the stable-dollar assumption. We also introduce Roberts Real Estate, a company used as a continuing example throughout the first four chapters. In Chapter 1, the activities of Roberts Real Estate are used to show how business transactions affect the balance sheet.

After studying this chapter you should be able to meet these Learning Objectives:

1 Define accounting and explain the purpose of an accounting system.

2 Recognize accounting as a field of challenging career opportunities.

3 Explain the phrase "generally accepted accounting principles."

4 Explain the function of the Financial Accounting Standards Board (FASB).

5 Give examples of business decisions for which accounting information is needed.

6 Describe a balance sheet; define assets, liabilities, and owner's equity.

7 Discuss the accounting principles involved in asset valuation.

8 Indicate the effects of various transactions upon the balance sheet.

WHAT IS ACCOUNTING?

Objective 1
Define accounting
and explain the
purpose of an
accounting
system.

Some people think of accounting as a highly technical field which can be understood only by professional accountants. Actually, nearly everyone practices accounting in one form or another on an almost daily basis. Accounting is the art of measuring, describing, and interpreting economic activity. Whether you are preparing a household budget, balancing your checkbook, preparing your income tax return, or running General Motors, you are working with accounting concepts and accounting information.

Accounting has often been called the "language of business." Such terms as assets, liabilities, revenue, expense, cash flow, inventory turnover, and earnings per share are but a few examples of technical accounting terms widely used in the business community. Every investor, manager, and business decision maker needs a clear understanding of accounting terms and concepts. At the end of each chapter in this book, the first exercise is devoted to enhancing your knowledge of accounting terminology.

We live in an era of accountability. Although accounting has made its most dramatic progress in the field of business, the accounting function is vital to every unit of our society. An individual must account for his or her income, and must file income tax returns. Often an individual must supply personal accounting information in order to buy a car or home, to qualify for a college scholarship, to secure a credit card, or to obtain a bank loan. Large corporations are accountable to their stockholders, to governmental agencies, and to the public. The federal government, the states, the cities, the school districts: all must use accounting as a basis for controlling their resources and measuring their accomplishments. Accounting is equally essential to the successful operation of a business, a university, a fraternity, a social program, or a city.

In every election the voters must make decisions at the ballot box on issues involving accounting concepts. Therefore, some knowledge of accounting is needed by all citizens if they are to act intelligently in meeting the challenges of our society. This book will help you develop your knowledge of accounting and your ability to use accounting information in making economic and political decisions.

The Purpose and Nature of Accounting

The underlying purpose of accounting is to provide financial information for decision making about an economic entity. In this book the economic entity we concentrate upon is a business enterprise. Business executives and managers need the financial information provided by an accounting system to help them *plan and control* the activities of the business. For example, management needs answers to such questions as the profitability of each department of the business, the adequacy of the company's cash position, and the trend of earnings.

Many businesses also compile nonfinancial information needed for decision making. An airline, for example, must have information about on-time arrivals, repair schedules, and physical examinations of flight crews. The use of computers makes possible the operation of a management information system (MIS) which provides decision makers with both financial and nonfinancial information. The accounting system is the most extensive and important component of a management information system because it is used by the entire business entity and by outsiders as well.

Financial information about a business is needed by many *outsiders*. These outsiders include owners, bankers, other creditors, potential investors, labor unions, government agencies, and the public, because all these groups have supplied money to the business or have some other interest in the business that will be served by information about its financial position and operating results. A labor union, for example, needs to be informed on a company's financial strength and profits before beginning negotiations for a new labor contract. Remember that every individual as well as every business must make economic decisions about the future. Therefore, everyone needs some understanding of accounting as a basis for making sound decisions.

To emphasize our basic concept, the goal of the accounting system is to provide useful information to decision makers. Thus, accounting is the connecting link between decision makers and business operations.

The Functions of an Accounting System

An accounting system consists of the methods and devices used by an entity to keep track of its financial activities and to summarize these activities in a manner useful to decision makers. To achieve these goals, an accounting system may make use of computers and video displays as well as handwritten records and reports printed on paper. In fact, the accounting system for any sizable business is likely to include all these records and devices. In every accounting system, whether simple or sophisticated, the data concerning each day's financial activities must be recorded, classified, and summarized.

Each day in the life of a business, goods and services are purchased and sold, credit is extended to customers, debts are incurred, and cash is received and paid out. These *transactions* must be recorded; that is, entered in accounting records. Notice that a transaction is a completed action, not an expected or possible future action. The recording of a transaction may be performed in many ways, such as writing with a pen or pencil, entering data through a computer keyboard, or passing machine-readable price tags over an optical scanner.

Of course, not all business events can be measured objectively and described in monetary terms. Therefore, we do not include in the accounting records such events as the death of a key executive or a threat by a labor union to call a strike.

To make the record of business transactions useful to management and other decision makers, the data must be classified into related groups of transactions. For example, grouping together all transactions in which cash is received or paid out provides useful information about the cash position of a business.

A complete listing of the sales transactions of a company such as Sears would be too long for anyone to read. Therefore, the detailed information is summarized to provide significant totals. Examples include: the sales of a given product, sales by department, sales by the entire store, by a regional group of stores, and by the entire company.

Communicating Accounting Information—Who Uses Accounting Reports?

The accounting process includes more than the *creating* of information. It also involves *communicating* this information to interested parties and *interpreting* accounting information to help in the making of specific business decisions.

Often we will want to compare the financial statements of Company A with those of Company B. From this comparison, we can determine which company is the more profitable, which is financially stronger, and which offers the better chance of future success. You can benefit personally by making this kind of analysis of a company you are considering investing in—or going to work for.

The major types of accounting reports which are developed by the accounting system of a business enterprise and the parties receiving this information are illustrated in the diagram shown below. The persons receiving accounting reports are termed the *users* of accounting information. The type of information that a specific user will require depends upon the kinds of decisions that person must make. For example, managers need detailed information about daily operating costs for the purpose of controlling the operations of the business and setting reasonable selling prices. Outsiders, on the other hand, need summarized information concerning resources on hand and information on operating results for the past year to use in making investment decisions, imposing income taxes, or making regulatory decisions.

As shown in the diagram, financial statements are the main source of financial information to persons outside the business organization, and also are of great importance to management. Financial statements show the financial position of the business at the end of the year (or other time period), and also the operating results by which the business arrived at this financial position. The basic purpose of financial statements is to assist decision makers in evaluating the financial strength, profitability, and future prospects of a business. Thus, management, the owners, bankers, the IRS, and other outside groups have a direct interest in financial statements.

Apart from financial statements, other types of accounting reports include income tax returns, reports to regulatory agencies, and management reports.

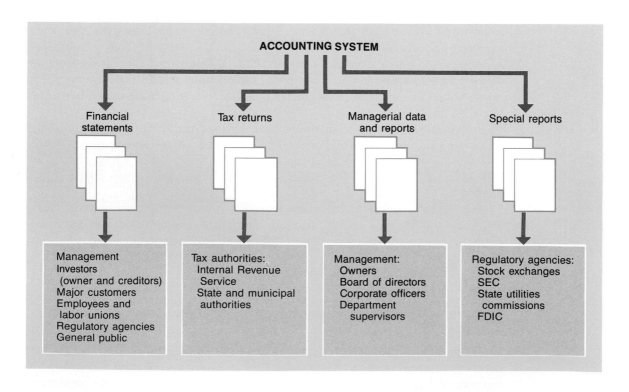

The Internal Revenue Service (IRS) requires businesses and individuals to file annual income tax returns designed to measure taxable income. *Taxable income* is a legal concept defined by laws which are frequently modified or changed. Thus the rules used in preparing income tax returns may vary from one year to the next. In general, however, there is a close parallel between income tax laws and the concepts underlying financial statements.

Certain types of business such as banks and telephone companies are regulated by government agencies. These regulated companies are often required to file special types of accounting reports specifically tailored to the needs of the regulatory agency. In large part, however, reports to regulatory agencies are based upon the same accounting principles as are financial statements.

The management of a business organization needs much detailed accounting data for use in planning and controlling the daily operations of the business. Management also needs specialized accounting information for long-range planning and for major decisions such as the introduction of a new product or the modernizing of an older plant. Accounting information being provided to managers need not conform to the rules for preparing financial statements. Rather, it should be tailored to the managers' specific information needs.

The Distinction between Accounting and Bookkeeping

Persons with little knowledge of accounting may fail to understand the difference between accounting and bookkeeping. *Bookkeeping* means the recording of transactions, the record-making phase of accounting. The recording of transactions tends to be mechanical and repetitive; it is only a small part of the field of accounting and probably the simplest part. *Accounting* includes not only the maintenance of accounting records, but also the design of efficient accounting systems, the performance of audits, the development of forecasts, income tax work, and the interpretation of accounting information. A person might become a reasonably proficient bookkeeper in a few weeks or months; however, to become a professional accountant requires several years of study and experience.

Careers in Accounting

Objective 2
Recognize accounting as a field of challenging career opportunities.

Accountants tend to specialize in a given sub-area of the discipline just as do attorneys and members of other professions. In terms of career opportunities, the field of accounting may be divided into four broad areas: (1) the public accounting profession, (2) private accounting, (3) governmental accounting, and (4) accounting education.

The Public Accounting Profession—the CPA

Certified public accountants (CPAs) are independent professional persons comparable to attorneys or physicians, who offer accounting services to clients for a fee. CPA firms vary in size from one-person practices to large, international organizations with several thousand professional accountants. The CPA certificate is a license to practice granted by the state on the basis of a rigorous examination and evidence of practical experience. All states require that candidates pass an examination prepared by the American Institute of Certified Public Accountants.

For professional accountants, education does not end at graduation time. CPAs are required to participate in continuing professional education programs throughout their careers. This commitment to staying proficient and to professional growth enables CPAs to advise their clients in a rapidly changing business environment. Public opinion polls indicate that most people have a high level of trust in certified public accountants. This attitude of trust reflects widespread public confidence in the competence, skills, and ethical standards of the accounting profession.

■ **Auditing**   The principal function of CPAs is auditing. How do people outside a business entity—owners, creditors, government officials, and other interested parties—know that the financial statements prepared by a company's management are reliable and complete? In large part, these outsiders rely upon *audits* performed by a CPA firm which is *independent* of the company issuing the financial statements.

To perform an audit of a business, a firm of certified public accountants makes a careful study of the company's accounting system and gathers evidence both from within the business and from outside sources. This evidence enables the CPA firm to express its professional *opinion* as to the fairness and reliability of the financial statements. Persons outside the business, such as bankers and investors, who rely upon financial statements for information, attach great importance to the annual *audit report* by the CPA firm.

There have long been eight very large CPA firms, known as the "Big Eight," which have audited many of the world's largest and best-known corporations.

CASE IN POINT   ■ The "Big Eight" public accounting firms and a few of their audit clients in recent years are listed below.

FIRM	SELECTED AUDIT CLIENTS
Arthur Andersen & Co.	ITT, Occidental Petroleum, Merck
Arthur Young & Co	Apple Computer, McDonald's, Mobile
Coopers & Lybrand	AT&T, Atlantic Richfield, Ford
DeLoitte, Haskins & Sells	General Motors, Procter & Gamble, Nissan
Ernst & Whinney	Blue Cross, Coca-Cola, Gulf & Western
KPMG Peat Marwick	General Electric, Squibb, Xerox
Price Waterhouse	Exxon, IBM, Sony
Touche Ross & Co.	Boeing, Prudential Insurance, Sears

The era of eight worldwide accounting firms is drawing to a close. To meet the demands of auditing giant international companies, several of the "Big Eight" are planning to merge, creating larger, but fewer international public accounting firms. Arthur Young intends to merge with Ernst & Whinney; DeLoitte, Haskins & Sells plans to merge with Touche Ross; and Arthur Andersen is discussing a possible merger with Price Waterhouse.

■ **Income Tax Services**   In making business decisions, executives consider the income tax consequences of each alternative course of action. The CPA is often called upon for "tax planning," which will show how a future transaction, such as the acquisition of expensive new equipment, may be arranged in a manner that will hold income taxes to a minimum amount. The CPA also may be retained by a business to prepare its federal and state income tax returns. To render tax services, the CPA must have extensive knowledge of tax statutes, regulations, and court decisions, as well as a thorough knowledge of accounting.

■ **Management Advisory Services**   Many CPA firms offer their clients a wide range of management consulting services. For example, a CPA firm might be engaged to study the feasibility of installing a computer-based accounting system, of introducing a new product line, or of merging with another company. The fact that business executives often seek their accountants' advice on a wide range of business problems illustrates the relevance of accounting information to virtually all business decisions.

Private Accounting

In contrast to the CPA in public practice who serves many clients, an accountant in private industry is employed by a single enterprise. The chief accounting officer of a medium-sized or large business is usually called the controller, in recognition of the use of accounting data to control business operations. The controller manages the work of the accounting staff. He or she is also a part of the top management team charged with the task of running the business, setting its objectives, and seeing that these objectives are met. Among other positions held by accountants in a business organization are assistant controller, chief accountant, internal auditor, plant accountant, systems analyst, financial forecaster, and tax accountant.

In a large business, accountants' work may be divided into such areas as:

1 Financial accounting   Financial accounting develops and communicates accounting information for internal use by management and also for external use by persons outside the business, such as owners, bankers, creditors, the IRS, and other government agencies. A principal purpose of financial accounting is the preparation of financial statements in accordance with the generally accepted accounting principles discussed later in this chapter.

To appreciate the importance of financial accounting and published financial statements, consider the millions of investors who own stock in IBM, General Electric, and other large companies. Financial accounting provides these millions of interested outsiders with information about the safety and the profitability of their investments. Financial statements may be viewed as the end product of financial accounting. In this book, we concentrate upon financial accounting.

2 Internal auditing   The internal auditing staff is responsible for evaluating the system of internal control to ensure that accounting reports are reliable, that the company's resources are safeguarded against theft or wasteful use, and that company policies are followed consistently at all levels of the business.

3 Tax accounting   As the laws defining taxable income have become more complex, both internal accountants and independent public accountants have devoted more time to problems of taxation. Although many companies rely largely on CPA firms for tax planning and the preparation of income tax returns, large companies also maintain their own tax departments.

4   Cost accounting   Knowing the cost of a particular product is vital to the efficient management of a business. For example, an automobile manufacturer needs to know the cost of each type of car produced. Knowing the cost of each manufacturing process (such as painting an automobile) or the cost of any business operation (such as an employee training program) is also essential to making sound business decisions. The phase of accounting concerned with collecting and interpreting cost data is called cost accounting.

5   Forecasting   A forecast (or budget) is a plan of financial operations for some future period expressed in monetary terms. By using a forecast, management is able to make comparisons between planned operations and actual results achieved. A forecast provides each division of the business with a specific goal, and thus gives management a means of measuring the efficiency of performance throughout the company.

6   Management accounting   An accounting system provides information for both external and internal use. The external reporting function has already been touched upon in our discussion of annual financial statements. The *internal* reporting function of an accounting system gives managers information needed for daily operations and also for long-range planning. Developing the types of information most relevant to specific managerial decisions and interpreting this information is called *management accounting* or *managerial accounting.* In short, management accounting is used by insiders rather than by outsiders. Both cost accounting and forecasting are often viewed as elements of management accounting. Keep in mind that financial accounting and managerial accounting are not two entirely separate disciplines. Much managerial accounting information is actually financial accounting information, rearranged to suit a particular managerial purpose.

■ **Certificate in Management Accounting**   The Institute of Management Accounting offers a program leading to a Certificate in Management Accounting. This certificate is a recognition of an individual's knowledge and competence in management accounting. To qualify, one must pass a professional examination and meet specified standards as to education and professional experience.

Governmental Accounting

Government officials rely on accounting information to help them direct the affairs of their agencies just as do the executives of corporations. However, accounting for governmental activities requires a somewhat different approach because the objective of earning a profit is absent from government agencies. Every agency of government at every level (federal, state, and local) must have accountants in order to carry out its responsibilities. Universities, hospitals, churches, and other not-for-profit institutions also follow a pattern of accounting that is similar to governmental accounting.

■ **Internal Revenue Service**   One of the governmental agencies which perform extensive accounting work is the Internal Revenue Service (IRS). The

IRS handles the millions of income tax returns filed by individuals and corporations, and frequently performs auditing functions relating to these returns and the accounting records on which they are based.

■ **Securities and Exchange Commission** Another governmental agency deeply involved in accounting is the Securities and Exchange Commission (SEC). The SEC establishes requirements regarding the content of financial statements and the reporting standards to be followed. All corporations which offer securities for sale to the public must file annually with the SEC audited financial statements meeting these requirements.

Accounting Education: Careers as Faculty Members

Many attractive career opportunities are open to accounting graduates. These openings are so attractive that most graduates move directly into public accounting, industry, or government. One interesting alternative, however, is to embark on the extensive graduate study and research required to qualify as an accounting faculty member. The demand for qualified accounting faculty is intense. Individuals with these qualifications are highly mobile—there are positions to be filled in virtually every state and country. Accounting faculty positions offer opportunities for research, consulting engagements, and an unusual degree of freedom in developing individual skills. Accounting educators contribute importantly to the accounting profession in many ways. One of these contributions lies in publishing in professional journals the results of their research concerning accounting practices. Another contribution consists of influencing top quality students to pursue careers in accounting.

Accounting—a Stepping Stone to Top Management

In the very largest corporations, many of the CEOs have had educational backgrounds in accounting. Such a background is invaluable because these top executives are working continuously with issues defined and described in accounting concepts. Thus, accounting enables individuals to practice as professionals in CPA firms or to rise to general management responsibilities in any field of business. Many people who begin their careers in accounting progress into top management levels of business organizations.

Generally Accepted Accounting Principles (GAAP)

Objective 3
Explain the phrase "generally accepted accounting principles."

To understand financial statements, one must first understand generally accepted accounting principles. These are the "ground rules," developed over a long span of years by the accounting profession. The purpose of these broad basic rules is to guide accountants in measuring and reporting the financial events that make up the life of a business. Briefly stated, generally accepted accounting principles are the accounting standards and concepts used in the measurement of financial activities and the preparation of financial statements.

If accountants consistently prepare financial statements in conformity with generally accepted accounting principles, then the current year's financial statements can be compared fairly with prior years' statements, and with the financial statements of other companies. When financial statements are comparable because they are all prepared under the same rules, then investors, bankers, and financial analysts can make better decisions in allocating capital to the most promising companies. The efficient allocation of capital is essential to the successful working of our economy. To summarize, we need a well-defined body of accounting principles to guide accountants in preparing financial statements that are relevant, reliable, understandable, and comparable.

In this chapter we will discuss five generally accepted accounting principles: the business entity concept, the cost principle, the going-concern assumption, the objectivity principle, and the stable-dollar assumption. These and other generally accepted accounting principles will be considered further at many points throughout this book.

Development of Generally Accepted Accounting Principles— the FASB

Objective 4
Explain the function of the FASB.

Research to develop accounting principles which will keep pace with changes in the economic and political environment is a major activity of professional accountants and accounting educators. In the United States four groups which have been influential in the improvement of financial reporting and accounting practices are the Financial Accounting Standards Board, the American Institute of Certified Public Accountants, the Securities and Exchange Commission, and the American Accounting Association.

Of special importance in establishing generally accepted accounting principles is the Financial Accounting Standards Board, known as the FASB. The FASB consists of seven full-time members, including representatives from public accounting, industry, and accounting education. In addition to conducting extensive research, the FASB issues *Statements of Financial Accounting Standards,* which represent authoritative expressions of generally accepted accounting principles.

Note that the FASB is part of the private sector of the economy and not a government agency. The development of accounting standards in the United States has traditionally been carried on in the private sector although the government, acting through the SEC, has exercised great influence on the FASB and other groups concerned with accounting research and standards of financial reporting.

The contribution of the FASB and the other groups mentioned above will be considered in later chapters. At this point we merely want to emphasize that accounting is not a closed system or a fixed set of rules, but a constantly evolving body of knowledge. As we explore accounting principles and related practices in this book, you will become aware of certain problems and conflicts for which fully satisfactory answers are yet to be developed. The need for further research is apparent despite the fact that present-day American accounting practices and standards of financial reporting are by far the best achieved anywhere at any time.

Accounting as the Basis for Business Decisions

To be successful, a business must make decisions that enable it to operate profitably and to stay solvent. A company that has sufficient cash to pay its debts promptly is said to be solvent. In contrast, a company that finds itself

Objective 5
Give examples of business decisions for which accounting information is needed.

unable to meet its obligations as they fall due is called insolvent. A business that becomes insolvent may be forced by its creditors to stop operations and end its existence.

How do business executives know whether a company is earning profits or incurring losses? How do they know whether the company is solvent or insolvent, and whether it probably will be solvent, say, a month from today? The answer to both these questions in one word is *accounting.* Accounting is the process by which the profitability and solvency of a company can be measured. Accounting also provides information needed as a basis for making business decisions that will enable management to guide the company on a profitable and solvent course.

For specific examples of these decisions, consider the following questions. What prices should the firm set on its products? If production is increased, what effect will this have on the cost of each unit produced? Will it be necessary to borrow from the bank? How much will costs increase if a pension plan is established for employees? Is it more profitable to produce and sell product A or product B? Shall a given part be manufactured or be bought from suppliers? Should an investment be made in new equipment? All these issues call for decisions that should depend, in part at least, upon accounting information. It might be reasonable to turn the question around and ask: What business decisions could be made intelligently *without* the use of accounting information? Examples would be hard to find.

We have already stressed that accounting is a means of measuring the results of business transactions and of communicating financial information. In addition, the accounting system must provide the decision maker with *predictive information* for making important business decisions in a changing environment.

Internal Control

The topic of internal control goes hand-in-hand with the study of accounting. We have stressed that business decisions of all types are based at least in part upon accounting information. Management needs assurance that the accounting information it receives is accurate and reliable. This assurance comes from the company's *system of internal control.*

A system of internal control consists of all the measures taken by an organization for the purpose of (1) protecting its resources against waste, fraud, and inefficiency; (2) ensuring accuracy and reliability in accounting and operating data; (3) securing compliance with company policies; and (4) evaluating the level of performance in all divisions of the company. In short, a system of internal control includes all of the measures designed to assure management that the entire business operates according to plan.

A basic principle of internal control is that no one person should handle all phases of a transaction from beginning to end. When business operations are so organized that two or more employees are required to participate in every transaction, the possibility of fraud is reduced and the work of one employee gives assurance of the accuracy of the work of another. The principal reason for many business documents and accounting procedures is to achieve strong internal control. Therefore, we shall discuss various internal control concepts and requirements throughout our study of accounting.

FINANCIAL STATEMENTS: THE STARTING POINT IN THE STUDY OF ACCOUNTING

The preparation of financial statements is not the first step in the accounting process, but it is a convenient point to begin the study of accounting. The financial statements are the means of conveying to management and to interested outsiders a concise picture of the profitability and financial position of the business. Since these financial statements are in a sense the end product of the accounting process, the student who acquires a clear understanding of the content and meaning of financial statements will be in an excellent position to appreciate the purpose of the earlier steps of recording and classifying business transactions.

The two most widely used financial statements are the *balance sheet* and the *income statement*.[1] Together, these two statements (perhaps a page each in length) summarize all the information contained in the hundreds or thousands of pages comprising the detailed accounting records of a business. In this introductory chapter and in Chapter 2, we shall explore the nature of the balance sheet, or statement of financial position, as it is sometimes called. Once we have become familiar with the form and arrangement of the balance sheet and with the meaning of technical terms such as *assets, liabilities,* and *owner's equity,* it will be as easy to read and understand a report on the financial position of a business as it is for an architect to read the blueprints of a proposed building. (We shall discuss the income statement in Chapter 3.)

The Balance Sheet

Objective 6
Describe a balance sheet; define assets, liabilities, and owner's equity.

The purpose of a balance sheet is to show the financial position of a business *at a particular date.* Every business prepares a balance sheet at the end of the year, and most companies prepare one at the end of each month. A balance sheet consists of a listing of the assets and liabilities of a business and of the owner's equity. The following balance sheet portrays the financial position of Vagabond Travel Agency at December 31.

VAGABOND TRAVEL AGENCY
Balance Sheet
December 31, 19___

Balance sheet shows financial position at a specific date

ASSETS		LIABILITIES & OWNER'S EQUITY	
Cash...........................	$ 7,500	Liabilities:	
Notes receivable	8,000	Notes payable...............	$ 52,000
Accounts receivable	57,000	Accounts payable	15,000
Supplies	1,500	Salaries payable.............	3,000
Land..........................	40,000	Total liabilities.............	$ 70,000
Building.......................	44,000	Owner's equity:	
Office equipment	12,000	Terry Crane, capital	100,000
Total.........................	$170,000	Total.........................	$170,000

---

[1] A third financial statement, called a *statement of cash flows,* will be discussed later.

Note that the balance sheet sets forth in its heading three items: (1) the name of the business, (2) the name of the financial statement "Balance Sheet," and (3) the date of the balance sheet. Below the heading is the body of the balance sheet, which consists of three distinct sections: assets, liabilities, and owner's equity. The remainder of this chapter is largely devoted to making clear the nature of these three sections.

Another point to note about the form of a balance sheet is that cash is always the first asset listed; it is followed by notes receivable, accounts receivable, supplies, and any other assets that will soon be converted into cash or consumed in operations. Following these items are the more permanent assets, such as land, buildings, and equipment.

The liabilities of a business are always listed before the owner's equity. Each liability (such as notes payable, accounts payable, and salaries payable) should be listed separately, followed by a total figure for liabilities.

The Concept of the Business Entity

The illustrated balance sheet above refers only to the financial affairs of the business entity known as Vagabond Travel Agency, and not to the personal financial affairs of the owner. Generally accepted accounting principles require that a set of financial statements describe a specific business entity. This concept is often called the entity principle.

For example, Vagabond is an economic unit operating as a travel agency. Its owner, Terry Crane, may have a personal bank account, a home, a car, and even another business, such as a cattle ranch. These items are not involved in the travel agency business and should not appear in Vagabond's financial statements.

In brief, a business entity is an economic unit which enters into business transactions that must be recorded, summarized, and reported. The entity is regarded as separate from its owner or owners. Consequently, for each business entity, there should be a separate set of accounting records and a separate set of financial statements.

Assets

Objective 7
Discuss the accounting principles involved in asset valuation.

Assets are economic resources which are owned by a business and are expected to benefit future operations. Assets may have definite physical form such as buildings, machinery, or merchandise. On the other hand, some assets exist not in physical or tangible form, but in the form of valuable legal claims or rights; examples are amounts due from customers, investments in government bonds, and patent rights.

One of the most basic and at the same time most controversial problems in accounting is determining the dollar values for the various assets of a business. At present, generally accepted accounting principles call for the valuation of assets in a balance sheet at *cost,* rather than at appraised market values. The specific accounting principles supporting cost as the basis for asset valuation are discussed below.

■ **The Cost Principle** Assets such as land, buildings, merchandise, and equipment are typical of the many economic resources that will be used in producing income for the business. The prevailing accounting view is that such assets should be recorded at their cost. When we say that an asset is shown in the balance sheet at its *historical cost,* we mean the dollar amount originally paid to acquire the asset; this amount may be very different from what we would have to pay today to replace it.

For example, let us assume that a business buys a tract of land for use as a building site, paying $100,000 in cash. The amount to be entered in the accounting records as the value of the asset will be the cost of $100,000. If we assume a booming real estate market, a fair estimate of the sales value of the land 10 years later might be $250,000. Although the market price or economic value of the land has risen greatly, the accounting value as shown in the accounting records and on the balance sheet would continue unchanged at the cost of $100,000. This policy of accounting for assets at their cost is often referred to as the *cost principle* of accounting.

In reading a balance sheet, it is important to bear in mind that the dollar amounts listed do not indicate the prices at which the assets could be sold, nor the prices at which they could be replaced. One useful generalization to be drawn from this discussion is that a balance sheet does *not* show "how much a business is worth."

■ **The Going-Concern Assumption**   It is appropriate to ask *why* accountants do not change the recorded values of assets to correspond with changing market prices for these properties. One reason is that the land and building being used to house the business were acquired for *use* and not for resale; in fact, these assets cannot be sold without disrupting the business. The balance sheet of a business is prepared on the assumption that the business is a continuing enterprise, a "going concern." Consequently, the present estimated prices at which the land and buildings could be sold are of less importance than if these properties were intended for sale.

■ **The Objectivity Principle**   Another reason for using cost rather than current market values in accounting for assets is the need for a definite, factual basis for valuation. Accountants use the term *objective* to describe asset valuations that are factual and can be verified by independent experts. For example, if land is shown on the balance sheet at cost, any CPA who performed an audit of the business would be able to find objective evidence that the land was actually valued at the cost incurred in acquiring it. Estimated market values, on the other hand, for assets such as buildings and specialized machinery are not factual and objective. Market values are constantly changing and estimates of the prices at which assets could be sold are largely a matter of personal opinion. Of course at the date an asset is acquired, the cost and market value are usually the same because the bargaining process which results in the sale of an asset serves to establish both the current market value of the property and the cost to the buyer. With the passage of time, however, the current market value of assets is likely to differ considerably from the cost recorded in the owner's accounting records.

■ **The Stable-Dollar Assumptions**   Severe inflation in several countries in recent years has raised serious doubts as to the adequacy of the conventional cost basis in accounting for assets. When inflation becomes very severe, historical cost values for assets simply lose their relevance as a basis for making business decisions. Much consideration has been given to the use of balance sheets which would show assets at current appraised values or at replacement costs rather than at historical cost.

Accountants in the United States by adhering to the cost basis of accounting are implying that the dollar is a *stable unit of measurement,* as is the gallon, the acre, or the mile. The cost principle and the stable-dollar assumption work very well in periods of stable prices, but are less satisfactory under conditions of rapid inflation. For example, if a company bought land 20 years ago for $100,000 and purchased a second similar tract of land today for $500,000, the total cost of land shown by the accounting records would be $600,000. This treatment ignores the fact that dollars spent 20 years ago had far greater purchasing power than today's dollar. Thus, the $600,000 total for cost of land is a mixture of two kinds of dollars with very different purchasing power.

After much research into this problem, the FASB required on a trial basis that large corporations report supplementary data showing current replacement costs and price-level adjusted data. However, after a few years, the cost of developing and disclosing such information in financial statements was judged to be greater than the benefits provided. Consequently, the disclosure requirement was eliminated. At the present time, the stable-dollar assumption continues in use in the United States—perhaps until challenged by more severe inflation sometime in the future.

Accounting concepts are not as exact and unchanging as many persons assume. To serve the needs of a fast-changing economy, accounting concepts and methods must undergo continuous evolutionary change. As of today, however, the cost basis of valuing assets is still the generally accepted method.

The problem of valuation of assets is one of the most complex in the entire field of accounting. It is merely being introduced at this point; in later chapters we shall explore carefully some of the valuation principles applicable to the major types of assets.

Liabilities

Liabilities are debts. All business concerns have liabilities; even the largest and most successful companies find it convenient to purchase merchandise and supplies on credit rather than to pay cash at the time of each purchase. The liability arising from the purchase of goods or services on credit is called an *account payable,* and the person or company to whom the account payable is owed is called a *creditor.*

A business concern frequently finds it desirable to borrow money as a means of supplementing the funds invested by the owner, thus enabling the business to expand more rapidly. The borrowed funds may, for example, be used to buy merchandise which can be sold at a profit to the firm's customers. Or, the borrowed money might be used to buy new and more efficient machinery, thus enabling the company to turn out a larger volume of products at lower cost. When a business borrows money for any reason, a liability is incurred and the lender becomes a creditor of the business. The form of the liability when money is borrowed is usually a *note payable,* a formal written promise to pay a certain amount of money, plus interest, at a definite future time.

An *account payable,* as contrasted with a *note payable,* does not involve the issuance of a formal written promise to the creditor, and it does not call for payment of interest. When a business has both notes payable and accounts payable, the two types of liabilities are shown separately in the balance sheet, with notes payable usually listed first. A figure showing the total of the liabilities should also be inserted, as shown by the illustrated balance sheet on page 14.

The creditors have claims against the assets of the business, usually not against any particular asset but against the assets in general. The claims of the creditors are liabilities of the business and have priority over the claims of owners. Creditors are entitled to be paid in full even if such payment should exhaust the assets of the business, leaving nothing for the owner.

Owner's Equity

The owner's equity in a business represents the resources invested by the owner; it is equal to the total assets minus the liabilities. The equity of the owner is a *residual claim* because the claims of the creditors legally come first. If you are the owner of a business, you are entitled to whatever remains after the claims of the creditors are fully satisfied.

For example, using the data from the illustrated balance sheet of Vagabond Travel Agency:

Vagabond Travel Agency has total assets of	*$170,000*
And total liabilities amounting to	*70,000*
Therefore, the owner's equity must equal	*$100,000*

Suppose that the Vagabond Travel Agency borrows $10,000 from a bank. After recording the additional asset of $10,000 cash and recording the new liability of $10,000 owed to the bank, we would have the following:

Vagabond Travel Agency now has total assets of	*$180,000*
And total liabilities are now	*80,000*
Therefore, the owner's equity still is equal to	*$100,000*

It is apparent that the total assets of the business were increased by the act of borrowing money from a bank, but the increase in assets was exactly offset by an increase in liabilities, and the owner's equity remained unchanged. The owner's equity in a business *is not increased* by borrowing from banks or other creditors.

■ **Increases in Owner's Equity** The owner's equity in a business comes from two sources:

1 Investment by the owner

2 Earnings from profitable operation of the business

Only the first of these two sources of owner's equity is considered in this chapter. The second source, an increase in owner's equity through earnings of the business, will be discussed in Chapter 3.

■ **Decreases in Owner's Equity** If you are the owner of a sole proprietorship, you have the right to withdraw cash or other assets from the business at any time. Because you want to see the business succeed, you will probably not make withdrawals that would handicap the business in operating efficiently. Withdrawals are most often made by writing a check drawn on the company's bank account and payable to the owner. Other types of withdrawals also occur, such as taking office equipment out of the business for personal use by the owner, or by causing cash belonging to the business to be used to pay a personal debt of the owner. Every withdrawal by the owner reduces the total assets of the business and reduces the owner's equity. In summary, decreases in the owner's equity in a business are caused in two ways:

1 *Withdrawals* of cash or other assets by the owner

2 *Losses* from unprofitable operation of the business

Only the first of these two causes of decreases in owner's equity is emphasized in this chapter. The second cause, a decrease in owner's equity through operating at a loss, will be considered in Chapter 3.

The Accounting Equation

A fundamental characteristic of every balance sheet is that the total figure for assets always equals the total for liabilities and owner's equity. This agreement or balance of total assets with the total of liabilities plus owner's equity is one reason for calling this statement of financial position a *balance sheet*. But *why* do total assets equal the total liabilities and owner's equity? The answer can be given in one short paragraph.

The dollar totals on the two sides of the balance sheet are always equal because these two sides are merely two views of the same business property. The listing of assets shows us *what resources* the business owns; the listing of liabilities and owner's equity tells us *who supplied these resources* to the business and how much each group supplied. Everything that a business owns has been supplied to it by the creditors or by the owner. Therefore, the total claims of the creditors plus the claim of the owner equal the total assets of the business.

The equality of assets on the one hand and of the claims of the creditors and the owner on the other hand is expressed in the equation:

■
Fundamental accounting equation

Assets = Liabilities + Owner's Equity
$170,000 = $70,000 + $100,000

The amounts listed in the equation were taken from the balance sheet illustrated on page 14. A balance sheet is simply a detailed statement of this equation. To illustrate this relationship, compare the balance sheet of Vagabond Travel Agency with the above equation.

To emphasize that the equity of the owner is a residual element, secondary to the claims of creditors, it is often helpful to transpose the terms of the equation, as follows:

■
Alternative form of equation

Assets − Liabilities = Owner's Equity
$170,000 − $70,000 = $100,000

Every business transaction, no matter how simple or how complex, can be expressed in terms of its effect on the accounting equation. A thorough understanding of the equation and some practice in using it are essential to the student of accounting.

Regardless of whether a business grows or contracts, this equality between the assets and the claims against the assets is always maintained. Any increase in the amount of total assets is necessarily accompanied by an equal increase on the other side of the equation, that is, by an increase in either the liabilities or the owner's equity. Any decrease in total assets is necessarily accompanied by a corresponding decrease in liabilities or owner's equity. The continuing equality of the two sides of the balance sheet can best be illustrated by taking a brand-new business as an example and observing the effects of various transactions upon its balance sheet.

Effects of Business Transactions upon the Balance Sheet

Objective 8
Indicate the effects of various transactions upon the balance sheet.

Assume that James Roberts, a licensed real estate broker, decided to start a real estate business of his own, to be known as Roberts Real Estate Company. The planned operations of the new business call for obtaining listings of houses being offered for sale by owners, advertising these houses, and showing them to prospective buyers. The listing agreement signed with each owner provides that Roberts Real Estate Company shall receive at the time of sale a commission equal to 6% of the sales price of the property.

The new business was begun on September 1, when Roberts deposited $180,000 in a bank account in the name of the business, Roberts Real Estate Company. The initial balance sheet of the new business then appeared as follows:

ROBERTS REAL ESTATE COMPANY
Balance Sheet
September 1, 19___

ASSETS		OWNER'S EQUITY	
Cash..........................	$180,000	James Roberts, capital........	$180,000

Beginning balance sheet of a new business

Observe that the equity of the owner in the assets is designated on the balance sheet by the caption, James Roberts, capital. The word *capital* is the traditional accounting term used in describing the equity of the proprietor in the assets of the business.

■ **Purchase of an Asset for Cash**   The next transaction entered into by Roberts Real Estate Company was the purchase of land suitable as a site for an office. The price for the land was $141,000 and payment was made in cash on September 3. The effect of this transaction on the balance sheet was twofold: first, cash was decreased by the amount paid out; and second, a new asset, Land, was acquired. After this exchange of cash for land, the balance sheet appeared as follows:

ROBERTS REAL ESTATE COMPANY
Balance Sheet
September 3, 19__

Balance sheet totals unchanged by purchase of land for cash

ASSETS		OWNER'S EQUITY	
Cash.........................	$ 39,000	James Roberts, capital	$180,000
Land.........................	141,000		
Total.........................	$180,000	Total.........................	$180,000

■ **Purchase of an Asset and Incurring of a Liability** On September 5 an opportunity arose to buy from Kent Company a complete office building which had to be moved to permit the construction of a freeway. A price of $36,000 was agreed upon, which included the cost of moving the building and installing it upon the Roberts Company's lot. As the building was in excellent condition and would have cost approximately $80,000 to build, Roberts considered this a very fortunate purchase.

The terms provided for an immediate cash payment of $15,000 and payment of the balance of $21,000 within 90 days. Cash was decreased $15,000, but a new asset, Building, was recorded at cost in the amount of $36,000. Total assets were thus increased by $21,000 but the total of liabilities and owner's equity was also increased as a result of recording the $21,000 account payable as a liability. After this transaction had been recorded, the balance sheet appeared as shown below. Remember that cash is always the first asset listed in a balance sheet.

ROBERTS REAL ESTATE COMPANY
Balance Sheet
September 5, 19__

Totals increased equally by purchase on credit

ASSETS		LIABILITIES & OWNER'S EQUITY	
Cash.........................	$ 24,000	Liabilities:	
Land.........................	141,000	Accounts payable	$ 21,000
Building......................	36,000	Owner's equity:	
		James Roberts, capital	180,000
Total.........................	$201,000	Total.........................	$201,000

Note that the building appears in the balance sheet at $36,000, its cost to Roberts Real Estate Company. The estimate of $80,000 as the probable cost to construct such a building is irrelevant. Even if someone should offer to buy the building from the Roberts Company for $80,000 or more, this offer, if refused, would have no bearing on the balance sheet. Accounting records are intended to provide a historical record of *costs actually incurred;* therefore, the $36,000 price at which the building was purchased is the amount to be recorded.

■ **Sale of an Asset** After the office building had been moved to the Roberts Company's lot, Roberts decided that the lot was larger than was needed. The adjoining business, Carter's Drugstore, wanted more room for a parking area so, on September 10, Roberts Company sold a small, unused corner of the lot to

Carter's Drugstore for a price of $11,000. Since the sales price was computed at the same amount per foot as Roberts Company had paid for the land, there was neither a profit nor a loss on the sale. No down payment was required but it was agreed that the full price would be paid within three months. By this transaction a new asset, Accounts Receivable, was acquired, but the asset Land was decreased by the same amount; consequently there was no change in the amount of total assets. After this transaction, the balance sheet appeared as follows:

ROBERTS REAL ESTATE COMPANY
Balance Sheet
September 10, 19__

ASSETS		LIABILITIES & OWNER'S EQUITY	
Cash.........................	$ 24,000	Liabilities:	
Accounts receivable	11,000	Accounts payable	$ 21,000
Land.........................	130,000	Owner's equity:	
Building.....................	36,000	James Roberts, capital	180,000
Total	$201,000	Total	$201,000

No change in totals by sale of land at cost

In the illustration thus far, Roberts Real Estate Company has an account receivable from only one debtor, and an account payable to only one creditor. As the business grows, the number of debtors and creditors will increase, but the Accounts Receivable and Accounts Payable designations will continue to be used. The additional records necessary to show the amount receivable from each individual debtor and the amount owing to each individual creditor will be explained in Chapter 6.

■ **Purchase of an Asset on Credit**   A complete set of office furniture and equipment was purchased on credit from General Equipment, Inc., on September 14 for $5,400. As the result of this transaction the business owned a new asset, Office Equipment, but it had also incurred a new liability in the form of Accounts Payable. The increase in total assets was exactly offset by the increase in liabilities. After this transaction the balance sheet appeared as follows:

ROBERTS REAL ESTATE COMPANY
Balance Sheet
September 14, 19__

ASSETS		LIABILITIES & OWNER'S EQUITY	
Cash.........................	$ 24,000	Liabilities:	
Accounts receivable	11,000	Accounts payable	$ 26,400
Land.........................	130,000	Owner's equity:	
Building.....................	36,000	James Roberts, capital	180,000
Office equipment	5,400		
Total	$206,400	Total	$206,400

Totals increased by acquiring asset on credit

■ **Collection of an Account Receivable**   On September 20, cash in the amount of $1,500 was received as partial settlement of the account receivable from Carter's Drugstore. This transaction caused cash to increase and the accounts receivable to decrease by an equal amount. In essence, this transaction was merely the exchange of one asset for another of equal value. Consequently, there was no change in the amount of total assets. After this transaction, the balance sheet appeared as follows:

ROBERTS REAL ESTATE COMPANY
Balance Sheet
September 20, 19___

	ASSETS		LIABILITIES & OWNER'S EQUITY	
	Cash	$ 25,500	Liabilities:	
	Accounts receivable	9,500	Accounts payable	$ 26,400
	Land	130,000	Owner's equity:	
	Building	36,000	James Roberts, capital	180,000
	Office equipment	5,400		
	Total	$206,400	Total	$206,400

■ Totals unchanged by collection of an account receivable

■ **Payment of a Liability**   On September 30 Roberts Real Estate Company paid $3,000 in cash to General Equipment, Inc. This payment caused a decrease in cash and an equal decrease in liabilities. Therefore the balance sheet totals were still in balance. After this transaction, the balance sheet appeared as follows:

ROBERTS REAL ESTATE COMPANY
Balance Sheet
September 30, 19___

	ASSETS		LIABILITIES & OWNER'S EQUITY	
	Cash	$ 22,500	Liabilities:	
	Accounts receivable	9,500	Accounts payable	$ 23,400
	Land	130,000	Owner's equity:	
	Building	36,000	James Roberts, capital	180,000
	Office equipment	5,400		
	Total	$203,400	Total	$203,400

■ Totals decreased by paying a liability

The transactions which have been illustrated for the month of September were merely preliminary to the formal opening for business of Roberts Real Estate Company on October 1. Since we have assumed that the business earned no commissions and incurred no expenses during September, the owner's equity at September 30 is shown in the above balance sheet at $180,000, unchanged from the original investment by Roberts on September 1. September was a month devoted exclusively to organizing the business and not to regular operations. In succeeding chapters we shall continue the example of Roberts Real Estate Company by illustrating operating transactions and considering how the net income of the business can be determined.

Effect of Business Transactions upon the Accounting Equation

A balance sheet is merely a detailed expression of the accounting equation, Assets = Liabilities + Owner's Equity. To emphasize the relationship between the accounting equation and the balance sheet, let us now repeat the September transactions of Roberts Real Estate Company to show the effect of each transaction upon the accounting equation. Briefly restated, the seven transactions were as follows:

Sept. 1 Began the business by depositing $180,000 in a company bank account.

     3 Purchased land for $141,000 cash.

     5 Purchased a building for $36,000, paying $15,000 cash and incurring a liability of $21,000.

   10 Sold part of the land at a price equal to cost of $11,000, collectible within three months.

   14 Purchased office equipment on credit for $5,400.

   20 Received $1,500 cash as partial collection of the $11,000 account receivable.

   30 Paid $3,000 on accounts payable.

The table below shows the effects of each of the September transactions on the accounting equation. The final line in the table corresponds to the amounts in the balance sheet at the end of September. Note that the equality of the two sides of the equation was maintained throughout the recording of the transactions.

	CASH	+	ACCOUNTS RECEIV-ABLE	+	LAND	+	BUILDING	+	OFFICE EQUIP-MENT	=	ACCOUNTS PAYABLE	+	JAMES ROBERTS, CAPITAL
					ASSETS					=	LIABIL-ITIES	+	OWNER'S EQUITY
Sept. 1	+$180,000		-0-		-0-		-0-		-0-		-0-		+$180,000
Sept. 3	−141,000				+$141,000								
Balances	$39,000		-0-		$141,000		-0-		-0-		-0-		$180,000
Sept. 5	−15,000						+$36,000				+$21,000		
Balances	$24,000		-0-		$141,000		$36,000		-0-		$21,000		$180,000
Sept. 10			+$11,000		−11,000								
Balances	$24,000		$11,000		$130,000		$36,000		-0-		$21,000		$180,000
Sept. 14									+$5,400		+5,400		
Balances	$24,000		$11,000		$130,000		$36,000		$5,400		$26,400		$180,000
Sept. 20	+1,500		−1,500										
Balances	$25,500		$9,500		$130,000		$36,000		$5,400		$26,400		$180,000
Sept. 30	−3,000										−3,000		
Balances	$22,500	+	$9,500	+	$130,000	+	$36,000	+	$5,400	=	$23,400	+	$180,000

Forms of Business Organization

A business enterprise may be organized as a *sole proprietorship,* a *partnership,* or a *corporation.*

■ **Sole Proprietorship**   An unincorporated business owned by one person is called a sole proprietorship. Often the owner also acts as the manager. This form of business organization is common for small retail stores and service enterprises, for farms, and for professional practices in law, medicine, and public accounting. The owner is *personally liable* for all debts incurred by the business. From an accounting viewpoint, however, the business is an entity separate from the proprietor. Sole proprietorships far outnumber both corporations and partnerships. The U.S. Bureau of the Census reports the existence of more than 13 million sole proprietorships, compared with less than 3 million corporations, and something over 1 million partnerships. However, virtually all large businesses are corporations. As a result, corporations carry on a far greater volume of business activities than do sole proprietorships and partnerships combined.

■ **Partnership** A business owned by two or more persons voluntarily associated as partners is called a partnership. Partnerships, like sole proprietorships, are widely used for small businesses and for professional practices. A great many CPA firms are organized as partnerships. As in the case of a sole proprietorship, a partnership is not legally an entity separate from its owners; consequently, a partner is personally responsible for the debts of the partnership. From an accounting standpoint, however, a partnership is a business entity separate from the personal activities of the partners.

■ **Corporation** A business organized as a separate legal entity with ownership divided into transferable shares of capital stock is called a corporation. Capital stock certificates are issued by the corporation to each stockholder showing the number of shares he or she owns. The stockholders are free to sell all or part of these shares to other investors at any time, and this ease of transfer adds to the attractiveness of investing in a corporation. Since a corporation is a separate legal entity, the owners (stockholders) are not personally liable for the debts of the corporation.

Persons wanting to form a new corporation must file an application with state officials for a corporate charter. The important role of the corporation in our economy is based on such advantages as the ease of gathering large amounts of money, transferability of shares in ownership, limited liability of owners, and continuity of existence.

Accounting principles and concepts of measurement apply to all three forms of business organization. In the first several chapters of this book, our study of basic accounting concepts will use as a model the sole proprietorship, which is the simplest and most common form of business organization.

USE OF FINANCIAL STATEMENTS BY OUTSIDERS
Through careful study of a company's financial statements, an outsider with a knowledge of accounting can gain an understanding of the financial position of the business and become aware of significant changes since the date of the preceding balance sheet. Bear in mind, however, that financial statements have limitations. Only those factors which can be reduced to monetary terms appear in the balance sheet. Let us consider for a moment some important business factors which are not set forth in financial statements. Perhaps a competing store has just opened for business across the street; the prospect of intensified competition in the future will not be described in the balance sheet. As another example, the health, experience, and managerial skills of the key people in the management group are extremely important in the success of a business, but these qualities cannot be measured and expressed in dollars in the financial statements.

Bankers and Other Creditors

Bankers who have loaned money to a business or who are considering making such a loan will be vitally interested in the balance sheet of the business. By studying the amount and kinds of assets in relation to the amount and payment dates of the liabilities, a banker can form an opinion as to the ability of the business to pay its debts promptly. The banker gives particular attention to the amount of cash and of other assets (such as accounts receivable) which will soon be converted into cash and then compares the amount of these assets with the amount of liabilities falling due in the near future.

The banker is also interested in the amount of the owner's equity, as this ownership capital serves as a protecting buffer between the banker and any losses which may befall the business. Bankers are seldom, if ever, willing to make a loan unless the balance sheet and other information concerning the prospective borrower offer reasonable assurance that the loan can and will be repaid promptly at the maturity date.

Another group making constant use of balance sheets consists of the credit managers of manufacturing and wholesaling firms, who must decide whether prospective customers are to be allowed to buy merchandise on credit. The credit manager, like the banker, studies the balance sheets of customers and prospective customers for the purpose of appraising their debt-paying ability. Credit agencies such as Dun & Bradstreet, Inc., make a business of obtaining financial statements from virtually all business concerns and establishing credit ratings for them. The conclusions reached by these credit agencies are available to business managers willing to pay for credit reports about prospective customers.

Owners

The financial statements of corporations listed on the stock exchanges are eagerly awaited by millions of stockholders. A favorable set of financial statements may cause the market price of the company's stock to rise dramatically; an unfavorable set of financial statements may cause the "bottom to fall out" of the market price. Current dependable financial statements are one of the essential ingredients for successful investment in securities. Of course, financial statements are equally important in a business organized as a sole proprietorship or as a partnership. The financial statements tell the owners just how successful the business has been and also summarize in concise form its present financial position.

Wide Distribution of Financial Statements

In addition to owners, managers, bankers, and merchandise creditors, other groups making use of accounting data include financial analysts, governmental agencies, employees, investors, and writers for business magazines. Some very large corporations have more than a million stockholders; these giant corporations send copies of their annual financial statements to each of these many owners and to anyone else who requests one. Financial statements are important not only to existing stockholders but also to potential investors and to the financial analysts and consultants who are constantly searching for promising investment opportunities. The wide distribution of financial statements marks an increasing awareness of the impact of corporate activities on all aspects of our lives and of the need for greater disclosure of information about the activities of business corporations.

End-of-Chapter Review

CONCEPTS INTRODUCED OR EMPHASIZED IN CHAPTER 1

The major concepts introduced in this chapter include:

■ The purpose and nature of accounting in terms of its use by a business enterprise.

■ The need for a knowledge of accounting by every business manager, public official, investor, financial analyst, banker, voter, and other decision makers.

■ Recognition of the many challenging career opportunities available to accounting graduates.

■ The preparation of a balance sheet as a means of showing the financial position of a business at a particular date.

■ The meaning of the term *generally accepted accounting principles* and the role of the Financial Accounting Standards Board in the development of these principles.

■ Definition and illustration of assets, liabilities, and owner's equity.

■ The effects of business transactions upon the balance sheet and upon the accounting equation.

The terminology introduced in this first chapter, including such basic terms as assets, accounting equation, generally accepted accounting principles, and balance sheet, will be used extensively throughout the book. At this point, you should feel comfortable with the balance sheet—its purpose and structure. In Chapter 2, you will become familiar with the journals and ledgers in which transactions are stored before they are summarized in financial statements. With this carefully planned approach, the introduction of the income statement in Chapter 3 will be a logical extension of concepts with which you have become quite familiar in Chapters 1 and 2.

KEY TERMS INTRODUCED OR EMPHASIZED IN CHAPTER 1

Accounting equation   Assets equal liabilities plus owner's equity. A = L + OE.

American Institute of Certified Public Accountants (AICPA)   The national professional association of certified public accountants (CPAs). Carries on extensive research and is influential in improving accounting standards and practices.

Assets   Economic resources owned by a business which are expected to benefit future operations.

Auditing   The principal activity of a CPA. Consists of an independent examination of the accounting records and other evidence relating to a business to support the expression of an impartial expert opinion about the reliability of the financial statements.

Balance sheet   A financial statement which shows the financial position of a business entity by summarizing the assets, liabilities, and owner's equity at a specific date.

Business entity   An economic unit that enters into business transactions that must be recorded, summarized, and reported. The entity is regarded as *separate from its owner or owners.*

Capital stock   Transferable units of ownership in a corporation.

Certificate in Management Accounting (CMA)   A designation granted to persons who have demonstrated competence in management accounting by passing an examination and meeting educational and professional requirements.

Certified public accountants (CPAs)   Independent professional accountants licensed by a state to offer auditing and accounting services to clients for a fee.

Corporation   A business organized as a separate legal entity and chartered by a state, with ownership divided into transferable shares of capital stock.

Cost principle   A widely used policy of accounting for assets at their original cost to the business.

Financial accounting   The area of accounting which emphasizes measuring and reporting the financial position and operating results of a business entity in conformity with generally accepted accounting principles.

Financial Accounting Standards Board (FASB)   An independent group which conducts research in accounting and issues authoritative statements as to proper accounting principles and methods for reporting financial information.

Financial statements   Reports which summarize the financial position and operating results of a business (balance sheet and income statement).

Generally accepted accounting principles (GAAP)   The accounting concepts, measurement techniques, and standards of presentation used in financial statements. Examples include the cost principle, the going-concern assumption, and the objectivity principle.

Going-concern assumption   An assumption by accountants that a business will continue to operate indefinitely unless specific evidence to the contrary exists, as, for example, impending bankruptcy.

Internal control   All measures used by a business to guard against errors, waste, and fraud; to assure the reliability of accounting data; to promote compliance with all company policies; and to evaluate the level of performance in all divisions of the company.

Liabilities   Debts or obligations of a business. The claims of creditors against the assets of a business.

Owner's equity   The excess of assets over liabilities. The amount of an owner's net investment in a business plus profits from successful operations which have been retained in the business.

Partnership   An unincorporated business owned by two or more persons voluntarily associated as partners.

Sole proprietorship   An unincorporated business owned by one person.

Solvency   Having enough money to pay debts as they fall due.

DEMONSTRATION PROBLEM FOR YOUR REVIEW

The accounting data (listed alphabetically) for Crystal Auto Wash at August 31, 19___, are shown on the next page. The figure for Don Johnson, capital is not given but it can be determined when all the available information is assembled in the form of a balance sheet.

Accounts payable	$ 9,000	Land	$40,000
Accounts receivable	800	Machinery & equipment	25,000
Building	35,000	Notes payable	49,000
Cash	4,200	Salaries payable	3,000
Don Johnson, capital	?	Supplies	400

Instructions Prepare a balance sheet at August 31, 19___.

SOLUTION TO DEMONSTRATION PROBLEM

CRYSTAL AUTO WASH
Balance Sheet
August 31, 19___

ASSETS		LIABILITIES & OWNER'S EQUITY	
Cash	$ 4,200	Liabilities:	
Accounts receivable	800	Notes payable	$ 49,000
Supplies	400	Accounts payable	9,000
Land	40,000	Salaries payable	3,000
Building	35,000	Total liabilities	$ 61,000
Machinery & equipment	25,000	Owner's equity:	
		Don Johnson, capital*	44,400
Total	$105,400	Total	$105,400

* Computed as total assets, $105,400 − total liabilities, $61,000 = Don Johnson, capital, $44,400

SELF-TEST QUESTIONS

The answers to these questions appear on page 40.

1 A balance sheet:

a Provides owners, investors, and other interested parties with all of the financial information they need to evaluate the financial strength, profitability, and future prospects of a given business entity.

b Shows the current market value of the owner's equity in the business at the balance sheet date.

c Assists creditors in evaluating the debt-paying ability of a business by showing the assets and liabilities of the business combined with those of its owner (or owners).

d Shows the assets, liabilities, and owner's equity of a business entity, valued in conformity with generally accepted accounting principles.

2 Which of the following statements is not consistent with current generally accepted accounting principles relating to asset valuation?

a Assets are originally recorded in accounting records at their cost to the business entity.

b Accountants assume no business will last forever; therefore, assets are never valued in a balance sheet in excess of their immediate resale value.

c Existing principles of asset valuation produce more reliable results during periods of stable prices than during periods of rapid inflation.

d Accountants prefer to base the valuation of assets upon objective, verifiable evidence rather than upon appraisals or personal opinion.

3 The balance sheet of Arrowhead Boat Shop includes the following items:

Accounts receivable   *Cash*
F. Houston, capital   *Accounts payable*
Equipment   *Supplies*
Notes payable   *Notes receivable*

This list includes:

a Four assets and three liabilities.

b Three liabilities and five assets.

c Five assets and two liabilities.

d Six assets and two liabilities.

4 During the current year, the assets of Clipper's Cuts increased by $29,000, and the liabilities decreased by $7,000. If the owner's equity in the business is $79,000 at the end of the year, the owner's equity at the beginning of the year must have been:

a $57,000   **b** $43,000   **c** $115,000   **d** $101,000

5 A transaction caused a $9,000 decrease in both assets and liabilities. This transaction could have been:

a Purchase of a delivery truck for $9,000 cash.

b Purchase of a delivery truck for $15,000, paying $9,000 cash and issuing a note payable for the balance.

c Repayment of a $9,000 bank loan.

d Collection of a $9,000 account receivable.

Assignment Material

REVIEW QUESTIONS

1 In broad general terms, what is the purpose of accounting?

2 Why is a knowledge of accounting terms and concepts useful to persons other than professional accountants?

3 What is meant by the term *business transaction?*

4 What are financial statements and how do they relate to the accounting system?

5 Explain briefly why each of the following groups is interested in the financial statements of a business:

   a Creditors

   b Potential investors

   c Labor unions

6 Distinguish between accounting and bookkeeping.

7 What is the purpose of an audit? Would a large corporation or a small sole proprietorship be more likely to retain a CPA firm to perform an annual audit? Explain.

8 After earning a degree in accounting, a college graduate might choose to enter any one of several fields or specialized areas of accounting. Which field would involve a work environment most similar to that of attorneys and physicians? Explain.

9 The following questions relate to the term, *generally accepted accounting principles:*

    a What type of accounting reports should be prepared in conformity with these principles?

    b Why is it important for these principles to be widely recognized?

    c Where do these principles come from?

    d List two examples of generally accepted accounting principles which relate to the valuation of assets.

10 What is the principal function of certified public accountants? What other services are commonly rendered by CPA firms?

11 Private accounting includes a number of subfields or specialized phases, of which cost accounting is one. Name three other such specialized phases of private accounting.

12 Is the Financial Accounting Standards Board (FASB) a government agency? What is its principal function?

13 Information available from the accounting records provides a basis for making many business decisions. List several examples of business decisions requiring the use of accounting information.

14 What are the objectives of a company's system of internal control?

15 State briefly the purpose of a balance sheet.

16 Define assets. List several examples.

17 Define liabilities. List examples.

18 Ray Company was offered $300,000 cash for the land and buildings occupied by the business. These assets had been acquired five years ago at a price of $200,000. Ray Company refused the offer, but is inclined to increase the land and buildings to a total valuation of $300,000 in the balance sheet in order to show more accurately "how much the business is worth." Do you agree? Explain.

19 Explain briefly the concept of the *business entity.*

20 The owner's equity in a business arises from what two sources?

21 State the accounting equation in two alternative forms.

22 Why are the total assets shown on a balance sheet always equal to the total of the liabilities and the owner's equity?

23 Can a business transaction cause one asset to increase or decrease without affecting any other asset, liability, or the owner's equity? Explain.

24 If a transaction causes total liabilities to decrease but does not affect the owner's equity, what change, if any, will occur in total assets?

25 Give examples of transactions that would:

    a Cause one asset to increase and another asset to decrease without any effect on the liabilities or owner's equity.

    b Cause both total assets and total liabilities to increase without any effect on the owner's equity.

26 Assume that a business becomes insolvent. Can the owner (or owners) of the business be held personally liable for the debts of the business? Give separate answers assuming that the business is organized as (a) a sole proprietorship, (b) a partnership, and (c) a corporation.

27 Not all the significant happenings in the life of a business can be expressed in monetary terms and entered in the accounting records. Identify two or more significant events affecting a business which could not be satisfactorily measured and entered in its accounting records.

EXERCISES

Exercise 1-1
Accounting
terminology

Listed below are nine technical accounting terms introduced in this chapter.

Cost principle	FASB	Audit
GAAP	Insolvent	Sole proprietorship
SEC	Corporation	Owner's equity

Each of the following statements may (or may not) describe one of these technical terms. For each statement, indicate the accounting term described, or answer "None" if the statement does not correctly describe any of the terms.

a A residual amount equal to total assets minus total liabilities.

b The organization which conducts extensive research in accounting and issues authoritative statements of generally accepted accounting principles.

c Ability to pay debts promptly as they come due.

d The "ground rules" for presenting accounting information in financial statements.

e A study of an accounting system and other evidence for the purpose of expressing a professional opinion on the reliability of a set of financial statements.

f The most common form of business organization in the American economy.

g A government agency concerned with corporate financial statements: their content and reporting standards.

h Valuation of land, buildings, and similar assets at the amount it would cost to replace them at present price levels.

Exercise 1-2
Prepare a
balance sheet

Listed below in alphabetical order are the balance sheet items of Long Company at December 31, 19__. You are to prepare a balance sheet (including a complete heading). The sequence of items should be similar to the illustrated balance sheet on page 14.

Accounts payable	$ 10,200	Jane Long, capital	$165,800
Accounts receivable	29,200	Land	67,000
Building	60,000	Office equipment	5,700
Cash	14,100		

Exercise 1-3
Prepare a
balance sheet

The items appearing in the balance sheet of Gray Company at December 31, 19__, are listed below in random order. You are to prepare a balance sheet (including a complete heading). Arrange the items in the sequence shown in the balance sheet illustrated on page 14 and include a figure for total liabilities. You must compute the amount for John Gray, capital.

Land	$135,000	Office equipment	$ 5,100
Cash	18,150	Accounts payable	21,900
Accounts receivable	28,350	Building	105,000
John Gray, capital	?	Notes payable	97,500

Exercise 1-4
Effect of
transactions on
total assets

The following transactions represent part of the activities of Malibu Company for the first month of its existence. Indicate the effect of each transaction upon the total assets of the business by use of the appropriate phrase: "increase total assets," "decrease total assets," "no change in total assets."

(1) The owner invested cash in the business.

(2) Purchased a typewriter for cash.

(3) Purchased a delivery truck at a price of $4,000, terms $500 cash and the balance payable in 24 equal monthly installments.

(4) Paid a liability.

(5) Borrowed money from a bank.

(6) Sold land for cash at a price equal to its cost.

(7) Sold land on account (on credit) at a price equal to its cost.

(8) Sold land for cash at a price in excess of its cost.

(9) Sold land for cash at a price less than its cost.

Exercise 1-5
Using the
accounting
equation

Compute the missing amount in each of the following three lines.

	ASSETS	LIABILITIES	OWNER'S EQUITY
a	$279,000	$171,000	?
b	?	112,500	$ 75,000
c	615,000	?	285,000

Exercise 1-6
Using the
accounting
equation

a The assets of Dale Company total $250,000 and the owner's equity amounts to $70,000. What is the amount of the liabilities?

b The balance sheet of Spark Company shows owner's equity of $85,000 which is equal to one-third the amount of total assets. What is the amount of liabilities?

c Morgan Company had assets in the amount of $225,000 on December 31, 1989. Assets increased to $315,000 by December 31 of 1990. During this same period, liabilities increased by $75,000. The owner's equity at December 31, 1989 amounted to $150,000. Compute the amount of owner's equity at December 31, 1990. Explain the basis for your answer.

Exercise 1-7
Effects of
business
transactions

For each of the following categories, state concisely a transaction that will have the required effect on the elements of the accounting equation.

a Increase an asset and increase a liability.

b Decrease an asset and decrease a liability.

c Increase one asset and decrease another asset.

d Increase an asset and increase owner's equity.

e Increase one asset, decrease another asset, and increase a liability.

Exercise 1-8
Effects of
business
transactions

A number of business transactions carried out by Green River Farms are shown below:

a Purchased a typewriter on credit.

b Owner invested cash in the business.

c Purchased office equipment for cash.

d Collected an account receivable.

e Owner withdrew cash from the business.

f Paid a liability.

g Returned for credit some of the office equipment previously purchased on credit but not yet paid for.

h Sold land for cash at a price in excess of cost.

i Borrowed money from a bank.

Indicate the effects of each of these transactions upon the total amounts of the company's assets, liabilities, and owner's equity. Organize your answer in tabular form, using the column headings shown below and the symbols + for increase, − for decrease, and NE for no effect. The answer for transaction (a) is provided as an example:

TRANSACTION	ASSETS	LIABILITIES	OWNER'S EQUITY
(a)	+	+	*NE*

PROBLEMS

Group A

Problem 1A-1
Preparing a balance sheet; computing owner's equity

Listed below in random order are the items to be included in the balance sheet of Mystery Mountain Lodge at December 31, 19___:

Accounts receivable	$ 6,200	Furniture	$ 47,800
Cash..........................	17,900	Snowmobiles..................	15,700
Accounts payable	35,800	Equipment	18,400
Daniel Craig, capital	?	Notes payable.................	352,000
Buildings.....................	296,000	Land..........................	115,000

Instructions

Prepare a balance sheet at December 31, 19___. Include a proper heading and organize your balance sheet similar to the illustration on page 14. (After "Buildings," you may list the remaining assets in any order.) You will need to compute the amount of owner's equity.

Problem 1A-2
Preparing a balance sheet; effects of a change in assets

Here Comes Tiger! is the name of a traveling circus owned by Tiger Hayes. The ledger accounts of the business at June 30 are listed below in alphabetical order.

Accounts payable	$ 16,900	Notes receivable	$ 2,000
Accounts receivable	9,100	Props and equipment..........	38,600
Animals	60,140	Salaries payable...............	6,700
Cages	15,800	Tents	43,400
Cash..........................	23,120	Tiger Hayes, capital	?
Costumes.....................	6,880	Trucks	46,480
Notes payable.................	118,000	Wagons	27,820

Instructions

a Prepare a balance sheet by using these items and computing the amount of the owner's capital. Organize your balance sheet similar to the one illustrated on page 14. (After "Accounts Receivable," you may list the remaining assets in any order.) Include a proper balance sheet heading.

b Assume that late in the evening of June 30, after your balance sheet had been prepared, a fire destroyed one of the tents, which had cost $12,100. The tent was not insured. Explain what changes would be required in your June 30 balance sheet to reflect the loss of this asset.

Problem 1A-3
Explaining effects of business transactions

Five transactions of Canyon Company are summarized in the table below. The effect of each transaction upon the accounting equation is shown, and also the new balance of each item in the equation. For each of the transactions (a) through (e), you are to write a sentence explaining the nature of the transaction.

		ASSETS				=	LIABILITIES	+	OWNER'S EQUITY
	CASH +	ACCOUNTS RECEIV- ABLE +	LAND +	BUILDING +	OFFICE EQUIP- MENT	=	ACCOUNTS PAYABLE	+	H. LEE, CAPITAL
Balances	$4,000	$7,000	$29,000	$50,000	$7,000		$8,000		$89,000
(a)	−2,600						−2,600		
Balances	$1,400	$7,000	$29,000	$50,000	$7,000		$5,400		$89,000
(b)	+800	−800							
Balances	$2,200	$6,200	$29,000	$50,000	$7,000		$5,400		$89,000
(c)					+700		+700		
Balances	$2,200	$6,200	$29,000	$50,000	$7,700		$6,100		$89,000
(d)	−300				+1,300		+1,000		
Balances	$1,900	$6,200	$29,000	$50,000	$9,000		$7,100		$89,000
(e)	+1,500								+1,500
Balances	$3,400 +	$6,200 +	$29,000 +	$50,000 +	$9,000 =		$7,100	+	$90,500

Problem 1A-4
Recording effects of business transactions

The items making up the balance sheet of Financial Planning Service at June 30 are listed below in tabular form similar to the illustration of the accounting equation on page 24.

		ASSETS			=	LIABILITIES		+	OWNER'S EQUITY
	CASH +	ACCOUNTS RECEIV- ABLE +	AUTO- MOBILES +	OFFICE EQUIP- MENT =	NOTES PAYABLE +	ACCOUNTS PAYABLE	+		D. HALL, CAPITAL
Balances	$6,500	$58,400	$8,000	$3,800	$20,000	$25,200			$31,500

During a short period after June 30, Financial Planning Service had the following transactions.

a Bought office equipment at a cost of $5,700. Paid cash.

b Borrowed $10,000 from a bank. Signed a note payable for that amount.

c Purchased an automobile for $10,500. Paid $3,000 cash and signed a note payable for the balance of $7,500.

d Paid $1,200 of accounts payable.

e Collected $4,000 of accounts receivable.

Instructions You are to construct a table similar to the one illustrated in Problem 1A-3. First, list the June 30 balances of assets, liabilities, and owner's equity in the tabular form shown above. Next, complete the table using a separate line for each transaction. Show the totals (balances) for all columns after each transaction.

Problem 1A-5
Preparing a balance sheet; effects of business transactions

The balance sheet items for Gremlin Car Wash (arranged in alphabetical order) were as follows at August 1, 19__:

Accounts payable	$ 4,000	Land...........................	$40,000
Accounts receivable	600	Notes payable..................	56,000
Building.......................	20,000	Supplies	2,700
Cash...........................	3,400	Susan Young, capital	?
Equipment	23,000		

During the next two days, the following transactions occurred:

Aug. 2   Young invested an additional $10,000 cash in the business. The accounts payable were paid in full. (No payment was made on the notes payable.)

3   Equipment was purchased at a cost of $6,000 to be paid within 10 days. Supplies were purchased for $500 cash from another car-washing concern which was going out of business. These supplies would have cost $900 if purchased through normal channels.

Instructions   **a** Prepare a balance sheet at August 1, 19__. Include a proper heading.

b Prepare a balance sheet at August 3, 19__. Include a proper heading.

Problem 1A-6
Preparing a
balance sheet;
discussion of
accounting
principles

Melonie Austin, owner and manager of Old Town Playhouse, needs to obtain a bank loan to finance the production of the company's next play. As part of the loan application, Austin was asked to prepare a balance sheet for the business. She prepared the following balance sheet, which is arranged correctly, but contains several errors with respect to such concepts as the business entity and the valuation of assets, liabilities, and owner's equity:

OLD TOWN PLAYHOUSE
Balance Sheet
September 30, 19__

ASSETS		LIABILITIES & OWNER'S EQUITY	
Cash	$ 17,900	Liabilities:	
Accounts receivable	153,100	Accounts payable	$ 4,900
Props and costumes	1,500	Salaries payable	31,600
Theater building	18,000	Total liabilities	$ 36,500
Lighting equipment	7,600	Owner's equity:	
Automobile	13,000	Melonie Austin, capital	9,000
Total	$211,100	Total	$ 45,500

In discussions with Austin and by reviewing the accounting records of Old Town Playhouse, you discover the following facts:

(1) The $17,900 amount for cash shown in the above balance sheet consists of $11,000 in the company's bank account, $1,900 on hand in the company's safe, and $5,000 in Austin's personal savings account.

(2) The accounts receivable, listed as $153,100, include $5,100 owed to the business by Artistic Tours. The remaining $148,000 is Austin's estimate of future ticket sales from September 30 through the end of the year (December 31).

(3) Austin explains to you that the props and costumes were purchased several days ago for $16,500. The business paid $1,500 of this amount in cash and issued a note payable to Actors' Supply Co. for the remainder of the purchase price ($15,000). As this note need not be paid until January of next year, it was not included among the company's liabilities.

(4) Old Town Playhouse rents the theater building from Kievits International at a rate of $2,000 a month. The $18,000 shown in the balance sheet represents the rent paid through September 30 of the current year. Kievits International acquired the building seven years ago at a cost of $135,000.

(5) The lighting equipment was purchased on September 26 at a cost of $7,600, but the stage manager says that it isn't worth a dime.

(6) The automobile is Austin's classic 1955 Porsche, which she purchased two years ago for $9,000. She recently saw a similar car advertised for sale at $13,000. She does not use the car in the business, but it has a personalized license plate which reads "PLAHOUS."

(7) The accounts payable include business debts of $3,800 and the $1,100 balance of Austin's personal Visa card.

(8) Salaries payable includes $28,000 offered to Mario Dane to play the lead role in a new play opening next December and also $3,600 still owed to stage hands for work done through September 30.

(9) When Austin founded Old Town Playhouse four years ago, she invested $9,000 in the business. She has shown this amount as her owner's equity in order to comply with the cost principle. However, Live Theater, Inc., has offered to buy her business for $35,000, and she believes that perhaps the owner's equity should be changed to this amount.

Instructions **a** Prepare a corrected balance sheet for Old Town Playhouse at September 30, 19___.

b For each of the nine numbered items above, explain your reasoning in deciding whether or not to include the items in the balance sheet and in determining the proper dollar valuation.

Group B

Problem 1B-1
Preparing a balance sheet; computing owner's equity

Listed below in random order are the items to be included in the balance sheet of Pearl Beach Resort at December 31, 19___:

Sailboats......................	$ 14,600	Buildings......................	$225,000
Land..........................	210,000	Cash..........................	12,200
Accounts receivable..........	4,800	Furnishings	29,100
Accounts payable	13,500	Notes payable.................	320,000
Equipment	9,200	Nancy Moore, capital..........	?

Prepare a balance sheet at December 31, 19___. Include a proper heading and organize your balance sheet similar to the illustration on page 14. (After "Buildings," you may list the remaining assets in any order.) You will need to compute the amount of owner's equity.

Problem 1B-2
Preparing a balance sheet; effect of a change in assets

Shown below in random order is a list of balance sheet items for Valencia Farms at September 30, 19___.

Land..........................	$305,000	Fences & gates	$ 18,650
Barns and sheds	43,500	Irrigation system	11,180
Notes payable.................	295,000	Cash..........................	9,285
Accounts receivable..........	12,425	Livestock	67,100
Citrus trees	42,600	Farm machinery	23,872
Accounts payable	42,830	Walter Berkeley, capital........	?
Property taxes payable	5,075	Wages payable	1,010

Instructions **a** Prepare a balance sheet by using these items and computing the amount for Walter Berkeley's capital. Use a sequence of assets similar to that illustrated on page 14. (After "Barns and sheds," you may list the remaining assets in any order.) Include a proper heading for your balance sheet.

b Assume that immediately after this September 30 balance sheet was prepared, a tornado completely destroyed one of the barns. This barn had a cost of $18,400, and was not insured against this type of disaster. Explain what changes would be required in your September 30 balance sheet to reflect the loss of this barn.

Problem 1B-3
Explaining effects
of business
transactions

Five selected transactions of JD Mortgage Co. are summarized in the table below. The effect of each transaction upon the accounting equation is shown, and also the new balance of each item in the equation. For each of the transactions (a) through (e), you are to write a sentence explaining the nature of the transaction.

	CASH	+	ACCOUNTS RECEIVABLE	+	LAND	+	BUILDING	+	OFFICE EQUIP- MENT	=	ACCOUNTS PAYABLE	+	J. DAY, CAPITAL
											LIABIL- ITIES		OWNER'S EQUITY
			ASSETS										
Balances	$3,000		$9,000		$35,000		$55,000		$3,000		$12,000		$93,000
(a)									+800		+800		
Balances	$3,000		$9,000		$35,000		$55,000		$3,800		$12,800		$93,000
(b)	−1,200										−1,200		
Balances	$1,800		$9,000		$35,000		$55,000		$3,800		$11,600		$93,000
(c)	+1,500		−1,500										
Balances	$3,300		$7,500		$35,000		$55,000		$3,800		$11,600		$93,000
(d)	−300								+900		+600		
Balances	$3,000		$7,500		$35,000		$55,000		$4,700		$12,200		$93,000
(e)	+5,000												+5,000
Balances	$8,000	+	$7,500	+	$35,000	+	$55,000	+	$4,700	=	$12,200	+	$98,000

Problem 1B-4
Recording effects
of business
transactions

Travel Connection was organized on September 1 and completed the following transactions within a short time.

a K. Bell deposited $35,000 of personal funds in a bank account in the name of the new company.

b Purchased land and a building for a total price of $80,000, of which $30,000 was the value of the land and $50,000 was the value of the building. Paid $20,000 in cash and signed a note payable for the remaining $60,000.

c Bought office equipment on credit for $9,500 (30-day open account).

d Obtained a bank loan in the amount of $8,000. Signed a note payable.

e Paid $6,000 of the accounts payable.

f K. Bell invested an additional $3,000 of personal funds in the business by depositing cash in the company bank account.

Instructions

Construct a tabular arrangement of the accounting equation as illustrated on page 24. The column headings should be as follows:

		ASSETS			=		LIABILITIES		+	OWNER'S EQUITY
CASH	+ LAND	+ BUILDING	+ OFFICE EQUIP- MENT	=	NOTES PAYABLE	+	ACCOUNTS PAYABLE	+	K. BELL, CAPITAL	

Use a separate line of the table to show the effects of each transaction on the assets, liabilities, and owner's equity. Identify each transaction by letter along the left margin of the table. Show totals for all columns after transaction (b) and after each subsequent transaction.

Problem 1B-5
Preparing a
balance sheet

At August 1, the balance sheet items (arranged in alphabetical order) for Gold Coast Restaurant were as follows:

Accounts payable	$ 9,500	Land	$55,000
Accounts receivable	1,250	Kay Martin, capital	?
Building	45,500	Notes payable	75,000
Cash	8,400	Supplies	3,440
Furniture	20,000		

The following transactions occurred during the next two days:

Aug. 2   Martin invested an additional $30,000 cash in the business. The accounts payable were paid in full. (No payment was made on the notes payable.)

Aug. 3   More furniture was purchased at a cost of $18,000 to be paid within 30 days. Supplies were purchased for $1,000 cash from a restaurant supply center which was going out of business. These supplies would have cost $1,875 if purchased under normal circumstances.

Instructions   **a**   Prepare a balance sheet at August 1, 19___.

  b   Prepare a balance sheet at August 3, 19___.

Problem 1B-6
Preparing a
balance sheet;
discussion of
accounting
principles

Hollywood Scripts is a service-type enterprise in the entertainment field, and its owner, Brad Jones, has only a limited knowledge of accounting. Jones prepared the following balance sheet, which, although arranged satisfactorily, contains certain errors with respect to such concepts as the business entity and asset valuation.

HOLLYWOOD SCRIPTS
Balance Sheet
November 30, 19___

ASSETS		LIABILITIES & OWNER'S EQUITY	
Cash	$ 690	Liabilities:	
Notes receivable	2,900	Notes payable	$ 67,000
Accounts receivable	2,465	Accounts payable	29,649
Land	70,000	Total liabilities	$ 96,649
Building	54,326	Owner's equity:	
Office furniture	6,947	Brad Jones, capital	63,080
Other assets	22,401		
Total	$159,729	Total	$159,729

By talking with Jones and inspecting the accounting records, you find the following:

(1) One of the notes receivable in the amount of $700 is an IOU which Jones received in a poker game about two years ago. The IOU bears only the initials B.K. and Jones does not know the name or address of the maker.

(2) Office furniture includes an antique desk purchased November 29 of the current year at a cost of $2,100. Jones explains that no payment is due for the desk until January and therefore this debt is not included among the liabilities.

(3) Also included in the amount for office furniture is a typewriter which cost $525 but is not on hand, because Jones gave it to a son as a birthday present.

(4) The "Other assets" of $22,401 represents the total amount of income taxes Jones has paid the federal government over a period of years. Jones believes the income tax law to be unconstitutional, and a friend who attends law school will help Jones recover the taxes paid as soon as he completes his legal education.

(5) The land had cost $34,000, but was increased to $70,000 when a friend of Jones offered to pay that much for it if Jones would move the building off the lot.

CHAPTER 1

Instructions **a** Prepare a corrected balance sheet at November 30, 19___.

b For each of the five numbered items above, use a separate numbered paragraph to explain whether the treatment followed by Jones is in accord with generally accepted accounting principles.

BUSINESS DECISION CASE

Case 1-1
Using a balance sheet in business decisions

Adams Company and Baker Company are in the same line of business and both were recently organized, so it may be assumed that the recorded costs for assets are close to current market values. Balance sheets for the two companies are as follows.

ADAMS COMPANY
Balance Sheet
July 31, 19___

ASSETS		LIABILITIES & OWNER'S EQUITY	
Cash..........................	$ 4,800	Liabilities:	
Accounts receivable	9,600	Notes payable	
Land..........................	96,000	(due in 60 days)	$ 22,400
Building.......................	60,000	Accounts payable	43,200
Office equipment	12,000	Total liabilities..............	$ 65,600
		Owner's equity:	
		Jill Adams, capital	116,800
Total..........................	$182,400	Total..........................	$182,400

BAKER COMPANY
Balance Sheet
July 31, 19___

ASSETS		LIABILITIES & OWNER'S EQUITY	
Cash..........................	$ 18,000	Liabilities:	
Accounts receivable	26,000	Notes payable	
Land..........................	37,200	(due in 60 days)	$ 12,400
Building.......................	38,000	Accounts payable	9,600
Office equipment	1,200	Total liabilities..............	$ 22,000
		Owner's equity:	
		Ed Baker, capital	98,400
Total..........................	$120,400	Total..........................	$120,400

Instructions **a** Assume that you are a banker and that each company has applied to you for a 90-day loan of $12,000. Which is the more favorable prospect? Explain fully.

b Assume that you are an investor considering the purchase of one or both of the companies. Both Jill Adams and Ed Baker have indicated to you that they would consider selling their respective businesses. In either transaction you would assume the existing liabilities. For which business would you pay the higher price? Explain fully. (It is recognized that for either decision, additional information would be useful, but you are to reach your decisions on the basis of the information available.)

ANSWERS TO SELF-TEST QUESTIONS
1 d   2 b   3 c   4 b   5 c

Recording Changes in Financial Position

In this chapter we explain the principles of double-entry accounting and introduce the accounting cycle—the procedures used by a business in recording, classifying, and summarizing business transactions. The activities of Roberts Real Estate Company, which were described in Chapter 1, are now recorded in the company's general journal and posted to the general ledger accounts. The preparation of a trial balance also is illustrated, and the uses and limitations of the trial balance are discussed. The chapter concludes by comparing the accounting procedures in manual accounting systems with those in computer-based systems.

After studying this chapter you should be able to meet these Learning Objectives:

1 Describe a ledger account and a ledger.

2 State the rules of debit and credit for balance sheet accounts.

3 Explain the double-entry system of accounting.

4 Explain the purpose of a journal and its relationship to the ledger.

5 Prepare journal entries to record common business transactions and post this information to ledger accounts.

6 Prepare a trial balance and explain its uses and limitations.

7 Describe the basic steps of the accounting cycle in both manual and computer-based accounting systems.

The Role of Accounting Records

Many businesses enter into hundreds or even thousands of business transactions each day. It would not be practical to prepare a balance sheet after each transaction, and it is quite unnecessary to do so. Instead, the many individual transactions are recorded in the accounting records, and, at the end of the month or other accounting period, a balance sheet is prepared from these records. In this chapter, we shall see how business transactions are analyzed, entered in the accounting records, and classified for use in preparing a balance sheet. In later chapters, we shall also see that the accounting records contain the data necessary to prepare an income statement, income tax returns, and other financial reports.

THE LEDGER

Objective 1
Describe a ledger
account and a
ledger.

An accounting system includes a separate record for each item that appears in the balance sheet. For example, a separate record is kept for the asset cash, showing all the increases and decreases in cash which result from the many transactions in which cash is received or paid. A similar record is kept for every other asset, for every liability, and for owner's equity. The form of record used to record increases and decreases in a single balance sheet item is called an *account,* or sometimes a *ledger account.* In a manual accounting system, these separate accounts are kept in a loose-leaf binder, and the entire group of accounts is called a *ledger.*

The concept of ledger accounts applies to computer-based accounting systems as well as to manual systems. Although computer-based systems store accounting data on magnetic discs rather than in loose-leaf binders, these systems all have the capability of maintaining ledger accounts.

An understanding of accounting concepts is most easily gained by studying a manual accounting system. The knowledge gained by working with manual accounting records is readily transferable to any type of automated accounting system. For these reasons, we shall use standard written accounting records such as ledger accounts in our study of basic accounting concepts. These written records continue to be used by a great many businesses, but for our purposes they should be viewed as *conceptual learning devices* rather than as physical components of an accounting system.

The Use of Ledger Accounts

A ledger account is a means of accumulating in one place all the information about changes in a specific asset, a liability, or owner's equity. For example, a ledger account for the asset cash provides a record of the amount of cash receipts, cash payments, and the current cash balance. By maintaining a Cash account, management can keep track of the amount of cash available for meeting payrolls and for making current purchases of assets or services. This record of cash is also useful in planning future operations and in advance planning of applications for bank loans.

In its simplest form, an account has only three elements: (1) a title, consisting of the name of the particular asset, liability, or owner's equity; (2) a left side, which is called the *debit* side; and (3) a right side, which is called the *credit* side. This form of account, illustrated below, is called a *T account* because of its resemblance to the letter T.

T account: a
ledger account in
simplified form

TITLE OF ACCOUNT

Left or debit side   *Right or credit side*

Debit and Credit Entries

What are debits and credits? Accountants use these terms simply to describe the left and right sides of a ledger account. An amount recorded on the *left* side of a ledger account is called a *debit,* or a *debit entry.* An amount entered on the *right* side of an account is called a *credit,* or a *credit entry.* Accountants also use the words "debit" and "credit" as verbs. The act of recording a debit entry is called *debiting* the account; recording a credit entry is called *crediting* the account.

Students beginning a course in accounting often have erroneous notions about the meanings of the terms debit and credit. For example, to some people unacquainted with accounting, the word credit may carry a more favorable connotation than does the word debit. Such connotations have no validity in the field of accounting. Accountants use *debit* to mean an entry on the left-hand side of an account, and *credit* to mean an entry on the right-hand side. Thus, debit and credit simply mean left and right, without any hidden or subtle implications.

To illustrate the recording of debits and credits in an account, let us go back to the cash transactions of Roberts Real Estate Company as illustrated in Chapter 1. When these cash transactions are recorded in an account, the receipts are listed in vertical order on the debit side of the account and the payments are listed on the credit side. The dates of the transactions may also be listed, as shown in the following illustration:

■
Cash transactions entered in ledger account

	CASH				
9/1		180,000	9/3		141,000
9/20		1,500	9/5		15,000
	181,500		9/30	159,000	3,000
9/30 Balance		22,500			

Each debit and credit entry in the Cash account represents a cash receipt or a cash payment. The amount of cash owned by the business at a given date is equal to the *balance* of the account on that date.

■ **Determining the Balance of a T Account**   The balance of a ledger account is the difference in dollars between the total debits and the total credits in the account. If the debit total exceeds the credit total, the account has a *debit balance;* if the credit total exceeds the debit total, the account has a *credit balance.*

In our illustrated Cash account, a rule has been drawn across the account following the last cash transaction recorded in September. The total cash receipts (debits) recorded in September amount to *$181,500* and the total cash payments (credits) amount to *$159,000.* These totals, called *footings,* are entered in small-size figures just above the rule. (Notice that these footings are written well to the left of the regular money columns so that they will not be mistaken for debit or credit entries.) By subtracting the credit total from the debit total ($181,500 − $159,000), we determine that the Cash account has a debit balance of *$22,500* on September 30.

This debit balance is entered in the debit side of the account just below the rule. In effect, the horizontal rule creates a "fresh start" in our T account, with the month-end balance representing the **net result** of all of the previous debit and credit entries. The Cash account now shows the amount of cash owned by the business on September 30. In a balance sheet prepared at this date, Cash in the amount of $22,500 would be listed as an asset.

Objective 2
State the rules of debit and credit for balance sheet accounts.

■ **Debit Balances in Asset Accounts** In the preceding illustration of a cash account, increases were recorded on the left or debit side of the account and decreases were recorded on the right or credit side. The increases were greater than the decreases and the result was a debit balance in the account.

All asset accounts **normally have debit balances;** in fact, the ownership of cash, land, or any other asset indicates that the increases (debits) to that asset have been greater than the decreases (credits). It is hard to imagine an account for an asset such as land having a credit balance, as this would indicate that the business had disposed of more land than it had acquired and had reached the impossible position of having a negative amount of land.

The fact that assets are located on the **left** side of the balance sheet is a convenient means of remembering the rule that an increase in an asset is recorded on the **left** (debit) side of the account, and also that an asset account normally has a debit **(left-hand)** balance.

■
Asset accounts normally have debit balances

ANY ASSET ACCOUNT	
(Debit) *Increase*	*(Credit)* *Decrease*

■ **Credit Balances in Liability and Owner's Equity Accounts** Increases in liability and owner's equity accounts are recorded by credit entries and decreases in these accounts are recorded by debits. The relationship between entries in these accounts and their position on the balance sheet may be summed up as follows: (1) liabilities and owner's equity belong on the **right** side of the balance sheet; (2) an increase in a liability or an owner's equity account is recorded on the **right** (credit) side of the account; and (3) liability and owner's equity accounts normally have credit **(right-hand)** balances.

■
Liability and owner's equity accounts normally have credit balances

ANY LIABILITY ACCOUNT OR OWNER'S EQUITY ACCOUNT	
(Debit) *Decrease*	*(Credit)* *Increase*

■ **Concise Statement of the Rules of Debit and Credit** The use of debits and credits to record changes in assets, liabilities, and owner's equity may be summarized as follows:

ASSET ACCOUNTS	LIABILITY & OWNER'S EQUITY ACCOUNTS
Increases are recorded by debits *Decreases are recorded by credits*	*Increases are recorded by* credits *Decreases are recorded by* **debits**

Double-Entry Accounting—the Equality of Debits and Credits

Objective 3
Explain the double-entry system of accounting.

The rules for debits and credits are designed so that *every transaction is recorded by equal dollar amounts of debits and credits.* The reason for this equality lies in the relationship of the debit and credit rules to the accounting equation:

$$\text{Assets} = \text{Liabilities} + \text{Owner's Equity}$$

If this equation is to remain in balance, any change in the left side of the equation (assets) *must be accompanied by an equal change* in the right-hand side (either liabilities or owner's equity). According to the debit and credit rules that we have just described, increases in the left side of the equation (assets) are recorded by *debits,* while increases in the right side (liabilities and owner's equity) are recorded by *credits.*

This system is often called *double-entry accounting.* The phrase "double-entry" refers to the need for both debit entries and credit entries (equal in dollar amount) to record every transaction. Virtually every business organization uses the double-entry system regardless of whether the company's accounting records are maintained manually or by computer. In addition, the double-entry system allows us to measure net income at the same time as we record the effects of transactions upon the balance sheet accounts. (The measurement of net income is discussed in Chapter 3.)

Double-entry accounting is not a new idea. The system has been in use for more than 600 years. The first systematic presentation of the double-entry system appears in a mathematics textbook written by Luca Pacioli, a friend of Leonardo da Vinci. This text was published in 1494—just two years after Columbus discovered America. Although Pacioli wrote the first textbook on this subject, surviving accounting records show that double-entry accounting had already been in use for at least 150 years.

Recording Transactions in Ledger Accounts: Illustration

The use of debits and credits for recording transactions in ledger accounts now will be illustrated using the September transactions of Roberts Real Estate Company. Each transaction will first be analyzed in terms of increases and decreases in assets, liabilities, and owner's equity. Then we shall follow the rules of debit and credit in entering these increases and decreases in T accounts. Asset accounts will be shown on the left side of the page; liability and owner's equity accounts on the right side. For convenience in following the transactions into the ledger accounts, the letter used to identify a given transaction will also appear opposite the debit and credit entries in the ledger. (This use of identifying letters is for illustrative purposes only and is not used in actual accounting practice.)

■ **Transaction (a)**   Roberts invested $180,000 cash in the business on September 1.

ANALYSIS	RULE	ENTRY
The asset Cash was increased	*Increases in assets are recorded by debits*	*Debit: Cash, $180,000*
The owner's equity was increased	*Increases in owner's equity are recorded by credits*	*Credit: James Roberts, Capital, $180,000*

CASH		JAMES ROBERTS, CAPITAL	
9/1 (a) 180,000			*9/1 (a) 180,000*

■ **Transaction (b)**   On September 3, Roberts Real Estate Company purchased land for cash in the amount of $141,000.

ANALYSIS	RULE	ENTRY
The asset Land was increased	*Increases in assets are recorded by debits*	*Debit: Land, $141,000*
The asset Cash was decreased	*Decreases in assets are recorded by credits*	*Credit: Cash, $141,000*

CASH		
9/1 180,000	*9/3*	*(b) 141,000*

LAND	
9/3 (b) 141,000	

■ **Transaction (c)**   On September 5, Roberts Real Estate Company purchased a building from Kent Company at a total price of $36,000. The terms of the purchase required a cash payment of $15,000 with the remainder of $21,000 payable within 90 days.

ANALYSIS	RULE	ENTRY
A new asset, Building, was acquired	*Increases in assets are recorded by debits*	*Debit: Building, $36,000*
The asset Cash was decreased	*Decreases in assets are recorded by credits*	*Credit: Cash, $15,000*
A new liability, Accounts Payable, was incurred	*Increases in liabilities are recorded by credits*	*Credit: Accounts Payable, $21,000*

CASH				ACCOUNTS PAYABLE		
9/1	180,000	9/3	141,000		9/5	(c) 21,000
		9/5	(c) 15,000			

BUILDING	
9/5	(c) 36,000

■ **Transaction (d)**   On September 10, Roberts Real Estate Company sold a portion of its land on credit to Carter's Drugstore for a price of $11,000. The land was sold at its cost, so there was no gain or loss on the transaction.

■
Sale of land on credit (no gain or loss)

ANALYSIS	RULE	ENTRY
A new asset, Accounts Receivable, was acquired	Increases in assets are recorded by debits	Debit: Accounts Receivable, $11,000
The asset Land was decreased	Decreases in assets are recorded by credits	Credit: Land, $11,000

ACCOUNTS RECEIVABLE	
9/10	(d) 11,000

LAND			
9/3	141,000	9/10	(d) 11,000

■ **Transaction (e)**   On September 14, Roberts Real Estate Company purchased office equipment on credit from General Equipment, Inc., in the amount of $5,400.

■
Purchase of an asset on credit

ANALYSIS	RULE	ENTRY
A new asset, Office Equipment, was acquired	Increases in assets are recorded by debits	Debit: Office Equipment, $5,400
A new liability, Accounts Payable, was incurred	Increases in liabilities are recorded by credits	Credit: Accounts Payable, $5,400

OFFICE EQUIPMENT		ACCOUNTS PAYABLE		
9/14	(e) 5,400		9/5	21,000
			9/14	(e) 5,400

■ Transaction (f) On September 20, cash of $1,500 was received as partial collection of the account receivable from Carter's Drugstore.

<table>
<tr><th>ANALYSIS</th><th>RULE</th><th>ENTRY</th></tr>
<tr><td>The asset Cash was increased</td><td>Increases in assets are recorded by debits</td><td>Debit: Cash, $1,500</td></tr>
<tr><td>The asset Accounts Receivable was decreased</td><td>Decreases in assets are recorded by credits</td><td>Credit: Accounts Receivable, $1,500</td></tr>
</table>

Collection of an account receivable

CASH

9/1	180,000	9/3		141,000
9/20	(f) 1,500	9/5		15,000

ACCOUNTS RECEIVABLE

9/10	11,000	9/20	(f) 1,500

■ Transaction (g) A cash payment of $3,000 was made on September 30 in partial settlement of the amount owing to General Equipment, Inc.

<table>
<tr><th>ANALYSIS</th><th>RULE</th><th>ENTRY</th></tr>
<tr><td>The liability Accounts Payable was decreased</td><td>Decreases in liabilities are recorded by debits</td><td>Debit: Accounts Payable, $3,000</td></tr>
<tr><td>The asset Cash was decreased</td><td>Decreases in assets are recorded by credits</td><td>Credit: Cash, $3,000</td></tr>
</table>

Payment of a liability

CASH

9/1	180,000	9/3		141,000
9/20	1,500	9/5		15,000
		9/30	(g)	3,000

ACCOUNTS PAYABLE

9/30	(g) 3,000	9/5		21,000
		9/14		5,400

Running Balance Form of Accounts

T accounts are widely used in the classroom and in accounting textbooks, because they provide a concise conceptual picture of the financial effects of a business transaction. In actual practice, however, most businesses prefer to use the ***running balance*** form of ledger account. This form of account has special columns for recording additional information, as illustrated below with the Cash account of Roberts Real Estate Company:

				CASH					Account No.	*1*
DATE		EXPLANATION	REF	DEBIT		CREDIT		BALANCE		
19__										
Sept	*1*			180 000 00				180 000 00		
	3					141 000 00		39 000 00		
	5					15 000 00		24 000 00		
	20			1 500 00				25 500 00		
	30					3 000 00		22 500 00		

The **Date** column shows the date of the transaction—which is not necessarily the same as the date the entry is recorded in the account. The **Explanation** column is needed only for unusual items, and in many companies it is seldom used. The **Ref** (Reference) column is used to list the page number of the journal in which the transaction is recorded, thus making it possible to trace ledger entries back to their source. (The use of a **journal** is explained later in this chapter.) In the **Balance** column of the account, the new balance is entered each time the account is debited or credited. Thus the current balance of the account can always be observed at a glance.

■ **The "Normal" Balance of an Account** The running balance form of ledger account does not indicate specifically whether the balance of the account is a debit or credit balance. However, this causes no difficulty because we know that asset accounts normally have debit balances and that accounts for liabilities and owner's equity normally have credit balances.

Occasionally an asset account may temporarily acquire a credit balance, either as the result of an accounting error or because of an unusual transaction. For example, an account receivable may acquire a credit balance because of overpayment by a customer. However, a credit balance in the Building account could be created only by an accounting error.

■ **Sequence and Numbering of Ledger Accounts** Accounts are usually arranged in the ledger in **financial statement order,** that is, assets first, followed by liabilities, owner's equity, revenue, and expenses. The number of accounts needed by a business will depend upon its size, the nature of its operations, and the extent to which management and regulatory agencies want detailed classification of information. An identification number is assigned to each account. A **chart of accounts** is a listing of the account titles and account numbers being used by a given business.

In the following list of accounts, certain numbers have not been assigned; these numbers are held in reserve so that additional accounts can be inserted in the ledger in proper sequence whenever such accounts become necessary. In this illustration, the numbers from 1 to 29 are used exclusively for asset accounts; numbers from 30 to 49 are reserved for liabilities; and numbers in the 50s signify owner's equity accounts. Numbers in the 60s represent revenue accounts and numbers from 70 to 99 designate expense accounts. Revenue and expense will be discussed in Chapter 3. The balance sheet accounts used thus far in our Roberts Real Estate illustration are numbered as shown in the following *chart of accounts:*

System for numbering ledger accounts

ACCOUNT TITLE	ACCOUNT NO.
Assets:	
Cash	*1*
Accounts Receivable	*4*
Land	*20*
Building	*22*
Office Equipment	*25*
Liabilities:	
Accounts Payable	*32*
Owner's Equity:	
James Roberts, Capital	*50*

In large businesses with hundreds or thousands of accounts, a more elaborate numbering system is used. Some companies use an eight or ten digit number for each ledger account; each of the digits carries special significance as to the classification of the account.

■ **Sequence of Asset Accounts**   As shown in all the balance sheets we have illustrated, cash is listed first among the assets. It is followed by such assets as marketable securities, short-term notes receivable, accounts receivable, inventories of merchandise, and supplies. These are the most common examples of current assets. The term *current assets* includes cash and those assets which will quickly be converted into cash or used up in operations. Next on the balance sheet come the relatively permanent assets used in the business (often called *plant assets*). Of this group, land is listed first and is followed by buildings. After these two items, any order is acceptable for other assets used in the business, such as automobiles, furniture and fixtures, computers, lighting equipment, store equipment, etc.

THE JOURNAL

Objective 4
Explain the purpose of a journal and its relationship to the ledger.

In our preceding discussion, we recorded business transactions directly in the company's ledger accounts. We did this in order to stress the effects of business transactions upon the individual asset, liability, and owner's equity accounts appearing in the company's balance sheet. In an actual accounting system, however, the information about each business transaction is initially recorded in an accounting record called the *journal.* After the transaction has been recorded in the journal, the debit and credit changes in the individual accounts are entered in the ledger. Since the journal is the accounting record in which transactions are *first recorded,* it is sometimes called the *book of original entry.*

The journal is a chronological (day-by-day) record of business transactions. The information recorded about each transaction includes the date of the transaction, the debit and credit changes in specific ledger accounts, and a brief explanation of the transaction. At convenient intervals, the debit and credit amounts recorded in the journal are transferred *(posted)* to the accounts in the ledger. The updated ledger accounts, in turn, serve as the basis for preparing the balance sheet and other financial statements.

Why Use a Journal?

Since it is technically possible to record transactions directly in the ledger, why bother to maintain a journal? The answer is that the unit of organization for the journal is the *transaction,* whereas the unit of organization for the ledger is the *account.* By having both a journal and a ledger, we achieve several advantages which would not be possible if transactions were recorded directly in ledger accounts:

1 The journal shows all information about a transaction in one place and also provides an explanation of the transaction In a journal entry, the debits and credits for a given transaction are recorded together, but when the transaction is recorded in the ledger, the debits and credits are entered in different accounts. Since a ledger may contain hundreds of accounts, it would be very difficult to locate all the facts about a particular transaction by looking in the ledger. The journal is the record which shows the complete story of a transaction in one entry.

2 The journal provides a chronological record of all the events in the life of a business If we want to look up the facts about a transaction of some months or years back, all we need is the date of the transaction in order to locate it in the journal.

3 The use of a journal helps to prevent errors If transactions were recorded directly in the ledger, it would be very easy to make errors such as omitting the debit or the credit, or entering the debit twice or the credit twice. Such errors are not likely to be made in the journal, since the offsetting debits and credits appear together for each transaction.

The General Journal: Illustration of Entries

Objective 5
Prepare journal entries to record common business transactions and post this information to ledger accounts.

Many businesses maintain several types of journals. The nature of operations and the volume of transactions in the particular business determine the number and type of journals needed. The simplest type of journal is called a *general journal* and is shown below. A general journal has only two money columns, one for debits and the other for credits; it may be used for all types of transactions.

The process of recording a transaction in a journal is called *journalizing* the transaction. To illustrate the use of the general journal, we shall now journalize the September transactions of Roberts Real Estate Company which have been discussed previously.

Efficient use of a general journal requires two things: (1) ability to analyze the effect of a transaction upon assets, liabilities, and owner's equity; and (2) familiarity with the standard form and arrangement of journal entries. Our primary interest is in the analytical phase of journalizing; the procedural steps can be learned quickly by observing the following points in the illustration of journal entries:

1 The year, month, and day of the first entry on the page are written in the

GENERAL JOURNAL			Page /	
DATE	ACCOUNT TITLES AND EXPLANATION	LP	DEBIT	CREDIT
19—				
Sept 1	Cash		180000	
	James Roberts, Capital			180000
	Invested cash in the business			
3	Land		141000	
	Cash			141000
	Purchased land for office site			
5	Building		36000	
	Cash			15000
	Accounts Payable			21000
	Purchased building to be moved			
	to our lot. Paid part cash;			
	balance payable within 90			
	days to Kent Company			
10	Accounts Receivable		11000	
	Land			11000
	Sold the unused part of our			
	lot at cost to Carter's Drugstore.			
	Due within 3 months.			
14	Office Equipment		5400	
	Accounts Payable			5400
	Purchased equipment on credit			
	from General Equipment, Inc.			
20	Cash		1500	
	Accounts Receivable			1500
	Collected part of receivable from			
	Carter's Drugstore.			
30	Accounts Payable		3000	
	Cash			3000
	Made partial payment of the lia-			
	bility to General Equipment, Inc			

date column. The year and month need not be repeated for subsequent entries until a new page or a new month is begun.

2 The name of the account to be debited is written on the first line of the entry and is customarily placed at the extreme left next to the date column. The amount of the debit is entered on the same line in the *left-hand* money column.

3 The name of the account to be credited is entered on the line below the debit entry and is *indented,* that is, placed about 1 inch to the right of the date column. The amount credited is entered on the same line in the *right-hand* money column.

4 A brief explanation of the transaction begins on the line immediately below the last account credited. This explanation includes any data needed to identify the transaction, such as the name of the customer or supplier. The explanation is not indented.

5 A blank line should be left after each entry. This spacing causes each journal entry to stand out clearly as a separate unit and makes the journal easier to read.

6 An entry which includes more than one debit or more than one credit (such as the entry on September 5) is called a *compound journal entry.* Regardless of how many debits or credits are contained in a compound journal entry, *all the debits* are entered *before any credits* are listed.

7 The LP (ledger page) column just to the left of the debit money column is left blank at the time of making the journal entry. When the debits and credits are later transferred to ledger accounts, the numbers of the ledger accounts will be listed in this column to provide a convenient cross reference with the ledger.

In journalizing transactions, remember that the *exact title* of the ledger accounts to be debited and credited should be used. For example, in recording the purchase of office equipment for cash, *do not* make a journal entry debiting "Office Equipment Purchased" and crediting "Cash Paid Out." There are no ledger accounts with such titles. The proper journal entry would consist of a debit to *Office Equipment* and a credit to *Cash.*

A familiarity with the general journal form of describing transactions is just as essential to the study of accounting as a familiarity with plus and minus signs is to the study of mathematics. The journal entry is a *tool* for *analyzing* and *describing* the impact of various transactions upon a business entity. The ability to describe a transaction in journal entry form requires an understanding of the nature of the transaction and its effects upon the financial position of the business.

Posting

The process of transferring the debits and credits from the general journal to the proper ledger accounts is called *posting.* Each amount listed in the debit column of the journal is posted by entering it on the debit side of an account in the ledger, and each amount listed in the credit column of the journal is posted to the credit side of a ledger account.

The mechanics of posting may vary somewhat with the preferences of the individual. The following sequence is commonly used:

1 Locate in the ledger the first account named in the journal entry.

2 Enter in the debit column of the ledger account the amount of the debit as shown in the journal.

3 Enter the date of the transaction in the ledger account.

4 Enter in the reference column of the ledger account the number of the journal page from which the entry is being posted.

5 The recording of the debit in the ledger account is now complete; as evidence of this fact, return to the journal and enter in the LP (ledger page) column the number of the ledger account or page to which the debit was posted.

6 Repeat the posting process described in the preceding five steps for the credit side of the journal entry.

■ **Illustration of Posting** To illustrate the posting process, the journal entry for the first transaction of Roberts Real Estate Company is repeated at this point along with the two ledger accounts affected by this entry.

Journal

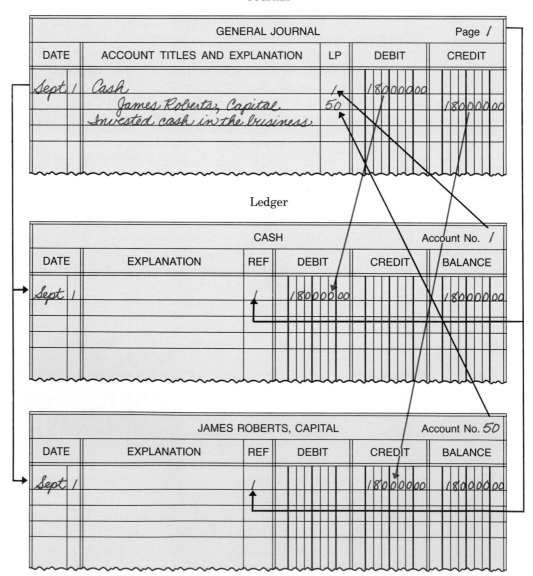

Ledger

Note that the **Ref** (Reference) column of each of the two ledger accounts contains the number 1, indicating that the posting was made from **page 1** of the journal. Entering the journal page number in the ledger account and listing the ledger account number in the journal provide a **cross reference** between these two records. It is often necessary to refer to the journal entry in order to obtain more information about an amount listed in a ledger account. A cross-reference between the ledger and journal is therefore essential to efficient use of the records. Another advantage gained from entering in the journal the number of the ledger account to which a posting has been made is to provide evidence throughout the posting work as to which items have been posted. Otherwise, any interruption in the posting might leave some doubt as to which entries had been posted.

Journalizing and posting by hand is a useful method for the study of accounting, both for problem assignments and for examinations. The manual approach is also followed in many small businesses. One shortcoming is the opportunity for error that exists whenever information is being copied from one record to another. In businesses having a large volume of transactions, the posting of ledger accounts is performed automatically by computer, which speeds up the work and reduces errors.

■ **Ledger Accounts after Posting** After all the September transactions have been posted, the ledger of Roberts Real Estate Company appears as shown below and on page 56. The accounts are arranged in the ledger in the same order as in the balance sheet, that is, assets first, followed by liabilities and owner's equity.

To conserve space in this illustration, several ledger accounts appear on a single page. In actual practice, however, each account occupies a separate page in the ledger.

■ Ledger showing September transactions

CASH					Account No. 1	
DATE	EXPLANATION	REF	DEBIT	CREDIT	BALANCE	
19—						
Sept 1		1	180000 00		180000 00	
3		1		141000 00	39000 00	
5		1		15000 00	24000 00	
20		1	1500 00		25500 00	
30		1		3000 00	22500 00	

ACCOUNTS RECEIVABLE					Account No. 4	
DATE	EXPLANATION	REF	DEBIT	CREDIT	BALANCE	
19—						
Sept 10		1	11000 00		11000 00	
20		1		1500 00	9500 00	

LAND					Account No. 20
DATE	EXPLANATION	REF	DEBIT	CREDIT	BALANCE
19—					
Sept 3		1	141 000 00		141 000 00
10		1		11 000 00	130 000 00

BUILDING					Account No. 22
DATE	EXPLANATION	REF	DEBIT	CREDIT	BALANCE
19—					
Sept 5		1	36 000 00		36 000 00

OFFICE EQUIPMENT					Account No. 25
DATE	EXPLANATION	REF	DEBIT	CREDIT	BALANCE
19—					
Sept 14		1	5400 00		5400 00

ACCOUNTS PAYABLE					Account No. 32
DATE	EXPLANATION	REF	DEBIT	CREDIT	BALANCE
19—					
Sept 5		1		21 000 00	21 000 00
14		1		5400 00	26 400 00
30		1	3000 00		23 400 00

JAMES ROBERTS, CAPITAL					Account No. 50
DATE	EXPLANATION	REF	DEBIT	CREDIT	BALANCE
19—					
Sept 1		1		180 000 00	180 000 00

THE TRIAL BALANCE

Since equal dollar amounts of debits and credits are entered in the accounts for every transaction recorded, the sum of all the debits in the ledger must be equal to the sum of all the credits. If the computation of account balances has been accurate, it follows that the total of the accounts with debit balances must be equal to the total of the accounts with credit balances.

Before using the account balances to prepare a balance sheet, it is desirable to *prove* that the total of accounts with debit balances is in fact equal to the total of accounts with credit balances. This proof of the equality of debit and credit balances is called a *trial balance*. A trial balance is a two-column schedule listing the names and balances of all the accounts *in the order in which they appear in the ledger;* the debit balances are listed in the left-hand column and the credit balances in the right-hand column. The totals of the two columns should agree. A trial balance taken from the ledger of Roberts Real Estate Company follows.

ROBERTS REAL ESTATE COMPANY
Trial Balance
September 30, 19___

Trial balance at month-end proves ledger is in balance

Cash	$ 22,500	
Accounts receivable	9,500	
Land	130,000	
Building	36,000	
Office equipment	5,400	
Accounts payable		$ 23,400
James Roberts, capital		180,000
	$203,400	$203,400

Uses and Limitations of the Trial Balance

The trial balance provides proof that the ledger is in balance. The agreement of the debit and credit totals of the trial balance gives assurance that:

1 Equal debits and credits have been recorded for all transactions.

2 The debit or credit balance of each account has been correctly computed.

3 The addition of the account balances in the trial balance has been correctly performed.

Suppose that the debit and credit totals of the trial balance do not agree. This situation indicates that one or more errors have been made. Typical of such errors are (1) the posting of a debit as a credit, or vice versa; (2) arithmetic mistakes in balancing accounts; (3) clerical errors in copying account balances into the trial balance; (4) listing a debit balance in the credit column of the trial balance, or vice versa; and (5) errors in addition of the trial balance.

The preparation of a trial balance does not prove that transactions have been correctly analyzed and recorded in the proper accounts. If, for example, a receipt of cash were erroneously recorded by debiting the Land account instead of the Cash account, the trial balance would still balance. Also, if a transaction were completely omitted from the ledger, the error would not be disclosed by the trial balance. In brief, *the trial balance proves only one aspect of the ledger, and that is the equality of debits and credits.*

Despite these limitations, the trial balance is a useful device. It not only provides assurance that the ledger is in balance, but it also serves as a convenient steppingstone for the preparation of financial statements. As explained in Chapter 1, the balance sheet is a formal statement showing the financial position of the business, intended for distribution to managers, owners, bankers, and various outsiders. The trial balance, on the other hand, is merely a working paper, useful to the accountant but not intended for distribution to others. The balance sheet and other financial statements can be prepared more conveniently from the trial balance than directly from the ledger, especially if there are a great many ledger accounts.

Locating Errors

In the illustration given, the trial balance was in balance. Every accounting student soon discovers in working problems, however, that errors are easily made which prevent trial balances from balancing. The lack of balance may be the result of a single error or a combination of several errors. An error may have been made in adding the trial balance columns or in copying the balances from the ledger accounts. If the preparation of the trial balance has been accurate, then the error may lie in the accounting records, either in the journal or in the ledger accounts. What is the most efficient approach to locating the error or errors? There is no single technique which will give the best results every time, but the following procedures, done in sequence, will often save considerable time and effort in locating errors.

1 Prove the addition of the trial balance columns by adding these columns in the opposite direction from that previously followed.

2 If the error does not lie in addition, next determine the exact amount by which the schedule is out of balance. The amount of the discrepancy is often a clue to the source of the error. If the discrepancy is *divisible by 9,* this suggests either a *transposition* error or a *slide.* For example, assume that the Cash account has a balance of $2,175, but in copying the balance into the trial balance the figures are *transposed* and written as $2,157. The resulting error is $18, and like all transposition errors is *divisible by 9.* Another common error is the slide, or incorrect placement of the decimal point, as when $2,175.00 is copied as $21.75. The resulting discrepancy in the trial balance will also be an amount *divisible by 9.*

To illustrate another method of using the amount of a discrepancy as a clue to locating the error, assume that the Office Equipment account has a *debit* balance of $420, but that it is erroneously listed in the *credit* column of the trial balance. This will cause a discrepancy of two times $420, or $840, in the trial balance totals. Since such errors as recording a debit in a credit column are not uncommon, it is advisable, after determining the discrepancy in the trial balance totals, to scan the columns for an amount equal to exactly *one-half* of the discrepancy. It is also advisable to look over the transactions for an item of the exact amount of the discrepancy. An error may have been made by recording the debit side of the transaction and forgetting to enter the credit side.

3 Compare the amounts in the trial balance with the balances in the ledger. Make sure that each ledger account balance has been included in the correct column of the trial balance.

4 Recompute the balance of each ledger account.

5 Trace all postings from the journal to the ledger accounts. As this is done, place a check mark in the journal and in the ledger after each figure verified. When the operation is completed, look through the journal and the ledger for unchecked amounts. In tracing postings, be alert not only for errors in amount but also for debits entered as credits, or vice versa.

Some Tips on Record-Keeping Procedures

Dollar signs are not used in journals or ledgers. Some accountants use dollar signs in trial balances; some do not. In this book, dollar signs are used in trial balances. Dollar signs should always be used in the balance sheet, the income statement, and other formal financial reports. In the balance sheet, for example, a dollar sign is placed by the first amount in each column and also by the final amount or total. Many accountants also place a dollar sign by each subtotal or other amount listed below an underlining. In the published financial statements of large corporations, the use of dollar signs is often limited to the first and last figures in a column.

When dollar amounts are being entered in the columnar paper used in journals and ledgers, commas and decimal points are not needed. On unruled paper, commas and decimal points should be used. Most of the problems and illustrations in this book are in even dollar amounts. In such cases the cents column can be left blank or, if desired, zeros or dashes may be used. A dollar amount that represents a final total within a schedule is underlined by a double rule.

THE ACCOUNTING CYCLE: AN INTRODUCTION

Objective 7
Describe the basic steps of the accounting cycle in both manual and computer-based accounting systems.

The sequence of accounting procedures used to record, classify, and summarize accounting information is often termed the *accounting cycle.* The accounting cycle begins with the initial recording of business transactions and concludes with the preparation of formal financial statements summarizing the effects of these transactions upon the assets, liabilities, and owner's equity of the business. The term "cycle" indicates that these procedures must be repeated continuously to enable the business to prepare new, up-to-date financial statements at reasonable intervals.

At this point, we have illustrated a complete accounting cycle as it relates to the preparation of a balance sheet for a service type business with a manual accounting system. The accounting procedures discussed to this point may be summarized as follows:

1 **Record transactions in the journal** As each business transaction occurs, it is entered in the journal, thus creating a chronological record of events. This procedure completes the recording step in the accounting cycle.

2 **Post to ledger accounts** The debit and credit changes in account balances are posted from the journal to the ledger. This procedure classifies the effects of the business transactions in terms of specific asset, liability, and owner's equity accounts.

3 Prepare a trial balance A trial balance proves the equality of the debit and credit entries in the ledger. The purpose of this procedure is to verify the accuracy of the posting process and the computation of ledger account balances.

4 Prepare financial statements At this point, we have discussed only one financial statement—the balance sheet. This statement shows the financial position of the business at a specific date. The preparation of financial statements summarizes the effects of business transactions occurring through the date of the statements and completes the accounting cycle.

In the next section of this chapter, and throughout this textbook, we shall extend our discussion to include computer-based accounting systems. In Chapters 3 and 4, we shall expand the accounting cycle to include the measurement of business income and the preparation of an income statement.

Manual and Computer-Based Systems: A Comparison

In our preceding discussion, we have assumed the use of a manual accounting system, in which all the accounting procedures are performed manually by the company's accounting personnel. The reader may wonder about the relevance of such a discussion in an era when even many small businesses use computer-based accounting systems. However, the concepts and procedures involved in the operation of manual and computer-based accounting systems are *essentially the same*. The differences are largely a question of whether specific procedures require human attention, or whether they can be performed automatically by machine.

Computers can be programmed to perform mechanical tasks with great speed and accuracy. For example, they can be programmed to read data, to perform mathematical computations, and to rearrange data into any desired format. However, computers cannot think. Therefore, they are not able to *analyze* business transactions. Without human guidance, computers cannot determine which events should be recorded in the accounting records, or which accounts should be debited and credited to properly record an event. With these abilities and limitations in mind, we will explore the effects of computer-based systems upon the basic accounting cycle.

■ **Recording Business Transactions** The recording of transactions requires two steps. First, the transaction must be *analyzed* to determine whether it should be recorded in the accounting records and, if so, which accounts should be debited and credited and for what dollar amounts. Second, the transaction must be *physically entered* (recorded) in the accounting system. As computers do not know which transactions should be recorded, or how to record them properly, these two functions must be performed by accounting personnel in both manual and computerized systems.

Differences do exist, however, in the manner in which data are physically entered into manual and computer-based systems. In manual systems, the data are entered in the form of handwritten journal entries. In a computer-based system, the data will be entered through a keyboard, an optical scanner, or other input device. Also, data entered into a computer-based system need *not* be arranged in the format of a journal entry. The data usually are entered into a *data base,* instead of a journal.

■ **What Is a Data Base?** A data base is a warehouse of information stored within a computer system. The purpose of the data base is to allow information that will be used for several different purposes to be entered into the computer system *only once.* Data are originally entered into the data base. Then, as data are needed, the computer refers to the data base, selects the appropriate data, and arranges them in the desired format.

The information that must be entered into the data base is the same as that contained in a journal entry—the date, the accounts to be debited and credited, the dollar amounts, and an explanation of the transaction. However, this information need not be arranged in the format of a journal entry. For example, in a data base, accounts usually are identified by number, rather than by title. Also, abbreviations such as "D" or "C" are used to indicate whether an account should be debited or credited. Once information has been entered in the data base, the computer can arrange this information into any desired format, such as journal entries, ledger accounts, and financial statements.

■ **Posting to Ledger Accounts** Posting merely transfers existing information from one accounting record to another—a function which can be easily performed by a computer. In a computer-based system, data posted to the ledger accounts come directly from the data base, rather than from the journal.

■ **Preparation of a Trial Balance** Preparation of a trial balance involves three steps: (1) determining the balances of ledger accounts, (2) arranging the account balances in the format of a trial balance, and (3) adding up the trial balance columns and comparing the column totals. All these functions involve information already contained in the data base and can be performed by the computer.

■ **Preparation of Financial Statements** The preparation of a balance sheet is similar to the preparation of a trial balance and can be readily performed by the computer. The preparation of an income statement involves additional procedures which will be discussed in Chapter 3.

■ **Summary** Computers can eliminate the need for copying and rearranging information which already has been entered into the system. They also can perform mathematical computations. In short, computers eliminate most of the "paper work" involved in the operation of an accounting system. However, they *do not* eliminate the need for accounting personnel who can analyze business transactions and explain these events in conformity with generally accepted accounting principles.

The differences in manual and computer-based systems with respect to the accounting procedures discussed in this chapter are summarized graphically in the flowcharts on the next page. Functions which are performed by accounting personnel are printed on a shaded background; tasks which can be performed automatically by the computer are printed on a white background.

End-of-Chapter Review

CONCEPTS INTRODUCED OR EMPHASIZED IN CHAPTER 2

The major concepts in this chapter include:

■ The use of journals and of ledger accounts.

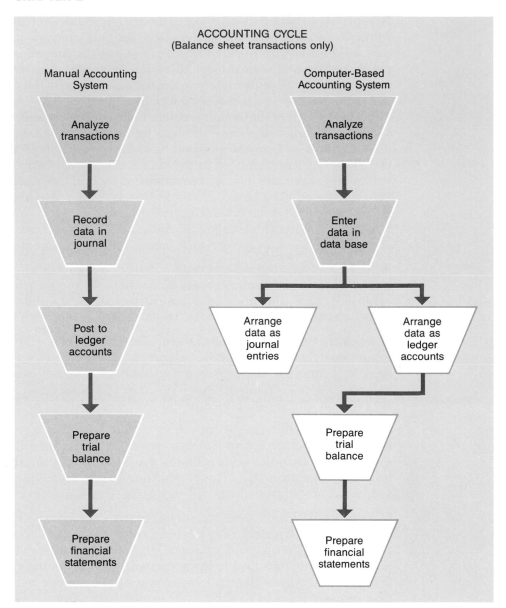

ACCOUNTING CYCLE
(Balance sheet transactions only)

Manual Accounting System

- Analyze transactions
- Record data in journal
- Post to ledger accounts
- Prepare trial balance
- Prepare financial statements

Computer-Based Accounting System

- Analyze transactions
- Enter data in data base
- Arrange data as journal entries
- Arrange data as ledger accounts
- Prepare trial balance
- Prepare financial statements

■ Double-entry accounting and the rules of debit and credit.

■ A brief introduction to the accounting cycle, including a comparison of manual and computer-based systems.

We will expand our discussion of the accounting cycle in the next two chapters to include steps relating to the measurement of net income. For the introductory student, Chapter 2 is one of the most important chapters in the textbook. Journal entries and T accounts will be used as instructional devices throughout the study of accounting. The topics of double-entry accounting and the accounting cycle serve as "building blocks" for much of the material presented in later chapters.

KEY TERMS INTRODUCED OR EMPHASIZED IN CHAPTER 2

Account A record used to summarize all increases and decreases in a particular asset, such as Cash, or any other type of asset, liability, owner's equity, revenue, or expense.

Accounting cycle The sequence of accounting procedures applied in recording, classifying, and summarizing accounting information. The cycle begins with the occurrence of business transactions and concludes with the preparation of financial statements. This concept will be expanded in later chapters.

Credit An amount entered on the right-hand side of an account. A credit is used to record a decrease in an asset and an increase in a liability or owner's equity.

Data base A storage center of information within a computer-based accounting system. The idea behind a data base is that data intended for a variety of uses may be entered into the computer system only once, at which time the information is stored in the data base. Then, as the information is needed, the computer can retrieve it from the data base and arrange it in the desired format.

Debit An amount entered on the left-hand side of an account. A debit is used to record an increase in an asset and a decrease in a liability or in owner's equity.

Double-entry accounting A system of recording every business transaction with equal dollar amounts of both debit and credit entries. As a result of this system, the accounting equation always remains in balance; in addition, the system makes possible the measurement of net income and also the use of error-detecting devices such as a trial balance.

Footing The total of amounts in a column.

Journal A chronological record of transactions, showing for each transaction the debits and credits to be entered in specific ledger accounts. The simplest type of journal is called a general journal.

Ledger A loose-leaf book, file, or other record containing all the separate accounts of a business.

Posting The process of transferring information from the journal to individual accounts in the ledger.

Trial balance A two-column schedule listing the names and the debit or credit balances of all accounts in the ledger.

DEMONSTRATION PROBLEM FOR YOUR REVIEW

Stadium Parking was organized on July 1 to operate a parking lot near a new sports arena. The following transactions occurred during July prior to the company beginning its regular business operations.

July 1 Martin Taylor opened a bank account in the name of the business with a deposit of $45,000 cash.

July 2 Purchased land to be used as the parking lot for a total price of $140,000. A cash down payment of $28,000 was made and a note payable was issued for the balance of the purchase price.

July 5 Purchased a small portable building for $4,000 cash. The purchase price included installation of the building on the parking lot.

July 12 Purchased office equipment on credit from Suzuki & Co. for $3,000.

July 28 Paid $2,000 of the amount owed to Suzuki & Co.

The account titles and account numbers used by Auto Parks, Inc., to record these transactions are as follows:

Cash..............................	1	Notes payable.......................	30
Land..............................	20	Accounts payable	32
Building..........................	22	Martin Taylor, capital	50
Office equipment	25		

Instructions **a** Prepare journal entries for the month of July.

b Post to ledger accounts of the three-column running balance form.

c Prepare a trial balance at July 31.

SOLUTION TO DEMONSTRATION PROBLEM

a General Journal Page 1

DATE		ACCOUNT TITLES AND EXPLANATIONS	LP	DEBIT	CREDIT
19__					
July	1	Cash..	1	45,000	
		Martin Taylor, Capital	50		45,000
		Owner invested cash to begin business.			
	2	Land..	20	140,000	
		Cash....................................	1		28,000
		Notes Payable	30		112,000
		Purchased land. Paid part cash and			
		issued a note payable for the balance.			
	5	Building......................................	22	4,000	
		Cash....................................	1		4,000
		Purchased a small portable building			
		for cash.			
	12	Office Equipment.............................	25	3,000	
		Accounts Payable	32		3,000
		Purchased office equipment on credit			
		from Suzuki & Co.			
	28	Accounts Payable	32	2,000	
		Cash....................................	1		2,000
		Paid part of account payable to Suzuki			
		& Co.			

b

	CASH				Account No. 1
DATE	EXPLANATION	REF	DEBIT	CREDIT	BALANCE
19—					
July 1		1	45000		45000
2		1		28000	17000
5		1		4000	13000
28		1		2000	11000

	LAND				Account No. 20
DATE	EXPLANATION	REF	DEBIT	CREDIT	BALANCE
19—					
July 2		1	140000		140000

	BUILDING				Account No. 22
DATE	EXPLANATION	REF	DEBIT	CREDIT	BALANCE
19—					
July 5		1	4000		4000

	OFFICE EQUIPMENT				Account No. 25
DATE	EXPLANATION	REF	DEBIT	CREDIT	BALANCE
19—					
July 12		1	3000		3000

	NOTES PAYABLE				Account No. 30
DATE	EXPLANATION	REF	DEBIT	CREDIT	BALANCE
19—					
July 2		1		112000	112000

	ACCOUNTS PAYABLE				Account No. 32
DATE	EXPLANATION	REF	DEBIT	CREDIT	BALANCE
19—					
July 12		1		3000	3000
28		1	2000		1000

	MARTIN TAYLOR, CAPITAL				Account No. 50
DATE	EXPLANATION	REF	DEBIT	CREDIT	BALANCE
19—					
July 1				45000	45000

c

STADIUM PARKING
Trial Balance
July 31, 19__

	DEBIT	CREDIT
Cash	$ 11,000	
Land	140,000	
Building	4,000	
Office equipment	3,000	
Notes payable		$112,000
Accounts payable		1,000
Martin Taylor, capital		45,000
	$158,000	$158,000

SELF-TEST QUESTIONS

Answers to these questions appear on page 80.

1 According to the rules of debit and credit for balance sheet accounts:

 a Increases in asset, liability, and owner's equity accounts are recorded by debits.

 b Decreases in asset and liability accounts are recorded by credits.

 c Increases in asset and owner's equity accounts are recorded by debits.

 d Decreases in liability and owner's equity accounts are recorded by debits.

2 Which of the following statements about accounting procedures is *not* correct?

 a The journal shows in one place all the information about specific transactions, arranged in chronological order.

 b A ledger account shows in one place all the information about changes in a specific asset or liability, or in owner's equity.

 c Posting is the process of transferring debit and credit changes in account balances from the ledger to the journal.

 d The end product of the accounting cycle consists of formal financial statements, such as the balance sheet and the income statement.

3 On March 31, the ledger for Manor House Cleaning Service consists of the following:

Cleaning Equipment	$1,780	Accounts Receivable	$2,100
Accounts Payable	1,570	Cash............................	690
M. Poppins, Capital..............	3,500	Salaries Payable................	960
Office Equipment................	1,200	Cleaning Supplies	260

In a trial balance prepared on March 31, the total of the credit column is:

 a $6,030   **b** $2,530   **c** $9,530   **d** $8,560

4 Sunset Tours has a $3,500 account receivable from the Del Mar Rotary. On January 20, the Rotary makes a partial payment of $2,100 to Sunset Tours. The journal entry made on January 20 by Sunset Tours to record this transaction includes:

 a A debit to the Cash Received account of $2,100.

 b A credit to the Accounts Receivable account of $2,100.

 c A debit to the Cash account of $1,400.

 d A debit to the Accounts Receivable account of $1,400.

5 The following journal entry was made in Dixie Stores' accounting records:

Cash...	12,000	
Notes Receivable...	48,000	
Land...		60,000

This transaction:

 a Involves the purchase of land for $60,000.

 b Involves a $12,000 cash payment.

 c Involves the sale of land for $60,000.

 d Causes an increase in total assets of $12,000.

Assignment Material

REVIEW QUESTIONS

1 In its simplest form, an account has only three elements or basic parts. What are these three elements?

2 At the beginning of the year, the Office Equipment account of Gulf Coast Airlines had a debit balance of *$126,900.* During the year, debit entries of *$23,400* and credit entries of *$38,200* were posted to the account. What was the balance of this account at the end of the year? (Indicate debit or credit balance.)

3 What relationship exists between the position of an account on the balance sheet and the rules for recording increases in that account?

4 State briefly the rules of debit and credit as applied to asset accounts. As applied to liability and owner's equity accounts.

5 Does the term *debit* mean increase and the term *credit* mean decrease? Explain.

6 What requirement is imposed by the double-entry system in the recording of any business transaction?

7 Explain precisely what is meant by each of the phrases listed below. Whenever appropriate, indicate whether the left or right side of an account is affected and whether an increase or decrease is indicated.

a A debit to the Land account

b Credit balance

c Credit side of an account

d A debit of $200 to the Cash account

e A debit of $600 to Accounts Payable

f A credit of $50 to Accounts Receivable

8 For each of the following transactions, indicate whether the account in parentheses should be debited or credited, and give the reason for your answer.

a Purchased a copying machine on credit, promising to make payment in full within 30 days. (Accounts Payable)

b Purchased land for cash. (Cash)

c Sold an old, unneeded typewriter on 30-day credit. (Office Equipment)

d Obtained a loan of $30,000 from a bank. (Cash)

e James Brown began the business of Brown Sporting Goods Shop by depositing $20,000 cash in a bank account in the name of the business. (James Brown, Capital)

9 For each of the following accounts, state whether it is an asset, a liability, or owner's equity; also state whether it would normally have a debit or a credit balance: (a) Office Equipment, (b) John Williams, Capital, (c) Accounts Receivable, (d) Accounts Payable, (e) Cash, (f) Notes Payable, (g) Land.

10 Why is a journal sometimes called the *book of original entry?*

11 Compare and contrast a *journal* and a *ledger.*

12 What is a *compound* journal entry?

13 Since it is possible to record the effects of business transactions directly in ledger accounts, why is it desirable for a business to maintain a journal?

14 What purposes are served by a trial balance?

15 In preparing a trial balance, an accounting student listed the balance of the Office Equipment account in the credit column. This account had a balance of $2,450. What would be the amount of the discrepancy in the trial balance totals? Explain.

16 Are dollar signs used in journal entries? In ledger accounts? In trial balances? In financial statements?

17 List the following five items in a logical sequence to illustrate the flow of accounting information through a manual accounting system:

 a Information entered in the journal

 b Preparation of financial statements

 c Occurrence of a business transaction

 d Debits and credits posted from journal to ledger

 e Preparation of a trial balance

18 Which step in the recording of transactions requires greater understanding of accounting principles: (a) the entering of transactions in the journal, or (b) the posting of entries to ledger accounts?

19 List the procedures in the *accounting cycle* as described in this chapter.

20 What is a *data base?* How does a data base relate to the preparation of journal entries and ledger accounts in a computer-based system?

EXERCISES

Exercise 2-1
Accounting
terminology

Listed below are nine technical accounting terms introduced in this chapter:

Ledger	*Account*	*Data base*
Posting	*Credit*	*Double-entry*
Trial balance	*Debit*	*Journal*

Each of the following statements may (or may not) describe one of these technical terms. For each statement, indicate the accounting term described, or answer "none" if the statement does not correctly describe any of the terms.

a The system of accounting in which all transactions are recorded both in the journal and in the ledger.

b An entry on the left-hand side of a ledger account.

c The process of transferring information from a journal to the ledger.

d The accounting record in which transactions are initially recorded in a manual accounting system.

e Information stored in a computer-based accounting system which can be arranged into any desired format.

f A device that proves the equality of debits and credits posted to the ledger.

g The accounting record from which a trial balance is prepared.

Exercise 2-2
Analysis of
transactions;
double-entry
accounting

Analyze separately each of the following transactions using the format illustrated at the end of the exercise. In each situation, explain the debit portion of the transaction before the credit portion.

a On August 1, Jeff Crane organized Coast Escrow Service by opening a bank account in the company name with a deposit of $80,000 cash.

b On August 3, land was acquired for $55,000. A cash payment of $15,000 was made and a note payable was issued for the balance of the purchase price.

c On August 5, a prefabricated building was purchased at a cost of $45,000 from Custom Company. A cash down payment of $25,000 was made and it was agreed that the balance should be paid in full within 30 days.

d On August 8, office equipment was purchased on credit from Taylor Office Supply Co. at a price of $8,500. The account payable was to be paid within 60 days.

e On August 31, a partial payment of $4,000 was made on the liability to Taylor Office Supply Co.

Note: The type of analysis to be made is shown by the following illustration, using transaction **(a)** as an example.

a (1) The asset Cash was increased. Increases in assets are recorded by debits. Debit Cash, $80,000.

(2) The owner's equity was increased. Increases in owner's equity are recorded by credits. Credit Jeff Crane, Capital, $80,000.

Exercise 2-3
Using ledger
accounts

Enter the following transactions in T accounts drawn on ordinary notebook paper. Enter the dates and amounts and label each debit and credit with the letter identifying the transaction. Prepare a trial balance at June 30.

a On June 10, Karen King opened a bank account in the name of her new business, King Realty Company, by making a deposit of $75,000 cash.

b On June 13, purchased land and an office building at a total price of $160,000, of which $120,000 was applicable to the land and $40,000 to the building. A cash payment of $50,000 was made and a note payable was issued for the balance.

c On June 20, office equipment was purchased at a cost of $8,400. A cash down payment of $2,800 was made, and it was agreed that the balance should be paid within 30 days.

d On June 30, paid $2,800 of the $5,600 liability arising from the purchase of office equipment on June 20.

Exercise 2-4
Effects of debits
and credits on
ledger account
balances

The first six transactions of South Pacific Travel Agency appear in the following T accounts.

CASH			
(1)	60,000	(2)	20,000
(6)	2,300	(5)	15,000

OFFICE EQUIPMENT			
(3)	20,000	(4)	5,000

ACCOUNTS RECEIVABLE			
(4)	5,000	(6)	2,300

NOTES PAYABLE			
		(2)	100,000

LAND			
(2)	72,000		

ACCOUNTS PAYABLE			
(5)	15,000	(3)	20,000

BUILDING			
(2)	48,000		

DANA LINDSEY, CAPITAL			
		(1)	60,000

For each of the six transactions in turn, indicate the type of accounts affected (asset, liability, or owner's equity) and whether the account was increased or decreased. Arrange your answers in the form illustrated for transaction *(1),* shown here as an example.

TRANSACTION	ACCOUNT(S) DEBITED		ACCOUNT(S) CREDITED	
	TYPE OF ACCOUNT(S)	INCREASE OR DECREASE	TYPE OF ACCOUNT(S)	INCREASE OR DECREASE
(1)	*Asset*	*Increase*	*Owner's equity*	*Increase*

Exercise 2-5
Preparing a trial
balance

Using the information in the ledger accounts presented in Exercise 2-4, prepare a trial balance for South Pacific Travel Agency at September 30, 19___.

Exercise 2-6
Recording
transactions in a
journal

Enter the following transactions in the two-column journal of Jenkins Sporting Goods. Include a brief explanation of the transaction as part of each journal entry.

Nov. 1   The owner, Dan Jenkins, invested an additional $40,000 cash in the business.

Nov. 3   Purchased an adjacent vacant lot for use as parking space. The price was $98,500, of which $28,500 was paid in cash; a note payable was issued for the balance.

Nov. 12   Collected an account receivable of $4,500 from a customer, Jean Krieger.

Nov. 17   Acquired office equipment from Tower Company for $7,600 cash.

Nov. 21   Issued a check for $764 in full payment of an account payable to Hampton Supply Co.

Nov. 28   Borrowed $25,000 cash from the bank by signing a 90-day note payable.

Exercise 2-7
Uses and
limitations of a
trial balance

Some of the following errors would cause the debit and credit columns of the trial balance to have unequal totals. For each of the four paragraphs, write a statement explaining whether the error would cause unequal totals in the trial balance. Each paragraph is to be considered independently of the others.

a A payment of $400 to a creditor was recorded by a debit to Accounts Payable of $400 and a credit to Cash of $40.

b A $540 payment for a new typewriter was recorded by a debit to Office Equipment of $54 and a credit to Cash of $54.

c An account receivable in the amount of $800 was collected in full. The collection was recorded by a debit to Cash for $800 and a debit to Accounts Payable for $800.

d An account payable was paid by issuing a check for $350. The payment was recorded by debiting Accounts Payable $350 and crediting Accounts Receivable $350.

Exercise 2-8
Steps in the
accounting cycle;
computerized
accounting
systems

Various steps and decisions involved in the accounting cycle are described in the seven lettered statements below. Indicate which of these procedures are mechanical functions that can be performed by machine in a computerized accounting system, and which require the judgment of people familiar with accounting principles and concepts.

a Decide whether or not events should be recorded in the accounting records.

b Determine which ledger accounts should be debited and credited to describe specific business transactions.

c Arrange recorded data in the format of journal entries.

d Arrange recorded data in the format of ledger accounts.

e Prepare a trial balance.

f Prepare financial statements (a balance sheet).

g Evaluate the debt-paying ability of one company relative to another.

PROBLEMS

Group A

Problem 2A-1
Recording transactions in a journal

In May, William Tanner, a physician, decided to open his own medical practice. During May, the new business engaged in the following transactions:

May 4 Tanner opened a bank account in the name of his medical practice, William Tanner, M.D., by depositing $30,000 cash.

May 16 Purchased a small medical office. The purchase price was $95,400, which included land valued at $50,000 and a building valued at $45,400. A cash down payment was made for $21,000, and a note payable was issued for the balance of the purchase price.

May 19 Purchased office furniture on account from Modern Office Co., $2,340.

May 22 Purchased medical supplies for cash from Denton Labs, $1,630.

May 23 Returned to Denton Labs $225 of the medical supplies purchased yesterday as these items were not exactly what Tanner had ordered. Denton Labs agreed to refund the $225 within 10 days.

May 30 Made an $1,170 partial payment on the account payable to Modern Office Co.

May 31 Received the $225 refund from Denton Labs for the supplies returned on May 23.

Instructions

Prepare journal entries to record the above transactions. Select the appropriate account titles from the following chart of accounts:

Cash	*Land*	*Notes payable*
Accounts receivable	*Building*	*Accounts payable*
Medical supplies	*Office furniture*	*William Tanner, capital*

Problem 2A-2
Analyzing transactions and preparing journal entries

Yoko Toyoda is the owner of Perfect Portraits, a photography studio. A few of the company's July business transactions are described below:

(1) On July 2, collected cash of $700 from accounts receivable.

(2) On July 7, purchased photographic equipment for $2,175, paying $800 in cash and charging the remainder on the company's 30-day account at Camera Supply Co.

(3) On July 9, returned to Camera Supply Co. $200 of photographic equipment which did not work properly. The return of this equipment reduced by $200 the amount owed to Camera Supply Co.

(4) On July 25, Yoko Toyoda made an additional investment in Perfect Portraits by depositing $3,500 cash in the company bank account.

(5) On July 31, paid the remaining $1,175 owed to Camera Supply Co.

Instructions

a Prepare an analysis of each of the above transactions. The form of analysis to be used is as follows, using transaction (1) as an example.

1(a) The asset Cash was increased. Increases in assets are recorded by debits. Debit Cash, $700.

(b) The asset Accounts Receivable was decreased. Decreases in assets are recorded by credits. Credit Accounts Receivable, $700.

b Prepare journal entries, including explanations, for the above transactions.

Problem 2A-3
Preparing a trial
balance and a
balance sheet

The ledger accounts of Black Mountain Golf Club at September 30 are shown below in an alphabetical listing.

Accounts payable	$ 5,340	Lighting equipment	$ 52,900
Accounts receivable	1,300	Maintenance equipment	36,500
Building	64,200	Notes payable	390,000
Robert Jones, capital	264,060	Notes receivable	24,000
Cash..........................	14,960	Office equipment	1,420
Fences........................	23,600	Office supplies	490
Golf carts	28,000	Sprinkler system	50,000
Land..........................	375,000	Taxes payable	12,970

Instructions

a Prepare a trial balance with the ledger accounts arranged in the usual financial statement order. Include a proper heading.

b Prepare a balance sheet at September 30, 19___. Include a subtotal showing total liabilities.

Problem 2A-4
Posting to ledger
accounts;
preparing a trial
balance and a
balance sheet

Susan Cole is a veterinarian. In January, she began organizing her own animal hospital, to be known as Animal Care Center. Cole has prepared the following journal entries to record all January business transactions. She has not posted these entries to ledger accounts. The ledger account numbers to be used are: Cash, 1; Office Supplies, 10; Land, 20; Building, 25; Medical Equipment, 27; Notes Payable, 30; Accounts Payable, 31; and Susan Cole, Capital, 50.

General Journal   Page 1

Jan	2	Cash..	60,000	
		Susan Cole, Capital		60,000
		Investment in business by owner.		
	4	Land..	45,000	
		Building	115,000	
		Cash.....................................		40,000
		Notes Payable...........................		120,000
		Purchased land and building.		
	7	Medical Equipment	7,480	
		Accounts Payable		7,480
		Bought equipment on credit from		
		Medco, Inc.		
	8	Office Supplies	590	
		Accounts Payable		590
		Bought supplies from Miller Supply.		
	13	Accounts Payable	1,400	
		Medical Equipment		1,400
		Returned defective medical equipment		
		to Medco, Inc., for credit on account.		
	18	Accounts Payable	590	
		Cash....................................		590
		Made payment of liability to Miller		
		Supply.		

74

Instructions

a Post the journal entries to ledger accounts of the three-column running balance form.

b Prepare a trial balance at January 31 from the ledger accounts completed in part **a**.

c Prepare a balance sheet at January 31, 19___.

Problem 2A-5
Preparing journal entries, posting, and preparing a trial balance

Coast Property Management was started on November 1 by Jean Klein to provide managerial services for the owners of apartment buildings. The organizational period extended throughout November and included the transactions listed below.

Nov. 1 Klein opened a bank account in the name of the business with a deposit of $40,000 cash.

Nov. 4 Purchased land and an office building for a price of $140,000, of which $75,000 was considered applicable to the land and $65,000 attributable to the building. A cash down payment of $30,000 was made and a note payable for $110,000 was issued for the balance of the purchase price.

Nov. 7 Purchased office equipment on credit from Harvard Office Equipment, $4,400.

Nov. 9 A typewriter (cost $560), which was part of the November 7 purchase of office equipment, proved defective and was returned for credit to Harvard Office Equipment.

Nov. 17 Sold one-third of the land acquired on November 4 to Regent Pharmacy at a price of $25,000. This price is equal to Coast Property's cost for this portion of the land, so there is no gain or loss on this transaction. Coast Property received a $5,000 cash down payment from Regent Pharmacy and a note receivable in the amount of $20,000, due in four monthly installments of $5,000 each, beginning on November 30 (ignore interest).

Nov. 28 Paid $1,600 in partial settlement of the liability to Harvard Office Equipment.

Nov. 30 Received cash of $5,000 as partial collection of the note receivable from Regent Pharmacy.

The account titles and account numbers to be used are

Cash	1	Office equipment	25
Notes receivable	5	Notes payable	31
Land	21	Accounts payable	32
Building	23	Jean Klein, capital	51

Instructions

a Prepare journal entries for the month of November.

b Post to ledger accounts of the three-column running balance form.

c Prepare a trial balance at November 30.

Problem 2A-6
Preparing journal entries, posting, and preparing a trial balance

Educational TV was organized in February 19___, to operate as a local television station. The account titles and numbers used by the business are listed below:

Cash	1	Telecasting equipment	24
Accounts receivable	5	Film library	25
Supplies	9	Notes payable	31
Land	21	Accounts payable	32
Building	22	Michael Turner, capital	51
Transmitter	23		

The transactions for February were as follows:

Feb. 1   Michael Turner deposited $300,000 cash in a bank checking account in the name of the business, Educational TV.

Feb. 2   Educational TV purchased the land, buildings, and telecasting equipment previously used by a local television station which had gone bankrupt. The total purchase price was $250,000, of which $100,000 was attributable to the land, $80,000 to the building, and the remainder to the telecasting equipment. The terms of the purchase required a cash payment of $160,000 and the issuance of a note payable for the balance.

Feb. 5   Purchased a transmitter at a cost of $200,000 from AC Mfg. Co., making a cash down payment of $56,000. The balance, in the form of a note payable, was to be paid in monthly installments of $12,000, beginning Feburary 15. (Interest expense is to be ignored.)

Feb. 9   Purchased a film library at a cost of $32,000 from Modern Film Productions, making a down payment of $15,000 cash, with the balance on account payable in 30 days.

Feb. 12   Bought supplies costing $3,000, paying cash.

Feb. 15   Paid $12,000 to AC Mfg. Co. as the first monthly payment on the note payable created on February 5. (Interest expense is to be ignored.)

Feb. 25   Sold part of the film library to City College; cost was $7,000 and the selling price also was $7,000. City College agreed to pay the full amount in 30 days.

Instructions   **a**   Prepare journal entries for the month of February.

b   Post to ledger accounts of the three-column running balance form.

c   Prepare a trial balance at February 28, 19__.

Group B

Problem 2B-1
Recording
transactions in a
journal

Patricia Matthews, a certified public accountant, resigned from her position with a large CPA firm in order to begin her own public accounting practice. The business transactions during September while the new venture was being organized are listed below.

Sept. 1   Matthews opened a bank checking account in the name of her firm, Patricia Matthews, Certified Public Accountant, by depositing $32,000 which she had saved over a period of years.

Sept. 10   Purchased a small office building located on a large lot for a total price of $91,200, of which $48,000 was applicable to the land and $43,200 to the building. A cash payment of $18,240 was made and a note payable was issued for the balance of the purchase price.

Sept. 15   Purchased a microcomputer system from Computer Stores, Inc., for $4,680 cash.

Sept. 19   Purchased office furniture, filing cabinets, and a typewriter from Davidson Office Supply Co. at a cost of $3,960. A cash down payment of $720 was made, the balance to be paid in three equal installments due September 28, October 28, and November 28. The purchase was on open account and did not require signing of a promissory note.

Sept. 26   A $140 monitor in the microcomputer system purchased on September 15 stopped working. The monitor was returned to Computer Stores, Inc., which promised to refund the $140 within five days.

Sept. 28   Paid Davidson Office Supply Co. $1,080 cash as the first installment due on the account payable for office equipment.

Sept. 30   Received $140 cash from Computer Stores, Inc., in full settlement of the account receivable created on September 26.

Instructions Prepare journal entries to record the above transactions. Select the appropriate account titles from the following chart of accounts:

Cash	Office equipment
Accounts receivable	Notes payable
Land	Accounts payable
Building	Patricia Matthews, capital

Problem 2B-2
Analyzing transactions and preparing journal entries

The Tool Shed was organized to rent trailers, tools, and other equipment to its customers. The organization of the business began on May 1 and the following transactions occurred in May before the company began regular operations on June 1.

(1) On May 1, Mark O'Brien opened a bank account in the name of his new company with a deposit of $70,000 cash.

(2) On May 3, The Tool Shed bought land for use in its operations at a total cost of $75,000. A cash down payment of $15,000 was made, and a note payable (payable within 90 days without interest) was issued for the balance.

(3) On May 5, a movable building was purchased for $16,000 cash and installed on the lot.

(4) On May 10, equipment was purchased on credit from Ace Tool Company at a cost of $14,100. The account payable was to be paid within 30 days. (The asset account is entitled Rental Equipment.)

(5) On May 31, a cash payment of $20,000 was made in partial settlement of the note payable issued on May 3.

Instructions **a** Prepare an analysis of each of the above transactions. The form of analysis to be used is as follows, using transaction **(1)** above as an example.

> **1(a)** The asset Cash was increased. Increases in assets are recorded by debits. Debit Cash, $70,000.
>
> **(b)** The owner's equity was increased. Increases in owner's equity are recorded by credits. Credit Mark O'Brien, Capital, $70,000.

b Prepare journal entries for the above five transactions. Include an explanation as a part of each journal entry.

Problem 2B-3
Preparing a trial balance and a balance sheet

Gayle Forbes & Associates is an investment advisory service. The account balances at November 30 are shown by the following alphabetical list:

Accounts payable	$ 4,800	Land	$ 85,000
Accounts receivable	16,700	Notes payable	145,000
Automobiles	12,600	Notes receivable	2,400
Building	110,000	Office furniture	12,900
Gayle Forbes, capital	129,650	Office supplies	850
Cash	17,650	Property taxes payable	1,060
Computer	18,800	Salaries payable	3,740
Computer software	5,450	Technical library	1,900

Instructions **a** Prepare a trial balance with the accounts arranged in financial statement order. Include a proper heading for your trial balance.

b Prepare a balance sheet. Include a subtotal for total liabilities.

Problem 2B-4
Posting to ledger accounts; preparing a trial balance and a balance sheet

After several seasons of professional tennis competition, Dave Farr had saved enough money to start his own tennis school, to be known as Winners' Tennis College. During July, while organizing the business, Farr prepared the following journal entries to record all July transactions. He has not posted these entries to ledger accounts. The ledger account numbers to be used are: Cash 1, Office Supplies 9, Land 20, Tennis Courts 22, Tennis Equipment 25, Notes Payable 30, Accounts Payable 31, and Dave Farr, Capital 50.

General Journal   Page 1

July	1	Cash..	30,000	
		Dave Farr, Capital		30,000
		Investment in business by owner.		
	3	Land..	28,400	
		Tennis Courts	75,000	
		Cash...................................		20,000
		Notes Payable.........................		83,400
		Purchased land and tennis courts.		
	6	Tennis Equipment	1,680	
		Accounts Payable		1,680
		Bought equipment on credit from		
		Rackets, Inc.		
	7	Office Supplies	315	
		Accounts Payable		315
		Bought supplies from Miller Supply.		
	12	Tennis Equipment	725	
		Accounts Payable		725
		Bought equipment from Rackets, Inc.		
	17	Accounts Payable	315	
		Cash...................................		315
		Made payment of liability to Miller		
		Supply.		
	22	Accounts Payable	725	
		Cash...................................		725
		Made payment of liability to Rackets,		
		Inc., for purchase of July 12.		

Instructions **a** Post the journal entries to ledger accounts of the three-column running balance form.

b Prepare a trial balance at July 31 from the ledger accounts completed in part **a**.

c Prepare a balance sheet at July 31, 19___.

Problem 2B-5
Preparing journal entries, posting, and preparing a trial balance

Ann Ryan, a licensed real estate broker, on October 1 began the organization of her own business to be known as Ryan Land Company. The following events occurred during October:

Oct. 2   Ann Ryan opened a bank account in the name of the business by depositing personal savings of $35,000.

Oct. 6   Purchased land and a small office building at a total price of $98,500 of which $64,000 was applicable to land and $34,500 to the building. The terms of the purchase required a cash payment of $29,500 and the issuance of a note payable for $69,000.

Oct. 15   Sold one-quarter of the land at its cost of $16,000 to a neighboring business, Village Medical Clinic, which wanted to expand its parking lot. No down payment was required; Village Medical Clinic issued a note promising payment of the $16,000 in a series of five monthly installments of $3,200 each, beginning October 30 (ignore interest). As the land was sold at the same price per square foot as Ryan Land Company had paid to acquire it, no gain or loss results on this transaction.

Oct. 20 Purchased office equipment on credit from Buffington Company in the amount of $5,280.

Oct. 30 Paid $3,440 as partial settlement of the liability to Buffington Company.

Oct. 31 Received the first $3,200 monthly installment on the note receivable from Village Medical Clinic.

The account titles and account numbers to be used are:

Cash.................................	1	Office equipment......................	26
Notes receivable	5	Notes payable........................	30
Land.................................	21	Accounts payable	32
Building.............................	23	Ann Ryan, capital....................	50

Instructions **a** Prepare journal entries for the month of October.

b Post to ledger accounts of the three-column running balance form.

c Prepare a trial balance at October 31, 19__.

Problem 2B-6
Preparing journal entries, posting, and preparing a trial balance

After playing several seasons of professional football, George Harris had saved enough money to start a business, to be called Number One Auto Rental. The transactions during March while the new business was being organized are listed below:

Mar. 1 George Harris invested $140,000 cash in the business by making a deposit in a bank account in the name of the new company.

Mar. 3 The new company purchased land and a building at a cost of $120,000, of which $72,000 was regarded as applicable to the land and $48,000 to the building. The transaction involved a cash payment of $41,500 and the issuance of a note payable for $78,500.

Mar. 5 Purchased 20 new automobiles at $8,600 each from Fleet Sales Company. Paid $40,000 cash, and agreed to pay $32,000 by March 31 and the remaining balance by April 15. The liability is viewed as an account payable.

Mar. 7 Sold an automobile at cost to Harris' father-in-law, Howard Facey, who paid $2,400 in cash and agreed to pay the balance within 30 days.

Mar. 8 One of the automobiles was found to be defective and was returned to Fleet Sales Company. The amount payable to this creditor was thereby reduced by $8,600.

Mar. 20 Purchased office equipment at a cost of $4,000 cash.

Mar. 31 Issued a check for $32,000 in partial payment of the liability to Fleet Sales Company.

The account titles and the account numbers used by the company are as follows:

Cash.................................	10	Automobiles.........................	22
Accounts receivable	11	Notes payable.......................	31
Land.................................	16	Accounts payable	32
Buildings............................	17	George Harris, capital	50
Office equipment	20		

Instructions **a** Journalize the March transactions.

b Post to ledger accounts. Use the running balance form of ledger account.

c Prepare a trial balance at March 31.

BUSINESS DECISION CASES

**Case 2-1
Computer-based
accounting
systems**

Farrah Moore is planning to create a computer-based accounting system for small businesses. Her system will be developed from a data base program and will be suitable for use on personal computers.

The idea underlying data base software is that data needed for a variety of uses is entered into the data base only once. The computer is programmed to arrange this data into any number of desired formats. In the case of Moore's accounting system, the company's accounting personnel must enter the relevant information about each business transaction into the data base. The program which Moore plans to write will then enable the computer operator to have the information arranged by the computer into the formats of (1) journal entries (with written explanations), (2) three-column running balance form ledger accounts, (3) a trial balance, and (4) a balance sheet.

Instructions

a Identify the relevant information about each business transaction that the company's accounting personnel must enter into the data base to enable Moore's program to prepare the four types of accounting records and statements described above.

b As described in this chapter, the accounting cycle includes the steps of (1) analyzing and recording business transactions, (2) posting the debit and credit amounts to ledger accounts, (3) preparing a trial balance, and (4) preparing financial statements (at this stage, only a balance sheet). Indicate which of these functions can be performed automatically by Moore's computer program and which must still be performed by the company's accounting personnel.

**Case 2-2
Preparing
balance sheets
and an
introduction to
measuring
income**

David Ray, a college student with several summers' experience as a guide on canoe camping trips, decided to go into business for himself. On June 1, Ray organized Birchbark Canoe Trails by depositing $1,600 of personal savings in a bank account in the name of the business. Also on June 1, the business borrowed an additional $3,200 cash from John Ray (David's father) by issuing a three-year note payable. To help the business get started, John Ray agreed that no interest would be charged on the loan. The following transactions were also carried out by the business on June 1:

(1) Bought a number of canoes at a total cost of $6,200; paid $2,000 cash and agreed to pay the balance within 60 days.

(2) Bought camping equipment at a cost of $3,400 payable in 60 days.

(3) Bought supplies for cash, $700.

After the close of the season on September 10, Ray asked another student, Sharon Lee, who had taken a course in accounting, to help determine the financial position of the business.

The only record Ray had maintained was a checkbook with memorandum notes written on the check stubs. From this source Lee discovered that Ray had invested an additional $1,200 of savings in the business on July 1, and also that the accounts payable arising from the purchase of the canoes and camping equipment had been paid in full. A bank statement received from the bank on September 10 showed a balance on deposit of $2,790.

Ray informed Lee that all cash received by the business had been deposited in the bank and all bills had been paid by check immediately upon receipt; consequently, as of September 10 all bills for the season had been paid. However, nothing had been paid on the note payable.

The canoes and camping equipment were all in excellent condition at the end of the season and Ray planned to resume operations the following summer. In fact, he had already accepted reservations from many customers who wished to return.

Lee felt that some consideration should be given to the wear and tear on the canoes and equipment but she agreed with Ray that for the present purpose the canoes and equipment should be listed in the balance sheet at the original cost. The supplies remaining on hand had cost $50 and Ray felt that these supplies could be used next summer.

Lee suggested that two balance sheets be prepared, one to show the condition of the business on June 1 and the other showing the condition on September 10. She also recommended to Ray that a complete set of accounting records be established.

Instructions

a Use the information in the first paragraph (including the three numbered transactions) as a basis for preparing a balance sheet dated June 1.

b Prepare a balance sheet at September 10. (Because of the incomplete information available, it is not possible to determine the amount of cash at September 10 by adding cash receipts and deducting cash payments throughout the season. The amount on deposit as reported by the bank at September 10 is to be regarded as the total cash belonging to the business at that date.)

c By comparing the two balance sheets, compute the change in owner's equity. Explain the sources of this change in owner's equity and state whether you consider the business to be successful. Also comment on the cash position at the beginning and end of the season. Has the cash position improved significantly? Explain.

ANSWERS TO SELF-TEST QUESTIONS

1 d   2 c   3 a   4 b   5 c

Measuring Business Income

In Chapter 3 our coverage of the accounting cycle is expanded to include the measurement of business income. Attention is focused on the accounting concepts of revenue, expense, net income, and owner's equity. Several important accounting principles are introduced, including the time period principle, the realization principle, and the matching principle. The continuing example of Roberts Real Estate Company is used to show how a business records revenue and expense transactions and prepares an income statement. As Roberts Real Estate Company owns depreciable assets, the concept of depreciation is introduced, and the recording of depreciation expense is illustrated. The procedures for closing the revenue and expense accounts at the end of the accounting period also are illustrated and explained. In summary, this chapter introduces and illustrates the basic concepts of accrual accounting.

After studying this chapter you should be able to meet these Learning Objectives:

1 Explain the nature of net income, revenue, and expenses.

2 Relate the realization principle and the matching principle to the recording of revenue and expenses.

3 Apply the rules of debit and credit to revenue and expense transactions.

4 Define and record depreciation expense.

5 Describe and prepare an income statement and a statement of owner's equity.

6 Prepare closing entries.

7 Describe the sequence of procedures in the accounting cycle.

8 Explain the accrual basis of accounting.

What Is Net Income?

In Chapter 1, we stated that a basic objective of every business is to earn a profit, or net income. Why? The answer lies in the very definition of net income: *an increase in owner's equity resulting from operation of the business.* The opposite of net income, a decrease in owner's equity resulting from operation of the business, is termed a *net loss.*

If you were to organize a small business of your own, you would do so with the hope and expectation that the business would operate at a profit, thereby increasing your ownership equity. Individuals who invest in the capital stock of a large corporation also expect the business to earn a profit which will increase the value of their investment.

The resources generated by profitable operations may be withdrawn by the owners, or retained in the business to finance growth. Some of the largest corporations have become large by retaining their earnings to finance expansion and new business activities.

The Income Statement: A Preview

To determine net income, a business must measure for a given time period (1) the price of goods sold and services rendered to customers and (2) the cost of goods and services used up. The technical accounting terms for these elements of net income are *revenue* and *expenses.* Therefore, we may state that *net income equals revenue minus expenses,* as shown in the following *income statement:*

ROBERTS REAL ESTATE COMPANY
Income Statement
For the Month Ended October 31, 19—

**Income statement
for October**

Revenue:		
Sales commissions earned..		$10,640
Expenses:		
Advertising expense	$ 630	
Salaries expense	7,100	
Telephone expense	144	
Depreciation expense: building.......................................	150	
Depreciation expense: office equipment	45	8,069
Net income		$ 2,571

When we measure the net income earned by a business we are measuring its economic performance—its success or failure as a business enterprise. The owner, managers, and major creditors are anxious to see the latest available income statement and thereby to judge how well the company is doing. If the business is organized as a corporation, the stockholders and prospective investors also will be keenly interested in each successive income statement.

We will show how this income statement is developed from the accounting records of Roberts Real Estate Company later in this chapter. For the moment, however, this illustration will assist us in discussing some of the basic concepts involved in measuring business income.

■ **Income Must Be Related to a Specified Period of Time**   Notice that our sample income statement covers a *period* of time—namely, the month of October. A balance sheet shows the financial position of a business at a *particular date.* An income statement, on the other hand, shows the results of business operations over a span of time. We cannot evaluate net income unless it is associated with a specific time period. For example, if an executive says, "My business earns a net income of $10,000," the profitability of the business is unclear. Does it earn $10,000 per week, per month, or per year?

CASE IN POINT   ■ The late J. Paul Getty, one of the world's first billionaires, was once interviewed by a group of business students. One of the students asked Getty to estimate the amount of his income. As the student had not specified a time period, Getty decided to have some fun with his audience and responded, "About $11,000 . . ." He paused long enough to allow the group to express surprise over this seemingly low amount, and then completed his sentence, ". . . an hour." Incidentally, $11,000 per hour (24 hours per day) amounts to about $100 million per year.

■ **Accounting Periods**   The period of time covered by an income statement is termed the company's *accounting period.* To provide the users of financial statements with timely information, net income is measured for relatively short accounting periods of equal length. This concept, called the *time period principle,* is one of the generally accepted accounting principles that guide the interpretation of financial events and the preparation of financial statements.

The length of a company's accounting period depends upon how frequently managers, investors, and other interested people require information about the company's performance. Every business prepares annual income statements, and most businesses prepare quarterly and monthly income statements as well. (Quarterly statements cover a three-month period and are prepared by all large corporations for distribution to their stockholders.)

The 12-month accounting period used by an entity is called its *fiscal year.* The fiscal year used by most companies coincides with the calendar year and ends on December 31. Some businesses, however, elect to use a fiscal year which ends on some other date. It may be convenient for a business to end its fiscal year during a slack season rather than during a time of peak activity.

CASE IN POINT   ■ Walt Disney Co. ends its fiscal year on September 30. Why? For one reason, September and October are relatively slow months at Disney's theme parks. For another, September financial statements provide timely information about the preceding summer, which is the company's busiest season.

As another example, many department stores, including K-Mart, Neiman-Marcus, Nordstrom, and J. C. Penney, end their fiscal years on January 31—after the rush of the holiday season.

Let us now explore the meaning of the accounting terms *revenue* and *expenses.*

Revenue

Revenue is the price of goods sold and services rendered during a given accounting period. Earning revenue causes owner's equity to increase. When a business renders services or sells merchandise to its customers, it usually receives cash or acquires an account receivable from the customer. The inflow of cash and receivables from customers increases the total assets of the company; on the other side of the accounting equation, the liabilities do not change, but owner's equity increases to match the increase in total assets. Thus revenue is the gross ***increase in owner's equity*** resulting from operation of the business.

Various terms are used to describe different types of revenue; for example, the revenue earned by a real estate broker might be called ***Sales Commissions Earned,*** or alternatively, ***Commissions Revenue.*** In the professional practice of lawyers, physicians, dentists, and CPAs, the revenue is called ***Fees Earned.*** A business which sells merchandise rather than services (General Motors, for example) will use the term ***Sales*** to describe the revenue earned. Another type of revenue is ***Interest Earned,*** which means the amount received as interest on notes receivable, bank deposits, government bonds, or other securities.

Objective 2
Relate the realization principle and the matching principle to the recording of revenue and expenses.

■ **When to Record Revenue: The Realization Principle**   When is revenue recorded in the accounting records? For example, assume that on May 24, a real estate company signs a contract to represent a client in selling the client's personal residence. The contract entitles the real estate company to a commission equal to 5% of the selling price, due 30 days after the date of sale. On June 10, the real estate company sells the house at a price of $120,000, thereby earning a $6,000 commission ($120,000 × 5%), to be received on July 10. When should the company record this $6,000 commission revenue—in May, June, or July?

The company should record this revenue on June 10—the day it ***rendered the service*** of selling the client's house. As the company will not collect this commission until July, it must also record an account receivable on June 10. In July, when this receivable is collected, the company must not record revenue a second time. Collecting an account receivable increases one asset, Cash, and decreases another asset, Accounts Receivable. Thus, collecting an account receivable ***does not increase owner's equity*** and does not represent revenue.

Our answer illustrates a generally accepted accounting principle called the ***realization principle.*** The realization principle states that a business should record revenue at the time ***services are rendered to customers*** or ***goods sold are delivered to customers.*** In short, revenue is recorded when it is ***earned,*** without regard as to when the cash is received.

Expenses

Expenses are the cost of the goods and services used up in the process of earning revenue. Examples include the cost of employees' salaries, advertising, rent, utilities, and the gradual wearing-out (depreciation) of such assets as buildings, automobiles, and office equipment. All these costs are necessary to attract and serve customers and thereby earn revenue. Expenses are often called the "costs of doing business," that is, the cost of the various activities necessary to carry on a business.

An expense always causes a *decrease in owner's equity.* The related changes in the accounting equation can be either (1) a decrease in assets, or (2) an increase in liabilities. An expense reduces assets if payment occurs at the time that the expense is incurred (or if payment has been made in advance). If the expense will not be paid until later, as, for example, the purchase of advertising services on account, the recording of the expense will be accompanied by an increase in liabilities.

■ **When to Record Expenses: The Matching Principle**   A significant relationship exists between revenue and expenses. Expenses are incurred for the *purpose of producing revenue.* In measuring net income for a period, revenue should be offset by *all the expenses incurred in producing that revenue.* This concept of offsetting expenses against revenue on a basis of "cause and effect" is called the *matching principle.*

Timing is an important factor in matching (offsetting) revenue with the related expenses. For example, in preparing monthly income statements, it is important to offset this month's expenses against this month's revenue. We should not offset this month's expenses against last month's revenue, because there is no cause and effect relationship between the two.

To illustrate the matching principle, assume that the salaries earned by sales personnel waiting on customers during July are not paid until early August. In which month should these salaries be regarded as an expense? The answer is *July,* because this is the month in which the sales personnel's services *helped to produce revenue.*

We previously explained that revenue and cash receipts are not one and the same thing. Similarly, expenses and cash payments are not identical. The cash payment for an expense may occur before, after, or in the same period that an expense helps to produce revenue. In deciding when to record an expense, the critical question is *"In what period will this expenditure help to produce revenue?"* not "When will the cash payment occur?"

■ **Expenditures Benefiting More Than One Accounting Period**
Many expenditures made by a business benefit two or more accounting periods. Fire insurance policies, for example, usually cover a period of 12 months. If a company prepares monthly income statements, a portion of the cost of such a policy should be allocated to insurance expense each month that the policy is in force. In this case, apportionment of the cost of the policy by months is an easy matter. If the 12-month policy costs $240, for example, the insurance expense for each month amounts to $20 ($240 cost ÷ 12 months).

Not all transactions can be so precisely divided by accounting periods. The purchase of a building, furniture and fixtures, machinery, a typewriter, or an automobile provides benefits to the business over all the years in which such an asset is used. No one can determine in advance exactly how many years of service will be received from such long-lived assets. Nevertheless, in measuring the net income of a business for a period of one year or less, the accountant must *estimate* what portion of the cost of the building and other long-lived assets is applicable to the current year. Since the allocations of these costs are estimates rather than precise measurements, it follows that income statements should be regarded as useful *approximations* of net income rather than as absolutely exact measurements.

For some expenditures, such as those for advertising or employee training programs, it is not possible to estimate objectively the number of accounting periods over which revenue is likely to be produced. In such cases, generally accepted accounting principles require that the expenditure be charged *immediately to expense*. This treatment is based upon the accounting principle of *objectivity* and the concept of *conservatism*. Accountants require *objective evidence* that an expenditure will produce revenue in future periods before they will view the expenditure as creating an asset. When this objective evidence does not exist, they follow the conservative practice of recording the expenditure as an expense. *Conservatism*, in this context, means applying the accounting treatment which results in the *lowest* (most conservative) estimate of net income for the current period.

Debit and Credit Rules for Revenue and Expense

Objective 3
Apply the rules of debit and credit to revenue and expense transactions.

We have stressed that revenue increases owner's equity and that expenses decrease owner's equity. The debit and credit rules for recording revenue and expenses in the ledger accounts are a natural extension of the rules for recording changes in owner's equity. The rules previously stated for recording increases and decreases in owner's equity were as follows:

■ *Increases* in owner's equity are recorded by *credits.*

■ *Decreases* in owner's equity are recorded by *debits.*

This rule is now extended to cover revenue and expense accounts:

■ Revenue *increases* owner's equity; therefore revenue is recorded by a *credit.*

■ Expenses *decrease* owner's equity; therefore expenses are recorded by *debits.*

Ledger Accounts for Revenue and Expenses

During the course of an accounting period, a great many revenue and expense transactions occur in the average business. To classify and summarize these numerous transactions, a separate ledger account is maintained for each major type of revenue and expense. For example, almost every business maintains accounts for advertising expense, telephone expense, and salaries expense. At the end of the period, all the advertising expenses appear as debits in the Advertising Expense account. The debit balance of this account represents the total advertising expense of the period and is listed as one of the expense items in the income statement.

Revenue accounts are usually much less numerous than expense accounts. A small business such as Roberts Real Estate Company in our continuing illustration may have only one or two types of revenue, such as commissions earned from arranging sales of real estate, and fees earned from managing properties in behalf of clients. In a business of this type, the revenue accounts might be called Sales Commissions Earned and Management Fees Earned.

Investments and Withdrawals by the Owner

The owner of an unincorporated business may at any time invest assets or withdraw assets from the business. These "investment transactions" cause changes in the amount of owner's equity, but they are *not* considered revenue or expenses of the business.

Investments of assets by the owner are recorded by debiting the asset accounts and crediting the owner's capital account. This transaction is not viewed as revenue, because the business has not sold any merchandise or rendered any service in exchange for the assets received.

The income statement of a sole proprietorship does not include any salary expense representing the managerial services rendered by the owner. One reason for not including a salary to the owner-manager is that individuals in such positions are able to set their salaries at any amount they choose. The use of an unrealistic salary to the proprietor would tend to destroy the usefulness of the income statement for measuring the profitability of the business. Thus, accountants regard the owner-manager as working to earn the *entire net income* of the business, rather than as working for a salary.

Even though the owner does not technically receive a salary, he or she usually makes withdrawals of cash from time to time for personal use. These withdrawals reduce the assets and owner's equity of the business, but they are *not* expenses. Expenses are incurred for the purpose of *generating revenue,* and withdrawals by the owner do not have this purpose.

Withdrawals could be recorded by debiting the owner's capital account. However, a clearer record is created if a separate Drawing account is debited. (In our Roberts Real Estate example, we will use an account entitled *James Roberts, Drawing* to record withdrawals by the owner.)

Debits to the owner's drawing account result from such transactions as:

1 Withdrawals of cash.

2 Withdrawals of other assets. The owner of a clothing store, for example, may withdraw merchandise for his or her personal use. The amount of the debit to the drawing account would be for the cost of the goods which were withdrawn.

3 Payment of the owner's personal bills out of company funds.

As investments and withdrawals by the owner are not classified as revenue and expenses, they are not included in the income statement. Instead, they are summarized in the statement of owner's equity, which will be discussed later in this chapter.

Recording Revenue and Expense Transactions: An Illustration

The organization of Roberts Real Estate Company during September has already been described. The illustration is now continued for October, during which the company earned commissions by selling several residences for its clients. Bear in mind that the company does not own any residential property; it merely acts as a broker or agent for clients wishing to sell their houses. A commission of 6% of the sales price of the house is charged for this service.

During October the company not only earned commissions but also incurred a number of expenses.

Note that each illustrated transaction which affects an income statement account also affects a balance sheet account. This pattern is consistent with our previous discussion of revenue and expenses. In recording revenue transactions, we debit the assets received and credit a revenue account. In recording expense transactions, we debit an expense account and credit the asset Cash, or a liability account if payment is to be made later. The transactions for October were as follows:

Oct. 1 Paid $360 for publication of newspaper advertising describing various houses offered for sale.

	ANALYSIS	RULE	ENTRY
Advertising expense incurred and paid	*The cost of advertising is an expense*	*Expenses decrease the owner's equity and are recorded by debits*	*Debit: Advertising Expense, $360*
	The asset Cash was decreased	*Decreases in assets are recorded by credits*	*Credit: Cash, $360*

Oct. 6 Earned and collected a commission of $2,250 by selling a residence previously listed by a client.

	ANALYSIS	RULE	ENTRY
Revenue earned and collected	*The asset Cash was increased*	*Increases in assets are recorded by debits*	*Debit: Cash, $2,250*
	Revenue was earned	*Revenue increases the owner's equity and is recorded by a credit*	*Credit: Sales Commissions Earned, $2,250*

Oct. 16 Newspaper advertising was purchased at a price of $270, payment to be made within 30 days.

	ANALYSIS	RULE	ENTRY
Advertising expense incurred; to be paid later	*The cost of advertising is an expense*	*Expenses decrease the owner's equity and are recorded by debits*	*Debit: Advertising Expense, $270*
	An account payable, a liability, was incurred	*Increases in liabilities are recorded by credits*	*Credit: Accounts Payable, $270*

Oct. 20 A commission of $8,390 was earned by selling a client's residence. The sales agreement provided that the commission would be received in 60 days.

	ANALYSIS	RULE	ENTRY
Revenue earned; to be collected later ■	*An asset in the form of an account receivable was acquired*	*Increases in assets are recorded by debits*	*Debit: Accounts Receivable, $8,390*
	Revenue was earned	*Revenue increases the owner's equity and is recorded by a credit*	*Credit: Sales Commissions Earned, $8,390*

Oct. 25 Roberts withdrew $2,800 for personal use.

	ANALYSIS	RULE	ENTRY
Withdrawal of cash by the owner ■	*Withdrawal of assets by the owner decreases the owner's equity*	*Decreases in owner's equity are recorded by debits*	*Debit: James Roberts, Drawing, $2,800*
	The asset Cash was decreased	*Decreases in assets are recorded by credits*	*Credit: Cash, $2,800*

Oct. 30 Roberts found that he did not need all of the $2,800 withdrawn on October 25, and he redeposited $1,000 of this amount in the company's bank account.

	ANALYSIS	RULE	ENTRY
Additional investment by the owner ■	*The asset Cash was increased*	*Increases in assets are recorded by debits*	*Debit: Cash, $1,000*
	The owner's equity was increased	*Increases in owner's equity are recorded by credits*	*Credit: James Roberts, Capital, $1,000*

Oct. 31 Paid salaries of $7,100 to employees for services rendered during October.

	ANALYSIS	RULE	ENTRY
Salaries expense incurred and paid ■	*Salaries of employees are an expense*	*Expenses decrease the owner's equity and are recorded by debits*	*Debit: Salaries Expense, $7,100*
	The asset Cash was decreased	*Decreases in assets are recorded by credits*	*Credit: Cash, $7,100*

Oct. 31 A telephone bill for October amounting to $144 was received. Payment was required by November 10.

	ANALYSIS	RULE	ENTRY
Telephone expense incurred; to be paid later	*The cost of telephone service is an expense*	*Expenses decrease the owner's equity and are recorded by debits*	*Debit: Telephone Expense, $144*
	An account payable, a liability, was incurred	*Increases in liabilities are recorded by credits*	*Credit: Accounts Payable, $144*

The journal entries to record the October transactions are as follows:

General Journal   Page 2

October journal entries for Roberts Real Estate Company

19—					
Oct	1	Advertising Expense..........................	70	360	
		Cash....................................	1		360
		Paid for newspaper advertising.			
	6	Cash...	1	2,250	
		Sales Commissions Earned.............	60		2,250
		Earned and collected commission by selling residence for client.			
	16	Advertising Expense..........................	70	270	
		Accounts Payable	32		270
		Purchased newspaper advertising; payable in 30 days.			
	20	Accounts Receivable	4	8,390	
		Sales Commissions Earned.............	60		8,390
		Earned commission by selling residence for client; commission to be received in 60 days.			
	25	James Roberts, Drawing	51	2,800	
		Cash....................................	1		2,800
		Withdrawal of cash by owner.			
	30	Cash...	1	1,000	
		James Roberts, Capital	50		1,000
		Additional investment by owner.			
	31	Salaries Expense.............................	72	7,100	
		Cash....................................	1		7,100
		Paid salaries for October.			
	31	Telephone Expense	74	144	
		Accounts Payable	32		144
		To record liability for October telephone service.			

The column headings at the top of the illustrated journal page (*Date, Account Titles and Explanation, LP, Debit,* and *Credit*) are seldom used in practice. They are included here as an instructional guide but will be omitted from some of the later illustrations of journal entries.

The Ledger

The ledger of Roberts Real Estate Company after the October transactions have been posted is now illustrated. The accounts appear in financial statement order. To conserve space in this illustration, several ledger accounts appear on a single page; in actual practice, however, each account occupies a separate page in the ledger.

		CASH			Account No.	
DATE	EXPLANATION	REF	DEBIT	CREDIT	BALANCE	
19—						
Sept 1		1	180000		180000	
3		1		141000	39000	
5		1		15000	24000	
20		1	1500		25500	
30		1		3000	22500	
Oct 1		2		360	22140	
6		2	2250		24390	
25		2		2800	21590	
30		2	1000		22590	
31		2		7100	15490	

		ACCOUNTS RECEIVABLE			Account No. 4	
DATE	EXPLANATION	REF	DEBIT	CREDIT	BALANCE	
19—						
Sept 10		1	11000		11000	
20		1		1500	9500	
Oct 20		2	8390		17890	

		LAND			Account No. 20										
DATE		EXPLANATION	REF	DEBIT		CREDIT		BALANCE	
19—									
Sept	3		1	141000				141000	
	10		1			11000		130000	

		BUILDING			Account No. 22										
DATE		EXPLANATION	REF	DEBIT		CREDIT		BALANCE	
19—									
Sept	5		1	36000				36000	

		OFFICE EQUIPMENT			Account No. 25										
DATE		EXPLANATION	REF	DEBIT		CREDIT		BALANCE	
19—									
Sept.	14		1	5400				5400	

		ACCOUNTS PAYABLE			Account No. 32										
DATE		EXPLANATION	REF	DEBIT		CREDIT		BALANCE	
19—									
Sept.	5		1			21000		21000	
	14		1			5400		26400	
	30		1	3000				23400	
Oct.	16		2			270		23670	
	31		2			144		23814	

	JAMES ROBERTS, CAPITAL				Account No. 50
DATE	EXPLANATION	REF	DEBIT	CREDIT	BALANCE
19—					
Sept 1		1		180000	180000
Oct 30		2		1000	181000

	JAMES ROBERTS, DRAWING				Account No. 51
DATE	EXPLANATION	REF	DEBIT	CREDIT	BALANCE
19—					
Oct 25		2	2800		2800

	SALES COMMISSIONS EARNED				Account No. 60
DATE	EXPLANATION	REF	DEBIT	CREDIT	BALANCE
19—					
Oct 6		2		2250	2250
20		2		8390	10640

	ADVERTISING EXPENSE				Account No. 70
DATE	EXPLANATION	REF	DEBIT	CREDIT	BALANCE
19—					
Oct 1		2	360		360
16		2	270		630

	SALARIES EXPENSE				Account No. 72
DATE	EXPLANATION	REF	DEBIT	CREDIT	BALANCE
19—					
Oct 31		2	7100		7100

TELEPHONE EXPENSE					Account No. 74
DATE	EXPLANATION	REF	DEBIT	CREDIT	BALANCE
19—					
Oct 31		2	144		144

The accounts in this illustration are listed in *financial statement order*—that is, balance sheet accounts first (assets, liabilities, and owner's equity), followed by income statement accounts. The sequence of accounts within the balance sheet categories was discussed in Chapter 2. Within the categories of revenue and expense, accounts may be listed in any order.

The Trial Balance

A trial balance prepared from the ledger accounts of Roberts Real Estate Company is shown below:

ROBERTS REAL ESTATE COMPANY
Trial Balance
October 31, 19__

Proving the equality of debits and credits

Cash	$ 15,490	
Accounts receivable	17,890	
Land	130,000	
Building	36,000	
Office equipment	5,400	
Accounts payable		$ 23,814
James Roberts, capital		181,000
James Roberts, drawing	2,800	
Sales commissions earned		10,640
Advertising expense	630	
Salaries expense	7,100	
Telephone expense	144	
	$215,454	$215,454

This trial balance proves the equality of the debit and credit entries in the company's ledger. Notice that the trial balance contains income statement accounts as well as balance sheet accounts.

ADJUSTING ENTRIES: THE NEXT STEP IN THE ACCOUNTING CYCLE

Many transactions affect the revenue or expenses of two or more accounting periods. For example, a business may purchase equipment that will last for many years, insurance policies that cover 12 months, or enough office supplies to last for several months. Each of these assets is gradually used up—that is, becomes expense. How do accountants allocate the cost of these assets to expense over a span of several accounting periods? The answer is *adjusting entries*.

Adjusting entries are made at the end of each accounting period. There are several different types of adjusting entries; in fact, many businesses make a dozen or more adjusting entries at the end of every accounting period. In this chapter, we introduce the concept of end-of-period adjustments with the entry to record *depreciation expense.* This is the most common of all adjusting entries; every business that owns a building or equipment must record depreciation expense at the end of each accounting period.

<table>
<tr><td>**Objective 4**
Define and record depreciation expense.</td><td>■ **Depreciation Expense**   Our definition of expense is the cost of goods and services used up in the process of earning revenue. Buildings and equipment are examples of goods that are purchased in advance, but which are used up gradually over many accounting periods. Each year a portion of the usefulness of these assets expires, and a portion of their total cost should be recognized as *depreciation expense.* The term *depreciation* means the *systematic allocation of the cost of an asset to expense* over the accounting periods making up the asset's useful life.</td></tr>
</table>

Although depreciation expense occurs each month, it does not involve monthly transactions. In effect, depreciation expense is paid in advance when the related asset is originally acquired. Thus, adjusting entries are needed at the end of each accounting period to record the appropriate amount of depreciation expense. Failure to make these adjusting entries would result in understating the expenses of the period and consequently overstating net income.

■ **Building**   The office building purchased by Roberts Real Estate Company at a cost of $36,000 is estimated to have a useful life of 20 years. The purpose of the $36,000 expenditure was to provide a place in which to carry on the business and thereby to obtain revenue. After 20 years of use the building is expected to be worthless and the original cost of $36,000 will have been entirely consumed. In effect, the company has purchased 20 years of "housing services" at a total cost of $36,000. A portion of this cost expires during each year of use of the building. If we assume that each year's operations should bear an equal share of the total cost (straight-line depreciation), the annual depreciation expense will amount to 1/20 of $36,000, or $1,800. On a monthly basis, depreciation expense is $150 ($36,000 cost ÷ 240 months). There are alternative methods of spreading the cost of a depreciable asset over its useful life, some of which will be considered in Chapter 10.

The journal entry to record depreciation of the building during October follows:

General Journal Page 2

	DATE		ACCOUNT TITLES AND EXPLANATION	LP	DEBIT	CREDIT

■
Recording depreciation of the building
	19__
	Oct
		31	*Depreciation Expense: Building* ....
			   Accumulated Depreciation:
			      Building ....
			To record depreciation for October. Cost of
			$36,000 ÷ 240 months = $150 a month.
				76
				
				23
					150	
						
						150

The depreciation expense account will appear in the income statement for October along with the other expenses of salaries, advertising, and telephone. The Accumulated Depreciation: Building account will appear in the balance sheet as a deduction from the Building account, as shown by the following illustration of a partial balance sheet:

ROBERTS REAL ESTATE COMPANY
Partial Balance Sheet
October 31, 19___

<table>
<tr><td>Building (at cost) ....</td><td>$36,000</td><td></td></tr>
<tr><td>Less: Accumulated depreciation ....</td><td>150</td><td>$35,850</td></tr>
</table>

Showing accumulated depreciation in the balance sheet

The end result of crediting the Accumulated Depreciation: Building account is much the same as if the credit had been made to the Building account; that is, the net amount shown on the balance sheet for the building is reduced from $36,000 to $35,850. Although the credit side of a depreciation entry *could* be made directly to the asset account, it is customary and more efficient to record such credits in a separate account entitled Accumulated Depreciation. The original cost of the asset and the total amount of depreciation recorded over the years can more easily be determined from the ledger when separate accounts are maintained for the asset and for the accumulated depreciation.

Accumulated Depreciation: Building is an example of a *contra-asset account,* because it has a credit balance and is offset against an asset account (Building) to produce the proper balance sheet amount for the asset.

■ **Office Equipment**   Depreciation on the office equipment of Roberts Real Estate Company must also be recorded at the end of October. This equipment cost $5,400 and is assumed to have a useful life of 10 years. Monthly depreciation expense on the straight-line basis is, therefore, $45, computed by dividing the cost of $5,400 by the useful life of 120 months. The journal entry is as follows:

General Journal   Page 2

DATE		ACCOUNT TITLES AND EXPLANATION	LP	DEBIT	CREDIT
19___					
Oct	31	Depreciation Expense: Office Equipment	78	45	
		Accumulated Depreciation: Office			
		Equipment	26		45
		To record depreciation for October. Cost of			
		$5,400 ÷ 120 months = $45 a month.			

Recording depreciation of office equipment

No depreciation was recorded on the building and office equipment for September, the month in which these assets were acquired, because regular operations did not begin until October. Generally, depreciation is not recognized until the business begins active operation and the assets are *placed in use.*

The journal entry by which depreciation is recorded at the end of the month is called an *adjusting entry.* The adjustment of certain asset accounts and related expense accounts is a necessary step at the end of each accounting period so that the information presented in the financial statements will be as accurate and complete as possible. In the next chapter, adjusting entries will be shown for some other items in addition to depreciation.

The Adjusted Trial Balance

After all the necessary adjusting entries have been journalized and posted, an *adjusted trial balance* is prepared to prove that the ledger is still in balance. It also provides a complete listing of the account balances to be used in preparing the financial statements. The following adjusted trial balance differs from the trial balance shown on page 94 because it includes accounts for depreciation expense and accumulated depreciation.

ROBERTS REAL ESTATE COMPANY
Adjusted Trial Balance
October 31, 19__

Adjusted trial balance

Cash..	$ 15,490	
Accounts receivable	17,890	
Land...	130,000	
Building...	36,000	
Accumulated depreciation: building		$ 150
Office equipment	5,400	
Accumulated depreciation: office equipment......................		45
Accounts payable		23,814
James Roberts, capital		181,000
James Roberts, drawing	2,800	
Sales commissions earned......................................		10,640
Advertising expense	630	
Salaries expense	7,100	
Telephone expense	144	
Depreciation expense: building.................................	150	
Depreciation expense: office equipment	45	
	$215,649	$215,649

FINANCIAL STATEMENTS

Now that Roberts Real Estate Company has been operating for a month, managers and outside parties will want to know more about the company than just its financial position. They will want to know the results of operations— whether the month's activities have been profitable or unprofitable. To provide this additional information, we will prepare a more complete set of financial statements, consisting of an income statement, a statement of owner's equity, and a balance sheet.[1] These statements are illustrated on page 98.

---

[1] A complete set of financial statements also includes a *statement of cash flows,* which will be discussed in Chapter 19.

ROBERTS REAL ESTATE COMPANY
Income Statement
For the Month Ended October 31, 19__

Revenue:		
Sales commissions earned...		$10,640
Expenses:		
Advertising expense	$ 630	
Office salaries expense	7,100	
Telephone expense	144	
Depreciation expense: building..	150	
Depreciation expense: office equipment	45	8,069
Net income		$ 2,571

Net income is an increase in owner's equity

ROBERTS REAL ESTATE COMPANY
Statement of Owner's Equity
For the Month Ended October 31, 19__

James Roberts, capital, Sept. 30, 19__	$180,000
Add: Net income for October	2,571
Additional investment by owner...	1,000
Subtotal...	$183,571
Less: Withdrawals by owner	2,800
James Roberts, capital, Oct. 31, 19__	$180,771

The ending balance of owner's equity appears in the balance sheet

ROBERTS REAL ESTATE COMPANY
Balance Sheet
October 31, 19__

ASSETS

Cash..		$ 15,490
Accounts receivable		17,890
Land..		130,000
Building..	$36,000	
Less: Accumulated depreciation	150	35,850
Office equipment	$ 5,400	
Less: Accumulated depreciation	45	5,355
Total assets		$204,585

LIABILITIES & OWNER'S EQUITY

Liabilities	
Accounts payable	$ 23,814
Owner's equity:	
James Roberts, capital, Oct. 31, 19__	180,771
Total liabilities & owner's equity..	$204,585

The Income Statement

Objective 5
Describe and
prepare an
income statement
and a statement
of owner's
equity.

The revenue and expenses shown in the income statement are taken directly from the company's adjusted trial balance. The income statement of Roberts Real Estate Company shows that revenue earned in October exceeded the expenses of the month, thus producing a net income of $2,571. Bear in mind, however, that our measurement of net income is not absolutely accurate or precise, because of the assumptions and estimates in the accounting process.

An income statement has certain limitations. Remember that the amounts shown for depreciation expense are based upon *estimates* of the useful lives of the company's building and office equipment. Also, the income statement includes only those events which have been *evidenced by business transactions.* Perhaps during October, Roberts Real Estate Company has made contact with many people who are right on the verge of buying or selling homes. Good business contacts are an important step toward profitable operations. However, such contacts are not reflected in the income statement because their value cannot be measured *objectively* until actual transactions take place. Despite these limitations, the income statement is of vital importance and indicates that the new business has been profitable during its first month of operation.

Alternative titles for the income statement include *earnings statement, statement of operations,* and *profit and loss statement.* However, *income statement* is by far the most popular term for this important financial statement. In summary, we can say that an income statement is used to summarize the *operating results* of a business by matching the revenue earned during a given time period with the expenses incurred in obtaining that revenue.

The Statement of Owner's Equity

This financial statement summarizes the increases and decreases during the accounting period in the amount of owner's equity. Increases result from earning net income and from additional investments by the owner; decreases result from net losses and from withdrawals of assets by the owner.

The owner's equity at the beginning of the period ($180,000) may be obtained from the ledger or from the balance sheet of the preceding period. As we have just illustrated, the amount of net income or net loss for the period is determined in the company's *income statement.* Additional investments by the owner may be determined by reviewing the credit column of the owner's capital account in the ledger. Withdrawals during the period are indicated by the balance in the owner's drawing account. By adjusting the beginning amount of owner's equity for the increases and decreases occurring during the period, we are able to determine the owner's equity at the end of the period. This amount, *$180,771* in our example, will also appear in the company's October 31 balance sheet.

The Balance Sheet

The balance sheet lists the amounts of the company's assets, liabilities, and owner's equity at the *end* of the accounting period. The balances of the asset and liability accounts are taken directly from the adjusted trial balance on page 97. The amount of owner's equity at the end of the period, $180,771, was determined in the *statement of owner's equity.*

Previous illustrations of balance sheets have been arranged in *account form*—that is, with assets on the left and liabilities and owner's equity on the right. The illustration on page 98 is arranged in *report form,* with the liabilities and owner's equity sections listed below rather than to the right of the asset section. Both the account form and the report form of balance sheet are widely used.

Relationship among the Financial Statements

A set of financial statements becomes easier to understand if we recognize that the income statement, statement of owner's equity, and balance sheet all are related to one another. These relationships are emphasized by the arrows in the right-hand margin of our illustration on page 98.

The balance sheet prepared at the end of the preceding period and the one prepared at the end of the current period each show the amount of owner's equity at the respective balance sheet dates. The statement of owner's equity summarizes the changes in owner's equity occurring between these two balance sheet dates. The income statement provides a detailed explanation of the most important change in owner's equity—the amount of net income or net loss for the accounting period. Thus, the income statement and the statement of owner's equity explain the change in the amount of owner's equity shown in successive balance sheets.

CLOSING THE TEMPORARY ACCOUNTS

Objective 6
Prepare closing entries.

As previously stated, revenue increases owner's equity, and expenses and withdrawals by the owner decrease owner's equity. If the only financial statement that we needed was a balance sheet, these changes in owner's equity could be recorded directly in the owner's capital account. However, owners, managers, investors, and others need to know amounts of specific revenues and expenses, and the amount of net income earned in the period. Therefore, we maintain separate ledger accounts to measure each type of revenue and expense, and the owner's drawings.

These revenue, expense, and drawing accounts are called *temporary* accounts, or *nominal* accounts, because they accumulate the transactions of *only one accounting period.* At the end of this accounting period, the changes in owner's equity accumulated in these temporary accounts are transferred into the owner's capital account. This process serves two purposes. First, it *updates the balance of the owner's capital account* for changes in owner's equity occurring during the accounting period. Second, it *returns the balances of the temporary accounts to zero,* so that they are ready for measuring the revenue, expenses, and drawings of the next accounting period.

The owner's capital account and other balance sheet accounts are called *permanent* or *real* accounts, because their balances continue to exist beyond the current accounting period. The process of transferring the balances of the temporary accounts into the owner's permanent capital account is called *closing* the accounts. The journal entries made for the purpose of closing the temporary accounts are called *closing entries.*

It is common practice to close the accounts only once a year, but for illustration, we shall now demonstrate the closing of the accounts of Roberts Real Estate Company at October 31 after one month's operation.

■ **Closing Entries for Revenue Accounts** Revenue accounts have credit balances. Closing a revenue account, therefore, means transferring its credit balance to the Income Summary account. This transfer is accomplished by a journal entry debiting the revenue account in an amount equal to its credit balance, with an offsetting credit to the Income Summary account. The debit portion of this closing entry returns the balance of the revenue account to zero; the credit portion transfers the former balance of the revenue account into the Income Summary account. The only revenue account of Roberts Real Estate Company is Sales Commission Earned, which had a credit balance of $10,640 at October 31. The closing entry is as follows:

General Journal   Page 3

	DATE		ACCOUNT TITLES AND EXPLANATION	LP	DEBIT	CREDIT
	19__					
Closing a revenue account	Oct	31	Sales Commissions Earned..................	60	10,640	
			Income Summary	53		10,640
			To close the Sales Commissions Earned			
			account.			

After this closing entry has been posted, the two accounts affected will appear as follows. A few details of account structure have been omitted to simplify the illustration; a directional arrow has been added to show the transfer of the $10,640 balance of the revenue account into the Income Summary account.

Sales Commissions Earned   80   Income Summary   53

DATE		EXP.	REF	DEBIT	CREDIT	BALANCE
Oct	6		2		2,250	2,250
	20		2		8,390	10,640
	31	To close	3	10,640		–0–

DATE		EXP.	REF	DEBIT	CREDIT	BALANCE
Oct	31		3		10,640	10,640

Closing Entries for Expense Accounts

Expense accounts have debit balances. Closing an expense account means transferring its debit balance to the Income Summary account. The journal entry to close an expense account, therefore, consists of a credit to the expense account in an amount equal to its debit balance, with an offsetting debit to the Income Summary account.

There are five expense accounts in the ledger of Roberts Real Estate Company. Five separate journal entries could be made to close these five expense accounts, but the use of one *compound journal entry* is an easier, time-saving method of closing all five expense accounts. A compound journal entry is an entry that includes debits to more than one account or credits to more than one account.

General Journal   Page 3

DATE		ACCOUNT TITLES AND EXPLANATION	LP	DEBIT	CREDIT
19__					
Oct	31	Income Summary	53	8,069	
		Advertising Expense....................	70		630
		Salaries Expense.......................	72		7,100
		Telephone Expense	74		144
		Depreciation Expense: Building.........	76		150
		Depreciation Expense: Office			
		Equipment	78		45
		To close the expense accounts.			

After this closing entry has been posted, the Income Summary account has a credit balance of $2,571, and the five expense accounts have zero balances, as shown on the following page.

Closing the Income Summary Account

The five expense accounts have now been closed and the total amount of $8,069 formerly contained in these accounts appears in the debit column of the Income Summary account. The commissions of $10,640 earned during October appear in the credit column of the Income Summary account. Since the credit entry of $10,640 representing October revenue is larger than the debit of $8,069 representing October expenses, the account has a credit balance of $2,571—the net income for October.

The net income of $2,571 earned during October causes the owner's equity to increase. The *credit* balance of the Income Summary account is, therefore, transferred to the owner's capital account by the following closing entry.

General Journal   Page 3

DATE		ACCOUNT TITLES AND EXPLANATION	LP	DEBIT	CREDIT
19__					
Oct	31	Income Summary	53	2,571	
		James Roberts, Capital	50		2,571
		To close the Income Summary account for			
		October by transferring the net income to			
		the owner's capital account.			

After this closing entry has been posted, the Income Summary account has a zero balance, and the net income for October will appear as an increase (or credit entry) in the owner's capital account as shown on page 104.

Expense accounts have zero balances after closing entries have been posted

INCOME SUMMARY   Account No. 53

DATE		EXPLANATION	REF	DEBIT	CREDIT	BALANCE
19__						
Oct	31		3		10,640	10,640
	31		3	8,069		2,571

ADVERTISING EXPENSE   Account No. 70

DATE		EXPLANATION	REF	DEBIT	CREDIT	BALANCE
19__						
Oct	2		2	360		360
	16		2	270		630
	31	To close	3		630	–0–

SALARIES EXPENSE   Account No. 72

DATE		EXPLANATION	REF	DEBIT	CREDIT	BALANCE
19__						
Oct	31		2	7,100		7,100
	31	To close	3		7,100	–0–

TELEPHONE EXPENSE   Account No. 74

DATE		EXPLANATION	REF	DEBIT	CREDIT	BALANCE
19__						
Oct	31		2	144		144
	31	To close	3		144	–0–

DEPRECIATION EXPENSE: BUILDING   Account No. 76

DATE		EXPLANATION	REF	DEBIT	CREDIT	BALANCE
19__						
Oct	31		2	150		150
	31	To close	3		150	–0–

DEPRECIATION EXPENSE: OFFICE EQUIPMENT   Account No. 78

DATE		EXPLANATION	REF	DEBIT	CREDIT	BALANCE
19__						
Oct	31		2	45		45
	31	To close	3		45	–0–

INCOME SUMMARY   Account No. 53

■
Income Summary
account is closed
into the owner's
capital account

19__						
Oct	31	Revenue	3		10,640	10,640
	31	Expenses	3	8,069		2,571
	31	To close	3	2,571		–0–

JAMES ROBERTS, CAPITAL   Account No. 50

19__						
Sept	1	Investment by owner	1		180,000	180,000
Oct	30	Additional investment by owner	2		1,000	181,000
	31	Net income for October	3		2,571	183,571

In our illustration the business has operated profitably with revenue in excess of expenses. Not every business is so fortunate: if the expenses of a business are larger than its revenue, the Income Summary account will have a debit balance, representing a **net loss** for the accounting period. In that case, the closing of the Income Summary account requires a debit to the owner's capital account and an offsetting credit to the Income Summary account. The owner's equity will, of course, be reduced by the amount of the loss debited to the capital account.

Note that the Income Summary account is used only at the end of the period when the accounts are being closed. The Income Summary account has no entries and no balance except during the process of closing the accounts at the end of the accounting period.

Closing the Owner's Drawing Account

As explained earlier in this chapter, withdrawals of cash or other assets by the owner are not considered as an expense of the business and, therefore, are not a factor in determining the net income for the period. Since drawings by the owner do not constitute an expense, the owner's drawing account is closed not into the Income Summary account but directly to the owner's capital account. The following journal entry serves to close the drawing account in the ledger of Roberts Real Estate Company at October 31.

General Journal   Page 3

■
Drawing account
is closed into the
owner's capital
account

DATE		ACCOUNT TITLES AND EXPLANATION	LP	DEBIT	CREDIT
19__					
Oct	31	James Roberts, Capital	50	2,800	
		James Roberts, Drawing	51		2,800
		To close the owner's drawing account.			

After this closing entry has been posted, the drawing account will have a zero balance, and the amount withdrawn by Roberts during October will appear as a deduction or debit entry in the capital account on page 105.

JAMES ROBERTS, DRAWING

19__							
Oct	31	Withdrawal	2	2,800		2,800
	31	To close	3		2,800	–0–

JAMES ROBERTS, CAPITAL

One account now shows the total equity of the owner

19__						
Sept	1	Investment by owner	1		180,000	180,000
Oct	30	Additional investment by owner	2		1,000	181,000
	31	Net income for October	3		2,571	183,571
	31	From owner's drawing account	3	2,800		180,771

Summary of the Closing Process

Let us now summarize the process of closing the accounts.

1 Close the various *revenue* accounts by transferring their balances into the Income Summary account.

2 Close the various *expense* accounts by transferring their balances into the Income Summary account.

3 Close the *Income Summary account* by transferring its balance into the owner's capital account.

4 Close the owner's *drawing* account into the owner's capital account. (The balance of the owner's capital account in the ledger will now be the same as the amount of owner's equity appearing in the balance sheet.)

The closing of the accounts may be illustrated graphically by use of T accounts as follows:

Flowchart of the closing process

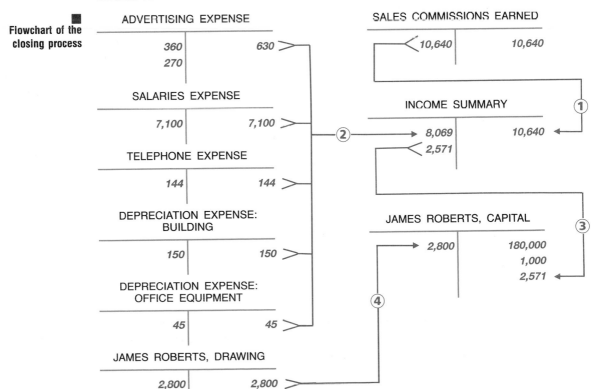

After-Closing Trial Balance

After the revenue and expense accounts have been closed, it is desirable to prepare an *after-closing trial balance,* which will consist of balance sheet accounts *only.* There is always the possibility that an error in posting the closing entries may have upset the equality of debits and credits in the ledger. The after-closing trial balance is prepared from the ledger. It gives assurance that the accounts are in balance and ready for the recording of the transactions of the new accounting period. The after-closing trial balance of Roberts Real Estate Company follows:

ROBERTS REAL ESTATE COMPANY

After-Closing Trial Balance

October 31, 19___

Only the balance sheet accounts remain open

Cash	$ 15,490	
Accounts receivable	17,890	
Land	130,000	
Building	36,000	
Accumulated depreciation: building		$ 150
Office equipment	5,400	
Accumulated depreciation: office equipment		45
Accounts payable		23,814
James Roberts, capital		180,771
	$204,780	$204,780

Sequence of Procedures in the Accounting Cycle

Objective 7
Describe the sequence of procedures in the accounting cycle.

The accounting procedures described to this point may be summarized in eight steps, as follows:

1 Journalize transactions   Enter all transactions in the general journal, thus creating a chronological record of events.

2 Post to ledger accounts   Post debits and credits from the general journal to the proper ledger accounts, thus creating a record classified by accounts.

3 Prepare a trial balance   Prove the equality of debits and credits in the ledger.

4 Make end-of-period adjustments   Draft adjusting entries in the general journal, and post to ledger accounts. Thus far we have illustrated only one type of adjustment: the recording of depreciation at the end of the period.

5 Prepare an adjusted trial balance   Prove again the equality of debits and credits in the ledger.

6 Prepare financial statements   An income statement is needed to show the results of operation for the period. A balance sheet is needed to show the financial position of the business at the end of the period.

7 Journalize and post closing entries   The closing entries clear the revenue, expense, and drawing accounts, making them ready for recording the events of the next accounting period. The closing entries also transfer the net income or loss of the completed period to the owner's capital account.

8 Prepare an after-closing trial balance This step ensures that the ledger remains in balance after posting of the closing entries.

These eight procedures represent a complete accounting cycle. In Chapter 4, however, we shall see that the preparation of a *work sheet* will enable us to consolidate several of these procedures.

Accounting Procedures in a Computer-Based System

The sequence of procedures performed in computer-based systems is essentially the same as in manual systems. Of course, the computer is programmed to perform a number of these steps automatically. In the preceding list, procedures **1** and **4** both involve the analysis of business transactions and judgmental decisions as to accounts to be debited and credited and the dollar amounts. These two steps in the accounting cycle require human judgment, regardless of whether the data is processed manually or by computer. As mentioned in Chapter 2, a computer-based system may call for recording transactions first in a data base, rather than in a journal. The computer then arranges the data into the format of journal entries, ledger accounts, trial balances, and financial statements.

Procedures such as posting and the preparation of trial balances and financial statements merely involve the *rearrangement* of recorded data and may easily be performed by computer. The preparation of closing entries also is a mechanical task, involving the transfer of recorded data from one ledger account to another. Thus, closing entries *may be performed automatically* in a computer-based system.

Accrual Basis of Accounting versus Cash Basis of Accounting

Objective 8
Explain the
accrual basis of
accounting.

A business which recognizes revenue in the period in which it is earned and which deducts in the same period the expenses incurred in generating this revenue is using the *accrual basis of accounting.* Because the accrual basis stresses the matching or offsetting of revenue and related expenses, it gives a realistic picture of the profitability of a business in each accounting period.

The alternative to the accrual basis of accounting is the *cash basis.* Under cash basis accounting, revenue is not recorded until received in cash; expenses are assigned to the period in which cash payment is made. Most business concerns use the accrual method of accounting, but individuals and professionals (such as physicians and lawyers) usually maintain their accounting records on a cash basis.

The cash basis of accounting does not give a good picture of profitability. For example, it ignores revenue that has been earned but not yet collected and expenses that have been incurred but not paid. Thus, we will emphasize the concepts of accrual accounting throughout most of this textbook.

End-of-Chapter Review

CONCEPTS INTRODUCED OR EMPHASIZED IN CHAPTER 3

The major concepts introduced in this chapter include:

■ The accrual basis of accounting, and the related definitions of net income, revenue, and expenses.

■ The time period principle, realization principle, matching principle, and the concept of conservatism.

■ The use of temporary (or nominal) accounts to record revenue and expense transactions, and withdrawals by the owner.

■ The nature of depreciation expense.

■ Expansion of the accounting cycle to include end-of-period adjustments and closing entries.

■ The form and content of the income statement and the statement of owner's equity, and the relationship of these statements to the balance sheet.

In Chapter 2, we introduced the double-entry system of accounting, but illustrated this system using only balance sheet accounts. In this third chapter, we have seen that the double-entry system also allows us to measure revenue and expenses as we record changes in assets and liabilities. In fact, it is this double-entry system that makes possible the measurement of revenue and expenses.

We have now illustrated the complete accounting cycle for a service-type business. In Chapter 4, we will look more closely at one important element of this cycle—end-of-period adjusting entries—and will also see how a work sheet can be used to consolidate several steps in the cycle. Accounting for merchandising activities will be discussed in Chapter 5.

KEY TERMS INTRODUCED OR EMPHASIZED IN CHAPTER 3

Accounting period The span of time covered by an income statement. One year is the accounting period for much financial reporting, but financial statements are also prepared by companies for each quarter of the year and also for each month.

Accrual basis of accounting Calls for recording revenue in the period in which it is earned and recording expenses in the period in which they are incurred. The effect of events on the business is recognized as services are rendered or consumed rather than when cash is received or paid.

Accumulated depreciation A contra-asset account shown as a deduction from the related asset account in the balance sheet. Depreciation taken throughout the useful life of an asset is accumulated in this account.

Adjusted trial balance A listing of all ledger account balances after the amounts have been changed to include the adjusting entries made at the end of the period.

Adjusting entries Entries required at the end of the period to update the accounts before financial statements are prepared. Adjusting entries serve to apportion transactions properly between the accounting periods affected and to record any revenue earned or expenses incurred which have not been recorded prior to the end of the period.

After-closing trial balance A trial balance prepared after all closing entries have been made. Consists only of accounts for assets, liabilities, and owner's equity.

Closing entries Journal entries made at the end of the period for the purpose of closing temporary accounts (revenue, expense, and drawing accounts) and transferring balances to the owner's capital account.

Conservatism The traditional accounting practice of resolving uncertainty by choosing the solution which leads to the lower (more conservative) amount of income being recognized in the current accounting period. This concept is designed to avoid overstatement of financial strength or earnings.

Contra-asset account An account with a credit balance which is offset against or deducted from an asset account to produce the proper balance sheet valuation for the asset.

Depreciation The systematic allocation of the cost of an asset to expense during the periods of its useful life.

Drawing account The account used to record the withdrawals of cash or other assets by the owner. Closed at the end of the period by transferring its balance to the owner's capital account.

Expenses The cost of the goods and services used up in the process of obtaining revenue.

Fiscal year *once a year* Any 12-month accounting period adopted by a business.

Income statement A financial statement summarizing the results of operations of a business by matching its revenue and related expenses for a particular accounting period. Shows the net income or net loss.

Income Summary account The summary account in the ledger to which revenue and expense accounts are closed at the end of the period. The balance (credit balance for a net income, debit balance for a net loss) is transferred to the owner's capital account.

Matching principle The revenue earned during an accounting period is matched (offset) with the expenses incurred in generating this revenue.

Net income An increase in owner's equity resulting from profitable operations. Also, the excess of revenue earned over the related expenses for a given period.

Realization principle The generally accepted accounting principle that determines when revenue should be recorded in the accounting records. Revenue is realized when services are rendered to customers or when goods sold are delivered to customers.

Revenue The price of goods sold and services rendered by a business.

Statement of owner's equity A financial statement summarizing the increases and decreases in owner's equity during an accounting period.

Time period principle To provide the users of financial statements with timely information, net income is measured for relatively short accounting periods of equal length. The period of time covered by an income statement is termed the company's accounting period.

DEMONSTRATION PROBLEM FOR YOUR REVIEW

Shown below is the adjusted trial balance of Lane Insurance Agency for the month ended June 30, 19   :

LANE INSURANCE AGENCY
Adjusted Trial Balance
June 30, 19___

Cash	$ 1,275	
Accounts receivable	605	
Office equipment	6,000	
Accumulated depreciation: office equipment		$ 150
Accounts payable		1,260
Richard Lane, capital		8,000
Richard Lane, drawing	1,000	
Commissions earned		3,710
Advertising expense	500	
Rent expense	870	
Telephone expense	120	
Salaries expense	2,700	
Depreciation expense: office equipment	50	
	$13,120	$13,120

Instructions **a** Prepare an income statement and a statement of owner's equity for the month ended June 30, and a balance sheet in report form at June 30.

b Prepare journal entries to close the accounts at June 30.

SOLUTION TO DEMONSTRATION PROBLEM

a
LANE INSURANCE AGENCY
Income Statement
For the Month Ended June 30, 19__

Revenue:		
Commissions earned		$3,710
Expenses:		
Advertising expense	$ 500	
Rent expense	870	
Telephone expense	120	
Salaries expense	2,700	
Depreciation expense: office equipment	50	4,240
Net Loss		$ 530

LANE INSURANCE AGENCY
Statement of Owner's Equity
For the Month Ended, June 30, 19__

Richard Lane, capital, May 31, 19__		$8,000
Less: Net loss for June	$ 530	
Withdrawals by owner	1,000	1,530
Richard Lane, capital, June 30, 19__		$6,470

LANE INSURANCE AGENCY
Balance Sheet
June 30, 19__

ASSETS

Cash		$1,275
Accounts receivable		605
Office equipment	$6,000	
Less: Accumulated depreciation	150	5,850
Total assets		$7,730

LIABILITIES & OWNER'S EQUITY

Liabilities:		
Accounts payable		$1,260
Owner's equity:		
Richard Lane, capital, June 30, 19__		6,470
Total liabilities & owner's equity		$7,730

b Closing entries:

Commissions Earned	3,710	
Income Summary		3,710
To close the revenue account.		

Income Summary	4,240	
Advertising Expense		500
Rent Expense		870
Telephone Expense		120
Salaries Expense		2,700
Depreciation Expense: Office Equipment		50
To close the expense accounts.		

Richard Lane, Capital	530	
Income Summary		530
To close the Income Summary account and reduce the owner's capital account by the amount of the net loss.		

Richard Lane, Capital	1,000	
Richard Lane, Drawing		1,000
To close the owner's drawing account.		

SELF-TEST QUESTIONS

Answers to these questions appear on page 126.

1 Net income:

    a Is computed in the income statement, appears in the statement of owner's equity, and also causes an increase in the amount of cash shown in the balance sheet.

    b Is equal to revenue minus expenses and withdrawals by the owner.

    c Is computed in the income statement, appears in the statement of owner's equity, and increases the amount of owner's equity shown in the balance sheet.

    d Appears in both the income statement and the statement of owner's equity, but has no effect upon any balance sheet account.

2 The wages earned by employees of Judy's Salon during the month of September will not be paid until Monday, October 3. The best rationale for recognizing these wages as expense in *September* is:

    a The realization principle—Judy's Salon should realize that these salaries are owed to employees as of Friday, September 30.

    b The time period principle—An equal amount of wages expense should be recognized in each month, regardless of when cash is paid or when services are performed by employees.

    c The matching principle—Wages expense is recognized in the period in which employees' services are used in the effort to produce revenue, regardless of when cash payments are made.

    d The principles of objectivity and conservatism—Judy's Salon is able to objectively measure the amount owed to employees at September 30, and is conserving cash by delaying payment until October 3.

3 The balance in the owner's capital account of Dayton Company at the beginning of the year was $65,000. During the year, the company earned revenue at $430,000, incurred expenses of $360,000, the owner withdrew $50,000 in assets, and the balance of the Cash account increased by $10,000. At year-end, the company's net income and the year-end balance in the owner's capital account were, respectively:

a $20,000 and $95,000.   **c** $60,000 and $75,000.

b $70,000 and $95,000.   **d** $70,000 and $85,000.

Use the following information in questions **4** and **5**:

Accounts appearing in the trial balance of Westside Plumbing at May 31 are listed below in alphabetical order:

Accounts payable................	$2,450	Equipment..................	$16,200
Accounts receivable	3,100	J. T. Golden, capital.........	11,000
Accumulated depreciation:		J. T. Golden, drawing........	2,100
equipment.....................	8,100	Other expenses	900
Advertising expense	150	Service revenue.............	4,800
Cash	2,900	Supplies expense	1,000

No adjusting entry has yet been made to record depreciation expense of $270 for the month of May.

4 The balance of J. T. Golden's capital account appearing in the May 31 balance sheet should be:

a $11,650   **b** $8,630   **c** $11,380   **d** Some other amount

5 In an **_after-closing_** trial balance prepared at May 31, the total of the credit column will be:

a $26,620   **b** $22,200   **c** $13,830   **d** Some other amount

Assignment Material

REVIEW QUESTIONS

1 What is the meaning of the term **_revenue?_** Does the receipt of cash by a business indicate that revenue has been earned? Explain.

2 What is the meaning of the term **_expenses?_** Does the payment of cash by a business indicate that an expense has been incurred? Explain.

3 Does net income represent an amount of cash that can be withdrawn by the owner of a business?

4 Explain the effect of operating profitably upon the **_balance sheet_** of a business entity.

5 A service enterprise performs services in the amount of $500 for a customer in May and receives payment in June. In which month is the $500 of revenue recognized? What is the journal entry to be made in May and the entry to be made in June?

6 When do accountants consider revenue to be realized? What basic question about recording revenue in accounting records is answered by the **_realization principle?_**

7 Late in March, Classic Auto Painters purchased paint on account, with payment due in 60 days. The company used the paint to paint customers' cars during the first three weeks of April. Late in May, the company paid the paint store from which the paint had been purchased. In which month should Classic Auto Painters recognize the cost of this paint as expense? What generally accepted accounting principle determines the answer to this question?

8 In what accounting period does the *matching principle* indicate that an expense should be recognized?

9 Explain the rules of debit and credit with respect to transactions recorded in revenue and expense accounts.

10 John Haley, owner of Haley Company, regularly withdraws cash from the business. Should these drawings by the owner be considered an expense of the business? Explain.

11 Britt Moore, owner of Moore Carpet Care, wrote a check for $1,700 on the business bank account to pay the monthly rent on her personal residence. Prepare a journal entry to record this transaction.

12 Why does any company that owns equipment or buildings need to make adjusting entries at the end of every accounting period?

13 Briefly describe the content and format of an income statement and of a statement of owner's equity.

14 Does a well-prepared income statement provide an exact measurement of net income for the period, or does it represent merely an approximation of net income? Explain.

15 Explain the relationships among the three financial statements discussed in this chapter—that is, the income statement, the statement of owner's equity, and the balance sheet.

16 How does *depreciation expense* differ from other operating expenses?

17 Which of the following accounts are closed at the end of the accounting period?

Donald Harris, Drawing	Salaries Expense
Fees Earned	Income Summary
Cash	Accumulated Depreciation
Donald Harris, Capital	Depreciation Expense

18 Supply the appropriate term (debit or credit) to complete the following statements.

a When a business is operating *profitably,* the journal entry to close the Income Summary account will consist of a _____ to that account and a _____ to the owner's capital account.

b When a business is operating at a *loss,* the journal entry to close the Income Summary account will consist of a _____ to that account and a _____ to the owner's capital account.

c The journal entry to close the owner's drawing account consists of a _____ to that account and a _____ to the owner's capital account.

19 How does the accrual basis of accounting differ from the cash basis of accounting? Which gives a more accurate picture of the profitability of a business? Explain.

EXERCISES

**Exercise 3-1
Accounting
terminology**

Listed below are nine technical accounting terms introduced in this chapter:

Depreciation	*Income statement*	*Matching*
Realization	*Adjusting entries*	*Revenue*
Closing entries	*Accrual basis of accounting*	*Expenses*

Each of the following statements may (or may not) describe one of these technical terms. For each statement, indicate the accounting term described, or answer "None" if the statement does not correctly describe any of the terms.

a Increases in owner's equity shown in the income statement.

b A financial statement that summarizes all increases and decreases in owner's equity during the accounting period.

c The procedures for transferring the balances of the revenue, expense, and owner's drawing account into the owner's capital account.

d The generally accepted accounting principle used in determining when to recognize expenses.

e The cost of goods and services used up in the process of earning revenue.

f The generally accepted accounting principle used in determining when to recognize revenue.

g Recognizing revenue when it is earned and expenses when the related goods or services are used in the effort to obtain revenue.

h The systematic allocation of the cost of a long-lived asset, such as a building or equipment, to expense over the useful life of the asset.

Exercise 3-2
Heading of an
income statement

On January 14, the accountant for Sunray Appliance Company prepared an income statement for the year ended December 31, 1991. The accountant used the following heading on this financial statement:

SUNRAY CO.
Profit and Loss Statement
January 14, 1992

Instructions

a Identify any errors in this heading.

b Prepare a corrected heading.

Exercise 3-3
When is revenue
realized?

The following transactions were carried out during the month of June by K. Davis and Company, a firm of real estate brokers. For each of the five transactions, you are to state whether the transaction represented revenue to the firm during the month of June. Give reasons for your decision in each case.

a Davis invested an additional $6,400 cash in the business.

b Borrowed $12,800 from Century Bank to be repaid in three months.

c Earned $63 interest on a company bank account during the month of June. No withdrawals were made from this account in June.

d Collected cash of $2,400 from an account receivable. The receivable originated in May from services rendered to a client.

e Arranged a sale of an apartment building owned by a client. The commission for making the sale was $14,400, but this amount will not be received until August 20.

Exercise 3-4
When are
expenses
incurred?

Evergreen Landscaping carried out the following transactions during May. Which of these transactions represented expenses in May? Explain.

a Paid an attorney $560 for legal services rendered in April.

b The owner withdrew $1,600 from the business for personal use.

c Purchased a copying machine for $2,750 cash.

d Paid $192 for gasoline purchases for a delivery truck during May.

e Paid $1,280 salary to an employee for time worked during May.

Exercise 3-5
Relationship between net income and owner's equity

Total assets and total liabilities of Yato Talent Agency as shown by the balance sheets at the beginning and end of the year were as follows:

	BEGINNING OF YEAR	END OF YEAR
Assets	$230,000	$295,000
Liabilities	110,000	140,000

Instructions

Compute the net income or net loss from operations for the year in each of the following independent cases.

a Yato made no withdrawals during the year and no additional investments.

b Yato made no withdrawals during the year but made an additional capital investment of $50,000.

c Yato made withdrawals of $20,000 during the year but made no additional investments.

d Yato made withdrawals of $80,000 during the year and made an additional capital investment of $25,000.

Exercise 3-6
Preparing journal entries to record revenue, expense, and drawings transactions

Shown below are selected transactions of the law firm of Emmons & Associates. You are to prepare journal entries to record the transactions in the firm's accounting records. The firm closes its accounts at the end of each calendar year.

Mar. 19 Drafted a prenuptial agreement for C. J. McCall. Sent McCall an invoice for $750, requesting payment within 30 days. (The appropriate revenue account is entitled Legal Fees Earned.)

May 31 Received a bill from Lawyers' Delivery Service for process service during the month of May, $1,150. Payment due by June 10. (The appropriate expense account is entitled Process Service Expense.)

Aug. 7 Ralph Emmons, owner of the law firm, withdrew $15,000 cash for personal purposes.

Dec. 31 Made a year-end adjusting entry to record depreciation expense on the firm's law library, $2,700.

Exercise 3-7
Adjusting entry for depreciation

Ahmed Pharmacy acquired a delivery truck at a cost of $9,600. Estimated life of the truck is four years. State the amount of depreciation expense per year and per month. Give the adjusting entry to record depreciation on the truck at the end of the first month, and explain where the accounts involved would appear in the financial statements.

Exercise 3-8
Preparing an income statement and statement of owner's equity

From the following account balances, prepare first an income statement and then a statement of owner's equity for Ross Painting Contractors for the year ended December 31, 1991. Include the proper headings on both financial statements.

T. Ross, Capital, Dec. 31, 1990 ..	$ 27,200	Rent Expense	$9,600
T. Ross, Drawing	18,000	Advertising Expense	3,200
Painting Fees Earned	140,000	Depreciation Expense: Painting	
Paint & Supplies Expense	27,500	Equipment	1,200
Salaries Expense	66,800		

Exercise 3-9
Preparing closing entries

Prepare the year-end closing entries for Ross Painting Contractors, using the data given in Exercise 3-8. Use four separate entries, as illustrated on pages 101–105. Indicate the balance in the owner's capital account that should appear in the balance sheet dated December 31, 1991.

PROBLEMS

Group A

Problem 3A-1
Preparing journal
entries

Reliable Plumbing performs repair work on both a cash and credit basis. Credit customers are required to pay within 30 days from date of billing. The ledger accounts used by the company include:

Cash	*Accounts payable*	*Advertising expense*
Accounts receivable	*David Cohen, drawing*	*Rent expense*
Tools	*Repair service revenue*	*Salaries expense*
Notes payable		

Among the June transactions were the following:

June 1   Performed repair work for Arden Hardware, a credit customer. Sent bill for $1,247.

June 2   Paid rent for June, $700.

June 3   Purchased tools with estimated life of 10 years for $1,200 cash.

June 10   Performed repairs for Harris Drugs and collected in full the charge of $510.

June 15   Newspaper advertising to appear on June 18 was arranged at a cost of $250. Received bill from *The Tribune* requiring payment within 30 days.

June 18   Received payment in full of the $1,247 account receivable from Arden Hardware for our services on June 1.

June 20   David Cohen, owner of Reliable Plumbing withdrew $1,000 cash from the business for personal use.

June 30   Paid salaries of $3,300 to employees for services rendered during June.

Instructions   Prepare a journal entry (including explanation) for each of the above transactions.

Problem 3A-2
Analyzing
transactions and
preparing journal
entries

Garwood Marine is a boat repair yard. During August its transactions included the following:

(1) On August 1, paid rent for the month of August, $4,000.

(2) On August 3, at request of Kiwi Insurance, Inc., made repairs on boat of Michael Fay. Sent bill for $4,680 for services rendered to Kiwi Insurance, Inc. (Credit Repair Service Revenue.)

(3) On August 9, made repairs to boat of Dennis Conner and collected in full the charge of $1,575.

(4) On August 14, placed advertisement in *Yachting World* to be published in issue of August 20 at cost of $95, payment to be made within 30 days.

(5) On August 25, received a check for $4,680 from Kiwi Insurance, Inc., representing collection of the receivable of August 3.

(6) On August 30, sent check to *Yachting World* in payment of the liability incurred on August 14.

(7) On August 31, Barbara Garwood, owner of Garwood Marine, withdrew $3,500 from the business for personal use.

Instructions **a** Write an analysis of each transaction. An example of the type of analysis desired is as follows:

(1)(a) Rent is an operating expense. Expenses are recorded by debits. Debit Rent Expense, $4,000.

(b) The asset Cash was decreased. Decreases in assets are recorded by credits. Credit Cash, $4,000.

b Prepare a journal entry (including explanation) for each of the above transactions.

Problem 3A-3
Preparing closing
entries

Family Fun Park is a miniature golf course. At year-end, the company prepared the following adjusted trial balance:

FAMILY FUN PARK
Adjusted Trial Balance
December 31, 19___

Cash..	$ 12,500	
Accounts receivable	1,800	
Buildings..	60,000	
Accumulated depreciation: buildings		$ 18,000
Golf course structures	30,000	
Accumulated depreciation: golf course structures		10,000
Roy Garcia, capital		72,000
Roy Garcia, drawing..	25,000	
Admissions revenue		175,000
Advertising expense	12,000	
Rent expense	34,000	
Repairs expense	5,200	
Salaries expense	79,000	
Light & power expense	4,500	
Depreciation expense: buildings...................................	6,000	
Depreciation expense: golf course structures......................	5,000	
	$275,000	$275,000

Instructions **a** Prepare journal entries to close the accounts. Use four entries: (1) to close the revenue account, (2) to close the expense accounts, (3) to close the Income Summary account, and (4) to close the owner's drawing account.

b Assume that in the following year, Family Fun Park again had $175,000 of admissions revenue, but that expenses increased to $190,000. Assuming that the revenue account and all the expense accounts had been closed into the Income Summary account at December 31, prepare a journal entry to close the Income Summary account.

Problem 3A-4
Preparing
financial
statements and
closing entries

Celebrity Caterers closes its accounts and prepares financial statements at the end of each calendar year. The following adjusted trial balance was prepared at December 31 of the most recent year.

CELEBRITY CATERERS
Adjusted Trial Balance
December 31, 19___

Cash	$ 7,300	
Notes receivable	6,000	
Accounts receivable	12,800	
Land	140,000	
Building	90,000	
Accumulated depreciation: building		$ 12,000
Office equipment	4,000	
Accumulated depreciation: office equipment		1,600
Notes payable		100,000
Accounts payable		16,200
Halley St. James, capital		132,300
Halley St. James, drawing	24,000	
Catering revenue		89,500
Advertising expense	12,500	
Insurance expense	2,800	
Utilities expense	2,600	
Salaries expense	46,200	
Depreciation expense: building	3,000	
Depreciation expense: office equipment	400	
	$351,600	$351,600

Instructions

a Prepare an income statement and a statement of owner's equity for the year ended December 31, and a balance sheet in report form as of December 31.

b Prepare closing entries at December 31. Use four entries as illustrated on pages 101–105.

**Problem 3A-5
Preparing journal entries, posting, and preparing a trial balance**

During the month of June, John Lane organized and began to operate an air taxi service to provide air transportation from a major city to a number of small towns not served by scheduled airlines. Transactions during the month of June were as follows:

June 1 John Lane deposited $55,000 cash in a bank account in the name of the business, Lane Air Service.

June 2 Purchased an aircraft for $225,000, paying $45,000 in cash and issuing a note payable for $180,000.

June 4 Paid $2,500 cash to rent a building for June.

June 10 Cash receipts from passenger fares revenue for the first 10 days amounted to $3,320.

June 14 Paid $1,850 to Ace Aircraft Co. for maintenance and repair services.

June 15 Paid $5,880 salaries to employees for services rendered during first half of June.

June 20 Cash receipts from passenger fares revenue for the second 10 days amounted to $7,800.

June 30 Cash receipts from passenger fares revenue for the last 10 days of June amounted to $9,100.

June 30 Paid $6,000 salaries to employees for services rendered during the second half of June.

June 30 Lane withdrew $2,000 from business for personal use.

June 30 Received a fuel bill from Phillips Oil Company amounting to $4,540 to be paid before July 10.

The account titles and numbers used by Lane Air Service are as follows:

Cash.............................	1	Passenger fares revenue...............	51
Aircraft..........................	15	Maintenance expense..................	61
Notes payable.....................	31	Fuel expense..........................	62
Accounts payable.................	32	Salaries expense......................	63
John Lane, capital................	41	Rent expense..........................	64
John Lane, drawing...............	42		

Instructions Based on the foregoing transactions:

a Prepare journal entries. (Number journal pages to permit cross reference to ledger.)

b Post to ledger accounts. (Number ledger accounts to permit cross reference to journal.) Enter ledger account numbers in the LP column of the journal as the posting work is done.

c Prepare a trial balance at June 30, 19___.

Problem 3A-6
End-of-period
adjusting and
closing
procedures;
preparing
financial
statements

Home Repair is a new business which began operations on July 1. The company follows a policy of closing its accounts and preparing financial statements at the end of each month. A trial balance at September 30 appears below.

HOME REPAIR
Trial Balance
September 30, 19___

Cash...	$ 2,500	
Accounts receivable..............................	1,500	
Land..	29,400	
Building..	50,400	
Accumulated depreciation: building...............		$ 336
Repair equipment.................................	7,500	
Accumulated depreciation: repair equipment........		250
Notes payable....................................		28,000
Accounts payable.................................		1,594
Paul Morgan, capital.............................		58,800
Paul Morgan, drawing.............................	1,400	
Repair service revenue............................		8,520
Advertising expense...............................	150	
Repair parts expense..............................	700	
Utilities expense..................................	170	
Wages expense....................................	3,780	
	$97,500	$97,500

Note that the trial balance includes two assets subject to depreciation: the building and the repair equipment. The accumulated depreciation accounts in the trial balance show the total depreciation for July and August; depreciation has not yet been recorded for September.

Instructions **a** Prepare adjusting entries at September 30 to record depreciation. Use one entry to record depreciation on the building and a second entry to record depreciation on the repair equipment. The amounts of depreciation for September are $168 on the building and $125 on the repair equipment.

b Prepare an *adjusted* trial balance at September 30. (This will differ from the trial balance only by inclusion of the depreciation recorded in part **a**.)

c Prepare an income statement and a statement of owner's equity for the month ended September 30, and a balance sheet in report form.

d Prepare journal entries to close the accounts. Use four entries: (1) to close the revenue account, (2) to close the expense accounts, (3) to close the Income Summary account, and (4) to close the owner's drawing account.

e Prepare an after-closing trial balance.

Problem 3A-7
Complete
accounting cycle

April Stein, M.D., after completing her medical education, established her own practice on May 1. The following transactions occurred during the first month.

May   1   Stein opened a bank account in the name of the practice, April Stein M.D., by making a deposit of $12,000.

May   1   Paid office rent for May, $1,700.

May   2   Purchased office equipment for cash, $7,200.

May   3   Purchased medical instruments from Niles Instruments, Inc., at a cost of $9,000. A cash down payment of $1,000 was made and a note payable was issued for the remaining $8,000.

May   4   Retained by Brandon Construction to be on call for emergency service at a monthly fee of $400. The fee for May was collected in cash.

May 15   Excluding the retainer of May 4, fees earned during the first 15 days of the month amounted to $1,600, of which $600 was in cash and $1,000 was in accounts receivable.

May 15   Paid Mary Hester, R.N., her salary for the first half of May, $1,000.

May 16   Dr. Stein withdrew $975 for personal use.

May 19   Treated Michael Tracy for minor injuries received in an accident during employment at Brandon Construction. No charge was made as these services were covered by Brandon's payment on May 4.

May 27   Treated Cynthia Knight, who paid $25 cash for an office visit and who agreed to pay $35 on June 1 for laboratory medical tests completed May 27.

May 31   Excluding the treatment of Cynthia Knight on May 27, fees earned during the last half of month amounted to $4,000, of which $2,100 was in cash and $1,900 was in accounts receivable.

May 31   Paid Mary Hester, R.N., $1,000 salary for the second half of month.

May 31   Received a bill from McGraw Medical Supplies in the amount of $640 representing the amount of medical supplies used during May.

May 31   Paid utilities for the month, $300.

Other Information

Dr. Stein estimated the useful life of medical instruments at 3 years and of office equipment at 5 years. The account titles to be used and the account numbers are as follows:

Cash	10	April Stein, drawing	41
Accounts receivable	13	Income summary	45
Medical instruments	20	Fees earned	49
Accumulated depreciation:		Medical supplies expense	50
medical instruments	21	Rent expense	51
Office equipment	22	Salaries expense	52
Accumulated depreciation:		Utilities expense	53
office equipment	23	Depreciation expense:	
Notes payable	30	medical instruments	54
Accounts payable	31	Depreciation expense:	
April Stein, capital	40	office equipment	55

Instructions

a Journalize the above transactions. (Number journal pages to permit cross-reference to ledger.)

b Post to ledger accounts. (Use running balance form of ledger account. Number ledger accounts to permit cross reference to journal.)

c Prepare a trial balance at May 31, 19___.

d Prepare adjusting entries to record depreciation for the month of May and post to ledger accounts. (For medical instruments, cost $9,000 ÷ 3 years × $\frac{1}{12}$. For office equipment, cost $7,200 ÷ 5 × $\frac{1}{12}$.)

e Prepare an adjusted trial balance.

f Prepare an income statement and statement of owner's equity for the month of May, and a balance sheet in report form at May 31. (As this is a new business, the first line in the statement of owner's equity should be: "Initial investment by owner, May 1, 19___ $12,000.")

g Prepare closing entries and post to ledger accounts.

h Prepare an after-closing trial balance.

Group B

Problem 3B-1
Preparing journal entries

Air Wolfe provides transportation by helicopter for skiers, backpackers, and others to remote mountainous areas. Among the ledger accounts used by the company are the following:

Cash	*Passenger fare revenue*	*Rent expense*
Accounts payable	*Advertising expense*	*Repair & maintenance expense*
Amy Wolfe, capital	*Fuel expense*	*Salaries expense*
Amy Wolfe, drawing		

Some of the January transactions of Air Wolfe are listed below.

Jan. **3** Paid $800 rent for the building for January.

Jan. **4** Placed advertising in local newspapers for publication during January. The agreed price of $270 was payable within 10 days after the end of the month.

Jan. 15 Cash receipts from passengers for the first half of January amounted to $4,825.

Jan. 16 Amy Wolfe, the owner, withdrew $1,800 cash for personal use.

Jan. 16 Paid salaries to employees for services rendered in first half of January, $2,750.

Jan. 29 Received a bill for fuel used from Western Oil Co., amounting to $985, and payable by February 10.

Jan. 31 Paid $843 to Stevens Aircraft for repair and maintenance work during January.

Instructions Prepare a journal entry (including an explanation) for each of the above transactions.

Problem 3B-2
Analyzing transactions and preparing journal entries

The July transactions of Auto Haus, an automobile repair shop, included the following:

(1) On July 1, paid rent for the month of July, $2,400.

(2) On July 3, at request of National Insurance, Inc., made repairs on car of Stanley West. Sent bill for $610 for services rendered to National Insurance, Inc. (Credit Repair Service Revenue.)

(3) On July 9, made repairs to car of H. F. Smith and collected in full the charge of $430.

(4) On July 14, placed advertisement in *Daily Star* to be published in issue of July 16 at cost of $150, payment to be made within 30 days.

(5) On July 25, received a check for $610 from National Insurance, Inc., representing collection of the receivable of July 3.

(6) On July 31, the owner, Hans Klauder, withdrew $3,600 cash for personal use.

(7) On July 31, obtained a loan from bank. Received $15,000 cash and signed a note payable for that amount.

Instructions **a** Write an analysis of each transaction. An example of the type of analysis desired is as follows for transaction (1) above.

(1)(a) Rent is an operating expense. Expenses are recorded by debits. Debit Rent Expense, $2,400.

(b) The asset Cash was decreased. Decreases in assets are recorded by credits. Credit Cash, $2,400.

b Prepare a journal entry (including explanation) for each of the above transactions.

Problem 3B-3
Preparing closing entries

An adjusted trial balance for Martin Insurance Agency at December 31 appears below.

MARTIN INSURANCE AGENCY
Adjusted Trial Balance
December 31, 19__

Cash	$ 10,200	
Accounts receivable	20,000	
Office equipment	15,000	
Accumulated depreciation: office equipment		$ 3,000
Accounts payable		6,000
Linda Martin, capital		19,700
Linda Martin, drawing	18,000	
Sales commissions earned		195,000
Advertising expense	38,500	
Rent expense	34,000	
Salaries expense	66,500	
Utilities expense	18,000	
Depreciation expense: office equipment	3,500	
	$223,700	$223,700

Instructions **a** Prepare journal entries to close the accounts. Use four entries: (1) to close the revenue account, (2) to close the expense accounts, (3) to close the Income Summary account, and (4) to close the owner's drawing account.

b Does the amount of net income or net loss appear in the closing entries? Explain fully.

Problem 3B-4
Preparing closing entries

During the absence of the regular accountant of Lawn Care Co., a new employee, Ralph Jones, prepared the closing entries for the year ended December 31, 19__. Jones had very little understanding of accounting and the closing entries he prepared were not satisfactory in several respects. The entries by Jones were:

Entry 1

Lawn service revenue	78,000	
Cash	8,000	
Accounts Receivable	27,000	
Income Summary		113,000

To close the revenue accounts.

Entry 2

Income Summary	*73,000*	
Salaries		*56,000*
J. Mallory, Drawing		*11,000*
Advertising		*4,000*
Depreciation Expense		*2,000*
To close the expense accounts.		

Entry 3

J. Mallory, Capital	*28,000*	
Income Summary		*28,000*
To close the owner's capital account.		

Instructions   **a**   Identify any errors which Jones made.

b   Prepare four correct closing entries, following the pattern illustrated on pages 101–105.

**Problem 3B-5
Preparing
financial
statements and
closing entries**   Adams Engineering prepares financial statements and closes its accounts at the end of each calendar year. The following adjusted trial balance was prepared at December 31 of the most recent year.

ADAMS ENGINEERING
Adjusted Trial Balance
December 31, 19___

Cash	$ *9,250*	
Notes receivable	*9,100*	
Accounts receivable	*48,450*	
Land	*140,000*	
Building	*90,000*	
Accumulated depreciation: building		$ *23,200*
Office equipment	*4,000*	
Accumulated depreciation: office equipment		*1,600*
Notes payable		*100,000*
Accounts payable		*16,200*
Sally Adams, capital		*134,800*
Sally Adams, drawing	*24,000*	
Consulting fees earned		*158,500*
Advertising expense	*22,500*	
Insurance expense	*4,800*	
Utilities expense	*3,600*	
Salaries expense	*75,200*	
Depreciation expense: building	*3,000*	
Depreciation expense: office equipment	*400*	
	$*434,300*	$*434,300*

Instructions   **a**   Prepare an income statement and a statement of owner's equity for the year ended December 31, and a balance sheet in report form as of December 31.

b   Prepare closing entries at December 31. Use four entries as illustrated on pages 101–105.

Problem 3B-6
Preparing journal
entries, posting,
and preparing a
trial balance

Metro Park was organized on March 1 for the purpose of operating an automobile parking lot. Included in the company's ledger are the following ledger accounts and their identification numbers.

Cash...............................	11	Tony Poletti, drawing	42
Land...............................	21	Parking fees earned	51
Notes payable.......................	31	Advertising expense	61
Accounts payable	32	Utilities expense.....................	63
Tony Poletti, capital	41	Salaries expense	65

The business was organized and operations were begun during the month of March. Transactions during March were as follows:

Mar. 1 Tony Poletti deposited $50,000 cash in a bank account in the name of the business.

Mar. 5 Purchased land for $160,000, of which $40,000 was paid in cash. A short-term note payable was issued for the balance of $120,000.

Mar. 6 An arrangement was made with the Century Club to provide parking privileges for its customers. Century Club agreed to pay $1,200 monthly, payable in advance. Cash was collected for the month of March.

Mar. 7 Arranged with Times Printing Company for a regular advertisement in the *Times* at a monthly cost of $390. Paid for advertising during March by check, $390.

Mar. 15 Parking receipts for the first half of the month were $1,836, exclusive of the monthly fee from Century Club.

Mar. 31 Received bill for light and power from Pacific Power Company in the amount of $78, to be paid by April 10.

Mar. 31 Paid $2,720 to employees for services rendered during the month. (Payroll taxes are to be ignored.)

Mar. 31 Parking receipts for the second half of the month amounted to $5,338.

Mar. 31 Poletti withdrew $2,000 for personal use.

Mar. 31 Paid $5,000 cash on the note payable incurred with the purchase of land. (You are to ignore any interest on the note.)

Instructions
a Journalize the March transactions.

b Post to ledger accounts. Enter ledger account numbers in the LP column of the journal as the posting work is done.

c Prepare a trial balance at March 31.

Problem 3B-7
End-of-period
adjusting and
closing
procedures;
preparing
financial
statements

The operations of Sunset Realty consist of obtaining listings of houses being offered for sale by owners, advertising these houses, and showing them to prospective buyers. The company earns revenue in the form of commissions. The building and office equipment used in the business were acquired on January 1 of the current year and were immediately placed in use. Useful life of the building was estimated to be 30 years and that of the office equipment five years. The company closes its accounts monthly; on March 31 of the current year, the trial balance is as follows:

SUNSET REALTY
Trial Balance
March 31, 19___

	DEBIT	CREDIT
Cash...	$ 6,500	
Accounts receivable	5,000	
Land...	25,000	
Building...	72,000	
Accumulated depreciation: building		$ 400
Office equipment	24,000	
Accumulated depreciation: office equipment........................		800
Notes payable..		81,000
Accounts payable		10,000
Ellen Norton, capital..		37,800
Ellen Norton, drawing..	2,000	
Commissions earned		20,000
Advertising expense	900	
Automobile rental expense..	700	
Salaries expense	13,300	
Telephone expense	600	
	$150,000	$150,000

Instructions From the trial balance and supplementary data given, prepare the following as of March 31, 19___.

a Adjusting entries for depreciation during March of building and of office equipment.

(Building: $72,000 cost ÷ 30 years × ¹/₁₂ = one month's depreciation)
(Office equipment: $24,000 cost ÷ 5 years × ¹/₁₂ = one month's depreciation)

b Adjusted trial balance.

c Income statement and a statement of owner's equity for the month of March, and a balance sheet at March 31 in report form.

d Closing entries.

e After-closing trial balance.

BUSINESS DECISION CASES

Case 3-1
Revenue
recognition
The realization principle determines when a business should recognize revenue. Listed below are three common business situations involving revenue. After each situation, we give two alternatives as to the accounting period (or periods) in which the business might recognize this revenue. Select the appropriate alternative by applying the realization principle, and explain your reasoning.

a Airline ticket revenue: most airlines sell tickets well before the scheduled date of the flight. (Period ticket sold, period of flight)

b Sales on account: in June 1989, a San Diego based furniture store had a big sale featuring "no payments until 1990." (Period furniture sold; periods that payments are received from customers)

c Magazine subscriptions revenue: most magazine publishers sell subscriptions for future delivery of the magazine. (Period subscription sold; periods that magazines are mailed to customers)

**Case 3-2
Expense
recognition**

As a basis for deciding when to recognize expense, we have discussed the *matching principle,* the need for *objective evidence* to recognize the existence of an asset, and the concept of *conservatism.* Shown below are three costs that ultimately become expenses. Each situation is followed by two alternatives as to when the business might record this expense. Select the appropriate alternative based upon the principles described above, and explain your answer.

a Computers: most businesses own them, and they are expensive. Due to the rapid advances in technology, it is very difficult to estimate in advance how long the business will keep them. (Period computers purchased; periods of an estimated useful life)

b Advertising: Apple Computer launched the MacIntosh with an expensive television advertising campaign. The MacIntosh line has been a major source of revenue for Apple ever since. (Period in which advertising was done; periods in estimated production life of the original model MacIntosh)

c Interest expense: on some loans, the borrower does not pay any interest until the end of the loan. This practice is very common on short-term loans, such as 60 or 90 days, but may also occur in some special types of long-term borrowing. (Periods comprising the life of the loan; period in which interest is paid)

ANSWERS TO SELF-TEST QUESTIONS

1 c   2 c   3 d   4 c   5 b

Completion of the Accounting Cycle

In Chapter 4 we complete our coverage of the accounting cycle for a service-type business. Emphasis is placed upon steps performed at the end of the cycle, including adjusting entries, preparation of a work sheet, and reversing entries. The continuing example of Roberts Real Estate Company is used to illustrate and explain the four basic types of adjusting entries and the preparation of a work sheet. In our discussion of reversing entries, we emphasize the optional nature of this final step in the accounting cycle. As in our earlier chapters on the accounting cycle, the procedures employed in computer-based accounting systems are compared with those in manual systems.

After studying this chapter you should be able to meet these Learning Objectives:

1 Explain how accounting periods of equal length are useful in evaluating the income of a business.

2 State the purpose of adjusting entries and explain how these entries are related to the concepts of accrual accounting.

3 Describe the four basic types of adjusting entries.

4 Prepare a work sheet and discuss its usefulness.

5 Describe the steps in the accounting cycle.

6 Explain when and why reversing entries may be used.

Accounting Periods and Financial Statements

Objective 1
Explain how accounting periods of equal length are useful in evaluating the income of a business.

For the purpose of measuring net income and preparing financial statements, the life of a business is divided into accounting periods of equal length. Because accounting periods are equal in length, we can compare the income of the current period with that of prior periods to see if our operating results are improving or declining.

As explained in Chapter 3, the **accounting period** means the span of time covered by an income statement. The usual accounting period for which complete financial statements are prepared and distributed to investors, bankers, and governmental agencies is one year. However, most businesses also prepare quarterly and monthly financial statements so that management will be currently informed on the profitability of the business from month to month.

Transactions Affecting More Than One Accounting Period

Dividing the life of a business into relatively short accounting periods requires the use of *adjusting entries* at the end of each period. Adjusting entries are required for those transactions which affect the revenue or the expenses of *more than one accounting period.* For example, assume that a company which prepares monthly financial statements purchases a one-year insurance policy at a cost of $1,200. Clearly, the entire $1,200 does not represent the insurance expense of the current month. Rather, it is the insurance expense for 12 months; only $\frac{1}{12}$ of this cost, or $100, should be recognized as expense in each month covered by the policy. The allocation of this cost to expense in 12 separate accounting periods is accomplished by making an adjusting entry at the end of each period.

Some transactions affect the revenue or expense of only one period. An example is the payment of a monthly salary to an employee on the last day of each month. Adjusting entries are not required for transactions of this type.

ADJUSTING ENTRIES: A CLOSER LOOK

Objective 2
State the purpose of adjusting entries and explain how these entries are related to the concepts of accrual accounting.

The *realization principle,* as explained in Chapter 3, requires that revenue be recognized and recorded in the period it is earned. The *matching principle* stresses that expenses are incurred in order to produce revenue. To measure net income for an accounting period, we must "match" or compare the revenue earned during the period with the expenses incurred to produce that revenue. At the end of an accounting period, adjusting entries are needed so that all revenue *earned* is reflected in the accounts regardless of whether it has been collected. Adjusting entries are also needed for expenses to assure that all expenses *incurred* are matched against the revenue of the current period regardless of when cash payment of the expense occurs.

Thus, adjusting entries help in achieving the goals of accrual accounting—recording revenue when it is *earned* and recording expenses when the related goods and services are *used.* The realization principle and the matching principle are key elements of accrual accounting. Adjusting entries are a technique of applying these principles to transactions which affect two or more accounting periods.

In Chapter 3, the concept of adjusting entries was introduced when Roberts Real Estate Company recorded depreciation for the month of October. Adjusting entries are necessary to record depreciation expense, because buildings and equipment are purchased in a single accounting period but are used over many periods. Some portion of the cost of these assets should be allocated to expense in each period of the asset's estimated life. In this chapter, we will see that the use of adjusting entries is not limited to recording depreciation expense. Adjusting entries are needed *whenever transactions affect the revenue or expense of more than one accounting period.*

Types of Adjusting Entries

A business may need to make a dozen or more adjusting entries at the end of each accounting period. The exact number of adjustments will depend upon the nature of the company's business activities. However, all adjusting entries fall into one of four general categories:

Objective 3
Describe the four basic types of adjusting entries.

1 **Entries to apportion recorded costs** A cost that will benefit more than one accounting period usually is recorded by debiting an asset account. In each period that benefits from the use of this asset, an adjusting entry is made to allocate a portion of the asset's cost to expense.

2 **Entries to apportion unearned revenue** A business may collect in advance for services to be rendered to customers in future accounting periods. In the period in which services are rendered, an adjusting entry is made to record the portion of the revenue earned during the period.

3 **Entries to record unrecorded expenses** An expense may be incurred in the current accounting period even though no bill has yet been received and payment will not occur until a future period. Such unrecorded expenses are recorded by an adjusting entry made at the end of the accounting period.

4 **Entries to record unrecorded revenue** Revenue may be earned during the current period, but not yet billed to customers or recorded in the accounting records. Such unrecorded revenue is recorded by making an adjusting entry at the end of the period.

Characteristics of Adjusting Entries

It will be helpful to keep in mind two important characteristics of all adjusting entries. First, every adjusting entry *involves the recognition of either revenue or expense.* Revenue and expenses represent changes in owner's equity. However, owner's equity cannot change by itself; there also must be a corresponding change in either assets or liabilities. *Thus, every adjusting entry affects both an income statement account* (revenue or expense) *and a balance sheet account* (asset or liability).

Second, adjusting entries are based upon the concepts of accrual accounting, *not upon monthly bills or month-end transactions.* No one sends us a bill saying, "Depreciation expense on your building amounts to $500 this month." Yet, we must be aware of the need to estimate and record depreciation expense if we are to measure net income properly for the period. Making adjusting entries requires a greater understanding of accrual accounting concepts than does the recording of routine business transactions. In many businesses, the adjusting entries are made by the company's controller or by a professional accountant, rather than by the regular accounting staff.

To demonstrate the various types of adjusting entries, the illustration of Roberts Real Estate Company will be continued for November. We shall consider in detail only those November transactions which require adjusting entries at the end of the month.

Apportioning Recorded Costs

When a business makes an expenditure that will benefit more than one accounting period, the amount usually is debited to an asset account. At the end of each period benefiting from this expenditure, an adjusting entry is made to transfer an appropriate portion of the cost from the asset account to an expense account. This adjusting entry reflects the fact that part of the asset has been used up—or become expense—during the current accounting period.

An adjusting entry to apportion a recorded cost consists of a debit to an expense account and a credit to an asset account (or a contra-asset account). Examples of these adjustments include the entries to record depreciation expense and to apportion the costs of *prepaid expenses.*

■ **Prepaid Expenses**   Payments in advance are often made for such items as insurance, rent, and office supplies. If the advance payment (or prepayment) will benefit more than just the current accounting period, the cost *represents an asset* rather than an expense. The cost of this asset will be allocated to expense in the accounting periods in which the services or the supplies are used. In summary, *prepaid expenses are assets;* they become expenses only as the goods or services are used up.

■ **Insurance**   To illustrate these concepts, assume that on November 1, Roberts Real Estate Company paid $600 for a one-year fire insurance policy covering the building. This expenditure was debited to an asset account by the following journal entry:

■
Expenditure for insurance policy recorded as asset

Unexpired Insurance...	*600*	
Cash...		*600*
Purchased a one-year fire insurance policy.		

Since this expenditure of $600 will protect the company against fire loss for one year, the insurance expense applicable to each month's operations is $\frac{1}{12}$ of the annual expense, or $50. In order that the accounting records for November show insurance expense of $50, the following *adjusting entry* is required at November 30:

■
Adjusting entry, portion of asset expires (becomes expense)

Insurance Expense	*50*	
Unexpired Insurance...		*50*
To record insurance expense for November.		

This adjusting entry serves two purposes: (1) it apportions the proper amount of insurance expense to November operations and (2) it reduces the asset account to $550 so that the correct amount of unexpired insurance will appear in the balance sheet at November 30.

What would be the effect on the income statement for November if the above adjustment were not made? The expenses would be understated by $50 and consequently the net income would be overstated by $50. The balance sheet also would be affected by failure to make the adjustment: the assets would be overstated by $50 and so would the owner's equity. The overstatement of the owner's equity would result from the overstated amount of net income transferred to the owner's equity account when the accounts were closed at November 30.

■ **Office Supplies**   On November 2, Roberts Real Estate Company purchased enough stationery and other office supplies to last for several months.

The cost of the supplies was $720, and this amount was debited to an asset account by the following journal entry:

Expenditure for office supplies recorded as asset

Office Supplies	720	
Cash		720
Purchased office supplies.		

No entries were made during November to record the day-to-day usage of office supplies, but on November 30 a count was made of the supplies still on hand. This physical count showed unused supplies with a cost of $500. Thus, supplies costing $220 were used during November. On the basis of the November 30 count, an adjusting entry is made debiting an expense account $220 (the cost of supplies consumed during November), and reducing the asset account by $220. The *adjusting entry* follows:

Adjusting entry. Portion of supplies used represents expense

Office Supplies Expense	220	
Office Supplies		220
To record consumption of office supplies in November.		

After this entry is posted the asset account, Office Supplies, will have a balance of $500, representing the cost of office supplies on hand at November 30. The Office Supplies account will appear in the balance sheet as an asset; the Office Supplies Expense account will be shown in the income statement.

How would failure to make this adjustment affect the financial statements? In the income statement for November, the expenses would be understated by $220 and the net income overstated by the same amount. Since the overstated amount for net income in November would be transferred into the owner's equity account in the process of closing the accounts, the owner's equity section of the balance sheet would be overstated by $220. Assets also would be overstated because Office Supplies would be listed at $220 too much.

■ **Recording Prepayments Directly in the Expense Accounts**   In our illustration, payments for insurance and office supplies which are expected to provide benefits for more than one accounting period are recorded by debiting an asset account, such as Unexpired Insurance or Office Supplies. However, some companies follow an alternative practice of debiting these prepayments directly to an expense account such as Insurance Expense. At the end of the period, the adjusting entry would then consist of a debit to Unexpired Insurance and a credit to Insurance Expense for the portion of the insurance cost *which has not yet expired.*

This alternative method leads to the same results in the balance sheet and income statement as does the method used in our illustration. Under both procedures, the cost of benefits consumed in the current period is treated as an expense, and the cost of benefits applicable to future periods is carried forward in the balance sheet as an asset.

In this text and in the end-of-chapter problem material, we will follow the practice of recording prepayments in *asset accounts* and then making adjusting entries to transfer these costs to expense accounts as the assets expire.

■ **Depreciation of Building**   The recording of depreciation expense at the end of an accounting period provides another example of an adjusting entry which *apportions a recorded cost.* The November 30 adjusting entry to record depreciation of the building used by Roberts Real Estate Company is exactly the same as the October 31 *adjusting entry* explained in Chapter 3.

■
**Adjusting entry.
Cost of building
is gradually
converted to
expense**

Depreciation Expense: Building	150	
Accumulated Depreciation: Building		150
To record depreciation for November.		

This allocation of depreciation expense to November operations is based on the following facts: the building cost $36,000 and is estimated to have a useful life of 20 years (240 months). Using the straight-line method of depreciation, the portion of the original cost which expires each month is $\frac{1}{240}$ of $36,000, or $150.

The Accumulated Depreciation: Building account now has a credit balance of $300 as a result of the October and November credits of $150 each. The book value of the building is $35,700; that is, the original cost of $36,000 minus the accumulated depreciation of $300. The term *book value* means the net amount at which an asset is shown in the accounting records, as distinguished from its market value. *Carrying value* is an alternative term, with the same meaning as book value.

■ **Depreciation of Office Equipment** The November 30 adjusting entry to record depreciation of the office equipment is the same as the *adjusting entry* for depreciation a month earlier, as shown in Chapter 3.

■
**Adjusting entry.
Cost of office
equipment
gradually
converted to
expense**

Depreciation Expense: Office Equipment	45	
Accumulated Depreciation: Office Equipment		45
To record depreciation for November.		

The original cost of the office equipment was $5,400, and the estimated useful life was 10 years (120 months). Depreciation each month under the straight-line method is therefore $\frac{1}{120}$ of $5,400, or $45.

What is the book value of the office equipment at this point? The original cost of $5,400, minus accumulated depreciation of $90 for two months, leaves a book value of $5,310.

Apportioning Unearned Revenue

In some instances, a business may *collect in advance* for services to be rendered to customers in later accounting periods. For example, a football team collects much of its revenue in advance through the sale of season tickets. Health clubs collect in advance by selling long-term membership contracts. Airlines sell many of their tickets well in advance of a scheduled flight.

For accounting purposes, amounts collected in advance *do not represent revenue,* because these amounts have *not yet been earned.* Amounts collected from customers in advance are recorded by debiting the Cash account and crediting an *unearned revenue* account. Unearned revenue also may be called *deferred revenue.*

When a company collects money in advance from its customers, it has an *obligation* to render services in the future. Therefore, the balance of an unearned revenue account is considered to be a liability; *it appears in the liability section of the balance sheet, not in the income statement.* Unearned revenue differs from other liabilities because it usually will be settled by rendering services, rather than by making payment in cash. In short, it will be *worked off* rather than *paid off.* Of course if the business is unable to render the service, it must discharge this liability by refunding money to its customers.

CASE IN POINT ■ One of the largest liabilities in the balance sheet of UAL, Inc., (United Air Lines) is "Advance ticket sales and customer deposits." This account, with a balance of approximately $500 million, represents unearned revenue resulting from the sale of tickets for future flights. Most of this unearned revenue will be earned as the future flights occur. Some customers, however, will change their plans and will return their tickets to United Airlines for a cash refund.

When the company renders the services for which customers have paid in advance, it is working off its liability to these customers and is earning the revenue. At the end of the accounting period in which the revenue is earned, an *adjusting entry* is made to transfer an appropriate amount from the unearned revenue account to a revenue account. This adjusting entry consists of a debit to a liability account (unearned revenue) and a credit to a revenue account.

To illustrate these concepts, assume that on November 1, Roberts Real Estate Company agreed to act as manager of some rental properties for a monthly fee of $300. The owner of the properties, Frank Day, was leaving the country on an extended trip and therefore paid the company for six months' service in advance. The journal entry by Roberts Real Estate Company to record the transaction on November 1 was:

Management fee collected but not yet earned

Cash..	1,800	
Unearned Management Fees......................................		1,800
Collected in advance six months' fees for management of properties		
owned by Frank Day.		

Remember that Unearned Management Fees is a *liability* account, not a revenue account. This management fee will be earned gradually over a period of six months as Roberts Real Estate Company performs the required services. At the end of each monthly accounting period, the company will make an adjusting entry transferring ⅙ of this management fee, or $300, from the unearned revenue account to a revenue account. The first in this series of monthly transfers will be made on November 30 by the following *adjusting entry:*

Adjusting entry to recognize earning of a part of management fee

Unearned Management Fees...	300	
Management Fees Earned		300
Fee earned by managing Frank Day property during November.		

After this entry has been posted, The Unearned Management Fees account will have a $1,500 credit balance. This balance represents the company's obligation to render $1,500 worth of services over the next five months and will appear in the liability section of the company's balance sheet. The Management Fees Earned account will be shown as revenue in the November income statement.

■ **Recording Advance Collections Directly in the Revenue Accounts** We have stressed that amounts collected from customers in advance represent liabilities, not revenue. However, some companies prefer to follow an accounting practice of crediting these advance collections directly to revenue accounts. Under this practice, the adjusting entry required at the end of the period would consist of a debit to the revenue account and a credit to the unearned revenue account for the portion of the advance payment *not yet earned.* This alternative accounting practice leads to the same results in the financial statements as does the method used in our Roberts Real Estate Company illustration.

Throughout this book, we will follow the originally described practice of crediting advance payments from customers to an unearned revenue account.

Recording Unrecorded Expenses

This type of adjusting entry recognizes expenses that will be paid in *future* transactions; thus, no cost has yet been recorded in the accounting records. Salaries of employees and interest on borrowed money are common examples of expenses which accumulate from day to day, but which usually are not recorded until they are paid. These expenses are said to *accrue* over time, that is, to grow or to accumulate. At the end of the accounting period, an adjusting entry should be made to record any expenses which have accrued, but which have not yet been recorded. Since these expenses will be paid at a future date, the adjusting entry consists of a debit to an expense account and a credit to a liability account. We shall now use the example of Roberts Real Estate Company to illustrate this type of adjusting entry.

■ **Accrual of Interest** On November 1, Roberts Real Estate Company borrowed the sum of $3,000 from a bank. Banks require every borrower to sign a *promissory note,* that is, a formal, written promise to repay the amount borrowed plus interest at an agreed future date. (Various forms of notes in common use and the accounting problems involved will be discussed more fully in Chapter 11.) The note signed by Roberts, with certain details omitted, is shown at the top of the next page.

The note payable is a liability of Roberts Real Estate Company, similar to an account payable but different in that a formal written promise to pay is required and interest is charged on the amount borrowed. A Notes Payable account is credited when the note is issued; the Notes Payable account will be debited three months later when the note is paid. Interest accrues throughout the life of the note payable, but it is not payable until the note matures on February 1. To the bank making the loan, the note signed by Roberts is an asset, a note receivable.

The journal entry made on November 1 by Roberts Real Estate Company to

**Note payable
issued to bank**

> $3,000   Los Angeles, California   November 1, 19__
>
> Three months _____ after date _____ I _____ promise to pay
>
> to the order of _____ American National Bank _____
>
> _____ ---Three thousand and no/100--- _____ dollars
>
> for value received, with interest at _____ 12 percent per year _____
>
> Roberts Real Estate Company
>
> By _____ *James Roberts* _____

record the borrowing of $3,000 from the bank was as follows:

**Entry when bank
loan is obtained**

Cash 3,000
    Notes Payable 3,000
Obtained from bank three-month loan with interest at 12% a year.

Three months later, Roberts Real Estate Company must pay the bank $3,090, representing repayment of the $3,000 note payable plus $90 interest ($3,000 × .12 × ³⁄₁₂). The $90 is the total interest expense for the three months. Although no payment will be made for three months, one-third of the interest expense ($30) is *incurred* each month, as shown in the chart below.

The following *adjusting entry* is made at November 30 to charge November operations with one month's interest expense and also to record the amount of interest owed to the bank at the end of November.

**Accrual of
interest**

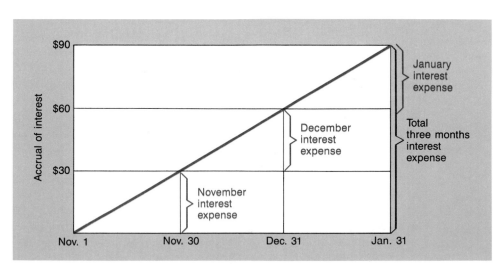

Adjusting entry
for interest
expense incurred
in November

Interest Expense 30
    Interest Payable 30
To record interest expense accrued during November on note payable
($3,000 × 12% × ¹⁄₁₂).

The debit balance in the Interest Expense account will appear in the November income statement; the credit balances in the Interest Payable and Notes Payable accounts will be shown in the balance sheet as liabilities. These two liability accounts will remain in the records until the maturity date of the loan, at which time a cash payment to the bank will wipe out both the Notes Payable account and the Interest Payable account.

■ **Accrual of Salary** On November 20, Roberts hired Carl Nelson as a part-time salesperson whose duties were to work evenings calling on property owners to secure listings of property for sale or rent. The agreed salary was $225 for a five-evening week, payable each Friday; payment for the first week was made on Friday, November 24. Personal income taxes and other taxes relating to payroll are ignored in this illustration.

Assume that the last day of the accounting period, November 30, fell on Thursday. Nelson had worked four evenings since being paid the preceding Friday and therefore had earned $180 (⁴⁄₅ × $225). In order that this $180 of November salary expense be reflected in the accounts before the financial statements are prepared, an ***adjusting entry*** is necessary at November 30.

Adjusting entry
for salaries
expense incurred
but unpaid at
November 30

Salaries Expense 180
    Salaries Payable... 180
To record salary expense and related liability to salesperson for last four
evenings' work in November.

The debit balance in the Salaries Expense account will appear as an expense in the November income statement; the credit balance of $180 in the Salaries Payable account is the amount owing to the salesperson for work performed during the last four days of November and will appear among the liabilities in the balance sheet at November 30.

The next regular payday for Nelson will be Friday, December 1, which is the first day of the new accounting period. Since the accounts were adjusted and closed on November 30, all the revenue and expense accounts have zero balances at the beginning of business on December 1. The payment of a week's salary to Nelson will be recorded by the following entry on December 1:

Payment of
salary
overlapping two
accounting
periods

Salaries Payable... 180
Salaries Expense 45
    Cash... 225
Paid weekly salary to salesperson.

Note that the net result of the November 30 accrual entry has been to split the salesperson's weekly salary expense between November and December. Four days of the work week fell in November, so four days' pay, or $180, was recognized as November expense. One day of the work week fell in December so $45 was recorded as December expense.

No accrual entry is necessary for other salaries in Roberts Real Estate

Company because everyone except Nelson is paid regularly on the last working day of the month.

Recording Unrecorded Revenue

A business may earn revenue during the current accounting period but might not bill the customer until a future accounting period. This situation is likely to occur if additional services will be performed for the same customer, in which case the bill might not be prepared until all services are completed. Any revenue which has been *earned but not recorded* during the current accounting period should be recorded at the end of the period by means of an adjusting entry. This adjusting entry consists of a debit to an account receivable and a credit to the appropriate revenue account. The term *accrued revenue* often is used to describe revenue which has been earned during the period but which has *not been recorded* prior to the making of adjusting entries.

To illustrate this type of adjusting entry, assume that on November 16, Roberts Real Estate Company entered into a management agreement with Angela Clayton, the owner of two small office buildings. The company agreed to manage the Clayton properties for a fee of $240 a month, payable on the fifteenth of each month. No entry is made in the accounting records at the time of signing a contract, because no services have yet been rendered and no change has occurred in assets or liabilities. The managerial duties are to begin immediately, but the first monthly fee will not be received until December 15. The following *adjusting entry* is therefore necessary at November 30:

■
Adjusting entry for fees earned but not yet billed

Management Fees Receivable	120	
Management Fees Earned		120
To record accrued revenue from services rendered to Angela Clayton during November.		

The debit balance in the Management Fees Receivable account will be shown in the balance sheet as an asset. The credit balance of the Management Fees Earned account, including earnings from both the Frank Day and the Angela Clayton contracts, will appear in the November income statement.

The collection of the first monthly fee from Clayton will occur in the next accounting period (December 15, to be exact). Of this $240 cash receipt, half represents collection of the asset account, Management Fees Receivable, created at November 30 by the adjusting entry. The other half of the $240 cash receipt represents revenue earned during December; this should be credited to the December revenue account for Management Fees Earned. The entry on December 15 is as follows:

■
Management fee applicable to two accounting periods

Cash	240	
Management Fees Receivable		120
Management Fees Earned		120
Collected commission from Angela Clayton for month ended December 15.		

The net result of the November 30 accrual entry has been to divide the revenue from managing the Clayton properties between November and December in accordance with the timing of the services rendered.

Adjusting Entries and the Accrual Basis of Accounting

Adjusting entries help make accrual basis accounting work successfully. By preparing adjusting entries, we can recognize revenue in the accounting period in which it is *earned* and also recognize any unrecorded expenses which helped to *produce that revenue.* For example, the adjusting entry to record revenue which has been earned but not yet recorded helps achieve our goal of including in the income statement all the revenue *realized* during the accounting period. The adjusting entries which recognize expenses help to achieve the *matching principle*—that is, offsetting revenues with all the expenses incurred in generating that revenue.

THE WORK SHEET

Objective 4
Prepare a work sheet and discuss its usefulness.

The work necessary at the end of an accounting period includes construction of a trial balance, journalizing and posting of adjusting entries, preparation of financial statements, and journalizing and posting of closing entries. So many details are involved in these end-of-period procedures that it is easy to make errors. If these errors are recorded in the journal and in the ledger accounts, considerable time and effort can be wasted in correcting them. Both the journal and the ledger are formal, permanent records. They may be prepared manually in ink or maintained electronically using a computer. One way of avoiding errors in the permanent accounting records and also of simplifying the work to be done at the end of the period is to use a *work sheet.*

In a manual accounting system, a work sheet is a large columnar sheet of paper, especially designed to arrange in a convenient systematic form all the accounting data required at the end of the period. The work sheet is not a part of the permanent accounting records; it is prepared in pencil by accountants for their own convenience. If an error is made on the work sheet, it may be erased and corrected much more easily than an error in the formal accounting records. Furthermore, the work sheet is so designed as to minimize errors by automatically bringing to light many types of discrepancies which otherwise might be entered in the journal and posted to the ledger accounts. Dollar signs, decimal points, and commas are not used with the amounts entered on work sheets, although commas are shown in this example. A work sheet for Roberts Real Estate appears on page 139.

The work sheet may be thought of as a testing ground on which the ledger accounts are adjusted, balanced, and arranged in the general form of financial statements. The satisfactory completion of a work sheet provides considerable assurance that all the details of the end-of-period accounting procedures have been properly brought together. After this point has been established, the work sheet then serves as the source from which the formal financial statements are prepared and the adjusting and closing entries are entered in the journal.

Preparing the Work Sheet

Notice that the heading of the work sheet illustrated for Roberts Real Estate consists of three parts: (1) the name of the business, (2) the title *Work Sheet,* and (3) the period of time covered. The body of the work sheet contains five pairs of money columns, each pair consisting of a debit and a credit column.

ROBERTS REAL ESTATE COMPANY
Work Sheet
For the Month Ended November 30, 19___

■ Trial balance is entered in first pair of columns on work sheet

	TRIAL BALANCE		ADJUSTMENTS		ADJUSTED TRIAL BALANCE		INCOME STATEMENT		BALANCE SHEET	
	DR	CR	DR	CR	DR	CR	DR	CR	DR	CR
Cash	21,740									
Accounts receivable	16,990									
Unexpired insurance	600									
Office supplies	720									
Land	130,000									
Building	36,000									
Accumulated depreciation: building		150								
Office equipment	5,400									
Accumulated depreciation: office equipment		45								
Notes payable		3,000								
Accounts payable		23,595								
Unearned management fees		1,800								
James Roberts, capital		180,771								
James Roberts, drawing	1,500									
Sales commissions earned		15,484								
Advertising expense	1,275									
Salaries expense	9,425									
Telephone expense	1,195									
	224,845	224,845								

The procedures to be followed in preparing a work sheet will now be illustrated in five simple steps.

1 Enter the ledger account balances in the Trial Balance columns The titles and balances of the ledger accounts at November 30 are copied into the Trial Balance columns of the work sheet, as illustrated on page 139. In practice these amounts may be taken directly from the ledger. It would be a duplication of work to prepare a trial balance as a separate schedule and then to copy this information into the work sheet. As soon as the account balances have been listed on the work sheet, these two columns should be added and the totals entered.

2 Enter the adjustments in the Adjustments columns The required adjustments for Roberts Real Estate Company were explained earlier in this chapter; these same adjustments are now entered in the Adjustments columns of the work sheet. (See page 141.)

As a cross reference, the debit and credit parts of each adjustment are keyed together by placing a key letter to the left of each amount. For example, the adjustment debiting Insurance Expense and crediting Unexpired Insurance is identified by the key letter (a). The use of the key letters makes it easy to match a debit entry in the Adjustments columns with its related credit. The identifying letters also key the debit and credit entries in the Adjustments columns to the brief explanations which appear at the bottom of the work sheet.

The titles of any accounts debited or credited in the adjusting entries but *not listed* in the trial balance should be written on the work sheet below the trial balance. For example, Insurance Expense does not appear in the trial balance; therefore it should be written on the first available line below the trial balance totals. After all the adjustment debits and credits have been entered in the Adjustments columns, this pair of columns must be totaled. Proving the equality of debit and credit totals helps to detect any arithmetical errors and to prevent them from being carried over into other columns of the work sheet.

3 Enter the account balances as adjusted in the Adjusted Trial Balance columns The work sheet as it appears after completion of the Adjusted Trial Balance columns is illustrated on page 142. Each account balance in the first pair of columns is combined with the adjustment, if any, in the second pair of columns, and the combined amount is entered in the Adjusted Trial Balance columns. This process of combining the items on each line throughout the first four columns of the work sheet requires horizontal addition or subtraction. It is called *cross footing,* in contrast to the addition of items in a vertical column, which is called *footing* the column.

For example, the Office Supplies account has a debit balance of $720 in the Trial Balance columns. This $720 debit amount is combined with the $220 credit appearing on the same line in the Adjustments column; the combination of a $720 debit with a $220 credit produces an adjusted debit amount of $500 in the Adjusted Trial Balance debit column. As another example, consider the Office Supplies Expense account. This account had no balance in the Trial Balance columns but shows a $220 debit in the Adjustments debit column. The combination of a zero starting balance and $220 debit adjustment produces a $220 debit amount in the Adjusted Trial Balance.

Explanatory footnotes keyed to adjustments

ROBERTS REAL ESTATE COMPANY
Work Sheet
For the Month Ended November 30, 19___

Account	Trial Balance DR	Trial Balance CR	Adjustments DR	Adjustments CR	Adjusted Trial Balance DR	Adjusted Trial Balance CR	Income Statement DR	Income Statement CR	Balance Sheet DR	Balance Sheet CR
Cash	21,740									
Accounts receivable	16,990									
Unexpired insurance	600			(a) 50						
Office supplies	720			(b) 220						
Land	130,000									
Building	36,000									
Accumulated depreciation: building		150		(c) 150						
Office equipment	5,400									
Accumulated depreciation: office equipment		45		(d) 45						
Notes payable		3,000								
Accounts payable		23,595								
Unearned management fees		1,800	(e) 300							
James Roberts, capital		180,771								
James Roberts, drawing	1,500									
Sales commissions earned		15,484								
Advertising expense	1,275									
Salaries expense	9,425		(g) 180							
Telephone expense	1,195									
	224,845	224,845								
Insurance expense			(a) 50							
Office supplies expense			(b) 220							
Depreciation expense: building			(c) 150							
Depreciation expense: office equipment			(d) 45							
Management fees earned				(e) 300 (h) 120						
Interest expense			(f) 30							
Interest payable				(f) 30						
Salaries payable				(g) 180						
Management fees receivable			(h) 120							
			1,055	1,095						

* Adjustments:
(a) Portion of insurance cost which expired during November.
(b) Office supplies used during November.
(c) Depreciation of building during November.
(d) Depreciation of office equipment during November.
(e) Earned one-sixth of the fee collected in advance on the Day properties.
(f) Interest expense accrued during November on note payable ($3,000 × 12% × 1/12).
(g) Salesperson's salary for last four days of November.
(h) Management fee accrued on Clayton contract in November.

Enter the adjusted amounts in columns 5 and 6 of work sheet

ROBERTS REAL ESTATE COMPANY
Work Sheet
For the Month Ended November 30, 19___

	TRIAL BALANCE DR	TRIAL BALANCE CR	ADJUSTMENTS DR	ADJUSTMENTS CR	ADJUSTED TRIAL BALANCE DR	ADJUSTED TRIAL BALANCE CR	INCOME STATEMENT DR	INCOME STATEMENT CR	BALANCE SHEET DR	BALANCE SHEET CR
Cash	21,740				21,740					
Accounts receivable	16,990				16,990					
Unexpired insurance	600			(a) 50	550					
Office supplies	720			(b) 220	500					
Land	130,000				130,000					
Building	36,000				36,000					
Accumulated depreciation: building		150		(c) 150		300				
Office equipment	5,400				5,400					
Accumulated depreciation: office equipment		45		(d) 45		90				
Notes payable		3,000				3,000				
Accounts payable		23,595				23,595				
Unearned management fees		1,800	(e) 300			1,500				
James Roberts, capital		180,771				180,771				
James Roberts, drawing	1,500				1,500					
Sales commissions earned		15,484				15,484				
Advertising expense	1,275				1,275					
Sales salaries expense	9,425		(g) 180		9,605					
Telephone expense	1,195				1,195					
	224,845	224,845								
Insurance expense			(a) 50		50					
Office supplies expense			(b) 220		220					
Depreciation expense: building			(c) 150		150					
Depreciation expense: office equipment			(d) 45		45					
Management fees earned				(e) 300 (h) 120		420				
Interest expense			(f) 30		30					
Interest payable				(f) 30		30				
Salaries payable				(g) 180		180				
Management fees receivable			(h) 120		120					
			1,095	1,095	225,370	225,370				

* Explanatory notes relating to adjustments are the same as on page 141.

Many of the accounts in the trial balance are not affected by the adjustments made at the end of the month; the balances of these accounts (such as Cash, Land, Building, or Notes Payable in the illustrated work sheet) are entered in the Adjusted Trial Balance columns in exactly the same amounts as shown in the Trial Balance columns. After all the accounts have been extended into the Adjusted Trial Balance columns, this pair of columns is totaled to prove that no arithmetical errors have been made up to this point.

4   Extend each amount in the Adjusted Trial Balance columns into the Income Statement columns or into the Balance Sheet columns   Assets, liabilities, and the owner's capital and drawing accounts are extended to the Balance Sheet columns; revenue and expense accounts are extended to the Income Statement columns.

The process of extending amounts horizontally across the work sheet should begin with the account at the top of the work sheet, which is usually Cash. The cash figure is extended to the Balance Sheet debit column. Then the accountant goes down the work sheet line by line, extending each account balance to the appropriate Income Statement or Balance Sheet column. The likelihood of error is much less when each account is extended in the order of its appearance on the work sheet, than if accounts are extended in random order. The work sheet as it appears after completion of this sorting process is illustrated on page 144. Note that each amount in the Adjusted Trial Balance columns is extended to one *and only one* of the four remaining columns.

5   Total the Income Statement columns and the Balance Sheet columns. Enter the net income or net loss as a balancing figure in both pairs of columns, and again compute column totals   The work sheet as it appears after this final step is shown on page 145.

The net income or net loss for the period is determined by computing the difference between the totals of the two Income Statement columns. In the illustrated work sheet, the credit column total is the larger and the excess represents net income:

Income Statement credit column total (revenue)	*$15,904*
Income Statement debit column total (expenses)	*12,570*
Difference: net income for period	*$ 3,334*

Note on the work sheet that the net income of $3,334 is entered in the Income Statement *debit* column as a balancing figure and also on the same line as a balancing figure in the Balance Sheet *credit* column. The caption *Net Income* is written in the space for account titles to identify and explain this item. New totals are then computed for both the Income Statement columns and the Balance Sheet columns. Each pair of columns is now in balance.

The reason for entering the net income of $3,334 in the Balance Sheet credit column is that the net income accumulated during the period in the revenue and expense accounts causes an increase in the owner's equity. If the balance sheet columns did not have equal totals after the net income had been recorded in the credit column, the lack of agreement would indicate that an error had been made in the work sheet.

Let us assume for a moment that the month's operations had produced a *loss* rather than a profit. In that case the Income Statement debit column

Extend each adjusted amount to columns for income statement or balance sheet

ROBERTS REAL ESTATE COMPANY
Work Sheet
For the Month Ended November 30, 19___

	TRIAL BALANCE DR	TRIAL BALANCE CR	ADJUSTMENTS* DR	ADJUSTMENTS* CR	ADJUSTED TRIAL BALANCE DR	ADJUSTED TRIAL BALANCE CR	INCOME STATEMENT DR	INCOME STATEMENT CR	BALANCE SHEET DR	BALANCE SHEET CR
Cash	21,740				21,740				21,740	
Accounts receivable	16,990				16,990				16,990	
Unexpired insurance	600			(a) 50	550				550	
Office supplies	720			(b) 220	500				500	
Land	130,000				130,000				130,000	
Building	36,000				36,000				36,000	
Accumulated depreciation: building		150		(c) 150		300				300
Office equipment	5,400				5,400				5,400	
Accumulated depreciation: office equipment		45		(d) 45		90				90
Notes payable		3,000				3,000				3,000
Accounts payable		23,595				23,595				23,595
Unearned management fees		1,800	(e) 300			1,500				1,500
James Roberts, capital		180,771				180,771				180,771
James Roberts, drawing	1,500				1,500				1,500	
Sales commissions earned		15,484				15,484		15,484		
Advertising expense	1,275				1,275		1,275			
Salaries expense	9,425		(g) 180		9,605		9,605			
Telephone expense	1,195				1,195		1,195			
	224,845	224,845								
Insurance expense			(a) 50		50		50			
Office supplies expense			(b) 220		220		220			
Depreciation expense: building			(c) 150		150		150			
Depreciation expense: office equipment			(d) 45		45		45			
Management fees earned				(e) 300 (h) 120		420		420		
Interest expense			(f) 30		30		30			
Interest payable				(f) 30		30				30
Salaries payable				(g) 180		180				180
Management fees receivable			(h) 120		120				120	
			1,095	1,095	225,370	225,370				

Completed work sheet

ROBERTS REAL ESTATE COMPANY
Work Sheet
For the Month Ended November 30, 19___

	Trial Balance DR	Trial Balance CR	Adjustments DR	Adjustments CR	Adjusted Trial Balance DR	Adjusted Trial Balance CR	Income Statement DR	Income Statement CR	Balance Sheet DR	Balance Sheet CR
Cash	21,740				21,740				21,740	
Accounts receivable	16,990				16,990				16,990	
Unexpired insurance	600			(a) 50	550				550	
Office supplies	720			(b) 220	500				500	
Land	130,000				130,000				130,000	
Building	36,000				36,000				36,000	
Accumulated depreciation: building		150		(c) 150		300				300
Office equipment	5,400				5,400				5,400	
Accumulated depreciation: office equipment		45		(d) 45		90				90
Notes payable		3,000				3,000				3,000
Accounts payable		23,595				23,595				23,595
Unearned management fees		1,800	(e) 300			1,500				1,500
James Roberts, capital		180,771				180,771				180,771
James Roberts, drawing	1,500				1,500				1,500	
Sales commissions earned		15,484				15,484		15,484		
Advertising expense	1,275				1,275		1,275			
Salaries expense	9,425		(g) 180		9,605		9,605			
Telephone expense	1,195				1,195		1,195			
	224,845	224,845								
Insurance expense			(a) 50		50		50			
Office supplies expense			(b) 220		220		220			
Depreciation expense: building			(c) 150		150		150			
Depreciation expense: office equipment			(d) 45		45		45			
Management fees earned				(e) 300 (h) 120		420		420		
Interest expense			(f) 30		30		30			
Interest payable				(f) 30		30				30
Salaries payable				(g) 180		180				180
Management fees receivable			(h) 120		120				120	
			1,095	1,095	225,370	225,370	12,570	15,904	212,800	209,465
Net income							3,334			3,334
							15,904	15,904	212,800	212,800

* Explanatory notes relating to adjustments are the same as on page 141.

would exceed the credit column. The excess of the debits (expenses) over the credits (revenue) would have to be entered in the *credit column* in order to bring the two Income Statement columns into balance. The incurring of a loss would decrease the owner's equity; therefore, the loss would be entered as a balancing figure in the Balance Sheet *debit column.* The Balance Sheet columns would then have equal totals.

■ **Self-Balancing Nature of the Work Sheet**   Why does the entering of the net income or net loss in one of the Balance Sheet columns bring this pair of columns into balance? The answer is short and simple. All the accounts in the Balance Sheet columns have November 30 balances with the exception of the owner's capital account, which still shows the October 31 balance. By bringing in the current month's net income as an addition to the October 31 capital, the capital account is brought up to date as of November 30 (except for the drawing account which is later closed to the capital account). The Balance Sheet columns now prove the familiar proposition that assets are equal to the total of liabilities and owner's equity.

Uses for the Work Sheet

■ **Preparing Financial Statements**   Preparing the formal financial statements from the work sheet is an easy step. All the information needed for both the income statement and the balance sheet has already been sorted and arranged in convenient form in the work sheet. For example, compare the amounts in the following income statement with the amounts listed in the Income Statement columns of the completed work sheet.

■ **Data taken from income statement columns of work sheet**

ROBERTS REAL ESTATE COMPANY
Income Statement
For the Month Ended November 30, 19___

Revenue:

Sales commissions earned		$15,484
Management fees earned		420
Total revenue		$15,904
Expenses:		
Advertising	$1,275	
Salaries	9,605	
Telephone	1,195	
Insurance	50	
Office supplies	220	
Depreciation: building	150	
Depreciation: office equipment	45	
Interest	30	
Total expenses		12,570
Net income		$ 3,334

Notice that in our November 30 work sheet, the owner's capital account still contains its November 1 balance of $180,771. This is because all the changes in owner's equity occurring in the month were recorded in the *temporary* proprietorship accounts (the revenue, expense, and drawing accounts), rather than in the owner's capital account. In the ledger, the owner's capital account will be brought up-to-date when the November closing entries are recorded and posted.

The work sheet provides us with all the information we need to compute the amount of owner's equity at November 30. During November, owner's equity was increased by the earning of net income ($3,334) and decreased by the withdrawal of assets by the owner ($1,500).

The November statement of owner's equity for Roberts Real Estate Company is shown below:

Net income exceeded withdrawals by owner

ROBERTS REAL ESTATE COMPANY
Statement of Owner's Equity
For the Month Ended November 30, 19__

James Roberts, capital, Nov. 1, 19__	$180,771
Add: Net income	3,334
Subtotal	$184,105
Less: Withdrawals	1,500
James Roberts, capital, Nov. 30, 19__	$182,605

Finally, the November 30 balance sheet for Roberts Real Estate contains the amounts for assets and liabilities listed in the Balance Sheet columns of the work sheet, along with the new balance of owner's equity.

Compare these amounts with figures in balance sheet columns of work sheet

ROBERTS REAL ESTATE COMPANY
Balance Sheet
November 30, 19__

ASSETS

Cash		$ 21,740
Accounts receivable		16,990
Management fees receivable		120
Unexpired insurance		550
Office supplies		500
Land		130,000
Building	$36,000	
Less: Accumulated depreciation	300	35,700
Office equipment	$ 5,400	
Less: Accumulated depreciation	90	5,310
Total assets		$210,910

LIABILITIES & OWNER'S EQUITY

Liabilities:		
Notes payable		$ 3,000
Accounts payable		23,595
Interest payable		30
Salaries payable		180
Unearned management fees		1,500
Total liabilities		$ 28,305
Owner's equity:		
James Roberts, capital		182,605
Total liabilities & owner's equity		$210,910

■ **Recording Adjusting Entries in the Accounting Records**   After the financial statements have been prepared from the work sheet at the end of the period, adjusting journal entries are prepared to bring the ledger accounts into agreement with the financial statements. This is an easy step because the adjustments have already been computed on the work sheet. The amounts appearing in the Adjustments columns of the work sheet and the related explanations at the bottom of the work sheet provide all the necessary information for the adjusting entries, as shown below. These adjusting entries are first entered in the journal and then posted to the ledger accounts.

General Journal   Page 5

DATE		ACCOUNT TITLES AND EXPLANATION	LP	DEBIT	CREDIT
19__					
Nov	30	Insurance Expense		50	
		Unexpired Insurance			50
		Insurance expense for November.			

Adjustments on work sheet are entered in general journal

General Journal   Page 5

DATE		ACCOUNT TITLES AND EXPLANATION	LP	DEBIT	CREDIT
19__					
Nov	30	Office Supplies Expense		220	
		Office Supplies..........................			220
		Office supplies used during November.			
	30	Depreciation Expense: Building...............		150	
		Accumulated Depreciation: Building			150
		Depreciation for November ($36,000 ÷ 240 = $150).			
	30	Depreciation Expense: Office Equipment.......		45	
		Accumulated Depreciation: Office Equipment			45
		Depreciation for November ($5,400 ÷ 120 = $45).			
	30	Unearned Management Fees		300	
		Management Fees Earned...............			300
		Earned one-sixth of fee collected in advance for management of the properties owned by Frank Day.			
	30	Interest Expense		30	
		Interest Payable.........................			30
		Interest expense accrued during November on note payable ($3,000 × 12% × 1/12).			
	30	Salaries Expense..............................		180	
		Salaries Payable			180
		To record expense and related liability to salesperson for last four evenings' work in November.			
	30	Management Fees Receivable		120	
		Management Fees Earned...............			120
		To record the receivable and related revenue earned for managing properties owned by Angela Clayton.			

■ **Recording Closing Entries** When the financial statements have been prepared, the revenue and expense accounts have served their purpose for the current period and should be closed. These accounts then will have zero balances and will be ready for the recording of revenue and expenses during the next fiscal period. The completed work sheet provides in convenient form all the information needed to make the closing entries. The preparation of closing entries from the work sheet may be summarized as follows:

1 To close the accounts listed in the Income Statement credit column, debit the revenue accounts and credit Income Summary.

2 To close the accounts listed in the Income Statement debit column, debit Income Summary and credit the expense accounts.

3 To close the Income Summary account, transfer the balancing figure in the Income Statement columns of the work sheet ($3,334 in the illustration) to the owner's capital account. A profit is transferred by debiting Income Summary and crediting the capital account; a loss is transferred by debiting the capital account and crediting Income Summary.

4 To close the owner's drawing account, debit the capital account and credit the drawing account. Notice on the work sheet that the account, James Roberts, Drawing, is extended from the Adjusted Trial Balance debit column to the Balance Sheet debit column. It does not appear in the Income Statement columns because a withdrawal of cash by the owner is not regarded as an expense of the business.

The closing entries at November 30 are shown as follows:

General Journal   Page 6

Closing entries derived from work sheet

DATE		ACCOUNT TITLES AND EXPLANATION	LP	DEBIT	CREDIT
19__					
Nov	30	Sales Commissions Earned...................		15,484	
		Management Fees Earned...................		420	
		Income Summary			15,904
		To close the revenue accounts.			
	30	Income Summary		12,570	
		Advertising Expense....................			1,275
		Salaries Expense......................			9,605
		Telephone Expense			1,195
		Insurance Expense			50
		Office Supplies Expense			220
		Depreciation Expense: Building.........			150
		Depreciation Expense: Office			
		Equipment			45
		Interest Expense			30
		To close the expense accounts.			
	30	Income Summary		3,334	
		James Roberts, Capital			3,334
		To close the Income Summary account.			
	30	James Roberts, Capital		1,500	
		James Roberts, Drawing			1,500
		To close the owner's drawing account.			

■ **Work Sheets in Computer-Based Systems** The "work sheet" in a computer-based accounting system usually consists of a display on the monitor screen rather than a sheet of columnar paper. Spreadsheet programs, such as Lotus 1-2-3 and VP Planner, are ideally suited to preparing a work sheet in a computerized accounting system.

Most of the steps involved in preparing a work sheet are mechanical and can be performed automatically in a computer-based system. Thus, the work sheet can be prepared faster and more easily than in a manual system. A trial balance, for example, is merely a listing of the ledger account balances, and can be prepared instantly by computer. Entering the adjustments, on the other hand, requires human judgment and analysis. Someone familiar with generally accepted accounting principles and with the unrecorded business activities of the company must decide what adjustments are necessary and must enter the adjustment data. Once the adjustments have been entered, the computer can instantly complete the work sheet. When the accountant is satisfied that the adjustments shown in the work sheet are correct, the adjusting and closing entries can be entered in the formal accounting records with the touch of a button.

The Accounting Cycle

Objective 5
Describe the steps in the accounting cycle.

As stated at the beginning of this chapter, the life of a business is divided into accounting periods of equal length. In each period we repeat a standard sequence of accounting procedures beginning with the journalizing of transactions and concluding with an after-closing trial balance.

Because the work sheet includes the trial balance, the adjusting entries in preliminary form, and an adjusted trial balance, the use of a work sheet will modify the sequence of procedures given in Chapter 3, as follows:

1 Journalize transactions Analyze business transactions as they occur and record them promptly in a journal.

2 Post to ledger accounts Transfer debits and credits from journal entries to ledger accounts.

3 Prepare a work sheet Begin with a trial balance of the ledger, enter all necessary adjustments, sort the adjusted account balances between income statement accounts and balance sheet accounts, and determine the net income or net loss.

4 Prepare financial statements Utilize the information in the work sheet to prepare an income statement, a statement of owner's equity, and a balance sheet.

5 Adjust and close the accounts Using the information in the work sheet as a guide, enter the adjusting entries in the journal. Post these entries to ledger accounts. Prepare and post journal entries to close the revenue and expense accounts into the Income Summary account and to transfer the net income or net loss to the owner's capital account. Also prepare and post a journal entry to close the owner's drawing account into the owner's capital account.

6 Prepare an after-closing trial balance Prove that equality of debit and credit balances in the ledger has not been upset by the adjusting and closing procedures.

The above sequence of accounting procedures constitutes a complete accounting process. The regular repetition of this standardized set of procedures in each accounting period is often referred to as the *accounting cycle.* The procedures of a complete accounting cycle are illustrated in the flowchart below. The white symbols indicate the accounting procedures; the shaded symbols represent accounting records, schedules, and statements.

Note that the preparing of financial statements (Step 4) comes before entering adjusting and closing entries in the journal and posting these entries to the

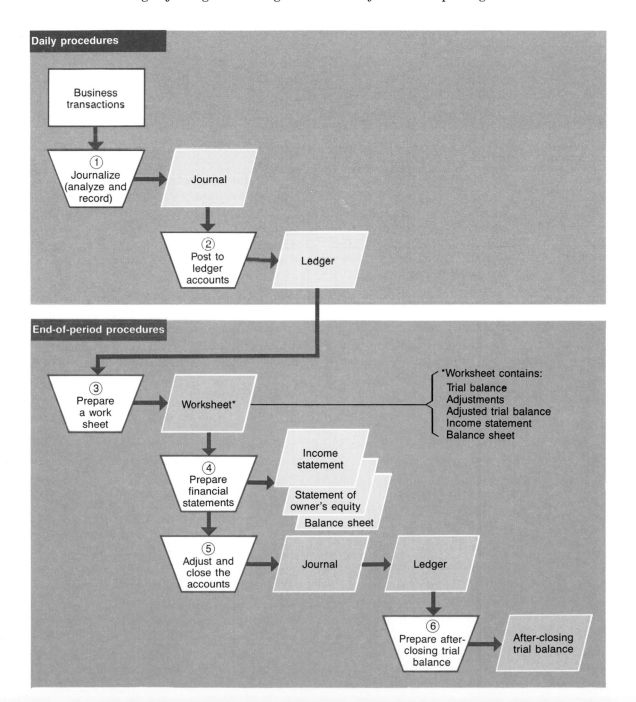

Daily procedures

Business transactions

① Journalize (analyze and record)

Journal

② Post to ledger accounts

Ledger

End-of-period procedures

③ Prepare a work sheet

Worksheet*

*Worksheet contains:
Trial balance
Adjustments
Adjusted trial balance
Income statement
Balance sheet

④ Prepare financial statements

Income statement
Statement of owner's equity
Balance sheet

⑤ Adjust and close the accounts

Journal

Ledger

⑥ Prepare after-closing trial balance

After-closing trial balance

ledger (Step 5). This sequence reflects the fact that *management wants the financial statements as soon as possible.* Once the work sheet is complete, all information required for the financial statements is available. Top priority then goes to preparation of the financial statements.

In most business concerns the accounts are closed only once a year; for these companies the accounting cycle is one year in length. For purposes of illustration in a textbook, however, it is often convenient to assume that the entire accounting cycle is performed within the time period of one month. The completion of the accounting cycle is the occasion for preparing financial statements and closing the revenue and expense accounts.

Preparing Monthly Financial Statements without Closing the Accounts

Many companies which close their accounts only once a year nevertheless prepare *monthly* financial statements for managerial use. These monthly statements are prepared from work sheets, but the adjustments indicated on the work sheets are not entered in the accounting records and no closing entries are made. Under this plan, the time-consuming operation of journalizing and posting adjustments and closing entries is performed only at the end of the fiscal year, but the company has the advantage of monthly financial statements. Monthly and quarterly financial statements are often referred to as *interim statements,* because they are in between the year-end statements. The annual or year-end statements are usually audited by a firm of certified public accountants; interim statements are usually unaudited.

Reversing Entries

Objective 6
Explain when and why reversing entries may be used.

Reversing entries are an optional procedure which may be carried out at year-end to simplify the recording of certain routine cash receipts and payments in the following period. As the name suggests, a *reversing entry* is the exact reverse of an adjusting entry. It contains the same account titles and dollar amounts as the related adjusting entry, but the debits and credits are the reverse of those in the adjusting entry and the date is the first day of the next accounting period.

Let us use as an example a small company on a five-day work week which pays its employees each Friday. Assume that the payroll is $600 a day or $3,000 for a five-day week. Throughout the year, a company employee makes a journal entry each Friday as follows:

■
Regular weekly entry for payroll

Salaries Expense	*3,000*	
Cash...		*3,000*
To record payment of salaries for the week.		

Next, let us assume that December 31, the last working day of the year 1991, falls on Wednesday. All expenses of the year must be recorded before the accounts are closed and financial statements prepared at December 31. Therefore, an adjusting entry must be made to record the salaries expense and the related liability to employees for the three days they have worked since the last payday. The adjusting entry for $1,800 (computed as 3 × $600 daily salary expense) is shown below:

Dec. 31 Salaries Expense	1,800	
Salaries Payable...		1,800
To record salaries expense and the related liability to employees		
for last three days worked in December.		

The closing of the accounts on December 31 will reduce the Salaries Expense account to zero, but the liability account, Salaries Payable, will remain open with its $1,800 credit balance at the beginning of the new year. On the next regular payday, Friday, January 2, an employee can record the $3,000 payroll by a debit of $1,800 to Salaries Payable, a debit of $1,200 to Salaries Expense, and a credit of $3,000 to Cash. However, splitting the debit side of the entry in this manner ($1,800 to the liability account and $1,200 to expense) requires more understanding and alertness from company personnel than if the entry were identical with the other 51 payroll entries made during the year.

By making a *reversing entry* as of the first day of the new accounting period, we can simplify the recording of routine transactions and avoid the need for the company's accounting staff to refer to prior adjusting entries for guidance. The reversing entry for the $1,800 year-end accrual of salaries would be dated January 1, 1992, and would probably be made under the direction of the accountant responsible for the year-end closing of the accounts and preparation of financial statements. The entry would be as follows:

Jan. 1 Salaries Payable	1,800	
Salaries Expense		1,800
To reverse the accrual of salaries made on Dec. 31, 1991.		

This reversing entry closes the Salaries Payable account by transferring the $1,800 liability to the credit side of the Salaries Expense account. Thus, the Salaries Expense account begins the new year with an abnormal credit balance of $1,800. On Friday, January 2, the normal payroll entry for $3,000 will be made to the same accounts as on every other Friday during the year.

**. . . regular
payroll entry for
first payday of
new year**

Jan. 2 Salaries Expense	3,000	
Cash		3,000
Paid salaries for week ended Jan. 2, 1992.		

After this January 2 entry has been posted, the ledger account for Salaries Expense will show a debit balance of $1,200, the result of this $3,000 debit and the $1,800 credit from the reversing entry on January 1. The amount of $1,200 is the correct expense for the two workdays of the new year at $600 a day. The results, of course, are *exactly the same* as if no reversing entry had been used and the company's accounting personnel had split the debit side of the January 2 payroll entry between Salaries Payable and Salaries Expense.

The ledger accounts for Salaries Expense and for Salaries Payable are shown below to illustrate the effect of posting the adjusting entry and the reversing entry.

SALARIES EXPENSE			DEBIT	CREDIT	BALANCE
1991					
Various	(51 weekly entries of $3,000)				153000
Dec. 31	Adjusting entry (3 days @ $600)		1800		154800
31	To close at year-end			154800	—0—
1992					
Jan. 1	Reversing entry			1800	1800 cr.
2	Weekly payroll		3000		1200

SALARIES PAYABLE			DEBIT	CREDIT	BALANCE
1991					
Dec. 31	Adjusting entry (3 days @ $600)			1800	1800
1992					
Jan. 1	Reversing entry		1800		—0—

■ **Which Adjusting Entries Should Be Reversed?** Even when a company follows a policy of making reversing entries, *not all adjusting entries should be reversed.* Only those adjustments which *create an account receivable or a short-term liability* should be reversed. These adjustments will be followed by cash receipts or cash payments within the near future. Reversing these adjusting entries will enable the company's personnel to record the upcoming cash transactions in a routine manner.

An adjusting entry which apportions an amount recorded in the past *should not be reversed.* Thus we do *not* reverse the adjusting entries which apportion recorded costs (such as depreciation), or which record the earning of revenue collected in advance.

In summary, reversing entries may be made for those adjusting entries which record *unrecorded expenses* or *unrecorded revenue.* Reversing entries are *not* made for adjustments which apportion recorded costs or recorded revenue.

■ **Reversing Entries in a Computer-Based System** Reversing entries do not require any analysis of transactions. Rather, they merely involve reversing the debit and credit amounts of specific adjusting entries. The adjusting entries to be reversed can be identified by a simple rule—namely, reverse those adjustments which increase accounts receivable or short-term liabilities. Thus, a computer may be programmed to prepare reversing entries automatically.

Finally, remember that reversing entries are *optional.* They are intended to simplify the accounting process, but they are *not essential* in the application of generally accepted accounting principles or in the preparation of financial statements.

End-of-Chapter Review

CONCEPTS INTRODUCED OR EMPHASIZED IN CHAPTER 4

The major concepts in this chapter include:

■ The use of accounting periods of equal length to facilitate comparison of the profitability and solvency of a business from one period to the next.

■ Adjusting entries as a means of applying the realization principle and the matching principle to transactions which affect two or more accounting periods.

■ Classification of adjusting entries into four types: (1) entries to apportion recorded costs; (2) entries to apportion unearned revenue; (3) entries to record unrecorded expenses; and (4) entries to record unrecorded revenue.

■ The use of a work sheet at the end of the accounting period to coordinate all the accounting work needed in preparing financial statements and in adjusting and closing ledger accounts.

■ The use of reversing entries—an optional year-end procedure designed to simplify the recording of certain routine cash receipts and payments in the following period.

■ Recognition of the steps comprising the accounting cycle: journalizing transactions, posting to ledger accounts, preparing a work sheet, preparing financial statements, adjusting and closing ledger accounts, and preparing an after-closing trial balance.

In Chapter 4 we have completed our study of the accounting cycle for a service-type business and have completed our continuing illustrated example of Roberts Real Estate Company. In Chapter 5 we will extend these concepts by focusing on some additional steps needed to account for the *inventories* which fill the sales counters and storerooms of a wholesale or retail merchandising business.

KEY TERMS INTRODUCED OR EMPHASIZED IN CHAPTER 4

Accounting cycle   The sequence of accounting procedures performed during an accounting period. The procedures include journalizing transactions, posting, preparation of a work sheet and financial statements, adjusting and closing the accounts, and preparation of an after-closing trial balance.

Accrued expenses   Expenses such as salaries of employees and interest on notes payable which have been accumulating day-by-day, but are unrecorded and unpaid at the end of the period. Also called *unrecorded expenses.*

Accrued revenue   Revenue which has been earned during the accounting period but has not been recorded or collected prior to the closing date. Also called *unrecorded revenue.*

Adjusting entries   Entries required at the end of the period to update the accounts before financial statements are prepared. Adjusting entries serve to apportion transactions properly between the accounting periods affected and to record any revenue earned or expenses incurred which have not been recorded prior to the end of the period.

Book value   The net amount at which an asset is shown in accounting records. For depreciable assets, book value equals cost minus accumulated depreciation. Also called *carrying value.*

Carrying value   See book value.

Deferred revenue   See unearned revenue.

Interim statements   Financial statements prepared at intervals of less than one year. Usually quarterly and monthly statements.

Prepaid expenses   Advance payments for such expenses as rent and insurance. The portion which has not been used up at the end of the accounting period is included in the balance sheet as an asset.

Promissory note   A formal written promise to repay an amount borrowed plus interest at a future date.

Reversing entries   An optional year-end procedure consisting of the reversal on the first day of the new accounting period of those year-end adjusting entries which accrue expenses or revenue and thus will be followed by later cash payments or receipts. Purpose is to permit company personnel to record routine transactions in a standard manner without referring to prior adjusting entries.

Unearned revenue   An obligation to render services or deliver goods in the future because of receipt of advance payment. Also called *deferred revenue.*

Unrecorded expenses   See accrued expenses.

Unrecorded revenue   See accrued revenue.

Work sheet   A large columnar sheet designed to arrange in convenient form all the accounting data required at the end of the period. Facilitates preparation of financial statements and the work of adjusting and closing the accounts.

DEMONSTRATION PROBLEM FOR YOUR REVIEW

Reed Geophysical Company adjusts and closes its accounts at the end of the calendar year. At December 31, 19__, the following trial balance was prepared from the ledger:

REED GEOPHYSICAL COMPANY
Trial Balance
December 31, 19__

Cash	$ 12,540	
Prepaid office rent	3,300	
Prepaid dues and subscriptions	960	
Supplies	1,300	
Equipment	20,000	
Accumulated depreciation: equipment		$ 1,200
Notes payable		5,000
Unearned consulting fees		35,650
Glen Reed, capital		17,040
Glen Reed, drawing	27,000	
Consulting fees earned		90,860
Salaries expense	66,900	
Telephone expense	2,550	
Rent expense	11,000	
Miscellaneous expenses	4,200	
	$149,750	$149,750

Other Data **(a)** For the first 11 months of the year, office rent had been charged to the Rent Expense account at a rate of $1,000 per month. On December 1, however, the company signed a new rental agreement and paid three months' rent in advance at a rate of $1,100 per month. This advance payment was debited to the Prepaid Rent account.

(b) Dues and subscriptions expired during the year in the total amount of $710.

(c) A count of supplies on hand was made at December 31; the cost of the unused supplies was $450.

(d) The useful life of the equipment has been estimated at 10 years from date of acquisition.

(e) Accrued interest on notes payable amounted to $100 at year-end. Set up accounts for Interest Expense and for Interest Payable.

(f) Consulting services valued at $32,550 were rendered during the year for clients who had made payment in advance.

(g) It is the custom of the firm to bill clients only when consulting work is completed or, in the case of prolonged engagements, at six-month intervals. At December 31, engineering services valued at $3,000 had been rendered to clients but not yet billed. No advance payments had been received from these clients.

(h) Salaries earned by employees but not yet paid amounted to $2,200 at December 31.

Instructions Prepare a work sheet for the year ended December 31, 19___.

SOLUTION TO DEMONSTRATION PROBLEM

REED GEOPHYSICAL COMPANY
Work Sheet
For the Year Ended December 31, 19___

	TRIAL BALANCE DR	TRIAL BALANCE CR	ADJUSTMENTS* DR	ADJUSTMENTS* CR	ADJUSTED TRIAL BALANCE DR	ADJUSTED TRIAL BALANCE CR	INCOME STATEMENT DR	INCOME STATEMENT CR	BALANCE SHEET DR	BALANCE SHEET CR
Cash	12,540				12,540				12,540	
Prepaid office rent	3,300			(a) 1,100	2,200				2,200	
Prepaid dues and subscriptions	960			(b) 710	250				250	
Supplies	1,300			(c) 850	450				450	
Equipment	20,000				20,000				20,000	
Accumulated depreciation: equipment		1,200		(d) 2,000		3,200				3,200
Notes payable		5,000				5,000				5,000
Unearned consulting fees		35,650	(f) 32,550			3,100				3,100
Glen Reed, capital		17,040				17,040				17,040
Glen Reed, drawing	27,000				27,000				27,000	
Consulting fees earned		90,860		(f) 32,550 (g) 3,000		126,410		126,410		
Salaries expense	66,900		(h) 2,200		69,100		69,100			
Telephone expense	2,550				2,550		2,550			
Rent expense	11,000		(a) 1,100		12,100		12,100			
Miscellaneous expense	4,200				4,200		4,200			
	149,750	149,750								
Dues and subscriptions expense			(b) 710		710		710			
Supplies expense			(c) 850		850		850			
Depreciation expense: equipment			(d) 2,000		2,000		2,000			
Interest expense			(e) 100		100		100			
Interest payable				(e) 100		100				100
Consulting fees receivable			(g) 3,000		3,000				3,000	
Salaries payable				(h) 2,200		2,200				2,200
			42,510	42,510	157,050	157,050	91,610	126,410	65,440	30,640
Net income							34,800			34,800
							126,410	126,410	65,440	65,440

* Adjustments:
(a) Rent expense for December.
(b) Dues and subscriptions expense for year.
(c) Supplies used for year ($1,300 − $450 = $850).
(d) Depreciation expense for year.
(e) Accrued interest on notes payable.
(f) Consulting services performed for clients who paid in advance.
(g) Services rendered but not billed.
(h) Salaries earned but not paid.

SELF-TEST QUESTIONS

Answers to these questions appear on page 175.

1 The purpose of adjusting entries is to:

a Adjust the owner's capital account for the revenue, expense, and withdrawal transactions which occurred during the year.

b Adjust daily the balances in asset, liability, revenue, and expense accounts for the effects of business transactions.

c Apply the realization principle and the matching principle to transactions affecting two or more accounting periods.

d Prepare revenue and expense accounts for recording the transactions of the next accounting period.

2 Before month-end adjustments are made, the January 31 trial balance of Rover Excursions contains revenue of $5,300 and expenses of $1,780. Adjustments are necessary for the following items:
   —portion of prepaid rent applicable to January, $900
   —depreciation for January, $480
   —portion of fees collected in advance earned in January, $1,100
   —fees earned in January, not yet billed to customers, $650

Net income in Rover Excursions' January income statement is:

a $3,520   **b** $5,690   **c** $2,590   **d** Some other amount

3 The CPA firm auditing Tucker's Studio found that owner's equity was understated and liabilities were overstated. Which of the following errors could have been the cause?

a Making the adjustment entry for depreciation expense twice.

b Failure to record interest accrued on a note payable.

c Failure to make the adjusting entry to record revenue which had been earned, but not yet billed to customers.

d Failure to record the earned portion of fees received in advance.

4 When a worksheet is prepared at year-end:

a Revenue and expense accounts do not have to be closed to the Income Summary account because the income statement is prepared from the worksheet and net income is already computed.

b Adjusting entries must be journalized and posted, even though the Adjustments column is properly completed.

c The amount of net income appears as a credit in the Income Statement column of the worksheet when revenue exceeds total expenses.

d The Income Statement columns and Balance Sheet columns of the worksheet eliminate the need to prepare formal financial statements.

5 On December 31, Elite Property Management made an adjusting entry to record $300 management fees earned but not yet billed to Marge Carson, a client. This entry was reversed on January 1. On January 15, Carson paid Elite $1,200, of which $900 was applicable to the period January 1 through January 15. The journal entry made by Elite to record receipt of the $1,200 on January 15 includes:

a A credit to Management Fees Earned of $1,200.

b A credit to Accounts Receivable of $300.

c A debit to Management Fees Earned of $300.

d A credit to Management Fees Earned of $900.

Assignment Material

REVIEW QUESTIONS

1 What is the purpose of making adjusting entries? Your answer should relate adjusting entries to the goals of accrual accounting.

2 Do all transactions involving revenue or expenses require adjusting entries at the end of the accounting period? If not, what is the distinguishing characteristic of those transactions which do require adjusting entries?

3 Do adjusting entries affect income statement accounts, balance sheet accounts, or both? Explain.

4 Why does the recording of adjusting entries require a better understanding of the concepts of accrual accounting than does the recording of routine revenue and expense transactions occurring throughout the period?

5 Why does the purchase of a one-year insurance policy four months ago give rise to insurance expense in the current month?

6 If services have been rendered during the current accounting period but no revenue has been recorded and no bill has been sent to the customers, why is an adjusting entry needed? What types of accounts should be debited and credited by this entry?

7 What is meant by the term *unearned revenue?* Where should an unearned revenue account appear in the financial statements? As the work is done, what happens to the balance of an unearned revenue account?

8 Crossroads Company forgot to record any depreciation on its building during the year just ended. What effects, if any, would this omission have upon the company's income statement? Upon its balance sheet? (You may find it convenient to use the terms "understated" and "overstated" in answering this question.)

9 The weekly payroll for employees of Card Company, which works a five-day week, amounts to $10,000. All employees are paid up-to-date at the close of business each Friday. If December 31 falls on Tuesday, what year-end adjusting entry is needed?

10 The Marvin Company purchased a one-year fire insurance policy on August 1 and debited the entire cost of $3,600 to Unexpired Insurance. The accounts were not adjusted or closed until the end of the year. Give the adjusting entry at December 31.

11 Office supplies on hand in the Melville Company amounted to $715 at the beginning of the year. During the year additional office supplies were purchased at a cost of $1,860 and debited to the asset account. At the end of the year a physical count showed that supplies on hand amounted to $540. Give the adjusting entry needed at December 31.

12 At year-end the adjusting entry to reduce the Unexpired Insurance account by the amount of insurance premium applicable to the current period was accidentally omitted. Which items in the income statement will be in error? Will these items be overstated or understated? Which items in the balance sheet will be in error? Will they be overstated or understated?

13 What is the purpose of a work sheet?

14 In performing the regular end-of-period accounting procedures, does the preparation of the work sheet precede or follow the posting of adjusting entries to ledger accounts? Why?

15 Assume that when the income statement columns of a work sheet are first totaled, the total of the debit column exceeds the total of the credit column by $60,000. Explain how the amount of net income (or net loss) should be entered in the work sheet columns.

16 Does the ending balance of the owner's capital account appear in the work sheet? Explain.

17 Can each step in the preparation of a work sheet be performed automatically in a computer-based accounting system? Explain.

18 List in order the procedures comprising the accounting cycle when a work sheet is used.

19 Is a work sheet ever prepared when there is no intention of closing the accounts?

20 The weekly payroll of Stevens Company, which has a five-day work week, amounts to $20,000 and employees are paid up to date every Friday. On January 1 of the current year, the Salaries Expense account showed a credit balance of $12,000. Explain the nature of the accounting entry or entries which probably led to this balance.

21 Four general types of adjusting entries were discussed in this chapter. If reversing entries are made, which of these types of adjusting entries should be reversed? Why?

EXERCISES

Exercise 4-1
Accounting terminology

Listed below are nine technical accounting terms used in this chapter:

Unrecorded revenue	*Adjusting entries*	*Accrued expenses*
Work sheet	*Reversing entries*	*Book value*
Unearned revenue	*Interim statements*	*Prepaid expenses*

Each of the following statements may (or may not) describe one of these technical terms. For each statement, indicate the accounting term described, or answer "None" if the statement does not correctly describe any of the terms.

a The net amount at which an asset is carried in the accounting records as distinguished from its market value.

b Expenses for such items as interest and salaries which have been incurred but not yet paid or recorded.

c A device for organizing all the data needed at the end of the period to prepare financial statements and to make entries to adjust and close the accounts.

d Revenue earned during the current accounting period but not yet recorded or billed, which requires an adjusting entry at the end of the period.

e Entries made at the end of the period to achieve the goals of accrual accounting by recording revenue when it is earned and by recording expenses when the related goods and services are used.

f A type of account credited when customers pay in advance for services to be rendered in the future.

g A balance sheet category used for advance payments of such items as insurance, rent, and office supplies.

h Entries made during the accounting period to correct errors in the original recording of complex transactions.

Exercise 4-2
Depreciation calculations

The adjusted trial balance of Rainbow Company at the end of the current year included the following account balances.

Building, $94,800
Depreciation Expense: Building, $4,740
Accumulated Depreciation: Building, $37,920

Assuming that Rainbow Company has owned the building since its original construction and has used straight-line depreciation, answer the following questions and show supporting calculations.

a What was the estimated useful life (in years) of the building at the date of its construction by Rainbow Company?

b What length of time (in years) has Rainbow Company owned the building?

Exercise 4-3
Notes payable
and interest

Venture Company adjusts and closes its accounts on December 31. On November 30, 1991, Venture Company signed a note payable and borrowed $12,000 from a bank for a period of six months at an annual interest rate of 10%.

a How much is the total interest expense over the life of the note? How much is the monthly interest expense?

b In the company's annual balance sheet at December 31, 1991, what is the amount of the liability to the bank?

c Prepare the journal entry to record issuance of the note payable on November 30, 1991.

d Prepare the adjusting entry to accrue interest on the note at December 31, 1991.

e Assume the company prepared a balance sheet at March 31, 1992: state the amount of the liability to the bank at this date.

Exercise 4-4
Effects of
adjusting entries

Information Services adjusts and closes its accounts at the end of each month. On November 30, adjusting entries are prepared to record:

a Interest expense that has accrued during November.

b Depreciation expense for November.

c The portion of the company's prepaid insurance which has expired during November.

d Earning a portion of the amount collected in advance from a customer, Harbor Restaurant.

e Salaries payable to company employees which have accrued since the last payday in November.

f Revenue earned during November which has not yet been billed to customers.

Indicate the effect of each of these adjusting entries upon the major elements of the company's financial statements—that is, upon revenue, expenses, net income, assets, liabilities, and owners' equity. Organize your answer in tabular form, using the column headings shown below and the symbols + for increase, − for decrease, and NE for no effect. The answer for adjusting entry *(a)* is provided as an example.

	INCOME STATEMENT			BALANCE SHEET		
ADJUSTING ENTRY	REVENUE	EXPENSES	NET INCOME	ASSETS	LIABILITIES	OWNERS' EQUITY
a	*NE*	+	−	*NE*	+	−

Exercise 4-5
Preparing
adjusting entries
for recorded
costs and
recorded revenue

The Outlaws, a professional football team, prepare financial statements on a monthly basis. Football season begins in August, but in July the team engaged in the following transactions:

a Paid $1,050,000 to Dodge City as advance rent for use of Dodge City Stadium for the five-month period from August 1 through December 31. This payment was debited to the asset account, Prepaid Rent.

b Collected $2,080,000 cash from sales of season tickets for the team's eight home games. This amount was credited to Unearned Ticket Revenue.

During the month of August, The Outlaws played one home game and two games on the road. Their record was two wins, one loss.

Instructions	Prepare the two adjusting entries required at August 31 to apportion this recorded cost and recorded revenue.
Exercise 4-6 **Preparing** **adjusting entries** **for unrecorded** **revenue and** **expenses**	The law firm of Dale & Clark prepares its financial statements on an annual basis at December 31. Among the situations requiring year-end adjusting entries were the following: **a** Salaries to staff attorneys are paid on the fifteenth day of each month. Salaries accrued since December 15 amount to $14,300 and have not yet been recorded. **b** The firm is defending J. R. Stone in a civil lawsuit. The agreed upon legal fees are $2,000 per day while the trial is in progress. The trial has been in progress for nine days during December and is not expected to end until late January. No legal fees have yet been billed to Stone. (Legal fees are recorded in an account entitled Legal Fees Earned.)
Instructions	Prepare the two adjusting entries required at December 31 to record the accrued salaries expense and the accrued legal fees revenue.
Exercise 4-7 **Adjusting entry** **and subsequent** **business** **transaction**	On Friday of each week, Relic Company pays its sales personnel weekly salaries amounting to $75,000 for a five-day work week. **a** Draft the necessary adjusting entry at year-end, assuming that December 31 falls on Wednesday. **b** Also draft the journal entry for the payment by Relic Company of a week's salaries to its sales personnel on Friday, January 2, the first payday of the new year. (Assume that the company does not use reversing entries.)
Exercise 4-8 **Preparing various** **adjusting entries**	Hill Corporation adjusts and closes its accounts at the end of the calendar year. Prepare the adjusting entries required at December 31 based on the following information. (Not all of these items may require adjusting entries.) **a** A bank loan had been obtained on September 1. Accrued interest on the loan at December 31 amounts to $4,800. No interest expense has yet been recorded. **b** Depreciation of office equipment is based on an estimated life of five years. The balance in the Office Equipment account is $25,000; no change has occurred in the account during the year. **c** Interest receivable on United States government bonds owned at December 31 amounts to $2,300. This accrued interest revenue has not been recorded. **d** On December 31, an agreement was signed to lease a truck for 12 months beginning January 1 at a rate of 35 cents a mile. Usage is expected to be 2,000 miles per month and the contract specifies a minimum payment equivalent to 18,000 miles a year. **e** The company's policy is to pay all employees up to date each Friday. Since December 31 fell on Monday, there was a liability to employees at December 31 for one day's pay amounting to $2,800.
Exercise 4-9 **Relationship of** **adjusting entries** **to business** **transactions**	Among the ledger accounts used by Glenwood Speedway are the following: Prepaid Rent, Rent Expense, Unearned Admissions Revenue, Admissions Revenue, Prepaid Printing, Printing Expense, Concessions Receivable, and Concessions Revenue. For each of the following items, write first the journal entry (if one is needed) to record the external transaction and second the adjusting entry, if any, required on May 31, the end of the fiscal year. **a** On May 1, borrowed $200,000 cash from National Bank by issuing a 12% note payable due in three months. **b** On May 1, paid rent for six months beginning May 1 at $25,000 per month. **c** On May 2, sold season tickets for a total of $700,000 cash. The season includes 70 racing days: 20 in May, 25 in June, and 25 in July. **d** On May 4, an agreement was reached with Snack-Bars, Inc., allowing that company

to sell refreshments at the track in return for 10% of the gross receipts from refreshment sales.

e On May 6, schedules for the 20 racing days in May and the first 10 racing days in June were printed and paid for at a cost of $9,000.

f On May 31, Snack-Bars, Inc., reported that the gross receipts from refreshment sales in May had been $145,000 and that the 10% owed to Glenwood Speedway would be remitted on June 10.

Exercise 4-10
Preparing
reversing entries

Blue Company closes its accounts at the end of each calendar year. The company operates on a five-day work week and pays its employees up to date each Friday. The weekly payroll is regularly $10,000. On Wednesday, December 31, 1991, an adjusting entry was made to accrue $6,000 salaries expense for the three days worked since the last payday. The company *did not* make a reversing entry. On Friday, January 2, 1992, the regular weekly payroll of $10,000 was paid and recorded by the usual entry debiting Salaries Expense $10,000 and crediting Cash $10,000.

Were Blue Company's accounting records correct for the year 1991? For 1992? Explain two alternatives the company might have followed with respect to payroll at year-end. One of the alternatives should include a reversing entry.

Exercise 4-11
Get your tickets
early

When TransWorld Airlines (TWA) sells tickets for future flights, it debits cash and credits an account entitled Advance Ticket Sales.

Instructions

With respect to this Advance Ticket Sales account:

a What does the balance of the account represent? Where should the account appear in TWA's financial statements?

b Explain the activity that normally reduces the balance of this account. Can you think of any other transaction that could reduce this account?

PROBLEMS

Group A

Problem 4A-1
Preparing
adjusting entries

The Inn by the Bay adjusts and closes its accounts once a year on December 31. Most guests of the motel pay at the time they check out, and the amounts collected are credited to Rental Revenue. A few guests pay in advance for rooms and these amounts are credited to Unearned Rental Revenue at the time of receipt. The following information is available as a source for preparing adjusting entries at December 31.

(a) Depreciation on The Inn's buildings is based upon an estimated useful life of 40 years. The original cost of the buildings was $1,660,000.

(b) Depreciation on furnishings is based upon a 10-year life. Total cost of furnishings is $296,000.

(c) On December 31, The Inn entered into an agreement to host the National Building Suppliers annual convention in June of the following year. The Inn expects to earn revenue of at least $60,000 from this convention.

(d) On November 1, The Inn had borrowed $100,000 for 90 days from Bayshore Bank. Interest on this loan is to be computed at the annual rate of 9% and is payable when the loan becomes due.

(e) On December 16, a suite of rooms was rented to a corporation on a long-term basis at a monthly rental of $4,800. Two months' rent of $9,600 was collected in advance and credited to Unearned Rental Revenue. At December 31, $2,400 of this amount, representing one-half month's rent, was considered to be earned and the remainder of $7,200 was considered to be unearned.

(f) As of December 31 the motel has earned $18,090 rental revenue from current guests who will not be billed until they are ready to check out. (Debit Rent Receivable.)

(g) Salaries earned by employees at December 31 but not yet paid amount to $11,640.

Instructions For each of the above numbered paragraphs, draft a separate adjusting journal entry (including explanation), if the information indicates that an adjusting entry is needed. One or more of the above paragraphs may not require any adjusting entry.

Problem 4A-2
Preparing
adjusting entries
from a trial
balance

Nick Charles operates a private investigating business called Nick Charles Investigations. Some clients are required to pay in advance for the company's services, while others are billed after the services have been rendered. Advance payments are credited to an account entitled Unearned Retainer Fees, which represents unearned revenue. The business adjusts and closes its accounts each month. At May 31, the trial balance appeared as follows:

NICK CHARLES INVESTIGATIONS
Trial Balance
May 31, 19__

Cash	$14,100	
Fees receivable	25,200	
Prepaid rent	3,600	
Office supplies	700	
Office equipment	11,400	
Accumulated depreciation: office equipment		$ 3,800
Accounts payable		2,600
Unearned retainer fees		16,000
Nick Charles, capital		32,400
Nick Charles, drawing	1,600	
Fees earned		17,900
Telephone expense	800	
Travel expense	2,300	
Salaries expense	13,000	
	$72,700	$72,700

Other Data **(a)** On May 1, the business moved into a new office and paid the first three months' rent in advance.

(b) Investigative services rendered during the month but not yet collected or billed to clients amounted to $1,800.

(c) Office supplies on hand May 31 amounted to $400.

(d) The useful life of the office equipment was estimated at five years.

(e) Fees of $4,300 were earned during the month by performing services for clients who had paid in advance.

(f) Salaries earned by employees during the month but not yet recorded or paid amounted to $1,100.

Instructions **a** Prepare the adjusting entries required at May 31.

b Determine the amount of revenue that should appear in the company's income statement for the month ended May 31.

Problem 4A-3
Making use of a
completed work
sheet

A 10-column work sheet for Reed Geophysical Company is illustrated on page 158.

Instructions
Using the information contained in the work sheet on page 158, prepare in journal entry form the adjusting and closing entries for Reed Geophysical Company at December 31, 19__.

Problem 4A-4
Format of a work
sheet

Shown below are the first four columns of the 10-column work sheet to be prepared for VCR Repair Service for the month ended April 30, 19__.

VCR REPAIR SERVICE
Work Sheet
For the Month Ended April 30, 19__

	TRIAL BALANCE		ADJUSTMENTS*	
	DR	CR	DR	CR
Cash......................................	4,200			
Accounts receivable	1,900			
Unexpired insurance........................	490			(a) 70
Supplies	1,460			(b) 560
Equipment	18,600			
Accumulated depreciation: equipment........		2,480		(c) 310
Notes payable..............................		10,000		
Unearned revenue		1,200	(e) 400	
Britt Miller, capital..........................		14,190		
Britt Miller, drawing	1,500			
Revenue from services		4,630		(e) 400
Rent expense	2,450			
Salaries expense	1,900		(f) 500	
	32,500	32,500		
Insurance expense			(a) 70	
Supplies expense...........................			(b) 560	
Depreciation expense: equipment			(c) 310	
Interest expense			(d) 80	
Interest payable				(d) 80
Salaries payable............................				(f) 500
			1,920	1,920

* Adjustments
(a) Insurance expired during April.
(b) Supplies used during the month.
(c) Depreciation for the month.
(d) Interest accrued on notes payable at April 30.
(e) Advance payments by customers earned during April.
(f) Salaries owed to employees at April 30.

Instructions

Prepare a 10-column work sheet utilizing the trial balance and adjustments shown above in the first four columns.

Problem 4A-5
Preparing a work
sheet

Ryan's Air Service operates several small airplanes providing passenger and freight service to small towns, oil fields, fishing lodges, and other remote locations in Alaska. The company adjusts and closes its accounts at the end of each month. At April 30, the following trial balance was prepared from the ledger:

RYAN'S AIR SERVICE
Trial Balance
April 30, 19__

Cash...	$ 24,850	
Accounts receivable	22,600	
Prepaid rent..	6,750	
Unexpired insurance..	30,600	
Airplanes...	684,000	
Accumulated depreciation: airplanes		$186,200
Notes payable..		360,000
Unearned passenger revenue		140,200
Sam Ryan, capital		145,400
Sam Ryan, drawing..	6,200	
Freight revenue		43,400
Fuel expense...	38,100	
Salaries expense	56,700	
Maintenance expense	5,400	
	$875,200	$875,200

Other Data

(a) One of Ryan's regular customers is Yukon Oil Co. The airline keeps track of the number of trips carrying freight for the oil company and sends a bill shortly after month-end. No entry has yet been made in the airline's accounting records to record $9,400 freight revenue earned in April from Yukon Oil Co.

(b) Three months' rent ($6,750) had been prepaid on April 1.

(c) On January 1, a 12-month insurance policy had been purchased for $40,800.

(d) Ryan's depreciates its airplanes over a period of 15 years (180 months).

(e) Accrued interest on notes payable amounts to $3,600 at April 30 and has not yet been recorded.

(f) The amount shown as unearned passenger revenue represents the price of tickets sold to customers in advance of flights. During April, $75,800 of this amount was earned by the airline. (Credit Passenger Revenue.)

(g) Salaries earned by airline employees but not yet recorded or paid amount to $1,300 at April 30.

Instructions

Prepare a 10-column work sheet using the trial balance and adjusting data provided. Include at the bottom of the work sheet a brief explanation keyed to each adjusting entry.

Problem 4A-6
A comprehensive work sheet problem

A trial balance and supplementary information needed for adjustments at September 30 are shown below for Cinemax Stage & Theater. The company follows a policy of adjusting and closing its accounts at the end of each month.

CINEMAX STAGE & THEATER
Trial Balance
September 30, 19___

Cash	$ 25,500	
Prepaid film rental	65,000	
Land	75,000	
Building	210,000	
Accumulated depreciation: building		$ 6,125
Projection equipment	90,000	
Accumulated depreciation: projection equipment		7,500
Notes payable		200,000
Accounts payable		8,500
Unearned admissions revenue		5,200
Helen James, capital		200,925
Helen James, drawing	10,500	
Admissions revenue		76,750
Salaries expense	21,250	
Light and power expense	7,750	
	$505,000	$505,000

Other Data

(a) Film rental expense for the month is $42,275, all of which had been paid in advance.

(b) The building is being depreciated over a period of 20 years (240 months).

(c) The projection equipment is being depreciated over a period of five years (60 months).

(d) No entry has yet been made to record interest payable accrued during September. At September 30, accrued interest totals $1,800.

(e) When tickets are sold to future performances, Cinemax credits its Unearned Admissions Revenue account. No entry has yet been made recording that $3,650 of these advance ticket sales were for performances given during September.

(f) Cinemax receives a percentage of the revenue earned by Variety Corp., the concessionaire operating the snack bar. For snack bar sales in September, Variety Corp. owes Cinemax $6,200, payable on October 10. No entry has yet been made to record this revenue. (Credit Concessions Revenue.)

(g) Salaries earned by employees, but unpaid as of September 30, amount to $3,750. No entry has yet been made to record this liability and expense.

Instructions Prepare

a A work sheet for the month ended September 30.

b An income statement.

c A statement of owner's equity.

d A balance sheet.

e Adjusting and closing entries.

Problem 4A-7
Use of reversing entries

Investors' Journal maintains its accounts on the basis of a fiscal year ending June 30. The company works a five-day week and pays its employees up-to-date each Friday. Weekly salaries have been averaging $20,000. At the June 30 fiscal year-end, the following events occurred relating to salaries.

June 26 (Friday) Paid regular weekly salaries of $20,000.

June 30 (Tuesday) Prepared an adjusting entry to record salaries expense for the last two work days in June.

July 1 (Wednesday) Prepared a reversing entry for accrued salaries.

July 3 (Friday) Paid regular weekly salaries of $20,000.

Instructions

a Prepare journal entries (with explanations) for the four above events relating to salaries.

b How much of the $20,000 in salaries paid on July 3 represents a July expense? Explain.

c Assume that no reversing entry had been made by Investors' Journal; prepare the journal entry for payment of salaries on July 3.

Group B

Problem 4B-1
Preparing adjusting entries

Red River Resort adjusts and closes its accounts once a year on December 31. Most guests of the resort pay at the time they check out, and the amounts collected are credited to Rental Revenue. A few guests pay in advance for rooms and these amounts are credited to Unearned Rental Revenue at the time of receipt. The following information is available as a source for preparing adjusting entries at December 31.

(a) Salaries earned by employees but not yet recorded or paid amount to $5,600.

(b) As of December 31 the resort has earned $9,040 rental revenue from current guests who will not be billed until they are ready to check out. (Debit Rent Receivable.)

(c) On November 1, a suite of rooms was rented to a corporation for six months at a monthly rental of $2,500. The entire six months' rent of $15,000 was collected in advance and credited to Unearned Rental Revenue. At December 31, the amount of $5,000, representing two months' rent, was considered to be earned and the remainder of $10,000 was considered to be unearned.

(d) A 60-day bank loan in the amount of $40,000 had been obtained on December 1. No interest has been paid and no interest expense has been recorded. The interest accrued at December 31 is $600.

(e) Depreciation on the resort's buildings amounted to $14,600 for the year ended December 31.

(f) Depreciation on a station wagon owned by the resort was based on a four-year life. The station wagon had been purchased new on September 1 of the current year at a cost of $12,600. Depreciation for four months should be recorded at December 31.

(g) On December 31, Red River Resort entered into an agreement to host the National Homebuilders' annual convention in June of next year. The resort expects to earn rental revenue of at least $15,000 from the convention.

Instructions

For each of the above lettered paragraphs, draft a separate adjusting journal entry (including explanation), if the information indicates that an adjusting entry is needed. One or more of the above paragraphs may not require any adjusting entry.

Problem 4B-2
Preparing
adjusting entries
from a trial
balance

In August 19__, Sherri DeLong, an attorney, opened her own legal practice, to be known as the Law Office of Sherri DeLong. The business adjusts and closes its accounts at the end of each month. The following trial balance was prepared at August 31, 19__, after one month of operations:

LAW OFFICE OF SHERRI DELONG
Trial Balance
August 31, 19__

Cash	$ 5,870	
Legal fees receivable	–0–	
Prepaid office rent	2,400	
Office supplies	730	
Office equipment	13,200	
Accumulated depreciation: office equipment		$ –0–
Notes payable		8,000
Interest payable		–0–
Salaries payable		–0–
Unearned retainer fees		7,510
Sherri DeLong, capital		10,000
Sherri DeLong, drawing	2,000	
Legal fees earned		790
Salaries expense	1,340	
Miscellaneous expense	760	
Office rent expense	–0–	
Office supplies expense	–0–	
Depreciation expense: office equipment	–0–	
Interest expense	–0–	
	$26,300	$26,300

Other Data

(a) The business rents an office at a monthly rate of $1,200. On August 1, two months' rent was paid in advance and charged to the Prepaid Rent account.

(b) Office supplies on hand at August 31 amounted to $400.

(c) The office equipment was purchased on August 1 and is being depreciated over an estimated useful life of 10 years.

(d) No interest has yet been paid on the note payable. Accrued interest at August 31 amounts to $100.

(e) Salaries earned by the office staff but not yet recorded or paid amounted to $520 at August 31.

(f) Many clients are asked to make an advance payment for the legal services to be rendered in future months. These advance payments are credited to the Unearned Retainer Fees account. During August, $2,350 of these advances were earned by the business.

(g) Some clients are not billed until all services relating to their matter have been rendered. As of August 31, services priced at $1,240 had been rendered to these clients but had not yet been recorded in the accounting records.

Instructions

a Prepare the adjusting entries required at August 31.

b Determine the amount of revenue that should appear in the company's income statement for the month ended August 31.

Problem 4B-3
Analysis of
adjusted data;
preparing
adjusting entries

Sea Cat, Inc., operates a large catamaran which takes tourists at several island resorts on diving and sailing excursions. The company adjusts and closes its accounts at the end of each month. Selected account balances appearing on the June 30 *adjusted* trial balance are as follows:

Prepaid rent..	$ 4,500	
Unexpired insurance...	900	
Catamaran	42,000	
Accumulated depreciation: catamaran..................................		$7,700
Unearned passenger revenue		180

Other Data **(1)** Four months' rent had been prepaid on June 1.

(2) The unexpired insurance is a 12-month fire insurance policy purchased on January 1.

(3) The catamaran is being depreciated over a 10-year estimated useful life, with no residual value.

(4) The unearned passenger revenue represents tickets good for future rides sold to a resort hotel for $12 per ticket on June 1. During June, 35 of the tickets were used.

Instructions **a** Determine

  (1) The monthly rent expense

  (2) The original cost of the 12-month fire insurance policy

  (3) The age of the catamaran in months

  (4) How many $12 tickets for future rides were sold to the resort hotel on June 1

b Prepare the adjusting entries which were made on June 30.

Problem 4B-4
Format of a work
sheet
Shown below are the first four columns of a 10-column work sheet to be prepared for Lakeside Executive Golf Course for the month ended October 31, 19___. The golf course operates on land rented from the city.

LAKESIDE EXECUTIVE GOLF COURSE
Work Sheet
For the Month Ended October 31, 19___

	TRIAL BALANCE		ADJUSTMENTS*	
	DR	CR	DR	CR
Cash..	20,900			
Unexpired insurance........................	7,200			(a) 800
Prepaid rent...............................	18,000			(b) 6,000
Equipment	24,000			
Accumulated depreciation: equipment........		7,600		(c) 400
Notes payable.............................		10,000		
Unearned greens' fees revenue		6,400	(d) 2,200	
Walter Nelson, capital		38,200		
Walter Nelson, drawing	5,900			
Greens' fees revenue		26,400		(d) 2,200
Salaries expense	8,600		(e) 1,900	
Water expense	1,200			
Advertising expense	600			
Repairs and maintenance expense	1,500			
Miscellaneous expense	700			
	88,600	88,600		
Insurance expense			(a) 800	
Rent expense			(b) 6,000	
Depreciation expense: equipment			(c) 400	
Salaries payable............................				(e) 1,900
Interest expense			(f) 100	
Interest payable				(f) 100
			11,400	11,400

* Adjustments:
(a) Insurance expiring during October.
(b) Prepaid rent applicable to October.
(c) Depreciation for the month.
(d) Portion of revenue collected in advance but earned during October.
(e) Salaries owed to employees, but unpaid as of month-end.
(f) Accrued interest on notes payable at October 31.

Instructions Prepare a 10-column work sheet utilizing the trial balance and adjustments shown above in the first four columns.

Problem 4B-5
Preparing a work sheet

Village Theater closes its accounts each month. At July 31, the trial balance and other information given below were available for adjusting and closing the accounts.

VILLAGE THEATER
Trial Balance
July 31, 19___

Cash..	$ 20,000	
Prepaid film rental..	31,200	
Land..	80,000	
Building..	168,000	
Accumulated depreciation: building		$ 10,500
Projection equipment...	36,000	
Accumulated depreciation: projection equipment		3,000
Notes payable..		190,000
Accounts payable		4,400
Unearned admissions revenue (YMCA)		1,000
Li Trong, capital...		103,400
Li Trong, drawing..	3,500	
Admissions revenue		36,900
Salaries expense	8,700	
Light and power expense..	1,800	
	$349,200	$349,200

Other Data

(a) Film rental expense for July amounts to $21,050. However, the film rental expense for several months had been paid in advance.

(b) The building is being depreciated over a period of 20 years (240 months).

(c) The projection equipment is being depreciated over five years (60 months).

(d) At July 31, accrued interest payable on the note payable amounts to $1,650. No entry has yet been made to record interest expense for the month of July.

(e) Village Theater allows the local YMCA to bring children attending summer camp to the movies on any weekday afternoon for a fixed fee of $500 per month. On May 28, the YMCA made a $1,500 advance payment covering the months of June, July, and August.

(f) Village Theater receives a percentage of the revenue earned by Tastie Corp., the concessionaire operating the snack bar. For snack bar sales in July, Tastie Corp. owes Village Theater $2,250, payable on August 10. No entry has yet been made to record this revenue. (Credit Concessions Revenue.)

(g) Salaries earned by employees, but not recorded or paid as of July 31, amount to $1,500. No entry has yet been made to record this liability and expense.

Instructions

Prepare a 10-column work sheet utilizing the trial balance and adjusting data provided. Include at the bottom of the work sheet a brief explanation keyed to each adjusting entry.

Problem 4B-6
Preparing a work sheet, financial statements, and adjusting and closing entries

Island Hopper is an airline providing passenger and freight service among some Pacific islands. The accounts are adjusted and closed each month. At June 30 the trial balance shown below was prepared from the ledger.

ISLAND HOPPER
Trial Balance
June 30, 19__

Cash	$ 23,600	
Accounts receivable	7,200	
Prepaid rent	9,600	
Unexpired insurance	21,000	
Aircraft	1,200,000	
Accumulated depreciation: aircraft		$ 380,000
Notes payable		600,000
Unearned passenger revenue		60,000
Mary Earhart, capital		230,850
Mary Earhart, drawing	7,000	
Freight revenue		130,950
Fuel expense	53,800	
Salaries expense	66,700	
Maintenance expense	12,900	
	$1,401,800	$1,401,800

Other Data **(a)** One of Island Hopper's regular customers is Pacific Trading Co. The airline keeps track of the weight of freight carried for the trading company during the month and sends a bill shortly after month-end. No entry has yet been made to record $4,600 earned in June carrying freight for Pacific Trading Co.

(b) Three months' rent ($9,600) had been prepaid on June 1.

(c) On April 1, a 12-month insurance policy had been purchased for $25,200.

(d) The aircraft is being depreciated over a period of 10 years (120 months).

(e) The amount shown as unearned passenger revenue represents tickets sold to customers in advance of flights. During June, $38,650 of this amount was earned by the airline. (Credit Passenger Revenue.)

(f) Salaries earned by employees but not yet paid amount to $3,300 at June 30.

(g) Accrued interest on notes payable amounts to $5,000 at June 30 and has not yet been recorded.

Instructions **a** Prepare a work sheet for the month ended June 30, 19__.

b Prepare an income statement, a statement of owner's equity, and a balance sheet. Follow the format illustrated on pages 146 and 147.

c Prepare adjusting and closing journal entries.

Problem 4B-7
Reversing entries Rodgers Construction Co. adjusts and closes its accounts at the end of each calendar year. The company works a five-day week and pays its employees up-to-date each Friday. The weekly salaries are $10,000 ($2,000 per day). Near year-end, the following events occurred relating to salaries:

Dec. 26 (Friday) Recorded payment of regular weekly salaries of $10,000.

Dec. 31 (Wednesday) Prepared an adjusting entry for accrued salaries of $6,000.

Jan. 1 (Thursday) Made a reversing entry for accrued salaries.

Jan. 2 (Friday) Recorded payment of regular weekly salaries of $10,000.

Instructions **a** Prepare journal entries (with explanations) for the four events relating to salaries.

b How much of the $10,000 in salaries paid on January 2 represents a January expense? Explain.

c Assume that no reversing entry was made by the company; prepare the journal entry required to record the payment of salaries on January 2.

BUSINESS DECISIONS CASES

Case 4-1
Alaska Airlines

Alaska Air Group, Inc. (Alaska Airlines), credits the proceeds from advance ticket sales to an account entitled "Air Traffic Liability." The company's 1987 annual report shows the following trend in the balance of this account over a three-year period:

	1985	1986	1987
Air traffic liability (in millions)	*$28.4*	*$35.5*	*$41.6*

Instructions **a** What does the balance in the Air Traffic Liability account represent?

b How does the airline normally discharge this liability?

c Explain the most probable reason for the increases in the amount of this liability from year-to-year.

d Based solely upon the trend in the amount of this liability, would you expect the annual amounts of passenger revenue earned by the airlines to be increasing or decreasing over this three-year period? Explain.

Case 4-2
Computer-based
accounting
systems

In Case 2-1, Farrah Moore used data base software to design a simple accounting system for use on personal computers. Moore's first system prepared only a balance sheet; she is now ready to design an enhanced system which will perform all of the steps in the accounting cycle and will produce a complete set of financial statements. This enhanced system also will utilize data base software.

The idea underlying data base software is that data intended for a variety of different uses must be entered into the data base only once. The computer can then arrange these data into any number of desired formats. It can also combine data and perform mathematical computations using data in the data base.

In Moore's new accounting system, the computer will arrange the data into the following formats: (1) journal entries (with explanations) for all transactions, (2) three-column running balance ledger accounts, (3) a 10-column work sheet, (4) a complete set of financial statements, (5) journal entries for all adjusting and closing entries, (6) an after-closing trial balance, and (7) reversing entries. As each of these records and statements is prepared, any totals or subtotals in the record are included automatically in the data base. For example, when ledger accounts are updated, the new account balances become part of the data base.

Instructions In Chapter 4, the steps of the accounting cycle were described as follows: (a) journalize transactions, (b) post to ledger accounts, (c) prepare a work sheet, (d) prepare financial statements, (e) adjust and close the accounts, (f) prepare an after-closing trial balance, and (g) prepare reversing entries. For each step in this cycle, briefly describe the types of data used in performing the step. Indicate whether this data is already contained in the data base, or whether the computer operator must enter data to enable the computer to perform the step.

ANSWERS TO SELF-TEST QUESTIONS

1 c   2 d ($3,890)   3 d   4 b   5 a

Comprehensive Problem for Part 1

FRIEND WITH A TRUCK

A short practice set, based upon a service business.

On September 1, 19__, Anthony Ferrara organized a business called Friend With A Truck for the purpose of operating an equipment rental yard. The new business was able to begin operations immediately by purchasing the assets and taking over the location of Rent-It, an equipment rental company that was going out of business.

Friend With A Truck uses the following chart of accounts:

Cash................................	1	Anthony Ferrara, Capital.............	30
Accounts Receivable	4	Anthony Ferrara, Drawing............	35
Prepaid Rent........................	6	Income Summary....................	40
Office Supplies......................	8	Rental Fees Earned..................	50
Rental Equipment	10	Salaries Expense	60
Accumulated Depreciation:		Maintenance Expense	61
Rental Equipment	12	Utilities Expense	62
Notes Payable.......................	20	Rent Expense	63
Accounts Payable	22	Office Supplies Expense	64
Interest Payable.....................	25	Depreciation Expense	65
Salaries Payable.....................	26	Interest Expense	66
Unearned Rental Fees	29		

The company closes its accounts and prepares financial statements at the end of each month. During September, the company entered into the following transactions:

Sept. 1   Anthony Ferrara deposited $100,000 cash in a bank account in the name of the business, Friend With A Truck.

Sept. 1   Paid $9,000 to Shapiro Realty as three months' advance rent on the rental yard and office formerly occupied by Rent-It.

Sept. 1   Purchased for $180,000 all of the equipment formerly owned by Rent-It. Paid $70,000 cash and issued a one-year note payable for $110,000, plus interest at the annual rate of 9%.

Sept. 4   Purchased office supplies on account from Modern Office Co., $1,630. Payment due in 30 days. (These supplies are expected to last for several months; debit the Office Supplies asset account.)

Sept. 8   Received $10,000 cash from McBryan Construction Co. as advance payment for equipment rental.

Sept. 12   Paid salaries for the first two weeks in September, $3,600.

Sept. 15   Excluding the McBryan advance, equipment rental fees earned during the first 15 days of September amounted to $6,100, of which $5,300 was received in cash and $800 was an account receivable.

Sept. 17   Purchased on account from Earth Movers, Inc., $340 in parts needed to repair a rental tractor. Payment is due in 10 days.

Sept. 23   Collected $210 of the accounts receivable recorded on September 15.

Sept. 25   Rented a backhoe to Mission Landscaping at a price of $100 per day, to be paid when the backhoe is returned. Mission Landscaping expects to keep the backhoe for about two or three weeks.

Sept. 26   Paid biweekly salaries, $3,600.

Sept. 27   Paid the account payable to Earth Movers, Inc., $340.

Sept. 28   Anthony Ferrara withdrew $2,000 cash from the business to pay the rent on his personal residence.

Sept. 30   Received a bill for utilities expense for the month of September, $270. Payment is due in 30 days.

Sept. 30   Cash received from equipment rental during the second half of September, $6,450.

Data for Adjusting Entries

(a) The advance payment of rent on September 1 covered a period of three months.

(b) Interest accrued on the note payable to Rent-It amounted to $825 at September 30.

(c) The rental equipment is being depreciated over a period of 10 years.

(d) Office supplies on hand at September 30 are estimated at $1,100.

(e) During September, the company earned $4,840 of the rental fees paid in advance by McBryan Construction Co. on September 8.

(f) As of September 30, Friend With A Truck has earned five days' rent on the backhoe rented to Mission Landscaping on September 25.

(g) Salaries earned by employees since the last payroll date (September 26) amounted to $900 at month-end.

Instructions

a Journalize the above transactions.

b Post to ledger accounts. (Use running balance form of ledger accounts. Enter numbers of journal pages and ledger accounts to complete the cross referencing between the journal and ledger.)

c Prepare a 10-column work sheet for the month ended September 30, 19__.

d Prepare an income statement and a statement of owner's equity for the month of September, and a balance sheet (in report form) as of September 30.

e Prepare adjusting and closing entries and post to ledger accounts.

f Prepare an after-closing trial balance as of September 30.

g Prepare appropriate reversing entries (dated October 1) and post to ledger accounts.

PART 2

Merchandising Concerns, Internal Control, and Accounting Systems

This part consists of two chapters. In the first, we explain the accounting concepts relating to merchandising activities. In the second chapter, we explore means of achieving internal control and of modifying an accounting system to handle efficiently a large volume of transactions.

5 **Accounting for Purchases and Sales of Merchandise**

6 **Internal Control and Accounting Systems**

Accounting for Purchases and Sales of Merchandise

In this chapter our discussion of the accounting cycle is expanded to include merchandising concerns—those businesses that sell goods rather than services. We illustrate and explain various types of merchandising transactions, the computation of net sales and the cost of goods sold, and a work sheet and closing entries for a merchandising company. Both the perpetual and periodic inventory systems are described. In addition, this chapter introduces several concepts of financial statement analysis, including evaluating the solvency of a business and the adequacy of its net income.

After studying this chapter you should be able to meet these Learning Objectives:

1 Account for sales, sales returns, and sales discounts.

2 Determine the cost of goods sold using the periodic inventory system.

3 Account for purchases of merchandise.

4 Analyze an income statement and evaluate the adequacy of net income.

5 Prepare a work sheet and closing entries for a merchandising company.

6 Distinguish between the periodic and the perpetual inventory systems.

7 Prepare a classified balance sheet and either a single-step or a multiple-step income statement.

8 Explain the purpose of the current ratio and the meaning of working capital.

MERCHANDISING COMPANIES

The preceding four chapters have illustrated step by step the complete accounting cycle for businesses rendering personal services. Service-type companies represent an important part of our economy. They include, for example, airlines, railroads, hotels, insurance companies, ski resorts, hospitals, and professional sports teams. These enterprises earn revenue by rendering services to their customers. The net income of a service-type business is equal to the excess of revenue over the operating expenses incurred.

In contrast to service-type businesses, merchandising companies—both wholesalers and retailers—earn revenue by selling goods or merchandise. The term *merchandise* refers to goods held for resale to customers. The accounting principles and methods we have studied for service-type businesses also apply to merchandising companies. However, some additional accounts and techniques are needed to account for purchases and sales of merchandise.

Selling merchandise introduces a new and major cost of doing business—the cost to the company of the merchandise being resold to customers. This cost is termed the *cost of goods sold* and is so important that it is shown separately from operating expenses in the income statement of a merchandising concern. Thus, the income statement of a merchandising company has *three main sections:* (1) the revenue section, (2) the cost of goods sold section, and (3) the operating expenses section.

A highly condensed income statement for a merchandising business is shown below. In comparison with the income statement of a service-type business, the new features of this statement are the inclusion of the cost of goods sold and a subtotal called *gross profit.*

OFFICE PRODUCTS
Condensed Income Statement
For the Year Ended December 31, 19___

Revenue from sales	$1,000,000
Less: Cost of goods sold	550,000
Gross profit on sales	$ 450,000
Less: Operating expenses	400,000
Net income	$ 50,000

Revenue from sales represents the selling price of merchandise sold during the period. The cost of goods sold, on the other hand, represents the cost to the merchandising concern of buying these goods. The difference between revenue from sales and the cost of goods sold is called *gross profit.* (Gross profit also may be called *gross margin.*)

If a merchandising business is to operate profitably, its gross profit must exceed its operating expenses. Thus, the net income of a merchandising company is the excess of revenue over the *sum* of (1) the cost of goods sold and (2) the operating expenses of the business.

Revenue from Sales

Objective 1
Account for sales, sales returns, and sales discounts.

Revenue earned by selling merchandise is credited to a revenue account entitled *Sales.* The figure shown in our condensed income statement, however, is the *net sales* for the accounting period. The term *net sales* means total sales revenue *minus* sales returns and allowances, and sales discounts. To illustrate this concept, let us now illustrate the revenue section of Office Products' income statement in greater detail:

OFFICE PRODUCTS
Partial Income Statement
For the Year Ended December 31, 19___

Revenue from sales:		
Sales		$1,012,000
Less: Sales returns and allowances	$8,000	
Sales discounts	4,000	12,000
Net sales		$1,000,000

The $1,012,000 figure labeled "sales" in the partial income statement is sometimes called *gross sales.* This amount represents the total of both cash and credit sales made during the year. When a business sells merchandise to its customers, it either receives immediate payment in cash or acquires an account receivable to be collected at a later date. Cash sales are rung up on cash registers as the transactions occur. At the end of the day, the total shown on all the company's cash registers represents total cash sales for the day and is recorded by a journal entry, as follows:

Journal entry for cash sales

Cash	900	
Sales		900
To record the sale of merchandise for cash.		

For a sale of merchandise on credit, a typical journal entry would be

Journal entry for sale on credit

Accounts Receivable	500	
Sales		500
Sold merchandise on credit to Kay's Gift Shop; payment due within 30 days.		

Sales revenue is earned in the period in which the merchandise is *delivered to the customer,* even though payment may not be received for a month or more after the sale. Consequently, the revenue earned in a given accounting period may differ considerably from the cash receipts of that period.

Sales Returns and Allowances

Most merchandising companies allow customers to obtain a refund or a credit by returning merchandise which is found to be unsatisfactory. When customers find that merchandise purchased has minor defects, they may agree to keep such merchandise if an allowance is made on the sales price. Refunds and allowances have the effect of nullifying previously recorded sales and reducing the amount of revenue earned by the business. The journal entry to record sales returns and allowances is shown below.

Journal entry for sales returns and allowances

Sales Returns and Allowances	100	
Cash (or Accounts Receivable)		100
Made refund for merchandise returned by customer.		

Sales Returns and Allowances is a *contra-revenue* account—that is, it appears in the income statement as a deduction from gross sales revenue.

Why use a separate Sales Returns and Allowances account rather than recording refunds by directly debiting the Sales account? The answer is that using a separate contra-revenue account enables management to see both the total amount of sales and the amount of sales returns. The relationship between these two amounts gives management an indication of customer satisfaction with the merchandise.

Credit Terms

For all sales of merchandise on credit, the terms of payment should be clearly stated, so that buyer and seller can avoid any misunderstanding as to the time and amount of the required payment. One common example of credit terms is "net 30 days" or "n/30," meaning that the net amount of the invoice or bill is due in 30 days. Another common form of credit terms is "10 eom," meaning payment is due 10 days after the end of the month in which the sale occurred.

Sales Discounts

Manufacturers and wholesalers usually sell on credit and require full payment within 30 or 60 days. Often these companies also offer the buyer a discount for paying earlier.

Perhaps the most common credit terms offered by manufacturers and wholesalers are "2/10, net/30." This expression is read "2, 10, net 30," and means that full payment is due in 30 days, but that the buyer may take a 2% discount if payment is made within 10 days. The 10-day period during which the discount is available is called the *discount period.* Because a sales discount provides an incentive to the customer to make an early cash payment, it is often referred to as a *cash discount.*

For example, assume that on November 3 Office Products sells merchandise for $1,000 on credit to Zipco, Inc., terms 2/10, n/30. At the time of the sale, the seller does not know if the buyer will take advantage of the discount by paying within the discount period; therefore, Office Products records the sale at the full price by the following entry:

Nov. 3 *Accounts Receivable*	*1,000*	
Sales		*1,000*
To record sale to Zipco, Inc., terms 2/10, n/30.		

The customer now has a choice between saving $20 by paying within the discount period, or waiting a full 30 days and paying the full price. If Zipco mails its check on or before November 13, it is entitled to deduct 2% of $1,000, or $20, and settle the obligation for $980. If Zipco decides to forgo the discount, it may postpone payment an additional 20 days until December 3 but must then pay $1,000.

Assuming that payment is made by Zipco on November 13, the last day of the discount period, the entry by Office Products to record collection of the receivable is

Nov. 13 *Cash*	*980*	
Sales Discounts	*20*	
Accounts Receivable		*1,000*
Collected from Zipco, Inc., for our sale of Nov. 3, less 2%		
cash discount.		

If a customer returns a portion of the merchandise before making payment, the discount applies only to the portion of the goods kept by the customer. In the above example, if Zipco had returned $300 worth of goods out of the $1,000 purchase, the discount would have been applicable only to the $700 portion of the order which the customer kept.

Sales Discounts is a contra-revenue account. In the income statement, sales discounts are deducted from gross sales revenue along with any sales returns and allowances. This treatment was illustrated in the partial income statement on page 183.

Cost of Goods Sold

Merchandising companies continuously buy and sell merchandise. The cost of merchandise sold during the year appears in the income statement as a deduction from the net sales revenue. The cost of merchandise still on hand at year-end appears in the balance sheet as an asset called *inventory.*

The cost of the inventory at year-end can be determined relatively easily. These goods are actually on hand, so they may be counted and their unit costs may be determined from the accounting records. Determining the cost of goods *sold* is a more challenging task, because the goods are no longer on hand. Two approaches may be used to measure the cost of goods sold: (1) the *periodic inventory system* or (2) the *perpetual inventory system.* We shall begin our discussion with the periodic inventory system. The perpetual inventory system will be discussed later in the chapter.

The Periodic Inventory System

Objective 2
Determine the cost of goods sold using the periodic inventory system.

The foundation of the periodic inventory system is a *physical count* of the goods on hand at the end of the period. This procedure, called *taking a physical inventory,* is both inconvenient and costly. Therefore, a physical inventory usually is taken only at year-end. Thus, the periodic inventory system is well suited to the preparation of annual financial statements, but not to preparing statements for shorter accounting periods, such as months or quarters.[1]

To determine the cost of goods sold by the periodic inventory system, the accounting records must show (1) the cost of the inventory at the beginning and at the end of the year, and (2) the cost of merchandise purchased throughout the year. Using this information, the cost of goods sold during the year may be computed as follows:

Inventory, beginning of the year	$180,000
Purchases	570,000
Cost of goods available for sale	$750,000
Less: Inventory, end of the year	200,000
Cost of goods sold	$550,000

In this example, the business had $180,000 of merchandise on hand at the beginning of the year. During the year, it purchased an additional $570,000 of merchandise. Thus, the total cost of goods offered for sale to customers during

---

[1] In Chapter 8 we discuss several estimating techniques that may be used in preparing monthly or quarterly financial statements.

the year was $750,000. At year-end, only $200,000 of these goods remained on hand. Consequently, the cost of goods sold during the year must have been $550,000.

In summary, the periodic inventory system works as follows:

1 A physical inventory is taken at the end of each year to determine the *ending inventory.* These physical counts also determine the *beginning inventory,* as the ending inventory from the prior year is the beginning inventory of the current year.

2 *Purchases* of merchandise during the year are recorded in the accounting records.

3 The beginning inventory is added to net purchases in order to determine the *cost of goods available for sale* during the period.

4 The cost of the *ending inventory* is *subtracted* from the *cost of goods available for sale.* The resulting figure represents the *cost of goods sold* during the period.

Computation of the cost of goods sold is an important concept that requires careful attention. To gain a thorough understanding of this concept, we need to consider the nature of the accounts and accounting procedures used in determining the cost of goods sold.

Beginning Inventory and Ending Inventory

The goods on hand at the beginning of an accounting period are called *beginning inventory;* the goods on hand at the end of the period are called *ending inventory.* Since a new accounting period begins as soon as the old one ends, the ending inventory of one accounting period becomes the beginning inventory of the next period.

A business using the periodic inventory system takes a physical inventory at the end of each period to determine the goods on hand. Taking inventory involves three basic steps:

1 All merchandise on hand is counted.

2 The quantity counted for each item is multiplied by the cost per unit shown in the accounting records.

3 The costs of the various kinds of merchandise are added together to determine the total cost of inventory on hand.

The resulting dollar amount for ending inventory appears as an asset in the balance sheet and also is used in computing the cost of goods sold for the period.

At the end of each accounting period, entries are made in the Inventory account to remove the cost of the beginning inventory and to enter the cost of the ending inventory, as determined by the physical count. (These entries are made during the closing process, and will be discussed later.) Notice that throughout the year, the Inventory account shows only the amount of the *beginning inventory.* The balance of this account *does not change* until the new ending inventory is recorded at year-end. Thus, *no entries are made in the Inventory account to record the costs of merchandise bought and sold during the period.*

Purchases of Merchandise

Objective 3
Account for purchases of merchandise.

Under the periodic inventory system, the cost of merchandise purchased for resale is recorded by debiting an account called Purchases, as shown below:

Nov. 3 Purchases *10,000*
       Accounts Payable *10,000*
      Purchased merchandise from ABC Supply Co. Credit terms 2/10,
      n/30.

The Purchases account *is used only for merchandise acquired for resale.* The Purchases account does not indicate whether the purchased goods have been sold or are still on hand. Assets acquired for *use in the business* (such as a delivery truck, a typewriter, or office supplies) are not recorded in the Purchases account; these asset acquisitions are recorded by debiting the appropriate asset accounts.

At the end of the period, the balance in the Purchases account represents the cost of all goods purchased during the period. This amount is added to the beginning inventory to determine the *cost of goods available for sale*—an important step in computing the cost of goods sold.

■ **Other Accounts Included in the Cost of Goods Sold**   In our illustration on page 185, we used only three items in computing the cost of goods sold: beginning inventory, purchases, and ending inventory. In most cases, however, some additional accounts are involved in this computation. These include accounts for Purchase Returns and Allowances, Purchase Discounts, and Transportation-in.

■ **Purchase Returns and Allowances**   When merchandise purchased from suppliers is found to be unsatisfactory, the goods may be returned, or a request may be made for an allowance on the price. A return of goods to the supplier is recorded as follows:

■
Journal entry for
return of goods
to supplier

Accounts Payable *1,200*
      Purchase Returns and Allowances *1,200*
To reduce liability to Jet Supply Co. by the cost of goods returned
for credit.

It is preferable to credit Purchase Returns and Allowances when merchandise is returned to a supplier rather than crediting the Purchases account directly. The accounts then show both the total amount of purchases and the amount of purchases which required adjustment or return. Management is interested in the percentage relationship between goods purchased and goods returned, because the returning of merchandise for credit is an expensive, time-consuming process. Excessive returns suggest inefficiency in the operation of the purchasing department and a need to find more dependable suppliers.

■ **Purchase Discounts**   As explained earlier, manufacturers and wholesalers frequently grant a cash discount to customers who will pay promptly for goods purchased on credit. The selling company regards a cash discount as a *sales discount;* the buying company calls the discount a *purchase discount.*

If the $10,000 purchase of November 3 shown on page 187 is paid for on or before November 13, the last day of the discount period, the purchasing company will save 2% of the price of the merchandise, or $200, as shown by the following entry:

■
Journal entry for payment within discount period

Nov. 13	Accounts Payable	10,000	
	Purchase Discounts		200
	Cash		9,800
	Paid ABC Supply Co. for purchases of Nov. 3, less 2% cash discount.		

The effect of the discount was to reduce the cost of the merchandise to the buying company. The credit balance of the Purchase Discounts account should therefore be deducted in the income statement from the debit balance of the Purchases account.

Do companies usually take advantage of available cash discounts? The answer is *yes.* The terms 2/10, n/30 offer the buyer a 2% discount for sending payment 20 days before it is otherwise due. Saving 2% by paying 20 days early is equivalent to earning an annual return of over 36% ($2\% \times \frac{365}{20} = 36.5\%$). Thus, taking cash discounts represents an excellent investment opportunity. Most companies take these discounts even if they must borrow from a bank in order to have the necessary cash available.

■ **Transportation-In**   The cost of merchandise acquired for resale logically includes any transportation charges necessary to bring the goods to the purchaser's place of business. A separate ledger account is used to accumulate transportation charges on merchandise purchased. The journal entry to record transportation charges on inbound shipments of merchandise is as follows:

■
Journalizing transportation charges on purchases of merchandise

Transportation-In	125	
Cash (or Accounts Payable)..		125
Air freight charges on merchandise purchased from Miller Brothers, Kansas City.		

Since transportation charges are part of the *delivered cost* of merchandise purchased, the Transportation-in account is combined with the Purchases account in the income statement to determine the cost of goods available for sale.

Transportation charges on inbound shipments of merchandise must not be confused with transportation charges on *outbound* shipments of goods to customers. Freight charges and other expenses incurred in making deliveries to customers are regarded as selling expenses; these outlays are debited to a separate account entitled Delivery Expense and are *not included* in the cost of goods sold.

Shoplifting and Inventory "Shrinkage" Losses

Under the periodic inventory system, it is assumed that all goods available for sale during the year are either sold or are on hand at year-end for the ending inventory. As a result of this assumption, the cost of merchandise lost because of shoplifting, employee theft, breakage, and spoilage will be included automatically in the cost of goods sold. For example, assume that a store has goods available for sale which cost $600,000. Assume that shoplifters steal $10,000 worth of goods and that the ending inventory is $100,000. (If the thefts had not occurred, the ending inventory would have been $10,000 larger.) The cost of goods sold is computed at $500,000 by subtracting the $100,000 ending inventory from the $600,000 cost of goods available for sale. The theft loss is not shown separately in the income statement. Technically, cost of goods sold was $490,000, and cost of goods stolen was $10,000.

Although the periodic inventory system causes inventory losses to be included automatically in the cost of goods sold, accountants have devised a method of estimating losses of merchandise from theft. This method is explained in Chapter 9.

Income Statement for a Merchandising Company

To pull together the various concepts discussed thus far in the chapter, we need to look at a detailed income statement for a merchandising business. The income statement of Olympic Sporting Goods is shown on the next page.

Notice that the income statement is divided into three major sections: revenue, the cost of goods sold, and operating expenses. We have already discussed the various accounts appearing in the first two sections. The operating expenses in the third section of the income statement are classified either as selling expenses or general and administrative expenses. *Selling expenses* include all expenses of storing and marketing merchandise, including advertising, sales salaries, and delivery expense. *General and administrative expenses* include those expenses relating to other business operations, such as expenses of the corporate headquarters, and of the accounting, finance, and personnel departments.

In many companies certain expenses, such as depreciation of the building, need to be divided, part to selling expense and part to general and administrative expenses. Olympic Sporting Goods divided its $8,000 of depreciation expense by allocating $6,000 to selling expenses and $2,000 to general and administrative expenses. This allocation can conveniently be made when the income statement is prepared from the work sheet; thus no additional ledger accounts are required. The amount for utilities expense, $3,100, was not divided because management did not consider the amount large enough to warrant such treatment.

Analyzing the Income Statement

Objective 4
Analyze an income statement and evaluate the adequacy of net income.

Perhaps the most important figure in an income statement is net income. The amount and the trend of net income are important to managers, investors, and others interested in the progress of a company. However, for merchandising companies, the trends in net sales and in gross profit are also of special importance.

A rising volume of sales is evidence of growth and suggests the probability of an increase in earnings. A declining trend in sales, on the other hand, is often the first signal of reduced earnings and of financial difficulties ahead. The amount of sales for each year is compared with the sales of the preceding

OLYMPIC SPORTING GOODS
Income Statement
For the Year Ending December 31, 19___

Revenue:			
Sales			$617,000
Less: Sales returns and allowances		$ 12,000	
Sales discounts		5,000	17,000
Net sales			$600,000
Cost of goods sold:			
Inventory, Jan. 1		$ 60,000	
Purchases	$367,000		
Less: Purchase returns and allowances	$6,700		
Purchase discounts	3,300	10,000	
Net purchases	$357,000		
Add: Transportation-in	13,000		
Cost of goods purchased		370,000	
Cost of goods available for sale		$430,000	
Less: Inventory, Dec. 31		70,000	
Cost of goods sold			360,000
Gross profit on sales			$240,000
Operating expenses:			
Selling expenses:			
Sales salaries		$ 74,000	
Advertising		29,000	
Delivery service		10,700	
Depreciation		6,000	
Total selling expenses		$119,700	
General & administrative expenses:			
Office salaries		$ 57,000	
Utilities		3,100	
Depreciation		2,000	
Total general & administrative expenses		62,100	
Total operating expenses			181,800
Income from operations			$ 58,200
Interest expense			8,200
Net income			$ 50,000

This income statement consists of three major sections

Nonoperating items can be a fourth (usually minor) section

year. The sales of each month may be compared with the sales of the preceding month and also with the corresponding month of the preceding year. These comparisons bring to light significant trends in the volume of sales.

■ **Gross Profit Rate: A Key Statistic** A useful step in evaluating the performance of a merchandising company is to express the gross profit as a percentage of net sales. For Olympic Sporting Goods, the gross profit amounts to 40% of net sales (gross profit, $240,000, divided by net sales, $600,000, equals 40%). This percentage is called the *gross profit rate.*

By computing the gross profit rate of a business for several years in a row, the user of financial statements gains insight into whether business is improving or declining. A rising gross profit rate is a sign of improved operating performance, indicating strong demand for the company's products. A falling gross profit rate, on the other hand, may indicate that the business is having to cut prices in order to sell its products, or that it is unable to pass cost increases on to its customers.

Of course, the gross profit rate will vary among different companies and different industries. Users of financial statements may compare the gross profit rate of one business to that of other companies in the same industry, or to the gross profit rate of the same company in prior years. In most merchandising companies, the rate of gross profit usually varies between 30% and 50% of net sales.

Accountants, investors, bankers, and business managers have the habit of mentally computing percentage relationships when they look at financial statements. Formation of this habit will be helpful throughout the study of accounting, as well as in many business situations. In analyzing an income statement, the amount of net sales is regarded as 100%, and every other item or subtotal in the statement is expressed as a percentage of net sales.

■ **Nonoperating Items**   Some expenses, such as interest expense, are not directly related to operating activities. These *nonoperating* expenses may be listed separately in the income statement after the subtotal *income from operations.* Interest is not considered an operating expense because it stems from the manner in which assets are financed, not from the daily operating activities of the business.

If nonoperating expenses are listed separately, *nonoperating revenue* (such as interest earned) also should be listed in this section of the income statement. Other nonoperating items include income or loss from investments, gains or losses arising from lawsuits, and (for corporations only) income taxes expense.

Classifying operating expenses into subcategories and showing nonoperating items separately are *optional accounting practices,* not required by generally accepted accounting principles. However, these practices assist management in identifying those departments within the business which are operating efficiently and those which are incurring excessive costs.

■ **Evaluating the Adequacy of Net Income**   Should the $50,000 net income of Olympic Sporting Goods for the current year be viewed as excellent, fair, or poor performance for a business of this size? In evaluating the net income of an unincorporated business, remember that no "salary" has been deducted for the value of the personal services rendered to the business by the owner. The reason for omitting the owner's "salary" from the expenses is that the owner could set this salary at any desired level. An unrealistic salary to the owner, whether too high or too low, would lessen the usefulness of the income statement as a measure of the earning power of the business.

Consider also that the owner may have a substantial amount of money invested in the business in the form of owner's equity. As no interest expense is recorded on equity investments, the income statement ignores the amount of the owner's financial investment in the business.

Finally, the net income of a business should be adequate to compensate the owner for taking significant risks. Some studies show that about half of all new businesses fail in their first year. Furthermore, Olympic's profitability in the current year is no guarantee of net income in future years. Losses might occur which could wipe out some or all of the owner's investment. This is especially true if the business has large liabilities.

In summary, the net income of an unincorporated business should be sufficient to compensate the owner for three factors: (1) personal services rendered to the business, (2) a return on capital invested, and (3) the degree of risk taken. Using these criteria, let us appraise the adequacy of the $50,000 net income of Olympic Sporting Goods.

Assume that Robert Riley, the owner of the company, works full time in the business. Also assume that if he were not running his own business, he could earn a salary of $35,000 per year managing a similar store. In addition, Riley had $115,000 invested in Olympic Sporting Goods at the beginning of the year. If this money had been invested in stocks and bonds, we might assume that Riley would have earned investment income of, say, $10,000. Thus, the two factors of the owner's personal services and financial investment indicate a need for the company to earn at least $45,000 per year to be considered successful. As the business actually earned $50,000, a $5,000 "cushion" is left to compensate Riley for the risks involved in running his own business. Whether or not $5,000 is adequate compensation for these risks depends upon the degree of risk involved in this type of business activity, and Riley's personal attitude toward risk taking.

Of course, some people simply enjoy owning their own business. Such people might prefer to own their own business even if they could earn more money by working for someone else.

Work Sheet for a Merchandising Business

Objective 5
Prepare a work sheet and closing entries for a merchandising company.

A merchandising company, like the service business discussed in Chapter 4, uses a work sheet at the end of the period to organize the information needed to prepare financial statements and to adjust and close the accounts. The new elements in the work sheet for Olympic Sporting Goods on the following page are the beginning inventory, the ending inventory, and the other merchandising accounts. The inventory accounts are shown in black to help focus your attention on their treatment.

■ **Trial Balance Columns**   The Trial Balance columns were prepared by listing the ledger account balances at December 31. Notice that the Inventory account in the Trial Balance debit column shows a balance of $60,000, the cost of merchandise on hand at the end of the prior year. No entries were made in the Inventory account during the current year despite the various purchases and sales of merchandise. The significance of the Inventory account in the trial balance is that it shows the amount of merchandise with which Olympic Sporting Goods began operations on January 1 of the current year.

■ **Adjustment Columns and Adjusted Trial Balance Columns**   The merchandising accounts usually do not require adjustment. Their balances are carried directly from the Trial Balance columns to the Adjusted Trial Balance columns.

In our illustration, the only adjustment needed at December 31 is the entry to record depreciation expense. Salaries to employees and interest on the note payable were paid on December 31, so no adjusting entries were needed for these items.

OLYMPIC SPORTING GOODS
Work Sheet
For the Year Ended December 31, 19____

	TRIAL BALANCE DR	TRIAL BALANCE CR	ADJUSTMENTS* DR	ADJUSTMENTS* CR	ADJUSTED TRIAL BALANCE DR	ADJUSTED TRIAL BALANCE CR	INCOME STATEMENT DR	INCOME STATEMENT CR	BALANCE SHEET DR	BALANCE SHEET CR
Cash	14,500				14,500				14,500	
Accounts receivable	43,500				43,500				43,500	
Inventory, Jan.	60,000				60,000		60,000 *Begin*		70,000 *End 70,000*	
Land	52,000				52,000				52,000	
Building	160,000				160,000				160,000	
Accumulated depreciation: building		56,000		(a) 8,000		64,000				64,000
Notes payable		82,000				82,000				82,000
Accounts payable		55,000				55,000				55,000
Robert Riley, capital		115,000				115,000				115,000
Robert Riley, drawing	26,000				26,000				26,000	
Sales		617,000				617,000		617,000		
Sales returns and allowances	12,000				12,000		12,000			
Sales discounts	5,000				5,000		5,000			
Purchases	367,000				367,000		367,000			
Purchase returns and allowances		6,700				6,700		6,700		
Purchase discounts		3,300				3,300		3,300		
Transportation-in	13,000				13,000		13,000			
Sales salaries	74,000				74,000		74,000			
Advertising expense	29,000				29,000		29,000			
Delivery service expense	10,700				10,700		10,700			
Office salaries	57,000				57,000		57,000			
Utilities expense	3,100				3,100		3,100			
Interest expense	8,200				8,200		8,200			
	935,000	935,000								
Depreciation expense: building			(a) 8,000		8,000		8,000			
			8,000	8,000	943,000	943,000				
Inventory, Dec. 31								70,000	70,000	
							647,000	697,000	366,000	316,000
Net income							50,000			50,000
Totals							697,000	697,000	366,000	366,000

Note the treatment of the beginning inventory

Note the treatment of the ending inventory

■ **Income Statement Columns**   The accounts which will appear in a company's income statement are the ones to be carried from the Adjusted Trial Balance columns to the Income Statement columns of the work sheet. These are the revenue accounts, cost of goods sold accounts, and expense accounts.

■ **Recording the Ending Inventory on the Work Sheet**   The key point to be observed in this work sheet is the method of recording the *ending inventory*. On December 31, Riley and his assistants took a physical inventory of all merchandise on hand. The entire inventory, priced at cost, amounted to $70,000. This ending inventory, dated December 31, does not appear in the trial balance; it is therefore written on the first available line below the trial balance totals. The amount of $70,000 is listed in the Income Statement credit column and also in the Balance Sheet debit column. By entering the ending inventory in the Income Statement *credit* column, we are in effect *deducting* it from the total of the beginning inventory, the purchases, and the transportation-in, all of which are extended from the trial balance to the Income Statement *debit* column.

One of the functions of the Income Statement columns is to bring together all the accounts involved in determining the cost of goods sold. The accounts with debit balances are the beginning Inventory, Purchases, and Transportation-in; these accounts total $440,000. Against this total the three credit items of Purchase Returns and Allowances, $6,700, Purchase Discounts, $3,300, and ending Inventory, $70,000, are offset. The three accounts with debit balances exceed in total the three credit balances by an amount of $360,000; this amount is the cost of goods sold, as shown in the income statement on page 190.

The ending inventory is also entered in the Balance Sheet debit column of the work sheet, because this inventory of merchandise on December 31 will appear as an asset in the year-end balance sheet.

■ **Completing the Work Sheet**   When all the accounts on the work sheet have been extended into the Income Statement or Balance Sheet columns, the final four columns are totaled. The net income is computed, and the work sheet completed in the same manner as illustrated in Chapter 4 for a service business.

Financial Statements

The work to be done at the end of the period is much the same for a merchandising business as for a service-type firm. First, the work sheet is completed; then, financial statements are prepared from the data in the work sheet; next, the adjusting and closing entries are entered in the journal and posted to the ledger accounts; and finally, an after-closing trial balance is prepared.[2] This completes the periodic accounting cycle.

■ **Income Statement**   The income statement on page 190 was prepared from the Olympic Sporting Goods work sheet. Note particularly the arrangement of items in the cost of goods sold section of the income statement; this

---

[2] The journalizing of the adjusting entry for Olympic Sporting Goods is not illustrated here because this entry is similar to those demonstrated in previous chapters.

portion of the income statement shows in summary form many of the essential accounting concepts covered in this chapter.

■ **Statement of Owner's Equity** The statement of owner's equity shows the increase in owner's equity from the year's net income and the decrease from the owner's withdrawals during the year. Note that the final amount in the statement of owner's equity also appears in the balance sheet as the new balance of the owner's capital account.

OLYMPIC SPORTING GOODS

Statement of Owner's Equity

For the Year Ended December 31, 19___

■

Which figure for owner's equity will appear in the balance sheet?

Robert Riley, capital, Jan. 1	$115,000
Add: Net income for the year	50,000
Subtotal	$165,000
Less: Withdrawals	26,000
Robert Riley, capital, Dec. 31	$139,000

■ **Balance Sheet** In studying the following balance sheet, note that all items are taken from the Balance Sheet columns of the work sheet, but that the amount for Robert Riley, Capital is the December 31 balance of $139,000, computed as shown in the preceding statement of owner's equity.

OLYMPIC SPORTING GOODS

Balance Sheet

December 31, 19___

ASSETS

Cash		$ 14,500
Accounts receivable		43,500
Inventory		70,000
Land		52,000
Building	$160,000	
Less: Accumulated depreciation	64,000	96,000
Total assets		$276,000

LIABILITIES & OWNER'S EQUITY

Liabilities:		
Notes payable		$ 82,000
Accounts payable		55,000
Total liabilities		$137,000
Owner's equity:		
Robert Riley, capital		139,000
Total liabilities & owner's equity		$276,000

Closing Entries

The entries used in closing revenue and expense accounts have been explained in preceding chapters. The only new elements in this illustration of closing entries for a merchandising business are the entries showing the *elimination* of the beginning inventory and the *recording* of the ending inventory. The beginning inventory is cleared out of the Inventory account by a debit to Income Summary and a credit to Inventory. A separate entry could be made for this purpose, but we can save time by making one compound entry which will debit the Income Summary account with the balance of the beginning inventory and with the balances of all temporary proprietorship accounts having debit balances.

The *temporary proprietorship accounts* are those which appear in the income statement. As the name suggests, the temporary proprietorship accounts are used to accumulate temporarily the increases and decreases in the proprietor's equity resulting from operation of the business. The entry to close out the beginning inventory and temporary proprietorship accounts with debit balances is illustrated below. (For emphasis, the accounts unique to a merchandising business are shown in black.)

Closing temporary proprietorship accounts with debit balances	Dec. 31 Income Summary	647,000
	Inventory (Jan. 1)..	**60,000**
	Sales Returns and Allowances	**12,000**
	Sales Discounts	**5,000**
	Purchases	**367,000**
	Transportation-in	**13,000**
	Sales Salaries	74,000
	Advertising Expense.....................................	29,000
	Delivery Service	10,700
	Office Salaries	57,000
	Utilities Expense	3,100
	Interest Expense	8,200
	Depreciation Expense: Building	8,000
	To close out the beginning inventory and the temporary proprietorship accounts with debit balances.	

The preceding closing entry closes all the operating expense accounts, as well as the accounts used to accumulate the cost of goods sold. It also closes the accounts for Sales Returns and Allowances and for Sales Discounts. After this first closing entry, the Inventory account has a zero balance. Therefore, it is time to record in this account the new inventory of $70,000 determined by a physical count at December 31.

To bring the ending inventory into the accounting records after the stock-taking on December 31, we could make a separate entry debiting Inventory and crediting the Income Summary account. It is more convenient, however, to combine this step with the closing of the Sales account and any other temporary proprietorship accounts having credit balances, as illustrated in the following closing entry:

Closing temporary proprietorship accounts with credit balances	Dec. 31 Inventory (Dec. 31)	70,000	
	Sales	617,000	
	Purchase Returns and Allowances	6,700	
	Purchase Discounts	3,300	
	Income Summary		697,000
	To record the ending inventory and to close all temporary proprietorship accounts with credit balances.		

The remaining closing entries serve to transfer the balance of the Income Summary account to the owner's capital account and to close the drawing account, as follows:

Closing the Income Summary account and Owner's Drawing account

Dec. 31	Income Summary	50,000
	Robert Riley, Capital	50,000
	To close the Income Summary account.	
Dec. 31	Robert Riley, Capital	26,000
	Robert Riley, Drawing	26,000
	To close the drawing account.	

After the preceding four closing entries have been posted to the ledger, the only ledger accounts left with dollar balances will be balance sheet accounts. An after-closing trial balance should be prepared to prove that the ledger is in balance after the year-end entries to adjust and close the accounts have been recorded.

Summary of Merchandising Transactions and Related Accounting Entries

The transactions regularly encountered in merchandising operations and the related accounting entries may be concisely summarized as follows:

	ACCOUNTING ENTRIES	
TRANSACTIONS	DEBIT	CREDIT
Sell merchandise to customers	Cash (or Accounts Receivable)	Sales
Permit customers to return merchandise, or grant them a reduction from original price	Sales Returns & Allowances	Cash (or Accounts Receivable)
Collect account receivable within discount period	Cash; Sales Discounts	Accounts Receivable
Purchase merchandise for resale	Purchases	Cash (or Accounts Payable)
Incur transportation charges on merchandise purchased for resale	Transportation-in	Cash (or Accounts Payable)
Return unsatisfactory merchandise to supplier, or obtain a reduction from original price	Cash (or Accounts Payable)	Purchase Returns and Allowances
Pay for merchandise within discount period	Accounts Payable	Cash; Purchase Discounts

INVENTORY PROCEDURES AT END OF PERIOD		
Transfer the balance of the beginning inventory to the Income Summary account	Income Summary	Inventory
Take a physical inventory of goods on hand at the end of the period, and price these goods at cost	Inventory	Income Summary

Sales Taxes

Sales taxes are levied by many states and cities on retail sales. Sales taxes actually are imposed upon the consumer, not upon the seller. However, the seller must collect the tax, file tax returns at times specified by law, and remit the taxes collected on all reported sales.

For cash sales, sales tax is collected from the customer at the time of the sales transaction. For credit sales, the sales tax is included in the amount charged to the customer's account. The liability to the governmental unit for sales taxes may be recorded at the time the sale is made as shown in the following journal entry:

Sales tax recorded at time of sale

Accounts Receivable (or Cash)...	1,050	
Sales Tax Payable		50
Sales		1,000

To record sales of $1,000 subject to 5% sales tax.

This approach requires a separate credit entry to the Sales Tax Payable account for each sale. At first glance, this may seem to require an excessive amount of bookkeeping. However, today's electronic cash registers can be programmed to record automatically the sales tax liability at the time of each sale.

■ **An Alternative Approach to Sales Taxes** Instead of recording the sales tax liability at the time of sale, some businesses prefer to credit the Sales account with the entire amount collected, including the sales tax, and to make an adjustment at the end of each period to reflect sales tax payable. For example, suppose that the total recorded sales for the period under this method were $315,000. Since the Sales account includes both the sales price and the sales tax (say, 5%), it is apparent that $315,000 is *105%* of the actual sales figure. Actual sales are $300,000 (computed $315,000 ÷ 1.05) and the amount of sales tax due is $15,000. (Proof: 5% of $300,000 = $15,000.) The entry to record the liability for sales taxes would be

Sales tax recorded as adjustment of sales

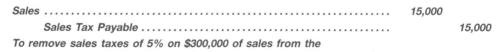

Sales	15,000	
Sales Tax Payable		15,000

To remove sales taxes of 5% on $300,000 of sales from the Sales account, and record as a liability.

This second approach is widely used in businesses which do not use electronic devices for recording each sales transaction.

If some of the products being sold are not subject to sales tax (such as food), the business must keep separate records of taxable and nontaxable sales.

Perpetual Inventory Systems

Objective 6
Distinguish between the periodic and the perpetual inventory systems.

In this chapter, we have emphasized the *periodic inventory system* as a means of valuing inventories and determining the cost of goods sold. Under this system, the amount of inventory is determined at the end of each accounting period by a physical count, and the cost of goods sold is determined by a computation. This system is in widespread use, especially by businesses that sell products of relatively low unit cost.

The *perpetual inventory system* provides a sharp contrast to the periodic inventory system. Under the perpetual inventory system, the Inventory account is kept continuously up-to-date; hence the name, *perpetual* inventory system. Under this system, a ledger account also is maintained showing the cost of goods sold during the period. The Inventory account is debited whenever merchandise is purchased. When merchandise is sold, two entries are made. The first entry records the sales revenue (debit Cash or Accounts Receivable, credit Sales). The second entry reduces the balance of the Inventory account *and records the cost of goods sold* (debit the Cost of Goods Sold account, credit Inventory).

Traditionally, the perpetual inventory system has been used by companies selling items of *high unit value,* such as automobiles, computers, or furniture. These businesses have relatively few sales transactions each day; thus, recording the cost of each sale is an easy matter.

In a business that sells large quantities of low cost merchandise, recording the cost of each sales transaction is not feasible without a computerized system. Therefore, businesses such as grocery stores, department stores, and most small retailers traditionally used the periodic inventory system. Today, however, "point-of-sale" computer terminals make it possible for almost every merchandising company to maintain a perpetual inventory system.

CASE IN POINT ■ A large supermarket may sell between 5,000 and 10,000 items per hour, each with a relatively low unit cost. Clearly, it would be impossible for clerks to look up and record the cost of each item sold. Thus, grocery stores traditionally have used the periodic inventory system. Now, however, electronic cash registers are able to read "product codes" (a pattern of thick and thin vertical bars) printed on each product. These product codes enable a computer to identify each item being sold, to record the sale, and to update perpetual inventory records and the cost of goods sold.

In summary, a perpetual inventory system is suited for use by businesses that (1) have a relatively low number of daily sales transactions, or (2) use point-of-sale computer terminals to determine and record the cost of each sale. Perpetual inventory systems are discussed further in Chapter 9.

Classified Financial Statements

Objective 7
Prepare a classified balance sheet and either a single-step or multiple-step income statement.

The financial statements illustrated up to this point have been rather short and simple because of the limited number of accounts used in these introductory chapters. Now let us look briefly at a more comprehensive balance sheet for a merchandising business.

In the balance sheet of Graham Company illustrated on the next page, the assets are classified into three groups: (1) current assets, (2) plant and equipment, and (3) other assets. The liabilities are classified into two types: (1) current liabilities and (2) long-term liabilities. This classification of assets and liabilities is virtually a standard one throughout American business.

The Purpose of Balance Sheet Classification

The purpose underlying a standard classification of assets and liabilities is to aid management, owners, creditors, and other interested persons in understanding the financial position of the business. Standard practices as to the order and arrangement of a balance sheet are a means of saving the time of the reader and of giving a clearer picture of the company's financial position.

■ **Current Assets** Current assets include cash, government bonds and other marketable securities, receivables, inventories, and prepaid expenses. To qualify for inclusion in the current asset category, an asset must be capable of being converted into cash within a relatively short period without interfering with the normal operation of the business. The period is usually one year, but it may be longer for businesses having an operating cycle in excess of one year.

GRAHAM COMPANY

Balance Sheet

December 31, 19___

ASSETS

Current assets:			
Cash			$ 25,000
Marketable securities			13,000
Notes receivable			30,000
Accounts receivable			70,000
Inventory			100,000
Prepaid expenses			12,000
Total current assets			$250,000
Plant and equipment:			
Land		$60,000	
Building	$140,000		
Less: Accumulated depreciation	56,000	84,000	
Store equipment	$ 24,000		
Less: Accumulated depreciation	18,000	6,000	
Delivery equipment	$ 19,000		
Less: Accumulated depreciation	10,000	9,000	
Total plant and equipment			159,000
Other assets:			
Land (future building site)			125,000
Total assets			$534,000

LIABILITIES & OWNER'S EQUITY

Current liabilities:		
Notes payable (due in 6 months)		$ 15,000
Accounts payable		59,900
Accrued expenses payable		14,100
Unearned revenue		11,000
Total current liabilities		$100,000
Long-term liabilities:		
Mortgage payable (due in 10 years)		181,000
Total liabilities		$281,000
Owner's equity:		
George Graham, capital		253,000
Total liabilities & owner's equity		$534,000

The term *operating cycle* means the average time period between the purchase of merchandise and the conversion of this merchandise back into cash. The series of transactions comprising a complete cycle often runs as follows: (1) purchase of merchandise, (2) sale of the merchandise on credit, (3) collection of the account receivable from the customer. The word *cycle* suggests the circular flow of capital from cash to inventory to receivables and back into cash again. This cycle of transactions in a merchandising business is portrayed in the following diagram:

The operating cycle repeats continuously

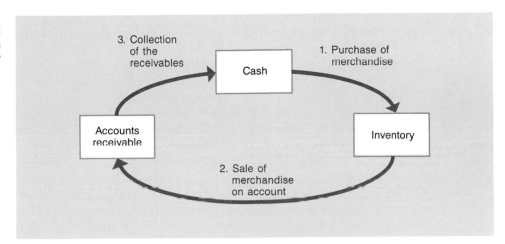

In a business handling fast-moving merchandise (a supermarket, for example) the operating cycle may be completed in a few weeks; for most merchandising businesses the operating cycle requires several months but less than a year.

Current assets are listed in order of liquidity; the closer an asset is to becoming cash the higher is its liquidity. The total amount of a company's current assets and the relative amount of each type give some indication of the company's short-run, debt-paying ability.

■ **Current Liabilities** Liabilities that must be paid within one year or the operating cycle (whichever is longer) are called *current liabilities.* Among the more common types of current liabilities are notes payable, accounts payable, taxes payable, salaries payable, interest payable, and unearned revenue. Notes payable are usually listed first, followed by accounts payable; any sequence of listing is acceptable for other current liabilities.

Settlement of most types of current liabilities requires writing a check to the creditor; in other words, use of the current asset cash. A somewhat different procedure for settlement is followed for the current liability of unearned revenue. As explained in Chapter 4, unearned revenue is a liability which arises when money is received from customers in advance for goods or services to be delivered in the future. To meet such obligations usually will require using up current assets either through delivering merchandise to the customer or making payments to employees or others to provide the agreed services.

The key point to recognize is the relationship between current liabilities and current assets. Current liabilities must be paid in the near future and current assets must be available to make these payments. Comparison of the amount of current liabilities with the amount of current assets is an important step in evaluating the ability of a company to pay its debts in the near future.

Objective 8
Explain the purpose of the current ratio and the meaning of working capital.

■ **Current Ratio** Many bankers and other users of financial statements believe that for a business to qualify as a good credit risk, the total current assets should be about twice as large as the total current liabilities. In studying a balance sheet, a banker or other creditor will compute the *current ratio* by dividing total current assets by total current liabilities. The current ratio is a convenient measure of the short-run debt-paying ability of a business.

In the illustrated balance sheet of Graham Company, the current assets of $250,000 are two and one-half times as great as the current liabilities of $100,000; the current ratio is therefore 2½ to 1, which would generally be regarded as a strong current position. The current assets could shrink substantially and still be sufficient for payment of the current liabilities. Although a strong current ratio is desirable, an extremely high current ratio (such as 4 to 1 or more) may signify that a company is holding too much of its resources in cash, marketable securities, and other current assets and is not pursuing opportunities for growth as aggressively as it might.

■ **Working Capital** The excess of current assets over current liabilities is called *working capital;* the relative amount of working capital is another indication of short-term financial strength. In the illustrated balance sheet of Graham Company, working capital is $150,000, computed by subtracting the current liabilities of $100,000 from the current assets of $250,000. The importance of *solvency* (ability to meet debts as they fall due) was emphasized in Chapter 1. Ample working capital permits a company to meet its short-term obligations, to qualify for favorable credit terms, and to take advantage of opportunities quickly. Many companies have been forced to suspend business because of inadequate working capital, even though total assets were much larger than total liabilities.

Classification and Format of Income Statements

There are two common forms of income statements: the *multiple-step income statement* and the *single-step income statement.* The multiple-step statement is more convenient in illustrating accounting principles and has been used consistently in our illustrations thus far. The income statement for Olympic Sporting Goods on page 190 is in multiple-step form. It is also a *classified* income statement because the various items of expense are classified into significant groups. The single-step form of income statement is illustrated on page 203.

■ **Multiple-Step Income Statement** The multiple-step income statement is so named because of the series of steps in which costs and expenses are deducted from revenue. As a first step, the cost of goods sold is subtracted from net sales to produce a subtotal for gross profit on sales. As a second step, operating expenses are deducted to obtain another subtotal called income from operations. As a final step, nonoperating revenue is added and nonoperating expenses are deducted to arrive at net income.

Variations may exist in the format of multiple-step income statements. For example, if a business has no nonoperating items, the subtotal for income from operations will not appear. Also, management may elect not to classify operating expenses into subcategories such as selling expenses and general and administrative expenses.

The multiple-step income statement is noted for its numerous sections and significant subtotals. These sections and subtotals assist managers in identifying important trends in various types of business activities. Therefore, the multiple-step format is widely used in small businesses and for the monthly (interim) income statements used by the managers of large businesses.

■ **Single-Step Income Statement** The income statements prepared by large corporations for distribution to thousands of stockholders often are greatly condensed because the public presumably is more interested in a concise report than in the details of operations. The single-step form of income statement takes its name from the fact that the total of all expenses (including the cost of goods sold) is deducted from total revenue in a single step. All types of revenue, such as sales, interest earned, and rent revenue, are added together to show the total revenue. Then all expenses are grouped together and deducted in one step without developing subtotals. A condensed income statement in single-step form is shown below for National Corporation, a large merchandising company.

NATIONAL CORPORATION
Income Statement
For the Year Ended December 31, 19__

■
Condensed single-step income statement

Revenue:		
Net sales		$90,000,000
Interest earned		1,800,000
Total revenue		$91,800,000
Expenses:		
Cost of goods sold	$60,000,000	
Selling expenses	10,200,000	
General & administrative expenses	9,750,000	
Interest expense	4,200,000	
Income taxes expense	3,150,000	
Total expenses		87,300,000
Net income		$ 4,500,000

Use of the single-step income statement has increased in recent years, perhaps because it is relatively simple and easy to read. A disadvantage of this format is that useful concepts such as the gross profit on sales are not readily apparent.

End-of-Chapter Review

CONCEPTS INTRODUCED OR EMPHASIZED IN CHAPTER 5

The major concepts in this chapter include:

■ Accounting for sales of merchandise, sales returns and allowances, and sales discounts.

■ Determining the cost of goods sold under the periodic inventory system.

■ Distinctive features of an income statement for a merchandising company.

■ Factors to be considered in evaluating the adequacy of a company's net income.

■ Perpetual inventory system—impact of computers.

■ Current assets, current liabilities, current ratio, and working capital as indicators of short-run, debt-paying ability.

In Chapter 5 your knowledge of accounting concepts and practices has been expanded to include the purchase and sale of merchandise. You are now familiar with all the steps in the accounting cycle for both service-type businesses and for merchandising companies. In addition you have made some important first steps toward proficiency in analyzing and interpreting financial statements. In the next chapter we will continue our discussion of merchandising transactions with emphasis on internal control and upon streamlining the accounting system to process efficiently a large volume of transactions.

KEY TERMS INTRODUCED OR EMPHASIZED IN CHAPTER 5

Cost of goods sold   A computation appearing as a separate section of an income statement showing the cost of goods sold during the period. Computed by adding net delivered cost of merchandise purchases to beginning inventory to obtain cost of goods available for sale, and then deducting from this total the amount of the ending inventory.

Current assets   Cash and other assets that can be converted into cash within one year or the operating cycle (whichever is longer) without interfering with the normal operation of the business.

Current liabilities   Liabilities that must be paid within one year or the operating cycle (whichever is longer). Among the most common are notes payable, accounts payable, taxes payable, salaries payable, interest payable, and unearned revenue.

Current ratio   Current assets divided by current liabilities. A measure of short-run debt-paying ability.

Gross profit on sales   Revenue from sales minus cost of goods sold.

Gross profit rate   Gross profit expressed as a percentage of net sales. Usually between 30% and 50% of net sales.

Inventory shrinkage   The loss of merchandise through such causes as shoplifting, employee theft, breakage, and spoilage. Under the periodic inventory system, losses from inventory shrinkage automatically are included in the cost of goods sold.

Multiple-step income statement   An income statement in which cost of goods sold and expenses are subtracted from revenue in a series of steps, thus producing significant subtotals prior to net income.

Net sales   Gross sales revenue minus sales returns and allowances and minus sales discounts.

Operating cycle   The average time period from the purchase of merchandise to its sale and conversion back into cash.

Periodic inventory system   A system of accounting for merchandise in which inventory at the balance sheet date is determined by counting and pricing the goods on hand. Cost of goods sold is computed by subtracting the ending inventory from the cost of goods available for sale.

Perpetual inventory system A system of accounting for merchandise that provides a continuous record showing the quantity and cost of all goods on hand.

Single-step income statement An income statement in which the cost of goods sold and all expenses are combined and deducted from total revenue in a single step to determine net income.

Working capital Current assets minus current liabilities. A measure of short-run debt-paying ability.

DEMONSTRATION PROBLEM FOR YOUR REVIEW

Ski America sells a wide variety of products and uses the periodic inventory method. During October, the company engaged in the following merchandising transactions. Terms of 2/10, n/30 are offered on all credit sales.

Oct. 3 Sold merchandise left over from last season to Freight Liquidators for $32,880 cash.

Oct. 9 Sold merchandise on account to Matterhorn Lodge, $24,820.

Oct. 12 Matterhorn Lodge returned $420 of the merchandise purchased on Oct. 9. Full credit was given to Matterhorn for this return.

Oct. 16 Purchased merchandise on account from Sports Fashions for $18,900; terms, 2/10, n/30.

Oct. 17 Paid freight charges on shipment received from Sports Fashions, $126.

Oct. 19 Received a check for $23,912 from Matterhorn Lodge in full settlement of the Oct. 9 sale, less the return on Oct. 12 and the allowable sales discount.

Oct. 22 Purchased merchandise on account from Outdoor Products, $17,100; terms, 5/10, n/60.

Oct. 24 Returned defective goods costing $900 to Outdoor Products. Received full credit on our account.

Oct. 26 Paid Sports Fashions for the purchase on Oct. 16, less 2%.

Instructions **a** Prepare journal entries to record these transactions.

b Prepare a partial income statement for October, showing the accounts included in computing net sales, the cost of goods sold, and gross profit. Assume that inventory was $31,400 on September 30, and $33,920 on October 31.

SOLUTION TO DEMONSTRATION PROBLEM

a   GENERAL JOURNAL

Oct	3	Cash...	32,880	
		Sales		32,880
		To record the sale of merchandise for cash.		
	9	Accounts Receivable	24,820	
		Sales		24,820
		To record sale to Matterhorn Lodge.		
	12	Sales Returns & Allowances	420	
		Accounts Receivable		420
		Gave credit to Matterhorn Lodge for merchandise returned.		

a   GENERAL JOURNAL

16	Purchases	18,900	
	Accounts Payable		18,900
	To record purchase from Sports Fashions, terms 2/10, n/30.		
17	Transportation-In	126	
	Cash..		126
	Paid transportation charges on goods purchased from Sports Fashions.		
19	Cash..	23,912	
	Sales Discounts	488	
	Accounts Receivable		24,400
	Collected from Matterhorn Lodge for our Oct. 9 sale, $24,820 less return of $420 and 2% discount on balance of $24,400.		
22	Purchases	17,100	
	Accounts Payable		17,100
	To record purchase from Outdoor Products, terms 5/10, n/60.		
24	Accounts Payable	900	
	Purchase Returns & Allowances...............		900
	Returned portion of Oct. 22 purchase from Outdoor Products because goods were defective.		
26	Accounts Payable	18,900	
	Purchase Discounts		378
	Cash..		18,522
	Paid Oct. 16 purchase invoice from Sports Fashions, less 2% discount.		

b

SKI AMERICA
Partial Income Statement
For the Month Ended October 31, 19__

Revenue:			
Sales			$57,700
Less: Sales returns and allowances		$ 420	
Sales discounts		488	908
Net sales			$56,792
Cost of goods sold:			
Inventory, Sept. 30		$31,400	
Purchases	$36,000		
Less: Purchase returns and allowances	$900		
Purchase discounts........................	378	1,278	
Net purchases	$34,722		
Add: Transportation-in	126		
Delivered cost of purchases		34,848	
Cost of goods available for sale......................................		$66,248	
Less: Inventory, Oct. 31..		33,920	
Cost of goods sold			32,328
Gross profit on sales			$24,464

SELF-TEST QUESTIONS

Answers to these questions appear on page 219.

1 A distinguishing characteristic of the financial statements for a merchandising concern is that:

a The balance sheet shows a subtotal for working capital.

b The income statement discloses the amount of cash paid for merchandise, net of any purchase discounts or returns.

c The income statement includes an amount for the cost of goods sold.

d The income statement must be prepared in the multiple-step format.

2 The accounting records of Fabric Outlet include the following for January:

Sales......................	$326,000	Transportation-in	$2,000
Purchases	260,000	Purchase Returns &	
Sales Discounts	6,000	Allowances....................	9,000

A physical count determined the cost of inventory on hand at January 31 to be $34,000. If gross profit amounts to 25% of net sales, compute the beginning inventory at January 1.

a $25,500   **b** $19,500   **c** $47,000   **d** $21,000

3 The closing entries for a merchandising company using a periodic inventory system would not include:

a A debit to Inventory (ending).

b A debit to Transportation-in.

c A credit to Purchases.

d A credit to Inventory (beginning).

4 When a perpetual inventory system is in use:

a The Inventory ledger account does not reflect the amount of merchandise on hand between financial statement dates.

b The ending inventory figure is more accurate than when a periodic inventory system is in use.

c A single ledger account is used to record the cost of goods sold.

d There is no need to perform a physical count of inventory.

5 Pisces Market presently has current assets totaling $300,000 and a current ratio of 2½ to 1. Compute the current ratio if Pisces Market pays off $30,000 of its accounts payable.

    a 3 to 1   **b** 3.33 to 1   **c** 2.2 to 1   **d** 2.25 to 1

Assignment Material

REVIEW QUESTIONS

1 During the current year, Green Bay Company made all sales of merchandise at prices in excess of cost. Will the business necessarily report a net income for the year? Explain.

2 Thornhill Company's income statement showed gross profit on sales of $432,000, operating expenses of $390,000, and cost of goods sold of $648,000. Compute the amount of net sales.

3 During its first year of operations Meadowland Market reported cost of goods sold of $672,000 and a gross profit equal to 40% of net sales. What was the dollar amount of net sales for the year?

4 Is the normal balance of the Sales Returns and Allowances account a debit or a credit? Is the normal balance of the Purchase Returns and Allowances account a debit or a credit?

5 Supply the proper terms to complete the following statements:

    a Net sales − cost of goods sold = __?__

    b Beginning inventory + purchases − purchase returns and allowances − purchase discounts + transportation-in = __?__

    c Cost of goods sold + ending inventory = __?__

    d Cost of goods sold + gross profit on sales = __?__

    e Net income + operating expenses = __?__

6 During the current year Broomfirth Corporation purchased merchandise with a cost of $600,000. State the cost of goods sold under each of the following alternative assumptions:

    a No beginning inventory; ending inventory $120,000

    b Beginning inventory $180,000; no ending inventory

    c Beginning inventory $174,000; ending inventory $234,000

    d Beginning inventory $270,000; ending inventory $201,000

7 Dell Labs purchased merchandise on account from Vita Products for $27,000, on terms of 2/10, n/30. Within the discount period, Dell Labs returned some of the merchandise and paid $19,600 in full settlement of the account. What was the cost of the merchandise returned by Dell Labs? Explain your reasoning.

8 Zenith Company uses the periodic inventory system and maintains its accounting records on a calendar-year basis. Does the beginning or the ending inventory figure appear in the trial balance prepared from the ledger on December 31?

9 Compute the amount of cost of goods sold, given the following account balances: beginning inventory $48,000, purchases $100,800, purchase returns and allowances $5,400, purchase discounts $1,800, transportation-in $1,200, and ending inventory $43,200.

10 In which columns of the work sheet for a merchandising company does the ending inventory appear?

11 State briefly the difference between the *perpetual* inventory system and the *periodic* inventory system.

12 When the periodic inventory method is in use, how is the amount of inventory determined at the end of the period?

13 What is the purpose of a closing entry consisting of a debit to the Income Summary account and a credit to the Inventory account?

14 Tireco is a retail store in a state that imposes a 5% sales tax. Would you expect to find an account entitled Sales Tax Expense and another account entitled Sales Tax Payable in Tireco's ledger? Explain your answer.

15 Explain the terms *current assets, current liabilities,* and *current ratio.*

16 Madison Corporation has current assets of $570,000 and current liabilities of $300,000. Compute the current ratio and the amount of working capital.

17 Barnes Imports has a current ratio of 3 to 1 and working capital of $60,000. What are the amounts of current assets and current liabilities?

18 Three items appearing in the annual income statement of Fashion House are: total operating expenses, $300,000; gross profit, $470,000; and income taxes expense, $50,000. Did Fashion House prepare a single-step or multiple-step income statement? Explain.

Now assume that Fashion House had prepared the *other type* of income statement. What would have been the amount of net income shown in the statement?

EXERCISES

Exercise 5-1
Accounting
terminology

Listed below are nine technical accounting terms introduced in this chapter:

Cost of goods available for sale	Periodic inventory system	Perpetual inventory system
Cost of goods sold	Gross profit on sales	Working capital
Purchase discount	Inventory	Current ratio

Each of the following statements may (or may not) describe one of these technical terms. For each statement, indicate the accounting term described, or answer "None" if the statement does not correctly describe any of the terms.

a Goods acquired and held for sale to customers.

b Current assets minus current liabilities.

c A reduction in revenue resulting from allowing a reduction in sales price to a customer whose purchases received slight damage during delivery.

d Accounting procedures which involve taking a physical inventory in order to determine the amount of inventory and the cost of goods sold.

e Net sales minus the cost of goods sold.

f Beginning inventory plus the delivered cost of net purchases.

g Beginning inventory minus gross profit.

**Exercise 5-2
Accounting for purchases and sales of merchandise**

Key Imports sold merchandise to Marine Systems for $75,000, terms 2/10, n/30. Marine Systems paid for the merchandise within the discount period.

a Prepare the journal entries by Key Imports to record the sale and the subsequent collection.

b Prepare the journal entries by Marine Systems to record the purchase and the subsequent payment.

**Exercise 5-3
Relationships among merchandising accounts**

The income statement of Magic Interiors included the items listed below.

Net sales	$600,000
Gross profit on sales	240,000
Beginning inventory	45,000
Purchase discounts	1,500
Purchase returns & allowances	6,000
Transportation-in	9,000
Operating expenses	120,000
Purchases	375,000

Use the appropriate items from this list as a basis for computing (a) the cost of goods sold, (b) the cost of goods available for sale, and (c) the ending inventory.

**Exercise 5-4
Income statement relationships in a merchandising business**

This exercise stresses the sequence and relationship of items in a multiple-step income statement for a merchandising business. Each of the five horizontal lines in the table represents a separate set of income statement items. You are to copy the table and fill in the missing amounts. A net loss in the right-hand column is to be indicated by placing brackets before and after the amount, as for example, in line e (25,000).

	NET SALES	BEGIN-NING INVENTORY	NET PURCHASES	ENDING INVENTORY	COST OF GOODS SOLD	GROSS PROFIT	EXPENSES	NET INCOME OR (LOSS)
a	300,000	95,000	130,000	44,000	?	119,000	90,000	?
b	600,000	90,000	340,000	?	330,000	?	?	25,000
c	700,000	230,000	?	185,000	490,000	210,000	165,000	?
d	900,000	?	500,000	150,000	?	260,000	300,000	?
e	?	260,000	?	255,000	660,000	225,000	?	(25,000)

**Exercise 5-5
Preparing closing entries from a worksheet**

The accountant for Village Ski Shop prepared a work sheet for the year ended December 31, 19__. Shown below are the Income Statement columns from that work sheet. During the year, Greta Lynn, owner of Village Ski Shop, withdrew assets of $22,000 from the business. Using this information, prepare four separate journal entries to close the accounts at December 31. Use the sequence of closing entries illustrated in this chapter.

Test

Do

	INCOME STATEMENT	
	DEBIT	CREDIT
Inventory, ~~Jan. 1~~	90,000	*81,000*
Sales		420,350
Sales returns & allowances	8,700	
Sales discounts	2,650	
Purchases	275,000	
Purchase returns & allowances		3,200
Purchase discounts		5,100
Transportation-in	4,300	
Selling expenses	48,000	
General and administrative expenses...........................	36,000	
Interest expense	7,000	
~~Inventory, Dec. 31~~		~~81,000~~
	471,650	509,650
Net income	38,000	
	509,650	509,650

Exercise 5-6
Multiple-step and
single-step
income
statements

Use the data from the Village Ski Shop work sheet in Exercise 5-5 to prepare:

a A multiple-step income statement in as much detail as the work sheet data will allow.

b A single-step income statement in condensed form. "Condensed form" means that net sales and the cost of goods sold will each be shown as a single amount, without showing the individual account balances which are used to compute these subtotals.

Exercise 5-7
Accounting for
sales taxes

Trophy Shop operates in an area in which a 5% sales tax is levied on all products handled by the store. On cash sales, the salesclerks include the sales tax in the amount collected from the customer and ring up the entire amount on the cash register without recording separately the tax liability. On credit sales, the customer is charged for the list price of the merchandise plus 5%, and the entire amount is debited to Accounts Receivable and credited to the Sales account. On sales of less than one dollar, the tax collected is rounded to the nearest cent.

Sales tax must be remitted to the government quarterly. At March 31 the Sales account showed a balance of $326,025 for the three-month period ended March 31.

a What amount of sales tax is owed at March 31?

b Give the journal entry to record the sales tax liability on the books.

Exercise 5-8
A quick look at
IBM's current
position

A recent balance sheet of IBM contained the following items among others. (Note: All amounts are stated in millions; thus Inventories of $8,645 may be read as 8 billion, 645 million.)

Cash..	$ 770
Investment in marketable securities (current asset)............................	6,197
Notes & accounts receivable (net)...	12,757
Other current receivables...	1,092
Inventories..	8,645
Prepaid expenses and other current assets......................................	1,559
Plant & other property (net of depreciation)....................................	20,082
Accounts payable	2,627
Loans payable (short term)	1,629
Taxes payable..	2,534
Other current liabilities	6,587
Long-term debt	3,858
Stockholders' equity...	38,263

Instructions

a From the above information, compute the amount of IBM's current assets and the amount of its current liabilities.

b How much working capital does IBM have?

c Compute the current ratio to the nearest tenth of a percent.

PROBLEMS

Group A

**Problem 5A-1
Recording
merchandising
transactions**

Westside Office Supply uses the periodic inventory system. A partial list of the company's transactions during July appears below.

July 5 Purchased merchandise on credit from Hayes Paper for $14,800. Terms, 2/10, n/30.

July 6 Paid inbound transportation charge of $120 on merchandise purchased from Hayes Paper on July 5.

July 7 Sold merchandise for cash, $1,120.

July 10 Sold merchandise on credit to Conway Realtors, $2,875. Terms, net 30 days.

July 10 Paid $72 freight charge on the outbound shipment of merchandise to Conway Realtors.

July 10 Found that some items of the merchandise received from Hayes Paper did not meet specifications. Returned these items to Hayes Paper and received full credit of $900.

July 12 Paid Hayes Paper Co. within discount period the remaining amount for the purchase of July 5 after allowing for the purchase return on July 10.

July 18 Sold merchandise on account to Meadowland Products for $2,800. Terms, 2/10, n/30.

July 19 Agreed to reduce the price $200 on merchandise sold to Meadowland Products on July 14, because of slight defects in the merchandise.

July 28 Received check from Meadowland Products within discount period in payment for transaction of July 18. Customer took discount on balance remaining after $200 allowance on July 19.

Instructions

Prepare a separate journal entry including an explanation for each of the July transactions listed above.

**Problem 5A-2
Preparing closing
entries and an
income statement**

The accounts listed below pertain to the income of Sonoma Distributors for the year ended December 31, 19___.

Sales	$1,500,000	Purchase discounts	$ 18,600
Sales returns &		Transportation-in...............	2,700
allowances.................	45,000	Inventory, Jan. 1	510,000
Sales discounts	23,400	Inventory, Dec. 31..............	492,300
Purchases	930,000	Operating expenses............	396,000
Purchase returns		Interest expense	77,100
& allowances..............	13,500		

Instructions

a Compute the amount of net sales for the year.

b Compute the cost of goods sold.

c Prepare a *condensed* multiple-step income statement. Show both net sales and the cost of goods sold as "one-line items," without showing the accounts used to compute these amounts. Interest expense should be shown after determining Income from Operations.

d Prepare closing entries for the year ended December 31. Only three closing entries are required, as the owner, Angel Cordero, made no withdrawals during the year.

Problem 5A-3
Preparing a work
sheet and
adjusting and
closing entries

A four-column schedule consisting of the first four columns of a 10-column work sheet for Marine Supplies appears below.

MARINE SUPPLIES
Work Sheet
For the Year Ended December 31, 19__

	TRIAL BALANCE		ADJUSTMENTS	
	DEBIT	CREDIT	DEBIT	CREDIT
Cash..	7,600			
Accounts receivable	19,500			
Inventory, Jan. 1	60,000			
Unexpired insurance........................	4,400			(b) 3,400
Equipment	22,000			
Accumulated depreciation:				
equipment		5,700		(a) 1,900
Accounts payable		20,400		
Anne Barr, Capital..........................		88,400		
Anne Barr, Drawing.........................	20,000			
Sales		529,000		
Sales returns & allowances	21,000			
Sales discounts	8,000			
Purchases	368,000			
Purchase returns & allowances		18,000		
Purchase discounts		6,000		
Transportation-in	12,000			
Advertising expense	32,000			
Rent expense	25,000			
Salaries expense	68,000			
	667,500	667,500		
Depreciation expense........................			(a) 1,900	
Insurance expense			(b) 3,400	
			5,300	5,300

The completed Adjustments columns have been included in the work sheet to minimize the detail work involved. These adjustments were derived from the following information available at December 31.

(a) Depreciation expense for the year on equipment, $1,900.

(b) Insurance premiums expired during the year, $3,400.

A physical inventory taken at December 31 showed the ending inventory to be $66,000.

Instructions   **a**   Prepare a 10-column work sheet following the format illustrated on page 193. Include at the bottom of the work sheet a legend consisting of a brief explanation keyed to each adjusting entry.

b   Prepare the two journal entries needed to adjust the accounts at December 31.

c   Prepare the necessary journal entries to close the accounts on December 31. Use four separate closing entries.

Problem 5A-4
Preparing a work
sheet, financial
statements, and
closing entries

The trial balance below was prepared from the ledger of Jessop's Boots & Saddles at December 31. The company maintains its accounts on a calendar-year basis and closes the accounts only once a year. The periodic inventory system is in use.

JESSOP'S BOOTS & SADDLES
Trial Balance
December 31, 19___

Cash..	$ 15,000	
Accounts receivable	76,000	
Inventory, Jan. 1	140,000	
Unexpired insurance..	4,000	
Office supplies	1,800	
Land..	35,000	
Buildings..	100,000	
Accumulated depreciation: buildings		$ 40,000
Notes payable..		80,000
Accounts payable		60,000
Tom Jessop, capital		119,800
Tom Jessop, drawing...	26,000	
Sales		633,000
Sales returns and allowances	42,000	
Sales discounts	16,000	
Purchases	381,000	
Purchase returns and allowances		23,000
Purchase discounts		8,000
Transportation-in	10,000	
Advertising expense	25,000	
Salaries expense	85,000	
Utilities expense..	7,000	
Totals..	$963,800	$963,800

Other Data   **(a)** *Unexpired* insurance at the end of the year amounted to $1,500.

(b) The buildings are being depreciated over a 25-year life.

(c) Office supplies unused and on hand at year-end amounted to $800, indicating that supplies costing $1,000 had been consumed.

(d) A physical inventory of merchandise at December 31, showed goods on hand of $120,000.

Instructions **a** Prepare a 10-column work sheet at December 31. Use the format illustrated on page 193.

b Prepare an income statement, a statement of owner's equity, and a *classified* balance sheet. The operating expenses need not be subdivided.

c Prepare adjusting entries and closing entries.

Problem 5A-5
Computing
current ratio and
working capital;
evaluating
solvency

A partial list of year-end account balances for Torino Products appears below.

Salaries payable...	$ 2,560
Accumulated depreciation: delivery equipment.................................	6,300
Inventory..	131,425
Cash..	21,210
Land..	95,000
Furniture & fixtures..	11,200
Mortgage payable (due in 20 years)	249,600
Anne Redgrave, capital	212,320
Delivery equipment	31,500
Interest payable	1,600
Advance payments from customers	5,760
Notes payable (due in 90 days)..	20,000
Marketable securities...	20,000
Accounts receivable	90,540
Accounts payable	75,430
Interest receivable...	200

Instructions **a** Prepare a partial balance sheet for Torino Products consisting of the current asset section and the current liability section *only*. Select the appropriate items from the above list.

b Compute the current ratio and the amount of working capital. Explain how each of these measurements is computed. State with reasons whether you consider the company to be in a strong or weak current position.

Group B

Problem 5B-1
Recording
merchandising
transactions

Apex Supply sells on a variety of credit terms to various customers and also makes sales for cash. The periodic inventory system is in use. The following transactions among others were completed in January.

Jan. 2 Sold merchandise on credit to Cable, Inc., $16,000. Terms, 2/10, n/30.

Jan. 4 Sold merchandise to Tucker Company on credit, $1,200. Terms, net 30.

Jan. 6 Paid transportation charges on shipment to Tucker Company, $375.

Jan. 12 Received check for $15,680 from Cable, Inc., as settlement within discount period for goods sold them on Jan. 2.

Jan. 14 Permitted Tucker Company to return for credit $630 of the merchandise purchased on Jan. 4 (no reduction in the transportation charges paid on Jan. 6).

Jan. 16 Refunded $390 to a customer who had made a prior cash purchase.

Jan. 20 Purchased merchandise from Selzer Company on credit, $15,000. Terms 2/10, n/30.

Jan. 21 Paid by check $240 in transportation charges on merchandise purchased from Selzer Company.

Jan. 23 Returned for credit of $1,000 merchandise purchased from Selzer Company (no reduction was allowed with respect to the transportation charges paid Jan. 21).

Jan. 30   Made payment within discount period to Selzer Company for merchandise purchased Jan. 20. (Note that a portion of the merchandise was returned for credit on Jan. 23.)

Instructions   Prepare a separate journal entry (including an explanation) for each of the above transactions.

Problem 5B-2
Preparing an income statement and closing entries

Listed below are the accounts relating to income of Leather Bandit for the year ended December 31, 19___.

Sales	$500,000	Transportation-in...........	$ 900
Sales returns & allowances	15,000	Inventory, Jan. 1, 19___	170,000
Sales discounts	7,800	Inventory, Dec. 31, 19___....	164,100
Purchases	310,000	Operating expenses........	121,400
Purchase returns & allowances	4,500	Interest expense	7,400
Purchase discounts	6,200		

Instructions   **a** Compute the amount of net sales for the year.

b Compute the cost of goods sold.

c Prepare a *condensed* multiple-step income statement. Show both net sales and the cost of goods sold as "one-line items," without showing the accounts used to compute these amounts. Interest expense should be shown after determining income from operations.

d Prepare closing entries for the year ended December 31, 19___. Only three closing entries are required as the owner, John Brown, made no withdrawals during the year.

Problem 5B-3
Preparing a work sheet and adjusting and closing entries

Westport Landing is a small company maintaining its accounts on a calendar-year basis and using a periodic inventory system. A four-column schedule consisting of the first four columns of a 10-column work sheet appears on the next page.

WESTPORT LANDING
Work Sheet
For the Year Ended December 31, 19___

	TRIAL BALANCE		ADJUSTMENTS	
	DEBIT	CREDIT	DEBIT	CREDIT
Cash..	6,400			
Accounts receivable	16,000			
Inventory, Jan. 1	60,000			
Unexpired insurance.........................	4,400			(b) 2,800
Equipment	22,000			
Accumulated depreciation: equipment........		6,600		(a) 2,200
Accounts payable		20,400		
Jane Hill, capital		83,800		
Jane Hill, drawing	21,000			
Sales		529,000		
Sales returns & allowances	21,000			
Sales discounts	8,000			
Purchases	368,000			
Purchase returns & allowances		18,000		
Purchase discounts		6,000		
Transportation-in	12,000			
Advertising expense	32,000			
Rent expense	25,000			
Salaries expense	68,000			
	663,800	663,800		
Depreciation expense........................			(a) 2,200	
Insurance expense			(b) 2,800	
			5,000	5,000

The completed Adjustments columns have been included in the work sheet to minimize the detail work involved. These adjustments were derived from the following information available at December 31.

(a) Depreciation expense for the year on equipment, $2,200.

(b) Insurance premiums expired during the year, $2,800.

A physical inventory taken at December 31 showed the ending inventory to be $66,000.

Instructions **a** Prepare a 10-column work sheet following the format illustrated on page 193. Include at the bottom of the work sheet a legend consisting of a brief explanation keyed to each adjusting entry.

b Prepare the two journal entries needed to adjust the accounts at December 31.

c Prepare the necessary journal entries to close the accounts on December 31.

Problem 5B-4
Preparing a work
sheet, financial
statements,
adjusting entries,
and closing
entries

Shown below is a trial balance prepared from the ledger of Western Supply at December 31, 19__. The accounts are maintained on a calendar-year basis and are adjusted and closed annually.

WESTERN SUPPLY
Trial Balance
December 31, 19__

Cash	$ 16,300	
Accounts receivable	49,200	
Inventory, Jan. 1, 19__	62,000	
Unexpired insurance	1,800	
Office supplies	800	
Land	17,000	
Buildings	60,000	
Accumulated depreciation: buildings		$ 2,400
Equipment	16,000	
Accumulated depreciation: equipment		4,800
Accounts payable		47,900
Mary Lane, capital		99,500
Mary Lane, drawing	18,000	
Sales		326,000
Sales returns & allowances	4,100	
Sales discounts	1,100	
Purchases	192,000	
Purchase returns & allowances		2,000
Purchase discounts		1,600
Transportation-in	4,800	
Salaries and wages expense	40,000	
Property taxes expense	1,100	
	$484,200	$484,200

Other Data

(a) Examination of policies showed $600 *unexpired* insurance on December 31.

(b) Supplies on hand at December 31 were estimated to amount to $300.

(c) The buildings are being depreciated over a 25-year useful life. The equipment is being depreciated over a 10-year useful life.

(d) Accrued salaries payable as of December 31 were $5,000.

(e) Inventory of merchandise on December 31 was $44,600.

Instructions

a Prepare a 10-column work sheet at December 31, 19__.

b Prepare an income statement, a statement of owner's equity, and a classified balance sheet.

c Prepare adjusting entries.

d Prepare closing entries.

Problem 5B-5
Computing
current ratio and
working capital;
evaluating
solvency

Some of the year-end ledger account balances of Mystic Gear are listed below.

Delivery equipment	$ 35,000
Interest payable	7,180
Advance payments from customers	3,320
Notes payable (due in 90 days)	62,000

Marketable securities	26,000
Accounts receivable	90,500
Accounts payable	37,340
Interest receivable	1,200
Inventory	105,580
Accumulated depreciation: delivery equipment	13,155
Salaries payable	2,560
Cash	24,000
Land	95,000
Furniture & fixtures	16,200
Mortgage payable (due in 20 years)	115,000
Buildings	290,000

Instructions   **a**   Prepare a partial balance sheet for Mystic Gear consisting of the current asset section and the current liability section *only.* Select the appropriate items from the above list.

b   Compute the current ratio and the amount of working capital. Explain how each of these measurements is computed. State with reasons whether you consider the company to be in a strong or weak current position.

BUSINESS DECISION CASE

Case 5-1
Hey, you! Put
that back!

Village Hardware is a retail store selling hardware, small appliances, and sporting goods. The business follows a policy of selling all merchandise at exactly twice the amount of its delivered cost to the store.

At year-end, the following information is taken from the accounting records:

Net sales	$500,000
Inventory, January 1	70,000
Delivered cost of purchases	255,000

A physical count indicates merchandise costing $64,000 on hand at December 31.

Instructions   **a**   Prepare a partial income statement showing computation of the gross profit for the year.

b   Upon seeing your income statement, the owner of the store makes the following comment. "Inventory shrinkage losses are really costing me. If it weren't for shrinkage losses, the store's gross profit would be 50% of net sales. I'm going to hire a security guard and put an end to shoplifting once and for all."

Determine the amount of loss from inventory "shrinkage" stated (1) at cost, and (2) at retail sales value. (Hint: Without any shrinkage losses, the cost of goods sold and the amount of gross profit would each amount to 50% of net sales.)

c   Assume that Village Hardware could virtually eliminate shoplifting by hiring a security guard at a cost of $1,500 per month. Would this strategy be profitable? Explain your reasoning.

ANSWERS TO SELF-TEST QUESTIONS

1 c   2 d   3 b   4 c   5 a

Internal Control and Accounting Systems

In the first part of Chapter 6, we explore the topic of internal control. After explaining the relationship between internal control and accounting, we discuss several methods of achieving strong internal control. These methods include the subdivision of duties, the use of various business documents, and the "net-price method" of recording merchandise purchases. In the second section of the chapter, we consider means of streamlining an accounting system to process a large volume of transactions. Special journals are illustrated and explained, along with subsidiary ledgers and controlling accounts. This discussion covers both manual and computer-based accounting systems.

After studying this chapter you should be able to meet these Learning Objectives:

1 Explain the purpose of a system of internal control.

2 Identify several specific measures useful in achieving strong internal control.

3 Explain the role of purchase orders and receiving reports in verifying a purchase invoice.

4 Describe the advantage of recording purchase invoices by the net-price method.

5 Explain the nature of special journals and the reasons for their use.

6 Use special journals to record credit sales, credit purchases, and cash transactions.

7 Explain the usefulness of a subsidiary ledger and its relationship to the controlling account in the general ledger.

8 Describe several advantages of a computer-based accounting system.

THE SYSTEM OF INTERNAL CONTROL

Objective 1
Explain the purpose of a system of internal control.

As defined in Chapter 1, a system of internal control includes all measures taken by an organization for the purposes of (1) protecting its resources against waste, fraud, or inefficient use, (2) ensuring the accuracy and reliability of accounting and operating data, (3) securing compliance with management's policies, and (4) evaluating the performance of all divisions of the company. In brief, the system of internal control includes all measures and procedures that enable an organization to operate in accordance with management's plans and policies.

Accounting Controls and Administrative Controls

Internal controls fall into two broad categories: accounting controls and administrative controls. *Accounting controls* are measures that relate directly to the protection of assets or to the reliability of accounting information. An example is the use of cash registers to create an immediate record of cash receipts. Another example is the policy of making an annual physical count of inventory even when a perpetual inventory system is in use.

Administrative controls are measures designed to increase operational efficiency; they have *no direct bearing* upon the reliability of the accounting records. An example of an administrative control is a requirement that traveling salespeople submit reports showing the names of customers called upon each day. Another example is the requirement that airline pilots have annual medical examinations.

In this textbook, we will emphasize *internal accounting controls*—those controls that have a *direct bearing* upon the reliability of accounting records, financial statements, and other accounting reports. Bear in mind, however, that sound administrative controls also play a vital role in the successful operation of a business.

Relationship between the Accounting System and the System of Internal Control

The primary objective of an accounting system is to provide useful financial information. The objective of the system of internal control is to keep the business "on track," operating in accordance with the policies and plans of management. These two systems are closely related; in fact, each depends greatly upon the other.

The accounting system depends upon internal control procedures to ensure the *reliability* of accounting data. Many internal control procedures, on the other hand, make use of accounting data in keeping track of assets and monitoring the performance of departments. The need for adequate internal control explains the nature and the very existence of many accounting records, reports, documents, and procedures. Thus, the topic of internal control and the study of accounting go hand-in-hand.

Objective 2
Identify several specific measures useful in achieving internal control.

Guidelines to Achieving Strong Internal Control

■ **Establish Clear Lines of Responsibility** Every organization should indicate clearly the persons or departments responsible for such functions as sales, purchasing, receiving incoming shipments, paying bills, and maintaining accounting records. The lines of authority and responsibility can be shown in an organization chart. (A partial organization chart is illustrated on the next page.) The organization chart should be supported by written job descriptions and by procedures manuals that explain in detail the authority and responsibilities of each person or department appearing in the chart.

■ **Establish Routine Procedures for Processing Each Type of Transaction** If management is to direct the activities of a business according to plan, every transaction should go through four separate steps; it should be authorized, approved, executed, and recorded. For example, consider the sale of merchandise on credit. Top management has the authority and responsibility to authorize credit sales to categories of customers who meet certain standards. The manager of the credit department is responsible for approving a credit sale of a given dollar amount to a particular customer. The transaction is executed by the shipping department which ships or delivers the merchandise to the customer. Finally, the transaction is recorded in the accounting department by debiting Accounts Receivable and crediting Sales.

■ **Subdivision of Duties** Perhaps the most important element in achieving internal control is an appropriate subdivision—or separation—of duties. Responsibilities should be assigned so that no one person or department handles a transaction completely from beginning to end. When duties are divided in this manner, the work of one employee serves to verify that of another and any errors which occur tend to be detected promptly.

To illustrate this concept, let us review the typical procedures followed by a wholesaler in processing a credit sale. The sales department of the company is responsible for securing the order from the customer; the credit department must approve the customer's credit before the order is filled; the stock room assembles the goods ordered; the shipping department packs and ships the goods; the billing department prepares the sales invoice; and the accounting department records the transaction. Each department receives written evidence of the action by the other departments and reviews the documents describing the transaction to see that the actions taken correspond in all details. The shipping department, for instance, does not release the merchandise until after the credit department has approved the customer as a credit risk. The accounting department does not record the sale until it has received documentary evidence that (1) an order was received from a customer, (2) the extension of credit was approved, (3) the merchandise was shipped to the customer, and (4) a sales invoice was prepared and mailed to the customer.

■ **Accounting Function Separate from Custody of Assets** Basic to the separation of duties is the concept that an employee who has custody of an asset (or access to an asset) should not maintain the accounting record for that asset. If one person has custody of assets and also maintains the accounting records, there is both opportunity and incentive to falsify the records to conceal a shortage. However, the person with custody of the asset will not be inclined to waste it, steal it, or give it away if he or she is aware that another employee is maintaining a record of the asset.

The diagram on page 224 illustrates how this separation of duties contributes to strong internal control.

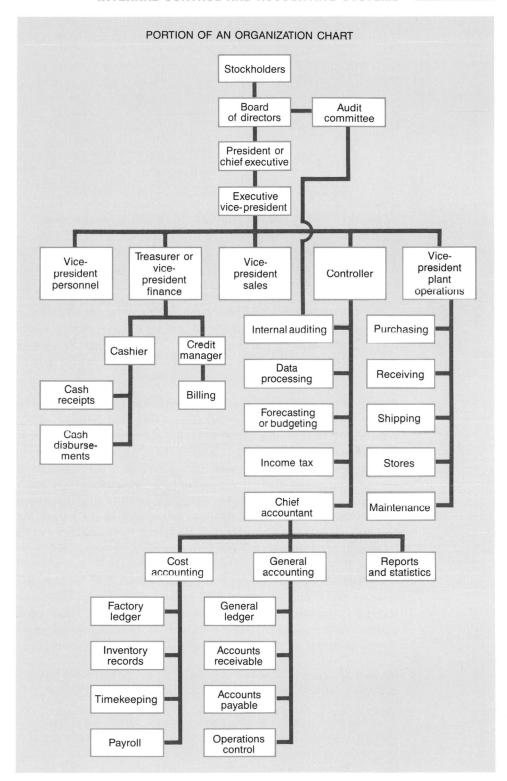

PORTION OF AN ORGANIZATION CHART

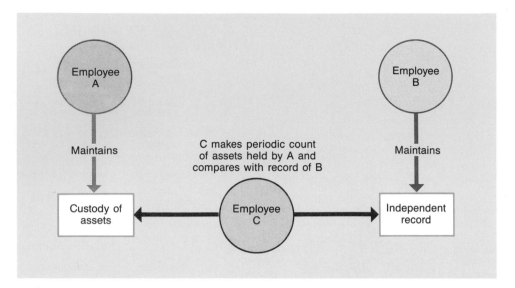

In this diagram Employee A has custody of assets and Employee B maintains an accounting record of the assets. Employee C periodically counts the assets and compares the count with the record maintained by B. This comparison should reveal any errors made by either A or B unless the two have collaborated to conceal an error or irregularity.

■ **Prevention of Fraud**   If one employee is permitted to handle all aspects of a transaction, the danger of fraud is increased. Studies of fraud cases suggest that many individuals may be tempted into dishonest acts if given complete control of company property. Most of these persons, however, would not engage in fraud if doing so required collaboration with another employee. Losses through employee dishonesty occur in a variety of ways: merchandise may be stolen; payments by customers may be withheld; suppliers may be overpaid with a view to kickbacks to employees; and lower prices may be allowed to favored customers. The opportunities for fraud are almost endless if all aspects of a sale or purchase transaction are concentrated in the hands of one employee.

Satisfactory internal control is more difficult to achieve in a small business than a large one because, with only a few employees, it is not possible to arrange extensive subdivision of duties. In many small businesses, internal control is unnecessarily weak, however, because management gives insufficient attention to the basic principles of internal control.

■ **Other Steps Toward Achieving Internal Control**   Other important internal control measures include the following:

1   Internal auditing   Virtually every *large* organization has an internal auditing staff. The objectives of the internal auditors are to monitor and improve the system of internal control. Internal auditors test and evaluate both accounting controls and administrative controls in all areas of the organization and prepare reports to top management on their findings and recommendations.

2   Financial forecasts   A plan of operations is prepared each year setting goals for each division of the business, as, for example, the expected volume of sales, amounts of expenses, and future cash balances. *Actual* results are compared with *forecast* amounts month by month. This comparison strengthens control because variations from planned results are investigated promptly.

3 Serially numbered documents Documents such as checks, purchase orders, and sales invoices should be serially numbered. If a document is misplaced or concealed, the break in the sequence of numbers will call attention to the missing item.

4 Competent personnel Even the best-designed system of internal control will not work well unless the people using it are competent. Competence and integrity of employees are in part developed through training programs, but they also are related to the policies for selection of personnel, and the adequacy of supervision.

The Role of Business Documents

Objective 3
Explain the role of purchase orders and receiving reports in verifying a purchase invoice.

We have made the point that strong internal control requires subdivision of duties among the departments of the business. How does each department know that the other departments have fulfilled their responsibilities? The answer lies in the use of carefully designed *business documents.* Some of the more important business documents used in controlling purchases of merchandise are summarized below:

BUSINESS DOCUMENT	INITIATED BY	SENT TO
Purchase requisition Issued when quantity of goods on hand falls below established reorder point	Departmental sales managers or stores department	Original to purchasing department, copy to accounting department
Purchase order Issued when order is placed. Indicates type, quantities, and prices of merchandise ordered.	Purchasing department	Original to selling company (vendor, supplier), copies to department requisitioning goods and the accounting department
Invoice Confirms that goods have been shipped and requests payment	Seller (supplier)	Accounting department of buying company
Receiving report Based on count and inspection of goods received	Receiving department of buying company	Original to accounting department, copies to purchasing department and to department requisitioning goods
Invoice approval form Based upon the documents listed above; authorizes payment of the purchase invoice	Accounting department of buying company	Finance department, to support issuance of check. Returned to accounting department with a copy of the check

■ **Purchase Requisition** A purchase requisition is a request from the sales department or stores department (warehousing) for the purchasing department to order merchandise. Thus, the purchasing department is not authorized to order goods **unless it has first received a purchase requisition.** A copy of the purchase requisition is sent to the accounting department.

■ **Purchase Orders** Once a purchase requisition has been received, the purchasing department determines the lowest-cost supplier of the merchandise and places an order. This order is documented in a **purchase order.** A purchase order issued by Fairway Pro Shop to Adams Manufacturing Company is illustrated below:

■
A serially numbered purchase order

	PURCHASE ORDER		Order no. 999	

FAIRWAY PRO SHOP
10 Fairway Avenue, San Francisco, California

To: Adams Manufacturing Company   Date Nov. 10, 19_

19 Union Street   Ship via Jones Truck Co.

Kansas City, Missouri   Terms: 2/10, n/30

Please enter our order for the following:

Quantity	Description	Price	Total
15 sets	Model S irons	$120.00	$1,800.00
50 dozen	X3Y Shur-Par golf balls	14.00	700.00
			$2,500.00

Fairway Pro Shop

By _PP McCarthy_

Several copies of a purchase order are usually prepared. The original is sent to the supplier; it constitutes an authorization to deliver the merchandise and to submit a bill based on the prices listed. A second copy is sent to the department that initiated the purchase requisition to show that the requisition has been acted upon. Another copy is sent to the accounting department of the buying company.

The issuance of a purchase order does not call for any entries in the accounting records of either the prospective buyer or seller. The company which receives an order does not consider that a sale has been made **until the merchandise is delivered.** At that point ownership of the goods changes, and both buyer and seller should make accounting entries to record the transaction.

■ **Invoices** When a manufacturer or wholesaler receives an order for its products, it takes two actions. One is to ship the goods to the customer and the other is to send the customer an invoice. By the act of shipping the merchandise, the seller is giving up ownership of one type of asset, inventory; by issuing the invoice the seller is recording ownership of another form of asset, an account receivable.

An invoice contains a description of the goods being sold, the quantities, prices, credit terms, and method of shipment. The illustration below shows an invoice issued by Adams Manufacturing Company in response to the previously illustrated purchase order from Fairway Pro Shop.

INVOICE
ADAMS MANUFACTURING COMPANY
19 Union Street
Kansas City, Missouri

Invoice no. 782

Sold to ___Fairway Pro Shop___   Invoice date ___Nov. 15, 19__

___10 Fairway Avenue___   Your sales no. ___999___

___San Francisco, Calif.___   Date shipped ___Nov. 15, 19__

Shipped to ___Same___   Shipped via ___Jones Truck Co.___

Terms ___2/10, n/30___

Quantity	Prescription	Price	Amount
15 sets	Model S irons	$12.00	$1,800.00
50 dozen	X3Y Shur-Par golf balls	14.00	700.00
			$2,500.00

From the viewpoint of the seller, an invoice is a *sales invoice;* from the buyer's viewpoint it is a *purchase invoice.* The invoice is the basis for an entry in the accounting records of *both* the seller and the buyer because it evidences the *transfer of ownership of goods.* At the time of issuing the invoice, the selling company makes an entry debiting Accounts Receivable and crediting Sales. The buying company however, does not record the invoice as a liability until the invoice has been approved for payment.

■ **Receiving Report**   Evidence that the merchandise has been received in good condition must be obtained from the receiving department. It is the function of the receiving department to receive all incoming goods, to inspect them as to quality and condition, and to determine the quantities received by counting, measuring, or weighing. The receiving department should prepare a serially numbered report for each shipment received; one copy of this *receiving report* is sent to the accounting department for use in approving the invoice for payment.

■ **Invoice Approval Form**   The approval of the invoice in the accounting department is accomplished by comparing the purchase requisition, purchase order, the invoice, and the receiving report. Comparison of these documents establishes that the merchandise described in the invoice was actually ordered, has been received in good condition, and was billed at the prices specified in the purchase order.

The person who performs these comparisons then records the liability (debit Purchases, credit Accounts Payable) and signs an *invoice approval form* authorizing payment of the invoice by the finance department. One type of invoice approval form, called a *voucher,* is illustrated in the following chapter.

■ **Debit and Credit Memoranda (Debit Memos, Credit Memos)** If merchandise purchased on account is unsatisfactory and is to be returned to the supplier (or if a price reduction is agreed upon), a *debit memorandum* may be prepared by the purchasing company and sent to the supplier. The debit memorandum informs the supplier that his or her account is being debited (reduced) by the buyer and explains the circumstances.

Upon being informed of the return of damaged merchandise (or having agreed to a reduction in price), the seller will send the buyer a *credit memorandum* indicating that the account receivable from the buyer has been credited (reduced).

Notice that issuing a credit memorandum has the same effect upon a customer's account as does receiving payment from the customer—that is, the account receivable is credited (reduced). Thus, an employee with authority to issue credit memoranda *should not be allowed to handle cash receipts from customers.* If both of these duties were assigned to the same employee, that person could abstract some of the cash collected from customers and conceal this theft by issuing credit memoranda.

Recording Purchase Invoices at Net Price

Objective 4
Describe the advantage of recording purchase invoices by the net-price method.

Most well-managed companies have a policy of taking all purchase discounts offered. The recording of purchase invoices at their *gross amount* and making payment of a reduced amount within the discount period was described in Chapter 5. Some companies which regularly take advantage of all available purchase discounts prefer the alternative method of recording purchase invoices at the *net amount* after discount rather than at the gross amount. If the amount which the buyer intends to pay is the invoice amount *minus a purchase discount,* why not record this net amount as the liability at the time the invoice is received? For example, if Fairway Pro Shop (the buyer) receives a $10,000 purchase invoice from Gator Sportswear bearing terms of 2/10, n/30, the entry could be

■
Entry for purchase: net-price method

Nov. 3 Purchases	9,800	
Accounts Payable		9,800
To record purchase invoice from Gator Sportswear less 2% cash discount available.		

Assuming that the invoice is paid within 10 days, the entry for the payment is as follows:

■
Entry for payment: net-price method

Nov. 13 Accounts Payable	9,800	
Cash		9,800
To record payment of $10,000 invoice from Gator Sportswear less 2% cash discount.		

Through oversight or carelessness, the purchasing company occasionally may fail to make payment of an invoice within the 10-day discount period. If such a delay occurred in paying the invoice from Gator Sportswear, the full amount of the invoice would have to be paid rather than the recorded liability of $9,800. The journal entry by Fairway Pro Shop to record the late payment on, say, December 3, is as follows:

```
Dec. 3  Accounts Payable ...........................................    9,800
        Purchase Discounts Lost .....................................     200
            Cash ...................................................              10,000
        To record payment of invoice and loss of discount by delaying
        payment beyond the discount period.
```

Under this method the cost of goods purchased is properly recorded at $9,800, and the additional payment of $200 caused by failure to pay the invoice promptly is placed in a special expense account designed to attract the attention of management. The gross-price method of recording invoices described in Chapter 5 shows the amount of purchase discounts taken each period; the net-price method now under discussion shows the amount of purchase discounts *lost* each period. The net-price method has the advantage of drawing the attention of management to a breakdown in internal control. The fact that purchase discounts have been taken does not require attention by management, but discounts lost because of inefficiency in processing accounts payable do call for managerial investigation.

Under the net-price method, inefficiency and delay in paying invoices is not concealed by including the lost discount in the cost of merchandise purchased. The purchases are stated at the net price available if all discounts had been taken; any purchase discounts lost are shown separately in the income statement as an operating expense.

Limitations and Cost of Internal Control

Although internal control is highly effective in increasing the reliability of accounting data and in protecting assets, no system of internal control provides complete protection against fraud or errors. Controls based upon a subdivision of duties may be defeated—at least temporarily by collusion among two or more dishonest employees. In a very small business, the opportunity for subdivision of duties is limited. Another limitation which exists to some extent in every business consists of carelessness by employees and misunderstanding of instructions. Such lapses can cause a breakdown in internal controls. Finally, the question of cost of controls cannot be ignored. Too elaborate a system of internal control may entail greater expense than is justified by the protection gained. For this reason, a system of internal control must be tailored to meet the needs of an individual business.

TAILORING AN ACCOUNTING SYSTEM TO THE NEEDS OF A LARGER BUSINESS

An accounting system consists of the business documents, journals, ledgers, procedures, and internal controls needed to produce reliable financial statements and other accounting reports. Accounting systems in common use range from simple systems in which accounting records are maintained by hand to sophisticated systems in which accounting records are maintained on magnetic discs. The accounting system used in any given company should be tailored to the size and to the information needs of the company.

In the early chapters of an introductory accounting book, basic accounting principles can be discussed most conveniently in terms of a small business with only a few customers and suppliers. This simplified model of a business has been used in preceding chapters to demonstrate the analysis and recording of the more common types of business transactions.

The recording procedures illustrated thus far call for recording each transaction by an entry in the general journal, and then posting each debit and credit from the general journal to the proper account in the ledger. We must now face the practical problem of streamlining and speeding up this basic accounting system so that the accounting department can keep pace with the rapid flow of transactions in a sizable business.

Two devices used in tailoring an accounting system to the needs of a business are *special journals* and *subsidiary ledgers.* These specialized accounting records are most easily illustrated in the context of a manual accounting system. However, special journals and subsidiary ledgers may be used to even greater advantage in computer-based accounting systems.

Special Journals

Objective 5
Explain the nature of special journals and the reasons for their use.

We have seen that any type of business transaction may be recorded in a general journal. A *special journal,* however, is an accounting record designed to handle the recording of *only one type* of business transaction. In order to record *all* types of business transactions, a business usually needs several special journals, as well as a general journal.

Why use a separate special journal to record a particular type of business transaction? The answer is that transactions may be recorded *much more quickly* in a journal that is specially designed for recording that particular type of transaction. Also, the amount of time spent posting transaction data may be greatly reduced. Finally, the use of special journals permits the work of recording transactions to be divided among several employees. Each special journal may be maintained by a different person.

The savings of time and effort are greatest when a separate special journal is designed to record each type of business transaction which *occurs frequently.* In most businesses, the great majority of transactions (perhaps 90 to 95%) fall into four types. These four types of transactions and the four corresponding special journals are listed below:

TYPE OF TRANSACTION	NAME OF SPECIAL JOURNAL
Sales of merchandise on account	*Sales journal*
Purchases of merchandise on account	*Purchases journal*
Receipts of cash	*Cash receipts journal*
Payments of cash	*Cash payments journal*

In addition to those special journals, a general journal still must be used to record those transactions which *do not fit* into any of the special journals. The general journal has been illustrated in preceding chapters. The adjective *"general"* is used to distinguish this multipurpose journal from the special journals.

We will now discuss the four special journals mentioned above, along with the related concept of subsidiary ledgers.

Sales Journal

Objective 6
Use special journals to record credit sales, credit purchases, and cash transactions.

Shown below is a *sales journal* containing entries for *all sales on account* made during November by the Seaside Company. Whenever merchandise is sold on credit, several copies of a sales invoice are prepared. The information listed on a sales invoice usually includes the date of the sale, the serial number of the invoice, the customer's name, the amount of the sale, and the credit terms. One copy of the sales invoice is used as the basis for entry in the sales journal.

Sales Journal   Page 1

DATE		ACCOUNT DEBITED	INVOICE NO.	✔	AMOUNT
19__					
Nov	2	Jill Adams	301	✔	450
	4	Harold Black	302	✔	1,000
	5	Robert Cross	303	✔	975
	11	H. R. Davis	304	✔	620
	18	C. D. Early	305	✔	900
	23	Mary Frost	306	✔	400
	29	D. H. Gray	307	✔	11,850
					16,195
					(5) (41)

Notice that the illustrated sales journal contains special columns for recording each of these aspects of the sales transaction, except the credit terms. If the business offers different credit terms to different customers, a column is inserted in the sales journal to show the terms of sale. Seaside Company, however, makes all credit sales on terms of 2/10, n/30; consequently, there is no need to write the credit terms as part of each entry.

Only sales on credit are entered in the sales journal. When merchandise is sold for cash, the transaction is recorded in a cash receipts journal, which is illustrated later in this chapter.

■ **Advantages of the Sales Journal**   Note that each of the seven sales transactions is recorded on a single line. Each entry consists of a debit to a customer's account; the offsetting credit to the Sales account is understood without being written, because sales on account are the only transactions recorded in this special journal.

An entry in a sales journal *need not include an explanation;* if more information about the transaction is desired it can be obtained by referring to the file copy of the sales invoice. The invoice number is listed in the sales journal as part of each entry. The one-line entry in the sales journal requires much less writing than would be necessary to record a sales transaction in the general journal. Since there may be several hundred or several thousand sales transactions each month, the time saved in recording transactions in this streamlined manner becomes quite important.

Another advantage of the special journal for sales is the great saving of time in posting credits to the Sales account. Remember that every amount entered in the sales journal represents a credit to Sales. In the illustrated sales journal on page 231, there are seven transactions (and in practice there might be 700). Instead of posting a separate credit to the Sales account for each sales transaction, we can wait until the end of the month and make *one posting* to the Sales account for the *total* of the amounts recorded in the sales journal.

In the illustrated sales journal for November, the sales on account totaled $16,195. On November 30 this amount is posted as a credit to the Sales account, and the ledger account number for Sales (41) is entered under the total figure in the sales journal to show that the posting operation has been performed. The total sales figure is also posted as a debit to ledger account no. 5, Accounts Receivable.

Notice the check marks (ν) in the column just to the left of the dollar amounts. These check marks indicate that the amount of the sale has been posted to the customer's account in the accounts receivable *subsidiary ledger.*

Controlling Accounts and Subsidiary Ledgers

Objective 7
Explain the usefulness of a subsidiary ledger and its relationship to the controlling account in the general ledger.

In preceding chapters all transactions involving accounts receivable from customers have been posted to a single account entitled Accounts Receivable. Under this procedure, however, it is not easy to look up the amount receivable from a given customer. In practice, a business which sell goods on credit *maintains a separate account receivable for each customer.* If there are 4,000 customers, this would require a ledger with 4,000 accounts receivable, in addition to the accounts for other assets, and for liabilities, owner's equity, revenue, and expenses. Such a ledger would be bulky and unwieldy. Also, the trial balance prepared from such a large ledger would be a very long one. If the trial balance showed the ledger to be out of balance, the task of locating the error or errors would be most difficult. All these factors indicate that it is not desirable to have too many accounts in one ledger. Fortunately, a simple solution is available; this solution is to *divide the ledger into several separate ledgers.*

In a business which has a large number of customers and a large number of creditors, it is customary to divide the ledger into three separate ledgers. All the accounts with *customers* are placed in alphabetical order in a separate ledger, called the *accounts receivable ledger.* All the accounts with *creditors* are arranged alphabetically in another ledger called the *accounts payable ledger.* Both of these ledgers are known as *subsidiary ledgers,* because they support and are controlled by the general ledger.

After placing the accounts receivable from customers in one subsidiary ledger and the accounts payable to creditors in a second subsidiary ledger, we have left in the original ledger all the revenue and expense accounts and also all the balance sheet accounts except those with individual customers and individual creditors. This ledger is called the *general ledger,* to distinguish it from the subsidiary ledgers.

When the numerous individual accounts receivable from customers are placed in a subsidiary ledger, an account entitled Accounts Receivable continues to be maintained in the general ledger. This account shows the *total amount due from all customers;* in other words, this single *controlling account* in the general ledger represents the numerous customers' accounts which make up the subsidiary ledger. The general ledger is still in balance because the controlling account, Accounts Receivable, has a balance equal to the total of the individual customers' accounts. Agreement of the controlling account with the sum of the accounts receivable in the subsidiary ledger also provides assurance of accuracy in the subsidiary ledger.

Relationship of subsidiary ledgers to controlling accounts in general ledger

A controlling account entitled Accounts Payable is also kept in the general ledger in place of the numerous accounts with creditors which form the accounts payable subsidiary ledger. Because the two controlling accounts represent the total amounts receivable from customers and payable to creditors, a trial balance can be prepared from the general ledger alone. The following illustration shows the relationship of the subsidiary ledgers to the controlling accounts in the general ledger.

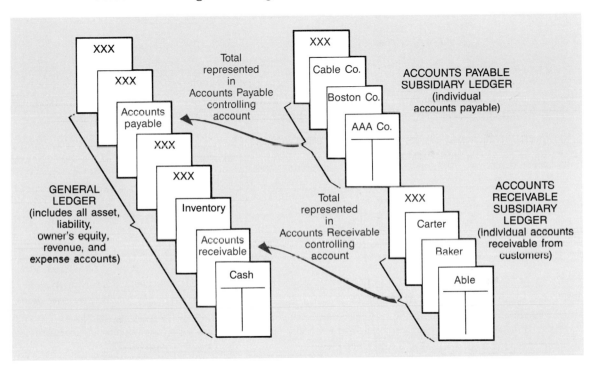

■ Posting to Subsidiary Ledgers and to Controlling Accounts To illustrate the posting of subsidiary ledgers and of controlling accounts, let us refer again to the sales journal illustrated on page 231. Each debit to a customer's account is posted currently during the month from the sales journal to the customer's account in the accounts receivable ledger. The accounts in this subsidiary ledger are usually kept in alphabetical order and are not numbered. When a posting is made to a customer's account, a check mark (✔) is placed in the sales journal as evidence that the posting has been made to the subsidiary ledger.

At month-end the sales journal is totaled. The total amount of sales for the month, *$16,195,* is posted as a credit to the Sales account and also as a debit to the controlling account, Accounts Receivable, in the general ledger. The controlling account will, therefore, equal the total of all the customers' accounts in the subsidiary ledger.

The diagram on the next page shows the day-to-day posting of individual entries from the sales journal to the subsidiary ledger. The diagram also shows the month-end posting of the total of the sales journal to the two general ledger accounts affected, Accounts Receivable and Sales. Note that the amount of the monthly debit to the controlling account is equal to the *sum of the debits* posted to the subsidiary ledger.

Subsidiary ledger posted daily; general ledger posted monthly

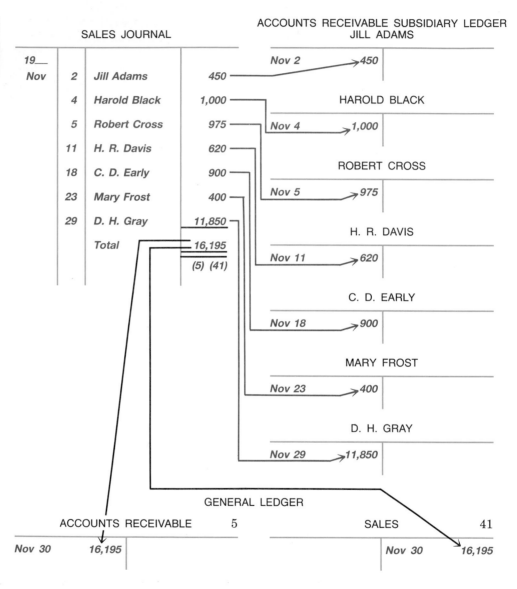

Other Subsidiary Ledgers In this chapter, we discuss only two subsidiary ledgers—accounts receivable and accounts payable. However, subsidiary ledgers are used for any account in which detailed information is needed about the *individual items that comprise the account balance.* The following schedule lists some of the general ledger accounts often supported by subsidiary ledgers and also indicates the unit of organization used within these subsidiary ledgers.

CONTROLLING ACCOUNT IN THE GENERAL LEDGER	UNIT OF ORGANIZATION WITHIN THE SUBSIDIARY LEDGER
Cash	*Each bank account*
Notes receivable	*Copy of each note receivable*
Inventory	*Each type of merchandise*
Plant assets	*Each asset (or category of assets)*
Notes payable	*Copy of each note payable*
Capital stock	*Individual stockholders (shows number of shares owned)*
	The revenue or expense on a departmental basis

These other subsidiary ledgers will be discussed in later chapters.

Purchases Journal

The handling of purchase transactions when a purchases journal is used follows a pattern quite similar to the one described for the sales journal.

The *purchases journal* shown on the next page includes *all purchases of merchandise on credit* during the month by the Seaside Company. The date of each purchase invoice is shown in a separate column, because the cash discount period begins on this date. Seaside Company follows a policy of recording purchase invoices at their gross amount. The five entries for purchases are posted as they occur during the month as credits to the creditors' accounts in the subsidiary ledger for accounts payable. As each posting is completed a check mark (✓) is placed in the purchases journal.

At the end of each month, the Amount column in the purchases journal is totaled. The total amount of purchases for the month, $7,250, is posted in the general ledger as a debit to the Purchases account and also as a credit to the Accounts Payable controlling account. The account numbers for Purchases (50) and for Accounts Payable (21) are then placed in parentheses below the column total of the purchases journal to show that the postings have been made.

The diagram on page 236 shows the day-to-day posting of individual entries from the purchases journal to the accounts with creditors in the subsidiary ledger for accounts payable. The diagram also shows how the column total of the purchases journal is posted at the end of the month to the general ledger accounts, Purchases and Accounts Payable. One objective of this diagram is to emphasize that the amount of the monthly credit to the controlling account is equal to the *sum of the credits* posted to the subsidiary ledger.

Under the particular system being described, the only transactions recorded in the purchases journal are *purchases of merchandise on credit*. The term *merchandise* means goods acquired for resale to customers. If merchandise is purchased for cash rather than on credit, the transaction should be recorded in the *cash payments journal,* not in the purchases journal.

When assets *other than merchandise* are being acquired, the journal to be used depends upon whether a cash payment is made. If assets of this type are purchased for cash, the transaction is entered in the *cash payments journal;* if the transaction is on credit, the *general journal* is used. The purchases journal is *not* used to record the acquisition of these assets because the total of this journal is posted to the Purchases account, which is used in determining the cost of goods sold.

Purchases Journal   Page 1

DATE		ACCOUNT CREDITED	INVOICE DATE		✔	AMOUNT
19__			19__			
Nov	2	Alabama Supply Co. (net 30)	Nov	2	✔	3,325
	4	Barker & Bright (2/10, n/30)		4	✔	700
	10	Canning & Sons (net 30)		9	✔	500
	17	Davis Co. (2/10, n/30)		16	✔	900
	27	Excelsior, Inc. (net 30)		25	✔	1,825
						7,250
						(50)(21)

Entries for purchases on credit during November

PURCHASES   50

Nov 30   7,250

ACCOUNTS PAYABLE   21

Nov 30   7,250

ACCOUNTS PAYABLE SUBSIDIARY LEDGER
ALABAMA SUPPLY CO.

Nov 2   3,325

BARKER & BRIGHT

Nov 4   700

CANNING & SONS

Nov 10   500

DAVIS CO

Nov 17   900

EXCELSIOR, INC.

Nov 27   1,825

Cash Receipts Journal

All transactions involving the receipt of cash are recorded in the cash receipts journal. One common example is the sale of merchandise for cash. As each cash sale is made, it is rung up on a cash register. At the end of the day the total of the cash sales is computed by striking the total key on the register. This total is entered in the cash receipts journal, which therefore contains one entry for the total cash sales of the day. For other types of cash receipts, such as the collection of accounts receivable from customers, a separate journal entry may be made for each transaction.

The cash receipts journal illustrated on the following page contains entries

Page 1

Cash Receipts Journal

| | | DEBITS | | | | | | CREDITS | | | | |
| | | | | OTHER ACCOUNTS | | | | ACCOUNTS RECEIVABLE | | | OTHER ACCOUNTS | |
DATE	EXPLANATION	CASH	SALES DISCOUNTS	NAME	LP	AMOUNT	ACCOUNT CREDITED	✓	AMOUNT	SALES	LP	AMOUNT
19												
Nov 1	Investment by owner	75,000					R. B. Jones, Capital				30	75,000
4	Cash sales	300								300		
5	Cash sales	400								400		
8	Invoice Nov. 2, less 2%	441	9				Jill Adams	✓	450			
10	Sale of land	7,000		Notes Receivable	3	10,000	Land				11	15,000
							Gain on Sale of Land				40	2,000
12	Invoice Nov. 4, less 2%	980	20				Harold Black	✓	1,000			
20	Invoice Nov. 18, less 2%	882	18				C. D. Early	✓	900			
27	Cash sales	125								125		
30	Obtained bank loan	4,000					Notes Payable				20	4,000
		89,128	47			10,000			2,350	825		96,000
		(1)	(43)			(X)			(5)	(41)		(X)

for all of the November transactions of Seaside Company which involved the receipt of cash. These transactions are listed below:

Nov. 1 The owner, R. B. Jones, made an additional investment in the business of $75,000 cash.

Nov. 4 Sold merchandise for cash, $300.

Nov. 5 Sold merchandise for cash, $400.

Nov. 8 Collected from Jill Adams for sales invoice of Nov. 2, $450 less 2% cash discount.

Nov. 10 Sold a small portion of land not needed in the business for a total price of $17,000, consisting of cash $7,000 and a note receivable for $10,000. The cost of the land sold was $15,000; thus, a $2,000 gain was realized on the sale.

Nov. 12 Collected from Harold Black for sales invoice of Nov. 4, $1,000 less 2% cash discount.

Nov. 20 Collected from C. D. Early for sales invoice of Nov. 18, $900 less 2% cash discount.

Nov. 27 Sold merchandise for cash, $125.

Nov. 30 Obtained $4,000 loan from bank. Issued a note payable in that amount.

Note that the cash receipts journal illustrated on page 237 has three debit columns and three credit columns as follows:

■ **Debits:**

1 Cash This column is used for every entry, because only those transactions which include the receipt of cash are entered in this special journal.

2 Sales discounts This column is used to accumulate the sales discounts allowed during the month. Only one line of the cash receipts book is required to record a collection from a customer who takes advantage of a cash discount.

3 Other accounts This third debit column is used for debits to any and all accounts other than cash and sales discounts, and space is provided for writing in the name of the account. For example, the entry of November 10 in the illustrated cash receipts journal shows that cash and a note receivable were obtained when land was sold. The amount of cash received, $7,000, is entered in the Cash debit column; the account title Notes Receivable is written in the Other Accounts debit column along with the amount of the debit to this account, $10,000. These two debits are offset by credit entries to Land, $15,000, and to Gain on Sale of Land, $2,000, in the Other Accounts credit column.

■ **Credits:**

1 Accounts receivable This column is used to list the credits to customers' accounts as receivables are collected. The name of the customer is written in the space entitled Account Credited to the left of the Accounts Receivable column.

2 Sales The existence of this column will save posting by permitting the accumulation of all sales for cash during the month and the posting of the column total at the end of the month as a credit to the Sales account.

3 Other accounts This column is used for credits to any and all accounts other than Accounts Receivable and Sales. In some instances, a transaction may require credits to two accounts. Such cases are handled by using two lines of the special journal, as illustrated by the transaction of November 10, which required credits to both the Land account and to Gain on Sale of Land.

■ **Posting the Cash Receipts Journal** It is convenient to think of the posting of a cash receipts journal as being divided into two phases. The first phase consists of the daily posting of individual amounts throughout the month; the second phase consists of the posting of column totals at the end of the month.

■ **Posting during the Month** Daily posting of the Accounts Receivable credit column is desirable. Each amount is posted to an individual customer's account in the accounts receivable subsidiary ledger. A check mark (✓) is placed in the cash receipts journal alongside each item posted to a customer's account to show that the posting operation has been performed. When debits and credits to customers' accounts are posted daily, the current status of each customer's account is available for use in making decisions as to further granting of credit and as a guide to collection efforts on past-due accounts.

The debits and credits in the Other Accounts sections of the cash receipts journal may be posted daily or at convenient intervals during the month. If this portion of the posting work is done on a current basis, less detailed work will be left for the busy period at the end of the month. As the postings of individual items are made, the number of the ledger account debited or credited is entered in the LP (ledger page) column of the cash receipts journal opposite the item posted. Evidence is thus provided in the special journal as to which items have been posted.

■ **Posting Column Totals at Month-End** At the end of the month, the cash receipts journal is ruled as shown above. Before posting any of the column totals, it is first important to prove that *the sum of the debit column totals is equal to the sum of the credit column totals.*

After the totals of the cash receipts journal have been crossfooted, the following columns totals are posted:

1 Cash debit column. Posted as a debit to the Cash account.

2 Sales Discounts debit column. Posted as a debit to the Sales Discounts account.

3 Accounts Receivable credit column. Posted as a credit to the controlling account, Accounts Receivable.

4 Sales credit column. Posted as a credit to the Sales account.

As each column total is posted to the appropriate account in the general ledger, the ledger account number is entered in parentheses just below the column total in the special journal. This notation shows that the column total has been posted and also indicates the account to which the posting was made. The totals of the Other Accounts columns in both the debit and credit sections of the special journal are not posted, because the amounts listed in the column affect various general ledger accounts and have already been posted as individual items. The symbol (**X**) is placed below the totals of these two columns to indicate that no posting is made.

Cash Payments Journal

Another widely used special journal is the cash payments journal, sometimes called the cash disbursements journal, in which *all payments of cash* are recorded. Among the more common of these transactions are payments of accounts payable to creditors, payment of operating expenses, and cash purchases of merchandise.

The cash payments journal illustrated on the following page contains entries for all November transactions of the Seaside Company which required the payment of cash. These transactions are:

Nov. 1   Paid to Westgate Mall rent on store building for November, $800.

Nov. 2   Purchased merchandise from Novelty Products for cash, $500.

Nov. 8   Paid Barker & Bright for invoice of Nov. 4, $700 less 2%.

Nov. 9   Bought land, $65,000, and building, $35,000, for future use in business. Paid cash of $70,000 to Admiralty Escrow Co. and signed a promissory note for the balance of $30,000. (Land and building were acquired in a single transaction.)

Nov. 17   Paid salaries, $3,600. (Issued one check for entire payroll to Payroll Services, Inc.)

Nov. 26   Paid Davis Co. for invoice of Nov. 16, $900 less 2%.

Nov. 27   Purchased merchandise from Coast Distributors, Inc., for cash, $400.

Nov. 28   Purchased merchandise from PaperWorld for cash, $650.

Nov. 29   Paid for newspaper advertising in the Daily Tribune, $50.

Nov. 29   Paid National Insurance Co. for one-year insurance policy, $720.

Note in the illustrated cash payments journal that the three credit columns are located to the left of the three debit columns; any sequence of columns is satisfactory in a special journal as long as the column headings clearly distinguish debits from credits. The Cash column is often placed first in both the cash receipts journal and the cash payments journal because it is the column used in every transaction.

Good internal control over cash disbursements requires that all payments be made by check. The checks are serially numbered and as each transaction is entered in the cash payments journal, the check number is listed in a special column provided just to the right of the date column. An unbroken sequence of check numbers in this column gives assurance that every check issued has been recorded in the accounting records.

■ **Posting the Cash Payments Journal**   The posting of the cash payments journal falls into the same two phases already described for the cash receipts journal. The first phase consists of the daily posting of entries in the Accounts Payable debit column to the individual accounts of creditors in the accounts payable subsidiary ledger. Check marks (✔) are entered opposite these items to show that the posting has been made. If a creditor telephones to inquire about any aspect of its account, information on all purchases and pay-

Includes all transactions involving payment of cash

Cash Payments Journal

DATE	CHECK NO.	PAYEE	CREDITS CASH	PURCHASE DISCOUNTS	OTHER ACCOUNTS NAME	LP	AMOUNT	ACCOUNT DEBITED	ACCOUNTS PAYABLE ✓	AMOUNT	PUR-CHASES	OTHER ACCOUNTS LP	AMOUNT
19__ Nov 1	420	Westgate Mall	800					Store Rent Expense				54	800
2	421	Novelty Products	500								500		
8	422	Barker & Bright	686	14				Barker & Bright	✓	700			
9	423	Admiralty Escrow Co.	70,000		Notes payable	20	30,000	Land				11	65,000
								Building				12	35,000
17	424	Payroll Services, Inc.	3,600					Salaries Expense				53	3,600
26	425	Davis Co.	882	18				Davis Co.	✓	900			
27	426	Coast Distributors, Inc.	400								400		
28	427	PaperWorld	650								650		
29	428	Daily Tribune	50					Advertising Expense				55	50
29	429	National Insurance Co.	720					Unexpired Insurance				6	720
			78,288	32			30,000			1,600	1,550		105,170
			(1)	(52)			(X)			(21)	(50)		(X)

ments made to date is readily available in the accounts payable subsidiary ledger.

The individual debit and credit entries in the Other Accounts columns of the cash payment journal may be posted daily or at convenient intervals during the month. As the posting of these individual items are made, the number of the ledger account debited or credited is entered in the LP (ledger page) column of the cash payments journal opposite the item posted.

The second phase of posting the cash payments journal is performed at the end of the month. When all the transactions of the month have been journalized, the cash payments journal is ruled as shown in our illustration, and the six money columns are totaled. The equality of debits and credits is then proved before posting.

After the totals of the cash payments journal have been proved to be in balance, the totals of the columns for Cash, Purchase Discounts, Accounts Payable, and Purchases are posted to the corresponding accounts in the general ledger. The numbers of the accounts to which these postings are made are listed in parentheses just below the respective column totals in the cash payments journal. The totals of the Other Accounts columns in both the debit and credit section of this special journal are not to be posted, and the symbol (X) is placed below the totals of these two columns to indicate that no posting is required.

The General Journal

When all transactions involving cash or the purchase and sale of merchandise are recorded in special journals, only a few types of transactions remain to be entered in the general journal. Examples include the declaration of dividends, the purchase or sale of plant and equipment on credit, the return of merchandise for credit to a supplier, and the return of merchandise by customers for credit to their accounts. The general journal is also used for adjusting and closing entries at the end of the accounting period.

The following transactions of the Seaside Company during November could not conveniently be handled in any of the four special journals and were therefore entered in the general journal.

Nov. 25   A customer, Mary Frost, returned for credit $50 worth of merchandise that had been sold to her on Nov. 23.

Nov. 28   The Seaside Company returned to a supplier, Excelsior, Inc., for credit $300 worth of the merchandise purchased on Nov. 27.

Nov. 29   Purchased for use in the business office equipment costing $1,225. Agreed to make payment within 30 days to XYZ Equipment Co.

General Journal   Page 1

Transactions which do not "fit" in any of the special journals

DATE		ACCOUNT TITLES AND EXPLANATION	LP	DR	CR
19__					
Nov	25	Sales Returns and Allowances	42	50	
		Accounts Receivable, Mary Frost......	5/✓		50
		Allowed credit to customer for return			
		of merchandise from sale of Nov. 23.			

DATE		ACCOUNT TITLES AND EXPLANATION	LP	DR	CR
	28	Accounts Payable, Excelsior, Inc............	21/✓	300	
		Purchase Returns and Allowances	51		300
		Returned to supplier for credit a portion			
		of merchandise purchased on Nov. 27.			
	29	Office Equipment...........................	14	1,225	
		Accounts Payable, XYZ Equipment Co.	21/✓		1,225
		Purchased office equipment on 30-day			
		credit.			

Each of the preceding three entries includes a debit or credit to a controlling account (Accounts Receivable or Accounts Payable) and also identifies by name a particular creditor or customer. When a *controlling account* is debited or credited by a general journal entry, the debit or credit must be posted *twice:* one posting to the controlling account in the *general ledger* and another posting to a customer's account or a creditor's account in a *subsidiary ledger.* This double posting is necessary to keep the controlling account in agreement with the subsidiary ledger.

For example, in the illustrated entry of November 25 for the return of merchandise by a customer, the credit part of the entry is posted twice:

1 To the Accounts Receivable controlling account in the general ledger; this posting is evidenced by listing the account number (5) in the LP column of the general ledger.

2 To the account of Mary Frost in the subsidiary ledger for accounts receivable; this posting is indicated by the check mark (✓) placed in the LP (ledger page) column of the general journal.

Showing the Source of Postings in Ledger Accounts

When a general journal and several special journals are in use, the ledger accounts should indicate the book of original entry from which each debit and credit was posted. An identifying symbol is placed opposite each entry in the reference column of the account. The symbols used in this text are as follows:

- *S1* meaning page 1 of the sales journal
- *P1* meaning page 1 of the purchases journal
- *CR1* Meaning page 1 of the cash receipts journal
- *CP1* meaning page 1 of the cash payments journal
- *J1* meaning page 1 of the general journal

The following illustration shows a typical customer's account in a subsidiary ledger for accounts receivable:

Aaron, Henry   Credit limit $2,000

DATE			REF	DEBIT	CREDIT	BALANCE
19__						
July	1		S2	400		400
	20		S3	200		600
Aug	4		CR2		400	200
	15		S6	120		320

Notice that the Reference column shows the source of each debit and credit entry. Similar references are entered in general ledger accounts.

Reconciling Subsidiary Ledgers with Controlling Accounts

We have made the point that the balance in a controlling account should be equal to the sum of the balances of the subsidiary ledger accounts. Proving the equality is termed *reconciling* the subsidiary ledger with its controlling account. This process may bring to light errors in either the subsidiary ledger or in the controlling account.

The first step in reconciling a subsidiary ledger is to prepare a schedule of the balances of the subsidiary ledger accounts. For example, the balances in Seaside Company's accounts receivable subsidiary ledger at November 30 are shown below. The total of this schedule should agree with the balance in the controlling account in the general ledger.

Schedule of Accounts Receivable
November 30, 19__

Robert Cross..	$ 975
H. R. Davis...	620
Mary Frost...	350
D. H. Gray	11,850
Total (should equal balance of the controlling account)	$13,795

Reconciling subsidiary ledgers with their controlling accounts is an important internal control procedure and should be performed at least once a month. This procedure may disclose such errors in the subsidiary ledger as failure to post transactions, transposition or slide errors, or mathematical errors in determining the balances of specific accounts receivable or accounts payable. However, this procedure will **not** disclose an entry which was posted to the wrong account within the subsidiary ledger.

If the subsidiary ledger and controlling account are **not** in agreement, the error may be difficult to find. The disagreement may be caused by an incorrect posting or by an error in the computation of an account balance. Thus, we may need to verify postings and recompute account balances until the error is found. Fortunately, most businesses use computer programs to maintain accounts receivable records. These programs have built-in internal control procedures that effectively prevent differences between amounts posted to the subsidiary ledger and to the related controlling account.

Variations in Special Journals

The number of columns to be included in each special journal and the number of special journals to be used will depend upon the nature of the particular business and especially upon the volume of the various kinds of transactions. For example, the desirability of including a Sales Discounts column in the cash receipts journal depends upon whether a business offers discounts to its customers for prompt payment.

A retail store may find that customers frequently return merchandise for credit. To record efficiently this large volume of sales returns, the store may establish a special sales returns and allowances journal. A special purchase returns and allowances journal may also be desirable if returns of goods to suppliers occur frequently.

Special journals should be regarded as laborsaving devices which may be designed with any number of columns appropriate to the needs of the particular business. A business will usually benefit by establishing a special journal for any type of transaction that *occurs quite frequently.*

COMPUTER-BASED ACCOUNTING SYSTEMS

The concepts of special journals and subsidiary ledgers apply to computer-based accounting systems as well as manual systems. In fact, special journals and subsidiary ledgers are far easier to maintain in computerized systems. We have stressed that two purposes of special journals are to reduce the amount of time involved in writing journal entries and posting to ledger accounts. In a computer-based system, the accountant need only enter the data needed for the computer to prepare journal entries. All the writing and all the posting to general ledger and subsidiary ledger accounts is then handled by machine with no further human effort.

Recording Retail Sales—Computers Reduce the Work

The *point-of-sale terminals* now prominent in many retail establishments greatly reduce the work involved in accounting for sales transactions. Many of these terminals use an optical scanner or other electronic device to "read" magnetically coded labels attached to the merchandise. As the merchandise is passed over the optical scanner, the code is sent instantaneously to the computer. From the code number, the computer is able to identify the item being sold, record the amount of the sale, and transfer the cost of the item from the Inventory account to the Cost of Goods Sold account. If the transaction is a credit sale, the salesclerk enters the customer's credit card number in the electronic register. This number enables the computer to update instantly the customer's account in the subsidiary ledger.

Note that all of the accounting is done automatically as the salesperson rings up the sale. Thus, any number of transactions can be recorded and posted with virtually no manual work. At the end of each day, the computer prints a complete sales journal along with up-to-date balances for the general ledger and subsidiary ledger accounts relating to sales transactions.

Advantages of Computer-Based Systems

The primary advantage of the computer is its incredible speed. The time needed for a computer to post a transaction or determine an account balance is but a few millionths of a second. This speed creates several advantages over manual accounting systems, including the following:

1 Large amounts of data can be processed quickly and efficiently Large businesses may engage in tens of thousands of transactions per day. In processing such a large volume of data, computers can save vast amounts of time in each step of the accounting process, including the recording of transactions, posting to ledger accounts, and preparing of accounting records, schedules, and reports.

2 Account balances may be kept up-to-date The speed with which data may be processed by a computer enables businesses to keep subsidiary ledger accounts, perpetual inventory records, and most general ledger accounts continually up-to-date.

3 Additional information may be developed at virtually no additional cost On page 231 we illustrated the type of sales journal that might be prepared in a manual accounting system. A similar journal can be maintained in a computerized system. However, the computer can also rearrange this information to show daily sales totals for each sales department, for each salesperson, and for specific products. Time and cost considerations often make the preparation of such supplementary information impractical in a manual accounting system.

4 Instant feedback may be available as transactions are taking place In *online, real-time (OLRT)* computer systems, the employee executing a transaction may have a terminal which is in direct communication with the computer. Thus, the employee has immediate access to accounting information useful in executing the current transaction.

CASE IN POINT ■ The electronic cash registers now found in many department stores are point-of-sale terminals in direct communication with the store's computer system. When a salesperson makes a credit sale to a customer who is using a store credit card, the salesperson enters the credit card number into the terminal. The computer compares this number to a list of cancelled or stolen credit cards and also determines whether the current sales transaction would cause the customer's account balance to exceed a predetermined credit limit. If any of these procedures indicate that credit should not be extended to the customer, the computer notifies the salesperson not to make the credit sale.

5 Additional internal control procedures may be possible in a computer-based system Approval of each credit sale, described in the preceding *Case in point,* is but one example of an internal control procedure that makes use of the unique capabilities of the computer. Such a control procedure may not be practical in a manual system, especially if the accounts receivable subsidiary ledger is not kept continually up-to-date.

End-of-Chapter Review

CONCEPTS INTRODUCED OR EMPHASIZED IN CHAPTER 6

The major concepts in this chapter include:

■ The purpose of a system of internal control and its relationship to the accounting system.

■ The subdivision of duties as an element of internal control.

■ The role of business documents in assuring that each department is fulfilling the responsibilities assigned to it by the organization plan.

■ The use of special journals to streamline accounting for those transactions which occur most frequently.

■ The use of controlling accounts and subsidiary ledgers for accounts receivable, accounts payable, and any other types of accounts for which detailed information is needed about the individual items comprising the account balance.

In the first six chapters of this book you have acquired a well-rounded understanding of the principles and guidelines used in preparing financial statements for both a service-type business and a merchandising company. In Chapter 6, you have become familiar with the elements of internal control and have gained an understanding of the importance of internal controls in avoiding fraud, accidental errors, and the waste of resources. With the completion of these six chapters, you are now at a strategic point to benefit from the use of a practice set to coordinate and pull together all the concepts covered in Parts 1 and 2 of this book.

In Part 3 we will focus on the fascinating and controversial topic of accounting principles used in the valuation of assets. These principles vitally affect the fairness and validity of both the balance sheet and the income statement.

KEY TERMS INTRODUCED OR EMPHASIZED IN CHAPTER 6

Accounting control An internal control procedure that *relates directly* to the protection of assets or to the reliability of accounting records.

Accounts payable ledger A subsidiary ledger containing an account with each supplier or vendor. The total of the ledger agrees with the general ledger controlling account, Accounts Payable.

Accounts receivable ledger A subsidiary ledger containing an account with each credit customer. The total of the ledger agrees with the general ledger controlling account, Accounts Receivable.

Administrative control An internal control procedure that has *no direct bearing* upon the reliability of the accounting records.

Cash payments journal A special journal used to record all payments of cash.

Controlling account A general ledger account which is supported by detailed information in a subsidiary ledger.

Credit memorandum A document issued by the seller to the buyer indicating the seller's willingness to reduce (credit) its account receivable from the buyer as the result of a sales return or allowance.

Debit memorandum   A document issued by the buyer to the seller indicating that the buyer intends to reduce (debit) its account payable to the seller in connection with a purchase return or allowance.

Internal auditors   Professional accountants employed by an organization to continually test and evaluate the system of internal control and to report their findings and recommendations to top management.

Internal control   All measures used by a business to guard against errors, waste, or fraud and to assure the reliability of accounting data. Designed to aid in the efficient operation of a business and to encourage compliance with company policies.

Invoice   An itemized statement of goods being bought or sold. Shows quantities, prices, and credit terms. Serves as the basis for an entry in the accounting records of both seller and buyer because it evidences the transfer of ownership of goods.

Invoice approval form   A business document prepared by a purchasing company's accounting department prior to recording or approving payment of a purchase invoice. Preliminary steps include comparing the purchase order and receiving report with the purchase invoice.

Net-price method   A policy of recording purchase invoices at amounts net of (reduced by) allowable cash discounts.

Point-of-sale terminal   Electronic cash registers used for computer-based processing of sales transactions. Widely used in large retail stores.

Purchase order   A serially numbered document sent by the purchasing department of a business to a supplier or vendor for the purpose of ordering materials or services.

Receiving report   An internal form prepared by the receiving department for each incoming shipment showing the quantity and condition of goods received.

Sales journal   A special journal used exclusively to record sales of merchandise on credit.

Subsidiary ledger   A supplementary record used to provide detailed information for a control account in the general ledger. The total of accounts in a subsidiary ledger equals the balance of the related control account in the general ledger.

SELF-TEST QUESTIONS

The answers to these questions appear on page 263.

1 Which of the following statements best describes the system of internal control? Measures intended to:

a Keep the business operating in accordance with the plans and policies of management.

b Prevent theft or misuse of company assets.

c Ensure the accuracy and reliability of the accounting records.

d Identify the person or persons responsible for errors or unauthorized activities.

2 One means of achieving strong internal control is an appropriate subdivision of duties. Identify all answers consistent with this concept.

a No one employee should handle all aspects of a transaction.

b Each employee's areas of responsibility should be carefully defined.

c Every task should be performed at least twice by different employees.

d Employees with custody of assets should not maintain the account records relating to those assets.

3 Morrison Company paid a purchase invoice for merchandise that was never received.

This error could have been prevented had Morrison's accounting department followed a practice of:

a Recording purchases by the net price method.

b Comparing purchase invoices to purchase orders.

c Accounting for the serial sequence of purchase requisitions.

d None of the above procedures would have prevented this error.

4 Garret Company is a small business that uses only a general journal. The company makes approximately 70 credit sales each month. If the company were to use a one-column sales journal in recording these transactions:

a The number of transactions to be journalized each month would be significantly reduced.

b The number of credit sales transactions posted to the general ledger each month would be reduced by almost two-thirds.

c Only one amount would be posted each month to the accounts receivable subsidiary ledger.

d Monthly credit sales could be entered in the general ledger by posting a single amount to two different accounts.

5 Which of the following statements about computer-based accounting systems is false?

a Sales transactions can be recorded in the accounting system at the time that the salesperson "rings-up" the transaction.

b The concepts of special journals and subsidiary ledgers do not apply to computer-based systems.

c The need for manual posting to ledger accounts may be eliminated entirely.

d Data economically may be rearranged in a number of different ways to assist in managerial decision making.

Assignment Material

REVIEW QUESTIONS

1 List four specific objectives of a system of internal control.

2 A system of internal control includes accounting controls and administrative controls. Describe each group and give an example of each.

3 Criticize the following statement: "In our company we get things done by requiring that a person who initiates a transaction follow it through in all particulars. For example, an employee who issues a purchase order is held responsible for inspecting the merchandise upon arrival, approving the invoice, and preparing the check in payment of the purchase. If any error is made, we definitely know whom to blame."

4 Suggest a control device to protect against the loss or nondelivery of invoices or other documents which are routed from one department to another.

5 Explain why the operations and custodianship functions should be separate from the accounting function.

6 Name three documents (business papers) which are needed by the accounting department to verify that a purchase of merchandise has occurred and that payment of the related liability should be made.

7 A company which has received a shipment of merchandise and a related invoice from the supplier sometimes finds it necessary to issue a debit memorandum. Describe a situation that would justify such action by the purchasing company.

8 Company A sells merchandise to Company B on credit and two days later agrees that B can return the merchandise. B does so. Should Company A issue a debit memorandum or a credit memorandum? Explain.

9 Briefly explain why a person who handles cash collections from customers should not also have authority to issue credit memoranda for sales returns and allowances.

10 Lap-Top Computer has a policy of taking all available purchase discounts. Explain how recording purchase invoices by the net-price method may assist management in enforcing this policy of taking all available purchase discounts.

11 What advantages are offered by the use of special journals?

12 Arrow Company uses a general journal and the four special journals described in this chapter. Which journal should the company use to record (a) cash sales, (b) depreciation, and (c) credit sales? Explain.

13 The column total of one of the four special journals described in this chapter is posted at month-end to two general ledger accounts. One of these two accounts is Accounts Payable. What is the name of the special journal? What account is debited and what account is credited with this total?

14 Pine Hill General Store makes about 500 sales on account each month, using only a two-column general journal to record these transactions. What would be the extent of the work saved by using a sales journal?

15 When accounts receivable and accounts payable are kept in separate ledgers, will the general ledger continue to be a self-balancing ledger with equal debits and credits? Explain.

16 Explain how, why, and when the cash receipts journal and cash payments journal are crossfooted.

17 July sales on credit by Jayco amounted to $41,625, but a $1,000 error was made in totaling the sales journal. When and how will the error be discovered?

18 For a large modern department store, such as a Sears or J.C. Penney, is it necessary to maintain a *manual single-column sales journal?* Explain.

19 Briefly describe some of the advantages of processing accounting information by computer rather than manually.

EXERCISES

**Exercise 6-1
Accounting
terminology**

Listed below are nine technical accounting terms emphasized in this chapter:

Internal auditing	*Net-price method*	*System of internal control*
Special journal	*Reconciling*	*Debit memorandum*
Subsidiary ledger	*Accounting system*	*Credit memorandum*

Each of the following statements may (or may not) describe one of these technical terms. For each statement, indicate the accounting term described, or answer "None" if the statement does not correctly describe any of the terms.

a The activity of conducting an investigation for the purpose of rendering an independent opinion upon the fairness of a company's financial statements.

b Responsibility for issuing this document should not be assigned to an employee who handles cash collections from customers.

c Measures intended to make all aspects of a business operate in accordance with management's plans and policies.

d A policy of originally recording purchase invoices at the amount that will be paid if payment is made within the discount period.

e A business document indicating the quantity of goods received and that the goods were in satisfactory condition.

f An accounting record used to record in an efficient manner a type of business transaction that occurs frequently.

g The activity of testing and evaluating internal controls throughout the organization and reporting the findings to top management.

Exercise 6-2
Subdivision of duties

Robert Hale, owner of Hale Equipment, a merchandising business, explains to you how duties have been assigned to employees. Hale states: "In order to have clearly defined responsibility for each phase of our operations, I have made one employee responsible for the purchasing, receiving, and storage of merchandise. Another employee has been charged with responsibility for maintaining the accounting records and for making all collections from customers. I have assigned to a third employee responsibility for maintaining personnel records for all our employees and for timekeeping, preparation of payroll records, and distribution of payroll checks. My goal in setting up this organization plan is to have a strong system of internal control."

You are to evaluate Hale's plan of organization and explain fully the reasoning underlying any criticism you may have.

Exercise 6-3
Business documents

Jet Auto Supply Store received from a manufacturer a shipment of 200 gasoline cans. Harold Abbott, who handles all purchasing activities, telephoned the manufacturer and explained that only 100 cans were ordered. The manufacturer replied that two separate purchase orders for 100 cans each had recently been received from Jet Auto Supply Store. Harold Abbott is sure that the manufacturer is in error and is merely trying to justify an excess shipment, but he can find no means of proving the point. What is the missing element in internal control over purchases by Jet Auto Supply Store?

Exercise 6-4
Using credit memoranda

James Company sold merchandise to Bay Company on credit. On the next day, James Company received a telephone call from Bay Company stating that one of the items delivered was defective. James Company immediately issued credit memorandum no. 163 for $100 to Bay Company.

a Give the accounting entry required in James Company's records to record the issuance of the credit memorandum.

b Give the accounting entry required in Bay Company's accounting records when the credit memorandum is received. (Assume that Bay Company had previously recorded the purchase at the full amount of the seller's invoice and had not issued a debit memorandum.)

Exercise 6-5
Recording purchase invoices

Taft Company received purchase invoices during July totaling $44,000, all of which carried credit terms of 2/10, n/30. It was the company's regular policy to take advantage of all available cash discounts, but because of employee vacations during July, there was confusion and delay in making payments to suppliers, and none of the July invoices was paid within the discount period.

a What was the amount of the additional cost incurred by Taft Company as a result of the company's failure to take the available purchase discounts?

b Explain briefly two alternative ways in which Taft Company's amount of purchases might be presented in the July income statement.

c What method of recording purchase invoices can you suggest that would call to the attention of the Taft Company management the inefficiency of operations in July?

Exercise 6-6
Recording transactions in special journals

Medical Supply Co. uses a cash receipts journal, a cash payments journal, a sales journal, a purchases journal, and a general journal. Indicate which journal should be used to record each of the following transactions.

a Payment of property taxes

b Purchase of office equipment on credit

c Sale of merchandise on credit

d Sale of merchandise for cash

e Cash refund to a customer who returned merchandise

f Return of merchandise to a supplier for credit

g Adjusting entry to record depreciation

h Purchase of delivery truck for cash

i Purchase of merchandise on account

j Return of merchandise by a customer company for credit to its account

Exercise 6-7
Using subsidiary
ledgers

Pacific Products uses a sales journal to record all sales of merchandise on credit. During July the transactions in this journal were as follows:

Sales Journal

DATE		ACCOUNT DEBITED	INVOICE NO.	AMOUNT
July	6	Robert Baker	437	3,600
	15	Minden Company	438	8,610
	17	Pell & Warden	439	1,029
	26	Stonewall Corporation	440	17,500
	27	Robert Baker	441	3,000
				33,739

Entries in the general journal during July include one for the return of merchandise by a customer, as follows:

July	18	Sales Returns and Allowances	500	
		Accounts Receivable, Minden		
		Company............................		500
		Allowed credit to customer for return of		
		merchandise from sale of July 15.		

a Prepare a subsidiary ledger for accounts receivable by opening a T account for each of the four customers listed above. Post the entries in the sales journal to these individual customers' accounts. From the general journal, post the credit to the account of Minden Company.

b Prepare a general ledger account in T form as follows: a controlling account for Accounts Receivable, a Sales account, and a Sales Returns and Allowances account. Post to these accounts the appropriate entries from the sales journal and general journal.

c Prepare a schedule of accounts receivable at July 31 to prove that this subsidiary ledger is in agreement with its controlling account.

Exercise 6-8
Posting from
special journals

The accounting system used by Adams Company includes a general journal and also four special journals for cash receipts, cash payments, sales, and purchases of merchandise. On January 31, after all January posting had been completed, the Accounts Receivable controlling account in the general ledger had a debit balance of $160,000, and the Accounts Payable controlling account had a credit balance of $48,000.

The February transactions recorded in the four special journals can be summarized as follows:

Sales journal	Total transactions, $96,000
Purchases journal	Total transactions, $56,000
Cash receipts journal	Accounts Receivable column total, $76,800 (credit)
Cash payments journal	Accounts Payable column total, $67,200 (debit)

a What posting would be made of the $76,800 total of the Accounts Receivable column in the cash receipts journal at February 28?

b What posting would be made of the $96,000 total of the sales journal at February 28?

c What posting would be made of the $56,000 total of the purchases journal at February 28?

d What posting would be made of the $67,200 total of the Accounts Payable column in the cash payments journal at February 28?

e Based on the above information, state the balances of the Accounts Receivable controlling account and the Accounts Payable controlling account in the general ledger after completion of posting at February 28?

Exercise 6-9
Locating errors in special journals and subsidiary ledgers

Keystone Company maintains a manual accounting system with the four special journals and general journal described in this chapter. During September, the following errors were made. For each of the errors you are to explain how and when the error will be brought to light.

a Incorrectly added the debit entries in a customer's account in the accounts receivable subsidiary ledger and listed the total as $950 when it should have been $550.

b A purchase of merchandise on credit from Rex Company in the amount of $1,000 was erroneously entered in the purchases journal as a $100 purchase.

c Recorded correctly in the sales journal a $400 sale of merchandise on credit but posted the transaction to the customer's account in the subsidiary ledger as a $40 sale.

Exercise 6-10
Internal control in a computer-based system

Mission Stores uses electronic registers to record its sales transactions. All merchandise bears a magnetic code number which can be read by an optical scanner. When merchandise is sold, the sales clerk passes each item over the scanner. The computer reads the code number, determines the price of the item from a master price list, and displays the price on a screen for the customer to see. After each item has been passed over the scanner, the computer displays the total amount of the sale and records the transaction in the company's accounting records.

If the transaction is a credit sale, the sales clerk enters the customer's credit card number into the register. The computer checks the customer's credit status and updates the accounts receivable subsidiary ledger.

Paragraphs **a** through **d** describe problems which may arise in a retailing business which uses manual cash registers and accounting records. Explain how the electronic registers used by Mission Stores will help reduce or eliminate these problems. If the electronic registers will not help to eliminate the problems, explain why not.

a A sales clerk is unaware of a recent change in the price of a particular item.

b Merchandise is stolen by a shoplifter.

c A sales clerk fails to record a cash sale and keeps the cash received from the customer.

d A customer buys merchandise on account using a stolen Mission Stores credit card.

PROBLEMS

Group A

Problem 6A-1
Internal control
measures

Listed below are eight possible errors or problems which might occur in a merchandising business. You are to list the letter (**a** through **h**) designating each of these errors or problems. Beside each letter, place the number indicating the internal control measure that would prevent this type of problem from occurring. If none of the specified control measures would be effective in preventing the problem, place "0" after the letter.

Possible Errors or Problems

a The cashier conceals the embezzlement of cash by reducing the balance of the Cash account.

b Management is unaware that the company often fails to pay its bills in time to take advantage of the cash discounts offered by its suppliers.

c Paid a supplier for goods that were never received.

d The purchasing department ordered goods from one supplier when a better price could have been obtained by ordering from another supplier.

e Paid an invoice in which the supplier had accidentally doubled the price of the merchandise.

f Paid a supplier for goods that were delivered, but that were never ordered.

g Purchased merchandise which turned out not to be popular with customers.

h Several sales invoices were misplaced and the accounts receivable department is therefore unaware of the unrecorded credit sales.

Internal Control Measures

1 Use of serially numbered documents

2 Comparison of purchase invoice with the receiving report

3 Comparison of purchase invoice with the purchase order

4 Separation of the accounting function from custody of assets

5 Separation of the responsibilities for approving and recording transactions

6 Use of the net-price method of recording purchases

0 None of the above control procedures can effectively prevent this error from occurring

Problem 6A-2
Internal control:
a short case
study

At the Uptown Theater, the cashier is located in a box office at the front of the building. The cashier receives cash from customers and operates a ticket machine which ejects serially numbered tickets. The serial number appears on each end of the ticket. The tickets come from the printer in large rolls which fit into the ticket machine and are removed at the end of each cashier's working period.

After purchasing a ticket from the cashier, in order to be admitted to the theater a customer must hand the ticket to a doorman stationed some 50 feet from the box office at the entrance to the theater lobby. The doorman tears the ticket in half, opens the door for the customer, and returns the ticket stub to the customer. The other half of the ticket is dropped by the doorman into a locked box.

Instructions

a Describe the internal controls present in Uptown Theater's method of handling cash receipts.

b What steps should be taken regularly by the theater manager or other supervisor to make these internal controls work most effectively?

c Assume that the cashier and the doorman decided to collaborate in an effort to abstract cash receipts. What action might they take?

d On the assumption made in *c* of collaboration between the cashier and the doorman, what features of the control procedures would be most likely to disclose the embezzlement?

<table>
<tr><td>

**Problem 6A-3
Recording
purchases by the
net-price method**

</td><td>

Rancho Furniture completed the following transactions relating to the purchase of merchandise during August, the first month of operation. It is the policy of the company to record all purchase invoices at the **net amount** and to pay invoices within the discount period.

</td></tr>
</table>

Aug. 1 Purchased merchandise from Carolina Corporation, invoice price, $21,000; terms 2/10, n/30.

Aug. 8 Purchased merchandise from Thomas Company, $36,000; terms 2/10, n/30.

Aug. 8 Merchandise with an invoice price of $3,000 purchased from Carolina Corporation on August 1 was found to be defective. It was returned to the supplier accompanied by debit memorandum no. 118, reducing the liability by the **net price** of the goods returned.

Aug. 18 Paid Thomas Company's invoice of August 8, less cash discount.

Aug. 25 Purchased merchandise from Thomas Company, $22,800; terms 2/10, n/30.

Aug. 30 Paid Carolina Corporation's invoice of August 1, taking into consideration the return of defective goods on August 8. (Remember that the August 1 purchase and the August 8 return were both recorded at **net amount** and not at invoice price.) Discount period expired on August 11.

Assume that the inventory of merchandise on August 1 was $79,400; on August 31, $87,800.

Instructions

a Journalize the above transactions, in general journal form, recording invoices at the net amount.

b Prepare the cost of goods sold section of the income statement.

c What is the amount of the account payable to Thomas Company at the end of August? What would be the amount of this account payable if Rancho Furniture followed the policy of recording purchase invoices at the gross amount?

<table>
<tr><td>

**\ Problem 6A-4
Using special
journals and
showing posting
references**

</td><td>

The accounting records of Video Games, a wholesale distributor of packaged software for computer games, include a general journal, four special journals, a general ledger, and two subsidiary ledgers. The chart of accounts includes the following accounts, among others:

</td></tr>
</table>

Cash	10	Sales	50
Notes receivable	15	Sales returns & allowances	52
Accounts receivable	17	Sales discounts	54
Notes payable	30	Purchase returns &	
Accounts payable	32	allowances	62

Transactions in June involving the sale of merchandise and the receipt of cash are shown below.

June 1 Sold merchandise to The Game Store for cash, $472. *CR-N*

June 4 Sold merchandise to Bravo Company, $8,500. Invoice no. 618; terms 2/10, n/30.

June 5 Received cash refund of $1,088 for merchandise returned to a supplier.

June 8 Sold merchandise to Micro Stores for $4,320. Invoice no. 619; terms 2/10, n/30.

June 11 Received $2,310 cash as partial collection of a $6,310 account receivable from Olympus Corporation. Also received a note receivable for the $4,000 remaining balance due.

June 13 Received check from Bravo Company in settlement of invoice dated June 4, less discount.

June 16 Sold merchandise to Books, Etc. for $4,040. Invoice no. 620; terms 2/10, n/30.

June 16 Returned $960 of merchandise to supplier, Software Co., for reduction of account payable.

June 20 Sold merchandise to Graphics, Inc., for $7,000. Invoice no. 621; terms 2/10, n/30.

June 21 Books, Etc. returned for credit $640 of merchandise purchased on June 16.

June 23 Borrowed $24,000 cash from a local bank, signing a six-month note payable.

June 25 Received $3,332 from Books, Etc., in full settlement of invoice dated June 16, less return on June 21 and 2% discount.

June 30 Collected from Graphics, Inc., amount of invoice dated June 20, less 2% discount.

June 30 Received a 60-day note receivable for $4,320 from Micro Stores in settlement of invoice dated June 8.

Instructions Record the above transactions in the appropriate journals. Use a single-column sales journal, a six-column cash receipts journal, and a two-column general journal. Foot and rule the special journals and indicate how postings would be made by placing ledger account numbers and check marks in the appropriate columns of the journals.

Problem 6A-5
Special journals;
purchases and
cash payments

Among the ledger accounts used by Poison Creek Drug Store are the following:

Cash	10	Purchases	50
Office supplies......................	18	Purchase returns	
Land................................	20	& allowances	52
Building............................	22	Purchase discounts	53
Notes payable	28	Salaries expense.....................	60
Accounts payable	30		

The August transactions relating to the purchase of merchandise for resale and to accounts payable are listed below along with selected other transactions. It is Poison Creek Drug's policy to record purchase invoices at their gross amount.

Aug. 1 Purchased merchandise from Medco Labs at a cost of $8,470. Invoice dated today; terms 2/10, n/30.

Aug. 4 Purchased merchandise from American Products for $19,300. Invoice dated August 3; terms 2/10, n/30.

Aug. 5 Returned for credit to Medco Labs defective merchandise having a list price of $1,220.

Aug. 6 Received shipment of merchandise from Tricor Corporation and their invoice dated August 5 in amount of $14,560. Terms net 30 days.

Aug. 8 Purchased merchandise from Vita-Life, Inc., $24,480. Invoice dated today; terms 1/10, n/60.

Aug. 10 Purchased merchandise from King Corporation, $30,000. Invoice dated August 9; terms 2/10, n/30.

Aug. 10 Issued check no. 631 for $7,105 to Medco Labs in settlement of balance resulting from purchase of August 1 and purchase return of August 5.

Aug. 11 Issued check no. 632 for $18,914 to American Products in payment of August 3 invoice, less 2%.

Aug. 18   Issued check no. 633 for $29,400 to King Corporation in settlement of invoice dated August 9, less 2% discount.

Aug. 20   Purchased merchandise for cash, $1,080. Issued check no. 634 to Candy Corp.

Aug. 21   Bought land and building for $208,800. Land was worth $64,800, and building, $144,000. Paid cash of $36,000 and signed a promissory note for the balance of $172,800. Check no. 635, in the amount of $36,000, was issued to Security Escrow Co.

Aug. 23   Purchased merchandise from Novelty Products for cash, $900. Issued check no. 636.

Aug. 26   Purchased merchandise from Ralston Company for $32,400. Invoice dated August 26, terms 2/10, n/30.

Aug. 28   Paid cash for office supplies, $270. Issued check no. 637 to Super Office, Inc.

Aug. 29   Purchased merchandise from Candy Corp. for cash, $1,890. Check no. 638.

Aug. 31   Paid salaries for August, $17,920. Issued check no. 639 to National Bank, which handles the distribution of the payroll to employees.

Instructions   **a**   Record the transactions in the appropriate journals. Use a single-column purchases journal, a six-column cash payments journal, and a two-column general journal. Foot and rule the special journals. Make all postings to the proper general ledger accounts and to the accounts payable subsidiary ledger.

b   Prepare a schedule of accounts payable at August 31 to prove that the subsidiary ledger is in balance with the controlling account for accounts payable.

Problem 6A-6
Cash journals   Marshall Ross wholesales designer sportswear to boutiques and other retail outlets. The company uses multicolumn cash receipts and cash payments journals similar to those illustrated in this chapter. The cash activities for May are listed below.

May 1   The owner, Marshall Ross, invested additional cash of $45,000 in the business.

May 2   Issued check no. 418 to Gaslamp Center in payment of store rent for May, $3,600.

May 4   Purchased store fixtures for $10,500 from Themes & Things, making a cash down payment of $1,500 (check no. 419) and issuing a 12%, 120-day note payable for the $9,000 balance. (Debit Fixtures.)

May 5   Sold merchandise for cash to Surprise Store, $12,300.

May 9   Received $2,100 as a partial collection of a $6,300 account receivable from Graffiti, Inc. Also received a $4,200 note receivable for the uncollected balance.

May 12   Paid Dallas at Night invoice of $9,000, less 2% discount. Check no. 420, in the amount of $8,820.

May 15   Received $3,822 from LA Stores in settlement of our $3,900 sales invoice, less allowable discount of 2%.

May 19   Purchased merchandise from Fashion World for cash, $7,200. Issued check no. 421.

May 25   Cash sales of merchandise, $8,045.

May 26   Paid Post Co. invoice, $9,900 less 2%. Check no. 422 for $9,702.

May 28   Purchased merchandise for cash from Albertson Corp., $6,450. Issued check no. 423.

May 30   Received check of $7,644 in full settlement of $7,800 sales invoice to Mix 'N Match dated May 21, less 2% discount for prompt payment.

May 31   Paid monthly salaries, $28,034. Issued one check, no. 424, to Third Street

Bank. The bank handles the distribution of the payroll to individual employees.

May 31   Paid Third Street Bank installment due today on a note payable. Issued check no. 425 in the amount of $1,440, representing interest expense of $702 and a reduction in the note payable of the remaining $738.

Instructions   Enter the above transactions in a six-column journal for cash receipts and a six-column journal for cash payments. Compute column totals and rule the journals. Determine the equality of debits and credits in column totals.

Group B

**Problem 6B-1
Internal control
measures—
emphasis upon
computer-based
systems**
The lettered paragraphs below describe eight possible errors or problems which might occur in a retail business. Also listed are seven internal control measures. List the letter (*a* through *h*) designating the errors or problems. Beside each letter, place the number indicating the internal control measure that should prevent this type of error or problem from occurring. If none of the specified internal control measures would effectively prevent the error or problem, place a "0" opposite the letter. Unless stated otherwise, assume that a computer-based accounting system is in use.

Possible Errors or Problems

a   A salesclerk unknowingly makes a credit sale to a customer whose account has already reached the customer's prearranged credit limit.

b   The cashier of a business conceals a theft of cash by adjusting the balance of the Cash account in the company's computer-based accounting records.

c   Certain merchandise proves to be so unpopular with customers that it cannot be sold except at a price well below its original cost.

d   A salesclerk rings up a sale at an incorrect price.

e   A salesclerk uses a point-of-sale terminal to improperly reduce the balance of a friend's account in the company's accounts receivable records.

f   One of the salesclerks is quite lazy and leaves most of the work of serving customers to the other salesclerks in the department.

g   A customer is never billed because through oversight the credit sale was never posted from the sales journal to the accounts receivable subsidiary ledger. (Assume that a manual accounting system is in use.)

h   A shoplifter steals merchandise while the salesclerk is busy with another customer.

Internal Control Measures

1   Limiting the types of transactions which can be processed from point-of-sale terminals to cash sales and credit sales.

2   All merchandise has a magnetically coded label which can be read automatically by a device attached to the electronic cash register. This code identifies to the computer the merchandise being sold.

3   Credit cards issued by the store have magnetic codes which can be read automatically by a device attached to the electronic cash register. Credit approval and posting to customers accounts are handled by the computer.

4   Subsidiary ledger accounts are periodically reconciled to the balance of the controlling account in the general ledger.

5   The computer prepares a report with separate daily sales totals for each sales person.

6   Employees with custody of assets do not have access to accounting records.

0   None of the above control measures effectively prevents this type of error from occurring.

Problem 6B-2
Internal control and fraud prevention

Golden Valley Farm Supply retained a firm of certified public accountants to devise a system of internal control especially designed for its operations. Assuming that the CPA firm has finished its work and the newly designed system of internal control is in use, answer fully the following:

a Will it be possible for any type of fraud to occur without immediate detection once the new system of internal control is in full operation?

b Describe two limitations inherent in a system of internal control that prevent it from providing absolute assurance against inefficiency and fraud.

Problem 6B-3
Recording purchases by the net-price method

The following transactions were completed by Data Tech during November, the first month of operation. The company uses the periodic inventory method and records purchase invoices at the **net amount**.

Nov. 1 Purchased merchandise from Hayes Company, $9,000; terms 2/10, n/30.

Nov. 7 Purchased merchandise from Joseph Corporation, $12,000; terms 2/10, n/30.

Nov. 8 Merchandise having a list price of $1,200, purchased from Hayes Company, was found to be defective. It was returned to the seller, accompanied by debit memorandum no. 382. (Note: This purchase return must be recorded at the **net** purchase price.)

Nov. 17 Paid Joseph Corporation's invoice of November 7, less cash discount.

Nov. 24 Purchased merchandise from Joseph Corporation, $7,600; terms 2/10, n/30.

Nov. 30 Paid Hayes Company's invoice of November 1, taking into consideration the return of goods on November 8. (Notice that this payment occurred **after** expiration of the discount period.)

Assume that the merchandise inventory on November 1 was $31,980; on November 30, $40,000.

Instructions

a Journalize the above transactions in general journal form, recording invoices at the **net amount**.

b Prepare the cost of goods sold section of the income statement.

c Based upon these November transactions, what is the amount of accounts payable at the end of November? What would the amount of accounts payable be at the end of November if Data Tech followed the policy of recording purchase invoices at the gross amount?

Problem 6B-4
Relationship between subsidiary ledgers and controlling accounts

Tyrolian Products sells skis and ski clothing. The company uses journals and ledgers similar to those illustrated in Chapter 6. At November 30, the subsidiary ledger for accounts receivable included accounts with individual customers as shown below and on the next page. Note that these accounts include postings from three different journals.

The purpose of this problem is to show the relationship between a controlling account and a subsidiary ledger. By studying the four subsidiary ledger accounts, you can determine what amounts should appear in the controlling account. (In actual practice, of course, both the controlling account and the subsidiary ledger would be completed by posting amounts from the various journals.)

NORDIC SPORTSWEAR

DATE	EXPLANATION	REF	DEBIT	CREDIT	BALANCE
19 —					
Oct. 31	Balance				1 2 4 0 0
Nov. 10		J1		6 3 0	1 1 7 7 0
11		S4	8 0 0 0		1 9 7 7 0
30		CR2		1 1 7 7 0	8 0 0 0

OLLIE'S SKI SHOP

DATE		EXPLANATION	REF	DEBIT	CREDIT	BALANCE
19—						
Nov.	4		S4	28160		28160
	29		S4	7680		35840
	29		CR2		28160	7680

PACIFIC SPORTS CENTER

DATE		EXPLANATION	REF	DEBIT	CREDIT	BALANCE
19—						
Nov.	3		S4	2240		2240
	9		S4	4160		6400
	27		CR2		2240	4160

QUALITY STORES, INC.

DATE		EXPLANATION	REF	DEBIT	CREDIT	BALANCE
19—						
Oct.	31	Balance				20736
Nov.	8		CR2		12800	7936
	8		J1		2560	5376
	28		CR2		5376	–0–

Instructions You are to make the necessary entries in the general ledger controlling account, Accounts Receivable, for the month of November. Use a three-column, running balance form of ledger account. (Remember that a controlling account is posted on a daily basis for transactions recorded in the general journal, but is posted only at the end of the month for the *monthly totals* of special journals such as the sales journal and the cash receipts journal.)

Include in the controlling account the balance at October 31, the transactions from the general journal during November in chronological order, and the running balance of the account after each entry. Finally, make one posting for all sales on credit during November and one posting for all cash collections from credit customers during November. For each amount entered in the Accounts Receivable controlling account, the date and source (name of journal and journal page) should be listed. Use the symbols shown on page 243 to identify the various journals.

Problem 6B-5
Special journals;
sales and cash
receipts

The accounting system of Springfield Express includes a general journal, four special journals, a general ledger, and two subsidiary ledgers. The chart of accounts includes the following accounts, among others.

Cash	10	Sales	50
Notes receivable	15	Sales returns & allowances	52
Accounts receivable.................	17	Sales discounts	54
Land................................	20	Purchases	60
Office equipment....................	25	Purchase returns & allowances	62
Notes payable	30	Interest revenue......................	82
Accounts payable	32	Gain on sale of land.................	85

Transactions in June involving the sale of merchandise and the receipt of cash are shown below, along with certain other selected transactions.

June 1   Sold merchandise to Williams Company for cash, $472.

June 4   Sold merchandise to Bravo Company, $8,500. Invoice no. 618; terms 2/10, n/30.

June 5   Received cash refund of $1,088 for merchandise returned to a supplier.

June 8   Sold merchandise to Bradley Company for $4,320. Invoice no. 619; terms 2/10, n/30.

June 9   Received a check from Kamlex Company in payment of a $2,400 invoice, less 2% discount.

June 11   Received $1,120 from Olympus Company in payment of a past-due invoice.

June 13   Received check from Bravo Company in settlement of invoice dated June 4, less discount.

June 16   Sold merchandise to XYZ Company, $4,040. Invoice no. 620; terms 2/10, n/30.

June 16   Returned $960 of merchandise to supplier, King Company, for reduction of account payable.

June 18   Purchased office equipment at a cost of $3,040, signing a 9%, 90-day note payable for the full amount.

June 20   Sold merchandise to Armstrong Co. for $7,000. Invoice no. 621; terms 2/10, n/30.

June 21   XYZ Company returned for credit $640 of merchandise purchased on June 16.

June 23   Borrowed $24,000 cash from a local bank, signing a six-month note payable.

June 25   Received payment in full from XYZ Company in settlement of invoice dated June 16, less return and discount.

June 29   Sold land costing $30,400 for $11,200 cash and a note receivable for $33,600. (Credit Gain on Sale of Land for $14,400.)

June 30   Collected from Armstrong Co. amount of invoice dated June 20, less 2% discount.

June 30   Collected $12,992 in full settlement of a $12,800 note receivable held since May 1. (No interest revenue has yet been recorded.)

June 30   Received a 60-day note receivable for $4,320 from Bradley Company in settlement of invoice dated June 8.

Instructions   Record the above transactions in the appropriate journals. Use a single-column sales journal, a six-column cash receipts journal, and a two-column general journal. Foot and rule the special journals and indicate how postings would be made by placing ledger account numbers and check marks in the appropriate columns of the journals.

Problem 6B-6
Using special
journals to record
cash transactions

J. D. Thomas Co. wholesales furniture to interior designers and retail furniture stores. The company uses multicolumn cash receipts and cash payments journals similar to those illustrated in this chapter. The cash activities for October are listed below:

Oct. 1 Issued check no. 734 to Furniture Trade Center in payment of store rent for October, $2,200.

Oct. 3 Purchased office equipment for $8,400 from MicroDesk, issuing check no. 735 as a $1,400 cash down payment and issuing a 10%, 90-day note payable for the $7,000 balance.

Oct. 4 The owner, J. D. Thomas, invested an additional $20,000 cash in the business.

Oct. 8 Paid a $15,000 account payable to Colonial House, taking the allowable 2% cash discount. Issued check no. 736 in the amount of $14,700.

Oct. 9 Sold merchandise for cash to Southwest Design Studios, $16,300.

Oct. 10 Received $3,600 as a partial collection of an $18,000 account receivable from Myra's Interiors. Also received a $14,400 note receivable for the uncollected balance.

Oct. 12 Received $7,742 from Furniture Gallery in settlement of our $7,900 sales invoice dated Oct. 2, less 2%.

Oct. 15 Cash sales of merchandise, $18,750.

Oct. 22 Purchased merchandise from Carolina Furniture Co. for cash, $11,200. Issued check no. 737.

Oct. 25 Paid $6,800 purchase invoice from Fabrics Unlimited, less 2%. Issued check no. 738 for $6,664.

Oct. 27 Purchased merchandise from Oak World, $16,700. Issued check no. 739.

Oct. 29 Received check for $17,836 from Lambert's in settlement of our $18,200 sales invoice dated Oct. 19, less 2%.

Oct. 31 Paid monthly salaries, $8,470. Issued one check, no. 740, to Merchants' Bank in the full amount of these salaries. (The bank handles the distribution of the payroll to individual employees.)

Oct. 31 Paid Merchants' Bank installment due today on a note payable. Issued check no. 741 in the amount of $1,630, representing $480 interest expense and a reduction in the balance of the note payable of the remaining $1,150.

Instructions Enter the above transactions in either a six-column cash receipts journal or a six-column cash payments journal. Total the money columns in each journal and determine the equality of the debit and credit column totals.

BUSINESS DECISION CASES

Case 6-1
The Baker Street
diversion

Printing Made Easy sells a variety of printers for use with personal computers. Last April, Arthur Doyle, the company's purchasing agent, discovered a weakness in internal control and engaged in a scheme to steal printers. Doyle issued a purchase order for 20 printers to one of the company's regular suppliers, but included a typewritten note requesting that the printers be delivered to 221B Baker Street, Doyle's home address.

The supplier shipped the printers to Baker Street and sent a sales invoice to Printing Made Easy. When the invoice arrived, an accounting clerk carefully complied with company policy and compared the invoice with a copy of the purchase order. After noting agreement between these documents as to quantities, prices, and model numbers, the clerk recorded the transaction in the accounting records and authorized payment of the invoice.

Instructions What is the weakness in internal control discovered by the purchasing agent to enable him to commit this theft? What changes would you recommend in the company's internal documentation and invoice approval procedures to prevent such problems in the future?

**Case 6-2
Designing a
special journal
and explaining
its use**

Leisure Clothing is a mail-order company which sells clothes to the public at discount prices. Recently Leisure Clothing initiated a new policy allowing a 10-day free trial on all clothes bought from the company. At the end of the 10-day period, the customer may either pay cash for the purchase or return the goods to Leisure Clothing. The new policy caused such a large boost in sales that, even after considering the many sales returns, the policy appeared quite profitable.

The accounting system of Leisure Clothing includes a sales journal, purchases journal, cash receipts journal, cash payments journal, and a general journal. As an internal control procedure, an officer of the company reviews and initials every entry in the general journal before the amounts are posted to the ledger accounts. Since the 10-day free trial policy has been in effect, hundreds of entries recording sales returns have been entered in the general journal each week. Each of these entries has been reviewed and initialed by an officer of the firm, and the amounts have been posted to Sales Returns & Allowances and to the Accounts Receivable controlling account in the general ledger, and also to the customer's account in the accounts receivable subsidiary ledger.

Since these sales return entries are so numerous, it has been suggested that a special journal be designed to handle them. This could not only save time in journalizing and posting the entries, but also eliminate the time-consuming individual review of each of these repetitive entries by an officer of the company.

Instructions

a How many amounts are entered in the general journal to describe a single sales return transaction? Are these amounts the same?

b Explain why these sales return transactions are suited to the use of a special journal. Explain in detail how many money columns the special journal should have, and what postings would have to be done either at the time of the transaction or at the end of the period.

c Assume that there were 3,000 sales returns during the month. How many postings would have to be made during the month if these transactions were entered in the general journal? How many postings would have to be made if the special journal you designed in b were used? (Assume a one-month accounting period.)

ANSWERS TO SELF-TEST QUESTIONS

1 a   **2 a, b,** and **d**   **3 d**   (The accounting department would need to compare the purchase invoice to a receiving report.)   **4 d**   **5 b**

Comprehensive Problem for Part 2

CRESTLINE LUMBER CO.

The use of special journals and subsidiary ledgers.

A partial chart of accounts for Crestline Lumber Co. is shown below:

Cash	1	Sales	60
Notes Receivable	2	Sales Returns and Allowances	62
Accounts Receivable	4	Sales Discounts	64
Supplies	6	Purchases	70
Unexpired Insurance	8	Purchase Returns and Allowances	72
Land	20	Purchase Discounts	74
Equipment	26	Transportation-in	76
Notes Payable	30	Salaries Expense	80
Accounts Payable	32		

The October 31 balances of the above ledger accounts appear in the partially completed working papers accompanying the text.

The schedules of accounts receivable and accounts payable for the company at October 31, 19__, are shown below:

Schedule of Accounts Receivable October 31, 19__		Schedule of Accounts Payable October 31, 19__	
Ace Contractors	$20,800	Northwest Mills	$30,000
Reliable Builders, Inc.	18,750		
Total	$39,550		

The accounting records of Crestline Lumber Co. include a general ledger and two subsidiary ledgers, one for accounts receivable and one for accounts payable. The company uses the four special journals illustrated in Chapter 6 as well as a two-column general journal. Crestline uses the periodic inventory system and records purchase invoices at their gross amount. All credit sales are on terms of 2/10, n/30.

The November transactions of the business are as follows:

Nov. 2 Purchased merchandise on account from Northwest Mills, $28,000. Invoice was dated today.

Nov. 3 Sold merchandise to Ace Contractors, $16,000. Invoice no. 428.

Nov. 4 Issued check no. 920 to Northwest Mills for $29,400, in full payment of balance at October 31, less 2% purchase discount.

Nov. 5 Sold merchandise for cash, $5,600.

Nov. 6 Collected $18,375 from Reliable Builders, Inc., representing the account receivable at October 31, less 2% cash discount.

Nov. 9 Purchased supplies for cash, $875. Issued check no. 921 to Aero Supply Co.

Nov. 10 Purchased merchandise from Tri-State Gypsum, $12,500. Invoice dated November 9, terms 2/10, n/30.

Nov. 11 Sold merchandise to Mountain Homes, $21,750. Invoice no. 429.

Nov. 12 Received $36,480 from Ace Contractors, representing collection of the October 31 balance receivable, upon which the discount has lapsed, and invoice no. 428 (see Nov. 3), less 2% cash discount.

Nov. 13   Paid transportation charges of $510 on goods purchased November 10 from Tri-State Gypsum. Issued check no. 922 to Cannonball Trucking.

Nov. 16   Sold a parcel of land not needed in the business at its cost of $25,000. Received $10,000 cash and a note receivable for $15,000.

Nov. 17   Issued credit memo. no. 78 in recognition of a $1,750 sales return by Mountain Homes of some of the merchandise purchased on November 11.

Nov. 17   Sold merchandise for cash, $4,675.

Nov. 18   Issued check no. 923 to Empire Insurance, $1,425, in full payment of a one-year fire insurance policy. (Debit Unexpired Insurance.)

Nov. 19   Bought merchandise for cash from Modern Tool Co., $2,625. Check no. 924.

Nov. 19   Issued check no. 925 for $12,250 to Tri-State Gypsum in payment of the purchase on November 10, less 2% cash discount.

Nov. 20   Received $19,600 from Mountain Homes in settlement of invoice no. 429 (Nov. 11), less sales return on Nov. 17, and less 2%.

Nov. 20   Sold merchandise on account to Ace Contractors, $13,650, invoice no. 430.

Nov. 23   Purchased merchandise from AAA Moldings for cash, $4,050, check no. 926.

Nov. 24   Sold goods on account to Lake Development Co., $39,950. Invoice no. 431.

Nov. 26   Purchased merchandise from Timber Products, $26,500. Invoice dated November 24.

Nov. 27   Returned to Timber Products merchandise costing $2,125. Issued debit memo. no. 42.

Nov. 30   Purchased equipment for $60,000. Issued check no. 927 to Electro-Lift for $10,000 as a cash down payment and issued a note payable for the $50,000 balance.

Nov. 30   Paid monthly salaries of $14,800. Issued one check (no. 928) to Payroll Service Co. in the amount of the entire payroll. Payroll Service Co. handles the preparation and distribution of paychecks to individual employees.

Instructions   **a** Record the November transactions in the appropriate journals and make all individual postings to the general ledger and subsidiary ledgers. Individual postings include:

(1) All entries in the general journal.

(2) Entries in the Other Accounts columns of the cash receipts journal and the cash payments journal.

(3) All entries in any journal which affect subsidiary ledger accounts.

In the journals, use check marks (✔) and ledger account numbers to indicate which amounts have been posted. In the ledger accounts, use the Ref column to indicate the source of each posting. (Assume that you are using page 7 of each journal.)

b Foot and rule the special journals and post the appropriate column totals to the general ledger. Make all appropriate posting cross-references.

c Prepare a schedule of the individual accounts receivable at November 30 and a separate schedule of the individual accounts payable. Determine that these schedules are in agreement with the related controlling accounts in the general ledger.

PART 3

Accounting for Assets

The manner in which a business records and values its assets affects both the balance sheet and the income statement. By studying the accounting principles involved in asset valuation, we will learn much about the content and limitations of financial statements.

7   The Control of Cash Transactions

8   Receivables

9   Inventories

10   Plant and Equipment, Depreciation, and Intangible Assets

The Control of Cash Transactions

Our chapter title suggests that internal control is especially needed to prevent fraud and theft relating to cash transactions. Cash is high in value, but light in weight and small in bulk—hence a fortune can be transported in a briefcase. The risk of fraud and related theft of cash are increased by the fact that currency bears no identifying data which can prove legal ownership. In this chapter, we emphasize that adequate internal control over cash transactions requires that each day's cash receipts be deposited intact in the bank and that all payments be made by check. We also illustrate and explain the use of a voucher system, a petty cash fund, and regular monthly bank reconciliations as means of achieving internal control over cash transactions.

After studying this chapter you should be able to meet these Learning Objectives:

1 Explain the objectives of cash management.

2 State the major steps in achieving internal control over cash transactions.

3 Explain how a voucher system can provide strong internal control over cash disbursements.

4 Describe the operation of a petty cash fund.

5 Prepare a bank reconciliation and explain its purpose.

Accountants define *cash* as money on deposit in banks and any items that a bank will accept for immediate deposit. These items include not only coins and paper money, but also checks, money orders, travelers' checks, and the charge slips signed by customers using bank credit cards, such as Visa and Master-Card.

Reporting Cash in the Balance Sheet

Cash is listed first in the balance sheet, because it represents a resource that can be used immediately to pay any type of obligation. The term *liquid assets* is used to describe assets that can be converted quickly into cash. In the current asset section of the balance sheet, assets are listed in the order of their *relative liquidity.* Thus, cash—being the ultimate in liquidity—is listed first.

■ **Cash Equivalents**   Some short-term investments are so liquid that they are termed *cash equivalents.* Examples include money market funds, U.S. Treasury bills, and commercial paper. These items are considered so similar to cash that they often are combined with the amount of cash in the balance sheet.[1] Therefore, many businesses call the first asset shown in the balance sheet *"Cash and cash equivalents."*

■ **Evaluating Solvency**   Bankers, credit managers, and other creditors who study a balance sheet always are interested in the amount of cash and cash equivalents as compared to other balance sheet items, such as accounts payable. These users of a company's financial statements are interested in evaluating the company's *solvency*—that is, its ability to pay its debts as they come due. They need to know the amount of liquid resources on hand. However, these users do not need such details as the number of separate bank accounts, or a breakdown of the amount of cash on hand as compared to cash in banks and amounts temporarily invested in cash equivalents.

■ **"Restricted" Cash**   Some bank accounts are restricted as to their use, so that they are not available to meet normal operating needs of the business. For example, a bank account may contain cash specifically earmarked for the acquisition of plant assets. Restricted bank accounts are not regarded as current assets if their balances are not available for use in paying current liabilities. Therefore, "restricted cash balances" may be listed just below the current asset section of the balance sheet in the section entitled long-term investments.

The Statement of Cash Flows

The balance sheet indicates the amount of cash owned by the business at a particular date. A separate financial statement, called the statement of cash flows, summarizes all of the cash *activity* (receipts and disbursements) during the accounting period. Interpreting the statement of cash flows requires an understanding of many types of business transactions, including the operating, investing, and financing activities of large corporations. Therefore, we will defer discussion of this financial statement to Chapter 19.

Management Responsibilities Relating to Cash

Objective 1
Explain the objectives of cash management.

Among the measures essential to the efficient management of cash are:

---

[1] Not all short-term investments are viewed as cash equivalents. Investments in stocks and bonds, for example, are *not* considered cash equivalents. Such investments appear in the balance sheet as "marketable securities," which usually is listed *second* among the current assets. Marketable securities are discussed in Chapter 17.

■ A cash budget (or forecast) of planned cash receipts, cash payments, and cash balances, scheduled month by month for a year in advance.

■ An accounting system that assures prompt and accurate recording of cash receipts, cash payments, and cash balances.

■ Internal controls that will prevent or minimize losses from fraud or theft.

■ Policies that anticipate the need for borrowing and assure the availability of a sufficient amount of cash at all times to make necessary payments plus a reasonable balance for emergencies.

■ Policies that prevent unnecessarily large amounts of cash from being held idle in bank accounts which produce little or no revenue.

Internal control over cash is sometimes regarded merely as a means of preventing fraud and theft. A good system of internal control, however, will also aid in achieving management's other objectives of anticipating the need for borrowing, accurate accounting for cash transactions, and the maintenance of adequate but not excessive cash balances.

Basic Requirements for Internal Control Over Cash

Objective 2
State the major steps in achieving internal control over cash transactions.

Cash is more susceptible to theft than any other asset. Furthermore, a large portion of the total transactions of a business involve the receipt or disbursement of cash. For both these reasons, internal control over cash is of great importance to management and also to the employees of a business. If a cash shortage arises in a small business in which internal controls are weak or nonexistent, every employee is under suspicion. Perhaps no one employee can be proved guilty of the theft, but neither can any employee prove his or her innocence.

On the other hand, if internal controls over cash are adequate, theft without detection is virtually impossible except through the collusion of two or more employees. To achieve internal control over cash or any other group of assets requires first of all that *the custody of assets be clearly separated from the recording of transactions.* Second, the recording function should be subdivided among employees, so that the work of one person is verified by that of another. This *subdivision of duties* discourages fraud, because collusion among employees would be necessary to conceal an irregularity. Internal control is more easily achieved in large companies than in small companies, because extensive subdivision of duties is more feasible in the larger business.

The major steps in establishing internal controls over cash include the following:

1 Separate the function of handling cash from the maintenance of accounting records. Employees who handle cash should not have access to the accounting records, and accounting personnel should not have access to cash.

2 Prepare a control listing of cash receipts at the time and place the money is received. For cash sales, this listing may be a cash register tape, created by ringing up each sale on a cash register. For checks received through the mail, a control listing of incoming checks should be prepared by the employee assigned to open the mail.

3 Require that all cash receipts be deposited daily in the bank.

4 Make all payments by check. The only exception should be for small payments to be made in cash from a petty cash fund. Payments should never be made out of cash receipts. Checks should never be drawn payable to Cash. A check drawn to a named payee requires endorsement by the payee on the back of the check before it can be cashed or deposited. This endorsement provides permanent evidence identifying the person who received the funds. On the other hand, a check payable to Cash can be deposited or cashed by anyone.

5 Require that the validity and amount of every expenditure be verified before a check is issued in payment.

6 Separate the function of approving expenditures from the function of signing checks.

The application of these principles in building an adequate system of internal control over cash can best be illustrated by considering separately the topics of cash receipts and cash disbursements. A company may supplement its system of internal control by obtaining a fidelity bond from an insurance company. Under a fidelity bond, the insurance company agrees to reimburse an employer for *proven* losses resulting from fraud or embezzlement by bonded employees.

Cash Receipts

Cash receipts consist primarily of two types: cash received through the mail as collections of accounts receivable, and cash received over the counter from cash sales.

■ **Cash Received through the Mail** Cash received through the mail should be in the form of checks made payable to the company. When the mail is first opened, an employee should stamp the back of each check with a restrictive endorsement stamp, indicating that the check is *"For Deposit Only"* into the company's bank account. This *restrictive endorsement* prevents anyone else from being able to cash the check or deposit it into another bank account.

Next, the employee should prepare a *control listing* of the checks received each day. This list shows each customer's name (or account number) and the amount received. One copy of this list is sent with the customers' checks to the cashier, who deposits the money in the bank. Another copy is sent to the accounting department, to be recorded in the cash receipts journal. Daily comparisons of this control listing with the amounts deposited by the cashier and with the receipts recorded by the accounting department should bring to light any cash shortages or recording errors.

■ **Cash Received over the Counter** Cash sales should be rung up on a cash register located so that the customer can see the amount recorded. The register has a locked-in tape, which serves as a control listing for cash sales. When the salesperson ends a workday, he or she will count the cash in the register and turn it over to the cashier. A representative of the accounting department will remove the tape from the cash register, compare the total shown on the tape with the amount turned in to the cashier, and record the cash sales in the cash receipts journal. In many larger stores, every cash register is linked directly to a computer, and each cash sale transaction immediately becomes part of the accounting records.

CASE IN POINT ■ Many large supermarkets have achieved faster checkout lines and stronger internal control by using electronic scanning equipment to read and record the price of all groceries passing the checkout counters. (The electronic scanning equipment replaces the traditional cash register.) All 12,000 or, so grocery items on the shelves bear a product code, consisting of a pattern of thick and thin vertical bars. At the checkout counter, the code on each item is read by a scanning laser. The code is sent instantaneously to a computer which locates the price and description of the item and flashes that information on a display panel in view of the customer and the checkout clerk. After all of the items have been passed through the scanner, the display panel shows the total amount of the sale. The clerk then enters the amount of cash received from the customer, and the display panel shows the amount of change that the customer should receive.

This system has many advantages. Not only is an immediate record made of all cash receipts, but the risk of errors in pricing merchandise or in making change is greatly reduced. This system also improves inventory control by giving management continuous information on what is being sold moment by moment, classified by product and by manufacturer. Comparison of these sales records with records of purchases will direct attention to any losses from theft or shoplifting.

■ **Use of Prenumbered Sales Tickets** Another means of establishing internal control over cash sales is by writing out a prenumbered sales ticket in duplicate at the time of each sale. The original is given to the customer and the carbon copy is retained. Prenumbered sales tickets are often used in businesses such as restaurants in which one central cashier rings up the sales made by all salespeople.

At the end of the day, an employee computes the total sales figure from these sales tickets and also makes sure that no tickets are missing from the series. This total sales figure is then compared with the cash register tape and the total cash receipts.

■ **Cash Over and Short** In handling over-the-counter cash receipts, a few errors in making change will inevitably occur. These errors will cause a cash shortage or overage at the end of the day, when the cash is counted and compared with the reading on the cash register.

For example, assume that the total cash sales for the day amount to $1,500 as recorded by the cash register, but that the cash in the drawer when counted amounts to only $1,490. The following entry would be made to record the day's sales and the cash shortage of $10.

■
**Recording cash
shortage**

Cash	*1,490*	
Cash Over and Short	*10*	
Sales		*1,500*

The account entitled Cash Over and Short is debited with shortages and credited with overages. If the cash shortages during an entire accounting period are in excess of the cash overages, the Cash Over and Short account will have a debit balance and will be shown as miscellaneous *expense* in the income statement. On the other hand, if the overages exceed the shortages, the Cash Over and Short account will show a credit balance at the end of the period and should be treated as an item of miscellaneous *revenue.*

■ **Subdivision of Duties**   Employees who handle cash receipts should *not have access to the accounting records.* This combination of duties might enable the employee to alter the accounting records and thereby conceal a cash shortage. For example, assume that an employee who serves as both the cashier and bookkeeper of a small business removes $500 from the day's cash sales receipts. By altering the accounting records, the employee could conceal this theft in any number of ways. One approach is simply to record the day's cash sales at $500 less than the actual amount. Another means of concealing the theft is to record cash sales correctly, but then record a fictitious sales return for $500 (debit Sales Returns & Allowances, credit Cash). In either case, the balance of the Cash account will not exceed the amount of cash on hand after the theft.

Employees who handle cash receipts also should *not have authority to issue credit memoranda for sales returns.* This combination of duties might enable the employee to conceal cash shortages by issuing fictitious credit memoranda. Assume, for example, that an employee with these responsibilities collects $100 cash from a customer as payment of the customer's account. The employee might remove this cash and issue a $100 credit memorandum, indicating that the customer had returned the merchandise instead of paying off the account. The credit memoranda would cause the customer's account to be credited. However, the offsetting debit would be to the Sales Returns & Allowances account, not to the Cash account. Thus, the books would remain in balance, the customer would receive credit for the abstracted payment, and there would be no record of cash having been received.

Cash Disbursements

An adequate system of internal control requires that each day's cash receipts be deposited intact in the bank and that *all disbursements be made by check.* Checks should be prenumbered. Any spoiled checks should be marked "Void" and filed in sequence so that all numbers in the series can be accounted for.

Every transaction requiring a cash disbursement should be verified and approved before payment is made. The official designated to *sign* checks should not be given authority to *approve* invoices for payment or to make entries in the accounting records. When a check is presented to a company official for signature, it should be accompanied by the approved invoice and voucher showing that the transaction has been fully verified and that payment is justified. When the check is signed, the supporting invoices and vouchers should be perforated or stamped "Paid" to eliminate any possibility of their being presented later in support of another check. If these rules are followed, it is almost impossible for a fraudulent cash disbursement to be concealed without the collusion of two or more persons.

In large companies which issue hundreds or thousands of checks daily, it is not practicable for a company official to sign each check manually. Instead, check-signing machines with various built-in control devices are used. This automation of the check-signing function does not weaken the system of internal control if attention is given to proper use of the machine and to control of the checks both before and after they pass through the check-signing machine.

CASE IN POINT ■ A large Boston-based construction company issued a great many checks every day but paid little attention to internal controls over its cash payments. Stacks of unissued checks were kept in an unlocked supply closet along with Styrofoam coffee cups. Because the number of checks issued was too great for the treasurer to sign them manually, a check-signing machine was used. This machine, after signing the checks, ejected them into a box equipped with a lock. In spite of warnings from the company's CPA firm, company officials found that it was "too inconvenient" to keep the box locked. The company also failed to make any use of the check-counting device built into the check-signing machine. Although the company maintained very large amounts on deposit in checking accounts, it did not bother to reconcile bank statements for weeks or months at a time.

These weaknesses in internal control led to a crisis when an employee was given a three-week-old bank statement and a bundle of paid checks and told to prepare a bank reconciliation. The employee found that the bundle of paid checks accompanying the bank statement was incomplete. No paid checks were on hand to support over $700,000 of charges deducted on the bank statement. Further investigation revealed that over $1 million in unauthorized and unrecorded checks had been paid from the corporation's bank accounts. These checks had been issued out of serial number sequence and had been run through the company check-signing machine. It was never determined who had carried out the theft and the money was not recovered.

The Voucher System

Objective 3
Explain how a voucher system can provide strong internal control over cash disbursements.

One widely used method of establishing control over cash disbursements is the voucher system. The basic idea of this system is that every transaction which will result in a cash disbursement must be verified, approved in writing, and recorded before a check is issued. A written authorization called a voucher is prepared for every transaction that will require a cash payment, regardless of whether the transaction is for payment of an expense, purchase of merchandise or a plant asset, or for payment of a liability. Remember that every purchase is treated as an independent transaction even though many purchases are made from the same supplier. Vouchers are serially numbered so that the loss or misplacement of a voucher would be immediately apparent.

To demonstrate the internal control inherent in a voucher system, consider the way a voucher is used in verifying an invoice received from a supplier. A serially numbered voucher is attached to each incoming invoice. The voucher (as illustrated on page 276) has spaces for listing the data from the invoice and showing the ledger accounts to be debited and credited in recording the transaction. Space is also provided for approval signatures for each step in the verification and approval process. A completed voucher provides a description of

Use of voucher
ensures
verification
of invoice

BROADHILL CORPORATION
Chicago, Illinois

Voucher No. 241 ← Serial number

Pay to *Black Company* Date *May 1, 19–*
3160 Main Street Date due *May 10, 19–*
Hilldale, Indiana

Date of Invoice *April 30, 19–* Gross amount $ *1,000.00*
Invoice number *847* Less: Cash discount *20.00*
Credit terms *2/10, n30* Net amount $ *980.00*

Approval

	Dates	Approved by
Extensions and footings verified	*May 1, 19–*	*RG*
Prices in agreement with purchase order	*May 1, 19–*	*RG*
Quantities in agreement with receiving report	*May 1, 19–*	*RG*
Credit terms in agreement with purchase order	*May 1, 19–*	*RG*
Account distribution & recording approved		*William Cross*
Approved for payment		*Judith Davis*

Verification procedures

Approved for payment

Accounting Supervisor

Reverse side
of voucher

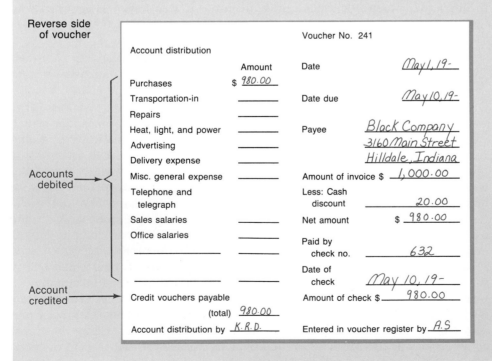

Account distribution

	Amount
Purchases	$ *980.00*
Transportation-in	
Repairs	
Heat, light, and power	
Advertising	
Delivery expense	
Misc. general expense	
Telephone and telegraph	
Sales salaries	
Office salaries	

Voucher No. 241

Date *May 1, 19–*

Date due *May 10, 19–*

Payee *Black Company*
3160 Main Street
Hilldale, Indiana

Amount of invoice $ *1,000.00*
Less: Cash discount *20.00*
Net amount $ *980.00*

Paid by check no. *632*

Date of check *May 10, 19–*
Amount of check $ *980.00*

Accounts debited →

Account credited →

Credit vouchers payable
(total) *980.00*

Account distribution by *K.R.D.* Entered in voucher register by *A.S*

the transaction and also of the work performed in verifying the liability and approving the cash disbursement.

■ **Preparing a Voucher** To illustrate the functioning of a voucher system, let us begin with the receipt of an invoice from a supplier. A voucher is prepared by filling in the appropriate blanks with information taken from the invoice, such as the invoice date, invoice number, amount, and the creditor's name and address. The voucher with the supplier's invoice attached is then sent to the employees responsible for verifying the extensions and footings on the invoice and for comparing prices, quantities, and terms with those specified in the purchase order and receiving report. When completion of the verification process has been evidenced by approval signatures of the persons performing these steps, the voucher and supporting documents are sent to an employee of the accounting department, who indicates on the voucher the accounts to be debited and credited. The voucher is then reviewed by an accounting official to provide assurance that the verification procedures have been satisfactorily completed and that the liability is a proper one.

Recording Approved Vouchers

After receiving the supervisory approval explained above, the voucher is entered in a journal called a *voucher register.* Entries in the voucher register indicate the nature of the expenditure by debiting the appropriate asset, expense, or liability accounts. The credit portion of each entry is always to a short-term liability account entitled *Vouchers Payable.* Note that the entry in the voucher register is not made until the liability has been verified and approved.

In a company using the voucher system, the ledger account, Vouchers Payable, replaces Accounts Payable. For purposes of balance sheet presentation, however, most companies continue to use the more widely understood term Accounts Payable.

Voucher systems are used principally by larger companies which process transactions by computer. Because our interest in voucher systems is in their internal control features and because manual voucher systems are rare, our discussion does not include illustration of a hand-operated voucher register.

■ **Paying the Voucher within the Discount Period** After the voucher has been entered in the voucher register, it is placed (with the supporting documents attached) in a tickler file according to the date of required payment. Cash discount periods generally run from the date of the invoice. Since a voucher is prepared for each invoice, the required date of payment is the last day on which a check can be prepared and mailed to the creditor in time to qualify for the discount.

When the payment date arrives, an employee in the accounting department removes the voucher from the unpaid file, draws a check for signature by the treasurer, and records payment of the voucher in a special journal called a *check register.* Since checks are issued only in payment of approved vouchers, every entry in the check register represents a debit to Vouchers Payable and a credit to Cash.

An important factor in achieving internal control is that the employee in the accounting department who prepares the check *is not authorized to sign it.*

The unsigned check and the supporting voucher are now sent to the treasurer or other designated official in the finance department. The treasurer reviews the voucher, especially the approval signatures, and signs the check. Thus, the invoice is *approved for payment* in the accounting department, but the actual cash disbursement is made by the finance department. *No one person or department is in a position both to approve invoices for payment and to issue signed checks.*

Once the check has been signed, the treasurer should mail it directly to the creditor. The voucher and all supporting documents are then perforated with a PAID stamp and are forwarded to the accounting department, which will note payment of the voucher in the voucher register and will file the paid voucher. The operation of a voucher system is illustrated in the flowchart on page 279. Notes have been made on the illustration identifying the most important internal control features in the system.

Petty Cash

Objective 4
Describe the operation of a petty cash fund.

As previously emphasized, adequate internal control over cash requires that all cash received be deposited in the bank and all disbursements be made by check. However, every business finds it convenient to have a small amount of cash on hand with which to make some minor expenditures. Examples include postage due, taxi fares, and small emergency purchases of office supplies. Internal control over these small cash payments can best be achieved through a petty cash fund. To issue checks for such items would be inconvenient, time-consuming, and expensive in relation to the amounts involved.

■ **Establishing the Petty Cash Fund**   To create a petty cash fund, a check is written payable to Petty Cash for a round amount such as $100 or $200, which will cover the small expenditures to be paid in cash for a period of two or three weeks. This check is cashed and the money kept on hand in a petty cash box or drawer in the office.

The entry for the issuance of the check is:

■
Creating the petty cash fund

Petty Cash	200	
Cash...		200
To establish a petty cash fund.		

■ **Making Disbursements from the Petty Cash Fund**   As cash payments are made from the petty cash box, the custodian of the fund is required to fill out a *petty cash receipt* or *voucher* for each expenditure. A petty cash receipt shows the date, the amount paid, the purpose of the expenditure, and the signature of the person receiving the money. A petty cash receipt should be prepared for every payment made from the fund. The petty cash box should, therefore, always contain cash and/or receipts totaling the exact amount of the fund.

The petty cash custodian should be informed that occasional surprise counts of the fund will be made and that he or she is personally responsible for the fund being intact at all times. Careless handling of petty cash has often been a first step toward large thefts; consequently, misuse of petty cash funds should not be tolerated.

OPERATION OF A VOUCHER SYSTEM

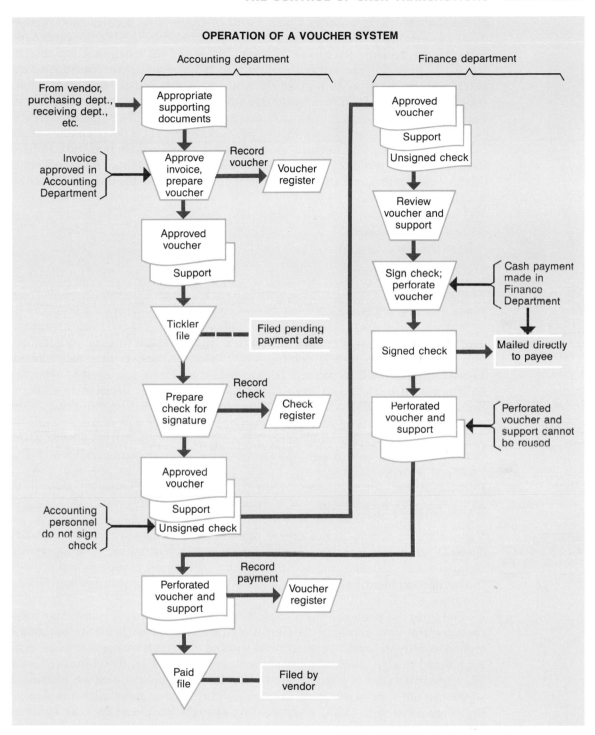

■ **Replenishing the Petty Cash Fund** Assume that a petty cash fund of $200 was established on June 1 and that payments totaling $174.95 were made from the fund during the next two weeks. Since the $200 originally placed in the fund is nearly exhausted, the fund should be replenished. To replenish a petty cash fund means to replace the amount of money that has been spent, thus restoring the fund to its original amount. A check is drawn payable to Petty Cash for the exact amount of the expenditures, $174.95. This check is cashed and the money placed in the petty cash box. The petty cash receipts (vouchers) totaling that amount are perforated to prevent their reuse and filed in support of the replenishment check. The journal entry to record the issuance of the check will debit the expense accounts indicated by inspection of the vouchers, as follows:

■ **Replenishment of petty cash fund**

Office Supplies Expense	80.60	
Transportation-In	16.00	
Postage Expense	45.25	
Miscellaneous Expense	33.10	
Cash		174.95

To replenish the petty cash fund.

Note that *expense accounts* are debited each time the fund is replenished. The Petty Cash account is debited only when the fund is first established. There ordinarily will be no further entries in the Petty Cash account after the fund is established, unless the fund is discontinued or a decision is made to change its size from the original $200 amount.

The petty cash fund is usually replenished at the end of an accounting period, even though the fund is not running low, so that all vouchers in the fund are charged to expense accounts before these accounts are closed and financial statements prepared.

Bank Checking Accounts

Objective 5
Prepare a bank reconciliation and explain its purpose.

Virtually every business has one or more bank checking accounts, which are opened and maintained in much the same way as a personal checking account. To open a personal checking account, you deposit money at a bank and provide the bank with identification data, such as a social security number and a driver's license.

For either a personal checking account or a business account, the bank requires the new depositor to sign a signature card, with his or her name signed exactly as it will be written in signing checks. If two persons are to be authorized to sign checks on the account, each must sign the signature card. The signature card is kept on file by the bank, so that any check bearing a signature not familiar to bank employees may be compared with the depositor's signature card. When a corporation opens a bank account, the board of directors will pass a resolution designating the officers or employees authorized to sign checks. A copy of the resolution must be given to the bank. Thus, access to cash is limited to those officers or employees designated by the board.

The bank provides the depositor with a book of checks and deposit tickets. Both the checks and the deposit tickets are imprinted with the depositor's name, address, and telephone number if desired. An identification number assigned by the bank to this new checking account is also printed on each check and each deposit ticket in magnetic ink so that transactions can be processed by computer. (See the illustrated deposit ticket and check on pages 282 and 283.)

Making Deposits

The depositor fills out a *deposit ticket* (usually in duplicate) for each deposit. The deposit ticket includes a listing of each check deposited and the code number of the bank on which it is drawn. Space is also provided for listing the amounts of coin and currency deposited. A bank teller signs the duplicate deposit ticket and returns it to the depositor. By keeping a file of duplicate deposit tickets, the depositor has *documentary evidence* of the amount of money turned over to the bank. Comparison of the duplicate deposit tickets with the cash receipts journal provides proof that the cashier has complied with company policy by making daily deposits of all cash received.

■ **Stop Payment Orders** Like other documents, checks are sometimes lost or stolen. The maker of a lost or stolen check should immediately issue a *stop payment order* to the bank, identifying the missing check by serial number and amount. Since a check itself is an order by the depositor instructing the bank to make a certain payment, a stop payment order is merely a reversal of the original order. After issuing a stop payment order for a missing check, the maker can cancel the original check in the record of cash payments and issue a replacement check.

If the bank should by accident pay a check after a stop payment has been filed by the depositor, this improper payment could not be deducted from the depositor's account. The bank would have to recover from the person who cashed the check or bear the loss itself.

Control Features of Bank Checking Accounts

We have already emphasized that all significant cash disbursements should be made by check. The use of checking accounts contributes to strong internal control in many ways. For example:

1 Checking accounts eliminate the need to keep large amounts of currency on hand.

2 The board of directors must notify the bank of the names of persons authorized to sign checks. Thus, access to cash is limited to those officers or employees designated by the board.

3 The person responsible for each cash disbursement is readily identified by the signature on the check.

4 The bank returns all checks which have been paid from the account. Thus, the depositor has documentary evidence showing the date and amount of each cash payment and the identity of the person who received the cash.

5 A comparison of the monthly *bank statement* with the depositor's accounting records will bring to light any errors made by the bank or by the depositor in accounting for cash transactions.

PARKVIEW COMPANY
109 Parkview Road
LOS ANGELES, CALIFORNIA 90034

DATE *July 12, 1991*

FOR CREDIT TO THE ACCOUNT

WESTERN NATIONAL BANK
Los Angeles, California 90064

Sign here for less cash

List checks by bank	Dollars	Cents
Currency	112	00
Coin		
Checks		
Checks from other side	911	77
SUBTOTAL		
Less cash received		
DEPOSIT TOTAL	1,023	77

00-000
0000

◄ If more than
2 checks list on
reverse side.
Enter totals here

1210·0035: 09991·2049·0124

DEPOSIT TICKET

PLEASE BE SURE THAT ALL ITEMS ARE PROPERLY
ENDORSED LIST EACH CHECK SEPARATELY

	DOLLARS	CENTS
CURRENCY		
COIN		
CHECKS (PROPERLY ENDORSED) LIST EACH SEPARATELY		
1 1-23/210	36	47
2 55-357/210	12	02
3 16-8/1220	155	15
4 11-35/210	100	00
5 2-3/1019	41	25
6 16-66/1220	15	00
7 5-2/220	90	00
8 16-66/1220	10	47
9 1-23/210	8	25
10 16-8/1220	37	69
11 16-941/1220	84	50
12 16-351/1220	98	00
13 16-21/119	68	47
14 1-67/1019	50	00
15 16-4/1220	104	50
16		
17		
18		
19		
20		
TOTAL	911	77

PLEASE ENTER THE TOTAL AMOUNT OF
DEPOSIT ON THE FRONT OF THIS TICKET

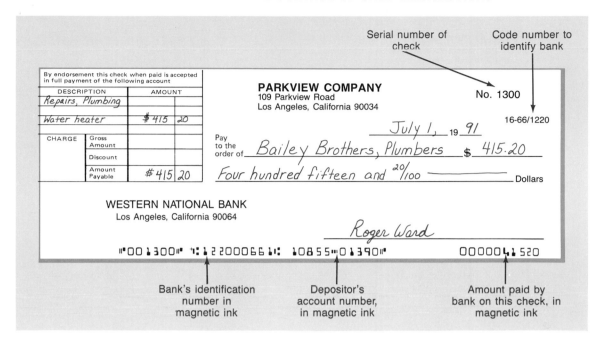

Serial number of check

Code number to identify bank

By endorsement this check when paid is accepted in full payment of the following account	
DESCRIPTION	AMOUNT
Repairs, Plumbing	
Water heater	$415 20

CHARGE	Gross Amount	
	Discount	
	Amount Payable	$415 20

PARKVIEW COMPANY
109 Parkview Road
Los Angeles, California 90034

No. 1300

16-66/1220

July 1, 19 91

Pay to the order of _Bailey Brothers, Plumbers_ $ 415.20

Four hundred fifteen and 20/100 _____ Dollars

WESTERN NATIONAL BANK
Los Angeles, California 90064

Roger Ward

⑈00⑆300⑈ ⑆⑆22000⑆⑆ ⑈⑆ ⑆0855⑈0⑆390⑈   00000⑆⑆520

Bank's identification number in magnetic ink

Depositor's account number, in magnetic ink

Amount paid by bank on this check, in magnetic ink

Bank Statements

Each month the bank will provide the depositor with a statement of the depositor's account, accompanied by the checks paid and charged to the account during the month.[2] As illustrated on the next page, a bank statement shows the balance on deposit at the beginning of the month, the deposits, the checks paid, any other debits and credits during the month, and the new balance at the end of the month. (To keep the illustration short, we have shown a limited number of deposits rather than one for each business day in the month.)

Reconciling the Bank Balance

A **bank reconciliation** is a schedule *explaining any differences* between the balance shown in the bank statement and the balance shown in the depositor's accounting records. Remember that both the bank and the depositor are maintaining independent records of the deposits, the checks, and the current balance of the bank account. Each month, the depositor should prepare a bank reconciliation to verify that these independent sets of records are in agreement. This reconciliation may disclose internal control failures, such as unauthorized cash disbursements or failures to deposit cash receipts, as well as errors in either the bank statement or the depositor's accounting records. In addition, the reconciliation helps to determine the "actual" amount of cash on deposit.

For strong internal control, the employee who reconciles the bank statement should not have any other responsibilities for cash.

■ **Normal Differences between Bank Records and Accounting Records** The balance shown in a monthly bank statement seldom equals the

---

[2] Large businesses may receive bank statements on a weekly basis.

WESTERN NATIONAL BANK
100 Olympic Boulevard
Los Angeles, California

Customer account no. 501390
Parkview Company
109 Parkview Road
Los Angeles, California

BANK STATEMENT
for the Month Ended July 31, 1991

DATE	CHECKS AND DEBITS		DEPOSITS		BALANCE
June 30					5,029.30
July 1			300.00		5,329.30
July 2	1,100.00		1,250.00		5,479.30
July 3	415.20	10.00			5,054.10
July 8			993.60		6,047.70
July 10	96.00	400.00			5,551.70
July 12	1,376.57		1,023.77		5,198.90
July 15	425.00				4,773.90
July 18	2,095.75		1,300.00		3,978.15
July 22	85.00	5.00 DM	500.00 CM		4,388.15
July 24	1,145.27		1,083.25		4,326.13
July 30	50.25 NSF		711.55		4,987.43
July 31	12.00 SC		24.74 INT		5,000.17

Explanation of symbols

CM Credit Memoranda   INT Interest on average balance
DM Debit Memoranda   NSF Not Sufficient Funds
E Error correction   SC Service Charge

Summary of activity:
Previous statement balance, June 30, 1991 .... $ 5,029.30
Checks and debit memoranda (13 items) .... (7,216.04)
Deposits and credit memoranda (9 items)............................. 7,186.91
Current statement balance, July 31, 1991 .... $ 5,000.17

balance appearing in the depositor's accounting records. Certain transactions recorded by the depositor may not have been recorded by the bank. The most common examples are:

1 Outstanding checks Checks issued and recorded by the company, but not yet presented to the bank for payment.

2 Deposits in transit Cash receipts recorded by the depositor, but which reached the bank too late to be included in the bank statement for the current month.

In addition, certain transactions appearing in the bank statement may not have been recorded by the depositor. For example:

1 Service charges Banks often charge a fee for handling small accounts. The amount of this charge usually depends upon both the average balance of the account and the number of checks paid during the month.

2 Charges for depositing NSF checks NSF stands for "Not Sufficient Funds." When checks are deposited, the bank increases (credits) the depositor's account. On occasion, one of these checks may prove to be uncollectible, because the maker of the check does not have sufficient funds in his or her account. In such cases, the bank will reduce the depositor's account by the amount of this uncollectible item and return the check to the depositor marked "NSF."

The depositor should view an NSF check as an account receivable from the maker of the check, not as cash. The accounting entry required consists of a debit to the account receivable from the customer and a credit to cash.

3 Credits for interest earned Most banks offer some checking accounts which earn interest. At month-end, this interest is credited to the depositor's account and reported on the bank statement.

4 Miscellaneous bank charges and credits Banks charge for services—such as printing checks, handling collections of notes receivable, and processing NSF checks. The bank deducts these charges from the depositor's account and notifies the depositor by including a debit memorandum in the monthly bank statement.[3] If the bank collects a note receivable on behalf of the depositor, it adds the money to the depositor's account and issues a credit memorandum.

In a bank reconciliation, the balances shown in the bank statement and in the accounting records both are adjusted for any unrecorded transactions. Additional adjustment may be required to correct any errors discovered in the bank statement or in the accounting records.

■ **Specific Steps in Preparing a Bank Reconciliation** To prepare a bank reconciliation, we determine those items which make up the difference between the ending *balance per the bank statement and the balance of cash according to the depositor's records.* By listing and studying these reconciling items we can determine the correct figure for cash owned. This is the amount which should appear on the balance sheet. The specific steps to be taken in preparing a bank reconciliation are:

1 Compare the deposits listed on the bank statement with the deposits shown in the company's records. Any deposits not yet recorded by the bank are deposits in transit and should be added to the balance shown in the bank statement. If there were any deposits in transit listed in the prior month's bank reconcilia-

[3] Banks view each depositor's account as a liability. Debit memoranda are issued for transactions that reduce this liability, such as bank service charges. Credit memoranda are issued to recognize an increase in this liability, as results, for example, from interest earned by the depositor.

tion, these amounts should appear as deposits in the current month's bank statement. If they do not appear, immediate investigation is necessary.

2 Arrange the paid checks in sequence by serial numbers and compare each check with the corresponding entry in the cash payments journal. Any checks issued but not yet paid by the bank should be listed as outstanding checks to be deducted from the balance reported in the bank statement. Determine whether the checks listed as outstanding in the bank reconciliation for the preceding month have been returned by the bank this month. If not, such checks should be listed as outstanding in the current reconciliation.

3 Add to the balance per the depositor's accounting records any credit memoranda issued by the bank which have not been recorded by the depositor. Examples in the illustrated bank reconciliation on page 287 are the $500 credit from collection of a note receivable and the $24.74 credit for interest earned.

4 Deduct from the balance per the depositor's records any debit memoranda issued by the bank which have not been recorded by the depositor. Examples in the illustrated bank statement on page 284 are the $5 collection fee, the $50.25 NSF check, and the $12 service charge.

5 Make appropriate additions or deductions to correct any errors in the balance per bank statement or the balance per depositor's records. An example in the illustrated bank reconciliation on page 287 is the $27 error by the company in recording check no. 875.

6 Determine that the adjusted balance of the bank statement is equal to the adjusted balance in the depositor's records.

7 Prepare journal entries to record any items in the bank reconciliation listed as adjustments to the balance per depositor's records.

■ **Illustration of a Bank Reconciliation** The July bank statement sent by the bank to Parkview Company was illustrated on page 284. This statement shows a balance of cash on deposit at July 31 of $5,000.17. Assume that on July 31, Parkview's ledger shows a bank balance of $4,262.83. The employee preparing the bank reconciliation has identified the following reconciling items:

1 A deposit of $410.90 made after banking hours on July 31 does not appear in the bank statement.

2 Four checks issued in July have not yet been paid by the bank. These checks are:

CHECK NO.	DATE	AMOUNT
801	June 15	$100.00
888	July 24	10.25
890	July 27	402.50
891	July 30	205.00

3 Two credit memoranda were included in the bank statement:

DATE	AMOUNT	EXPLANATION
July 22	$500.00	Proceeds from collection of a non-interest-bearing note receivable from J. David. Parkview Company had left this note with the bank's collection department.
July 31	24.74	Interest earned on average account balance during July.

4 Three debit memoranda accompanied the bank statement:

DATE	AMOUNT	EXPLANATION
July 22	$ 5.00	Fee charged by bank for handling collection of note receivable.
July 30	50.25	Check from customer J. B. Ball deposited by Parkview Company charged back as NSF.
July 31	12.00	Service charge by bank for the month of July.

5 Check no. 875 was issued July 20 in the amount of $85 but was erroneously recorded in the cash payments journal as $58. The check, in payment of telephone expense, was paid by the bank and correctly listed at $85 in the bank statement. In Parkview's ledger, the Cash account is *overstated* by $27 because of this error ($85 − $58 = $27).

The July 31 bank reconciliation for Parkview Company is shown below. (The numbered arrows coincide both with the steps in preparing a bank reconciliation listed on pages 285–286 and with the reconciling items listed above.)

PARKVIEW COMPANY
Bank Reconciliation
July 31, 19___

Balance per bank statement, July 31, 19___			$5,000.17
(1) Add: Deposit of July 31 not recorded by bank			410.90
			$5,411.07
(2) Deduct: Outstanding checks:			
No. 801		$100.00	
No. 888		10.25	
No. 890		402.50	
No. 891		205.00	717.75
Adjusted cash balance			**$4,693.32**
Balance per depositor's records, July 31, 19___			$4,262.83
(3) Add: Note receivable collected for us by bank		$500.00	
Interest earned during July		24.74	524.74
			$4,787.57
(4) Deduct: Collection fee		$ 5.00	
NSF check of J. B. Ball		50.25	
Service charge		12.00	
(5) Error on check stub no. 875		27.00	94.25
Adjusted cash balance (as above)			**$4,693.32**

(6)

■ **Updating the Accounting Records** The last step in reconciling a bank statement is to update the depositor's accounting records for any unrecorded cash transactions brought to light. In the bank reconciliation, every adjustment to the *balance per depositor's records* is a cash receipt or a cash payment that has not been recorded in the depositor's accounts. Therefore, *each of these items should be recorded.*

In this illustration and in our assignment material, we will follow a policy of making one journal entry to record the unrecorded cash receipts, and another to record the unrecorded cash reductions. (Acceptable alternatives would be to make separate journal entries for each item or to make one compound entry for all items.) Based on our recording policy, the entries to update the accounting records of Parkview Company are:

■
Per bank credit memoranda . . .

Cash	*524.74*	
Notes Receivable		*500.00*
Interest Revenue		*24.74*

To record collection of note receivable from J. David collected by bank and interest earned on bank account in July.

. . . per bank debit memoranda (and correction of an error)

Bank Service Charges	*17.00*	
Accounts Receivable, J. B. Ball	*50.25*	
Telephone Expense	*27.00*	
Cash		*94.25*

To record bank charges (service charge, $12; collection fee, $5), to reclassify NSF check from customer J. B. Ball as an account receivable, and to correct understatement of cash payment for telephone expense.

End-of-Chapter Review

CONCEPTS INTRODUCED OR EMPHASIZED IN CHAPTER 7

The major concepts in this chapter are:

■ The objectives of cash management.

■ Internal control measures for cash receipts.

■ The role of a voucher system in maintaining internal control over cash disbursements.

■ The reconciliation of bank checking accounts as an overall internal control over cash transactions.

With respect to the asset cash, internal control is of special importance and balance sheet valuation is not a major problem. As we discuss other assets (such as receivables, inventory, and plant and equipment) in the following chapters, we will see that the *valuation* of these assets is an issue of prime importance and materially affects the measurement of net income.

KEY TERMS INTRODUCED OR EMPHASIZED IN CHAPTER 7

Bank reconciliation   An analysis that explains the difference between the balance of cash shown on the bank statement and the balance of cash shown in the depositor's records.

Cash   Currency, coins, checks, money orders, and any other medium of exchange which a bank will accept for deposit.

Cash over and short   A ledger account used to accumulate the cash overages and shortages resulting from errors in making change.

Check register   A simplified version of the cash payments journal used for recording cash payments when a voucher system is in use.

Deposit ticket   A form filled out by the depositor listing the checks and currency being deposited. Each check is listed separately and identified by the code number of the bank on which it is drawn.

Deposits in transit   Cash receipts which have been entered in the depositor's accounting records and mailed to the bank or left in the bank's night depository, but which reached the bank too late to be included in the current monthly bank statement.

NSF check   A customer's check which was deposited but returned because of a lack of funds (Not Sufficient Funds) in the account on which the check was drawn.

Outstanding checks   Checks issued by a business to suppliers, employees, or other payees but not yet presented to the bank for payment.

Petty cash fund   A small amount of cash set aside for making minor cash payments for which writing of checks is not practicable.

Voucher   A written authorization used in approving a transaction for recording and payment.

Voucher register   A book of original entry used to record vouchers which have been approved for payment.

Voucher system   An accounting system designed to provide strong internal control over cash disbursements. Requires that every transaction which will result in a cash payment be verified, approved, and recorded before a check is prepared.

DEMONSTRATION PROBLEM FOR YOUR REVIEW

The information listed below is available in reconciling the bank balance for the White River Company on November 30, 19__.

(1) The bank statement at November 30 indicated a balance of $9,734.70. The ledger account for Cash showed a balance at November 30 of $12,761.94.

(2) The November 30 cash receipts of $5,846.20 had been mailed to the bank on that date and did not appear among the deposits on the November bank statement.

(3) Of the checks issued in November, the following were not included among the paid checks returned by the bank:

CHECK NO.	AMOUNT	CHECK NO.	AMOUNT
924	$136.25	944	$ 95.00
940	105.00	945	716.15
941	11.46	946	60.00
943	826.70		

(4) A service charge for $340 by the bank had been made in error against the White River Company account.

(5) The paid checks returned with the November bank statement disclosed two errors in the company's cash records. Check no. 936 for $504.00 had been erroneously recorded as $50.40 in the cash payments journal, and check no. 942 for $245.50 had been recorded as $254.50. Check no. 936 was issued in payment of advertising expense and check no. 942 was for the acquisition of office equipment.

(6) Included with the November bank statement was an NSF check for $220 signed by a customer, J. Wilson. This amount had been charged against the bank account on November 30.

(7) A non-interest-bearing note receivable for $1,890 owned by the White River Company had been left with the bank for collection. On November 30 the company received a memorandum from the bank indicating that the note had been collected and credited to the company's account after deduction of a $5 collection charge. No entry has been made by the company to record collection of the note.

(8) A debit memorandum for $12 was enclosed with the paid checks at November 30. This charge covered the printing of checkbooks bearing the White River Company name and address.

Instructions **a** Prepare a bank reconciliation at November 30.

b Prepare journal entries required at November 30 to bring the company's records up-to-date.

SOLUTION TO DEMONSTRATION PROBLEM

a

WHITE RIVER COMPANY
Bank Reconciliation
November 30, 19___

Balance per bank statement, Nov. 30...			$ 9,734.70
Add: Deposit of Nov. 30 not recorded by			
bank..		$5,846.20	
Service charge made by bank in			
error..		340.00	6,186.20
Subtotal...			$15,920.90
Less: Outstanding checks on Nov. 30:			
No. 924		$ 136.25	
No. 940		105.00	
No. 941		11.46	
No. 943		826.70	
No. 944		95.00	
No. 945		716.15	
No. 946		60.00	1,950.56
Adjusted cash balance			$13,970.34

Balance per depositor's records, Nov. 30......................................			$12,761.94
Add: Error in recording check no. 942			
for office equipment:			
Recorded as	$254.50		
Correct amount	245.50	$ 9.00	
Note receivable collected by bank,			
$1,890, less collection charge, $5		1,885.00	1,894.00
			$14,655.94

Less: Error in recording check no. 936
     for advertising expense:
          Correct amount $504.00
          Recorded as .... 50.40 $ 453.60
          NSF check, J. Wilson 220.00
          Charge by bank for printing checks 12.00   685.60
Adjusted cash balance (as above) $13,970.34

b Journal entries required at November 30 to bring the company's records up-to-date.

19—
Nov. 30   Cash 1,894.00
          Miscellaneous Expense....................................   5.00
               Office Equipment.....................................   9.00
               Notes Receivable 1,890.00
          To record increase in Cash account as indicated by
          bank reconciliation.

Nov. 30   Advertising Expense.......................................   453.60
          Miscellaneous Expense....................................   12.00
          Accounts Receivable, J. Wilson 220.00
               Cash 685.60
          To record decreases in Cash account as indicated
          by bank reconciliation.

SELF-TEST QUESTIONS

The answers to these questions appear on page 303.

1 Which of the following practices contributes to efficient cash management?

a Never borrow money—maintain a cash balance sufficient to make all necessary payments.

b Record all cash receipts and cash payments at the end of the month when reconciling the bank statements.

c Prepare monthly forecasts of planned cash receipts, payments and anticipated cash balances up to a year in advance.

d Pay each bill as soon as the invoice arrives.

2 Each of the following measures strengthens internal control over cash receipts *except:*

a The use of a voucher system.

b Preparation of a daily listing of all checks received through the mail.

c The deposit of cash receipts intact in the bank on a daily basis.

d The use of cash registers.

3 When a voucher system is in use:

a The voucher and supporting documents are perforated when the check is prepared for signature.

b The finance department signs the check and perforates the voucher and supporting documents.

c The accounting department does not have access to the perforated vouchers and support.

d The finance department signs the check and returns the signed check to the accounting department to be mailed.

Use the following data for questions 4 and 5.

Quinn Company's bank statement at January 31 shows a balance of $13,360, while the ledger account for Cash in Quinn's ledger shows a balance of $12,890 at the same date. The only reconciling items are the following:
—Deposit in transit, $890.
—Bank service charge, $24.
—NSF check from customer Greg Denton in the amount of $426.
—Error in recording check No. 389 for rent: check was written in the amount of $1,320, but was recorded in the bank statement as $1,230.
—Outstanding checks, $?????

4 What is the total amount of outstanding checks at January 31?

   a $1,048   **b** $868   **c** $1,900   **d** $1,720

5 Assuming a single journal entry is made to adjust Quinn Company's accounting records at January 31, the journal entry includes:

a A debit to Rent Expense for $90.

b A credit to Accounts Receivable, G. Denton, for $426.

c A credit to Cash for $450.

d A credit to Cash for $1,720.

Assignment Material

REVIEW QUESTIONS

1 If a company has checking accounts in three banks, should it maintain a separate ledger account for each? Should the company's balance sheet show as three separate items the amounts on deposit in the three banks? Explain.

2 Does the expression "efficient management of cash" mean anything more than procedures to prevent losses from fraud or theft? Explain.

3 Among the various assets owned by a business, cash is probably the one for which strong internal control is most urgently needed. What specific attributes of cash cause this special need for internal control?

4 The accountant's work in verifying the amount of cash which should appear in a balance sheet is aided by the existence of two independent records of the deposits, the checks, and the running balance of cash. Identify these two independent records of cash transactions.

5 Mention some principles to be observed by a business in establishing strong internal control over cash receipts.

6 Explain how internal control over cash transactions is strengthened by compliance with the following rule: "Deposit each day's cash receipts intact in the bank, and make all disbursements by check."

7 Ringo Store sells only for cash and records all sales on cash registers before delivering merchandise to the customers. On a given day the cash count at the close of business indicated $10.25 less cash than was shown by the totals on the cash register tapes. In what account would this cash shortage be recorded? Would the account be debited or credited?

8 Name three internal control practices relating to cash which would be practicable even in a small business having little opportunity for division of duties.

9 With respect to a *voucher system,* what is meant by the terms *voucher, voucher register,* and *check register?*

10 Randall Company uses a voucher system to control its cash disbursements. With respect to a purchase of merchandise, what three documents would need to be examined to verify that the voucher should be approved?

11 Suggest an internal control procedure to prevent the documents supporting a paid voucher from being resubmitted later in support of another cash disbursement.

12 Pico Stationery Shop has for years maintained a petty cash fund of $75, which is replenished twice a month.

    a How many debit entries would you expect to find in the Petty Cash account each year?

    b When would expenditures from the petty cash fund be entered in the ledger accounts?

13 A check for $455 issued in payment of an account payable was erroneously listed in the cash payments journal as $545. The error was discovered early in the following month when the paid check was returned by the bank. What corrective action is needed?

14 It is standard accounting practice to treat as cash all checks received from customers. When a customer's check is received, recorded, and deposited, but later returned by the bank marked NSF, what accounting entry or entries would be appropriate?

15 List two items often encountered in reconciling a bank account which may cause cash per the bank statement to be larger than the balance of cash shown in the accounts.

16 In the reconciliation of a bank account, what reconciling items necessitate a journal entry in the depositor's accounting records?

17 On January 10 Susan Jones wrote a check for $500 and mailed it to Joe Smith in payment of a debt. On January 25, Smith called and asked to be paid, stating that no check had been received. Jones placed a stop payment order with her bank and wrote another check which she delivered personally to Smith.

    a What information should Jones have given the bank in connection with the stop payment order in order that the bank could guard against paying the first check?

    b In preparing a bank reconciliation at January 31, should Jones include on the outstanding check list the check on which payment had been stopped? Explain.

    c If the first check was presented to the bank by a third person on February 15 and was cashed by the bank despite the existence of the stop payment order, would the loss fall on Jones, Smith, or the bank?

18 What information usually appears on a bank statement?

19 Evaluate the following statement. "The purpose of preparing a bank reconciliation is to determine which of two independent records of cash is correct. If both records are incorrect, the reconciliation cannot be completed."

EXERCISES

Exercise 7-1
Accounting
terminology

Listed below are nine technical accounting terms introduced in this chapter:

NSF checks	*Duplicate deposit*	*Cash management*
Voucher system	*ticket*	*Stop payment order*
Cash over and short	*Bank reconciliation*	*Petty cash fund*
Cash equivalents		

Each of the following statements may (or may not) describe one of these technical terms. For each statement, indicate the accounting term described, or answer "None" if the statement does not correctly describe any of the terms.

a Instruction to be issued by maker of a check which has been lost or stolen.

b Documentary evidence of the amount of money the owner of a bank checking account has placed in the account.

c Includes measures to prevent the maintenance of excessively large balances in non-interest-bearing bank accounts.

d The account in which errors in making change for cash customers are recorded.

e Short-term liquid investments (such as U.S. Treasury bills) which produce revenue.

f Checks issued by a business which have not yet been presented for payment.

g Documents which an employee handling cash receipts should not have authority to issue.

h Provides control of cash disbursements by requiring written authorization for every transaction that will require a cash payment.

**Exercise 7-2
Internal control;
identifying
strength and
weakness**

Some of the following practices are suggestive of strength in internal controls; others are suggestive of weakness. Identify each of the eight practices with the term Strength or Weakness. Give reasons for your answers.

a Accounting department personnel are not authorized to prepare bank reconciliations. This procedure is performed in the finance department and the accounting department is notified of any required adjustments to the accounts.

b Checks received through the mail are recorded daily by the person maintaining accounts receivable records.

c All cash receipts are deposited daily.

d Any difference between a day's over-the-counter cash receipts and the day's total shown by the cash register is added to or removed from petty cash.

e After the monthly bank reconciliation has been prepared, any difference between the adjusted balance per the depositor's records and the adjusted balance per the bank statement is entered in the Cash Over and Short account.

f Employees who handle cash receipts are not authorized to issue credit memoranda or to write off accounts receivable as uncollectible.

g Vouchers and all supporting documents are perforated with a "PAID" stamp before being sent to the finance department for review and signing of checks.

h Personnel in the accounting department are not authorized to handle cash receipts. Therefore, accounts receivable records are maintained by the credit manager, who handles all collections from customers.

**Exercise 7-3
Subdivision of
duties**

Certain subdivisions of duties are highly desirable for the purpose of achieving a reasonable degree of internal control. For each of the following five responsibilities, explain whether or not assigning the duty to an employee who also handles cash receipts would represent a significant weakness in internal control. Briefly explain your reasoning.

a Responsibility for issuing credit memoranda for sales returns.

b Responsibility for preparing a control listing of all cash collections.

c Responsibility for preparing monthly bank reconciliations.

d Responsibility for executing both cash and credit sales transactions.

e Responsibility for maintaining the general ledger.

f Responsibility for maintaining the accounts receivable subsidiary ledger.

Exercise 7-4
Voucher system

Laser Optic, Inc., uses a voucher system. The following transactions occurred early this month.

(a) Voucher no. 100 prepared to purchase office equipment at cost of $4,000 from Coast Furniture Co.

(b) Check no. 114 issued in payment of voucher no. 100.

(c) Voucher no. 101 prepared to establish a petty cash fund of $150.

(d) Check no. 115 issued in payment of voucher no. 101.

(e) Voucher no. 102 prepared to replenish the petty cash fund which contained $40 cash, and receipts for postage $38, miscellaneous expense $54, and delivery service $18.

(f) Check no. 116 issued in payment of voucher no. 102. Check cashed and proceeds placed in petty cash fund.

You are to record the transactions in general journal form (without explanations). Also indicate after each entry the journal (or book of original entry) in which in actual practice the transaction would be recorded. For example, your treatment of transaction **(a)** should be as follows:

(a) Office Equipment *4,000*
         Vouchers Payable *4,000*
    (Voucher register)

Exercise 7-5
Petty cash

Test

Sunset Plaza established a petty cash fund of $150 on June 1. On June 20 the fund was replenished for the payments made to date as shown by the following petty cash vouchers: freight-in, $9.30; postage, $46; telephone expense, $8.20; repairs, $34.70; miscellaneous expense, $27. Prepare journal entries in *general journal form* to record the establishment of the fund on June 1 and its replenishment on June 20.

Exercise 7-6
Short bank
reconciliation

The following information relating to the bank checking account is available for Music Hall at July 31:

Balance per bank statement at July 31	$19,893.25
Balance per depositor's records	18,681.35
Outstanding checks	2,102.50
Deposits in transit...	872.60
Service charge by bank...	18.00

Prepare a bank reconciliation for Music Hall at July 31.

Exercise 7-7
Bank
reconciliation and
entries to update
the accounting
records

Test

Shown below is the information needed to prepare a bank reconciliation for Data Flow, Inc., at December 31.

(1) At December 31, cash per the bank statement was $15,981; cash per the company's records was $17,445.

(2) Two debit memoranda accompanied the bank statement: service charges for December of $24, and a $600 check drawn by Jane Jones marked NSF.

(3) Cash receipts of $4,353 on December 31 were not deposited until January.

(4) The following checks had been issued in December but were not included among the paid checks returned by the bank: no. 620 for $978, no. 630 for $2,052, and no. 641 for $483.

Instructions

a Prepare a bank reconciliation at December 31.

b Prepare the necessary journal entry or entries to update the accounting records of Data Flow, Inc.

Exercise 7-8
Updating the
cash account

In this exercise we focus on some of the basic computations required in almost all bank reconciliations. At the end of November, Glacier Lodge received a bank statement showing a balance of $105,000. The balance included interest earned during November of $450. All checks issued by Glacier Lodge were returned with the November bank statement except for 10 checks totaling $16,000 issued on November 30. Also, a deposit of $8,000 mailed to the bank by Glacier Lodge on November 30 did not appear on the bank statement.

Instructions

a Compute the amount of cash to appear on the November 30 balance sheet of Glacier Lodge. Show all computations.

b Compute the amount of cash shown by Glacier Company's records *before* any month-end entries were made to update the company's records.

PROBLEMS

Group A

Problem 7A-1
Internal control
procedures

Listed below are nine errors or problems which might occur in the processing of cash transactions. Also shown is a separate list of internal control procedures.

Possible Errors or Problems

a Joy Hart, an employee of Center Hardware, frequently has trouble in getting the bank reconciliation to balance. If the book balance is more than the bank balance, she writes a check payable to Cash and cashes it. If the book balance is less than the bank balance, she makes an accounting entry debiting Cash and crediting Cash Over and Short.

b Without fear of detection, the cashier sometimes abstracts cash forwarded to him from the mailroom or the sales department instead of depositing these receipts in the company's bank account.

c The monthly bank reconciliation continually shows a difference between the adjusted bank balance and the adjusted book balance because the cashier regularly deposits actual cash receipts but the debits to the Cash account reflect cash register readings which differ by the amount of errors in making change in cash sales transactions.

d All cash received from Monday through Thursday was lost in a burglary on Thursday night.

e A salesclerk occasionally makes an error in the amount of change given to a customer.

f The official designated to sign checks is able to steal blank checks and issue them for unauthorized purposes without fear of detection.

g In serving customers who do not appear to be attentive, a salesclerk often rings up a sale at less than the actual sales amount and then removes the additional cash collected from the customer.

h John Davis, who has prepared bank reconciliations for Marlo Corporation for several years has noticed that some checks issued by the company are never presented for payment. Davis, therefore, has formed the habit of dropping any checks outstanding for more than six months from the outstanding checklist and removing a corresponding amount of cash from the cash receipts. These actions taken together have left the ledger account for cash in agreement with the adjusted bank balance and have enriched Davis substantially.

i A voucher was circulated through the system twice, causing the supplier to be paid twice for the same invoice.

Internal Control Procedures

1 Periodic reconciliation of bank statements to accounting records.

2 Use of a Cash Over and Short account.

3 Adequate subdivision of duties.

4 Use of prenumbered sales tickets.

5 Depositing each day's cash receipts intact in the bank.

6 Use of electronic cash registers equipped with optical scanners to read magnetically coded labels on merchandise.

7 Immediate preparation of a control listing when cash is received, and the comparison of this listing to bank deposits.

8 Cancellation of paid vouchers.

9 Requirement that a voucher be prepared as advance authorization of every cash disbursement.

0 None of the above control procedures can effectively prevent this type of error from occurring.

Instructions   List the letters (**a** through **i**) designating each possible error or problem. Beside this letter, place the number indicating the internal control procedure that should prevent this type of error or problem from occurring. If none of the specified internal control procedures would effectively prevent the error, place an "0" opposite the letter.

**Problem 7A-2
Operating a petty
cash fund**   On September 1 Bay City Graphics established a petty cash fund of $200. The company does not use a voucher system. The petty cash fund was established by writing a check for $200 payable to Petty Cash. This check was cashed and the money placed in a lockbox in the custody of the cashier.

During September small payments from the petty cash fund totaled $176.20, as shown below.

Transportation-in	$ 37.10
Postage expense	72.00
Automobile expense	12.50
Telephone expense	19.00
Parking expense	35.60
Total of petty cash vouchers	$176.20

A check was issued and cashed to replenish the petty cash fund on September 30.

Instructions   **a** Prepare a journal entry (in general journal form) to record the establishment of the petty cash fund on September 1.

b Prepare a journal entry to record the replenishment of the petty cash fund at September 30.

c Net income for September for Bay City Graphics amounted to $2,412.80 as shown by the September income statement. What amount of net income would have appeared on the September income statement if Bay City Graphics had failed to replenish the petty cash fund at September 30?

**Problem 7A-3
Preparing a bank
reconciliation**   The information necessary for preparing a bank reconciliation for Chapel School at November 30, 19___, appears below.

(1) As of November 30, cash per the accounting records was $32,406; per bank statement, $27,754.

(2) Cash receipts of $6,244 on November 30 were not deposited until December 1.

(3) Among the paid checks returned by the bank was a stolen check for $1,008 paid in error by the bank after Chapel School had issued a stop payment order to the bank. Note that the bank was at fault.

(4) The following memoranda accompanied the bank statement:

(a) A debit memo for service charges for the month of November, $14.

(b) A debit memo attached to a $778 check of Frank Miller, marked NSF.

(c) A credit memo showing that interest of $90 had been earned on the bank account during November.

(5) The following checks had been issued but were not included in the paid checks returned by the bank: no. 921 for $1,564, no. 924 for $964, and no. 925 for $774.

Instructions Prepare a bank reconciliation for Chapel School at November 30, 19__, in the form illustrated on page 287.

Problem 7A-4
A more
comprehensive
bank
reconciliation

During July the cash transactions and cash balances of Custom Harvest were as follows:

(1) The cash balance per the bank statement at July 31 was $28,945.27.

(2) The ledger account for Cash had a balance at July 31 of $26,686.95.

(3) Cash receipts on July 31 amounted to $4,000. These cash receipts were left at the bank in the night depository chute after banking hours on July 31 and therefore were not included by the bank in the July bank statement.

(4) Included with the July bank statement was a credit memorandum showing interest earned by the depositor on this account in the amount of $80.

(5) Another credit memorandum enclosed with the July bank statement showed that a non-interest-bearing note for $4,545 from Ralph Warde, left with the bank for collection, had been collected and the proceeds credited to the account of Custom Harvest.

(6) Also included with the July bank statement was a debit memorandum from the bank for $7.65 representing service charges for July.

(7) Comparison of the paid checks returned by the bank with the entries in the cash payments journal revealed that check no. 821 for $835.02 issued July 15 in payment for office equipment had been erroneously entered in the cash payments journal as $853.02.

(8) Examination of the paid checks also revealed that three checks, all issued in July, had not yet been paid by the bank: no. 811 for $861.12; no. 814 for $640.80; no. 823 for $301.05.

(9) Included with the July bank statement was a $180 check drawn by Edward Jones, a customer of Custom Harvest. This check was marked NSF. It had been included in the deposit of July 27 but had been charged back against the company's account on July 31.

Instructions **a** Prepare a bank reconciliation for Custom Harvest at July 31.

b Prepare journal entries (in general journal form) to adjust the accounts at July 31. Assume that the accounts have not been closed.

c State the amount of cash which should appear on the balance sheet at July 31.

Problem 7A-5
Internal control—
a short case
study

John Smith, a trusted employee of Bluestem Products, found himself in personal financial difficulties and decided to "borrow" (steal) $3,000 from the company and to conceal his theft.

As a first step, Smith removed $3,000 in currency from the cash register. This amount represented the bulk of the cash received in over-the-counter sales during the three business days since the last bank deposit. Smith then removed a $3,000 check from the day's incoming mail; this check had been mailed in by a customer, Michael Adams, in full payment of his account. Smith made no entry in the cash receipts journal for the $3,000 collection from Adams but deposited the check in Bluestem Products' bank account in place of the $3,000 over-the-counter cash receipts he had stolen.

In order to keep Adams from protesting when his month-end statement reached him, Smith made a general journal entry debiting Sales Returns and Allowances and crediting Accounts Receivable—Michael Adams. Smith posted this entry to the two general ledger accounts affected and also to Adams's account in the subsidiary ledger for accounts receivable.

Instructions   **a** Did these actions by Smith cause the general ledger to be out of balance or the subsidiary ledger to disagree with the controlling account? Explain.

b Assume that Bluestem Products prepares financial statements at the end of the month without discovering the theft. Would any items in the balance sheet or the income statement be in error? Explain.

c Several weaknesses in internal control apparently exist in Bluestem Products. Indicate three specific changes needed to strengthen internal control over cash receipts.

Group B

**Problem 7B-1
Internal control
procedures**

Listed below are nine errors or problems which might occur in the processing of cash transactions. Also shown is a list of internal control procedures.

Possible Errors or Problems

a A salesclerk often rings up a sale at less than the actual sales price and then removes the additional cash collected from the customer.

b The cashier conceals a shortage of cash by making an entry in the general ledger debiting Miscellaneous Expense and crediting Cash.

c A salesclerk occasionally makes an error in the amount of change given to a customer.

d The employee designated to sign checks is able to steal blank checks and issue them for unauthorized purposes without fear of detection.

e All cash received during the last four days is lost in a burglary on Thursday night.

f An employee steals the cash collected from a customer for an account receivable and conceals this theft by issuing a credit memorandum indicating that the customer returned the merchandise.

g The same voucher was circulated through the system twice, causing the supplier to be paid twice for the same invoice.

h Without fear of detection, the cashier sometimes abstracts cash forwarded to him from the mailroom or the sales department instead of depositing these receipts in the company's bank account.

i A purchase invoice was paid even though the merchandise was never received.

Internal Control Procedures

1 Monthly reconciliation of bank statements to accounting records.

2 Use of a Cash Over and Short account.

3 Adequate subdivision of duties.

4 Use of prenumbered sales tickets.

5 Depositing each day's cash receipts intact in the bank.

6 Use of electronic cash registers equipped with optical scanners to read magnetically coded labels on merchandise.

7 Immediate preparation of a control listing when cash is received, and the comparison of this listing to bank deposits.

8 Cancellation of paid vouchers.

9 Requirement that a voucher be prepared as advance authorization of every cash disbursement.

0 None of the above control procedures can effectively prevent this type of error from occurring.

Instructions

List the letters (**a** through **i**) designating each possible error or problem. Beside this letter, place the number indicating the internal control procedure that should prevent this type of error or problem from occurring. If none of the specified internal control procedures would effectively prevent the error, place an "0" opposite the letter.

Problem 7B-2
Operating a petty
cash fund

Shore Line Times controls its small cash payments by use of a petty cash fund. The company does not use a voucher system. Shown below are the transactions involving the establishment of the fund and its replenishment at September 30, the end of the company's fiscal year:

Sept. 12   A check for $360 was issued and cashed to establish a petty cash fund.

Sept. 30   The fund was replenished. Petty cash vouchers in the fund were as follows:

Office supplies expense	$119.10
Postage expense	73.92
Telephone and telegraph expense	23.10
Miscellaneous expense	66.44

Sept. 30   Management wished to replenish the fund before the accounts were closed for the fiscal year. A check was therefore issued and cashed on this date in the amount necessary to replenish the fund.

Instructions

a Prepare journal entries in general journal form to record the establishment of the fund on September 12 and its replenishment on September 30.

b What would have been the effect, if any, on net income for the fiscal year ended September 30 if the company had forgotten to replenish the fund on September 30? Explain.

Problem 7B-3
Preparing a bank
reconciliation

The information required to prepare a bank reconciliation for Arrowhead Boat Works at November 30 is listed below.

(1) At November 30, the balance of cash per the bank statement was $56,637. Cash per the accounting records was $63,750.

(2) The November 30 cash receipts of $9,366 were deposited on December 1.

(3) The bank statement showed that $250.50 interest had been earned on this checking account during November.

(4) The outstanding checks at November 30 were no. 645 for $1,446 and no. 647 for $1,627.50.

(5) Two debit memoranda were enclosed with the November bank statement: these items were:

(a) Service charge, $21

(b) An NSF check for $1,050 drawn by customer Hayes Kent.

Instructions

a Prepare a bank reconciliation at November 30.

b Update the accounting records at November 30 by preparing two adjusting journal entries. One entry should record the interest earned and the other should deal with the bank service charge and the NSF check.
Explain

Problem 7B-4
A more
comprehensive
bank
reconciliation

Holden, Inc., reports the following information concerning cash balances and cash transactions for the month of September:

(1) Cash balance per bank statement as of September 30 was $20,793.25.

(2) Two debit memoranda accompanied the bank statement: one for $4 was for service charges for the month; the other for $64.60 was attached to an NSF check from A. Smith.

(3) Included with the bank statement was a $9 credit memorandum for interest earned on the bank account in September.

(4) The paid checks returned with the September bank statement disclosed an error in Holden's cash records. Check no. 851 for $77.44 for telephone expense had erroneously been listed in the cash payments journal as $44.77.

(5) A collection charge for $126.00 (not applicable to Holden, Inc.) was erroneously deducted from the account by the bank. Notice that this was the bank's error.

(6) Cash receipts of September 30 amounting to $585.25 were mailed to the bank too late to be included in the September bank statement.

(7) Checks outstanding as of September 30 were as follows: no. 860 for $151.93, no. 867 for $82.46, and no. 869 for $123.61.

(8) The Cash account showed the following entries during September:

CASH

Sept	1	Balance		18,341.82	Sept	30			CD7	11,514.63
	30		CR5	14,411.58						

Instructions   **a** Prepare a bank reconciliation at September 30.

b Prepare the necessary adjusting entries in general journal form.

Problem 7B-5
Weak internal
control and a
fraudulent bank
reconciliation

Bayview Company, a successful small business, had never given much consideration to internal control concepts and the internal controls over cash transactions were not adequate. Betty Jones, the cashier-bookkeeper, handled cash receipts, made small disbursements from the cash receipts, maintained accounting records, and prepared the monthly reconciliations of the bank account.

The bank statement for the month ended April 30 showed a balance on deposit of $29,500. The outstanding checks were as follows: no. 6052 for $431.16, no. 6173 for $366.00, no. 6174 for $530.61, no. 7611 for $316.13, no. 7613 for $614.04, and no. 7622 for $310.01. The balance of cash shown by the company's ledger account for Cash was $34,824.96, which included the cash on hand.

Recognizing the weakness existing in internal control over cash transactions, Jones removed all the cash on hand in excess of $6,365.14, and then prepared the following reconciliation in an effort to conceal this theft. In studying this reconciliation, you should take nothing for granted and keep in mind that Jones is trying to mislead anyone who reviews her work.

Balance per accounting records, Apr. 30		*$34,824.96*
Add: Outstanding checks:		
No. 7611	*$316.13*	
No. 7613	614.04	
No. 7622	310.01	1,040.18
		$35,865.14
Deduct: Cash on hand		6,365.14
Balance per bank statement, Apr. 30		$29,500.00

Instructions   **a** Determine how much cash Jones took. Prepare a bank reconciliation in a form which shows

(1) The balance per the accounting records

(2) The balance per the bank statement

(3) A deduction from the bank statement balance of the proper amount of outstanding checks

(4) The adjusted bank balance after deducting the outstanding checks

The adjusted bank balance will not agree with the balance per the accounting records; the difference is the amount of undeposited cash which should be on hand. Comparison of the undeposited cash which should be on hand with the actual amount on hand of $6,365.14 will indicate the amount of the cash shortage.

b Explain how Jones attempted to conceal her theft in the improper bank reconciliation shown above. Your explanation may be in the form of a list of dollar amounts which add up to the total dollar amount stolen by Jones.

c Suggest some specific internal control measures for Bayview Company.

BUSINESS DECISION CASE

**Case 7-1
Internal control—
a challenging
case study**

June Davis inherited a highly successful business, Solano, Inc., shortly after her twenty-second birthday and took over the active management of the business. A portion of the company's business consisted of over-the-counter sales for cash, but most sales were on credit and were shipped by truck. Davis had no knowledge of internal control practices and relied implicitly upon the bookkeeper-cashier, John Adams, in all matters relating to cash and accounting records. Adams, who had been with the company for many years, maintained the accounting records and prepared all financial statements with the help of two assistants, made bank deposits, signed checks, and prepared bank reconciliations.

The monthly income statements submitted to Davis by Adams showed a very satisfactory rate of net income; however, the amount of cash in the bank declined steadily during the first 18 months after Davis took over the business. To meet the company's weakening cash position, a bank loan was obtained and a few months later when the cash position again grew critical, the loan was increased.

On April 1, two years after Davis assumed the management of the company, Adams suddenly left town, leaving no forwarding address. Davis was immediately deluged with claims of creditors who stated their accounts were several months past due and that Adams had promised all debts would be paid by April 1. The bank telephoned to notify Davis that the company's account was overdrawn and that a number of checks had just been presented for payment.

In an effort to get together some cash to meet this emergency, Davis called on two of the largest customers of the company, to whom substantial sales on account had recently been made, and asked if they could pay their accounts at once. Both customers informed her that their accounts were paid in full. They produced paid checks to substantiate their payments and explained that Adams had offered them reduced prices on merchandise if they would pay within 24 hours after delivery.

To keep the business from insolvency, Davis agreed to sell at a bargain price a half interest in the company. The sale was made to Helen Smith, who had had considerable experience in the industry. One condition for the sale was that Smith should become the general manager of the business. The cash investment by Smith for her half interest was sufficient for the company to meet the demands on it and continue operations.

Immediately after Smith entered the business, she launched an investigation of Adams's activities. During the course of this investigation the following irregularities were disclosed:

(1) During the last few months of Adams's employment with the company, bank deposits were much smaller than the cash receipts. Adams had abstracted most of the receipts and substituted for them a number of worthless checks bearing fictitious signatures. These checks had been accumulated in an envelope marked "Cash Receipts—For Deposit Only."

(2) Numerous legitimate sales of merchandise on account had been charged to fictitious customers. When the actual customer later made payment for the goods, Adams abstracted the check or cash and made no entry. The account receivable with the fictitious customer remained in the records.

(3) When checks were received from customers in payment of their accounts, Adams had frequently recorded the transaction by debiting an expense account and crediting Accounts Receivable. In such cases Adams had removed from the cash receipts an equivalent amount of currency, thus substituting the check for the currency and causing the bank deposit to agree with the recorded cash receipts.

(4) More than $3,000 a month had been stolen from petty cash. Fraudulent petty cash vouchers, mostly charged to the Purchases account, had been created to conceal these thefts and to support the checks cashed to replenish the petty cash fund.

(5) For many sales made over the counter, Adams had recorded lesser amounts on the cash register or had not rung up any amount. He had abstracted the funds received but not recorded.

(6) To produce income statements that showed profitable operations, Adams had recorded many fictitious sales. The recorded accounts receivable included many from nonexistent customers.

(7) In preparing bank reconciliations, Adams had omitted many outstanding checks, thus concealing the fact that the cash in the bank was less than the amount shown by the ledger.

(8) Inventory had been recorded at inflated amounts in order to increase reported profits from the business.

Instructions   **a** For each of the numbered paragraphs, describe one or more internal control procedures you would recommend to prevent the occurrence of such fraud.

b Apart from specific internal controls over cash and other accounts, what general precaution could June Davis have taken to assure herself that the accounting records were properly maintained and the company's financial statements complete and dependable? Explain fully.

ANSWERS TO SELF-TEST QUESTIONS
1 c   2 a   3 b   4 d   5 c

Receivables

When a business sells goods or services on credit, it does so in the belief that the customer will make payment in accordance with the terms of sale. This confidence in the collectibility of receivables is the basis for showing accounts receivable and notes receivable as assets in the balance sheet and for including credit sales as revenue in the income statement. Along with our overall confidence in receivables, however, is a recognition that a few customers will fail to pay as agreed. Making sales on credit inevitably leads to some credit losses. In this chapter, we explore methods of measuring the expense of uncollectible accounts receivable and of reflecting this expense in the financial statements. We also consider various forms of notes receivable and the calculation of interest. In the final pages of the chapter, we show how the concept of present value is applied to long-term notes receivable.

After studying this chapter you should be able to meet these Learning Objectives:

1 Prepare estimates of uncollectible accounts receivable, write off any accounts known to be uncollectible, and record any later recoveries.

2 Apply the balance sheet approach and the income statement approach to estimating uncollectible accounts.

3 Compare the allowance method and the direct write-off method of accounting for uncollectible accounts.

4 Account for sales to customers using credit cards.

5 Explain promissory notes and the nature of interest.

6 Describe measures useful in evaluating the quality of receivables.

7 Account for notes receivable with the interest charges included in the face amount.

8 Discuss the concept of present value in accounting for long-term notes receivable.

One of the key factors underlying the growth of the American economy is the trend toward selling goods and services *on credit.*

CASE IN POINT ■ Henry Ford is often recognized as a pioneer of the assembly line which was designed for mass production and lower unit cost of automobiles. However, production on this scale would not have been possible had Ford not also been a pioneer in the introduction of consumer credit. The key to volume sales of automobiles was the installment plan calling for a small down payment followed by a series of weekly or monthly payments. Thus, consumer credit put the purchase of an automobile within the grasp of millions of people who could never have purchased an automobile for cash. These two related concepts (the low unit cost of assembly-line production and the huge sales potential created by consumer credit) transformed American society into a new era of mass production, expanded sales, and higher wages—and a mountain of consumer debt.

ACCOUNTS RECEIVABLE

Accounts receivable are very liquid assets, usually being converted into cash within a period of 30 to 60 days. Therefore, accounts receivable from customers (and notes receivable as well) are classified as current assets, appearing in the balance sheet immediately after cash and cash equivalents.

Sometimes companies sell merchandise on longer-term installment plans, requiring 12, 24, or even 48 months to collect the entire amount receivable from the customer. By definition, the normal period of time required to collect accounts receivable is part of a company's *operating cycle.* Therefore, accounts receivable arising from "normal" sales transactions usually are classified as current assets, even if the credit terms extend beyond one year.[1]

Uncollectible Accounts

No business wants to sell on credit to a customer who will prove unable or unwilling to pay his or her account. Therefore, most businesses have a credit department that investigates the credit worthiness of each prospective customer. This investigation usually includes obtaining a credit report from a national credit-rating agency such as *Dun & Bradstreet, Inc.* If the prospective customer is a business concern, its financial statements will be obtained and analyzed to determine its financial strength and the trend of its operating results.

A business that sells its goods or services on credit will inevitably find that some of its accounts receivable are uncollectible. Regardless of how thoroughly the credit department investigates prospective customers, some uncollectible

---

[1] As explained in Chapter 5, the period used to define current assets and current liabilities is one year or the company's operating cycle, whichever is longer. The *operating cycle* is the period of time needed to convert cash into inventory, the inventory into accounts receivable, and the accounts receivable back into cash.

accounts will arise as a result of errors in judgment or because of unexpected developments. In fact, a limited amount of uncollectible accounts is evidence of a sound credit policy. If the credit department should become too cautious and conservative in rating customers, it might avoid all credit losses but, in so doing, lose profitable business by rejecting many acceptable customers.

Objective 1
Prepare estimates of uncollectible accounts receivable, write off any accounts known to be uncollectible, and record any later recoveries.

■ Reflecting Uncollectible Accounts in the Financial Statements

An account receivable that has been determined to be uncollectible is no longer an asset. The loss of this asset represents an *expense,* termed uncollectible accounts expense.

In measuring business income, one of the most fundamental principles of accounting is that revenue should be *matched* with (offset by) the expenses incurred in generating that revenue. Uncollectible accounts expense is *caused by selling goods* on credit to customers who fail to pay their bills. Therefore, this expense is incurred in the month in which the *related sales* are made, even though specific accounts receivable may not be determined to be uncollectible until a later accounting period. Thus, an account receivable that originates from a sale on credit in January and is determined to be uncollectible in August represents an expense in *January.* Unless each month's uncollectible accounts expense is *estimated* and reflected in the month-end income statement and balance sheet, these financial statements may show overstated earnings and overvalued assets.

To illustrate, assume that World Famous Toy Co. begins business on January 1, 1991, and makes most of its sales on account. At January 31, accounts receivable amount to $250,000. On this date, the credit manager reviews the accounts receivable and estimates that approximately $10,000 of these accounts will prove to be uncollectible. The following adjusting entry should be made at January 31:

■
Provision for uncollectible accounts

Uncollectible Accounts Expense	10,000	
Allowance for Doubtful Accounts.................................		10,000
To record the portion of total accounts receivable estimated		
to be uncollectible.		

The *Uncollectible Accounts Expense* account created by the debit part of this entry is closed into the Income Summary account in the same manner as any other expense account. The *Allowance for Doubtful Accounts* which was credited in the above journal entry will appear in the balance sheet as a deduction from the face amount of the accounts receivable. It serves to reduce the accounts receivable to their *net realizable value* in the balance sheet, as shown by the following illustration:

WORLD FAMOUS TOY CO.
Partial Balance Sheet
January 31, 1991

■
How much is the estimated net realizable value of the accounts receivable?

Current assets:		
Cash...		$ 75,000
Accounts receivable	$250,000	
Less: Allowance for Doubtful Accounts...........................	10,000	240,000
Inventory..		300,000
Total current assets		$615,000

The Allowance for Doubtful Accounts

There is no way of telling in advance *which* accounts receivable will prove to be uncollectible. It is therefore not possible to credit the accounts of specific customers for our estimate of probable uncollectible accounts. Neither should we credit the Accounts Receivable controlling account in the general ledger. If the Accounts Receivable controlling account were to be credited with the estimated amount of doubtful accounts, this controlling account would no longer be in balance with the total of the numerous customers' accounts in the subsidiary ledger. The only practical alternative, therefore, is to credit a separate account called *Allowance for Doubtful Accounts* with the amount estimated to be uncollectible.

The Allowance for Doubtful Accounts often is described as a *contra-asset* account or a *valuation* account. Both of these terms indicate that the Allowance for Doubtful Accounts has a credit balance, which is offset against the asset Accounts Receivable to produce the proper balance sheet value for this asset.

■ **Estimating the Amount of Uncollectible Accounts** Before financial statements are prepared at the end of the accounting period, an estimate of the expected amount of uncollectible accounts receivables should be made. This estimate is based upon past experience and modified in accordance with current business conditions. Losses from uncollectible receivables tend to be greater during periods of recession than in periods of growth and prosperity. Because the allowance for doubtful accounts is necessarily an estimate and not a precise calculation, the factor of personal judgment may play a considerable part in determining the size of this valuation account.

■ **Conservatism as a Factor in Valuing Accounts Receivable** The larger the allowance established for doubtful accounts, the lower the net valuation of accounts receivable will be. Some accountants and some business executives tend to favor the most conservative valuation of assets that logically can be supported. *Conservatism* in the preparation of a balance sheet implies a tendency to resolve uncertainties in the valuation of assets by reporting assets at the lower end of the range of reasonable values rather than by establishing values in a purely objective manner.

The valuation of assets at conservative amounts is a long-standing tradition in accounting, stemming from the days when creditors were the major users of financial statements. From the viewpoint of bankers and others who use financial statements as a basis for granting loans, conservatism in valuing assets has long been regarded as a desirable policy.

Assume that the balance sheet of Company A presents optimistic, exaggerated values for the assets owned. Assume also that this "unconservative" balance sheet is submitted to a banker in support of an application for a loan. The banker studies the balance sheet and makes a loan to Company A in reliance upon the values listed. Later the banker finds it impossible to collect the loan and also finds that the assets upon which the loan was based had been greatly overstated in the balance sheet. The banker will undoubtedly consider the overly optimistic character of Company A's balance sheet as partially responsible for the loss incurred by the bank. Experiences of this type have led creditors as a group to stress the desirability of conservatism in the valuation of assets.

In considering the argument for balance sheet conservatism, it is important to recognize that the income statement also is affected by the estimate made of uncollectible accounts. The act of providing a relatively large allowance for doubtful accounts involves a correspondingly heavy charge to expense. Setting asset values at a minimum in the balance sheet has the related effect of minimizing the amount of net income reported in the current period.

■ **Monthly Adjustments of the Allowance Account**   In the adjusting entry made by World Famous Toy Co. at January 31, the amount of the adjustment ($10,000) was equal to the estimated amount of uncollectible accounts. This is true because January was the first month of operations and this was the company's first estimate of its uncollectible accounts. In future months, the amount of the adjusting entry will depend upon two factors: (1) the estimate of uncollectible accounts, and (2) the *current balance* in the Allowance for Doubtful Accounts. Before we illustrate the adjusting entry for a future month, let us first see why the balance in the allowance account may change during the accounting period.

Writing Off an Uncollectible Account Receivable

Whenever an account receivable from a specific customer is determined to be uncollectible, it no longer qualifies as an asset and should be written off. To *write off* an account receivable is to reduce the balance of the customer's account to zero. The journal entry to accomplish this consists of a credit to the Accounts Receivable controlling account in the general ledger (and to the customer's account in the subsidiary ledger), and an offsetting debit to the *Allowance for Doubtful Accounts.*

To illustrate, assume that on February 15, World Famous Toy Co. learns that a customer, Discount Stores, has gone out of business and that the $4,000 account receivable from this customer is now worthless. The entry to write off this uncollectible account receivable is:

■
**Writing off a
receivable
"against the
allowance"**

Allowance for Doubtful Accounts.......................................	*4,000*	
* Accounts Receivable, Discount Stores ....*		*4,000*
To write off the receivable from Discount Stores as uncollectible.		

The important thing to note in this entry is that the debit is made to the *Allowance for Doubtful Accounts* and *not* to the Uncollectible Accounts Expense account. The estimated expense of credit losses is charged to the Uncollectible Accounts Expense account at the end of each accounting period. When a particular account receivable is later determined to be worthless and is written off, this action does not represent an additional expense but merely confirms our previous estimate of the expense. If the Uncollectible Accounts Expense account were first charged with *estimated* credit losses and then later charged with *proven* credit losses, we would be double counting the actual uncollectible accounts expense.

After the entry writing off Discount Stores' account has been posted, the Accounts Receivable controlling account and the Allowance for Doubtful Accounts appear as follows:

ACCOUNTS RECEIVABLE

1991		1991	
Jan. 31	250,000	Feb. 15 (write-off)	4,000

ALLOWANCE FOR DOUBTFUL ACCOUNTS

1991		1991	
Feb. 15 (write-off)	4,000	Jan. 31	10,000

Note that the *net* amount of the accounts receivable was unchanged by writing off the receivable from Discount Stores against the Allowance for Doubtful Accounts. The write-off reduced the asset account and the allowance account by the same amount.

BEFORE THE WRITE-OFF		AFTER THE WRITE-OFF	
Accounts receivable	$250,000	Accounts receivable	$246,000
Less: Allowance for		Less: Allowance for	
doubtful accounts	10,000	doubtful accounts	6,000
Net value of receivables	$240,000	Net value of receivables	$240,000

The fact that writing off a worthless receivable against the Allowance for Doubtful Accounts does not change the net carrying value of accounts receivable shows that no expense is entered in the accounting records when an account receivable is written off. This example bears out the point stressed earlier in the chapter. *Credit losses belong in the period in which the sale is made, not in a later period in which the account receivable is discovered to be uncollectible.* This is another example of the use of the *matching principle* in determining net income.

■ **Write-Offs Seldom Agree with Previous Estimates** The total amount of accounts receivable actually written off will seldom, if ever, be exactly equal to the estimated amount previously credited to the Allowance for Doubtful Accounts.

If the amounts written off as uncollectible turn out to be less than the estimated amount, the Allowance for Doubtful Accounts will continue to show a credit balance. If the amounts written off as uncollectible are greater than the estimated amount, the Allowance for Doubtful Accounts will acquire a *temporary debit balance,* which will be eliminated by the adjustment at the end of the period.

Recovery of an Account Receivable Previously Written Off

Occasionally a receivable which has been written off as worthless will later be collected in full or in part. Such collections are often referred to as *recoveries* of bad debts. Collection of an account receivable previously written off is evidence that the write-off was an error; the receivable should therefore be reinstated as an asset.

Let us assume, for example, that a past-due account receivable in the amount of $200 from J. B. Barker was written off on February 16 by the following entry:

Barker account considered uncollectible

Allowance for Doubtful Accounts..	200	
Accounts Receivable, J. B. Barker		200
To write off the receivable from J. B. Barker as uncollectible.		

On February 27, the customer, J. B. Barker, pays the account in full. The entry to restore Barker's account will be:

Barker account reinstated

Accounts Receivable, J. B. Barker	200	
Allowance for Doubtful Accounts....................................		200
To reinstate as an asset an account receivable previously written off.		

Notice that this entry is *exactly the opposite* of the entry made when the account was written off as uncollectible. A separate entry will be made in the cash receipts journal to record the collection from Barker. This entry will debit Cash and credit Accounts Receivable, J. B. Barker.

Monthly Estimates of Credit Losses

At the end of each month, management should again estimate the probable amount of uncollectible accounts *and adjust the Allowance for Doubtful Accounts to this new estimate.*

To illustrate, assume that at the end of February the credit manager of World Famous Toy Co. analyzes the accounts receivable and estimates that approximately $11,000 of these accounts will prove uncollectible. Currently, the Allowance for Doubtful Accounts has a credit balance of only $6,000, determined as follows:

Current balance in the allowance account

Balance at January 31 (credit)			$10,000
Less: Write-offs of accounts considered worthless:			
Discount Stores		$4,000	
J. B. Barker		200	4,200
Subtotal..			$ 5,800
Add: Recoveries of accounts previously written off: J. B. Barker			200
Balance at end of February (prior to adjusting entry)...........................			$ 6,000

To increase the balance in the allowance account to $11,000 at February 28, the month-end adjusting entry must add $5,000 to the allowance. The entry will be:

Increasing the allowance for doubtful accounts

Uncollectible Accounts Expense	5,000	
Allowance for Doubtful Accounts.....................................		5,000
To increase the Allowance for Doubtful Accounts to $11,000,		
computed as follows:		

Required allowance at Feb. 28	*$11,000*
Credit balance prior to adjustment	*6,000*
Required adjustment	*$ 5,000*

Objective 2
Apply the balance sheet approach and the income statement approach to estimating uncollectible accounts.

■ **Estimating Credit Losses—the "Balance Sheet" Approach** In our discussion thus far of estimating credit losses, we have used the balance sheet approach. As the name "balance sheet approach" suggests, this method emphasizes the proper balance sheet valuation of accounts receivable. A key factor in applying the balance sheet approach is an *aging* of the accounts receivable.

"Aging" accounts receivable means classifying each receivable according to its age. An aging schedule for the accounts receivable of Valley Ranch Supply is illustrated below:

Analysis of Accounts Receivable by Age
December 31, 19__

	TOTAL	NOT YET DUE	1–30 DAYS PAST DUE	31–60 DAYS PAST DUE	61–90 DAYS PAST DUE	OVER 90 DAYS PAST DUE
Animal Care Center	*$ 9,000*	*$ 9,000*				
Butterfield, John D.	*2,400*			*$ 2,400*		
Citrus Groves, Inc.	*4,000*	*3,000*	*$ 1,000*			
Dairy Fresh Farms	*1,600*				*$ 600*	*$1,000*
Eastlake Stables	*13,000*	*7,000*	*6,000*			
(Other customers)	*70,000*	*32,000*	*22,000*	*9,600*	*2,400*	*4,000*
Totals	*$100,000*	*$51,000*	*$29,000*	*$12,000*	*$3,000*	*$5,000*
Percentage	*100*	*51*	*29*	*12*	*3*	*5*

This analysis of accounts receivable gives management a useful picture of the status of collections and the probabilities of credit losses. Almost half the total accounts receivable are past due. The question "How long past due?" is pertinent, and is answered by the bottom line of the aging analysis. About 29% of the total receivables are past due from 1 to 30 days; another 12% are past due from 31 to 60 days; about 3% are past due from 61 to 90 days; and 5% of the total receivables consist of accounts past due more than three months. If an analysis of this type is prepared at the end of each month, management will be informed continuously on the trend of collections and can take appropriate action to ease or to tighten credit policy. Moreover, a yardstick is available to measure the performance of the persons responsible for collection activities.

The longer past due an account receivable becomes, the greater the likelihood that it will not be collected. Utilizing past experience, the credit manager estimates the percentage of credit losses likely to occur in each age group of accounts receivable. This percentage, when applied to the total dollar amount in the age group, gives the estimated uncollectible portion for that group. By adding together the estimated uncollectible portions for all age groups, the *required balance* in the Allowance for Doubtful Accounts is determined. The following schedule lists the group totals from the aging schedule and shows how the estimated total amount of uncollectible accounts is computed:

Estimated Uncollectible Accounts Receivable
December 31, 19___

	AGE GROUP TOTAL	PERCENTAGE CONSIDERED UNCOLLECTIBLE*	ESTIMATED UNCOLLECTIBLE ACCOUNTS
Not yet due	$ 51,000	1	$ 510
1–30 days past due	29,000	3	870
31–60 days past due	12,000	10	1,200
61–90 days past due	3,000	20	600
Over 90 days past due.......	5,000	50	2,500
Totals....................	$100,000		$5,680

*These percentages are estimated each month by the credit manager, based upon recent experience and current economic conditions.

At December 31, Valley Ranch Supply has total accounts receivable of $100,000, of which $5,680 are estimated to be uncollectible. Thus, an adjusting entry is needed to increase the Allowance for Doubtful Accounts from its present level to $5,680. If the allowance account currently has a credit balance of, say, $4,000, the month-end adjusting entry should be in the amount of *$1,680.*[2]

■ **An Alternative Approach to Estimating Credit Losses** The procedures above describe the *balance sheet* approach to estimating and recording credit losses. This approach is based upon an aging schedule, and the Allowance for Doubtful Accounts is *adjusted to a required balance.* An alternative method, called the *income statement* approach, focuses upon estimating the uncollectible accounts *expense* for the period. Based upon past experience, the uncollectible accounts expense is estimated at some percentage of net credit sales. The adjusting entry is made in the *full amount of the estimated expense,* without regard for the current balance in the Allowance for Doubtful Accounts.

To illustrate, assume that a company's past experience indicates that about 2 percent of its credit sales prove to be uncollectible. If credit sales for September amount to $150,000, the month-end adjusting entry to record uncollectible accounts expense is:

The "income statement" approach

Uncollectible Accounts Expense	3,000	
Allowance for Doubtful Accounts...................................		3,000

To record uncollectible accounts expense, estimated at 2% of credit sales ($150,000 × 2% = $3,000).

[2] If accounts receivable written off during the period *exceed* the Allowance for Doubtful Accounts at the last adjustment date, the allowance account temporarily acquires a *debit balance.* This situation seldom occurs if the allowance is adjusted each month, but often occurs if adjusting entries are made only at year-end.

If Valley Ranch Supply makes only an annual adjustment for uncollectible accounts, the allowance account might have a debit balance of, say, $10,000. In this case, the year-end adjusting entry should be for *$15,680* in order to bring the allowance to the required credit balance of $5,680.

Regardless of how often adjusting entries are made, the balance in the allowance account of Valley Ranch Supply should be *$5,680 at year-end.* Uncollectible accounts expense will be the same for the year regardless of whether adjusting entries are made annually or monthly. The only difference is in whether this expense is recognized in one annual adjusting entry or in 12 monthly adjusting entries, each for a smaller amount.

This approach is fast and simple—no aging schedule is required and no consideration is given to the existing balance in the Allowance for Doubtful Accounts. The aging of accounts receivable, however, provides a more reliable estimate of uncollectible accounts because of the consideration given to the age and collectibility of specific accounts receivable at the balance sheet date.

In past years, many small companies used the income statement approach as a shortcut in preparing monthly financial statements but used the balance sheet method in preparing annual financial statements. Today, however, most businesses have computer software that quickly and easily prepares monthly aging schedules of accounts receivable. Thus, most businesses today use the *balance sheet approach* in their monthly as well as annual financial statements.

Direct Write-Off Method

Objective 3
Compare the allowance method and the direct write-off method of accounting for uncollectible accounts.

Some companies do not use any valuation allowance for accounts receivable. Instead of making end-of-period adjusting entries to record uncollectible accounts expense on the basis of estimates, these companies recognize no uncollectible accounts expense until specific receivables are determined to be worthless. This method makes no attempt to match revenue and related expenses. Uncollectible accounts expense is recorded in the period in which individual accounts receivable are determined to be worthless rather than in the period in which the sales were made.

When a particular customer's account is determined to be uncollectible, it is written off directly to Uncollectible Accounts Expense, as follows:

Uncollectible Accounts Expense	250	
Accounts Receivable, Bell Products		250
To write off the receivable from Bell Products as uncollectible.		

When the direct write-off method is in use, the accounts receivable will be listed in the balance sheet at their gross amount, and *no valuation allowance* will be used. The receivables, therefore, are not stated at estimated net realizable value.

In some situations, use of the direct write-off method is acceptable. If a company makes most of its sales for cash, the amount of its accounts receivable will be small in relation to other assets. The expense from uncollectible accounts should also be small. Consequently, the direct write-off method is acceptable because its use does not have a *material* effect on the reported net income. Another situation in which the direct write-off method works satisfactorily is in a company which sells all or most of its output to a few large companies which are financially strong. In this setting there may be no basis for making advance estimates of any credit losses.

For many years, income tax rules permitted the use of either the direct write-off method or the allowance method of measuring uncollectible accounts expense. However, the Tax Reform Act of 1986 made the direct write-off method the *only* acceptable means of determining taxable income. From the standpoint of accounting theory, the allowance method is better, for it enables expenses to be *matched with the related revenue* and thus aids in making a logical measurement of net income.

Credit Card Sales

Objective 4
Account for sales
to customers
using credit
cards.

Many retailing businesses avoid the risk of uncollectible accounts by making credit sales to customers who use well-known credit cards, such as American Express, Visa, and MasterCard. A customer who makes a purchase using one of these cards must sign a multiple-copy form, which includes a *credit card draft.* A credit card draft is similar to a check which is drawn upon the funds of the credit card company rather than upon the personal bank account of the customer. The credit card company promptly pays cash to the merchant to redeem these drafts. At the end of each month, the credit card company bills the credit card holder for all the drafts it has redeemed during the month. If the credit card holder fails to pay the amount owed, it is the credit card company which sustains the loss.

By making sales through credit card companies, merchants receive cash more quickly from credit sales and avoid uncollectible accounts expense. Also, the merchant avoids the expenses of investigating customers' credit, maintaining an accounts receivable subsidiary ledger, and making collections from customers.

■ **Bank Credit Cards** Some widely used credit cards (such as Visa and MasterCard) are issued by banks. When the credit card company is a bank, the retailing business may deposit the signed credit card drafts directly in its bank account, along with the currency and personal checks received from customers. Since banks accept these credit card drafts for immediate deposit, sales to customers using bank credit cards are recorded as *cash sales.*

In exchange for handling the credit card drafts, the bank makes a monthly service charge which usually runs between $1\frac{1}{4}$ and $3\frac{1}{2}\%$ of the amount of the drafts deposited by the merchant during the month. This monthly service charge is deducted from the merchant's bank account and appears with other bank service charges in the merchant's monthly bank statement.

■ **Other Credit Cards** When customers use nonbank credit cards (such as American Express, Diners' Club, and Carte Blanche), the retailing business cannot deposit the credit card drafts directly in its bank account. Instead of debiting Cash, the merchant records an account receivable from the credit card company. Periodically, the credit card drafts are mailed to the credit card company, which then sends a check to the merchant. Credit card companies, however, do not redeem the drafts at the full sales price. The agreement between the credit card company and the merchant usually allows the credit card company to take a discount of between $3\frac{1}{2}$ and 5% when redeeming the drafts.

To illustrate the procedures in accounting for these credit card sales, assume that Bradshaw Camera shop sells a camera for $200 to a customer who uses a Quick Charge credit card. The entry would be:

■
**This receivable is
from the credit
card company**

Accounts Receivable, Quick Charge Co.	*200*	
Sales		*200*
To record sale to customer using Quick Charge credit card.		

At the end of the week, Bradshaw Camera Shop mails credit card drafts totaling $1,200 to Quick Charge Co., which redeems the drafts after deducting a 5% discount. When payment is received by Bradshaw, the entry is

Cash...	*1,140*	
Credit Card Discount Expense	*60*	
Accounts Receivable, Quick Charge Co............................		*1,200*
To record collection of account receivable from Quick Charge Co.,		
less 5% discount.		

The expense account, Credit Card Discount Expense, should be included among the selling expenses in the income statement of Bradshaw Camera Shop.

Internal Controls for Receivables

One of the most important principles of internal control is that employees who have custody of cash or other negotiable assets must not maintain accounting records. In a small business, unfortunately, it is not uncommon to find that one employee has responsibility for handling cash receipts from customers, maintaining the accounts receivable records, issuing credit memos for goods returned by customers, and writing off receivables judged to be uncollectible. Such a combination of duties is a virtual invitation to fraud. The employee in this situation is able to remove the cash collected from a customer without making any record of the collection. The next step is to dispose of the balance in the customer's account. This can be done by issuing a credit memo indicating that the customer has returned merchandise, or by writing off the customer's account as uncollectible. Thus, the employee has the cash, the customer's account shows a zero amount, and the books are in balance.

To avoid fraud in the handling of receivables, some of the most important rules are that employees who maintain the accounts receivable subsidiary ledger must **not have access** to cash receipts, and employees who handle cash receipts must not have access to the records of receivables. Furthermore, **neither** the employees who maintain records of receivables **nor** those who handle cash receipts should have authority to issue credit memoranda or to authorize the write-off of receivables as uncollectible. These are classic examples of incompatible duties.

NOTES RECEIVABLE

Objective 5
Explain promissory notes and the nature of interest.

A promissory note is an unconditional promise in writing to pay on demand or at a future date a definite sum of money.

The person who signs the note and thereby promises to pay is called the *maker* of the note. The person to whom payment is to be made is called the *payee* of the note. In the illustration on the next page, G. L. Smith is the maker of the note and A. B. Davis is the payee.

From the viewpoint of the maker, G. L. Smith, the illustrated note is a liability and is recorded by crediting the Notes Payable account. However, from the viewpoint of the payee, A. B. Davis, this same note is an asset and is recorded by debiting the Notes Receivable account. The maker of a note expects to pay cash at the maturity date; the payee expects to receive cash at that date.

Simplified form
of promissory
note

$1,000   Los Angeles, California   July 10, 19__

_____One month_____ after date _____I_____ promise to pay

to the order of _____A. B. Davis_____

_____-----One thousand and no/100-----_____ dollars

payable to _____First National Bank of Los Angeles_____

for value received, with interest at _____12% per annum_____

G. L. Smith

Nature of Interest

Interest is a charge made for the use of money. A borrower incurs interest expense. A lender earns interest revenue. When you encounter notes payable in a company's financial statements, you know that the company is borrowing and you should expect to find interest expense. When you encounter notes receivable, you should expect interest revenue.

■ **Computing Interest**   A formula used in computing interest is as follows:

$$\text{Principal} \times \text{Rate of Interest} \times \text{Time} = \text{Interest}$$

(Often expressed as $P \times R \times T = I$)

Interest rates are usually stated on an annual basis. For example, the interest on a $1,000, one-year, 12% note is computed as follows:

$$\$1,000 \times 0.12 \times 1 = \$120$$

If the term of the note were only four months instead of a year, the interest charge would be $40, computed as follows:

$$\$1,000 \times 0.12 \times \tfrac{4}{12} = \$40$$

If the term of the note is expressed in days, the exact number of days must be used in computing the interest. *The day on which a note is dated is not included; the day on which a note falls due is included.* Thus, a note dated today and maturing tomorrow involves only one day's interest. In making calculations, it is convenient to assume that a year contains 360 days.[3] Sup-

_____

[3] In calculating interest, banks and other businesses traditionally assumed that a year contained 360 days rather than 365. Consequently, one day's interest was treated as $\tfrac{1}{360}$ of a year, rather than $\tfrac{1}{365}$. This assumption causes the interest amount for a short-term note to be slightly higher, but makes interest computations much simpler. In recent years, however, most banks have changed to the use of a 365-day year for interest calculations.

pose, for example, that a 60-day, 12% note for $1,000 is drawn on June 10. The interest charge could be computed as follows:

$$\$1{,}000 \times 0.12 \times {}^{60}\!/_{360} = \$20$$

The principal of the note ($1,000) plus the interest ($20) equals $1,020 and this amount (the *maturity value*) will be payable on August 9. The computation of days to maturity is as follows:

Days remaining in June (30 – 10; date of origin is not included)	20
Days in July	31
Days in August to maturity date (date of payment is included)........................	9
Total days called for by note	60

Accounting for Notes Receivable

In some fields of business, notes receivable are seldom encountered; in other fields they occur frequently and may constitute an important part of total assets. Business concerns that sell high-priced durable goods such as automobiles and farm machinery often accept notes receivable from their customers. Many companies obtain notes receivable in settlement of past-due accounts receivable.

All notes receivable are usually posted to a single account in the general ledger. A subsidiary ledger is not essential because the notes themselves, when filed by due dates, are the equivalent of a subsidiary ledger and provide any necessary information as to maturity, interest rates, collateral pledged, and other details. The amount debited to Notes Receivable is always the *face amount* of the note, regardless of whether or not the note bears interest. When an interest-bearing note is collected, the amount of cash received may be larger than the face amount of the note. The interest collected is credited to an Interest Revenue account, and only the face amount of the note is credited to the Notes Receivable account.

■ **Illustrative Entries** Assume that on December 1 a 12%, 90-day note receivable is acquired from a customer, Marvin White, in settlement of an existing account receivable of $30,000. The entry for acquisition of the note is as follows:

Note received to replace account receivable

Notes Receivable	*30,000*	
Accounts Receivable, Marvin White		*30,000*
Accepted 12%, 90-day note in settlement of account receivable.		

At December 31, the end of the company's fiscal year, the interest earned to date on notes receivable should be accrued by an adjusting entry as follows:

Adjusting entry for interest revenue earned in December

Interest Receivable	*300*	
Interest Revenue		*300*
To accrue interest for the month of December on Marvin White note ($30,000 × 12% × $\frac{1}{12}$ = $300).		

On March 1 (90 days after the date of the note), the note matures. The entry to record collection of the note will be:

Collection of principal and interest

Cash	*30,900*	
Notes Receivable		*30,000*
Interest Receivable		*300*
Interest Revenue		*600*

Collected 12%, 90-day note from Marvin White ($30,000 × 12% × ³⁄₁₂
= $900 interest of which $600 was earned in current year).

The preceding three entries show that interest is being earned throughout the life of the note and that the interest should be apportioned between years on a time basis. The revenue of each year will then include the interest actually earned in that year.

■ **If the Maker of a Note Defaults** A note receivable which cannot be collected at maturity is said to have been *defaulted* by the maker. Immediately after the default of a note, an entry should be made by the holder to transfer the amount due from the Notes Receivable account to an account receivable from the debtor.

To illustrate, assume that on March 1, our customer, Marvin White, had defaulted on the note used in the preceding example. In this case, the entry on March 1 would have been:

Accounts Receivable, Marvin White	*30,900*	
Notes Receivable		*30,000*
Interest Receivable		*300*
Interest Revenue		*600*

To record default by Marvin White on 12%, 90-day note.

Notice that the interest earned on the note is recorded through the maturity date and is included in the account receivable from the maker. The interest receivable on a defaulted note is just as valid a claim against the maker as is the principal amount of the note.

If the account receivable from White cannot be collected, it ultimately will be written off against the Allowance for Doubtful Accounts. Therefore, the balance in the Allowance for Doubtful Accounts should provide for estimated uncollectible *notes* receivable as well as uncollectible *accounts* receivable.

CASE IN POINT ■ For many companies, the provision for doubtful accounts is small and does not have a material effect upon net income for the period. Notes receivable, however, are the largest and most important asset for nearly every bank. Interest on these notes is a bank's largest and most important type of revenue. Thus, the collectibility of notes owned by a bank is a key factor in determining the success or failure of that bank.

Citicorp, the nation's largest bank, recently added a staggering $3 billion to its allowance for doubtful loans to developing countries. The related debit to expense caused Citicorp to report one of the largest net losses for a single quarter (three-month period) in the history of American business. Citicorp is not alone in having problems with uncollectible loans. In recent years, uncollectible loans have been the largest expense in the income statements of many American banks and savings and loan associations.

■ **Renewal of a Note Receivable** Sometimes the two parties to a note agree that the note shall be renewed rather than paid at the maturity date. In this situation a new note should be prepared and the old one canceled. If the old note does not bear interest, the entry could be made as follows:

■
Renewal of note should be recorded

Notes Receivable..	10,000	
Notes Receivable..		10,000

A 60-day, non-interest-bearing note from Bell Company renewed today with new 60-day, 14% note.

Since the above entry causes no change in the balance of the Notes Receivable account, a question may arise as to whether the entry is necessary. The renewal of a note is an important transaction requiring managerial attention; a general journal entry is needed to record the action taken by management and to provide a permanent record of the transaction. If journal entries were not made to record the renewal of notes, confusion might arise as to whether some of the notes included in the balance of the Notes Receivable account were current or defaulted.

Discounting Notes Receivable

Many business concerns which obtain notes receivable from their customers prefer to sell the notes to a bank for cash rather than to hold them until maturity. Selling a note receivable to a bank or finance company is often called *discounting* a note receivable. The holder of the note endorses the back of the note (as in endorsing a check) and delivers the note to the bank. The bank expects to collect the *maturity value* (principal plus interest) from the maker of the note at the maturity date, but if the maker fails to pay, the bank can demand payment from the endorser.

When a business endorses a note and turns it over to a bank for cash, the business (as endorser) is contingently liable to the bank. A *contingent liability* is a potential liability which either will develop into a full-fledged liability or will be eliminated entirely by a future event. The future event in the case of a discounted note receivable is the payment (or default) of the note by the maker. If the maker pays, the contingent liability of the endorser is thereby ended. If the maker fails to pay, the endorser must pay in his or her stead. In either case the period of contingent liability ends at the maturity date of the note.

The amount of cash obtained from the bank by discounting a note receivable is called the *proceeds* from discounting the note. The proceeds are always less than the maturity value of the note; the difference represents the return that the bank expects to earn on the transaction. The company discounting the note recognizes any difference between the proceeds and the carrying value of the note as *interest revenue* or *interest expense.*

To illustrate, assume that Retail Sales Co. receives a 60-day, 12% note for $10,000 from Chris Kelly. Several days later, Retail Sales Co. discounts this note to its bank, receiving cash of $9,970. The entry to record discounting this note is:

Cash	9,970	
Interest Expense	30	
Notes Receivable		10,000
To record discounting the Chris Kelly note receivable to Security Bank.		

In this illustration, the proceeds of $9,970 were less than the $10,000 face amount of the note. The proceeds received from discounting a note may be *either* more or less than the face amount of the note, depending upon interest rates and the amount of time left until the note matures. If the proceeds are less than the face amount, the difference is debited to Interest Expense. However, if the proceeds exceed the face amount of the note, the difference is credited to interest revenue.

■ **Discounted Note Receivable Paid by its Maker**   Before the maturity date of the discounted note, the bank will notify the maker, Chris Kelly, that it now holds the note. Kelly will therefore make payment directly to the bank. Kelly's payment of the note will require no entries in the accounting records of Retail Sales Co.

■ **Discounted Note Receivable Defaulted by its Maker**   Now let us assume that when the note matures, Kelly is unable to pay the bank. Retail Sales Co. would then be obligated to "make the note good"—that is, to immediately pay the bank the full $10,200 maturity value of the note.[4] Thus, the company's contingent liability becomes a real liability. The entry to record payment of this note in the event of Kelly's default is shown below:

Accounts Receivable, Chris Kelly	10,200	
Cash		10,200
To record payment to bank of maturity value of discounted Kelly note,		
defaulted by maker.		

■ **Disclosure of Contingent Liabilities**   Since contingent liabilities are potential liabilities rather than full-fledged liabilities, they are not included in the liability section of the balance sheet. However, these potential liabilities may affect the financial position of the business if future events cause them to become real liabilities. Therefore, contingent liabilities should be *disclosed in footnotes to the financial statements.* The contingent liability arising from the discounting of notes receivable could be disclosed by the following footnote:

Note 1: Contingencies and commitments

At December 31, the Company was contingently liable for notes receivable discounted with maturity values in the amount of $700,000.

---

[4] The maturity value of the note includes both the principal amount of the note plus any interest due at the maturity date. The maturity value of the 12%, 60-day note receivable from Chris Kelly may be computed as follows:

Principal amount	$10,000
Interest ($10,000 × 12% × $\frac{2}{12}$)	200
Maturity value	$10,200

Evaluating the Quality of Notes and Accounts Receivable

Objective 6
Describe measures useful in evaluating the quality of receivables.

In the annual audit of a company by a CPA firm, the independent auditors will verify receivables by communicating directly with the customers of the company and with the makers of notes receivable. This *confirmation* process is designed to provide evidence that the customers and other debtors actually exist, and that they acknowledge the indebtedness. The CPA firm may also verify the credit rating of debtors.

Any company with large amounts of receivables needs the assurance of an annual audit to guard against the possibility that worthless notes and accounts receivable from bankrupt firms or fictitious customers may have been disguised as genuine assets. The quality of receivables may also be appraised by an internal auditing staff which will study the adequacy of the internal controls over such activities as the granting of credit, accounting for receivables, and the prompt recognition of credit losses.

■ **Accounts Receivable Turnover** Collecting accounts receivable *on time* is important; it spells the success or failure of a company's credit and collection policies. A past-due receivable is a candidate for write-off as a credit loss. To help us judge how good a job a company is doing in granting credit and collecting its receivables, we compute the ratio of average receivables to sales. The accounts receivable turnover ratio tells us how many times the receivables were converted into cash during the year. The ratio is computed by dividing annual net sales by average accounts receivable. For example, recent financial statements of 3M (Minnesota Mining and Manufacturing Company) show net sales of $9.4 billion. Receivables were $1.6 billion at the beginning of the year and $1.4 billion at the end of the year. Adding these two amounts and dividing the total by 2 gives us average receivables of $1.5 billion. Now we divide the year's net sales by the average receivables ($9.4 ÷ $1.5 = 6.3); the result indicates an accounts receivable turnover rate of 6.3 times per year for 3M. The higher the turnover rate the more liquid the company's receivables.

Another step that will help us judge the liquidity of a company's accounts receivable is to convert the accounts receivable turnover rate to average days' sales uncollected. This is a simple calculation: divide the number of days in the year by the turnover rate. Continuing our 3M example, divide 365 days by turnover of 6.3 (365 ÷ 6.3 = 57.9). This calculation tells us that on average, 3M waited approximately 58 days to make collection of a sale on credit.

The data described above for computing the accounts receivable turnover rate and the average days' sales uncollected can be concisely stated as shown in the following equations:

Accounts Receivable Turnover

$$\frac{\text{Net sales}}{\text{Average accounts receivable}} = \frac{\$9.4}{(\$1.6 + \$1.4) \div 2} = \frac{\$9.4}{\$1.5} = 6.3 \text{ times}$$

Average Days' Sales Uncollected

$$\frac{\text{Days in year}}{\text{Accounts receivable turnover}} = \frac{365}{6.3} = 58 \text{ days}$$

These ratios are of special interest to short-term creditors, including bankers and merchandise suppliers, who analyze the financial statements of their customers as a basis for decisions to approve bank loans or to authorize sales of merchandise on credit.

Notes Receivable with Interest Included in the Face Amount

Objective 7
Account for notes receivable with the interest charges included in the face amount.

In our discussion to this point, we have used notes receivable with the interest rate *stated separately.* We now want to compare this form of note with an alternative form in which the interest charge is *included in the face amount* of the note. For example, assume that Genetic Services has a $10,000 account receivable from a customer, Biolab. The customer is short of cash and wants to postpone payment, so Genetic Services agrees to accept a six-month promissory note from Biolab with interest at the rate of 12% a year to replace the $10,000 account receivable. The interest for six months will amount to $600 and the total amount to be received at maturity will be $10,000 principal plus $600 interest, or $10,600 altogether.

If the note is drawn with interest stated separately, as in the first illustration below, the wording will be ". . . Biolab promises to pay to Genetic Services the sum of $10,000 with interest at the rate of 12% a year."

This note is for the principal amount with interest stated separately

Miami, Florida   November 1, 19__

Six months   after this date_____ Biolab

promises to pay to Genetic Services the sum of $_____ 10,000

with interest at the rate of __12% a year__

                              Signed_____ George Harr

                              Title_____ Treasurer, Biolab

If the alternative form of note is used, the $600 interest will be included in the face amount and the note will appear as shown below:

Interest is included in face amount of this note

Miami, Florida   November 1, 19__

Six months   after this date_____ Biolab

promises to pay to Genetic Services the sum of $_____ 10,600

                              Signed_____ George Harr

                              Title_____ Treasurer, Biolab

Notice that the face amount of the note ($10,600) is greater than the $10,000 account receivable which it replaces. However, the value of the note receivable at November 1 is only $10,000; the other $600 included in the face amount of the note represents *unearned* interest. As this interest is earned over the life of the note, the value of the note will rise to $10,600 at maturity.

The journal entry by Genetic Services at November 1 to record the acquisition of the note will be as follows:

Interest included in face of note

Notes Receivable...	10,600	
Discount on Notes Receivable		600
Accounts Receivable		10,000

Obtained from Biolab a six-month note with interest at 12% included in the face amount.

The asset account, Notes Receivable, was debited with the full face amount of the note ($10,600). It is, therefore, necessary to credit a contra-asset, Discount on Notes Receivable, for the $600 of unearned interest included in the face amount of the note. The Discount on Notes Receivable will appear in the balance sheet as a deduction from Notes Receivable. In our illustration, the amounts in the balance sheet will be Notes Receivable, $10,600 minus Discount on Notes Receivable, $600, or a net asset value of $10,000 on November 1.

■ **Discount on Notes Receivable** The $600 balance of the account Discount on Notes Receivable at November 1 represents *unearned interest.* As the interest is earned over the life of the note, the amount in the discount account will be gradually transferred into Interest Revenue. Thus, at the maturity date of the note, Discount on Notes Receivable will have a zero balance and the value of the note receivable will have increased to $10,600. The process of transferring the amount in the Discount on Notes Receivable account into the Interest Revenue account is called *amortization* of the discount.

■ **Amortization of the Discount** The discount on short-term notes receivable usually is amortized by the straight-line method, which allocates the same amount of discount to interest revenue for each month of the note's life.[5] Thus, the $600 discount on the Biolab note will be transferred from Discount on Notes Receivable into Interest Revenue at the rate of $100 per month ($600 ÷ 6 months).

Adjusting entries should be made to amortize the discount at the end of the year and at the date the note matures. At December 31, 1991, Genetic Services will make the following adjusting entry to recognize the two months' interest revenue earned since November 1:

Amortization of discount

Discount on Notes Receivable	200	
Interest Revenue		200

To record interest revenue earned to end-of-year on six-month note dated Nov. 1 ($600 discount × 2/6).

[5] When an interest charge is included in the face amount of a long-term note, the effective interest method of amortizing the discount is often used instead of the straight-line method. The effective interest method of amortization is introduced later in this chapter and discussed more fully in Chapter 16.

At December 31, the net valuation of the note receivable will appear in the balance sheet of Genetic Services as shown below:

■
Asset shown net
of discount

Current assets:

Notes receivable	$10,600	
Less: Discount on notes receivable	400	$10,200

The net asset valuation of $10,200 consists of the $10,000 principal amount receivable from Biolab plus the $200 interest which has accrued since November 1.

When the note matures on May 1, 1992, Genetic Services will recognize the $400 interest revenue earned since year-end and will collect $10,600 from Biolab. The entry is:

■
Two-thirds of
interest
applicable to
second year

Cash...	10,600	
Discount on Notes Receivable	400	
Interest Revenue		400
Notes Receivable...		10,600

To record collection of six-month note due today and to recognize interest revenue earned since year-end ($10,000 × 12% × ⅔ = $400).

Comparison of the Two Forms of Notes Receivable

We have illustrated two alternative methods which Genetic Services could use in accounting for its $10,000 receivable, depending upon the form of the note. Journal entries for both methods, along with the resulting balance sheet presentations of the asset at November 1 and December 31, are summarized on the next page. Notice that both methods result in Genetic Services recognizing the same amount of interest revenue and the same asset valuation in the balance sheet. The form of the note does not change the economic substance of the transaction.

The Concept of Present Value

Objective 8
Discuss the concept of present value in accounting for long-term notes receivable.

Assume that you receive three offers for an automobile you are trying to sell. One offer is for $4,000 cash; the second offer is a one-year note for $4,100; and the third offer is a two-year note for $4,250. Assume also that the offers are from financially responsible persons. Which of the three is the best offer?

We can make this decision by using the concept of present value. This concept is based upon the "time value" of money—the idea that an amount of money received today is equivalent to a larger amount of money which will not be received until some time in the future. Money available today can be invested to earn interest and thereby become equivalent to a larger amount in the future. The more distant the future cash receipt, the smaller its *present value.*

If we apply this present value concept to decide among the three offers for the automobile, it is apparent that the $4,000 cash is the best offer. Assume that the current rate of interest on an insured bank savings account is 8% a year. The amount of $4,000 invested today would grow to $4,320 within one year, significantly more than the $4,100 one-year note. Turning to the third

Comparison of the Two Forms of Notes Receivable

NOTE WRITTEN FOR $10,000 PLUS 12% INTEREST

Entry to record acquisition of notes on Nov. 1

Notes Receivable	10,000	
Accounts Receivable		10,000

Partial balance sheet at Nov. 1

Current assets:

Notes receivable	$10,000

Adjusting entry at Dec. 31

Interest Receivable	200	
Interest Revenue		200

Partial balance sheet at Dec. 31

Current assets:

Notes receivable	$10,000	
Interest receivable	200	$10,200

Entry to record collection of note on May 1

Cash	10,600	
Notes Receivable		10,000
Interest Receivable		200
Interest Revenue		400

NOTE WRITTEN WITH INTEREST INCLUDED IN FACE AMOUNT

Entry to record acquisition of notes on Nov. 1

Notes Receivable	10,600	
Discount on Notes Receivable		600
Accounts Receivable		10,000

Partial balance sheet at Nov. 1

Current assets:

Notes receivable	$10,600	
Less: Discount on notes receivable	600	$10,000

Adjusting entry at Dec. 31

Discount on Notes Receivable	200	
Interest Revenue		200

Partial balance sheet at Dec. 31

Current assets:

Notes receivable	$10,600	
Less: Discount on notes receivable	400	$10,200

Entry to record collection of note on May 1

Cash	10,600	
Discount on Notes Receivable	400	
Interest Revenue		400
Notes Receivable		10,600

offer, if we invest $4,000 today for a two-year period at an annual interest rate of 8%, our investment will grow to about $4,666 within the two years. We can conclude, therefore, that the two offers in the form of notes are not attractive. They offer us far less than the going rate of interest to wait for a future cash receipt.

If a realistic rate of interest is stated separately in a long-term note, we may assume that no interest charge is included in the face amount. If no interest rate is stated, however, or if the stated interest rate is unrealistically low (such as 2% a year), a portion of the face amount of the note must be assumed to represent an interest charge. The note should be valued at its ***present value*** rather than at the face amount.

When a note does not call for the payment of interest, the present value of the note is less than its face amount, because the face amount of the note will not be received until the maturity date. The difference between the present value of a note and its face amount should be viewed as an interest charge included in the face amount. Often we can determine the present value of a note by the fair market value of the asset acquired when the note is issued. As an alternative, we can compute the present value by using the mathematical techniques illustrated in Appendix A following Chapter 16.

The ***effective rate of interest*** associated with a note is that interest rate which will cause the note's present value to increase to the full maturity value of the note by the due date.

An Illustration of Notes Recorded at Present Value

To illustrate the use of present value in transactions involving long-term notes receivable, let us assume that on September 1, Tru-Tool, Inc., sells equipment to Everts Company and accepts as payment a one-year note in the face amount of $230,000 with no mention of an interest rate. It is not logical to assume that Tru-Tool, Inc., would extend credit for one year without charging any interest. Therefore, some portion of the $230,000 face amount of the note should be regarded as a charge for interest.

Let us assume that the regular sales price of the equipment sold in this transaction is $200,000. In this case the present value of the note is apparently $200,000, and the remaining $30,000 of the face amount represents a charge for interest. The rate of interest which will cause the $200,000 present value of the note to increase to the $230,000 maturity value in one year is 15%. Thus, the face amount of the note actually includes an interest charge computed at the effective interest rate of 15%.

The selling company, Tru-Tool, Inc., should use the present value of the note in determining the amount of revenue to be recognized from the sale. The $30,000 interest charge included in the face amount of the note receivable from Everts Company represents ***unearned interest*** to Tru-Tool, Inc., and is ***not part of the sales price of the equipment.*** If Tru-Tool, Inc., were to treat the entire face amount of the note receivable as the sales price of the equipment, the result would be to overstate sales revenue and notes receivable by $30,000, and also to understate interest revenue by this amount over the life of the note. Tru-Tool, Inc., should record the sale at the present value of the note received, as follows:

Present value of this note receivable is $200,000

Notes Receivable...	230,000	
Discount on Notes Receivable		30,000
Sales		200,000

Sold equipment to Everts Company and received a one-year note with a 15% interest charge included in the face amount.

As the $30,000 interest is earned over the life of the note, this amount will be transferred into Interest Revenue. At December 31, Tru-Tool, Inc., will have earned four months' interest revenue and will make the following entry:

Present value has increased $10,000 by Dec. 31

Discount on Notes Receivable	10,000	
Interest Revenue		10,000

To record interest earned from Sept. 1 through Dec. 31 on Everts Company note ($200,000 × 15% × 4/12).

On September 1 of the following year, when the note receivable is collected from Everts Company, the required entry will be:

Present value has risen to $230,000 by maturity date

Cash..	230,000	
Discount on Notes Receivable	20,000	
Interest Revenue		20,000
Notes Receivable..		230,000

To record collection of Everts Company note and to recognize interest earned since year-end.

In an earlier era of accounting practice, failure to use the concept of present value in recording transactions involving long-term notes sometimes resulted in large overstatements of assets and sales revenue, especially by real estate development companies. In recognition of this problem, the Financial Accounting Standards Board now requires the use of present value in recording transactions involving *long-term* notes receivable or payable which do not bear reasonable stated rates of interest.[6]

When a note is issued for a short period of time, any interest charge included in its face amount is likely to be relatively small. Therefore, the use of present value is not required in recording normal transactions with customers or suppliers involving notes due in less than one year. Notes given or received in such transactions which do not specify an interest rate may be considered non-interest-bearing.

Installment Receivables

Another application of present value is found in the recording of *installment sales.* Many retailing businesses sell merchandise on installment sales plans, which permit customers to pay for their credit purchases through a series of monthly payments. The importance of installment sales is emphasized by a recent balance sheet of Sears, Roebuck, and Co., which shows about $17 billion of receivables, nearly all of which call for collection in monthly installments.

---

[6] APB Opinion No. 21, "Interest on Receivables and Payable," AICPA (New York: 1971).

When merchandise is sold on an installment plan, substantial interest charges are usually added to the "cash selling price" of the product in determining the total dollar amount to be collected in the series of installment payments. The amount of sales revenue recognized at the time of sale, however, is limited to the *present value* of these installment payments. In most cases, the present value of these future payments is equal to the regular sales price of the merchandise. The portion of the installment account receivable which represents unearned finance charges is credited to the contra-asset account, Discount on Installment Receivables. Thus, the entry to record an installment sale consists of a debit to Installment Contracts Receivable, offset by a credit to Discount on Installment Receivables for the unearned finance charges and a credit to Sales for the regular sales price of the merchandise. The balance of the contra-asset account, Discount on Installment Receivables, is then amortized into Interest Revenue over the length of the collection period.

Although the collection period for an installment receivable often runs as long as 24 to 36 months, such receivables are regarded as current assets if they correspond to customary credit terms of the industry. In published balance sheets, the Discount on Installment Receivables is often called Deferred Interest Income or Unearned Finance Charges. A typical balance sheet presentation of installment accounts receivable is illustrated below:

Trade accounts receivable:

Accounts receivable	$ 75,040,000
Installment contracts receivable, including $31,000,000 due after one year .	52,640,000
	$127,680,000
Less: Deferred interest income ($8,070,000) and allowance for doubtful	
accounts ($1,872,000)	9,942,000
Total trade accounts and notes receivable	$117,738,000

■ **Income Tax Aspects of Installment Sales**   Current provisions of the federal income tax law permit sellers to spread the recognition of the gross profit from installment sales over the years in which collections are received. The result of this treatment is to postpone the recognition of taxable income and the payment of income tax. In financial statements, however, the entire gross profit from installment sales is recognized *in the period in which the sale occurs.* The method of recognizing gross profit from installment sales for income tax purposes will be illustrated in Chapter 13. There are a number of other more complex issues relating to installment sales; these are covered in advanced accounting courses.

End-of-Chapter Review

CONCEPTS INTRODUCED OR EMPHASIZED IN CHAPTER 8

Major concepts in this chapter include:

■ The importance of sales on credit in achieving a high volume of production and a high level of earnings.

■ Estimating the amount of uncollectible accounts.

■ Accounting for uncollectible accounts expense; write-off of uncollectible accounts; and later recovery of accounts written off.

■ The allowance for doubtful accounts and its use in reporting the net realizable value of accounts receivable.

■ Aging accounts receivable—the "balance sheet approach."

■ Accounting for credit card sales.

■ The direct write-off method of accounting for uncollectible accounts expense.

■ Promissory notes and the nature of interest.

■ The concept of present value—notes receivable with interest included in the face amount.

■ The role of the matching principle and of conservatism in the valuation of receivables.

In this chapter we have explored the valuation of accounts receivable and notes receivable in financial statements. The current threat of large-scale insolvencies of many banks and savings and loan associations is dramatic evidence that the valuation of notes receivable can be of critical importance. In the following chapter, we will again explore the issue of asset valuation—this time in the area of inventories.

KEY TERMS INTRODUCED OR EMPHASIZED IN CHAPTER 8

Accounts receivable turnover   A ratio used to measure the liquidity of accounts receivable and the reasonableness of the accounts receivable balance. Computed by dividing net sales by average receivables.

Aging the accounts receivable   The process of classifying accounts receivable by age groups such as current, past due 1–30 days, past due 31–60 days, etc. A step in estimating the uncollectible portion of the accounts receivable.

Allowance for Doubtful Accounts   A valuation account or contra account relating to accounts receivable and showing the portion of the receivables estimated to be uncollectible.

Conservatism   A traditional practice of resolving uncertainties by choosing an asset valuation at the lower point of the range of reasonableness. Also refers to the policy of postponing recognition of revenue to a later date when a range of reasonable choice exists. Designed to avoid overstatement of financial strength and earnings.

Contingent liability   A potential liability which either will develop into a full-fledged liability or will be eliminated entirely by a future event.

Contra-asset account   A ledger account which is deducted from or offset against a related account in the financial statements, for example, Allowance for Doubtful Accounts and Discount on Notes Receivable.

Default   Failure to pay interest or principal of a promissory note at the due date.

Direct write-off method   A method of accounting for uncollectible receivables in which no expense is recognized until individual accounts are determined to be worthless. At that point the account receivable is written off with an offsetting debit to uncollectible accounts expense. Fails to match revenue and related expenses.

Discount on Notes Receivable   A contra-asset account representing any unearned interest included in the face amount of a note receivable. Over the life of the note, the balance of the Discount on Notes Receivable account is amortized into Interest Revenue.

Discounting notes receivable Selling a note receivable prior to its maturity date.

Effective interest rate The rate of interest which will cause the present value of a note to increase to the maturity value by the maturity date.

Interest A charge made for the use of money. The formula for computing interest is Principal × Rate of interest × Time = Interest $(P \times R \times T = I)$.

Maker (of a note) A person or entity who issues a promissory note.

Maturity date The date on which a note becomes due and payable.

Maturity value The value of a note at its maturity date, consisting of principal plus interest.

Payee The person named in a promissory note to whom payment is to be made (the creditor).

Present value of a future cash receipt The amount of money which an informed investor would pay today for the right to receive that future cash receipt. The present value is always less than the future amount, because money available today can be invested to earn interest and thereby become equivalent to a larger amount in the future.

Proceeds The amount received from selling a note receivable prior to its maturity. Maturity value minus discount equals proceeds.

SELF-TEST QUESTIONS

The answers to these questions appear on page 342.

1 Which of the following best describes the application of generally accepted accounting principles to the valuation of accounts receivable?

a Realization principle—Accounts receivable are shown at their net realizable value in the balance sheet.

b Matching principle—The loss due to an uncollectible account is recognized in the period in which the sale is made, not in the period in which the account receivable is determined to be worthless.

c Cost principle—Accounts receivable are shown at the initial cost of the merchandise to customers, less the cost the seller must pay to cover uncollectible accounts.

d Principle of conservatism—Accountants favor using the lowest reasonable estimate for the amount of uncollectible accounts shown in the balance sheet.

2 On January 1, Dillon Company had a $3,100 balance in the Allowance for Doubtful Accounts. During the year, sales totaled $780,000 and $6,900 of accounts receivable were written off as uncollectible. A December 31 aging of accounts receivable indicated the amount probably uncollectible to be $5,300. (No recoveries of accounts previously written off were made during the year.) Dillon's financial statements for the current year should include:

a Uncollectible accounts expense of $9,100.

b Uncollectible accounts expense of $5,300.

c Allowance for Doubtful Accounts with a credit balance of $1,500.

d Allowance for Doubtful Accounts with a credit balance of $8,400.

3 Under the *direct write-off* method of accounting for uncollectible accounts:

a The current year uncollectible accounts expense is less than the expense would be under the income statement approach.

b The relationship between the current period net sales and current period uncollectible accounts expense illustrates the matching principle.

c The Allowance for Doubtful Accounts is debited when specific accounts receivable are determined to be worthless.

d Accounts receivable are not stated in the balance sheet at net realizable value, but at the balance of the Accounts Receivable ledger account.

4 On October 1, 1991 Blaine Company sold a parcel of land in exchange for a 12%, 9-month note receivable in the amount of $300,000. Interest is not included in the face amount of this note and the proper adjusting entry was made with respect to this note at December 31, 1991. Blaine's journal entry to record collection of this note at July 1, 1992 (maturity date) includes:

a A debit to Cash for $318,000.

b A credit to Interest Revenue of $18,000.

c A debit to Interest Receivable of $9,000.

d A credit to Notes Receivable of $327,000.

5 On September 1, 1991, Vickers Industries sold machinery in exchange for a 6-month note receivable. An interest charge, computed at an annual rate of 12%, was included in the face amount of the note. In its December 31, 1991, balance sheet, Vickers correctly presented the note receivable as follows:

Note Receivable, due March 1, 1992	$143,100	
Less: Discount on note receivable	(2,700)	$140,400

What was the total amount of interest charge included in the face amount of the note on *September 1,* 1991?

a $2,700   **b** $5,400   **c** $8,100   **d** $8,586

Assignment Material

REVIEW QUESTIONS

1 Jones Company, a retailer, makes most of its sales on credit. In the first 10 years of operation, the company incurred some bad debts or uncollectible accounts expense each year. Does this record indicate that the company's credit policies are in need of change?

2 Company A and Company B are virtually identical in size and nature of operations, but Company A is more conservative in valuing accounts receivable. Will this greater emphasis on conservatism cause A to report higher or lower net income than Company B? Assume that you are a banker considering identical loan applications from A and B and you know of the more conservative policy followed by A. In which set of financial statements would you feel more confidence? Explain.

3 Adams Company determines at year-end that its Allowance for Doubtful Accounts should be increased by $6,500. Give the adjusting entry to carry out this decision.

4 In making the annual adjusting entry for uncollectible accounts, a company may utilize a **balance sheet approach** to make the estimate or it may use an **income statement approach.** Explain these two alternative approaches.

5 At the end of its first year in business, Baxter Laboratories had accounts receivable totaling $148,500. After careful analysis of the individual accounts, the credit manager estimated that $146,100 would ultimately be collected. Give the journal entry required to reflect this estimate in the accounts.

6 In February of its second year of operations, Baxter Laboratories (Question **5** above) learned of the failure of a customer, Sterling Corporation, which owed Baxter $800. Nothing could be collected. Give the journal entry to recognize the uncollectibility of the receivable from Sterling Corporation.

7 Bell Company, which uses the allowance method of accounting for uncollectible accounts, wrote off as uncollectible a $1,200 receivable from Dailey Company. Several months later, Dailey Company obtained new long-term financing and promptly paid all its old debts in full. Give the journal entry or entries (in general journal form) which Bell Company should make to record this recovery of $1,200.

8 What is the direct write-off method of handling credit losses as opposed to the allowance method? What is its principal shortcoming?

9 Morgan Corporation has decided to write off its account receivable from Brill Company because the latter has declared bankruptcy. What general ledger accounts should be debited and credited, assuming that the allowance method is in use? What general ledger accounts should be debited and credited if the direct write-off method is in use?

10 Mill Company, which has accounts receivable of $309,600 and an allowance for doubtful accounts of $3,600, decides to write off as worthless a past-due account receivable for $1,500 from J. D. North. What effect will the write-off have upon total current assets? Upon net income for the period? Explain.

11 What information can an aging analysis of accounts receivable make available to management each month?

12 What are the advantages to a retailer of making credit sales only to customers who use nationally recognized credit cards?

13 Alta Mine Co., a restaurant that had always made cash sales only, adopted a new policy of honoring several nationally known credit cards. Sales did not increase, but many of Alta Mine Co.'s regular customers began charging dinner bills on the credit cards. Has the new policy been beneficial to Alta Mine Co.? Explain.

14 Determine the maturity date of the following notes:

   a A three-month note dated March 10

   b A 30-day note dated August 15

   c A 90-day note dated July 2

15 X Company acquires a 9%, 60-day note receivable from a customer, Robert Waters, in settlement of an existing account receivable of $4,000. Give the journal entry to record acquisition of the note and the journal entry to record its collection at maturity.

16 Williams Gear sold merchandise to Dayco in exchange for a one-year note receivable. The note was drawn with a face amount of $13,310, *including* a 10% interest charge. Compute the amount of sales revenue to be recognized by Williams Gear.

17 Maxline Stores sells merchandise with a sales price of $1,260 on an installment plan requiring 12 monthly payments of $120 each. How much revenue will this sale ultimately generate for Maxline Stores? Explain the nature of this revenue and when it should be recognized in the accounting records.

18 With reference to Question **17** above, make the journal entries required in the accounting records of Maxline Stores to record:

   a Sale of the merchandise on the installment plan.

   b Collection of the first monthly installment payment. (Assume that an equal portion of the discount is amortized at the time that each installment payment is received.)

19 Explain the nature of a contingent liability. What is the contingent liability that arises when notes receivable are discounted with a bank?

20 Does a contingent liability appear on a balance sheet? If so, in what part of the balance sheet?

21 How does an annual audit by a CPA firm provide assurance that a company's accounts receivable and notes receivable are of satisfactory quality?

EXERCISES

Exercise 8-1
Accounting
terminology

Listed below are nine technical accounting terms introduced in this chapter:

Accounts receivable turnover	*Writing off receivables*	*Conservatism*
Direct write-off method	*Aging schedule*	*Default*
Discounting a note receivable	*Present value*	*Contingent liability*

Each of the following statements may (or may not) describe one of these technical terms. For each statement, indicate the accounting term described or answer "None" if the statement does not correctly describe any of the terms.

a Recognition of credit losses only when specific accounts receivable are determined to be worthless.

b The value today of a non-interest-bearing note receivable which matures one year from today.

c Sale of a note receivable to a bank rather than holding the note to maturity.

d Cost of plant equipment minus accumulated depreciation.

e Resolving uncertainties in the valuation of assets by reporting assets at the lower end of the range of reasonable values rather than by establishing values in a purely objective manner.

f The obligation of the endorser of a discounted note receivable to make payment if the maker fails to pay at the due date.

g Failure to make payment of the principal or interest per the terms of a promissory note.

h A ratio useful in judging how good a job a business is doing in granting credit and collecting its receivables.

Exercise 8-2
Balance sheet
approach

Laser Products follows the balance sheet approach to estimating uncollectible accounts expense. At May 31, the accounts receivable totaled $882,000. An aging analysis of these accounts indicated an expected loss of $21,960. Prepare the adjusting entry at May 31 under each of the following independent assumptions:

a The Allowance for Doubtful Accounts had a credit balance of $15,840.

b The Allowance for Doubtful Accounts had a debit balance of $5,328.

Exercise 8-3
Income statement
approach

The income statement approach to estimating uncollectible accounts expense is used by Thornhill Brothers. On January 31 the firm had accounts receivable in the amount of $750,000. The Allowance for Doubtful Accounts had a credit balance of $5,250. The controller estimated that uncollectible accounts expense would amount to one-half of 1% of the $4,500,000 of net sales made during January. This estimate was entered in the accounts by an adjusting entry on January 31. On February 12, an account receivable from Carlotta Smith of $4,125 was determined to be worthless and was written off. However, on February 24, Smith won several million dollars in the state lottery and immediately paid the $4,125 past-due account. Prepare four journal entries in general journal form to record the above four events.

Exercise 8-4
Uncollectible
accounts expense

The credit manager of Road Warrior Tires has gathered the following information about the company's accounts receivable and credit losses during the current year:

Net credit sales for the year		$2,000,000
Accounts receivable at year-end		240,000
Uncollectible accounts receivable:		
Actually written off during the year	$29,100	
Estimated portion of year-end receivables expected to prove uncollectible (per aging schedule)	12,000	41,100

Prepare one journal entry summarizing the recognition of uncollectible accounts expense for the entire year under each of the following independent assumptions:

(1) Uncollectible accounts expense is estimated at an amount equal to 1½% of net credit sales.

(2) Uncollectible accounts expense is recognized by adjusting the balance in the Allowance for Doubtful Accounts to the amount indicated in the year-end aging schedule. The balance in the allowance account at the beginning of the current year was $10,000. (Consider the effect of the write-offs during the year upon the balance in the Allowance for Doubtful Accounts.)

(3) The company uses the direct write-off method of accounting for uncollectible accounts.

Exercise 8-5
Write-offs and recoveries

The balance sheet of Maps, Inc., at the end of last year included the following items:

Notes receivable from customers	$ 36,000
Accrued interest on notes receivable	720
Accounts receivable	151,200
Less: Allowance for doubtful accounts	3,600

You are to record the following events of the current year in general journal entries:

a Accounts receivable of $3,456 are written off as uncollectible.

b A customer's note for $990 on which interest of $54 has been accrued in the accounts is deemed uncollectible, and both balances are written off against the Allowance for Doubtful Accounts.

c An account receivable for $468 previously written off is collected.

d Aging of accounts receivable at the end of the current year indicates a need for an $5,400 allowance to cover possible failure to collect accounts currently outstanding. (Consider the effect of entries for **a, b,** and **c** on the amount of the Allowance for Doubtful Accounts.)

Exercise 8-6
How fast are accounts receivable collected?

In your analysis of the financial statements of Rayscan, Inc., you note that net sales for the year were $17,000,000; accounts receivable were $1,500,000 at the beginning of the year and $1,900,000 at the end of the year.

a Compute the accounts receivable turnover rate for the year.

b Compute the average days's sales uncollected.

c Assume that during the following year sales increase and the accounts receivable turnover rate also increases. Would you regard this as a favorable development. Explain.

Exercise 8-7
Notes and interest

On November 1, a 12%, 90-day note receivable is acquired from Sharon Rogers, a customer, in settlement of her $10,000 account receivable. Prepare journal entries to record (a) the receipt of the note on November 1, (b) the adjustment to record 60 days' interest revenue on December 31, and (c) collection of the principal and interest on January 30.

Exercise 8-8
Discounting notes receivable

Morgan Company received a 9%, 6-month note receivable from John Ross in the face amount of $20,000. Soon thereafter, Morgan Company discounted this note at National Bank.

Instructions

a Prepare the journal entry to record the discounting of this note under each of the following assumptions:

(1) The proceeds amounted to $19,915.

(2) The proceeds amounted to $20,210.

b Draft a footnote to Morgan Company's financial statement to disclose the contingent liability from discounting this note.

c Prepare the journal entry that would be made at the maturity date if John Ross defaults and Morgan Company must pay off the note.

Exercise 8-9
Two forms of notes receivable

On November 1, Bannister Company made a loan of $600,000 to a supplier, Mohawk Fabrics. The loan agreement provided for repayment of the $600,000 in six months plus interest at an annual rate of 12%. You are to prepare two different presentations of the note receivable from Mohawk Fabrics on Bannister Company's balance sheet at December 31, assuming that the note was drawn as follows:

a For $600,000 with interest stated separately and payable at maturity.

b With the total interest charge included in the face amount of the note.

Exercise 8-10
Interest included in face amount of note

West Motors, a truck dealer, sold three trucks to Day & Night Truck Lines on July 1, for a total price of $81,600. Under the terms of the sale, West Motors received $24,000 cash and a promissory note due in full in 18 months. The face amount of the note was $64,512, which included interest on the note for the 18 months.

Prepare entries in general journal form for West Motors relating to this transaction and to the note for the year ended December 31. Include the adjusting entry needed to record interest earned to December 31.

PROBLEMS

Group A

Problem 8A-1
Hey, Pal . . . When you gonna pay for this beer?

Shown below are the net sales and the average amounts of accounts receivable of two beverage companies in a recent year:

	(DOLLARS IN MILLIONS)	
	AVERAGE ACCOUNTS RECEIVABLE	NET SALES
Adolph Coors	$ 95	$1,315
Anheuser-Busch Cos., Inc.............................	337	7,677

Instructions

a For each of these companies, compute:

(1) The number of times that the average balance of accounts receivable turned over during this fiscal year. (Round to the nearest tenth.)

(2) The number of days (on average) that each company must wait to collect its accounts receivable. (Round to the nearest day.)

b Based upon your computations in part **a**, which company's accounts receivable appear to be the more "liquid" asset? Explain briefly.

**Problem 8A-2
Aging accounts
receivable; write-
offs**

Tell Services uses the balance sheet approach to estimate uncollectible accounts expense. At year-end an aging of the accounts receivable produced the following classification:

Not yet due	*$111,000*
1–30 days past due	*45,000*
31–60 days past due	*19,500*
61–90 days past due	*4,500*
Over 90 days past due..	*7,500*
Total	*$187,500*

On the basis of past experience, the company estimated the percentages probably uncollectible for the above five age groups to be as follows: Group 1, 1%; Group 2, 3%; Group 3, 10%; Group 4, 20%; and Group 5, 50%.

The Allowance for Doubtful Accounts before adjustment at December 31 showed a credit balance of $2,700.

Instructions

a Compute the estimated amount of uncollectible accounts based on the above classification by age groups.

b Prepare the adjusting entry needed to bring the Allowance for Doubtful Accounts to the proper amount.

c Assume that on January 10 of the following year, Tell Services learned that an account receivable which had originated on September 1 in the amount of $2,850 was worthless because of the bankruptcy of the customer, Ball Company. Prepare the journal entry required on January 10 to write off this account.

**Problem 8A-3
Estimating bad
debts: income
statement
approach and
balance sheet
approach**

Rivero Graphics, owned by Maria Rivero, sells paper novelty goods to retail stores. All sales are made on credit and the company has regularly estimated its uncollectible accounts expense as a percentage of net sales. The percentage used has been ½ of 1% of net sales. However, it appears that this provision has been inadequate because the Allowance for Doubtful Accounts has a debit balance of $3,900 at May 31 prior to making the monthly provision. Rivero has therefore decided to change the method of estimating uncollectible accounts expense and to rely upon an analysis of the age and character of the accounts receivable at the end of each month.

At May 31, the accounts receivable totaled $260,000. This total amount included past-due accounts in the amount of $46,000. None of these past-due accounts was considered worthless; all accounts regarded as worthless had been written off as rapidly as they were determined to be uncollectible. After careful investigation of the $46,000 of past-due accounts at May 31, Rivero decided that the probable loss contained therein was 10%. In addition she decided to provide for a loss of 1% of the current accounts receivable.

Instructions

a Compute the probable uncollectible accounts expense applicable to the $260,000 of accounts receivable at May 31, based on the analysis by the owner.

b Prepare the journal entry necessary to carry out the change in company policy with respect to providing for uncollectible accounts expense.

**Problem 8A-4
Accounts
receivable: a
comprehensive
problem**

Specialty Products has 250 accounts receivable in its subsidiary ledger. All accounts are due in 30 days. On June 30, an aging schedule was prepared. The results are summarized below:

CUSTOMER	TOTAL	NOT YET DUE	1–30 DAYS PAST DUE	31–60 DAYS PAST DUE	61–90 DAYS PAST DUE	OVER 90 DAYS PAST DUE
(248 names)						
Subtotals	*$345,250*	*$183,590*	*$94,680*	*$43,340*	*$9,000*	*$14,640*

Two accounts receivable were accidentally omitted from this schedule. The following data is available regarding these accounts:

(1) R. Jones owes $4,250 from two invoices; invoice no. 218, dated March 14, in the amount of $2,980; and invoice no. 568, dated May 9, in the amount of $1,270.

(2) F. Smith owes $3,760 from two invoices; invoice no. 574, dated May 19, in the amount of $1,350; and invoice no. 641, dated June 5, in the amount of $2,410.

Instructions

a Complete the aging schedule as of June 30 by adding to the column subtotals an aging of the accounts of Jones and Smith.

b Prepare a schedule to compute the estimated portion of each age group that will prove uncollectible and the required balance in the Allowance for Doubtful Accounts. Arrange your schedule in the format illustrated on page 312. The following percentages of each age group are estimated to be uncollectible: Not yet due, 1%; 1–30 days, 4%; 31–60 days, 10%; 61–90 days, 30%; over 90 days, 50%.

c Prepare the journal entry to bring the Allowance for Doubtful Accounts up to its required balance at June 30, 19___. Prior to making this adjustment, the account has a credit balance of $13,800.

d Show how accounts receivable would appear in the company's balance sheet at June 30, 19___.

e On July 7, the credit manager of Specialty Products learns that the $4,250 account receivable from R. Jones is uncollectible because Jones has declared bankruptcy. Prepare the journal entry to write off this account.

Problem 8A-5
Note receivable:
entries for
collection and for
default

Hanover Mills sells merchandise to retail stores on 30-day credit, but insists that any customer who fails to pay an invoice when due must replace it with an interest-bearing note. The company adjusts and closes its accounts at December 31. Among the transactions relating to notes receivable were the following.

Nov. 1   Received from a customer (Jones Brothers) a 12%, 6-month note for $30,000 in settlement of an account receivable due today.

May 1   Collected in full the 12%, 6-month note receivable from Jones Brothers, including interest.

Instructions

a Prepare journal entries (in general journal form) to record: (1) the receipt of the note on November 1; (2) the adjustment for interest on December 31; and (3) collection of principal and interest on the following May 1. Assume that the company does not use reversing entries.

b Assume that instead of paying the note on the following May 1, the customer (Jones Brothers) had defaulted. Give the journal entry by Hanover Mills to record the default. Assume that Jones Brothers has sufficient resources that the note will eventually be collected.

Problem 8A-6
Notes receivable—
including
discounting

Union Square, a wholesaler, sells merchandise on 30-day open account, but requires customers who fail to pay invoices within 30 days to substitute promissory notes for their past-due accounts. No sales discount is offered. Among recent transactions were the following:

Mar. 17   Sold merchandise to S. R. Davis on account, $72,000, terms n/30.

Apr. 16   Received a 60-day, 10% note from Davis dated today in settlement of the open account of $72,000.

May 26   Discounted the Davis note at the bank, receiving proceeds of $72,712. The bank discount rate was 12% applied to the maturity value of the note for the 20 days remaining to maturity.

June 15   Received notice from the bank that the Davis note due today was in default. Paid the bank the maturity value of the note. Since Davis has extensive business interests, the management of Union Square is confident that no loss will be incurred on the defaulted note.

June 25 Made a $48,000 loan to John Raymond on a 30-day, 15% note.

Instructions **a** Prepare in general journal form the entries necessary to record the above transactions. (In making interest calculations, assume a 360-day year.)

b Prepare the adjusting journal entry needed at June 30, the end of the company's fiscal year, to record interest accrued on the two notes receivable. [Accrue interest at 10% per annum from date of default (June 15) on the maturity value of the Davis note.]

Problem 8A-7
Long-term note
receivable with
interest included
in face amount

On April 1, 1991, Merrimac Corporation sold merchandise to West Supply Co. in exchange for a note receivable due in *one year.* The note was drawn in the face amount of $189,200, which included the principal amount and an interest charge. In its December 31, 1991, balance sheet, Merrimac Corporation correctly presented the note receivable as follows:

Note receivable, due Mar. 31, 1992	$189,200	
Less: Discount on note receivable	3,300	$185,900

Instructions **a** Determine the monthly interest revenue earned by Merrimac Corporation from this note receivable. (Hint: The balance in the discount account represents unearned interest as of December 31, 1991. This is a one-year note with three months remaining before it matures.)

b Compute the amount of interest revenue recognized by Merrimac Corporation from the note during 1991.

c Compute the amount of sales revenue recognized by Merrimac Corporation on April 1, 1991, when this note was received.

d Compute the effective annual rate of interest (stated as a percentage) represented by the interest charge originally included in the face amount of the note.

e Prepare all journal entries relating to this note in the accounting records of Merrimac Corporation for 1991 and 1992. Assume that adjusting entries are made only at December 31 and that reversing entries are not used. Assume also that the note was collected on the maturity date.

Group B

Problem 8B-1
Turnover of
accounts
receivable

Shown below are the net sales and the average amounts of accounts receivable of two computer makers in a recent year:

	(DOLLARS IN MILLIONS)	
	AVERAGE ACCOUNTS RECEIVABLE	NET SALES
Hewlett-Packard Company............................	$1,297	$7,102
Digital Equipment Corporation	2,108	9,390

Instructions **a** For each of these companies, compute:

(1) The number of times that the average balance of accounts receivable turned over during this fiscal year. (Round to the nearest tenth.)

(2) The number of days (on average) that each company must wait to collect its accounts receivable. (Round to the nearest day.)

b Based upon your computations in part **a**, which company's accounts receivable appear to be the more "liquid" asset? Explain briefly.

Problem 8B-2
Aging accounts
receivable; write-
offs

Brom Bones & Co. uses the balance sheet approach to estimate bad debts and maintains an allowance account to reduce accounts receivable to realizable value. An analysis of the accounts receivable at year-end produced the following age groups:

Not yet due	$174,000
1–30 days past due	90,000
31–60 days past due	39,000
61–90 days past due	9,000
Over 90 days past due...	15,000
Total accounts receivable..	$327,000

In reliance upon its past experience with collections, the company estimated the percentages probably uncollectible for the above five age groups to be as follows: Group 1, 1%; Group 2, 4%; Group 3, 10%; Group 4, 30%; and Group 5, 50%.

Prior to adjustment at December 31, the Allowance for Doubtful Accounts showed a credit balance of $6,300.

Instructions

a Compute the estimated amount of uncollectible accounts based on the above classification by age groups.

b Prepare the adjusting entry needed to bring the Allowance for Doubtful Accounts to the proper amount.

c Assume that on February 2 of the following year, Brom Bones & Co. learned that an account receivable which had originated on October 6 in the amount of $5,000 was worthless because of the bankruptcy of the customer, Crane Company. Prepare the journal entry required on February 2 to write off this account receivable.

Problem 8B-3
Estimating bad
debts: balance
sheet approach

At December 31 last year, the balance sheet prepared by Pedro Montoya included $504,000 in accounts receivable and an allowance for doubtful accounts of $26,400. During January of the current year selected transactions are summarized as follows:

(1) Sales on account	$368,000
(2) Sales returns & allowances	7,360
(3) Cash collections from customers (no cash discounts)	364,800
(4) Account receivable from Acme Company written off as worthless............	9,280

After a careful aging and analysis of all customers' accounts at January 31, it was decided that the allowance for doubtful accounts should be adjusted to a balance of $29,280 in order to reflect accounts receivable at net realizable value in the January 31 balance sheet.

Instructions

a Give the appropriate entry in general journal form for each of the four numbered items above and the adjusting entry at January 31 to provide for uncollectible accounts.

b Show the amounts of accounts receivable and the allowance for doubtful accounts as they would appear in a partial balance sheet at January 31.

c Assume that three months after the receivable from Acme Company had been written off as worthless, Acme Company won a large award in the settlement of patent litigation and immediately paid the $9,280 debt to Pedro Montoya. Give the journal entry or entries (in general journal form) to reflect this recovery of a receivable previously written off.

Problem 8B-4
Estimating bad
debts: income
statement
approach and
balance sheet
approach

Snowwhite, Inc., owned by Linda Snow, had for the past three years been engaged in selling paper novelty goods to retail stores. Sales are made on credit and each month the company has estimated its uncollectible accounts expense as a percentage of net sales. The percentage used has been ½ of 1% of net sales. However, it appears that this provision has been inadequate because the Allowance for Doubtful Accounts has a debit balance of $3,100 at May 31 prior to making the monthly provision. Snow has therefore decided to change the method of estimating uncollectible accounts expense and to rely upon an analysis of the age and character of the accounts receivable at the end of each month.

At May 31, the accounts receivable totaled $190,000. This total amount included past-due accounts in the amount of $43,000. None of these past-due accounts was considered hopeless; all accounts regarded as worthless had been written off as rapidly as they were determined to be uncollectible. After careful investigation of the past-due accounts at May 31, Linda Snow decided that the probable loss contained therein was 10%, and that in addition she should anticipate a loss of 1% of the current accounts receivable.

Instructions

a Compute the probable uncollectible accounts expense applicable to the accounts receivable at May 31, based on the analysis by the owner.

b Prepare the journal entry necessary to carry out the change in company policy with respect to providing for uncollectible accounts expense.

**Problem 8B-5
Note receivable:
entries for
collection and for
default**

Tower Imports sells a variety of merchandise to retail stores on open account, but insists that any customer who fails to pay an invoice when due must replace it with an interest-bearing note. The company adjusts and closes its accounts at December 31. Among the transactions relating to notes receivable were the following:

Nov. 1 Received from a customer (Hill Stores) a 9%, six-month note for $30,000 in settlement of an account receivable due today.

May 1 Collected in full the 9%, six-month note receivable from Hill Stores, including interest.

Instructions

a Prepare journal entries (in general journal form) to record: (1) the receipt of the note on November 1; (2) the adjustment for interest on December 31; and (3) collection of principal and interest on May 1. Assume that the company does not use reversing entries.

b Assume that instead of paying the note on May 1, the customer (Hill Stores) had defaulted. Give the journal entry by Tower Imports to record the default. Assume that Hill Stores has sufficient resources that the note eventually will be collected.

**Problem 8B-6
Accounting for
notes receivable:
a comprehensive
problem**

On December 1, 19__, the accounting records of Oak Tree Corporation showed the following information on receivables. (In calculating interest, the company's policy is to assume a 360-day year.)

Notes receivable:

Jill Barnes, 10% 45-day note dated Nov. 4	$18,000
C. D. Dawson, 12%, 90-day note dated Dec. 1	32,000
Total	$50,000

Accounts receivable:

Judi Morgan	$ 7,275
T. J. Peppercorn	6,700
Mia Greenberg	9,000
Total	$22,975

Installment contracts receivable:

Jay Dallas (monthly payment $450)	$ 8,550

Unearned interest on installment contracts:

Applicable to Jay Dallas contract	$ 1,140

During the month of December selected transactions affecting receivables were as follows:

Dec. 7   T. J. Peppercorn paid $700 on account and gave a 30-day, 10% note to cover the $6,000 balance.

Dec. 12   Received a 60-day, 12% note from Judi Morgan in full settlement of her account.

Dec. 19   Jill Barnes wrote that she would be unable to pay the note due today and enclosed a check for the interest due along with a new 30-day, 10% note replacing the old note. No accrued interest had been recorded in November.

Dec. 28   Discounted the Judi Morgan note at the bank and received proceeds of $7,302.

Dec. 31   Received the monthly payment on the Jay Dallas installment contract. The payment of $450 includes $60 of interest earned during December. The interest charges included in the face amount of the installment contract had originally been credited to the contra-asset account, Unearned Interest on Installment Contracts.

Instructions **a** Prepare five journal entries (in general journal form) for the five December transactions listed above.

b Prepare an adjusting entry at December 31 to accrue interest on the three notes receivable on hand (the Peppercorn, Barnes, and Dawson notes). Include in the explanation portion of the adjusting entry the computations to determine the accrued interest on each of the three notes. Add these three accrued amounts to find the total amount for the adjusting entry.

c Prepare a partial balance sheet for Oak Tree Corporation at December 31 showing under the heading of current assets the notes receivable, accounts receivable, installment contracts receivable, unearned interest on installment contracts, and interest receivable. Also add a footnote to disclose the amount of the contingent liability for the discounted note receivable.

Problem 8B-7
Long-term note receivable with interest included in face amount

On April 1, 1991, Monitor Corporation sold merchandise to Gear Box Co. in exchange for a note receivable due in *one year*. The note was drawn in the face amount of $58,240, which included the principal amount and an interest charge. In its December 31, 1991, balance sheet, Monitor Corporation correctly presented the note receivable as follows:

Note receivable, due Mar. 31, 1992	$58,240	
Less: Discount on note receivable	1,560	$56,680

Instructions **a** Determine the monthly interest revenue earned by Monitor Corporation from this note receivable. (Hint: The balance in the discount account represents unearned interest as of December 31, 1991. This is a one-year note with three months remaining before it matures.)

b Compute the amount of interest revenue recognized by Monitor Corporation from the note during 1991.

c Compute the amount of sales revenue recognized by Monitor Corporation on April 1, 1991, when this note was received.

d Compute the effective annual rate of interest (stated as a percentage) represented by the interest charge originally included in the face amount of the note.

e Prepare all journal entries relating to this note in the accounting records of Monitor Corporation for 1991 and 1992. Assume that adjusting entries are made only at December 31, and that the note was collected on the maturity date.

BUSINESS DECISION CASE

Case 8-1
How did he do it?

Allan Carter was a long-time employee in the accounting department of Marston Company. Carter's responsibilities included the following:

(1) Maintain the accounts receivable subsidiary ledger.

(2) Prepare vouchers for cash disbursements. The voucher and supporting documents were forwarded to John Marston, owner of the company.

(3) Compute depreciation on all plant assets.

(4) Authorize all sales returns and allowances given to credit customers and prepare the related credit memoranda. The credit memoranda were forwarded to Howard Smith, who maintains the company's journals and general ledger.

John Marston personally performs the following procedures in an effort to achieve strong internal control:

(1) Prepare monthly bank reconciliations.

(2) Prepare monthly trial balances from the general ledger and reconcile the accounts receivable controlling account with the subsidiary ledger.

(3) Prepare from the subsidiary ledger all monthly bills sent to customers and investigate any complaints from customers about inaccuracies in these bills.

(4) Review all vouchers and supporting documents before signing checks for cash disbursements.

Carter became terminally ill and retired. Shortly thereafter, he died. However, he left a letter confessing that over a period of years he had embezzled over $300,000 from Marston Company. As part of his scheme, he had managed to obtain both a bank account and a post office box in the name of Marston Company. He had then contacted customers whose accounts were overdue and offered them a 20% discount if they would make payment within five days. He instructed them to send their payments to the post office box. When the payments arrived, he deposited them in his "Marston Company" bank account. Carter stated in his letter that he had acted alone, and that no other company employees knew of his dishonest actions.

Marston cannot believe that Carter committed this theft without the knowledge and assistance of Howard Smith, who maintained the journals and the general ledger. Marston reasoned that Carter must have credited the customers' accounts in the accounts receivable subsidiary ledger, because no customers had complained about not receiving credit for their payments. Smith must also have recorded these credits in the general ledger, or Marston would have discovered the problem by reconciling the subsidiary ledger with the controlling account. Finally, Smith must have debited some other account in the general ledger to keep the ledger in balance. Thus, Marston is about to bring criminal charges against Smith.

Instructions **a** Explain how Carter might have committed this theft without Smith's knowledge and without being detected by Marston's control procedures. (Assume that Carter had no personal access to the journals or general ledger.)

b Which of the duties assigned to Carter should not have been assigned to an employee responsible for maintaining accounts receivable? Would internal control be strengthened if this duty were assigned to the company's cashier? Explain.

ANSWERS TO SELF-TEST QUESTIONS
1 b   **2 a**   **3 d**   **4 b**
5 c [($2,700 ÷ 2 months) × 6 months]

Inventories

In accounting for inventories, our first objective is the proper determination of income. The matching principle is our guideline in determining what portion of the cost of goods available for sale should be deducted from the year's revenue and what portion should be included in the balance sheet as inventory. The valuation of the year-end inventory also establishes the cost of goods sold. Thus, the validity of both the income statement and the balance sheet rests on accuracy in the valuation of inventory. Our second goal in this chapter is to stress that inventory is valued at cost, but that several alternative methods are acceptable in measuring cost. Four methods are illustrated and evaluated: specific identification; average cost; first-in, first-out (FIFO); and last-in, first-out (LIFO). Both the gross profit method and the retail method are introduced as examples of techniques for estimating inventories. We conclude the chapter by emphasizing the importance of internal control over inventories and the advantages of using the perpetual inventory system whenever feasible.

After studying this chapter you should be able to meet these Learning Objectives:

1 Define inventory and explain how the valuation of inventory relates to the measurement of income.

2 Describe the effects of an inventory error on the income statement of the current year and of the following year.

3 Explain why and how a business takes a physical inventory at the end of a fiscal year.

4 Determine the cost of inventory by using (a) specific identification; (b) average cost; (c) first-in, first-out (FIFO); and (d) last-in, first-out (LIFO). Discuss the merits and shortcomings of these methods.

5 Explain the lower-of-cost-or-market rule.

6 Estimate ending inventory by the gross profit method and by the retail method.

7 Explain how a perpetual inventory system operates.

Inventory Defined

Objective 1
Define inventory
and explain how
the valuation of
inventory relates
to the
measurement of
income.

One of the largest assets in a retail store or in a wholesale business is the inventory of merchandise, and the sale of this merchandise is the major source of revenue. For a merchandising company, *the inventory consists of all goods owned and held for sale in the regular course of business.* Merchandise held for sale will normally be converted into cash within less than a year's time and is therefore regarded as a current asset. In the balance sheet, inventory is listed immediately after accounts receivable, because it is just one step further removed from conversion into cash than are the accounts receivable.

In manufacturing businesses there are three major types of inventories: *raw materials, goods in process of manufacture,* and *finished goods.* All three classes of inventories are included in the current asset section of the balance sheet.

To expand our definition of inventory to fit manufacturing companies as well as merchandising companies, we can say that inventory means "the aggregate of those items of tangible personal property which (1) are held for sale in the ordinary course of business, (2) are in process of production for such sale, or (3) are to be currently consumed in the production of goods or services to be available for sale."[1]

Periodic Inventory System versus Perpetual Inventory System

The distinction between a periodic inventory system and a perpetual inventory system was explained earlier in Chapter 5. To summarize briefly, a periodic system of inventory accounting requires that acquisitions of merchandise be recorded by debits to a Purchases account. When merchandise is sold to a customer, the only accounting entry is a debit to Cash or Accounts Receivable and a credit to Sales for the sales price of the goods sold. No entry is made to reduce the inventory by the *cost* of the goods sold. Under the periodic inventory system, the Inventory account remains *unchanged* until the end of the accounting period. At year-end, all the goods on hand are counted and priced at cost; the total cost figure is then entered in the accounts as the amount of the year-end inventory.

The periodic inventory system is likely to be used by a business that sells a variety of merchandise with low unit prices, such as a hardware store or a drugstore. To maintain perpetual inventory records in such a business may be considered too time-consuming and expensive. However, the growing use of computers and electronic price tags is enabling some businesses with merchandise of low unit cost to adopt perpetual inventory systems.

Companies that sell products of high unit value such as automobiles and television sets usually maintain a perpetual inventory system that shows at all times the amount of inventory on hand. As merchandise is acquired, its cost is added to an inventory account; as goods are sold, their cost is transferred out of inventory and into a cost of goods sold account. This continuous updating of the inventory account explains the name *perpetual* inventory system.

In the early part of this chapter we will use the periodic inventory system as a point of reference; in the latter part we will emphasize perpetual inventories.

[1] AICPA, *Accounting Research and Terminology Bulletins,* Final Edition (New York: 1961), p. 27.

The Matching Principle as Applied to Inventories

The matching principle, as explained in Chapter 3, is fundamental to the measurement of net income for an accounting period. *Matching* revenue and related expenses means that the revenue for the period must be offset by all the expenses incurred in producing that revenue. In a merchandising business, the cost of goods sold is the largest single deduction from revenue. The huge size of this deduction makes accuracy in its measurement of special importance in producing a reliable income statement.

The American Institute of Certified Public Accountants has summarized the relationship between inventory valuation and the measurement of income in the following words: "A major objective of accounting for inventories is the proper determination of income through the process of matching appropriate costs against revenues."[2] The expression "matching costs against revenues" means determining what portion of the cost of goods available for sale should be deducted from the revenue of the current period and what portion should be carried forward (as inventory) to be matched against the revenue of the following period. The above quotation from the AICPA indicates that in accounting for inventories the proper determination of income *takes precedence over other goals.* As explained later in this chapter, an inventory valuation method which leads to a realistic value for the cost of goods sold may not produce the most realistic balance sheet valuation for inventories.

Inventory Valuation and the Measurement of Income

In measuring the gross profit on sales earned during an accounting period, we subtract the *cost of goods sold* from the total *sales* of the period. The figure for sales is easily accumulated from the daily record of sales transactions, but in many businesses no day-to-day record is maintained showing the cost of goods sold.[3] The figure representing the cost of goods sold during an entire accounting period is computed at the end of the period by separating the *cost of goods available for sale* into two elements:

1 The cost of the goods sold

2 The cost of the goods not sold, which therefore comprise the ending inventory

This idea, with which you are already quite familiar, may be concisely stated in the form of an equation as follows:

Finding cost of goods sold

$$\text{Cost of Goods Available for Sale} - \text{Ending Inventory} = \text{Cost of Goods Sold}$$

Determining the amount of ending inventory is the key step in establishing the cost of goods sold. In separating the *cost of goods available for sale* into its components of *goods sold* and *goods not sold,* we are as much or more interested in establishing the proper amount for cost of goods sold as in determining a proper figure for inventory. Throughout this chapter you should bear in mind

---

[2] AICPA, *Accounting Research and Terminology Bulletins,* Final Edition (New York: 1961), p. 28.

[3] As explained in Chap. 5, a company that maintains perpetual inventory records will have a day-to-day record of the cost of goods sold and of goods in inventory. Our present discussion, however, is based on the assumption that the periodic system of inventory is being used.

that the procedures for determining the amount of the ending inventory are also the means for determining the cost of goods sold. The valuation of inventory and the determination of the cost of goods sold are in effect the two sides of a single coin.

Importance of an Accurate Valuation of Inventory

The most important current assets in the balance sheets of most companies are cash, accounts receivable, and inventory. Of these three, the inventory of merchandise is usually by far the largest. Because of the relatively large size of the inventory, an error in the valuation of this asset may not be readily apparent. However, a large error in inventory can cause a material misstatement of financial position and of net income. An error of 20% in valuing the inventory may have as much effect on the financial statements as would the complete omission of the asset cash.

An error in inventory will of course lead to other erroneous figures in the balance sheet, such as the total current assets, total assets, owner's equity, and the total of liabilities and owner's equity. The error will also affect key figures in the income statement, such as the cost of goods sold, the gross profit on sales, and the net income for the period. Finally, it is important to recognize that *the ending inventory of one year is also the beginning inventory of the following year.* Consequently, the income statement of the second year will also be in error by the full amount of the original error in inventory valuation.

Objective 2
Describe the effects of an inventory error on the income statement of the current year and of the following year.

■ **Effects of an Error in Valuing Inventory: Illustration** Assume that on December 31, 1990, the inventory of the Hillside Company is actually $100,000 but, through an accidental error, it is recorded as $90,000. The effects of this $10,000 error on the income statement for 1990 are indicated in the first illustration shown below, showing two income statements side by side. The left-hand set of figures shows the inventory of December 31 at the *proper value of $100,000* and represents a correct income statement. The right-hand set of figures represents an incorrect income statement, because the ending inventory is *erroneously listed as $90,000.* For emphasis, amounts affected by this error are shown in black. Note the differences between the two income statements with respect to net income, gross profit on sales, and cost of goods sold. Income taxes have purposely been omitted in this illustration.

HILLSIDE COMPANY
Income Statement
For the Year Ended December 31, 1990

■
Effects of error in inventory

	WITH CORRECT ENDING INVENTORY		WITH INCORRECT ENDING INVENTORY	
Sales		$240,000		$240,000
Cost of goods sold:				
Beginning inventory, Jan. 1, 1990	$ 75,000		$ 75,000	
Purchases	210,000		210,000	
Cost of goods available for sale........	$285,000		$285,000	
Less: Ending inventory, Dec. 31, 1990	100,000		90,000	
Cost of goods sold		185,000		195,000
Gross profit on sales		$ 55,000		$ 45,000
Operating expenses		30,000		30,000
Net income		$ 25,000		$ 15,000

This illustration shows that an understatement of $10,000 in the ending inventory caused an understatement of $10,000 in the net income for 1990. Next, consider the effect of this error on the income statement of the following year. The ending inventory of 1990 is, of course, the beginning inventory of 1991. The preceding illustration is now continued to show side by side a correct income statement and an incorrect statement for 1991. Amounts affected by this error are shown in black. The ending inventory of $120,000 for 1991 is the same in both statements and is to be considered correct. Note that the $10,000 error in the beginning inventory of the right-hand statement causes an error in the cost of goods available for sale, in cost of goods sold, in gross profit, and in net income for 1991.

HILLSIDE COMPANY
Income Statement
For the Year Ended December 31, 1991

		WITH CORRECT BEGINNING INVENTORY		WITH INCORRECT BEGINNING INVENTORY
Sales			$265,000	$265,000
Cost of goods sold:				
Beginning inventory, Jan. 1, 1991	$100,000			$ 90,000
Purchases	230,000			230,000
Cost of goods available for sale..........	$330,000			$320,000
Less: Ending inventory, Dec. 31, 1991	120,000			120,000
Cost of goods sold			210,000	200,000
Gross profit on sales			$ 55,000	$ 65,000
Operating expenses			33,000	33,000
Net income			$ 22,000	$ 32,000

■ **Effects on succeeding year**

■ **Counterbalancing Errors** The illustrated income statements for 1990 and 1991 show that an understatement of the ending inventory in 1990 caused an understatement of net income in that year and an offsetting overstatement of net income for 1991. Over a period of two years the effects of an inventory error on net income will *counterbalance,* and the total net income for the two years together will be the same as if the error had not occurred. Since the error in reported net income for the first year is exactly offset by the error in reported net income for the second year, it might be argued that an inventory error has no serious consequences. Such an argument is not sound, for it disregards the fact that accurate yearly figures for net income are a primary objective of the accounting process. Moreover, many actions by management and many decisions by creditors and owners are based upon *trends* indicated in the financial statements for two or more years. Note that the inventory error has made the 1991 net income appear to be more than twice as large as the 1990 net income, when in fact *less* net income was earned in 1991 than in 1990. Anyone relying on the erroneous financial statements would be greatly misled as to the trend of Hillside Company's earnings.

■ **Relation of Inventory Errors to Net Income** The effects of errors in inventory upon net income may be summarized as follows:

1 When the *ending* inventory is understated, the net income for the period will be understated.

2 When the *ending* inventory is overstated, the net income for the period will be overstated.

3 When the *beginning* inventory is understated, the net income for the period will be overstated.

4 When the *beginning* inventory is overstated, the net income for the period will be understated.

A few companies (usually small and unaudited) intentionally understate their ending inventory year after year for the purpose of evading income taxes. This type of fraud is discussed further at a later point in this chapter.

Taking a Physical Inventory

Objective 3
Explain why and how a business takes a physical inventory at the end of a fiscal year.

To establish a dollar value for the ending inventory, a business conducts a count of all merchandise owned. This count includes all goods on shelves and sales counters, and in storerooms and warehouses. The quantity counted of each item is multiplied by its unit cost; then the costs for all the various kinds of merchandise are added together to arrive at the total value for the ending inventory.

The physical inventory is usually taken at the end of the fiscal year. Often a business selects a fiscal year ending in a season of low activity. Thus, many department stores have a fiscal year ending in January or February. It is common practice to take inventory after regular business hours. By taking inventory while business operations are suspended, a more accurate count is possible than if goods were being sold or received while the count was in process.

■ **Planning the Physical Inventory** Unless the taking of a physical inventory is carefully planned and supervised, serious errors are likely to occur which will invalidate the results of the count. The goal is to prevent such errors as the double counting of items, the omission of goods from the count, the inclusion of damaged goods, and other quantitative errors. If the business is audited each year by a CPA firm, the independent auditors will review the plans for the physical count and will be on hand during the taking of the inventory to perform test counts and to determine that the count is performed in accordance with the written plans developed in advance.

The first step in carrying out an accurate physical inventory is to designate one person to be responsible for all aspects of planning and controlling the count. Written instructions should be distributed to all supervisors and employees who are to participate, and meetings should be conducted to ensure that every supervisor and employee understands his or her role in carrying out the year-end inventory.

There are various methods of counting merchandise. One of the simplest procedures is carried out by the use of two-member teams. One member of the team counts and calls the description and quantity of each item. The other person lists the descriptions and quantities on an inventory sheet. (In some situations a tape recorder is useful in recording quantities counted.) When all goods have been counted and listed, the items on the inventory sheets are priced at cost, and the unit cost prices are multiplied by the quantities to determine the valuation of the inventory.

The Year-End Cutoff of Transactions

A proper *cutoff* of transactions at year-end is essential to the preparation of accurate financial statements. Our goal is to prepare financial statements that reflect all transactions occurring through the last day of the period and none that occur thereafter.

The term *cutoff* as applied to inventory means that all purchases of merchandise through the last day of the period are included in the ending inventory and all goods sold on or before the last day of the period are excluded from ending inventory. A sale of merchandise occurs *when title to the goods passes from the seller to the buyer.* Title passes when the goods are delivered.

■ **Passage of Title to Merchandise** A sale of merchandise is recorded by the seller as a debit to Accounts Receivable and an offsetting credit to the Sales account. This entry should be made when title to the goods passes to the customer. Obviously it would be improper for the seller to set up an account receivable and at the same time to include the goods in question in inventory. Sometimes, in an effort to meet sales quotas, companies have recorded sales on the last day of the accounting period, when in fact the merchandise was not shipped until early in the next period. Such practices lead to an overstatement of the year's earnings and are not in accordance with generally accepted principles of accounting.

Merchandise in inventory is valued at *cost,* whereas accounts receivable are stated at the *sales price* of the merchandise sold. Consequently, the recording of a sale prior to delivery of the goods results in an unjustified increase in the total assets of the company. The increase will equal the difference between the cost and the selling price of the goods in question. The amount of the increase will also be reflected in the income statement, where it will show up as additional earnings. An unscrupulous company, which wanted to make its financial statements present a more favorable picture than actually existed, might do so by treating year-end orders from customers as sales even though the goods were not yet shipped.

■ **Goods in Transit** Do goods in transit belong in the inventory of the seller or of the buyer? If the selling company makes delivery of the merchandise in its own trucks, the merchandise remains its property while in transit. If the goods are shipped by rail, air, or other public carrier, the question of ownership of the goods while in transit depends upon whether the public carrier is acting as the agent of the seller or of the buyer. If the terms of the shipment are *F.O.B.* (free on board) *shipping point,* title passes at the point of shipment and the goods are the property of the buyer while in transit. If the terms of the shipment are *F.O.B. destination,* title does not pass until the shipment reaches the destination, and the goods belong to the seller while in transit. In deciding whether goods in transit at year-end should be included in inventory, it is therefore necessary to refer to the terms of the agreement with vendors (suppliers) and customers.

Pricing the Inventory

One of the most interesting and widely discussed issues in accounting is the pricing of inventory. Even those business executives who have little knowledge of accounting are usually interested in the various methods of pricing inventory, because inventory valuation may have a significant effect upon reported net income.

Accounting for inventories involves determination of cost and of current fair value or replacement cost. An understanding of the meaning of the term *cost* as applied to inventories is a first essential in dealing with the question of inventory valuation.

Cost Basis of Inventory Valuation

In the words of the AICPA's Committee on Accounting Procedure, "The primary basis of accounting for inventory is cost, which has been defined generally as the price paid or consideration given to acquire an asset. As applied to inventories, cost means in principle the sum of the applicable expenditures and charges directly or indirectly incurred in bringing an article to its existing condition and location."[4] A number of interesting questions arise in determining the *cost* of inventory. For example, should any expenditures other than the invoice price of purchased goods be considered as part of inventory cost? Another provocative question—if identical items of merchandise are purchased at different prices during the year, which of these purchase prices represent the cost of the items remaining in inventory at year-end? We will now address these and other questions involved in determining the cost of inventory.

■ **Inclusion of Additional Incidental Costs in Inventory—a Question of Materiality** From a theoretical point of view, the cost of an item of inventory includes the invoice price, minus any discount, plus all expenditures necessary to place the article in the proper location and condition for sale. Among these additional incidental costs are import duties, transportation-in, storage, insurance of goods being shipped or stored, and costs of receiving and inspecting the goods.

In determining the cost of the ending inventory, some companies add to the net invoice price of the goods a reasonable share of the charges for transportation-in incurred during the year. However, in other lines of business, it is customary and logical to price the year-end inventory *without* adding transportation-in or any other incidental costs because these charges *are not material in amount.* Although this practice results in a slight understatement of inventory cost, the understatement is so small that it does not affect the usefulness or reliability of the financial statements. Thus, the omission of transportation and other incidental charges from the cost of inventory often may be justified by the factors of convenience and economy. Accounting textbooks stress theoretical concepts of cost and income determination. The student of accounting should be aware, however, that in many business situations a close *approximation* of cost will serve the purpose at hand. The extra work involved in developing more precise accounting data must be weighed against the benefits that will result.

To sum up, we can say that in theory a portion of all the incidental costs of acquiring goods should be assigned to each item in the year-end inventory. However, the expense of computing cost in such a precise manner would usu-

---

[4] AICPA, *Accounting Research and Terminology Bulletins,* Final Edition (New York: 1961), p. 28.

ally outweigh the benefits to be derived. Consequently, these incidental costs relating to the acquisition of merchandise are usually treated as expense of the period in which incurred, rather than being carried forward to another accounting period by inclusion in the balance sheet amount for inventory. Thus, the accounting principle of *materiality* may at times take priority over the principle of *matching costs and revenue.*

Inventory Valuation Methods

Objective 4
Determine the cost of inventory by using (a) specific identification; (b) average cost; (c) FIFO; and (d) LIFO. Discuss the merits and shortcomings of these methods.

The prices of many kinds of merchandise are subject to frequent change. When *identical* lots of merchandise are purchased at various dates during the year, each lot may be acquired at a different cost price.

To illustrate the several alternative methods in common use for determining which purchase prices apply to the identical units remaining in inventory at the end of the period, assume the data shown below.

	NUMBER OF UNITS	COST PER UNIT	TOTAL COST
Beginning inventory	100	$ 80	$ 8,000
First purchase (Mar. 1)...................................	50	90	4,500
Second purchase (July 1)	50	100	5,000
Third purchase (Oct. 1)	50	120	6,000
Fourth purchase (Dec. 1).................................	50	130	6,500
Available for sale	300		$30,000
Units sold..	180		
Units in ending inventory	120		

This schedule shows that 180 units were sold during the year and that 120 identical units are on hand at year-end to make up the ending inventory. In order to establish a dollar amount for cost of goods sold and for the ending inventory, we must make an assumption as to which units were sold and which units remain on hand at the end of the year. There are several acceptable assumptions on this point; four of the most common will be considered. Each assumption made as to the cost of the units in the ending inventory leads to a different method of pricing inventory and to different amounts in the financial statements. The four assumptions (and inventory valuation methods) to be considered are known as (1) specific identification, (2) average cost, (3) first-in, first-out, and (4) last-in, first-out.

Although each of these four methods will produce a different answer as to the cost of goods sold and the cost of the ending inventory, the valuation of inventory in each case is said to be at "cost." In other words, *these methods represent alternative definitions of inventory cost.*

■ **Specific Identification Method** The specific identification method is best suited to inventories of high-priced, low-volume items. If each item in inventory is different from all others, as in the case of valuable paintings, custom jewelry, estate homes, and most other types of real estate, the specific identification method is clearly the logical choice. This type of inventory presents quite different problems from an inventory composed of large quantities of identical items.

If the units in the ending inventory can be identified as coming from specific purchases, they **may** be priced at the amounts listed on the purchase invoices. Continuing the example already presented, if the ending inventory of 120 units can be identified as, say, 50 units from the purchase of March 1, 40 units from the purchase of July 1, and 30 units from the purchase of December 1, the cost of the ending inventory may be computed as follows:

Specific identification method and . . .	

50 units from the purchase of Mar. 1 @ $90 .... *$ 4,500*
40 units from the purchase of July 1 @ $100 .... *4,000*
30 units from the purchase of Dec. 1 @ $130 .... *3,900*
  Ending inventory (specific identification) *$12,400*

The cost of goods sold during the period is determined by subtracting the ending inventory from the cost of goods available for sale.

. . . cost of goods sold computation	

Cost of goods available for sale *$30,000*
Less: Ending inventory *12,400*
  Cost of goods sold (specific identification method) *$17,600*

The specific identification method has an intuitive appeal because it assigns actual purchase costs to the specific units purchased. For decision-making purposes, however, this approach does not always provide the most useful accounting information for a company handling a large volume of identical units.

As a simple example, assume that a coal dealer purchased 100 tons of coal at $60 a ton and a short time later made a second purchase of 100 tons of the same grade of coal at $80 a ton. The two purchases are in separate piles and it is a matter of indifference as to which pile is used in making sales to customers. Assume that the dealer makes a retail sale of one ton of coal at a price of $100. In measuring the gross profit on the sale, which cost figure should be used, $60 or $80? To insist that the cost depended on which of the two identical piles of coal was used in filling the delivery truck is an argument of questionable logic.

A situation in which the specific identification method is more likely to give meaningful results is in the purchase and sale of such high-priced articles as boats, automobiles, and jewelry.

■ **Average-Cost Method** Average cost is computed by dividing the total cost of goods available for sale by the number of units available for sale. This computation gives a **weighted-average unit cost,** which is then applied to the units in the ending inventory.

Average-cost method and . . .	

Cost of goods available for sale *$30,000*
Number of units available for sale *300*
Average unit cost .... *$ 100*
  Ending inventory (at average cost, 120 units @ $100) *$12,000*

Note that this method, when compared with the specific identification method, leads to a different amount for cost of goods sold as well as a different amount for the ending inventory.

■
. . . cost of
goods sold
computation

Cost of goods available for sale	$30,000
Less: Ending inventory	12,000
Cost of goods sold (average-cost method)	$18,000

When the average-cost method is used, the cost figure of $12,000 determined for the ending inventory is influenced by all the various prices paid during the year. The price paid early in the year may carry as much weight in pricing the ending inventory as a price paid at the end of the year. A common criticism of the average-cost method of pricing inventory is that it attaches no more significance to current prices than to prices which prevailed several months earlier.

■ **First-In, First-Out Method**   The first-in, first-out method, which is often referred to as *FIFO,* is based on the assumption that the first merchandise acquired is the first merchandise sold. In other words, each sale is made out of the *oldest* goods in stock; *the ending inventory therefore consists of the most recently acquired goods.* The FIFO method of determining inventory cost may be adopted by any business, regardless of whether or not the physical flow of merchandise actually corresponds to this assumption of selling the oldest units in stock. Using the same data as in the preceding illustrations, the 120 units in the ending inventory would be regarded as consisting of the most recently acquired goods as follows:

■
First-in, first-out
method and . . .

50 units from the Dec. 1 purchase @ $130	$ 6,500
50 units from the Oct. 1 purchase @ $120	6,000
20 units from the July 1 purchase @ $100	2,000
Ending inventory, 120 units (at FIFO cost)	$14,500

During a period of *rising prices* the first-in, first-out method will result in a larger amount ($14,500) being assigned as the cost of the ending inventory than would be assigned under the average-cost method. When a relatively large amount is allocated as cost of the ending inventory, a relatively small amount will remain as cost of goods sold, as indicated by the following calculation:

■
. . . cost of
goods sold
computation

Cost of goods available for sale	$30,000
Less: Ending inventory	14,500
Cost of goods sold (first-in, first-out method)	$15,500

It may be argued in support of the first-in, first-out method that the inventory valuation reflects recent costs and is therefore a realistic value in the light of conditions prevailing at the balance sheet date.

■ **Last-In, First-Out Method**   The last-in, first-out method, commonly known as *LIFO,* is one of the most interesting methods of pricing inventories. The title of this method suggests that the most recently acquired goods are sold first, and that *the ending inventory consists of "old" goods acquired in the earliest purchases.* Although this assumption is not in accord with the physical movement of merchandise in most businesses, there is a strong logical argument to support the LIFO method.

For the purpose of measuring income, the *flow of costs* may be more significant than the physical flow of merchandise. Supporters of the LIFO method contend that the measurement of income should be based upon *current* market conditions. Therefore, current sales revenue should be offset by the *current* cost of the merchandise sold. Under the LIFO method, the costs assigned to the cost of goods sold are relatively current, because they stem from the most recent purchases. Under the FIFO method, on the other hand, the cost of goods sold is based on "older" costs.

Using the same data as in the preceding illustrations, the 120 units in the ending inventory would be priced as if they were the oldest goods available for sale during the period, as follows:

Last-in, first-out method and . . .

100 units from the beginning inventory @ $80	$8,000
20 units from the purchase of Mar. 1 @ $90	1,800
Ending inventory, 120 units (at LIFO cost)	$9,800

Note that the LIFO cost of the ending inventory ($9,800) is very much lower than the FIFO cost ($14,500) of ending inventory in the preceding example. Since a relatively small part of the cost of goods available for sale is assigned to ending inventory, it follows that a relatively large portion must have been assigned to cost of goods sold, as shown by the following computation:

. . . cost of goods sold computation

Cost of goods available for sale..	$30,000
Less: Ending inventory...	9,800
Cost of goods sold (last-in, first-out method)	$20,200

■ **Comparison of the Alternative Methods** We have now illustrated four widely used methods of pricing inventory at cost: specific identification; average cost; first-in, first-out (FIFO); and last-in, first-out (LIFO). The resulting valuations of ending inventory and of the cost of goods sold are summarized below. In this comparison, we assume net sales of $27,500 in order also to show the effects of the different methods upon gross profit.

Different inventory pricing methods produce different results

	SPECIFIC IDENTIFI-CATION	AVERAGE-COST	FIRST-IN, FIRST-OUT	LAST-IN, FIRST-OUT
Sales	$27,500	$27,500	$27,500	$27,500
Cost of goods sold:				
Beginning Inventory	$ 8,000	$ 8,000	$ 8,000	$ 8,000
Purchases	22,000	22,000	22,000	22,000
Cost of goods available for sale..	$30,000	$30,000	$30,000	$30,000
Less: Ending inventory...........	12,400	12,000	14,500	9,800
Cost of goods sold	$17,600	$18,000	$15,500	$20,200
Gross profit on sales	$ 9,900	$ 9,500	$12,000	$ 7,300

Why does each inventory pricing method produce different results? The answer stems from our assumption that merchandise purchased at different dates is acquired at *different costs*.[5] Each of the four inventory methods is

[5] If the purchase cost of merchandise never changes, all four inventory pricing methods result in the same valuation of ending inventory and of the cost of goods sold.

based on a different assumption as to *which of these purchase costs* should be assigned to the ending inventory and which should be included in the cost of goods sold. Thus, each method results in a different value for ending inventory, cost of goods sold, gross profit, and, eventually, net income.

Evaluation of the Methods

All four of the inventory methods described above are acceptable for financial reporting purposes and also for the purpose of computing taxable income.[6] Different inventory methods may be used in accounting for different types of inventory (such as different product lines), or for inventories in different geographical locations. As discussed below, each inventory method has certain advantages and shortcomings. In the final analysis, the selection of inventory methods is a managerial decision. The method (or methods) used in the valuations of inventories should be disclosed in a footnote to the financial statements.

Let us now look briefly at the major advantages and shortcomings of each inventory pricing method.

■ **Specific Identification**   This is the only method in which the allocation of costs between ending inventory and the cost of goods sold *exactly parallels* the physical flow of merchandise. As stated earlier, if each unit of merchandise is unique and has a different cost, this is the only practical method.

When the inventory consists of many *identical items,* however, the specific identification method has a number of shortcomings. First, if the items are identical, it may be difficult to make the "specific identification" necessary to apply the method. In addition, this method assigns different costs to identical items. This, in turn, permits the manipulation of reported net income merely by selecting which items to deliver in filling sales orders.

■ **Average Cost**   Identical items will have the same accounting values only under the average-cost method. Assume for example that a hardware store sells a given size nail for 65 cents per pound. The hardware store buys the nails in 100-pound quantities at different times at prices ranging from 40 to 50 cents per pound. Several hundred pounds of nails are always on hand, stored in a large bin. The average-cost method properly recognizes that when a customer buys a pound of nails it is not necessary to know exactly which nails the customer happened to select from the bin in order to measure the gross profit on the sale. Therefore, the average-cost method avoids the shortcomings of the specific identification method. It is not necessary to keep track of the specific items sold and of those still in inventory. Also, it is not possible to manipulate income merely by selecting the items to be delivered to customers.

A shortcoming in the average-cost method is that changes in current replacement costs of inventory are concealed because these costs are averaged with older costs. Thus, neither the valuation of ending inventory nor the cost of goods sold will quickly reflect changes in the current replacement cost of merchandise.

---

[6] *Taxable income* is a term describing the amount of income subject to income taxes. Taxable income is computed in a manner somewhat similar to the computation of *net income,* although significant differences in these computations do exist. The computation of taxable income is discussed in greater detail in Chap. 20.

■ **FIFO**   The first-in, first-out method assigns the "oldest" purchase costs to the cost of goods sold and the costs of the most recent purchases to ending inventory. As a result, inventory is valued relatively close to its current replacement cost. During a period of rising prices, however, the "older" costs assigned to the cost of goods sold may be less than the cost actually paid by the company to restock its inventory. Thus, some accountants feel that the FIFO method tends to understate the cost of goods sold and overstate net income.

Whether or not this method actually "overstates" net income is a value judgment. Notice, however, that in our comparison of inventory pricing methods on page 354, FIFO results in the lowest cost of goods sold and the highest amount of gross profit. This outcome is characteristic of the FIFO method during a period of rising prices.

■ **LIFO**   A recent survey of large corporations shows the last-in, first-out (LIFO) to be the most widely used of all inventory pricing methods.[7] The authors of this textbook consider LIFO to be theoretically preferable to the other methods. Sales revenue reflects current prices; therefore, we believe that the cost of goods sold should reflect the current costs of merchandise. The LIFO method comes closest to this objective by assigning to the cost of goods sold the prices paid for the most recent purchases of merchandise.

Income tax considerations, however, provide another reason for the popularity of the LIFO method. Remember that the LIFO method assigns the most recent inventory purchase costs to the cost of goods sold. In the common situation of rising prices, these "most recent" costs are also the highest costs. By reporting a higher cost of goods sold than results from the other inventory valuation methods, the LIFO method usually results in *lower taxable income.* In short, if inventory costs are rising, a company can reduce the amount of its income tax obligation by using the LIFO method in its income tax returns.

For the reason stated above, most companies use LIFO in their income tax returns. However, income tax regulations allow a corporation to use LIFO in its income tax return only if the company also uses LIFO in its financial statements. Thus, income tax considerations often provide an important reason for selecting the LIFO method.

There is one significant shortcoming to the LIFO method. The valuation of the asset inventory is based upon the company's "oldest" inventory acquisition costs. After the company has been in business for many years, these "oldest" costs may greatly understate the current replacement cost of the inventory. Thus, when an inventory is valued by the LIFO method, the company also should disclose the current replacement cost of the inventory in a note to the financial statements.

During periods of rising inventory replacement costs, the LIFO method results in the lowest valuation of inventory and measurement of net income. Therefore, LIFO is regarded as the most *"conservative"* of the inventory pricing methods. FIFO, on the other hand, is the "least conservative" method.[8]

---

[7] American Institute of Certified Public Accountants, *Accounting Trends & Techniques* (New York: 1987), p. 126.

[8] During a prolonged period of declining inventory replacement costs, this situation reverses: FIFO becomes the most conservative method, and LIFO the least conservative.

Consistency in the Valuation of Inventory

The principle of *consistency* is one of the basic concepts underlying reliable financial statements. This principle means that once a company has adopted a particular accounting method, it should follow that method consistently, rather than switching methods from one year to the next. (Remember, however, that a company may use different inventory pricing methods to account for different types of inventory, or for inventories in different geographical locations.)

The principle of consistency does *not* prohibit a company from *ever* changing its method of pricing inventory. If such a change is made, however, the reasons for the change must be explained and the effects of the change upon the company's net income must be fully disclosed.[9]

The Environment of Inflation

We have previously discussed the relationship between the valuation of assets in the balance sheet and the recognition of costs and expenses in the income statement. As assets are sold or used up, their cost is removed from the balance sheet and recognized in the income statement as a cost or expense. In the case of inventory, the cost of units sold is transferred from the balance sheet to the income statement as cost of goods sold. In the case of depreciable assets, such as a building, the cost is gradually transferred to the income statement as depreciation expense. This flow of costs is illustrated in the chart below.

A period of sustained inflation causes some distortion in financial statements which are based upon *historical costs*. (As explained in Chapter 1, historical cost means the dollar cost originally paid to acquire the asset.) Rising price levels may cause the current replacement cost of assets to be substantially higher than the amounts at which these assets are valued in the balance sheet. Furthermore, the cost assigned to the income statement as these assets

"Flow" of historical costs through the balance sheet into the income statement

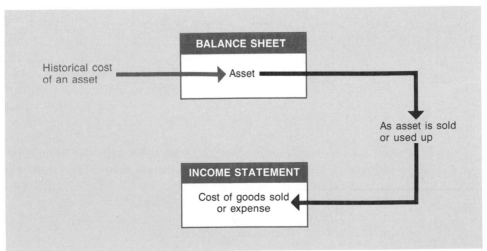

---

[9] A change in the method of inventory pricing also requires the approval of the Internal Revenue Service.

are sold or used up tends to understate the cost to the business of replacing these assets.

Some accountants believe that the use of FIFO or of average cost during a period of inflation results in the reporting of overstated profits and in the payment of more income taxes than would be required under the LIFO method. Profits are considered overstated under both the FIFO and average-cost methods because the gross profit is computed by subtracting "old" inventory costs rather than current replacement costs from sales revenue. These old costs are relatively low, resulting in a larger reported gross profit. However, the company must pay the higher current cost to replenish its inventory.

Inflation and high income tax rates have stimulated the interest of business management in the choice of inventory methods. Although the rate of inflation slowed significantly in the 1980s, most business executives and government officials expect the trend of rising prices to continue. In other words, an environment of inflation has come to be considered as normal. The LIFO method of inventory valuation causes reported net income to reflect the increasing cost of replacing the merchandise sold during the year and also tends to avoid basing income tax payments on an exaggerated measurement of income. Therefore, many companies have switched to the LIFO method in recent years.

The Lower-of-Cost-or-Market Rule (LCM)

Objective 5
Explain the lower-of-cost-or-market rule.

Although cost is the primary basis for valuation of inventories, circumstances may arise under which inventory may properly be valued at less than its cost. If the *utility* of the inventory has fallen below cost because of a decline in the price level, a loss has occurred. This loss may appropriately be recognized as a loss of the current period by reducing the accounting value of the inventory from cost to a lower level designated as *market.* The word *market* as used in this context means *current replacement cost.* For a merchandising company, *market* is the amount which the concern would have to pay at the present time for the goods in question, purchased in the customary quantities through the usual sources of supply and including transportation-in. To avoid misunderstanding, the rule might better read "lower of actual cost or replacement cost."

A restriction of the lower-of-cost-or-market rule is that inventory should never be carried at an amount greater than *net realizable value,* which may be defined as prospective selling price minus anticipated selling expenses. Assume, for example, that because of unstable market conditions, it is believed that goods acquired at a cost of $5,000 and having a current replacement cost of $4,500 will probably have to be sold for no more than $5,200 and that the selling expenses involved will amount to $1,200. The inventory should then be reduced to a carrying value (net realizable value) of $4,000, which is less than current replacement cost. The lower-of-cost-or-market rule is another example of the accounting concept of conservatism. A conservative valuation of inventory requires prompt recognition of losses, even though the exact amount of the loss cannot be conclusively determined.

■ **Application of the Lower-of-Cost-or-Market Rule** The lower of cost or market for inventory is often computed by determining the cost and the market figures for each item in inventory and using the lower of the two amounts in every case. If, for example, item A cost $100 and replacement cost is $90, the item should be priced at $90. If item B cost $200 and replacement cost is $225, this item should be priced at $200. The total cost of the two items is $300 and total replacement cost is $315, but the total inventory value determined by applying the lower-of-cost-or-market rule to each item in inventory is only $290. This application of the lower-of-cost-or-market rule is illustrated by the tabulation shown below:

Application of Lower-of-Cost-or-Market Rule, Item-by-Item Method

Pricing inventory at lower of cost or market

ITEM	QUANTITY	UNIT COST COST	UNIT COST MARKET	TOTAL COST COST	TOTAL COST MARKET	LOWER OF COST OR MARKET
A	10	$100	$ 90	$ 1,000	$ 900	$ 900
B	8	200	225	1,600	1,800	1,600
C	50	50	60	2,500	3,000	2,500
D	80	90	70	7,200	5,600	5,600
Totals ...				$12,300	$11,300	$10,600

If the lower-of-cost-or-market rule is applied item by item, the carrying value of the above inventory would be $10,600. However, an alternative and less rigorous version of the lower-of-cost-or-market rule calls for applying it to the total of the entire inventory rather than to the individual items. Under this approach, the balance sheet amount for inventory is determined merely by comparing the total cost of $12,300 with the total replacement cost of $11,300 and using the lower of the two figures. Still another alternative method of using the lower-of-cost-or-market concept is to apply it to categories of the inventory rather than item by item. Each of these alternative methods of applying the lower-of-cost-or-market rule is acceptable in current accounting practice, although once a method has been selected it should be followed consistently from year to year.

■ **Other Writedowns of Inventory** Big writedowns of inventory are more likely to arise because merchandise has become obsolete or has been damaged by water, smoke, heat, or other factors. Inventory which becomes unsalable because it is damaged or obsolete should be written down to zero, or to scrap value, if any. Writedowns of this type are not an application of the lower-of-cost-or-market rule, because the inventory is being written off as unsalable rather than being reduced to a current replacement cost for salable merchandise.

CASE IN POINT ■ An automobile dealership operating as a partnership retained a CPA firm to make a first audit of the business. During the audit the CPAs observed the taking of a physical inventory of repair parts. They noticed a large number of new fenders of a design and shape not used in current model automobiles. Investigation revealed that the fenders (with a total inventory valuation of many thousands of dollars) were for a model of automobile discontinued seven years earlier. The records showed that only one of these fenders had been sold during recent years. The partners explained to the CPAs that these fenders had been included in the parts inventory when they purchased the business and they had no idea why such a large supply had originally been acquired. The partners agreed that few, if any, of this model of fender would ever be sold. It had not occurred to the partners to write down the carrying value of these obsolete parts, but they agreed with the CPA firm's suggestion that the fenders, being virtually unsalable, should be reduced to scrap value.

Estimating Ending Inventory and Cost of Goods Sold

Objective 6
Estimate ending inventory by the gross profit method and by the retail method.

A physical inventory taken at the end of the year provides the inventory amount needed for the preparation of annual financial statements. Many business managers, however, also want monthly and quarterly financial statements. To take a physical inventory every month would be very expensive and time-consuming. Consequently, it is common practice to use an estimated amount for inventory in preparing monthly or quarterly financial statements. One method of *estimating* inventories is the *gross profit method;* another method used by retail stores is called the *retail inventory method.*

The Gross Profit Method of Estimating Ending Inventory

The gross profit method is a quick, simple technique for estimating inventories, and can be used in almost all types and sizes of business. In using this method, it is assumed that the rate of gross profit earned in the preceding year will remain the same for the current year. When we know the rate of gross profit, we can divide the dollar amount of net sales into two elements: (1) the gross profit and (2) the cost of goods sold. We view net sales as 100%. If gross profit, for example, is 40%, the cost of goods sold must be 60%. In other words, the cost of goods sold percentage (cost percentage) is determined by deducting the gross profit percentage from 100%.

When the gross profit percentage is known, the ending inventory can be estimated by the following procedures:

1 Determine the *cost of goods available for sale* from the general ledger records of beginning inventory and net purchases.

2 Estimate the *cost of goods sold* by multiplying the net sales by the cost percentage.

3 Deduct the *cost of goods sold* from the *cost of goods available for sale* to find the estimated ending inventory.

To illustrate, assume that Metro Hardware has a beginning inventory of $50,000 on January 1. During the month of January, net purchases amount to $20,000 and net sales total $30,000. Assume that the company's normal gross profit rate is 40% of net sales; it follows that the cost percentage is 60%. Using these facts, the inventory on January 31 may be estimated as follows:

Goods available for sale:

Beginning inventory, Jan. 1	*$50,000*
Net purchases	*20,000*
Cost of goods available for sale	*$70,000*

Step 1 . . .

	Deduct: Estimated cost of goods sold:		
	Net sales	*$30,000*	
Step 2 . . .	*Cost percentage (100% − 40%) ....*	*60%*	
	Estimated cost of goods sold		*18,000*
Step 3 . . .	*Estimated ending inventory, Jan. 31 ....*		*$52,000*

The gross profit method of estimating inventory has several uses apart from the preparation of monthly financial statements. If an inventory is destroyed by fire, the company must determine the amount of the inventory on hand at the date of the fire in order to file an insurance claim. The most convenient way to determine this inventory amount is often the gross profit method.

The gross profit method is also used at year-end after the taking of a physical inventory to confirm the overall reasonableness of the amount determined by the counting and pricing process.

The Retail Method of Estimating Ending Inventory

The retail method of inventory is widely used by department stores and other types of retail business. To use the retail inventory method, a store must maintain records showing the beginning inventory *at cost* and *at retail*. The term "at retail" means the marked selling prices of all items in the store. The records also must show the purchases during the period both *at cost* and *at retail*. The only other information needed is the net sales for the month. The amount of net sales, of course, is equal to the amount recorded in the Sales revenue account during the period minus any sales returns and sales discounts.

The records described above enable us to know the amount of goods available for sale, stated both at cost and at retail selling prices. (As you know, goods available for sale are the total of beginning inventory and net purchases.) With this information, all we need to do is to deduct the net sales for the month from the retail sales value of the goods available for sale. The result will be the ending inventory at retail selling price. A final step is to convert the ending inventory at retail selling price to a cost basis by multiplying it by the *cost percentage*. The cost percentage is the *ratio of cost to selling price for the current period*. To compute the cost percentage, divide the cost of goods available for sale by the retail sales value of these goods. The end result of these procedures is that we have an estimated cost value for inventory without going through the extensive work of taking a physical inventory.

The following illustration shows the calculation of an ending inventory of $280,000 by the retail inventory method.

Estimating inventory for monthly financial statements

	COST PRICE	RETAIL SELLING PRICE
Goods available for sale:		
Beginning inventory	*$415,000*	*$ 560,000*
Net purchases	*285,000*	*440,000*
Goods available for sale	*$700,000*	*$1,000,000*
Cost percentage: $700,000 ÷ $1,000,000 = 70%		
Deduct: Net sales at retail		*600,000*
Ending inventory at retail selling price............................		*$ 400,000*
Ending inventory at cost ($400,000 × 70%)........................	*$280,000*	

■ **Reducing a Physical Inventory to Cost by the Retail Method**   A second use for the retail inventory method is to aid in the completion of the annual physical inventory. Goods on sale in retail stores have price tags attached, showing retail prices. When the annual physical inventory is taken, it is more convenient to list the retail prices from the price tags than to look up purchase invoices to find the unit cost of each item in the store. The total of the inventory at retail selling price is then reduced to cost by applying the cost percentage, that is, the ratio between cost and selling price during the current period. The following illustration shows a year-end physical inventory amounting to $170,000 at retail selling price. This amount is reduced to a cost basis of $102,000 by applying the cost percentage of 60%.

	COST PRICE	RETAIL SELLING PRICE
Goods available for sale:		
Beginning inventory	$ 98,000	$160,000
Net purchases	262,000	440,000
Goods available for sale	$360,000	$600,000
Cost percentage: $360,000 ÷ $600,000 = 60%		
Ending inventory at retail selling price (per physical inventory)		$170,000
Ending inventory at cost ($170,000 × 60%)	$102,000	

Take year-end physical inventory at retail; then reduce it to cost

In this illustration we have shown the calculation of inventory by the retail inventory method without going into the complications which would arise from markups and markdowns in the original retail selling prices. Such changes in price are considered in advanced accounting courses.

Although the inventory amount is an estimate, experience has shown this retail inventory method to be a reliable one. An inventory amount established in this manner is acceptable in audited financial statements and also in federal income tax returns.

Internal Control of Inventories

Inventories are usually the largest current asset of a merchandising or manufacturing business. Furthermore, the very nature of inventories makes them subject to theft and to major errors and misstatement. The large dollar amounts involved, coupled with the rapid turnover of inventory items, and the variety of alternative valuation methods make it possible for a major shortage to occur in inventories without attracting immediate attention. Thus, the accountant's approach to inventories should stress an awareness of the possibility of large intentional errors as well as major accidental errors in establishing inventory quantities and amounts. If one or more members of a company's management is determined to evade income taxes, to conceal shortages arising from irregularities, or to mislead absentee owners, inventories constitute the most likely area for such fraudulent action to take place.

To provide the strong internal control procedures needed to protect inventories, the various physical functions involved in acquiring and handling merchandise should be assigned to separate departments. These functions may include purchasing, receiving, storing, issuing, and shipping the items which comprise the inventory. Thus, the organizational structure of a company should include a purchasing department with exclusive authority to make all purchases. All merchandise received by the company should be cleared through a receiving department. This department will count the merchandise received, detect any damaged items, issue a receiving report to the accounts payable department and other departments, and transmit the merchandise to the stores department.

In addition to the protection afforded by extensive subdivision of duties, another important approach to assuring reliability in the amounts reported as inventory and cost of goods sold is an annual audit by a CPA firm. Every independent audit includes first-hand observation of the annual taking of a physical inventory. Such observation by a competent outsider provides assurance that the physical inventory is carefully counted and priced, thus leading to valid amounts for inventory and cost of goods sold in the financial statements. In addition, the independent auditors will study and test the system of internal control.

Many small companies have too few employees to permit the extensive subdivision of duties described above. Moreover, these small concerns usually are unwilling to incur the cost of an annual audit by a CPA firm. Under these circumstances, the amounts shown in the financial statements (especially inventory, cost of goods sold, gross profit, and net income) should be viewed with caution by absentee owners, bankers, creditors, IRS agents, and other outsiders.

CASE IN POINT ■ The Internal Revenue Service (IRS) conducts audits of the income tax returns of most business organizations to see that these companies have not understated taxable income and thereby evaded income taxes. The IRS has found that a business which wants to understate its taxable income is likely to do so by understating inventory. Small businesses, in particular, which are not audited by CPA firms, may make a practice of regularly understating the ending inventory year after year in order to understate taxable income. In income tax audits, therefore, the IRS makes it standard practice to verify as fully as possible the determination of the amount of ending inventory. An ending inventory which is quite small in relation to the year's sales volume is a "red flag signal" to the tax auditor.

Perpetual Inventory System

Objective 7
Explain how a perpetual inventory system operates.

Companies which deal in merchandise of high unit cost, such as automobiles, television sets, or expensive jewelry, find a perpetual inventory system worthwhile and efficient. Since inventory is often one of the largest assets in a business and has a rapid rate of turnover, strong internal control is especially important. A perpetual inventory system, if properly designed and operated, can provide the strongest possible internal control over the inventory of merchandise. The key feature of a perpetual inventory system is that the records show continuously the amount of inventory on hand and the cost of goods sold. Companies with computer-based accounting records including point-of-sale terminals are in a good position to carry on continuous updating of inventory records.

Internal Control and Perpetual Inventory Systems

A perpetual inventory system has the potential of providing excellent internal control. However, the fact that perpetual inventory records are in use does not automatically guarantee strong internal control. Such basic internal control concepts as the subdivision of duties, the control of documents by serial numbers, and separation of the accounting function from the custody of assets are essential elements with either the perpetual or periodic inventory systems.

CASE IN POINT ■ Par-Flite, a manufacturer of golf equipment, maintained an inventory of several thousand sets of golf clubs. The clubs were kept in a storeroom with barred windows and doors under the supervision of John Adams. Adams was also responsible for maintaining detailed perpetual inventory records of the golf clubs in the storeroom. Another employee acquired an unauthorized key to the storeroom and began stealing large numbers of clubs. Adams discovered that the quantities on hand did not agree with the perpetual records he maintained. Afraid that his records would be criticized as highly inaccurate, he made numerous changes in the records so they would agree with the quantities of golf clubs on hand. The theft of clubs continued and large losses were sustained before the inventory shortage came to the attention of management.

If the person maintaining records had not also been responsible for physical custody of the merchandise, there would have been no incentive or opportunity to conceal a shortage by falsifying the records. Satisfactory internal control over inventories requires that the accounting function be separate from the custody of assets. Frequent comparison of quantities of merchandise on hand with the quantities shown by the perpetual inventory records should be made by employees who do not have responsibility either for custody of assets or for maintenance of records.

Perpetual Inventory Records

The information required for a perpetual system can be processed electronically or manually. In a manual system a subsidiary record card, as shown below, is used for each type of merchandise on hand. If the company has 100 different kinds of products in stock, then 100 inventory record cards will make up the subsidiary inventory record. Shown on the next page is an inventory record card for item XL-2000.

On this card, the quantity and cost of units received will be listed at the date of receipt; the quantity and cost of units sold will be recorded at the date of sale; and after each purchase or sales transaction, the balance remaining on hand will be shown. This running balance will be shown in number of units, cost per unit, and total dollar amount.

The information on the illustrated inventory record shows that the first-in, first-out basis of pricing the inventory is being used. After the sale of two units on January 7, the remaining inventory consisted of 10 units at a cost of $50 each. The purchase on January 9 of 10 units carried a unit cost of $55, rather than $50, hence must be accounted for separately. The balance on hand after the January 9 purchase appears on two lines: 10 units at $50 and 10 units at

**Perpetual
inventory record
card**

| Item | XL-2000 | | Minimum | 8 |
| Location | Storeroom 2 | | Maximum | 20 |

	PURCHASED			SOLD			BALANCE		
Date	Units	Unit Cost	Total	Units	Unit Cost	Total	Units	Unit Cost	Balance
Jan. 1							12	$50.00	$600.00
7				2	$50.00	$100.00	10	50.00	500.00
9	10	$55.00	$550.00				10	50.00	
							10	55.00	1,050.00
12				8	50.00	400.00	2	50.00	
							10	55.00	650.00
31				2	50.00	100.00			
				1	55.00	55.00	9	55.00	495.00

$55. When eight units were sold on January 12, they were treated as coming from the oldest stock on hand and therefore had a cost of $50 each. The balance remaining on hand then consisted of two units at $50 and 10 units at $55. When three units were sold on January 31, the cost consisted of two units at $50 and one unit at $55. The ending inventory of nine units consists of the most recently acquired units with a cost of $55 each.

Perpetual inventory records may also be maintained on a last-in, first-out basis or on an average-cost basis, but these systems involve some complexities which are considered in advanced accounting courses.

Control over the amount invested in inventory can be strengthened by listing on each inventory card the maximum and minimum quantities that should be kept in stock. By maintaining quantities within these limits, overstocking and out-of-stock situations can be avoided.

■ **General Ledger Entries for a Perpetual Inventory System** The general ledger controlling account entitled *Inventory* is continuously (perpetually) updated when a perpetual inventory system is in use. This Inventory account controls the many subsidiary record cards discussed above. A continuously updated Cost of Goods Sold account is also maintained in the general ledger.

The purchase of merchandise by a company using a perpetual inventory system requires a journal entry affecting general ledger controlling accounts as follows:

Inventory 1,500
   Accounts Payable, Lake Company 1,500
To record purchase of merchandise on credit.

This purchase transaction would also be recorded in the subsidiary ledger (the perpetual inventory cards) showing the quantity of each kind of merchandise purchased. The $1,500 purchase from Lake Company might affect only one or perhaps a dozen of the subsidiary records, depending on how many types of merchandise were included in this purchase transaction.

For every sales transaction, we can determine the cost of the goods sold by referring to the appropriate perpetual inventory card record. Therefore, at the time of a sale, we can record both the amount of the selling price and the *cost* of the goods sold, as illustrated in the following pair of related entries.

Accounts Receivable, J. Williams....................................	140	
Sales		140
To record the sale of merchandise on credit.		

Cost of Goods Sold	100	
Inventory...		100
To record the cost of goods sold and the related decrease in inventory.		

To avoid making a large number of entries in the general journal, a special column can be entered in the sales journal to show the cost of the goods involved in each sales transaction. At the end of the month the total of this "Cost" column can be posted as a debit to Cost of Goods Sold and a credit to Inventory.

When a perpetual inventory system is in use, the Inventory account is increased by purchases of merchandise. It is decreased by the cost of goods sold, by purchase returns and allowances, and by purchase discounts. At the end of the year the dollar balances of all the subsidiary inventory record cards should be added to see that the total is in agreement with the general ledger controlling account. The only adjustment necessary at year-end will be to correct the Inventory controlling account and the subsidiary records for any discrepancies indicated by the taking of a physical inventory.

The advantages of a perpetual inventory system as indicated in the preceding discussion include:

1 Stronger internal control. By comparing the physical inventory with the perpetual records, management will be made aware of any shortages or errors and can take corrective action.

2 The accounting records provide information about the cost and quantity of goods on hand. This information is useful in avoiding overstocking and out-of-stock situations.

3 Quarterly or monthly financial statements can be prepared more readily because of the availability of dollar amounts for inventory and cost of goods sold in the accounting records.

Need for an Annual Physical Inventory

An annual physical inventory is essential in every merchandising business even though a perpetual inventory system is in use. The perpetual inventory records show the amount of merchandise which *should be* on hand; the physical count shows the amount of merchandise which actually *is* on hand. The taking of a physical inventory usually discloses significant differences from the perpetual records. These discrepancies may be the result of errors in the accounting process, or from shrinkage of inventory because of shoplifting, employee theft, or other factors. The discrepancies should be disposed of by adjusting the perpetual inventory records to agree with the physical count.

For example, assume that the perpetual inventory records of Baxter Corporation show an inventory of $290,000 at year-end. A physical inventory taken at December 31 shows merchandise on hand of $279,100. The adjusting entry to correct the perpetual inventory records is:

Cost of Goods Sold	*10,900*	
Inventory...		*10,900*

To adjust the perpetual inventory records to the amount indicated by the year-end physical inventory.

End-of-Chapter Review

CONCEPTS INTRODUCED OR EMPHASIZED IN CHAPTER 9

The major concepts in this chapter include:

■ The matching principle—determining what portion of the cost of goods available for sale should be deducted from the revenue of the current period and what portion should be carried forward (as inventory) to be matched against the revenue of the following period.

■ Four alternative methods of inventory valuation: specific identification, average cost, FIFO, and LIFO.

■ Inflation as an argument for the LIFO method.

■ The principle of consistency applied to the use of an inventory valuation method.

■ The lower-of-cost-or-market rule: an application of the concept of conservatism.

■ Estimating inventory: the gross profit method and the retail method.

■ Perpetual inventory systems as a means of stronger internal control.

In this chapter we have shown that different inventory methods can have significant effects on net income as reported in the financial statements, and on income tax returns as well. In the following chapter, we will extend this concept to the depreciation of plant and equipment. The choice of depreciation methods can influence reported net income to a significant degree.

KEY TERMS INTRODUCED OR EMPHASIZED IN CHAPTER 9

Average-cost method   A method of inventory valuation. Weighted-average unit cost is computed by dividing the total cost of goods available for sale by the number of identical units available for sale.

Consistency in inventory valuation   An accounting standard that calls for the use of the same method of inventory pricing from year to year, with full disclosure of the effects of any change in method. Intended to make financial statements comparable.

First-in, first-out (FIFO) method   A method of computing the cost of inventory and the cost of goods sold based on the assumption that the first merchandise acquired is the first merchandise sold, and that the ending inventory consists of the most recently acquired goods.

F.O.B. destination   A term meaning the seller bears the cost of shipping goods to the buyer's location. Title to the goods remains with the seller while the goods are in transit.

F.O.B. shipping point   The buyer of goods bears the cost of transportation from the seller's location to the buyer's location. Title to the goods passes at the point of shipment and the goods are the property of the buyer while in transit.

Gross profit method   A method of estimating the cost of the ending inventory based on the assumption that the rate of gross profit remains approximately the same from year to year.

Last-in, first-out (LIFO) method   A method of computing the cost of goods sold by use of the prices paid for the most recently acquired units. Ending inventory is valued on the basis of prices paid for the units first acquired.

Lower-of-cost-or-market method   A method of inventory pricing in which goods are valued at original cost or replacement cost (market), whichever is lower.

Net realizable value   The prospective selling price minus anticipated selling expenses. Inventory should not be carried at more than net realizable value.

Perpetual inventory system   Provides a continuous (perpetual) running record of the goods on hand. As goods are sold their cost is transferred to a Cost of Goods Sold account.

Physical inventory   A systematic count of all goods on hand, followed by the application of unit prices to the quantities counted and development of a dollar value for ending inventory.

Retail method   A method of estimating inventory in a retail store based on the assumption that the cost of goods on hand bears the same percentage relationship to retail prices as does the cost of all goods available for sale to the original retail prices. Inventory is first priced at retail and then converted to cost by application of a cost-to-retail percentage.

Specific identification method   A method of pricing inventory by identifying the units in the ending inventory as coming from specific purchases.

DEMONSTRATION PROBLEM FOR YOUR REVIEW

Information relating to the inventory quantities, purchases, and sales of a certain type of capacitor by Morton Electronics during the year is shown below:

	NUMBER OF UNITS	COST PER UNIT	TOTAL COST
Inventory, Jan. 1	4,000	$5.89	$ 23,560
First purchase (Mar. 15)	5,150	6.20	31,930
Second purchase (June 6)	6,200	6.60	40,920
Third purchase (Sept. 20)	4,800	6.80	32,640
Fourth purchase (Dec. 31)	3,850	7.00	26,950
Goods available for sale	24,000		$156,000
Units sold during the year	18,600		
Inventory, Dec. 31	5,400		

Instructions Compute the cost of the December 31 inventory and the cost of goods sold for the capacitors during the year using:

a The first-in, first-out method

b The last-in, first-out method

c The average-cost method

SOLUTION TO DEMONSTRATION PROBLEM

a FIFO method

Inventory:

3,850 units from the Dec. 31 purchase @ $7.00	$ 26,950
1,550 units from the Sept. 20 purchase @ $6.80	10,540
Ending inventory, 5,400 units (at FIFO cost)...................................	$ 37,490

Cost of goods sold:

Cost of goods available for sale...	$156,000
Less: Ending inventory (FIFO)	37,490
Cost of goods sold (FIFO)	$118,510

b LIFO method

Inventory:

4,000 units from beginning inventory @ $5.89..................................	$ 23,560
1,400 units from the Mar. 15 purchase @ $6.20	8,680
Ending inventory, 5,400 units (at LIFO cost)...................................	$ 32,240

Cost of goods sold:

Cost of goods available for sale...	$156,000
Less: Ending inventory (LIFO)	32,240
Cost of goods sold (LIFO)	$123,760

c Average-cost method

Inventory:

Cost of goods available for sale...	$156,000
Number of units available for sale..	24,000
Average cost per unit ($156,000 ÷ 24,000 units)	$ 6.50
Ending inventory (at average cost, 5,400 units × $6.50)........................	$ 35,100

Cost of goods sold:

Cost of goods available for sale...	$156,000
Less: Ending inventory (average cost)	35,100
Cost of goods sold (average cost)	$120,900

Alternative computation of cost of goods sold:

Cost of goods sold (18,600 units at $6.50)	$120,900

SELF-TEST QUESTIONS

The answers to these questions appear on page 382.

1 The primary objective in the selection of an inventory valuation method is to:

a Show inventory in the balance sheet at the figure that most closely approximates replacement cost.

b Parallel the physical flow of merchandise through the business.

c Offset against revenue an appropriate cost of goods sold.

d Report the most conservative (lowest) figure for net income.

2 Trent Retail uses a periodic inventory system. Merchandise kept in a rented storage facility was accidentally omitted from the physical inventory taken at December 31, 1990 ($13,000 cost of merchandise omitted) and again at December 31, 1991 ($19,000 cost of merchandise omitted). In addition, a credit sale of merchandise for $3,200 was made on December 31, 1991, but the entry recording this transaction was dated January 3, 1992. If these errors are not corrected:

a Cost of goods sold for 1991 will be understated by $6,000.

b Cost of goods sold for 1991 will be overstated by $2,800.

c Net income for 1991 will be overstated by $2,800.

d Net income for 1991 will be understated by $9,200.

3 T-Shirt City made four purchases of a particular item during the first year of operations. Each purchase was for 500 units and the prices paid were: $9 per unit in the first purchase, $10 per unit in the second purchase, $12 per unit in the third purchase, and $13 per unit in the fourth purchase. At year-end, 650 of these units remained unsold. Compute the cost of goods sold under the FIFO method and LIFO method, respectively.

a $13,700 (FIFO) and $16,000 (LIFO).

b $8,300 (FIFO) and $6,000 (LIFO).

c $16,000 (FIFO) and $13,700 (LIFO).

d $6,000 (FIFO) and $8,300 (LIFO).

4 In July, 1992, the accountant for LBJ Imports is in the process of preparing financial statements for the quarter ended June 30, 1992. The physical inventory, however, was last taken on June 5 and the accountant must establish the approximate cost at June 30 from the following data:

Physical inventory, June 5, 1992	$900,000
Transactions for the period June 5–June 30:	
Sales	700,000
Purchases	400,000

The gross profit on sales has consistently averaged 40% of sales. Using the gross profit method, compute the approximate inventory cost at June 30, 1992.

a $420,000   b $880,000   c $480,000   d $1,360,000

5 When a perpetual inventory system is in use:

a The balance in the Inventory ledger account is at all times an accurate figure for the amount of merchandise actually on hand.

b The specific identification method of inventory valuation must be used.

c The purchase of merchandise involves a debit to the Cost of Goods Available for Sale account.

d The sale of merchandise requires an entry which debits the Cost of Goods Sold account and credits the Inventory account.

Assignment Material

REVIEW QUESTIONS

1 Which of the seven items listed below are used in computing the *cost of goods available for sale?*

a Ending inventory   **e** Transportation-in
b Sales   **f** Purchase returns and allowances
c Beginning inventory   **g** Delivery expense
d Purchases

2 Through an error in counting of merchandise at December 31, 1989, the Trophy Company overstated the amount of goods on hand by $8,000. Assuming that the error was not discovered, what was the effect upon net income for 1989? Upon owners' equity at December 31, 1989? Upon net income for 1990? Upon owners' equity at December 31, 1990?

3 Is the establishment of an appropriate valuation for the merchandise inventory at the end of the year more important in producing a dependable income statement, or in producing a dependable balance sheet?

4 Explain the meaning of the term *physical inventory.*

5 Near the end of December, Hadley Company received a large order from a major customer. The work of packing the goods for shipment was begun at once but could not be completed before the close of business on December 31. Since a written order from the customer was on hand and the goods were nearly all packed and ready for shipment, Hadley felt that this merchandise should not be included in the physical inventory taken on December 31. Do you agree? What is probably the reason behind Hadley's opinion?

6 During a prolonged period of rising prices, will the FIFO or LIFO method of inventory valuation result in higher reported profits?

7 Throughout several years of strongly rising prices, Company A used the LIFO method of inventory valuation and Company B used the FIFO method. In which company would the balance sheet figure for inventory be closer to current replacement cost of the merchandise on hand? Why?

8 You are making a detailed analysis of the financial statements and accounting records of two companies in the same industry, Adams Company and Bar Company. Price levels have been rising steadily for several years. In the course of your investigation, you observe that the inventory value shown on the Adams Company balance sheet is quite close to the current replacement cost of the merchandise on hand. However, for Bar Company, the carrying value of the inventory is far below current replacement cost. What method of inventory valuation is probably used by Adams Company? By Bar Company? If we assume that the two companies are identical except for the inventory valuation method used, which company has probably been reporting higher net income in recent years?

9 Apex Corporation operates in two locations: New York and Oregon. The LIFO method is used in accounting for inventories at the New York facility and the specific identification method for inventories at the Oregon location. Does this concurrent use of two inventory methods indicate that Apex is violating the accounting principle of consistency? Explain.

10 Why do some accountants consider the net income reported by businesses during a period of rising inventory prices to be overstated?

11 Assume that a business uses the first-in, first-out method of accounting for inventories during a prolonged period of inflation and that the owner makes withdrawals equal to the amount of reported net income. Suggest a problem that may arise in continued successful operation of the business.

12 Explain the meaning of the term *market* as used in the expression "lower of cost or market."

13 One of the items in the inventory of Grayline Stores is marked for sale at $125. The purchase invoice shows the item cost $95, but a newly issued price list from the manufacturer shows the present replacement cost to be $90. What inventory valuation should be assigned to this item if Grayline follows the lower-of-cost-or-market rule?

14 Explain the usefulness of the *gross profit method* of estimating inventories.

15 A store using the *retail inventory method* takes its physical inventory by applying current retail prices as marked on the merchandise to the quantities counted. Does this procedure indicate that the inventory will appear in the financial statements at retail selling price? Explain.

16 Estimate the ending inventory by the gross profit method, given the following data: beginning inventory $40,000, net purchases $100,000, net sales $106,667, average gross profit rate 25% of net sales.

17 Summarize the difference between the *periodic system* and the *perpetual system* of accounting for inventory. Which system would usually cost more to maintain? Which system would be most practicable for a restaurant, a retail drugstore, a new car dealer?

18 Identify each of the four statements shown below as true or false. Also, give a brief explanation. In the accounting records of a company using a perpetual inventory system:

a The Inventory account will ordinarily remain unchanged until the end of an accounting period.

b The Cost of Goods Sold account is debited with the sales price of merchandise sold.

c The Inventory account and the Cost of Goods Sold account will both normally have debit balances.

d The Inventory account and the Cost of Goods Sold account will normally have equal but offsetting balances.

19 A large art gallery has in inventory several hundred paintings. No two are alike. The least expensive is priced at more than $1,000 and the higher priced items carry prices of $100,000 or more. Which of the four methods of inventory valuation discussed in this chapter would you consider to be most appropriate for this business? Give reasons for your answer.

20 Assume that during the first year of Hatton Corporation's operation, there were numerous purchases of identical items of merchandise. However, there was no change during the year in the prices paid for this merchandise. Under these special circumstances how would the financial statements be affected by the choice between the FIFO and LIFO methods of inventory valuation?

EXERCISES

Exercise 9-1
Accounting
terminology

Listed below are nine technical accounting terms introduced in this chapter:

Taking a physical inventory	*LIFO method*	*Average-cost method*
Retail method	*FIFO method*	*Gross profit method*
Lower-of-cost-or-market rule	*Periodic inventory system*	*Perpetual inventory system*

Each of the following statements may (or may not) describe one of these technical terms. For each statement, indicate the accounting term described, or answer "None" if the statement does not correctly describe any of the terms.

a Procedures which provide a continuous running record of the inventory on hand and the cost of goods sold.

b Establishing a balance sheet valuation for the ending inventory by a process of counting and pricing merchandise on hand.

c A pricing method in which inventory appears in the balance sheet at expected sales price, rather than at cost.

d A pricing method in which the oldest goods on hand are assumed to be the first ones sold.

e The pricing method most appropriate for an inventory of unique items, such as oil paintings or custom jewelry.

f The pricing method most likely to minimize income taxes during a period of rising prices.

g A method of estimating inventory and the cost of goods sold which does not require recording purchases at two separate amounts.

Exercise 9-2
Effects of errors in inventory valuation

Norfleet Company prepared the following condensed income statements for two successive years:

	1991	1990
Sales	$1,500,000	$1,440,000
Cost of goods sold	879,600	914,400
Gross profit on sales	$ 620,400	$ 525,600
Operating expenses	460,500	447,000
Net income	$ 159,900	$ 78,600

At the end of 1990 (right-hand column above) the inventory was understated by $50,400, but the error was not discovered until after the accounts had been closed and financial statements prepared at the end of 1991. The balance sheets for the two years showed owner's equity of $214,200 at the end of 1990 and $260,400 at the end of 1991.

a Compute the corrected net income figures for 1990 and 1991.

b Compute the gross profit amounts and the gross profit percentages for each year based on corrected data.

c What correction, if any, should be made in owner's equity at the end of 1990 and at the end of 1991?

Exercise 9-3
F.O.B. shipping point and F.O.B. destination

Fraser Company had two large shipments in transit at December 31. One was a $90,000 inbound shipment of merchandise (shipped December 28, F.O.B. shipping point) which arrived at the Fraser receiving dock on January 2. The other shipment was a $55,000 outbound shipment of merchandise to a customer which was shipped and billed by Fraser on December 30 (terms F.O.B. shipping point) and reached the customer on January 3.

In taking a physical inventory on December 31, Fraser counted all goods on hand and priced the inventory on the basis of average cost. The total amount was $480,000. In developing this figure, Fraser gave no consideration to goods in transit.

What amount should appear as inventory on the company's balance sheet at December 31? Explain. If you indicate an amount other than $480,000, state what asset or liability other than inventory would also be changed in amount.

Exercise 9-4
LIFO, FIFO, and average cost

The records of Harbor, Inc., showed the beginning inventory balance of Item T12 on January 1 and the purchases of this item during the current year to be as follows:

Jan. 1 Beginning inventory	900 units @ $10.00	$ 9,000
Feb. 23 Purchase	1,200 units @ $11.00	13,200
Apr. 20 Purchase	3,000 units @ $11.20	33,600
May 4 Purchase	4,000 units @ $11.60	46,400
Nov. 30 Purchase	900 units @ $13.00	11,700
Totals	10,000 units	$113,900

At December 31 the ending inventory consisted of 1,500 units.

Determine the cost of the ending inventory, based on each of the following methods of inventory valuation:

a Average cost

b First-in, first-out

c Last-in, first-out

Exercise 9-5
Again: FIFO,
LIFO, and
average cost

One of the inventory items sold by Pacific Plumbing is a ¾-inch brass gate valve. The company purchases these valves several times a year and makes sales of the item daily. Shown below are the inventory quantities, purchases, and sales for the year.

	NUMBER OF UNITS	COST PER UNIT	TOTAL COST
Beginning inventory (Jan. 1).............................	9,100	$4.00	$ 36,400
First purchase (Feb. 20)..................................	20,000	4.10	82,000
Second purchase (May 10)..............................	30,000	4.25	127,500
Third purchase (Aug. 24).................................	50,000	4.60	230,000
Fourth purchase (Nov. 30)	10,900	5.00	54,500
Goods available for sale	120,000		$530,400
Units sold during the year	106,000		
Ending inventory (Dec. 31)	14,000		

Compute the cost of the ending inventory of gate valves, using the following inventory valuation methods:

a First-in, first-out

b Last-in, first-out

c Average cost

Exercise 9-6
Applying the LCM
rule

Valley Company has compiled the following information concerning items in its inventory at December 31:

ITEM	QUANTITY	UNIT COST COST (FIFO)	UNIT COST MARKET
A	120	$ 46	$ 50
B	70	160	136
C	62	100	110
D	81	280	290

Determine the total inventory value to appear on Valley Company's balance sheet under the lower-of-cost-or-market rule, assuming (a) that the rule is applied to inventory as a whole and (b) that the rule is applied on an item-by-item basis.

Exercise 9-7
Conservatism in
inventory pricing

The concept of conservatism sometimes enters into the valuation of inventory. This concept indicates that when some doubt exists about the valuation of merchandise, the accountant should favor the accounting option which produces a lower net income for the current period and a less favorable financial position. For each of the following pairs of options, indicate which is the more conservative practice.

1 a Inventory items are priced at net invoice price plus all additional incidental costs incurred to transport, store, and insure the goods until they reach the place and condition for sale.

b All incidental costs relating to the purchase of merchandise (such as transportation-in, import duties, storage, and insurance of goods in storage or in transit) are treated as period costs; that is, they are treated as expense of the period in which incurred.

2 a Inventory is priced by the lower-of-cost-or-market rule, applied on an item-by-item basis.

　b Inventory is priced by the lower-of-cost-or-market rule, applied to the inventory as a whole.

3 a During a long period of rising prices, inventory is priced by the average-cost method.

　b During a long period of rising prices, inventory is priced by the first-in, first-out method.

Exercise 9-8
Estimating inventory by the gross profit method

When Anne Blair arrived at her store on the morning of January 29, she found empty shelves and display racks; thieves had broken in during the night and stolen the entire inventory. Blair's accounting records showed that she had $55,000 inventory on January 1 (cost value). From January 1 to January 29, she had made net sales of $200,000 and net purchases of $141,800. The gross profit during the last several years had consistently averaged 30% of net sales. Blair wishes to file an insurance claim for the theft loss. You are to use the *gross profit method* to estimate the cost of her inventory at the time of the theft. Show computations.

Exercise 9-9
Estimating inventory by the retail method

Westlake Accessories needs to determine the approximate amount of inventory at the end of each month without taking a physical inventory of merchandise in the shop. From the following information, you are to estimate the cost of the July 31 inventory by the *retail method* of inventory valuation.

	COST PRICE	RETAIL SELLING PRICE
Inventory of merchandise, June 30	$264,800	$400,000
Purchases (net) during July	170,400	240,000
Sales (net) during July		275,200

Exercise 9-10
Using the perpetual inventory system

Caliente Products uses a perpetual inventory system. On January 1, the Inventory account had a balance of $93,500. During the first few days of January the following transactions occurred.

Jan. 2　Purchased merchandise on credit from Bell Company for $12,500.

Jan. 3　Sold merchandise for cash, $9,000. The cost of this merchandise was $6,300.

a Prepare entries in general journal form to record the above transactions.

b What was the balance of the Inventory account at the close of business January 3?

PROBLEMS

Group A

Problem 9A-1
Inventory errors: effects on earnings

The owners of Auto Toy are offering the business for sale as a going concern. The income statements of the business for the three years of its existence are summarized below.

	1992	1991	1990
Net sales	$860,000	$850,000	$800,000
Cost of goods sold	481,600	486,000	480,000
Gross profit on sales	$378,400	$364,000	$320,000
Gross profit percentage	44%	43%*	40%

* Rounded to nearest full percentage point.

In negotiations with prospective buyers of the business, the owners of Auto Toy are calling attention to the rising trends of the gross profit and of the gross profit percentage as very favorable elements.

Assume that you are retained by a prospective purchaser of the business to make an investigation of the fairness and reliability of Auto Toy's accounting records and financial statements. You find everything in order except for the following: (1) An arithmetical error in the computation of inventory at the end of 1990 had caused a $24,000 understatement in that inventory; and (2) a duplication of figures in the computation of inventory at the end of 1992 had caused an overstatement of $43,000 in that inventory. The company uses the periodic inventory system and these errors had not been brought to light prior to your investigation.

Instructions   **a** Prepare a revised three-year schedule similar to the one illustrated above.

b Comment on the trend of gross profit and gross profit percentage before and after the revision.

Problem 9A-2
FIFO, LIFO, and
average cost

One of the most popular items carried in stock by Audio Shop is an 8-inch speaker unit. The inventory quantities, purchases, and sales of this unit for the most recent year are shown below.

	NUMBER OF UNITS	COST PER UNIT	TOTAL COST
Inventory, Jan. 1	2,700	$30.00	$ 81,000
First purchase (May 12)...............................	3,540	30.60	108,324
Second purchase (July 9)	2,400	31.05	74,520
Third purchase (Oct. 4)	1,860	32.10	59,706
Fourth purchase (Dec. 18)	3,000	32.55	97,650
Goods available for sale	13,500		$421,200
Units sold during the year	9,600		
Inventory, Dec. 31	3,900		

Instructions   **a** Compute the cost of the December 31 inventory and the cost of goods sold for the 8-inch speaker units during the year using:

(1) The first-in, first-out method

(2) The last-in, first-out method

(3) The average-cost method

b Which of the three inventory pricing methods provides the most realistic balance sheet valuation of inventory in light of the current replacement cost of the speaker units? Does this same method also produce the most realistic measure of income in light of the costs being incurred by Audio Shop to replace the speakers when they are sold? Explain.

Problem 9A-3
More on FIFO,
LIFO, and
average cost

Pacific Rim concentrates on the sale of a single product. Sales for the year consisted of 79,000 units for a total dollar amount of $600,000. The January 1 inventory contained 10,000 units with a total inventory value of $40,000. During the year, purchases were as follows: 5,000 units at $4.40; 25,000 units at $5.00; 40,000 units at $5.20; and 20,000 units at $6.00 each.

Instructions   **a** Compute the December 31 inventory using:

(1) The first-in, first-out method

(2) The last-in, first-out method

(3) The average-cost method

b Prepare partial income statements for each of the above three methods of pricing inventory. The income statements are to be carried only to the determination of gross profit on sales.

c Which of the three methods of pricing inventory would be most advantageous from an income tax standpoint during a period of rising prices? Comment on the significance of the inventory figure under the method you recommend with respect to current replacement cost.

Problem 9A-4
Evaluating
different
inventory
methods

A note to the financial statements of *The Quaker Oats Company* includes the following information:

Inventories Inventories are valued at the lower of cost or market, using various cost methods. The percentage of year-end inventories valued using each of the methods is as follows:

June 30 (fiscal year-end)	1988
Average cost	54%
Last-in, first-out (LIFO)	29%
First-in, first-out (FIFO)	17%

Instructions

a Does the company's use of three different inventory methods violate the accounting principle of consistency?

b Assuming that the replacement cost of inventories has been steadily rising, would the company's reported net income be higher or lower if all inventories were valued by the FIFO method?

c Assume that management's primary objective is to minimize income taxes. Which inventory valuation method would you recommend? Would this recommendation influence your choice of inventory valuation methods used in the financial statements? Explain your answers.

Problem 9A-5
Wanted: a more
efficient inventory
method

Helen Morgan, a CPA, was retained by Plaza North, a retail store, to review its methods of accounting for inventories. Plaza North has an inventory of several thousand low-priced items. Each item is plainly marked with the retail selling price. A physical inventory is taken at the end of each year; after the merchandise has been counted, it is then priced at cost by looking up purchase invoices to determine the cost of each item. The store manager is interested in finding a more economical method of assigning cost prices to the merchandise on hand at year-end. Under the existing system, more time is used in pricing the inventory than in counting the goods on hand.

Helen Morgan made an analysis of the accounting records which showed that net purchases for the year totaled $1,995,000. The retail selling price of this merchandise was $2,625,000. The physical inventory taken at the end of the year showed goods on hand priced to sell at $408,000. This represented a considerable increase over the inventory of a year earlier. At December 31 a year ago, the inventory on hand had appeared in the balance sheet at a cost of $255,000, although it had a retail sales value of $375,000.

Instructions

a Outline a plan whereby the inventory can be computed without the necessity of looking up individual purchase invoices. List step by step the procedures to be followed. Ignore the possibility of markups and markdowns in the original retail price of merchandise.

b Compute the cost of the inventory at December 31 of the current year, using the method described in a.

c Explain how the inventory method you have described can be modified for the preparation of monthly financial statements when no physical count of inventory is taken.

Problem 9A-6
Entries for
perpetual
inventory

Halley's Space Scope sells state-of-the-art telescopes to individuals and organizations interested in studying the solar system. At December 31, the end of the fiscal year, the company's inventory amounted to $90,000. During the first week of January, the company made only one purchase and one sale. These transactions were as follows:

Jan. 3 Sold one telescope costing $28,000 to Eastern State University for cash, $40,000.

Jan. 6 Purchased merchandise on account from Solar Optics, $18,500. Terms, net 30 days.

Instructions

a Prepare journal entries to record these transactions assuming that Halley's Space Scope uses the perpetual inventory system. Use separate entries to record the sales revenue and the cost of goods sold for the sale on January 3.

b Compute the balance of the Inventory account on January 7.

c Prepare journal entries to record the two transactions assuming that Halley's Space Scope uses the periodic inventory system.

d Compute the cost of goods sold for the first week of January assuming use of a periodic inventory system. Use your answer to part b as the ending inventory.

e Which inventory system do you believe that a company such as Halley's Space Scope would probably use. Explain your reasoning.

Problem 9A-7
Perpetual inventory records in a small business

Executive Suites, Inc., uses a perpetual inventory system. This system includes a perpetual inventory record card for each of the 60 types of products the company keeps in stock. The following transactions show the purchases and sales of a particular desk chair (product code DC-SB2) during September.

Sept. 1	Balance on hand, 50 units, cost $60 each	$3,000
Sept. 4	Purchase, 20 units, cost $65 each	1,300
Sept. 8	Sale, 35 units, sales price $100 each	3,500
Sept. 9	Purchase, 40 units, cost $65 each	2,600
Sept. 20	Sale, 60 units, sales price $100 each	6,000
Sept. 25	Purchase, 40 units, cost $70 each	2,800
Sept. 30	Sale, 5 units, sales price $110 each	550

Instructions

a Record the beginning inventory, the purchases, the cost of goods sold, and the running balance on an inventory record card like the one illustrated on page 365. Use the first-in, first-out method.

b Assume that all sales were made on credit. Compute the total sales and total cost of goods sold of this product for September. Prepare an entry in general journal form to record these sales and a second entry to record the cost of goods sold for September.

c Compute the gross profit on sales of this product for the month of September.

Group B

Problem 9B-1
Inventory errors: effect on earnings

Three years after organizing Fashion Fair, the owners decided to offer the business for sale as a going concern. The income statements of the business for the last three years include the following key figures.

Net sales	$540,000	$520,000	$500,000
Cost of goods sold	356,400	348,800	345,000
Gross profit on sales	$183,600	$171,200	$155,000
Gross profit percentage	34%	33%*	31%

*Rounded to the nearest full percentage point.

In discussions with prospective buyers, the owners are emphasizing the rising trends of gross profit and gross profit percentage as very favorable factors.

Assume that you are retained by a prospective purchaser of the business to make an investigation of the fairness and reliability of Fashion Fair's accounting records and financial statements. You find everything in order except for the following: (1) An arithmetical error in the computation of inventory at the end of 1990 had caused a $10,000 understatement in that inventory; and (2) a duplication of figures in the computation of inventory at the end of 1992 had caused an overstatement of $27,000 in that inventory. The company uses the periodic inventory system and these errors had not been brought to light prior to your investigation.

Instructions **a** Prepare a revised three-year schedule along the lines of the one illustrated above.

b Comment on the trend of gross profit and gross profit percentage before and after the revision.

Problem 9B-2
Comparison of
FIFO, LIFO, and
average cost
methods

Sky Ring derives much of its revenue from sale of a specialized type of valve. For the most recent year, the inventory quantities, purchases, and sales of this valve are summarized as follows:

	NUMBER OF UNITS	COST PER UNIT	TOTAL COST
Inventory, Jan. 1	2,500	$30.00	$ 75,000
First purchase (Mar. 10)	3,600	31.00	111,600
Second purchase (June 9)	2,500	32.00	80,000
Third purchase (Sept. 30)	2,000	32.90	65,800
Fourth purchase (Dec. 16)	3,400	34.00	115,600
Goods available for sale	14,000		$448,000
Units sold during the year	10,000		
Inventory, Dec. 31	4,000		

Instructions **a** Compute the cost of the December 31 inventory and the cost of goods sold for the above valve during the year, using each of the following three methods.

(1) The first-in, first-out method

(2) The last-in, first-out method

(3) The average-cost method

b Which of the above three inventory pricing methods provides the most realistic balance sheet valuation of inventory in light of the current replacement cost of the valve? Does this same method also produce the most realistic measure of income in light of the costs being incurred by Sky Ring to replace the valves when they are sold? Explain.

Problem 9B-3
More FIFO, LIFO,
and average cost

Much of the revenue earned by Fluid Power, Inc., comes from the sale of a single product. During the year, the inventory quantities, purchases, and sales of this product were as follows:

	NUMBER OF UNITS	COST PER UNIT	TOTAL COST
Inventory, Jan. 1	8,000	$5.89	$ 47,120
First purchase (Mar. 15)	10,300	6.20	63,860
Second purchase (June 6)	12,400	6.60	81,840
Third purchase (Sept. 20)	9,600	6.80	65,280
Fourth purchase (Dec. 31)	7,700	7.00	53,900
Goods available for sale	48,000		$312,000
Units sold during the year	37,200		
Inventory, Dec. 31	10,800		

Instructions **a** Compute the cost of the December 31 inventory and the cost of goods sold for the product during the year using:

(1) The first-in, first-out method

(2) The last-in, first-out method

(3) The average-cost method

b Which of the three inventory pricing methods provides the most realistic balance sheet valuation of inventory in light of the current replacement cost of the product? Does this same method also produce the most realistic measure of income in light of the costs being incurred by Fluid Power to replace the product as it is sold? Explain.

c Which of the three methods of pricing inventory would be the *least* advantageous from an income tax standpoint during a period of rising prices? Explain.

Problem 9B-4
Evaluating alternative inventory methods

Notes to the financial statements of two well-known clothing manufacturers are shown below:

J. P. Stevens & Co., Inc.
Inventories: The inventories are stated at the lower of cost, determined principally by the LIFO method, or market.

Bobbie Brooks, Incorporated
Inventories: Inventories are stated at the lower of cost (first-in, first-out method) or market value.

Instructions

Assuming a period of rising prices:

a Which company is using the more "conservative" method of pricing its inventories? Explain.

b Based upon the inventory methods in use in their financial statements, which company is in the better position to minimize the amount of income taxes that it must pay? Explain.

Problem 9B-5
Retail inventory method

Armstrong's, a retail store, had net sales during January of $48,900. Purchases of merchandise from suppliers during January amounted to $30,930. Of these January purchases, invoices totaling $20,430 were paid during the month; the remaining January invoices totaling $10,500 were still unpaid at January 31. The merchandise purchased during January had a retail selling value of $44,250.

The merchandise on hand on January 1 represented a cost of $31,800 as determined by the year-end physical inventory. The retail sales value of this inventory was $48,000. The retail selling price was plainly marked on every item of merchandise in the store.

At January 31 the manager of Armstrong's wanted to estimate the cost of inventory on hand without taking time to count the merchandise and look up the cost prices as shown on purchase invoices.

Instructions

a Use the retail inventory method to estimate the cost of the inventory at January 31.

b What effect, if any, does the fact that January purchase invoices in the amount of $10,500 were unpaid at January 31 have upon the determination of the amount of inventory at January 31? Explain.

Problem 9B-6
Entries for perpetual inventory

Satellite Trackers sells satellite tracking systems for receiving television broadcasts from satellites in outer space. At December 31 last year, the company's inventory amounted to $22,000. During the first week of January this year, the company made only one purchase and one sale. These transactions were as follows:

Jan. 3 Sold one tracking system costing $11,200 to Mystery Mountain Resort for cash, $18,900.

Jan. 6 Purchased merchandise on account from Yamaha, $9,600. Terms, net 30 days.

Instructions

a Prepare journal entries to record these transactions assuming that Satellite Trackers uses the perpetual inventory system. Use separate entries to record the sales revenue and the cost of goods sold for the sale on January 3.

b Compute the balance of the Inventory account on January 7.

c Prepare journal entries to record the two transactions assuming that Satellite Trackers uses the periodic inventory system.

d Compute the cost of goods sold for the first week of January assuming use of a periodic inventory system. Use your answer to part b as the ending inventory.

e Which inventory system do you believe that a company such as Satellite Trackers would probably use? Explain your reasoning.

Problem 9B-7
Perpetual inventory records

A perpetual inventory system is used by Black Hawk, Inc., and an inventory record card is maintained for each type of product in stock. The following transactions show beginning inventory, purchases, and sales of product KR9 for the month of May:

May 1	Balance on hand, 20 units, cost $40 each	$800
May 5	Sale, 8 units, sales price $60 each	480
May 6	Purchase, 20 units, cost $45 each..	900
May 21	Sale, 10 units, sales price $60 each	600
May 31	Sale, 15 units, sales price $65 each	975

Instructions

a Record the beginning inventory, the purchases, the cost of goods sold, and the running balance on an inventory record card like the one illustrated on page 365. Use the first-in, first-out method.

b Assume that all sales were made on credit. Compute the total sales and the total cost of goods sold of product KR9 for May. Prepare an entry in general journal form to record these sales and a second entry to record the cost of goods sold for the month of May.

c Compute the gross profit on sales of product KR9 for the month of May.

BUSINESS DECISION CASE

Case 9-1
Have I got a deal for you!

You are the sales manager of Continental Motors, an automobile dealership specializing in European imports. Among the automobiles in Continental Motors' showroom are two Italian sports cars, which are identical in every respect except for color; one is red and the other white. The red car had been ordered last February, at a cost of $13,300 American dollars. The white car had been ordered early last March, but because of a revaluation of the Italian lira relative to the dollar, the white car had cost only $12,000 American dollars. Both cars arrived in the United States on the same boat and had just been delivered to your showroom. Since the cars were identical except for color and both colors were equally popular, you had listed both cars at the same suggested retail price, $18,000.

Smiley Miles, one of your best salesmen, comes into your office with a proposal. He has a customer in the showroom who wants to buy the red car for $18,000. However, when Miles pulled the inventory card on the red car to see what options were included, he happened to notice the inventory card of the white car. Continental Motors, like most automobile dealerships, uses the specific identification method to value inventory. Consequently, Miles noticed that the red car had cost $13,300, while the white one had cost Continental Motors only $12,000. This gave Miles the idea for the following proposal.

"Have I got a deal for you! If I sell the red car for $18,000, Continental Motors makes a gross profit of $4,700. But if you'll let me discount that white car $500, I think I can get my customer to buy that one instead. If I sell the white car for $17,500, the gross profit will be $5,500, so Continental Motors is $800 better off than if I sell the red car for $18,000. Since I came up with this plan, I feel I should get part of the benefit, so Continental Motors should split the extra $800 with me. That way, I'll get an extra $400 commission, and the company still makes $400 more than if I sell the red car."

Instructions

a Prepare a schedule which shows the total revenue, cost of goods sold, and gross profit to Continental Motors if *both* cars are sold for $18,000 each.

b Prepare a schedule showing the revenue, cost of goods sold, and gross profit to Continental Motors if both cars are sold but Miles' plan is adopted and the white car is sold for $17,500. Assume the red car is still sold for $18,000. To simplify comparison of this schedule to the one prepared in part a, include the extra $400 commission to Miles in the cost of goods sold of the part b schedule.

c Write out your decision whether or not to accept Miles' proposal, and explain to Miles why the proposal either would or would not be to the advantage of Continental Motors. (Hint: Refer to your schedules prepared in parts **a** and **b** in your explanation.)

ANSWERS TO SELF-TEST QUESTIONS

1 c   2 d   3 a   4 b   5 d

Plant and Equipment, Depreciation, and Intangible Assets

Our primary goal in this chapter is to illustrate and explain the accounting concepts relating to the acquisition, use, and disposal of plant assets. An important element of this discussion is our coverage of alternative depreciation methods, including the straight-line, units-of-output, double-declining-balance, and sum-of-the-years'-digits methods. In the final portions of the chapter, we address the special topics of accounting for intangible assets and for natural resources.

After studying this chapter you should be able to meet these Learning Objectives:

1 Determine the cost of plant assets.

2 Distinguish between capital expenditures and revenue expenditures.

3 Explain the relationship between depreciation and the matching principle.

4 Compute depreciation by the straight-line, units-of-output, declining-balance, and sum-of-the-years'-digits methods.

5 Explain why depreciation based upon historical costs may cause an overstatement of net income.

6 Record the sale, trade-in, or scrapping of a plant asset.

7 Explain the nature of goodwill and indicate when this asset should appear in the accounting records.

8 Account for the depletion of natural resources.

PLANT AND EQUIPMENT

The term *plant and equipment* is used to describe long-lived assets acquired for use in the operation of the business and not intended for resale to customers. Among the more common examples are land, buildings, machinery, furniture and fixtures, office equipment, and automobiles. A delivery truck in the showroom of an automobile dealer is inventory; when this same truck is sold to a drugstore for use in making deliveries to customers, it becomes a unit of plant and equipment.

The term *fixed assets* has long been used in accounting literature to describe all types of plant and equipment. This term, however, has virtually disappeared from the published financial statements of large corporations. *Plant and equipment* appears to be a more descriptive term. Another alternative title used on many corporation balance sheets is *property, plant, and equipment.*

Plant and Equipment—A Stream of Services

It is convenient to think of a plant asset as a stream of services to be received by the owner over a period of years. Ownership of a delivery truck, for example, may provide about 100,000 miles of transportation. The cost of the delivery truck is customarily entered in a plant and equipment account entitled Delivery Truck, which in essence represents the advance purchase of many years of transportation service. Similarly, a building may be regarded as advance purchase of many years' supply of housing services. As the years go by, these services are utilized by the business and the cost of the plant asset gradually is transferred into depreciation expense.

An awareness of the similarity between plant assets and prepaid expenses is essential to an understanding of the accounting process by which the cost of plant assets is allocated to the accounting periods in which the benefits of ownership are received.

Major Categories of Plant and Equipment

Plant and equipment items are often classified into the following groups:

1 Tangible plant assets. The term *tangible* denotes physical substance, as exemplified by land, a building, or a machine. This category may be subdivided into two distinct classifications:

a Plant property subject to depreciation; included are plant assets of limited useful life such as buildings and office equipment.

b Land. The only plant asset not subject to depreciation is land, which has an unlimited term of existence.

2 Intangible assets. The term *intangible assets* is used to describe assets which are used in the operation of the business but have no physical substance, and are noncurrent. Examples include patents, copyrights, trademarks, franchises, and goodwill. Current assets such as accounts receivable or prepaid rent are not included in the intangible classification, even though they are lacking in physical substance.

3 Natural resources. A site acquired for the purpose of extracting or removing some valuable resource such as oil, minerals, or timber is classified as a *natural resource,* not as land. This type of plant asset is gradually converted into inventory as the natural resource is extracted from the site.

Determining the Cost of Plant and Equipment

Objective 1
Determine the
cost of plant
assets.

The cost of plant and equipment includes all expenditures reasonable and necessary in acquiring the asset and placing it in a position and condition for use in the operations of the business. Only *reasonable* and *necessary* expenditures should be included. For example, if the company's truck driver receives a traffic ticket while hauling a new machine to the plant, the traffic fine is *not* part of the cost of the new machine. If the machine is dropped and damaged while being unloaded, the cost of repairing the damage should be recognized as expense in the current period and should *not* be added to the cost of the machine.

Cost is most easily determined when an asset is purchased for cash. The cost of the asset is then equal to the cash outlay necessary to acquire the asset plus any expenditures for freight, insurance while in transit, installation, trial runs, and any other costs necessary to make *the asset ready for use.* If plant assets are *purchased* on the installment plan or by issuance of notes payable, the interest element or carrying charge should be recorded as interest expense and *not* as part of the cost of the plant assets. However, if a company *constructs* a plant asset for its own use, interest costs incurred *during the construction period* are viewed as part of the cost of the asset.[1]

This principle of including in the cost of a plant asset all the incidental charges necessary to put the asset in use is illustrated by the following example. A factory in Minneapolis orders a machine from a San Francisco tool manufacturer at a list price of $10,000, with terms of 2/10, n/30. Sales tax of $588 must be paid, as well as freight charges of $1,250. Transportation from the railroad station to the factory costs $150, and installation labor amounts to $400. The cost of the machine to be entered in the Machinery account is computed as follows:

Items included in cost of machine

List price of machine	$10,000
Less: Cash discount (2% × $10,000)	200
Net cash price	$ 9,800
Sales tax	588
Freight	1,250
Transportation from railroad station to factory	150
Installation labor	400
Cost of machine	$12,188

[1] *FASB Statement No. 34,* "Capitalization of Interest Costs" (Stamford, Conn.: 1979).

Why should all the incidental charges relating to the acquisition of a machine be included in its cost? Why not treat these incidental charges as expenses of the period in which the machine is acquired?

The answer is to be found in the basic accounting principle of **matching costs and revenue.** The benefits of owning the machine will be received over a span of years, for example, 10 years. During those 10 years the operation of the machine will contribute to revenue. Consequently, the total costs of the machine should be recorded in the accounts as an asset and allocated against the revenue of the 10 years. All costs incurred in acquiring the machine are costs of the services to be received from using the machine.

■ **Land** When land is purchased, various incidental costs are generally incurred, in addition to the purchase price. These additional costs may include commissions to real estate brokers, escrow fees, legal fees for examining and insuring the title, delinquent taxes paid by the purchaser, and fees for surveying, draining, clearing, and grading the property. All these expenditures become part of the cost of the land.

■ **Apportionment of a Lump-Sum Purchase** Separate ledger accounts are necessary for land and buildings, because buildings are subject to depreciation and land is not. The treatment of land as a nondepreciable asset is based on the premise that land used as a building site has an unlimited life. When land and building are purchased for a lump sum, the purchase price must be apportioned between the land and the building. An appraisal may be necessary for this purpose. Assume, for example, that land and a building are purchased for a bargain price of $400,000. The apportionment of this cost on the basis of an appraisal may be made as follows:

	VALUE PER APPRAISAL	PERCENTAGE OF TOTAL	APPORTIONMENT OF COST
Land................................	$200,000	40%	$160,000
Building............................	300,000	60%	240,000
Total..............................	$500,000	100%	$400,000

■ Apportioning cost between land and building

Sometimes a tract of land purchased as a building site has on it an old building which is not suitable for the buyer's use. The Land account should be charged with the entire purchase price *plus any costs incurred in tearing down or removing the building.* Proceeds received from sale of the materials salvaged from the old building are recorded as a credit in the Land account.

■ **Land Improvements** Improvements to real estate such as driveways, fences, parking lots, and sprinkler systems have a limited life and are therefore subject to depreciation. For this reason they should be recorded not in the Land account but in a separate account entitled Land Improvements.

■ **Buildings** Old buildings are sometimes purchased with the intention of repairing them prior to placing them in use. Repairs made under these circumstances are charged to the Buildings account. After the building has been placed in use, ordinary repairs are considered as maintenance expense when incurred.

Capital Expenditures and Revenue Expenditures

Objective 2
Distinguish between capital expenditures and revenue expenditures

Expenditures for the purchase or expansion of plant assets are called *capital expenditures* and are recorded in asset accounts. Expenditures for ordinary repairs, maintenance, fuel, and other items necessary to the ownership and use of plant and equipment are called *revenue expenditures* and are recorded by debits to expense accounts. The charge to an expense account is based on the assumption that the benefits from the expenditure will be used up in the current period, and the cost should therefore be deducted from the revenue of the current period in determining the net income.

A business may purchase many small items which will benefit several accounting periods, but which have a relatively low cost. Examples of such items include auto batteries, wastebaskets, and pencil sharpeners. Such items are theoretically capital expenditures, but if they are recorded as assets in the accounting records it will be necessary to compute and record the related depreciation expense in future periods. We have previously mentioned the idea that the extra work involved in developing more precise accounting information should be weighed against the benefits that result. Thus, for reasons of convenience and economy, expenditures which are *not material* in dollar amount are treated in the accounting records as expenses of the current period. In brief, *any material expenditure that will benefit several accounting periods is considered a capital expenditure. Any expenditure that will benefit only the current period or that is not material in amount is treated as a revenue expenditure.*

Many companies develop formal policy statements defining capital and revenue expenditures as a guide toward consistent accounting practice from year to year. These policy statements often set a minimum dollar limit for a capital expenditure (such as $100 or $200).

■ **Effect of Errors in Distinguishing between Capital and Revenue Expenditures**   Because a capital expenditure is recorded by debiting an asset account, the transaction has no immediate effect upon net income. However, the depreciation of the amount entered in the asset account will be reflected as an expense in future periods. A revenue expenditure, on the other hand, is recorded by debiting an expense account and therefore represents an immediate deduction from earnings in the current period.

Assume that the cost of a new delivery truck is erroneously debited to the Repairs Expense account. The result will be to overstate repairs expense, thereby understating the current year's net income. If the error is not corrected, the net income of subsequent years will be overstated because no depreciation expense will be recognized during the years in which the truck is used.

On the other hand, assume that ordinary truck repairs are erroneously debited to the asset account, Delivery Truck. The result will be to understate repairs expense, thereby overstating the current year's net income. If the error is not corrected, the net income of future years will be understated because of excessive depreciation charges based upon the inflated balance of the Delivery Truck account.

These examples indicate that a careful distinction between capital and revenue expenditures is essential to attainment of one of the most fundamental objectives of accounting—the determination of net income for each year of operation of a business.

DEPRECIATION

Allocating the Cost of Plant and Equipment over the Years of Use

Objective 3
Explain the relationship between depreciation and the matching principle.

Tangible plant assets, with the exception of land, are of use to a company for only a limited number of years. *Depreciation,* as the term is used in accounting, is the ***allocation of the cost of a tangible plant asset to expense in the periods in which services are received from the asset.*** In short, the basic purpose of depreciation is to achieve the ***matching principle***—that is, to offset the revenue of an accounting period with the costs of the goods and services being consumed in the effort to generate that revenue.

Earlier in this chapter, we described a delivery truck as a "stream of transportation services" to be received over the years that the truck is owned and used. The cost of the truck initially is debited to an asset account, because this purchase of these "transportation services" will benefit many future accounting periods. As these services are received, however, the cost of the truck gradually is removed from the balance sheet and allocated to expense, through the process called "depreciation." This "flow of costs" is illustrated below. The red arrow indicates the process of "depreciation."

■
Depreciation: a process of allocating the cost of an asset to expense

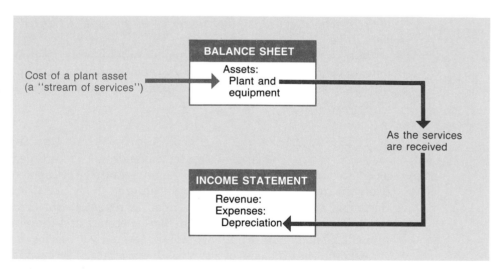

The journal entry to record depreciation expense consists of a debit to Depreciation Expense and a credit to Accumulated Depreciation. The credit portion of the entry removes from the balance sheet that portion of the asset's cost estimated to have been used up during the current period. The debit portion of the entry allocates this expired cost to expense.

Separate Depreciation Expense and Accumulated Depreciation accounts are maintained for different types of depreciable assets, such as factory buildings, delivery equipment, and office equipment. These separate accounts help accountants to measure separately the costs of different business activities, such as manufacturing, sales, and administration.

■ **Depreciation Is Not a Process of Valuation** Depreciation is a process of ***cost allocation,*** not a process of valuation. Accounting records do not attempt to show the current market values of plant assets. The market value of a building, for example, may increase during some accounting periods within the building's useful life. The recognition of depreciation expense continues, however, without regard to such temporary increases in market value. Accountants recognize that the building will render useful services only for a limited number of years, and that the full cost of the building should be *systematically allocated to expense* during these years.

■ **Book Value** Plant assets are shown in the balance sheet at their book values (or *carrying values*). The *book value* of a plant asset is its *cost minus the related accumulated depreciation.* Accumulated depreciation is a contra-asset account, representing that portion of the asset's cost that has *already* been allocated to expense. Thus, book value represents the portion of the asset's cost that remains to be allocated to expense in future periods.

■ **Depreciation and Cash Flows** Depreciation differs from most expenses in that it does not depend upon a cash payment at or near the time the expense is recorded. For this reason, depreciation sometimes is called a "non-cash" expense. Bear in mind, however, that "payment" of many years' depreciation expense may be made in advance, when the plant asset is purchased. Also, when the asset eventually wears out, an even larger cash payment may be required to replace it.

Some people mistakenly believe that accumulated depreciation represents a fund of cash being accumulated for the purpose of replacing the plant assets when they wear out. This is a misconception. Accumulated depreciation is *not an asset*—it is the portion of the asset's cost that *already has been allocated to expense.* The amount of cash owned by a company is shown in the asset account, Cash and Cash Equivalents.

Causes of Depreciation

The two major causes of depreciation are physical deterioration and obsolescence.

■ **Physical Deterioration** Physical deterioration of a plant asset results from use, as well as from exposure to sun, wind, and other climatic factors. When a plant asset has been carefully maintained, it is not uncommon for the owner to claim that the asset is as "good as new." Such statements are not literally true. Although a good repair policy may greatly lengthen the useful life of a machine, every machine eventually reaches the point at which it must be discarded. In brief, the making of repairs does not lessen the need for recognition of depreciation.

■ **Obsolescence** The term *obsolescence* means the process of becoming out of date or obsolete. An airplane, for example, may become obsolete even though it is in excellent physical condition; it becomes obsolete because better planes of superior design and performance have become available.

The usefulness of plant assets may also be reduced because the rapid growth of a company renders such assets inadequate. *Inadequacy* of a plant asset may necessitate replacement with a larger unit even though the asset is in good physical condition. Obsolescence and inadequacy are often closely associated; both relate to the opportunity for economical and efficient use of an asset rather than to its physical condition.

Methods of Computing Depreciation

Objective 4
Compute depreciation by the straight-line, units-of-output, declining-balance, and sum-of-the-years'-digits methods.

There are several alternative methods of computing depreciation. A business need not use the same method of depreciation for all its various assets. For example, a company may use straight-line depreciation on some assets and a declining-balance method for other assets. Furthermore, the methods used for computing depreciation expense in financial statements *may differ* from the methods used in the preparation of the company's income tax return.

■ **Straight-Line Method** The simplest and most widely used method of computing depreciation is the straight-line method. This method was described in Chapter 3 and has been used repeatedly in problems throughout this book. Under the straight-line method, an equal portion of the cost of the asset is allocated to each period of use; consequently, this method is most appropriate when usage of an asset is fairly uniform from year to year.

The computation of the periodic charge for depreciation is made by deducting the estimated *residual* or *salvage value* from the cost of the asset and dividing the remaining *depreciable cost* by the years of estimated useful life. For example, if a delivery truck has a cost of *$17,000,* a residual value of *$2,000,* and an estimated useful life of *five years,* the annual computation of depreciation expense will be as follows:

$$\frac{\text{Cost} - \text{Residual Value}}{\text{Years of Useful Life}} = \frac{\$17,000 - \$2,000}{5} = \$3,000$$

This same depreciation computation is shown below in tabular form.

■
Computing depreciation by straight-line method

Cost of the depreciable asset	$17,000
Less: Estimated residual value (amount to be realized by sale of asset	
when it is retired from use)	2,000
Total amount to be depreciated (depreciable cost)	$15,000
Estimated useful life	5 years
Depreciation expense each year ($15,000 ÷ 5)	$ 3,000

The following schedule summarizes the accumulation of depreciation over the useful life of the asset. The amount to be depreciated is *$15,000* (cost of $17,000 minus estimated residual value of $2,000).

Depreciation Schedule: Straight-Line Method

■
Constant annual depreciation expense

YEAR	COMPUTATION	DEPRECIATION EXPENSE	ACCUMULATED DEPRECIATION	BOOK VALUE
				$17,000
First	(⅕ × $15,000)	$ 3,000	$ 3,000	14,000
Second	(⅕ × $15,000)	3,000	6,000	11,000
Third....................	(⅕ × $15,000)	3,000	9,000	8,000
Fourth	(⅕ × $15,000)	3,000	12,000	5,000
Fifth	(⅕ × $15,000)	3,000	15,000	2,000
		$15,000		

Depreciation rates for various types of assets can conveniently be stated as percentages. In the above example the asset had an estimated life of five years, so the depreciation expense each year was ⅕ of the depreciable amount. The fraction "⅕" is of course equivalent to an annual rate of *20%*. Similarly, a 10-year life indicates a depreciation rate of ¹⁄₁₀, or 10% and an 8-year life a depreciation rate of ⅛, or 12½%.

In the preceding illustration we assumed that the company maintained its accounts on a calendar-year basis and that the asset was acquired on January 1, the beginning of the accounting period. If the asset had been acquired sometime during the year, on October 1 for example, it would have been in use for only three months, or ³⁄₁₂ of a year. Consequently, the depreciation to be recorded at December 31 would be only ³⁄₁₂ of $3,000, or *$750*. Stated more precisely, the depreciation expense in this situation is computed as follows: 20% × $15,000 × ³⁄₁₂ = $750.

In practice, the possibility of residual value is sometimes ignored and the annual depreciation charge computed by dividing the total cost of the asset by the number of years of estimated useful life. This practice may be justified in those cases in which residual value is not material and is difficult to estimate accurately.

■ **Units-of-Output Method** For certain kinds of assets, more equitable allocation of the cost can be obtained by dividing the cost (minus salvage value, if significant) by the estimated units of output rather than by the estimated years of useful life. A truck line or bus company, for example, might compute depreciation on its vehicles by a mileage basis. If we assume that the delivery truck in our example has an estimated useful life of 100,000 miles, the depreciation rate *per mile of operation* is *15 cents* ($15,000 ÷ 100,000 miles). This calculation of the depreciation rate may be stated as follows:

$$\frac{\text{Cost} - \text{Residual Value}}{\text{Estimated Units of Output (Miles)}} = \frac{\text{Depreciation per}}{\text{Unit of Output (Mile)}}$$

or

$$\frac{\$17,000 - \$2,000}{100,000 \text{ miles}} = \$.15 \text{ depreciation per mile}$$

At the end of each year, the amount of depreciation to be recorded would be determined by multiplying the 15-cent rate by the number of miles the truck had been driven during the year. This method is suitable only when the total units of output of the asset over its entire useful life can be estimated with reasonable accuracy.

■ **Accelerated Depreciation Methods** The term *accelerated depreciation* means recognition of relatively large amounts of depreciation in the early years of use and reduced amounts in the later years. Many types of plant and equipment are most efficient when new and therefore provide more and better services in the early years of useful life. If we assume that the benefits derived from owning an asset are greatest in the early years when the asset is relatively new, then the amount of the asset's cost which we allocate as depreciation expense should be greatest in these same early years. This is consistent with the basic accounting concept of matching costs with related revenue. Accelerated depreciation methods have been widely used in income tax returns because they reduce the current year's tax burden by recognizing a relatively large amount of depreciation expense.

■ **Declining-Balance Method** The accelerated depreciation method which allocates the largest portion of the cost of an asset to the early years of its useful life is called *double-declining-balance*. This method consists of doubling the straight-line depreciation rate and applying this doubled rate to the *undepreciated cost* (book value) of the asset.

To illustrate, consider our example of the $17,000 delivery truck. The estimated useful life of the truck is five years; therefore, the depreciation rate under the straight-line method would be 20%. To depreciate the truck by the double-declining-balance method, we double the straight-line rate of 20% and apply the doubled rate of *40%* to the *$17,000* book value. Depreciation expense in the first year would then amount to $6,800 ($17,000 × 40% = $6,800). In the second year the depreciation expense would drop to $4,080, computed at 40% of the *remaining* book value of $10,200. In the third year depreciation would be $2,448, in the fourth year $1,469, and in the fifth year only $881. The following table shows the computation of each year's depreciation expense by the declining-balance method (rounded to the nearest dollar).

Depreciation Schedule: Declining-Balance Method

<table>
<tr><td>YEAR</td><td>COMPUTATION</td><td>DEPRECIATION EXPENSE</td><td>ACCUMULATED DEPRECIATION</td><td>BOOK VALUE</td></tr>
<tr><td></td><td></td><td></td><td></td><td>*$17,000*</td></tr>
<tr><td>*First* ....</td><td>*(40% × $17,000)*</td><td>*$6,800*</td><td>*$ 6,800*</td><td>*10,200*</td></tr>
<tr><td>*Second* ....</td><td>*(40% × $10,200)*</td><td>*4,080*</td><td>*10,880*</td><td>*6,120*</td></tr>
<tr><td>*Third*..................</td><td>*(40% × $ 6,120)*</td><td>*2,448*</td><td>*13,328*</td><td>*3,672*</td></tr>
<tr><td>*Fourth* ....</td><td>*(40% × $ 3,672)*</td><td>*1,469*</td><td>*14,797*</td><td>*2,203*</td></tr>
<tr><td>*Fifth* ....</td><td>*(40% × $ 2,203)*</td><td>*881*</td><td>*15,678*</td><td>*1,322*</td></tr>
</table>

■
Accelerated depreciation: declining-balance

Notice that the estimated residual value of the delivery truck *does not* enter into the computation of depreciation expense by the declining-balance method. This is because the declining-balance method provides an *"automatic"* residual value. As long as each year's depreciation expense is equal to only a portion of the undepreciated cost of the asset, the asset *will never be entirely written off.* However, if the asset has a significant residual value, depreciation should *stop at this point.* Since our delivery truck has an estimated residual value of *$2,000,* the depreciation expense for the fifth year should be *limited to $203,* rather than the $881 computed in the table. By limiting the last year's depreciation expense in this manner, the book value of the truck at the end of the fifth year will be equal to its $2,000 estimated residual value.

If the asset in the above illustration had been acquired on October 1 rather than on January 1, depreciation for only three months would be recorded in the first year. The computation would be 40% × $17,000 × 3/12, or $1,700. For the next calendar year the calculation would be 40% × ($17,000 − $1,700), or $6,120.

■ **Sum-of-the-Years'-Digits Method** This is another method of allocating a large portion of the cost of an asset to the early years of its use. The depreciation rate to be used is a fraction, of which the numerator is the remaining years of useful life (as of the beginning of the year) and the denominator is the sum of the years of useful life. Consider again the example of the delivery truck costing $17,000 having an estimated life of five years and an estimated residual value of $2,000. Since the asset has an estimated life of five years, the denominator of the fraction will be **15,** computed as follows:[2] $1 + 2 + 3 + 4 + 5 = 15$. For the first year, the depreciation will be $5/15 \times (\$17,000 - \$2,000)$, or $5,000. (Notice that we reduced the cost of the truck by the estimated residual value in determining the amount to be depreciated.) For the second year, the depreciation will be $4/15 \times \$15,000$, or $4,000; in the third year $3/15 \times \$15,000$, or $3,000; in the fourth year, $2/15 \times \$15,000$, or $2,000; and in the fifth year, $1/15 \times \$15,000$, or $1,000. In tabular form, this depreciation program will appear as follows:

Depreciation Schedule: Sum-of-the-Years'-Digits Method

YEAR	COMPUTATION	DEPRECIATION EXPENSE	ACCUMULATED DEPRECIATION	BOOK VALUE
				$17,000
First	($5/15 × $15,000)	$ 5,000	$ 5,000	12,000
Second	($4/15 × $15,000)	4,000	9,000	8,000
Third...................	($3/15 × $15,000)	3,000	12,000	5,000
Fourth	($2/15 × $15,000)	2,000	14,000	3,000
Fifth	($1/15 × $15,000)	1,000	15,000	2,000
		$15,000		

Accelerated depreciation: sum-of-the-years' digits

Assume that the asset being depreciated by the sum-of-the-years'-digits method was acquired on October 1 and the company maintains its accounts on a calendar-year basis. Since the asset was in use for only three months during the first accounting period, the depreciation to be recorded in this first period will be for only $3/12$ of a full year, that is, $3/12 \times \$5,000$, or $1,250. For the second accounting period the depreciation computation will be:

$9/12 \times (5/15 \times \$15,000)$	$3,750
$3/12 \times (4/15 \times \$15,000)$	1,000
Depreciation expense, second period	$4,750

A similar pattern of allocation will be followed for each accounting period of the asset's life.

■ **Depreciation for Fractional Periods** When an asset is acquired in the middle of an accounting period, it is not necessary to compute depreciation

---

[2] Alternatively, the denominator may be computed by using the formula $n\left(\dfrac{n+1}{2}\right)$, where n is the useful life of the asset. According to this formula, the sum of the years' digits for an asset with a five-year life is computed as follows: $5\left(\dfrac{5+1}{2}\right) = 5(3) = 15$. Similarly, the sum of the years' digits for an asset with a 10-year life would be computed as follows: $10\left(\dfrac{10+1}{2}\right)10(5.5) = 55$.

expense to the nearest day or week. In fact, such a computation would give a misleading impression of great precision. Since depreciation is based upon an estimated useful life of many years, the depreciation applicable to any one year is only an approximation at best.

One widely used method of computing depreciation for part of a year is to round the calculation to the nearest whole month. Thus, if an asset is acquired on July 12, depreciation is computed for the six months beginning July 1. If an asset is acquired on July 16 (or any date in the latter half of July), depreciation is recorded for only five months (August through December) in the current calendar year.

Another acceptable approach, called the *half-year convention,* is to record six months' depreciation on all assets acquired during the year. This approach is based upon the assumption that the actual purchase dates will "average out" to approximately midyear. The half-year convention is widely used for assets such as office equipment, automobiles, and machinery. For buildings, however, income tax rules require that depreciation be computed for the actual number of months that the building is owned.

The half-year convention enables us to treat similar assets acquired at different dates during the year as a single group. For example, assume that an insurance company purchases hundreds of desk-top computers throughout the current year at a total cost of $600,000. The company depreciates these computers by the straight-line method, assuming a five-year life and no residual value. Using the half-year convention, the depreciation expense on all of the computers purchased during the year may be computed as follows: $600,000 ÷ 5 years × $6/12$ = $60,000. If we did not use the half-year convention, depreciation would have to be computed separately for computers purchased in different months.

Management's Responsibility for Depreciation Methods and Related Estimates

Management is responsible for selecting the methods to be used in depreciating company assets. For purposes of financial reporting, management usually elects to use the straight-line method, because this method allows the company to report higher earnings. In fact, a recent survey of 600 large corporations shows that more than 90% of these companies used straight-line depreciation in their financial statements for at least some of their plant assets. In contrast, only about 23% of the companies surveyed used an accelerated method in depreciating some or all of their plant assets.[3]

■ **The Principle of Consistency** The *consistent* application of accounting methods is a generally accepted accounting principle. With respect to depreciation methods, this principle means that a company should *not change* from year to year the method used in computing the depreciation expense for a given plant asset. However, management *may* use different methods in computing depreciation for different assets. Also, management may use different depreciation methods in the company's financial statements and in its income tax returns.

[3] AICPA, "Accounting Trends & Techniques" (New York: 1987), p. 296.

■ **Financial Statement Disclosures**   A company should *disclose* in notes to its financial statements the methods used to depreciate plant assets. Readers of these statements should recognize that accelerated depreciation methods transfer the costs of plant assets to expense more quickly than does the straight-line method. Thus, accelerated methods result in more *conservative* (lower) balance sheet valuations of plant assets and measurements of net income.

■ **Estimates of Useful Life and Residual Value**   Estimating the useful lives and residual values of plant assets also is a responsibility of management. These estimates usually are based upon the company's past experience with similar assets, but also reflect the company's current circumstances and management's future plans. Thus, the estimated lives of similar assets may vary from one company to another.

The estimated lives of plant assets affect the amount of net income reported each period. The longer the estimated useful life, the smaller the amount of cost transferred each period to depreciation expense, and the larger the amount of reported net income. Bear in mind, however, that all large corporations are *audited* annually by a firm of independent public accountants. One of the responsibilities of these auditors is to determine that management's estimates of the useful lives of plant assets are reasonable under the circumstances.

Automobiles typically are depreciated over relatively short estimated lives—say, from three to five years. Most other types of equipment are depreciated over a period of from five to 15 years. Buildings are depreciated over much longer lives—perhaps 30 to 50 years for a new building, and 15 years or more for a building acquired used.

■ **Revision of Estimated Useful Lives**   What should be done if, after a few years of using a plant asset, management decides that the asset actually is going to last for a considerably longer or shorter period than was originally estimated? When this situation arises, a *revised estimate* of useful life should be made and the periodic depreciation expense decreased or increased accordingly.

The procedure for correcting the depreciation program is to spread the remaining undepreciated cost of the asset *over the years of remaining useful life.* This correction affects only the amount of depreciation expense that will be recorded in the current and future periods. The financial statements of past periods are *not* revised to reflect changes in the estimated useful lives of depreciable assets.

To illustrate, assume that a company acquires a $10,000 asset which is estimated to have a 10-year useful life and no residual value. Under the straight-line method, the annual depreciation expense is $1,000. At the end of the sixth year, accumulated depreciation amounts to $6,000, and the asset has an undepreciated cost (or book value) of $4,000.

At the beginning of the seventh year, it is decided that the asset will last for eight more years. The revised estimate of useful life is, therefore, a total of 14 years. The depreciation expense to be recognized for the seventh year and for each of the remaining years is $500, computed as follows:

Undepreciated cost at end of sixth year ($10,000 − $6,000)	*$4,000*
Revised estimate of remaining years of useful life	*8 years*
Revised amount of annual depreciation expense ($4,000 ÷ 8)	*$ 500*

Depreciation and Income Taxes

The depreciation methods used in preparing income tax returns usually differ from the methods used in preparing financial statements. Many companies use straight-line depreciation in their financial statements because this permits reporting higher earnings. In preparing tax returns, however, most companies use *accelerated depreciation methods.* The accelerated depreciation methods result in larger amounts of depreciation expense, which reduces taxable income and the amount of income taxes due in the current period.

Income tax rules are changed frequently by Congress, and the rules relating to depreciation seem especially subject to change. For assets acquired prior to 1981, taxpayers were permitted to choose among straight-line depreciation and accelerated methods, such as double-declining-balance and sum-of-the-years'-digits. For assets acquired after 1981, taxpayers were required to use either straight-line depreciation or a special new accelerated method called the Accelerated Cost Recovery System *(ACRS).*

An important feature of ACRS was that it replaced the traditional concept of making reasonable estimates of useful life with shorter, arbitrary, "recovery periods" for allocating the cost of depreciable assets to expense. Automobiles, for example, were to be written off in only three years, and buildings in only 15 years. The recovery periods established by ACRS were modified by the Tax Reform Act of 1986, and the Modified Accelerated Cost Recovery System *(MACRS)* lengthened the recovery periods for the various classes of property.

ACRS and MACRS are used *only in income tax returns.* These systems generally are not used in financial statements, because the "recovery periods" usually are much shorter than the assets' useful lives.

Inflation and Depreciation

Objective 5
Explain why
depreciation
based upon
historical costs
may cause an
overstatement of
net income.

The valuation of plant and equipment on a cost basis and the computation of depreciation in terms of cost will work very well during periods of relatively stable price levels. However, the substantial rise in the price level in recent years has led some government officials and business executives to suggest that a more realistic measurement of net income could be achieved by basing depreciation on the *estimated current replacement cost* of plant assets rather than on the original cost of the assets presently in use.

As a specific illustration, assume that a manufacturing company purchased machinery in 1983 at a cost of $1,000,000. Estimated useful life was 10 years and straight-line depreciation was used. During this 10-year period the price level rose sharply. By 1993 the machinery purchased in 1983 was fully depreciated; it was scrapped and replaced by new machinery in 1993. Although the new machines were not significantly different from the old, they cost $3,000,000, or three times as much as the old machinery. Some accountants would argue that the depreciation expense for the 10 years was in reality $3,000,000, because this was the outlay required for new machinery if the company was merely to "stay even" in its productive facilities. It also may be argued that reported profits are *overstated* during a period of rising prices if depreciation is based on the lower plant costs of some years ago.

Historical Cost versus Replacement Cost

Historical cost means the cost actually incurred by a business in acquiring an asset, as evidenced by paid checks and other documents. The preceding criticism of depreciation accounting based on historical cost does not mean that American business is about to abandon the cost principle in accounting for assets and computing depreciation. To substitute estimated current replacement cost for the historical cost of plant and equipment would create many new difficulties and much confusion. For many assets, current replacement cost cannot be determined easily or with precision. For example, the current cost of replacing a steel mill with its great variety of complex, made-to-order machinery would involve making many assumptions and unprovable estimates. Or, as another example, consider the difficulty of estimating the replacement cost of a large tract of timber or of a gold mine.

Another difficulty in substituting replacement cost for historical cost of plant assets would be that the whole process of establishing estimated cost data would presumably need to be repeated each year. In contrast, historical cost (which we presently use as the basis of accounting for plant and equipment) is determined at the time of acquiring an asset and remains unchanged throughout the useful life of the asset.

These difficulties connected with the possible adoption of replacement cost as a basis of accounting for assets do not mean that such a change cannot or should not be attempted. However, these difficulties do explain why American business has continued to use historical cost as a primary basis of accounting for assets even during periods of continued inflation.

DISPOSAL OF PLANT AND EQUIPMENT

Objective 6
Record the sale, trade-in, or scrapping of a plant asset.

When depreciable assets are disposed of at any date other than the end of the year, an entry should be made to record depreciation for the *fraction of the year* ending with the date of disposal. If the half-year convention is in use, six months' depreciation should be recorded on all assets disposed of during the year. In the following illustrations of the disposal of items of plant and equipment, it is assumed that any necessary entries for fractional-period depreciation have been recorded.

As units of plant and equipment wear out or become obsolete, they must be scrapped, sold, or traded in on new equipment. Upon the disposal or retirement of a depreciable asset, the cost of the property is removed from the asset account, and the accumulated depreciation is removed from the related contra-asset account. Assume, for example, that office equipment purchased 10 years ago at a cost of $5,000 has been fully depreciated and is no longer useful. The entry to record the scrapping of the worthless equipment is as follows:

■
Scrapping fully depreciated asset

Accumulated Depreciation: Office Equipment	*5,000*	
Office Equipment		*5,000*

To remove from the accounts the cost and the accumulated depreciation on fully depreciated office equipment now being scrapped. No salvage value.

Once an asset has been fully depreciated, no more depreciation should be recorded on it, even though the property is in good condition and is still in use. The objective of depreciation is to spread the *cost* of an asset over the periods of its usefulness; in no case can depreciation expense be greater than the amount paid for the asset. When a fully depreciated asset remains in use beyond the original estimate of useful life, the asset account and the Accumulated Depreciation account should remain in the accounting records without further entries until the asset is retired.

Gains and Losses on Disposal of Plant and Equipment

Since the residual value and useful life of plant assets are only estimates, it is not uncommon for plant assets to be sold at a price which differs from their book value at the date of disposal. When plant assets are sold, any gain or loss on the disposal is computed by comparing the *book value with the amount received from the sale.* A sales price in excess of the book value produces a gain; a sales price below the book value produces a loss. These gains or losses, if material in amount, should be shown separately in the income statement in computing the income from operations.

■ **Disposal at a Price Above Book Value**   Assume that a machine which cost $10,000 and has a book value of $2,000 is sold for $3,000. The journal entry to record this disposal is as follows:

Gain on disposal of plant asset

Cash	3,000	
Accumulated Depreciation: Machinery	8,000	
Machinery		10,000
Gain on Disposal of Plant Assets		1,000

To record sale of machinery at a price above book value.

■ **Disposal at a Price Below Book Value**   Now assume that the same machine is sold for $500. The journal entry in this case would be as follows:

Loss on disposal of plant asset

Cash	500	
Accumulated Depreciation: Machinery	8,000	
Loss on Disposal of Plant Assets	1,500	
Machinery		10,000

To record sale of machinery at a price below book value.

The disposal of a depreciable asset at a price equal to book value would result in neither a gain nor a loss. The entry for such a transaction would consist of a debit to Cash for the amount received, a debit to Accumulated Depreciation for the balance accumulated, and a credit to the asset account for the original cost.

Gains and Losses for Income Tax Purposes

Keep in mind that a business may use one depreciation method in its financial statements and *another method* for income tax purposes. As a result of using different depreciation methods, the asset's book value for income tax purposes may differ from its book value in the financial statements. Since the gain or loss on disposal is determined by comparing the disposal price to the asset's book value, the amount of gain or loss computed for income tax purposes *may differ* from that reported in the company's financial statements.

Trading in Used Assets on New

Certain types of depreciable assets, such as automobiles and trucks, are often traded in on new assets of the same kind. The trade-in allowance granted by the dealer may differ substantially from the book value of the asset being traded in. This raises the question of whether or not gains and losses should be recognized on the disposal of assets being traded in.

For financial reporting purposes, the answer to this question depends upon whether the trade-in allowance suggests a gain or a loss on the disposal of the old asset. Under generally accepted accounting principles, *no gains are recognized* when plant assets are traded in on similar plant assets. However, material *losses* on such transactions *are recognized.*

■ **Nonrecognition of Gains** A trade-in appears to result in a gain if the trade-in allowance offered by the dealer *exceeds* the book value of the asset being given in trade. Why, then, is this "gain" not recognized? The answer lies in the fact that the "list price" of the new asset may be inflated to allow the dealer to offer discounts to cash customers and excessively high trade-in allowances to customers exchanging a used asset.

CASE IN POINT ■ Offering customers a discount from the "factory sticker price" is a common practice among auto dealers. Some dealerships follow the policy of offering customers an "overallowance" on trade-ins, instead of discounting the price of the new automobile. The overallowance is simply an overly generous trade-in allowance for the customer's old car. The dealer hopes that by offering high trade-in allowances, it will convince customers that they are getting a good deal. In recording sales, however, the auto dealer treats the overallowances as sales discounts. The cars taken in trade are recorded in the dealer's inventory records at a realistic wholesale value.

The Financial Accounting Standards Board has taken the position that a high trade-in allowance does *not* provide sufficient evidence to justify the recognition of a gain. Revenue is not realized merely by substituting a new productive asset for an old one. Rather, revenue flows from the production of goods and services which productive assets make possible.[4]

The fact that no gain is recognized when a trade-in allowance exceeds the book value of the old asset makes recording the transaction relatively simple. The cost assigned to the asset being acquired is determined as follows:

$$\text{Cost of New Asset} = \text{Book Value of Old Asset Being Traded In} + \text{Additional Amount Paid (or to Be Paid)}$$

---

[4] *APB Opinion No. 29,* "Accounting for Nonmonetary Transactions," AICPA (New York: 1973).

To illustrate, assume that a delivery truck is being traded in on a new truck. The old truck was originally purchased for $8,000 cash, and has been depreciated by the straight-line method with the assumption of a five-year life and no salvage value. Annual depreciation expense is ($8,000 ÷ 5) or $1,600. After four years of use, the truck is traded in on a new model having a list price of $10,000. The truck dealer grants a trade-in allowance of $2,400 for the old truck; the additional amount to be paid to acquire the new truck is, therefore, $7,600 ($10,000 list price minus $2,400 trade-in allowance). The cost of the new truck is computed as follows:

Trade-in: cost of new equipment

Cost of the old truck	$8,000
Less: Accumulated depreciation ($1,600 × 4)...................................	6,400
Book value of the old truck	$1,600
Add: Cash payment for the new truck (list price, $10,000 − $2,400	
trade-in allowance)	7,600
Cost of the new truck	$9,200

The trade-in allowance and the list price of the new truck are ***not recorded*** in the purchaser's accounting records. These amounts are only used in order to determine the amount the purchaser must pay in addition to turning in the old truck. The journal entry to record this transaction is:

Delivery Truck (new)	9,200	
Accumulated Depreciation: Delivery Truck (old)	6,400	
Delivery Truck (old)		8,000
Cash..		7,600

To remove from the accounts the cost of old truck and accumulated depreciation thereon, and to record new truck at cost equal to book value of old truck traded in plus cash paid.

Notice that no gain is recognized on this trade-in, even though the trade-in allowance exceeds the book value of the old truck.

■ **Recognition of Losses** When the trade-in allowance offered by a dealer is *less* than the book value of the asset being traded-in, the transaction implies a *loss* on disposal of the old asset. If this loss is material in dollar amount, it ***should be recognized*** by the company trading in the used asset.

For example, assume that a company receives a trade-in allowance of only $10,000 for old machinery which has a book value of $100,000. A journal entry illustrating this situation follows:

Notice recognition of loss on trade-in

Machinery (new)...	600,000	
Accumulated Depreciation: Machinery (old)..........................	300,000	
Loss on Trade-in of Plant Assets....................................	90,000	
Machinery (old)...		400,000
Cash..		590,000

To recognize for financial reporting purposes a material loss on trade-in of machinery. Loss not recognized in determining taxable income.

■ **Different Rules for Gains and Losses** Notice that in recording trade-ins, accountants apply different criteria for recognizing gains and losses. This is but one illustration of the accounting concept of conservatism. *Conservatism* refers to a deliberate effort by accountants to avoid overstating earnings and asset values. Thus, accountants are willing to recognize losses based upon less evidence than they require for the recognition of gains. In fact, the concept of conservatism is sometimes summarized by the adage, "Recognize all losses, but anticipate no gains."

■ **Income Tax Rules** *Neither gains nor losses* on trade-in transactions may be recognized in the determination of taxable income. Thus, for income tax purposes, the cost assigned to the new asset is always equal to the sum of (1) the book value of the old asset traded in, plus (2) any additional amount paid or to be paid.

Notice that income tax rules parallel generally accepted accounting principles with respect to not recognizing gains on trade-ins, but they differ with respect to the recognition of losses. In practice, however, this difference is seldom important. If the trade-in allowance is below the book value of the old asset, the company disposing of this asset probably will sell it, rather than trading it in. By structuring the disposal of the old asset as a sale, the company will be able to deduct the loss for income tax purposes.

INTANGIBLE ASSETS

Characteristics

As the word *intangible* suggests, assets in this classification have no physical substance. Leading examples are goodwill, patents, and trademarks. Intangible assets are classified in the balance sheet as a subgroup of plant assets. However, not all assets which lack physical substance are regarded as intangible assets. An account receivable, for example, or a short-term prepayment is of nonphysical nature but is classified as a current asset and is not regarded as an intangible. In brief, *intangible assets are assets which are used in the operation of the business but which have no physical substance and are noncurrent.*

The basis of valuation for intangible assets is cost. In some companies, certain intangible assets such as trademarks may be of great importance but may have been acquired without the incurring of any cost. An intangible asset should appear in the balance sheet *only* if a cost of acquisition or development has been incurred.

Operating Expenses versus Intangible Assets

For an expenditure to qualify as an intangible asset, there must be reasonable evidence of future benefits. Many expenditures offer some prospects of yielding benefits in subsequent years, but the existence and life-span of these benefits is so uncertain that most companies treat these expenditures as operating expenses. Examples are the expenditures for intensive advertising campaigns to introduce new products, and the expense of training employees to work with new types of machinery or office equipment. There is little doubt that some benefits from these outlays continue beyond the current period, but because of the uncertain duration of the benefits, it is almost universal practice to treat expenditures of this nature as expense of the current period.

Amortization

The term *amortization* is used to describe the write-off to expense of the cost of an intangible asset over its useful life. The usual accounting entry for amortization consists of a debit to Amortization Expense and a credit to the intangible asset account. There is no theoretical objection to crediting an accumulated amortization account rather than the intangible asset account, but this method is seldom encountered in practice.

Although it is difficult to estimate the useful life of an intangible such as a trademark, it is highly probable that such an asset will not contribute to future earnings on a permanent basis. The cost of the intangible asset should, therefore, be deducted from revenue during the years in which it may be expected to aid in producing revenue. Under the current rules of the Financial Accounting Standards Board, the maximum period for amortization of an intangible asset cannot exceed *40 years.*[5] The straight-line method normally is used for amortizing intangible assets.

Goodwill

Objective 7
Explain the nature of goodwill and indicate when this asset should appear in the accounting records.

Business executives used the term *goodwill* in a variety of meanings before it became part of accounting terminology. One of the most common meanings of goodwill in a nonaccounting sense concerns the benefits derived from a favorable reputation among customers. To accountants, however, goodwill has a very specific meaning not necessarily limited to customer relations. It means the *present value of future earnings in excess of the normal return on net identifiable assets.* Above-average earnings may arise not only from favorable customer relations but also from such factors as superior management, manufacturing efficiency, and weak competition.

The phrase *normal return on net identifiable assets* requires explanation. Net assets means the owner's equity in a business, or assets minus liabilities. Goodwill, however, is not an *identifiable* asset. The existence of goodwill is implied by the ability of a business to earn an above-average return; however, the cause and precise dollar value of goodwill are largely matters of personal opinion. Therefore, *net identifiable assets* mean all assets *except goodwill,* minus liabilities. A *normal return* on net identifiable assets is the rate of return which investors demand in a particular industry to justify their buying a business at the *fair market value* of its net identifiable assets. A business has goodwill when investors will pay a higher price because the business earns more than the normal rate of return.

Assume that two similar restaurants are offered for sale and that the normal return on the fair market value of the net identifiable assets of restaurants of this type is 15% a year. The relative earning power of the two restaurants during the past five years is shown on the next page.

---

[5] *APB Opinion No. 17,* "Intangible Assets," AICPA (New York: 1970), par. 29.

	MANDARIN COAST	GOLDEN DRAGON
Fair market value of net identifiable assets	$1,000,000	$1,000,000
Normal rate of return on net assets	15%	15%
Average net income for past five years	$ 150,000	$ 190,000
Normal earnings, computed as 15% of net identifiable assets	150,000	150,000
Earnings in excess of normal	$ –0–	$ 40,000

An investor presumably would be willing to pay $1,000,000 to buy Mandarin Coast, because this restaurant earns the normal 15% return which justifies the fair market value of its net identifiable assets. Although Golden Dragon has the same amount of net identifiable assets, an investor would be willing to pay *more* for Golden Dragon than for Mandarin Coast, because Golden Dragon has a record of superior earnings which will presumably continue for some time in the future. The *extra amount* that a buyer would pay to purchase Golden Dragon represents the value of this business' *goodwill.*

■ **Estimating Goodwill** How much will an investor pay for goodwill? Above-average earnings in past years are of significance to prospective purchasers only if they believe that these earnings *will continue* after they acquire the business. Investors' appraisals of goodwill, therefore, will vary with their estimates of the future earning power of the business. Very few businesses, however, are able to maintain above-average earnings for more than a few years. Consequently, the purchaser of a business will usually limit any amount paid for goodwill to not more than four or five times the amount by which annual earnings exceed normal earnings.

Arriving at a fair value for the goodwill of an ongoing business is a difficult and subjective process. Any estimate of goodwill is in large part a matter of personal opinion. The following are several methods which a prospective purchaser might use in estimating a value for goodwill:

1 Agreement on the amount of goodwill may be reached through negotiation between buyer and seller. For example, it might be agreed that the fair market value of net identifiable assets is $1,000,000 and that the total purchase price for the business will be $1,180,000, thus providing a $180,000 payment for goodwill.

2 Goodwill may be determined as a multiple of the amount by which average annual earnings exceed normal earnings. Referring to our example involving Golden Dragon, a prospective buyer might be willing to pay four times the amount by which average earnings exceed normal earnings, indicating a value of $160,000 (4 × $40,000) for goodwill. The purchase price of the business, therefore, would be $1,160,000.

The multiple applied to the excess annual earnings will vary widely from perhaps 1 to 10. An investor who pays four times the excess earnings for goodwill must, of course, expect these earnings to continue for at least four years.

3 Goodwill may be estimated by *capitalizing* the amount by which average earnings exceed normal earnings. Capitalizing an earnings stream means dividing those earnings by the investor's required rate of return. The result is the maximum amount which the investor could pay for the earnings in order to achieve the required rate of return on the investment. To illustrate, assume that the prospective buyer decides to capitalize the $40,000 annual excess earnings of Golden Dragon at a rate of 20%. This approach results in a $200,000 estimate ($40,000 ÷ .20 = $200,000) for the value of goodwill. (Note that $40,000 per year represents a 20% return on a $200,000 investment.)

A weakness in the capitalization method is that *no provision is made for the recovery* of the investment. If the prospective buyer is to earn a 20% return on the $200,000 investment in goodwill, either the excess earnings must continue *forever* (an unlikely assumption) or the buyer must be able to recover the $200,000 investment at a later date by selling the business at a price above the fair market value of net identifiable assets.

■ **Recording Goodwill in the Accounting Records** Goodwill is recorded in the accounting records *only when it is purchased;* this situation usually occurs only when a going business is purchased in its entirety. After the fair market values of all identifiable assets have been recorded in the accounting records of the new owners, any additional amount paid for the business may properly be debited to an asset account entitled Goodwill. This intangible asset must then be amortized over a period not to exceed 40 years, although a much shorter amortization period is usually appropriate.

Many businesses have never purchased goodwill but have generated it internally through developing good customer relations, superior management, or other factors which result in above-average earnings. Because there is no objective means of determining the dollar value of goodwill unless the business is sold, internally developed goodwill is *not recorded* in the accounting records. Thus, goodwill may be a very important asset of a successful business but may not even appear in the company's balance sheet.

Patents

A patent is an exclusive right granted by the federal government for manufacture, use, and sale of a particular product. The purpose of this exclusive grant is to encourage the invention of new machines and processes. When a company acquires a patent by purchase from the inventor or other holder, the purchase price should be recorded by debiting the intangible asset account Patents.

Patents are granted for a period of 17 years, and the period of amortization must not exceed that period. However, if the patent is likely to lose its usefulness in less than 17 years, amortization should be based on the shorter period of estimated useful life. Assume that a patent is purchased from the inventor at a cost of $100,000, after five years of the legal life have expired. The remaining *legal* life is, therefore, 12 years, but if the estimated *useful* life is only four years, amortization should be based on this shorter period. The entry to be made to record the annual amortization expense would be:

■
Entry for amortization of patent

Amortization Expense: Patents	*25,000*	
Patents		*25,000*
To amortize cost of patent on a straight-line basis and estimated life of four years.		

Trademarks and Trade Names

Coca-Cola's distinctive bottle was for years the classic example of a trademark known around the world. A trademark is a word, symbol, or design that identifies a product or group of products. A permanent exclusive right to the use of a trademark, brand name, or commercial symbol may be obtained by registering it with the federal government. The costs of developing a trademark or brand name often consist of advertising campaigns which should be treated as expense when incurred. If a trademark or trade name is *purchased,* however, the cost may be substantial. Such cost should be capitalized and amortized to expense over a period of not more than 40 years. If the use of the trademark is discontinued or its contribution to earnings becomes doubtful, any unamortized cost should be written off immediately.

Franchises

A franchise is a right granted by a company or a governmental unit to conduct a certain type of business in a specific geographical area. An example of a franchise is the right to operate a McDonald's restaurant in a specific neighborhood. The cost of franchises varies greatly and often may be quite substantial. When the cost of a franchise is small, it may be charged immediately to expense or amortized over a short period such as five years. When the cost is material, amortization should be based upon the life of the franchise (if limited); the amortization period, however, may not exceed 40 years.

Copyrights

A copyright is an exclusive right granted by the federal government to protect the production and sale of literary or artistic materials for the life of the creator plus 50 years. The cost of obtaining a copyright in some cases is minor and therefore is chargeable to expense when paid. Only when a copyright is *purchased* will the expenditure be *material enough* to warrant its being capitalized and spread over the useful life. The revenue from copyrights is usually limited to only a few years, and the purchase cost should, of course, be amortized over the years in which the revenue is expected.

Other Intangibles and Deferred Charges

Among the other intangibles found in the published balance sheets of large corporations are moving costs, plant rearrangement costs, organization costs, formulas, processes, name lists, and film rights. Some companies group items of this type under the title of Deferred Charges, meaning expenditures that will provide benefits beyond the current year and will be written off to expense over their useful economic lives. It is also common practice to combine these items under the heading of Other Assets, which is listed at the bottom of the balance sheet.

Research and Development (R&D) Costs

The spending of billions of dollars a year on research and development leading to all kinds of new products is a striking characteristic of American industry.

In the past, some companies treated all research and development costs as expense in the year incurred; other companies in the same industry recorded these costs as intangible assets to be amortized over future years. This diversity of practice prevented the financial statements of different companies from being comparable.

The lack of uniformity in accounting for R&D was ended when the Financial Accounting Standards Board ruled that all research and development expenditures should be charged to expense *when incurred*.[6] This action by the FASB had the beneficial effect of reducing the number of alternative accounting practices and helping to make financial statements of different companies more comparable.

NATURAL RESOURCES

Accounting for Natural Resources

Objective 8
Account for the depletion of natural resources.

Mining properties, oil and gas reserves, and tracts of standing timber are leading examples of natural resources or "wasting assets." The distinguishing characteristics of these assets are that they are physically consumed and converted into inventory. Theoretically, a coal mine might be regarded as an underground "inventory" of coal; however, such an "inventory" is certainly not a current asset. In the balance sheet, mining property and other natural resources are classified as property, plant, and equipment.

We have explained that plant assets such as buildings and equipment depreciate because of physical deterioration or obsolescence. A mine or an oil reserve does not "depreciate" for these reasons, but it is gradually *depleted* as the natural resource is removed from the ground. Once all of the coal has been removed from a coal mine, for example, the mine is "fully depleted" and will be abandoned or sold for its residual value.

To illustrate the depletion of a natural resource, assume that Rainbow Minerals pays $45 million to acquire the Red Valley Mine, which is believed to contain 10 million tons of coal. The residual value of the mine after all of the coal is removed is estimated to be $5 million. The depletion that will occur over the life of the mine is the original cost minus the residual value, or $40 million. This depletion will occur at the rate of *$4 per ton* ($40 million ÷ 10 million tons) as the coal is removed from the mine. If we assume that 2 million tons are mined during the first year of operations, the entry to record the depletion of the mine would be as follows:

Recording depletion

Depletion of Coal Deposits *8,000,000*
    Accumulated Depletion: Red Valley Mine *8,000,000*
To record depletion of the Red Valley Mine for the year; 2,000,000
tons mined @ $4 per ton.

Accumulated Depletion is a contra-asset account similar to the Accumulated Depreciation account; it represents the portion of the mine which has

---

[6] *FASB Statement No. 2,* "Accounting for Research and Development Costs" (Stamford, Conn.: 1974), par. 12.

been used up (depleted) to date. In Rainbow Mineral's balance sheet, the Red Valley Mine now appears as follows:

Property, Plant, & Equipment:
Mining properties: Red Valley Mine $45,000,000
Less: Accumulated depletion 8,000,000 $37,000,000

The **Depletion of Coal Deposits** account may be viewed as similar to the **Purchases** account of a merchandising business. This account is added to any other mining costs and any beginning inventory of coal to arrive at the cost of goods (coal) available for sale. If all of the coal has been sold by year-end, these costs are deducted from revenue as the cost of goods sold. If some of the coal is still on hand at year-end, a portion of these costs is assigned to the ending inventory of coal, which is a current asset.

■ **Depreciation of Buildings and Equipment Closely Related to Natural Resources** Buildings and equipment installed at a mine or drilling site may be useful only at that particular location. Consequently, such assets should be depreciated over their normal useful lives, or over the life of the natural resource, **whichever is shorter.** Often depreciation on such assets is computed using the units-of-output method, thus relating the depreciation expense to the rate at which units of the natural resource are removed.

Depreciation, Amortization, and Depletion—a Common Goal

The processes of depreciation, amortization, and depletion discussed in this chapter all have a common goal. That goal is to **allocate the acquisition cost of a long-lived asset to expense over the years in which the asset contributes to revenue.** By allocating the acquisition cost of long-lived assets over the years which benefit from the use of these assets, we stress again the importance of the **matching principle.** The determination of income requires the matching of revenue with the expenses incurred to produce that revenue.

End-of-Chapter Review

CONCEPTS INTRODUCED IN CHAPTER 10

The major concepts in this chapter include:

■ The nature of plant and equipment; plant assets as a stream of future services.

■ Determining the cost of plant assets.

■ The distinction between revenue expenditures and capital expenditures.

■ Depreciation as a cost allocation procedure; computation of depreciation expense by the straight-line, units-of-output, sum-of-the-years'-digits, and declining-balance methods.

■ Why basing depreciation upon historical costs may cause an overstatement of net income.

■ Accounting for disposals of plant assets, including trade-ins.

■ The nature of intangible assets; amortization.

■ The nature of natural resources; depletion.

This chapter completes our discussion of the valuation of the major types of business assets. To review, we have seen that cash is valued at its face amount, receivables at their net realizable value, inventories at the lower of cost or market, and plant assets at cost less accumulated depreciation. Two ideas that are consistently reflected in each of these valuation bases are the matching principle and the concept of conservatism. In the coming chapters, we will turn our attention to the measurement of liabilities and owner's equity.

KEY TERMS INTRODUCED OR EMPHASIZED IN CHAPTER 10

Accelerated depreciation Methods of depreciation that call for recognition of relatively large amounts of depreciation in the early years of an asset's useful life and relatively small amounts in the later years.

Amortization The systematic write-off to expense of the cost of an intangible asset over the periods of its economic usefulness.

Book value The cost of a plant asset minus the total recorded depreciation, as shown by the Accumulated Depreciation account. The remaining undepreciated cost is also known as *carrying value*.

Capital expenditure A cost incurred to acquire a long-lived asset. An expenditure that will benefit several accounting periods.

Declining-balance depreciation An accelerated method of depreciation in which the rate is a multiple of the straight-line rate, which is applied each year to the *undepreciated cost* of the asset. Most commonly used is double the straight-line rate.

Deferred charge An expenditure expected to yield benefits for several accounting periods and therefore capitalized and written off during the periods benefited.

Depletion Allocating the cost of a natural resource to the units removed as the resource is mined, pumped, cut, or otherwise consumed.

Depreciation The systematic allocation of the cost of an asset to expense over the years of its estimated useful life.

Goodwill The present value of expected future earnings of a business in excess of the earnings normally realized in the industry. Recorded when a business entity is purchased at a price in excess of the fair value of its net identifiable assets (excluding goodwill) less liabilities.

Half-year convention The practice of taking six months' depreciation in the year of acquisition and the year of disposition, rather than computing depreciation for partial periods to the nearest month. This method is widely used and is acceptable for both income tax reporting and financial reports, as long as it is applied to *all* assets of a particular type acquired during the year. The half-year convention generally is *not* used for buildings.

Intangible assets Those assets which are used in the operation of a business but which have no physical substance and are noncurrent.

Natural resources Mines, oil fields, standing timber, and similar assets which are physically consumed and converted into inventory.

Net identifiable assets Total of all assets *except goodwill* minus liabilities.

Present value The amount that a knowledgeable investor would pay today for the right to receive future cash flows. The present value is always less than the sum of the future cash flows because the investor requires a return on the investment.

Replacement cost The estimated cost of replacing an asset at the current balance sheet date.

Residual (salvage) value The portion of an asset's cost expected to be recovered through sale or trade-in of the asset at the end of its useful life.

Revenue expenditure Any expenditure that will benefit only the current accounting period.

Straight-line depreciation A method of depreciation which allocates the cost of an asset (minus any residual value) equally to each year of its useful life.

Sum-of-the-years'-digits depreciation An accelerated method of depreciation. The depreciable cost is multiplied each year by a fraction of which the numerator is the remaining years of useful life (as of the beginning of the current year) and the denominator is the sum of the years of useful life.

Units-of-output depreciation A depreciation method in which cost (minus residual value) is divided by the estimated units of lifetime output. The unit depreciation cost is multiplied by the actual units of output each year to compute the annual depreciation expense.

SELF-TEST QUESTIONS

The answers to these questions appear on page 422.

1 In which of the following situations should the named company not record any depreciation expense on the asset described?

a Commuter Airline is required by law to maintain its aircraft in "as good as new" condition.

b Metro Advertising owns an office building that has been increasing in value each year since it was purchased.

c Computer Sales Co. has in inventory a new type of computer designed "never to become obsolete."

d None of the above answers is correct—in each case, the named company should record depreciation on the asset described.

2 Each of the following statements is false, *except:*

a Accumulated depreciation represents a fund being accumulated for the replacement of plant assets.

b The cost of a machine includes the cost of repairing damage to the machine during the installation process.

c A company may use different depreciation methods in its financial statements and its income tax return.

d The use of an accelerated depreciation method causes an asset to wear out more quickly than does use of the straight-line method.

3 On April 1, 1991, Sanders Construction paid $10,000 for equipment with an estimated useful life of ten years and a residual value of $2,000. The company uses the double-declining-balance method of depreciation, and applies the half-year convention to fractional periods. In *1992,* the amount of depreciation expense to be recognized on this equipment is:

a $1,600   **b** $1,440   **c** $1,280   **d** Some other amount

4 Delta Co. sold a plant asset that originally had cost $50,000 for $22,000 cash. If Delta correctly reports a $5,000 gain on this sale, the *accumulated depreciation* on the asset at the date of sale must have been:

a $33,000   **b** $28,000   **c** $23,000   **d** Some other amount

5 In which of the following situations would Burton Industries include goodwill in its balance sheet?

a The fair market value of Burton's net identifiable assets amounts to $2,000,000. Normal earnings for this industry is 15% of net identifiable assets. Burton's net income for the past five years has averaged $390,000.

b Burton spent $800,000 during the current year for research and development for a new product which promises to generate substantial revenue for at least 10 years.

c Burton acquired Baxter Electronics at a price in excess of the fair market value of Baxter's net identifiable assets.

d A buyer wishing to purchase Burton's entire operation has offered a price in excess of the fair market value of Burton's net identifiable assets.

Assignment Material

REVIEW QUESTIONS

1 Which of the following characteristics would prevent an item from being included in the classification of plant and equipment? (a) Intangible, (b) limited life, (c) unlimited life, (d) held for sale in the regular course of business, (e) not capable of rendering benefits to the business in the future.

2 The following expenditures were incurred in connection with a large new machine acquired by a metals manufacturing company. Identify those which should be included in the cost of the asset. (a) Freight charges, (b) sales tax on the machine, (c) payment to a passing motorist whose car was damaged by the equipment used in unloading the machine, (d) wages of employees for time spent in installing and testing the machine before it was placed in service, (e) wages of employees assigned to lubrication and minor adjustments of machine one year after it was placed in service.

3 What is the distinction between a *capital expenditure* and a *revenue expenditure?*

4 If a capital expenditure is erroneously treated as a revenue expenditure, will the net income of the current year be overstated or understated? Will this error have any effect upon the net income reported in future years? Explain.

5 Which of the following statements best describes the nature of depreciation?

a Regular reduction of asset value to correspond to the decline in market value as the asset ages.

b A process of correlating the carrying value of an asset with its gradual decline in physical efficiency.

c Allocation of cost in a manner that will ensure that plant and equipment items are not carried on the balance sheet at amounts in excess of net realizable value.

d Allocation of the cost of a plant asset to the periods in which services are received from the asset.

6 Should depreciation continue to be recorded on a building when ample evidence exists that the current market value is greater than original cost and that the rising trend of market values is continuing? Explain.

7 What connection exists between the choice of a depreciation method used to depreciate expensive new machinery for income tax reporting and the amount of income taxes payable in the near future?

8 Criticize the following quotation:

"We shall have no difficulty in paying for new plant assets needed during the coming year because our estimated outlays for new equipment amount to only $80,000, and we have more than twice that amount in our accumulated depreciation account at present."

9 A factory machine acquired at a cost of $94,200 was to be depreciated by the sum-of-the-years'-digits method over an estimated life of eight years. Residual salvage value was estimated to be $15,000. State the amount of depreciation during the *first* year and during the *eighth* year.

10 Explain two approaches to computing depreciation for a fractional period in the year in which an asset is purchased. (Neither of your approaches should require the computation of depreciation to the nearest day or week.)

11 a Does the accounting principle of consistency require a company to use the same method of depreciation for all of its plant assets?

b Is it acceptable for a corporation to use different depreciation methods in its financial statements and its income tax returns?

12 After four years of using a machine acquired at a cost of $15,000, Ohio Construction Company determined that the original estimated life of 10 years had been too short and that a total useful life of 12 years was a more reasonable estimate. Explain briefly the method that should be used to revise the depreciation program, assuming that straight-line depreciation has been used. Assume that the revision is made after recording depreciation and closing the accounts at the end of four years of use of the machine.

13 "The terms ACRS and MACRS refer to accelerated cost recovery systems established by the IRS for use in computing depreciation on income tax returns. Such endorsement of a depreciation system by the IRS automatically makes it acceptable for use in the published financial statements of major corporations." Do you agree with these two statements? Explain.

14 Explain what is meant by the following quotation: "In periods of rising prices companies do not recognize adequate depreciation expense, and reported corporate profits are substantially overstated."

15 Century Company traded in its old computer on a new model. The trade-in allowance for the old computer is greater than its book value. Should Century Company recognize a gain on the exchange in computing its taxable income or in determining its net income for financial reporting? Explain.

16 Newton Products purchased for $2 million a franchise making it the exclusive distributor of Gold Creek Beer in three western states. This franchise has an unlimited legal life and may be sold by Newton Products to any buyer who meets with Gold Creek Beer's approval. The accountant at Newton Products believes that this franchise is a permanent asset, which should appear in the company's balance sheet indefinitely at $2 million, unless it is sold. Is this treatment in conformity with generally accepted accounting principles, as prescribed by the FASB?

17 Define *intangible assets.* Would an account receivable arising from a sale of merchandise under terms of 2/10, n/30 qualify as an intangible asset under your definition?

18 Over what period of time should the cost of various types of intangible assets be amortized by regular charges against revenue? (Your answer should be in the form of a principle or guideline rather than a specific number of years.) What method of amortization is generally used?

19 Several years ago March Metals purchased for $120,000 a well-known trademark for padlocks and other security products. After using the trademark for three years, March Metals discontinued it altogether when the company withdrew from the lock business and concentrated on the manufacture of aircraft parts. Amortization of the trademark at the rate of $3,000 a year is being continued on the basis of a 40-year life, which the owner of March Metals says is required by accounting standards. Do you agree? Explain.

20 Under what circumstances should *goodwill* be recorded in the accounts?

21 In reviewing the financial statements of Digital Products Co. with a view to investing in the company's stock, you notice that net tangible assets total $1 million, that goodwill is listed at $400,000, and that average earnings for the past five years have been $50,000 a year. How would these relationships influence your thinking about the company?

22 Mineral King recognizes $20 depletion for each ton of ore mined. During the current year the company mined 600,000 tons but sold only 500,000 tons, as it was attempting to build up inventories in anticipation of a possible strike by employees. How much depletion should be deducted from revenue of the current year?

EXERCISES

Exercise 10-1
Accounting terminology

Listed below are nine technical accounting terms introduced in this chapter:

Intangible asset	Revenue expenditure	Amortization
Book value	Accumulated depletion	Declining-balance
Goodwill	Research & development	ACRS or MACRS

Each of the following statements may (or may not) describe one of these technical terms. For each statement, indicate the accounting term described, or answer "None" if the statement does not correctly describe any of the terms.

a A type of asset usually found only in the financial statements of a company which has purchased another going business in its entirety.

b Noncurrent assets lacking in physical substance.

c A depreciation method which often consists of doubling the straight-line rate and applying this doubled rate to the undepreciated cost of the asset.

d A depreciation method designed for use in income tax returns but not in conformity with generally accepted accounting principles.

e The cost of a plant asset minus the total recorded depreciation on the asset.

f A material expenditure that will benefit several accounting periods.

g The systematic allocation to expense of the cost of an intangible asset.

h The portion of the cost of a natural resource which has been consumed or used up.

Exercise 10-2
Identifying costs to be capitalized

New office equipment was purchased by Valley Company at a list price of $36,000; the credit terms were 2/10, n/30. Payment of the invoice was made within the discount period. The payment included 5% sales tax on the *net price*. Valley Company also paid transportation charges of $430 on the new equipment as well as $760 for installing the equipment in the appropriate locations. During the unloading and installation work, some of the equipment fell from a loading platform and was damaged. Repair of the damaged parts cost $2,180. After the equipment had been in use for three months, it was thoroughly cleaned and lubricated at a cost of $260. Prepare a list of the items which should be capitalized by a debit to the Office Equipment account and state the total cost of the new equipment.

Exercise 10-3
Distinguishing capital expenditures from revenue expenditures

Identify the following expenditures as capital expenditures or revenue expenditures:

a Immediately after acquiring a new delivery truck at a cost of $5,500, paid $125 to have the name of the store and other advertising material painted on the truck.

b Painted delivery truck at a cost of $175 after two years of use.

c Purchased new battery at a cost of $40 for two-year-old delivery truck.

d Installed an escalator at a cost of $12,500 in a three-story building which had previously been used for some years without elevators or escalators.

e Purchased a pencil sharpener at a cost of $3.50.

f Original life of the delivery truck had been estimated at four years and straight-line depreciation of 25% yearly had been recognized. After three years' use, however, it was decided to recondition the truck thoroughly, including a new engine and transmission, at a cost of $4,000. By making this expenditure it was believed that the useful life of the truck would be extended from the original estimate of four years to a total of six years.

Exercise 10-4
Units-of-output
method

During the current year, Western Auto Rentals purchased 50 new automobiles at a cost of $11,400 per car. After the cars have been driven 40,000 miles each in the rental business, they will be sold to a wholesale automobile dealer at an estimated $5,000 each. Western Auto Rentals computes depreciation expense on its automobiles by the units-of-output method, based upon mileage.

a Compute the amount of depreciation to be recognized for each mile that a rental automobile is driven.

b Assuming that the 50 rental cars are given a total of 1,500,000 miles during the current year, compute the total amount of depreciation expense that Western Auto Rentals should recognize on the fleet of cars for the year.

Exercise 10-5
Double-declining-
balance method

Merril Products acquired machinery with an estimated life of five years and a cost of $60,000. Estimated residual value of the machinery is $6,000. Compute the annual depreciation on the machinery for each of the five years using the double-declining-balance method. Limit the depreciation recognized in the fifth year to an amount that will cause the book value of the machinery to equal the estimated $6,000 residual value at year-end.

Exercise 10-6
Depreciation for
fractional years

On June 7, Adair Enterprises purchased equipment at a cost of $900,000. Useful life of the equipment was estimated to be six years and the residual value $90,000. Compute the depreciation expense to be recognized in each calendar year during the life of the equipment under each of the following methods:

a Straight-line (round computations for a partial year to the nearest full month).

b Straight-line (use the half-year convention).

Exercise 10-7
Trade-in and cost
basis

Olin Quarry traded in an old machine on a similar new one. The original cost of the old machine was $45,000 and the accumulated depreciation was $36,000. The new machine carried a list price of $60,000 and the trade-in allowance was $12,000. What amount must Olin Quarry pay? Compute the indicated gain or loss regardless of whether it should be recorded in the accounts. Compute the cost basis of the new machine to be used in figuring depreciation for determination of income subject to federal income tax.

Exercise 10-8
Disposal of
equipment by
sale, trade-in, or
as scrap

A tractor which cost $25,000 had an estimated useful life of five years and an estimated salvage value of $5,000. Straight-line depreciation was used. Give the entry (in general journal form) required by each of the following alternative assumptions:

a The tractor was sold for cash of $13,500 after two years' use.

b The tractor was traded in after three years on another tractor with a list price of $37,000. Trade-in allowance was $15,000. The trade-in was recorded in a manner acceptable for income tax purposes.

c The tractor was scrapped after four years' use. Since scrap dealers were unwilling to pay anything for the tractor, it was given to a scrap dealer for his services in removing it.

Exercise 10-9
Estimating
goodwill

During the past several years the annual net income of Bell Optics Company has averaged $378,000. At the present time the company is being offered for sale. Its accounting records show net assets (total assets minus all liabilities) to be $2,100,000.

An investor negotiating to buy the company offers to pay an amount equal to the book value for the net assets and to assume all liabilities. In addition, the investor is willing to pay for goodwill an amount equal to net earnings in excess of 15% on net assets, capitalized at a rate of 25%.

On the basis of this agreement, what price is the investor offering for Bell Optics Company? Show computations.

King Mining Company purchased the Lost Creek Mine for $15,000,000 cash. The mine was estimated to contain 2 million tons of ore and to have a residual value of $3,000,000.

During the first year of mining operations at the Lost Creek Mine, 400,000 tons of ore were mined, of which 300,000 tons were sold.

a Prepare a journal entry to record depletion of the Lost Creek Mine during the year.

b Show how the mine and the accumulated depletion would appear in King Mining Company's balance sheet after the first year of operations.

c Will the entire balance of the account debited in part **a** be deducted from revenue in determining the income for the year? Explain.

PROBLEMS

Group A

Early this summer, Crystal Car Wash purchased new "brushless" car washing equipment for all 10 of its car washes. The following information refers to the purchase and installation of this equipment.

(1) The list price of the brushless equipment was $7,500 for the equipment needed at each car wash. Because Crystal Car Wash purchased 10 sets of equipment at one time, it was given a special "package price" of $63,000 for all of the equipment. Crystal paid $23,000 of this amount in cash (no cash discount was allowed) and issued a 9%, 90-day note payable for the remaining $40,000. Crystal paid this note promptly at its maturity date, along with $900 in accrued interest charges.

(2) In addition to the amounts described above, Crystal paid sales taxes of $3,150 at the date of purchase.

(3) Freight charges for delivery of the equipment totaled $4,810.

(4) Crystal paid a contractor $2,600 per location to install the equipment at six of Crystal's car washes. Management was able to find a less expensive contractor who installed the equipment in the remaining four car washes at a cost of $2,000 per location.

(5) During installation, one of the new machines was accidentally damaged by an employee of Crystal Car Wash. The cost to repair this damage, $914, was paid by Crystal.

(6) As soon as the machines were installed, Crystal Car Wash paid $6,400 for a series of radio commercials advertising the fact that it now uses brushless equipment in all of its car washes.

a In one sentence, make a general statement summarizing the nature of the expenditures properly included in the cost of plant and equipment.

b For each of the six numbered paragraphs, indicate which items should be included by Crystal Car Wash in the cost debited to the Equipment account. Also briefly indicate the accounting treatment that should be accorded to any items that you *do not* regard as part of the cost of the equipment.

c Prepare a list of the expenditures that should be included in the cost of the equipment. (Determine the total cost of the equipment at all 10 locations; do not attempt to separate costs by location.)

d Prepare a journal entry at the end of the current year to record depreciation on this equipment. Crystal depreciates this equipment by the straight-line method over an estimated useful life of 10 years, assumes zero salvage value, and applies the half-year convention.

Problem 10A-2
Three depreciation methods

Werner Engineering purchased new equipment with an estimated useful life of four years. Cost of the equipment was $100,000 and the residual salvage value was estimated to be $10,000.

Instructions

Compute the annual depreciation expense throughout the four-year life of the equipment under each of the following methods of depreciation:

a Straight-line

b Sum-of-the-years'-digits

c Double-declining-balance. Limit the depreciation expense in the fourth year to an amount that will cause the book value of the equipment at year-end to equal the $10,000 estimated residual value.

Problem 10A-3
Three depreciation methods

New machinery was acquired by Chilton Manufacturing at a cost of $400,000. Useful life of the machinery was estimated to be five years, with residual salvage value of $37,000.

Instructions

Compute the annual depreciation expense throughout the five-year life of the machinery under each of the following methods of depreciation:

a Straight-line

b Sum-of-the-years'-digits

c Double-declining-balance. Limit the amount of depreciation recognized in the fifth year to an amount that will cause the book value of the machinery to equal the $37,000 estimated residual value.

Problem 10A-4
Evaluation of disclosures in annual reports

A recent annual report of **H. J. Heinz Company** includes the following note:

Depreciation: For financial reporting purposes, depreciation is provided on the straight-line method over the estimated useful lives of the assets. Accelerated depreciation methods generally are used for income tax purposes.

Instructions

a Identify four "accelerated depreciation" methods that the company might be using in its income tax returns. (Note: Because tax laws change from year-to-year, the company is using different accelerated methods on assets acquired in different years.)

b Is the company violating the accounting principle of consistency by using different depreciation methods in its financial statements and in its income tax returns? Explain.

c Why do you think that the company uses accelerated depreciation methods in its income tax returns?

d Would the use of accelerated depreciation methods in the financial statements be more "conservative," or less "conservative," than the current practice of using the straight-line method? Explain.

Problem 10A-5
Disposal of plant assets

During 19__, Festival Productions disposed of plant assets in the following transactions:

Feb. 10   Office equipment costing $14,000 was given to a scrap dealer. No proceeds were received from the scrap dealer. At the date of disposal, accumulated depreciation on the office equipment amounted to $11,900.

Apr. 1   Festival sold land and a building to MeriMar Development Co. for $630,000, receiving $200,000 in cash and a 10% five-year note receivable for $430,000. Festival's accounting records showed the following amounts: land, $120,000; building, $350,000; accumulated depreciation: building (as of April 1), $115,000.

Aug. 15   Festival traded in an old truck for a new one. The old truck had cost $11,000, and accumulated depreciation amounted to $7,000. The list price of the new truck was $17,000; Festival received a $5,000 trade-in allowance for the old truck and paid the $12,000 balance in cash. (Trucks are included in the Vehicles account.)

Oct. 1 Festival traded in its old computer system as part of the purchase of a new system. The old computer had cost $150,000 and, as of October 1, accumulated depreciation amounted to $110,000. The new computer had a list price of $90,000. Festival was granted a $10,000 trade-in allowance for the old computer system, paid $30,000 in cash, and issued a $50,000, 9%, two-year note payable to Action Computers for the balance. (Computers are included in the Office Equipment account.)

Instructions Prepare journal entries to record each of these transactions. Assume that depreciation expense on each asset already has been recorded up to the date of disposal. Thus, you need not update the accumulated depreciation figures stated in the problem.

Problem 10A-6
Depletion of an
oil field

On March 17, 1991, Wildcat Oil Company began operations at its Southfork Oil Field. The oil field had been acquired several years earlier at a cost of $14.4 million. The field is estimated to contain 4 million barrels of oil and to have a residual value of $2 million after all of the oil has been pumped out. Equipment costing $560,000 was purchased for use at the Southfork Field. This equipment will have no economic usefulness once Southfork is depleted; therefore, it is depreciated on a units-of-output basis.

Wildcat Oil also built a pipeline at a cost of $3,400,000 to serve the Southfork Field. Although this pipeline is physically capable of being used for many years, its economic usefuless is limited to the productive life of the Southfork Field and there is no residual value. Therefore, depreciation of the pipeline also is based upon the estimated number of barrels of oil to be produced.

Production at the Southfork Field amounted to 460,000 barrels in 1991 and 530,000 barrels in 1992.

Instructions **a** Compute the per-barrel depletion rate of the oil field and the per-barrel depreciation rates of the equipment and the pipeline.

b Make the year-end adjusting entries required at December 31, 1991, and December 31, 1992, to record depletion of the oil field and the related depreciation. (Make separate entries to record depletion of the oil field, depreciation of the equipment, and depreciation of the pipeline.)

c Show how the Southfork Field should appear in Wildcat Oil's balance sheet at the end of 1992. (Use "Oil Reserves: Southfork Field" as the title of the asset account; show accumulated depletion, but do not include the equipment or pipeline.)

Problem 10A-7
Intangible assets
or operating
expenses: GAAP

During the current year, Home Sales Corporation incurred the following expenditures which should be recorded either as operating expenses of the current year or as intangible assets:

a Expenditures for the training of new employees. The average employee remains with the company for seven years, but is retrained for a new position every three years.

b Purchased from another company the trademark to a household product. The trademark has an unlimited legal life, and the product is expected to contribute to revenue indefinitely.

c Incurred significant research and development costs to develop a dirt-resistant fiber. The company expects that the fiber will be patented, and that sales of the resulting products will contribute to revenue for at least 50 years. The legal life of the patent, however, will be 17 years.

d An expenditure to acquire the patent on a popular video game. The patent has a remaining life of 14 years, but Home Sales expects to produce and sell the game for only three years.

e Spent a large amount to sponsor a television mini-series about the French Revolution. The purpose in sponsoring the program was to make television viewers more aware of the company's name and its product lines.

Instructions Explain whether each of the above expenditures should be recorded as an operating expense or an intangible asset. If you view the expenditure as an intangible asset, indicate the number of years over which the asset should be amortized. Explain your reasoning.

Problem 10B-1
Determining cost
of plant assets

Brenner Graphics, a newly organized St. Louis corporation, purchased typesetting equipment having a list price of $204,000 from a manufacturer in the New England area. Credit terms for the transaction were 2/10, n/30. Included on the seller's invoice was an additional amount of $13,994 for sales tax. Brenner Graphics paid the invoice within the discount period. (The sales tax is not subject to the cash discount.) Other payments relating to the acquisition of the equipment were a freight bill of $2,600 and a labor cost for installing the equipment of $4,200. During the installation process, an accident caused damage ·to the equipment which was repaired at a cost of $5,900. As soon as the equipment was in place, the company obtained insurance on it for a premium of $1,800. All the items described above were charged to the Typesetting Equipment account. No entry for depreciation has yet been made and the accounts have not yet been closed.

Instructions **a** Prepare a list of the expenditures which should have been capitalized by debiting the Typesetting Equipment. Show the correct total cost for this asset.

b Prepare one compound journal entry to correct the error or errors by the company in recording these transactions.

c In one sentence state the accounting principle or concept which indicates the nature of expenditures properly included in the cost of equipment. (Do not list individual types of expenditure.)

Problem 10B-2
Three
depreciation
methods

New machinery was acquired by Southland Vending at a cost of $200,000. Useful life of the machinery was estimated to be five years, with residual salvage value of $17,000.

Instructions

Compute the annual depreciation expense throughout the five-year life of the machinery under each of the following methods of depreciation:

a Straight-line

b Sum-of-the-years'-digits

c Double-declining-balance. Limit the amount of depreciation recognized in the fifth year to an amount that will cause the book value of the machinery to equal the $17,000 estimated residual value.

Problem 10B-3
Three
depreciation
methods

Troy Industries purchased new equipment with an estimated useful life of four years. Cost of the equipment was $300,000 and the residual salvage value was estimated to be $33,000.

Instructions Compute the annual depreciation expense throughout the four-year life of the equipment under each of the following methods of depreciation:

a Straight-line

b Sum-of-the-years'-digits

c Double-declining-balance. Limit the depreciation expense in the fourth year to an amount that will cause the book value of the equipment at year-end to equal the $33,000 estimated residual value.

Problem 10B-4
Depreciation
policies in
annual reports

Shown below is a note accompanying recent financial statements of *International Paper Company:*

Plant, Properties, and Equipment
   Plant, properties, and equipment are stated at cost less accumulated depreciation.

For financial reporting purposes, the Company uses the units-of-production method of depreciating its major pulp and paper mills and certain wood products facilities, and the straight-line method for other plants and equipment.

Annual straight-line depreciation rates for financial reporting purposes are as follows: buildings 2½% to 8%; machinery and equipment 5% to 33%; woods equipment 10% to 16%. For tax purposes, depreciation is computed utilizing accelerated methods.

Instructions

a Are the depreciation methods used in the company's financial statements determined by current income tax laws? If not, who is responsible for selecting these methods? Explain.

b Does the company violate the consistency principle by using different depreciation methods for its paper mills and wood products facilities than it uses for its other plant and equipment? If not, what does the principle of consistency mean? Explain.

c What is the estimated useful life of the machinery and equipment being depreciated with a straight-line depreciation rate of:

(1) 5%.

(2) 33% (round to the nearest year).

Who determines the useful lives over which specific assets are to be depreciated?

d Why do you think the company uses accelerated depreciation methods for income tax purposes, rather than using the straight-line method? Explain.

Problem 10B-5
Disposal of plant assets

During 19__, Cabrillo Moving and Storage disposed of plant assets in the following transactions:

Mar. 12   Cabrillo traded in an old moving van for a new one. The old moving van had cost $27,000 and accumulated depreciation amounted to $19,000. The list price of the new moving van was $38,000. Cabrillo received a $12,000 trade-in allowance for the old moving van and paid the $26,000 balance in cash. (Moving vans are included in the Vehicles account.)

May 23   Cabrillo sold land and an unused storage facility to Self-Store, Inc., for $850,000, receiving $300,000 in cash and a 10% five-year note receivable for $550,000. Cabrillo's accounting records showed the following amounts: land, $120,000; building, $570,000; accumulated depreciation: building (as of May 23), $230,000.

Sept. 20   Cabrillo traded in its old computer system as part of the purchase of a new system. The old computer had cost $126,000 and, as of September 20, accumulated depreciation amounted to $98,000. The new computer had a list price of $95,000. Cabrillo was granted a $10,000 trade-in allowance for the old computer system, paid $35,000 in cash, and issued a $50,000, 12%, two-year note payable to Business Systems for the balance. (Computers are included in the Office Equipment account.)

Nov. 8   Office equipment costing $11,000 was given to a scrap dealer. No proceeds were received from the scrap dealer. At the date of disposal, accumulated depreciation on the office equipment amounted to $8,900.

Instructions

Prepare journal entries to record each of these transactions. Assume that depreciation expense on each asset already has been recorded up to the date of disposal. Thus, you need not update the accumulated depreciation figures stated in the problem.

Problem 10B-6
Depletion of a mine

Early in 1991, Gemini Minerals began operation at its Lost Hills Mine. The mine had been acquired several years earlier at a cost of $14,100,000. The mine is expected to contain 3 million tons of ore and to have a residual value of $1,500,000. Before beginning mining operations, the company installed equipment costing $3,750,000 at the mine. This equipment will have no economic usefulness once the mine is depleted. Therefore, depreciation of the equipment is based upon the estimated number of tons of ore produced each year (units-of-output method).

Ore removed from the Lost Hills Mine amounted to 572,000 tons in 1991 and 690,000 tons in 1992.

Instructions **a** Compute the per-ton depletion rate of the mine and the per-ton depreciation rate of the mining equipment.

b Make the year-end adjusting entries at December 31, 1991, and December 31, 1992, to record depletion of the mine and the related depreciation. (Use separate entries to record depletion of the mine and depreciation of the equipment.)

c Show how the Lost Hills Mine should appear in Gemini's balance sheet at the end of 1992. (Use "Mineral Deposits: Lost Hills Mine" as the title of the asset account; show accumulated depletion but do not include the equipment.)

Problem 10B-7
Intangible assets
or operating
expense: GAAP

During the current year Magnum Industries incurred the following expenditures which should be recorded either as operating expenses of the current year, or as intangible assets.

a Expenditure to acquire a franchise as one of four American distributors of an Italian automobile. The franchise expires in 49 years.

b Incurred research and development costs in an effort to produce a 100,000 mile tire. At year-end, the project looks promising. If successful, the product will be patented for 17 years, but should contribute to revenue for at least 20 years.

c Purchased a patent on a fuel-saving device. The patent has a remaining legal life of 13 years, but Magnum Industries expects to produce and sell the device for a period of five years.

d Expenditures to advertise a new product. The product is patented and is expected to contribute to company revenue for the entire 17-year life of the patent.

e Expenditures for management training programs. The average manager stays with the company for a period of 9½ years, but attends a management training program every two years.

Instructions Explain whether each of the above expenditures should be recorded as an operating expense of the current year or as an intangible asset. If you view the expenditure as creating an intangible asset, indicate the number of years over which the asset should be amortized. Explain your reasoning.

BUSINESS DECISION CASES

Case 10-1
Effects of
depreciation
policies upon
earnings

Two independent cases are described below. You are to comment separately on each case.

Case A Assume that Adams Company and Barnes Company are in the same line of business, have similar plant assets, and each report the same amount of net income. In their financial statements, Adams Company uses straight-line depreciation and Barnes Company uses an accelerated method.

Instructions Do you have any reason for considering one of these companies to be more profitable than the other? Explain.

Case B The income statement of Morris Foods includes depreciation expense of $200,000 and net income of $100,000. A note accompanying the financial statements discloses the following information about the company's depreciation policies:

Depreciation For financial statement purposes, depreciation is computed by the straight-line method using the following estimated useful lives:

Automobiles...	*12 years*
Furniture and equipment..	*25 to 30 years*
Buildings...	*60 to 90 years*

For tax purposes, depreciation is computed using accelerated methods.

Instructions In general terms, evaluate the effects of these depreciation policies upon the net income reported by the company in its income statement.

Case 10-2
Did I do this
right?

Protein Plus is a processor and distributor of frozen foods. The company's management is anxious to report the maximum amount of net income allowable under generally accepted accounting principles, and therefore uses the longest acceptable lives in depreciating or amortizing the company's plant assets. Depreciation and amortization computations are rounded to the nearest full month.

Near year-end the company's regular accountant was in an automobile accident, so a clerk with limited accounting experience prepared the company's financial statements. The income statement prepared by the clerk indicated a net loss of $45,000. However, the clerk was unsure that he had properly accounted for the following items:

(1) On April 4, the company purchased a small food processing business at a cost $80,000 above the value of that business's net identifiable assets. The clerk classified this $80,000 as goodwill on Protein Plus's balance sheet and recorded no amortization expense because the food processor's superior earnings are expected to continue indefinitely.

(2) During the year the company spent $32,000 on a research project to develop a method of freezing avocados. The clerk classified these expenditures as an intangible asset on the company's balance sheet and recorded no amortization expense because it was not yet known whether the project would be successful.

(3) Two gains from the disposal of plant assets were included in the income statement. One gain, in the amount of $4,300, resulted from the sale of a plant asset at a price above its book value. The other gain, in the amount of $2,700 on December 31, was based on receiving a trade-in allowance higher than the book value of an old truck that was traded in on a new one.

(4) A CPA firm had determined that the company's depreciation expense for income tax purposes was $51,400, using accelerated methods such as ACRS and MACRS. The clerk used this figure as depreciation expense in the income statement, although in prior years the company had used the straight-line method of depreciation in its financial statements. Depreciation for the current year amounts to $35,600 when computed by the straight-line method over realistic estimates of useful lives.

(5) On January 4, the company paid $90,000 to purchase a 10-year franchise to become the exclusive distributor in three eastern states for a brand of Mexican frozen dinners. The clerk charged this $90,000 to expense in the current year because the entire amount had been paid in cash.

(6) During the year, the company incurred advertising costs of $22,000 to promote the newly acquired line of frozen dinners. The clerk did not know how many periods would be benefited from these expenditures, so he included the entire amount in the selling expenses of the current year.

Instructions

a For each of the numbered paragraphs, explain whether the clerk's treatment of the item is in conformity with generally accepted accounting principles.

b Prepare a schedule determining the correct net income (or net loss) for the year. Begin with "Net loss originally reported . . . $45,000," and indicate any adjustments that you consider appropriate. If you indicate adjustments for the amortization of intangible assets acquired during the year, round the amortization to the nearest month.

ANSWERS TO SELF-TEST QUESTIONS

1 c (Depreciation is not recorded on inventory.)   **2 c**   **3 d** [$1,800, computed as 20% of ($10,000 − ½ of 20% of $10,000)]   **4 a** (Book value = $22,000 − $5,000 = $17,000; accumulated depreciation = $50,000 cost − $17,000 book value)   **5 c**

Comprehensive Problem for Part 3

ALPINE VILLAGE AND NORDIC SPORTS

Concepts of asset valuation and effects upon net income.

Chris Scott, a former Olympic skier, wants to purchase an established ski equipment and clothing shop in Aspen, Colorado. Two such businesses currently are available for sale: Alpine Village and Nordic Sports. Both businesses are organized as sole proprietorships and have been in operation for three years. Shown below is a summary of the current balance sheet data for both shops.

ALPINE VILLAGE AND NORDIC SPORTS
Summary of Current Balance Sheet Data

ASSETS	ALPINE VILLAGE	NORDIC SPORTS
Cash..	$ 38,700	$ 32,100
Accounts receivable	187,300	174,800
Inventory...	151,400	143,700
Plant and equipment:		
Land...	40,000	35,000
Building (net of accumulated depreciation)	99,900	72,900
Equipment (net of accumulated depreciation).....................	7,600	8,200
Goodwill	18,500	
Total assets	$543,400	$466,700

LIABILITIES & OWNER'S EQUITY		
Total liabilities..	$199,900	$206,300
Owner's equity	343,500	260,400
Total liabilities & owner's equity.................................	$543,400	$466,700

Income statements for the last three years show that Alpine Village has reported total net income of *$238,500* since the business was started. The income statements of Nordic Sports show total net income of *$199,400* for the same three-year period.

With the permission of the owners of the two businesses, Scott arranges for a certified public accountant to review the accounting records of both companies. This investigation discloses the following information:

Accounts receivable Alpine Village uses the direct write-off method of recording uncollectible accounts expense. The accountant believes that the $187,300 of accounts receivable appearing in the company's balance sheet includes about $15,000 in uncollectible accounts. Nordic Sports makes monthly estimates of its uncollectible accounts and shows accounts receivable in its balance sheet at estimated net realizable value.

Inventories Alpine Village uses the first-in, first-out *(FIFO)* method of pricing its inventory. Had the company used the last-in, first-out method *(LIFO),* the balance sheet valuation of inventory would be about $10,000 lower. Nordic Sports uses the LIFO method to value inventory; if it had used FIFO, the balance sheet valuation of inventory would be about $9,000 greater.

Buildings Alpine Village depreciates its building over an estimated life of 40 years using the straight-line method. Nordic Sports depreciates its building over 20 years using the double-declining-balance method. Nordic has owned its building for three years, and the accumulated depreciation on the building now amounts to $27,100.

Goodwill Three years ago, each business provided $20,000 in prize money for ski races held in the area. Alpine Village charged this expenditure to goodwill, which it is amortizing over a period of 40 years. Nordic Sports charged its $20,000 prize money expenditure directly to advertising expense.

Instructions

a Prepare a revised summary of the balance sheet data in a manner that makes the information about the two companies more comparable. Use the format illustrated at the beginning of this problem. However, you are to adjust the asset values shown for one company or the other so that the balance sheet data of each company meets the following standards:

(1) Accounts receivable are valued at estimated net realizable value.

(2) Inventories are valued by the method that will minimize income taxes during a period of rising prices.

(3) Depreciation on the buildings is based upon the straight-line method and an estimated useful life of 40 years.

(4) The cost of the $20,000 payment of prize money is treated in the manner required by generally accepted accounting principles.

After making the indicated adjustments to the valuation of certain assets, show "owner's equity" at the amount needed to bring total liabilities & owner's equity into agreement with total assets.

When you revalue an asset of either company, *show supporting computations.*

b Revise the *cumulative amount* of net income reported by each company during the last three years, taking into consideration the changes in accounting methods and policies called for in part **a.**

c Assume that Scott is willing to buy either company at a price equal to the revised amount of owner's equity as determined in part **a,** plus an amount for goodwill. For goodwill, Scott is willing to pay four times the amount by which average annual net income exceeds a 20% return on this revised owner's equity.

Determine the price that Scott is willing to pay for each of the two companies. Base your computations on the revised data about owner's equity and net income that you developed in parts **a** and **b.** (Hint: Remember that the cumulative net income in part **b** was earned over a *three-year period.* To find average *annual* net income, divide this amount by *3.*)

Current Liabilities, Partnerships, and Accounting Principles

Part 4 consists of three chapters. In Chapter 11 we deal with current liabilities; in Chapter 12 we discuss accounting for partnerships; and in Chapter 13 we review the accounting principles introduced in earlier chapters.

11 Current Liabilities and Payroll Accounting

12 Partnerships

13 Accounting Principles and Concepts

Current Liabilities and Payroll Accounting

In this chapter we concentrate on current liabilities, with special attention to notes payable. An important element of current liabilities arises from the payroll accounting system; consequently, the basic concepts of payroll accounting are discussed in the final section of this chapter. Long-term liabilities will be considered in Chapter 16.

After studying this chapter you should be able to meet these Learning Objectives:

1 Explain how the prompt recognition of liabilities relates to the matching principle of accounting.

2 Define current liabilities and explain how this classification is used in interpreting a balance sheet.

3 Account for the issuance of notes payable, the accrual of interest, and the payment of a note at maturity.

4 Explain the accounting treatment of notes payable which have interest included in the face amount.

5 Define loss contingencies and explain how they are presented in financial statements.

6 Describe the basic separation of duties in a payroll system and explain how this plan contributes to strong internal control.

7 Account for a payroll, including computation of amounts to be withheld, and payroll taxes on the employer.

The Nature of Liabilities

Liabilities are obligations arising from past transactions and requiring the future payment of assets or future performance of services. The dollar amount of a liability is usually clearly stated in a written or oral agreement between the debtor and the creditor. For example, assume that we make a $10,000 credit purchase of merchandise for our inventory, terms net 30 days. We should immediately record a $10,000 liability, the amount stated in our purchase order and in the invoice issued by the seller.

Examples of transactions calling for the future performance of services are a professional football team selling season tickets, and an airline selling tickets for travel at a future date. The organization receiving such payments in advance from customers must immediately record a liability, such as Unearned Ticket Revenue or Unearned Passenger Revenue. This liability will be discharged by rendering future services rather than by making a cash payment.

■ **Liabilities of Definite Amount vs. Estimated Liabilities** Most liabilities are of definite dollar amount clearly stated by contract. Examples are accounts payable, notes payable, bonds payable, dividends payable, sales taxes payable, accrued liabilities such as interest payable, and revenue collected in advance such as unearned passenger revenue. Our principal responsibility in accounting for these liabilities is to see that they are identified promptly as they come into existence and are properly recorded in the accounts.

Estimated liabilities have two key characteristics: The liability is known to exist, but the precise dollar amount cannot be determined until a later date. A common example is the liability of a manufacturer to honor a warranty on products sold. For instance, assume that a company manufactures and sells television sets which carry a two-year warranty. To achieve the objective of offsetting current revenue with all related expenses, the liability for future warranty repairs on television sets sold during the current period should be estimated and recorded at the balance sheet date. This estimate will be based upon the company's past experience.

Another common example of estimated liabilities is income tax on corporations. The income earned by a corporation is subject to tax by the federal government, as well as by most states and by some cities. Because of the complexities and frequent changes in the income tax laws, a corporation often needs several weeks or months after the year-end to determine the precise amount of the income tax liability. If disputes arise between a corporation and the tax authorities over the amount of the tax owed, the issues sometimes take years to resolve. However, income tax is a major expense of the year in which income is earned. Consequently, the tax liability must be estimated. The estimated amount is entered in the accounts and appears in the financial statements both as an expense and as a liability.

Timely Recognition of Liabilities

Objective 1
Explain how the prompt recognition of liabilities relates to the matching principle of accounting.

Correct timing in the recognition of liabilities is essential to producing dependable financial statements. An omission of a liability from the balance sheet is usually accompanied by the understatement of an expense in the income statement. For example, if advertising expense is not recorded in the period it is incurred, liabilities will be understated and advertising expense will be understated. This understatement of expenses causes net income to be overstated along with the owner's equity. The essential rule is that *a liability must be recognized in the accounting period in which it comes into being.* For purchases of merchandise on credit, the recognition of the liability (as evidenced by the purchase order, purchase invoice, and receiving report) is a routine procedure subject to strong internal controls. However, the recognition of unrecorded liabilities, such as product warranty expense, professional fees, interest, and salaries owed at the end of the period, requires the use of adjusting entries and is more subject to errors and omissions. An important reason for making adjusting entries at the end of the fiscal period is to recognize any unrecorded liabilities.

The need for prompt recognition of all liabilities stems from the *matching principle* of accounting. This principle requires that we recognize in each period all the expenses incurred in producing the revenue of the period. For expenses which do not require payment until some time after they are incurred, we must record the expense when incurred and credit a liability account to show our obligation to make this later payment. In performing an audit, CPA firms are especially alert to detect any omission of a liability from the balance sheet. Frauds involving the theft of assets have often been concealed by the deliberate omission of a liability.

CASE IN POINT ▪ King Building Supply, a small but profitable business, frequently issued notes payable to suppliers when its cash position did not permit prompt payment for purchases of materials. John Smith, office manager, usually prepared these notes payable for signature by the owner, Roy King. King relied heavily on Smith for all accounting and financial activities of the company.

Smith decided to take advantage of this situation to defraud the company through theft of inventory. He prepared a note for $100,000 payable to a regular supplier and obtained King's signature on it. He then ordered $100,000 worth of building materials to be delivered to a warehouse which he (Smith) had rented. Smith paid for the materials with the note signed by King, but made no accounting entry for the transaction. Smith felt sure that when the note matured, he could use company funds to pay it and charge the payment to the Purchases account. However, his fraud was disclosed during the year-end audit. The CPA firm discovered the existence of the unrecorded note payable by obtaining month-end statements from the company's suppliers. One of these statements showed a $100,000 sale, settled by a note received from King Building Supply, whereas the company's books showed no such purchase and no $100,000 note outstanding.

Current Liabilities

Objective 2
Define current liabilities and explain how this classification is used in interpreting a balance sheet

Current liabilities are obligations that must be paid within one year or within the operating cycle whichever is longer. Another requirement for classification as a current liability is the expectation that the debt will be paid from current assets. Occasionally, a current liability may be replaced with a new short-term liability rather than being paid in cash. For example, a company short of cash may issue a short-term note payable to settle a past-due account payable. Liabilities that do not fall due within one year or within the operating cycle are classified as long-term liabilities.

The current liability classification parallels the current asset classification. As explained in Chapter 5, the amount of working capital (current assets less current liabilities) and the current ratio (current assets divided by current liabilities) are valuable indicators of a company's ability to pay its debts in the near future. In other words, these indicators help us to judge a company's solvency.

Among the more common current liabilities are accounts payable, notes payable, dividends payable, current portion of long-term debt (such as this year's required principal payments on a long-term mortgage), sales taxes payable, accrued liabilities (such as interest payable), revenue collected in advance (such as unearned ticket revenue), payroll liabilities, and estimated liabilities, including product warranty liability and corporate income taxes.

Accounts Payable

Accounts payable are sometimes subdivided into trade accounts payable and other accounts payable. Trade accounts payable are short-term obligations to suppliers for purchases of merchandise. Other accounts payable include the liability for acquisition of assets such as office equipment and for any goods and services other than merchandise. We have previously discussed in Chapter 6 the guidelines for maintaining strong internal control over accounts payable. These guidelines include the locating of the purchasing function in a separate purchasing department and making payment only of liabilities which have been approved after comparison of invoice, purchase order, and receiving report. The voucher system is especially useful in providing assurance of the integrity of the system for approving and paying invoices.

NOTES PAYABLE

Objective 3
Account for the issuance of notes payable, the accrual of interest, and the payment of a note at maturity.

Notes payable are issued whenever bank loans are obtained. Other transactions which may give rise to notes payable include the purchase of real estate or costly equipment, the purchase of merchandise, and the substitution of a note for a past-due account payable.

Notes Payable Issued to Banks

Assume that on November 1 Porter Company borrows $10,000 from its bank for a period of six months at an annual interest rate of 12%. Six months later on May 1, Porter Company will have to pay the bank the *principal* amount of $10,000 plus $600 interest ($10,000 $\times$ .12 $\times$ $^6/_{12}$.) The owners of Porter Company have authorized John Caldwell, the company's treasurer, to sign notes payable issued by the company. The note issued by Porter Company is shown at the top of the next page.

The journal entry in Porter Company's accounting records for this November 1 borrowing is:

Face amount of note

Cash..	10,000	
Notes Payable..		10,000
Borrowed $10,000 for six months at 12% interest per year.		

Notice that no liability is recorded for the interest charges when the note is issued. At the date that money is borrowed, the borrower has a liability *only for the principal amount of the loan;* the liability for interest accrues day by day over the life of the loan. At December 31, two months' interest expense has been incurred, and the following year-end adjusting entry is made:

This note is for the principal amount with interest stated separately

```
    Miami, Florida                              November 1, 19_
   _____                        _____

    Six months                                 Porter Company
   _____  after this date _____

   promises to pay to Security National Bank the sum of $_____10,000_____

   with interest at the rate of _____12%_____ per annum.

                              Signed____ John Caldwell ____

                              Title____ Treasurer ____
```

A liability for interest accrues day by day

Interest Expense 200
     Interest Payable 200
To record interest expense incurred through year-end on 12%, six-month
note dated Nov. 1 ($10,000 × .12 × ²⁄₁₂ = $200).

If we assume that the company does not use reversing entries, the entry on May 1 when the note is paid will be:

Payment of principal and interest

Notes Payable.. 10,000
Interest Payable 200
Interest Expense 400
     Cash.. 10,600
To record payment of 12%, six-month note on maturity date and to
recognize interest expense incurred since year-end
($10,000 × .12 × ⁴⁄₁₂ = $400).

Notes Payable with Interest Charges Included in the Face Amount

Objective 4
Explain the accounting treatment of notes payable which have interest included in the face amount.

Instead of stating the interest rate separately as in the preceding illustration, the note payable issued by Porter Company could have been drawn to include the interest charge in the face amount of the note, as shown below:

This note shows interest included in face amount

```
    Miami, Florida                              November 1, 19_
   _____                        _____

    Six months                                 Porter Company
   _____  after this date _____

   promises to pay to Security National the sum of $_____$10,600_____

                              Signed____ John Caldwell ____

                              Title____ Treasurer ____
```

Notice that the face amount of this note ($10,600) is greater than the $10,000 amount borrowed. Porter Company's liability at November 1 is only $10,000—the present value of the note.[1] The other $600 included in the face amount of the note represents *future interest charges.* As interest expense is incurred over the life of the note, Porter Company's liability will grow to $10,600, just as in the preceding illustration.

The entry to record Porter Company's $10,000 borrowing from the bank at November 1 will be as follows for this type of note payable:

Interest included in face of note

Cash...	10,000	
Discount on Notes Payable	600	
Notes Payable...		10,600
Issued to bank a 12%, six-month note payable with interest charge		
included in the face amount of note.		

The liability account, Notes Payable, was credited with the full face amount of the note ($10,600). It is therefore necessary to debit a *contra-liability* account, *Discount on Notes Payable,* for the future interest charges included in the face amount of the note. Discount on Notes Payable is shown in the balance sheet as a deduction from Notes Payable. In our illustration, the amounts in the balance sheet would be Notes Payable, $10,600, minus Discount on Notes Payable, $600, or a net liability of $10,000 at November 1.

■ **Discount on Notes Payable**   The balance of the account Discount on Notes Payable represents *interest charges applicable to future periods.* As this interest expense is incurred, the balance of the discount account gradually is transferred into the Interest Expense account. Thus, at the maturity date of the note, Discount on Notes Payable will have a zero balance, and the net liability will have increased to $10,600. The process of transferring the amount in the Discount on Notes Payable account into the Interest Expense account is called *amortization* of the discount.

■ **Amortization of the Discount**   The discount on *short-term* notes payable usually is amortized by the straight-line method, which allocates the same amount of discount to interest expense for each month the note is outstanding.[2] Thus, the $600 discount on the Porter Company note payable will be transferred from Discount on Notes Payable into Interest Expense at the rate of $100 per month ($600 ÷ 6 months).

Adjusting entries should be made to amortize the discount at the end of the year and at the date the note matures. At December 31, Porter Company will make the following adjusting entry to recognize the two months' interest expense incurred since November 1:

---

[1] The concept of present value was introduced in Chapter 8. The mechanics of computing present value when the amount is not specifically stated are discussed in Appendix A following Chapter 16.

[2] When an interest charge is included in the face amount of a long-term note, the effective interest method of amortizing the discount is often used instead of the straight-line method. The effective interest method of amortization is discussed in Chapter 16.

■
Amortization of discount

Interest Expense	200	
Discount on Notes Payable		200

To record interest expense incurred to end of year on 12%, six-month note dated Nov. 1 ($600 discount × ⅓).

Notice that the liability for accrued interest is recorded by crediting Discount on Notes Payable rather than Interest Payable. The credit to Discount on Notes Payable reduces the debit balance in this contra-liability account from $600 to $400, thereby increasing the *net liability* for notes payable by $200.

At December 31, Porter Company's net liability for the bank loan will appear in the balance sheet as shown below:

■
Liability shown net of discount

Current liabilities:		
Notes payable...	$10,600	
Less: Discount on notes payable	400	$10,200

The net liability of $10,200 consists of the $10,000 principal amount of the debt plus the $200 interest which has accrued since November 1.

When the note matures on May 1, Porter Company will recognize the four months' interest expense incurred since year-end and will pay the bank $10,600. The entry is:

■
Two-thirds of interest applicable to second year

Notes Payable...	10,600	
Interest Expense	400	
Discount on notes payable.................................		400
Cash...		10,600

To record payment of six-month note due today and recognize interest expense incurred since year-end ($10,000 × 12% × 4/12 = $400).

Comparison of the Two Forms of Notes Payable

We have illustrated two alternative methods which Porter Company could use in accounting for its $10,000 bank loan, depending upon the form of the note payable. The journal entries for both methods, along with the resulting balance sheet presentations of the liability at November 1 and December 31, are summarized on the next page. Notice that both methods result in Porter Company recognizing the same amount of interest expense and the same total liability in its balance sheet. The form of the note does not change the economic substance of the transaction.

Loss Contingencies

Objective 5
Define loss contingencies and explain how they are presented in financial statements.

In Chapter 8, we discussed the contingent liability which arises when a business discounts a note receivable to a bank. The business endorses the note and thereby promises to pay the note if the maker fails to do so. The contingent liability created by discounting the note is a potential liability which will become a full-fledged liability or will be eliminated altogether by a future event. Contingent liabilities are also called *loss contingencies.* Loss contingencies, however, is a broader term, which includes the possible impairment of assets. Assume, for example, that an American company with operations overseas faces threats by a foreign country to seize American-owned assets in that

Comparison of the Two Forms of Notes Payable

	NOTE WRITTEN FOR $10,000 PLUS 12% INTEREST		NOTE WRITTEN WITH INTEREST INCLUDED IN FACE AMOUNT	
Entry to record borrowing on Nov. 1	Cash............ 10,000 　Notes Payable 10,000		Cash............ 10,000 Discount on Notes Payable .... 600 　Notes Payable 10,600	
Partial balance sheet at Nov. 1	*Current liabilities:* Notes Payable $10,000		*Current liabilities:* Notes payable .... $10,600 Less: Discount on notes payable .... 600　$10,000	
Adjusting entry at Dec. 31	Interest Expense .... 200 　Interest Payable............ 200		Interest Expense .... 200 　Discount on Notes Payable 200	
Partial balance sheet at Dec. 31	*Current liabilities:* Notes payable .... $10,000 Interest Payable............ 200　$10,200		*Current liabilities:* Notes payable .... $10,600 Less: Discount on notes payable .... 400　$10,200	
Entry to record payment of note on May 1	Notes Payable .... 10,000 Interest Payable............ 200 Interest Expense .... 400 　Cash............ 10,600		Notes Payable .... 10,600 Interest Expense .... 400 　Discount on Notes Payable............ 400 　Cash............ 10,600	

country. The possible loss is clearly a potential impairment of assets rather than a contingent liability.

A loss contingency may be defined as a possible loss, stemming from **past events,** that will be resolved as to existence and amount by some future event. Central to the definition of a loss contingency is the element of **uncertainty**—uncertainty as to the amount of loss and, on occasion, uncertainty as to whether or not any loss actually has been incurred. A common example of a loss contingency is the risk of loss from a lawsuit pending against a company. The lawsuit is based on past events, but until the suit is resolved, uncertainty exists as to the amount of the company's liability.

Loss contingencies are recorded in the accounting records at estimated amounts only when both of the following criteria are met: (1) it is **probable** that a loss has been incurred, and (2) the amount of loss can be **reasonably estimated.**[3] An example of a loss contingency which meets these criteria and is recorded in the accounts is the estimated loss from doubtful accounts receivable. Loss contingencies which do not meet both of these criteria should be **disclosed in footnotes** to the financial statements whenever there is at least a **reasonable possibility** that a loss has been incurred. Pending lawsuits, for example, almost always are disclosed in footnotes, but the loss, if any, is not entered in the accounting records until the lawsuit is settled.

When loss contingencies are disclosed in footnotes to the financial statements, the footnote should describe the nature of the contingency and, if possible, provide an estimate of the amount of possible loss. If a reasonable estimate of the amount of possible loss cannot be made, the footnote should include the range of possible loss or a statement that an estimate cannot be made. The following footnote is typical of the disclosure of the loss contingency arising from pending litigation:

■
Footnote disclosure of a loss contingency

Note 8: Contingencies

In October of the current year, the Company was named as defendant in a lawsuit alleging patent infringement and claiming damages of $408 million. The Company denies all charges in this case and is preparing its defenses against them. The Company is advised by legal counsel that it is not possible at this time to determine the ultimate legal or financial responsibility with respect to this litigation.

Users of financial statements should pay close attention to the footnote disclosure of loss contingencies. Even though no loss has been recorded in the accounting records, some loss contingencies may be so material in amount as to threaten the continued existence of the company.

CASE IN POINT ■ In August 1982, Manville Corp. surprised the financial community by filing for bankruptcy. Manville Corp., with its worldwide mining and manufacturing operations, had a long record of profitability and financial strength. In fact, the corporation was one of the 30 "blue chip" companies whose stock prices are used in the computation of the famous Dow-Jones Industrial Average. As late as 1981, the dollar amounts in

---

[3] *FASB Statement No. 5,* "Accounting for Contingencies" (Stamford, Conn.: 1975).

the company's financial statements showed Manville Corp. to be both profitable and solvent.

A clue to the company's impending problems, however, could be found in the notes accompanying the statements. Beginning in 1979, the statements included a note disclosing that the company was a defendant in "numerous legal actions alleging damage to the health of persons exposed to dust from asbestos-containing products manufactured or sold by the Company. . . ." It was these pending lawsuits, which numbered over 50,000 by August of 1982, which caused the company to file for bankruptcy.

Finally, notice that loss contingencies relate only to possible losses from *past events.* In the Manville case, the past events were exposing people to asbestos. The risk that losses might be incurred as a result of *future* events is *not* a loss contingency. The risk of *future* losses is *not* disclosed in financial statements for several reasons. For one, any disclosure of possible future losses would be sheer speculation. For another, it is not possible to foresee all the events which might give rise to future losses.

■ **Commitments** Contracts for future transactions are called commitments. They are not liabilities, but, if material, may be disclosed by footnotes to the financial statements. For example, a professional baseball club may issue a three-year contract to a player at an annual salary of, say, $1 million. This is a commitment to pay for services to be rendered in the future. There is no obligation to make payment until the services are received. Because there is no present obligation, no liability exists. Other examples of commitments include a corporation's long-term employment contract with a key officer, a contract for construction of a new plant, and a contract to buy inventory over a period of years. The common quality of all these commitments is an intent to enter into transactions in the future. Commitments that are material in amount should be disclosed in notes to the financial statements.

PAYROLL ACCOUNTING

Labor costs and related payroll taxes constitute a large and constantly increasing portion of the total costs of operating most business organizations. In the commercial airlines, for example, labor costs traditionally have represented 40 to 50% of total operating costs.

The task of accounting for payroll costs would be an important one simply because of the large amounts involved; however, it is further complicated by the many federal and state laws which require employers to maintain certain specific information in their payroll records not only for the business as a whole but also for each individual employee. Frequent reports of wages paid and amounts withheld must be filed with government agencies. These reports are prepared by every employer and must be accompanied by *payment* to the government of the amounts withheld from employees and of the payroll taxes levied on the employer.

A basic rule in most business organizations is that every employee must be paid on time, and the payment must be accompanied by a detailed explanation of the computations used in determining the net amount received by the employee. The payroll system must therefore be capable of processing the input data (such as employee names, social security numbers, hours worked, pay rates, overtime, and taxes) and producing a prompt and accurate output of paychecks, payroll records, withholding statements, and reports to government agencies. In addition, the payroll system must have built-in safeguards against overpayments to employees, the issuance of duplicate paychecks, payments to fictitious employees, and the continuance on the payroll of persons who have been terminated as employees.

Instead of distributing paychecks to employees, many companies have adopted the practice of making direct deposits to employees' bank accounts. Payroll information is sent to the bank by an electronic funds transfer system (EFTS). With this information, the bank debits the employer's account and credits the bank account of each employee, without any paper changing hands.

Internal Control over Payrolls

Payroll fraud has a long history. Before the era of social security records and computers, payroll records were often handwritten and incomplete. Employees were commonly paid in cash and documentary evidence was scanty. Some specific characteristics of present-day payroll accounting make payroll fraud more difficult. These helpful factors include the required frequent filing of payroll data with the government, and the universal use of employer identification numbers and employees' social security numbers. For example, "padding" a payroll with fictitious names is more difficult when social security numbers must be on file for every employee, individual earnings records must be created, and quarterly reports must be submitted to the Internal Revenue Service, showing for every employee the gross earnings, social security taxes, and income tax withheld.

Objective 6
Describe the basic separation of duties in a payroll system and explain how this plan contributes to strong internal control.

However, neither automation of the accounting process nor extensive reporting of payroll data to the government has caused payroll fraud to disappear. Satisfactory internal control over payrolls still requires separation and subdivision of duties. In a computer-based system, this means clear separation of the functions of systems analysts, programmers, computer operators, and control group personnel.

In many organizations the payroll activities include the functions of (1) employing workers, (2) timekeeping, (3) payroll preparation and record keeping, and (4) the distribution of pay to employees. Internal control will be strengthened if each of these functions is handled by a separate department.

■ **Employment (Personnel) Department** The work of the employment or personnel department begins with interviewing and hiring job applicants. When a new employee is hired, the personnel department prepares records showing the date of employment, the authorized rate of pay, and payroll deductions. The personnel department sends a written notice to the payroll department to place the new employee on the payroll. Changes in pay rates and termination of employees will be recorded in personnel department records. When a person's employment is terminated, the personnel department should conduct an exit interview and notify the payroll department to remove the employee's name from the payroll.

■ **Timekeeping** For employees paid by the hour, the time of arrival and departure should be punched on time cards. A new time card should be placed in the rack by the time clock at the beginning of each week or other pay period.

Control procedures should exist to ensure that each employee punches his or her own time card and no other. The timekeeping function should be lodged in a separate department which will control the time cards and transmit these source documents to the payroll department.

■ **The Payroll Department**   The input of information to the payroll department consists of hours reported by the timekeeping department, and authorized names, pay rates, and payroll deductions received from the personnel department. The output of the payroll department includes (1) payroll checks, (2) individual employee records of earnings and deductions, and (3) regular reports to the government showing employee earnings and taxes withheld.

■ **Distribution of Paychecks**   The paychecks prepared in the payroll department are transmitted to the *paymaster,* who distributes them to the employees. The paymaster should not have responsibility for hiring or firing employees, timekeeping, or preparation of the payroll.

Paychecks for absent employees should never be turned over to other employees or to supervisors for delivery. Instead, the absent employee should later pick up the paycheck from the paymaster after presenting proper identification and signing a receipt. The distribution of paychecks by the paymaster provides assurance that paychecks will not continue to be issued to fictitious employees or employees who have been terminated.

The operation of a typical payroll system is illustrated on the flowchart below. Notes have been made indicating the major internal control points within the system.

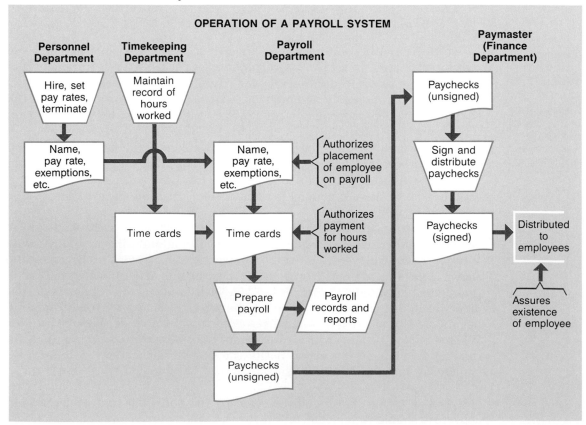

■ **Weaknesses in Internal Control** There is seldom justification for paying employees in cash. The use of paychecks provides better evidence that payments were made only to existing employees at authorized rates. Even in companies with numerous small branches, it is urgent that branch managers *not* be authorized to combine such duties as hiring and firing employees with the preparation of payrolls, or the distribution of paychecks. Much better internal control can be achieved by lodging in the headquarters office the work outlined above relating to employment, pay rates, pay changes, deductions, terminations, payroll preparation, and distribution of paychecks.

CASE IN POINT ■ Minox, Inc., a manufacturer with several hundred employees, permitted weaknesses in internal control that led to a large-scale payroll fraud. Supervisors in the factory had access to time cards and they also distributed W-2 forms to employees at the end of each year. This combination of duties enabled the supervisors to maintain more than 20 fictitious names on the payroll. Paychecks for these nonexistent employees were taken by the supervisors and endorsed for their own use.

This fraud was disclosed by chance when a temporary summer employee applied for a college loan and was refused on the grounds of excessive earnings. The employee's parents wrote to the president of Minox, Inc., complaining that the company had reported to the IRS much larger earnings than he had really received. The president of the company ordered an investigation which revealed that a factory supervisor had punched the temporary employee's time card daily, thus keeping him on the payroll after his termination. The supervisor had kept and endorsed the paychecks issued in the student's name.

Deductions from Earnings of Employees

Objective 7
Account for a payroll including computation of amounts to be withheld, and payroll taxes on the employer.

The take-home pay of most employees is much less than the gross earnings. Major factors explaining this difference between the amount earned and the amount received are social security taxes, federal income taxes withheld, and other deductions discussed in the following pages.

Social Security Taxes (FICA)

Under the terms of the Social Security Act, qualified workers who retire after reaching a specified age receive monthly retirement payments and Medicare benefits. Benefits are also provided for the family of a worker who dies before or after reaching this retirement age. Funds for the operation of this program are obtained through taxes levied under the Federal Insurance Contributions Act, often referred to as FICA taxes, or simply as *social security taxes.*

Employers are required by the Federal Insurance Contributions Act to withhold a portion of each employee's earnings as a contribution to the social security program. A tax at the same rate is levied against the employer. For example, assume that an employee earns $20,000 subject to FICA taxes of 7½%. The employer will withhold $1,500 ($20,000 × .075) from the employee's earnings. The employer will then pay to the government the amount of $3,000, consisting of the $1,500 withheld from the employee plus an additional $1,500 of FICA tax on the employer.

Two factors are involved in computing the FICA tax: the *base* or amount of earnings subject to the tax; and the *rate* which is applied to the base. Both the *base* and the *rate* have been increased many times in recent years and probably will continue to be changed in future years.

CASE IN POINT ■ The enormous increase in social security taxes is revealed in the following table.

YEAR	BASE (EARNINGS SUBJECT TO FICA TAX)	TAX RATE	AMOUNT OF TAX
1937	$ 3,000	1.0%	$ 30
1951	3,600	1.5%	54
1966	6,600	4.2%	277
1972	9,000	5.2%	468
1977	16,500	5.85%	965
1983	35,700	6.70%	2,392
1986	42,000	7.15%	3,003
1996	?	?	?

We can see from the table that individuals with earnings greater than the base were required to pay approximately 100 times as much in 1986 as they were in 1937 when the social security plan was started.

These changes in rates and in the base do not affect the accounting principles or procedures involved. For illustrative purposes in this book, we shall assume the rate of tax to be 7½% on both the employee and the employer, applicable to a *base of $45,000* (the first $45,000 of wages received by each employee in each calendar year). This assumption of round amounts for both the tax and the base is a convenient one for the purpose of illustrations and for the solution of problems by the student, regardless of frequent changes in the rate and base.

An example may clarify the expression "subject to FICA tax." Assume that during a year when a $45,000 base prevails, you earn $48,000 in salary. You would have to pay the 7½% FICA tax on $45,000 of your salary. You would *not* pay FICA tax on the $3,000 by which your salary exceeded the $45,000 base.

Federal Income Taxes

Our pay-as-you-go system of federal income tax requires employers to withhold a portion of the earnings of their employees. The amount withheld depends upon the amount of the earnings and upon the number of income tax exemptions claimed by the employee. On a federal income tax return, one exemption is allowed for oneself, one for a spouse, and one for each dependent. Each exemption causes a specified amount of yearly earnings to be exempt from income tax. An employee is required to file with the employer a Withholding Allowance Certificate (Form W-4) showing the number of exemptions claimed.

Present regulations provide a graduated system of withholding, designed to make the amount of income tax withheld approximate the individual's tax liability at the end of the year. Because persons in higher income brackets are subject to *higher rates* of taxation, the withholding rates are correspondingly higher for them. There is no ceiling with respect to the amount of salary subject to income tax.

For more extensive consideration of federal income taxes, see Chapter 18, Income Taxes and Business Decisions.

Most states and cities which levy income taxes also require the employer to withhold the tax from employees' earnings. Because such situations involve a variety of rates, they will not be discussed here.

Other Deductions from Employees' Earnings

In addition to the compulsory deductions for taxes, many other deductions are voluntarily authorized by employees. Union dues and insurance premiums already have been mentioned as examples of payroll deductions. Others include charitable contributions, retirement programs, savings bond purchases, and pension plans.

Employer's Responsibility for Amounts Withheld

In withholding amounts from an employee's earnings for either voluntary or involuntary deductions, the employer acts merely as a collection agent. The amounts withheld are paid to the designated organization, such as a government agency or labor union. The employer is also responsible for maintaining accounting records which will enable it to file required reports and make timely payments of the amounts withheld. From the employer's viewpoint, the amounts withheld from employees' earnings represent current liabilities.

Payroll Records and Procedures

Although payroll records and procedures vary greatly according to the number of employees and the extent of automation in processing payroll data, there are a few fundamental steps common to payroll work in most organizations. One of these steps taken at the end of each pay period is the preparation of a *payroll register* showing for each employee the gross earnings, amounts withheld, and net pay. When the computation of the payroll register has been completed, the next step is to reflect the expense and the related liabilities in the ledger accounts. A general journal entry as shown below may be used to bring into the accounts the information summarized in the payroll register. (This entry does not include payroll taxes on the employer.)

■ **Journal entry to record payroll**		
Sales Salaries Expense	4,800	
Office Salaries Expense..	3,200	
FICA Tax Payable (7½% of $8,000)		600
Liability for Income Tax Withheld....................................		1,330
Liability for Insurance Premiums Withheld		150
Salaries Payable...		5,920
To record the payroll for the period Jan. 1–Jan. 15.		

The two debits to expense accounts indicate that the business has incurred salaries expense of $8,000; however, only $5,920 of this amount will be paid to the employees on payday. The payment will be recorded by a debit to Salaries Payable and a credit to Cash. The remaining $2,080 (consisting of deductions for taxes and insurance premiums withheld) is lodged in liability accounts. Payment of these liabilities must be made at frequent intervals.

■ **Wage and Tax Statement** By January 31 each year, employers are required to furnish every employee with a Wage and Tax Statement (Form W-2). This form shows gross earnings for the preceding calendar year and the amounts withheld for FICA tax and income taxes. The employer sends one copy of this form to the federal government, one copy to the state government, and gives three copies to the employee. When the employee files a federal income tax return, he or she must attach a copy of the withholding statement. A copy also must be attached to the state income tax return.

Payroll Taxes on the Employer

The discussion of payroll taxes up to this point has dealt with taxes levied on employees and withheld from their pay. From the viewpoint of the employing company, such withheld taxes are significant because they must be accounted for and remitted in a timely manner to the appropriate government agencies. However, *payroll taxes are also levied on the employer.* These taxes on the employer are expenses of the business and *are recorded by debits to expense accounts,* just as in the case of property taxes or license fees for doing business.

■ **Social Security (FICA) Tax** The employer is taxed to help finance the social security program. The tax is figured at the same rate and on the same amount of earnings used to compute FICA tax on employees. (In all problems and illustrations in this book, the tax is assumed to be 7½% on the first $45,000 of gross earnings by each employee in each calendar year.)

■ **Federal Unemployment Insurance Tax** Unemployment insurance is another part of the national social security program designed to offer temporary relief to unemployed persons. The FUTA tax (Federal Unemployment Tax Act) is levied on *employers only* and is not deducted from the wages of employees. The rates of tax and the wage base subject to the tax are changed from time to time. For purposes of illustration in this book, we shall assume that employers are subject to federal unemployment tax at the rate of 6.2% on the first $7,000 of each employee's earnings in each calendar year. However, the employer may take a credit against this tax (not in excess of 5.4% of the first $7,000 of each employee's wages) for amounts that are paid into state unemployment funds. As a result, an employer may be subject to a *federal* tax of only .8% on wages up to $7,000 per employee.

■ **State Unemployment Insurance Tax** All the states participate in the federal-state unemployment insurance program. The usual rate of tax is 5.4% of the first $7,000 of earnings by each employee during the calendar year. Under this provision, the employer actually makes payment of the larger part of the FUTA tax directly to state governments which carry out the federal-state unemployment insurance program. This arrangement means that the

FUTA tax is divided into two parts: the larger part, or 5.4%, of the first $7,000 of wages paid going to the state and the remainder (.8%) to the federal government.

■ **Accounting Entry for Employer's Payroll Taxes** The entry to record the employer's payroll taxes is usually made at the same time the payroll is recorded. To illustrate, let us use again the $8,000 payroll first used on page 439 in the discussion of amounts withheld from employees. This time, however, we are illustrating taxes levied on the *employer*. (None of the employees has earned over $7,000 since this is the first pay period of the current year.)

■
Journal entry to record payroll taxes on employer

Payroll Taxes Expense	*1,096*	
FICA Tax Payable (7½% of $8,000)		*600*
State Unemployment Tax Payable (5.4% of $8,000)		*432*
Federal Unemployment Tax Payable (0.8% of $8,000)		*64*

To record payroll taxes on employer for period ended Jan. 15.

Thus the total payroll expense for the employer is $9,096, which consists of wages of $8,000 and payroll taxes of $1,096.

Distinction between Employees and Independent Contractors

Every business obtains personal services from *employees* and also from *independent contractors*. The employer-employee relationship exists when the company paying for the services has a right to direct and supervise the person rendering the services. Independent contractors, on the other hand, are retained to perform a specific task and exercise their own judgment as to the best methods for performing the work. Examples of independent contractors include CPAs engaged to perform an audit, attorneys retained to represent a company in a law suit, and a plumber called in to repair a broken pipe. The *fees* paid to independent contractors are not included in payroll records and are not subject to withholding or payroll taxes.

End-of-Chapter Review

CONCEPTS INTRODUCED OR EMPHASIZED IN CHAPTER 11

The major concepts in this chapter include:

■ Prompt recognition of liabilities in accordance with the matching principle.

■ Current liabilities: a factor in judging debt-paying ability.

■ Notes payable with interest stated separately, and notes payable with interest included in the face amount.

■ Loss contingencies and commitments.

■ Internal control over the payroll system.

■ Withholding: social security taxes and income taxes.

■ Payroll taxes on the employer.

■ Employees and independent contractors.

In this chapter we have emphasized current liabilities; that is, liabilities that must be paid within one year or the operating cycle, whichever is longer. Long-term liabilities, such as bonds payable, will be discussed in Chapter 16, following an introduction to the corporate form of business organization.

KEY TERMS INTRODUCED OR EMPHASIZED IN CHAPTER 11

Amortization of discount The process of systematically writing off to interest expense each period a portion of the discount on a note payable. Causes the carrying value of the liability to rise to the face value of the note by the maturity date.

Commitments Agreements to carry out future transactions. Not a liability because the transaction has not yet been performed, but may be disclosed in footnotes to the financial statements.

Contingent liability A potential liability which either will develop into a full-fledged liability or will be eliminated entirely by a future event.

Contra-liability account A ledger account which is deducted from or offset against a related liability account in the balance sheet. For example, Discount on Notes Payable.

Discount on Notes Payable A contra-liability account representing any interest charges applicable to future periods included in the face amount of a note payable. Over the life of the note, the balance of the Discount on Notes Payable account is amortized into Interest Expense.

Federal Unemployment Insurance Tax (FUTA) A tax imposed on the employer by the Federal Unemployment Tax Act based on amounts of payrolls. Designed to provide temporary payments to unemployed persons.

FICA tax Payroll tax imposed by the Federal Insurance Contribution Act on both employer and employees. Used to finance the social security program of monthly retirement payments and Medicare benefits. Benefits also are paid to the family of a worker who dies before reaching retirement age.

Gross earnings Total amount earned by an employee before deductions such as social security taxes, federal income tax withheld, and any voluntary deductions.

Independent contractor A person or firm providing services to a company for a fee or commission. Not controlled or supervised by the client company. Not subject to payroll taxes.

Loss contingency A situation involving uncertainty as to whether or not a loss has occurred. The uncertainty will be resolved by a future event. An example of a loss contingency is the possible loss relating to a lawsuit pending against a company. Although loss contingencies are sometimes recorded in the accounts, they are more frequently disclosed only in footnotes to the financial statements.

Maturity value The value of a note at its maturity date, consisting of principal plus any interest payable at that date.

Note payable A liability evidenced by issuance of a formal written promise to pay a certain amount of money, usually with interest, at a future date.

Payroll A record listing the names of employees during a given pay period, the rates of pay, time worked, gross earnings, deductions for taxes and any other amounts withheld, and net pay.

Payroll register A form of payroll record showing for each pay period all payroll information for employees individually and in total.

Principal amount That portion of the maturity value of a note which is attributable to the amount borrowed or to the cost of the asset acquired when the note was issued, rather than being attributable to interest charges.

State unemployment insurance tax   A tax generally levied on employers only and based on payrolls. A part of the joint federal-state program to provide payments to unemployed persons. (In a few states a tax is also levied on employees.)

Wage and Tax Statement (W-2 Form)   A form furnished by the employer to every employee showing the employee's gross earnings for the calendar year and the amounts withheld for FICA taxes and income taxes.

SELF-TEST QUESTIONS

The answers to these questions appear on page 453.

1 Which of the following situations require recording a liability in 1991? (More than one answer may be correct.)

a In 1991, a company manufactures and sells stereo equipment which carries a three-year warranty.

b In 1991, a theater group receives payments in advance from season ticket holders for productions to be performed in 1992.

c A company is a defendant in a legal action. At the end of 1991, the company's attorney feels it is possible the company will lose, and that the amount of the loss might be material.

d During 1991, a midwest agricultural co-operative is concerned about the risk of loss if inclement weather destroys the crops.

Use the following data for questions 2 and 3.
On May 1, 1991, Thompkins Company borrowed $350,000 from the bank and agreed to repay that amount plus 12% interest at the end of one year.

2 Assume the note payable is drawn in the amount of $350,000 with interest stated separately. With respect to this note, Thompkins' financial statements for the year ended December 31, 1991 include:

a Interest expense of $42,000.

b An overall current liability for this loan of $392,000.

c An overall current liability for this loan of $378,000.

d Unamortized Discount on Notes Payable of $14,000.

3 Assume the note payable is drawn with interest included in the face of the note. Thompkins' adjusting entry on December 31, 1991 with regard to this note includes:

a A credit to Notes Payable of $14,000.

b A debit to Interest Expense of $14,000.

c A credit to Interest Payable of $28,000.

d A credit to Discount on Notes Payable of $28,000.

4 Each of the following indicates a significant weakness in internal control over payrolls, *except:*

a The paymaster is responsible for preparing, signing, and distributing paychecks to employees.

b The personnel department is responsible for firing and hiring employees, and for the distribution of paychecks.

c The payroll department is responsible for preparing payroll checks for signature by the paymaster, maintaining individual employee records of earnings and deductions, and filing required payroll reports with the government.

d The payroll department prepares paychecks for signature by the paymaster; signed checks are returned to the payroll department for distribution to employees.

5 Hennesey receives a salary of $60,000 per year from Carling Company. Federal income taxes withheld amounted to $9,000. FICA taxes (7.5% each on employee and employer) apply to wages up to $45,000. The state unemployment tax is 5.4% of earnings up to $7,000, and the federal unemployment tax is 0.8% of earnings up to $7,000. Hennesey's take-home pay and the total cost to Carling of having Hennesey on the payroll are, respectively:

a $47,625 and $63,809.

c $46,891 and $63,809.

b $51,000 and $67,184.

d $47,625 and $60,434.

Assignment Material

REVIEW QUESTIONS

1 Evaluate the following statement: "A transaction which consists of the receipt of cash from a customer in payment for the performance of services in the future does not create a liability because there is no intent to make a cash payment to the customer at any time in the future."

2 A liability should be recognized in the period it is incurred. The omission of a liability from the balance sheet is most likely to be accompanied by which of the following:

a The overstatement of an expense

b The understatement of an expense

c The understatement of owner's equity

d The overstatement of an asset

Give reasons for your answer.

3 Define current liabilities, long-term liabilities, and estimated liabilities. Give an example of an estimated liability.

4 Jonas Company issues a 90-day, 12% note payable to replace an account payable to Smith Supply Company in the amount of $8,000. Draft the journal entries (in general journal form) to record the issuance of the note payable and the payment of the note at the maturity date.

5 Howard Benson applied to the City Bank for a loan of $20,000 for a period of three months. The loan was granted at an annual interest rate of 12%. Write a sentence illustrating the wording of the note signed by Benson if

a Interest is stated separately in the note.

b Interest is included in the face amount of the note.

6 With reference to Question **5** above, give the journal entry required on the books of Howard Benson for issuance of each of the two types of notes.

7 What kind of account is Discount on Notes Payable? Where and how should it appear in the financial statements? What is the eventual disposition of amounts in Discount on Notes Payable?

8 Define the term loss contingency, give an example relating to litigation, and state how (if at all) a loss contingency should be reported in the financial statements.

9 Should commitments appear on a balance sheet? If so, in what part of the balance sheet?

10 The personnel department of Meadow Company failed to notify the payroll department that five hourly factory workers had been terminated at the end of the last pay period. Assuming a normal subdivision of duties regarding personnel, timekeeping, preparation of payroll, and distribution of paychecks, what control procedure will prevent the payroll department from preparing paychecks for these five employees in the current period?

11 That type of payroll fraud known as "padding" a payroll is a more difficult maneuver under today's payroll accounting practices than it was a generation or more ago. What present-day factors make the padding of payrolls a complex and more difficult type of fraud?

12 Name the federal taxes that most employers are required to withhold from employees. What account or accounts would be credited with the amounts withheld?

13 Explain which of the following taxes relating to an employee's wages are borne by the employee and which by the employer:

    a FICA taxes

    b Federal unemployment compensation taxes

    c State unemployment compensation taxes

    d Federal income taxes

14 Is the Salary Expense account equal to "take-home" pay or to gross earnings? Why?

15 Distinguish between an employee and an independent contractor. Why is this distinction important with respect to payroll accounting?

EXERCISES

Exercise 11-1
Accounting
terminology

Listed below are nine technical accounting terms introduced in this chapter:

Estimated liabilities	Payroll register	Maturity value of note
FUTA tax	Independent contractor	Contingent liabilities
Commitments	FICA tax	Discount on Notes Payable

Each of the following statements may (or may not) describe one of these technical terms. For each statement, indicate the accounting term described, or answer "None" if the statement does not correctly describe any of the terms.

a The principal amount of a promissory note plus any interest payable at the maturity date.

b A federal tax based on payrolls and imposed on employers but not on employees.

c Legal obligations which are known to exist but for which the dollar amount is presently uncertain.

d Information presented in footnotes to financial statements concerning agreements to carry out certain transactions in the future.

e Interest charges included in the face amount of a note payable.

f An employee whose compensation is based on units of output rather than an hourly wage or a monthly salary.

g A federal tax based on payrolls and imposed on both employers and employees.

Exercise 11-2
Two forms for
notes payable

On November 1, Metals Exchange, Inc., borrowed $250,000 from a bank, and promised to repay that amount plus 12% interest (per year) at the end of six months. (Remember that the interest is stated at an annual rate.) You are to prepare two different presentations of the liability to the bank on Metals Exchange's December 31 balance sheet, assuming that the note payable to the bank was drawn as follows:

a For $250,000, with interest stated separately and payable at maturity.

b With the total interest charge included in the face amount of the note.

Exercise 11-3
Interest included
in face amount of
note payable

On April 1, Tiger Truck Lines bought four trucks from Freeway Motors for a total price of $272,000. The transactions required Tiger Truck Lines to pay $80,000 cash and to issue a promissory note due in full 18 months later. The face amount of the note was $215,040, which included interest on the note for the 18 months.

Prepare all entries (in general journal form) for Tiger Truck Lines relating to the purchase of the trucks and the note for the current fiscal year ended December 31. Include the adjusting entries to record interest expense and depreciation expense to December 31. (The trucks are to be depreciated over an eight-year service life by the straight-line method. There is no estimated salvage value.)

Exercise 11-4
Internal control
over payroll

A supervisor in the factory of Barton Products, a large manufacturing company, discharged an employee but did not notify the personnel department of this action. The supervisor then began forging the employee's signature on time cards. When giving out paychecks, the supervisor diverted to his own use the paychecks drawn payable to the discharged worker. What internal control measure would be most effective in preventing this fraudulent activity?

Exercise 11-5
Internal control
over payroll

Ames Company had 60 employees throughout the current year. The lowest-paid employee had gross earnings of $10,000. Assume that Federal Unemployment Tax Act specifies a rate of 6.2% on the first $7,000 of gross earnings and that the state unemployment tax is 5.4% of the same base. The employer is permitted to take as a credit against the federal tax the 5.4% of wages paid to the state. Compute the following:

a The state unemployment tax for the year

b The federal unemployment tax for the year

c The total unemployment tax for the year

Exercise 11-6
Payroll taxes on
employer

Wedge Company had the following payroll data for the year:

Gross earnings of employees	*$1,200,000*
Employee earnings not subject to FICA tax	*144,000*
Employee earnings not subject to FUTA tax	*675,000*

Assuming that the payroll is subject to a FICA tax rate of 7.5%, a 5.4% state unemployment tax rate, and a federal FUTA tax rate of .8 of 1%, compute the amount of Wedge Company's *payroll tax expense* for the year, showing separately the amount of each of the three taxes. (Note: Taxes on employees are not involved in this exercise.)

Exercise 11-7
Entries for
payroll and
payroll taxes

For the week ended January 7, the payroll records of Foursome Company showed the following amounts for total earnings: sales employees, $35,200; office employees, $28,800. Amounts withheld consisted of FICA taxes at a rate of 7.5% on all earnings for this period; federal income taxes, $7,680; and group insurance premiums, $2,400.

a After computing the amount of FICA taxes withheld, prepare a general journal entry to record the payroll. Do not include taxes on the employer.

b Prepare a general journal entry to record the payroll taxes expense to Foursome Company relating to this payroll. Assume that the federal unemployment tax rate is 6.2% of the first $7,000 paid each employee, and that 5.4% of this tax is payable to the state. No employee received more than $7,000 in this first pay period of the year.

PROBLEMS

Group A

Problem 11A-1
Liabilities:
recognition and
disclosure

The events described below occurred at Redford Grain Corporation on December 31, the last day of the company's fiscal year.

a The company was named as defendant in a $30 million lawsuit. Redford's legal counsel stated that the lawsuit was without merit and that Redford would defend itself vigorously in court. However, the legal counsel also stated that it was impossible at this time to predict the outcome of the litigation, or the liability, if any, which might eventually be determined.

b Signed a note payable to obtain a bank loan. The note was in the principal amount of $300,000, to mature in nine months, plus interest of $22,500 (computed at 10% per year).

c Discounted a note receivable at a bank and received cash of $205,000. The note was in the face amount of $200,000, had a total life of one year, and a stated interest rate of 11%.

d The general ledger included an account entitled Income Taxes Withheld with a balance at December 31 of $16,500.

e Purchased land for use in the business at a price of $500,000. Signed a note payable due nine months from today (December 31) in the total amount of $533,750. The note constituted payment in full for the land.

f On December 31 signed a contract with another grain dealer calling for the purchase by Redford of 50,000 bushels of wheat per month for six months at a price of $4 per bushel.

g Signed a contract with a labor union on December 31 specifying annual increases in wage rates of 5% for the next three years. The increase in labor costs for the first year of the agreement was estimated to be $1,200,000.

For each of the above seven events, you are to state the dollar amount (if any) which should appear in the current liability section of Redford Corporation's balance sheet at December 31. For any event which does not affect current liabilities, you are to indicate whether it should appear in the balance sheet and the proper location and amount.

Problem 11A-2
Notes payable;
adjusting entries
for interest

In the fiscal year ended October 31, Harbor Corporation carried out several transactions involving notes payable. The company uses a 360-day year in making all interest calculations. Listed below are the transactions relating to notes payable.

June 1 Borrowed $20,000 from Holden Investments, by issuing a 60-day, 12% note payable to Holden as evidence of the indebtedness.

July 19 Bought office equipment from Western Office Supply. The invoice amount was $18,000 and Western Office Supply accepted as full payment a 10%, three-month note for this amount.

July 31 Paid the Holden note for $20,000 plus interest.

Sept. 1 Borrowed $240,000 from Midwest Bank at an annual interest rate of 8%; signed a 90-day note with interest included in the face amount of the note.

Oct. 1 Purchased merchandise for $16,200 from Earthware Imports. Gave in settlement a 90-day note bearing interest at 10%.

Oct. 19 The $18,000 note payable to Western Office Supply matured today. Paid the interest accrued and issued a new 30-day, 12% note to replace the matured note.

Instructions

a Prepare journal entries (in general journal form) to record the above transactions.

b Prepare the adjusting entries needed at October 31, prior to closing the accounts. Use one adjusting entry to accrue interest on the two notes in which interest is stated separately (the Earthware Imports note and the Western Office Supply note). Use a separate adjusting entry to record interest expense accrued on the note with interest included in the face amount (the Midwest Bank note).

Problem 11A-3
Notes payable
and interest
computations

Lane Products had the following transactions relating to notes payable during the fiscal year ending June 30 and shortly thereafter.

Feb. 9 Obtained a loan of $25,000 from Horizon Finance and signed a 45-day, 12% note payable.

Mar. 12 Purchased delivery truck from E-Z Company. Issued a 12%, three-month note payable for $15,000, the full cost of the truck.

Mar. 26 Paid the note due today to Horizon Finance, plus accrued interest.

May 1 Borrowed the amount of $200,000 for 90 days from First Bank at an interest rate of 14% per year; signed a note payable with the interest included in the face amount of the note.

May 31 Purchased merchandise for $7,500 from Patten Co. Issued a 90-day note bearing interest at 16% annually.

June 12 The $15,000 note payable to E-Z Company matured today. Paid in cash the interest accrued and issued a new 30-day note bearing interest at 14% per annum to replace the maturing note. (Use one compound journal entry for this transaction.)

June 30 End of fiscal year.

July 12 Paid principal and interest of the 30-day, 14% note to E-Z Company dated June 12 which matured today.

July 30 Paid in full the 90-day note to First Bank dated May 1 and maturing today.

Instructions
a Prepare journal entries (in general journal form) to record the six transactions dated prior to June 30. All interest rates quoted are annual rates. Use a 360-day year for interest computations.

b Prepare two adjusting entries at June 30 relating to interest expense. The first entry should accrue interest on the two notes with interest stated separately (the note to Patten Co. and the note to E-Z Company). The explanation should include computations showing the amount of interest accrued on each note. The second adjusting entry should record interest on the First Bank note in which interest was included in the face amount.

c Prepare journal entries for the two transactions occurring in July.

Problem 11A-4
Notes payable: a
comprehensive
problem

During the three months ended June 30, Optics, Inc., had the following transactions relating to notes payable.

Apr. 1 Purchased office equipment for use in the business from Eastern Gear, Inc., for $13,000, making an $1,800 cash down payment and issuing a one-year note payable for the balance. The face amount of the note was $12,992, which included a 16% interest charge. (Use one compound journal entry which includes discount on Notes Payable.)

Apr. 16 Gave $5,000 cash and a 90-day, 8% note to Lees Company in settlement of open account due today in the amount of $14,000.

Apr. 25 Purchased office equipment from Hale Company for $17,400, giving a 60-day, 9% note in settlement thereof.

May 11 Borrowed $72,000 from First State Bank, giving a 90-day note as evidence of indebtedness. An interest charge computed at 17% per annum was included in the face amount of the note.

June 15 Purchased merchandise on account from Phoenix Co., $18,000.

June 18 Issued a 60-day note bearing interest at 9% in settlement of the Phoenix Co. account.

June 24 Paid the 60-day, 9% note due to Hale Company, which matured today.

Instructions **a** Prepare journal entries (in general journal form) to record the listed transactions for the three months ended June 30. (Use a 360-day year in computing interest.)

b Prepare adjusting entries to record the interest expense on notes payable through June 30. Prepare one adjusting entry to record the interest payable on the two notes for which interest is stated separately (the Lees Company note and the Phoenix Co. note). The other adjusting entry should record the amortization of discount on the two notes in which interest is included in the face amount (the Eastern Gear, Inc., note and the First State Bank note).

c Prepare a partial balance sheet at June 30 reflecting the above transactions. Show Notes Payable to Bank (minus the discount) as one item and Notes Payable: Other (minus the discount) as a separate liability. Also include the interest payable in the current liability section of the balance sheet.

Problem 11A-5
Internal control
over payrolls

Char Burger, a chain of 10 drive-in hamburger stands, is a sole proprietorship owned by Betty Lee. Although Lee has other business interests, she devotes a portion of her time to management of the drive-in chain. A manager is employed at each of the 10 locations and the number of employees at each location varies from six to twelve.

The manager of each unit prepares payroll sheets each week showing hours worked as reported by the employees on time cards which are approved by the manager. Each manager's salary is also listed on the weekly payroll. Upon completion of the payroll, the manager pays all employees and him- or herself in cash. Each employee acknowledges receipt of payment by signing the payroll sheet.

Employees at each branch are employed and terminated by the local managers, who also set wage rates. The salaries of the managers are authorized by Betty Lee.

Each week the payroll sheets are mailed by the managers to Lee, whose secretary prepares individual earnings records for each employee and compiles federal and state tax returns from the weekly payroll sheets.

Instructions **a** Write a paragraph evaluating the adequacy of internal controls over payrolls. State the specific practices, if any, which you think should be changed.

b List four specific ways in which payroll fraud could be carried on by the manager of any of the 10 drive-ins.

Problem 11A-6
Recording payroll
and payroll taxes

Hudson Company incurred salaries expense during January of $28,000, classified as follows: $20,000 of salaries for the sales staff and $8,000 salaries expense for office personnel.

FICA taxes were withheld from employees' earnings at an assumed rate of 7.5%. Other amounts withheld were $3,750 for federal income taxes and $700 for group insurance premiums.

Instructions **a** Prepare a general journal entry to record the payroll and deductions from employees' earnings. Do not include payroll taxes on the employer in this journal entry.

b Prepare a general journal entry to record the payroll taxes on the employer as a result of the above payroll. Assume an FICA tax of 7.5%, a state unemployment tax of 5.4%, and a federal unemployment tax of .8% on the entire payroll.

c What is the total payroll expense of Hudson Company for January? Show computations.

Problem 11A-7
Employees'
earnings records:
payroll taxes

Individual earnings records for all employees of Crown Point are as follows so far in the current year.

EMPLOYEE	CUMULATIVE EARNINGS	EMPLOYEE	CUMULATIVE EARNINGS
Adams, A. B.	$10,000	Hale, T. R.	$ 5,261
Carline, M. A.	15,000	Kent D. C.	51,890
Fox, L. M.	11,530	Land, S. B.	2,358
Grant, N. P.	6,701	Paul, R. M.	26,039

The FICA taxes are assumed to be 7½% on the first $45,000 of gross earnings. The rate of federal unemployment tax is assumed to be 6.2% on the first $7,000 of gross earnings, but with credit to the employer for a maximum of 5.4% of gross earnings for state unemployment taxes.

Instructions

a Prepare a three-column schedule showing for each employee the following accounts: cumulative earnings (as given), earnings subject to unemployment compensation tax, and earnings subject to FICA taxes. As an example, the first line of the schedule would show for Adams, A. B. the following three amounts: $10,000, $7,000, and $10,000.

b Some payroll taxes are levied on the employee and some on the employer. Use the information shown in part a above to compute the total payroll taxes *deducted* from the earnings of the employees as a group. (Income taxes are not involved in this problem.)

c Compute the total payroll taxes levied on the employer, Crown Point, and the percentage of the total payroll ($128,779) represented by this payroll tax. Round amounts to the nearest tenth of a percent.

Group B

Problem 11B-1
Liabilities:
recognition and
disclosure

The six events listed below occurred at Capitol Products on or near the end of the fiscal year, December 31.

a On December 15, signed a contract for purchase of 50,000 barrels of oil a month for the next 18 months at a price of $15 a barrel.

b On December 31, discounted a $200,000 note receivable at a bank and received cash of $198,000. The note bears interest at 9% a year and has a total life of one year.

c On October 31, borrowed $500,000 from a bank and signed a 6-month note payable for $530,000 with interest included in the face amount.

d On December 31, purchased machinery at a price of $200,000 and signed a note payable due six months from today in the total amount of $210,000. Interest of $10,000 was included in the face amount of the note.

e On December 31, signed a two-year contract with a labor union providing for a 4% increase in wage rates each year. The increase in wages for the first year was estimated at $1,300,000.

f At December 31, the ledger account Salaries Payable had a balance of $220,000.

Instructions

For each of the six events, you are to indicate the dollar amount, if any, which should appear in the current liability section of the December 31 balance sheet. If an event does not affect current liabilities, indicate whether it should appear in the balance sheet and the proper location and dollar amount.

Problem 11B-2
Current
liabilities: journal
entries

During the year ended December 31, Rockport Associates had a number of transactions relating to accounts payable and notes payable. Among these transactions were the following:

Mar. 6 Purchased merchandise from A. B. Hayes on open account, $25,200.

Apr. 8 Informed A. B. Hayes that it was unable to make payment as previously agreed. Issued to Hayes a 14%, eight-month note to replace the open account payable.

Apr. 20 Borrowed $48,000 from Third National Bank today and signed a six-month, 16% note as evidence of indebtedness. The interest was added to the $48,000 amount borrowed and included in the face amount of the note.

May 15 Purchased merchandise from Birmingham, Incorporated, on 30-day open account, $19,200.

Oct. 20 Paid note (principal and interest) due today at Third National Bank.

Dec. 8 Paid note (principal and interest) due today to A. B. Hayes.

Instructions

Prepare all necessary journal entries (in general journal form) to record the above transactions in the accounts of Rockport Associates. Show all supporting computations as part of the explanations of the journal entries. Adjusting entries are not required.

Problem 11B-3
Notes payable;
accruing interest

During the fiscal year ended October 31, Dunleer Corporation carried out the following transactions involving notes payable.

June 6 Borrowed $11,200 from Tom Hutchins, issuing to him a 45-day, 12% note payable.

July 13 Purchased office equipment from Harper Company. The invoice amount was $16,800 and Harper Company agreed to accept as full payment a 12%, three-month note for the invoiced amount.

July 21 Paid the Hutchins note plus accrued interest.

Sept. 1 Borrowed $235,200 from Sun National Bank at an interest rate of 12% per annum; signed a 90-day note with interest included in the face amount of the note. (Use Discount on Notes Payable account.)

Oct. 1 Purchased merchandise in the amount of $3,000 from Kramer Co. Gave in settlement a 90-day note bearing interest at 14%.

Oct. 13 The $16,800 note payable to Harper Company matured today. Paid the interest accrued and issued a new 30-day, 12% note to replace the maturing note.

Instructions

a Prepare journal entries (in general journal form) to record the above transactions. Use a 360-day year in making the interest calculations.

b Prepare the adjusting entries needed at October 31, prior to closing the accounts. Use one entry for the two notes on which interest is stated separately and a separate entry for the Sun National Bank note in which interest is included in the face amount of the note.

Problem 11B-4
Notes payable: a
comprehensive
problem

The following transactions relating to notes payable were completed by Desktop Graphics during the three months ended June 30.

Apr. 1 Bought office equipment for use in the business from Stylecraft, Inc., for $39,000, making a $5,400 cash down payment and issuing a one-year note payable for the balance. The face amount of the note was $38,976, which included a 16% interest charge. Use one compound journal entry which includes Discount on Notes Payable.

Apr. 16 Paid $15,000 cash and issued a 90-day, 8%, $27,000 note to Hall Company in settlement of open account payable in the amount of $42,000.

Apr. 25 Purchased office equipment from ADM Company for $52,200, issuing a 60-day, 9% note payable in settlement.

May 11 Borrowed $216,000 from Manufacturers Bank, issuing a 90-day note payable as evidence of indebtedness. An interest charge computed at 17% per year was included in the face amount of the note.

June 15 Purchased merchandise on account from Texas Co., $54,000.

June 18 Issued a 60-day note bearing interest at 9% in settlement of the account payable to Texas Co.

June 24 Paid the 60-day, 9% note due to ADM Company, which matured today.

Instructions

a Prepare journal entries (in general journal form) to record the listed transactions for the three months ended June 30. (Use a 360-day year in computing interest.)

b Prepare adjusting entries to record the interest expense on notes payable through June 30. Prepare one adjusting entry to record the accrued interest payable on the two notes for which interest is stated separately (the Hall Company note and the Texas Co. note). The other adjusting entry should record the amortization of discount on the two notes in which interest is included in the face amount (the Stylecraft, Inc., note and the Manufacturers Bank note).

c Prepare a partial balance sheet at June 30 reflecting the above transactions. Show Notes Payable to Bank (minus the discount) as one item and Notes Payable: Other (minus the discount) as a separate liability. Also include the interest payable in the current liability section of the balance sheet.

Problem 11B-5
Payroll fraud

Friendly Finance Company makes small loans through a network of more than 100 branch offices in several states. A branch manager is in charge of each office and the number of employees under the manager's supervision is usually from four to seven. Each branch manager prepares a weekly payroll sheet, including his or her own salary. All employees are paid from cash on hand. The employees sign the payroll sheet signifying receipt of their salaries. Hours worked by hourly personnel are inserted in the payroll sheet from time cards prepared by the employees and approved by the manager.

The weekly payroll sheets are sent to the home office along with other accounting statements and reports. The home office compiles employee earnings records and prepares all federal and state salary reports from the payroll sheets.

Salaries are established by home office job evaluation schedules. Salary adjustments, promotions, and transfers of full-time employees are approved by a home office salary committee based upon recommendations of branch managers and area supervisors. Branch managers advise the salary committee of new full-time employees and terminations. Part-time and temporary employees are hired without referral to the salary committee.

Instructions

You are to evaluate the company's payroll system, especially the internal control features, and then suggest five ways in which the branch managers might carry out payroll fraud.

Problem 11B-6
Recording payroll
and payroll taxes

The payroll records of Copper Kettle for the first week in January showed total salaries earned by employees of $12,000. This total included $7,000 of salaries to sales employees and $5,000 to office employees.

The amounts withheld from employees' pay consisted of FICA taxes computed at an assumed rate of 7.5%, federal income taxes of $1,150, and insurance premiums of $140.

Instructions

a Prepare a general journal entry to summarize the above payroll and the deductions from the earnings of employees. Payroll taxes on the employer are not to be included in this entry.

b Prepare a general journal entry to summarize the payroll taxes on the *employer* associated with the above payroll. Assumed tax rates are as follows: FICA tax of 7.5%, state unemployment tax of 5.4%, and a federal unemployment tax of .8%.

c What is the amount of the total payroll expense of Copper Kettle for the first week in January? Show computations.

Problem 11B-7
Employees'
earnings records:
payroll taxes

The employees' earnings records thus far in the current year for Data Services are as follows:

EMPLOYEE	CUMULATIVE EARNINGS	EMPLOYEE	CUMULATIVE EARNINGS
Arthur, D. S.	$14,322	Hamilton, A. J.	$16,771
Barnett, S. T.	21,868	Monday, M. D.	17,328
Darwin, E. G.	2,550	Saunders, K. U.	3,930
Greer, C. K.	6,167	Taylor, M. E.	47,265

FICA taxes are assumed to be 7.5% on the first $45,000 of an employee's gross earnings. The federal unemployment tax is assumed to be 6.2% of the first $7,000 of gross earnings, but with credit to the employer for a maximum of 5.4% of gross earnings for state unemployment taxes.

Instructions

a Prepare a schedule showing for each employee the cumulative earnings, the earnings subject to unemployment compensation tax, and the earnings subject to FICA taxes for the year to date. Columnar headings for the schedule should be as follows:

		EARNINGS SUBJECT TO	
EMPLOYEE	CUMULATIVE EARNINGS	UNEMPLOYMENT TAXES	FICA TAXES

b Compute the total payroll taxes *deducted* from the earnings of employees as a group for the year to date.

c Compute the total payroll taxes expense of Data Services and the percentage of total payroll ($130,201) represented by payroll taxes expense. (Round off to the nearest tenth of a percent.)

BUSINESS DECISION CASES

Case 11-1 Loss contingencies?

Discuss each of the following situations, indicating whether the situation is a loss contingency which should be recorded or disclosed in the financial statements of Aztec Airlines. If the situation is not a loss contingency, explain how (if at all) it should be reported in the company's financial statements. (Assume that all dollar amounts are material.)

a Aztec estimates that $100,000 of its accounts receivable will prove to be uncollectible.

b The company's president is in poor health and has previously suffered two heart attacks.

c As any airline, Aztec faces the risk that a future airplane crash could cause considerable loss.

d Aztec is being sued for $2 million for failing to adequately provide for passengers whose reservations were cancelled as a result of the airline overbooking certain flights. This suit will not be resolved for a year or more.

Case 11-2 Internal control over payrolls

The payroll procedures of Metals, Inc., a manufacturing concern with 80 factory employees, may be summarized as follows:

1 Applicants are interviewed and hired by Carl Olson, the factory superintendent. He obtains an employee's Withholding Allowance Certificate (a W-4 form) from each new employee and writes on it the hourly rate of pay to be used. The superintendent gives this certificate to a payroll clerk as notice that a new employee has been added.

2 When hourly pay rate changes are made, the superintendent advises the payroll clerk verbally of the new rate for the employee(s) affected.

3 Blank time cards are kept in a box at the factory entrance. On Mondays each employee takes a time card, writes in his or her name, and makes pencil notations during the week of hours of arrival and departure. At the end of the week, the employee returns the card to the box.

4 The completed cards are taken from the box on Monday mornings. Two payroll clerks divide the cards alphabetically between them; compute the gross pay, deductions, and net pay; post the information to the employees' individual earnings records; and prepare and number the payroll checks.

5 The payroll checks are signed by the chief accountant and given to the superintendent, who distributes them to employees and holds those for any absent employees.

6 The payroll bank account is reconciled by the chief accountant, who also prepares the quarterly and annual payroll tax reports.

Instructions

With the objective of improving the system of internal control over the hiring practices and payroll procedures of Metals, Inc., you are to recommend any basic changes needed in organization, equipment, forms, and procedures. Then list at least six specific hiring practices and payroll procedures which you believe should be instituted.

ANSWERS TO SELF-TEST QUESTIONS

1 a and b   **2** c   **3** d   **4** c   **5** a

Partnerships

In prior chapters we have used the sole proprietorship as a model in our study of basic accounting concepts. In this chapter we focus on the partnership and the accounting issues related to this form of business organization. Among these topics are the maintenance of a separate capital account for each partner, the equitable division of partnership income or loss among the partners, the admission and the withdrawal of individual partners, and finally the liquidation of a partnership business.

After studying this chapter you should be able to meet these Learning Objectives:

1 Describe the basic characteristics of a partnership.

2 Discuss the advantages and disadvantages of the partnership as a form of business organization.

3 Distinguish between a regular partnership and a limited partnership.

4 Account for the formation of a partnership.

5 Divide the net income of a partnership among the partners.

6 Account for the admission of a new partner, and the withdrawal of a partner.

7 Account for the liquidation of a partnership.

Three types of business organization are common to American business: the sole proprietorship, the partnership, and the corporation. Partnerships are a popular form of organization because they provide a convenient, inexpensive means of combining the capital and the special abilities of two or more persons. The partnership form of organization is widely used in all types of small business and also in the professions. The Uniform Partnership Act, which has been adopted by most states, defines a partnership as "an association of two or more persons to carry on, as co-owners, a business for profit." A partnership is often referred to as a *firm;* the name of the firm often includes the word "company," as, for example, "Adams, Barnes, and Company."

Significant Features of a Partnership

Before taking up the accounting problems peculiar to partnerships, it will be helpful to consider briefly some of the distinctive characteristics of the partnership form of organization. These characteristics (such as limited life and unlimited liability) all stem from the concept that a partnership is not a separate legal entity in itself but merely a voluntary association of individuals.

Objective 1
Describe the basic characteristics of a partnership.

■ **Ease of Formation** A partnership can be created without any legal formalities. When two or more persons agree to become partners, such agreement constitutes a contract and a partnership is automatically created. The contract should be in writing in order to lessen the chances for misunderstanding and future disagreement. The voluntary aspect of a partnership agreement means that no one can be forced into a partnership or forced to continue as a partner.

CASE IN POINT ■ Richard and Mike were friends and employees of the same large corporation. They became interested in forming a partnership to acquire a nearby small business being offered for sale for a down payment of $50,000. They felt that they could manage the business (which had two employees) in their spare time. Richard and Mike agreed that each would deposit $25,000 in a partnership bank account. There was no written agreement of partnership. Richard made his deposit from his personal savings; Mike had only $10,000 of his own but was able to obtain the other $15,000 from his brother-in-law, Joe, to whom he described the business with great enthusiasm. Mike then deposited $25,000 in the partnership bank account and the business was purchased. Richard had never met Joe and was not aware of his $15,000 investment.

A few months later, Joe became annoyed because he had received no return on his investment. He appeared suddenly at the business while Richard was there, stating that he was a partner and demanding to see the accounting records and the bank statements. Richard refused, and after an angry argument, Joe was forcibly ejected. The question of whether Joe was a "silent partner" caused bitter disagreement among all three of the principals. During this dispute, the business was forced to shut down because of lack of working capital. Richard, Mike, and Joe each retained an attorney to seek damages from the others.

Although a partnership may be at times a somewhat unstable form of organization, a written agreement of partnership might have avoided the problems encountered by Richard and Mike—and by Joe.

■ **Limited Life** A partnership may be ended at any time by the death or withdrawal of any member of the firm. Other factors which may bring an end to a partnership include the bankruptcy or incapacity of a partner, the expiration of the period specified in the partnership contract, or the completion of the project for which the partnership was formed. The admission of a new partner or the retirement of an existing member means an end to the old partnership, although the business may be continued by the formation of a new partnership.

■ **Mutual Agency**   Each partner acts as an agent of the partnership, with authority to enter into contracts for the purchase and sale of goods and services. The partnership is bound by the acts of any partner as long as these acts are within the scope of normal operations. The factor of mutual agency suggests the need for exercising great caution in the selection of a partner. To be in partnership with an irresponsible person or one lacking in integrity is an intolerable situation.

■ **Unlimited Liability**   Each partner is personally responsible for all the debts of the firm. The lack of any ceiling on the liability of a partner may deter a wealthy person from entering a partnership.

A new member joining an existing partnership may or may not assume liability for debts incurred by the firm prior to his or her admission. A partner withdrawing from membership must give adequate public notice of withdrawal; otherwise the former partner may be held liable for partnership debts incurred subsequent to his or her withdrawal. The retiring partner remains liable for partnership debts existing at the time of withdrawal unless the creditors agree to a release of this obligation.

■ **Co-ownership of Partnership Property and Profits**   When a partner invests a building, inventory, or other property in a partnership, he or she does not retain any personal right to the assets contributed. The property becomes jointly owned by all partners. Each member of a partnership also has an ownership right in the profits.

Advantages and Disadvantages of a Partnership

Objective 2
Discuss the advantages and disadvantages of the partnership as a form of business organization.

Perhaps the most important advantage of most partnerships is the opportunity to bring together sufficient capital to carry on a business. The opportunity to combine special skills, as, for example, the specialized talents of an engineer and an accountant, may also induce individuals to join forces in a partnership. To form a partnership is much easier and less expensive than to organize a corporation. Members of a partnership enjoy more freedom from government regulation and more flexibility of action than do the owners of a corporation. The partners may withdraw funds and make business decisions of all types without the necessity of formal meetings or legalistic procedures.

Operating as a partnership *may* in some cases produce income tax advantages as compared with doing business as a corporation. The partnership itself is not a legal entity and does not have to pay income taxes as does a corporation, although the individual partners pay taxes on their respective shares of the firm's income.

Offsetting these advantages of a partnership are such serious disadvantages as limited life, unlimited liability, and mutual agency. Furthermore, if a business is to require a large amount of capital, the partnership is a less effective device for raising funds than is a corporation. Many persons who invest freely in common stocks of corporations are unwilling to enter a partnership because of the unlimited liability imposed on partners.

Limited Partnerships

In recent years a number of businesses have been organized as "limited partnerships." This form of organization is widely used for businesses which provide tax sheltered income to investors, such as real estate syndications and oil

Objective 3
Distinguish
between a
regular
partnership and a
limited
partnership.

drilling ventures. However, limited partnerships are **not** appropriate for businesses in which the owners intend to be active managers. Recent tax legislation has also reduced greatly the income tax advantages formerly available to investors in limited partnerships.

A limited partnership must have at least one **general partner** as well as one or more **limited partners.** The general partners are partners in the traditional sense, with unlimited liability for the debts of the business and the right to make managerial decisions. The limited partners, however, are basically **investors** rather than traditional partners. They have the right to participate in profits of the business, but their liability for losses is limited to the amount of their investment. Also, limited partners do not actively participate in management of the business. Thus, the concepts of unlimited liability and mutual agency apply only to the general partners in a limited partnership.

In this chapter, we emphasize the characteristics and accounting practices of conventional partnerships rather than limited partnerships. Limited partnerships are discussed in depth in courses on business law and federal income taxes.

The Partnership Contract

Although a partnership can be formed by an oral agreement, it is highly desirable that a written partnership agreement be prepared, summarizing the partners' mutual understanding on such points as:

1 Names of the partners

2 The duties and rights of each partner, effective the specified date of formation of the partnership

3 Amount to be invested by each partner, including the procedure for valuing any noncash assets invested or withdrawn by partners

4 Methods of sharing profits and losses

5 Withdrawals to be allowed each partner

Partnership Accounting

As mentioned earlier in this chapter, a partnership **does not** constitute a **legal** entity with an identity separate from its owners. However, from a record-keeping and reporting point of view, a partnership does constitute a **separate and distinct accounting entity.**

An adequate accounting system and an accurate measurement of income are needed by every business, but they are especially important in a partnership because the net income is divided among two or more owners. Each partner needs current, accurate information on profits so that he or she can make intelligent decisions on such questions as additional investments, expansion of the business, or sale of an interest in the partnership.

CASE IN POINT ■ Rowe and Davis were partners in an automobile dealership and auto repair shop. Rowe was the active manager of the business, but Davis had supplied nearly all the capital. Aware that the firm was quite profitable, Rowe devised a scheme to become the sole owner by buying out his partner. In order to persuade Davis to sell his interest at a bargain price, Rowe deliberately began falsifying the accounting records and financial statements in a manner to understate the earnings of the business. Much of the revenue from auto repair work was not recorded at all; depreciation expense was overstated; ending inventories were understated; and the cost of new items of plant and equipment were charged to expense. The result was a series of monthly income statements which showed the business operating at a larger loss each month. Faced with these discouraging financial statements, Davis became pessimistic over the prospects for the business and was on the verge of selling his interest to Rowe at a price far below the balance in his capital account.

However, a friend suggested that before selling out, Davis should insist upon an audit of the business by a CPA firm. An audit was performed and revealed that the business was in fact highly profitable. When confronted by Davis with the auditors' findings, Rowe withdrew from the partnership and Davis became the sole owner.

Opening the Accounts of a New Partnership

Objective 4
Account for the formation of a partnership.

When a partner contributes assets other than cash, a question always arises as to the value of such assets. The valuations assigned to noncash assets should be their *fair market values* at the date of transfer to the partnership. The valuations assigned must be agreed to by all partners.

To illustrate the opening entries for a newly formed partnership, assume that on January 1 Joan Blair and Richard Cross, who operate competing retail stores, decide to form a partnership by consolidating their two businesses. A capital account will be opened for each partner and credited with the agreed valuation of the *net assets* (total assets less total liabilities) that the partner contributes. The journal entries to open the accounts of the partnership of Blair and Cross are as follows:

Entries for formation of partnership

Cash	40,000	
Accounts Receivable	60,000	
Inventory	90,000	
Accounts Payable		30,000
Joan Blair, Capital		160,000
To record the investment by Joan Blair in the partnership of Blair and Cross.		
Cash	10,000	
Inventory	60,000	
Land	60,000	
Building	100,000	
Accounts Payable		70,000
Richard Cross, Capital		160,000
To record the investment by Richard Cross in the partnership of Blair and Cross.		

Partnership accounting is similar to that in a sole proprietorship, except that separate capital and drawing accounts are maintained for each partner. These capital and drawing accounts show for each partner the amounts invested, the amounts withdrawn, and the appropriate share of partnership net income. In brief, each partner is provided with a history of his or her equity in the firm.

The values assigned to assets in the accounts of the new partnership may be quite different from the amounts at which these assets were carried in the accounts of their previous owners. For example, the land contributed by Cross and valued at $60,000 might have appeared in his accounting records at a cost of $20,000. The building which he contributed was valued at $100,000 by the partnership, but it might have cost Cross only $80,000 some years ago and might have been depreciated on his records to a net value of $60,000. Assuming that market values of land and buildings had risen sharply while Cross owned this property, it is only fair to recognize the *current market value* of these assets at the time he transfers them to the partnership and to credit his capital account accordingly. Depreciation of the building in the partnership accounts will be based on the assigned value of $100,000 at the date of acquisition by the partnership.

Additional Investments

Assume that after six months of operation the firm is in need of more cash, and the partners make an additional investment of $10,000 each on July 1. These additional investments are credited to the capital accounts as shown below:

Entry for additional investment

Cash...	*20,000*	
* Joan Blair, Capital...*		*10,000*
* Richard Cross, Capital..*		*10,000*
To record additional investments.		

Drawing Accounts

The drawing account maintained for each partner serves the same purpose as the drawing account of the owner of a sole proprietorship. The transactions calling for debits to the drawing accounts of partners may be summarized as follows:

1 Cash or other assets withdrawn by a partner

2 Payments from partnership funds of the personal debts of a partner

3 Partnership cash collected on behalf of the firm by a partner but retained by the partner personally

Loans from Partners

Ordinarily any funds furnished to the firm by a partner are recorded by crediting that partner's capital account. Occasionally, however, a partnership may be in need of funds but the partners do not wish to increase their permanent capital investment in the business, or perhaps one partner is willing to advance funds when the others are not. Under these circumstances, the advance of funds may be designated as a loan from the partner and credited to a partner's loan account. Partnership liabilities to outsiders always take precedence over any loans from partners.

Closing the Accounts of a Partnership at Year-End

At the end of the accounting period, the balance in the Income Summary account is closed into the partners' capital accounts. The profits or losses of a partnership may be divided among the partners in ***any manner agreed upon*** by the partners. However, this agreement should be carefully explained in the partnership contract. In the event that the partners ***do not*** have a formal profit-and-loss sharing agreement, the law requires all profits or losses to be ***divided equally*** among the partners.

In our illustration, let us assume that Blair and Cross have agreed to share profits equally. (We will discuss other profit-and-loss sharing arrangements later in this chapter.) Assuming that the partnership earns net income of $60,000 in the first year of operations, the entry to close the Income Summary account is as follows:

Closing income summary: profits shared equally

Income Summary	60,000	
Joan Blair, Capital		30,000
Richard Cross, Capital		30,000

To divide net income for the year in accordance with partnership agreement to share profits equally.

The next step in closing the accounts is to transfer the balance of each partner's drawing account to his capital account. Assuming that withdrawals during the year amounted to $24,000 for Blair and $16,000 for Cross, the entry at December 31 to close the drawing accounts is as follows:

Closing the drawing accounts to capital accounts

Joan Blair, Capital	24,000	
Richard Cross, Capital	16,000	
Joan Blair, Drawing		24,000
Richard Cross, Drawing		16,000

To transfer debit balances in partners' drawing accounts to their respective capital accounts.

■ **Income Statement for a Partnership**   The income statement for a partnership differs from that of a sole proprietorship in only one respect: a final section may be added to show the division of the net income between the partners, as illustrated below for the firm of Blair and Cross. The income statement of a partnership is consistent with that of a sole proprietorship in showing no income taxes expense and no salaries expense relating to services rendered by partners.

BLAIR AND CROSS
Income Statement
For the Year Ended December 31, 19___

Note distribution of net income

Sales		$600,000
Cost of goods sold:		
Inventory, Jan. 1	$150,000	
Purchases	460,000	
Cost of goods available for sale.................................	$610,000	
Less: Inventory, Dec. 31	210,000	
Cost of goods sold		400,000
Gross profit on sales		$200,000
Operating expenses:		
Selling expenses	$100,000	
General & administrative expenses	40,000	140,000
Net income		$ 60,000
Division of net income:		
To Joan Blair (50%)...	$ 30,000	
To Richard Cross (50%)	30,000	$ 60,000

■ **Statement of Partners' Capital** The partners will usually want an explanation of the change in their capital accounts from one year-end to the next. A supplementary schedule called a ***statement of partners' capital*** is prepared to show this information. A statement of partners' capital for Blair and Cross appears below:

BLAIR AND CROSS
Statement of Partners' Capital
For the Year Ended December 31, 19___

Changes in capital accounts during the year

	BLAIR	CROSS	TOTAL
Balances, Jan. 1, 19	$160,000	$160,000	$320,000
Add: Additional investments	10,000	10,000	20,000
Net income for the year	30,000	30,000	60,000
Subtotals	$200,000	$200,000	$400,000
Less: Drawings......................................	24,000	16,000	40,000
Balances, Dec. 31, 19___	$176,000	$184,000	$360,000

The balance sheet of Blair and Cross would show the capital balance for each partner, as well as the total capital of $360,000.

Partnership Profits and Income Taxes

■ **Partnerships Are Not Required to Pay Income Taxes** However, a partnership is required to file an information tax return showing the amount of the partnership net income, and the share of each partner in the net income. Partners must include their shares of the partnership profit (after certain technical adjustments) on their individual income tax returns. Partnership net income is thus taxable to the partners individually in the year in which it is earned. The income tax rules applicable to investment in a partnership are quite complex; those complexities are appropriate to advanced accounting courses.

Note that partners report and pay tax on their respective shares of the net income earned by the partnership during the year and *not* on the amounts which they have drawn out of the business during the year. ***The net income of the partnership is taxable to the partners each year,*** even though there may have been no withdrawals. This treatment is consistent with that accorded a sole proprietorship.

The Nature of Partnership Profits

Profits earned by partnerships, like those earned by sole proprietorships, compensate the owners for (1) personal services rendered to the business, (2) capital invested in the business, and (3) "entrepreneurial risk"—that is, taking the risk that the investments of personal services and of capital may be lost if the business is unsuccessful. Recognition of these three factors is helpful in developing an equitable plan for the division of partnership profits.

If one partner devotes full time to the business while another devotes little or no time, the difference in the partners' contributions of time and effort should be reflected in the profit-sharing agreement. If one partner possesses special skills, the profit-sharing agreement should reward this partner's talent. Also, partners may each provide different amounts of capital to the business entity. Again, the differences in the value of the partners' contributions to the business should be reflected in the profit-and-loss sharing agreement.

To recognize the particular contributions of each partner to the business, partnership profit-and-loss sharing agreements often include "salary allowances" to partners, and "interest" on the balances of partners' capital accounts. These "salaries" and "interest" are *not expenses* of the business; rather, they are ***steps in the computation made to divide partnership net income among the partners.***

In the preceding illustrations of the partnership of Blair and Cross, we assumed that the partners invested equal amounts of capital, rendered equal services, and divided net income equally. We are now ready to consider cases in which the partners invest ***unequal*** amounts of capital and services.

Dividing Partnership Net Income among the Partners

Partners can share net income or loss in any manner they decide upon; however, most profit-sharing agreements fall under one of the following types:

Objective 5
Divide the net income of a partnership among the partners

1 A fixed ratio. The fixed ratio method has already been illustrated in the example of the Blair and Cross partnership in which profits were shared equally, that is, 50% and 50%. Partners may agree upon any fixed ratio such as 60% and 40%, or 70% and 30%.

2 Salary allowances to the partners, with remaining net income or loss divided in a fixed ratio.

3 Interest allowances on partners' capital balances, with remaining net income or loss divided in a fixed ratio.

4 Salary allowances to the partners, interest allowances on partners' capital balances, and remaining net income or loss divided in a fixed ratio.

All these methods of sharing partnership net income are intended to recognize differences in the personal services rendered by partners and in the amounts of capital invested in the firm. For example, if one partner invests twice as much capital as another, this needs to be considered in the plan for sharing profits. If one partner works full time in the business and the other only half time, this difference can be compensated for by setting different salary allowances. Different salary allowances are also reasonable when one partner is more experienced or has a special skill not possessed by other partners.

In the illustrations which follow, it is assumed that beginning balances in the partners' capital accounts were Brooke Adams, $160,000, and Ben Barnes, $40,000. At year-end, the Income Summary account showed a credit balance of $96,000, representing the net income for the year before any partners' salaries or interest on capital account balances.

■ **Salaries to Partners, with Remainder in a Fixed Ratio** Because partners often contribute different amounts of personal services, partnership agreements often provide for partners' salaries as a factor in the division of profits.

For example, assume that Adams and Barnes agree to annual salary allowances of $24,000 for Adams and $48,000 for Barnes. These salaries, which total $72,000 per year, are agreed upon by the partners in advance. Of course, the net income of the business is not likely to be exactly $72,000 in a given year. Therefore, the profit-and-loss sharing agreement should also specify a fixed ratio for dividing any profit or loss remaining after giving consideration to the agreed-upon salary allowances. We will assume that Adams and Barnes agree to divide any remaining profit or loss equally.

The division of the $96,000 in partnership net income between Adams and Barnes is illustrated in the schedule shown below. The first step is to allocate to each partner his or her agreed-upon salary allowance. This step allocates $72,000 of the partnership net income. The remaining $24,000 is then divided in the agreed-upon fixed ratio (50-50 in this example).

Division of Net Income

Profit sharing; salary allowances and remainder in a fixed ratio

	ADAMS	BARNES	NET INCOME
Net income to be divided			*$96,000*
Salary allowances to partners.....................	*$24,000*	*$48,000*	*(72,000)*
Remaining income after salary allowances			*$24,000*
Allocated in a fixed ratio:			
Adams (50%)...................................	*12,000*		
Barnes (50%)..................................		*12,000*	*(24,000)*
Total share to each partner	*$36,000*	*$60,000*	*$ –0–*

Under this agreement, Adams' share of the $96,000 profit amounts to $36,000 and Barnes' share amounts to $60,000. The entry to close the Income Summary account would be:

Income Summary	*96,000*	
Brooke Adams, Capital		*36,000*
Ben Barnes, Capital		*60,000*

To close the Income Summary account by crediting each partner
with agreed upon salary allowance and dividing the remaining
profits equally.

The "salary allowances" used in dividing partnership net income are sometimes misinterpreted, even by the partners. These salary allowances are merely an agreed-upon device for dividing net income; they are *not expenses* of the business and are *not recorded in any ledger account.* A partner is considered an owner of the business, not an employee. Therefore, the services that a partner renders to the firm are assumed to be rendered in anticipation of earning a share of the profits, not a salary.

The amount of cash or other assets that a partner withdraws from the partnership may be greater than or less than the partner's salary allowance. Even if a partner decides to withdraw an amount of cash equal to his or her "salary allowance," the withdrawal should be recorded by debiting the partner's drawing account, *not by debiting an expense account.* Let us repeat the main point: *"salary allowances" to partners should not be recorded as expenses of the business.*[1]

Because of this treatment of salary allowances, the net income reported by a partnership will differ from the net income that would be reported if the business were organized as a corporation. Corporations do record as expenses any salaries paid to owners.[2]

■ Interest Allowances on Partners' Capital, with Remainder in a Fixed Ratio

Next we shall assume a business situation in which the partners spend very little time in the business and net income depends primarily on the amount of money invested. The profit-sharing plan then might emphasize invested capital as a basis for the first step in allocating income.

For example, assume that Adams and Barnes agree that both partners are to be allowed interest at *15%* on their beginning capital balances, with any remaining profit or loss to be divided equally. Net income to be divided is $96,000 and the beginning capital balances are Adams, *$160,000,* and Barnes, *$40,000.*

---

[1] Some exceptions to this general rule will be discussed in advanced accounting courses.
[2] The net income reported by a corporation also differs from that reported by an unincorporated business because the corporation is subject to income taxes on its earnings. Accounting practices of corporations are discussed in later chapters.

Division of Net Income

	ADAMS	BARNES	NET INCOME
Net income to be divided			$96,000
Interest allowances on beginning capital:			
Adams ($160,000 × 15%)........................	$24,000		
Barnes ($40,000 × 15%)		$ 6,000	
Total allocated as interest			(30,000)
Remaining income after interest on capital			$66,000
Allocated in a fixed ratio:			
Adams (50%)...................................	33,000		
Barnes (50%)...................................		33,000	(66,000)
Total share to each partner	$57,000	$39,000	$ –0–

The entry to close the Income Summary account in this example would be:

Income Summary...	96,000	
Brooke Adams, Capital		57,000
Ben Barnes, Capital		39,000

To close the Income Summary account by crediting each partner with interest at 15% on beginning capital and dividing the remaining profits equally.

Interest allowances on partners' capital, like partners' salary allowances, are computational devices used in dividing partnership net income. This "interest" is not recorded as an expense of the business.

■ **Salary Allowances, Interest on Capital, and Remainder in a Fixed Ratio** The preceding example took into consideration the difference in amounts of capital provided by Adams and Barnes but ignored any difference in personal services performed. In the next example, we shall assume that the partners agree to a profit-sharing plan providing for salaries and for interest on beginning capitals. Salary allowances, as before, are authorized at $24,000 for Adams and $48,000 for Barnes. Beginning capital balances are $160,000 for Adams and $40,000 for Barnes. Partners are to be allowed interest at 10% on their beginning capital balances, and any profit or loss remaining after authorized salary and interest allowances is to be divided equally.

Division of Net Income

	ADAMS	BARNES	NET INCOME
Net income to be divided			$96,000
Salary allowances to partners......................	$24,000	$48,000	(72,000)
Income after salary allowances			$24,000
Interest allowances on beginning capital:			
Adams ($160,000 × 10%).........................	16,000		
Barnes ($40,000 × 10%).........................		4,000	
Total allocated as interest			(20,000)
Remaining income after salary and interest allowances			$ 4,000
Allocated in a fixed ratio:			
Adams (50%).....................................	2,000		
Barnes (50%)....................................		2,000	(4,000)
Total share to each partner	$42,000	$54,000	$ –0–

Profit sharing; salaries, interest, and remainder in a fixed ratio

The journal entry to close the Income Summary account in this case will be:

Income Summary..	96,000	
Brooke Adams, Capital		42,000
Ben Barnes, Capital		54,000

To close the Income Summary account by crediting each partner with authorized salary, interest at 10% on beginning capital, and dividing the remaining profits equally.

■ Authorized Salary and Interest Allowance in Excess of Net Income

In the preceding example the total of the authorized salaries and interest was $92,000 and the net income to be divided was $96,000. Suppose that the net income had been only *$80,000;* how should the division have been made?

If the partnership contract provides for salaries and interest on invested capital, these provisions are to be followed even though the net income for the year is *less* than the total of the authorized salaries and interest. If the net income of the firm of Adams and Barnes amounted to only $80,000, this amount would be distributed as shown below:

Division of Net Income

	ADAMS	BARNES	NET INCOME
Net income to be divided			$ 80,000
Salary allowances to partners......................	$24,000	$48,000	(72,000)
Income after salary................................			$ 8,000
Interest allowances on beginning capital:			
Adams ($160,000 × 10%).........................	16,000		
Barnes ($40,000 × 10%).........................		4,000	
Total allocated as interest allowances			(20,000)
Residual loss after salary and			
interest allowances...............................			$(12,000)
Allocated in a fixed ratio:			
Adams (50%).....................................	(6,000)		
Barnes (50%)....................................		(6,000)	12,000
Total share to each partner	$34,000	$46,000	$ –0–

Authorized salary and interest allowances in excess of net income

Notice that after allowing for the specified partners' salaries and interest on partners' capital, the partnership has a residual *loss of $12,000.* Since the partnership contract states that any residual profit or loss is to be divided equally between Adams and Barnes, the entry to close the Income Summary account will be as follows:

Income Summary *80,000*
      Brooke Adams, Capital *34,000*
      Ben Barnes, Capital *46,000*
To close the Income Summary account by crediting each partner
with authorized salary and with interest on invested capital and
by dividing the residual loss equally.

Admission of a New Partner

Objective 6
Account for the admission of a new partner and the withdrawal of a partner.

An individual may gain admission to an existing partnership in either of two ways: (1) by buying an equity interest from one or more of the present partners, or (2) by making an investment in the partnership. When an incoming partner purchases an equity interest from a present member of the firm, the payment goes personally to the old partner, and there is no change in the assets or liabilities of the partnership. On the other hand, if the incoming partner acquires an equity interest by making an investment in the partnership, the assets of the firm are increased by the amount paid in by the new partner.

■ **By Purchase of an Interest**   When a new partner buys an equity interest from a present member of a partnership, the only change in the accounts will be a transfer from the capital account of the selling partner to the capital account of the incoming partner.

Assume, for example, that Pam Lee has an $80,000 equity interest in the partnership of Lee, Martin, and Nash. Lee arranges to sell her entire interest to Paul Trent for $100,000 cash. Partners Martin and Nash agree to the admission of Trent, and the transaction is recorded in the partnership accounts by the following entry:

■
Incoming partners buys interest from present partner

Pam Lee, Capital *80,000*
      Paul Trent, Capital *80,000*
To record the transfer of Pam Lee's equity interest to the
incoming partner, Paul Trent.

Note that the entry in the partnership accounts is for *$80,000,* the balance of Lee's capital account. The entry does *not* indicate the price paid by Trent to the retiring partner. The payment of $100,000 by Trent to Lee was a *personal transaction* between these two individuals; it does not affect the assets or liabilities of the partnership and, therefore, is *not* entered in the partnership accounting records.

As a separate but related example, assume that Trent is to gain admission to the firm of Lee, Martin, and Nash by purchasing one-fourth of the equity interest of each partner. The present capital accounts are as follows: Lee $80,000; Martin, $60,000; Nash, $100,000. Assume also that Trent makes payment directly to the old partners, *not to the partnership.* The amount paid to each existing partner for one-fourth of his or her equity interest is a privately negotiated matter, and the amounts of these payments are ***not*** recorded in the partnership records. The only entry required in the partnership accounting records is the following:

Pam Lee, Capital	*20,000*	
Pat Martin, Capital	*15,000*	
Tom Nash, Capital	*25,000*	
Paul Trent, Capital		*60,000*

This entry transfers to Paul Trent one-fourth of the balance formerly appearing in the capital accounts of each of the existing partners. The amounts actually paid to these partners by Trent are ***not recorded*** in the partnership accounts, because these payments did not flow into the partnership business entity. Thus, the transfer of ownership equity among the partners does not affect the assets, liabilities, or ***total*** partners' equity in the business.

■ **By Investing in the Firm**   Now let us assume that an incoming partner acquires his or her equity by making an investment directly into the firm. In this case the payment by the new partner goes to the partnership and not to the partners as individuals; the investment therefore increases the partnership assets and also the total owners' equity of the firm.

Assume that Ann Phillips and Judy Ryan are partners, each having a capital account of $100,000. They agree to admit Bart Smith to a one-half interest in the business upon his investment of $200,000 in cash. The entry to record the admission of Smith would be as follows:

■
Investment in business by new partner

Cash	*200,000*	
Bart Smith, Capital		*200,000*
To record the admission of Bart Smith to a one-half interest in the firm.		

Although Smith has a one-half equity interest in the net assets of the new firm of Phillips, Ryan, and Smith, he is not necessarily entitled to receive one-half of the profits. Profit sharing is a matter for agreement among the partners; if the new partnership contract contains no mention of profit sharing, the assumption is that the three partners intended to share profits and losses equally.

■ **Allowing a Bonus to Former Partners**   If an existing partnership has exceptionally high earnings year after year, the present partners may demand a ***bonus*** as a condition for admission of a new partner. In other words, to acquire an interest of, say, $80,000, the incoming partner may be required to invest $120,000 in the partnership. The excess investment of $40,000 may be regarded as a bonus to the old partners and credited to their capital accounts in the established ratio for profit sharing.

To illustrate the recording of a bonus to the old partners, let us assume that Janet Rogers and Richard Steel are members of a highly successful partnership. Their partnership agreement calls for profits and losses to be divided 60% to Rogers and 40% to Steel. As a result of profitable operations, the partners' capital accounts have doubled within a few years and presently stand at

$100,000 each. David Taylor desires to join the firm and offers to invest $100,000 for a one-third interest. Rogers and Steel refuse this offer but extend a counteroffer to Taylor of $120,000 for a one-fourth interest in the capital of the firm and a one-fourth interest in profits. Taylor accepts these terms because of his desire to share in the unusually large profits of the business. The recording of Taylor's admission to the partnership is based on the following calculations:

Calculation of bonus to old partners	Net assets (owners' equity) of old partnership	$200,000
	Cash investment by Taylor	120,000
	Net assets (owners' equity) of new partnership	$320,000
	Taylor's one-fourth interest	$ 80,000

To acquire an interest of $80,000 in the net assets of $320,000, Taylor has invested $120,000. His *excess investment* or *bonus* of $40,000 will be allocated 60% to Rogers ($24,000) and 40% to Steel ($16,000), in accordance with the profit-sharing arrangement in effect prior to Taylor's admission.

The entry to record Taylor's admission to the partnership follows:

Recording bonus to old partners	Cash	120,000	
	David Taylor, Capital		80,000
	Janet Rogers, Capital		24,000
	Richard Steel, Capital		16,000

To record admission of David Taylor as a partner with a one-fourth interest in capital and profits.

The total capital of the new partnership is now $320,000, in which Taylor has a one-fourth interest ($80,000). Rogers' capital account is $124,000 and Steel's capital account is $116,000 after admission of Taylor. Although in this case Taylor was also granted a one-fourth share of future partnership profits, *the equity interest and the profit-sharing ratio of a partner are not necessarily the same.* Old partners Rogers and Steel will set a new profit-sharing arrangement for the remaining 75% of profits to be divided between themselves.

■ **Allowing a Bonus to New Partner**   An existing partnership may sometimes be very anxious to bring in a new partner who can bring needed cash to the firm. In other instances the new partner may possess special talents or may have advantageous business contacts that will add to the profitability of the partnership. Under either of these sets of circumstances, the old partners may offer the new member a bonus in the form of a capital account larger than the amount of the incoming partner's investment.

Assume, for example, that John Bryan and Merle Davis are partners in an existing partnership. Their partnership agreement calls for partnership profits and losses to be divided 70% to Bryan and 30% to Davis. Capital account balances are presently $120,000 for Bryan and $100,000 for Davis. Since the firm is in desperate need of cash, they offer to admit Kay Grant to a one-third equity interest in the firm upon her investment of only $80,000 in cash. The recording of Grant's admission to the partnership is based on the following calculations:

Total capital of old partnership:

John Bryan, capital	$120,000	
Merle Davis, capital	100,000	$220,000
Cash invested by Kay Grant		80,000
Total capital of new three-member partnership		$300,000
Grant's one-third interest		$100,000

To acquire an equity interest of $100,000 in the new partnership's net assets of $300,000, Grant has invested only $80,000. The $20,000 excess allocated to Grant's capital account is a bonus to Grant from the existing partners, Bryan and Davis. A bonus granted to a new partner is charged to the old partners' capital accounts according to the profit-sharing arrangement in effect *prior to* admission of the new partner.

The following journal entry records the admission of Grant to a one-third equity interest in the business, with allowance of the $20,000 bonus to Grant from the two old partners:

■
Entry for bonus to new partner

Cash...	80,000	
John Bryan, Capital	14,000	
Merle Davis, Capital	6,000	
Kay Grant, Capital...		100,000

To record admission of Grant to a one-third interest, and the allowance of a $20,000 bonus to Grant: 70% from Bryan and 30% from Davis.

Withdrawal of a Partner

To illustrate the withdrawal or retirement of a partner, assume the following data for the partnership of Acres, Bundy, and Coe:

	CAPITAL ACCOUNT	SHARE OF PROFITS
Chris Acres	$ 75,000	20%
Brit Bundy	125,000	30%
John Coe	100,000	50%
Total partners' capital	$300,000	

We will use this data to illustrate the retirement of Coe and the treatment accorded the partners' capital accounts under several different assumptions.

■ **Coe Sells His Interest to Someone Else** The simplest case is when Coe, with the consent of Acres and Bundy, sells his equity in the business to a new partner. In this case, the payment by the incoming partner goes directly to Coe, and there is *no change* in the assets or liabilities of the partnership. Regardless of the price received by Coe, the only entry required in the partnership accounts is to transfer the $100,000 balance in Coe's capital account into the capital account of the new partner. This transaction is virtually the same as the one described on page 467 for the admission of a new partner by purchase of an interest.

Now let us change this situation slightly and assume that Coe sells equal amounts of his equity in the business to his fellow partners, Acres and Bundy. If Acres and Bundy pay Coe from their *personal funds,* the assets and liabilities of the partnership are again unchanged. Regardless of the price Acres and Bundy pay to Coe, the transaction is recorded in the partnership accounting records merely by transferring the $100,000 in Coe's capital account into the capital accounts of the remaining two partners, as follows:

■
**Notice there is
no change in
total capital**

John Coe, Capital	*100,000*	
Chris Acres, Capital		*50,000*
Brit Bundy, Capital		*50,000*
To record the sale of Coe's interest in equal portions to Acres and Bundy.		

■ **Coe's Interest Is Purchased by the Partnership**   Now let us assume that the partnership pays Coe in cash for his equity in the business. (The distribution of assets other than cash to a retiring partner will be discussed in advanced accounting courses.) If the partnership pays Coe exactly $100,000 cash for his equity—an amount equal to the balance in his capital account—the entry is simple: debit Coe's capital account $100,000 and credit cash $100,000. However, the payment to Coe may be greater or less than the balance in his capital account.

■ **Partnership Pays Coe More Than the Balance in His Capital Account**   A partner withdrawing from a partnership naturally expects to receive an amount for his or her equity that reflects the *current market value* of the partnership's net assets. Often, current market values exceed the book values appearing in the firm's balance sheet. For example, assets such as real estate may have appreciated greatly in value since they were acquired by the business. Also, if the business has been successful, it may have developed *un-recorded goodwill.*[3] Thus, the settlement paid to a retiring partner often is greater than the balance in that partner's capital account.

An amount paid to a retiring partner in excess of the balance in his or her capital account is treated as a *bonus to the withdrawing partner* and comes out of the capital accounts of the continuing partners. This bonus is charged against (debited to) the continuing partners' capital accounts in proportion to their *relative* profit- and loss-sharing ratio.

The term *relative profit-sharing ratio* describes the relationship between the profit- and loss-sharing ratios of the continuing partners, excluding the share formerly received by the retiring partner. The relative profit- and loss-sharing ratio of each continuing partner is computed by the following formula:

$$\frac{\text{Percentage formerly received by this partner}}{\text{Total percentage formerly received by all continuing partners}}$$

Based upon this formula, the relative profit- and loss-sharing ratios of Acres and Bundy are as follows:

Acres (20% ÷ 50%)	*40%*
Bundy (30% ÷ 50%)	*60%*

[3] As discussed in Chapter 10, goodwill is recorded only when it is purchased.

Assume now that Coe receives *$140,000* in cash from the partnership in full settlement of his equity in the firm. As Coe's capital account has a balance of only $100,000, he is receiving a *$40,000 bonus* from Acres and Bundy. This bonus is charged against the capital accounts of Acres and Bundy in relation to their relative profit- and loss-sharing ratios (Acres, 40%; Bundy, 60%). Thus, Coe's withdrawal from the firm is recorded as follows:

Bonus paid to withdrawing partner

John Coe, Capital (retiring partner)	*100,000*	
Chris Acres, Capital	*16,000*	
Brit Bundy, Capital	*24,000*	
Cash		*140,000*

To record the withdrawal of partner Coe, and payment of his capital account plus a bonus of $40,000. Bonus charged 40% to Acres, 60% to Bundy.

■ **Partnership Pays Coe Less Than the Balance in His Capital Account** Now assume that Coe is willing to accept a cash payment of *only $80,000* in full settlement of his $100,000 capital account. This situation might arise if, for example, Coe has a pressing need for cash, or the future of the firm is jeopardized by loss contingencies not yet recorded in its balance sheet accounts. In our example, the continuing partners' equity in the firm will *increase* by a total of $20,000 as a result of Coe's withdrawal. Acres and Bundy should divide this *"bonus to the continuing partners"* in their relative profit- and loss-sharing ratios. The entry is:

Payment to withdrawing partner of less than book equity

John Coe, Capital	*100,000*	
Cash		*80,000*
Chris Acres		*8,000*
Brit Bundy		*12,000*

To record the withdrawal of Coe, and settlement in full for $20,000 less than the balance of his capital account. Bonus to continuing partners allocated 40% to Acres, 60% to Bundy.

Death of a Partner

A partnership is dissolved by the death of any member. To determine the amount owing to the estate of the deceased partner, it is usually necessary to close the accounts and prepare financial statements. This serves to credit all partners with their individual shares of the net income earned during the fractional accounting period ending with the date of *dissolution.*

The partnership agreement may prescribe procedures for making settlement with the estate of a deceased partner. Such procedures often include an audit by certified public accountants, appraisal of assets, and computation of goodwill. If payment to the estate must be delayed, the amount owed should be carried in a liability account replacing the deceased partner's capital account.

■ **Insurance on Lives of Partners** Members of a partnership often obtain life insurance policies which name the partnership as the beneficiary. Upon the death of a partner, the cash collected from the insurance company is used to pay the estate of the deceased partner. In the absence of insurance on the lives of partners, there might be insufficient cash available to pay the deceased partner's estate without disrupting the operation of the business.

Liquidation of a Partnership

Objective 7
Account for the liquidation of a partnership.

A partnership is terminated or dissolved whenever a new partner is added or an old partner withdraws. The termination or dissolution of a partnership, however, does not necessarily indicate that the business is to be discontinued. Often the business continues with scarcely any outward evidence of the change in membership of the firm. Termination of a partnership indicates a change in the membership of the firm, which may or may not be followed by liquidation.

The process of breaking up and discontinuing a partnership business is called *liquidation.* Liquidation of a partnership spells an end to the business. If the business is to be discontinued, the assets will be sold, the liabilities paid, and the remaining cash distributed to the partners.

■ **Sale of the Business**   The partnership of Royal, Simms, and Tate sells its business to the North Corporation. The balance sheet appears as follows:

ROYAL, SIMMS, AND TATE
Balance Sheet
December 31, 19__

■
Partnership at time of sale

Cash...........................	$ 50,000	Accounts payable	$100,000
Inventory......................	200,000	Ann Royal, capital	140,000
Other assets	150,000	Ed Simms, capital	120,000
		Jon Tate, capital	40,000
Total	$400,000	Total	$400,000

The terms of sale provide that the inventory and other assets will be sold to the North Corporation for a consideration of $230,000, a price resulting in a loss of $120,000. The liabilities will not be transferred to North Corporation, but will be paid by the partnership out of existing cash plus the proceeds of the sale, prior to any distribution of cash to the partners. The entry to record the sale of the inventory and other assets to North Corporation is:

■
Entry to record the sale of the business

Cash..	230,000	
Loss on Sale of Business	120,000	
Inventory..		200,000
Other Assets		150,000
To record the sale of all assets other than cash to North Corporation.		

■ **Division of the Gain or Loss from Sale of the Business**   The gain or loss from the sale of the business must be divided among the partners in the agreed profit- and loss-sharing ratio *before* any cash is distributed to them. The amount of cash to which each partner is entitled in liquidation cannot be determined until each capital account has been increased or decreased by the proper share of the gain or loss on disposal of the assets. Assuming that Royal, Simms, and Tate share profits and losses equally, the entry to allocate the $120,000 loss on the sale of the business will be as follows:

Entry to divide loss on sale

Ann Royal, Capital..	40,000	
Ed Simms, Capital..	40,000	
Jon Tate, Capital	40,000	
Loss on Sale of Business		120,000

*To divide the loss on the sale of the business among the partners
in the established ratio for sharing profits and losses.*

■ **Distribution of Cash** The balance sheet of Royal, Simms, and Tate appears as follows after the loss on the sale of the assets has been entered in the partners' capital accounts:

ROYAL, SIMMS, AND TATE
Balance Sheet
(After the Sale of All Assets Except Cash)

Balance sheet after sale of assets

Cash..........................	$280,000	Accounts payable	$100,000
		Ann Royal, capital	100,000
		Ed Simms, capital	80,000
		Jon Tate, capital	–0–
Total..........................	$280,000	Total..........................	$280,000

The creditors must be paid in full before cash is distributed to the partners. The sequence of entries will be as follows:

(1) Pay creditors

Accounts Payable	100,000	
Cash..		100,000

To pay the creditors in full.

(2) Pay partners

Ann Royal, Capital..	100,000	
Ed Simms, Capital..	80,000	
Cash..		180,000

*To complete liquidation of the business by distributing the remaining
cash to the partners according to the balances in their capital accounts.*

Note that the equal division of the $120,000 loss on the sale of the business reduced the capital account of Jon Tate to zero; therefore, Tate received nothing when the cash was distributed to the partners. This action is consistent with the original agreement of the partners to share profits and losses equally. In working partnership liquidation problems, accounting students sometimes make the error of dividing the cash among the partners in the profit- and loss-sharing ratio. A profit- and loss-sharing ratio means just what the name indicates; it is a ratio for sharing profits and losses, ***not a ratio for sharing cash or any other asset.*** The amount of cash which a partner should receive in liquidation will be indicated by the balance in his or her capital account ***after*** the gain or loss from the disposal of assets has been divided among the partners in the agreed ratio for sharing profits and losses.

■ **Treatment of Debit Balance in a Capital Account** To illustrate this situation, let us change our assumptions concerning the sale of the assets by the firm of Royal, Simms, and Tate, and say that the loss incurred on the sale of assets was *$144,000* rather than the *$120,000* previously illustrated. Tate's one-third share of a $144,000 loss would be $48,000, which would wipe out the $40,000 credit balance in his capital account and create an *$8,000 debit balance*. After the liabilities had been paid, a balance sheet for the partnership would appear as follows:

ROYAL, SIMMS, AND TATE
Balance Sheet
(After the Sale of All Assets Except Cash)

<table>
<tr><td>**Tate now owes $8,000 to the partnership** ■</td><td>Cash............................</td><td align="right">$156,000</td><td>Ann Royal, capital ....</td><td align="right">$ 92,000</td></tr>
<tr><td></td><td></td><td></td><td>Ed Simms, capital ....</td><td align="right">72,000</td></tr>
<tr><td></td><td></td><td></td><td>Jon Tate, capital (deficiency)...</td><td align="right">(8,000)</td></tr>
<tr><td></td><td>Total ....</td><td align="right">$156,000</td><td>Total ....</td><td align="right">$156,000</td></tr>
</table>

To eliminate the debit balance in his capital account, Tate should pay $8,000 to the partnership. If Tate makes this payment, the balance in his capital account will become zero, and the cash on hand will be increased to $164,000, which is just enough to pay Royal and Simms the balances shown in their capital accounts.

If Tate is unable to pay the $8,000 due to the firm, how should the $156,000 of cash on hand be divided between Royal and Simms, whose capital accounts stand at $92,000 and $72,000, respectively? Failure of Tate to pay in the debit balance means an additional loss to Royal and Simms; according to the original partnership agreement, Royal and Simms have equal profit- and loss-sharing ratios. Therefore, each must absorb $4,000 additional loss resulting from Tate's inability to pay the $8,000 due to the partnership.[4] The $156,000 of cash on hand should be divided between Royal and Simms in such a manner that the capital account of each will be paid down to $4,000, their respective shares of the additional loss. The journal entry to record this distribution of cash to Royal and Simms is as follows:

<table>
<tr><td>**Entry to record distribution of cash on hand** ■</td><td>Ann Royal, Capital...</td><td align="right">88,000</td><td></td></tr>
<tr><td></td><td>Ed Simms, Capital...</td><td align="right">68,000</td><td></td></tr>
<tr><td></td><td>   Cash...</td><td></td><td align="right">156,000</td></tr>
</table>

To divide the remaining cash by paying down the capital accounts
of Royal and Simms to a balance of $4,000 each, representing
the division of Tate's loss between them.

After this entry has been posted, the only accounts still open in the partnership records will be the capital accounts of the three partners. A trial balance of the ledger will appear as follows:

▬▬▬▬▬▬

[4] If the profit- and loss-sharing ratios of Royal and Simms were not equal, the $8,000 loss would be absorbed by Royal and Simms according to their *relative* profit- and loss-sharing ratios. The computation of each partner's share of the additional loss would be similar to the allocation of the bonus paid by or received by remaining partners illustrated on page 472.

ROYAL, SIMMS, AND TATE
Trial Balance
(After Distribution of Cash)

Trial balance after cash distribution

Ann Royal, capital		$4,000
Ed Simms, capital		4,000
Jon Tate, capital (deficiency)	$8,000	
	$8,000	$8,000

If Tate is later able to pay in the $8,000 debit balance, Royal and Simms will then receive the additional $4,000 each indicated by the credit balances in their accounts. If Tate is not able to make good the debit balance, the distribution of cash to Royal and Simms will have been equitable under the circumstances.

End-of-Chapter Review

CONCEPTS INTRODUCED OR EMPHASIZED IN CHAPTER 12

The major concepts introduced in this chapter are:

■ The significant characteristics of a partnership, and the advantages and disadvantages of this form of business entity.

■ The vital role of a partnership contract in clarifying the rights and responsibilities of each partner.

■ Techniques of dividing partnership net income or net loss among the partners in an equitable manner.

■ Accounting for the admission of a new partner, either by the new partner purchasing an interest from the existing partners or investing assets directly into the partnership.

■ Accounting for the withdrawal of a partner, including payments to the retiring partner that are greater or smaller than the balance of that partner's capital acount.

■ Accounting for the liquidation of a partnership and the distribution of cash to the partners.

This chapter completes our discussion of accounting for unincorporated businesses—that is, sole proprietorships and partnerships. Beginning with Chapter 14, we will shift our emphasis to the special accounting problems of businesses organized as corporations. Now, however, you are probably approaching the end of the first semester in accounting. Therefore, in Chapter 13 we will pause and review the accounting concepts introduced in the first half of this textbook. These concepts also serve as the foundation for many topics that will be introduced in later chapters.

KEY TERMS INTRODUCED OR EMPHASIZED IN CHAPTER 12

Dissolution (of a partnership) Termination of an existing partnership by any change in the personnel of the partners or by liquidating the business.

General partner   A partner in a limited partnership who has the traditional rights and responsibilities of a partner, including mutual agency and unlimited personal liability for the debts of the business.

Limited partner   A partner in a limited partnership who has the right to participate in profits, but whose liability for losses is limited to the amount he or she has invested and who does not have the right to participate in management of the business. A limited partner's role is that of an investor rather than that of a traditional partner.

Limited partnership   A partnership which has one or more *limited partners* as well as one or more *general partners.* Limited partnerships are used primarily to attract investment capital from the limited partners for such ventures as exploratory oil drilling and real estate development.

Liquidation of a partnership   The process of breaking up and discontinuing a partnership, including the sale of assets, payment of creditors, and distribution of remaining assets to the partners.

Mutual agency   Authority of each partner to act as agent for the partnership within its normal scope of operations and to enter into contracts which bind the partnership.

Partnership contract   An agreement among partners on the formation and operation of the partnership. Usually includes such points as a plan for sharing profits, amounts to be invested, and provision for dissolution.

Statement of partners' capital   A financial statement which shows for each partner and for the firm the amounts of beginning capitals, additional investments, net income, drawings, and ending capitals.

Uniform Partnership Act   Uniform legislation enacted by most states. Governs the formation, operation, and liquidation of partnerships.

SELF-TEST QUESTIONS

The answers to these questions appear on page 518.

1 When a partnership is formed,

a A written partnership agreement, signed by all partners, must be filed in the state in which the partnership is formed.

b Each partner may bind the business to contracts and may withdraw an unlimited amount of assets from the partnership, unless these rights are limited in the partnership contract.

c Each member of the partnership is entitled to participate equally in the earnings of and management of the partnership, unless the partnership is a limited partnership.

d The partnership must file an income tax return and pay income taxes on its net income.

2 Carter and Dixie have capital account balances of $80,000 and $100,000, respectively, at the beginning of 1991. Their partnership agreement provides for interest on beginning capital account balances, 10%; salaries to Carter, $30,000, and to Dixie, $24,000; residual profit or loss divided 60% to Carter, and 40% to Dixie. Partnership net income for 1991 is $62,000. Neither partner made any additional investment in the partnership during 1991, but Carter withdrew $1,500 monthly and Dixie withdrew $1,000 monthly throughout 1991. The partnership balance sheet at December 31, 1991 should include:

a Capital, Carter, $94,000.

b Capital, Carter, $112,000.

c Capital, Dixie, $30,000.

d Total partners' equity, $242,000.

3 Quinn and Ryan are partners who divide profits and losses 30% to Quinn and 70% to Ryan. At the present time, Quinn's capital account balance is $80,000 and Ryan's capital account balance is $160,000. Stone is admitted to a one-third equity interest in the partnership for an investment of $60,000. Each of the following statements relating to the admission of Stone is true with the exception of:

a Quinn has a capital account balance of $68,000 after recording Stone's admission.

b Stone has a capital account balance of $60,000 upon his admission to the partnership.

c Stone received a "bonus" of $40,000 from Quinn and Ryan.

d Total capital (equity) of the new partnership is $300,000 after Stone's admission is recorded.

4 Link, Martin, and Nolan are partners dividing profits and losses 30% to Link, 40% to Martin, and 30% to Nolan. Their capital accounts are as follow: Link, $500,000; Martin, $100,000; Nolan, $400,000. Nolan decides to retire and receives $393,000 from the partnership in exchange for his equity interest. Recording Nolan's withdrawal involves:

a A debit to Nolan's capital account for $393,000.

b Debits to Link's and to Martin's capital accounts for $3,500 each.

c A credit to Link's capital account for $3,000 and a credit to Martin's capital account for $4,000.

d Credits to Link's and to Martin's capital accounts for $200,000 each.

5 When a partnership is liquidated:

a Any cash distribution to partners is allocated according to the profit- and loss-sharing ratios.

b Cash is distributed to each partner in an amount equal to his capital account balance prior to the sale of partnership assets.

c Any gain or loss on disposal of partnership assets is divided among the partners according to their relative capital account balances.

d A partner who maintained a credit balance in his capital account prior to liquidation may end up owing cash to the partnership if partnership assets are sold at a loss.

Assignment Material

REVIEW QUESTIONS

1 Jane Miller is the proprietor of a small manufacturing business. She is considering the possibility of joining in partnership with Mary Bracken, whom she considers to be thoroughly competent and congenial. Prepare a brief statement outlining the advantages and disadvantages of the potential partnership to Miller.

2 Allen and Baker are considering forming a partnership. What do you think are the two most important factors for them to include in their partnership agreement?

3 What is meant by the term *mutual agency?*

4 A real estate development business is managed by two experienced developers and is financed by 50 investors from throughout the state. To allow maximum income tax benefits to the investors, the business is organized as a partnership. Explain why this type of business would probably be a limited partnership rather than a regular partnership.

5 What factors should be considered in drawing up an agreement as to the way in which income shall be shared by two or more partners?

6 Scott has land having a book value of $50,000 and a fair market value of $80,000 and a building having a book value of $70,000 and a fair market value of $60,000. The land and building become Scott's sole capital contribution to a partnership. What is Scott's capital balance in the new partnership? Why?

7 Is it possible that a partnership agreement containing interest and salary allowances as a step toward dividing net income could cause a partnership net loss to be distributed so that one partner's capital account would be decreased by more than the amount of the entire partnership net loss?

8 Partner John Young has a choice to make. He has been offered by his partners a choice between no salary allowance and a one-third share in the partnership income or a salary of $16,000 per year and a one-quarter share of residual profits. Write a brief memorandum explaining the factors he should consider in reaching a decision.

9 Helen Lee withdraws $25,000 from a partnership during the year. When the financial statements are prepared at the end of the year, Lee's share of the partnership income is $15,000. Which amount must Lee report on her income tax return?

10 What factors should be considered when comparing the net income figure of a partnership to that of a corporation of similar size?

11 Explain the difference between being admitted to a partnership by buying an interest from an existing partner and by making an investment in the partnership.

12 If C is going to be admitted to the partnership of A and B, why is it first necessary to determine the current fair market value of the assets of the partnership of A and B?

13 Shirley Bray and Carl Carter are partners who share profits and losses equally. The current balances in their capital accounts are: Bray, $50,000; Carter, $35,000. If Carter sells his interest in the firm to Deacon for $70,000 and Bray consents to the sale, what entry should be made in the partnership accounting records?

14 Farley invests $80,000 cash in the partnership of Dale and Erskin, but is granted a capital interest of only $60,000 upon his admission to the partnership. What is the nature of the $20,000 difference between the amount invested by Farley and the equity interest he received? How is this $20,000 difference handled in the partnership accounting records?

15 Majors, who has a capital account balance of $90,000, received cash of $120,000 from the partnership of Linden, Majors, & Napp upon his retirement. Discuss the nature of the $30,000 paid to Majors in excess of his capital account balance and how this excess payment is handled in the partnership books upon Majors' withdrawal.

16 Describe how a *dissolution* of a partnership may differ from a *liquidation* of a partnership.

17 What measure can you suggest to prevent a partnership from having insufficient cash available to pay the estate of a deceased partner without disrupting the operation of the business?

18 Upon the death of Robert Bell, a partner in the firm of Bell, Cross, and Davis, Charles Bell, the son of Robert Bell, demanded that he replace his father as a member of the partnership. Can Charles Bell enforce this demand? Explain.

EXERCISES

Exercise 12-1
Accounting
terminology

Listed below are nine technical accounting terms introduced in this chapter:

Unlimited liability	*Partnership contract*	*Termination of partnership*
Liquidation	*Fair market value*	*Interest on partners' capital*
General partner	*Limited partner*	*Partnership net income*

Each of the following statements may (or may not) describe one of these technical terms. For each statement, indicate the accounting term described, or answer "None" if the statement does not correctly describe any of the terms.

a Serves to identify partners, specify capital contributions, and establish profit-sharing formula.

b The process of breaking up and discontinuing a partnership business.

c Amounts to be entered in asset accounts of a partnership to record the investment by partners of noncash assets.

d A method of dividing partnership net income to ensure that a partner's share of profits will not be less than the prime rate of interest applied to his or her capital account.

e A characteristic of the partnership type of organization which causes many wealthy investors to choose investments in limited partnerships or corporations rather than in regular partnerships.

f Results from the retirement of a partner from the firm or the admission of a new partner.

g A partner whose financial responsibility does not exceed the amount of his or her investment and who does not actively participate in management.

h A profit-sharing provision designed to compensate for differences in dollar amounts contributed by different partners.

Exercise 12-2
Formation of a
partnership

A business owned by Megan Rogers was short of cash and Rogers therefore decided to form a partnership with Steve Wilson, who was able to contribute cash to the new partnership. The assets contributed by Rogers appeared as follows in the balance sheet of her business: cash, $500; accounts receivable, $28,900, with an allowance for doubtful accounts of $800; inventory, $38,000; and store equipment, $18,000. Rogers had recorded depreciation of $1,500 during her use of the store equipment in her sole proprietorship.

Rogers and Wilson agreed that the allowance for doubtful accounts was inadequate and should be $1,500. They also agreed that a fair value for the inventory was its replacement cost of $45,000 and that the fair value of the store equipment was $16,000. You are to open the partnership accounts by making a general journal entry to record the investment by Rogers.

Exercise 12-3
Partners' capital
and drawing
accounts

Explain briefly the effect of each of the transactions given below on a partner's capital and drawing accounts:

a Partner borrows funds from the business.

b Partner collects a partnerhip account receivable while on vacation and uses the funds for personal purposes.

c Partner receives in cash the salary allowance provided in the partnership agreement.

d Partner takes home merchandise (cost $80, selling price $120) for personal use.

e Partner has loaned money to the partnership. The principal together with interest at 15% is now repaid to the partner in cash.

Exercise 12-4
Dividing
partnership
income

Redmond and Adams, both of whom are CPAs, form a partnership, with Redmond investing $50,000 and Adams $40,000. They agree to share net income as follows:

(1) Salary allowances of $40,000 to Redmond and $30,000 to Adams.

(2) Interest allowances at 15% of beginning capital account balances.

(3) Any partnership earnings in excess of the amount required to cover the interest and salary allowances to be divided 60% to Redmond and 40% to Adams.

The partnership net income for the first year of operations amounted to $123,500 before interest and salary allowances. Show how this $123,500 should be divided between the two partners. Use a three-column schedule of the type illustrated on page 466. List on separate lines the amounts of interest, salaries, and the residual amount divided.

Exercise 12-5
Admission of a
new partner;
bonus to old
partners

Able and Burns are partners having capital balances of $68,000 and $42,000. They share profits equally. The partnership has been quite profitable and has an excellent reputation. Able and Burns agree to admit Cole to a one-third equity interest in the partnership for an investment of $70,000. The assets of the business are not to be revalued. Explain how the bonus to the old partners is computed and prepare a general journal entry to record the admission of Cole.

Exercise 12-6
Admission of a
new partner;
bonus to new
partner

Reed and Dumas are partners who divide profits and losses 60% to Reed and 40% to Dumas. At the present time, each partner's capital account balance is $70,000. Reed and Dumas agree to admit Franklin to a one-fourth equity interest in the partnership for an investment of $40,000. Prepare a general journal entry to record the admission of Franklin. Explain how any bonus (to existing partners *or* to the incoming partner) is computed.

Exercise 12-7
Withdrawal of a
partner

The capital accounts of the Triple D partnership are as follows: Drake, $30,000; Dunlap, $70,000; Dyson, $60,000. Profits and losses are allocated 10% to Drake, 40% to Dunlap, and 50% to Dyson. Dyson is withdrawing from the partnership and it is agreed that he shall be paid $80,000 for his interest because the earnings of the business are high in relation to the assets of the firm. Assuming that the excess of the settlement over the amount of Dyson's capital account is to be recorded as a bonus to Dyson, prepare a general journal entry to record Dyson's retirement from the firm.

Exercise 12-8
Liquidation of a
partnership

The CDE partnership is being liquidated. After all liabilities have been paid and all assets sold, the balances of the partners' capital accounts are as follows: Cooley, $42,000 credit balance; Dean, $16,000 *debit* balance; Emmett, $53,000 credit balance. The partners share profits equally.

a How should the available cash (the only remaining asset) be distributed if it is impossible to determine at this date whether Dean will be able to pay the $16,000 he owes the firm?

b Draft the journal entries to record a partial payment of $13,000 to the firm by Dean, and the subsequent distribution of this cash.

PROBLEMS

Group A

Problem 12A-1
Formation of a
partnership

The partnership of Kelley and Reed was formed on January 1, when Tom Kelley and Pat Reed agreed to invest equal amounts and to share profits equally. The investment by Kelley consists of *$44,000* cash and an inventory of merchandise valued at *$96,000*. Reed is also to contribute a total of $140,000. However, it is agreed that her contribution will consist of the following assets of her business along with the transfer to the partnership of her business liabilities. The agreed value of the various items as well as their carrying values on Reed's records are listed below:

	INVESTMENT BY REED	
	BALANCES IN REED'S RECORDS	AGREED VALUE
Cash..	$ 9,400	$ 9,400
Accounts receivable	127,600	127,600
Allowance for doubtful accounts	8,040	11,500
Inventory..	17,900	19,800
Office equipment (net)	18,200	24,500
Accounts payable	29,800	29,800

Instructions

a Draft general journal entries to record the investments of Kelley and Reed in the new partnership.

b Prepare the beginning balance sheet of the partnership (in report form) at the close of business January 1, reflecting the above transfers to the firm.

c On the following December 31 after one year of operations, the Income Summary account had a credit balance of $98,000 and the Drawing account for each partner showed a debit balance of $41,000. Prepare journal entries to close the Income Summary and the drawing accounts at December 31.

Problem 12A-2
Dividing income;
statement of
partners' capital

Xclass

The adjusted trial balance of Design Associates indicates the following account balances at the end of the current year:

	DEBIT	CREDIT
Cash	$ 25,800	
Accounts receivable	105,200	
Allowance for doubtful accounts		$ 2,000
Inventory (beginning of the year)	27,700	
Showroom fixtures	32,400	
Accumulated depreciation		6,400
Notes payable		9,000
Accounts payable		38,000
Baylor, capital		80,000
Baylor, drawing	40,000	
Finley, capital		70,000
Finley, drawing	32,000	
Sales		652,000
Purchases	391,800	
Selling expenses	110,000	
Administrative expenses	92,500	
Totals	$857,400	$857,400

There were no changes in partners' capital accounts during the year. The inventory at the end of the year was $39,500. The partnership agreement provided that partners are to be allowed 15% interest on invested capital as of the beginning of the year and that the residual net income is to be divided equally.

Instructions

a Prepare a multiple-step income statement for the current year, using the appropriate accounts from the above list. At the bottom of the income statement, prepare a schedule showing the division of net income between the partners.

b Prepare a statement of partners' capital for the current year.

c Prepare a balance sheet at the end of the current year.

Problem 12A-3
Sharing
partnership net
income: various
methods

A small nightclub called Comedy Tonight was organized as a partnership with Lewis investing $40,000 and Martin investing $60,000. During the first year, net income amounted to $65,000.

Instructions

a Determine how the $65,000 net income would be divided under each of the following three independent assumptions as to the agreement for sharing profits and losses. Use schedules of the type illustrated in this chapter to show all steps in the division of net income between the partners.

(1) Net income is to be divided in a fixed ratio: 40% to Lewis and 60% to Martin.

(2) Interest allowances at 15% to be allowed on beginning capital investments and balance to be divided equally.

(3) Salary allowances of $23,000 to Lewis and $33,000 to Martin, interest at 15% to be allowed on beginning capital investments, balance to be divided equally.

b Prepare the journal entry to close the Income Summary account, using the division of net income developed under the last assumption (a, 3) above.

Problem 12A-4
Dividing
partnership profit
and loss

Research Consultants has three partners—Axle, Brandt, and Conrad. During the current year their capital balances were: Axle, $180,000; Brandt, $140,000; and Conrad, $80,000. The partnership agreement provides that partners shall receive salary allowances as follows: Axle, $10,000; Brandt, $50,000; Conrad, $28,000. The partners shall also be allowed 12% interest annually on their capital balances. Residual profit or loss is to be divided: Axle, ½; Brandt, ⅓; Conrad, ⅙.

Instructions

Prepare separate schedules showing how income will be divided among the three partners in each of the following cases. The figure given in each case is the annual partnership net income or loss to be allocated among the partners.

a Income of $502,000

b Income of $79,000

c Loss of $20,000

Problem 12A-5
Admission of a
new partner

wed.

A condensed balance sheet for the partnership of Modern Art Gallery, owned by Hale and Kent, at September 30 is shown below. On this date the two partners agreed to admit a new partner, Lee. Hale and Kent have been dividing profits in a ratio of 3:2 (that is 60% and 40%). The new partnership will have a profit- and loss-sharing ratio of Lee, 50%; Hale, 25% and Kent, 25%.

MODERN ART GALLERY
Balance Sheet
September 30

Current assets	$180,000	Liabilities		$160,000
Plant & equipment		Partners'		
(net)	420,000	capitals:		
		Hale, capital......	$280,000	
		Kent, capital	160,000	440,000
Total..........................	$600,000	Total..........................		$600,000

Instructions

Described below are four different situations under which Lee might be admitted to the partnership. Considering each independently, prepare the journal entries necessary to record the admission of Lee to the firm.

a Lee purchases a one-half interest (50% of the entire ownership equity) in the partnership from Hale for $290,000. Payment is made to Hale as an individual.

b Lee purchases one-half of Hale's interest and one-half of Kent's interest, paying Hale $172,000 and Kent $98,000.

c Lee invests $320,000 in the partnership and receives a one-half interest in capital and income. It is agreed that there will be no change in the valuation of the present net assets. (Bonus to Lee is charged against Hale and Kent in a 3:2 ratio.)

d Lee invests $540,000 in the partnership and receives a one-half interest in capital and income. The bonus to the old partners indicated by the amount of the investment by Lee for a one-half interest will be divided between Hale and Kent in the 3:2 ratio.

Problem 12A-6
Withdrawal of a
partner

Century City Brokers is a partnership of three individuals. At the end of the current year, the firm had the following balance sheet.

friday

CENTURY CITY BROKERS
Balance Sheet
December 31, 19___

Cash..........................	$ 65,000	Liabilities	$ 99,000
Receivables	75,000	Partners'	
Inventory.....................	160,000	capitals:	
Land..........................	105,000	Swartz, capital ... $132,000	
		Cross, capital 90,000	
		Dart, capital...... 84,000	306,000
Total.........................	$405,000	Total.........................	$405,000

The partners share profits and losses in the ratio of 50% to Swartz, 30% to Cross, and 20% to Dart. It is agreed that Dart is to withdraw from the partnership on this date.

Instructions Listed below are a number of different assumptions involving the withdrawal of Dart from the firm. For each case you are to prepare the general journal entry or entries needed to record Dart's withdrawal.

a Dart, with the permission of the other partners, gives his equity to his brother-in-law, Jones, who is accepted as a partner in the firm.

b Dart sells one-fourth of his interest to Cross for $28,000 cash and sells the other three-fourth to Swartz for $84,000 cash. The payments are made by Cross and Swartz personally and not by the partnership.

c Dart is paid $80,000 from partnership funds for his interest. The bonus indicated by this payment is allocated to the continuing partners according to their *relative* profit-sharing ratios: Swartz, ⅝; Cross, ⅜.

d Dart is paid $60,000 cash and given inventory having a book value of $66,000. These assets come from the firm. The partners agree that no revaluation of assets will be made. (Ratio for sharing profits and losses between Swartz and Cross is 5:3, or Swartz, ⅝ and Cross, ⅜.)

Problem 12A-7
Liquidation;
insolvent partners
The December 31 balance sheet of Data Survey, a partnership appears below. In order to focus attention on the principles involved in liquidating a partnership, the balance sheet has been shortened by combining all assets other than cash under the caption of Other assets.

Hand, Trent, and Dell share the profits in a ratio of 3:2:1, respectively. At the date of the balance sheet the partners decided to liquidate the business.

DATA SURVEY
Balance Sheet
December 31, 19___

Cash..........................	$ 60,000	Liabilities	$120,000
Other assets	300,000	Partners'	
		capitals:	
		Hand, capital..... $ 90,000	
		Trent, capital..... 80,000	
		Dell, capital 70,000	240,000
Total.........................	$360,000	Total.........................	$360,000

Instructions For each of the three independent situations shown below, prepare journal entries to record the sale of the "other assets," payment of liabilities, division of the loss on the sale of "other assets" among the partners, and distribution of the available cash to the partners. Support all entries with adequate explanation; the entries for distribution of cash to the partners should have explanations showing how the amounts were determined.

a Other assets are sold for $252,000.

b Other assets are sold for $96,000. Each partner has personal assets and will contribute the amount necessary to cover any debit balance in his or her capital account that may arise in the liquidation process.

c Other assets are sold for $78,000. Trent has personal assets and will contribute any necessary amount. Hand and Dell are both personally bankrupt; any deficit in either capital account must be absorbed by remaining partners.

Group B

Problem 12B-1
Formation of a partnership; closing the Income Summary account

The partnership of Avery and Kirk was formed on July 1, when George Avery and Dinah Kirk agreed to invest equal amounts and to share profits and losses equally. The investment by Avery consists of $30,000 cash and an inventory of merchandise valued at $56,000.

Kirk also is to contribute a total of $86,000. However, it is agreed that her contribution will consist of the following assets of her business along with the transfer to the partnership of her business liabilities. The agreed values of the various items as well as their carrying values on Kirk's records are listed below. Kirk also contributes enough cash to bring her capital account to $86,000.

	INVESTMENT BY KIRK	
	BALANCES ON KIRK'S RECORDS	AGREED VALUE
Accounts receivable	$87,600	$87,600
Allowance for doubtful accounts	5,920	8,000
Inventory..	11,400	12,800
Office equipment (net)	14,300	9,000
Accounts payable	24,800	24,800

Instructions

a Draft entries (in general journal form) to record the investments of Avery and Kirk in the new partnership.

b Prepare the beginning balance sheet of the partnership (in report form) at the close of business July 1, reflecting the above transfers to the firm.

c On the following June 30 after one year of operation, the Income Summary account showed a credit balance of $74,000 and the Drawing account for each partner showed a debit balance of $31,000. Prepare journal entries to close the Income Summary account and the drawing accounts at June 30.

Problem 12B-2
Dividing partnership income; financial statements

The adjusted trial balance of A&F Distributors indicates the following account balances at the end of the current year:

	DEBIT	CREDIT
Cash..	$ 21,620	
Accounts receivable (net)...............................	84,000	
Inventory (beginning of year).........................	27,360	
Prepaid expenses......................................	3,900	
Equipment...	98,000	
Accumulated depreciation.............................		$ 18,000
Notes payable...		9,600
Accounts payable.....................................		38,520
Accrued expenses.....................................		2,880
Adams, capital (beginning of year)..................		70,000
Adams, drawing.......................................	10,080	
Farlow, capital (beginning of year)..................		60,000
Farlow, drawing......................................	7,200	
Sales...		648,960
Purchases...	391,800	
Selling expenses......................................	112,380	
Administrative expenses..............................	91,620	
Totals...	$847,960	$847,960

There were no changes in partners' capital accounts during the year. The inventory at the end of the year was $38,200. The partnership agreement provided that partners are to be allowed 10% interest on invested capital as of the beginning of the year and that the residual net income is to be divided equally.

Instructions

a Prepare an income statement for the current year, using the appropriate accounts from the above list. At the bottom of the income statement, prepare a schedule showing the division of net income.

b Prepare a statement of partners' capital for the current year.

c Prepare a balance sheet at the end of the current year.

Problem 12B-3
Various methods for dividing partnership net income

Elizabeth Dyer and Robert McGraw, both real estate appraisers, formed a partnership, with Dyer investing $60,000 and McGraw investing $80,000. During the first year, the net income of the partnership amounted to $55,000.

Instructions

a Determine how the $55,000 net income would be divided under each of the following four independent assumptions as to the agreement for sharing profits and losses. Use schedules of the types illustrated in the chapter and show all steps in the division of net income between the partners.

(1) The partnership agreement does not mention profit sharing.

(2) Interest at 15% to be allowed on beginning capital investments and balance to be divided 70% to Dyer and 30% to McGraw.

(3) Salaries of $28,000 to Dyer and $21,000 to McGraw, balance to be divided equally.

(4) Salaries of $24,000 to Dyer and $20,000 to McGraw, interest at 15% to be allowed on beginning capital investments, balance to be divided 60% to Dyer and 40% to McGraw.

b Prepare the journal entry to close the Income Summary account, using the division of net income developed under the last assumption (**a, 4**) above.

Problem 12B-4
Dividing
partnership profit
and loss

Financial Planners has three partners—Reed, Stein, and Trump. During the current year their capital balances were: Reed, $140,000; Stein, $100,000; and Trump, $60,000. The partnership agreement provides that partners shall receive salary allowances as follows: Reed, none; Stein, $60,000; and Trump, $38,000. The partners shall also be allowed 12% interest annually on their capital balances. Residual profit or loss is to be divided: Reed, 50%; Stein, 30%; Trump, 20%.

Instructions

Prepare separate schedules showing how income or loss will be divided among the three partners in each of the following cases. The figure given in each case is the annual partnership net income or loss to be allocated among the partners.

a Income of $554,000

b Income of $83,000

c Loss of $19,000

Problem 12B-5
A new partner
joins the firm

Aspen Lodge is a partnership with a record of profitable operations. At the end of the current year the capital accounts of the three partners and the ratio for sharing profits and losses are as shown in the following schedule. At this date, it is agreed that a new partner, Wolfgang Ritter, is to be admitted to the firm.

	CAPITAL	PROFIT-SHARING RATIO
Olga Svenson	$300,000	60%
Jill Kidd	240,000	30%
Miles Kohl	180,000	10%

Instructions

For each of the following situations involving the admission of Ritter to the partnership, give the necessary journal entry to record his admission.

a Ritter purchases one-half of Kidd's interest in the firm, paying Kidd personally $150,000.

b Ritter buys a one-quarter interest in the firm for $200,000 by purchasing one-fourth of the present interest of each of the three partners. Ritter pays the three individuals directly.

c Ritter invests $360,000 in the firm and receives a one-quarter interest in capital and profits of the business. Give the necessary journal entries to record Ritter's admission as a partner and the division of the bonus to the old partners in their relative ratios for profit-sharing prior to Ritter's admission.

Problem 12B-6
Retirement of a
partner

In the partnership of World Travel Agency, the partners' capital accounts at the end of the current year were as follows: Roy Kim, $220,000; Susan John, $152,000; and Mark Ray, $90,000. The partnership agreement provides that profits will be shared 40% to Kim, 50% to John, and 10% to Ray. At this time Kim decides to retire from the firm.

Instructions

Described below are a number of independent situations involving the retirement of Kim. In each case prepare the journal entries necessary to reflect the withdrawal of Kim from the firm.

a Kim sells three-fourths of his interest to Ray for $201,000 and the other one-fourth to John for $69,000. The payments to Kim are made from the personal funds of Ray and John, not from the partnership.

b Kim accepts $100,000 in cash and a patent having a book value of $96,000 in full payment for his interest in the firm. This payment consists of a transfer of partnership assets to the retiring partner. The continuing partners agree that a revaluation of assets is not needed. The excess of Kim's capital account over the payment to him for withdrawal should be credited to the continuing partners according to their *relative* profit-sharing ratios (⅚ to John and ⅙ to Ray).

c Kim receives $100,000 in cash and a 10-year, 12% note for $150,000 in full payment for his interest. Assets are not to be revalued. The bonus to Kim is to be charged against the capital accounts of the continuing partners in their *relative* profit-sharing ratios prior to Kim's withdrawal (⅚ and ⅙).

Problem 12B-7
Liquidation of a partnership

The partnership of Talent Scouts has ended its operations and is in the process of liquidation. All assets except for cash and accounts receivable have already been sold. The task of collecting the accounts receivable is now to be carried out as rapidly as possible. The general ledger balances are as follows:

	DEBIT	CREDIT
Cash..	$ 27,200	
Accounts receivable	116,800	
Allowance for doubtful accounts		$ 6,400
Liabilities		36,800
May, capital (profit-loss share 30%)		43,200
Nix, capital (profit-loss share 50%)		33,600
Peat, capital (profit-loss share 20%)................................		24,000

Instructions

For each of the two independent situations shown below, prepare journal entries to record the collection or sale of the receivables, the payment of liabilities, and the distribution of all remaining cash to the partners. Support all entries with adequate explanation; the entries for distribution of cash to the partners should have explanations showing how the amounts were determined.

a Collections of $66,400 are made on receivables, and the remainder are deemed uncollectible. Debit the uncollectible receivables in excess of the allowance to an account entitled Loss on Sale of Business.

b Receivables are sold to a collection agency; the partnership receives in cash as a final settlement 30% of the gross amount of its receivables. The personal financial status of the partners is uncertain, but all available cash is to be distributed at this time. (Nix's deficiency will be charged to May and Peat in a 30:20 ratio.)

BUSINESS DECISION CASES

Case 12-1
Developing an equitable plan for dividing partnership income

Juan Ramirez and Robert Cole are considering forming a partnership to engage in the business of aerial photography. Ramirez is a licensed pilot, is currently earning $48,000 a year, and has $50,000 to invest in the partnership. Cole is a professional photographer who is currently earning $20,000 a year. He has recently inherited $70,000 which he plans to invest in the partnership.

Both partners will work full time in the business. After careful study, they have estimated that expenses are likely to exceed revenue by $10,000 during the first year of operations. In the second year, however, they expect the business to become profitable, with revenue exceeding expenses by an estimated $90,000. (Bear in mind that these estimates of expenses do not include any salaries or interest to the partners.) Under present market conditions, a fair rate of return on capital invested in this type of business is 20%.

Instructions

a On the basis of this information, prepare a brief description of the income-sharing agreement which you would recommend for Ramirez and Cole. Explain the basis for your proposal.

b Prepare a separate schedule for each of the next two years showing how the estimated amounts of net income would be divided between the two partners under your plan. (Assume that the original capital balances for both partners remain unchanged during the two-year period. This simplifying assumption allows you to ignore the changes which would normally occur in capital accounts as a result of divisions of profits, or from drawings or additional investments.)

c Write a brief statement explaining the differences in allocation of income to the two partners and defending the results indicated by your income-sharing proposal.

**Case 12-2
An offer of
partnership**

Upon graduation from college, Ray Bradshaw began work as a staff assistant for a Big Eight CPA firm. During the next few years, Bradshaw received his CPA certificate and was promoted to the level of senior on the firm's audit staff.

At this time, Bradshaw received an offer from a small local CPA firm, Ames and Bolt, to join that firm as a third partner. Both Ames and Bolt have been working much overtime and they would expect a similar workload from Bradshaw. Ames and Bolt draw salaries of $50,000 each and share residual profits equally. They offer Bradshaw a $50,000 salary plus one-third of residual profits. The offer provides for Bradshaw to receive a one-third equity in the firm and requires him to make a cash investment of $100,000. Balance sheet data for the firm of Ames and Bolt are as follows:

Current assets	$ 60,000	Current liabilities	$ 30,000
Property & equipment	240,000	Long-term liabilities	145,000
		Ames, capital	62,500
		Bolt, capital	62,500
Total...........................	$300,000	Total...........................	$300,000

Projected net income of the CPA firm for the next four years is estimated below. These estimated earnings are before partners' salaries and are based on the assumption that Bradshaw joins the firm and makes possible an increased volume of business.

1st year......................	$159,000	3rd year......................	$186,000
2nd year	$168,000	4th year......................	$198,000

If Bradshaw decides to continue in his present position with the national CPA firm rather than join the local firm, he estimates that his salary over the next four years will be as follows:

1st year......................	$51,000	3rd year......................	$60,000
2nd year	$54,000	4th year......................	$66,000

Instructions

a Assuming that Bradshaw accepts the offer from Ames and Bolt, determine the amount of his beginning capital and prepare the entry in the partnership accounts to record Bradshaw's admission to the firm.

b Compute the yearly amounts of Bradshaw's income from the partnership for the next four years. Compare these amounts with the salary that he will receive if he continues in his present employment and write a memo explaining the factors Bradshaw should consider in deciding whether to accept or decline the offer from Ames and Bolt.

c Assuming that Bradshaw declines the offer, suggest some alternatives that he might propose if he decides to present a counteroffer to Ames and Bolt.

ANSWERS TO SELF-TEST QUESTIONS

1 b   **2** a   **3** b   **4** c   **5** d

Accounting Principles and Concepts

Throughout this text, we have tried to explain the theoretical rationale for each new accounting concept, practice, and procedure as it has first come under discussion. In this chapter, we look back and review some of the major ideas, concepts, and assumptions that represent the theoretical framework for financial reporting. We also explain the nature and purpose of independent audits of financial statements, and discuss the crucial role of professional judgment in the financial reporting process.

After studying this chapter you should be able to meet these Learning Objectives:

1 Explain the need for recognized accounting standards.

2 Discuss the nature and the sources of generally accepted accounting principles.

3 Discuss the accounting principles, assumptions, and concepts presented on pages 494–498.

4 Explain the percentage-of-completion method of income recognition.

5 Define an independent audit and discuss the assurances provided by the auditors' report.

6 Discuss the primary factors considered by the FASB in establishing new accounting standards.

7 Describe the role of professional judgment in the financial reporting process.

The Need for Recognized Accounting Standards

Objective 1
Explain the need for recognized accounting standards.

The basic purpose of financial statements is to provide information about a business entity—information that will be *useful in making economic decisions.* Investors, managers, creditors, financial analysts, economists, and government policy makers all rely upon financial statements and other accounting reports in making the decisions which shape our economy. Therefore, it is of vital importance that the information contained in financial statements possess certain characteristics. The information should be:[1]

1 *Relevant* to the information needs of the decision makers.

2 As *reliable* as possible.

3 *Comparable* to the financial statements of prior accounting periods and also to the statements of other companies.

4 *Understandable* to the users of the financial statements.

We need a well-defined body of accounting principles or standards to guide accountants in preparing financial statements which possess these characteristics. The users of financial statements also must be familiar with these principles in order to interpret properly the information contained in these statements.

Generally Accepted Accounting Principles (GAAP)

Objective 2
Discuss the nature and the sources of generally accepted accounting principles.

The principles which constitute the ground rules for financial reporting are called *generally accepted accounting principles.* Accounting principles may also be termed *standards, assumptions, conventions, or concepts.* The various terms used to describe accounting principles stem from the many efforts that have been made to develop a satisfactory framework of accounting theory.[2] For example, the word *standards* was chosen rather than *principles* when the Financial Accounting Standards Board replaced the Accounting Principles Board as the top rule-making body in the accounting profession. The effort to construct a satisfactory body of accounting theory is an ongoing process, because accounting theory must continually change with changes in the business environment and changes in the needs of financial statement users.

■ **Nature of Accounting Principles** Accounting principles are not like physical laws; they do not exist in nature to be "discovered" by man. Rather, they are developed by man, in the light of what we consider to be the most important objectives of financial reporting. In some ways, generally accepted accounting principles may be compared to the rules established for an organized sport, such as football or basketball. For example, accounting principles, like sports rules:

■ Originate from a combination of tradition, experience, and official decree.

■ Require authoritative support and some means of enforcement.

■ Must be clearly understood and observed by all participants in the process.

---

[1] Adapted from *Statement of Financial Accounting Concepts No. 2,* "Qualitative Characteristics of Accounting Information," FASB (Stamford, Conn.: 1980).

[2] See, for example, *Accounting Research Study No. 3,* "A Tentative Set of Broad Accounting Principles for Business Enterprises," AICPA (New York: 1962); *APB Statement No. 4,* "Basic Concepts and Accounting Principles Underlying Financial Statements of Business Enterprises," AICPA (New York: 1970); and *Statements of Financial Accounting Concepts Nos. 1–6,* FASB (Stamford, Conn.: 1978–1985).

■ Are sometimes arbitrary.

■ May change as gaps or shortcomings in the existing rules come to light, in response to technological innovation, or simply in response to a widespread belief that a change in rules would "improve the game."

An important aspect of accounting principles is the *need for consensus* within the economic community. If these principles are to provide a useful framework for financial reporting, they must be understood and observed by the participants in the financial reporting process. Thus, the words *"generally accepted"* are an important part of the phrase, generally accepted accounting principles.

As accounting principles are closely related to the needs, objectives, and traditions of a society, they vary somewhat from one country to another. Our discussion is limited to accounting principles "generally accepted" within the United States. An effort is underway to create greater uniformity in accounting principles among nations, but this effort will be a long, slow process.

Authoritative Support for Accounting Principles

To qualify as generally accepted, an accounting principle must have "substantial authoritative support." Principles, standards, and rules set forth by the official rule-making bodies of the accounting profession automatically qualify as generally accepted accounting principles. However, a concept or practice may gain substantial authoritative support from unofficial sources, such as widespread use, or recognition in textbooks and other "unofficial" accounting literature. Thus, the phrase generally accepted accounting principles includes more concepts and practices than appear in the "official" literature.

■ **Official Sources of GAAP**   Over the years, the official sources of accounting principles in this country have included (1) the American Institute of Certified Public Accountants, (2) the Financial Accounting Standards Board, and (3) the Securities and Exchange Commission. Also important in the development of accounting theory has been the American Accounting Association (AAA), an organization of accounting educators.

■ **American Institute of Certified Public Accountants (AICPA)**   The AICPA is a professional organization of certified public accountants (CPAs). Prior to the organization of the Financial Accounting Standards Board, committees of the AICPA were responsible for stating and defining generally accepted accounting principles. One such committee was the *Accounting Principles Board (APB),* which issued 31 formal *Opinions* on specific accounting issues. The positions expressed in these Opinions are considered to be generally accepted accounting principles.

The APB has been replaced by the Financial Accounting Standards Board, and the AICPA is no longer the official rule-making organization of the accounting profession. However, the Opinions of the APB *remain in effect,* and continue to represent an important part of generally accepted accounting principles.

■ **Financial Accounting Standards Board (FASB)**   Today, the most authoritative source of generally accepted accounting principles is the FASB.

The FASB is a highly independent rule-making body, consisting of seven members from public accounting, industry, government, and accounting education. Lending support to the FASB are an advisory council and a large research staff.

The FASB is authorized to issue *Statements of Financial Accounting Standards,* which represent authoritative expressions of generally accepted accounting principles. To date, the FASB has issued over 100 such *Statements,* along with a number of *Interpretations* and *Technical Bulletins.*

■ **Securities and Exchange Commission (SEC)**   The SEC is a governmental agency with the legal power to set accounting principles and disclosure requirements for all large, publicly owned corporations. In the past, the SEC has tended to adopt the recommendations of the FASB, rather than to develop its own set of accounting principles. Thus, accounting principles continue to be developed in the private sector, but are given the force of law by the SEC.

To assure widespread acceptance of new accounting standards, the FASB needs the support of the SEC. Therefore, these two organizations work closely together in developing new accounting standards.

The SEC also reviews the financial statements of all large corporations to assure compliance with the Commission's reporting requirements. In the event that a publicly owned corporation fails to comply with the SEC's requirements, the SEC may initiate legal action against the company and the responsible individuals. Thus, the SEC does much to enforce compliance with generally accepted accounting principles.

■ **Unofficial Sources of GAAP**   Not all of what we call generally accepted accounting principles can be found in the "official pronouncements" of the standard-setting organizations. The business community is too complex and changes too quickly for every possible type of transaction to be covered by an official pronouncement. Thus, practicing accountants often must account for situations that have never been addressed by the APB or the FASB.

When the method of accounting for a particular situation is not explained in any official literature, generally accepted accounting principles are based upon such considerations as:

■ Accounting practices that are in widespread use.

■ Accounting practices recommended in authoritative, but "unofficial" accounting literature.[3]

■ Broad theoretical concepts that underlie most accounting practices.

Thus, an understanding of generally accepted accounting principles requires a familiarity with (1) authoritative accounting literature, (2) accounting practices in widespread use, and (3) the broad theoretical concepts that

---

[3] Authoritative, but unofficial, accounting literature includes the *Accounting Guides, Audit Guides,* and *Statements of Position* published by the AICPA; "unofficial" publications by the FASB and the SEC; research studies published by the American Accounting Association (AAA), other professional associations, trade associations, and individuals engaged in accounting research; and accounting textbooks.

underlie accounting practices. We will discuss these "broad theoretical concepts" in the following sections of this chapter.

The Accounting Entity Concept

Objective 3
Discuss the
accounting
principles,
assumptions, and
concepts
presented on
page 488.

One of the basic principles of accounting is that information is compiled for a clearly defined accounting entity. An *accounting entity* is any economic unit which controls resources and engages in economic activities. An individual is an accounting entity. So is a business enterprise, whether organized as a proprietorship, partnership, or corporation. Governmental agencies are accounting entities, as are nonprofit clubs and organizations. An accounting entity may also be defined as an identifiable economic unit *within a larger accounting entity.* For example, the Chevrolet Division of General Motors Corporation may be viewed as an accounting entity separate from GM's other activities.

The basic accounting equation, Assets = Liabilities + Owner's Equity, reflects the accounting entity concept because the elements of the equation relate **to the *particular entity* whose economic activity is being reported in the financial statements.** Although we have considerable flexibility in defining our accounting entity, we must be careful to use the *same definition* in the measurement of assets, liabilities, owner's equity, revenue, and expense. An income statement would not make sense, for example, if it included all the revenue of General Motors Corporation but listed only the expenses of the Chevrolet Division.

Although the entity concept appears straightforward, it can pose some judgmental allocation problems for accountants. Assume, for example, that we want to prepare an income statement for only the Chevrolet Division of General Motors. Also assume that a given plant facility is used in the production of Chevrolets, Pontiacs, and school buses. How much of the depreciation on this factory building should be regarded as an expense of the Chevrolet Division? We will discuss the solution to such problems in later chapters; however, the importance of the entity concept in developing meaningful financial information should be clear.

The Going-Concern Assumption

An underlying assumption in accounting is that an accounting entity will continue in operation for a period of time sufficient to carry out its existing commitments. The assumption of continuity, especially in the case of corporations, is in accord with experience in our economic system. This assumption leads to the concept of the *going concern.* In general, the going-concern assumption justifies ignoring immediate liquidating values in presenting assets and liabilities in the balance sheet.

For example, suppose that a company has just purchased a three-year insurance policy for $5,000. If we assume that the business will continue in operation for three years or more, we will consider the $5,000 cost of the insurance as an asset which provides services (freedom from risk) to the business over a three-year period. On the other hand, if we assume that the business is likely to terminate in the near future, the insurance policy should be recorded at its cancellation value—the amount of cash which can be obtained from the insurance company as a refund on immediate cancellation of the policy, which may be, say, $3,500.

Although the assumption of a going concern is justified in most normal situations, it should be dropped when it is not in accord with the facts. Accountants are sometimes asked to prepare a statement of financial position for an enterprise that is about to liquidate. In this case the assumption of continuity is no longer valid and the accountant drops the going-concern assumption and reports assets at their current liquidating value and liabilities at the amount required to settle the debts immediately.

The Time Period Principle

The users of financial statements need information that is reasonably current, and that is comparable to the information relating to prior accounting periods. Therefore, for financial reporting purposes, the life of a business must be divided into a series of relatively short accounting periods of equal length. This concept is called the time period principle.

The need for periodic reporting creates many of the accountant's most challenging problems. Dividing the life of an enterprise into relatively short time segments, such as a year or a quarter of a year, requires numerous estimates and assumptions. For example, estimates must be made of the useful lives of depreciable assets and assumptions must be made as to appropriate depreciation methods. Thus periodic measurements of net income and financial position are at best only informed estimates. The tentative nature of periodic measurements should be understood by those who rely on periodic accounting information.

The Stable-Dollar Assumption

The stable-dollar assumption means that money is used as the basic measuring unit for financial reporting. The dollar, or any other monetary unit, is a measure of value—that is, it indicates the relative price (or value) of different goods and services.

When accountants add or subtract dollar values originating in different years, they imply that the dollar is a **stable unit of measure,** just as the gallon, the acre, and the mile are stable units of measure. Unfortunately, the dollar is **not** a stable measure of value.

To illustrate, assume that in 1970, you purchased land for $20,000. In 1990, you sell this land for $30,000. Under generally accepted accounting principles, which include the stable-dollar assumption, you have made a $10,000 "gain" on the sale. Economists would point out, however, that $30,000 in 1990 represents less "buying power" than did $20,000 in 1970. When the relative buying power of the dollar in 1970 and 1990 is taken into consideration, you came out behind on the purchase and the sale of this land.

To compensate for the shortcomings of the stable-dollar assumption, the FASB asks large corporations to prepare voluntarily **supplementary information** disclosing the effects of inflation upon their financial statements.[4] Accounting for the effects of inflation is explained and illustrated in Appendix D, which follows Chapter 20.

Let us stress, however, that despite its shortcomings, the stable-dollar as-

---

[4] *FASB Statement No. 89,* "Financial Reporting and Changing Prices" (Stamford, Conn.: 1986).

sumption remains a generally accepted accounting principle. In periods of low inflation, this assumption does not cause serious problems. During periods of severe inflation, however, the assumption of a stable dollar may cause serious distortions in accounting information.

The Objectivity Principle

The term *objective* refers to measurements that are *unbiased* and subject to verification by independent experts. For example, the price established in an arm's-length transaction is an objective measure of exchange value at the time of the transaction. Exchange prices established in business transactions constitute much of the raw material from which accounting information is generated. Accountants rely on various kinds of evidence to support their financial measurements, but they seek always the most objective evidence available. Invoices, contracts, paid checks, and physical counts of inventory are examples of objective evidence.

If a measurement is objective, 10 competent investigators who make the same measurement will come up with substantially identical results. However, 10 competent accountants who set out independently to measure the net income of a given business would *not* arrive at an identical result. Despite the goal of objectivity, *it is not possible to insulate accounting information from opinion and personal judgment.* For example, the cost of a depreciable asset can be determined objectively but not the periodic depreciation expense. Depreciation expense is merely an estimate, based upon estimates of the useful life and the residual value of the asset, and a judgment as to which depreciation method is most appropriate. Such estimates and judgments can produce significant variations in the measurement of net income.

Objectivity in accounting has its roots in the quest for reliability. Accountants want to make their economic measurements reliable and, at the same time, as relevant to decision makers as possible. Where to draw the line in the trade-off between *reliability* and *relevance* is one of the crucial issues in accounting theory. Thus, accountants are constantly faced with the necessity of compromising between what users of financial information would like to know and what it is possible to measure with a reasonable degree of reliability.

Asset Valuation: The Cost Principle

Both the balance sheet and the income statement are affected by the cost principle. Assets are initially recorded in the accounts at cost, and no adjustment is made to this valuation in later periods, except to allocate a portion of the original cost to expense as the assets expire. At the time an asset is originally acquired, cost represents the "fair market value" of the goods or services exchanged, as evidenced by an arm's-length transaction. With the passage of time, however, the fair market value of such assets as land and buildings may change greatly from their historical cost. These later changes in fair market value generally have been ignored in the accounts, and the assets have continued to be valued in the balance sheet at historical cost (less the portion of that cost which has been allocated to expense).

Many accountants and users of financial statements believe that current market value, rather than historical cost, should be used as the basis for asset valuation. This group argues that the use of current values would result in a more meaningful balance sheet. Also, they claim that expenses shown in the income statement should reflect the current market values of the goods and services consumed in the effort to generate revenue.

The cost principle is derived, in large part, from the principle of objectivity. Those who support the cost principle argue that it is important that users have confidence in financial statements, and that this confidence can best be maintained if accountants recognize changes in assets and liabilities only on a basis of completed transactions. Objective evidence generally exists to support cost; current market values, however, may be largely a matter of personal opinion.

The question of whether to value assets at cost or estimated market value is a classic illustration of the "trade-off" between the relevance and the reliability of accounting information.

Revenue Recognition: The Realization Principle

When should revenue be recognized? Under the assumptions of accrual accounting, revenue should be recognized "when it is earned." However, the "earning" of revenue usually is an extended *economic process* and does not actually take place at a single point in time.

Some revenue, such as interest earned, is directly related to time periods. For this type of revenue, it is easy to determine how much revenue has been earned by computing how much of the earning process is complete. However, the earning process for sales revenue relates to *economic activity* rather than to a specific period of time. In a manufacturing business, for example, the earning process involves (1) acquisition of raw materials, (2) production of finished goods, (3) sale of the finished goods, and (4) collection of cash from credit customers.

In the manufacturing example, there is little objective evidence to indicate how much revenue has been earned during the first two stages of the earning process. Accountants therefore usually do not recognize revenue until the revenue has been *realized*. Revenue is realized when both of the following conditions are met: (1) the earning process is *essentially complete* and (2) *objective evidence* exists as to the amount of revenue earned.

In most cases, the realization principle indicates that revenue should be recognized *at the time goods are sold or services are rendered.* At this point the business has essentially completed the earning process and the sales value of the goods or services can be measured objectively. At any time prior to sale, the ultimate sales value of the goods or services sold can only be estimated. After the sale, the only step that remains is to collect from the customer, and this is usually a relatively certain event.

In Chapter 3, we described a *cash basis* of income measurement whereby revenue is recognized only when cash is collected from customers and expenses are recorded only when cash is actually paid out. Cash basis accounting *does not conform* to generally accepted accounting principles, but it is widely used by individuals in determining their *taxable* income. (Remember that the accounting methods used in income tax returns often differ from those used in financial statements.)

■ **The Installment Method**   Companies selling goods on the installment plan sometimes use the installment method of accounting for income tax purposes. Under the installment method, the seller recognizes the gross profit on sales gradually over an extended time span as the cash is actually collected from customers. If the gross profit rate on installment sales is 30%, then out of every dollar collected on installment receivables, the sum of 30 cents represents gross profit.

To illustrate, assume that on December 15, 1990, a retailer sells for $400 a television set which cost $280, or 70% of the sales price. The terms of the sale call for a $100 cash down payment with the balance payable in 15 monthly installments of $20 each, beginning on January 1, 1990. (Interest charges are ignored in this illustration.) The collections of cash and recognition of profit under the installment method are summarized below:

YEAR	CASH COLLECTED	− COST RECOVERY, 70%	= PROFIT EARNED, 30%
1990	$100	$ 70	$ 30
1991	240	168	72
1992	60	42	18
Totals........	$400	$280	$120

Installment method illustrated

This method of profit recognition exists largely because it is allowed for income tax purposes; it postpones the payment of income taxes until cash is collected from customers. From an accounting viewpoint, there is little theoretical justification for delaying the recognition of profit beyond the point of sale. Therefore, the installment method is seldom used in financial statements.[5]

Objective 4
Explain the percentage-of-completion method of income recognition.

■ **Percentage-of-Completion: An Exception to the Realization Principle**   Under certain circumstances, accountants may depart from the realization principle and recognize income during the production process. An example arises in the case of long-term construction contracts, such as the building of a dam over a period of 10 years. Clearly the income statements of a company engaged in such a project would be of little use to managers or investors if no profit or loss were reported until the dam was finally completed. The accountant therefore estimates the portion of the dam completed during each accounting period, and recognizes the gross profit on the project *in proportion* to the work completed. This is known as the percentage-of-completion method of accounting for long-term contracts.

The percentage-of-completion method works as follows:

1   An estimate is made of the total costs to be incurred and the total profit to be earned over the life of the project.

2   Each period, an estimate is made of the portion of the total project completed during the period. This estimate is usually made by expressing the costs incurred during the period as a percentage of the estimated total cost of the project.

3   The percentage figure determined in step **2** is applied to the estimated total

[5] Under generally accepted accounting principles, use of the installment method is permissible only when the amounts likely to be collected on installment sales are *so uncertain* that no reasonable basis exists for estimating an allowance for doubtful accounts.

profit on the contract to compute the amount of profit applicable to the current accounting period.

4 No estimate is made of the percentage of work during the final period. In the period in which the project is completed, any remaining profit is recognized.

To illustrate, assume that Reed Construction Company enters into a contract with the government to build an irrigation canal at a price of $50,000,000. The canal will be built over a three-year period at an estimated total cost of $40,000,000. Therefore, the estimated total profit on the project is $10,000,000. The following schedule shows the actual costs incurred and the amount of profit to be recognized in each of the three years using the percentage-of-completion method:

■ **Profit recognized as work progresses**

YEAR	(A) ACTUAL COSTS INCURRED	(B) PERCENTAGE OF WORK DONE IN YEAR (COLUMN A ÷ $40,000,000)	(C) PROFIT CONSIDERED EARNED ($10,000,000 × COLUMN B)
1	$ 6,000,000	15	$1,500,000
2	20,000,000	50	5,000,000
3	14,520,000	*	2,980,000 balance
Totals	$40,520,000		$9,480,000

* Balance required to complete the contract.

The percentage of the work completed during Year 1 was estimated by dividing the actual cost incurred in the year by the estimated total cost of the project ($6,000,000 ÷ $40,000,000 = 15%). Because 15% of the work was done in Year 1, 15% of the estimated total profit of $10,000,000 was considered earned in that year ($10,000,000 × 15% = $1,500,000). Costs incurred in Year 2 amounted to 50% of the estimated total costs ($20,000,000 ÷ $40,000,000 = 50%); thus, 50% of the estimated total profit was recognized in Year 2 ($10,000,000 × 50% = $5,000,000). Note that no percentage of work completed figure was computed for Year 3. In Year 3, the total actual cost is known ($40,520,000), and the actual total profit on the contract is determined to be $9,480,000 ($50,000,000 − $40,520,000). Since profits of $6,500,000 were previously recognized in Years 1 and 2, the *remaining* profit ($9,480,000 − $6,500,000 = $2,980,000) must be recognized in Year 3.

Although an expected *profit* on a long-term construction contract is recognized in proportion to the work completed, a different treatment is accorded to an expected *loss.* If at the end of any accounting period it appears that a loss will be incurred on a contract in progress, the *entire loss should be recognized at once.*

The percentage-of-completion method should be used only when the total profit expected to be earned can be *reasonably estimated in advance.* If there are substantial uncertainties in the amount of profit which will ultimately be earned, no profit should be recognized until *production is completed.* This approach is often referred to as the *completed-contract method.* If the completed-contract method had been used in the preceding example, no profit would have been recognized in Years 1 and 2; the entire profit of $9,480,000 would have been recorded in Year 3 when the contract was completed and actual costs known.

Expense Recognition: The Matching Principle

The relationship between expenses and revenue is one of *cause and effect.* Expenses are *causal factors* in the earning of revenue. To measure the profitability of an economic activity, we must consider not only the revenue earned, but also all the expenses incurred in the effort to produce this revenue. Thus, accountants attempt to *match* (or *offset*) the revenue appearing in an income statement with all the expenses incurred in generating that revenue. This concept, called the *matching principle,* governs the timing of expense recognition in financial statements.

To illustrate, assume that in June a painting contractor purchases paint on account. The contractor uses the paint on jobs completed in July, but does not pay for the paint until August. In which month should the contractor recognize the cost of the paint as expense? The answer is *July,* because this is the month in which the paint was *used in the process of earning revenue.*

Because of the matching principle, costs that are expected to benefit future accounting periods are debited to asset accounts. These costs are then allocated to expense in the periods that the costs contribute to the production of revenue. The matching principle underlies such accounting practices as depreciating plant assets, computing the cost of goods sold each period, and amortizing the cost of unexpired insurance policies. All end-of-the-period adjusting entries involving recognition of expense are applications of the matching principle.

Costs are matched with revenue in one of two ways:

1 Direct association of costs with specific revenue transactions The ideal method of matching revenue with expenses is to determine the amount of expense associated with the specific revenue transactions occurring during the period. However, this approach works only for those costs and expenses that can be directly associated with specific revenue transactions. The cost of goods sold and commissions paid to salespeople are examples of costs and expenses that can be *directly associated* with the revenue of a specific accounting period.

2 Systematic allocation of costs over the "useful life" of the expenditure Many expenditures contribute to the earning of revenue for a number of accounting periods, but cannot be directly associated with specific revenue transactions. Examples include the costs of insurance policies, depreciable assets, and intangible assets such as goodwill. In these cases, accountants attempt to match revenue and expenses by *systematically allocating the cost to expense* over its useful life. Straight-line amortization and the various methods of depreciation are examples of the "systematic allocation" techniques used to match revenue with the related costs and expenses.

Unfortunately, it is not possible to objectively apply the matching principle to every type of expenditure. Many expenditures offer at least some hope of producing revenue in future periods; however, there may be little or no objective evidence to support these hopes. Accountants defer recognition of an expense to the future only when there is *reasonable evidence* that the expenditure will, in fact, benefit future operations. If this evidence is not available, or is not convincing, accountants do not attempt to apply the matching principle; rather, they charge the expenditure *immediately to expense.* Expenditures generally considered "too subjective" for accountants to apply the matching principle include advertising, research and development, and the cost of employee training programs.

CASE IN POINT ■ Large pharmaceutical companies such as Merck, Squibb, and Marion Labs spend hundreds of millions of dollars each year in research and development (R&D). Ten or more years may be spent developing and testing a new product. During this time, no revenue is received from the product, but related R&D costs totaling hundreds of millions are charged to expense. Every now and then, these companies discover a "blockbuster" drug, which can bring in revenue of perhaps $1 billion per year for a decade or more. The costs of manufacturing pharmaceutical products are relatively small; the primary costs incurred in generating the companies' revenues are the R&D expenditures incurred in prior years.

As a result of accountants' inability to match R&D costs against the subsequent revenue, the income of pharmaceutical companies is understated during the years of product development and is overstated in the years that a successful product brings in revenue. Unfortunately, there is no simple solution to this problem. How are accountants to determine objectively whether or not today's research expenditures will result in a "blockbuster" product 10 years down the road?

The Consistency Principle

The principle of *consistency* implies that a particular accounting method, once adopted, will not be changed from period to period. This assumption is important because it assists users of financial statements in interpreting changes in financial position and changes in net income.

Consider the confusion which would result if a company ignored the principle of consistency and changed its method of depreciation every year. The company could cause its net income for any given year to increase or decrease merely by changing its depreciation method.

The principle of consistency does not mean that a company should *never* make a change in its accounting methods. In fact, a company *should* make a change if a proposed new accounting method will provide more useful information than does the method presently in use. But when a significant change in accounting methods does occur, the fact that a change has been made and the dollar effects of the change should be *fully disclosed* in the financial statements.

Consistency applies to a single accounting entity and increases the comparability of financial statements from period to period. Different companies, even those in the same industry, may follow different accounting methods. For this reason, it is important to determine the accounting methods used by companies whose financial statements are being compared.

The Disclosure Principle

Adequate disclosure means that all *material* and *relevant facts* concerning financial position and the results of operations *are communicated to users.* This can be accomplished either in the financial statements or in the notes accompanying the statements. Such disclosure should make the financial statements more useful and less subject to misinterpretation.

Adequate disclosure does not require that information be presented in great detail; it does require, however, that no important facts be withheld. For example, if a company has been named as a defendant in a large lawsuit, this information must be disclosed. Other examples of information which should be disclosed in financial statements include:

1 A summary of the *accounting methods* used in the preparation of the statements

2 Dollar effects of any *changes* in these accounting methods during the current period.

3 Any *loss contingencies* that may have a material effect upon the financial position of the business.

4 Contractual provisions that will affect future cash flows, including the terms and conditions of borrowing agreements, employee pension plans, and commitments to buy or sell material amounts of assets.

Even significant events which occur *after* the end of the accounting period but before the financial statements are issued may need to be disclosed.

Naturally, there are practical limits to the amount of disclosure that can be made in financial statements and the accompanying notes. The key point to bear in mind is that the supplementary information should be *relevant to the interpretation* of the financial statements.

Materiality

The term *materiality* refers to the *relative importance* of an item or an event. An item is "material" if knowledge of the item might reasonably *influence the decisions* of users of financial statements. Accountants must be sure that all material items are properly reported in the financial statements.

However, the financial reporting process should be *cost effective*—that is, the value of the information should exceed the cost of its preparation. By definition, the accounting treatment accorded to *immaterial* items is of little or no value to decision makers. Therefore, accountants should not waste time accounting for immaterial items; these items may be treated in the *easiest and most convenient manner.* In short, the concept of materiality allows accountants to *ignore other accounting principles* with respect to items that are not material.

An example of the materiality concept is found in the manner in which most companies account for low-cost plant assets, such as pencil sharpeners or wastebaskets. Although the matching principle calls for depreciating plant assets over their useful lives, these low-cost items usually are charged immediately to an expense account. The resulting "distortion" in the financial statement is too small to be of any importance.

If a large number of immaterial items occur in the same accounting period, accountants should consider the *cumulative effect* of these items. Numerous "immaterial" items may, in aggregate, *have a material effect upon the financial statements.* In these situations, the numerous immaterial events must be properly recorded to avoid a material distortion of the financial statements.

We must recognize that the materiality of an item is a relative matter; what is material in a small business organization may not be material in a larger one. The materiality of an item depends not only upon its dollar amount, but also upon its nature. In a large corporation, for example, it may be immaterial whether a given $50,000 expenditure is classified as an asset or as an expense. However, if the $50,000 item is a misuse of corporate funds, such as an unauthorized payment of the personal living expenses of the chief executive, the *nature* of the item may make it quite material to users of the financial statements.

Conservatism as a Guide in Resolving Uncertainties

We have previously referred to the use of *conservatism* in connection with the measurement of net income and the reporting of accounts receivable and inventories in the balance sheet. Although the concept of conservatism may not qualify as an accounting principle, it has long been a powerful influence upon asset valuation and income determination. Conservatism is most useful when matters of judgment or estimates are involved. Ideally, accountants should base their estimates on sound logic and select those accounting methods which neither overstate nor understate the facts. When some doubt exists about the valuation of an asset or the realization of a gain, however, accountants traditionally select the accounting option which produces a lower net income for the current period and a less favorable financial position.

An example of conservatism is the traditional practice of pricing inventory at the lower of cost or market (replacement cost). Decreases in the market value of the inventory are recognized as a part of the cost of goods sold in the current period, but increases in market value of inventory are ignored. Failure to apply conservatism when valuations are especially uncertain may produce misleading information and result in losses to creditors and stockholders.

Audited Financial Statements

Objective 5
Define an independent audit and discuss the assurances provided by the auditors' report.

The annual financial statements of large corporations are used by great numbers of stockholders, creditors, government regulators, and members of the general public. What assurance do these people have that the information in these statements is reliable and is presented in conformity with generally accepted accounting principles? The answer is that the annual financial statements of large corporations are *audited* by independent certified public accountants (CPAs).

An audit is a thorough investigation of every item, dollar amount, and disclosure which appears in the financial statements. (Keep in mind that many ledger balances and other types of information are combined and condensed in preparing financial statements. Consequently, only material items appear in the financial statements.) After completing the audit, the CPAs express their opinion as to the *fairness* of the financial statements. This opinion, called the *auditors' report,* is published with the financial statements in the company's annual report to its stockholders. A report by a CPA firm might read as follows:

To the Board of Directors and Stockholders
XYZ Company

We have audited the accompanying balance sheet of XYZ Company as of December 31, 19___, and the related statements of income, retained earnings, and cash flow for the year then ended. These financial statements are the responsibility of the Company's management. Our responsibility is to express an opinion on these financial statements based on our audit.

We conducted our audit in accordance with generally accepted auditing standards. Those standards require that we plan and perform the audit to obtain reasonable assurance about whether the financial statements are free of material misstatement. An audit includes examining, on a test basis, evidence supporting the amounts and disclosures in the financial statements. An audit also includes assessing the accounting principles used and significant estimates made by management, as well as evaluating the overall financial statement presentation. We believe that our audit provides a reasonable basis for our opinion.

In our opinion, the financial statements referred to above present fairly, in all material respects, the financial position of XYZ Company as of December 31, 19___, and the results of its operations and its cash flows for the year then ended in conformity with generally accepted accounting principles.

Springfield, Mo.   *Blue, White & Company*
January 29, 19___

                                    Certified Public Accountants

Over many decades, audited financial statements have developed an excellent track record of reliability. Note, however, that the CPAs ***do not guarantee*** the accuracy of financial statements; rather, they render their ***professional opinion*** as to the overall ***fairness*** of the statements. "Fairness," in this context, means that the financial statements are ***not misleading.*** However, just as a physician may make an error in the diagnosis of a particular patient, there is always a possibility that an auditor's opinion may be in error. The primary responsibility for the reliability of financial statements rests with the management of the issuing company, not with the independent CPAs.

Setting New Accounting Standards

Objective 6
Discuss the primary factors considered by the FASB in establishing new accounting standards.

As mentioned earlier, accounting principles are not "laws of nature" that await discovery. Rather, these principles are developed and shaped by man, for the purpose of meeting the needs of economic decision makers. As the business environment changes, the need for new principles (or standards) often becomes apparent. In fact, the FASB typically issues several new standards each year.

In an effort to meet the needs of the entire economic community, the FASB invites all elements of the community to express their views during the standard-setting process. For example, the Board issues a ***Discussion Memorandum*** explaining the issue under consideration, and encouraging all interested parties to comment and to express their views. After considering the responses to the Discussion Memorandum, the Board issues an ***Exposure Draft*** of the proposed new standard and again encourages public response. These responses also are considered carefully before the Board issues a formal new *Statement of Financial Accounting Standards.*

By inviting the public to participate in the standard-setting process, the FASB tries to develop the understanding and support which will cause the new standard to be "generally accepted."

The Conceptual Framework Project

In addition to responding to the needs of the economic community, the FASB tries to make each new accounting standard consistent with the general framework of accounting theory set forth by the Board in a series of *Statements of Financial Accounting Concepts.* These "concepts statements" explain the interrelationships among the:

■ Objectives of financial reporting.

■ Desired characteristics of accounting information (such as relevance, reliability, and understandability).

■ Elements of financial statements (such as assets, liabilities, revenue, and expenses).

■ Criteria for deciding what information to include in financial statements.

■ Valuation concepts relating to the determination of financial statement amounts.

The primary purpose of the conceptual framework is to provide guidance to the FASB in developing future accounting standards.[6] By making each new standard consistent with this framework, the Board hopes that the standards will resolve accounting problems in a logical and consistent manner.

The concepts statements do not represent "official" generally accepted accounting principles, as do the FASB's *Statements of Financial Accounting Standards.* However, these concepts statements are very useful to practicing accountants in accounting for situations that are not specifically addressed by one of the FASB's standards.

Professional Judgment: An Essential Element in Financial Reporting

Objective 7
Explain the role of professional judgment in the financial reporting process.

Judgment plays a major role in financial reporting. For those situations not specifically covered by an official pronouncement, accountants must exercise professional judgment in determining the treatment that is most consistent with generally accepted accounting principles. Judgment also is exercised in selecting appropriate accounting methods (as for example, deciding whether to use the FIFO or LIFO method of inventory valuation), in estimating the useful lives of depreciable assets, and in deciding what events are "material" to a given business entity.

Judgment is a personal matter; competent accountants often will make

---

[6] *FASB Statement of Financial Accounting Concepts No. 1,* "Objectives of Financial Reporting by Business Enterprises" (Stamford, Conn.: 1978), p. 4.

different judgments. This explains why the financial statements of different companies are not likely to be directly comparable in all respects.

End-of-Chapter Review

CONCEPTS INTRODUCED OR EMPHASIZED IN CHAPTER 13

The major concepts emphasized in this chapter include the:

■ Need for and the sources of generally accepted accounting principles as a framework for developing financial statements that are relevant, reliable, comparable, and understandable.

■ Idea that generally accepted accounting principles are manmade rules that may change with changes in the economic environment and in the needs of decision makers.

■ Basic concepts of asset valuation, revenue recognition, and expense recognition, including the:
  Concept of an accounting entity.
  Going-concern assumption.
  Stable-dollar assumption (and why this assumption is technically not valid).
  Objectivity principle.
  Cost principle as the basis for asset valuation.
  Realization principle as the basis for revenue recognition.
  Matching principle as the basis for expense recognition.
  Consistency principle.
  Disclosure principle.
  Concept of materiality.
  Concept of conservatism as a guide to resolving uncertainty.

■ Nature of audited financial statements and the purpose of the independent auditors' report.

■ Goal of public participation in the process of developing new accounting standards.

■ Role of professional judgment in the financial reporting process.

The concepts discussed in this chapter form the theoretical framework of the financial reporting process. Thus, an understanding of these concepts will be useful throughout the study of accounting. In the preceding chapters, we have focused primarily upon unincorporated business—that is, sole proprietorships and partnerships. In the remaining chapters, we will emphasize the corporate form of business entity. You will find that generally accepted accounting principles are equally applicable to all three forms of business organizations.

KEY TERMS INTRODUCED OR EMPHASIZED IN CHAPTER 13

Accounting Principles Board (APB) Formerly the top standard-setting body in accounting. Although the APB has since been replaced by the *FASB*, many of the APB's Opinions remain in effect as generally accepted accounting principles.

American Institute of Certified Public Accountants (AICPA) A professional organization of Certified Public Accountants (CPAs) that has long been influential in the development of accounting principles.

Auditors' report The report issued by a firm of certified public accountants after auditing the financial statements of a business. Expresses an opinion on the fairness of the financial statements and indicates the nature and limits of the responsibility being assumed by the independent auditors.

Conservatism A traditional practice of resolving uncertainties by choosing an asset valuation at the lower point of the range of reasonableness. Also refers to the policy of postponing recognition of revenue to a later date when a range of reasonable choice exists. Designed to avoid overstatement of financial strength and earnings.

Consistency An assumption that once a particular accounting method is adopted, it will not be changed from period to period. Intended to make financial statements of a given company comparable from year to year.

Disclosure principle Financial statements should disclose all material and relevant information about the financial position and operating results of a business. The notes accompanying financial statements are an important means of disclosure.

Financial Accounting Standards Board (FASB) The organization with primary responsibility for formulating new accounting standards. The FASB is part of the private sector and is not a governmental agency.

Generally accepted accounting principles (GAAP) The "ground rules" for financial reporting. Includes principles, concepts, and methods that have received authoritative support (such as from the *FASB*), or which have become "generally accepted" through widespread use.

Going-concern assumption An assumption that a business entity will continue in operation indefinitely and thus will carry out its existing commitments.

Installment method An accounting method used principally in the determination of taxable income. It provides for recognition of realized profit on installment contracts in proportion to cash collected.

Matching principle The accounting principle that governs the timing of expense recognition. This principle indicates that expenses should be offset against revenue on a basis of cause and effect. That is, the revenue of an accounting period should be offset by those costs and expenses that were causal factors in producing that revenue.

Materiality The relative importance of an amount or item. An item which is not significant enough to influence the decisions of users of financial statements is considered as *not* material. The accounting treatment of immaterial items may be guided by convenience rather than by theoretical principles.

Objectivity (objective evidence) The valuation of assets and the measurement of income are to be based as much as possible on objective evidence, such as exchange prices in arm's-length transactions.

Percentage-of-completion method A method of accounting for long-term construction projects which recognizes revenue and profits in proportion to the work completed, based on an estimate of the portion of the project completed each accounting period.

Realization principle The principle of recognizing revenue in the accounts only when the earning process is virtually complete, which is usually at the time of sale of goods or rendering service to customers.

Securities and Exchange Commission (SEC) A governmental agency with the legal power to set accounting principles. However, the SEC traditionally has adopted the principles developed by the FASB, rather than developing its own set of principles. The SEC enforces accounting principles by giving the weight of law to standards developed by the FASB. The SEC reviews the financial statements of publicly owned corporations for compliance with the Commission's reporting requirements.

Stable-dollar assumption In using money as a measuring unit and preparing financial statements expressed in dollars, accountants make the assumption that the dollar is a stable unit of measurement. This assumption is obviously faulty in an environment of continued inflation.

Time period principle The idea that to be useful, financial statements should be prepared for relatively short accounting periods of equal length. While this principle contributes to the timeliness of financial statements, it conflicts with the objectivity principle by forcing accountants to make many estimates, such as the useful lives of depreciable assets.

SELF-TEST QUESTIONS

The answers to these questions appear on page 518.

1 Generally accepted accounting principles (GAAP)

a Include only the official pronouncements of the standard-setting organizations, such as the AICPA, SEC, and the FASB.

b May include customary accounting practices in widespread use even if not mentioned specifically in official pronouncements.

c Eliminate the need for professional judgment in the areas in which an official pronouncement exists.

d Are laws issued by the FASB and the SEC, based upon a vote by the CPAs in the United States.

2 Which of the following situations best illustrates the application of the realization principle?

a A company sells merchandise on the installment method and recognizes gross profit as the cash is collected from customers.

b A construction company engaged in a three-year project determines the portion of profit to be recognized each year using the percentage-of-completion method.

c A construction company engaged in a three-month project recognizes no profit until the project is completed under the completed-contract method.

d A manufacturer that sells washing machines with a three-year warranty recognizes warranty expense related to current year sales, based upon the estimated future liability.

3 Which of the following concepts has the *least* influence in determining the depreciation expense reported in the income statement under current GAAP?

a Reliability—The price of a depreciable asset established in an exchange transaction can be supported by verifiable, objective evidence.

b Cost principle—Assets are initially recorded in the account at cost and no adjustment is made to this valuation in subsequent periods, except to allocate a portion of the original cost to expense as assets expire.

c Relevance—Amounts shown in the financial statements should reflect current market values, as these are the most relevant to decision makers.

d Matching principle—Accountants attempt to match revenue with the expenses incurred in generating that revenue by systematically allocating an asset's cost to expense over its useful life.

4 The existence of generally accepted accounting principles has eliminated the need for professional judgment in:

a Estimating the useful lives and residual values of depreciable plant assets.

b Selecting an appropriate inventory valuation method, such as LIFO, FIFO, average cost, or specific identification.

c Determining which events are "material" to a given entity.

d None of the above is correct; each of the above situations requires the use of professional judgment.

5 The fact that a corporation's financial statements have been audited means that:

a In the opinion of the CPAs who performed the audit, the financial statements are not misleading.

b The IRS has examined the financial statements to investigate compliance with tax laws.

c The financial statements are guaranteed to be accurate by the CPAs who prepared them.

d The financial statements were prepared by a CPA firm, rather than by the company itself.

Assignment Material

REVIEW QUESTIONS

1 What is the basic purpose of financial statements?

2 Briefly explain the meaning of the term *generally accepted accounting principles*.

3 Why is it important that the accounting principles be "generally accepted"?

4 Name the three groups in the United States that have been the most influential in developing generally accepted accounting principles.

5 To be "generally accepted," must an accounting method be set forth in the official pronouncements of an accounting rule-making organization? Explain.

6 Are generally accepted accounting principles in worldwide use? Explain.

7 Why is it necessary for accountants to assume the existence of a clearly defined *accounting entity?*

8 What is the *time period principle?* Does this principle tend to increase or decrease the objectivity of accounting information? Explain.

9 What is meant by the term *stable-dollar assumption?* Is this assumption completely valid? Explain.

10 What is the meaning of the term *objectivity* as it is used by accountants? Is accounting information completely objective? Explain.

11 An argument has long existed as to whether assets should be valued in financial statements at cost or at estimated market value. Explain the implications of the *objectivity principle* in this controversy.

12 Explain what is meant by the expression "trade-off between *reliability* and *relevance*" in connection with the preparation of financial statements.

13 Barker Company has at the end of the current period an inventory of merchandise which cost $500,000. It would cost $600,000 to replace this inventory, and it is estimated that the goods will probably be sold for a total of $700,000. If the firm were to terminate operations immediately, the inventory could probably be sold for $480,000. Discuss the relative reliability and relevance of each of these dollar measurements of the ending inventory.

14 What two conditions should be met before accountants consider revenue to be *realized?*

15 Long-term construction projects often are accounted for by the percentage-of-completion method.

    a Is this method consistent with the realization principle? Explain.

    b What is the justification for the use of this method?

16 Briefly explain the *matching principle.* Indicate two approaches that accountants follow in attempting to "match" revenue with expense.

17 In the valuation of depreciable assets, such as buildings and equipment, the logic of matching revenue with expenses is dependent upon the assumption of a going concern. Explain this statement.

18 Does the concept of *consistency* mean that all companies should use the same accounting methods? Explain.

19 Briefly define the principle of *disclosure.* List four examples of information that should be disclosed in financial statements or in notes accompanying the statements.

20 Publicly owned corporations are required to include in their annual reports a description of the accounting methods followed in the preparation of their financial statements. What advantages do you see in this practice?

21 Briefly explain the concept of *materiality.* If an item is not material, how is the item treated for financial reporting purposes?

22 Does *conservatism* mean that assets should be deliberately understated in accounting records? Explain fully.

23 Indicate how the concept of conservatism would apply to:

    a Estimating the allowance for doubtful accounts receivable.

    b Estimating the useful lives of depreciable assets.

24 What are *audited* financial statements? Is the auditing of financial statements made easier or more difficult by the principle of objectivity? Explain.

25 What organization is primarily responsible for the development of new accounting standards? Why does this organization encourage all elements of the economic community to express their views during the standard-setting process?

26 Professional judgment plays an important role in financial reporting. Explain at least three areas in which the accountant preparing financial statements must make professional judgments that will affect the content of the statements.

EXERCISES

**Exercise 13-1
Accounting
terminology**

Listed below are nine technical accounting terms introduced or emphasized in this chapter:

GAAP	Professional judgment	Realization
SEC	Materiality	Matching
Objectivity	Conservatism	Consistency

Each of the following statements may (or may not) describe one of these technical terms. For each statement, indicate the accounting term described, or answer "None" if the statement does not correctly describe any of the terms.

    a The concept of associating expenses with revenue on a basis of cause and effect.

    b An essential element for an accountant making estimates, selecting appropriate accounting methods, and resolving trade-offs between the goals of conflicting accounting principles.

c The organization which is primarily responsible for developing new accounting standards in the United States.

d The goal of having all companies use the same accounting methods.

e The list of acceptable accounting principles developed by the SEC as part of its conceptual framework project.

f The accounting principle used in determining when revenue should be recognized in financial statements.

g An accounting concept that may justify departure from other accounting principles for purposes of convenience and economy.

Exercise 13-2
Asset valuation

Milestone Mfg. Co. has just purchased expensive equipment that was custom-made to suit the firm's manufacturing operations. Because of the custom nature of this machinery, it would be of little value to any other company. Therefore, the controller of Milestone is considering writing these machines down to their estimated resale value in order to provide a conservative valuation of assets in the company's balance sheet. In the income statement, the write-down would appear as a "loss on revaluation of machinery."

Separately discuss the idea of writing down the carrying value of the machinery in light of each of the following accounting concepts:

a The going-concern assumption.

b The matching principle.

c Objectivity.

d Conservatism.

Exercise 13-3
Revenue
recognition

In deciding when to recognize revenue in financial statements, accountants normally apply the realization principle.

a Revenue is considered realized when two conditions are met. What are these conditions?

b Indicate when the conditions for recognition of revenue have been met in each of the following situations. (Assume that financial statements are prepared monthly.)

(1) An airline sells tickets several months in advance of its flights.

(2) An appliance dealer sells merchandise on 24-month payment plans.

(3) A professional sports team sells season tickets in July for eight home games to be played in the months of August through December.

(4) Interest revenue relating to a two-year note receivable is all due at the maturity of the note.

Exercise 13-4
Expense
recognition

Mystery Playhouse prepares monthly financial statements. At the beginning of its three-month summer season, the company has programs printed for each of its 48 upcoming performances. Under certain circumstances, either of the following accounting treatments of the costs of printing these programs would be acceptable. Justify both of the accounting treatments using accounting principles discussed in this chapter.

a The cost of printing the programs is recorded as an asset and is allocated to expense in the month in which the programs are distributed to patrons attending performances.

b The entire cost of printing the programs is charged to expense when the invoice is received from the printer.

Exercise 13-5
Violations of accounting principles

For each situation described below, indicate the principle of accounting that is being violated. You may choose from the following:

Accounting entity   Materiality
Consistency   Objectivity
Disclosure   Realization
Matching   Stable monetary unit

a The bookkeeper for a large, metropolitan auto dealership depreciates metal waste-baskets over a period of five years.

b Upon completion of the construction of a condominium project which will soon be offered for sale, Townhome Developers increased the balance sheet valuation of the condominiums to their sales value and recognized the expected profit on the project.

c Plans to dispose of a major segment of the business are not communicated to readers of the financial statements.

d The cost of expensive, custom-made machinery installed in an assembly line is charged to expense, because it is doubtful that the machinery would have any resale value if the assembly line were shut down.

e A small commuter airline recognizes no depreciation on its aircraft because the planes are maintained in "as good as new" condition.

Exercise 13-6
Profit recognition: installment method

On September 15, 1990, Susan Moore sold a piece of property which cost her $56,000 for $80,000, net of commissions and other selling expenses. The terms of sale were as follows: down payment, $8,000; balance, $3,000 on the fifteenth day of each month for 24 months, starting October 15, 1990. Compute the gross profit to be recognized by Moore in 1990, 1991, and 1992 (a) on the *accrual basis* of accounting and (b) on the *installment basis* of accounting. Moore uses a fiscal year ending December 31.

Exercise 13-7
Profit recognition: percentage of completion method

The Clinton Corporation recognizes the profit on a long-term construction project as work progresses. From the information given below, compute the profit that should be recognized each year, assuming that the original cost estimate on the contract was $6,000,000 and that the contract price is $7,500,000.

YEAR	COSTS INCURRED	PROFIT CONSIDERED REALIZED
1989	$1,800,000	$?
1990	3,000,000	?
1991	1,171,000	?
Total............................	$5,971,000	$1,529,000

Exercise 13-8
Audits of financial statements

The annual financial statements of all large, publicly owned corporations are audited.

a What is an audit of financial statements?

b Who performs these audits?

c What is the basic purpose of an audit?

Exercise 13-9
Developing new accounting standards

Answer the following questions relating to the creation of new accounting standards:

a Why will a need for new standards always exist?

b What organization has primary responsibility for setting new accounting standards?

c What role is played by the SEC in the standard-setting process?

d Why are all elements of the economic community invited to comment and to express their views during the standard-setting process?

Exercise 13-10
The conceptual
framework

The FASB recently issued a series of *Statements of Financial Accounting Concepts* intended to set forth a broad "conceptual framework" of accounting theory. Explain how an understanding of accounting theory is useful to:

a Members of the FASB.

b Accountants involved in the preparation of financial statements.

c Users of financial statements.

PROBLEMS

Group A

Problem 13A-1
Rationale behind
acceptable
practices

Paragraphs **a** through **e** describe accounting practices which *are in accord* with generally accepted accounting principles. From the following list of accounting principles, identify those principles which you believe justify or explain each described accounting practice. (Most of the described practices are explained by a single principle; however, more than one principle may relate to a given practice.) Briefly explain the relationship between the described accounting practice and the underlying accounting principle.

Accounting Principles

Consistency	Accounting entity concept
Materiality	Matching revenue with expense
Objectivity	Going-concern assumption
Realization	Adequate disclosure
Conservatism	Stable-dollar assumption

Accounting Practices

a If land costing $60,000 were sold for $65,000, a $5,000 gain would be reported regardless of inflation during the years that the land has been owned.

b When equipment is purchased an estimate is made of its useful life, and the equipment is then depreciated over this period.

c The personal assets of the owner of a sole proprietorship are not disclosed in the financial statements of the business, even when these personal assets are sufficient to assure payment of all the business's liabilities.

d In estimating the appropriate size of the allowance for doubtful accounts, most accountants would rather see this allowance be a little too large rather than a little too small.

e The methods used in the valuation of inventory and for the depreciation of plant assets are described in a footnote to the financial statements.

Problem 13A-2
Violations of
GAAP

Six independent situations are described below.

a Morris Construction, Inc., does not have sufficient current assets to qualify for a much needed loan. Therefore, the corporation included among its current assets the personal savings accounts of several major stockholders, as these stockholders have promised to invest more money in the corporation if necessary.

b First Bank incurred large losses on uncollectible agricultural loans. On average, these loans call for payments to be received over a period of 10 years. Therefore, First Bank is amortizing its losses from the uncollectible loans against the revenue that will be earned over this 10-year period.

c The Ghost of 42nd Street, a Broadway play, has sold out in advance for the next two years. These ticket sales were recognized as revenue at the time cash was received from the customers.

d Wall Street Advisory Service has been sued by clients for engaging in illegal securities transactions. No mention is made of this lawsuit in the company's financial statements, as the suit has not been settled and the company cannot objectively estimate the extent of its liability.

e Carver Company sold for $200,000 land that had been purchased 10 years ago for $150,000. As the general price level had doubled during this period, Carver Company restated the cost of the land at $300,000 and recognized a $100,000 loss.

f In recent years, many savings and loan associations have become bankrupt. Although Red River Savings Bank was in no danger of bankruptcy, it reduced the carrying value of its assets to liquidation value to make its financial statements more comparable to those of other companies in the industry.

Instructions For each situation, identify the accounting principle that has been violated and explain the nature of the violation.

Problem 13A-3
Alternative
methods of
income
recognition

Early in 1990, Roadbuilders, Inc., was notified that it was the successful bidder on the construction of a section of state highway. The bid price for the project was $24 million. Construction began in 1990 and will take about 27 months to complete; the deadline for completion is in April of 1992.

The contract calls for payments of $6 million per year to Roadbuilders, Inc., for four years, beginning in 1990. (After the project is complete, the state will also pay a reasonable interest charge on the unpaid balance of the contract.) The company estimates that construction costs will total $16 million, of which $6 million will be incurred in 1990, $8 million in 1991 and $2 million in 1992.

The controller of the company, Joe Morgan, recognizes that there are a number of ways he might account for this contract. He might recognize income at the time the contract is completed (completed-contract method), in April of 1992. Alternatively, he might recognize income during construction (percentage-of-completion method), in proportion to the percentage of the total cost incurred in each of the three years. Finally, he might recognize income in proportion to the percentage of the total contract price collected in installment receipts during the four-year period (installment method).

Instructions **a** Prepare a schedule (in millions of dollars) showing the profit that would be recognized on this project in each of the four years under each of the three accounting methods being considered by the controller. Assume that the timing and construction costs go according to plan. (Ignore the interest revenue relating to the unpaid balance of the contract.)

b Explain which accounting method you consider to be *most* appropriate in this situation. Also explain why you consider the other two methods less appropriate.

Problem 13A-4
Applying
accounting
principles

In each of the situations described below, indicate the accounting principle or concept, if any, that has been violated and explain briefly the nature of the violation. If you believe the treatment *is in accord with generally accepted accounting principles,* state this as your position and briefly defend it.

a Pearl Cove Hotel recognizes room rental revenue on the date that a reservation is received. For the summer season, many guests make reservations as much as a year in advance of their intended visit.

b In prior years Regal Corporation had used the straight-line method of depreciation for both financial reporting purposes and for income tax purposes. In the current year, Regal continued to use straight-line depreciation on all assets for financial reporting purposes, but began depreciating newly acquired assets by an accelerated method for income tax purposes.

c The liabilities of Ellis Construction Co. are substantially in excess of the company's assets. In order to present a more impressive balance sheet for the business, Roy Ellis, the owner of the company, included in the company's balance sheet such personal assets as his savings account, automobile, and real estate investments.

d On January 9, 1992, Gable Company's only plant was badly damaged by a tornado and will be closed for much of the coming year. No mention was made of this event in the financial statements for the year ended December 31, 1991, as the tornado occurred after year-end.

e Friday Production follows a policy of valuing its plant assets at liquidation values in the company's balance sheet. No depreciation is recorded on these assets. Instead, a loss is recognized if the liquidation values decline from one year to the next. If the liquidation values increase during the year, a gain is recognized.

Problem 13A-5
GAAP from an
auditor's
perspective

Assume that you are an independent CPA performing audits of financial statements. In the course of your work, you encounter the following situations:

a Gala Magazine receives most of its revenue in the form of 12-month subscriptions. Even though this subscription revenue has already been received in cash, the company's controller defers recognition in the income statement; the revenue is recognized on a monthly basis as the monthly issues of the magazine are mailed to subscribers.

b Due to the bankruptcy of a competitor, Regis Trucking was able to buy plant assets worth at least $400,000 for the "bargain price" of $300,000. In order to reflect the benefits of this bargain purchase in the financial statements, the company recorded the assets at a cost of $400,000 and reported a $100,000 "gain on purchase of plant assets."

c Metro Development Co. built a 400-unit furnished apartment complex. All materials and furnishings used in this project that had a unit cost of less than $200 were charged immediately to expense. The total cost of these items amounted to $6 million.

d In January 1991, the main plant of Hillside Mfg. Co. was destroyed in a fire. As this event happened in 1991, no loss was shown in the income statement for 1990. However, the event was thoroughly disclosed in notes to the 1990 financial statements.

e In an effort to match revenue with all related expenses in an objective manner, Brentwood Company has established "useful life" standards for all types of expenditures. For example, expenditures for advertising are amortized over 12 months; the costs of employee training programs, 24 months; and research and development costs, 10 years.

Instructions

Discuss each of the above situations. If you consider the treatment to be in conformity with generally accepted accounting principles, explain why. If you do not, explain which principle or principles have been violated, and also explain how the situation should have been reported.

Group B

Problem 13B-1
Accounting
principles

Paragraphs **a** through **e,** below, describe accounting practices which *are in accord* with generally accepted accounting principles. From the following list of accounting principles, identify those principles which you believe justify or explain each described accounting practice. (Most of the practices are explained by a single principle; however, more than one principle may relate to a particular practice.) Briefly explain the relationship between the described accounting practice and the underlying accounting principle.

Accounting Principles

Consistency	*Accounting entity*
Materiality	*Matching revenue with expense*
Objectivity	*Going-concern assumption*
Realization	*Adequate disclosure*
Conservatism	*Stable-dollar assumption*

Accounting Practices

a The purchase of a two-year fire insurance policy is recorded by debiting an asset account even though no refund will be received if the policy is canceled.

b Hand tools with a small unit cost are charged to expense when purchased even though the individual tools have a useful life of several years.

c An airline records depreciation on its aircraft even though an excellent maintenance program keeps the planes in "as good as new" condition.

d A lawsuit filed against a company is described in footnotes to the company's financial statements even though the lawsuit was filed with the court shortly after the company's balance sheet date.

e A real estate developer carries an unsold inventory of condominiums in its accounting records at cost rather than at estimated sales value.

Problem 13B-2
Applications of
accounting
principles

In each of the situations described below, indicate the accounting principles or concepts, if any, that have been violated and explain briefly the nature of the violation. If you believe the treatment *is in accord with generally accepted accounting principles,* state this as your position and defend it.

a Holly Manufacturing purchased an expensive special-purpose machine with an estimated useful life of 10 years. Proper installation of the machine required that it be set in the concrete of the factory floor. Once the machine was installed, Holly's controller felt that it had no resale value, so he charged the entire cost of the machine to expense in the current period.

b Lee Oil Co. reported on its balance sheet as an intangible asset the total of all wages, supplies, depreciation on equipment, and other costs related to the drilling of a producing oil well and then amortized this asset as oil was produced from the well.

c A large lawsuit pending against Consumer Products Co. was not mentioned in the footnotes to the company's financial statements because the lawsuit had not actually been filed with the court until seven days after the end of the current year.

d Bob Standish is president of Dutchman Mines. During the current year, geologists and engineers revised upward the estimated amount of ore deposits on the company's property. Standish instructed the company's accountant to record goodwill of $2 million, representing the estimated value of unmined ore in excess of previous estimates. The offsetting credit was made to a revenue account.

e Aspen Airlines follows the practice of charging the purchase of hand tools with a unit cost of less than $50 to an expense account rather than to an asset account. The average life of these tools is about three years.

Problem 13B-3
Alternative
methods of
income
recognition

Nantucket Boat Works builds custom sailboats. During the first year of operations, the company built four boats for Island Charter Company. The four boats had a total cost of $216,000 and were sold for a total price of $360,000, due on an installment basis. Island Charter Company paid $120,000 of this sales price during the first year, plus an additional amount for interest charges.

At year-end, work is in progress on two other boats which are 40% complete. The contract price for these two boats totals $250,000 and costs incurred on these boats during the year total $60,000 (40% of estimated total costs of $150,000).

Instructions

Compute the gross profit for Nantucket Boat Works during its first year of operations under each of the following assumptions. (Interest earned from Island Charter Company does not enter into the computation of gross profit.)

a The entire profit is recognized on the four boats completed and profit on the two boats under construction is recognized on a percentage-of-completion basis.

b Profit on the four boats completed is recognized on the installment basis and no portion of the profit on the two boats under construction will be recognized until the boats are completed, delivered to customers, and cash is collected.

Problem 13B-4
Evaluating
applications of
accounting
principles

Assume that you are an independent CPA performing audits of financial statements. In the course of your work, you encounter the following situations:

a Reliable Appliance Co. sells appliances on long-term payment plans. The company uses the installment method of recognizing revenue in its income tax returns and in its financial statements. Uncollectible accounts consistently range between 1.5% and 2.0% of net sales.

b Akron Labs has spent $700,000 during the year in a very imaginative advertising campaign. The controller is sure that the advertising will generate revenue in future periods, but he has no idea how much revenue will be produced, or over what period of time it will be earned. Therefore, he has decided to follow the "conservative" policy of charging the advertising expenditures to expense in the current period.

c Taylor Corp. has purchased special-purpose equipment, designed to work with other machinery already in place in Taylor's assembly line. Due to the special nature of this machinery, it has virtually no resale value to any other company. Therefore, Taylor's accountant has charged the entire cost of this special-purpose machinery to expense in the current period.

d Architectural Associates charges all purchases of drafting supplies directly to expense. At year-end, the company makes no entry to record the fact that $100 to $200 of these supplies remain on hand.

e Newton Company prepares financial statements four times each year. For convenience, these statements are prepared when business is slow and the accounting staff is not busy with other matters. Last year, financial statements were prepared for the two-month period ended February 28, the five-month period ended July 31, the three-month period ended October 31, and the one-month period ended November 30.

Instructions   Discuss each of the above situations. If you consider the treatment to be in conformity with generally accepted accounting principles, explain why. If you do not, explain which principle or principles have been violated, and also explain how the situation should have been reported.

Problem 13B-5 "Trade-offs" among accounting principles   It is not possible to be consistent with all accounting principles all the time. Sometimes trade-offs are necessary; accountants may need to compromise one accounting principle or goal in order to achieve another more fully.

Instructions   Describe a situation that requires a trade-off between the following sets of principles or goals:

a The relevance of accounting information to decision makers and the need for this information to be reliable.

b The comparability of information reported by different companies and the idea that a company should consistently apply the same accounting methods from year-to-year.

c The realization principle and the need for relatively timely information.

d The desire to match revenue with expenses and the quest for objectivity.

BUSINESS DECISION CASE

Case 13-1 Gotta match?   In determining when to recognize an expenditure as expense, accountants attempt to apply the matching principle. If there is insufficient evidence to apply this principle in a meaningful manner, the expenditure is charged immediately to expense.

Instructions   Listed below are 10 types of costs frequently encountered by business organizations. Indicate in which period or periods these costs should be recognized as expense.

Types of Costs

1 The cost of merchandise purchased for resale.

2 The cost to an auto dealer of a training program for mechanics. On average, mechanics stay with the dealership for four years.

3 Sales commissions owed to employees for sales in the current period, but which are payable next period.

4 The cost of a two-year insurance policy.

5 The cost of accounts receivable estimated to be uncollectible.

6 Cost of expensive factory equipment with an estimated life of 10 years.

7 Research and development costs that may benefit the company for a decade or more if successful products are discovered and brought to market.

8 Cost of four wastebaskets with an estimated useful life of 10 years.

9 Interest on notes payable that has accrued during one period but is not payable until a future period.

10 Cost of an advertising campaign promoting the opening of a new store that is expected to remain in operation for 20 years.

ANSWERS TO SELF-TEST QUESTIONS

1 b   **2 c**   **3 c**   **4 d**   **5 a**

PART 5

Corporations

The next four chapters and two appendixes focus on accounting issues which primarily affect corporations. Although single proprietorships and partnerships are more numerous than corporations, it is the corporation which plays the dominant role in our economy. Corporations own more assets, earn more revenue, provide more jobs, and attract more investment capital than all other forms of business organization combined.

14 Corporations: Organization and Stockholders' Equity

15 Corporations: Operations, Earnings per Share, and Dividends

16 Bonds Payable, Leases, and Other Liabilities

Appendix A: Applications of Present Value

17 Investments in Corporate Securities

Appendix B: International Accounting and Foreign Currency Transactions

Corporations: Organization and Stockholders' Equity

This chapter begins our study of businesses organized as corporations. First, we describe the nature of a corporation, explain the concept of a "separate legal entity," and discuss the advantages and disadvantages of the corporate form of organization. Next, we focus attention upon the stockholders' equity section of a corporate balance sheet. Paid-in capital is distinguished from retained earnings, and preferred stock is contrasted with common stock. Distinctions are drawn among the concepts of par value, book value, and market value. Various stockholders' equity transactions are illustrated and explained, including the issuance of capital stock and the declaration and payment of cash dividends. Also covered are such topics as subscriptions to capital stock, accounting for donated capital, and the computation of book value per share.

After studying this chapter you should be able to meet these Learning Objectives:

1 Discuss the advantages and disadvantages of organizing a business as a corporation.

2 Explain the rights of stockholders and the roles of corporate directors and officers.

3 Contrast the balance sheet presentation of the ownership equity in a corporation and in a sole proprietorship.

4 Explain the nature of par value and of additional paid-in capital; account for the issuance of capital stock.

5 Contrast preferred stock and common stock.

6 Discuss the factors affecting the market price of preferred stock and of common stock.

7 Account for stock subscriptions and for donated capital.

8 Explain why the book value of common stock may differ significantly from market price.

Who owns General Motors Corporation? The owners of a corporation are called *stockholders.* Stockholders in General Motors include over one million men and women, as well as many pension funds, mutual investment funds, labor unions, banks, universities, and other organizations. Because a corporation can be used to pool the savings of any number of investors, it is an ideal means of obtaining the capital necessary for large-scale business activities.

Nearly all large businesses and many small ones are organized as corporations. There are many more sole proprietorships and partnerships than corporations, but in dollar volume of business activity, corporations hold an impressive lead. Because of the dominant role of the corporation in our economy, it is important for everyone interested in business, economics, or politics to have an understanding of corporations and their accounting practices.

What Is a Corporation?

A corporation is a *legal entity* having an existence separate and distinct from that of its owners. In the eyes of the law a corporation is an "artificial person," having many of the rights and responsibilities of a real person.

A corporation, as a separate legal entity, may own property in its own name. Thus, the assets of a corporation belong to the corporation itself, *not to the stockholders.* A corporation has legal status in court—that is, it may sue and be sued as if it were a person. As a legal entity, a corporation may enter into contracts, is responsible for its own debts, and pays income taxes on its earnings.

Advantages of the Corporate Form of Organization

The corporation offers a number of advantages not available in other forms of organization. Among these advantages are the following:

Objective 1
Discuss the advantages and disadvantages of organizing a business as a corporation.

1 No personal liability for stockholders   Creditors of a corporation have a claim against the assets of the corporation, not against the personal property of the stockholders. Thus, the amount of money which stockholders risk by investing in a corporation is *limited to the amount of their investment.* To many investors, this is the most important advantage of the corporate form.

2 Ease of accumulating capital   Ownership of a corporation is evidenced by transferable *shares of stock.* The sale of corporate ownership in units of one or more shares permits both large and small investors to participate in ownership of the business. Some corporations actually have more than a million individual stockholders. For this reason, large corporations are often said to be *publicly owned.* Of course not all corporations are large. Many small businesses are organized as corporations and are owned by a limited number of stockholders. Such corporations are said to be *closely held.*

3 Ownership shares are readily transferable   Shares of stock may be sold by one investor to another without dissolving or disrupting the business organization. The shares of most large corporations may be bought or sold by investors in organized markets, such as the *New York Stock Exchange.* Investments in these shares have the advantage of *liquidity,* because investors may easily convert their corporate ownership into cash by selling their stock.

4 Continuous existence A corporation is a separate legal entity with a perpetual existence. The continuous life of the corporation, despite changes in ownership, is made possible by the issuance of transferable shares of stock. By way of contrast, a partnership is a relatively unstable form of organization which is dissolved by the death or retirement of any of its members. The continuity of the corporate entity is essential to most large-scale business activities.

5 Professional management The stockholders own the corporation, but they do not manage it on a daily basis. To administer the affairs of the corporation, the stockholders elect a *board of directors.* The directors, in turn, hire a president and other corporate officers to manage the business. There is no mutual agency in a corporation; thus, an individual stockholder has no right to participate in the management of the business unless he or she has been hired as a corporate officer.

Disadvantages of the Corporate Form of Organization

Among the disadvantages of the corporation are:

1 Heavy taxation The income of a partnership or a sole proprietorship is taxable only as personal income to the owners of the business. The income of a corporation, on the other hand, is subject to income taxes which must be paid by the corporation. The combination of federal and state corporate income taxes often takes a major share of a corporation's before-tax income. If a corporation distributes its earnings to stockholders, the stockholders must pay personal income taxes on the amounts they receive. This practice of first taxing corporate income to the corporation and then taxing distributions of that income to the stockholders is sometimes called *double taxation.*

2 Greater regulation A corporation comes into existence under the terms of state laws and these same laws may provide for considerable regulation of the corporation's activities. For example, the withdrawal of funds from a corporation is subject to certain limits set by law. Federal laws administered by the Securities and Exchange Commission require publicly owned corporations to make extensive disclosure of their affairs.

3 Separation of ownership and control The separation of the functions of ownership and management may be an advantage in some cases but a disadvantage in others. On the whole, the excellent record of growth and earnings in most large corporations indicates that the separation of ownership and control has benefited rather than injured stockholders. In a few instances, however, a management group has chosen to operate a corporation for the benefit of insiders. The stockholders may find it difficult in such cases to take the concerted action necessary to oust the officers.

Income Taxes in Corporate Financial Statements

Since a corporation is a separate legal entity subject to taxes upon its income, the ledger of a corporation should include accounts for recording income taxes. No such accounts are needed for a business organized as a sole proprietorship or partnership.

Income taxes are based on a corporation's earnings. At year-end, before preparing financial statements, income taxes are recorded by an adjusting entry such as the following:

Recording corporate income taxes

Income Taxes Expense	72,750	
Income Taxes Payable		72,750

To record the income taxes payable for the year ended Dec. 31.

The account debited in this entry, Income Taxes Expense, is an expense account and usually appears as the very last deduction in the income statement as follows:

Final step in income statement

Income before income taxes	$200,000
Income taxes expense	72,750
Net income	$127,250

The liability account, Income Taxes Payable, will ordinarily be paid within a few months and should, therefore, appear in the current liability section of the balance sheet. More detailed discussion of corporate income taxes is presented in Chapter 18.

Formation of a Corporation

A corporation is created by obtaining a corporate *charter* from the state in which the company is to be incorporated. To obtain a corporate charter, an application called the *articles of incorporation* is submitted to the state corporations commissioner or other designated official. Once the charter is obtained, the stockholders in the new corporation hold a meeting to elect *directors* and to pass *bylaws* as a guide to the company's affairs. The directors in turn hold a meeting at which officers of the corporation are appointed.

■ **Organization Costs** The formation of a corporation is a much more costly step than the organization of a partnership. The necessary costs include the payment of an incorporation fee to the state, the payment of fees to attorneys for their services in drawing up the articles of incorporation, payments to promoters, and a variety of other outlays necessary to bring the corporation into existence. These costs are charged to an asset account called Organization Costs. In the balance sheet, organization costs appear under the "Other assets" caption, as illustrated on page 541.

The incurring of these organization costs leads to the existence of the corporate entity; consequently, the benefits derived from these costs may be regarded as extending over the entire life of the corporation. Since the life of a corporation may continue indefinitely, one might argue that organization costs are an asset with an unlimited life. However, income tax rules have permitted organization costs to be written off over a period of five years or more; consequently, most companies have elected to write off organization costs over a five-year period. Accountants have been willing to accept this practice, because organization costs are not material in dollar amount. The accounting principle of *materiality* permits departures from theoretical concepts on the grounds of convenience if the practice in question will not cause any material distortion of net income or financial position.

■ **Rights of Stockholders** The ownership of stock in a corporation usually carries the following basic rights:

Objective 2

Explain the rights of stockholders and the roles of corporate directors and officers.

1 To vote for directors, and thereby to be represented in the management of the business. The approval of a majority of stockholders may also be required for such important corporate actions as mergers and acquisitions, the selection of independent auditors, the incurring of long-term debts, the establishment of stock option plans, or the splitting of capital stock into a larger number of shares.

When a corporation issues both common stock and preferred stock, voting rights generally are granted only to the holders of common stock. These two different types of capital stock will be discussed in detail later in this chapter.

2 To share in profits by receiving *dividends* declared by the board of directors. Stockholders in a corporation may not make withdrawals of company assets, as may an owner of an unincorporated business. However, the earnings of a profitable corporation may be distributed to stockholders in the form of cash dividends. The payment of a dividend always requires formal authorization by the board of directors.

3 To share in the distribution of assets if the corporation is liquidated. When a corporation ends its existence, the creditors of the corporation must first be paid in full; any remaining assets are divided among stockholders in proportion to the number of shares owned.

Stockholders' meetings usually are held once a year. Each share of stock is entitled to one vote. In large corporations, these annual meetings are usually attended by relatively few persons, often by less than 1% of the stockholders. Prior to the meeting, the management group will request stockholders who do not plan to attend in person to send in *proxy statements* assigning their votes to the existing management. Through this use of the proxy system, management may secure the right to vote as much as, perhaps, 80% or more of the total outstanding shares.

■ **Functions of the Board of Directors** The primary functions of the board of directors are to manage the corporation and to protect the interests of the stockholders. At this level, management may consist principally of formulating policies and reviewing acts of the officers. Specific duties of the directors include declaring dividends, setting the salaries of officers, reviewing the system of internal control with the internal auditors and with the company's independent auditors, and authorizing important contracts of various kinds.

In recent years increasing importance has been attached to the inclusion of outside directors on the boards of large corporations. The term *outside directors* refers to individuals who are not officers of the company and who thus have a view independent of that of the corporate officers.

■ **Functions of Corporate Officers** Corporate officers are the top level of the professional managers appointed by the board of directors to run the business. These officers usually include a president or chief executive officer (CEO), one or more vice-presidents, a controller, a treasurer, and a secretary. A vice-president is often made responsible for the sales function; other vice-presidents may be given responsibility for such important functions as personnel, finance, and production.

The responsibilities of the controller, treasurer, and secretary are most directly related to the accounting phase of business operation. The *controller,* or chief accounting officer, is responsible for the maintenance of adequate internal control and for the preparation of accounting records and financial statements. Such specialized activities as budgeting, tax planning, and preparation of tax returns are usually placed under the controller's jurisdiction. The *treasurer* has custody of the company's funds and is generally responsible for planning and controlling the company's cash position. The *secretary* represents the corporation in many contractual and legal matters and maintains minutes of the meetings of directors and stockholders. Another responsibility of the secretary is to coordinate the preparation of the annual report, which includes the financial statements and other information relating to corporate activities. In small corporations, one officer frequently acts as both secretary and treasurer. The following organization chart indicates lines of authority extending from stockholders to the directors to the president and other officers.

■
Typical corporate organization

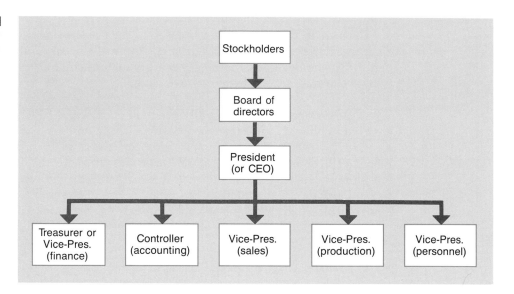

Stockholders' Equity

Objective 3
Contrast the balance sheet presentation of the ownership equity in a corporation and in a sole proprietorship.

The sections of the balance sheet showing assets and liabilities are much the same for a corporation as for a sole proprietorship. The owner's equity section is the principal point of contrast. In the balance sheet of a corporation, the term *stockholders' equity* is used instead of owner's equity.

The owners' equity in a corporation, as in other types of business organizations, is equal to the assets of the business minus the liabilities. However, state laws require that the stockholders' equity section of a corporate balance sheet clearly indicate the *source* of the owners' equity. The two basic sources of owners' equity are (1) investment by the stockholders *(paid-in capital),* and (2) earnings from profitable operation of the business *(retained earnings).*

When stockholders invest cash or other assets in the business, the corporation issues in exchange shares of capital stock as evidence of the stockholders' equity ownership. In the simplest case, capital invested by the stockholders is recorded in the corporation's accounting records by a credit to an account entitled **Capital Stock.** The capital paid in by stockholders is regarded as permanent capital not ordinarily subject to withdrawal.

The increase in stockholders' equity arising from profitable operations is called **retained earnings.** At the end of the year the balance of the Income Summary account is closed into the Retained Earnings account. For example, if net income for the year is $70,000, the closing entry will be as follows:

Income Summary...	70,000	
Retained earnings		70,000
To close the Income Summary account by transferring the year's net		
income into the Retained Earnings account.		

If the company operates at a loss of, say, $25,000, the Income Summary account will have a debit balance. The account must then be credited to close it. The closing entry will be:

Retained Earnings...	25,000	
Income Summary..		25,000
To close the Income Summary account by transferring the year's net		
loss into the Retained Earnings account.		

If a corporation has sufficient cash, a distribution of profits may be made to stockholders. Distributions of this nature are termed **dividends** and decrease both total assets and total stockholders' equity. Since dividends are regarded as distributions of earnings the decrease in stockholders' equity is recorded in the Retained Earnings account. Thus, the amount of retained earnings at any balance sheet date represents the **accumulated earnings of the company since the date of incorporation, minus any losses, and minus all dividends.**

Some people mistakenly believe that retained earnings represents a fund of cash available to a corporation. **Retained earnings is not an asset; it is an element of stockholders' equity.** Although the amount of retained earnings indicates the portion of total assets which are **financed** by earning and retaining net income, it does **not** indicate the **form** in which these resources are currently held. The resources generated by retaining profits may have been invested in land, buildings, equipment, or any other kind of asset. The total amount of cash owned by a corporation is shown by the balance of the Cash account, which appears in the asset section of the balance sheet.

■ **Stockholders' Equity on the Balance Sheet** For a corporation with $100,000 of capital stock and $40,000 of retained earnings, the stockholders' equity section of the balance sheet (omitting certain details) will appear as follows:

■
**Paid-in capital
and retained
earnings**

Stockholders' equity:		
Capital stock...	*$100,000*	
Retained earnings	*40,000*	*$140,000*

If this same company had been unprofitable and had incurred losses aggregating $30,000 since its organization, the stockholders' equity section of the balance sheet would be as follows:

Paid-in capital less losses incurred

Stockholders' equity:

Capital stock	*$100,000*	
Less: Deficit	*30,000*	*$70,000*

This second illustration tells us that $30,000 of the original $100,000 invested by stockholders has been lost. Note that the capital stock in both illustrations remains at the fixed amount of $100,000, the stockholders' original investment. The accumulated profits or losses since the organization of the corporation are shown as *retained earnings* or as a *deficit* and are not intermingled with the paid-in capital. The term *deficit* indicates a negative amount of retained earnings.

Cash Dividends

The term *dividend,* when used by itself, is generally understood to mean a distribution of cash by a corporation to its stockholders. Dividends are stated as a specific amount per share of capital stock, as, for example, a dividend of $1 per share. The amount received by each stockholder is in proportion to the number of shares owned. A stockholder who owns 100 shares will receive a check for $100.

Dividends are paid only through action by the board of directors. The board has full discretion to declare a dividend or to refrain from doing so. Once the declaration of a dividend has been announced, the obligation to pay the dividend is a current liability of the corporation and cannot be rescinded.

Because a dividend is declared on one date by the board of directors and paid at a later date, two separate journal entries are necessary. To illustrate the entries for declaration and payment of a cash dividend, assume that a corporation declares a dividend of $1 a share on 100,000 shares of outstanding stock. The dividend is declared on December 15 and is payable on January 25. The two entries would be as follows:

Dec. 15	*Retained Earnings*	*100,000*	
	Dividends Payable		*100,000*
	To record declaration by the board of directors of a cash dividend of $1 per share on the 100,000 shares of stock outstanding.		

Jan. 25	*Dividends Payable*	*100,000*	
	Cash		*100,000*
	To record payment of the $1 per share dividend declared Dec. 15 on the 100,000 shares of stock outstanding.		

The account *Dividends Payable,* which was credited at the date of declaring the dividend, is a current liability. If a company has more than one issue of capital stock (such as both common stock and preferred stock), it may use a separate Dividends Payable account for each issue.

Some companies in recording the declaration of a dividend will debit an account entitled Dividends instead of debiting the Retained Earnings account. Whenever a Dividends account is used, a closing entry will be required at the end of the year to transfer the debit balance in the Dividends account into the Retained Earnings account. Under either method the end result is a reduction in retained earnings for the amount of the dividends declared. (In our end-of-chapter material we will debit the Retained Earnings account, as illustrated above.)

What Is Capital Stock?

As previously mentioned, the caption *capital stock* in the balance sheet of a corporation represents the amount invested by the owners of the business. When the owners of a corporation invest cash or other assets in the business, the corporation issues capital stock as evidence of the investors' ownership equity.

The basic unit of capital stock is called a *share,* but a corporation may issue capital stock certificates in denominations of 1 share, 100 shares, or any other number. The total number of shares of capital stock outstanding at any given time represents 100% ownership of the corporation. *Outstanding* shares are those in the hands of stockholders. The number of shares owned by an individual investor determines the extent of his or her ownership of the corporation.

Assume, for example, that Star Corporation issues a total of 50,000 shares of capital stock to investors in exchange for cash. If you were to acquire 5,000 shares of the 50,000 shares, you would own a 10% interest in the corporation.

Authorization and Issuance of Capital Stock

The articles of incorporation specify the number of shares of capital stock which a corporation is authorized to issue and the *par value,* if any, per share. Large issues of capital stock to be offered for sale to the general public must be approved by the SEC as well as by state officials. The corporation may choose not to issue immediately all the authorized shares; in fact, it is customary to secure authorization for a larger number of shares than presently needed. In future years, if more capital is needed, the previously authorized shares will be readily available for issue; otherwise, the corporation would be forced to apply to the state for permission to increase the number of authorized shares.

Objective 4
Explain the nature of par value and of additional paid-in capital; account for the issuance of capital stock.

■ **Par Value**   Par value (or stated value) represents the *legal capital* per share—the amount below which stockholders' equity cannot be reduced except by losses from business operations or special legal action. A dividend cannot be declared by a corporation if such action would cause the stockholders' equity to fall below the par value of the outstanding shares. Par value, therefore, may be regarded as a minimum cushion of equity capital existing for the protection of creditors.

Par value may be $1 per share, $5, $100, or any other amount decided upon by the corporation. The par value of the stock is *no indication of its market value;* the par value merely indicates the amount per share to be entered in the *Capital Stock* account. The par value of most common stocks is relatively low. Polaroid Corporation common stock, for example, has a par value of $1; Sears, Roebuck & Co. common stock has a par value of 75 cents, American Home Products common stock has a par value of $33\frac{1}{3}$ cents per share. The market value of all these securities is far above their par value.

■ **Issuance of Par Value Stock**   Mere authorization of a stock issue does not bring an asset into existence, nor does it give the corporation any capital.

The obtaining of authorization from the state for a stock issue merely affords a legal opportunity to obtain assets through the sale of stock.

When par value stock is *issued,* the Capital Stock account is credited with the par value of the shares issued, regardless of whether the issuance price is more or less than par. Assuming that 10,000 shares of $10 par value stock have been authorized and that 5,000 of these authorized shares are issued at a price of $10 each, Cash would be debited and Capital Stock would be credited for $50,000. When stock is sold for more than par value, the Capital Stock account is credited with the par value of the shares issued, and a separate account, ***Additional Paid-in Capital,*** is credited for the excess of selling price over par. If, for example, our 5,000 shares were issued at a price of *$15* per share, the entry would be:

■
**Stockholders'
investment in
excess of par
value**

Cash...	*75,000*	
Capital Stock..		*50,000*
Additional Paid-in Capital		*25,000*
Issued 5,000 shares of $10 par value stock at a price of $15 a share.		

The additional paid-in capital does not represent a profit to the corporation. It is part of the invested capital and it will be added to the capital stock on the balance sheet to show the total paid-in capital. The stockholders' equity section of the balance sheet is illustrated below. (The existence of $10,000 in retained earnings is assumed in order to have a complete illustration.)

■
**Corporation's
capital classified
by source**

Stockholders' equity:	
Capital stock, $10 par value, authorized 10,000 shares, issued and	
outstanding 5,000 shares	*$50,000*
Additional paid-in capital	*25,000*
Total paid-in capital	*$75,000*
Retained earnings	*10,000*
Total stockholders' equity...	*$85,000*

If stock is issued by a corporation for less than par, the account Discount on Capital Stock should be debited for the difference between the issuance price and the par value. The issuance of stock at a discount is seldom encountered; it is illegal in many states.

■ **No-Par Stock** Some states allow corporations to issue stock without designating a par or stated value. When this "no-par" stock is issued, the *entire issue price* is credited to the Capital Stock account and is viewed as legal capital not subject to withdrawal.

Preferred Stock and Common Stock

**Objective 5
Contrast
preferred stock
and common
stock.**

In order to appeal to as many investors as possible, a corporation may issue more than one kind of capital stock. The basic type of capital stock issued by every corporation is called ***common stock.*** Common stock has the three basic rights previously mentioned. Whenever these rights are modified, the term ***preferred stock*** (or sometimes Class B Common) is used to describe this second type of capital stock. A few corporations issue two or more classes of preferred stock, each class having certain distinctive features designed to interest a particular type of investor. In summary, we may say that every business corporation has common stock; a good many corporations also issue preferred stock; and some companies have two or more types of preferred stock.

Common stock may be regarded as the basic, residual element of ownership. It carries voting rights and, therefore, is the means of exercising control over the business. Common stock has unlimited possibilities of increasing in value; during periods of business expansion the market prices of common stocks of some leading corporations may rise to many times their former values. On the other hand, common stocks lose value more rapidly than other types of securities when corporations encounter periods of unprofitable business.

The following stockholders' equity section illustrates the balance sheet presentation for a corporation having both preferred and common stock; note that separate additional paid-in capital accounts are used for each type of capital stock.

Balance sheet presentation

Stockholders' equity	
9% cumulative preferred stock, $100 par value, authorized 100,000 shares, issued 50,000 shares	$ 5,000,000
Common stock, $5 par value, authorized 3 million shares, issued 2 million shares	10,000,000
Additional paid-in capital:	
Preferred	200,000
Common	20,000,000
Total paid-in capital	$35,200,000
Retained earnings	13,500,000
Total stockholders' equity	$48,700,000

Characteristics of Preferred Stock

Most preferred stocks have the following distinctive features:

1 Preferred as to dividends

2 Cumulative dividend rights

3 Preferred as to assets in event of the liquidation of the company

4 Callable at the option of the corporation

5 No voting power

Another very important but less common feature is a clause permitting the *conversion* of preferred stock into common at the option of the holder. Preferred stocks vary widely with respect to the special rights and privileges granted. Careful study of the terms of the individual preferred stock contract is a necessary step in the evaluation of any preferred stock.

■ **Stock Preferred as to Dividends** Stock preferred as to dividends is entitled to receive each year a dividend of specified amount before any dividend is paid on the common stock. The dividend is usually stated as a dollar amount per share. Some preferred stocks state the dividend preference as a *percentage of par value.* For example, a *9%* preferred stock with a par value of $100 per share would mean that $9 must be paid yearly on each share of preferred stock before any dividends are paid on the common.

CASE IN POINT ■ Consolidated Edison has three issues of preferred stock which are publicly traded on the New York Stock Exchange. The first issue is a $5 preferred stock, which pays annual dividends of $5 per share. The other two issues include a 4.65% preferred and a 6% preferred. As both of these issues have $100 par values, they pay annual dividends of $4.65 and $6.00 per share, respectively.

Dividends on all three issues of preferred stock must be paid in full before Consolidated Edison pays any dividend on its common stock.

The holders of preferred stock have no assurance that they will always receive the indicated dividend. A corporation is obligated to pay dividends to stockholders only when the board of directors declares a dividend. Dividends must be paid on preferred stock before anything is paid to the common stockholders, but if the corporation is not prospering, it may decide not to pay dividends on either preferred or common stock. For a corporation to pay dividends, profits must be earned and cash must be available. However, preferred stocks in general offer *more assurance* of regular dividend payments than do common stocks.

■ **Cumulative Preferred Stock**   The dividend preference carried by most preferred stocks is a *cumulative* one. If all or any part of the regular dividend on the preferred stock is omitted in a given year, the amount omitted is said to be *in arrears* and must be paid in a subsequent year before any dividend can be paid on the common stock. Assume that a corporation was organized January 1, 1990, with 10,000 shares of $8 cumulative preferred stock and 50,000 shares of common stock. Dividends paid in 1990 were at the rate of $8 per share of preferred stock and $2 per share of common. In 1991, earnings declined sharply and the only dividend paid was $2 per share on the preferred stock. No dividends were paid in 1992. What is the status of the preferred stock at December 31, 1992? Dividends are in arrears in the amount of $14 a share ($6 omitted during 1991 and $8 omitted in 1992). On the entire issue of 10,000 shares of preferred stock, the dividends in arrears amount to $140,000.

Dividends in arrears *are not listed among the liabilities of a corporation, because no liability exists until a dividend is declared by the board of directors.* Nevertheless, the amount of any dividends in arrears on preferred stock is an important factor to investors and should always be *disclosed.* This disclosure is usually made by a note accompanying the balance sheet such as the following:

■
**Footnote
disclosure of
dividends in
arrears**

Note 6: Dividends in arrears

As of December 31, 1992, dividends on the $8 cumulative preferred stock were in arrears to the extent of $14 per share and amounted in total to $140,000.

In 1993, we shall assume that the company earned large profits and wished to pay dividends on both the preferred and common stocks. Before paying a dividend on the common, the corporation must pay the $140,000 in arrears on the cumulative preferred stock *plus* the regular $8 a share applicable to the current year. The preferred stockholders would, therefore, receive a total of $220,000 in dividends in 1993; the board of directors would then be free to declare dividends on the common stock.

For a *noncumulative* preferred stock, any unpaid or omitted dividend is lost forever. Because of this factor, investors view the noncumulative feature as an unfavorable element, and very few noncumulative preferred stocks are issued.

■ **Stock Preferred as to Assets**   Most preferred stocks carry a preference as to assets in the event of liquidation of the corporation. If the business is terminated, the preferred stock is entitled to payment in full of its par value or a higher stated liquidation value before any payment is made on the common stock. This priority also includes any dividends in arrears.

■ **Callable Preferred Stock**   Most preferred stocks include a *call provision.* This provision grants the issuing corporation the right to repurchase the stock from the stockholders at a stipulated *call price.* The call price is usually slightly higher than the par value of the stock. For example, $100 par value preferred stock may be callable at $105 or $110 per share. In addition to paying the call price, a corporation which redeems its preferred stock must pay any dividends in arrears. A call provision gives a corporation flexibility in adjusting its financial structure, for example, by eliminating a preferred stock and replacing it with other securities if future growth of the company makes such change advantageous.

■ **Convertible Preferred Stock**   In order to add to the attractiveness of preferred stock as an investment, corporations sometimes offer a *conversion privilege* which entitles the preferred stockholders to exchange their shares for common stock in a stipulated ratio. If the corporation prospers, its common stock will probably rise in market value, and dividends on the common stock will probably increase. The investor who buys a convertible preferred stock rather than common stock has greater assurance of regular dividends. In addition, through the conversion privilege, the investor is assured of sharing in any substantial increase in value of the company's common stock.

As an example, assume that Remington Corporation issued a 9%, $100 par, convertible preferred stock on January 1, at a price of $100 a share. Each share was convertible into four shares of the company's $10 par value common stock at any time. The common stock had a market price of $20 a share on January 1, and an annual dividend of $1 a share was being paid. During the next few years, Remington Corporation's earnings increased, the dividend on the common stock was raised to an annual rate of $3, and the market price of the common stock rose to $40 a share. At this point the preferred stock would have a market value of *at least $160,* since it could be converted at any time into four shares of common stock with a market value of $40 each. In other words, the market value of a convertible preferred stock will tend to move in accordance with the price of the common.

When the dividend rate is increased on the common stock, some holders of the preferred stock may convert their holdings into common stock in order to obtain a higher cash return on their investments. If the holder of 100 shares of the preferred stock presented these shares for conversion, Remington Corporation would make the following journal entry:

■
Conversion of preferred stock into common

9% Convertible Preferred Stock...	*10,000*	
Common Stock..		*4,000*
Additional Paid-in Capital: Common Stock........................		*6,000*
To record the conversion of 100 shares of preferred stock, par $100, into		
400 shares of $10 par value common stock.		

Note that the issue price recorded for the 400 shares of common stock is based upon the carrying value of the preferred stock in the accounting records, not upon market prices at the date of conversion.

■ **Participating Clauses in Preferred Stock**   Since participating preferred stocks are very seldom issued, discussion of them will be brief. A fully participating preferred stock is one which, in addition to the regular specified dividend, is entitled to participate in some manner with the common stock in any additional dividends paid. For example, a $5 participating preferred stock would be entitled to receive $5 a share before the common stock received anything. After $5 a share had been paid to the preferred stockholders, a $5 dividend could be paid on the common stock. If the company desired to pay an additional dividend to the common, say, an extra $3 per share, the preferred stock would also be entitled to receive an extra $3 dividend. In brief, a fully participating preferred stock participates dollar for dollar with the common stock in any dividends paid in excess of the stated rate on the preferred stock.

It is important to remember that most preferred stocks are *not* participating. Although common stock dividends may increase year after year if the corporation prospers, the dividends on most preferred stocks are fixed in amount. A $6 preferred stock, unless it is participating, *will never pay an annual dividend in excess of $6*.

Market Price of Preferred Stock

Objective 6
Discuss the factors affecting the market price of preferred stock and of common stock.

Investors buy preferred stocks primarily to receive the dividends that these shares pay. Thus, the dividend rate is one important factor in determining the market price of a preferred stock.

But what happens to the market price of an 8% preferred stock, originally issued at a par value of $100, if government policies and other factors cause long-term interest rates to rise to, say, 15 or 16%? If investments offering a return of 16% are readily available, investors will no longer pay $100 for a share of preferred stock which provides a dividend of only $8 per year. Thus, the market price of the preferred stock will fall to about half of its original issue price, or about $50 per share. At this market price, the stock offers a 16% return (called the *dividend yield*) to an investor purchasing the stock ($8 per year ÷ $50 = 16%). However, if the prevailing long-term interest rates should again decline to the 8% range, the market price of an 8% preferred stock should quickly rise to approximately par value.

In conclusion, the market price of preferred stock *varies inversely with interest rates.* As interest rates rise, preferred stock prices decline; as interest rates fall, preferred stock prices rise.

CASE IN POINT ■ The preceding point is illustrated by the performance of Philadelphia Electric's 9½%, $100 par value, preferred stock as interest rates have fluctuated over the years:

	LONG-TERM INTEREST RATES*	STOCK PRICE
September 1978	9½%	$99
August 1981	15¼%	60
March 1983	12½%	76
April 1985	13½%	68
August 1987	9¾%	102
June 1989	10½%	95

* The long-term interest rates cited in this example are the market yields of federally insured 30-year fixed-rate mortgages.

Market Price of Common Stock

Interest rates also affect the market price of common stock. However, dividends paid to common stockholders are not fixed in amount. Both the amount of the dividend and the market price of stock may increase dramatically if the corporation is successful. Therefore, the most important factor in the market price of common stock is **investors' expectations** as to the profitability of future operations.

CASE IN POINT ■ In early 1982, things looked bad for Ford Motor Company. The country was in the midst of a recession and auto sales were down. In each of the two preceding years, Ford had lost over $1 billion, and the company recently had stopped paying dividends. Investors were pessimistic about the company's future, and Ford's common stock traded for less than $4 per share.*

Over the next five years, an improving economy, a weak dollar, and such popular new models as the Taurus helped to turn Ford around. Earnings and dividends increased steadily. By 1987, Ford was among the most profitable corporations in the world, earning net income of more than $4½ billion and paying a substantial dividend. In mid-1987, the company's common stock was trading for more than $50 per share.*

* Per share prices have been adjusted for stock splits. Stock splits are discussed in Chapter 15.

Bear in mind that after shares have been issued they belong to the *stockholders,* not to the issuing corporation. Therefore, changes in the market price of the shares *do not affect the financial statements of the corporation,* and these changes are not recorded in the corporation's accounting records. The paid-in capital shown in a corporate balance sheet represents the amount *received when the stock was issued,* not the current market value of shares.

The Role of an Underwriter

When a large amount of stock is to be issued, most corporations use the services of an investment banking firm, frequently referred to as an *underwriter.* The underwriter guarantees the issuing corporation a specific price for the stock and makes a profit by selling the shares to the investing public at a slightly higher price. The corporation records the issuance of the stock at the net amount received from the underwriter. The use of an underwriter assures the corporation that the entire stock issue will be sold without delay, and the entire amount of funds to be raised will be available on a specific date.

The price that a corporation will ask for a new issue of stock is based upon such factors as (1) expected future earnings and dividends, (2) the financial strength of the company, and (3) the current state of the investment markets. However, if the corporation asks too much, it simply will not find an underwriter or other buyers willing to purchase the shares.

Stock Issued for Assets Other Than Cash

Corporations generally sell their capital stock for cash and use the cash to buy the various types of assets needed in the business. Sometimes, however, a corporation may issue shares of its capital stock in a direct exchange for land, buildings, or other assets. Stock may also be issued in payment for services rendered by attorneys and promoters in the formation of the corporation.

When a corporation issues capital stock in exchange for services or for assets other than cash, the transaction should be recorded at the current *market value* of the goods or services received. For some types of assets such as land or buildings, the services of a firm of professional appraisers may be useful in establishing current market value. Often, the best evidence as to the market value of these goods or services is the market value of the shares issued in exchange. For example, assume that a company issues 10,000 shares of its $1 par value common stock in exchange for land. Competent appraisers may have differing opinions as to the market value of the land. But let us assume that the company's stock is currently selling on a stock exchange for $90 per share. It is logical to say that the cost of the land to the company is $900,000, the market value of the shares issued in exchange.

Once the valuation has been decided, the entry to record the issuance of the stock in exchange for the land is as follows:

Notice the use of current market values

Land...	900,000	
Common Stock...		10,000
Additional Paid-in Capital: Common Stock.........................		890,000

To record the issuance of 10,000 shares of $1 par value common stock in exchange for land. Current market value of stock ($90 per share) used as basis for valuing the land.

Subscriptions to Capital Stock

Objective 7
Account for stock subscriptions and for donated capital.

Small corporations sometimes sell stock on a *subscription plan,* in which the investor agrees to pay the subscription price at a future date or in a series of installments. When the subscription contract is signed, Stock Subscriptions Receivable is debited and Capital Stock Subscribed is credited. Later, as installments are collected, the entry is a debit to Cash and a credit to Stock Subscriptions Receivable. When the entire subscription price has been collected, the stock certificates are issued. The issuance of the stock is recorded by debiting Capital Stock Subscribed and crediting Capital stock. The following illustration demonstrates the accounting procedures for stock subscriptions.

In this example, 10,000 shares of $1 par value capital stock are subscribed at a price of $15. Subscriptions for 6,000 of these shares are then collected in full. A partial payment is received on the other 4,000 shares.

Subscription price above par

Stock Subscriptions Receivable	150,000	
Capital Stock Subscribed		10,000
Additional Paid-in Capital		140,000

Received subscriptions for 10,000 shares of $1 par value stock at price of $15 a share.

When the subscriptions for 6,000 shares are collected in full, certificates for 6,000 shares will be issued. The following entries are made:

Certificates issued for fully paid shares

Cash...	90,000	
Stock Subscriptions Receivable		90,000

Collected subscriptions in full for 6,000 shares at $15 each.

Capital Stock Subscribed	6,000	
Capital Stock...		6,000

Issued certificates for 6,000 fully paid $1 par value shares.

The subscriber to the remaining 4,000 shares paid only half of the amount of the subscription but promised to pay the remainder within a month. Stock certificates will not be issued until the subscription is collected in full, but the partial collection is recorded by the following entry:

Partial collection of subscription

Cash...	30,000	
Stock Subscriptions Receivable		30,000

Collected partial payment on subscription for 4,000 shares.

From the corporation's point of view, Stock Subscriptions Receivable is a current asset, which ordinarily will be collected within a short time. If financial statements are prepared between the date of obtaining subscriptions and the date of issuing the stock, the Capital Stock Subscribed account is regarded as legal capital and will appear in the stockholders' equity section of the balance sheet.

Donated Capital

On occasion, a corporation may receive assets as a gift. To increase local employment, for example, some cities have given corporations the land upon which to build factories. When a corporation receives such a gift, both total assets and total stockholders' equity increase by the market value of the assets received. *No profit is recognized when a gift is received;* the increase in stockholders' equity is regarded as paid-in capital. The receipt of a gift is recorded by debiting the appropriate asset accounts and crediting an account entitled

Donated Capital. Donated capital appears in the stockholders' equity section of the balance sheet, as illustrated on page 541.

Stockholder Records in a Corporation

A large corporation with shares listed on the New York Stock Exchange usually has millions of shares outstanding and several hundred thousand stockholders. Each day many stockholders sell their shares; the buyers of these shares become new members of the company's family of stockholders. An investor purchasing stock in a corporation receives a ***stock certificate*** from the company indicating the number of shares acquired. If the investor later sells these shares, this stock certificate must be surrendered to the corporation for cancellation before a new certificate is issued to the new owner of the shares.

A corporation must have an up-to-date record of the names and addresses of this constantly changing army of stockholders so that it can send dividend checks, financial statements, and voting forms to the right people. Also, the corporation must make sure that old stock certificates are canceled as new ones are issued so that no excess certificates become outstanding.

■ **Stockholders' Ledger**   When there are numerous stockholders, it is not practical to include a separate account for each stockholder in the general ledger. Instead, a single controlling account entitled Capital Stock appears in the general ledger, and a subsidiary stockholders' ledger is maintained. This ledger contains a page for each individual stockholder. Entries in the stockholders' ledger are made in number of shares rather than in dollars. Thus, each stockholder's account shows the number of shares owned, and the dates of acquisitions and sales. This record enables the corporation to send each stockholder a single dividend check, even though the stockholder may have acquired several stock certificates at different dates.

A corporation which has one or more issues of preferred stock outstanding, as well as common stock, will maintain a separate set of stockholders' records for each issue.

■ **Stock Transfer Agent and Stock Registrar**   Large, publicly owned corporations use an independent stock transfer agent and a stock registrar to maintain their stockholder records and to establish strong internal control over the issuance of stock certificates. These transfer agents and registrars usually are large banks or trust companies. When stock certificates are to be transferred from one owner to another, the old certificates are sent to the transfer agent, who cancels them, makes the necessary entries in the stockholders' ledger, and prepares a new certificate for the new owner of the shares. This new certificate then must be registered with the stock registrar before it represents valid and transferable ownership of stock in the corporation.

Small, closely held corporations generally do not use the services of independent registrars and transfer agents. In these companies, the stockholder records usually are maintained by a corporate officer. To prevent the accidental or fraudulent issuance of an excessive number of stock certificates, even a small corporation should require that each certificate be signed by at least two designated corporate officers.

Book Value per Share of Common Stock

Because the equity of each stockholder in a corporation is determined by the number of shares he or she owns, an accounting measurement of interest to many stockholders is book value per share of common stock. Book value per share is equal to the *net assets* represented by one share of stock. The term *net assets* means total assets minus total liabilities; in other words, net assets are equal to total stockholders' equity. Thus in a corporation which has issued common stock only, the book value per share is computed by dividing total stockholders' equity by the number of shares outstanding (or subscribed).

For example, assume that a corporation has 4,000 shares of capital stock outstanding and the stockholders' equity section of the balance sheet is as follows:

■
How much is book value per share?

Capital stock, $1 par value (4,000 shares outstanding)	$ 4,000
Additional paid-in capital	40,000
Retained earnings	76,000
Total stockholders' equity	$120,000

The book value per share is $30; it is computed by dividing the stockholders' equity of $120,000 by the 4,000 shares of outstanding stock. In computing book value, we are not concerned with the number of authorized shares but merely with the *outstanding* shares, because the total of the outstanding shares represents 100% of the stockholders' equity.

■ **Book Value When a Company Has Both Preferred and Common Stock** Book value is usually computed only for common stock. If a company has both preferred and common stock outstanding, the computation of book value per share of common stock requires two steps. First, the redemption value or *call price* of the entire preferred stock issue and any dividends in arrears are deducted from total stockholders' equity. Second, the remaining amount of stockholders' equity is divided by the number of common shares outstanding to determine book value per common share. This procedure reflects the fact that the common stockholders are the residual owners of the corporate entity.

To illustrate, assume that the stockholders' equity of Video Company at December 31 is as follows:

■
Two classes of stock

8% preferred stock, $100 par, callable at $110	$1,000,000
Common stock, $10 stated value; authorized 100,000 shares, issued and outstanding 50,000 shares	500,000
Additional paid-in capital: common stock	750,000
Retained earnings	130,000
Total stockholders' equity	$2,380,000

Because of a weak cash position, Video Company has paid no dividends during the current year. As of December 31, dividends in arrears on the cumulative preferred stock total *$80,000.*

All the equity belongs to the common stockholders, except the $1.1 million call price ($110 × 10,000 shares) applicable to the preferred stock and the $80,000 of dividends in arrears on preferred stock. The calculation of book value per share of common stock is shown below:

Total stockholders' equity		*$2,380,000*
Less: Equity of preferred stockholders:		
Call price of preferred stock	*$1,100,000*	
Dividends in arrears	*80,000*	*1,180,000*
Equity of common stockholders		*$1,200,000*
Number of common shares outstanding		*50,000*
Book value per share of common stock		
($1,200,000 ÷ 50,000 shares)		*$24*

Objective 8
Explain why the book value of common stock may differ significantly from market price.

■ **Book Value and Market Price** To some extent, book value is used in evaluating the reasonableness of the market price of a stock. However, it must be used with great caution; the fact that a stock is selling at less than book value does not necessarily indicate a bargain.

Book value is a historical concept, representing the amounts invested by stockholders plus the amounts earned and retained by the corporation. If a stock is selling at a price well ***above*** book value, investors believe that management has created a business worth substantially more than the historical cost of the resources entrusted to its care. This, in essence, is the sign of a successful corporation. If the excess of market price over book value becomes very great, however, investors should consider whether the company's prospects really justify a market price so much above the underlying book value of the company's resources.

On the other hand, if the market price of a stock is ***less than*** book value, investors believe that the company's resources are worth less than their cost while under the control of current management. Thus, the relationship between book value and market price is one measure of investors' confidence in a company's management.

Balance Sheet for a Corporation Illustrated

A fairly complete balance sheet for a corporation is illustrated on the following page. Note the inclusion in this balance sheet of liabilities for income taxes payable and dividends payable. These liabilities do not appear in the balance sheet of an unincorporated business. Note also that the caption for each capital stock account indicates the type of stock, the par value per share, and the number of shares authorized and issued. The caption for preferred stock also indicates the dividend rate, call price, and other important features.

Bear in mind that current practice includes many alternatives in the choice of terminology and the arrangement of items in financial statements.

DEL MAR CORPORATION
Balance Sheet
December 31, 1991

ASSETS

Current assets:

Cash		$ 305,600
Accounts receivable (net)		1,105,200
Stock subscriptions receivable		110,000
Inventories		1,300,800
Short-term prepayments		125,900
Total current assets		$2,947,500
Plant and equipment:		
Land		900,000
Buildings and equipment	$5,283,000	
Less: Accumulated depreciation	1,250,000	4,033,000
Other assets: Organization costs		14,000
Total assets		$7,894,500

LIABILITIES & STOCKHOLDERS' EQUITY

Current liabilities:

Accounts payable		$ 998,100
Income taxes payable		324,300
Dividends payable		109,700
Interest payable		20,000
Total current liabilities		$1,452,100
Long-term liabilities: Bonds payable, 12%, due Oct. 1, 1999		1,000,000
Total liabilities		$2,452,100

Stockholders' equity:

Cumulative 8% preferred stock, $100 par, callable at $104, authorized and issued 10,000 shares		$1,000,000
Common stock, $1 par, authorized 1,000,000 shares, issued 600,000 shares		600,000
Common stock subscribed, 20,000 shares		20,000
Additional paid-in capital: common		2,070,000
Donated capital		210,000
Total paid-in capital		$3,900,000
Retained earnings		1,542,400
Total stockholders' equity		$5,442,400
Total liabilities & stockholders' equity		$7,894,500

End-of-Chapter Review

CONCEPTS INTRODUCED OR EMPHASIZED IN CHAPTER 14

The major concepts introduced in this chapter include:

■ The nature, advantages, and disadvantages of the corporate form of business organization.

■ The "limited liability" of a corporation's owners (stockholders).

■ The distinction between paid-in capital and retained earnings.

■ Accounting for the issuance of capital stock and for the declaration and payment of dividends to stockholders.

■ The characteristics and features of preferred stock and of common stock.

■ The presentation of stockholders' equity in the balance sheet of a corporation.

■ The meaning and significance of different "values" of capital stock, including par value, market value, and book value.

We will continue our discussion of corporate accounting issues over the next three chapters, concluding with a discussion of corporate securities (stocks and bonds) from the viewpoint of the investor. Throughout the remainder of this textbook, and in later accounting courses, the corporation will be the form of organization used in most illustrations and assignment material.

KEY TERMS INTRODUCED OR EMPHASIZED IN CHAPTER 14

Additional paid-in capital   Amounts invested in a corporation by stockholders (or as donated capital) in excess of the par value or stated value of any shares issued in exchange. In short, *paid-in capital* in excess of *legal capital.*

Board of directors   Persons elected by common stockholders to direct the affairs of a corporation.

Book value per share   The stockholders' equity represented by each share of common stock, computed by dividing common stockholders' equity by the number of common shares outstanding.

Call price   The price to be paid by a corporation for each share of callable preferred stock if the corporation decides to call (redeem) the preferred stock.

Capital stock   Transferable units of ownership in a corporation. A broad term which may refer to common stock, preferred stock, or both.

Common stock   A type of capital stock which possesses the basic rights of ownership including the right to vote. Represents the residual element of ownership in a corporation.

Deficit   Accumulated losses incurred by a corporation. A negative amount of retained earnings.

Dividend   A distribution of cash by a corporation to its stockholders.

Donated capital   Capital given to a corporation, with no payment being made or capital stock being issued in exchange. Shown in the balance sheet as an element of paid-in capital.

Legal capital   Equal to the *par value* or *stated value* of capital stock issued. This amount represents a "permanent commitment" of capital by the owners of a corporation and cannot be removed without special legal action. Of course, it may be eroded by losses.

Organization costs   Costs incurred to form a corporation.

Paid-in capital   The amounts invested in a corporation by its stockholders (also includes donated capital).

Par value or stated value   The *legal capital* of a corporation. Represents the minimum amount per share to be invested in the corporation by its owners and cannot be withdrawn except by special legal action.

Preferred stock   A class of capital stock usually having preferences as to dividends and in the distribution of assets in event of liquidation.

Retained earnings   That portion of stockholders' equity resulting from profits earned and retained in the business. Retained earnings is increased by the earning of net income and is decreased by the incurring of net losses and by the declaration of dividends.

Stock certificate   A document issued by a corporation (or its transfer agent) as evidence of the ownership of the number of shares stated on the certificate.

Stock registrar   An independent fiscal agent, usually a large bank, retained by a corporation to provide assurance against overissuance of stock certificates.

Stock transfer agent   A bank or trust company retained by a corporation to maintain its records of capital stock ownership and make transfers from one investor to another.

Stockholder   Someone with an ownership interest in a corporation. The percentage of this ownership interest is determined by the percentage of the outstanding shares owned.

Stockholders' ledger   A subsidiary record showing the number of shares owned by each stockholder.

Subscriptions to capital stock   Formal promises to buy shares of stock from a corporation with payment at a later date. Stock certificates are delivered when full payment is received.

Underwriter   An investment banking firm which handles the sale of a corporation's stock to the public.

DEMONSTRATION PROBLEM FOR YOUR REVIEW

At the close of the current year, the stockholders' equity section of Rockhurst Corporation's balance sheet was as follows:

Stockholders' equity:		
$6 preferred stock, $100 par value, callable at $102, 200,000		
shares authorized		$12,000,000
Common stock, $5 par value, 5,000,000 shares authorized:		
Issued	$10,000,000	
Subscribed..	4,000,000	14,000,000
Additional paid-in capital:		
Preferred..	$ 360,000	
Common (including subscribed shares)....................	30,800,000	31,160,000
Retained earnings		2,680,000
Total stockholders' equity..		$59,840,000

Assets of the corporation include *subscriptions receivable, $7,200,000.*

Instructions   On the basis of this information, answer the following questions and show any necessary supporting computations.

a   How many shares of preferred stock have been issued?

b   What is the total annual dividend requirement on the outstanding preferred stock?

c   How many shares of common stock have been issued or subscribed?

d   What was the average price per share received by the corporation for its common stock, including shares subscribed?

e What is the average amount per share that subscribers to common stock have yet to pay on their subscriptions?

f What is the total amount of legal capital, including shares subscribed?

g What is the total paid-in capital, including shares subscribed?

h What is the book value per share of common stock? (Assume no dividends in arrears.)

SOLUTION TO DEMONSTRATION PROBLEM

a 120,000 shares ($12,000,000 total par value, divided by $100 par value per share)

b $720,000 (120,000 shares × $6 per share)

c 2,800,000 shares ($14,000,000 total par value, divided by $5 par value per share)

d

Par value of common shares issued and subscribed	$14,000,000
Additional paid-in capital on common shares	30,800,000
Total issue price of common shares (including subscribed)	$44,800,000
Shares issued and subscribed (part c)	2,800,000
Average issue price per share ($44,800,000 ÷ 2,800,000 shares)	$16

e

Subscriptions receivable	$ 7,200,000
Shares subscribed ($4,000,000 total par value, divided by	
$5 par value per share)	800,000
Average amount due per share ($7,200,000 ÷ 800,000 shares)	$9

f $26,000,000 ($12,000,000 preferred, $14,000,000 common)

g $57,160,000 ($26,000,000 legal capital, plus $31,160,000 additional paid-in capital)

h

Total stockholders' equity	$59,840,000
Less: Claims of preferred stockholders (120,000 shares	
× $102 call price)	12,240,000
Equity of common stockholders	$47,600,000
Common shares outstanding or subscribed (part c)	2,800,000
Book value per share ($47,600,000 ÷ 2,800,000 shares)	$17

SELF-TEST QUESTIONS

The answers to these questions appear on page 555.

1 When a business is organized as a corporation:

a Stockholders are liable for the debts of the business only in proportion to their percentage ownership of capital stock.

b Stockholders do **not** have to pay personal income taxes on dividends received, because the corporation is subject to income taxes on its earnings.

c Fluctuations in the market value of outstanding shares of capital stock do **not** affect the amount of stockholders' equity shown in the balance sheet.

d Each stockholder has the right to bind the corporation to contracts and to make other managerial decisions.

2 Great Plains Corporation was organized with authorization to issue 100,000 shares of $1 par value common stock. Forty thousand shares were issued to Tom Morgan, the company's founder, at a price of $5 per share. No other shares have yet been issued.

a Morgan owns **40%** of the stockholders' equity of the corporation.

b The corporation should recognize a $160,000 gain on the issuance of these shares.

c If the balance sheet includes retained earnings of $50,000, total *paid-in* capital amounts to $250,000.

d In the balance sheet, the Additional Paid-in Capital account will have a $160,000 balance, regardless of the profits earned or losses incurred since the corporation was organized.

3 Which of the following is *not* a characteristic of the *common stock* of a large, publicly owned corporation?

a The shares may be transferred from one investor to another without disrupting the continuity of business operations.

b Voting rights in the election of the board of directors.

c A cumulative right to receive dividends.

d After issuance, the market value of the stock is unrelated to its par value.

4 Tri-State Electric is a profitable utility company that has increased its dividend to *common* stockholders every year for 62 consecutive years. Which of the following is *least* likely to affect the market price of the company's *preferred* stock?

a The company's earnings are expected to increase significantly over the next several years.

b An increase in long-term interest rates.

c The annual dividend paid to preferred shareholders.

d Whether or not the preferred stock carries a conversion privilege.

5 The following information is taken from the balance sheet and related disclosures of Blue Oyster Corporation:

Total paid-in capital	$5,400,000
Outstanding shares:	
Common stock, $5 par value..	100,000 shares
6% preferred stock, $100 par value, callable at	
$108 per share	10,000 shares
Preferred dividends in arrears..	2 years
Total stockholders' equity..	$4,700,000

For this question, more than one answer may be correct.

a The preferred dividends in arrears amount to $120,000 and should appear as a liability in the corporate balance sheet.

b The book value per share of common stock is $35.

c The stockholders' equity section of the balance sheet should include a deficit of $700,000.

d The company has paid no dividend on its *common* stock during the past two years.

Assignment Material

REVIEW QUESTIONS

1 Why are large corporations often said to be *publicly owned?*

2 Distinguish between corporations and partnerships in terms of the following characteristics:

a Owners' liability for debts of the business

b Transferability of ownership interest

c Continuity of existence

d Federal taxation on income

3 What are the basic rights of the owner of a share of corporate stock? In what way are these basic rights commonly modified with respect to the owner of a share of preferred stock?

4 Explain the meaning of the term *double taxation* as it applies to corporate profits.

5 Distinguish between *paid-in capital* and *retained earnings* of a corporation. Why is such a distinction useful?

6 If the Retained Earnings account has a debit balance, how is it presented in the balance sheet and what is it called?

7 Explain the significance of *par value.* Does par value indicate the reasonable market price for a share of stock? Explain.

8 Describe the usual nature of the following features as they apply to a share of preferred stock: (a) cumulative, (b) convertible, and (c) callable.

9 Why is noncumulative preferred stock considered a very unattractive form of investment?

10 When stock is issued by a corporation in exchange for assets other than cash, accountants face the problem of determining the dollar amount at which to record the transaction. Discuss the factors to be considered and explain their significance.

11 State the classification (asset, liability, stockholders' equity, revenue, or expense) of each of the following accounts:

a Subscriptions receivable   **e** Capital stock subscribed

b Organization costs   **f** Additional paid-in capital

c Preferred stock   **g** Income taxes payable

d Retained earnings

12 A professional baseball team received as a gift from the city the land upon which to build a stadium. What effect, if any, will the receipt of this gift have upon the baseball team's balance sheet and income statement? Explain.

13 Explain the following terms:

a Stock transfer agent   **c** Underwriter

b Stockholders' ledger   **d** Stock registrar

14 What does *book value per share* of common stock represent? Does it represent the amount common stockholders would receive in the event of liquidation of the corporation? Explain briefly.

15 How is book value per share of common stock computed when a company has both preferred and common stock outstanding?

16 What would be the effect, if any, on book value per share of common stock as a result of each of the following independent events: **(a)** a corporation obtains a bank loan; **(b)** a dividend is declared (to be paid in the next accounting period).

17 In the great stock market crash of October 19, 1987, the market price of IBM's capital stock fell by over $31 per share. Explain the effects, if any, of this decline in share price on IBM's balance sheet.

EXERCISES

**Exercise 14-1
Accounting
terminology**

Listed below are nine technical accounting terms introduced or emphasized in this chapter:

Par value	*Retained earnings*	*Preferred stock*
Book value	*Deficit*	*Common stock*
Market value	*Dividend in arrears*	*Paid-in capital*

Each of the following statements may (or may not) describe one of these technical terms. For each statement, indicate the term described, or answer "None" if the statement does not correctly describe any of the terms.

a The type of capital stock for which the dividend usually is fixed in amount.

b Cash provided by profitable operations that is available for distribution to stockholders as dividends.

c The per-share value of common stock that reflects investors' expectations of future profitability.

d A dividend paid to common stockholders that is smaller than the dividend paid in the prior year.

e That portion of stockholders' equity arising from the issuance of capital stock.

f The type of capital stock most likely to increase in value as a corporation becomes increasingly profitable.

g The net assets represented by one share of common stock.

h A distribution of cash by a corporation to its owners.

**Exercise 14-2
Computing
retained earnings**

Plastic Pipe Corporation began operations in 1990. In that year, the corporation earned net income of $170,000 and paid dividends of $2.00 per share on its 60,000 outstanding shares of capital stock. In 1991, the corporation incurred a net loss of $95,000 and paid no dividends.

Instructions

a Prepare the journal entry to close the Income Summary account at December 31, 1991 (the year of the $95,000 net loss).

b Compute the amount of retained earnings or deficit which will appear in the company's balance sheet at December 31, 1991.

**Exercise 14-3
Recording
dividends**

Showboat Corporation has only one issue of capital stock, consisting of 50,000 outstanding shares. The net income in the first year of operations was $96,000. No dividends were paid in the first year. On January 15 of the second year, a dividend of $1.10 per share was declared by the board of directors payable February 15.

Instructions

a Prepare the journal entry at December 31 of the first year to close the Income Summary account.

b Prepare the journal entries for declaration of the dividend on January 15 and payment of the dividend on February 15 of the second year.

**Exercise 14-4
Stockholders'
equity section of
a balance sheet**

When Heritage Corporation was formed, the company was authorized to issue 2,000 shares of $100 par value, 9% cumulative preferred stock, and 100,000 shares of $1 stated value common stock. The preferred stock is callable at $106.

All of the preferred stock was issued at a price of $102 per share, and 40,000 shares of the common stock were sold for $10 per share. At the end of the current year, Heritage Corporation has retained earnings of $216,000. Prepare the stockholders' equity section of the company's balance sheet at the end of the current year.

Exercise 14-5
Analyzing stockholders' equity

The year-end balance sheet of Maui Corporation includes the following stockholders' equity section (with certain details omitted):

Stockholders' equity:
  Capital stock:
    7% cumulative preferred stock, $100 par value, callable at $105 . . . . $ 15,000,000
    Common stock, $5 par value, 5,000,000 shares authorized,
      4,000,000 shares issued.   20,000,000
    Additional paid-in capital:
      Preferred.   300,000
      Common   44,000,000
    Retained earnings   64,450,000
      Total stockholders' equity. $143,750,000

Instructions

From this information, compute answers to the following questions:

a How many shares of preferred stock have been issued?

b What is the total amount of the annual dividends paid to preferred stockholders?

c What was the average issuance price per share of common stock?

d What is the amount of legal capital and the amount of total paid-in capital?

e What is the book value per share of common stock?

Exercise 14-6
Computing book value

Presented below is the information necessary to compute the net assets (stockholders' equity) and book value per share of common stock for Ringside Corporation:

8% cumulative preferred stock, $100 par (callable at $110) $200,000
Common stock, $5 par, authorized 100,000 shares, issued 60,000 shares   300,000
Additional paid-in capital   452,800
Deficit   146,800
Dividends in arrears on preferred stock, 1 full year   16,000

Instructions

a Compute the amount of net assets (stockholders' equity).

b Compute the book value per share of common stock.

Exercise 14-7
Issuing stock for assets other than cash

Roto Corporation issued 25,000 shares of common stock in exchange for land with a fair market value of $650,000. Prepare the journal entry to record this transaction under each of the following independent assumptions:

a The stock has a $2 par value.

b The stock has a $30 par value. (Disregard possible violation of state laws.)

c The stock has no par value or stated value.

Exercise 14-8
Stock subscriptions

To raise capital for a new polo field, Santa Fe Polo Club offered shares of its common stock to club members on a subscription plan. Prepare journal entries in the club's accounting records to record the following transactions:

Sept. 15   Members subscribed to 10,000 shares of $2 par value common stock at a subscription price of $30 per share.

Dec. 20   Collected $240,000 cash in full payment of 8,000 of the subscribed shares. Issued stock certificates for these shares.

Exercise 14-9
Nature of market,
par, and book
values

SmithKline Beckman, the large pharmaceutical company that manufactures the cold-remedy *Contac,* had a stated goal of increasing its net income by 10% each year. As of mid-1988, the company's earnings growth had been "right on target" for several years, and most investors thought the company would again achieve its goal in 1988. In June 1988, however, the company surprised investors by announcing that earnings probably would not increase in 1988. In fact, management estimated that earnings for 1988 might be about 10% below the earnings of 1987. The reduced level of earnings, however, would not affect the company's ability to continue paying dividends at the current rate.

What would you expect the immediate effect of this announcement to be upon the following values of SmithKline's common stock? Explain.

a Par value

b Market value

c Book value

PROBLEMS

Group A

Problem 14A-1
Journal entries
for corporate
transactions

Shown below are selected transactions of St. Claire Vineyards for the year ended December 31, 1991:

Jan. 19 Issued 10,000 shares of $1 par value capital stock to Martin DiBello in exchange for land. The fair market value of the land and of the issued shares is $190,000.

June 10 At their June meeting, the board of directors declared a dividend of $0.20 per share, payable on July 15 to the owners of the corporation's 200,000 outstanding shares of capital stock.

July 15 Paid the dividend declared on June 10.

Dec. 31 Recorded income tax expense for the three months ended December 31, 1991, $34,900. These taxes will be paid on January 15, 1992. (Income taxes for the first nine months of 1991 have already been recorded and paid.)

Dec. 31 Closed the Income Summary account at the end of a profitable period. Net income, $365,000.

Instructions Prepare journal entries to record the above transactions.

Problem 14A-2
Stockholders'
equity in a
balance sheet

Early in 1988, Scott Industries was organized with authorization to issue 10,000 shares of $100 par value preferred stock and 500,000 shares of $5 par value common stock. All of the preferred stock was issued at par, and 120,000 shares of common stock were sold for $15 per share. The preferred stock pays a 9% cumulative dividend and is callable at $110.

During the first four years of operations (1988 through 1991), the corporation earned a total of $725,000 and paid dividends of 50 cents per share each year on the common stock. In 1992, however, the corporation reported a net loss of $340,000 and paid no dividends.

Instructions **a** Prepare the stockholders' equity section of the balance sheet at December 31, 1992. Include a supporting schedule showing your computation of the amount of retained earnings or deficit.

b Draft a footnote to accompany the financial statements disclosing any dividends in arrears at the end of 1992.

Problem 14A-3
Stockholders'
equity section—a
more challenging
problem

Maria Martinez organized Manhattan Transport Co. in January 1989. The corporation immediately issued at $15 per share one-half of its 100,000 authorized shares of $5 par common stock. On January 2, *1990*, the corporation sold at par the entire 5,000 authorized shares of 8%, $100 par value, cumulative preferred stock. On January 2, *1991*, the company again needed money and issued 5,000 shares of an authorized 10,000 shares of $9, no-par, cumulative preferred stock for a total of $494,000. The company suffered losses in its first two years reporting a deficit of $290,000 at the end of 1990. During 1991 and 1992 combined, the company earned a total of $950,000. Dividends of $1 per share were paid on common stock in 1991 and $3.20 per share in 1992.

Instructions

Prepare the stockholders' equity section of the balance sheet at December 31, 1992. Include a supporting schedule showing your computation of retained earnings or deficit at the balance sheet date.

Problem 14A-4
Stockholders'
equity: a short,
comprehensive
problem

Early in the year Jack LaVayne and several friends organized a corporation called Fitness Centers, Inc. The corporation was authorized to issue 50,000 shares of $100 par value, $10 cumulative preferred stock and 400,000 shares of $5 par value common stock. The following transactions (among others) occurred during the year:

Jan. 6   Issued for cash 20,000 shares of common stock at $24 per share. The shares were issued to LaVayne and 10 other investors.

Jan. 7   Issued an additional 500 shares of common stock to LaVayne in exchange for his services in organizing the corporation. The stockholders agreed that these services were worth $12,000.

Jan. 12   Issued 2,500 shares of preferred stock for cash of $250,000.

June 4   Acquired land as a building site in exchange for 12,000 shares of common stock. In view of the appraised value of the land and the progress of the company, the directors agreed that the common stock was to be valued for purposes of this transaction at $25 per share.

Nov. 15   The first annual dividend of $10 per share was declared on the preferred stock to be paid December 20.

Dec. 20   Paid the cash dividend declared on November 15.

Dec. 31   After the revenue and expenses (except income taxes) were closed into the Income Summary account, that account showed a before-tax profit of $180,000. Income taxes were determined to be $49,500.

Instructions

a Prepare journal entries in general journal form to record the above transactions. Include entries at December 31 to (1) record the income tax liability; (2) close the Income Taxes Expense account into the Income Summary account; and (3) close the Income Summary account.

b Prepare the stockholders' equity section of the Fitness Centers, Inc., balance sheet at December 31.

Problem 14A-5
Starting a new
corporation;
includes stock
subscriptions

Pancho's Cantina is the best Mexican restaurant in town—maybe the best anywhere. For years, the restaurant was a sole proprietorship owned by Wayne Label. Many of Label's friends and customers had offered to invest in the business if he ever decided to open new locations. So, early this year, Label decided to expand the business. He formed a new corporation, called Pancho's Cantinas, Inc., which planned to issue stock and use the money received to open new Pancho's restaurants in various locations.

The new corporation is authorized to issue 100,000 shares of $1 par value capital stock. In April the corporation entered into the following transactions:

Apr. 1   Received subscriptions from various investors for 25,000 shares of capital stock to be issued at a price of $30 per share.

Apr. 24   Received an invoice from an attorney for $6,200 for services relating to the formation of the new corporation. This invoice is due in 30 days.

Apr. 28   Received $60,000 cash as full payment from Shirley Long, an investor who had subscribed to 2,000 shares of capital stock. A stock certificate was immediately issued to Long for 2,000 shares. (No payments have been received from the subscribers to the other 23,000 shares.)

Apr. 30 Issued 25,000 shares of capital stock to Label in exchange for the assets of the original Pancho's Cantina. These assets and their current market values on this date are listed below.

Inventory	$ 20,000
Land	305,000
Building	280,000
Equipment and fixtures	145,000

Apr. 30 Issued 100 shares of capital stock to Label in exchange for $3,000 cash, thus assuring Label voting control of the corporation even after the other investors pay for their subscribed shares.

The new corporation will begin operation of the original Pancho's Cantina on May 1. Therefore, the corporation had no revenue or expenses relating to restaurant operations during April. No depreciation of plant assets or amortization of organization costs will be recognized until May when operations get under way.

Instructions **a** Prepare journal entries to record the April transactions in the accounting records of the new corporation.

b Prepare a classified balance sheet for the corporation as of April 30, 19___.

Problem 14A-6
Analysis of an
equity section of
a balance sheet

The year-end balance sheet of DeskTop Products includes the following stockholders' equity section (with certain details omitted):

Stockholders' equity:

Capital stock:

8% cumulative preferred stock, $100 par value, callable at $110,	
30,000 shares authorized	$ 1,600,000
Common stock, $2 par value, 500,000 shares authorized,	
400,000 shares issued	800,000
Additional paid-in capital: common stock	9,600,000
Donated capital	500,000
Retained earnings	4,060,000
Total stockholders' equity	$16,560,000

Instructions From this information, compute answers to the following questions:

a How many shares of preferred stock have been issued?

b What is the total amount of the annual dividends paid to preferred stockholders?

c What was the average issuance price per share of common stock?

d What is the amount of legal capital?

e What is the total amount of paid-in capital?

f What is the book value per share of common stock? (There are no dividends in arrears.)

g Assume that retained earnings at the beginning of the year amounted to $3,208,000, and that net income for the year was $2,500,000. What was the dividend declared during the year on each share of common stock?

Group B

Shown below are five selected transactions of Evergreen Growers for the year ended December 31, 1991.

Mar. 15   The board of directors declared a dividend of $0.30 per share, payable on April 10, to the owners of the corporation's 150,000 outstanding shares of capital stock.

June 19   Issued an additional 20,000 shares of $5 par value capital stock to Sunrise Nurseries in exchange for land. The fair market value of the land and of the issued shares both were considered to be $310,000 on this date.

Oct. 10   Paid a cash dividend totaling $51,000, declared on September 15.

Dec. 31   Recorded income tax expense for the three-month period ended December 31, 1991, $54,200. These taxes will be paid on January 15, 1992. (Income taxes for the first nine months of 1991, amounting to $184,600, have already been recorded and paid.)

Dec. 31   Closed the Income Summary account at the end of a profitable year. Net income, $472,000.

Prepare journal entries to record the above transactions.

Banner Publications was organized early in 1987 with authorization to issue 20,000 shares of $100 par value preferred stock and 1 million shares of $1 par value common stock. All of the preferred stock was issued at par per share, and 300,000 shares of common stock were sold for $20 per share. The preferred stock pays a 10% cumulative dividend and is callable at $105.

During the first five years of operations (1987 through 1991), the corporation earned a total of $4,460,000 and paid dividends of $1 per share each year on the common stock. In 1992, however, the corporation reported a net loss of $1,600,000 and paid no dividends.

a Prepare the stockholders' equity section of the balance sheet at December 31, 1992. Prepare a separate supporting schedule showing your computation of the amount of retained earnings or deficit.

b Draft a footnote to accompany the financial statements disclosing any dividends in arrears at the end of 1992.

Tomahawk Tools, Inc., was organized in January 1989. The corporation issued at $18 per share one-half of its 100,000 authorized shares of $2 par common stock. On January 2, *1990*, the company sold at par the entire 10,000 authorized shares of $50 par value, 8% cumulative preferred stock. On January 2, *1991*, the company again needed money and issued 5,000 shares of an authorized 20,000 shares of $11, no-par, cumulative preferred stock for a total of $518,000. The company suffered losses and paid no dividends during 1989 and 1990, reporting a deficit of $200,000 at the end of 1990. During 1991 and 1992 combined, the company earned a total of $800,000. Dividends of $1.50 per share were paid on common stock in 1991 and $3.00 per share in 1992.

Prepare the stockholders' equity section of the balance sheet at December 31, 1992. Include a separate supporting schedule showing your computation of retained earnings or deficit at this balance sheet date.

Hua Lai organized Pacific Rim Corporation early in 1991. On January 9, the corporation issued to Hua Lai and other investors 50,000 of its 200,000 authorized shares of $5 par value common stock at a price of $18 per share.

After the revenue and expense accounts (except income tax expense) were closed into the Income Summary account at the end of the year, that account showed a before-tax profit of $144,000. Income taxes were determined to be $32,000. No dividends were paid during 1991.

On June 15, 1992, the board of directors declared a cash dividend of 90 cents per share, payable July 31.

a Prepare the journal entries for 1991, to (1) record the issuance of the common stock,

(2) record the income tax liability at December 31, (3) close the Income Tax Expense account into the Income Summary account, and (4) close the Income Summary account.

b Prepare the journal entries in 1992 for the declaration of the dividend on June 15 and payment of the dividend on July 31.

c Operations in 1992 resulted in a $79,400 net loss. Prepare the journal entry to close the Income Summary account at December 31, 1992.

d Prepare the stockholders' equity section of the balance sheet at December 31, 1992. Include a separate supporting schedule showing your determination of retained earnings at that date. Disregard the possibility of an income tax refund.

Problem 14B-5
Issuance of
capital stock and
stock
subscriptions

For several years, Heather Dansk has operated a successful business organized as a sole proprietorship. In order to raise the capital to operate on a larger scale, she decided to organize a new corporation to continue in the same line of business. In January, Dansk organized Heather's Touch, Inc., which was authorized to issue 250,000 shares of $2 par value common stock. During January, Heather's Touch, Inc., completed the following transactions:

Jan. 9 Issued 10,000 shares of common stock to various investors for cash at $27 per share.

Jan. 12 Issued 25,000 shares of common stock to Dansk in exchange for assets with a current market value as follows:

Inventory	$186,000
Land	170,000
Equipment	107,000
Building	212,000

Jan. 14 Received an invoice from an attorney for $9,800 for services relating to the formation of Heather's Touch, Inc. The invoice will be paid in 30 days.

Jan. 15 Received subscriptions for 5,000 shares of common stock at $27 per share; 1,000 of the shares were subscribed by Dansk and 4,000 were subscribed by other investors.

Jan. 31 Collected from Dansk the full amount of her subscription to 1,000 shares of common stock and issued a stock certificate for these shares. (No collection has yet been made from the subscribers to the other 4,000 shares.)

The corporation will begin operations in February; no revenue was earned and no expenses were incurred during January. No depreciation of plant assets and no amortization of organization cost will be recognized until February when operations get under way.

Instructions

a Prepare journal entries to record the transactions for January in the accounting records for Heather's Touch, Inc.

b Prepare a classified balance sheet for the corporation at January 31.

Problem 14B-6
Analysis of
stockholders'
equity

The year-end balance sheet of U-Drive Truck Rentals includes the following stockholders' equity section (with certain details omitted):

Stockholders' equity:	
$8.50 cumulative preferred stock, $100 par value, callable at $110, authorized 30,000 shares	$ 1,200,000
Common stock, $5 par value, authorized 500,000 shares	1,550,000
Additional paid-in capital: common	6,200,000
Donated capital	710,000
Retained earnings	4,680,000
Total stockholders' equity	$14,340,000

Instructions On the basis of this information, answer the following questions and show any necessary supporting computations:

a How many shares of preferred stock are outstanding?

b What is the amount of the annual dividend requirement on preferred stock?

c How many shares of common stock are outstanding?

d What was the average issuance price of a share of common stock?

e What is the current book value per share of common stock?

f What is the total legal capital of the corporation?

g What is the total paid-in (or contributed) capital?

h Total dividends of $722,000 were declared on the preferred and common stock during the year, and the balance of retained earnings at the beginning of the year was $3,302,000. What was the amount of net income for the year?

BUSINESS DECISION CASES

Case 14-1
Factors affecting
the market prices
of preferred and
common stocks

ADM Labs is a publicly owned company with several issues of capital stock outstanding. Over the past decade, the company has consistently earned modest profits and has increased its common stock dividend annually by 5 or 10 cents per share. Recently the company introduced several new products which you believe will cause future sales and profits to increase dramatically. You also expect a gradual increase in long-term interest rates from their present level of about 11% to, perhaps, 12 or 12½%. Based upon these forecasts, explain whether you would expect to see the market prices of the following issues of ADM capital stock increase or decrease. Explain your reasoning in each answer.

a 10%, $100 par value, preferred stock (currently selling at $90 per share).

b $5 par value common stock (currently paying an annual dividend of $2.50 and selling at $40 per share).

c 7%, $100 par value, convertible preferred stock (currently selling at $125 per share).

Case 14-2
Whether or not to
incorporate

Mario Valenti owns Valenti Ford, a successful automobile dealership. For twenty five years, Valenti has operated the business as a sole proprietorship and has acted as both owner and manager. Now, he is seventy years old and is planning on retiring from active management. However, he wants the dealership to stay in the family; his long-term goal is to leave the business to his two children and five grandchildren.

Valenti is wondering whether or not he should incorporate his business. If he were to reorganize Valenti Ford as a corporation, he could then leave an appropriate number of shares of stock to each of his heirs. Otherwise, he could leave the entire business to his heirs to be operated as a partnership. In selecting the appropriate form of business entity, Valenti has formulated the following objectives:

1 Ownership: Valenti wants each of his two children to own 25% of the business and each of his five grandchildren to own 10%.

2 Continuity of existence: Valenti wants the business to continue indefinitely, even if one or more of the heirs should die or should no longer want to participate in ownership.

3 Management: When Valenti retires, he plans to give Joe Heinz, a long-time employee, responsibility for managing the business. Although Valenti wants to keep the ownership of the business in the family, he does not believe that any of his family members have the time or experience to manage the business on a daily basis. In fact, Valenti believes that two of his grandchildren simply have no "business sense," and he does not want them to participate in management.

4 Income taxes: Valenti wants to organize the business in a manner which will minimize the income taxes to be paid by his heirs. He expects that all the earnings of the business will normally be distributed to its owners on an annual basis.

5 Owners' liability: Valenti recognizes that an automobile dealership might become liable for vast amounts of money, if, for example, improper repairs caused a customer's car to be involved in an accident. Although the business carries insurance, he wants to be sure that his heirs' equity in the business does not place their personal assets at risk in the event of business losses.

Instructions   **a** For each of the five numbered paragraphs above, explain how the choice of business organization (partnership or corporation) relates to Valenti's stated objective.

b In light of your analysis in part **a**, above, would you recommend that Valenti reorganize Valenti Ford as a corporation, or leave the business unincorporated so that his heirs may operate it as a partnership?

ANSWERS TO SELF-TEST QUESTIONS
1 c   2 d   3 c   4 a   5 b, c, and d

Corporations: Operations, Earnings per Share, and Dividends

In this chapter, we explore special topics relating primarily to the financial statements of large, publicly owned corporations. We illustrate how the results of discontinued operations and other "unusual events" are presented in the income statement. We also illustrate and explain the presentation of earnings per share, with emphasis upon the interpretation of the different per-share amounts. In the remainder of the chapter we discuss a variety of transactions affecting stockholders' equity, including cash dividends, stock dividends, stock splits, prior period adjustments, and treasury stock transactions.

After studying this chapter you should be able to meet these Learning Objectives:

1 Describe how discontinued operations and other "unusual events" are presented in the income statement.

2 Compute earnings per share.

3 Distinguish between primary and fully diluted earnings per share.

4 Account for stock dividends and stock splits, and explain the probable effect of these transactions upon market price.

5 Describe and prepare a statement of retained earnings.

6 Define prior period adjustments and explain how they are presented in financial statements.

7 Account for treasury stock transactions.

8 Describe and prepare a statement of stockholders' equity.

REPORTING THE RESULTS OF OPERATIONS

The most important aspect of corporate financial reporting, in the view of most stockholders, is the determination of periodic net income. Both the market price of common stock and the amount of cash dividends per share depend to a considerable extent on the current level of earnings (net income). Even more important than the absolute amount of net income is the *trend* of earnings over time.

Developing Predictive Information

An income statement tells us a great deal about the performance of a company over the past year. For example, study of the income statement makes clear the types and amounts of revenue earned and expenses incurred as well as the amounts of gross profit and net income. But can we expect the income statement for *next year* to indicate about the same level of performance? If the transactions summarized in the income statement for the year just completed were of a normal recurring nature, such as selling merchandise, paying employees, and incurring other normal expenses, we can reasonably assume that the operating results were typical and that somewhat similar results can be expected in the following year. However, in any business, unusual and nonrecurring events may occur which cause the current year's net income to be quite different from the income we should expect the company to earn in the future. For example, the company may have sustained large losses in the current year from an earthquake or some other event which is not likely to recur in the near future.

Ideally, the results of unusual and nonrecurring transactions should be shown in a separate section of the income statement *after* the income or loss from normal business activities has been determined. Income from *normal and recurring* activities presumably should be a more useful figure for *predicting future earnings* than is a net income figure which includes the results of nonrecurring events. The problem in creating such an income statement, however, is in determining which events are so unlikely to recur that they should be excluded from the results of "normal" operations. Three categories of events that require special treatment in the income statement are (1) the results of discontinued operations, (2) extraordinary items, and (3) the cumulative effects of changes in accounting principles.

Reporting Unusual Items—an Illustration

Objective 1
Describe how discontinued operations and other "unusual events" are presented in the income statement.

To illustrate the presentation of these items, assume that Ross Corporation operates both a small chain of retail stores and two motels. Near the end of the current year, the company sells both motels to a national hotel chain. In addition, Ross Corporation reports two "extraordinary items" and also changes the method used in computing depreciation expense. An income statement reporting these events appears on the next page.

ROSS CORPORATION
Income Statement
For the Year Ended December 31, 1991

Net sales		$8,000,000
Costs and expenses:		
Cost of goods sold	$4,500,000	
Selling expenses	1,500,000	
General and administrative expenses	920,000	
Loss on settlement of lawsuit	80,000	
Income taxes (on continuing operations)	300,000	7,300,000
Income from continuing operations		$ 700,000
Discontinued operations:		
Operating loss on motels (net of $90,000 income tax benefit)	$ (210,000)	
Gain on sale of motels (net of $195,000 income taxes)	455,000	245,000
Income before extraordinary items and cumulative effect of		
accounting change		$ 945,000
Extraordinary items:		
Gain on condemnation of land by State Highway Department		
(net of $45,000 income taxes)	$ 105,000	
Loss from earthquake damage to Los Angeles store (net of		
$75,000 income tax benefit)	(175,000)	(70,000)
Cumulative effect of change in accounting principle:		
Effect on prior years' income of change in method of computing		
depreciation (net of $60,000 applicable income taxes)		140,000
Net income		$1,015,000

The preceding income statement is designed to illustrate the presentation of "unusual events." Rarely, if ever, will all these types of events appear in the income statement of one company within a single year.

Continuing Operations

The first section of the income statement contains only the results of *continuing business activities*—that is, the retail stores. Notice that the income taxes expense shown in this section relates *only to continuing operations*. The income taxes relating to the "special items" are shown separately in the income statement as adjustments to the amounts of these items.

■ **Income from Continuing Operations** The subtotal *income from continuing operations* measures the profitability of the ongoing operations. This subtotal should be helpful in making predictions of the company's future earnings. For example, if we predict no significant change in the profitability of its retail stores, we would expect Ross Corporation to earn a net income of approximately $700,000 next year.

Discontinued Operations

If management enters into a formal plan to sell or discontinue a *segment* of the business, the results of that segment's operations are shown separately in the income statement. This enables users of the financial statements to better evaluate the performance of the company's ongoing (continuing) operations.

Two items are included in the "discontinued operations" section of the income statement: (1) the income or loss from *operating* the segment prior to its disposal, and (2) the gain or loss on *disposal* of the segment. Notice also that the income taxes relating to the discontinued operations are *shown separately* from the income tax expense relating to continuing business operations.

■ **Discontinued Operations Must Be a "Segment" of the Business** To qualify for separate presentation in the income statement, the discontinued operations must represent an *entire segment* of the business. A "segment" of a business is a separate line of business activity or an operation that services a distinct category of customers.

For example, Allstate Insurance Company is a segment of Sears, Roebuck & Co. From time to time, Sears closes individual Allstate offices. Such office closures do *not* qualify as "discontinued operations," because Sears remains in the insurance business. If, however, Sears were to sell the entire Allstate Insurance Company, insurance activities would be shown in Sears' income statement as discontinued operations.

■ **Discontinued Operations Are Not Really "Unusual"** In recent years, a characteristic of the American economy has been the "restructuring" of many large corporations. As part of this restructuring, corporations often sell one or more segments of the business. Thus, the presence of "discontinued operations" is not uncommon in the income statements of large corporations.

CASE IN POINT ■ In one recent year, TWA sold Hilton International, the hotel chain, to Allegis (parent company of United Airlines). Later that year, Allegis disposed of several segments of its business, including Hilton hotels and Hertz rental cars. In the same year, Sears sold its savings bank segment, RJR Nabisco sold its Heublein (wine and spirits) segment, Owens-Illinois sold its forest products division, and Metromedia sold its cellular telephone operations. All in all, several hundred large corporations reported discontinued operations.

Extraordinary Items

The second category of events requiring disclosure in a separate section of the income statements is extraordinary items. An extraordinary item is a gain or loss that is *(1) material in amount, (2) unusual in nature, and (3) not expected to recur in the foreseeable future.* By definition, extraordinary items are extremely rare; hence, they seldom appear in financial statements. Examples of extraordinary items include the effects of unusual casualties such as earthquakes or tornadoes; expropriation or condemnation of assets by a governmental agency; and gains or losses that may result from a newly enacted law or from the early retirement of long-term debt.

When a gain or loss qualifies as an extraordinary item, it appears at or near the bottom of the income statement following the subtotal, *Income before Ex-*

traordinary Items. Since the extraordinary item is so unusual, this subtotal is considered necessary to show investors what the net income *would have been* if the unusual event had not occurred. Extraordinary items are shown net of any related income tax effects.

■ **Other "Unusual" Gains and Losses**   Some transactions are not typical of normal operations but also do not meet the criteria for separate presentation as extraordinary items. Among such events are losses incurred because of strikes and the gains or losses resulting from sales of plant assets. Such items, if material, should be individually listed as items of revenue or expense, rather than being combined with other items in broad categories such as sales revenue or general and administrative expenses.

In the illustrated income statement of Ross Corporation (page 558), the $80,000 loss resulting from the settlement of a lawsuit was disclosed separately in the income statement but was *not* listed as an extraordinary item. This loss was important enough to bring to the attention of readers of the financial statements, but most lawsuits are not so unusual or infrequent as to be considered extraordinary items.

Changes in Accounting Principle

The accounting principle of *consistency* means that a business should continue to use the same accounting principles and methods from one period to the next. However, this principle does not mean that a business can *never* make a change in its accounting methods. A change may be made if the need for the change can be justified and the effects of the change are *properly disclosed* in the financial statements.

■ **The "Cumulative Effect" of an Accounting Change**   In reporting most changes in accounting principle, the *cumulative effect* of the change upon the income of prior years is shown in the income statement when the change is made. To compute this "cumulative effect," we recompute the income of prior years *as if the new accounting method had always been in use.* The difference between this recomputed net income and the net income actually reported in those periods is the "cumulative effect" of the accounting change.

To illustrate, assume that Ross Corporation has been using the double-declining-balance method of depreciation, but decides in the current year to change to the straight-line method. The company determines that if the straight-line method had always been in use, the total net income of prior years would have been $140,000 higher than was actually reported. This $140,000 is the *cumulative effect* of the change in accounting principle and is shown as a separate item in the current year's income statement. Depreciation expense in the current year's income statement is computed by the straight line method, just as if this method had always been in use.

■ **Changes in Principle versus Changes in Estimate**   A change in accounting principle refers to a change in the *method* used to compute financial statements amounts, not to a change in the underlying estimates. For example, a switch from straight-line to another method of computing depreciation is regarded as a change in accounting principle. However, a change in the estimated useful life used in computing depreciation expense is a *change in estimate.* This distinction is an important one. When we change an accounting *principle* (method), we determine the cumulative effect of the change upon the income reported in prior years. Changes in *estimate,* however, affect only the current year and future years; no effort is made to recompute the income of prior years.

Earnings per Share (EPS)

Objective 2
Compute
earnings per
share.

Perhaps the most widely used of all accounting statistics is *earnings per share* of common stock. Everyone who buys or sells stock in a corporation needs to know the annual earnings per share. Stock market prices are quoted on a per-share basis. If you are considering investing in IBM stock at a price of, say, $120 per share, you need to know the earnings per share and the annual dividend per share in order to decide whether this price is reasonable. In other words, how much earning power and how much dividend income would you be getting for each share you buy?

To compute earnings per share, the annual net income applicable to the common stockholders is divided by the average number of common shares outstanding. The concept of earnings per share applies *only to common stock;* preferred stock has no claim to earnings beyond the stipulated preferred stock dividends.

Many financial analysts express the relationship between earnings per share and market price per share as a *price-earnings ratio* (p/e ratio). This ratio is computed by dividing the market price per share of common stock by the annual earnings per share.

■ **Weighted-Average Number of Shares Outstanding** The simplest example of computing earnings per share is found when a company has issued only common stock and the number of shares outstanding has not changed during the year. In this situation, the net income for the year divided by the number of shares outstanding at year-end equals earnings per share.

In many companies, however, the number of shares of stock outstanding is changed one or more times during the year. When additional shares are issued in exchange for assets during the year, the computation of earnings per share is based upon the *weighted-average* number of shares outstanding.[1]

The weighted-average number of shares for the year is determined by multiplying the number of shares outstanding by the fraction of the year that said number of shares outstanding remained unchanged. For example, assume that 100,000 shares of common stock were outstanding during the first nine months of 1991 and 140,000 shares during the last three months. Assume also that the increase in shares outstanding resulted from the sale of 40,000 shares for cash. The weighted-average number of shares outstanding during 1991 would be *110,000* determined as follows:

100,000 shares × 9/12 of a year	*75,000*
140,000 shares × 3/12 of a year	*35,000*
Weighted-average number of common shares outstanding	*110,000*

---

[1] When the number of shares outstanding changes as a result of a stock split or a stock dividend (discussed later in this chapter), the computation of the weighted-average number of shares outstanding should be adjusted *retroactively* rather than weighted for the period the new shares were outstanding. Earnings per share data for prior years thus will be consistently stated in terms of the current capital structure.

This procedure gives more meaningful earnings per share data than if the total number of shares outstanding at the end of the year were used in the calculations. By using the weighted-average number of shares, we recognize that the proceeds from the sale of the 40,000 shares were available to generate earnings only during the last three months of the year.

■ **Preferred Dividends and Earnings per Share** When a company has preferred stock outstanding, the preferred stockholders participate in net income to the extent of the preferred stock dividends. To determine the earnings *applicable to the common stock,* we must first deduct from net income the amount of any preferred stock dividends. To illustrate, let us assume that Tanner Corporation has 200,000 shares of common stock and 10,000 shares of $6 preferred stock outstanding throughout the year. Net income for the year totals $560,000. Earnings per share of common stock would be computed as follows:

Net income	$560,000
Less: Dividends on preferred stock (10,000 shares × $6)	60,000
Earnings applicable to common stock	$500,000
Weighted-average number of common shares outstanding	200,000
Earnings per share of common stock ($500,000 ÷ 200,000 shares)	$2.50

■ **Presentation of Earnings per Share in the Income Statement** All publicly owned corporations are required to present earnings per share data in their income statements.[2] If an income statement includes subtotals for income from continuing operations, or for income before extraordinary items, per-share figures are shown for these amounts as well as for net income. These additional per-share amounts are computed by substituting the amount of the appropriate subtotal for the net income figure in the preceding calculation.

To illustrate all of the potential per-share computations, we will expand our Tanner Corporation example to include income from continuing operations and income before extraordinary items. We should point out, however, that all of these figures seldom appear in the same income statement. Very few companies have both discontinued operations and an extraordinary item to report in the same year. The following condensed income statement is intended to illustrate the proper format for presenting earnings per share figures and to provide a review of the calculations.

TANNER CORPORATION
Condensed Income Statement
For the Year Ended December 31, 1991

Net sales	$9,000,000
Costs and expenses (including income taxes on continuing operations).......	8,340,000
Income from continuing operations	$ 660,000
Loss from discontinued operations (net of income tax benefits)	(60,000)
Income before extraordinary items and cumulative effect of account- ing change...	$ 600,000
Extraordinary loss (net of income tax benefit) .... $(120,000)	
Cumulative effect of accounting change (net of related income taxes)... 80,000	(40,000)
Net income	$ 560,000
Earnings per share of common stock:	
Earnings from continuing operations	$3.00[a]
Loss from discontinued operations..	(.30)
Earnings before extraordinary items and cumulative effect of ac- counting change	$2.70[b]
Extraordinary loss	(.60)
Cumulative effect of accounting change...................................	.40
Net earnings	$2.50[c]

[a] ($660,000 − $60,000 preferred dividends) ÷ 200,000 shares
[b] ($600,000 − $60,000) ÷ 200,000 shares
[c] ($560,000 − $60,000) ÷ 200,000 shares

■ **Interpreting the Different Per-Share Amounts** To informed users of financial statements, each of these figures has a different significance. Earnings per share from continuing operations represents the results of continuing and ordinary business activity. This figure is the most useful one for predicting future operating results. *Net earnings* per share, on the other hand, shows the overall operating results of the current year, including any discontinued operations or extraordinary items.

Unfortunately the term *earnings per share* often is used without qualification in referring to various types of per-share data. When using per-share information, it is important to know exactly which per-share statistic is being presented. For example, the price-earnings ratios (market price divided by earnings per share) for common stocks listed on major stock exchanges are reported daily in *the Wall Street Journal* and many other newspapers. Which earnings per share figures are used in computing these ratios? If a company reports an extraordinary gain or loss, the price-earnings ratio is computed using the per-share *earnings before the extraordinary item.* Otherwise, the ratio is based upon *net earnings* per share.

Primary and Fully Diluted Earnings per Share

Objective 3
Distinguish between primary and fully diluted earnings per share.

Let us assume that a company has an outstanding issue of preferred stock that is convertible into shares of common stock at a rate of, say, two shares of common for each share of preferred. The conversion of this preferred stock would increase the number of common shares outstanding and might *dilute* (reduce) earnings per share. Any common stockholder interested in the trend of earnings per share will want to know what effect the conversion of the preferred stock would have upon this statistic.

To inform investors of the potential dilution which might occur, two figures are presented for each earnings per share statistic. The first figure, called *primary* earnings per share, is based upon the weighted-average number of common shares actually outstanding during the year. Thus, this figure ignores the potential dilution represented by the convertible preferred stock.[3] The second figure, called *fully diluted* earnings per share, shows the impact that conversion of the preferred stock would have upon primary earnings per share.

Primary earnings per share are computed in the same manner illustrated in our preceding example of Tanner Corporation. Fully diluted earnings per share, on the other hand, are computed on the assumption that all the preferred stock *had been converted into common stock at the beginning of the current year.*[4] (The mechanics of computing fully diluted earnings per share are covered in the intermediate accounting course.)

It is important to remember that fully diluted earnings per share represent a *hypothetical case.* This statistic is computed even though the preferred stock actually was *not* converted during the year. The purpose of showing fully diluted earnings per share is to warn common stockholders what *could* have happened. When the difference between primary and fully diluted earnings per share becomes significant, investors should recognize the *risk* that future earnings per share may be reduced by conversions of other securities into common stock.

When a company reports both primary and fully diluted earnings per share, the price-earnings ratio shown in newspapers is based upon the *primary* figure.

OTHER STOCKHOLDERS' EQUITY TRANSACTIONS

Cash Dividends

The prospect of receiving cash dividends is a principal reason for investing in the stocks of corporations. An increase or decrease in the established rate of dividends will usually cause an immediate rise or fall in the market price of the company's stock. Stockholders are keenly interested in prospects for future dividends and as a group are strongly in favor of more generous dividend payments. The board of directors, on the other hand, is primarily concerned with the long-run growth and financial strength of the corporation; it may prefer to restrict dividends to a minimum in order to conserve cash for the purchase of plant and equipment or for other needs of the company. Many of the so-called "growth companies" plow back into the business most of their earnings and pay only very small cash dividends.

---

[3] If certain criteria are met, convertible securities qualify as *common stock equivalents* and enter into the computation of primary earnings per share. Common stock equivalents and other complex issues relating to earnings per share are discussed in intermediate accounting courses and in *APB Opinion No. 15,* "Earnings per Share," AICPA (New York: 1969).

[4] If the preferred stock had been issued during the current year, we would assume that it was converted into common stock on the date it was issued.

The preceding discussion suggests three requirements for the payment of a cash dividend. These are:

1 Retained earnings Since dividends represent a distribution of earnings to stockholders, the theoretical maximum for dividends is the total undistributed net income of the company, represented by the credit balance of the Retained Earnings account. As a practical matter, many corporations limit dividends to somewhere near 40% of annual net income, in the belief that a major portion of the net income must be retained in the business if the company is to grow and to keep pace with its competitors.

2 An adequate cash position The fact that the company reports large earnings does not mean that it has a large amount of cash on hand. Cash generated from earnings may have been invested in new plant and equipment, or in paying off debts, or in acquiring a larger inventory. There is no necessary relationship between the balance in the Retained Earnings account and the balance in the Cash account. The traditional expression of "paying dividends out of retained earnings" is misleading. Cash dividends can be paid only "out of" cash.

3 Dividend action by the board of directors Even though a company's net income is substantial and its cash position seemingly satisfactory, dividends are not paid automatically. A formal action by the board of directors is necessary to declare a dividend.

Dividend Dates

Four significant dates are involved in the distribution of a dividend. These dates are:

1 Date of declaration On the day on which the dividend is declared by the board of directors, a liability to make the payment comes into existence.

2 Date of record The date of record always follows the date of declaration, usually by a period of two or three weeks, and is always stated in the dividend declaration. In order to be eligible to receive the dividend, a person must be listed as the owner of the stock on the date of record.

3 Ex-dividend date The ex-dividend date is significant for investors in companies with stocks traded on the stock exchanges. To permit the compilation of the list of stockholders as of the record date, it is customary for the stock to go **ex-dividend** three business days before the date of record. A stock is said to be selling ex-dividend on the day that it loses the right to receive the latest declared dividend. A person who buys the stock before the ex-dividend date is entitled to receive the dividend; conversely, a stockholder who sells shares before the ex-dividend date does not receive the dividend.

4 Date of payment The declaration of a dividend always includes announcement of the date of payment as well as the date of record. Usually the date of payment comes from two to four weeks after the date of record.

The journal entries to record the declaration and payment of a cash dividend were illustrated in Chapter 14 but are repeated here with emphasis on the date of declaration and date of payment.

■
**Entries made on
declaration date
and . . .**

June 1	Retained Earnings	100,000	
	Dividends Payable		100,000
	To record declaration of a cash dividend of $1 per share on		
	the 100,000 shares of common stock outstanding. Payable		
	July 10 to stockholders of record on June 20.		

■
**. . . on payment
date**

July 10	Dividends Payable	100,000	
	Cash		100,000
	To record payment of $1 per share dividend declared June 1		
	to stockholders of record on June 20.		

As mentioned in Chapter 14, some companies record the declaration of a dividend by debiting a Dividends account instead of debiting Retained Earnings. In this case, a closing entry is required at the end of the year to transfer the debit balance of the Dividends account into the Retained Earnings account. Under either method, the balance of the Retained Earnings account ultimately is reduced by the amount of all dividends declared during the period.

Most dividends are paid in cash, but occasionally a dividend declaration calls for payment in assets other than cash. A large distillery once paid a dividend consisting of a bottle of whiskey for each share of stock. When a corporation goes out of existence (particularly a small corporation with only a few stockholders), it may choose to distribute noncash assets to its owners rather than to convert all its assets into cash.

Liquidating Dividends

A *liquidating dividend* occurs when a corporation pays a dividend that *exceeds the balance in the Retained Earnings account.* Thus, the dividend returns to stockholders all or part of their paid-in capital investment. Liquidating dividends are usually paid only when a corporation is going out of existence or is making a permanent reduction in the size of its operations. Normally dividends are paid as a result of profitable operations; stockholders may assume that a dividend represents a distribution of profits unless they are notified by the corporation that the dividend is a return of invested capital.

Stock Dividends

Objective 4
Account for stock
dividends and
stock splits, and
explain the
probable effect
of these
transactions upon
market price.

Stock dividend is a term used to describe a distribution of *additional shares of stock* to a company's stockholders in proportion to their present holdings. In brief, the dividend is payable in *additional shares of stock* rather than in cash. Most stock dividends consist of additional shares of common stock distributed to holders of common stock, and our discussion will be limited to this type of stock dividend.

An important distinction must be drawn between a cash dividend and a stock dividend. In a *cash dividend,* assets are distributed by the corporation to the stockholders. Thus, a cash dividend reduces both assets and stockholders' equity. In a *stock dividend,* however, *no assets are distributed.* Thus, a stock dividend causes *no change* in assets or in total stockholders' equity. Each stockholder receives additional shares, but his or her total ownership in the corporation is *no larger than before.*

To illustrate this point, assume that a corporation with 2,000 shares of stock is owned equally by James Davis and Susan Miller, each owning 1,000 shares of stock. The corporation declares a stock dividend of 10% and distributes 200 additional shares (10% of 2,000 shares), with 100 shares going to each of the two stockholders. Davis and Miller now hold 1,100 shares apiece, but each *still owns one-half of the business.* Furthermore, the corporation has not changed in size; its assets and liabilities and its total stockholders' equity are exactly the same as before the dividend.

Now let us consider the logical effect of this stock dividend upon the *market price* of the company's stock. Assume that before the stock dividend, the outstanding 2,000 shares in our example had a market price of $110 per share. This price indicates a total market value for the corporation of $220,000 (2,000 shares × $110 per share). As the stock dividend does not change total assets or total stockholders' equity, the total market value of the corporation *should remain $220,000* after the stock dividend. As 2,200 shares are now outstanding, the market price of each share *should fall* to $100 ($220,000 ÷ 2,200 shares). In short, the market value of the stock *should fall in proportion* to the number of new shares issued. Whether the market price per share *will* fall in proportion to a small increase in number of outstanding shares is another matter. The market prices of common stocks are influenced by many different factors.

■ **Reasons for Issuing Stock Dividends** Although stock dividends cause no change in total assets or total stockholders' equity, they are popular both with management and with stockholders. Management likes stock dividends because they do not cost anything (other than administrative costs)—the corporation does not have to surrender any assets. Stockholders enjoy stock dividends because often the market price of the stock *does not fall enough* to reflect fully the increased number of shares. While this failure of the stock price to fall proportionately is not logical, it is nonetheless a common phenomenon. In such cases, the stock dividend actually does increase the total market value of the corporation and of each stockholder's investment.

■ **Entries to Record a Stock Dividend** In accounting for *small* stock dividends (say, less than 20%), the *market value* of the new shares is transferred from the Retained Earnings accounts to the paid-in capital accounts. This process sometimes is called *capitalizing* retained earnings. The overall effect is the same as if the dividend had been paid in cash, and the stockholders had immediately reinvested the cash in the business in exchange for additional shares of stock. Of course, no cash actually changes hands—the new shares of stock are sent directly to the stockholders.

To illustrate, Aspen Corp., on June 1, has outstanding 100,000 shares of $5 par value common stock with a market value of $22 per share. On this date, the company declares a 10% stock dividend, distributable on July 15 to stockholders of record on June 20. The entry at June 1 to record the *declaration* of this dividend is:

**Stock dividend
declared; note
use of market
price of stock**

Retained Earnings	220,000	
Stock Dividend to Be Distributed.................................		50,000
Additional Paid-in Capital: Stock Dividends		170,000

*Declared a 10% stock dividend consisting of 10,000 shares
(100,000 shares × 10%) of $5 par value common stock, market
price $22 per share. Distributable July 15 to stockholders' of record on
June 20.*

The Stock Dividend to Be Distributed account is ***not a liability,*** because there is no obligation to distribute cash or any other asset. If a balance sheet is prepared between the date of declaration of a stock dividend and the date of distribution of the shares, this account, as well as Additional Paid-in Capital: Stock Dividends, should be presented in the stockholders' equity section of the balance sheet.

Notice that the Retained Earnings account was debited for the ***market value*** of the shares to be issued (10,000 shares × $22 per share = $220,000). Notice also that ***no change*** occurs in the total amount of stockholders' equity. The amount removed from the Retained Earnings account was simply transferred into two other stockholders' equity accounts.

On July 15, the entry to record the ***distribution*** of the dividend shares is:

Stock Dividend to Be Distributed.......................................	50,000	
Common Stock..		50,000

Distributed 10,000 share stock dividend declared June 1.

Large stock dividends (for example, those in excess of 20 to 25%) should be recorded by transferring ***only the par or stated value*** of the dividend shares from the Retained Earnings account to the Common Stock account. Large stock dividends generally have the effect of proportionately reducing the market price of the stock. For example, a 100% stock dividend would reduce the market price by about 50%, because twice as many shares would be outstanding. A 100% stock dividend is very similar to the 2 for 1 ***stock split*** discussed in the following section of this chapter.

Stock Splits

A corporation may split its stock by increasing the number of outstanding shares of common stock and reducing the par or stated value per share in proportion. The purpose of the split is to reduce substantially the market price of the common stock, with the intent of making the stock more attractive to investors.

For example, assume that Pelican Corporation has outstanding 1 million shares of $10 par value stock. The market price is $90 per share. The corporation now reduces the par value from $10 to $5 per share and increases the number of shares from 1 million to 2 million. This action would be called a 2 for 1 stock split. A stockholder who owned 100 shares of the stock before the split would own 200 shares after the split. Since the number of outstanding shares has been doubled without any change in total assets or total stockholders' equity, the market price of the stock should drop from $90 to approximately $45 a share.

A stock split does not change the balance of any ledger account; consequently, the transaction may be recorded merely by *a memorandum entry* in the general journal and in the Common Stock account. For Pelican Corporation, this memorandum entry might read:

■
Memorandum
entry to record a
stock split

Sept. 30   Memorandum: Issued additional 1 million shares of common stock in a 2 for 1 stock split. Par value reduced from $10 per share to $5 per share.

The description of common stock also is changed in the balance sheet to reflect the lower par value and the greater number of shares outstanding.

Stock may be split in any desired ratio. Among the more common ratios are 2 for 1, 3 for 2, and 3 for 1. The determining factor is the number of shares needed to bring the price of the stock into the desired trading range. For example, assume that a stock is selling at a price of $150 per share, and that management wants to reduce the price to approximately $30 per share. This objective may be accomplished with a *5 for 1* stock split ($150 ÷ 5 = $30).

■ Distinction between Stock Splits and Large Stock Dividends
What is the difference between a 2 for 1 stock split and a 100% stock dividend? There is very little difference; both will double the number of outstanding shares without changing total stockholders' equity, and both should serve to cut the market price of the stock approximately in half. The stock dividend, however, will cause a transfer from the Retained Earnings account to the Common Stock account equal to the par or stated value of the dividend shares, whereas the stock split does not change the dollar balance of any account.

After an increase in the number of shares as a result of a stock split or stock dividend, earnings per share are computed in terms of the increased number of shares. In presenting five- or ten-year summaries, the earnings per share for earlier years are *retroactively restated* to reflect the increased number of shares currently outstanding and thus make the trend of earnings per share from year to year a valid comparison.

CASE IN POINT ■ In 1980, Mylan Laboratories, Inc., reported earnings of $0.54 per share. Over the next six years, the company declared a 100% stock dividend and five separate stock splits. By 1986, each share outstanding in 1980 had been split into 27 shares. Thus, each share outstanding in 1986 represented only $\frac{1}{27}$ of an original 1980 share. In the 10-year summary appearing in the company's 1986 annual report, the 1980 earnings were restated at $0.02 per share ($0.54 × $\frac{1}{27}$ = $0.02).

Statement of Retained Earnings

Objective 5
Describe and
prepare a
statement of
retained
earnings.

The term retained earnings refers to the portion of stockholders' equity derived from profitable operations. Retained earnings is increased by earning net income and is reduced by incurring net losses and by the declaration of dividends.

In addition to a balance sheet and an income statement, a complete set of financial statements includes a statement of retained earnings, and a statement of cash flows. The statement of cash flows will be discussed in Chapter

19; a statement of retained earnings is illustrated below:

SHORE LINE CORPORATION
Statement of Retained Earnings
For the Year Ended December 31, 1991

Retained earnings, December 31, 1990		$600,000
Net income for 1991		180,000
Subtotal		$780,000
Less: Cash dividends:		
Preferred stock ($5 per share)	$ 17,500	
Common stock ($1 per share)	55,300	
10% stock dividend	140,000	212,800
Retained earnings, December 31, 1991		$567,200

Prior Period Adjustments

Objective 6
Define prior period adjustments and explain how they are presented in financial statements.

On occasion, a company may discover that a material error was made in the measurement of net income in a prior year. Since net income is closed into the Retained Earnings account, an error in reported net income will cause an error in the amount of retained earnings shown in all subsequent balance sheets. When such errors come to light, they should be corrected. The correction, called a ***prior period adjustment,*** is shown in the ***statement of retained earnings*** as an adjustment to the balance of retained earnings at the beginning of the current year. The amount of the adjustment is shown net of any related income tax effects.

To illustrate, assume that late in 1991 Shore Line Corporation discovers that it failed to record depreciation on certain assets in 1990. After considering the income tax effects of this error, the company finds that the net income reported in 1990 was overstated by $35,000. Thus, the current balance of retained earnings ($600,000 at December 31, 1990) also is overstated by $35,000. Correction of this error leads to a revised 1991 statement of retained earnings as follows:

SHORE LINE CORPORATION
Statement of Retained Earnings
For the Year Ended December 31, 1991

Notice the adjustment to beginning retained earnings

Retained earnings, December 31, 1990:		
As originally reported		$600,000
Less: Prior period adjustment for error in recording 1989 depreciation		
expense (net of $15,000 income taxes)		35,000
As restated		$565,000
Net Income for 1991		180,000
Subtotal		$745,000
Less: Cash dividends:		
Preferred stock ($5 per share)	$ 17,500	
Common stock ($1 per share)	55,300	
10% stock dividend	140,000	212,800
Retained earnings, December 31, 1991		$532,200

Prior period adjustments rarely appear in the financial statements of large, publicly owned corporations. The financial statements of these corporations are audited annually by certified public accountants and are not likely to contain material errors which subsequently will require correction by prior period adjustments. Such adjustments are much more likely to appear in the financial statements of closely held corporations that are not audited on an annual basis.

■ **Restrictions of Retained Earnings**   Some portion of retained earnings may be restricted because of various contractual agreements. A "restriction" of retained earnings prevents a company from declaring a dividend that would cause retained earnings to fall below a designated level. Most companies disclose restrictions of retained earnings in notes accompanying the financial statements. For example, a company with retained earnings of $10 million might include the following note in its financial statements:

Footnote disclosure of restrictions placed on retained earnings

Note 7: Restriction of retained earnings
As of December 31, 1992, certain long-term debt agreements prohibited the declaration of cash dividends that would reduce the amount of retained earnings below $5,200,000. Retained earnings not so restricted amounted to $4,800,000.

Treasury Stock

Corporations frequently reacquire shares of their own capital stock by purchase in the open market. Paying out cash to reacquire shares will reduce the assets of the corporation and reduce the stockholders' equity by the same amount. One reason for such purchases is to have stock available to reissue to officers and employees under bonus plans. Other reasons may include a desire to increase the reported earnings per share or to support the current market price of the stock.

Treasury stock may be defined as shares of a corporation's own capital stock that have been issued and later *reacquired by the issuing company,* but that have not been canceled or permanently retired. Treasury shares may be held indefinitely or may be issued again at any time. Shares of capital stock held in the treasury are not entitled to receive dividends, to vote, or to share in assets upon dissolution of the company. In the computation of earnings per share, shares held in the treasury are not regarded as outstanding shares.

Recording Purchases of Treasury Stock

Objective 7
Account for treasury stock transactions.

Purchases of treasury stock should be recorded by debiting the Treasury Stock account with the cost of the stock.[5] For example, if Torrey Corporation reacquires 1,500 shares of its own $5 par stock at a price of $100 per share, the entry is as follows:

Treasury stock recorded at cost

Treasury Stock	150,000	
Cash...		150,000
Purchased 1,500 shares of $5 par treasury stock at $100 per share.		

---

[5] State laws may prescribe different methods of accounting for treasury stock transactions. In this text, we illustrate only the widely used "cost method."

Note that the Treasury Stock account is debited for the *cost* of the shares purchased, not their par value.

■ **Treasury Stock Is Not an Asset**   When treasury stock is purchased, the corporation is eliminating part of its stockholders' equity by a payment to one or more stockholders. The purchase of treasury stock should be regarded as a *reduction of stockholders' equity,* not as the acquisition of an asset. For this reason, the Treasury Stock account should appear in the balance sheet *as a deduction in the stockholders' equity section.*[6] The presentation of treasury stock in a corporate balance sheet is illustrated at the bottom of page 554.

Reissuance of Treasury Stock

When treasury shares are reissued, the Treasury Stock account is credited for the cost of the shares reissued and Paid-in Capital from Treasury Stock Transactions is debited or credited for any difference between *cost* and the reissue price. To illustrate, assume that 1,000 of the treasury shares acquired by Torrey Corporation at a cost of $100 per share are now reissued at a price of $115 per share. The entry to record the reissuance of these shares at a price above cost would be:

■
Reissued at a price above cost

Cash...	*115,000*	
* Treasury Stock ....*		*100,000*
* Additional Paid-in Capital: Treasury Stock Transactions ....*		*15,000*
Sold 1,000 shares of treasury stock, which cost $100,000 at a price		
of $115 per share.		

If treasury stock is reissued at a price below cost, paid-in capital from previous treasury stock transactions is reduced (debited) by the excess of cost over the reissue price. To illustrate, assume that Torrey Corporation reissues its remaining 500 shares of treasury stock (cost $100 per share) at a price of $90 per share. The entry would be:

■
Reissued at a price below cost

Cash...	*45,000*	
Additional Paid-in Capital: Treasury Stock Transactions	*5,000*	
* Treasury Stock ....*		*50,000*
Sold 500 shares of treasury stock, which cost $50,000 at a price of		
$90 each.		

If there is no additional paid-in capital from previous treasury stock transactions, the excess of the cost of the treasury shares over the reissue price may be recorded as a debit to Retained Earnings.

■ **No Profit or Loss on Treasury Stock Transactions**   Note that *no gain or loss is recognized on treasury stock transactions,* even when the shares

---

[6] Despite a lack of theoretical support, a few corporations do classify treasury stock as an asset, on the grounds that the shares could be sold for cash just as readily as shares owned in another corporation. The same argument could be made of treating unissued shares as assets. Treasury shares are basically the same as unissued shares, and an unissued share of stock is definitely not an asset.

are reissued at a price above or below cost. A corporation earns profits by selling goods and services to outsiders, not by issuing or reissuing shares of its own capital stock. When treasury shares are reissued at a price above cost the corporation receives from the new stockholder an amount of paid-in capital larger than the reduction in stockholders' equity when the corporation acquired the treasury shares. Conversely, if treasury shares are reissued at a price below cost, the corporation ends up with less paid-in capital as a result of the purchase and reissuance of the shares. Thus, any changes in stockholders' equity resulting from treasury stock transactions are regarded as changes in *paid-in capital* and are *not* included in the measurement of net income.

■ Restriction of Retained Earnings for Treasury Stock Owned

Purchases of treasury stock, like cash dividends, are distributions of assets to the stockholders in the corporation. Many states have a legal requirement that distributions to stockholders (including purchases of treasury stock) cannot exceed the balance in the Retained Earnings account. Therefore, retained earnings usually are restricted by an amount equal to the cost of any shares held in the treasury.

Statement of Stockholders' Equity

Objective 8
Describe and prepare a statement of stockholders' equity.

Many corporations expand their statement of retained earnings to show the changes during the year in all of the stockholders' equity accounts. This expanded statement, called a *statement of stockholders' equity,* is illustrated for Shore Line Corporation on the next page.

The top line of this statement shows the beginning balance in each stockholders' equity account. All of the transactions affecting these accounts during the year then are listed in summary form, along with the related changes in the balances of specific stockholders' equity accounts. The bottom line of the statement shows the ending balance in each stockholders' equity account and should agree with the amounts shown in the year-end balance sheet.

A statement of stockholders' equity is not a required financial statement. However, it is widely used as a substitute for the *statement of retained earnings* because it presents a more complete description of the transactions affecting stockholders' equity. Notice that the Retained Earnings column of this statement contains the same items shown in the statement of retained earnings illustrated on page 570.

SHORE LINE CORPORATION
Statement of Stockholders' Equity
For the Year Ended December 31, 1991

	5% Convertible preferred stock ($100 par value)	Common stock ($10 par value)	Additional paid-in capital	Retained earnings	Treasury stock	Total stockholders' equity
Balances, Dec. 31, 1990 ..	$400,000	$200,000	$300,000	$600,000	$ –0–	$1,500,000
Prior period adjustment (net of $15,000 taxes)				(35,000)		(35,000)
Issued 5,000 common shares @ $52		50,000	210,000			260,000
Conversion of 1,000 preferred into 3,000 common shares	(100,000)	30,000	70,000			
Distributed 10% stock dividend (2,800 shares at $50; market price)		28,000	112,000	(140,000)		
Purchased 1,000 shares of common stock for the treasury at $47 a share ..					(47,000)	(47,000)
Net income				180,000		180,000
Cash dividends:						
Preferred ($5 a share) ..				(17,500)		(17,500)
Common ($2 a share)...				(55,300)		(55,300)
Balances, Dec. 31, 1991 ..	$300,000	$308,000	$692,000	$532,200	$(47,000)	$1,785,200

Illustration of Stockholders' Equity Section

The following illustration of a stockholders' equity section of a balance sheet shows the various elements of corporate capital. You should be able to explain the nature and origin of each account and disclosure printed in black.

Stockholders' equity:		
Capital stock:		
Preferred stock, $100 par value, call price $110 per share, authorized and issued 2,000 shares		$200,000
Common stock, $5 par value, authorized 100,000 shares, issued 32,000 shares (of which 2,000 are held in the treasury)		160,000
Additional paid-in capital:		
From issuance of common stock	$240,000	
From stock dividends..	50,000	
From treasury stock transactions	10,000	300,000
Total paid-in capital		$660,000
Retained earnings (of which $50,000, an amount equal to the cost of treasury stock owned, is not available for dividends).........................		210,000
Subtotal..		$870,000
Less: Treasury stock (2,000 shares of common, at cost)......................		50,000
Total stockholders' equity...		$820,000

End-of-Chapter Review

CONCEPTS INTRODUCED OR EMPHASIZED IN CHAPTER 15

Major concepts in this chapter include:

- Reporting the results of normal and continuing operations.

- Reporting the effects of unusual and nonrecurring events.

- Earnings per share.

- The declaration and distribution of cash dividends

- The nature of stock dividends and stock splits, and the probable effects of these transactions upon market price.

- Accounting for treasury stock transactions; why treasury stock is not an asset.

- The form and content of the statement of retained earnings, and the statement of stockholders' equity.

This chapter—the second in our unit on corporate accounting—completes our discussion of capital stock and stockholders' equity. When a corporation needs to raise vast amounts of capital, it may elect to issue **bonds payable** as an alternative to issuing additional shares of capital stock. The next chapter addresses the topics of bonds payable and other forms of long-term debt financing.

KEY TERMS INTRODUCED OR EMPHASIZED IN CHAPTER 15

Date of record   The date on which a person must be listed as a shareholder in order to be eligible to receive a dividend. Follows the date of declaration of a dividend by two or three weeks.

Discontinued operations   The net operating results (revenue and expenses) of a segment of a company which has been or is being sold.

Earnings per share   Net income applicable to the common stock divided by the weighted-average number of common shares outstanding during the year.

Ex-dividend date   A date three days prior to the date of record specified in a dividend declaration. A person buying a stock prior to the ex-dividend date also acquires the right to receive the dividend. The three-day interval permits the compilation of a list of stockholders as of the date of record.

Extraordinary items   Transactions and events that are material in dollar amount, unusual in nature, and occur infrequently; for example, a large earthquake loss. Such items are shown separately in the income statement after the determination of Income before Extraordinary Items.

Fully diluted earnings per share   Earnings per share computed under the assumption that all convertible securities had been converted into additional common shares at the beginning of the current year. The purpose of this hypothetical computation is to warn common stockholders of the risk that future earnings per share might be diluted by the conversion of other securities into common stock.

Price-earnings ratio   Market price of a share of common stock divided by annual earnings per share.

Primary earnings per share Net income applicable to the common stock divided by weighted-average number of common shares outstanding during the year.

Prior period adjustment A correction of a material error in the earnings reported in the financial statements of a prior year. Prior period adjustments are recorded directly in the Retained Earnings account and are not included in the income statement of the current period.

Segment of a business Those elements of a business that represent a separate and distinct line of business activity or that service a distinct category of customers.

Statement of retained earnings A basic financial statement explaining the change during the year in the amount of retained earnings. May be expanded into a *statement of stockholders' equity.*

Statement of stockholders' equity An expanded version of a *statement of retained earnings.* Summarizes the changes during the year in all stockholders' equity accounts. Not a required financial statement, but widely used as a substitute for the statement of retained earnings.

Stock dividend A distribution of additional shares to common stockholders in proportion to their holdings.

Stock split An increase in the number of shares outstanding with a corresponding decrease in par value per share. The additional shares are distributed proportionately to all common shareholders. Purpose is to reduce market price per share and encourage wider public ownership of the company's stock. A 2 for 1 stock split will give each stockholder twice as many shares as previously owned.

Treasury stock Shares of a corporation's stock which have been issued and then reacquired, but not canceled.

DEMONSTRATION PROBLEM FOR YOUR REVIEW

The stockholders' equity of Sutton Corporation at January 1, 19__, is shown below:

Stockholders' equity:	
Common stock, $10 par, 100,000 shares authorized, 40,000 shares issued	$ 400,000
Additional paid-in capital: common stock	200,000
Total paid-in capital	$ 600,000
Retained earnings	1,500,000
Total stockholders' equity	$2,100,000

Transactions affecting stockholders' equity during the year are as follows:

Mar. 31 A 5 for 4 stock split proposed by the board of directors was approved by vote of the stockholders. The 10,000 new shares were distributed to stockholders.

Apr. 1 The company purchased 2,000 shares of its common stock on the open market at $37 per share.

July 1 The company reissued 1,000 shares of treasury stock at $45 per share.

July 1 Issued for cash 20,000 shares of previously unissued $8 par value common stock at a price of $45 per share.

Dec. 1 A cash dividend of $1 per share was declared, payable on December 30, to stockholders of record at December 14.

Dec. 22 A 10% stock dividend was declared; the dividend shares to be distributed on January 15 of the following year. The market price of the stock on December 22 was $48 per share.

The net income for the year ended December 31, 19__, amounted to $177,000, after an extraordinary loss of $35,400 (net of related income tax benefits).

Instructions   **a** Prepare journal entries (in general journal form) to record the transactions relating to stockholders' equity that took place during the year.

b Prepare the lower section of the income statement for the year, beginning with the *income before extraordinary items* and showing the extraordinary loss and the net income. Also illustrate the presentation of earnings per share in the income statement, assuming that earnings per share is determined on the basis of the *weighted-average* number of shares outstanding during the year.

SOLUTION TO DEMONSTRATION PROBLEM

a   GENERAL JOURNAL

Mar. 31	Memorandum: Stockholders approved a 5 for 4 stock split. This action increased the number of shares of common stock outstanding from 40,000 to 50,000 and reduced the par value from $10 to $8 per share. The 10,000 new shares were distributed.		
Apr. 1	Treasury Stock	74,000	
	Cash		74,000
	Acquired 2,000 shares of treasury stock at $37 per share.		
July 1	Cash	45,000	
	Treasury Stock		37,000
	Additional Paid-in Capital: Treasury Stock Transactions		8,000
	Sold 1,000 shares of treasury stock at $45 per share.		
1	Cash	900,000	
	Common Stock, $8 par		160,000
	Additional Paid-in Capital: Common Stock		740,000
	Issued 20,000 shares of previously unissued $8 par value stock for cash of $45 per share.		
Dec. 1	Retained Earnings	69,000	
	Dividends Payable		69,000
	To record declaration of cash dividend of $1 per share on 69,000 shares of common stock outstanding (1,000 shares in treasury are not entitled to receive dividends).		

Note: Entry to record the payment of the cash dividend is not shown here since the action does not affect the stockholders' equity.

22	Retained Earnings	331,200	
	Stock Dividends to Be Distributed		55,200
	Additional Paid-in Capital: Stock Dividends....................		276,000
	To record declaration of 10% stock dividend consisting of 6,900 shares of $8 par value common stock to be distributed on Jan. 15 of next year.		
31	Income Summary	177,000	
	Retained Earnings		177,000
	To close Income Summary account.		

b

SUTTON CORPORATION
Partial Income Statement
For Year Ended December 31, 19___

Income before extraordinary items	$212,400
Extraordinary loss (net of income tax benefits)	(35,400)
Net income	$177,000

Earnings per share.*	
Income before extraordinary items	$3.60
Extraordinary loss	(0.60)
Net income	$3.00

* On 59,000 weighted-average number of shares of common stock outstanding during 19___, determined as follows:

Jan. 1–Mar. 31: (40,000 + 10,000 shares issued pursuant to a 5 for 4 split) × ¼ of year .	12,500
Apr. 1–June 30: (50,000 − 2,000 shares of treasury stock) × ¼ of year	12,000
July 1–Dec. 31: (50,000 + 20,000 shares of new stock − 1,000 shares of treasury stock) × ½ of year	34,500
Weighted-average number of shares outstanding	59,000

SELF-TEST QUESTIONS

The answers to these questions appear on page 590.

1 The primary purpose of showing special types of events separately in the income statement is to:

a Increase earnings per share.

b Assist users of the income statement in evaluating the profitability of normal, ongoing operations.

c Minimize the income taxes paid on the results of ongoing operations.

d Prevent unusual losses from recurring.

2 Which of the following situations would **not** be presented in a separate section of the current year's income statement of Marlow Corporation? During the current year:

a Marlow's St. Louis headquarters are destroyed by a tornado.

b Marlow sells its entire juvenile furniture operations and concentrates upon its remaining children's clothing segment.

c Marlow changes from the straight-line method of depreciation to the double-declining-balance method.

d Marlow's accountant discovers that the entire price paid several years ago to purchase company offices in Texas had been charged to a Land account; consequently, no depreciation has ever been taken on these buildings.

3 When a corporation has outstanding both common and preferred stock:

a Primary and fully diluted earnings per share are reported only if the preferred stock is cumulative.

b Earnings per share is reported for each type of stock outstanding.

c Earnings per share may be computed without regard to the amount of dividends declared on common stock.

d Earnings per share may be computed without regard to the amount of the annual preferred dividends.

4 The statement of retained earnings:

a Need not be prepared if a separate statement of stockholders' equity accompanies the financial statements.

b Indicates the amount of cash available for the payment of dividends.

c Includes prior period adjustments and cash dividends, but not stock dividends.

d Shows revenue, expenses, and dividends for the accounting period.

5 On December 10, 1990, Totem Corporation reacquired 2,000 of its own $5 par stock at a price of $60 per share. In 1991, 500 of the treasury shares are reissued at a price of $70 per share. Which of the following statements is correct?

a The treasury stock purchased is recorded at cost and is shown in Totem's December 31, 1990 balance sheet as an asset.

b The two treasury stock transactions result in an overall reduction in Totem's stockholders' equity of $85,000.

c Totem recognizes a gain of $10 per share on the reissuance of the 500 treasury shares in 1991.

d Totem's stockholders' equity was increased by $110,000 when the treasury stock was acquired.

Assignment Material

REVIEW QUESTIONS

1 What is the purpose of arranging an income statement to show subtotals for *Income from Continuing Operations* and for *Income before Extraordinary Items?*

2 Pappa Joe's owns 30 pizza parlors and a minor league baseball team. During the current year, the company sold three of its pizza parlors and closed another when the lease on the building expired. Should any of these events be classified as "discontinued operations" in the company's income statement? Explain.

3 Define *extraordinary items.* Give three examples of losses which qualify as extraordinary items and three examples of losses which would *not* be classified as extraordinary.

4 In past years, the management of St. Thomas Medical Supply had consistently estimated the allowance for doubtful accounts at 2% of total accounts receivable. At the end of the current year, management estimated that uncollectible accounts would equal 4% of accounts receivable. Should the uncollectible accounts expense of prior years be recomputed in order to show in the income statement the cumulative effect of this change in accounting estimate?

5 Both the *cumulative effect of a change in accounting principle* and a *prior period adjustment* affect the income of past accounting periods. Distinguish between these two items and explain how each is shown in the financial statements.

6 In the current year, Garden Products decided to switch from use of an accelerated method of depreciation to the straight-line method. Will the cumulative effect of this change in accounting principle increase or decrease the amount of net income reported in the current year? Explain.

7 Explain how each of the following is computed:

a Price-earnings ratio

b Primary earnings per share

c Fully diluted earnings per share

8 Throughout the year, Gold Seal Co. had 4 million shares of common stock and 120,000 shares of convertible preferred stock outstanding. Each share of preferred is convertible into four shares of common. What number of shares should be used in the computation of (a) primary earnings per share, and (b) fully diluted earnings per share?

9 A financial analyst notes that Baxter Corporation's earnings per share have been rising steadily for the last five years. The analyst expects the company's net income to continue to increase at the same rate as in the past. In forecasting future primary earnings per share, what special risk should the analyst consider if Baxter's primary earnings are significantly larger than its fully diluted earnings?

10 Explain the significance of the following dates relating to dividends: date of declaration, date of record, date of payment, ex-dividend date.

11 What is the purpose of a *stock split?*

12 Distinguish between a *stock split* and a *stock dividend.* Is there any reason for the difference in accounting treatment of these two events?

13 What are *prior period adjustments?* How are they presented in financial statements?

14 Identify three items that may appear in a statement of retained earnings as changes in the amount of retained earnings.

15 A *statement of stockholders' equity* sometimes is called an "expanded" statement of retained earnings. Why?

16 What is *treasury stock?* Why do corporations purchase their own shares? Is treasury stock an asset? How should it be reported in the balance sheet?

17 In many states, the corporation law requires that retained earnings be restricted for dividend purposes to the extent of the cost of treasury shares. What is the reason for this legal rule?

EXERCISES

Listed below are nine technical accounting terms introduced or emphasized in this chapter:

Treasury stock	*Discontinued operations*	*Ex-dividend*
Extraordinary item	*Prior period adjustment*	*Stock dividend*
Cumulative effect of	*Fully diluted earnings*	*Primary earnings*
an accounting change	*per share*	*per share*

Each of the following statements may (or may not) describe one of these technical terms. For each statement, indicate the term described, or answer "None" if the statement does not correctly describe any of the terms.

a An adjustment to the beginning balance of retained earnings to correct an error previously made in the measurement of net income.

b Earnings per share of cumulative preferred stock.

c A separate section sometimes included in an income statement as a step in helping investors to evaluate the profitability of ongoing business activities.

d A hypothetical figure indicating what earnings per share would have been if all securities convertible into common stock had been converted at the beginning of the current year.

e A gain or loss that is material in amount, unusual in nature, and not expected to recur in the foreseeable future.

f The asset represented by shares of capital stock that have not yet been issued.

g A distribution of additional shares of stock that reduces retained earnings but causes no change in total stockholders' equity.

h The effect that retroactive application of a newly adopted accounting principle has upon the amount of net income reported in prior accounting periods.

Exercise 15-2
Discontinued
operations

During the current year, SunSports, Inc., operated two business segments: a chain of surf and dive shops and a small chain of tennis shops. The tennis shops were not profitable and were sold near year-end to another corporation. SunSports' operations for the current year are summarized below. The first two captions, "Net sales" and "Costs and expenses," relate only to the company's continuing operations.

Net sales	$9,600,000
Costs and expenses (including applicable income taxes)	8,600,000
Operating loss from tennis shops (net of income tax benefit)..................	160,000
Loss on sale of tennis shops (net of income tax benefit)	290,000

The company had 100,000 shares of a single class of capital stock outstanding throughout the year.

Instructions

Prepare a condensed income statement for the year. At the bottom of the statement, show any appropriate earnings-per-share figures. (A *condensed* income statement is illustrated on page 563.)

Exercise 15-3
Reporting an
extraordinary
item

For the year ended December 31, Union Chemical had net sales of $9,000,000, costs and other expenses (including income taxes) of $8,060,000, and an extraordinary loss (net of income tax) of $400,000. Prepare a condensed income statement (including earnings per share), assuming that 200,000 shares of common stock were outstanding throughout the year.

Exercise 15-4
Computing
earnings per
share: changes in
number of shares
outstanding

In the year just ended, Sunshine Citrus earned net income of $4,510,000. The company has issued only one class of capital stock, of which 1 million shares were outstanding at January 1. Compute the company's earnings per share under each of the following *independent* assumptions:

a No change occurred during the year in the number of shares outstanding.

b On October 1, the company issued an additional 100,000 shares of capital stock in exchange for cash.

c On July 1, the company distributed an additional 100,000 shares of capital stock as a 10% stock dividend. (No additional shares are issued on October 1.)

Exercise 15-5
Computing
earnings per
share: effect of
preferred stock

The net income of Carriage Trade Clothiers amounted to $2,550,000 for the current year. Compute the amount of earnings per share assuming that the shares of capital stock outstanding throughout the year consisted of:

a 300,000 shares of $10 par value common stock and no preferred stock.

b 200,000 shares of 9%, $100 par value preferred stock and 300,000 shares of $5 par value common stock.

Exercise 15-6
Cash dividends,
stock dividends
and stock splits

Glass Corporation has 500,000 shares of $10 par value capital stock outstanding. You are to prepare the journal entries to record the following transactions:

Apr. 30 Distributed an additional 500,000 shares of capital stock in a 2-for-1 stock split.

June 1 Declared a cash dividend of 60 cents per share.

July 1 Paid the 60-cent cash dividend to stockholders.

Aug. 1 Declared a 5% stock dividend. Market price of stock was $19 per share.

Sept. 10 Issued 50,000 shares pursuant to the 5% stock dividend.

Dec. 1 Declared a 50% stock dividend. Market price of stock was $23 per share.

Exercise 15-7
Effect of stock
dividends on
stock price

Jiffy Tool Co. has a total of 40,000 shares of common stock outstanding and no preferred stock. Total stockholders' equity at the end of the current year amounts to $2 million and the market value of the stock is $72 per share. At year-end, the company declares a stock dividend of one share for each five shares held. If all parties concerned clearly recognize the nature of the stock dividend, what should you expect the market price per share of the common stock to be on the ex-dividend date?

Exercise 15-8
Recording
treasury stock
transactions

Cable Transmissions engaged in the following transactions involving treasury stock:

Nov. 10 Purchased for cash 12,500 shares of treasury stock at a price of $20 per share.

Dec. 4 Reissued 5,000 shares of treasury stock at a price of $24 per share.

Dec. 22 Reissued 4,000 shares of treasury stock at a price of $19 per share.

Instructions

a Prepare general journal entries to record these transactions.

b Compute the amount of retained earnings that should be restricted because of the treasury stock still owned at December 31.

Exercise 15-9
Restating
earnings per
share after a
stock split

The 1985 annual report of **PepsiCo., Inc.,** included the following comparative summary of earnings per share over the last three years:

	1983	1984	1985
Earnings per share	*$3.00*	*$3.45*	*$4.50*

Early in 1986, PepsiCo., Inc., split its common stock 3 for 1. Following this stock split, the company reported earnings per share of $1.75 in 1986 and $2.23 in 1987.

Instructions

a Prepare a three-year schedule similar to the one above, but compare earnings per share during the years 1985, 1986, and 1987. (Hint: All per-share amounts in your schedule should be based on the number of shares outstanding *after* the stock split.)

b In preparing your schedule, which figure (or figures) did you have to restate? Why? Explain the logic behind your computation.

PROBLEMS

Group A

Problem 15A-1
Unusual events
affecting publicly
owned
corporations

The following events have been reported in the financial statements of large, publicly owned corporations.

a *Atlantic Richfield Company* (ARCO) sold or abandoned the entire "noncoal minerals" segment of its operations. In the year of disposal, this segment had an operating loss. ARCO also incurred a loss of $514 million on disposal of its noncoal minerals segment of the business.

b *American Airlines* increased the estimated useful life used in computing depreciation on its aircraft. If the new estimated life had always been in use, the net income reported in prior years would have been substantially higher.

c *Union Carbide Corp.* sustained a large loss as a result of the explosion of a chemical plant.

Instructions

Indicate whether each event should be classified as a discontinued operation, an extraordinary item, the cumulative effect of an accounting change, or included among the revenue and expenses of normal and recurring business operations. Briefly explain your reasons for each answer.

Problem 15A-2
Reporting unusual events; using predictive subtotals

Sea Quest Corporation operated both a fleet of commercial fishing vessels and a chain of six seafood restaurants. The restaurants continuously lost money and were sold to a large restaurant chain near year-end. The operating results of Sea Quest Corporation for the year ended December 31, 1991 are shown below:

Continuing operations (fishing fleet):	
Net sales	$4,800,000
Costs and expenses (including related income taxes)	4,040,000
Other data:	
Operating loss from restaurants (net of income tax benefit)	380,000
Gain on sale of restaurant properties (net of income taxes)	230,000
Extraordinary loss (net of income tax benefit)	400,000

The extraordinary loss resulted from the expropriation of a fishing vessel by a foreign government.

Sea Quest Corporation had 200,000 shares of capital stock outstanding throughout the year.

Instructions

a Prepare a condensed income statement including proper presentation of the discontinued restaurant operations and the extraordinary loss. Include all appropriate earnings per share figures.

b Assume that you expect the profitability of Sea Quest's fishing operations to increase by 5% next year. What is your estimate of the company's net earnings per share next year?

Problem 15A-3
Format of an Income statement and a statement retained earnings

Shown below is data relating to the operations of Suma Electronics Corporation during 1991:

Continuing operations:	
Net sales	$21,000,000
Costs and expenses (including applicable income taxes)	18,300,000
Other data:	
Operating loss during 1991 on segment of the business discontinued near year-end (net of income tax benefit)	300,000
Loss on disposal of discontinued segment (net of income tax benefit)	900,000
Extraordinary gain (net of income tax)	630,000
Cumulative effect of change in accounting principle (decrease in net income, net of related income tax benefit)	150,000
Prior period adjustment (increase in 1990 research and development expense, net of income tax benefit)	240,000
Cash dividends declared ($4 per share)	1,200,000

Instructions

a Prepare a condensed income statement for 1991, including earnings per share statistics. Suma Electronics had 300,000 shares of a single class of capital stock outstanding throughout the year.

b Prepare a statement of retained earnings for the year ended December 31, 1991. As originally reported, retained earnings at December 31, 1990 amounted to $7,400,000.

**Problem 15A-4
Reporting the
results of
operations—a
comprehensive
problem**

Katherine McCall, the accountant for Alternative Energy Systems, was injured in a skiing accident, and the following income statement was prepared by a temporary employee with little knowledge of accounting:

ALTERNATIVE ENERGY SYSTEMS
Income Statement
For the Year Ended December 31, 1991

Net sales		$5,400,000
Gain on sale of treasury stock		30,000
Excess of issuance price over par value of capital stock		120,000
Operating income from segment of business discontinued during the year (net of income taxes)		200,000
Cumulative effect of change in accounting principle (net of income taxes)		75,000
Total revenue		$5,825,000
Less:		
Prior period adjustment (net of income tax benefit)	$ 250,000	
Cost of goods sold	2,480,000	
Selling expenses	1,160,000	
General and administrative operations	820,000	
Income taxes on continuing operations	270,000	
Extraordinary loss (net of income tax benefit)	230,000	
Loss on sale of discontinued segment (net of income tax benefit)	450,000	
Dividends declared on capital stock	300,000	5,960,000
Net loss		$ 135,000

Instructions

a Prepare a corrected income statement for the year ended December 31, 1991, using the format illustrated on page 558. Include at the bottom of your income statement all appropriate earnings per share figures. Assume that throughout the year the company had outstanding a weighted average of 50,000 shares of a single class of capital stock.

b Prepare a statement of retained earnings for 1991. Assume that retained earnings at December 31, 1990, were originally reported at $2,300,000.

**Problem 15A-5
Preparing a
statement of
stockholders'
equity**

Shown below is a summary of the transactions affecting the stockholders' equity of North County Dinner Theater, Inc., during 19__:

Prior period adjustment (net of income taxes)	$ 25,000
Declaration and distribution of a 10% stock dividend (2,000 shares, market price $40 per share)	80,000
Issuance of 5,000 shares of $5 par value capital stock at $42 per share	210,000
Purchased 1,000 shares of treasury stock at $38 per share	(38,000)
Reissued 500 shares of treasury stock at $43 per share	21,500
Net income	164,600
Cash dividends declared ($2 per share)	(53,000)

Brackets ( ) indicate a debit change—a reduction in stockholders' equity.

Instructions

Prepare a statement of stockholders' equity for the year ended December 31, 19__. Use the column headings and beginning balances shown below. (Notice that one column is used to combine the additional paid-in capital from all sources.)

■ Balances, January 1, 19__	CAPITAL STOCK $5 PAR VALUE $100,000	ADDITIONAL PAID-IN CAPITAL $420,000	RETAINED EARNINGS $340,000	TREASURY STOCK –0–	TOTAL STOCKHOLDERS' EQUITY $860,000

Problem 15A-6
Recording stock
dividends and
treasury stock
transactions

The stockholders' equity of Martin Cole Productions, Inc., at January 1, 1991, is as follows:

Stockholders' equity:
  Common stock, $5 par value, 500,000 shares authorized,
    260,000 issued $1,300,000
  Additional paid-in capital: common stock................................... 4,065,000
    Total paid-in capital $5,365,000
  Retained earnings 1,610,000
  Total stockholders' equity.. $6,975,000

During the year the following transactions relating to stockholders' equity occurred:

Jan. 15   Paid a $1 per share cash dividend declared in December of the preceding year. This dividend was properly recorded at the declaration date and was the only dividend declared during the preceding year.

June 10   Declared a 5% stock dividend to stockholders of record on June 30, to be distributed on July 15. At June 10, the market price of the stock was $35 per share.

July 15   Distributed the stock dividend declared on June 10.

Aug. 4   Purchased 5,000 shares of treasury stock at a price of $30 per share.

Oct. 15   Reissued 3,000 shares of treasury stock at a price of $32 per share.

Dec. 10   Reissued 1,000 shares of treasury stock at a price of $28.50 per share.

Dec. 15   Declared a cash dividend of $1 per share to be paid on January 15 to stockholders of record on December 31.

Dec. 31   The Income Summary account, showing net income of $810,000, was closed into the Retained Earnings account.

Instructions

a Prepare in general journal form the entries necessary to record these transactions.

b Prepare the stockholders' equity section of the balance sheet at December 31, 1991, following the format illustrated on page 574. Include a note following your stockholders' equity section indicating any portion of retained earnings which is not available for dividends. Also include a supporting schedule showing your computation of the balance of retained earnings at year-end.

c Comment on whether Martin Cole Productions, Inc., increased or decreased the total amount of cash dividends declared during the year in comparison with dividends declared in the preceding year.

Problem 15A-7
Preparing the
stockholders'
equity section of
a balance sheet

David Klein was a free-lance engineer who developed and patented a highly efficient turbocharger for automotive engines. In 1990, Klein and Scott Harris organized Performance, Inc., to manufacture the turbocharger. The corporation was authorized to issue 150,000 shares of $10 par value capital stock. Presented below is the information necessary to prepare the stockholders' equity section of the company's balance sheet at the end of 1990 and at the end of 1991.

1990. On January 20, the corporation issued 80,000 shares of common stock to Harris and other investors for cash at $34 per share. In addition, 10,000 shares of common stock were issued on that date to Klein in exchange for his patents. In November, Klein was killed while auto racing in Europe. At the request of Klein's heirs, Performance, Inc., purchased the 10,000 shares of its stock from Klein's estate at $45 per share. Because of the unexpected cash outlay to acquire treasury stock, the directors decided against declaring any cash dividends in 1990. Instead, they declared a 5% stock dividend which was distributed on December 31. The stock price at the declaration date was $42 per share. (The treasury shares did not participate in the stock dividend.) Net income for the year was $415,000.

1991. In March, the 10,000 treasury shares were reissued at a price of $52 per share. In August, the stock was split four shares for one, with a reduction in the par value to $2.50 per share and an increase in the number of shares authorized to 600,000. On December 20, the directors declared a cash dividend of 70 cents per share, payable in January of 1992. Net income for the year was $486,000.

Instructions   Prepare the stockholders' equity section of the balance sheet at:

a December 31, 1990

b December 31, 1991

Use the format illustrated on page 574 and show any necessary supporting computations.

Group B

Problem 15B-1
Unusual events
reported by
publicly owned
corporations

The following events have been reported in the financial statements of large, publicly owned corporations:

a *AT&T* changed the method used to depreciate certain assets. Had the new method always been in use, the net income of prior years would have been $175 million lower than was actually reported.

b *Georgia Pacific Corporation* realized a $10 million gain as a result of condemnation proceedings in which a governmental agency purchased assets from the company in a "forced sale."

c Squibb Corporation sold or abandoned much of its animal health business segment. The company remains in the animal health business, but on a greatly reduced scale.

Instructions   Indicate whether each event should be classified as a discontinued operation, an extraordinary item, the cumulative effect of an accounting change, or included among the revenue and expenses of normal and recurring business operations. Briefly explain your reasons for each answer.

Problem 15B-2
Reporting
unusual events;
using predictive
subtotals

Gulf Coast Airlines operated both an airline and several motels located near airports. During the year just ended, all motel operations were discontinued and the following operating results were reported:

Continuing operations (airlines):	
Net sales	*$42,600,000*
Costs and expenses (including income taxes on continuing operations).....	*36,100,000*
Other data:	
Operating income from motels (net of income taxes)......................	*720,000*
Gain on sale of motels (net of income taxes)	*4,130,000*
Extraordinary loss (net of income tax benefit).........................	*2,800,000*

The extraordinary loss resulted from the destruction of an airliner by terrorists.

Gulf Coast Airlines had 1 million shares of capital stock outstanding throughout the year.

Instructions   **a** Prepare a condensed income statement including proper presentation of the discontinued motel operations and the extraordinary loss. Include all appropriate earnings per share figures.

b Assume that you expect the profitability of Gulf Coast's airlines operations to *de-*

cline by 2% next year. What is your estimate of the company's net earnings per share next year?

Problem 15B-3
Format of an
income statement
and a statement
retained earnings

Shown below is data relating to the operations of Ocean Transport Corp. during 1991:

Continuing operations:

Net sales	$14,000,000
Costs and expenses (including applicable income taxes)	12,200,000

Other data:

Operating income during 1991 on segment of the business dis-continued near year-end (net of income taxes)...........................	150,000
Loss on disposal of discontinued segment (net of income tax benefit)	450,000
Extraordinary loss (net of income tax benefit).............................	520,000
Cumulative effect of change in accounting principle (increase in net income, net of related income taxes)	90,000
Prior period adjustment (increase in 1989 depreciation expense, net of income tax benefit)	100,000
Cash dividends declared ($3 per share)....................................	600,000

Instructions

a Prepare a condensed income statement for 1991, including earnings per share statistics. Ocean Transport had 200,000 shares of a single class of capital stock outstanding throughout the year.

b Prepare a statement of retained earnings for the year ended December 31, 1991. As originally reported, retained earnings at December 31, 1990 amounted to $4,300,000.

Problem 15B-4
Reporting
unusual events: a
comprehensive
problem

The following income statement was prepared by a new and inexperienced employee in the accounting department of Thomas Furniture Co.:

THOMAS FURNITURE CO.
Income Statement
For the Year Ended December 31, 1991

Net sales		$9,000,000
Gain on sale of treasury stock		45,000
Excess of issuance price over par value of common stock		425,000
Prior period adjustment (net of income taxes)		50,000
Extraordinary gain (net of income taxes).............................		30,000
Total revenue		$9,550,000
Less:		
Cost of goods sold	$5,000,000	
Selling expenses	920,000	
General and administrative expenses..........................	1,580,000	
Loss from settlement of litigation	20,000	
Income taxes on continuing operations........................	600,000	
Operating loss on discontinued operations (net of income tax benefit).....................................	210,000	
Loss on disposal of discontinued oper-ations (net of income tax benefit)	350,000	
Cumulative effect of change in accounting principle (net of income tax benefit)	70,000	
Dividends declared on capital stock..........................	300,000	
Total costs and expenses..		9,050,000
Net income		$ 500,000

Instructions   **a** Prepare a corrected income statement for the year ended December 31, 1991, using the format illustrated on page 558. Include at the bottom of your income statement all appropriate earnings per share figures. Assume that throughout the year, the company had outstanding a weighted average of 100,000 shares of a single class of capital stock.

b Prepare a statement of retained earnings for 1991. (As originally reported, retained earnings at December 31, 1990 amounted to $1,400,000.)

Problem 15B-5
Preparing a
statement of
stockholders'
equity

Shown below is a summary of the transactions affecting the stockholders' equity of Sonoma Valley Corporation during the current year:

Prior period adjustment (net of income tax benefit)	*$(50,000)*
Issuance of common stock: 10,000 shares of $10 par value	
capital stock at $62 per share	*620,000*
Distribution of 5% stock dividend (6,000 shares, market price	
$60 per share)...	*360,000*
Purchased 1,000 shares of treasury stock at $58	*(58,000)*
Reissued 500 shares of treasury stock at a price of $64 per	
share	*32,000*
Net income	*510,000*
Cash dividends declared ($1 per share)......................................	*126,000*

Brackets ( ) indicate a debit change—a reduction—in stockholders' equity.

Instructions   Prepare a statement of stockholders' equity for the year. Use the column headings and beginning balances shown below. (Notice that all additional paid-in capital accounts are combined into a single column.)

	CAPITAL STOCK ($10 PAR VALUE)	ADDITIONAL PAID-IN CAPITAL	RETAINED EARNINGS	TREASURY STOCK	TOTAL STOCK-HOLDERS' EQUITY
Balances,					
January 1, 19___	*$1,100,000*	*$1,800,000*	*$900,000*	*$ –0–*	*$3,800,000*

Problem 15B-6
Recording stock
dividends and
treasury stock
transactions

At the beginning of 1991, OverNight Letter showed the following amounts in the stockholders' equity section of its balance sheet:

Stockholders' equity:	
Capital stock, $2 par value, 500,000 shares authorized,	
191,000 issued	*$ 382,000*
Additional paid-in capital: capital stock......................................	*3,140,000*
Total paid-in capital	*$3,522,000*
Retained earnings	*1,386,000*
Total stockholders' equity...	*$4,908,000*

The transactions relating to stockholders' equity accounts during the year are as follows:

Jan.   3   Declared a dividend of $1 per share to stockholders of record on January 31, payable on February 15.

Feb. 15   Paid the cash dividend declared on January 3.

Apr. 12   The corporation purchased 3,000 shares of its own capital stock at a price of $40 per share.

May   9   Reissued 2,000 shares of the treasury stock at a price of $44 per share.

June	1	Declared a 5% stock dividend to stockholders of record at June 15, to be distributed on June 30. The market price of the stock at June 1 was $42 per share. (The 1,000 shares remaining in the treasury do not participate in the stock dividend.)
June	30	Distributed the stock dividend declared on June 1.
Aug.	4	Reissued 500 of the 1,000 remaining shares of treasury stock at a price of $37 per share.
Dec.	31	The Income Summary account, showing net income for the year of $964,000, was closed into the Retained Earnings account.

Instructions **a** Prepare in general journal form the entries to record the above transactions.

b Prepare the stockholders' equity section of the balance sheet at December 31, 1991. Use the format illustrated on page 574. Include a supporting schedule showing your computation of retained earnings at that date.

c Compute the maximum cash dividend per share which legally could be declared at December 31, 1991, without impairing the paid-in capital of OverNight Letter. (Hint: The availability of retained earnings for dividends is restricted by the cost of treasury stock owned.)

Problem 15B-7
Preparing the stockholders' equity section: a challenging case

The Mandella family decided early in 1991 to incorporate their family-owned vineyards under the name Mandella Corporation. The corporation was authorized to issue 200,000 shares of a single class of $10 par value capital stock. Presented below is the information necessary to prepare the stockholders' equity section of the company's balance sheet at the end of 1991 and at the end of 1992.

1991. In January the corporation issued to members of the Mandella family 75,000 shares of capital stock in exchange for cash and other assets used in the operation of the vineyards. The fair market value of these assets indicated an issue price of $30 per share. In December, Joe Mandella died, and the corporation purchased 5,000 shares of its own capital stock from his estate at $34 per share. Because of the large cash outlay to acquire this treasury stock, the directors decided not to declare cash dividends in 1991 and instead declared a 10% stock dividend to be distributed in January of 1992. The stock price at the declaration date was $35 per share. (The treasury shares do not participate in the stock dividend.) Net income for 1991 was $470,000.

1992. In January the corporation distributed the stock dividend declared in 1991, and in February, the 5,000 treasury shares were sold to Maria Mandella at $39 per share. In June, the capital stock was split, two shares for one. (Approval was obtained to increase the authorized number of shares to 400,000.) On December 15, the directors declared a cash dividend of $2 per share, payable in January of 1993. Net income for 1992 was $540,000.

Instructions Using the format illustrated on page 574, prepare the stockholders' equity section of the balance sheet at

a December 31, 1991

b December 31, 1992

Show any necessary computations in supporting schedules.

BUSINESS DECISION CASES

Case 15-1
The case of the extraordinarily ordinary loss

In 1986 *Squibb Corporation* recognized a $68 million loss from the write-off of certain foreign-based assets due to "escalating war, social upheaval, the weakening economies of oil-producing nations, and growing political instability." (Squibb's operations in these foreign countries were not discontinued.) Squibb originally classified this loss as an extraordinary item. Upon reviewing the company's financial statements, however, the Securities and Exchange Commission requested that Squibb reclassify this item as a normal operating loss. In 1987, Squibb revised its 1986 income statement to comply with the SEC's request.

Instructions Indicate the effect of the reclassification of this loss upon Squibb's:

a Net income for 1986.

b Income before extraordinary items for 1986.

c Income from continuing operations in 1986.

d Price-earnings ratio as shown in financial newspapers such as *The Wall Street Journal*.

e 1987 financial statements.

f Ability to pay cash dividends.

Explain the reasoning behind your answers.

Case 15-2
Is there life
without baseball?

Midwestern Publishing, Inc., publishes two newspapers and until recently owned a professional baseball team. The baseball team had been losing money for several years and was sold at the end of 1991 to a group of investors who plan to move it to a larger city. Also in 1991, Midwestern suffered an extraordinary loss when its Raytown printing plant was damaged by a tornado. The damage has since been repaired. A condensed income statement is shown below:

MIDWESTERN PUBLISHING, INC.
Income Statement
For the Year Ended December 31, 1991

Net revenue		$41,000,000
Costs and expenses		36,500,000
Income from continuing operations		$ 4,500,000
Discontinued operations:		
Operating loss on baseball team	$(1,300,000)	
Gain on sale of baseball team	4,700,000	3,400,000
Income before extraordinary items		$ 7,900,000
Extraordinary loss:		
Tornado damage to Raytown printing plant		(600,000)
Net income		$ 7,300,000

Instructions On the basis of this information, answer the following questions. Show any necessary computations and explain your reasoning.

a What would Midwestern's net income have been for 1991 if it **had not** sold the baseball team?

b Assume that for 1992, you expect a 7% increase in the profitability of Midwestern's newspaper business, but had projected a $2,000,000 operating loss for the baseball team if Midwestern had continued to operate the team in 1992. What amount would you forecast as Midwestern's 1992 net income *if the company had continued to own and operate the baseball team?*

c Given your assumptions in part **b**, but given that Midwestern *did* sell the baseball team in 1991, what would you forecast as the company's estimated net income for 1992?

d Assume that the expenses of operating the baseball team in 1991 amounted to $32,200,000, net of any related income tax effects. What was the team's *net revenue* for the year?

ANSWERS TO SELF-TEST QUESTIONS

1 b   2 d   3 c   4 a   5 b

Bonds Payable, Leases, and Other Liabilities

In this chapter, we describe various types of long-term debt. Large corporations borrow vast amounts of money; Exxon Corporation, for example, has liabilities totaling more than $30 billion. Our emphasis in this chapter is upon the issuance of bonds payable—a form of borrowing which enables large corporations to raise hundreds of millions of dollars from thousands of individual investors. Both the straight-line and effective interest methods of amortizing bond discount and premium are illustrated and explained. Other long-term liabilities covered in this chapter include mortgages, lease payment obligations, and pension plans.

After studying this chapter you should be able to meet these Learning Objectives:

1 Describe the typical characteristics of corporate bonds.

2 Explain the advantage of raising capital by issuing bonds instead of stock.

3 Account for the issuance of bonds, payment of interest, and retirement of the bonds.

4 Explain how bond discount or premium affects the cost of borrowing.

5 Amortize bond discount or premium by the straight-line and effective interest methods.

6 Discuss the relationship between interest rates and the market price behavior of bonds.

7 Describe convertible bonds and explain the possible benefits to the issuing corporation and to the bondholder.

8 Explain the accounting treatment of operating leases and of capital leases.

BONDS PAYABLE

Financially sound corporations may arrange some long-term loans by issuing a note payable to a bank or an insurance company. But to finance a large project, such as building a refinery or acquiring a fleet of jumbo jets, a corporation may need more capital than any single lender can supply. When a corporation needs to raise large amounts of long-term capital—perhaps 10, 50, or 100 million dollars or more—it generally sells additional shares of capital stock or issues *bonds payable.*[1]

What Is a Bond Issue?

Objective 1
Describe the typical characteristics of corporate bonds.

The issuance of bonds payable is a technique of splitting a large loan into a great many units, called bonds. Each bond is a long-term interest-bearing note payable, usually in the face amount of $1,000. The bonds are sold to the investing public, thus allowing many different investors to participate in the loan. An example of a corporate bond issue is the 8% bond issue of the Singer Corporation, due January 15, 1999. With this bond issue, the Singer Corporation borrowed $100 million by issuing 100,000 bonds of $1,000 each.

Bonds payable differ from capital stock in several ways. First, bonds payable are a liability; thus, bondholders are *creditors* of the corporation, not owners. Bondholders generally do not have voting rights and do not participate in the earnings of the corporation beyond receiving contractual interest payments. Next, bond interest payments are *contractual obligations* of the corporation. Dividends, on the other hand, do not become legal obligations of the corporation until they have been formally declared by the board of directors. Finally, bonds have a specified *maturity date,* upon which the corporation must redeem the bonds at their face amount ($1,000 each). Capital stock, on the other hand, does not have a maturity date and may remain outstanding indefinitely.

■ **Authorization of a Bond Issue** Formal approval of the board of directors and the stockholders is usually required before bonds can be issued. If the bonds are to be sold to the general public, approval must also be obtained from the SEC, just as for an issue of capital stock which is offered to the public.

The issuing corporation also selects a *trustee* to represent the interests of the bondholders. This trustee generally is a large bank or trust company. A contract is drawn up indicating the terms of the bond issue and the assets (if any) which are pledged as collateral for the bonds. Sometimes this contract places limitations on the payment of dividends to stockholders during the life of the bonds. For example, dividends may be permitted only when working capital is above specified amounts. If the issuing corporation defaults on any of the terms of this contract, the trustee may foreclose upon the assets which secure the bonds or may take other legal action on behalf of the bondholders.

■ **The Role of the Underwriter in Marketing a Bond Issue** An investment banker or underwriter is usually employed to market a bond issue, just as in the case of capital stock. The corporation turns the entire bond issue over to the underwriter at a specified price; the underwriter sells the bonds to the

---

[1] Bonds payable also are issued by the federal government and by many other governmental units such as states, cities, and school districts. In this chapter, our discussion is limited to corporate bonds, although the concepts also apply to the bond issues of governmental agencies.

public at a slightly higher price. By this arrangement the corporation is assured of receiving the entire proceeds on a specified date.

■ **Transferability of Bonds** Corporate bonds, like capital stocks, are traded daily on organized securities exchanges. The holders of a 25-year bond issue need not wait 25 years to convert their investment into cash. By placing a telephone call to a broker, an investor may sell bonds within a matter of minutes at the going market price. This quality of *liquidity* is one of the most attractive features of an investment in corporate bonds.

■ **Quoted Market Prices** The market price of stocks is quoted in terms of dollars per share. Bond prices, however, are quoted as a *percentage* of their face value or *maturity* value, which is usually $1,000. The maturity value is the amount the issuing company must pay to redeem the bond at the date it matures (becomes due). A bond quoted at *102* would therefore have a market price of $1,020 (102% of $1,000). Bond prices are quoted at the nearest one-eighth of a percentage point. The following line from the financial page of a daily newspaper summarizes the previous day's trading in bonds of Sears, Roebuck and Co.

■
What is the market value of this bond?

BONDS	SALES	HIGH	LOW	CLOSE	NET CHANGE
Sears R 7⅞'07	45	89½	87½	89	+1

This line of condensed information indicates that 45 of Sears, Roebuck and Co.'s 7⅞, $1,000 bonds maturing in 2007 were traded. The highest price is reported as 89½, or $895 for a bond of $1,000 face value. The lowest price was 87½, or $875 for a $1,000 bond. The closing price (last sale of the day) was 89, or $890. This was one point above the closing price of the previous day, an increase of $10 in the price of a $1,000 bond.

The primary factors which determine the market value of a bond are (1) the relationship of the bond's interest rate to other investment opportunities, (2) the length of time until the bond matures, and (3) investors' confidence that the issuing company has the financial strength to make all future interest and principal payments promptly. Thus, a bond with a 12% interest rate will command a higher market price than a 10% bond with the same maturity date if the two companies issuing the bonds are of equal financial strength.

A bond selling at a market price greater than its maturity value is said to be selling at a *premium;* a bond selling at a price below its maturity value is selling at a *discount.* As a bond nears its maturity date, the market price of the bond moves toward the maturity value. At the maturity date the market value of the bond will be exactly equal to its maturity value, because the issuing corporation will redeem the bond for that amount.

■ **Types of Bonds** Bonds secured by the pledge of specific assets are called *mortgage bonds.* An unsecured bond is called a *debenture bond;* its value rests upon the general credit of the corporation. A debenture bond issued by a very large and strong corporation may have a higher investment rating than a secured bond issued by a corporation in less satisfactory financial condition. For example, the $500 million of debenture bonds recently issued by IBM are rated AAA, the highest possible rating.

Some bonds have a single fixed maturity date for the entire issue. Other bond issues, called *serial bonds,* provide for varying maturity dates to lessen the problem of accumulating cash for payment. For example, serial bonds in the amount of $20 million issued in 1980 might call for $2 million of bonds to mature in 1990, and an additional $2 million to become due in each of the succeeding nine years. Almost all bonds are *callable,* which means that the corporation has the right to pay off the bonds *in advance* of the scheduled maturity date. To compensate the bondholders for being forced to give up their investments, the call price is usually somewhat higher than the face value of the bonds.

Most corporation bonds issued in recent years have been *registered bonds;* that is, the name of the owner is registered with the issuing corporation. Payment of interest is made by semiannual checks mailed to the registered owners. *Coupon bonds* were more popular some years ago and many are still outstanding. Coupon bonds have interest coupons attached; each six months during the life of the bond one of these coupons becomes due. The bondholder detaches the coupon and deposits it with a bank for collection. The names of the bondholders are not registered with the corporation.

As an additional attraction to investors, corporations sometimes include a conversion privilege in the bond indenture. A *convertible bond* is one which may be exchanged for common stock at the option of the bondholder. The advantages to the investor of the conversion feature in the event of increased earnings for the company were described in Chapter 14 with regard to convertible preferred stock.

Tax Advantage of Bond Financing

Objective 2
Explain the advantage of raising capital by issuing bonds instead of stock.

A principal advantage of raising money by issuing bonds instead of stock is that interest payments are *deductible* in determining income subject to corporate income taxes. Dividends paid to stockholders, however, are *not deductible* in computing taxable income.

To illustrate, assume that a corporation pays income taxes at a rate of *30%* on its taxable income. If this corporation issues $10 million of 10% bonds payable, it will incur interest expense of $1 million per year. This interest expense, however, will *reduce taxable income* by $1 million, thus reducing the corporation's annual income taxes by $300,000. As a result, the *after-tax* cost of borrowing the $10 million is only *$700,000,* as shown below:[2]

Interest expense ($10 million × 10%)	*$1,000,000*
Less: Income tax savings ($1,000,000 deduction × 30%)	*300,000*
After-tax cost of borrowing	*$ 700,000*

The Issuance of Bonds Payable

Objective 3
Account for the issuance of bonds, payment of interest, and retirement of the bonds.

Assume that Wells Corporation on January 1, 1991, after proper authorization by the board of directors and approval by the stockholders, issues $1,000,000 of

---

[2] A short-cut approach to computing the after-tax cost of borrowing is simply to multiply the interest expense by *one minus the company's tax rate,* as follows: *$1,000,000 × (1 − .30) = $700,000.*

12%, 20-year bonds payable. All the bonds bear the January 1, 1991 date, and interest is computed from this date. Interest on the bonds is payable semiannually, each July 1 and January 1. If all the bonds are sold at par value (face value), the sale will be recorded by the following entry on January 1, 1991:

Cash	*1,000,000*	
Bonds Payable		*1,000,000*
Issued at 12%; 20-year bonds payable at a price of 100.		

At each semiannual interest payment date, Wells Corporation must pay $60,000 to the bondholders ($1,000,000 × 12% × ½ = $60,000). Each semiannual interest payment will be recorded as shown below:

Bond Interest Expense	*60,000*	
Cash		*60,000*
Semiannual payment of bond interest.		

When the bonds mature 20 years later on January 1, 2011, repayment of the principal amount of the bond issue will be recorded as follows:

Bonds Payable	*1,000,000*	
Cash		*1,000,000*
Paid face amount of bonds at maturity.		

Bonds Issued between Interest Dates

The semiannual interest dates (such as January 1 and July 1, or April 1 and October 1) are printed on the bond certificates. However, bonds are often issued between the specified interest dates. The *investor* is then required to pay the interest accrued to the date of issuance *in addition* to the stated price of the bond. This practice enables the corporation to pay a full six months' interest on all bonds outstanding at the semiannual interest payment date. The accrued interest collected from investors purchasing bonds between interest payment dates is thus returned to them on the next interest payment date.

To illustrate, let us modify our illustration to assume that Wells Corporation issues its $1,000,000 of 12% bonds at a price of 100 on *March 1*—two months after the date printed on the bonds. The amount received from the bond purchasers now will include two months' accrued interest, as shown below:

Bonds issued between interest dates

Cash	*1,020,000*	
Bonds Payable		*1,000,000*
Bond Interest Payable		*20,000*
Issued $1,000,000 face value of 12%, 20-year bonds at 100 plus		
accrued interest for two months ($1,000,000 × 12% × ²⁄₁₂ = $20,000).		

Four months later on the regular semiannual interest payment date, a full six months' interest ($60 per each $1,000 bond) will be paid to all bondholders, regardless of when they purchased their bonds. The entry for the semiannual interest payment is illustrated below:

Notice only part
of the interest
payment is
charged to
expense

Bond Interest Payable	20,000	
Bond Interest Expense	40,000	
Cash		60,000

Paid semiannual interest on $1,000,000 face value of 12% bonds.

Now consider these interest transactions from the standpoint of the *investors.* They paid for two months' accrued interest at the time of purchasing the bonds, and they received checks for six months' interest after holding the bonds for only four months. They have, therefore, been reimbursed properly for the use of their money for four months.

When bonds are subsequently sold by one investor to another, they sell at the quoted market price *plus accrued interest* since the last interest payment date. This practice enables the issuing corporation to pay all the interest for an interest period to the investor owning the bond at the interest date. Otherwise, the corporation would have to make partial payments to every investor who bought or sold the bond during the interest period.

The amount which investors will pay for bonds is the *present value* of the principal and interest payments they will receive. Before going further in our discussion of bonds payable, it will be helpful to review the concepts of present value and effective yield.

The Concept of Present Value

The concept of present value is based upon the "time value" of money—the idea that receiving money today is preferable to receiving money at some later date. Assume, for example, that a bond will have a maturity value of $1,000 five years from today but will pay no interest in the meantime. Investors would not pay $1,000 for this bond today, because they would receive no return on their investment over the next five years. There are prices less than $1,000, however, at which investors would buy the bond. For example, if the bond could be purchased for $600, the investor could expect a return (interest) of $400 from the investment over the five-year period.

The *present value* of a future cash receipt is the amount that a knowledgeable investor will pay *today* for the right to receive that future payment. The exact amount of the present value depends upon (1) the amount of the future payment, (2) the length of time until the payment will be received, and (3) the rate of return required by the investor. However, the present value will always be *less* than the future amount. This is because money received today can be invested to earn interest and thereby becomes equivalent to a larger amount in the future.

The rate of interest which will cause a given present value to grow to a given future amount is called the discount rate or *effective interest rate.* The effective interest rate required by investors at any given time is regarded as the going *market rate* of interest. The procedures for computing the present value of a future amount are illustrated in an appendix following this chapter.

The Present Value Concept and Bond Prices

The price at which bonds will sell is the present value to investors of the future principal and interest payments. If the bonds sell at par, the effective interest rate is equal to the ***contract interest rate*** (or nominal rate) printed on the bonds. The higher the effective interest rate investors require, the less they will pay for bonds with a given contract rate of interest. For example, if investors insist upon a 10% return, they will pay less than $1,000 for a 9%, $1,000 bond. Thus, if investors require an effective interest rate ***greater*** than the contract rate of interest for the bonds, the bonds will sell at a ***discount*** (price less than face value). On the other hand, if investors require an effective interest rate of ***less*** than the contract rate, the bonds will sell at a ***premium*** (price above face value).

A corporation wishing to borrow money by issuing bonds must pay the going market rate of interest. The "market rate" of interest for a given bond issue depends upon many factors, including the financial strength of the corporation and the length of time until the bonds mature. (Normally investors require a higher rate of return on long-term bonds than upon bonds that will mature in the near future.)

Market rates of interest are fluctuating constantly. It must be expected, therefore, that the contract rate of interest may vary somewhat from the market rate at the date the bonds are issued. Thus, bonds often are issued at either a ***discount*** or a ***premium***.

Bonds Issued at a Discount

To illustrate the sale of bonds at a discount, assume that a corporation plans to issue $1,000,000 face value of 9%, 10-year bonds. At the issuance date of January 1, the going market rate of interest is slightly above 9% and the bonds sell at a price of only *98* ($980 for each $1,000 bond). The issuance of the bonds will be recorded by the following entry:

■
Issuance of bonds at a discount

Cash..	*980,000*	
Discount on Bonds Payable.......................................	*20,000*	
Bonds Payable		*1,000,000*
Issued $1,000,000 face value of 9%, 10-year bonds at 98.		

If a balance sheet is prepared immediately after the issuance of the bonds, the liability for bonds payable will be shown as follows:

■
Reporting the net liability

Long-term liabilities:		
9% bonds payable, due in 10 years	*$1,000,000*	
Less: Discount on bonds payable	*20,000*	*$980,000*

The amount of the discount is deducted from the face value of the bonds payable to show the ***carrying value*** or book value of the liability. At the date of issuance, the carrying value of bonds payable is equal to the amount for which the bonds were sold. In other words, the amount of the company's liability at the date of issuing the bonds is equal to the amount of money borrowed. Over the life of the bonds, however, we shall see that this carrying value gradually increases until it reaches the face value of the bonds at the maturity date.

Objective 4
Explain how bond discount or premium affects the cost of borrowing.

■ **Bond Discount as Part of the Cost of Borrowing**   In Chapter 11, we illustrated two ways in which interest charges can be specified in a note payable: the interest may be stated as an annual percentage rate of the face amount of the note, or it may be included in the face amount. Bonds issued at a discount include *both* types of interest charge. The $1,000,000 bond issue in our example calls for cash interest payments of $90,000 per year ($1,000,000 × 9% contract interest rate), payable semiannually. In addition to making the semiannual interest payments, the corporation must redeem the bond issue for $1 million on the maturity date. This maturity value is $20,000 greater than indicated by $980,000 received when the bonds were issued. Thus, the $20,000 discount in the issue price may be regarded as an *interest charge included in the maturity value of the bonds.*

Although the interest charge represented by the discount will not be paid to bondholders until the bonds mature, the corporation benefits from this cost during the entire period that it has the use of the bondholders' money. Therefore, the cost represented by the discount should be allocated over the life of the bond issue. The process of allocating bond discount to interest expense is termed *amortization* of the discount.

Bonds are sometimes issued between interest dates. In this situation the bonds are outstanding for a shorter time, therefore, the amortization period is shorter. For example, if a 10-year bond issue dated January 1, 1991, is issued on March 1, 1991, the bonds will be outstanding for 9 years and 10 months, or a total of 118 months. Under the straight-line method of amortization, the discount amortized per month will be 1/118 of the total discount.

Whenever bonds are issued at a discount, the total interest cost over the life of the bonds is equal to the total of the regular cash interest payments *plus the amount of the discount.* For the $1 million bond issue in our example, the total interest cost over the 10-year life of the bonds is $920,000, of which $900,000 represents the 20 semiannual cash interest payments and $20,000 represents the discount. The average annual interest expense, therefore, is $92,000 ($920,000 ÷ 10 years), consisting of $90,000 paid in cash and $2,000 amortization of the bond discount. This analysis is illustrated below:

Total cash interest payments to bondholders		
($1,000,000 × 9% × 10 years)		*$900,000*
Add: Interest charge included in face amount of bonds:		
Maturity value of bonds	*$1,000,000*	
Amount borrowed	*980,000*	*20,000*
Total cost of borrowing over life of bond issue		*$920,000*
Average annual interest expense ($920,000 ÷ 10 years)		*$ 92,000*

Objective 5
Amortize bond discount or premium by the straight-line and effective interest methods.

■ **Amortization of Bond Discount**   The simplest method of amortizing bond discount is the *straight-line method,* which allocates an equal portion of the discount to Bond Interest Expense in each period.[3] In our example, the Discount on Bonds Payable account has a beginning debit balance of $20,000; each year one-tenth of this amount, or $2,000, will be amortized into Bond

---

[3] An alternative method of amortization, called the *effective interest method,* is illustrated later in this chapter. Although the effective interest method is theoretically preferable to the straight-line method, the resulting differences generally are not material in dollar amount.

Interest Expense. Assuming that the interest payment dates are June 30 and December 31, the entries to be made each six months to record bond interest expense are as follows:

■
Payment of bond interest and straight-line amortization of bond discount

Bond Interest Expense...	45,000	
Cash..		45,000
Paid semiannual interest on $1,000,000 of 9%, 10-year bonds.		
Bond Interest Expense...	1,000	
Discount on Bonds Payable....................................		1,000
Amortized discount for six months on 10-year bond issue		
($20,000 discount × 1/20).		

The two entries shown above to record the cash payment of bond interest and to record the amortization of bond discount can conveniently be combined into one compound entry, as follows:

Bond Interest Expense...	46,000	
Cash..		45,000
Discount on Bonds Payable....................................		1,000
To record payment of semiannual interest on $1,000,000 of 9%,		
10-year bonds ($1,000,000 × 9% × 1/2) and to amortize 1/20 of the		
discount on the 10-year bond issue.		

Regardless of whether the cash payment of interest and the amortization of bond discount are recorded in separate entries or combined in one entry, the amount recognized as Bond Interest Expense is the same—$46,000 each six months, or a total of $92,000 a year. An alternative accounting procedure that will produce the same results is to amortize the bond discount only at year-end rather than at each interest-payment date.

Note that the additional interest expense resulting from amortization of the discount does not require any additional cash payment. The credit portion of the entry is to the contra-liability account, Discount on Bonds Payable, rather than to the Cash account. Crediting this contra-liability account *increases the carrying value of bonds payable.* The original $20,000 discount will be completely amortized by the end of the tenth year, and the net liability (carrying value) will be the full face value of the bonds.

In this example, the bonds were outstanding for the full term of 10 years or 120 months. If the bonds had been issued between interest dates, say, March 1, rather than January 1, the amortization period would have been the shortened life of 118 months.

Bonds Issued at a Premium

Bonds will sell above par if the contract rate of interest specified on the bonds is higher than the current market rate for bonds of this grade. Let us now change our basic illustration by assuming that the $1 million issue of 9%, 10-year bonds is sold at a price of 102 ($1,020 for each $1,000 bond). The entry is shown on the following page.

Cash	*1,020,000*	
Bonds Payable		*1,000,000*
Premium on Bonds Payable		*20,000*

Issued $1,000,000 face value of 9%, 10-year bonds at price of 102.

If a balance sheet is prepared immediately following the sale of the bonds, the liability will be shown as follows:

Long-term liabilities:

9% bonds payable, due in 10 years	*$1,000,000*	
Add: Premium on bonds payable	*20,000*	*$1,020,000*

The amount of any unamortized premium is **added** to the maturity value of the bonds payable to show the current carrying value of the liability. Over the life of the bond issue, this carrying value will be reduced toward the maturity value of $1,000,000.

■ **Bond Premium as Reduction in the Cost of Borrowing**   We have illustrated how issuing bonds at a discount increases the cost of borrowing above the amount of the regular cash interest payments. Issuing bonds at a premium, on the other hand, *reduces the cost of borrowing below the amount of the regular cash interest payments.*

The amount received from issuance of the bonds is $20,000 greater than the amount which must be repaid at maturity. This $20,000 premium is not a gain but is to be offset against the periodic interest payments in determining the net cost of borrowing. Whenever bonds are issued at a premium, the total interest cost over the life of the bonds is equal to the regular cash interest payments *minus the amount of the premium.* In our example, the total interest cost over the life of the bonds is computed as $900,000 of cash interest payments minus $20,000 of premium amortized, or a net borrowing cost of $880,000. The average annual interest expense will be $88,000, consisting of $90,000 paid in cash less an offsetting $2,000 transferred from the Premium on Bonds Payable account to the credit side of the Bond Interest Expense account.

The semiannual entries on June 30 and December 31 to record the payment of bond interest and amortization of bond premium (by the straight-line method) are as follows:

Bond Interest Expense	*45,000*	
Cash		*45,000*

Paid semiannual interest on $1,000,000 of 9%, 10-year bonds.

Premium on Bonds Payable	*1,000*	
Bond Interest Expense		*1,000*

Amortized premium for six months on 10-year bond issue ($20,000 premium × ¹⁄₂₀).

In our prior discussion of bond discount, we stated that if bonds are issued between interest dates, the amortization period will be shortened. This concept also applies to bonds issued at a premium. In brief, the period for amortization of premium is determined by the number of years and months the bonds are actually outstanding.

Year-End Adjustments for Bond Interest Expense

In the preceding illustration, it was assumed that one of the semiannual dates for payment of bond interest coincided with the end of the company's accounting year. In most cases, however, the semiannual interest payment dates will fall during an accounting period rather than on the last day of the year.

For purposes of illustration, assume that $1 million of 12%, 10-year bonds are issued at a price of 97 on *October 1,* 1991. Interest payment dates are April 1 and October 1. The total discount to be amortized amounts to $30,000, or $1,500 in each six-month interest period. (Notice that the discount is amortized at a rate of $250 per month.) Now also assume that the corporation closes its accounts at the end of each calendar year. At December 31, an *adjusting entry* will be needed to (1) record accrued interest at the 12% contract rate for the three months since October 1, and (2) amortize the bond discount for the three months since October 1. This adjusting entry will be:

Bond Interest Expense..	30,750	
Bond Interest Payable		30,000
Discount on Bonds Payable.................................		750

*To adjust for accrued interest on bonds and to amortize
discount for period from Oct. 1 to Dec. 31. Accrued
interest: $1,000,000 × .12 × 3/12 = $30,000. Amortization:
$30,000 × 3/120 = $750.*

A similar adjusting entry will be required every December 31 throughout the life of the bond issue.

In the December 31, 1991 balance sheet, the accrued interest payable of $30,000 will appear as a current liability. The long-term liability for bonds payable will appear as follows:

Long-term liabilities:
12% Bonds payable, due Oct. 1, 2001	$1,000,000	
Less: Discount on bonds payable	29,250	$970,750

When the bonds were issued on October 1, the net liability for bonds payable was $970,000. Notice that the carrying value of the bonds has *increased* over the three months by the amount of discount amortized. When the entire discount has been amortized, the carrying value of the bonds will be $1,000,000, which is equal to their maturity value.

On April 1, we must record interest expense and discount amortization only for the *three-month period since year-end.* Of the semiannual $60,000 cash payment to bondholders, one-half, or $30,000, represents payment of the liability for bond interest payable recorded on December 31. The entry on April 1 is:

Bond Interest Expense...	30,750	
Bond Interest Payable	30,000	
Discount on Bonds Payable.................................		750
Cash..		60,000

*To record bond interest expense and amortization of discount
for three-month period since year-end and to record semiannual
payment to bondholders.*

Straight-Line Amortization: A Theoretical Shortcoming

Although the straight-line method of amortizing bond discount or premium recognizes the full cost of borrowing over the life of a bond issue, the method has one conceptual weakness: The same dollar amount of interest expense is recognized each year. Amortizing a discount, however, causes a gradual increase in the liability for bonds payable; amortizing a premium causes a gradual decrease in the liability. If the uniform annual interest expense is expressed as a *percentage* of either an increasing or a decreasing liability, it appears that the borrower's cost of capital is changing over the life of the bonds.

This problem can be avoided by using the *effective interest method* of amortizing bond discount or premium. The effective interest method recognizes annual interest expense equal to a *constant percentage of the carrying value of the related liability.* This percentage is the effective rate of interest incurred by the borrower. For this reason, the effective interest method of amortization is considered theoretically preferable to the straight-line method. Whenever the two methods would produce *materially different* annual results, the Financial Accounting Standards Board requires the use of the effective interest method.

Over the life of the bonds, both amortization methods recognize the same total amount of interest expense. Even on an annual basis, the results produced by the two methods usually are very similar. Thus, both methods usually meet the requirements of the FASB.

Effective Interest Method of Amortization

When bonds are sold at a discount, the effective interest rate incurred by the issuing corporation is *higher* than the contract rate printed on the bonds. Conversely, when bonds are sold at a premium, the effective rate of interest is *lower* than the contract rate.

When the effective interest method is used, bond interest expense is determined by multiplying the *carrying value of the bonds* at the beginning of the period by the *effective rate of interest* for the bond issue. The amount of discount or premium to be amortized is the *difference* between the interest expense computed in this manner and the amount of interest paid (or payable) to bondholders for the period. The computation of effective interest expense and the amount of discount or premium amortization for the life of the bond issue is made in advance on a schedule called an *amortization table.*

■ **Sale of Bonds at a Discount** To illustrate the effective interest method, assume that on May 1 a corporation issues $1,000,000 face value, 9%, 10-year bonds with interest dates of November 1 and May 1. The bonds sell for *$937,689,* a price resulting in an effective interest rate of 10%.[4] An amortiza-

---

[4] Computation of the exact effective interest rate involves mathematical techniques beyond the scope of this discussion. A very close estimate of the effective interest rate can be obtained by dividing the *average* annual interest expense by the *average* carrying value of the bonds. Computation of average annual interest expense was illustrated on page 598. The average carrying value of the bonds is found by adding the issue price and the maturity value of the bond issue and dividing this sum by 2. Applying these procedures to the bond issue in our example provides an estimated effective interest rate of 9.93%, computed [($900,000 interest + $62,311 discount) ÷ 10 years] divided by [($937,689 + $1,000,000) ÷ 2].

tion table for this bond issue is shown below. (Amounts of interest expense have been *rounded to the nearest dollar.*)

This amortization table can be used to illustrate the concepts underlying the effective interest method of determining interest expense and discount amortization. Note that the "interest periods" in the table are the *semiannual* (six-month) interest periods. Thus, the interest payments (column A), interest expense (column B), and discount amortization (column C) are for six-month periods. Similarly, the balance of the Discount on Bonds Payable account (column D) and the carrying value of the liability (column E) are shown as of each semiannual interest payment date.

The original issuance price of the bonds ($937,689) is entered at the top of column E. This represents the carrying value of the liability throughout the first six-month interest period. The semiannual interest payment, shown in column A, is 4½% (one-half of the original contract rate) of the $1,000,000 face value of the bond issue. The semiannual cash interest payment does not change over the life of the bonds. The interest expense shown in column B, however, *changes every period*. This expense is always a *constant percentage* of the carrying value of the liability as of the end of the preceding period. The

Amortization Table for Bonds Sold at a Discount
($1,000,000, 10-year bonds, 9% interest payable semiannually,
sold at $937,689 to yield 10% compounded semiannually)

SIX-MONTH INTEREST PERIOD	(A) INTEREST PAID SEMIANNUALLY (4½% OF FACE VALUE)	(B) EFFECTIVE SEMIANNUAL INTEREST EXPENSE (5% OF BOND CARRYING VALUE)	(C) DISCOUNT AMORTI-ZATION (B − A)	(D) BOND DISCOUNT BALANCE	(E) CARRYING VALUE OF BONDS, END OF PERIOD ($1,000,000 − D)
Issue date				$62,311	$ 937,689
1	$45,000	$46,884	$1,884	60,427	939,573
2	45,000	46,979	1,979	58,448	941,552
3	45,000	47,078	2,078	56,370	943,630
4	45,000	47,182	2,182	54,188	945,812
5	45,000	47,291	2,291	51,897	948,103
6	45,000	47,405	2,405	49,492	950,508
7	45,000	47,525	2,525	46,967	953,033
8	45,000	47,652	2,652	44,315	955,685
9	45,000	47,784	2,784	41,531	958,469
10	45,000	47,923	2,923	38,608	961,392
11	45,000	48,070	3,070	35,538	964,462
12	45,000	48,223	3,223	32,315	967,685
13	45,000	48,384	3,384	28,931	971,069
14	45,000	48,553	3,553	25,378	974,622
15	45,000	48,731	3,731	21,647	978,353
16	45,000	48,918	3,918	17,729	982,271
17	45,000	49,114	4,114	13,615	986,385
18	45,000	49,319	4,319	9,296	990,704
19	45,000	49,535	4,535	4,761	995,239
20	45,000	49,761*	4,761	−0−	1,000,000

* In the last period, interest expense is equal to interest paid to bondholders plus the remaining balance on the bond discount. This compensates for the accumulated effects of rounding amounts.

"constant percentage" is the effective interest rate of the bond issue. The bonds have an effective annual interest rate of 10%, indicating a semiannual rate of 5%. Thus, the effective interest expense for the first six-month period is $46,884 (5% of $937,689). The discount amortization for period 1 is the difference between this effective interest expense and the contract rate of interest paid to bondholders.

After the discount is reduced by $1,884 at the end of period 1, the carrying value of the bonds in column E *increases* by $1,884 (from $937,689 to $939,573). In period 2, the effective interest expense is determined by multiplying the effective semiannual interest rate of 5% by this new carrying value of $939,573 (5% × $939,573 = $46,979).

Semiannual interest expense may be recorded every period directly from the data in the amortization table. For example, the entry to record bond interest expense at the end of the first six-month period is:

Bond Interest Expense...	*46,884*	
Discount on Bonds Payable...................................		*1,884*
Cash..		*45,000*
To record semiannual interest payment and amortize discount		
for six months.		

Similarly, interest expense at the end of the **fifteenth** six-month period would be recorded by the following journal entry:

Bond Interest Expense...	*48,731*	
Discount on Bonds Payable...................................		*3,731*
Cash..		*45,000*
To record semiannual interest payment and amortize discount		
for six months.		

When bond discount is amortized, the carrying value of the liability for bonds payable *increases* every period toward the maturity value. Since the effective interest expense in each period is a constant percentage of this increasing carrying value, the interest expense also increases from one period to the next. This is the basic difference between the effective interest method and straight-line amortization.

■ **Sale of Bonds at a Premium** Let us now change our illustration by assuming that the $1,000,000 issue of 9%, 10-year bonds is sold on May 1 at a price of $1,067,952, resulting in an effective interest rate of 8% annually (4% per six-month interest period). An amortization table for this bond issue follows:

Amortization Table for Bonds Sold at a Premium
($1,000,000, 10-year bonds, 9% interest payable semiannually,
sold at $1,067,952 to yield 8% compounded semiannually)

SIX-MONTH INTEREST PERIOD	(A) INTEREST PAID SEMIANNUALLY (4½% OF FACE VALUE)	(B) EFFECTIVE SEMIANNUAL INTEREST EXPENSE (4% OF BOND CARRYING VALUE)	(C) PREMIUM AMORTI- ZATION (A − B)	(D) BOND PREMIUM BALANCE	(E) CARRYING VALUE OF BONDS, END OF PERIOD ($1,000,000 + D)
Issue date				$67,952	$1,067,952
1	$45,000	$42,718	$2,282	65,670	1,065,670
2	45,000	42,627	2,373	63,297	1,063,297
3	45,000	42,532	2,468	60,829	1,060,829
4	45,000	42,433	2,567	58,262	1,058,262
5	45,000	42,330	2,670	55,592	1,055,592
6	45,000	42,224	2,776	52,816	1,052,816
7	45,000	42,113	2,887	49,929	1,049,929
8	45,000	41,997	3,003	46,926	1,046,926
9	45,000	41,877	3,123	43,803	1,043,803
10	45,000	41,752	3,248	40,555	1,040,555
11	45,000	41,622	3,378	37,177	1,037,177
12	45,000	41,487	3,513	33,664	1,033,664
13	45,000	41,347	3,653	30,011	1,030,011
14	45,000	41,200	3,800	26,211	1,026,211
15	45,000	41,048	3,952	22,259	1,022,259
16	45,000	40,890	4,110	18,149	1,018,149
17	45,000	40,726	4,274	13,875	1,013,875
18	45,000	40,555	4,445	9,430	1,009,430
19	45,000	40,377	4,623	4,807	1,004,807
20	45,000	40,193*	4,807	–0–	1,000,000

* In the last period, interest expense is equal to interest paid to bondholders minus the remaining balance of the bond premium. This compensates for the accumulated effects of rounding amounts.

In this amortization table, the interest expense for each six-month period is equal to 4% of the carrying value at the beginning of that period. This amount of interest expense is less than the amount of cash being paid to bondholders, illustrating that the effective interest rate is less than the contract rate.

Based upon this amortization table, the entry to record the interest payment and amortization of the premium for the first six months of the bond issue is:

■
Amortization of premium decreases interest expense

Bond Interest Expense...	42,718	
Premium on Bonds Payable..	2,282	
Cash..		45,000

To record semiannual interest payment and amortization of premium.

As the carrying value of the liability declines, so does the amount recognized as bond interest expense.

■ **Year-End Adjusting Entries**   Since the amounts recognized as interest expense change from one period to the next, we must refer to the appropriate interest period in the amortization table to obtain the dollar amounts for use in year-end adjusting entries. To illustrate, consider our example of the bonds sold at a premium on May 1. The entry shown above records interest and amortization of the premium through November 1. If the company keeps its accounts on a calendar-year basis, two months' interest has accrued as of December 31, and the following adjusting entry is made at year-end:

■ Year-end adjusting entry

Bond Interest Expense..	*14,209*	
Premium on Bonds Payable..	*791*	
Bond Interest Payable		*15,000*

To record two months' accrued interest and amortize
one-third of the premium for the interest period.

This adjusting entry covers one-third (two months) of the second interest period. Consequently, the amounts shown as bond interest expense and amortization of premium are *one-third* of the amounts shown in the amortization table for the second interest period. Similar adjusting entries must be made at the end of every accounting period while the bonds are outstanding. The dollar amounts of these adjusting entries will vary, however, because the amounts of interest expense and premium amortization change in every interest period. The amounts applicable to any given adjusting entry will be the appropriate fraction of the amounts for the interest period then in progress.

Following the year-end adjusting entry illustrated above, the interest expense and premium amortization on May 1 of the second year, are recorded as follows:

■ Interest payment in the following year

Bond Interest Expense..	*28,418*	
Bond Interest Payable	*15,000*	
Premium on Bonds Payable..	*1,582*	
Cash..		*45,000*

To record semiannual interest payment, a portion of which had
been accrued, and amortize remainder of premium applicable
to interest period.

Retirement of Bonds Payable

Bonds are sometimes retired before the maturity date. The principal reason for retiring bonds early is to relieve the issuing corporation of the obligation to make future interest payments. If interest rates decline to the point that a corporation can borrow at an interest rate below that being paid on a particular bond issue, the corporation may benefit from retiring those bonds and issuing new bonds at a lower interest rate.

Most bond issues contain a call provision, permitting the corporation to redeem the bonds by paying a specified price, usually a few points above par. Even without a call provision, the corporation may retire its bonds before maturity by purchasing them in the open market. If the bonds can be purchased by the issuing corporation at less than their carrying value, a *gain* is realized on the retirement of the debt. If the bonds are reacquired by the issuing corporation at a price in excess of their carrying value, a *loss* must be recognized. The FASB has ruled that these gains and losses, if material in amount, should be classified in the income statement as ***extraordinary items*** and shown net of any income tax effects.[5]

For example, assume that the Briggs Corporation has outstanding a $1 million bond issue with unamortized premium in the amount of $20,000. The bonds are callable at 105 and the company exercises the call provision on 100 of the bonds, or 10% of the issue. The entry would be as follows:

Bonds called at price above carrying value

Bonds Payable	100,000	
Premium on Bonds Payable...	2,000	
Loss on Retirement of Bonds	3,000	
Cash...		105,000

To record retirement of $100,000 face value of bonds, carrying value of $102,000, at call price of 105.

The carrying value of each of the 100 called bonds was $1,020, whereas the call price was $1,050. For each bond called the company incurred a loss of $30, or a total loss of $3,000. Notice that when 10% of the total issue was called, 10% of the unamortized premium was written off.

When bonds remain outstanding until the maturity date, the discount or premium is completely amortized and the accounting entry to retire the bonds (assuming that interest is paid separately) consists of a debit to Bonds Payable and a credit to Cash.

One year before the maturity date, the bonds payable should be reclassified from long-term debt to a current liability in the balance sheet if payment is to be made from current assets rather than from a ***bond sinking fund***.

Bond Sinking Fund

To make a bond issue attractive to investors, corporations may agree to create a sinking fund, exclusively for use in paying the bonds at maturity. A bond sinking fund is created by setting aside a specified amount of cash at regular intervals. The cash is usually deposited with a trustee, who invests it and adds the earnings to the amount of the sinking fund. The periodic deposits of cash plus the earnings on the sinking fund investments should cause the fund to equal approximately the amount of the bond issue by the maturity date. When the bond issue approaches maturity, the trustee sells all the securities in the fund and uses the cash proceeds to pay the holders of the bonds. Any excess cash remaining in the fund will be returned to the corporation by the trustee.

A bond sinking fund is not included in current assets because it is not available for payment of current liabilities. The cash and securities comprising the fund are usually shown as a single amount under a caption such as Long-Term Investments, which is placed just below the current asset section. Interest earned on sinking fund securities constitutes revenue to the corporation.

[5] FASB *Statement No. 4,* "Reporting Gains and Losses from Extinguishment of Debt" FASB (Stamford, Conn.: 1975).

Market Prices of Bonds

Objective 6
Discuss the relationship between interest rates and the market price behavior of bonds.

As stated earlier, many corporate bonds are traded daily on organized securities exchanges at quoted market prices. After bonds are issued, their market prices vary *inversely* with changes in market interest rates. As interest rates rise, investors will be willing to pay less money to own a bond that pays a given contract rate of interest. Conversely, as interest rates decline, the market prices of bonds rise.

CASE IN POINT ■ IBM sold to underwriters $500 million of 9⅜%, 25-year debenture bonds. The underwriters planned to sell the bonds to the public at a price of 99⅝. Just as the bonds were offered for sale, however, a change in Federal Reserve credit policy started an upward surge in interest rates. The underwriters encountered great difficulty selling the bonds. Within one week, the market price of the bonds had fallen to 94½. The underwriters dumped their unsold inventory at this price and sustained one of the largest underwriting losses in Wall Street history.

During the months ahead, interest rates soared to record levels. Within five months, the price of the bonds had fallen to 76⅜. Thus, nearly one-fourth of the market value of these bonds evaporated in less than half a year. The financial strength of IBM was never in question; this dramatic loss in market value was caused entirely by rising interest rates.

In addition to the current level of interest rates, the market prices of bonds are strongly influenced by the *length of time remaining until the bonds mature*—that is, are redeemed at their maturity value (par value) by the issuing corporation. As a bond nears its maturity date, its market price normally moves closer and closer to the maturity value.

CASE IN POINT ■ Commonwealth Edison has outstanding two issues of 8¼% bonds, one issue maturing in 1993 and the other in 2007. Recently, the going market rate of interest was greater than 8¼% and both bonds were selling at a discount. The bonds maturing in 1993, however, were selling at a market price of 98, whereas the bonds maturing in 2007 were selling at a price of only 85. Both bonds pay the same amount of interest, were issued by the same company, and have identical credit ratings. Thus, the difference in the market prices is caused solely by the differences in the bonds' maturity dates.

■ **Volatility of Short-Term and Long-Term Bond Prices** When interest rates fluctuate, the market prices of long-term bonds are affected to a far greater extent than are the market prices of bonds due to mature in the near future. To illustrate, assume that market interest rates suddenly soar from 9% to 12%. A 9% bond scheduled to mature in but a few days will still have a market value of approximately $1,000—the amount to be collected in a few days from the issuing corporation. However, the market price of a 9% bond maturing in 10 years will drop significantly. Investors who must accept these "below market" interest payments for many years will only buy the bonds at a discounted price.

In summary, fluctuations in interest rates have a far greater effect upon the market prices of long-term bonds than upon the prices of short-term bonds.

Remember that after bonds have been issued, they belong to the bondholders, *not to the issuing corporation.* Therefore, changes in the market price of bonds subsequent to their issuance *do not* affect the financial statements of the issuing corporation, and these changes are not recorded in the corporation's accounting records. However, the corporation must maintain a subsidiary *bondholders' ledger,* similar to the stockholders' ledger discussed in Chapter 14. The bondholders' ledger contains a separate account showing the *number of bonds owned by each bondholder.* This record provides the information for determining the amount of interest owed to each bondholder and for notifying the bondholder if his or her bonds have been called.

Convertible Bonds Payable

Objective 7
Describe convertible bonds and explain the possible benefits to the issuing corporation and to the bondholder.

Convertible bonds represent a popular form of financing, particularly during periods when common stock prices are rising. The conversion feature gives bondholders an opportunity to profit from a rise in the market price of the issuing company's common stock while still maintaining their status of creditors rather than stockholders. Because of this potential gain, convertible bonds generally carry lower interest rates than nonconvertible bonds.

The number of shares of common stock into which each bond may be converted is termed the *conversion ratio.* The market value of this number of shares represents the *stock value* of the bond. When the bond is originally issued, a conversion ratio is selected that sets the stock value well below the face value of the bond. In future periods, however, both the price of the stock and the stock value of the bond may increase without limit.

For example, assume that the current market rate of interest on long-term bonds is 9%, and that the common stock of Ling Corporation has a current market price of *$27* per share. Instead of issuing 9% bonds payable, the company might issue *7% convertible bonds,* with a conversion ratio of 20 to 1. At the issuance date, the stock value of each convertible bond would be only $540 (20 shares × $27). If the value of the common stock rises above *$50* per share, however, the stock value will rise above the $1,000 face value of the bond. (The per-share stock price that causes the stock value and maturity value of the bond to be equal—$50 in our example—is called the *conversion price.*)

When the price of the common stock rises above the conversion price, the stock value of the bond becomes far more important than the current level of interest rates in establishing the market price of a convertible bond. (See, for example, the Case in Point on the following page.)

Ling Corporation benefits from issuing these convertible bonds because it is able to pay less than the going market rate of interest. The bondholders also may benefit from the conversion feature, *but only if the price of the common stock rises above the conversion price* ($50 per share) during the life of the bonds.

Let us assume that Ling Corporation issues $5 million of these convertible bonds at par. Some years later, when the price of the common stock has risen to

$90 per share, holders of 100 bonds decide to convert their bonds into common stock (which has a par value of $1 per share). Ling Corporation will record this conversion as follows:

Convertible Bonds Payable	*100,000*	
Common Stock, $1 par		*2,000*
Additional Paid-in Capital		*98,000*

To record the conversion of 100 bonds payable into 2,000 shares of $1 par value common stock.

Notice that the current market price of the stock ($90 per share) *does not* affect this entry. The carrying value of the bonds is simply assigned to the common stock issued in exchange. Thus, the effect of the entry is to transfer the carrying value of the bonds from the liability section to the stockholders' equity section of the balance sheet. (If the bonds had been issued at a price above or below the face amount, any unamortized premium or discount relating to the converted bonds would be written off at the time of conversion in order to assign the *net* carrying value of the bonds to the common stock.)

Conversion of Bonds from the Investor's Viewpoint

Investors do not always convert their investment in convertible bonds into capital stock as soon as the market value of the capital stock they would receive rises above the $1,000 maturity value of their bonds. As the bonds easily can be converted into capital stock, their market value *rises right along* with that of the capital stock.

CASE IN POINT ■ Walgreen Co. recently had an outstanding issue of bonds payable in which each bond was convertible into 247.98 shares of the company's capital stock. The company's capital stock was selling at $40 per share, indicating a market value for 247.98 shares of $9,919.20. The market value of the convertible bonds was quoted at 992, even though the bonds would mature at a price of only 100 in the near future.

In fact, there may be several good reasons for *not* converting an investment in bonds into capital stock. First, the periodic interest payments received from the investment in bonds may exceed the dividends that would be received from the shares of capital stock into which the bonds could be converted. Second, an investment in bonds has less *downside risk* than an investment in capital stock. (The term "downside risk" means the threat of possible loss to the investor from a drop in market price.) Bonds ultimately mature and are redeemed by the issuing corporation at their maturity value (usually $1,000 per bond). Capital stock, on the other hand, has no maturity value. The price of a company's capital stock may decline dramatically even though the company is not in such financial difficulty that it might default upon its obligations to bondholders.

In conclusion, when are the owners of convertible bonds likely to exchange their bonds for shares of capital stock? The exchange point is reached when the dividends that would be received from the capital stock *exceed the interest payments* currently being received from the investment in bonds. When the capital stock dividends increase to this level, the bondholders can *increase their cash receipts* by converting their bonds into shares of capital stock. Regardless of the relationship between interest and dividends, convertible bonds should be converted prior to their maturity date if the market price of the common stock exceeds the conversion price.

LEASES

A company may purchase the assets needed in its business operations or, as an alternative, it may lease them. A *lease* is a contract in which the lessor gives the lessee the right to use an asset for a specified period of time in exchange for periodic rental payments. The *lessor* is the owner of the property; the *lessee* is a tenant or renter. Examples of assets frequently acquired by lease include automobiles, building space, computers, and equipment.

Operating Leases

Objective 8
Explain the accounting treatment of operating leases and of capital leases.

When the lessor gives the lessee the right to use leased property for a limited period of time, but retains the usual risks and rewards of ownership, the contract is known as an *operating lease.* An example of an operating lease is a contract leasing office space in an office building. If the building increases in value, the *lessor* can receive the benefits of this increase by either selling the building or increasing the rental rate once the lease term has expired. On the other hand, if the building declines in value, it is the lessor who bears the loss.

In accounting for an operating lease, the lessor views the monthly lease payments received as rental revenue, and the lessee regards these payments as rental expense. No asset or liability (other than a short-term liability for accrued rent payable) relating to the lease appears in the lessee's balance sheet. Thus, operating leases are sometimes termed *off-balance-sheet financing.*

Capital Leases

Some lease contracts are intended to provide financing to the lessee for the eventual purchase of the property, or provide the lessee with use of the property over most of its useful life. These lease contracts are called *capital leases* (or financing leases). In contrast to an operating lease, a capital lease transfers most of the risks and rewards of ownership from the lessor to the *lessee.* Assume, for example, that City Realty leases a new automobile for a period of three years. Also assume that at the end of the lease, title to the automobile transfers to City Realty at no additional cost. Clearly, City Realty is not merely "renting" the use of the automobile; rather, it is using the lease agreement as a means of *financing the purchase* of the car.

From an accounting viewpoint, capital leases are regarded as *essentially equivalent to a sale* of the property by the lessor to the lessee, even though title to the leased property has not been transferred. Thus, a capital lease should be recorded by the *lessor as a sale* of property and by the *lessee as a purchase.* In such lease agreements, an appropriate interest charge usually is added to the regular sales price of the property in determining the amount of the lease payments.

Some companies frequently use capital lease agreements as a means of financing the sale of their products to customers. In accounting for merchandise "sold" through a capital lease, the lessor *debits Lease Payments Receivable* and *credits Sales* for an amount equal to the present value of the future lease payments.[6] In most cases, the present value of these future payments is equal to the regular sales price of the merchandise. In addition, the lessor transfers the cost of the leased merchandise from the Inventory account to the Cost of Goods Sold account (assuming a perpetual inventory system is in use). When lease payments are received, the lessor should recognize an appropriate portion of the payment as representing interest revenue and the remainder as a reduction in Lease Payments Receivable.

When equipment is acquired through a capital lease, the lessee should *debit an asset account,* Leased Equipment, and *credit a liability account,* Lease Payment Obligation, for the present value of the future lease payments. Lease payments made by the lessee are allocated between Interest Expense and a reduction in the liability, Lease Payment Obligation. *No rent expense is involved in a capital lease.* The asset account, Leased Equipment, is depreciated over the life of the equipment rather than the life of the lease. (The journal entries used in accounting for a capital lease are illustrated on pages 632–633 of the appendix to this chapter.)

■ Distinguishing between Capital Leases and Operating Leases

The FASB requires that a lease which meets any one of the following criteria be accounted for as a capital lease.[7]

1 The lease transfers ownership of the property to the lessee at the end of the lease term.

2 The lease contains a "bargain purchase option."

3 The lease term is equal to 75% or more of the estimated economic life of the leased property.

4 The present value of the minimum lease payments amounts to 90% or more of the fair value of the leased property.

Only those leases which meet *none* of the above criteria may be accounted for as operating leases.

---

[6] We have elected to record the present value of the future lease payments by a single debit entry to Lease Payments Receivable. An alternative is to debit Lease Payments Receivable for the total amount of the future payments and to credit Discount on Lease Payments Receivable, a contra-asset account, for the unearned finance charges included in the contractual amount. Either approach results in the lessor recording a net receivable equal to the present value of the future lease payments.

[7] *FASB Statement No. 13,* "Accounting for Leases" (Stamford, Conn.: 1976), pp. 9–10.

OTHER LONG-TERM LIABILITIES

Mortgage Notes Payable

Purchases of real estate and certain types of equipment often are financed by the issuance of mortgage notes payable. When a mortgage note is issued, the borrower pledges title to specific assets as collateral for the loan. If the borrower defaults on the note, the lender may foreclose upon these assets. Mortgage notes usually are payable in equal monthly installments. These monthly installments may continue until the loan is completely repaid, or the note may contain a "due date" at which the remaining unpaid balance of the loan must be repaid in a single, lump-sum payment.

A portion of each monthly payment represents interest on the unpaid balance of the loan and the remainder of the monthly payment reduces the amount of the liability (Mortgage Payable). Since the liability is being *reduced each month,* the portion of each successive payment representing interest will *decrease,* and the portion of the payment going toward repayment of the liability will *increase.* To illustrate, assume that on June 30 a company issues a $100,000 mortgage note to finance the purchase of a warehouse. The note bears interest at the annual rate of 12% (or 1% per month) and will be paid in monthly installments of $1,200 over a period of 15 years. The following partial *amortization table* shows the allocation of the first three monthly payments between interest and principal (amounts are rounded to the nearest dollar):

	(A) PAYMENT DATE	MONTHLY PAYMENT	(B) MONTHLY INTEREST EXPENSE (1% OF UNPAID BALANCE)	(C) REDUCTION IN MORTGAGE PAYABLE (A − B)	(D) BALANCE OF MORTGAGE PAYABLE
Monthly payments on a mortgage note	June 30—Issue date				$100,000
	July 31	$1,200	$1,000	$200	99,800
	Aug. 31	1,200	998	202	99,598
	Sept. 30	1,200	996	204	99,394

The entry to record the first monthly mortgage payment on July 31 would be:

Payment is allocated between interest and principal

Interest Expense	1,000	
Mortgage Payable	200	
Cash...		1,200

To record interest expense and reduction in principal included in July 31 mortgage payment.

That portion of the mortgage which will be paid off within one year (the sum of column C for the next 12 months) should be classified in the balance sheet as a *current liability.* The caption used for this current liability may be "Current Portion of Long-Term Debt." The remaining balance of the mortgage payable should appear as a long-term liability.

Liabilities for Pension Plans

A pension plan is a contract between a company and its employees under which the company agrees to pay retirement benefits to eligible employees. Most employers meet their pension plan obligations by making regular cash payments into a **pension fund** managed by a trustee. This type of arrangement is called a **funded** pension plan.

If a pension plan is **fully funded,** the trustee assumes all responsibility for paying retirement benefits to employees from the assets of the pension fund. Thus, **no liability** for payment of retirement benefits appears in the employer's balance sheet. The employer simply records each payment to the trustee by debiting Pension Expense and crediting Cash. Most pension plans are fully funded; therefore, most corporations do not report any pension liability. However, an employer must show as a liability any portion of its pension plan that is **unfunded.**

In addition to pension plans, many companies have promised their employees other types of retirement benefits, such as health insurance. Most companies have not funded their obligation for payment of retirement benefits other than pensions. In the past, most employers recognized the expense of these benefits on a "pay-as-you-go" basis—that is, recognizing the expense at the time of making the cash payments. Under this "pay-as-you-go" approach, no liability for future payments appears in the employer's balance sheet.

Recently the FASB has proposed extending the accounting method used for pensions to all forms of retirement benefits.[8] Under this proposal, the expense of retirement plans is recognized as employees earn the right to the benefits, not in the periods that payments are made to retired persons. Also, the employing company includes in its balance sheet a liability for any accrued benefits that have not been funded. This liability is shown at the present value of the estimated future benefit payments.

There are many complex issues involved in computing and reporting unfunded liabilities for retirement benefits. These issues will be discussed in more advanced accounting courses.

End-of-Chapter Review

CONCEPTS INTRODUCED OR EMPHASIZED IN CHAPTER 16

The major concepts in this chapter include:

■ The nature of bonds payable and the income tax advantage of issuing bonds rather than capital stock.

■ Accounting for the issuance of bonds, the payment of interest, and the retirement of bonds.

■ The concept of present value and other factors affecting bond prices.

---

[8] *FASB Proposed Statement of Financial Accounting Standards,* "Employers' Accounting for Postretirement Benefits Other Than Pensions" (Stamford, Conn.: 1989).

■ Bond discount and premium as elements of the cost of borrowing.

■ Amortization of bond discount and premium by both the straight-line and the effective interest methods of amortization.

■ The preparation and use of an amortization table.

■ Convertible bonds payable: the advantages to the issuing corporation and possible advantages to the bondholder.

■ Accounting for operating leases and capital leases; the economic distinction between these two types of lease agreements.

This chapter completes our discussion of corporate securities (stocks and bonds) from the perspective of the issuing company. In the following chapter, we will discuss accounting for investments in these types of securities.

KEY TERMS INTRODUCED OR EMPHASIZED IN CHAPTER 16

Amortization of discount or premium on bonds payable   The process of systematically writing off a portion of bond discount to increase interest expense or writing off a portion of bond premium to decrease interest expense each period the bonds are outstanding.

Bond sinking fund   Cash set aside by the corporation at regular intervals (usually with a trustee) to be used to pay the bonds at maturity.

Capital lease   A lease contract which, in essence, finances the eventual purchase by the lessee of leased property. The lessor accounts for a capital lease as a sale of property; the lessee records an asset and a liability equal to the present value of the future lease payments. Also called a *financing lease*.

Contract interest rate   The contractual rate of interest printed on bonds. The contract interest rate, applied to the face value of the bonds, determines the amount of the annual cash interest payments to bondholders. Also called the *nominal interest rate.*

Convertible bond   A bond which may be exchanged (at the bondholders' option) for a specified number of shares of the company's capital stock.

Discount on bonds payable   Amount by which the face amount of the bond exceeds the price received by the corporation at the date of issuance. Indicates that the contractual rate of interest is lower than the market rate of interest.

Effective interest method of amortization   A method of amortizing bond discount or premium which causes bond interest expense to be a constant percentage of the carrying value of the liability.

Effective interest rate   The actual rate of interest expense to the borrowing corporation, taking into account the contractual cash interest payments and the discount or premium to be amortized.

Lessee   The tenant, user, or renter of leased property.

Lessor   The owner of property leased to a lessee.

Off-balance-sheet financing   An arrangement in which the use of resources is financed without the obligation for future payments appearing as a liability in the balance sheet. An operating lease is a common example of off-balance-sheet financing.

Operating lease   A lease contract which is in essence a rental agreement. The lessee has the use of the leased property, but the lessor retains the usual risks and rewards of ownership. The periodic lease payments are accounted for as rent expense by the lessee and as rental revenue by the lessor.

Pension fund   A fund managed by an independent trustee into which an employer company makes periodic payments. The fund is used for the purpose of paying retirement benefits to company employees.

Premium on bonds payable   Amount by which the issuance price of a bond exceeds the face value. Indicates that the contractual rate of interest is higher than the market rate.

Present value of a future amount   The amount of money that an informed investor would pay today for the right to receive the future amount, based upon a specific rate of return required by the investor.

SELF-TEST QUESTIONS

Answers to these questions appear on page 625.

1 Which of the following statements are correct? (More than one statement may be correct.)

a A bond issue is a technique for subdividing a very large loan into a great many small, transferable units.

b Bond interest payments are contractual obligations, whereas the board of directors determines whether or not dividends will be paid.

c As interest rates rise, the market prices of bonds fall; as interest rates fall, bond prices tend to rise.

d Bond interest payments are deductible in determining income subject to income taxes, whereas dividends paid to stockholders are not deductible.

2 On September 1, 1991, Reese Corporation issued at par $100 million in 12% bonds payable, due September 1, 2011. Interest payment dates are September 1 and March 1. (More than one of the following answers may be correct.)

a In 1991, Reese will make no interest payments to bondholders, but will incur bond interest expense.

b In 1992, the amount of cash paid to bondholders by Reese will exceed the bond interest expense incurred during that year.

c If interest rates increase over the life of this bond issued, the amount of interest expense recognized by Reese each year will decline.

d In 2011, Reese makes total payments to bondholders of $112 million.

3 On May 1, Exeter Corporation issued $2,000,000 face amount of 12% bonds and received total proceeds of $2,050,000. If the bonds pay interest semiannually each June 30 and December 31, which of the following is *not* true?

a Exeter must make an interest payment on June 30 in the amount of $120,000.

b The journal entry to record issuance of these bonds involves a debit to Discount on Bonds Payable of $30,000.

c These bonds were issued at a premium of $50,000.

d The effective rate of interest (the market rate) on May 1 was higher than 12%.

4 On July 1, 1990, Collier Corporation issued $6,000,000 face value, 12%, 20-year bonds with interest dates of January 1 and July 1. The bonds sell for $7,030,000, a price resulting in an effective interest rate of 10%. As a result:

a Total interest expense recognized by Collier over the life of the bonds is $14,400,000.

b Collier recognizes bond interest expense of $351,500 for 1990, using the effective interest method of amortizing the premium.

c Collier recognizes bond interest expense of $385,750 for 1990 using the straight-line method of amortizing the premium.

d The amortization of premium for 1990, using the effective interest method of amortization, is $51,500.

5 Lawton International leases its manufacturing equipment from Atlas under an arrangement that qualifies as a capital lease. Lawton's financial statements should include:

a Depreciation expense on the leased equipment.

b Rent expense each period for the amount of the lease payment made.

c Lease payments receivable for the present value of all future lease payments.

d A liability for the total amount of all future lease payments.

Assignment Material

REVIEW QUESTIONS

1 Distinguish between the two terms in each of the following pairs:

a Mortgage bond; debenture bond

b Contract (or nominal) interest rate; effective interest rate

c Callable bond; convertible bond

d Coupon bond; registered bond

2 K Company has decided to finance expansion by issuing $10 million of 20-year debenture bonds and will ask a number of underwriters to bid on the bond issue. Discuss the factors that will determine the amount bid by the underwriters for these bonds.

3 Briefly explain the income tax advantage of raising capital by issuing bonds rather than by capital stock.

4 Bell Company pays federal income taxes at a rate of 30% on taxable income. Compute the company's annual *after-tax* cost of borrowing on a 10%, $5 million bond issue. Express this after-tax cost as a percentage of the borrowed $5 million.

5 The following excerpt is taken from an article in a leading business periodical: "In the bond market high interest rates mean low prices. Bonds pay out a fixed percentage of their face value, usually $1,000; an 8% bond, for instance, will pay $80 a year. In order for its yield to rise to 10%, its price would have to drop to $800." Give a critical evaluation of this quotation.

6 Discuss the advantages and disadvantages of a *call provision* in a bond contract from the viewpoint of (a) the bondholder and (b) the issuing corporation.

7 Some bonds now being bought and sold by investors on organized securities exchanges were issued when interest rates were much lower than they are today. Would you expect these bonds to be trading at prices above or below their face values? Explain.

8 The 6% bonds of Central Gas & Electric are selling at a market price of 72, whereas the 6% bonds of Interstate Power are selling at a price of 97. Does this mean that Interstate Power has a better credit rating than Central Gas & Electric? Explain. (Assume current long-term interest rates are in the 11 to 13% range.)

9 Explain why the effective rate of interest differs from the contract rate when bonds are issued (a) at a discount and (b) at a premium.

10 When the effective interest method is used to amortize bond discount or premium, the amount of bond interest expense will differ in each period from that of the preceding period. Explain how the amount of bond interest expense changes from one period to another when the bonds are issued (a) at a discount and (b) at a premium.

11 Explain why the effective interest method of amortizing bond discount or premium is considered to be theoretically preferable to the straight-line method.

12 What is a *convertible bond?* Discuss the advantages and disadvantages of convertible bonds from the standpoint of (a) the investor and (b) the issuing corporation.

13 What situation or condition is most likely to cause the holders of convertible bonds to convert their bonds into shares of common stock? (Do not assume that the bonds have been called or that they are about to mature.)

14 Explain how the lessee accounts for an operating lease and a capital lease. Why is an operating lease sometimes called *off-balance-sheet financing?*

15 A friend of yours has just purchased a house and has incurred a $50,000, 11% mortgage, payable at $476.17 per month. After making the first monthly payment, he received a receipt from the bank stating that only $17.84 of the $476.17 had been applied to reducing the principal amount of the loan. Your friend computes that at the rate of $17.84 per month, it will take over 233 years to pay off the $50,000 mortgage. Do you agree with your friend's analysis? Explain.

16 Ortega Industries has a fully funded pension plan. Each year, pension expense runs in excess of $10 million. At the present time, employees are entitled to receive pension benefits with a present value of $125 million. Explain what liability, if any, Ortega Industries should include in its balance sheet as a result of this pension plan.

EXERCISES

**Exercise 16-1
Accounting
terminology**

Listed below are nine technical accounting terms introduced in this chapter:

Amortization of bond premium	Amortization of bond discount	Effective interest method of amortization
Present value	Operating lease	Effective interest rate
Convertible bond	Capital lease	Contract interest rate

Each of the following statements may (or may not) describe one of these technical terms. For each statement, indicate the accounting term described, or answer "None" if the statement does not correctly describe any of the terms.

a A lease agreement which does not require the lessee to include any long-term lease payment obligation in its balance sheet.

b An adjusting entry which reduces the amount of semiannual interest expense below the amount of the semiannual cash payment to bondholders.

c Amortizing bond discount or premium in a manner that the amount of interest expense remains the same in every period in which bonds are outstanding.

d The amount that a knowledgeable investor would pay today for the right to receive a given amount of cash at a given future date.

e The interest rate which determines the dollar amount of the semiannual payments to bondholders.

f A lease which requires the lessee to record both a depreciable asset and a long-term liability.

g The going market rate of interest at the time that bonds are issued.

h A bond in which past interest payments are in default.

Exercise 16-2
Bond interest
(bonds issued at par)

On March 31, Bancor Corporation received authorization to issue $30,000,000 of 12%, 30-year debenture bonds. Interest payment dates were March 31 and September 30. The bonds were all issued at par on April 30, one month after the interest date printed on the bonds.

Instructions

a Prepare the journal entry at April 30, to record the sale of the bonds.

b Prepare the journal entry at September 30, to record the semiannual bond interest payment.

c Prepare the adjusting entry at December 31, to record bond interest accrued since September 30.

Exercise 16-3
Amortizing bond discount and premium: straight-line method

North Company issued $80 million of 12%, 10-year bonds on January 1. Interest is payable semiannually on June 30 and December 31. The bonds were sold to an underwriting group at 105.

South Company issued $80 million of 11%, 10-year bonds on January 1. Interest is payable semiannually on June 30 and December 31. The bonds were sold to an underwriting group at 95.

Prepare journal entries to record all transactions during the year for (a) the North Company bond issue and (b) the South Company bond issue. Assume that both companies amortize bond discount or premium by the straight-line method at each interest payment date.

Exercise 16-4
Basic entries for a bond issue: issuance, interest payment, and retirement

La Paloma Corp. issued $10,000,000 of 15-year, 10½% bonds on July 1, 1991, at 98½. Interest is due on June 30 and December 31 of each year, and the bonds mature on June 30, 2006. The fiscal year ends on December 31; bond discount is amortized by the straight-line method. Prepare the following journal entries:

a July 1, 1991, to record the issuance of the bonds.

b December 31, 1991, to pay interest and amortize the bond discount (make two entries).

c June 30, 2006, to pay interest, amortize the bond discount, and retire the bonds at maturity (make three entries).

Exercise 16-5
Using an amortization table

Three Flags Corporation issued on the authorization date $1,000,000 of 10-year, 9% bonds payable and received proceeds of $937,689, resulting in an effective interest rate of 10%. The discount is amortized by the effective interest method; the amortization table for this bond issue is illustrated on page 603. Interest is payable semiannually.

Instructions

a Show how the liability for the bonds would appear on a balance sheet prepared immediately after issuance of the bonds.

b Show how the liability for the bonds would appear on a balance sheet prepared after *14* semiannual interest periods (three years prior to maturity).

c Show the necessary calculations to determine interest expense by the effective interest method for the *second* six-month period, the discount amortized at the end of that second period, and the cash interest payment. Round all amounts to the nearest dollar.

Exercise 16-6
Using an amortization table; adjusting entries

On April 1, Financial Publications issued $1,000,000 of 10-year, 9% bonds payable and received proceeds of $1,067,952 resulting in an effective interest rate of 8%. Interest is payable on September 30 and March 31. The effective interest method is used to amortize bond premium; an amortization table for this bond issue is illustrated on page 605.

Instructions

Prepare the necessary journal entries (rounding all amounts to the nearest dollar) on:

a April 1, to record the issuance of the bonds

b September 30, to record the payment of interest and amortization of premium at the first semiannual interest payment date

c December 31, to accrue bond interest expense through year-end

d March 31, to record the payment of interest and amortization of bond premium at the second semiannual interest payment date

Exercise 16-7
Convertible bonds

A recent annual report of **McGraw-Hill, Inc.,** shows that 406 of the company's 3⅞%, $1,000 face amount, convertible bonds are still outstanding. These bonds mature in 1992, and have a conversion ratio of 32 to 1. The company's common stock has a par value of $1 per share, a current market price of $60 per share, and pays dividends of $1.68 per share.

Instructions

a Prepare the journal entry that would be made by McGraw-Hill to record the conversion of these outstanding convertible bonds into shares of common stock. (Assume the bonds originally were issued at par.)

b Under the circumstances described above, would it be advantageous for the bondholders to exchange the bonds for shares of McGraw-Hill's common stock? Explain.

Exercise 16-8
Accounting for leases

On July 1, City Hospital leased equipment from MedTech Instruments for a period of five years. The lease calls for monthly payments of $2,000, payable in advance on the first day of each month, beginning July 1.

Instructions

Prepare the journal entry needed to record this lease in the accounting records of City Hospital on July 1 under each of the following independent assumptions:

a The lease represents a simple rental arrangement.

b At the end of five years, title to this equipment will be transferred to City Hospital at no additional cost. The present value of the 60 monthly lease payments is $90,809, $2,000 of which is paid in cash on July 1.

Exercise 16-9
Accounting for mortgage payments

Shown on page 613 is a partial amortization table for the first three monthly payments on a 12%, $100,000 mortgage payable. You are to continue this amortization table for one more month—that is, enter in each column the effects of the $1,200 payment to be made on October 31. Show supporting computations for the amounts that you enter in columns B, C, and D. (Enter as your starting point the $99,394 balance of the mortgage at Sept. 30.)

PROBLEMS

Group A

Problem 16A-1
Bond interest (bonds issued at par)

Plaza Hotels obtained all necessary approvals to issue $20,000,000 face value of 9%, 20-year bonds dated April 1, 1991. Interest payment dates were October 1 and April 1. The bonds were not issued, however, until two months later, June 1, 1991. On this date the entire bond issue was sold to an underwriter at a price of 100 plus accrued interest.

Instructions

Prepare the required entries in general journal form on:

a June 1, to record the issuance of the bonds

b October 1, to record the first semiannual interest payment on the bonds

c December 31, to accrue bond interest expense through year-end

d April 1, 1992, to record the second semiannual interest payment

Problem 16A-2
Amortizing bond discount and premium: straight-line method

On November 1, 1991, Festival Cruise Ships, Inc., issued $60,000,000 face value of 11% debenture bonds, with interest payable on May 1 and November 1. The bonds mature 10 years from the date of issuance. Company policy is to amortize bond discount or premium by the straight-line method at each interest payment date; the company's fiscal year ends at December 31.

Instructions

a Make the necessary adjusting entries at December 31, 1991, and the journal entry to record the payment of bond interest on May 1, 1992, under each of the following assumptions:

(1) The bonds were issued at 96. $\subset 96\%$

(2) The bonds were issued at 102.

b Compute the net bond liability at December 31, 1991, under assumptions (1) and (2) above.

Problem 16A-3
Comprehensive
problem: straight-
line amortization

Test

Liberty Broadcasting Corporation obtained authorization to issue $16,000,000 of 12%, 10-year bonds, dated May 1, 1991. Interest payment dates were May 1 and November 1. Issuance of the bonds did not take place until July 1, 1991. On this date, the entire bond issue was sold to an underwriter at a price which included the two months' accrued interest. Liberty Broadcasting follows the policy of amortizing bond discount or premium by the straight-line method at each interest date as well as for year-end adjusting entries at December 31.

Instructions

a Prepare all journal entries necessary to record the issuance of the bonds and bond interest expense during 1991, assuming that the sales price of the bonds on July 1 was $16,792,000 including accrued interest. (Note that the bonds will be outstanding for a period of only 9 years and 10 months.)

b Assume that the sales price of the bonds on July 1 had been $15,966,000, including accrued interest. Prepare journal entries for 1991 parallel to those in part **a** above.

c Show the proper balance sheet presentation of the liability for bonds payable in the balance sheet prepared at December 31, *1996,* assuming that the original sales price of the bonds (including accrued interest) had been:

(1) $16,792,000, as described in part **a**

(2) $15,966,000, as described in part **b**

Problem 16A-4
Preparing and
using an
amortization
table (discount)

On December 31, 1991, Rocky Mountain Railroad sold a $10,000,000 face value, 9%, 10-year bond issue to an underwriter at a price of 93¾. This price results in an effective annual interest rate of 10%. Interest is payable semiannually on June 30 and December 31. Rocky Mountain Railroad amortizes bond discount by the effective interest method.

Instructions

a Prepare an amortization table for the first two years (four interest periods) of this bond issue. Round all amounts to the nearest dollar and use the following column headings for your table:

Six-Month Interest Period	(A) Interest Paid Semi-Annually ($10,000,000 × 4½%)	(B) Effective Semi-Annual Interest Expense (Carrying Value × 5%)	(C) Discount Amorti-zation (B − A)	(D) Bond Discount Balance	(E) Carrying Value of Bonds, End of Period ($10,000,000 − D)

b Using the information from your amortization table, prepare all journal entries necessary to record issuance of the bonds in 1991 and bond interest expense for 1992. (Use a compound entry for the interest payment and amortization of bond discount at each semiannual interest payment date.)

c Show the proper balance sheet presentation of Bonds Payable and Discount on Bonds Payable at December 31, *1993.*

Problem 16A-5
A second
problem on an
amortization
table (premium)

On December 31, 1991, Crescent Bay Gas & Electric sold a $6,000,000, 9½%, 12-year bond issue to an underwriter at a price of 103½. This price results in an effective annual interest rate of 9%. The bonds were dated December 31, and the interest payment dates were June 30 and December 31. The company follows a policy of amortizing the bond premium by the effective interest method at each semiannual payment date.

Instructions

a Prepare an amortization table for the first two years (four interest periods) of the life of this bond issue. Round all amounts to the nearest dollar and use the following column headings:

Six-Month Interest Period	(A) Interest Paid Semi- Annually ($6,000,000 × 4¾%)	(B) Effective Semi- Annual Interest Expense (Carrying Value × 4½%)	(C) Premium Amortization (A − B)	(D) Bond Premium Balance	(E) Carrying Value of Bonds, End of Period ($6,000,000 + D)

b Using the information in your amortization table, prepare all journal entries necessary to record issuance of the bonds in 1991 and the bond interest expense during *1992*. (Use a compound entry for the interest payment and amortization of bond premium at each semiannual interest payment date.)

c Show the proper balance sheet presentation of the liability for bonds payable at December 31, *1993*.

Problem 16A-6
Factors affecting
bond prices

Shown below are three independent cases, each involving two bond issues of a publicly owned corporation. In each case, both bond issues have identical credit ratings.

a *Citicorp* has outstanding two issues of 10½% bonds—one issue maturing in 1995, and the other in 2016.

b *BellSouth Corp.* has issued 3⅛% bonds maturing in 1989 and 4⅜% bonds maturing in 1998.

c *COMPAQ Computer* has issued the following convertible bonds: (1) 5¼% bonds maturing in 2012, with a conversion ratio of 25.22 to 1, and (2) 6½% bonds maturing in 2013, with conversion ratio of 15.38 to 1. In June 1988, the market price of COMPAQ's common stock was $66 per share.

Instructions

For each case, explain which of the two bonds you would expect to have been selling at the higher market price in *June 1988*. Also indicate whether each bond should have been selling at a premium or a discount at that time. Explain the reasoning behind your answers. Assume that in June 1988, market interest rates for bonds of this quality were as follows:

MATURITY DATE	MARKET INTEREST RATE
Years 1989–1994	*9%*
Years 1995–2000	*10%*
Year 2001 and beyond	*11%*

Group B

Problem 16B-1
Bond interest
(bonds issued
at par)

Gulf Coast Telephone Co. obtained authorization to issue $60,000,000 face value of 10% 20-year bonds, dated May 1, 1991. Interest payment dates were November 1 and May 1. Issuance of the bonds did not take place until August 1, 1991. On this date all the bonds were sold at a price of 100 plus three months' accrued interest.

Instructions

Prepare the necessary entries in general journal form on:

a August 1, 1991, to record the issuance of the bonds

b November 1, 1991, to record the first semiannual interest payment on the bond issue

c December 31, 1991, to accrue bond interest expense through year-end

d May 1, 1992, to record the second semiannual interest payment

Problem 16B-2
Amortizing bond
discount and
premium: straight-
line method

On September 1, 1991, American Farm Equipment issued $30 million in 12% debenture bonds. Interest is payable semiannually on March 1 and September 1, and the bonds mature in 10 years. Company policy is to amortize bond discount or premium by the straight-line method at each interest payment date; the company's fiscal year ends at December 31.

Instructions

a Make the necessary adjusting entries at December 31, 1991, and the journal entry to record the payment of bond interest on March 1, 1992, under each of the following assumptions:

(1) The bonds were issued at 98.

(2) The bonds were issued at 103.

b Compute the net bond liability at December 31, 1991 under assumptions (1) and (2) above.

Problem 16B-3
Comprehensive problem: straight-line amortization

Drexal Laboratories, Inc., obtained the necessary approvals to issue $6 million of 10%, 10-year bonds, dated March 1, 1991. Interest payment dates were September 1 and March 1. Issuance of the bonds did not occur until June 1, 1991. On this date, the entire bond issue was sold to an underwriter at a price which included three months' accrued interest. Drexal Laboratories, Inc., follows the policy of amortizing bond discount or premium by the straight-line method at each interest date as well as for year-end adjusting entries at December 31.

Instructions

a Prepare all journal entries necessary to record the issuance of the bonds and bond interest expense during 1991, assuming that the sales price of the bonds on June 1 was $6,618,000, including accrued interest.

b Assume that the sales price of the bonds on June 1 had been $5,799,000, including accrued interest. Prepare journal entries for 1991 parallel to those in part **a** above.

c Show the proper balance sheet presentation of the liability for bonds payable in the balance sheet prepared at December 31, *1995,* assuming that the original sales price of the bonds (including accrued interest) had been:

(1) $6,618,000, as described in part **a**

(2) $5,799,000, as described in part **b**

Problem 16B-4
Preparing and using an amortization table (bonds at a discount)

On December 31, 1990, Roadside Inns sold a $6,000,000 face value, 10%, 10-year bond issue to an underwriter at a price of 94. This price results in an effective annual interest rate of 11%. Interest is payable semiannually on June 30 and December 31. Roadside Inns amortizes bond discount by the effective interest method.

Instructions

a Prepare an amortization table for the first two years (four interest periods) of this bond issue. Round all amounts to the nearest dollar and use the following column headings for your table:

Six-Month Interest Period	(A) Interest Paid Semi-Annually ($6,000,000 × 5%)	(B) Effective Semi-Annual Interest Expense (Carrying Value × 5½%)	(C) Discount Amorti- zation (B − A)	(D) Bond Discount Balance	(E) Carrying Value of Bonds, End of Period ($6,000,000 − D)

b Using the information from your amortization table, prepare all journal entries necessary to record issuance of the bonds on December 31, 1990, and bond interest for 1991. (Use a compound entry for interest payment and amortization of bond discount at each semiannual interest payment date.)

c Show the proper balance sheet presentation of Bonds Payable and Discount on Bonds Payable at December 31, 1992.

Problem 16B-5
Another amortization table (bonds at a premium)

On December 31, 1991, Glenview Hospital sold an $8,000,000, 9½%, 12-year bond issue to an underwriter at a price of 103½. This price results in an effective annual interest rate of 9%. The bonds were dated December 31, 1991, and the interest payment dates were June 30 and December 31. Glenview Hospital follows a policy of amortizing the bond premium by the effective interest method at each semiannual payment date.

Instructions

a Prepare an amortization table for the first two years (four interest periods) of the life of this bond issue. Round all amounts to the nearest dollar and use the following column headings:

(A) Six-Month Interest Period	(B) Interest Paid Semi- Annually ($8,000,000 × 4¾%)	(C) Effective Semi- Annual Interest Expense (Carrying Value × 4½%)	(D) Premium Amortization (A − B)	(E) Bond Premium Balance	Carrying Value of Bonds, End of Period ($8,000,000 + D)

b Using the information in your amortization table, prepare all journal entries necessary to record issuance of the bonds on December 31, 1991, and the bond interest expense during 1992.

c Show the proper balance sheet presentation of the liability for bonds payable at December 31, 1993.

Problem 16B-6
Factors affecting bond prices

Shown below are three independent cases, each involving two bond issues of a publicly owned corporation. In each case, both bond issues have identical credit ratings.

a *Pacific Gas & Electric Co.* has two bond issues maturing in the year 2020; one has a contract interest rate of 8½%; and the other, a contract rate of 10%.

b *Columbia Gas System, Inc.,* has outstanding 9⅝% bonds maturing in 1989, and 9⅞% bonds maturing in 1999.

c *McKesson Corp.* has issued the following convertible bonds: (1) 6% bonds maturing in 1994, with a conversion ratio of 65.23 to 1, and (2) 9¾% bonds maturing in 2006, with conversion ratio of 45.70 to 1. In June 1988, the market price of McKesson's common stock was $35 per share.

Instructions

For each case, explain which of the two bonds you would expect to have been selling at the higher market price in *June 1988*. Also indicate whether each bond should have been selling at a premium or a discount at that time. Explain the reasoning behind your answers. Assume that in June 1988, market interest rates for bonds of this quality were as follows:

MATURITY DATE	MARKET INTEREST RATE
Years 1989–1994	9%
Years 1995–2000	10%
Year 2001 and beyond	11%

BUSINESS DECISION CASES

Case 16-1
Don't call us . . .
we'll call you

On December 31 of the current year, SYNEX Corp. has outstanding $10 million of 14½% bonds payable that mature in 15 years. These bonds were issued at par and are callable at a price of 106. Because of a recent decline in market interest rates, the company today can issue $10 million of 15-year bonds with an interest rate of only 12% and use the proceeds to call the 14½% bonds.

Instructions

a Compute the reduction in the company's annual bond interest expense that would result from issuing 12% bonds to replace the 14½% bonds.

b Compute the gain or loss in the current year that will result from calling the 14½% bond issue on December 31.

c In light of your answers to parts **a** and **b,** would you recommend that SYNEX replace the 14½% bond issue, or leave it outstanding? Justify your recommendation.

d If the 14½% bonds are called, how will the related gain or loss be classified in the company's financial statements?

e Assume that you are an investor willing to earn the current market rate of return of

12%. If you were to purchase the SYNEX 14½% bonds at a price of 113 and hold these bonds until their maturity date, you would earn a return slightly greater than 12%. Does this investment sound attractive? Explain.

Case 16-2
Convertible bonds

Dreyer's Grand Ice Cream, Inc., has outstanding $50 million face value of 6½% convertible bonds payable, callable at 106½, maturing in 2011. Each $1,000 bond is convertible into 31.25 shares of the company's $1 par value common stock. Today's newspaper indicates a market price for the company's common stock, which pays no dividend, of $15 per share. On this date, the market rate of interest for bonds of similar quality and maturity date but ***without*** a conversion feature is approximately 13%.

Instructions

a Compute the conversion price and the stock value for one of these bonds.

b Prepare journal entries in the company's accounting records to record the following alternative possibilities:

(1) Dreyer's calls the bonds (assume the bonds were originally issued at par).

(2) Bondholders convert the entire bond issue into common stock.

c Given the circumstances described above, would you expect:

(1) The bonds to be selling at a discount or a premium?

(2) Dreyer's to call the bonds in the immediate future?

(3) Bondholders to convert the bonds into common stock in the immediate future?

Explain the reasons for your answers to each question in part **c.**

Case 16-3
Accounting for leases

At the beginning of the current year, Cable TV entered into the two long-term lease agreements described below:

Building Lease

Leased from Lamden Properties the use of an office building for a period of five years. The monthly lease payments are based upon the square footage of the building and increase by 5% each year. The estimated useful life of the building is 40 years.

Satellite Lease

Leased from SpaceNet, Inc., the use of a communications satellite for a period of five years. The monthly payments are intended to pay SpaceNet the current sales price of the satellite, plus a reasonable charge for interest. At the end of the lease, ownership of the satellite will transfer to Cable TV at no additional cost. The estimated useful life of the satellite is 15 years.

Instructions

Answer each of the following questions as they relate to the building lease. After answering all four questions, answer them again as they relate to the satellite lease.

a Is this agreement an operating lease or a capital lease? Why?

b Will this lease result in any assets or liabilities being included in Cable TV's future balance sheets? If so, identify these assets and liabilities.

c Indicate the nature of any expenses that will appear in Cable TV's future income statements as a result of the lease, and indicate the number of years for which the expense will be incurred.

d Briefly explain how the ***lessor*** should account for this lease agreement, including the receipt of future lease payments. Indicate whether the lessor should recognize depreciation on the leased asset.

ANSWERS TO SELF-TEST QUESTIONS

1 a, b, c, and d   2 a and d   3 c   4 b   5a

Appendix A
Applications of Present Value

Several preceding chapters have included brief references to the concept of present value in discussions of the valuation of certain assets and liabilities. The purpose of this appendix is to discuss this concept more fully and also to demonstrate the use of present value tables as an aid in making present value computations. In addition, the appendix summarizes in one location the various applications of the present value concept which have been discussed throughout the book. These applications include the valuation of long-term notes receivable and payable, estimation of goodwill, computation of bond prices, and accounting for capital lease transactions.

After studying this appendix you should be able to meet these Learning Objectives:

1 Explain the concept of present value.

2 Identify the three factors that affect the present value of a future amount.

3 Compute the present value of a future amount and of an annuity using present value tables.

4 Discuss accounting applications of the present value concept.

THE CONCEPT OF PRESENT VALUE

Objective 1
Explain the concept of present value.

The concept of present value has many applications in accounting, but it is most easily explained in the context of evaluating investment opportunities. In this context, the present value of an expected future cash receipt is the amount that a knowledgeable investor would pay *today* for the right to receive that future amount. The present value is always *less* than the future amount, because the investor will expect to earn a return on the investment. The amount by which the future cash receipt exceeds its present value represents the investor's profit; in short, this difference may be regarded as *interest revenue* included in the future amount.

Objective 2
Identify the three factors that affect the present value of a future amount.

The present value of a particular investment opportunity depends upon three factors: (1) the expected dollar amount to be received in the future, (2) the length of time until the future amount will be received, and (3) the rate of return (called the *discount rate*) required by the investor. The process of determining the present value of a future cash receipt or payment is called *discounting* the future amount.

To illustrate the present value concept, assume that a specific investment is expected to result in a $1,000 cash receipt at the end of one year. An investor requiring a 10% annual rate of return would be willing to pay $909 today (computed as $1,000 ÷ 1.10) for the right to receive this future amount. This computation may be verified as follows (amounts rounded to the nearest dollar):

Amount to be invested (present value)	$ 909
Required return on investment ($909 × 10%)	91
Amount to be received in one year (future value)	$1,000

If the $1,000 is to be received *two years* in the future, the investor would pay only $826 for the investment today [($1,000 ÷ 1.10) ÷ 1.10]. This computation may be verified as follows (amounts rounded to the nearest dollar):

Amount to be invested (present value)	$ 826
Required return on investment in first year ($826 × 10%)	83
Amount invested after one year	$ 909
Required return on investment in second year ($909 × 10%)	91
Amount to be received in two years (future value)	$1,000

The amount that our investor would pay today, $826, is the *present value* of $1,000 to be received two years later, discounted at an annual rate of 10%. The $174 difference between the $826 present value and the $1,000 future amount may be regarded as the return (interest revenue) to be earned by the investor over the two-year period.

Present Value Tables

Although we can compute the present value of future amounts by a series of divisions as illustrated above, a more convenient method is available. We can use a *table of present values* to find the present value of *$1* at a specified discount rate and then multiply this value by the future amount. For example, in *Table 1* on the next page, the present value of $1 to be received in two years, discounted at an annual rate of 10%, is *$0.826*. If we multiply *.826* by the expected future cash receipt of $1,000, we get an answer of *$826*, the same amount produced by the series of divisions in our previous illustration.

Selecting an Appropriate Discount Rate

The *discount rate* may be viewed as the investor's required rate of return. All investments involve some degree of risk that actual future cash flows may turn out to be less than expected. Investors usually will expect a rate of return which justifies taking this risk. Under today's market conditions, investors require annual returns of between 6% and 9% on low-risk investments, such as government bonds and certificates of deposit. For relatively high-risk investments, such as the introduction of a new product line, investors may expect to earn an annual return of perhaps 15% or more.

TABLE 1
Present Values of $1 Due in n Periods*

NUMBER OF PERIODS (n)	DISCOUNT RATE								
	1%	1½%	5%	6%	8%	10%	12%	15%	20%
1	.990	.985	.952	.943	.926	.909	.893	.870	.833
2	.980	.971	.907	.890	.857	.826	.797	.756	.694
3	.971	.956	.864	.840	.794	.751	.712	.658	.579
4	.961	.942	.823	.792	.735	.683	.636	.572	.482
5	.951	.928	.784	.747	.681	.621	.567	.497	.402
6	.942	.915	.746	.705	.630	.564	.507	.432	.335
7	.933	.901	.711	.665	.583	.513	.452	.376	.279
8	.923	.888	.677	.627	.540	.467	.404	.327	.233
9	.914	.875	.645	.592	.510	.424	.361	.284	.194
10	.905	.862	.614	.558	.463	.386	.322	.247	.162
20	.820	.742	.377	.312	.215	.149	.104	.061	.026
24	.788	.700	.310	.247	.158	.102	.066	.035	.013
36	.699	.585	.173	.123	.063	.032	.017	.007	.001

* The present value of $1 is computed by the formula $p = 1/(1 + i)^n$, where p is the present value of $1, i is the discount rate, and n is the number of periods until the future cash flow will occur. Amounts in this table have been rounded to three decimal places and are shown for a limited number of periods and discount rates. Many calculators are programmed to use this formula and can compute present values when the future amount is entered along with values for i and n.

In addition to the amount of risk involved, the "appropriate" discount rate for determining the present value of a specific investment depends upon the investor's cost of capital and the returns available from other investment opportunities. When a higher discount rate is used, the resulting present value will be lower and the investor, therefore, will be interested in the investment only at a lower price.

Discounting Annual Cash Flows

Let us now assume that an investment is expected to produce an annual net cash flow of $10,000 for each of the next three years. If Camino Company expects a 12% return on this type of investment, it may compute the present value of these cash flows as follows:

YEAR	EXPECTED NET CASH FLOW	×	PRESENT VALUE OF $1 DISCOUNTED AT 12%	=	PRESENT VALUE OF NET CASH FLOWS
1	$10,000		.893		$ 8,930
2	10,000		.797		7,970
3	10,000		.712		7,120
Total present value of the investment.....................................					$24,020

This analysis indicates that the present value of the expected net cash flows from the investment, discounted at an annual rate of 12%, amounts to $24,020. This is the maximum amount that Camino Company could afford to pay for this investment and still expect to earn the 12% required rate of return.

In the preceding schedule, we multiplied each of the expected annual cash flows by the present value of $1 in the appropriate future period, discounted at 12% per year. The present values of the annual cash flows were then added to determine the total present value of the investment. Separately discounting each annual cash flow to its present value is necessary only when the cash flows vary in amount from one year to the next. Since the annual cash flows in our example are *uniform in amount,* there are two easier ways to compute the total present value.

One way is to add the three decimal figures representing the present value of $1 in the successive years (.893 + .797 + .712) and then to multiply this total (2.402) by the $10,000 annual cash flow. This approach produces the same result ($10,000 × 2.402 = $24,020) we obtained by determining the present value of each year's cash flow separately and adding the results.

Objective 3
Compute the present value of a future amount and of an annuity using present value tables.

An even easier approach to determining the present value of uniform annual cash flows is to refer to an *annuity table,* which shows the present value of *$1 to be received periodically* for a given number of periods. An annuity table is shown below:

TABLE 2
Present Values of $1 to Be Received Periodically for *n* Periods

NUMBER OF PERIODS (*n*)	1%	1½%	5%	6%	8%	10%	12%	15%	20%
					DISCOUNT RATE				
1	0.990	0.985	0.952	0.943	0.926	0.909	0.893	0.870	0.833
2	1.970	1.956	1.859	1.833	1.783	1.736	1.690	1.626	1.528
3	2.941	2.912	2.723	2.673	2.577	2.487	2.402	2.283	2.106
4	3.902	3.854	3.546	3.465	3.312	3.170	3.037	2.855	2.589
5	4.853	4.783	4.329	4.212	3.993	3.791	3.605	3.352	2.991
6	5.795	5.697	5.076	4.917	4.623	4.355	4.111	3.784	3.326
7	6.728	6.598	5.786	5.582	5.206	4.868	4.564	4.160	3.605
8	7.652	7.486	6.463	6.210	5.747	5.335	4.968	4.487	3.837
9	8.566	8.361	7.108	6.802	6.247	5.759	5.328	4.772	4.031
10	9.471	9.222	7.722	7.360	6.710	6.145	5.650	5.019	4.192
20	18.046	17.169	12.462	11.470	9.818	8.514	7.469	6.259	4.870
24	21.243	20.030	13.799	12.550	10.529	8.985	7.784	6.434	4.937
36	30.108	27.661	16.547	14.621	11.717	9.677	8.192	6.623	4.993

Note that the present value of $1 to be received periodically (annually) for three years, discounted at 12% per year, is *$2.402.* Thus, $10,000 received annually for three years, discounted at 12%, is *$24,020* ($10,000 × 2.402).

Discount Periods of Less Than One Year

The interval between regular periodic cash flows is termed the *discount period.* In our preceding examples we have assumed annual cash flows and, therefore, discount periods of one year. Often a note or a contract may call for cash payments on a more frequent basis, such as monthly, quarterly, or semi-annually. The illustrated present value tables can be used with discount periods at any length, *but the discount rate must relate to the time interval of the discount period.* Thus, if we use the annuity table to find the present value of a series of equal monthly cash payments, the discount rate must be expressed as a monthly interest rate.

To illustrate, assume that StyleMart purchases merchandise from Western Fashions, issuing in exchange a $9,600 note payable to be paid in 24 monthly installments of $400 each. As discussed in earlier chapters, both companies should record this transaction at the present value of the note. If a reasonable *annual* interest rate for this type of note is 12%, we should discount the monthly cash payments at the *monthly* rate of 1%. The annuity table shows the present value of $1 to be received (or paid) for 24 monthly periods, discounted at 1% per month, is 21.243. Thus, the present value of the installment note issued by StyleMart is $8,497 ($400 × 21.243, rounded to the nearest dollar).

ACCOUNTING APPLICATIONS OF THE PRESENT VALUE CONCEPT

Objective 4
Discuss accounting applications of the present value concept

Accounting applications of the concept of present value have been discussed at appropriate points throughout this textbook. We will now demonstrate these applications with examples which make use of our present value tables.

Valuation of Long-Term Notes Receivable and Payable (Chapters 8 and 11)

When a long-term note receivable or payable does not bear a realistic stated rate of interest, a portion of the face amount of the note should be regarded as representing an interest charge. The amount of this interest charge can be determined by discounting the note to its present value using as a discount rate a realistic rate of interest.

To illustrate, consider our preceding example in which StyleMart purchases merchandise from Western Fashions by issuing an installment note payable with a face amount of $9,600 and no stated rate of interest. The present value of this note, discounted at the realistic market interest rate of 1% per month, was $8,497. The difference between the $9,600 face amount of the note and its present value of $8,497 is $1,103, which represents the interest charge included in the face amount. StyleMart should use the *present value* of the note in determining the cost of the merchandise and the amount of the related net liability, as shown by the following entry:

Purchases	8,497	
Discount on Notes Payable	1,103	
Notes Payable..		9,600

Purchased merchandise by issuing a 24-month installment note payable with a 1% monthly interest charge included in the face amount.

Assuming that StyleMart uses the effective interest method to amortize the discount on the note, the entry to record the first monthly payment and the related interest expense is as follows:

Notes Payable..	400	
Interest Expense	85	
Discount on Notes Payable		85
Cash..		400

To record first monthly payment on installment note payable and recognize one month's interest expense ($8,497 × 1%, rounded to nearest dollar).

Estimating the Value of Goodwill (Chapter 10)

The asset goodwill may be defined as the present value of expected future earnings in excess of the normal return on net identifiable assets. One method of estimating goodwill is to estimate the annual amounts by which earnings are expected to exceed a normal return and then to discount these amounts to their present value.

For example, assume that John Reed is negotiating to purchase a small but very successful business. In addition to paying the fair market value of the company's net identifiable assets, Reed is willing to pay an appropriate amount for goodwill. He believes that the business will probably earn at least $40,000 in excess of "normal earnings" in each of the next five years. If Reed requires a 20% annual return on purchased goodwill, he would be willing to pay $119,640 for this expected five-year $40,000 annuity, computed as follows: $40,000 × 2.991 (from Table 2) = $119,640.

Market Prices of Bonds (Chapter 16)

The market price of bonds may be regarded as the *present value* to bondholders of the future principal and interest payments. To illustrate, assume that a corporation issues $1,000,000 face value of 9%, 10-year bonds when the going market rate of interest is 10%. Since bond interest is paid semiannually, we must use 20 *semiannual* periods as the life of the bond issue and a 5% *semiannual* market rate of interest in our present value calculations. The expected issuance price of this bond issue may be computed as follows:

Present value of future principal payments:
   $1,000,000 due after 20 semiannual periods, discounted at 5% per period:
     $1,000,000 × .377 (from Table 1, page 628)................................... **$377,000**
Present value of future interest payments:
   $45,000 per period ($1,000,000 × 9% × ½) for 20 semiannual periods,
     discounted at 5%: $45,000 × 12.462 (from Table 2, page 629)................. **560,790**
Expected issuance price of bond issue* **$937,790**

* The terms of this bond issue correspond with those of the bond issue illustrated in the amortization table on page 603 in Chapter 16. In the amortization table, however, the issuance price of the bonds is $937,689, or $101 less than indicated by our computations above. The difference results from our rounding the present value of $1 to only three decimal places. Rounding to three decimal places may cause an error of up to $500 per $1 million.

Capital Lease (Chapter 16)

A capital lease is regarded as a sale of the leased asset by the lessor to the lessee. At the date of this sale, the lessor recognizes sales revenue equal to the *present value* of the future lease payments receivable, discounted at a realistic rate of interest. The lessee also uses the present value of the future payments to determine the cost of the leased asset and the valuation of the related liability.

To illustrate, assume that on December 1, Pace Tractor uses a *capital lease* to finance the sale of a tractor to Kelly Grading Co. The tractor was carried in Pace Tractor's perpetual inventory records at a cost of $15,000. Terms of the lease call for Kelly Grading Co. to make *24* monthly payments of *$1,000* each, beginning on December 31. These lease payments include an interest charge of *1%* per month. At the end of the 24-month lease, title to the tractor will pass to Kelly Grading Co. at no additional cost.

■ **Accounting by the Lessor (Pace Tractor)**   *Table 2* on page 629 shows that the present value of $1 to be received monthly for 24 months, discounted at 1% per month, is *21.243*. Therefore, the present value of the 24 future lease payments is $1,000 × 21.243, or *$21,243*. Pace Tractor should record this capital lease as a sale of the tractor at a price equal to the present value of the lease payments, as follows:

Lease Payment Receivable (net)...	21,243	
Cost of Goods sold...	15,000	
Inventory..		15,000
Sales		21,243

*Financed sale of a tractor to Kelly Grading Co. using a capital lease
requiring 24 monthly payments of $1,000. Payments include a
1% monthly interest charge.*

Notice that the sales price of the tractor is only $21,243, even though the gross amount to be collected from Kelly Grading Co. amounts to $24,000 ($1,000 × 24 payments). The difference between these two amounts, $2,757, will be recognized by Pace Tractor as interest revenue over the life of the lease.[1]

To illustrate the recognition of interest revenue, the entry on December 31 to record collection of the first monthly lease payment (rounded to the nearest dollar) is:

Cash..	1,000	
Interest Revenue		212
Lease Payments Receivable (net)		788

Received first lease payment from Kelly Grading Co.:

Lease payment received	$1,000
Interest revenue ($21,243 × 1%).................................	(212)
Reduction in lease payments receivable	$ 788

---

[1] We have elected to record the present value of the future lease payments by a single debit entry to Lease Payments Receivable. An alternative is to debit Lease Payments Receivable for the total amount of the future payments and to credit Discount on Lease Payments Receivable, a contra-asset account, for the unearned finance charges included in the contractual amount. Either approach results in the lessor recording a net receivable equal to the present value of the future lease payments.

After this first monthly payment is collected, the present value of the lease payments receivable is reduced to $20,455 ($21,243 original balance, less $788). Therefore, the interest revenue earned during the *second* month of the lease (rounded to the nearest dollar) will be *$205* ($20,455 × 1%).[2]

■ **Accounting by the Lessee (Kelly Grading Co.)** Kelly Grading Co. also should use the present value of the lease payments to determine the cost of the tractor and the amount of the related liability, as shown below:

Leased Equipment..	*21,243*	
* Lease Payment Obligation ....*		*21,243*
To record acquisition of a tractor through a capital lease from Pace		
Tractor. Terms call for 24 monthly payments of $1,000, which include		
a 1% monthly interest charge.		

The entry on December 31 to record the first monthly lease payment (rounded to the nearest dollar) is:

Interest Expense	*212*	
Lease Payment Obligation	*788*	
* Cash...*		*1,000*
To record first monthly lease payment to Pace Tractor:		
* Amount of payment ....*	*$1,000*	
* Interest expense ($21,243 × 1%) ....*	*(212)*	
* Reduction in lease payment obligation ....*	*$ 788*	

PROBLEMS

Problem 1
Using present
value tables

Use the tables on pages 628 and 629 to determine the present value of the following cash flows:

a $10,000 to be paid annually for seven years, discounted at an annual rate of 10%.

b $7,500 to be received today, assuming that money can be invested to earn 15% annually.

c $350 to be paid monthly for 24 months, with an additional "balloon payment" of $15,000 due at the end of the twenty-fourth month, discounted at a monthly interest rate of 1½%.

d $30,000 to be received annually for the first three years, followed by $20,000 to be received annually for the next two years (total of five years in which collections are received, discounted at an annual rate of 12%.

Problem 2
Present value
and bond prices

On June 30 of the current year, Rural Gas & Electric Co. issued $10,000,000 face value, 11%, 10-year bonds payable, with interest dates of December 31 and June 30. The bonds were issued at a discount, resulting in an effective *semiannual* interest rate of 6%. The company maintains its accounts on a calendar-year basis and amortizes the bond discount by the effective interest method.

Instructions

a Compute the issuance price for the bond issue which results in an effective semiannual interest rate of 6%. (Hint: Discount both the interest payments and the maturity value over 20 semiannual periods.)

---

[2] Both Pace Tractor and Kelly Grading Co. would prepare amortization tables showing the allocation of each lease payment between interest and the amount due.

b Prepare all journal entries necessary to record the issuance of the bonds and bond interest expense during the current year, assuming that the sales price of the bonds on June 30 was the amount you computed in part **a.**

Problem 3
Valuation of a
note payable

On December 1, Showcase Interiors purchased a shipment of furniture from Colonial House by paying $10,500 cash and issuing an installment note payable in the face amount of $28,800. The note is to be paid in 24 monthly installments of $1,200 each. Although the note makes no mention of an interest charge, the rate of interest usually charged to Showcase Interiors in such transactions is 1½% per month.

Instructions

a Compute the present value of the note payable, using a discount rate of 1½% per month.

b Prepare the journal entries in the accounts of Showcase Interiors on:

(1) December 1, to record the purchase of the furniture (debit Purchases).

(2) December 31, to record the first $1,200 monthly payment on the note and to recognize interest expense for one month by the effective interest method. (Round interest expense to the nearest dollar.)

c Show how the liability for this note would appear in the balance sheet at December 31. (Assume that the note is classified as a current liability.)

Problem 4
Discounting lease
agreements to
present value

Metropolitan Transit District (MTD) plans to acquire a large computer system by entering into a long-term lease agreement with the computer manufacturer. The manufacturer will provide the computer system under either of the following lease agreements:

Five-Year Lease

MTD is to pay $2,500,000 at the beginning of the lease (delivery date) and $1,000,000 annually at the end of each of the next five years. At the end of the fifth year, MTD may take title to the system for an additional payment of $3,000,000.

Ten-Year Lease

MTD is to pay $2,000,000 at the beginning of the lease and $900,000 annually at the end of each of the next 10 years. At the end of the tenth year, MTD may take title for an additional payment of $1,300,000.

Under either proposal, MTD will buy the computer at the end of the lease. MTD is a governmental agency which does not seek to earn a profit and is not evaluating alternative investment opportunities. However, MTD does attempt to minimize its costs and it must borrow the money to finance either lease agreement at an annual interest rate of 10%.

Instructions

a Determine which lease proposal results in the lower cost for the computer system when the future cash outlays are discounted at an annual interest rate of 10%.

b Prepare a journal entry to record the acquisition of the computer system under the lowest cost lease agreement as determined in part **a.** (This journal entry will include the initial cash payment to the computer manufacturer required at the beginning of the lease.)

Problem 5
Valuation of a
note receivable
with an
unrealistic
interest rate

On December 31, Richland Farms sold a tract of land, which had cost $310,000, to Skyline Developers in exchange for $50,000 cash and a five-year, 4%, note receivable for $300,000. Interest on the note is payable annually, and the principal amount is due in five years. The accountant for Richland Farms did not notice the unrealistically low interest rate on the note and made the following entry on December 31 to record this sale:

Cash	*50,000*	
Notes Receivable	*300,000*	
Land		*310,000*
Gain on Sale of Land		*40,000*
Sold land to Skyline Developers in exchange for cash and a		
five-year note with interest due annually.		

Instructions **a** Compute the present value of the note receivable from Skyline Developers at the date of sale, assuming that a realistic rate of interest for this transaction is 12%. (Hint: Consider both the annual interest payments and the principal amount of the note.)

b Prepare the journal entry on December 31 to record the sale of the land correctly. Show supporting computations for (1) the gain or loss on the sale, and (2) the discount on the note receivable.

c Explain what effects the error made by Richland Farms' accountant will have upon (1) the net income in the year of the sale, and (2) the combined net income of the next five years. Ignore income taxes.

Problem 6
Capital leases: a
comprehensive
problem

Custom Truck Builders frequently uses long-term lease contracts to finance the sale of its trucks. On November 1, 1991, Custom Truck Builders leased to Interstate Van Lines a truck carried in the perpetual inventory records at $33,520. The terms of the lease call for Interstate Van Lines to make 36 monthly payments of $1,400 each, beginning on November 30, 1991. The present value of these payments, after considering a built-in interest charge of 1% per month, is equal to the regular $42,150 sales price of the truck. At the end of the 36-month lease, title to the truck will transfer to Interstate Van Lines.

Instructions **a** Prepare journal entries for 1991 in the accounts of Custom Truck Builders on:

(1) November 1 to record the sale financed by the lease and the related cost of goods sold. (Debit Lease Payments Receivable for the $42,150 present value of the future lease payments.)

(2) November 30, to record receipt of the first $1,400 monthly payment. (Prepare a compound journal entry which allocates the cash receipt between interest revenue and reduction of Lease Payments Receivable. The portion of each monthly payment recognized as interest revenue is equal to 1% of the balance of the account Lease Payments Receivable, at the beginning of that month. Round all interest computations to the nearest dollar.)

(3) December 31, to record receipt of the second monthly payment.

b Prepare journal entries for 1991 in the accounts of Interstate Van Lines on:

(1) November 1, to record acquisition of the leased truck.

(2) November 30, to record the first monthly lease payment. (Determine the portion of the payment representing interest expense in a manner parallel to that described in part **a**.)

(3) December 31, to record the second monthly lease payment.

(4) December 31, to recognize depreciation on the leased truck through year-end. Compute depreciation expense by the straight-line method, using a 10-year service life and an estimated salvage value of $6,150.

c Compute the net carrying value of the leased truck in the balance sheet of Interstate Van Lines at December 31, 1991.

d Compute the amount of Interstate Van Lines' lease payment obligation at December 31, 1991.

Investments in Corporate Securities

In this chapter, we discuss investments in corporate securities (stocks and bonds) from the viewpoint of the investor. We first focus upon short-term investments in marketable securities—that is, highly liquid investments made primarily for the purpose of earning dividend or interest revenue. Next, we discuss long-term investments in common stock made for the purpose of exercising influence or control over the issuing corporation. We illustrate the equity method of accounting for these investments and explain how a parent company and its subsidiaries function as one economic entity. The chapter concludes with a discussion of consolidated financial statements. Following the chapter is an optional appendix discussing the special accounting problems of multinational corporations.

After studying this chapter you should be able to meet these Learning Objectives:

1 Account for short-term investments in stocks and bonds.

2 Account for an investment in common stock by the equity method.

3 Explain how a parent company "controls" its subsidiaries.

4 Describe the distinctive feature of consolidated financial statements.

5 Explain why intercompany transactions must be eliminated as a step in preparing consolidated financial statements.

6 Prepare a consolidated balance sheet.

The term *corporate securities* refers to the stocks and bonds issued by corporations. The securities issued by large, publicly owned corporations such as IBM or General Motors are owned by literally millions of different investors. On the other hand, all of the common stock issued by a small, closely held corporation may be owned by one individual or by a small group of investors, such as the members of a family. From the investor's point of view, most investments in corporate securities fall into one of two broad categories: (1) investments in *marketable securities*, and (2) investments for purposes of *influence or control*.

INVESTMENTS IN MARKETABLE SECURITIES

Marketable securities consist primarily of U.S. government bonds and the bonds and stocks of large corporations. These securities are traded on organized securities exchanges, such as the New York Stock Exchange. Thus, they are easily purchased or sold at quoted market prices. Investments in marketable securities earn a return for the investor, yet are almost as liquid as cash itself. For this reason, marketable securities usually are listed in the balance sheet second among current assets, immediately after cash.

To qualify as a current asset, an investment in marketable securities must be readily marketable. *Readily marketable* means immediately salable at a quoted market price. In addition, management must be *willing* to use the invested funds to pay current liabilities. Investments which are not readily marketable, or which management intends to hold on a long-term basis, are *not* current assets. Such investments should be shown in the balance sheet just below the current asset section under the caption, Long-Term Investments.

The current market prices of most marketable securities are quoted daily by securities exchanges, brokerage houses, and in the financial pages of major newspapers. The market prices of stocks are quoted in terms of dollars per share. As illustrated in Chapter 16, bond prices are stated as a percentage of the bond's maturity value, which usually is $1,000. Thus, a bond with a quoted price of *87* has a market value of *$870* ($1,000 × 87%).

Accounting for Marketable Securities

Objective 1
Account for short-term investments in stocks and bonds.

Accounting principles differ somewhat between investments in marketable *equity* securities (stocks) and in marketable *debt* securities (bonds). For this reason, separate controlling accounts are used in the general ledger for each type of investment. For each controlling account, a subsidiary ledger is maintained which shows for each security owned the acquisition date, total cost, number of shares (or bonds) owned, and the cost per share (or bond). This subsidiary ledger provides the information necessary to determine the amount of gain or loss when an investment in a particular stock or bond is sold.

The principal distinction in accounting for investments in stocks and in bonds is that *interest on bonds accrues* from day to day. An investor in bonds must account for this accrued interest when the bonds are purchased, at the end of each accounting period, and when the bonds are sold. Dividends on stock, however, *do not accrue*.

Marketable Debt Securities (Bonds)

The amount of interest paid annually to bondholders is equal to a stated percentage of the bond's maturity value. Thus, the owner of a 10% bond receives $100 interest ($1,000 × 10%) every year. Since bond interest usually is paid semiannually, the bondholder receives two semiannual interest payments of $50 each.

When bonds are purchased between interest dates, the purchaser pays the quoted market price for the bond *plus* the interest accrued since the last interest payment date. By this arrangement the new owner becomes entitled to receive in full the next semiannual interest payment. An account called Bond Interest Receivable should be debited for the amount of accrued interest purchased.

To illustrate the accounting entries for an investment in bonds, assume that on August 1 an investor purchases ten 9%, $1,000 bonds of Rider Co. which pay interest on June 1 and December 1. The investor buys the bonds on August 1 at a price of 98 (or $9,800), plus a brokerage commission of $50 and two months' accrued interest of $150 ($10,000 × 9% × 2/12 = $150). The brokerage commission is viewed as part of the cost of the bonds. However, the accrued interest receivable at the time of purchase must be accounted for separately. Therefore, the journal entry made by the investor on August 1 is:

■
Separate account for accrued bond interest purchased

Marketable Debt Securities	9,850	
Bond Interest Receivable	150	
Cash..		10,000

Purchased ten 9% bonds of Rider Co. for $9,800 plus a brokerage
commission of $50 and two months' accrued interest.

On December 1, the semiannual interest payment date, the investor will receive an interest check for $450, which will be recorded as follows:

■
Note portion of interest check earned

Cash..	450	
Bond Interest Receivable		150
Bond Interest Revenue		300

Received semiannual interest on Rider Co. bonds.

The $300 credit to Bond Interest Revenue represents the amount actually earned during the four months the bonds were owned by the investor (9% × $10,000 × 4/12 = $300).

If the investor's accounting records are maintained on a calendar-year basis, the following adjusting entry is required at December 31 to record bond interest earned since December 1:

Bond Interest Receivable	75	
Bond Interest Revenue		75

To accrue one month's interest earned (Dec. 1–Dec. 31) on
Rider Co. bonds ($10,000 × 9% × 1/12 = $75).

■ **Amortization of Bond Discount or Premium from the Investor's Viewpoint** We have discussed the need for the corporation issuing bonds payable to amortize any bond discount or premium to measure correctly the bond interest expense. But what about the *purchaser* of the bonds? Should an investor in bonds amortize any difference between the cost of the investment and its future maturity value in order to measure investment income correctly? The answer to this question depends upon whether the investor considers the bonds to be a current asset or a long-term investment.

When an investment in bonds is classified as a current asset, the investor usually *does not* amortize discount or premium. The justification for this practice is the accounting principle of *materiality*. Given that the investment may be held for but a short period of time, amortization of bond discount or premium probably will not have a material effect upon reported net income. When an investment in bonds will be held for the long term, however, the investor should amortize discount or premium. Amortization of a discount will increase the amount of interest revenue recognized by the investor; amortization of a premium will reduce the amount of interest revenue recognized.

Marketable Equity Securities (Stocks)

Since dividends on stock do not accrue, the ***entire cost*** of purchasing stock (including brokerage commissions) is debited to the Marketable Equity Securities account. Dividend revenue usually is recognized when the dividend check arrives; the entry consists of a debit to Cash and a credit to Dividend Revenue. No adjusting entries are needed to recognize dividend revenue at the end of an accounting period.

Additional shares of stock received in stock splits or stock dividends ***are not income*** to the stockholder, and only a ***memorandum entry*** is used to record the increase in the number of shares owned. The ***cost basis per share*** is decreased, however, because of the larger number of shares comprising the investment after receiving additional "free" shares from a stock split or a stock dividend.

As an example, assume that an investor purchases 100 shares of Delta Co. common stock at a total cost of $7,200, including commission. The investor's original cost basis is $72 per share ($7,200 ÷ 100 shares). Later the investor receives an additional 20 shares as the result of a 20% stock dividend. The investor's cost basis per share is thereby reduced to ***$60*** per share, computed by dividing the total cost of $7,200 by the ***120*** shares owned after the stock dividend. The memorandum entry to be made in the investor's general journal would be:

July 10   Memorandum: Received 20 additional shares of Delta Co. common
stock as a result of 20% stock dividend. Now own 120 shares with a
cost basis of $7,200, or $60 per share.

Gains and Losses from Sales of Investments

The sale of an investment in ***stocks*** is recorded by debiting Cash for the amount received and crediting the Marketable Equity Securities account for the cost of the securities sold. Any difference between the proceeds of the sale and the cost of the investment is recorded by a debit to Loss on Sale of Marketable Securities or by a credit to Gain on Sale of Marketable Securities.

At the date of sale of an investment in ***bonds***, any interest which has accrued since the last interest payment date (or year-end) should be recognized as interest revenue. For example, assume that 10 bonds of the Elk Corporation carried in the accounts of an investor at $9,600 are sold at a price of ***94***, plus accrued interest of ***$90***, and less a brokerage commission of ***$50***. The gain or loss may be computed as follows:

Proceeds from sale ($9,400 + $90 − $50)	$9,440
Less: Proceeds representing interest revenue	90
Sales price of investment in bonds	$9,350
Cost of investment in bonds	9,600
Loss on sale	$ 250

This sale should be recorded by the following journal entry:

Cash..	9,440	
Loss on Sale of Marketable Securities......................................	250	
Marketable Debt Securities		9,600
Bond Interest Revenue		90

*Sold 10 bonds of Elk Corporation at 94 and accrued interest of $90, less
broker's commission of $50.*

Balance Sheet Valuation of Marketable Securities

Although the market price of a bond may fluctuate from day to day, we can be
reasonably certain that when the maturity date arrives the market price will
be equal to the bond's maturity value. Stocks, on the other hand, do not have
maturity values. When the market price of a stock declines, there is no way we
can be certain whether the decline will be temporary or permanent. For this
reason, different valuation standards are applied in accounting for investments in marketable *debt* securities (bonds) and investments in marketable
equity securities (stocks).

■ **Valuation of Marketable Debt Securities**   A short-term investment
in bonds is generally carried in the accounting records at *cost* and a gain or loss
is recognized when the investment is sold. If bonds are held as a long-term
investment and the difference between the cost of the investment and its maturity value is substantial, the valuation of the investment is adjusted each
year by amortization of the discount or premium.

■ **Valuation of Marketable Equity Securities**   The market values of
stocks may rise or fall dramatically during an accounting period.

CASE IN POINT   ■ In a single day, the market price of IBM's capital stock
dropped over $31 per share, falling from $135 to $103.25.
Of course, this was not a "typical" day. The date—October 19, 1987—will long
be remembered as "Black Monday." On this day, stock prices around the world
suffered the greatest one-day decline in history. Those stocks listed on the New
York Stock Exchange lost about 20% of their total value in six hours. Given
that annual dividends on these stocks amounted to about 2% of market value,
this one-day "market loss" was approximately equal to the loss by investors of
all dividend revenue for a period of 10 years.

An investor who sells an investment at a price above or below cost will recognize a gain or loss on the sale. But what if the investor continues to hold
securities after a significant change in their market value? In this case, should
any gain or loss be recognized in the financial statements?

The FASB has stated that a portfolio[1] of marketable equity securities should be shown in the investor's balance sheet at the *lower of* the portfolio's total cost or current market value. If the market value of the portfolio *falls below cost*, the decline in value is *reported as a loss* in the investor's income statement. Recoveries in the market value of the portfolio are reported in the income statement as gains, but only as the market value rises back up to cost.[2] Increases in market value above cost are *not shown* in the income statement.

The lower-of-cost-or-market rule produces *conservative results* in both the balance sheet and the income statement. In the balance sheet, the portfolio of marketable equity securities is shown at the lowest justifiable amount—that is, the lower of its cost or its market value. In the income statement, declines in market value below cost immediately are recognized as losses. Increases in market value above cost, however, are not recognized until the securities are sold.

Accountants traditionally have applied different criteria in recognizing gains and losses. One of the basic principles in accounting is that gains shall not be recognized until they are *realized*, and the usual test of realization is the sale of the asset in question. Losses, on the other hand, are recognized as soon as *objective evidence* indicates that a loss has been incurred.

Applying the Lower-of-Cost-or-Market Rule: An Illustration

In applying the lower-of-cost-or-market rule, the total cost of the *portfolio* of marketable equity securities is compared with its current market value, and the *lower* of these two amounts is used as the balance sheet valuation. If the market value of the portfolio is below cost, an entry is made to reduce the carrying value of the portfolio to current market value and to recognize an *unrealized loss* for the amount of the market decline. The write-down of an investment in marketable equity securities to a market value below cost is an end-of-period adjusting entry and should be based upon market prices at the balance sheet date.

To illustrate the lower-of-cost-or-market adjustment, assume the following facts for the investment portfolio of Eagle Corporation at December 31, 1991:

	COST	MARKET VALUE
Common stock of Adams Corporation	*$100,000*	*$106,000*
Common stock of Barnes Company	*60,000*	*52,000*
Preferred stock of Parker Industries	*200,000*	*182,000*
Other marketable equity securities	*25,000*	*25,000*
Totals	*$385,000*	*$365,000*

[1] In this context, a "portfolio" of securities includes all investments that are accorded similar accounting treatment and similar balance sheet classification. Those marketable equity securities classified as current assets and those classified as long-term investments represent *two separate portfolios*. Other "portfolios" of investment securities include debt securities classified as current assets, and debt securities classified as long-term investments.

[2] Recognition of these gains and losses in the income statement assumes that the investor classifies the marketable equity securities as current assets. Treatment of these gains and losses on a portfolio classified as a long-term investment is discussed on pages 644–646.

Because the total market value of the securities in our example is less than their cost to Eagle Corporation, the balance sheet valuation would be the lower amount of *$365,000*. This downward adjustment of $20,000 means that an *unrealized loss* of $20,000 will be included in the determination of the year's net income. The accounting entry would be as follows:

```
Dec. 31   Unrealized Loss on Marketable Equity Securities ...............   20,000
                   Valuation Allowance for Marketable Equity Securities ......        20,000
              To reduce the carrying value of the investment
              in marketable equity securities to the lower of cost
              or market.
```

The loss from the decline in the market value of securities owned is termed an *unrealized loss* to distinguish it from a loss which is realized by an actual sale of securities.

■ **The Valuation Account**   The Valuation Allowance for Marketable Equity Securities is a *contra-asset* account or *valuation* account. In the balance sheet, this valuation account is offset against the asset Marketable Equity Securities in the same manner as the Allowance for Doubtful Accounts is offset against Accounts Receivable. The following partial balance sheet illustrates the use of the Valuation Allowance for Marketable Equity Securities:

EAGLE CORPORATION
Partial Balance Sheet
December 31, 1991

Current assets:		
Cash..		$ 80,000
Marketable securities...	$385,000	
Less: Valuation allowance for marketable equity securities	20,000	365,000
Accounts receivable	$573,000	
Less: Allowance for doubtful accounts	9,000	564,000

■ **The Valuation Account Is Adjusted Every Period**   At the end of every period, the balance of the valuation account is adjusted so that marketable equity securities will be shown in the balance sheet at the lower of cost or current market value. If the valuation allowance must be increased because of further declines in market value, the adjusting entry will recognize an additional unrealized loss. On the other hand, if market prices have gone up since the last balance sheet date, the adjusting entry will reduce or eliminate the valuation allowance and recognize an *unrealized gain*.

To illustrate the adjustment of the valuation account, let us assume that by the end of 1992 the market value of Eagle Corporation's portfolio *increases* to an amount greater than cost. Since market value is no longer below cost, the valuation allowance, which has a credit balance of $20,000, is no longer needed. Thus, the following entry would be made to eliminate the balance of the valuation allowance:

Unrealized gain is limited to former balance of the valuation account

Dec. 31 *Valuation Allowance for Marketable Equity Securities* *20,000*

   Unrealized Gain on Marketable Equity Securities *20,000*

   To increase the carrying value of marketable
   equity securities to original cost following recovery
   of market value.

Note that the amount of unrealized gain recognized is limited to the amount in the valuation account. ***Increases in market value above cost are not recognized in the accounting records.*** In brief, when marketable equity securities have been written down to the lower of cost or market, they can be written back up ***to original cost*** if the market prices recover. However, current rules of the FASB do not permit recognition of a market rise above the original cost of the portfolio.

Because the valuation allowance is based upon a comparison of total ***portfolio*** cost and market value, the allowance cannot be directly associated with individual investments. The valuation allowance reduces the carrying value of the total portfolio but does not affect the individual carrying values of the investments which comprise the portfolio. Lower-of-cost-or-market adjustments, therefore, have ***no effect*** upon the gain or loss recognized when an investment is sold. When specific securities are sold, the gain or loss realized from the sale is determined by comparing the ***cost*** of the securities (without regard to lower-of-cost-or-market adjustments) to their selling price.[3]

■ **Income Tax Rule for Marketable Securities**   The FASB rules described above are not acceptable in determining income subject to income tax. The only gains or losses recognized for income tax purposes are ***realized*** gains and losses resulting from sale of an investment.

Presentation of Marketable Securities in Financial Statements

Gains and losses on the sale of investments, as well as interest and dividend revenue, are types of nonoperating income. These items should be specifically identified in the income statement and shown after the determination of operating income.

We have explained that different accounting principles are involved in accounting for marketable ***debt*** securities and marketable ***equity*** securities. In the balance sheet, however, these two types of investments generally are combined and shown under a single caption, such as ***Marketable Securities.***

Although marketable securities are usually classified as current assets in the balance sheet, they may alternatively be classified as long-term investments if management has a definite intention to hold the securities for more than one year. Regardless of how marketable ***equity*** securities are classified in the balance sheet, they are shown at the lower-of-cost-or-market value.

---

[3] The reader may notice that a decline in the market value of securities owned could be reported in the income statement on two separate occasions: first, as an unrealized loss in the period in which the price decline occurs; and second, as a realized loss in the period in which the securities are sold. However, after securities with market values below cost have been sold, the valuation allowance may be reduced or eliminated. The entry to reduce the valuation allowance involves the recognition of an unrealized gain, which offsets the unrealized losses reported in earlier periods.

The unrealized gains and losses resulting from application of the lower-of-cost-or-market rule, however, are presented differently in the financial statements depending upon whether the securities portfolio is classified as a current asset or a long-term investment. When the portfolio is viewed as a *current* asset, the unrealized gains and losses are closed into the Income Summary account and shown in the income statement along with other types of investment income.

The FASB has ruled that unrealized gains and losses on *long-term* investments should *not* be included in the measurement of the current year's net income, because management does not intend to sell these securities in the near future. Therefore, any net unrealized loss relating to long-term investments is shown in the balance sheet as a *reduction in stockholders' equity* and is *not* included in the income statement.

■ Presentation of Investments That Are Not Readily Marketable

Securities issued by small businesses may not be traded on securities exchanges and, therefore, may not have quoted market prices. These securities are not "readily marketable"; an investor owning such securities should classify the investment as long-term, rather than as a current asset. Also, such investments should be identified as "Other Long-Term Investments," rather than as marketable securities. As these securities do not have quoted market prices, the lower-of-cost-or-market rule is not applied. These investments normally are shown in the investor's balance sheet at *cost*.[4]

INVESTMENTS FOR PURPOSES OF INFLUENCE OR CONTROL

An investor may acquire enough of a company's common stock to *influence or control* that company's activities through the voting rights of the shares owned. Such large holdings of common stock create an important business relationship between the investor and the issuing company (called the *investee*). Since investments of this type cannot be sold without disrupting this relationship, they are not "readily marketable" and are *not* classified as marketable securities. Such investments are shown in the investor's balance sheet under the caption Long-Term Investments and are accounted for quite differently from an investment in marketable equity securities.

If an investor is able to exercise *significant influence* over the investee's management, dividends paid by the investee may no longer be a good measure of the investor's income from the investment. This is because the investor may influence the investee's dividend policy. In such cases, dividends paid by the investee are likely to reflect the *investor's* cash needs and income tax considerations, rather than the profitability of the investment.

For example, assume that Sigma Company owns all the common stock of Davis Company. For three years Davis Company is very profitable but pays no dividends, because Sigma Company has no need for additional cash. In the fourth year, Davis Company pays a large cash dividend to Sigma Company despite operating at a loss for that year. Clearly, it would be misleading for

[4] As with any asset valued at cost, the asset should be written down to an estimated recoverable amount if it becomes apparent that the original cost cannot be recovered.

Sigma Company to report no investment income while the company it owns is operating profitably, and then to show large investment income in a year when Davis Company incurred a net loss.

The investor does not have to own 100% of the common stock of the investee to exercise a significant degree of influence. An investor with much less than 50% of the voting stock may have influence or even effective control, since the remaining shares are not likely to vote as an organized block. In the absence of other evidence (such as another large stockholder), ownership of *20% or more* of the investee's common stock is viewed as giving the investor significant influence over the investee's policies and operations. In such cases, the investor should account for the investment by using the *equity method.*

The Equity Method

Objective 2
Account for an investment in common stock by the equity method.

When the equity method is used, an investment in common stock is first recorded at cost but later is adjusted each year for changes in the stockholders' equity in the investee. As the investee earns net income, the stockholders' equity in the company increases. An investor using the equity method recognizes its *proportionate share of the investee's net income* as an increase in the carrying value of its investment. A proportionate share of a net loss reported by the investee is recognized as a decrease in the investment.

When the investee pays dividends, the stockholders' equity in the company is reduced. The investor, therefore, treats dividends received from the investee as a conversion of the investment into cash, thus reducing the carrying value of the investment. Investments accounted for by the equity method are *not* adjusted to the lower of cost or market value. In effect, the equity method causes the carrying value of the investment to rise and fall with changes in the book value of the shares.

■ **Illustration of the Equity Method** Assume that Cove Corporation purchases 25% of the common stock of Bay Company for $200,000, which corresponds to the underlying book value. During the following year, Bay Company earns net income of $120,000 and pays dividends of $80,000. Cove Corporation would account for its investment as follows:

Investment in Bay Company	*200,000*	
Cash		*200,000*
To record acquisition of 25% of the common stock of Bay Company.		

Investment in Bay Company	*30,000*	
Investment Income		*30,000*
To increase the investment for 25% share of net income earned by Bay Company (25% × $120,000).		

Cash	*20,000*	
Investment in Bay Company		*20,000*
To reduce investment for dividends received from Bay Company (25% × $80,000).		

The net result of these entries by Cove Corporation is to increase the carrying value of the investment in Bay Company account by $10,000. This corresponds to 25% of the increase reported in Bay Company's retained earnings during the period [25% × ($120,000 − $80,000) = $10,000].

In this illustration of the equity method, we have made several simplifying assumptions: (1) Cove Corporation purchased the stock of Bay Company at a price equal to the underlying book value; (2) Bay Company had issued common stock only and the number of shares outstanding did not change during the year; and (3) there were no intercompany transactions between Cove Corporation and Bay Company. If we were to change any of these assumptions, the computations in applying the equity method would become more complicated. Application of the equity method in more complex situations is discussed in advanced accounting courses.

Parent and Subsidiary Companies

Objective 3
Explain how a parent company "controls" its subsidiaries.

A corporation which owns **all or a majority** of another corporation's capital stock is called a **parent** company, and the corporation which is wholly owned or majority-held is called a **subsidiary**.[5] Through the voting rights of the owned shares, the parent company can elect the board of directors of the subsidiary company and thereby control the subsidiary's resources and activities. In effect, the **affiliated companies** (the parent and its subsidiaries) function as a **single economic unit** controlled by the directors of the parent company. This relationship is illustrated in the diagram on the next page.

For simplicity, our illustration shows a parent company with only two subsidiaries. It is not unusual, however, for a parent company to own and control a dozen or more subsidiaries.

There are a number of economic, legal, and income tax advantages which encourage large business organizations to operate through subsidiaries rather than through a single legal entity. Although we think of Sears, General Electric, or IBM as single companies, each of these organizations is really a parent company with many subsidiaries. Since the parent company in each case controls the resources and activities of its subsidiaries, it is logical for us to consider an organization such as IBM as one **economic** entity.

Growth through the Acquisition of Subsidiaries

A parent company may acquire another corporation as a subsidiary by purchasing more than 50% of the other corporation's voting stock. The purchase of one corporation by another may be termed a **merger,** a **business combination,** an **acquisition,** or a **takeover.** The acquisition of new subsidiaries is a fast and effective way for a company to grow, to diversify into new product lines, and to acquire new technology. In one recent year, more than 2,500 existing corporations were acquired by other companies at a total cost of over $120 billion.

CASE IN POINT ■ Just a few of the large business combinations in recent years: Chevron Corporation greatly increased the size of its oil reserves by acquiring as a subsidiary one of its largest competitors, Gulf

---

[5] Ownership of a majority of a company's voting stock means holding at least 50% plus one share.

Corporation. R. J. Reynolds, a tobacco company, expanded its product line by acquiring the well-known food company, Nabisco Brands. Mobil Oil went into the department store business by acquiring the giant retailer, Montgomery Ward. Eli Lilly, a manufacturer of pharmaceutical products, acquired a "high tech" medical research company called Hybritech, Inc., in hopes that Hybritech's research will lead to important new pharmaceutical products.

PARENT COMPANY AND TWO SUBSIDIARIES

The acquisition of one corporation by another is, perhaps, the largest and most interesting of all business transactions. Such transactions may involve billions of dollars, bidding wars among prospective buyers, and dramatic increases in the value of a sought-after company's capital stock. Sometimes a company borrows vast amounts of money and acquires a corporation much larger than itself, thus doubling or tripling the size of the parent company overnight. For example, ABC, a major television network, recently was acquired by Capital Communications, Inc. Prior to the acquisition, Capital Communications was about one-fourth the size of ABC.

Financial Statements for a Consolidated Economic Entity

Objective 4
Describe the distinctive feature of consolidated financial statements.

Because the parent company and its subsidiaries are separate legal entities, separate financial statements are prepared for each company. In the *separate* financial statements of the parent company, the subsidiaries appear only as assets classified as long-term investments. Since the affiliated companies function as a single economic unit, the parent company also prepares *consolidated financial statements* which show the financial position and operating results of the *entire group of companies.*[6] It is these consolidated financial statements which are of greatest interest to the investing public and which are included in the parent company's annual report to its stockholders.

In consolidated financial statements, the parent company and its subsidiaries are viewed as *one business entity.* The distinctive feature of these statements is that the assets, liabilities, revenue, and expenses of *two or more separate legal entities* are combined in a single set of financial statements. For example, the amount shown as cash in a consolidated balance sheet is the total of the cash owned by all of the affiliated companies. Liabilities of the parent and subsidiary companies also are combined. Similarly, in a consolidated income statement, the revenue and expenses of the affiliated companies are combined to show the operating results of the consolidated economic entity.

Stockholders and creditors of the parent company have a vital interest in the financial results of all operations under the parent company's control, including those conducted by subsidiaries. Therefore, it is the consolidated financial statements which are included in the parent company's annual and quarterly reports to stockholders. (The separate financial statements of certain major subsidiaries sometimes are presented in footnotes to the consolidated financial statements.)

There are many interesting accounting issues involved in the preparation of consolidated financial statements. A brief introduction to some of these issues is provided in the following section of this chapter. However, *no special problems are posed in reading a set of consolidated financial statements.* The number of separate legal entities within the consolidated organization is an unimportant detail. For most purposes, consolidated financial statements may be interpreted as if the parent companies and its subsidiaries *were just one organization.*

CONSOLIDATED FINANCIAL STATEMENTS: CONCEPTS AND MECHANICS

Methods of Consolidation

The purchase of an entire corporation usually is a very big investment. To accumulate the money necessary to buy another corporation, the parent company often needs to issue capital stock or bonds payable. If the parent company pays cash or issues debt securities to purchase the other corporation's capital stock, the business combination is accounted for by the *purchase method.*

A second method of accounting for a business combination is called a *pooling of interests.* The pooling method may be appropriate if the stock of a subsidiary is acquired in direct exchange for shares of the parent company's capi-

---

[6] In the past, some subsidiaries were omitted from the consolidated financial statements for such reasons as the subsidiaries being engaged in business activities substantially different from those of the parent company. New rules, however, require every subsidiary controlled by the parent company to be included in the consolidated statements unless this control will be temporary. In this case, the investment in the subsidiary is shown in the balance sheet at cost and is classified as a long-term investment; dividends received are recorded as revenue.

tal stock.[7] A key aspect of such a transaction is that the former stockholders of the subsidiary *become stockholders in the parent corporation.* The vast majority of business combinations are viewed as purchases, rather than poolings. In this textbook, we shall illustrate only the purchase method of accounting for business combinations. The special case of a pooling-of-interests will be covered in more advanced accounting courses.

Consolidated financial statements are prepared by combining the amounts that appear in the separate financial statements of the parent and subsidiary companies. In the combining process, however, certain adjustments are made to *eliminate the effects of intercompany transactions* and thus to reflect the assets, liabilities, and stockholders' equity as those of a single economic entity.

Objective 5
Explain why intercompany transactions must be eliminated as a step in preparing consolidated financial statements.

■ **Intercompany Transactions**   The term *intercompany transactions* refers to transactions between affiliated companies. These transactions may include, for example, the sale of merchandise, the leasing of property, and the making of loans. When the affiliated companies are viewed separately, these transactions may create assets and liabilities for the individual companies. However, when the affiliated companies are viewed as a single business entity, these assets and liabilities are merely the result of internal transfers within the business organization and should *not appear* in the consolidated financial statements.

For example, if a subsidiary borrows money from the parent company, a note payable will appear as a liability in the balance sheet of the subsidiary company and a note receivable will appear as an asset in the separate balance sheet of the parent. When the two companies are viewed as a single consolidated entity, however, this "loan" is nothing more than a transfer of cash from one part of the business to another. Transferring assets between two parts of a single business entity does not create either a receivable or a payable for that entity. Therefore, the parent company's note receivable and the subsidiary's note payable should not appear in the consolidated financial statements.

■ **Preparing Consolidated Financial Statements**   Separate accounting records are maintained for each company in an affiliated group, but no accounting records are maintained for the consolidated entity. The amounts shown in consolidated financial statements *do not come from a ledger;* they are determined on a *working paper* by combining the amounts of like items on the financial statements of the affiliated companies. For example, the inventories of all the affiliated companies are combined into one amount for inventories. Entries to eliminate the effects of intercompany transactions are made *only* on this working paper. These elimination entries are *not recorded in the accounting records* of either the parent company or its subsidiaries.

---

[7] In addition to the parent company issuing only common stock in exchange for the subsidiary's shares, other specific criteria must be met for the affiliation to qualify as a pooling of interests. For example, at least 90% of the subsidiary's stock must be acquired within one year following the beginning of negotiations. For a more complete discussion of the differences between a purchase and a pooling of interests, see *APB Opinion No. 16,* "Business Combinations," AICPA (New York: 1970).

Consolidation at the Date of Acquisition

Objective 6
Prepare a consolidated balance sheet.

To illustrate the basic principles of consolidation, we will now prepare a consolidated balance sheet. Assume that on January 1 Post Corporation purchases for cash 100% of the capital stock of Sun Company at its book value of $300,000. (The shares are purchased from Sun Company's former stockholders.) Also on this date, Post Corporation lends $40,000 cash to Sun Company, receiving a note as evidence of the loan. Immediately after these two transactions, the separate balance sheet accounts of Post Corporation and Sun Company are as shown in the first two columns of the following working paper:

POST CORPORATION AND SUBSIDIARY
Working Paper—Consolidated Balance Sheet
January 1, 19__ (Date of Acquisition)

	POST CORPO-RATION	SUN COMPANY	INTERCOMPANY ELIMINATIONS		CONSOL-IDATED BALANCE SHEET
			DEBIT	CREDIT	
Cash.........................	60,000	45,000			105,000
Notes receivable	40,000			(b) 40,000	
Accounts receivable (net)	70,000	50,000			120,000
Inventories	110,000	95,000			205,000
Investment in Sun Company	300,000			(a) 300,000	
Plant & equipment (net)........	210,000	180,000			390,000
Totals.....................	790,000	370,000			820,000
Notes payable.................		40,000	(b) 40,000		
Accounts payable	125,000	30,000			155,000
Capital stock—Post Corporation	400,000				400,000
Capital stock—Sun Company		200,000	(a) 200,000		
Retained earnings— Post Corporation	265,000				265,000
Retained earnings— Sun Company		100,000	(a) 100,000		
Totals.....................	790,000	370,000	340,000	340,000	820,000

Explanation of elimination:
(a) To eliminate the Investment in Sun Company against Sun Company's stockholders' equity.
(b) To eliminate intercompany note receivable against related note payable.

Intercompany Eliminations

Before the balance sheet amounts of Post Corporation and Sun Company are combined, entries are made in the working paper to eliminate the effects of intercompany transactions. Intercompany eliminations may be classified into three basic types:

1 Elimination of intercompany stock ownership

2 Elimination of intercompany debt

3 Elimination of intercompany revenue and expenses

The first two types of eliminations are illustrated in our example of Post Corporation and Sun Company. The elimination of intercompany revenue and expenses will be discussed later in this chapter.

To understand the need for elimination entries, we must adopt the viewpoint of the consolidated entity, in which Post Corporation and Sun Company are regarded as two departments within a single company.

■ **Entry (a): Elimination of Intercompany Stock Ownership** The purpose of entry (a) in the working paper on page 650 is to eliminate from the consolidated balance sheet both the asset account and the stockholders' equity accounts representing the parent company's ownership of the subsidiary.

Post Corporation's ownership interest in Sun Company appears in the *separate* balance sheets of both corporations. In the parent's balance sheet, this ownership interest is shown as the asset, Investment in Sun Company. In the separate balance sheet of the subsidiary, the parent company's ownership interest is represented by the stockholders' equity accounts, Capital Stock and Retained Earnings. In the *consolidated* balance sheet, however, this "ownership interest" is neither an asset nor a part of stockholders' equity.

From the viewpoint of the single consolidated entity, *there are no stockholders in Sun Company.* "Stockholders" are outside investors who have an ownership interest in the business. All of Sun Company's capital stock is "internally owned" by another part of the consolidated entity. A company's "ownership" of its own stock does not create either an asset or stockholders' equity. Therefore the asset account, Investment in Sun Company, and Sun Company's related stockholders' equity accounts must be eliminated from the consolidated balance sheet.

■ **Entry (b): Elimination of Intercompany Debt** When Post Corporation loaned $40,000 to Sun Company, the parent company recorded a note receivable and the subsidiary recorded a note payable. This "receivable" and "payable" exist only when Post Corporation and Sun Company are viewed as two separate entities. When both corporations are viewed as a single company, this "loan" is merely a transfer of cash from one part of the business to another. Such internal transfers of assets do not create either a receivable or a payable for the consolidated entity. Therefore, entry (b) is made to eliminate Post Corporation's note receivable and Sun Company's note payable from the consolidated balance sheet.

After the necessary eliminations have been entered in the working paper, the remaining balance sheet amounts of Post Corporation and Sun Company are combined to determine the assets, liabilities, and stockholders' equity of the consolidated entity. The following consolidated balance sheet is then prepared from the last column of the working paper.

POST CORPORATION AND SUBSIDIARY
Consolidated Balance Sheet
January 1, 19__

ASSETS

Current assets:		
Cash...		$105,000
Accounts receivable (net)......................................		120,000
Inventories...		205,000
Total current assets..		$430,000
Plant & equipment (net)..		390,000
Total assets...		$820,000

LIABILITIES & STOCKHOLDERS' EQUITY

Current liabilities:		
Accounts payable...		$155,000
Stockholders' equity:		
Capital stock..	$400,000	
Retained earnings..	265,000	
Total stockholders' equity.................................		665,000
Total liabilities & stockholders' equity.......................		$820,000

■
Notice the stockholders' equity is that of the parent company

Acquisition of Subsidiary's Stock at a Price Above Book Value

When a parent company purchases a controlling interest in a subsidiary, it usually pays a price for the shares in excess of their book value.[8] We cannot ignore a difference between the cost of the parent company's investment and the underlying book value of these shares. In consolidation, the parent's investment is offset against the stockholders' equity accounts of the subsidiary, and if the two amounts are not equal, we must determine what the difference between them represents.

To illustrate, assume that C Company purchases all of the outstanding shares of D Company for $980,000. At the date of acquisition, D Company's balance sheet shows total stockholders' equity of $700,000, consisting of capital stock of $300,000 and retained earnings of $400,000. In preparing the elimination entry on the working papers for a consolidated balance sheet, we must determine what to do with the $280,000 difference between the price paid, $980,000, and the stockholders' equity of D Company, $700,000.

Why would C Company pay a price in excess of book value for D Company's stock? C Company's management must believe that either (1) the fair market value of certain specific assets of D Company (such as land or buildings) is in excess of book value, or (2) D Company's future earnings prospects are so favorable as to justify paying $280,000 for D Company's unrecorded *goodwill.*

If we assume that the $280,000 represents unrecorded goodwill, the entry in the working papers to eliminate C Company's investment account against the stockholders' equity accounts of D Company would be:

---

[8] The parent company also might acquire the shares of the subsidiary at a price below book value. This situation will be discussed in an advanced accounting course.

**Note: This entry
is made only in
the working
papers not in the
accounting
records of either
company**

Capital Stock—D Company	300,000	
Retained Earnings—D Company	400,000	
Goodwill	280,000	
Investment in D Company (C Company's asset account)		980,000

*To eliminate the cost of C Company's 100% interest in D Company
against D's stockholders' equity accounts and to recognize D Company's
unrecorded goodwill.*

(Although we have shown this entry in general journal form, it actually would be made only in the Intercompany Eliminations columns of the working paper for a consolidated balance sheet.)

The $280,000 of goodwill will appear as an asset only in the **consolidated** balance sheet.[9] This asset will be amortized to expense over its useful life.

Less Than 100% Ownership in Subsidiary

If a parent company owns a majority interest in a subsidiary but less than 100% of the outstanding shares, a new kind of ownership equity known as the *minority interest* will appear in the consolidated balance sheet. This minority interest represents the ownership interest in the subsidiary held by stockholders other than the parent company.

When there are minority stockholders, only the portion of the subsidiary's stockholders' equity owned by the parent company is eliminated. The remainder of the stockholders' equity of the subsidiary is included in the consolidated balance sheet under the caption Minority Interest.

To illustrate, assume that on December 31, Park Company purchases 75% of the outstanding capital stock of Sims Company for $150,000 cash, an amount equal to the book value of the stock acquired. The working paper to prepare a consolidated balance sheet on the date that control of Sims Company is acquired appears on the next page. Entry (*a*) in this working paper offsets Park Company's asset, Investment in Sims Company, against 75% of Sims Company's capital stock and retained earnings. The purpose of this entry is to eliminate intercompany stock ownership from the assets and stockholders' equity shown in the consolidated balance sheet. Entry (*b*) reclassifies the remaining 25% of Sims Company's capital stock and retained earnings into a special stockholders' equity account entitled Minority Interest. The FASB recommends that the minority interest appear in the stockholders' equity section of the consolidated balance sheet as follows:[10]

Stockholders' equity:	
Capital stock	$500,000
Minority interest	50,000
Retained earnings	100,000
Total stockholders' equity	$650,000

---

[9] If specific assets of D Company had been undervalued, the $280,000 would be allocated to increase the valuation of those assets in the consolidated working papers. The revaluation of specific assets is beyond the scope of our introductory discussion.

[10] Some companies emphasize the limited ownership of the minority stockholders by showing the minority interest in a special section of the balance sheet between liabilities and stockholders' equity. However, the FASB supports the classification of minority interest as stockholders' equity. See *FASB Statement of Financial Accounting Concepts No. 3*, "Elements of Financial Statements of Business Enterprise" (Stamford, Conn.: 1980), para. 179.

PARK COMPANY AND SUBSIDIARY
Working Paper—Consolidated Balance Sheet
December 31, 19__ (Date of Acquisition)

	PARK COMPANY	SIMS COMPANY	INTERCOMPANY ELIMINATIONS		CONSOL-IDATED BALANCE SHEET
			DEBIT	CREDIT	
Cash..........................	200,000	50,000			250,000
Other assets	500,000	210,000			710,000
Investment in Sims Company	150,000			(a) 150,000	
Totals.....................	850,000	260,000			960,000
Liabilities	250,000	60,000			310,000
Capital stock—Park Company	500,000				500,000
Capital stock—Sims Company		120,000	(a) 90,000 (b) 30,000		
Retained earnings— Park Company	100,000				100,000
Retained earnings— Sims Company		80,000	(a) 60,000 (b) 20,000		
Minority interest (25% of $200,000)....................				(b) 50,000	50,000
Totals.....................	850,000	260,000	200,000	(b) 200,000	960,000

Explanation of elimination:
(a) To eliminate Park Company's investment in 75% of Sims Company's stockholders' equity.
(b) To classify the remaining 25% of Sims Company's stockholders' equity as a minority interest.

■ **Minority Interest** Why is the minority interest shown separately in the consolidated balance sheet instead of being included in the amounts shown for capital stock and retained earnings? The reason for this separate presentation is to distinguish between the ownership equity of the controlling stockholders and the equity of the minority stockholders.

The stockholders in the parent company own the controlling interest in the consolidated entity. Because these stockholders elect the directors of the parent company, they control the entire group of affiliated companies. The minority interest, however, has *no control* over any of the affiliated companies. Because they own shares only in a subsidiary, they cannot vote for the directors of the parent company. Also, they can never outvote the majority stockholder (the parent company) in electing the directors or establishing the policies of the subsidiary.

The minority stockholders receive 25% of the dividends declared by Sims Company but do not participate in dividends declared by the parent company. The controlling stockholders, on the other hand, receive all the dividends declared by Park Company but do not receive dividends declared by the subsidiary.

Consolidated Income Statement

A consolidated income statement is prepared by combining the revenue and expense accounts of the parent and subsidiary. Revenue and expenses arising from *intercompany transactions* are eliminated because they reflect transfers of assets from one affiliated company to another and do not change the net assets from a consolidated viewpoint.

■ **Elimination of Intercompany Revenue and Expenses** Some of the more common examples of intercompany items that should be eliminated in preparing a consolidated income statement are:

■ Sales to affiliated companies

■ Cost of goods sold resulting from sales to affiliated companies

■ Interest expense on loans from affiliated companies

■ Interest revenue on loans made to affiliated companies

■ Rent or other revenue received for services rendered to affiliated companies

■ Rent or other expenses paid for services received from affiliated companies

Because of the complexity of the intercompany eliminations, the preparation of a consolidated income statement and a consolidated statement of retained earnings are topics appropriately deferred to an advanced accounting course.

Accounting for Investments in Corporate Securities: A Summary

In this chapter, we have discussed the accounting principles applied to investments in corporate securities under various circumstances. The accounting treatment accorded to investments in *bonds* depends upon whether the investment is viewed as a current asset or a long-term investment. The accounting treatment of an investment in *stock* depends primarily upon the *degree of control* which the investor is able to exercise over the issuing corporation. These relationships are summarized below and on page 656.

SITUATION	ACCOUNTING PRACTICE
Investments in bonds:	
Classified as current asset	*Combined with current asset portfolio of stocks and shown as Marketable Securities. Interest revenue accrues each period. Difference between cost and maturity value (discount or premium) generally not amortized.*
Classified as a long-term investment	*Combined with long-term portfolio of stocks and shown as marketable securities, under the classification, Long-Term Investments. Interest revenue accrues each period. Difference between cost and maturity value is amortized.*

Investments in stocks:

Noninfluential interest (ownership of less than 20% of the voting stock)	*(Readily marketable) Shown as a marketable security (may be classified as a current asset or a long-term investment). Each portfolio valued at lower-of-cost-or-market. Dividends recorded as revenue when received.*
	(Not readily marketable) Shown as a long-term investment and carried at cost. Dividends recorded as revenue when received.
Influential but noncontrolling interest (ownership from 20% to 50% of the voting stock)	*Shown as a long-term investment, accounted for by the equity method.*
Controlling interest (ownership of more than 50% of voting stock)	*The assets, liabilities, revenue, and expenses of controlled subsidiary are combined with those of the parent corporation in consolidated financial statements.*

End-of-Chapter Review

CONCEPTS INTRODUCED IN CHAPTER 17

The major concepts introduced in this chapter include:

■ The reason for different accounting principles in recognizing interest revenue from investments in bonds and dividend revenue from investments in stocks.

■ Accounting for purchases and sales of marketable debt securities (bonds), the accrual of interest revenue, and the possible need to amortize the difference between cost and maturity value.

■ Accounting for purchases and sales of marketable equity securities (stocks), the receipt of dividend revenue, and application of the lower-of-cost-or-market rule.

■ The reasons for using different methods in accounting for investments in marketable equity securities and investments held for the purpose of exercising influence or control over the issuing corporation.

■ The use of the equity method in accounting for influential (but noncontrolling) investments in common stock.

■ How one corporation may "control" other corporations.

■ The nature of consolidated financial statements.

■ The need for eliminating the effects of intercompany transactions from consolidated financial statements.

This chapter concludes our four-chapter introduction to the corporate form of business organization. Because of the dominant role of corporations in our economy, this form of organization will be emphasized in the remainder of this textbook and in most following accounting courses.

KEY TERMS INTRODUCED OR EMPHASIZED IN CHAPTER 17

Business combination   The combining of two or more companies into a single economic entity. Also called a *merger, acquisition,* or *takeover.*

Consolidated financial statements   A set of statements presenting the combined financial position and operating results of a consolidated entity consisting of a parent company and one or more subsidiaries.

Equity method   The method of accounting used when the investment by one corporation in another is large enough to influence the policies of the *investee.* The investor recognizes as investment income its proportionate share of the investee's net income, rather than considering dividends received as income.

Intercompany transactions   Transactions between two affiliated companies. The effects of intercompany transactions, such as intercompany loans, are eliminated as a step in preparing consolidated financial statements.

Marketable securities   A highly liquid type of investment which can be sold at any time without interfering with normal operation of the business. Usually classified as a current asset second only to cash in liquidity.

Minority interest   Shares of a subsidiary owned by investors other than the parent.

Parent company   A corporation which owns a controlling interest in another company.

Purchase method   The method used in preparing consolidated financial statements when the parent company has purchased the shares of its subsidiary by paying cash or issuing debt securities. The purchase method is not used for those special transactions which qualify as a *pooling-of-interests.*

Subsidiary   A corporation in which a controlling stock interest is held by another corporation (the parent).

Unrealized gains and losses   Increases and decreases in the market value of an asset which have not yet been realized through sale of the asset. Unrealized losses and some unrealized gains on a portfolio of marketable equity securities are recognized in the accounting records.

SELF-TEST QUESTIONS

The answers to these questions appear on page 669.

1 During 1990, Bonner Company bought and sold a short-term investment in $200,000 face value, 9% bonds which pay interest each April 1 and October 1. Bonner purchased the bonds at 98 plus accrued interest on February 1, 1990, and held the bonds until December 1, 1990, when the entire investment was sold for $200,000, including accrued interest. Each of the following is true, *except:*

   a Bonner recognizes bond interest revenue of $15,000 for 1990.

   b Bonner paid a total of $202,000 to acquire the investment on February 1, 1990.

   c Bonner recognizes a gain of $1,000 on the sale of these marketable securities on December 1, 1990.

   d Bonner received semiannual interest checks in the amounts of $3,000 on April 1 and $9,000 on October 1.

2 Early in 1991, Rodgers Corp. purchased for $1,000,000 a portfolio of several marketable equity securities as a short-term investment. The market value of this portfolio was $900,000 at the end of 1991, $990,000 at the end of 1992, and $1,180,000 at the end of 1993. Based on these facts: (more than one answer may be correct)

a Rodgers will recognize in its income statement an unrealized loss of $100,000 in 1991, and unrealized gains of $90,000 in both 1992 and 1993.

b At the end of 1992, Rodgers' ledger account Valuation Allowance for Marketable Equity Securities should have a $10,000 credit balance.

c In 1993, Rodgers' income statement should include an unrealized gain of $10,000.

d If the entire portfolio is sold in 1994 for $1,200,000, Rodgers' income statement for 1994 will include a realized gain of $20,000.

3 Which of the following is *true* with regard to investments in corporate securities?

a When an investor acquires more than 20% of the common stock of a company, the investment is no longer classified as a marketable equity security even if it is traded on the stock exchanges.

b An investor who owns more than 20% of the outstanding bonds of a company should account for this investment by using the equity method.

c Whenever an investor owns less than 50% of the common stock of a corporation, the investment is valued at the lower of cost or market value.

d Regardless of percentage ownership, an investor in the common stock of another corporation records dividends as revenue when they are received.

4 On January 1, 1990, Stockdale Company purchased 30% (30,000 shares) of the common stock of Equus, Inc., for $600,000. At December 31, 1990, Equus reported net income of $200,000 and paid cash dividends of $80,000. At December 31, 1990, Equus' stock is trading at $19 per share. With regard to this investment, Stockdale's financial statements for 1990 should report:

a Dividend revenue of $24,000.

b Investment in Equus, Inc., of $636,000.

c Investment income of $36,000.

d Unrealized loss on marketable equity securities of $30,000.

5 When consolidated financial statements are issued by a parent and a subsidiary:

a The consolidated balance sheet includes the stockholders' equity accounts of both the parent and the subsidiary.

b Intercompany transactions are reported in separate sections of the income statement and the balance sheet.

c There is no need for the parent and the subsidiary to maintain separate accounting records or prepare separate financial statements.

d Minority interest appears in the consolidated balance sheet whenever the parent does not own 100% of the outstanding shares of the subsidiary.

Assignment Material

REVIEW QUESTIONS

1 Why are investments in marketable securities usually regarded as current assets?

2 Why must an investor who owns numerous marketable securities maintain a marketable securities subsidiary ledger?

3 If an investor buys a bond between interest dates, he or she pays as a part of the purchase price the accrued interest since the last interest date. On the other hand, if the investor buys a share of common or preferred stock, no "accrued dividend" is added to the quoted price. Explain why this difference exists.

4 Should stock dividends received be considered revenue to an investor? Explain.

5 Because of a decline in market prices, National Corporation had to write down the carrying value of its investment in marketable securities by $70,000 in the current year. In the determination of net income for the current year, does it make any difference if National Corporation's investment portfolio is classified as a current asset or a long-term investment? Explain fully.

6 In the current asset section of its balance sheet, Delta Industries shows marketable equity securities at a market value $120,000 below cost. If the market value of these securities rises by $190,000 during the next accounting period, how large an unrealized gain (if any) should Delta Industries include in its next income statement? Explain fully.

7 How does the financial reporting requirement of valuing marketable equity securities at the lower-of-cost-or-market value compare with income tax rules concerning marketable securities?

8 When should investors use the equity method to account for an investment in common stock?

9 Dividends on stock owned are usually recognized as income when they are received. Does an investor using the *equity method* to account for an investment in common stock follow this policy? Explain fully.

10 Alexander Corporation owns 80% of the outstanding stock of Benton Company. Explain the basis for the assumption that these two companies constitute a single economic entity operating under unified control.

11 What are consolidated financial statements? Explain briefly how these statements are prepared.

12 List the three basic types of intercompany eliminations which should be made as a step in the preparation of consolidated financial statements.

13 Explain why the price paid to acquire a controlling interest in a subsidiary company may be different from the book value of the equity acquired.

14 The following items appear on a consolidated balance sheet: "Minority interest in subsidiary . . . $620,000." Explain the nature of this item, and where you would expect to find it on the consolidated balance sheet.

15 Briefly explain when a business combination is viewed as a *purchase* and when it might be viewed as a *pooling of interests.*

16 As a general rule, when are consolidated financial statements appropriate?

17 What groups of investors are likely to be primarily interested in consolidated financial statements? Why?

EXERCISES

**Exercise 17-1
Accounting
terminology**

Listed below are nine technical accounting terms introduced in this chapter:

Lower of cost or market	*Consolidated financial statements*	*Elimination of intercompany transactions*
Subsidiary	*Minority interest*	*Marketable debt securities*
Investee	*Equity method*	*Parent company*

Each of the following statements may (or may not) describe one of these technical terms. For each statement, indicate the accounting term described, or answer "None" if the statement does not correctly describe any of the terms.

a A single set of financial statements showing the assets, liabilities, revenue, and expenses of all companies in a given industry.

b A corporation which owns at least 20% of the voting shares of another company, but which does not have controlling interest in that company.

c Procedures used to account for an investment which gives the investor significant influence over the policies of the other corporation.

d An investment in voting stock of a large corporation that is too small to give the investor significant influence within the issuing company and that is almost as liquid an asset as cash.

e A corporation that owns and controls other corporate entities.

f Method used in the balance sheet valuation of a portfolio of marketable equity securities.

g A separate legal entity owned and controlled by another corporation.

h An accounting procedure which is a necessary step in preparing consolidated financial statements, but which does not involve making entries in the ledger accounts.

Exercise 17-2
Investment in bonds

Yamato Company purchased as a short-term investment $100,000 face value of the 9% bonds of Lorenzo, Inc., on March 31 of the current year, at a total cost of $101,250, including interest accrued since January 1. Interest is paid by Lorenzo, Inc., on June 30 and December 31. On July 31, four months after the purchase, Yamato Company sold the bonds and interest accrued since July 1 for a total price of $101,050.

Prepare in general journal form all entries required in the accounting records of Yamato Company relating to the investment in Lorenzo, Inc., bonds. (Commissions are to be ignored.)

Exercise 17-3
Investment in stocks

Prepare the journal entries in the accounting records of Axel Masters, Inc., to record the following transactions. Include a memorandum entry on July 9 to show the change in the cost basis per share.

Jan. 7   Purchased as a temporary investment 1,000 shares of Reed Company common stock at a price of $62.50 per share, plus a brokerage commission of $500.

Feb. 12   Received a cash dividend of $1 per share on the investment in Reed Company stock.

July 9   Received an additional 50 shares of Reed Company common stock as a result of a 5% stock dividend.

Aug. 14   Sold 500 shares of Reed Company common stock at a price of $65 per share, less a brokerage commission of $290.

Exercise 17-4
Valuation at lower-of-cost-or-market

The cost and market value of Edgebrook Corporation's portfolio of marketable equity securities at the end of 1991 and 1992 are shown below. The marketable equity securities are viewed as a current asset.

	COST	MARKET VALUE
1991	$79,000	$66,800
1992	87,000	91,600

Show how the portfolio would appear in the balance sheet at the end of 1991 and at the end of 1992. If appropriate, use a valuation account in your presentation.

Exercise 17-5
The equity method

On Jan 1, 1991, City Broadcasting purchases 40% of the common stock of News Service, Inc., for $300,000, which corresponds to the underlying book value. News Service, Inc., has issued common stock only. At December 31, 1991, News Service, Inc., reported net income for the year of $140,000 and paid cash dividends of $60,000. City Broadcasting uses the equity method to account for this investment.

Instructions

a Prepare all journal entries in the accounting records of City Broadcasting relating to the investment during 1991.

b During 1992, News Service, Inc., reports a net loss of $110,000 and pays no dividends. Compute the carrying value of City Broadcasting's investment in News Service, Inc., at the end of 1992.

Exercise 17-6
Eliminating intercompany stock ownership; recording goodwill

Midtown Cafeteria has purchased all the outstanding shares of Ballpark Caterers for $290,000. At the date of acquisition, Ballpark Caterers' balance sheet showed total stockholders' equity of $240,000, consisting of $100,000 capital stock and $140,000 retained earnings. The excess of this purchase price over the book value of Ballpark Caterers' shares is regarded as payment for Ballpark Caterers' unrecorded goodwill.

In general journal entry form, prepare the eliminating entry necessary on the working paper to consolidate the balance sheets of these two companies.

Exercise 17-7
Computing consolidated amounts

Selected account balances from the separate balance sheets of Adams Company and its wholly owned subsidiary, Baker Company, are shown below:

	ADAMS COMPANY	BAKER COMPANY	CONSOLIDATED
Accounts receivable	$ 400,000	$ 160,000	$
Accrued rent receivable—Adams Company ..		4,000	
Investment in Baker Company	1,240,000		
Accounts payable	320,000	120,000	
Accrued expenses payable.................	11,000		
Bonds payable	1,400,000	900,000	
Capital stock.............................	2,000,000	1,000,000	
Retained earnings	1,820,000	240,000	

Adams Company owes Baker Company $4,000 in accrued rent payable and Baker Company owes Adams Company $30,000 on account for services rendered. Show the amount that should appear in the consolidated balance sheet for each of these selected accounts. If the account would not appear in the consolidated balance sheet, indicate "None" as the consolidated account balance.

Exercise 17-8
Preparing a consolidated balance sheet; minority interest

On June 30, P Company *purchased* 80% of the stock of S Company for $480,000 in cash. The separate condensed balance sheets immediately after the purchase are shown below:

	P COMPANY	S COMPANY
Cash...	$ 140,000	$ 90,000
Investment in S Company...................................	480,000	
Other assets	2,180,000	710,000
	$2,800,000	$800,000
Liabilities	$ 600,000	$200,000
Capital stock..	1,200,000	400,000
Retained earnings	1,000,000	200,000
	$2,800,000	$800,000

Instructions Prepare a consolidated balance sheet immediately after P Company acquired control of S Company.

PROBLEMS

Group A

**Problem 17A-1
Investments in
bonds (includes
amortization of
discount)**

On May 1, 1991, Dillon Press purchased $60,000 face value of the 9% bonds of Southern Gas Co. at a price of 95, plus accrued interest. The bonds pay interest semiannually on June 30 and December 31, and mature on June 30, 1995 (50 months from the date of purchase). Dillon Press views these bonds as a long-term investment and follows the policy of amortizing the difference between the cost of the bonds and their maturity value by the straight-line method at the end of each year.

Instructions

a Prepare the journal entries to record the following transactions in 1991:

(1) Purchase of the bonds on May 1

(2) Receipt of semiannual bond interest on June 30

(3) Receipt of semiannual bond interest on December 31 and amortization of the difference between cost of the bonds and their maturity value for 8 months.

b Assume that an unexpected need for cash forces Dillon Press to sell the entire investment in Southern Gas Co. bonds for $57,190 plus accrued interest on January 31, 1992. Prepare the journal entries to:

(1) Accrue bond interest receivable at January 31, 1992, and to amortize the difference between cost and maturity value for the one month since year-end.

(2) Record the sale of the bonds on January 31.

**Problem 17A-2
Investments in
marketable equity
securities**

During the current year, Overnight Air Freight (OAF) engaged in the following transactions relating to marketable equity securities:

Feb. 28 Purchased 1,000 shares of National Products common stock for $63 per share plus a broker's commission of $600.

Mar. 15 National Products paid a cash dividend of 50 cents per share which had been declared on February 20 payable on March 15 to stockholders of record on March 6.

May 31 National Products distributed a 20% stock dividend.

Nov. 15 National Products distributed additional shares as the result of a 2 for 1 stock split.

Dec. 5 OAF sold 600 shares of its National Products stock at $28 per share, less a broker's commission of $150.

Dec. 10 National Products paid a cash dividend of 25 cents per share. Dividend was declared November 20 payable December 10 to stockholders of record on November 30.

As of December 31, National Products common stock had a market value of $24 per share. OAF classifies its National Products stock as a current asset and owns no other marketable equity securities.

Instructions

Prepare journal entries to account for this investment in OAF's accounting records. Include memorandum entries when appropriate to show changes in the cost basis per share. Also include the year-end adjusting entry, if one is necessary, to reduce the investment to the lower-of-cost-or-market value. For journal entries involving computations, the explanation portion of the entry should include the computation.

**Problem 17A-3
Accounting for
marketable
securities: a
comprehensive
problem**

The portfolio of marketable securities owned by Bar Harbor Corporation at January 1 consisted of the three securities listed below. All marketable securities are classified as current assets.

*$50,000 maturity value Copper Products Co. 9% bonds due
Apr. 30, 2002. Interest is payable on Apr. 30 and Oct. 31 of each
year. Cost basis $990 per bond* 49,500

1,500 shares of Aztec Corporation common stock. Cost basis

  $38.50 share 57,750

800 shares of Donner-Pass, Inc., $6.00 cumulative preferred stock.

  Cost basis $55 per share 44,000

Jan. 10   Acquired 500 shares of Rhodes Co. common stock at $71½ per share. Broker-age commissions paid amounted to $250.

Jan. 21   Received quarterly dividend of $1.50 per share on 800 shares of Donner-Pass, Inc., preferred stock.

Mar. 5   Sold all 800 shares of Donner-Pass, Inc., preferred stock at $58 per share less a brokerage commission of $200.

Apr. 1   Received additional 1,000 shares of Rhodes Co. common stock as a result of a 3 for 1 split.

Apr. 30   Received semiannual interest on Copper Products Co. 9% bonds. Accrued interest of $750 had been recorded on December 31 of last year in the Bond Interest Receivable account.

June 30   Sold $25,000 face value of Copper Products Co. 9% bonds at 93, plus two months' accrued interest, less a commission of $125.

July 10   Received additional 150 shares of Aztec Corporation common stock as a result of 10% stock dividend.

Sept. 24   Sold 650 shares of Aztec Corporation common stock at $40 per share, less a brokerage commission of $150.

Oct. 31   Received semiannual interest payment on remaining $25,000 face value of Copper Products Co. 9% bonds.

At December 31, 19__ , the quoted market prices of the marketable equity securities owned by Bar Harbor Corporation were as follows: Aztec Corporation common stock, $37; and Rhodes Co. common stock, $18.

Instructions

a Prepare journal entries to record the transactions listed above. Include an adjusting entry to record accrued interest on the remaining Copper Products Co. bonds through December 31. (Do not consider a lower-of-cost-or-market adjustment in part **a**.)

b Prepare a schedule showing the cost and market value of the marketable *equity* securities owned by Bar Harbor Corporation at December 31. Prepare an adjusting entry, if one is required, to reduce the portfolio to the lower of cost or market. (At the beginning of the current year, the market value of the portfolio was above cost and the Valuation Allowance for Marketable Equity Securities account had a zero balance.)

Problem 17A-4
Basic elements
of a consolidated
balance sheet

On December 31, 1992, Northwest Building Materials purchased for cash 80% of the capital stock of Corning Electrical Supply. The separate year-end balance sheets of the two companies include the following items:

	NORTHWEST BUILDING MATERIALS	CORNING ELECTRICAL SUPPLY
Accounts receivable—Corning Electrical Supply	*160,000*	*–0–*
Investment in Corning Electrical Supply	*1,200,000*	*–0–*
Total assets	*9,800,000*	*1,700,000*
Accounts payable—Northwest Building Materials	*–0–*	*160,000*
Total liabilities	*3,600,000*	*700,000*
Total stockholders' equity	*6,200,000*	*1,000,000*

The excess of the $1,200,000 purchase price over the book value of Corning's shares is regarded as a purchase of Corning's unrecorded goodwill.

Instructions   Showing your computations, compute the amounts to appear in the year-end consolidated balance sheet for each of the following:

a Goodwill

b Minority interest

c Total assets

d Total liabilities

e Total stockholders' equity (including minority interest)

Problem 17A-5
Preparing a
consolidated
balance sheet

On June 30, 19__, American Sportswear paid $1 million cash to acquire all the outstanding capital stock of Jeans by Jorge. Immediately *before* this acquisition, the condensed separate balance sheets of the two companies were as shown below. (As these balance sheets were prepared immediately *before* the acquisition, the current assets of American Sportswear still include the $1 million in cash which will be paid to acquire Jeans by Jorge.

ASSETS	AMERICAN SPORTSWEAR	JEANS BY JORGE
Current assets	$1,880,000	$ 320,000
Plant and equipment	1,520,000	900,000
Total assets	$3,400,000	$1,220,000

LIABILITIES & STOCKHOLDERS' EQUITY		
Current liabilities	$ 540,000	$ 280,000
Long-term debt	1,200,000	200,000
Capital stock	600,000	300,000
Retained earnings	1,060,000	440,000
Total liabilities & stockholders' equity	$3,400,000	$1,220,000

The excess of the $1 million purchase price over the book value of Jeans by Jorge shares is regarded as payment for unrecorded goodwill.

Instructions   Prepare a consolidated balance sheet for American Sportswear and its newly acquired subsidiary (Jeans by Jorge) on June 30, 19__, the date of acquisition.

Problem 17A-6
Working paper
for a
consolidated
balance sheet

On September 30, 1991, Wheelhouse Restaurants purchased 80% of the stock of Cajun Jack's for cash. The separate balance sheets of the two companies immediately after this purchase are shown below:

ASSETS	WHEELHOUSE RESTAURANTS	CAJUN JACK'S
Cash	$ 35,000	$ 18,000
Note receivable from Cajun Jack's	50,000	
Accounts receivable	90,000	50,000
Inventories	100,000	145,000
Investment in Cajun Jack's	475,000	
Plant and equipment	350,000	450,000
Accumulated depreciation	(140,000)	(83,000)
Total assets	$960,000	$580,000

LIABILITIES & STOCKHOLDERS' EQUITY

Notes payable	$100,000	$ 50,000
Accounts payable	120,000	60,000
Accrued liabilities	30,000	20,000
Common stock	400,000	200,000
Retained earnings	310,000	250,000
Total liabilities & stockholders' equity	$960,000	$580,000

Other information

(1) Wheelhouse Restaurants' asset account, Investment in Cajun Jack's, represents ownership of 80% of Cajun Jack's stockholders' equity, which has a book value of $360,000 [80% × ($200,000 + $250,000) = $360,000]. The remainder of the Investment account balance represents the purchase of Cajun Jack's unrecorded goodwill.

(2) Cajun Jack's $50,000 note payable is owed to Wheelhouse Restaurants. (All interest has been paid through September 30.)

(3) The accounts payable of Wheelhouse Restaurants include $9,000 owed to Cajun Jack's. This amount also is included in the accounts receivable of Cajun Jack's.

Instructions

Prepare a working paper for a consolidated balance sheet at September 30, 1991—immediately after the purchase of Cajun Jack's. Include at the bottom of the working paper explanations of the elimination entries.

Group B

**Problem 17B-1
Investments in
bonds (includes
amortization of
premium)**

On March 1, 1991, Allied Chemical purchased $50,000 face value of the 12% bonds of Tiger Trucking at a price of 104 plus accrued interest. The bonds pay interest semiannually on June 30 and December 31, and mature on June 30, 1994 (40 months from the date of purchase). Allied Chemical views these bonds as a long-term investment and follows the policy of amortizing the difference between the cost of the bonds and their maturity value by the straight line method at the end of each year.

Instructions

a Prepare the journal entries to record the following transactions in 1991:

(1) Purchase of the bonds on March 1

(2) Receipt of semiannual bond interest on June 30

(3) Receipt of semiannual bond interest on December 31 and amortization of the difference between cost of the bonds and their maturity value for 10 months.

b Assume that an unexpected need for cash forces Allied Chemical to sell the entire investment in Tiger Trucking bonds for $51,800, plus accrued interest on January 31, 1992. Prepare the journal entries to:

(1) Accrue bond interest receivable at January 31, 1992, and to amortize the difference between cost and maturity value for the one month since year-end.

(2) Record the sale of the bonds on January 31.

**Problem 17B-2
Investments in
marketable equity
securities**

On January 31, Talley Mfg. Co. purchased as a temporary investment 1,000 shares of Reese Company common stock at $52 per share plus broker's commission of $500. Reese Company declared a cash dividend of $1.50 per share on February 15, payable on March 31 to stockholders of record on March 15.

On June 30, Reese Company distributed a 5% stock dividend. On July 31, the shares were split 2 for 1 and the additional shares distributed to stockholders. On August 25, a cash dividend of $1 per share was declared, payable on September 30 to stockholders of record on September 15. Talley Mfg. Co. sold 1,000 shares of Reese Company stock at $34 a share on December 31. Commission charges on the sale amounted to $400.

Instructions

Prepare journal entries to record the above events in the accounts of Talley Mfg. Co. Include memorandum entries when appropriate, even though ledger accounts are not affected. For journal entries involving computations, the explanation portion of the entry should include the computations.

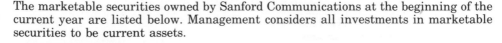

**Problem 17B-3
Accounting for
marketable
securities: a
comprehensive
problem**

The marketable securities owned by Sanford Communications at the beginning of the current year are listed below. Management considers all investments in marketable securities to be current assets.

$60,000 maturity value of Micro Computer Co. 12% bonds due
  Apr. 30, 1999. Interest payable on Apr. 30 and Oct. 31 of each
  year. Cost basis $990 per bond $59,400
2,000 shares of Ryan Corporation common stock. Cost basis $42
  per share 84,000

Transactions relating to marketable securities during the current year were as follows:

Jan. 21 Received semiannual cash dividend of $1.10 per share on the 2,000 shares of Ryan Corporation common stock.

Feb. 8 Purchased 1,000 shares of Gramm Co. common stock at $39¾ per share. Brokerage commissions amounted to $250.

Mar. 15 Received an additional 1,000 shares of Gramm Co. common stock as a result of a 2 for 1 split.

Apr. 30 Received semiannual interest on Micro Computer Co. 12% bonds. Accrued interest of $1,200 had been recorded on December 31 of last year in the Bond Interest Receivable account.

May 31 Sold $40,000 face value of Micro Computer Co. 12% bonds at a price of 103, plus one month's accrued interest, less a brokerage commission of $200.

July 21 Received cash dividend on 2,000 shares of Ryan Corporation common stock. Amount of dividend has increased to $1.20 per share.

Oct. 18 Received an additional 100 shares of Ryan Corporation common stock as a result of a 5% stock dividend.

Oct. 19 Sold 600 shares of Ryan Corporation common stock at $37 per share, less a brokerage commission of $150.

Oct. 31 Received semiannual interest payment on remaining $20,000 face value of Micro Computer Co. 12% bonds.

At December 31 of the current year, the quoted market prices of the marketable equity securities owned by Sanford Communications were as follows: Ryan Corporation, $33 per share; Gramm Co., $21.50 per share.

Instructions **a** Prepare journal entries to record the transactions listed above. Include an adjusting entry to record the accrued interest on the remaining Micro Computer Co. bonds through December 31. (Do not consider a lower-of-cost-or-market adjustment in part **a.**)

b Prepare a schedule showing the cost and market value of the marketable *equity* securities owned by Sanford Communications at December 31. Prepare an adjusting entry, if one is required, to reduce the portfolio to the lower of cost or market. (At the beginning of the current year, the market value of the portfolio was above cost and the Valuation Allowance for Marketable Equity Securities account had a zero balance.)

On December 31, 1992, Old Towne Furniture purchased for cash 70% of the capital stock of Marvelous Mattress Co. The separate year-end balance sheets of the two companies include the following items:

	OLD TOWNE FURNITURE	MARVELOUS MATTRESS CO.
Accounts receivable—Old Towne Furniture	–0–	380,000
Investment in Marvelous Mattress Co.	950,000	–0–
Total assets	6,100,000	1,900,000
Accounts payable—Marvelous Mattress Co.	380,000	–0–
Total liabilities	4,100,000	900,000
Total stockholders' equity	2,000,000	1,000,000

The excess of the $950,000 purchase price over the book value of the acquired shares in Marvelous Mattress Co. is regarded as a purchase of Marvelous Mattress Co.'s unrecorded goodwill.

Instructions   Showing your computations, compute the amounts to appear in the year-end consolidated balance sheet for each of the following:

a Goodwill

b Minority interest

c Total assets

d Total liabilities

e Total stockholders' equity (including minority interest)

Problem 17B-5
Preparing a
consolidated
balance sheet

Just *before* Morris Theaters purchased Video Rentals on December 31, 19__, the condensed balance sheets of the two companies were as follows:

ASSETS	MORRIS THEATERS	VIDEO RENTALS
Current assets	$1,630,000	$240,000
Other assets	1,970,000	660,000
Total assets	$3,600,000	$900,000

LIABILITIES & STOCKHOLDERS' EQUITY		
Current liabilities	$ 580,000	$120,000
Long-term debt	900,000	208,000
Capital stock	1,000,000	200,000
Retained earnings	1,120,000	372,000
Total liabilities & stockholders' equity	$3,600,000	$900,000

Instructions   Assume that on December 31, 19__, Morris Theaters purchased (using current assets) all the outstanding capital stock of Video Rentals for $800,000. The excess of this purchase price over the book value of Video Rentals' acquired shares is regarded as payment for Video Rentals' unrecorded goodwill. Prepare a consolidated balance sheet for Morris Theaters and its new subsidiary (Video Rentals) at the date of acquisition.

Problem 17B-6
Working papers
for a
consolidated
balance sheet

On March 31, 1991, Cross Yacht Design purchased for $162,000 cash 90% of the capital stock of Wing Sails, Inc. Shown on page 668 are the separate balance sheets of the two corporations immediately *after* this purchase:

ASSETS	CROSS YACHT DESIGN	WING SAILS, INC.
Cash..	$ 50,000	$ 20,000
Accounts receivable	85,000	30,000
Inventories	60,000	40,000
Investment in Wing Sails, Inc.....................................	162,000	
Plant and equipment	250,000	180,000
Accumulated depreciation	(50,000)	(40,000)
Total assets	$557,000	$230,000

LIABILITIES & STOCKHOLDERS' EQUITY		
Accounts payable	$ 40,000	$ 40,000
Accrued liabilities	25,000	10,000
Common stock..	300,000	100,000
Retained earnings	192,000	80,000
Total liabilities & stockholders' equity	$557,000	$230,000

Additional Information

(1) Cross Yacht purchased the stock in Wing Sails at a price equal to its book value ($180,000 × 90% = $162,000).

(2) Wing Sails owes Cross Yacht Design $7,000 in accrued rent payable. This amount is included in the accrued liabilities of the subsidiary and the accounts receivable of the parent company.

(3) Cross Yacht Design owes Wing Sails $16,000 for services rendered. This amount is included in the parent company's accounts payable and the subsidiary's accounts receivable.

Instructions Prepare a working paper for a consolidated balance sheet at March 31, 1991—the date of this business combination. Include at the bottom of the working paper explanations of the elimination entries.

BUSINESS DECISION CASE

Case 17-1 Apples and oranges Dane Electronics has the following investments in the securities of other corporations:

a 2,000 shares of the common stock of Apple Computer. Apple is a large publicly owned corporation and sells at a quoted market price in excess of Dane's cost. Dane's management stands ready to sell these shares at any time.

b $100,000 face amount of Central Telephone's 3⅝% bonds maturing in 10 years. The bonds were acquired at a substantial discount. These bonds are readily marketable, and Dane's management stands ready to sell them to meet any current cash requirements.

c 5 million of the 15 million voting shares in Micro-Desk, Inc. Micro-Desk is a publicly owned corporation, and its quoted stock price recently has declined to a level below Dane's cost.

d $300,000 face value of Carver Stores 12¼% bonds maturing in 10 years. These bonds are readily marketable at a quoted price. However, Dane intends to hold these bonds until their maturity date. The bonds were acquired at a premium.

e 90% of the voting stock in Consumer Finance Corp. Consumer Finance is a profitable company, but it is not publicly owned. There is no quoted market price for Consumer's capital stock.

f 50,000 of the 1 million outstanding shares of SIMCO Products, a publicly owned corporation. The market price of SIMCO's shares has declined steadily since Dane purchased its shares. Dane's management, however, believes in the long-run prospects of SIMCO and intends to hold this investment for at least 10 years.

g 5,000 shares of voting stock of Orange Express. Orange Express operates profitably, but is not publicly owned and has no quoted market value. This investment does not give Dane an influential interest in Orange Express. Dane's management stands ready to sell these shares at any time that an attractive offer is received.

Instructions Explain how Dane Electronics should account for each of these investments. Your explanations should include discussion of the three topics listed below. You may find the summary on page 655 helpful in preparing your answers to this case.

(1) Whether the investment qualifies for consolidation and, if not, the appropriate balance sheet classification of the investment account.

(2) The basis for balance sheet valuation (e.g., consolidation, equity method, cost, cost adjusted for amortization of bond discount or premium, or lower-of-cost-or-market).

(3) The factors involved in the recognition of income (or loss) from the investment (e.g., Do lower-of-cost-or-market adjustments enter into the determination of net income? Is bond discount or premium amortized? Are dividends recorded as income when received? Is the equity method in use?).

ANSWERS TO SELF-TEST QUESTIONS
1 d   2 b and c   3 a   4 b   5 d

Appendix B
International Accounting and Foreign Currency Transactions

This appendix addresses some special accounting issues encountered by companies which conduct part of their business in foreign countries or in foreign currencies. First, we discuss the meaning of currency exchange rates and the reasons that cause these rates to fluctuate. The accounting for purchases and sales of merchandise in transactions that span national boundaries is illustrated and explained. Special attention is given to gains and losses caused by fluctuations in exchange rates.

After studying this appendix you should be able to meet these Learning Objectives:

1 Translate an amount of foreign currency into the equivalent number of U.S. dollars.

2 Explain why exchange rates fluctuate and what is meant by a "strong" or a "weak" currency.

3 Compute the gain or loss on a receivable or payable stated in terms of a foreign currency when exchange rates fluctuate.

4 Explain how fluctuations in foreign exchange rates affect companies with receivables or with payables stated in terms of foreign currencies.

From what geographical area does Bank of America—the largest bank in California—earn most of its revenue? The answer is abroad—that is, from its operations in foreign countries. Bank of America is not alone in its pursuit of business on a worldwide basis. Most large corporations, such as Exxon, IBM, Volkswagen, and Sony, do business in many countries. Coca-Cola, for example, has operations in more than 150 countries throughout the world. Companies that do business in more than one country often are described as *multinational* corporations. The extent to which foreign sales contributed to the revenue of several well-known multinational corporations in a recent year is shown below:

COMPANY	HEADQUARTERS	TOTAL REVENUE (IN MILLIONS)	% EARNED FROM FOREIGN OPERATIONS
Nestles	Switzerland	$13,626	97.2
Sony	Japan	4,528	74.5
Exxon	USA	97,173	71.4
Volkswagen	W. Germany	15,427	67.9
Bank of America	USA	14,955	53.8
British Petroleum	Great Britain	51,353	52.3
IBM	USA	34,364	44.6
Coca-Cola	USA	6,250	42.7

Most large and well-known multinational corporations are headquartered in the highly industrialized countries, such as the United States, Japan, Great Britain, and the countries of Western Europe. Virtually every country, however, has many companies that engage in international business activity.

What Is International Accounting?

Accounting for business activities that span national borders comprises the field of international accounting. In this appendix, we emphasize accounting for transactions with foreign companies. We also briefly discuss some of the problems of preparing consolidated financial statements for American-based companies with subsidiaries located in foreign countries. Our discussion is limited to basic concepts; the details and complexities of international accounting will be covered in advanced accounting courses.

Foreign Currencies and Exchange Rates

One of the principal problems in international accounting arises because every country uses a different currency. Assume, for example, that a Japanese company sells merchandise to an American corporation. The Japanese company will want to be paid in Japanese currency—yen, but the American company's bank account contains U.S. dollars. Thus, one currency must be converted into another.

Most banks participate in an international currency exchange, which enables them to buy foreign currencies at the prevailing *exchange rate.* Thus, our American corporation can pay its liability to the Japanese company through the international banking system. The American company will pay its bank in dollars. The bank will then use these dollars to purchase the required amount of yen on the international currency exchange and will arrange for delivery of the yen to the Japanese company's bank.[1]

---

[1] Alternatively, the American company may send the Japanese company a check (or a bank draft) stated in dollars. The Japanese company can then arrange to have the dollars converted into yen through its bank in Japan.

■ **Exchange Rates** A currency exchange rate is the ratio at which one currency may be converted into another. Thus, the exchange rate may be viewed as the "price" of buying units of foreign currency, stated in terms of the domestic currency (which for our purpose is U.S. dollars). Exchange rates fluctuate daily, based upon the worldwide supply and demand for particular currencies. The current exchange rate between the dollar and most major currencies is published daily in the financial press. For example, a few of the exchange rates recently listed in *The Wall Street Journal* are shown below:

COUNTRY	CURRENCY	EXCHANGE RATE (IN DOLLARS)
Britain	*Pound (£)*	*$1.7730*
France	*French franc (FF)*	*.1772*
Japan	*Yen (¥)*	*.0080*
Mexico	*Peso ($)*	*.0005*
West Germany	*Deutsche mark (DM)*	*.5974*

Objective 1
Translate an amount of foreign currency into the equivalent number of U.S. dollars.

Exchange rates may be used to determine how much of one currency is equivalent to a given amount of another currency. Assume that the American company in our preceding example owes the Japanese company 1 million yen (expressed ¥1,000,000). How many dollars are needed to settle this obligation, assuming that the current exchange rate is $.0080 per yen? To restate an amount of foreign currency in terms of the equivalent amount of U.S. dollars, we multiply the foreign currency amount by the exchange rate, as illustrated below.[2]

Amount Stated in Foreign Currency	× Exchange Rate (in Dollars) =	Equivalent Number of U.S. Dollars
¥1,000,000	× $.0080 per yen =	$8,000

This process of restating an amount of foreign currency in terms of the equivalent number of dollars is called *translating* the foreign currency.

Objective 2
Explain why exchange rates fluctuate and what is meant by a "strong" or a "weak" currency.

■ **Why Exchange Rates Fluctuate** An exchange rate represents the "price" of one currency, stated in terms of another. These prices fluctuate, based upon supply and demand, just as do the prices of gold, silver, soybeans, and other commodities. When the demand for a particular currency exceeds supply, the price (exchange rate) rises. If supply exceeds demand, the exchange rate falls.

What determines the demand and supply for particular currencies? In short, it is the quantities of the currency that traders and investors seek to buy or to sell. Buyers of a particular currency include purchasers of that country's exports and foreign investors seeking to invest in the country's capital markets. Sellers of a currency include companies within the country that are importing goods from abroad and investors within the country who would prefer

---

[2] To convert an amount of dollars into the equivalent amount of a foreign currency, we would *divide* the dollar amount by the exchange rate. For example, $8,000 ÷ $.0080 per yen = ¥1,000,000.

to invest their funds abroad. Thus, two major factors in the demand and supply for a currency are (1) the ratio of the country's imports to its exports, and (2) the real rate of return available in the country's capital markets.

To illustrate the first of these points, let us consider Japan and Great Britain. Japan exports far more than it imports. As a result, Japan's customers must buy yen in the international currency market in order to pay for their purchases. This creates a strong demand for the yen and has caused its price (exchange rate) to rise relative to most other currencies. Great Britain, on the other hand, imports more than it exports. Thus, British companies must sell British pounds in order to acquire the foreign currencies needed to pay for their overseas purchases. This has increased the supply of pounds in the currency markets, and the price of the pound has declined substantially over the last several decades.

The second factor—the international attractiveness of a country's capital markets—depends upon both political stability and the country's interest rates relative to its internal rate of inflation. When a politically stable country offers high interest rates relative to inflation, foreign investors will seek to invest their funds in that country. First, however, they must convert their funds into that country's currency. This demand tends to raise the exchange rate for that currency. High interest rates relative to the internal rate of inflation were the major reason for the strength of the U.S. dollar during the early 1980s. Later in the decade, however, lower interest rates, along with large trade deficits (imports in excess of exports), significantly reduced the value of the dollar.

■ **Exchange Rate "Jargon"** In the financial press, currencies are often described as "strong," "weak," or as rising or falling against one another. For example, an evening newscaster might say that "A strong dollar rose sharply against the weakening British pound, but fell slightly against the Japanese yen and the Swiss franc." What does this mean about exchange rates?

To understand such terminology, we must remember that an exchange rate is simply the price of one currency *stated in terms of another currency.* Throughout this appendix, we refer to the prices of various foreign currencies stated in terms of *U.S. dollars.* In other countries, however, the U.S. dollar is a foreign currency, and its price is stated in terms of the local (domestic) currency.

To illustrate, consider our table from *The Wall Street Journal,* which shows the exchange rate for the Japanese yen to be $.0080. At this exchange rate, ¥125 is equivalent to $1 (¥125 × $.0080 per yen = $1). Thus, while we would say that the exchange rate for the Japanese yen is *$.0080,* the Japanese would say that the exchange rate for the U.S. dollar is *¥125.*

Now let us assume that the exchange rate for the yen (stated in dollars) rises to $.0082. At this exchange rate, ¥122 is approximately equivalent to $1 (¥122 × $.0082 = $1). In the United States, we would say that the exchange rate for the yen has *risen* from $.0080 to $.0082. In Japan, however, they would say that the exchange rate for the dollar has *fallen* from ¥125 to ¥122. In the financial press, it might be said that "the yen has risen against the dollar," or that "the dollar has fallen against the yen." The two statements mean the same thing—that the yen has become more valuable relative to the dollar.

Now let us return to our original phrase, "A strong dollar rose sharply against the weakening British pound, but fell slightly against the Japanese yen and the Swiss franc." When exchange rates are stated in terms of U.S. dollars, this statement means that the price (exchange rate) of the British pound fell sharply, but the prices of the Japanese yen and the Swiss franc rose slightly. A currency is described as "strong" when its exchange rate is rising relative to most other currencies and as "weak" when its exchange rate is falling.

Accounting for Transactions with Foreign Companies

Objective 3
Compute the gain or loss on a receivable or payable stated in terms of a foreign currency when exchange rates fluctuate.

When an American company buys or sells merchandise in a transaction with a foreign company, the transaction price may be stipulated either in U.S. dollars or in units of the foreign currency. If the price is stated in *dollars,* the American company encounters no special accounting problems. The transaction may be recorded in the same manner as are similar transactions with domestic suppliers or customers.

If the transaction price is stated in terms of the *foreign currency,* the American company encounters two accounting problems. First, since the American company's accounting records are maintained in dollars, the transaction price must be translated into dollars before the transaction can be recorded. The second problem arises when (1) the purchase or sale is made *on account,* and (2) the exchange rate *changes* between the date of the transaction and the date that the account is paid. This fluctuation in the exchange rate will cause the American company to experience either a gain or a loss in the settlement of the transaction.

■ **Credit Purchases with Prices Stated in a Foreign Currency**
Assume that on August 1 an American company buys merchandise from a British company at a price of 10 thousand British pounds (£10,000), with payment due in 60 days. The exchange rate on August 1 is $1.80 per British pound. The entry on August 1 to record this purchase (assuming use of the periodic inventory system) is shown below:

Purchases	18,000	
Accounts Payable		18,000

To record the purchase of merchandise from a British company for £10,000 when the exchange rate is $1.80 per pound (£10,000 × $1.80 = $18,000).

Let us now assume that by September 30, when the £10,000 account payable must be paid, the exchange rate has fallen to $1.78 per British pound. If the American company had paid for the merchandise on August 1, the cost would have been $18,000. On September 30, however, only $17,800 is needed to pay off the £10,000 liability (£10,000 × $1.78 = $17,800). Thus, *the decline in the exchange rate has saved the company $200.* This savings is recorded in the accounting records as a *Gain on Fluctuations in Foreign Exchange Rates.* The entry on September 30 to record payment of the liability and recognition of this gain would be:

Accounts Payable	18,000	
Cash..		17,800
Gain on Fluctuations in Foreign Exchange Rates.....................		200

To record payment of £10,000 liability to British company and to recognize gain from decline in exchange rate:

Original liability (£10,000 × $1.80)	$18,000
Amount paid (£10,000 × $1.78)...............................	17,800
Gain from decline in exchange rate...........................	$ 200

Now let us assume that instead of declining, the exchange rate had *increased* from $1.80 on August 1 to $1.83 on September 30. Under this assumption, the American company would have to pay $18,300 in order to pay off the £10,000 liability on September 30. Thus, the company would be paying *$300 more* than if the liability had been paid on August 1. This additional $300 cost was caused by the increase in the exchange rate and should be recorded as a loss. The entry on September 30 would be:

Accounts Payable...	18,000	
Loss on Fluctuations in Foreign Exchange Rates	300	
Cash		18,300

To record payment of £10,000 liability to British company and to recognize loss from increase in exchange rate:

Original liability (£10,000 × $1.80)	$18,000
Amount paid (£10,000 × $1.83)...............................	18,300
Loss from increase in exchange rate	$ 300

In summary, having a liability that is fixed in terms of a foreign currency results in a gain for the debtor if the exchange rate falls between the date of the transaction and the date of payment. The gain results because fewer dollars will be needed to repay the debt than had originally been owed. An increase in the exchange rate, on the other hand, causes the debtor to incur a loss. In this case, the debtor will have to spend more dollars than had originally been owed in order to purchase the foreign currency needed to pay the debt.

■ **Credit Sales with Prices Stated in a Foreign Currency**   A company that makes credit sales at prices stated in a foreign currency also will experience gains or losses from fluctuations in the exchange rate. To illustrate, let us change our preceding example to assume that the American company *sells* merchandise on August 1 to the British company at a price of £10,000. We shall again assume that the exchange rate on August 1 is $1.80 per British pound and that payment is due in 60 days. The entry on August 1 to record this sale is:

Accounts Receivable	18,000	
Sales		18,000

To record sale to British company with sales price set at £10,000 (£10,000 ×$1.80) = $18,000. To be collected in 60 days.

In 60 days (September 30), the American company will collect from the British company the U.S. dollar equivalent of £10,000. If the exchange rate on September 30 has fallen to $1.78 per pound, the American company will collect only $17,800 (£10,000 × $1.78 = $17,800) in full settlement of its account receivable. Since the receivable had originally been equivalent to $18,000, the decline in the exchange rate has caused a loss of $200 to the American company. The entry to be made on September 30 is:

Cash	17,800	
Loss on Fluctuations in Foreign Exchange Rates	200	
Accounts Receivable		18,000

To record collection of £10,000 receivable from British company and to recognize loss from fall in exchange rate since date of sale:

Original sales price (£10,000 × $1.80)	$18,000
Amount received (£10,000 × $1.78)	17,800
Loss from decline in exchange rate	$ 200

Now consider the alternative case, in which the exchange rate rises from $1.80 at August 1 to $1.83 at September 30. In this case, the British company's payment of £10,000 will convert into $18,300, creating a gain for the American company. The entry on September 30 would then be:

Cash	18,300	
Accounts Receivable		18,000
Gain on Fluctuations in Foreign Exchange Rates		300

To record collection of £10,000 receivable from British company and to recognize gain from increase in exchange rate:

Original sales price (£10,000 × $1.80)	$18,000
Amount received (£10,000 × $1.83)	18,300
Gain from increase in exchange rate	$ 300

■ **Adjustment of Foreign Receivables and Payables at the Balance Sheet Date**   We have seen that fluctuations in exchange rates may cause gains or losses for companies with accounts payable or receivable in foreign currencies. The fluctuations in the exchange rates occur on a daily basis. For convenience, however, the company usually waits until the account is paid or collected before recording the related gain or loss. An exception to this convenient practice occurs at the end of the accounting period. An *adjusting entry* must be made to recognize any gains or losses that have accumulated on any foreign payables or receivables through the balance sheet date.

To illustrate, assume that on November 10 an American company buys equipment from a Japanese company at a price of 10 million yen (¥10,000,000), payable on January 10 of the following year. If the exchange rate is $.0080 per yen on November 10, the entry to record the purchase would be:

Equipment	80,000	
Accounts Payable		80,000

To record purchase of equipment from Japanese company at a price of ¥10,000,000, payable January 10 (¥10,000,000 × $.0080 = $80,000).

Now assume that on December 31, the exchange rate has fallen to $.0077 per yen. At this exchange rate, the American company's account payable is equivalent to only $77,000 (¥10,000,000 × $.0077). Gains and losses from changes in exchange rates are recognized in the period *in which the change occurs*. Therefore, the American company should make an adjusting entry to restate its liability at the current dollar-equivalent and to recognize any related gain or loss. This entry, which would be dated December 31, is as follows:

Accounts Payable	3,000	
Gain on Fluctuations in Foreign Exchange Rates....................		3,000
To adjust balance of ¥10,000,000 account payable to amount indicated by		
year-end exchange rate:		
Original account balance	$80,000	
Adjusted balance (¥10,000,000 × $.0077).....................	77,000	
Required adjustment	$ 3,000	

Similar adjustments should be made for any other accounts payable or receivable at year-end that are fixed in terms of a foreign currency.

If the exchange rate changes again between the date of this adjusting entry and the date that the American company pays the liability, an additional gain or loss must be recognized. Assume, for example, that on January 10 the exchange rate has risen to $.0078 per yen. The American company must now spend $78,000 to buy the ¥10,000,000 needed to pay its liability to the Japanese company. Thus, the rise in the exchange rate has caused the American company a $1,000 loss since year-end. The entry to record payment of the account on January 10 would be:

Accounts Payable	77,000	
Loss on Fluctuations in Foreign Exchange Rates	1,000	
Cash...		78,000
To record payment of ¥10,000,000 payable to Japanese company and to		
recognize loss from rise in exchange rate since year-end:		
Account payable, December 31	$77,000	
Amount paid, January 10	78,000	
Loss from increase in exchange rate	$ 1,000	

Gains and losses from fluctuations in foreign exchange rates should be shown in the income statement following the determination of income from operations. This treatment is similar to that accorded to gains and losses from the sale of plant assets or investments.

Currency Fluctuations—Who Wins and Who Loses?

Objective 4
Explain how fluctuations in foreign exchange rates affect companies with receivables or payables stated in terms of foreign currencies.

Gains and losses from fluctuations in exchange rates are sustained by companies (or individuals) that have either payables or receivables that are *fixed in terms of a foreign currency*. American companies that import foreign products usually have large foreign liabilities. Companies that export American products to other countries are likely to have large receivables stated in foreign currencies.

As foreign exchange rates (stated in dollars) fall, American-based importers will gain and exporters will lose. When a foreign exchange rate falls, the foreign currency becomes *less expensive*. Therefore, importers will have to spend fewer dollars to pay their foreign liabilities. Exporters, on the other hand, will have to watch their foreign receivables become worth fewer and fewer dollars.

When foreign exchange rates rise, this situation reverses. Importers will lose, because more dollars are required to pay the foreign debts. Exporters will gain, because their foreign receivables become equivalent to an increasing number of dollars.

■ **Exchange Rates and Competitive Prices**   Up to this point, we have discussed only the gains and losses incurred by companies that have receivables or payables stated in terms of a foreign currency. However, fluctuations in exchange rates change the *relative prices* of goods produced in different countries. Exchange rate fluctuations may make the prices of a country's products more or less competitive both at home and to customers throughout the world. Even a small store with no foreign accounts receivable or payable may find its business operations greatly affected by fluctuations in foreign exchange rates.

Consider, for example, a small store in Kansas that sells an American-made brand of television sets. If foreign exchange rates fall, which happens when the dollar is strong, the price of foreign-made television sets will decline. Thus, the store selling American-made television sets may have to compete with stores selling imported television sets at lower prices. Also, a strong dollar makes American goods *more expensive to customers in foreign countries.* Thus, an American television manufacturer will find it more difficult to sell its products abroad.

The situation reverses when the dollar is weak—that is, when foreign exchange rates are relatively high. A weak dollar makes foreign imports more expensive to American consumers. Also, a weak dollar makes American products less expensive to customers in foreign countries.

In summary, we may say that a strong U.S. dollar *helps companies that sell foreign-made goods in the American market.* A weak dollar, on the other hand, *gives a competitive advantage to companies that sell American products both at home and abroad.*

Consolidated Financial Statements That Include Foreign Subsidiaries

In Chapter 17, we discussed the principles of preparing consolidated financial statements. These statements view the operations of the parent company and its subsidiaries as if the affiliated companies were a single business entity. Several special accounting problems arise in preparing consolidated financial statements when subsidiaries operate in foreign countries. First, the accounting records of the foreign subsidiaries must be translated into U.S. dollars. Second, the accounting principles in use in the foreign countries may differ significantly from American generally accepted accounting principles.

These problems pose interesting challenges to professional accountants and will be addressed in later accounting courses. Readers of the financial statements of American-based corporations, however, need not be concerned with these technical issues. The consolidated financial statements of these companies are expressed in U.S. dollars and conform to American generally accepted accounting principles.

Assignment Material

REVIEW QUESTIONS

1 Translate the following amounts of foreign currency into an equivalent number of U.S. dollars using the exchange rates in the table on page 672.

    a £300,000

    b ¥275,000

    c DM25,000

2 Assume that an American company makes a purchase from a West German company and agrees to pay a price of 2 million deutsche marks.

    a How will the American company determine the cost of this purchase for the purpose of recording it in the accounting records?

    b Briefly explain how an American company can arrange the payment of deutsche marks to a West German company.

3 A recent newspaper shows the exchange rate for the British pound at $1.78 and for the yen at $.0083. Does this indicate that the pound is a stronger currency than the yen? Explain.

4 Identify two factors that tend to make the exchange rate for a country's currency rise.

5 Explain how an increase in a foreign exchange rate will affect a U.S. company that makes:

    a Credit sales to a foreign company at prices stated in the foreign currency.

    b Credit purchases from a foreign company at prices stated in the foreign currency.

    c Credit sales to a foreign company at prices stated in U.S. dollars.

6 You are the purchasing agent for an American business that purchases merchandise on account from companies in Mexico. The exchange rate for the Mexican peso has been falling against the dollar and the trend is expected to continue for at least several months. Would you prefer that the prices for purchases from the Mexican companies be specified in U.S. dollars or in Mexican pesos? Explain.

7 CompuTech is an American-based multinational corporation. Foreign sales are made at prices set in U.S. dollars, but foreign purchases are often made at prices stated in foreign currencies. If the exchange rate for the U.S. dollar has risen against most foreign currencies throughout the year, would CompuTech have recognized primarily gains or losses as a result of exchange rate fluctuations? Explain.

PROBLEMS

Problem 1
Currency fluctuations: who wins and who loses?

Indicate whether each of the companies or individuals in the following independent cases would benefit more from a strong U.S. dollar (relatively low foreign exchange rates) or a weak U.S. dollar (relatively high foreign exchange rates). Provide a brief explanation of your reasoning.

    a An American tourist visiting England.

    b A small store that sells American-made video recorders in Toledo, Ohio. The store has no foreign accounts receivable or payable.

    c Toyota (the Japanese auto manufacturer).

    d The Mexico City dealer for Caterpillar tractors (made in the U.S.).

e Boeing (an American aircraft manufacturer that sells many planes to foreign customers).

f A Nikon camera store in Beverly Hills, California. (Nikon cameras are made in Japan.)

Problem 2
Gains and losses from exchange rate fluctuations

Europa-West is an American corporation that purchases automobiles from European manufacturers for distribution in the United States. A recent purchase involved the following events:

Nov. 12 Purchased automobiles from West Berlin Motors for DM2,000,000, payable in 60 days. Current exchange rate, $.5975 per deutsche mark. (Europa-West uses the perpetual inventory system; debit the Inventory account.)

Dec. 31 Made year-end adjusting entry relating to the DM2,000,000 account payable to West Berlin Motors. Current exchange rate, $.6150 per deutsche mark.

Jan. 11 Issued a check to World Bank for $1,220,000 in full payment of the account payable to West Berlin Motors.

Instructions

a Prepare in general journal form the entries necessary to record the preceding events.

b Compute the exchange rate (price) of the deutsche mark in U.S. dollars on January 11.

Problem 3
Gains and losses from rate fluctuations: an alternative problem

IronMan, Inc., is an American company that manufactures exercise machines and also distributes several lines of imported bicycles. Selected transactions of the company are listed below:

Oct. 4 Purchased manufacturing equipment from Rhine Mfg. Co., a West German company. The purchase price was DM150,000, due in 60 days. Current exchange rate, $.6000 per deutsche mark. (Debit the Equipment account.)

Oct. 18 Purchased 4,000 racing bicycles from Ninja Cycles, a Japanese company, at a price of ¥80,000,000. Payment is due in 90 days; the current exchange rate is $.0080 per yen. (IronMan uses the perpetual inventory system; debit the Inventory account.)

Nov. 15 Purchased 1,000 touring bicycles from Royal Lion Ltd., a British corporation. The purchase price was £199,500, payable in 30 days. Current exchange rate, $1.80 per British pound.

Dec. 3 Issued check to First Bank for the U.S. dollar-equivalent of DM150,000 in payment of the account payable to Rhine Mfg. Co. Current exchange rate, $.6150 per deutsche mark.

Dec. 15 Issued check to First Bank for dollar-equivalent of £199,500 in payment of the account payable to Royal Lion Ltd. Current exchange rate, $1.77 per British pound.

Instructions

a Prepare entries in general journal form to record the preceding transactions.

b Prepare the December 31 adjusting entry relating to the account payable to Ninja Cycles. The year-end exchange rate is $.0082 per Japanese yen.

Problem 4
A comprehensive problem on exchange rate fluctuations

Wolfe Computer is an American company that manufactures portable personal computers. Many of the components for the computer are purchased abroad, and the finished product is sold in foreign countries as well as in the United States. Among the recent transactions of Wolfe are the following:

Oct. 28 Purchased from Mitsutonka, a Japanese company, 20,000 disc drives. The purchase price was ¥200,000,000, payable in 30 days. Current exchange rate, $.0082 per yen. (Wolfe uses the perpetual inventory method; debit the Inventory of Raw Materials account.)

Nov. 9   Sold 700 personal computers to the Bank of England for £510,000 due in 30 days. The cost of the computers, to be debited to the Cost of Goods Sold account, was $518,000. Current exchange rate, $1.75 per British pound. (Use one compound journal entry to record the sale and the cost of goods sold. In recording the cost of goods sold, credit Inventory of Finished Goods.)

Nov. 27   Issued a check to Inland Bank for $1,720,000 in full payment of account payable to Mitsutonka.

Dec. 2   Purchased 10,000 amber monitors from German Optical for DM1,200,000, payable in 60 days. Current exchange rate, $.6000 per deutsche mark. (Debit Inventory of Raw Materials.)

Dec. 9   Collected dollar-equivalent of £510,000 from the Bank of England. Current exchange rate, $1.73 per British pound.

Dec. 11   Sold 10,000 personal computers to Computique, a French retail chain, for FF75,000,000, due in 30 days. Current exchange rate, $.1700 per French franc. The cost of the computers, to be debited to Cost of Goods Sold and credited to Inventory of Finished Goods, is $7,400,000.

Instructions   **a** Prepare in general journal form the entries necessary to record the preceding transactions.

b Prepare the adjusting entries needed at December 31 for the DM1,200,000 account payable to German Optical and the FF75,000,000 account receivable from Computique. Year-end exchange rates, $.5950 per deutsche mark and $.1710 per French franc. (Use a separate journal entry to adjust each account balance.)

c Compute the unit sales price of computers in U.S. dollars in either the November 9 or December 11 sales transactions. (The sales price is the same in each transaction.)

d Compute the exchange rate for the yen, stated in U.S. dollars, on November 27.

ANSWERS TO SELF-TEST QUESTIONS

1 d   **2 b and c**   **3 a**   **4 b**   **5 d**

PART 6

Special Reports and Analysis of Financial Statements

In the next three chapters we discuss several specialized uses of accounting information, including the determination of taxable income, the measurement of cash flows, and the analysis of financial statements by investors. Part 6 also includes two appendixes. In the first, we illustrate and explain a popular alternative to the method recommended by the FASB for measuring and reporting cash flows. In the second, we show how accounting information can be modified to reflect the effects of inflation.

The Comprehensive Problem for Part 6 provides an opportunity to analyze and evaluate the financial statements of a well-known corporation.

18 Income Taxes and Business Decisions

19 Measuring Cash Flows

Appendix C: The Indirect Method

20 Analysis and Interpretation of Financial Statements

Appendix D: Accounting for the Effects of Inflation

Income Taxes and Business Decisions

For many college students, this chapter may be their only academic exposure to the truly remarkable system known as federal income taxes. The early part of the chapter presents a brief history and rationale of the federal income tax structure, including the Tax Reform Act of 1986. This introduction stresses the pervasive influence of income taxes upon economic activity. The next section portrays the basic process of determining taxable income and the tax liability for individual taxpayers. The income tax computations for a small corporation are also explained and illustrated. The final section of the chapter gives students an understanding of the important role that tax planning can play in the affairs of individuals and also in the decision-making of a business entity.

After studying this chapter you should be able to meet these Learning Objectives:

1 Describe the history of the federal income tax and the highlights of the Tax Reform Act of 1986.

2 Discuss the advantages of the cash basis of accounting for preparation of individual income tax returns.

3 State the formula for determining the taxable income of an individual.

4 Explain the recent changes in the taxation of capital gains and losses.

5 Contrast the determination of taxable income for a corporation with that for an individual.

6 Discuss the concept of interperiod income tax allocation.

7 Explain how tax planning is used in choosing the form of business organization and the capital structure.

Tax Reform Act of 1986

The United States Congress spent much of the year 1986 in writing a new tax bill—a bill that brought sweeping changes in income tax rules and rates. Although annual changes in the income tax laws have become normal practice, the changes made by the Tax Reform Act of 1986 were the most drastic in the history of the federal income tax. Annual changes however, will continue. In fact, this 1986 bill prescribed changes in rules and rates effective in 1987, further changes in 1988, and still more changes in 1989. In other words, the drastic changes created by the 1986 law were phased in over a period of years. Three striking characteristics of recent tax legislation are the lowering of tax rates, the elimination of numerous deductions, and a shifting of the tax burden from individuals to corporations.

Objective 1
Describe the history of the federal income tax and the highlights of the Tax Reform Act of 1986.

Income tax returns are based on accounting information. In many respects this information is consistent with the accounting concepts we have discussed in earlier chapters. However, the measurement of *taxable income* includes some unique principles and computations which differ from those used for published financial statements. An understanding of the unique aspects of taxable income can assist an individual or a business in minimizing the amount of income taxes owed.

Tax Planning versus Tax Evasion

Individuals who plan their business affairs in a manner that will result in the lowest possible income tax are acting rationally and legally. They are using the techniques called *tax planning.* In the words of a distinguished jurist, Judge Learned Hand:

Over and over again courts have said that there is nothing sinister in so arranging one's affairs as to keep taxes as low as possible. Everybody does so, rich or poor, and all do right, for nobody owes any public duty to pay more than the law demands: taxes are enforced exactions, not voluntary contributions. To demand more in the name of morals is mere cant.

To reduce and to postpone income taxes are the goals of tax planning. Almost every business decision involves a choice among alternative courses of action with different tax consequences. For example, should we lease or buy business automobiles; should we obtain needed capital by issuing bonds or preferred stock; should we use straight-line depreciation or an accelerated method? Some of these alternatives will lead to much lower income taxes than others. Tax planning, therefore, means *determining in advance the income tax effect* of every proposed business action and then making business decisions which will lead to the smallest tax liability. Tax practice is an important element of the services furnished to clients by CPA firms. This tax work includes not only the computing of taxes and preparing of tax returns, but also tax planning.

Tax planning must begin early. Unfortunately, some wait until the end of the year and then, faced with the prospect of paying a large amount of income tax, ask their accountants what can be done to reduce the tax liability. If we are to arrange transactions in a manner that will lead to the minimum income tax liability, the tax planning must be carried out *before* the date of a transaction, not after it is an accomplished fact. Because it is important for everyone to recognize areas in which tax savings may be substantial, a few of the major opportunities for tax planning are discussed in the final section of this chapter.

Newspaper stories tell us each year of some taxpayers who have deliberately understated their taxable income by failing to report a portion of income received or by claiming fictitious deductions such as an excess number of personal exemptions. Such purposeful understatement of taxable income is called *tax evasion* and is, of course, illegal. On the other hand, *tax avoidance* (the arranging of business and financial affairs in a manner that will minimize tax liability) is entirely legal.

The Critical Importance of Income Taxes

Taxes levied by federal, state, and local governments are a significant part of the cost of operating a typical household, as well as a business enterprise. Every manager who makes business decisions, and every individual who makes personal investments, urgently needs some knowledge of income taxes. A general knowledge of income taxes will help any business manager or owner to benefit more fully from the advice of the professional tax accountant.

Some understanding of income taxes will also aid the individual citizen in voting intelligently, because a great many of the issues decided in every election have tax implications. Such issues as pollution, inflation, foreign policy, and employment are closely linked with income taxes. For example, one approach to protection of the environment is to offer special tax incentives that encourage businesses to carry on pollution-control programs.

In terms of revenue generated, the four most important kinds of taxes in the United States are *income taxes, sales taxes, property taxes,* and *excise taxes.* Income taxes exceed all others in terms of the amounts involved, and they also exert a pervasive influence on all types of business decisions. For this reason we shall limit our discussion to the basic federal income tax rules applicable to individuals, partnerships, and corporations.

Income taxes are usually determined from information contained in accounting records. The amount of income tax is computed by applying the appropriate tax rates to *taxable income.* As explained later in this chapter, *taxable income* is not necessarily the same as *accounting income* even though both are derived from the accounting records. Business managers can influence the amount of taxes they pay by their choice of form of business organization, methods of financing, and alternative accounting methods. Thus income taxes are inevitably an important factor in reaching business decisions.

The Federal Income Tax: History and Objectives

The present federal income tax dates from the passage of the Sixteenth Amendment to the Constitution in 1913.[1] This amendment, only 30 words in

---

[1] A federal income tax was proposed as early as 1815, and an income tax law was actually passed and income taxes collected during the Civil War. This law was upheld by the Supreme Court, but it was repealed when the need for revenue subsided after the war. In 1894 a new income tax law was passed, but the Supreme Court declared this law invalid on constitutional grounds.

length,[2] removed all questions of the constitutionality of income taxes and paved the way for the more than 50 revenue acts passed by Congress since that date. In 1939 these tax laws were first combined into what is known as the Internal Revenue Code. The administration and enforcement of the tax laws are duties of the Treasury Department, operating through a division known as the Internal Revenue Service (IRS). The Treasury Department publishes its interpretation of the tax laws in Treasury regulations; the final word in interpretation lies with the federal courts.

Originally the purpose of the federal income tax was simply to obtain revenue for the government. And at first, the tax rates were quite low—by today's standards. In 1913 a married person with taxable income of $15,000 would have been subject to a tax rate of 1%, resulting in a tax liability of $150. The maximum federal income tax rate in 1913 was 7%. By the 1970s, the maximum tax rate had risen to 70%; and for most of the 1980s the top rate was 50%. Recent Congressional action lowered the top rate to 28% beginning with the year 1988.

The purpose of federal income tax now includes *several goals apart from raising revenue.* Examples of these other goals are: influencing the rate of economic growth, encouraging full employment, combatting inflation, favoring small businesses, and redistributing national income on a more equal basis.

Classes of Taxpayers

In the eyes of the income tax law, there are four major classes of taxpayers: *individuals, corporations, estates,* and *trusts.* A business organized as a sole proprietorship or as a partnership is not taxed as a separate entity; its income is taxed directly to the individual proprietor or partners, *whether or not the income is withdrawn from the business.* However, a partnership must file an *information return* showing the computation of total partnership net income and the allocation of this income among the partners.

A sole proprietor reports his or her income from ownership of a business on an individual tax return (Form 1040); the members of a partnership include on their individual income tax returns their respective shares of the partnership net income. Of course, an individual's income tax return must include not only any business income from a proprietorship or partnership, but also any interest, dividends, salary, or other forms of income received.

A corporation is a separate taxable entity; it must file a corporate income tax return (Form 1120) and pay a tax on its annual taxable income. In addition, individual stockholders must report dividends received from corporations as part of their personal taxable income. The taxing of corporate dividends has led to the charge that there is "double taxation" of corporate income—once to the corporation and again when it is distributed to stockholders. This double impact of tax is particularly apparent when a corporation is owned by one person or one family.

To illustrate, let us use the tax rates in effect during the early 1980s to consider the tax impact on one dollar of corporate earnings. The *income before*

---

[2] It reads "The Congress shall have power to lay and collect taxes on incomes, from whatever source derived, without apportionment among the several States, and without regard to any census or enumeration."

taxes earned by a corporation was (in general) subject to a federal corporate income tax rate of 46%. First, the corporation paid 46%, or 46 cents, out of the dollar to the Internal Revenue Service. That left 54 cents for the corporation. Next, assume that the 54 cents was distributed as dividends to individual stockholders. The dividend was taxable to the stockholders personally at rates varying from 12 to 50%, depending on their individual tax brackets. Thus, the 54 cents of after-tax income to the corporation could be reduced by 50%, or 27 cents of individual income tax, leaving 27 cents of the original dollar for the shareholder. In summary, *federal income taxes could take as much as 73 cents out of a dollar earned by a corporation and distributed as a dividend to a shareholder.* The remaining 27 cents could be reduced further by state income taxes. This example would, of course, appear less extreme if we used the lower rates effective in 1988.

Special and complex rules apply to the determination of taxable income for estates and trusts. These rules will not be discussed in this chapter.

INCOME TAXES: INDIVIDUALS

Cash Basis of Accounting for Income Tax Returns

Objective 2
Discuss the advantages of the cash basis of accounting for preparation of individual income tax returns.

Almost all *individual* income tax returns are prepared on the cash basis of accounting. Many small service-type business concerns and professional firms also choose to prepare their tax returns on the cash basis. Revenue is recognized when collected in cash; expenses (except depreciation) are recognized when a cash payment is made. The cash basis (as prescribed in IRS rules) does not permit expenditures for plant and equipment to be deducted in the year of purchase. These capital expenditures are capitalized and depreciated for tax purposes. Also, the income tax laws do not permit use of the cash basis by companies in which inventories and the sale of merchandise are significant factors.

Although the cash basis of accounting does not measure income satisfactorily in the context of generally accepted accounting principles, it has much merit in the area of taxation. From the government's viewpoint, the logical time to collect tax on income is when the taxpayer receives the income in cash. At any earlier date, the taxpayer may not have the cash to pay income taxes; at any later date, the cash may have been used for other purposes.

The cash basis is advantageous for the individual taxpayer and for service-type businesses for several reasons. It is relatively simple, and requires a minimum of records. The income of most individuals comes in the form of salaries, interest, and dividends. At the end of each year, an individual receives from his or her employer a W-2 form showing the salary earned and income tax withheld during the year. This report is prepared on a cash basis without any accrual of unpaid wages. Persons receiving interest or dividends also receive from the paying companies Form 1099 showing amounts received for the year. Thus, most individuals are provided with *reports prepared on a cash basis* for use in preparing their individual tax returns.

The cash basis has other advantages for the individual taxpayer and for many professional firms and service-type businesses. It often permits tax savings by individuals who deliberately shift the timing of revenue and expense transactions from one year to another. For example, a dentist whose taxable income is higher than usual in the current year may decide in December to delay billing patients until January 1, and thus postpone the receipt of gross income to the next year. The timing of *expense payments* near year-end is also controllable by a taxpayer using the cash basis. A taxpayer who has received a bill for a deductible expense item in December may choose to pay it before or after December 31 and thereby influence the amount of taxable income in each year. However, a cash-basis taxpayer is not permitted to deduct rent paid in advance on business property. Such an advance payment must be treated as an asset and amortized over the rental period.

Any taxpayer who maintains a set of accounting records may *elect* to use the accrual basis in preparing a tax return, but very few taxpayers (individual or corporate) choose to do so if they are eligible to use the cash basis.

Tax Rates

All taxes may be characterized as progressive, proportional, or regressive with respect to any given base. A *progressive* tax becomes a larger portion of the base as that base increases. Federal income taxes are *progressive* with respect to income, since a higher tax *rate* applies as the amount of taxable income increases. A *proportional* tax remains a constant percentage of the base no matter how that base changes. For example, a 6% sales tax remains a constant percentage of sales regardless of changes in the dollar amount of sales. A *regressive* tax becomes a smaller percentage of the base as the base increases. Regressive taxes, however, are extremely rare.

Keep in mind that tax rates have been changed many times in the past and no doubt will continue to be changed in the future. The present tax structure for individuals provides for only two brackets of 15% and 28%. The 15% rate is applicable to all taxable income of single individuals up to $17,850, and the 28% rate to income above that amount. For married couples filing joint returns, the 15% rate applies to taxable income up to $29,750. The 28% rate applies to taxable income above that amount.

Tax Rate Schedules

	TAXABLE INCOME	TAX RATE
Single taxpayers:	First $17,850	15%
....	Amount over $17,850	28%*
Married taxpayers filing joint returns:................	First $29,750	15%
....	Amount over $29,750	28%*

* High-income taxpayers are subject to surtaxes which cause some portion of their income to be taxed at an effective rate of 33%. These surtaxes are discussed on page 698.

Example: Find the tax for a single person having taxable income of $25,000.

Answer: Tax on first $17,850 at 15%	$2,677.50
Tax on $7,150 excess at 28%..	2,002.00
Tax on $25,000 for a single person	$4,679.50

The top rate of 28% stipulated in the current law is perhaps misleading, because high-income taxpayers must pay a rate of 33% on a portion of their income. This 33% effective rate results from adding a 5% surcharge to the 28%

ratc. Thc purposc of this 5% surcharge is to deny high-income taxpayers any benefit from the 15% rate. The result is that high-income taxpayers are required to pay an average tax rate of 28% on their entire taxable income.

Income Tax Formula for Individuals

Objective 3
State the formula for determining the taxable income of an individual.

The federal government supplies standard income tax forms on which taxpayers are guided to a proper computation of their taxable income and the amount of the tax. It is helpful to visualize the computation in terms of an income tax formula as diagrammed on the next page. The sequence of material on income tax forms differs somewhat from the arrangement in this formula. However, it is easier to understand the structure and logic of the federal income tax by referring to the tax formula rather than to tax forms.

Total Income and Gross Income

Total income as defined for tax purposes is a very broad concept that includes in the words of the law, "all income from whatever source derived." *Gross income* is computed by deducting from *total income* certain items excluded by the tax laws; the leading cxamplc is intcrcst rcccivcd on state and municipal bonds. A concise definition of gross income is "all income not excluded by law." Gross income therefore includes salaries, commissions, bonuses, dividends, interest, rent, and gains from sale of securities, real estate, and other property. To determine whether any given income item is included in gross income, one must ask, "Is thcrc a provision in thc tax law cxcluding this item of income from gross income?" Among the items *excluded from gross income* by statute are interest on state and municipal bonds, gifts and inheritances, life insurance proceeds, workmen's compensation, social security benefits (subject to certain limits), thc portion of receipts from annuities that represents return of cost, pensions to veterans, and compensation for actual damages.

Among the items of miscellaneous incomc which must bc *included* in gross income are prizes and awards won, tips received, and gains from sale of personal property. The fact that income arises from an illegal transaction does not keep it from being taxable.

Deductions to Arrive at Adjusted Gross Income

Some of the more common deductions from *gross income* in computing *adjusted gross income* are listed below.

1 Business expenses of a sole proprietorship   These include all ordinary and necessary expenses of carrying on a trade, business, or profession (other than as an employee). For the actual tax computation, business expenses are deducted from business revenue, and net business income is then included in adjusted gross income on the proprietor's tax return.

2 Expenses attributable to rental properties   The owner of rental property, such as an apartment building, incurs a variety of operating expenses. Depreciation, property taxes, repairs, maintenance, interest on indebtedness related to property, and other expenses incurred in connection with the earn-

General Federal Income Tax Formula for Individuals

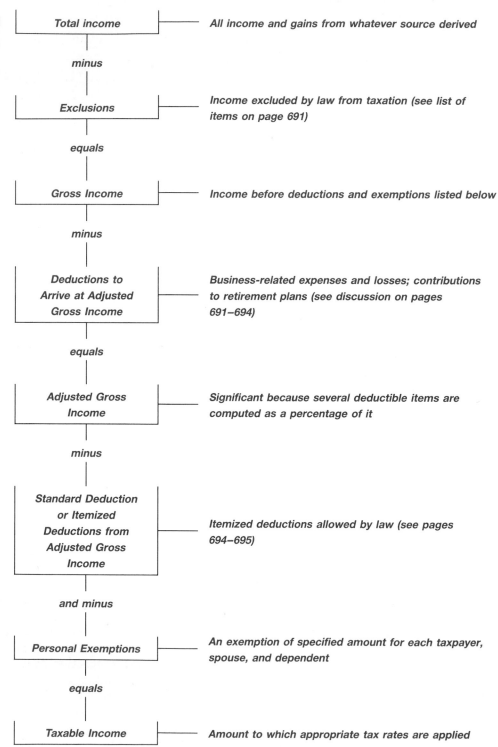

Use this formula to compute taxable income for individuals

Total income — All income and gains from whatever source derived

minus

Exclusions — Income excluded by law from taxation (see list of items on page 691)

equals

Gross Income — Income before deductions and exemptions listed below

minus

Deductions to Arrive at Adjusted Gross Income — Business-related expenses and losses; contributions to retirement plans (see discussion on pages 691–694)

equals

Adjusted Gross Income — Significant because several deductible items are computed as a percentage of it

minus

Standard Deduction or Itemized Deductions from Adjusted Gross Income — Itemized deductions allowed by law (see pages 694–695)

and minus

Personal Exemptions — An exemption of specified amount for each taxpayer, spouse, and dependent

equals

Taxable Income — Amount to which appropriate tax rates are applied

ing of rental income are allowed as deductions. This means that only the *net income* derived from rental property is included in adjusted gross income.

3 Losses from the sale of property used in business Any loss resulting from the sale of property used in a trade or business may be deducted against other items of gross income.[3]

4 Net capital losses Up to $3,000 of *net capital losses* may be deducted to arrive at adjusted gross income. Capital gains and losses are discussed on pages 696–697.

5 Contributions to retirement plans: IRA and Keogh plans A retirement plan known as IRA (Individual Retirement Arrangement) is one that you set up and contribute to yourself, without any participation by your employer. The purpose is to encourage you to set money aside for your retirement in a personal savings plan. The incentive offered is that your contributions may be fully or partially deductible in computing your current taxable income—that is, not taxable until withdrawn upon your retirement. Moreover, the *income earned* on amounts in the IRA are not taxable until the time of withdrawal. Thus, an IRA may grow more rapidly than most investments because the entire current earnings go to increase the amount invested without any current taxation.

The present law permits a person who is *not covered by an employer-sponsored pension plan* to contribute up to $2,000 a year to an IRA, and to deduct this contribution in arriving at taxable income. At a 28% tax rate, this deduction creates an immediate tax saving of 28% × $2,000 or $560. Persons covered by an employer-sponsored retirement plan are not permitted to take a deduction for an IRA contribution if their incomes are above specified levels. Partial deductions are permitted for certain income levels. As a result of these restrictive provisions, deductions for IRA contributions are available principally to persons not covered by a retirement plan at work. However, persons not eligible to take a deduction may still choose to make an annual IRA contribution without claiming a deduction, because the earnings from an IRA plan accumulate tax-free until retirement.

If you are self-employed, a Keogh H.R. 10 plan is a valuable device for reducing your income taxes and building assets for retirement. Individuals who are self-employed are permitted to deduct from gross income the amounts they contribute to a Keogh plan. The present limit on such contributions is the lower of $30,000 or 15% of your annual earnings. The amounts contributed, plus earnings on the fund assets, are not taxable until the taxpayer retires and begins making withdrawals from the fund. The Keogh plan is intended to provide self-employed persons with opportunities similar to those of persons employed by companies with pension plans. A self-employed person may contribute to both an IRA and a self-employed retirement plan. However, the IRA contribution will be deductible only if income is within specified limits.

---

[3] Losses arising from the sale of personal property, such as a home or personal automobile, are not deductible. On the other hand, gains from the sale of personal property are taxable. This appears inconsistent, until one realizes that a loss on the sale of personal property usually reflects depreciation through use, which is a personal expense.

6 Other deductions to arrive at adjusted gross income Among other deductions are alimony paid, and penalties on early withdrawals from long-term savings deposits.

■ **Adjusted Gross Income** By deducting from gross income the various items described in the preceding section, we arrive at a very significant total called ***adjusted gross income*** (AGI). This amount is significant because several deductible items such as medical expense and charitable contributions are limited by their percentage relationship to adjusted gross income. For example, medical expense is deductible only to the extent it ***exceeds*** 7½% of adjusted gross income.

Deductions from Adjusted Gross Income

Taxpayers have a choice with respect to deductions from adjusted gross income. They may choose to take a lump-sum ***standard deduction,*** or they may choose to ***itemize*** their deductions, in which case they can deduct a number of expenses specified in the tax law as itemized deductions.

■ **Standard Deduction** Most taxpayers choose to take the standard deduction from adjusted gross income rather than to itemize their deductions by listing such items as mortgage interest payments and state income taxes. Effective in 1988, the amounts of the standard deduction were increased substantially to the following levels: $5,000 for married couples filing jointly, $4,400 for heads of households, and $3,000 for single taxpayers. As a matter of convenience, these round amounts are to be used in all exercises and problems in this book which involve the standard deduction. However, the law provides that the amounts of the standard deduction will continue to be adjusted annually for inflation. Originally the standard deduction was based on the concept that everyone could claim some deductions and the computation of a person's tax liability could be simplified by providing the option of a standard deduction. Now, however, a major reason for the recent large increases in the standard deduction appears to be a desire to free millions of lower-income individuals from paying any income tax.

■ **Does It Pay to Itemize?** Should you itemize your deductions or claim the standard deduction? If you can qualify to itemize your deductions, it pays to do so. To find out if you qualify, add up your deductible expenses to see if the total exceeds the standard deduction. If it does, you will save taxes by itemizing. If the total is less than the standard deduction, you will benefit by claiming the standard deduction.

■ **Itemized Deductions** The major types of itemized deductions allowable under the Tax Reform Act of 1986 are described below.

1 Mortgage interest Interest on mortgages on a first and a second home continue to be deductible. However, consumer interest charges, as on credit cards, auto loans, and boat loans, were phased out during the years from 1988 through 1990.

2 Taxes State income taxes and taxes by local government on real estate and personal property continue to be deductible. Sales taxes no longer may be deducted. No federal taxes qualify as itemized deductions.

3 Contributions Contributions by individuals to charitable, religious, educational, and certain nonprofit organizations are deductible within certain limits, but only for taxpayers who itemize deductions. In other words, a taxpayer who takes the standard deduction cannot also take deductions for charitable contributions. Gifts to friends, relatives, and other persons are not deductible.

4 Medical expenses Medical and dental expenses may be deducted only to the extent that they exceed 7½% of adjusted gross income.

5 Casualty losses Losses in excess of $100 from any fire, storm, earthquake, theft, or other sudden, unexpected, or unusual causes are deductible only to the extent that they exceed 10% of adjusted gross income. For example, assume that a taxpayer with adjusted gross income of $45,000 sustains an uninsured fire loss of $10,100. First, we eliminate $100 of the loss, leaving the amount of $10,000. Next, we reduce the loss by 10% of the adjusted gross income of $45,000, a reduction of $4,500. This leaves $5,500 as the net deduction from adjusted gross income in arriving at the amount subject to tax.

6 Miscellaneous deductions Such items as union dues, investment expenses, professional journals, and deductions for employee business expenses are allowable only to the extent that they exceed 2% of adjusted gross income.

Personal Exemptions

A deduction from adjusted gross income is allowed for one or more *personal exemptions,* as well as for the standard deduction discussed above. An unmarried individual is entitled to one personal exemption, provided that he or she is not listed as a dependent on some other person's tax return. In addition, a taxpayer can claim a personal exemption for each dependent.

For 1989, the personal exemption was $2,000. An indexing plan provides for an annual inflation adjustment for 1990 and thereafter. As a matter of convenience in illustrations and problems in this book, we assume the round amount of $2,000 for each personal exemption.

The term dependent means a person who (1) receives over one-half of his or her support from the taxpayer, (2) is closely related to the taxpayer or lives in the taxpayer's home, (3) has gross income during the year of less than the current exemption amount unless he or she is a child of the taxpayer and is under 19 years of age or is a full-time student, (4) meets a citizenship test, and (5) does not file a joint return. For any dependent five years of age or more, the taxpayer must list the dependent's social security number. To summarize the tax savings from personal exemptions, we can say that each personal exemption reduces taxable income by $2,000. With a tax rate of 28%, the tax saving is $560, computed as $2,000 × 28%.

Taxable Income—Individuals

We have now traced the steps required to determine the taxable income of an individual: In brief, this process includes:

1 Computation of total income

2 Exclusion of certain items specified by law to determine gross income

3 Deduction of business-related expenses to arrive at adjusted gross income

4 Deduction of the standard deduction (or itemized deductions) and personal exemptions to arrive at the key figure of taxable income.

The concept of taxable income is important because it is the amount to which the appropriate tax rate is applied to determine the tax liability.

Capital Gains and Losses

Objective 4
Explain the recent changes in the taxation of capital gains and losses.

As indicated on page 693, an individual taxpayer may deduct up to $3,000 of *net capital losses* in computing adjusted gross income. To understand this step, we need first to understand the nature of capital gains and losses. Certain kinds of property are defined under the tax laws as capital assets. For most individuals, investments in securities and real estate (including a personal residence) are the most important capital assets. However, almost everything you own and use for personal purposes is considered a capital asset. Included are household furniture, an automobile, jewelry, and stamp and coin collections. However, capital assets do not include assets used in a trade or business, such as inventory, plant and equipment, and accounts receivable. If you sell a capital asset for a price higher than the basis of the property, you will recognize a capital gain. If you sell at a price lower than the basis of the property, you will suffer a capital loss. The *basis* for purchased property is its cost, reduced by any accumulated depreciation.

Capital gains and losses were an important element of the income tax structure for many decades until the Tax Reform Act of 1986 eliminated favorable treatment of long-term capital gains. Capital gains and losses are classified as long-term when the investor owns the asset for more than one year. To investors, one of the most attractive features of the "old tax law" was the favorable treatment of long-term capital gains. For example, assume that you bought common stock in a newly organized business. Subsequently, the business grew rapidly and the value of your shares increased greatly. After holding your investment for a few years, you sold the shares at a large profit. Under the pre-1986 law, you would have been taxed on only 40% of your profit. Thus, the tax on long-term capital gains was only 40% as high as the tax on an equal amount of income from other sources, such as salaries, interest, or dividends received. In other words, in 1986 and prior years, 60% of a long-term capital gain was not subject to tax.

The rationale underlying the favorable treatment of long-term capital gains was to encourage investment capital to flow into new growth industries and thus to stimulate the economy. In brief, a tax incentive was offered to encourage investors to take risks rather than to invest in "risk-free" securities, such as government bonds. Despite the elimination of this tax incentive by the Tax Reform Act of 1986, taxpayers are still required to identify capital gains and losses and to report them separately, because only a limited amount of net capital losses can be deducted from other income.

■ **Limited Deductibility of Capital Losses** Not every investment is a winner, thus investors have capital losses as well as capital gains. The term *net short-term gains* means short-term gains in excess of short-term losses. Net short-term gains have for years been taxed the same as ordinary income. Capital losses, whether long-term or short-term, are deductible against capital gains. A taxpayer whose total capital losses exceed total capital gains in a given year has a *net capital loss.* On the individual's tax return, this net capital loss can be deducted from other income up to a maximum of $3,000 a year. To illustrate the limitation on deducting capital losses, let us assume that an individual incurred a capital loss of $100,000 and also had an annual salary of $50,000. He or she would have adjusted gross income of $47,000. The unused capital loss could be carried forward and offset against capital gains, if any, in future years, or against other income at the rate of $3,000 a year. Thus, a great many years might be required to offset the $100,000 loss against other income.

■ **Tax Strategy for Capital Gains and Losses** One widely used tax strategy is to "defer income and accelerate deductions." A first step in carrying out this strategy is to review one's security holdings as the year-end approaches. Identify any investments for which the current market price is less than the taxpayer's cost basis. Consider selling this investment before year-end in order to generate a capital loss which can be offset against any capital gains already realized in the current year or against other income (subject to the $3,000 limitation previously discussed). The sale of an investment in securities to generate a capital loss must not be accompanied by the purchase of the same security within 30 days or the IRS will disallow the loss on grounds that it was part of a "wash transaction."

■ **Long-Term Capital Gains—In Perspective** One of the most significant changes brought by the Tax Reform Act of 1986 was the elimination of favorable tax treatment of long-term capital gains. *Both* long-term and short-term capital gains are now taxed at the same rates as ordinary income. However, anyone seeking a perspective on the American experience with income taxes needs to be familiar with the concept of capital gains and losses because it has been used for decades as a means of influencing the direction and growth of economic activity. Remember that income taxation has other objectives in addition to raising revenue for the government. Considerable support is presently being expressed for reinstatement of some form of the capital gains concept, and a study of the issue is being made by the Treasury Department. Some officials suggest that favorable tax treatment of capital gains may stimulate economic activity sufficiently to increase the total revenue provided by income taxes.

The present tax status of capital gains can be summarized as follows: (1) the taxpayer must identify and report separately long-term and short-term capital gains and losses; (2) capital gains are taxed at the same rates as other income; (3) a net capital loss can be deducted from an individual's other income to the extent of $3,000 a year; (4) the distinction between long-term and short-term capital gains and losses is a reporting requirement, but under current law has no economic significance to taxpayers.

■ **Business Plant and Equipment** Buildings, machinery, and other depreciable property used in a trade or business *are not capital assets* under the tax law. This means that a net loss realized on the sale or disposal of such business property is fully deductible.

698

CHAPTER 18

Computing the Tax Liability

After determining the amount of taxable income, we are ready to compute the gross tax liability. For a single taxpayer with taxable income less than $43,150, we apply the 15% rate to the first $17,850, and then the 28% rate to the excess above $17,850. For example, assume that Edward Jones is single and has taxable income of $22,850. The computation produces a tax of $4,078 (rounded to the nearest dollar) as shown below.

TAXABLE INCOME		TAX RATE		TAX
$17,850	×	.15	=	$2,678
5,000	×	.28	=	1,400
$22,850				$4,078

For a married couple filing a joint return, we apply the 15% rate to the first $29,750 of taxable income, and then the 28% rate to any excess above $29,750. For example, assume that John and Mary Smith have taxable income of $60,000. The computation produces a tax (rounded to the nearest dollar) of $12,933, as shown below.

TAXABLE INCOME		TAX RATE		TAX
$29,750	×	.15	=	$ 4,463
30,250	×	.28	=	8,470
$60,000				$12,933

■ **Surtaxes** For single persons with taxable income above $43,150 (and for married couples with taxable income above $71,900), one or two surtaxes are imposed and the calculations become more complex. The purpose of the first surtax of 5% is to take back the benefit derived by the taxpayer from using the lower 15% rate on the first layer of taxable income. This "rate" surtax is 5% of the amount by which a single person's taxable income exceeds $43,150, up to a maximum surtax amount of $2,321. For married couples, the rate surcharge is 5% of the amount by which taxable income exceeds $71,900, up to a maximum surtax amount of $3,868. The result of this rate surcharge is that higher-income taxpayers must pay tax of 28% on their entire taxable incomes.

Another 5% surcharge designed to take back the benefit of the personal exemption is imposed upon higher-income taxpayers. This surcharge equals 5% of the amount by which the taxable income of a single person exceeds $89,560. For married couples, the surtax is 5% of the excess of taxable income over $149,250. The maximum dollar amount of the surcharge is $546 for each personal exemption shown on the tax returns of both single taxpayers and married couples. For example, the maximum surcharge for a married couple with two dependent children would be 4 × $546 or $2,184. One conclusion which might be drawn from the creation of the two surcharges described above is that the new tax structure is somewhat more progressive in nature than is suggested by the much discussed rates of 15% and 28%.

■ **Tax Credits** The gross tax liability as computed by the methods described above is reduced by subtracting any tax credits. Note that a tax credit is subtracted directly from the tax owed, whereas a deduction (as for charitable contributions) is subtracted from adjusted gross income and thus leads to a smaller amount of taxable income to which the tax rate is applied. Tax credits were important to many individuals and to virtually every business prior to the Tax Reform Act of 1986. Under the present tax law, however, most types of tax credits have been eliminated. The few remaining tax credits include a credit for qualifying low-income taxpayers and a small credit for certain child care expenses of working parents.

■ **Tax Prepayments**   The most common example of tax prepayments is the withholding of income taxes from a person's salary. Another common example is the quarterly payment of estimated income taxes on dividend income or interest income not subject to withholding. The gross tax liability computed at the end of the year is reduced by subtracting these tax prepayments. The remaining amount is the *net tax liability*—the amount to be paid with the tax return.

Quarterly Payments of Estimated Tax

We have seen that the federal income tax law stresses a pay-as-you-go system for all taxpayers. The tax must be paid as the taxpayer receives income during the year. There are two methods of carrying out the pay-as-you-go principle: one is *withholding* and the other is payment of *estimated taxes* on a current basis.

Income in the form of salaries has long been subject to withholding. However, for self-employed persons, such as doctors, dentists, and owners of small unincorporated business concerns, there is no salary and no withholding. Other examples of income on which no withholding occurs are interest, dividends, rental income, and capital gains.

To equalize the treatment of self-employed persons and salaried employees, the tax law requires persons having taxable income not subject to withholding to pay *estimated taxes* in advance quarterly installments. One-quarter of the current year's estimated income tax must be paid by April 15 and the remainder in three equal quarterly installments. Thus, a self-employed person may write two checks to the IRS on April 15; one for any balance due with last year's tax return and one for one-quarter of the estimated tax for the current year.

Tax Returns, Tax Refunds, and Payment of the Tax

The tax return must be filed within 3½ months after the close of the taxable year. Most taxpayers are on a calendar-year basis; therefore, the deadline for filing is April 15. However, the taxpayer has the alternative of paying the tax due at April 15 and requesting an extension of time to August 15 for filing of the return.

■ **Withholding Makes the System Work**   Without the withholding feature, the present income tax system would probably be unworkable. The high rate of income taxes would pose an impossible collection problem if employees received their total earnings in cash and were later called upon at the end of the year to pay the government a major portion of a year's salary.

The amounts withheld from an employee's salary for income tax can be considered as payments on account. If the amount of income tax as computed by preparing a tax return at the end of the year is less than the amount withheld during the year; the taxpayer is entitled to a refund. On the other hand, if the tax as computed at year-end is more than the amount withheld, the taxpayer must pay the additional amount with the tax return.

■ **The Deceptive Lure of a Tax Refund Check**   Most American taxpayers receive tax refunds each year. Apparently these 60 million or more persons so enjoy receiving a refund check that they are willing to have the government withhold excessive amounts of tax from their paychecks throughout the year. The IRS reports that millions of individual taxpayers declare fewer personal exemptions than they expect to claim at year-end. The result is over-withholding of billions of dollars on which the government pays no interest. It is interesting that even during periods of inflation and high interest rates, American taxpayers would choose to have the government hold their money throughout the year with no interest in order to be paid back at year-end in dollars worth less in purchasing power than when earned.

Computation of Individual Income Tax Illustrated

The computation of the federal income tax for Mary and John Reed is illustrated below.

MARY AND JOHN REED

Illustrative Federal Income Tax Computation

Gross income (excluding $700 interest on municipal bonds):		
Gross fees from John Reed's law practice	$81,000	
Less: Expenses incurred in law practice.........................	32,000	
Net income from law practice.................................		$ 49,000
Salary received by Mary Reed		54,400
Dividends received		7,240
Interest received		1,120
Long-term capital gain		1,000
Gross income		$112,760
Deductions to arrive at adjusted gross income:		
Contribution to Keogh retirement plan		3,000
Adjusted gross income		$109,760
Deductions from adjusted gross income:		
Itemized deductions	$12,920	
Personal exemptions (4 × $2,000)	8,000	20,920
Taxable income		$ 88,840
Computation of tax:		
Tax on $29,750 at 15%...............................	$ 4,463	
Tax on $59,090 at 28%...............................	16,545	
Rate surtax on ($88,840 − $71,900) at 5%..........................	847	
Total tax		$ 21,855
Less: Quarterly payments of estimated tax and amounts withheld:		
Quarterly payments of estimated tax	$ 9,000	
Tax withheld from salary...	11,000	20,000
Tax to be paid with return		$ 1,855

In this example it is assumed that the Reeds provide over one-half the support of their two children. John Reed is a practicing attorney who received $81,000 in gross fees from his law practice and incurred $32,000 of business expenses. Mary Reed earned $54,400 during the year as a CPA working for a national firm of accountants. During the year, $11,000 was withheld from her salary for federal income taxes. Just before the end of the year, John Reed contributed $3,000 to a Keogh retirement plan. The Reeds received $700 interest on municipal bonds, and $1,120 interest on savings accounts. Dividends received on stock jointly owned amounted to $7,240. During the year, stock purchased several years ago by John Reed for $2,600 was sold for $3,600, net of brokerage fees, thus producing a $1,000 long-term capital gain.

The Reeds have total itemized deductions of $12,920, including contributions, mortgage interest expense, property taxes, etc. They paid a total of $9,000 on their declaration of estimated tax during the year. In this illustration, as in the problems at the end of the chapter, we have for convenience used the amount of $2,000 for each personal exemption.

On the basis of these facts, the taxable income for the Reeds is shown to be $88,840, and the total tax is $21,855. Taking withholdings and quarterly payments of estimated tax into account, the Reeds have already paid income taxes of $20,000 and thus owe $1,855 at the time of filing their tax return.

Alternative Minimum Tax

You may have read newspaper stories about a few individuals with very high incomes who were able, through extensive use of tax shelters, tax preferences, and various loopholes, to avoid paying any income tax. Although such cases are extremely rare, they create strong adverse reaction by the public and by Congress. One goal of the Tax Reform Act of 1986 was to assure that every person with a large income pays a significant amount of income tax. The approach taken was to strengthen the Alternative Minimum Tax (AMT). This minimum tax requires that you add back to adjusted gross income a long list of deductions (such as state income tax) and tax preferences (such as accelerated depreciation). The total resulting from these adjustments is your Alternative Minimum Tax income. You apply a 21% rate to this total. If your Alternative Minimum Tax is higher than your tax under the regular computation, you must pay the Alternative Minimum Tax.

Partnerships

Partnerships are not taxable entities. Although a partnership pays no income tax, it must file an *information return* showing the computation of net income or loss and the share of net income or loss allocable to each partner. The partners must include in their personal tax returns their respective shares of the net income or loss of the partnership.

INCOME TAXES: CORPORATIONS

Objective 5
Contrast the determination of taxable income for a corporation with that for an individual.

A corporation is a separate taxable entity. Our discussion is focused on the general business corporation and does not cover certain other types of corporations for which special tax treatment applies. Every corporation, unless specifically exempt from taxation, must file an income tax return whether or not it has taxable income or owes any tax.

The earning of taxable income inevitably creates a liability to pay income taxes. This liability and the related charge to expense must be entered in the accounting records before financial statements are prepared. For example:

Income Taxes Expense	60,000	
Income Taxes Payable		60,000
To record corporate income taxes for the current period.		

Corporation Tax Rates

The Tax Reform Act of 1986 reduced the top corporate tax rate from 46% to 34% and continued the practice of allowing lower rates for small companies. The following table shows the three brackets provided by the current law.

Corporate Income Tax Rates

TAXABLE INCOME	RATES
Up to $50,000	15%
Over $50,000 but not over $75,000	25%
Over $75,000	34%

The benefits from the 15% and 25% tax rates on the first two layers of corporate income are phased out for larger companies with earnings over $100,000. The 5% surtax applies to taxable earnings between $100,000 and $335,000.

To illustrate, let us compute the tax for a corporation with taxable income of $1,000,000.

	TAXABLE INCOME	TAX RATE	TAX
First	$ 50,000	15%	$ 7,500
Next	25,000	25%	6,250
Next	25,000	34%	8,500
Next	235,000	39%*	91,650
Next	665,000	34%	226,100
Total	$1,000,000		$340,000

* Includes a 5% surtax designed to deny high-income corporations any benefit from the lower tax rates on the first $75,000 of corporate income.

The total tax of $340,000 is exactly 34% of the entire $1,000,000 of taxable income, indicating that the use of the 5% surtax has nullified the benefits of the 15% and 25% rates for this corporation. Any corporation with taxable income of $335,000 or more pays tax at a flat rate of 34%.

Taxable Income of Corporations

In many respects, the taxable income of corporations is computed by following the same concepts we employ in preparing an income statement. The starting point is total revenue. From this amount, we deduct ordinary and necessary business expenses. However, net income determined by generally accepted accounting principles usually differs from taxable income. The difference is caused by specific rules in the tax laws which prescribe for certain items of revenue and expense a treatment different from that called for by GAAP. Another difference is the fact that from time to time, Congress makes drastic changes in the rules for determining taxable income. Some of the special factors to be considered in preparing a corporation tax return are considered below.

1 Dividends received Dividends received by a corporation on investments in stocks of other domestic corporations are included in gross income, but at least 70% of such dividends can be deducted from gross income.[4] As a result, only 30% or less of dividend income is taxable to the receiving corporation.

2 Capital gains and losses The net capital gains of corporations are taxed as ordinary income. Thus, rates may vary from 15% to 34%. Capital gains are treated the same as any other form of income in determining the extent, if any, to which the 5% surtax is applied. Corporations may deduct capital losses only by offsetting them against capital gains.

3 Other variations from taxation of individuals The concept of adjusted gross income is not applicable to a corporation. There is no standard deduction and no personal exemption. Gross income minus the deductions allowed to corporations equal *taxable income.*

4 Repeal of the Investment Tax Credit For many years in the past, businesses were eligible for an Investment Tax Credit, often equal to as much as 10% of the cost of new equipment. The Investment Tax Credit (ITC) is no longer in effect; however, the possibility of its reinstatement remains. This is not the first time the Investment Tax Credit has been eliminated. In the past the elimination of the ITC was followed by its reinstatement. Present congressional concern over budget deficits suggests that Congress will look closely at the tax laws. Issues such as favorable treatment for capital gains and tax credits to stimulate investment will probably be among the topics considered.

5 Alternative Minimum Tax A major political reason for passage of the Tax Reform Act of 1986 was that a few large corporations had paid little or no income tax in certain years. The new bill contains a strong new minimum tax designed to prevent such extremes of tax avoidance. The starting point in calculating the Alternative Minimum Tax is the corporation's regular taxable income. This amount is adjusted by recalculating various deductions and deferrals, such as deferred gain on installment sales and any excess of income reported to stockholders over reported taxable income. A 20% minimum tax

---

[4] The percentage of dividends received that may be deducted in arriving at taxable income increases to 80% if the investor corporation owns 20% or more of the other company's stock, and to 100% if the investor owns 80% or more of the stock. Thus, a parent company is not taxed upon dividends received from a wholly owned subsidiary.

(AMT) is applied to this recalculated base. The minimum tax must be paid if it is higher than the tax calculated by regular procedures.

Illustrative Tax Computation for Corporation

Shown below and on the next page is an income statement for Stone Corporation, along with a separate supporting schedule for the tax computation. In this supporting schedule, we compute the amount of income taxes to appear in the income statement and also show the payments of estimated tax, thus arriving at the amount of tax payable with the tax return.

Accounting Income versus Taxable Income

Objective 6
Discuss the concept of interperiod income tax allocation.

In the determination of *accounting income,* the objective is to measure business operating results as accurately as possible in accordance with generally accepted accounting principles. *Taxable income,* on the other hand, is a legal concept governed by statute and subject to sudden and frequent change by Congress. In setting the rules for determining taxable income, Congress is interested not only in meeting the revenue needs of government but in achieving certain public policy objectives. Since accounting income and taxable income are determined with different purposes in mind, it is not surprising that they often differ by material amounts.

Differences between taxable income and accounting income may result from special tax rules which are unrelated to accounting principles.

1 Some items included in accounting income are not taxable. For example, interest on state or municipal bonds is excluded from taxable income.

2 Some business expenses are not deductible. The Tax Reform Act of 1986 banned the reserve method of determining the amount of the deduction for bad debts. Only the direct write-off method is accepted for use by taxpayers other than certain banks. As another example, the amortization of goodwill is not allowed for tax purposes. Goodwill must be treated as a capital asset of indefinite life.

3 Special deductions in excess of actual business expenses are allowed some taxpayers. For example, depletion deductions in excess of actual cost are allowed taxpayers in some mining industries.

STONE CORPORATION
Income Statement
For the Year Ended December 31, 19___

Revenue:		
Sales		$800,000
Dividends received from domestic corporations		20,000
Total revenue		$820,000
Expenses:		
Cost of goods sold	$537,000	
Other expenses (includes capital loss of $13,000)	100,000	637,000
Income before income taxes		$183,000
Income taxes expense		54,230
Net income		$128,770

SCHEDULE A
Computation of Income Tax

Income before income taxes	$183,000
Add back: Items not deductible for tax purposes:	
Capital loss deducted as operating expense	13,000
Subtotal	$196,000
Deduct: Dividends received credit ($20,000 × 80%)	14,000
Taxable income	$182,000

Income tax:		
15% of first $50,000	$ 7,500	
25% of next $25,000	6,250	
34% of next $25,000	8,500	
39% of $82,000 (includes 5% surtax)	31,980	
Total income tax		$ 54,230
Deduct: Quarterly payments of estimated tax		50,000
Balance of tax payable with tax return		$ 4,230

In addition, the *timing* of the recognition of certain revenue and expenses under tax rules differs from that under accounting principles. Some items of income received in advance may be taxed in the year of receipt while certain accrued expenses may not be deductible for income tax purposes until they are actually paid in cash.

Alternative Accounting Methods Offering Possible Tax Advantages

There are many examples of elective methods which postpone income taxes. Taxpayers engaged in exploration of natural resources may use a one-year write-off of the costs of drilling for oil and gas rather than capitalizing these costs for later depreciation. Ranchers may treat the cost of cattle feed as expense in the year of purchase rather than in the year the feed is consumed.

The accelerated cost recovery system (ACRS) created by Congress in 1981 replaced for tax purposes the useful-life depreciation concept which had been followed since the beginning of the federal income tax. For some types of plant and equipment, depreciation under ACRS is based on a recovery period shorter than useful life. The Tax Reform Act of 1986 modified ACRS by setting longer recovery periods (less liberal write-offs). This modified system is known as Modified Accelerated Cost Recovery System (MACRS) and applies to tangible property placed in service after 1986. Neither ACRS nor MACRS is in accord with generally accepted accounting principles. Consequently, the amount of depreciation expense in a corporate income statement will differ from that in the tax return. Thus, another factor exists to cause taxable income to differ from accounting income. Under present tax laws, taxpayers have the option of using straight-line depreciation rather than the rapid write-off provided by ACRS or MACRS. However, taxpayers generally choose for income tax purposes those accounting methods which cause expenses to be recognized as soon as possible and revenue to be recognized as late as possible.

Interperiod Income Tax Allocation

We have seen that differences between generally accepted accounting principles and income tax rules can be material. Some businesses might consider it more convenient to maintain their accounting records in conformity with the tax rules, but the result would be to distort financial statements. It is clearly preferable to maintain accounting records by the principles that produce relevant information about business operations. The data contained in the records can then be adjusted by use of work sheets to arrive at taxable income.

When a corporation follows one method in its accounting records and financial statements but uses a different method for its income tax return, a financial reporting problem arises. The difference in method will usually have the effect of postponing the recognition of income on the tax return (either because an expense deduction is accelerated or because revenue recognition is postponed). The question is whether the income tax expense to appear in the financial statements should be accrued when the income is recognized in the accounting records, or when it is actually subject to taxation.

To illustrate the problem, let us consider a very simple case. Suppose the Pryor Company has before-tax accounting income of $600,000 in each of two years. However, the company takes as a tax deduction in the first year an expense of $200,000 which is reported for accounting purposes in the second year. The company's accounting income, taxable income, and the actual income taxes due (assuming an average tax rate of 34%) are shown below.

	1ST YEAR	2D YEAR
Accounting income (before income taxes)	$600,000	$600,000
Taxable income	400,000	800,000
Actual income taxes due each year at 34% rate	136,000	272,000

Let us assume the Pryor Company reports as an expense in its income statement each year the amount of income taxes due for that year. The effect on reported net income as shown in the company's financial statements would be as follows:

	1ST YEAR	2D YEAR
Accounting income (before income taxes)	$600,000	$600,000
Income taxes expense (amount actually due)	136,000	272,000
Net income	$464,000	$328,000

Company reports actual taxes

The readers of Pryor Company's income statement might well wonder why the same $600,000 accounting income before income taxes in the two years produced such widely varying amounts of tax expense and net income.

To deal with this distortion between pretax income and after-tax income, an accounting policy known as **_interperiod income tax allocation_** is required for financial reporting purposes.[5] Briefly, the objective of income tax allocation is to accrue income taxes in relation to accounting income, whenever differences between accounting and taxable income are caused by differences in the **_tim-_**

---

[5] For a more complete discussion of tax allocation procedures, see *APB Opinion No. 11,* "Accounting for Income Taxes," AICPA (New York: 1967).

ing of revenue or expenses. In the Pryor Company example, this means we would report in the first year income statement a tax expense based on $600,000 of accounting income even though a portion of this income ($200,000) will not be subject to income tax until the second year. The effect of this accounting procedure is demonstrated by the following journal entries to record the income tax expense in each of the two years:

Entries to record income tax allocation

1st Year	Income Taxes Expense	204,000	
	Current Income Tax Liability		136,000
	Deferred Income Tax Liability		68,000
	To record current and deferred income taxes at 34% of accounting income of $600,000.		

2d Year	Income Taxes Expense	204,000	
	Deferred Income Tax Liability	68,000	
	Current Income Tax Liability		272,000
	To record income taxes at 34% of accounting income of $600,000 and to record actual income taxes due.		

Using tax allocation procedures, Pryor Company's financial statements would report net income during the two-year period as follows:

Company uses tax allocation procedure

	1ST YEAR	2D YEAR
Income before income taxes	$600,000	$600,000
Income taxes expense (tax allocation basis)	204,000	204,000
Net income	$396,000	$396,000

In this example, the difference between taxable income and accounting income (caused by the accelerated deduction of an expense) was fully offset in a period of two years. In practice, differences between accounting and taxable income may persist over extended time periods and deferred tax liabilities may accumulate to significant amounts. For example, in a recent balance sheet of Sears, Roebuck and Co., deferred taxes of almost $2.5 billion were reported. This huge deferral of tax payments resulted from the use of the installment sales method for income tax purposes while reporting the net income in financial statements by the usual accrual method.

In contrast to the example for the Pryor Company in which income taxes were deferred, income taxes *may be prepaid* when taxable income exceeds accounting income because of timing differences. The portion of taxes paid on income deferred for accounting purposes would be reported as prepaid taxes in the balance sheet. When the income is reported as earned for accounting purposes in a later period, the *prepaid taxes are recognized as tax expense* applicable to the income currently reported but *taxed in an earlier period.*[6]

---

[6] A good example of this treatment is found in the annual report of the Ford Motor Company. A recent balance sheet showed "Income Taxes Allocable to the Following Year," $206.5 million, as a current asset. This large prepaid tax came about as a result of estimated car warranty expense being deducted from revenue in the period in which cars were sold; for income tax purposes, this expense is deductible only when it is actually incurred.

TAX PLANNING

Federal income tax laws have become so complex that detailed tax planning is now a way of life for most business firms. Almost all companies today engage professional tax specialists to review the tax aspects of major business decisions and to develop plans for legally minimizing income taxes. We will now consider some areas in which tax planning may offer substantial benefits.

Form of Business Organization

Objective 7
Explain how tax planning is used in choosing the form of business organization and the capital structure.

Tax factors should be carefully considered at the time a business is organized. As a sole proprietor or partner, a business owner will pay taxes at individual rates, ranging currently from 15 to 33% (including surtax), on the business income earned in any year *whether or not it is withdrawn from the business.* Corporations, on the other hand, are taxed on earnings at rates varying from 15 to 39% (including surtax). In determining taxable income, corporations deduct salaries paid to owners for services but cannot deduct dividends paid to stockholders. Both *salaries and dividends* are taxable income to the persons receiving them.

These factors must be weighed in deciding in any given situation whether the corporate or noncorporate form of business organization is preferable. There is no simple rule of thumb, even considering only these basic differences. To illustrate, suppose that Able, a married man, starts a business which he expects will produce, before any compensation to himself and before income taxes, an average annual income of $80,000. Able plans to withdraw $20,000 yearly from the business. The combined corporate and individual taxes under the corporate and sole proprietorship form of business organization are summarized below.

Form of Business Organization

	CORPORATION	SOLE PROPRIETORSHIP
Business income	$80,000	$80,000
Salary to Able	20,000	
Taxable income	$60,000	$80,000
Corporate Tax:		
15% of first $50,000 .... $7,500		
25% of next $10,000 2,500	10,000	
Net income	$50,000	$80,000
Combined corporate and individual tax:		
Corporate tax on $60,000 income*	$10,000	
Individual tax—joint return		
On Able's $20,000 salary......................	3,000	
On Able's $80,000 business income		$18,938
Total tax on business income	$13,000	$18,938

* Able's personal exemptions and deductions have been ignored, on the assumption that his other income equals personal exemptions and deductions. We have rounded amounts to the nearest dollar.

Under these assumptions, the formation of a corporation is favorable from an income tax viewpoint. If the business is incorporated, the combined tax on the corporation and on Able personally will be $13,000. If the business is not incorporated, the tax will be $18,938, or almost 50% more. The key to the advantage indicated for choosing the corporate form of organization is that Able did not take much of the earnings out of the corporation.

If Able decides to operate as a corporation, the $50,000 of net income retained in the corporation will be taxed to Able as ordinary income *when and if* it is distributed as dividends. In other words, Able cannot get the money out of the corporation without paying personal income tax on it. An advantage of the corporation as a form of business organization is that Able can *postpone* payment of a significant amount of tax as long as the earnings remain invested in the business.

■ **If All Earnings of the Business Are to Be Withdrawn** Now let us change one of our basic assumptions and say that Able plans to withdraw all net income from the business each year. Under this assumption the sole proprietorship form of organization would be better than a corporation from an income tax standpoint. If the business is incorporated and Able again is to receive a $20,000 salary plus dividends equal to the $50,000 of corporate net income, the total tax will be much higher. The corporate tax of $10,000 plus personal tax of $15,733 (based on $20,000 salary and $50,000 in dividends) would amount to $25,733. This is considerably higher than the $18,938 which we previously computed as the tax liability if the business operated as a proprietorship.

We have purposely kept our example as short as possible. You can imagine some variations which would produce different results. Perhaps Able might incorporate and set his salary at, say, $75,000 instead of $20,000. If this salary were considered reasonable by the IRS, the corporation's taxable income would drop to $5,000 rather than the $60,000 used in our illustration. This and other possible assumptions should make clear that the choice between a corporation and a sole proprietorship requires careful consideration of a number of factors in each individual case. Both the marginal rate of tax to which individual business owners are subject and the extent to which profits are to be withdrawn are always basic issues in studying the relative advantages of one form of business organization over another.

Under certain conditions, small, closely held corporations may elect to be Subchapter S corporations, in which case the corporation pays no tax but the individual shareholders are taxed directly on the corporation's earnings.

Tax Planning in the Choice of Financial Structure

In deciding upon the best means of raising capital to start or expand a business, consideration should be given to income taxes. Different forms of business financing produce different amounts of tax expense. Interest paid on debt, for example, is *fully deductible* in computing taxable income, but dividends paid on preferred or common stock are not. This factor operates as a strong incentive to finance expansion by borrowing.

Let us assume that a corporation subject to a 39% marginal tax rate needs $100,000 to invest in productive assets on which it can earn a 20% annual return. If the company obtains the needed money by issuing $100,000 in 14% preferred stock, it will earn *after taxes* only $12,200, which is not even enough to cover the $14,000 preferred dividend. (This after-tax amount is computed as $20,000 income less taxes at 39% of $20,000.)

Now let us assume, on the other hand, that the company borrowed $100,000 at 14% interest. The additional gross income would be $20,000 but interest expense of $14,000 would be deducted, leaving taxable income of $6,000. The tax on the $6,000 at 39% would be $2,340, leaving after-tax income of $3,660. Analysis along these lines is also needed in choosing between debt financing and financing by issuing common stock.

The choice of financial structure should be considered from the viewpoint of investors, especially in the case of a small, closely held corporation.

CASE IN POINT ■ The owners of a small incorporated business decided to invest an additional $100,000 in the business to finance expanding operations. They were undecided whether to make a $100,000 loan to the corporation or to purchase $100,000 worth of additional capital stock. Finally, the owners turned to a CPA firm for advice. The CPAs suggested that the loan would be better because the $100,000 cash invested could be returned by the corporation at the maturity date of the loan without imposing any individual income tax on the owners. The loan could be arranged to mature in installments or at a single fixed date. Renewal of the note could be easily arranged if desired.

On the other hand, if the $100,000 investment were made by purchase of additional shares of capital stock, the return of these funds to the owners would be more difficult. If the $100,000 came back to the owners in the form of dividends, a considerable portion would be consumed by individual income taxes. If the corporation repurchased $100,000 worth of its stock from the owners, the retained earnings account would become restricted by this amount. In summary, the CPAs pointed out that it is easier for persons in control of a small corporation to get their money back if the investment takes the form of a loan rather than the purchase of additional capital stock.

Tax Shelters

A tax shelter is an investment which produces a loss for tax purposes in the near term but hopefully proves profitable in the long run. The reason for seeking a tax loss is to offset this loss against other income and, by so doing, lower both taxable income and the income tax owed for the current year. Near the close of each year, many newspaper advertisements offer an opportunity to invest in a program which promises to reduce the investor's present tax liability yet produce future profits. These programs have a particular appeal to persons in high tax brackets who face the prospect of paying much of a year's net income as taxes.

A limited partnership organization has often been used for tax shelter ventures, so that each investor may claim his or her share of the immediate losses. Typical of the types of ventures are oil and gas drilling programs and real estate investments offering high leverage and accelerated depreciation. The real estate limited partnership appears to have been virtually wiped out by the Tax Reform Act of 1986, but no doubt the promoters of tax shelters will find new loopholes to exploit. A principal appeal of real estate tax shelters has been their use of rapid depreciation to produce losses in early years of the partnership. The change in the law drastically curtails rapid depreciation. A major goal of the Tax Reform Act of 1986 was to curtail or eliminate tax shelters in general. Among the heaviest blows to tax shelters were: (1) the elimination of favorable treatment of long-term capital gains; (2) the strengthening of the Alternative Minimum Tax to catch investors deeply involved in sheltering income; and (3) the change to less liberal depreciation. The depreciation of rental residential property is limited to the straight-line method over a period of 27.5 years and other real estate to 31.5 years.

Unfortunately, many so-called tax shelters have proved to be merely unprofitable investments, in which the investors saved taxes but lost larger amounts of capital. A sound approach to tax shelters should probably be based on the premise that if an investment does not appear *worthwhile without the promised tax benefits, it should be avoided.*

Some tax shelters, on the other hand, are not of a high-risk nature. State and municipal bonds offer a modest rate of interest which is tax exempt. Investment in real estate with deductions for mortgage interest, property taxes, and depreciation will often show losses which offset other taxable income, yet eventually prove profitable because of rising market value, especially in periods of inflation.

End-of-Chapter Review

CONCEPTS INTRODUCED OR EMPHASIZED IN CHAPTER 18

The major concepts in this chapter include:

- A brief history of the federal income tax.

- Advantages of the cash basis of accounting for preparing individual income tax returns.

- Formula for determining the taxable income of an individual.

- The on-again, off-again taxation of capital gains.

- The pay-as-you-go plan: withholding and payments of estimated tax.

- The Alternative Minimum Tax.

- Determining the taxable income of a corporation.

- Interperiod income tax allocation.

- Tax planning: legally minimizing income taxes.

In this chapter we have emphasized the pervasive influence of income taxes on the economic decisions of both individuals and corporations. The basic elements of determining taxable income and computing the tax liability have been discussed and illustrated. Our attention has been focused on these basic concepts rather than on the step-by-step mechanics of filling out a tax return.

KEY TERMS INTRODUCED OR EMPHASIZED IN CHAPTER 18

Accelerated cost recovery system (ACRS)   An accelerated depreciation method for income tax purposes for depreciable assets acquired after 1980. This method is used in income tax returns but not in financial statements prepared in accordance with generally accepted accounting principles.

Adjusted gross income   A subtotal in an individual's tax return computed by deducting from gross income any business-related expenses and other deductions authorized by law. A key figure to which many measurements are linked.

Capital asset   Stocks, bonds, and real estate not used in a trade or business.

Capital gain or loss   The difference between the cost basis of a capital asset and the amount received from its sale.

Cash basis of accounting   Revenue is recorded when received in cash and expenses are recorded in the period in which payment is made. Widely used for individual tax returns and for tax returns of professional firms, farms, and service-type businesses. Gives taxpayers a degree of control over taxable income by deliberate timing of collections and payments. Not used in most financial statements because it fails to match revenue with related expenses.

Declaration of estimated tax   Self-employed persons and others with income not subject to withholding must file by April 15 each year a declaration of estimated tax for the current year and must make quarterly payments of such tax.

Gross income   All income and gains from whatever source derived unless specifically excluded by law, such as interest on state and municipal bonds.

Interperiod tax allocation   Allocation of income tax expense among accounting periods because of timing differences between accounting income and taxable income. Causes income tax expense reported in financial statements to be in logical relationship to accounting income.

Itemized deductions   Personal expenses deductible from adjusted gross income, such as mortgage interest, property taxes, contributions, and medical expenses and casualty losses in excess of certain amounts.

Marginal tax rate   The rate to which a taxpayer is subject on the top dollar of income received.

Modified accelerated cost recovery system (MACRS)   A modified ACRS to be used for tax purposes in depreciating tangible property placed in service after 1986. Provides less liberal write-offs than ACRS.

Personal exemption   A deduction of specified amount from adjusted gross income for the taxpayer, the taxpayer's spouse, and each dependent.

Standard deduction   A specified amount to be deducted from adjusted gross income. An alternative to listing itemized deductions, such as mortgage interest and property taxes.

Tax credit   An amount to be subtracted from the tax itself. Examples are the earned income credit and the credit for child-care expenses.

Tax planning   A systematic process of minimizing income taxes by considering in advance the tax consequences of alternative business or investment actions. A major factor in choosing the form of business organization and capital structure, in lease-or-buy decisions, and in timing of transactions.

Tax shelters   Investment programs designed to show losses in the short term to be offset against other taxable income, but offering the hope of long-run profits.

Taxable income   The computed amount to which the appropriate tax rate is to be applied to arrive at the tax liability.

DEMONSTRATION PROBLEM FOR YOUR REVIEW

Ralph and Jennifer Lane own and operate a restaurant and an apartment building. They file a joint income tax return. The Lanes furnish over one-half the support of their son who attends college and who earned $2,560 in part-time jobs and summer employment. They also support Ralph's father who has no taxable income of his own.

The depreciation basis of the apartment building is $160,000; depreciation is recorded at the rate of 4% per year on a straight-line basis. During the current year, the Lanes had the following cash receipts and cash expenditures applicable to the restaurant business, the apartment building, other investments, and personal activities.

Cash receipts:	
Cash withdrawn from restaurant (net income, $48,000)	$36,000
Gross rentals from apartment building	28,800
Cash dividends on stock owned jointly	2,760
Interest on River City bonds	976
Received from sale of stock purchased two years ago for $10,000	16,000
Received from sale of motorboat purchased three years ago for $4,792 and used entirely for pleasure	2,712
Cash expenditures:	
Expenditures relating to apartment building:	
Interest on mortgage	7,200
Property taxes	4,720
Insurance (one year)	560
Utilities	2,368
Repairs and maintenance	3,872
Gardening	640
Other cash expenditures:	
Mortgage interest on residence	3,160
Property taxes on residence	1,700
Insurance on residence	400
State income tax paid	1,900
State sales taxes	700
Charitable contributions	1,200
Medical expenses	1,376
Payment by Ralph to a Keogh H.R.10 plan	3,000
Payment by Jennifer to an IRA	2,000
Payments on declaration of estimated tax for current year	7,000

Instructions **a** Determine the amount of taxable income Ralph and Jennifer Lane would report on their federal income tax return for the current year. In your computation of taxable income, first list the net income of the restaurant business. Second, show the revenue and expenses of the apartment building and the amount of net income from this source. Third, show the data for dividends and capital gains. After combining the above amounts and appropriate deductions to determine adjusted gross income, list the itemized deductions and personal exemptions to arrive at taxable income. Assume that the personal exemption is $2,000 each.

b Compute the income tax liability for Ralph and Jennifer Lane using the tax rate information on page 698. Indicate the amount of tax due (or refund to be received).

SOLUTION TO DEMONSTRATION PROBLEM

a *Computation of taxable income:*

Net income from restaurant business...			$48,000
Net rental income from apartment building:			
Gross rentals..		$28,800	
Depreciation (4% of $160,000)............................	$6,400		
Interest on mortgage	7,200		
Property taxes	4,720		
Insurance (one year)......................................	560		
Utilities	2,368		
Repairs and maintenance.................................	3,872		
Gardening...	640	25,760	
Net rental income (amount included			
in adjusted gross income).......................................			3,040
Dividends...			2,760
Capital gain on sale of stock			6,000
Subtotal..			$59,800
Deductions to arrive at adjusted gross income:			
Contribution to Keogh plan		$ 3,000	
Contribution to IRA...		2,000	5,000
Adjusted gross income...			$54,800
Deductions from adjusted gross income:			
Itemized deductions:			
Mortgage interest on residence	$3,160		
Property taxes on residence	1,700		
State income taxes paid	1,900		
Charitable contributions	1,200	$ 7,960	
Personal exemptions ($2,000 × 4)................................		8,000	
Total deductions from adjusted gross income:			15,960
Taxable income..			$38,840

Explanation of omitted items:

  Cash withdrawn from business ($36,000) is irrelevant;
    entire business income is taxed.

  Interest on River City bonds is excluded from gross income.

  Loss on sale of motorboat is personal and is not deductible.

  Insurance on residence is not deductible.

  Medical expenses are less than 7½% of adjusted gross
    income ($54,800), and therefore none is deductible.

b *Computation of income tax liability on joint return:*

Taxable income (see **a**)		$38,840
Tax on first $29,750 at 15%	$4,463	
Tax on next $9,090 at 28%	2,545	
Total tax..		$ 7,008
Less: Payments on estimated tax...		7,000
Tax remaining to be paid with return		$ 8

SELF-TEST QUESTIONS

Answers to these questions appear on page 727.

1 Which of the following is applicable to the federal income tax system in the United States?

a A taxpayer who structures a transaction so as to lower or avoid income taxes is guilty of tax evasion.

b The major classes of taxpayers are individuals, sole proprietorships, partnerships, and corporations.

c One result of the Tax Reform Act of 1986 was lower tax rates for both individual taxpayers and for corporations.

d The original United States Constitution provided for a federal income tax system and authorized the Treasury Department to pass new tax legislation as necessary.

2 In preparing the income tax return for an individual taxpayer:

a Federal income taxes withheld from an individual's salary are deducted from taxable income before computing the tax liability.

b A cash basis taxpayer may postpone paying an expense in order to receive a tax deduction in a subsequent year.

c Individual taxpayers may choose to itemize their deductions, or to deduct the personal exemptions, but are not allowed to deduct both.

d Receipt of a large refund each year indicates better tax planning than does receipt of a very small refund.

3 Following the Tax Reform Act of 1986, the status of capital gains and losses is as follows: (More than one answer may be correct.)

a In computing adjusted gross income for individuals, only $3,000 of capital losses may be offset against capital gains.

b Capital gains, whether long term or short term, are taxed at the same rate as other income.

c An individual taxpayer who has a net capital gain of $10,000 in 1990 will be taxed on the entire amount in 1990; a taxpayer who has a net capital loss of $10,000 in 1990 may deduct only $3,000 in 1990.

d Capital assets include assets used for a trade or business, but not items such as a personal residence or automobile used for personal use.

4 When a business is organized as a corporation:

a Income taxes expense recorded in the accounting records is based upon accounting income and may differ from the income tax liability shown in the corporate income tax return.

b The treatment of capital gains and losses is the same as for individuals—capital gains are taxed at ordinary income rates; net capital losses of $3,000 may be deducted in computing taxable income.

c The amount of the standard deduction is greater than the amount of standard deduction for individuals.

d Taxable income is the same as net income before taxes in the income statement.

5 Which of the following are valid statements regarding tax planning and the choice of business organization? (More than one answer may be correct.)

a When a business is organized as a corporation, no income tax is paid on earnings that remain invested in the business.

b In computing a corporation's taxable income, the corporation may deduct salaries paid to owners, but may not deduct dividends.

c When a business is organized as a sole proprietorship, the owner must pay taxes at individual rates on the entire amount of business income, regardless of amounts withdrawn by the owner.

d An individual who organizes a business as a corporation must pay individual income taxes on any salary received from the corporation, as well as on any dividends received.

Assignment Material

REVIEW QUESTIONS

1 How did the income tax rates for individuals during the 1980s compare with the rates prevailing in the 1970s? Explain.

2 State two goals of tax planning.

3 "The increase in the standard deduction by the Tax Reform Act of 1986 was primarily of benefit to those individuals who usually did not itemize their deductions." Do you agree with this statement? Explain.

4 What are the four major classes of taxpayers under the federal income tax law?

5 List three of the principal changes affecting individual taxpayers made by the tax legislation of the later 1980s.

6 It has been claimed that corporate income is subject to "double taxation." Explain the meaning of this expression.

7 Taxes are characterized as *progressive, proportional,* or *regressive* with respect to any given base. Describe an income tax rate structure that would fit each of these characterizations.

8 State whether you agree with the following statements and explain your reasoning.

a A person in a very high tax bracket who makes a cash contribution to a college will reduce his or her tax liability by more than the amount of the gift.

b Newspaper stories occasionally tell of very wealthy individuals who are so deeply involved in tax sheltered ventures that they are not required to pay any income tax. Does the Tax Reform Act of 1986 deal with such situations? Explain.

9 State in equation form the federal income tax formula for individuals, beginning with total income and ending with taxable income.

10 List some differences between the tax rules for corporations and the tax rules for individuals.

11 What are some objectives of the federal income tax structure other than providing revenue for the government?

12 Explain the difference between *tax avoidance* and *tax evasion,* and give an example of each.

13 Peggy Bame, M.D., files her income tax return on a cash basis. During the current year she collected $12,600 from patients for medical services rendered in prior years, and billed patients $77,000 for services rendered this year. She has accounts receivable of $16,400 relating to this year's billings at the end of the year. What amount of gross income from her practice should Bame report on her tax return?

14 Joe Gilmore, a single man, files his income tax return on a cash basis. During the current year $800 of interest was credited to him on his savings account; he withdrew his interest on January 18 of the following year. No other interest and no dividends were received by Gilmore.

In December of the current year Gilmore purchased some business equipment having an estimated service life of 10 years. He also paid a year's rent in advance on certain business property on December 29 of the current year. Explain how these items would be treated on Gilmore's income tax return for the current year.

15 Which of the following is not a capital asset according to the Internal Revenue Code? (a) an investment in General Motors stock; (b) a personal residence; (c) equipment used in the operation of a business; (d) an investment in Krugerrands (gold coins).

16 An individual with a yearly salary of $40,000 had a capital loss of $60,000. To what extent, if any, could this capital loss be offset against the salary in computing taxable income? Explain.

17 Even when a taxpayer uses the accrual method of accounting, taxable income may differ from accounting income. Give four examples of differences between the tax treatment and accounting treatment of items that are included in the determination of income.

18 Under what circumstances is the accounting procedure known as *income tax allocation* appropriate? Explain the purpose of this procedure.

19 List some tax factors to be considered in deciding whether to organize a new business as a corporation or as a partnership.

20 Explain how the corporate income tax makes debt financing in general more attractive than financing through the issuance of preferred stock.

21 The depreciation expense computed by Farr Company under the modified accelerated cost recovery system (MACRS) appeared in the tax return as $150,000. In the accounting records and financial statements, Farr's depreciation was computed on the straight-line basis and amounted to $100,000. Under interperiod tax allocation procedures, would Farr Company's balance sheet show prepaid income taxes or deferred income taxes? Explain.

22 Some of the decisions that business owners must make in organizing and operating a business will affect the amount of income taxes to be paid. List some of these decisions which affect the amount of income taxes legally payable.

EXERCISES

Exercise 18-1
Accounting
terminology

Listed below are nine technical accounting terms introduced in this chapter:

Alternative Minimum Tax	Itemized deductions	Tax credit
Adjusted gross income	Tax shelter	Personal exemption
Interperiod tax allocation	Reserve method	Cash basis of accounting

Each of the following statements may (or may not) describe one of these technical terms. For each statement, indicate the accounting term described, or answer "None" if the statement does not correctly describe any of the terms.

a Important to individual taxpayers who pay large amounts of state income tax, and make large charitable contributions.

b An amount subtracted from the gross tax liability.

c Assures that profitable corporations and high-income individuals do not escape taxation altogether through any combination of tax shelters and tax preferences.

d A subtotal in an individual's tax return, computed by deducting from gross income any business-related expenses, contributions to retirement plans, and other deductions authorized by law.

e Revenue recorded when received in cash and expenses recorded in period payment is made.

f Income tax recognized each period as a constant percentage of net sales.

g An investment program designed to show losses in the short run to be offset against other taxable income, but offering the hope of long-run profits.

h Causes income tax expense reported in financial statements to be in logical relationship to accounting income.

i A method of accounting for bad debts no longer permitted in determining taxable income.

Exercise 18-2
Cash basis or
accrual basis

Individual taxpayers have the choice of preparing their income tax returns on the cash basis of accounting or on the accrual basis. However, nearly all tax returns filed by individuals are prepared on the cash basis. Many small corporations in service-type businesses also file on the cash basis. How do you explain:

a The strong preference by taxpayers for the cash basis of accounting?

b The government's willingness to accept tax returns prepared on the cash basis in an era in which the accrual basis is the standard approach underlying generally accepted accounting principles?

Exercise 18-3
Tax strategy:
investments

Margaret Stuart, an executive earning an annual salary of $75,000, is a strong believer in income tax planning. One of her regular practices each December 1 is to review her income and expenses for the first 11 months of the current year. After estimating her income tax liability, she then considers what transactions, if any, she might carry out in December which would reduce her tax payable for the current year. Thus far in the first 11 months of the year, Stuart has had no capital gains or losses. In this December 1 review, Stuart notes that four of her five security investments are currently trading on the New York Stock Exchange at prices above her cost. The fifth stock (of which Stuart holds 300 shares) is trading at $50 per share, and Stuart's cost is $60 per share. Stuart believes that the stock may decline a little further, but she feels confident that it will eventually trade much higher.

You are to suggest what action Stuart might take with respect to her security investments that would reduce her tax liability for the current year. Explain fully both the advantages and the possible disadvantages of the action you suggest.

Exercise 18-4
Impact of the Tax
Reform Act of
1986

Explain briefly the impact of the Tax Reform Act of 1986 on each of the following:

a Tax rates on individuals

b Tax rates on corporations

c Capital gains of individuals

d The standard deduction and low-income taxpayers

Exercise 18-5
Gross income:
items to include
and items to
exclude

You are to consider the income tax status of the items listed below. List the numbers 1 to 15 on your answer sheet. For each item state whether it is *included in gross income* or *excluded from gross income* for federal income tax on individuals. Add explanatory comments if needed.

(1) Inheritance of ranch from estate of deceased uncle

(2) Amount received as damages for injury in automobile accident

(3) Tips received by waiter

(4) Pension received by veteran from U.S. government for military service

(5) Dividends received on investment in Ford Motor stock

(6) Trip to London received by employee as award for outstanding performance

(7) Rent received on personal residence while on an extended European tour

(8) First prize of $14,000,000 won in California state lottery

(9) Gain on the sale of a 1953 Jaguar purchased 10 years ago

(10) Proceeds of life insurance policy received on death of spouse

(11) Share of income from partnership in excess of drawings

(12) Gain on sale of Super Bowl tickets by season ticket holder

(13) Interest received on bonds of state of Texas

(14) Value of U.S. Savings Bonds received as a gift

(15) Salary received from corporation by a stockholder who owns directly or indirectly all of the corporation's capital stock

Exercise 18-6
Is it deductible?

You are to determine the deductibility status, for federal income tax purposes, of each of the items listed below. List the numbers 1 to 10 on your answer sheet. For each item state whether the item *is deducted to arrive at adjusted gross income; deducted from adjusted gross income;* or *not deductible.*

(1) Sales taxes

(2) Medical expense of $2,000 incurred by a taxpayer with adjusted gross income of $50,000

(3) State income tax paid

(4) Property taxes paid on personal residence

(5) Interest paid on mortgage on personal residence

(6) Loss on sale of equipment used in a business

(7) Capital loss on sale of an investment in securities

(8) Contribution to a Keogh H.R.10 retirement plan

(9) Payment to an IRA

(10) Damage by storm to motorboat used for pleasure

Exercise 18-7
Computing taxable income

Listed below is income tax data for Arthur and Jane Brown, a married couple filing a joint tax return. You are to compute the *taxable income,* using *only* the relevant data.

Total income, including gifts, inheritances, interest on municipal bonds, etc.	*$56,000*
Exclusions (gifts, inheritances, interest on municipal bonds, etc.)	*8,300*
Deductions to arrive at adjusted gross income	*1,700*
Itemized deductions	*7,100*
Personal exemptions ($2,000 each)	*4,000*
Income taxes withheld from salary	*7,300*

Exercise 18-8
Computing tax on individuals

Use the tax rate information on page 690 to compute the tax for each of the following. Round amounts to the nearest dollar.

	TAXABLE INCOME
a Single taxpayer	*$24,000*
b Married couple filing joint return	*$48,050*

Exercise 18-9
Computing tax liability of a corporation

Raintree Corporation reports the following income for the year:

Income from operations	*$260,000*
Capital gain	*90,000*

In computing the tax, assume that corporate tax rates are as follows:

On first $50,000 of taxable income	15%
On second $25,000 of taxable income	25%
On taxable income over $75,000	34%
A surtax on taxable income between $100,000 and $335,000	5%

Compute Raintree's tax liability for the year.

**Exercise 18-10
Interperiod tax
allocation**

Mission Bay Corporation deducted on its tax return for 1990 an expense of $100,000 which was not recognized as an expense for accounting purposes until 1991. The corporation's accounting income before income taxes in each of the two years was $525,000. The company uses tax allocation procedures.

a Prepare the journal entries required at the end of 1990 and 1991 to record income tax expense. To compute the tax, multiply the entire amount of taxable income by 34%.

b Prepare a two-column schedule showing the net income to appear on the financial statements for 1990 and 1991, assuming that tax allocation procedures are used. Also prepare a similar schedule on the assumption that tax allocation procedures are not used.

PROBLEMS

Group A

**Problem 18A-1
Computing the
tax: joint return**

Fred and Kay Johnson are married and file a joint tax return. They claim one exemption each, plus two exemptions for dependents. Both Fred and Kay are employed; each earns an annual salary of $30,000. During the year Fred contributed $2,000 to an IRA. This contribution was fully deductible because neither Fred nor Kay is covered by an employer-sponsored pension plan. The following information has been gathered by Fred and Kay in getting ready to prepare their tax return. Assume the standard deduction is $5,000.

Federal income tax withheld from salaries	$ 8,000
Payments of estimated tax	2,800
Total income (including $60,000 salaries, $1,000 in municipal bond interest, and $9,000 income from other sources)	70,000
Itemized deductions	5,250
Payment to an IRA	2,000
Personal exemptions ($2,000 × 4)	8,000

Instructions

a Compute gross income.

b Compute adjusted gross income.

c Compute taxable income.

d Compute the amount of tax remaining to be paid or the refund to be claimed.

**Problem 18A-2
Determining
adjusted gross
income and
taxable income**

The following two cases are independent of each other. The instructions for preparing your solutions appear at the end of the second case.

Case A

Fernando Rivero, an independent photographer conducting his own practice, had total income of $56,000 for the year just ended. This amount included $1,100 of interest on municipal bonds; the remainder was from self-employment. During the year Rivero contributed $7,000 to a Keogh H.R.10 retirement plan. His itemized deductions amounted to $2,300, and he was entitled to one personal exemption of $2,000. Assume the standard deduction is $3,000 for a single taxpayer.

Case B
Janet Raymond, a real estate broker conducting her own real estate practice, uses the accrual basis of accounting in maintaining accounting records and financial statements. However, for income tax purposes, she uses the cash basis of accounting. During the current year, her business net income (computed on an accrual basis) was $80,000. Between the beginning and end of the current year, her financial statements showed that receivables from clients increased by $13,000, and current liabilities for rent and other operating expenses decreased by $8,000. The net income for the business included $2,000 of interest received on municipal bonds.

Raymond has a personal savings account to which $800 in interest was credited during the year, none of which was withdrawn from the bank. In addition to business expenses taken into account in computing the net income of her real estate practice, Raymond has $2,000 in deductions to arrive at adjusted gross income. Her personal exemption amounts to $2,000 and her itemized deductions are $6,200. Assume the standard deduction is $3,000.

Instructions
For each of the two cases described above, prepare a separate schedule showing in appropriate order all the steps necessary to determine the taxpayer's *adjusted gross income* and the *taxable income* for the year. For Case B, your solution would show: (1) business net income (accrual basis), (2) the increases and/or decreases for conversion to the cash basis, (3) the amount of business net income on a cash basis, and (4) the steps to determine taxable income.

Problem 18A-3
Joint return: a
comprehensive
problem

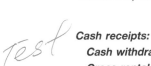

Charles and Lisa Castillo file a joint income tax return. They provide more than one-half the support of their son who attends college and who earned $4,000 during the year in part time jobs and summer employment. The Castillos also support Lisa's father who has no taxable income of his own.

The principal income of the Castillos is from a hardware store which they own and operate. They also own a small apartment building. The depreciation basis of the apartment building is $200,000; depreciation is recorded at the rate of 4% on a straight-line basis. During the current year, the Castillos had the following cash receipts and cash expenditures applicable to the hardware business, the apartment building, other investments, and personal activities.

Cash receipts:

Cash withdrawn from hardware store (net income, $60,000)	45,000
Gross rentals from apartment building	40,000
Cash dividends on stock owned jointly	3,400
Interest on River City bonds	1,220
Received from sale of stock purchased two years ago for $12,500	20,000
Received from sale of motorboat purchased three years ago for $5,000 and used entirely for pleasure	3,000

Cash expenditures:

Expenditures relating to apartment building:

Interest on mortgage	9,000
Property taxes	5,900
Insurance (one year)	700
Utilities	3,000
Repairs and maintenance	5,000
Gardening	1,000

Other cash expenditures:

Mortgage interest on residence	4,000
Property taxes on residence	2,100
Insurance on residence	1,200
State income tax paid	2,400
State sales taxes	800
Charitable contributions	1,300
Medical expenses	1,500
Payment by Charles to a Keogh H.R.10 plan	4,000
Payment by Lisa to an IRA	2,000
Payments on declaration of estimated tax for current year	10,000

Instructions

a Determine the amount of taxable income Charles and Lisa Castillo would report on their federal income tax return for the current year. In your computation of taxable income, first list the net income of the hardware business. Second, show the revenue and expenses of the apartment building and the amount of net income from this source. Third, show the data for dividends and capital gains. After combining the above amounts and appropriate deductions to determine adjusted gross income, list the itemized deductions and personal exemptions to arrive at taxable income. Assume that the standard deduction is $5,000 and the personal exemption is $2,000 each.

b Compute the income tax liability for Charles and Lisa Castillo using the tax rate information on page 698. Indicate the amount of tax due (or refund to be received).

Problem 18A-4
Corporation tax
return

Riverbend Corporation had total revenue for the year of $304,000, including dividends of $6,000 from domestic corporations. Expenses were as follows:

Advertising expense	$ 18,800
Depreciation expense	6,400
Property taxes expense	4,500
Rent expense	34,000
Salaries expense	110,000
Travel expense	8,400
Utilities expense	6,900

Instructions

a Prepare an income statement for the corporation. Show Dividends Received as a separate item following Income from Operations. Reference the amount for Income Tax Expense to a separate supporting schedule as called for in **b** below.

b Compute Riverbend's total income tax for the year in a schedule which begins with "Income before income taxes," and shows all details of the tax computation. Use the 70% rate to compute the dividends received deduction.

Problem 18A-5
Interperiod
income tax
allocation

The following summary amounts reflect the operations of Dunleer Corporation for the year 1990.

Net sales	$1,185,000
Cost of goods sold	630,000
Selling expenses	100,000
Administrative expenses	50,000

In addition to the selling expenses shown above, Dunleer Corporation incurred a cost of $65,000 during the year for a sales promotion campaign for a new line of products. The $65,000 cost of this sales campaign will be deducted in computing taxable income for 1990, but the company has chosen to defer this $65,000 expenditure for accounting purposes so that it may be charged against revenue during 1991 when sales of the new product line will be reflected in revenue. The company will follow tax allocation procedures in reporting the income taxes expense in the income statement during 1990.

In 1991, revenue was $1,400,000. The total of cost of goods sold and expenses (including the $65,000 of sales promotion cost deferred from 1990) amounted to $1,000,000.

Instructions   **a**   Prepare an income statement for Dunleer Corporation for 1990. In a separate supporting schedule, show your computation of the provision for federal income taxes for 1990. In computing the tax, use the short-cut method of multiplying the entire taxable income by 34%.

b   Prepare the journal entry which should be made to record Dunleer's current income taxes expense, the current income tax liability, and the deferred income tax liability at the end of 1990.

c   Prepare the journal entry needed at December 31, 1991, to record the company's current income taxes expense for 1991. (Again, use the short-cut method to compute income tax expense.)

Group B

Problem 18B-1
Joint return:
computing tax

Marc and Carol Levine are married and file a joint tax return. They claim one personal exemption each, plus an exemption for their young daughter. Marc's salary for the year was $20,000 and he contributed $2,000 to an IRA. Carol's salary was $22,000. Neither Marc nor Carol is covered by an employer-sponsored pension plan.

Assume that a personal exemption is $2,000 and the standard deduction for a married couple is $5,000. Marc and Carol have compiled the following information as a preliminary step toward preparing their joint tax return. (Some of the information may not be required.)

Total income, (including $42,000 salaries, $600 in muncipal bond interest, and $6,000 income from other sources)	$48,600
Federal income taxes withheld from salaries	4,000
Payments of estimated tax	1,000
Itemized deductions	3,560
Payment to an IRA (Marc)	2,000

Instructions   **a**   Compute gross income.

b   Compute adjusted gross income.

c   Compute taxable income.

d   Compute the amount of tax remaining to be paid or the refund to be claimed.

Problem 18B-2
Adjusted gross
income and
taxable income

The following two cases are independent of each other. See the instructions following the second case.

Case A   The following information related to the income tax situation of Rick Jones, an unmarried taxpayer, for the current year:

Total income	$96,000
Personal exemption	2,000
Deductions to arrive at adjusted gross income	7,680
Itemized deductions	9,740
Exclusions from gross income	1,920

Case B   Jill Friday, a self-employed psychiatrist, uses the accrual basis of accounting in maintaining records for her business and in preparing financial statements, but uses cash basis accounting in determining her income subject to federal income tax. For the current year, her business net income (computed on an accrual basis) was $90,480. A comparison of the current balance sheet for the business with a balance sheet prepared a year earlier showed an increase of $14,400 in accounts receivable from clients during the current year. Current liabilities for rent, salaries owed to employees, and other operating expenses were $8,160 less at year-end than they were one year ago. The business income of $90,480 included $1,440 of interest received on municipal bonds.

Apart from the business, Friday has a personal savings account to which $864 of interest was credited during the year, none of which was withdrawn. During the year Friday contributed $8,000 to a Keogh plan and $2,000 to an IRA. She has one personal exemption of $2,000 and her itemized deductions are $7,740.

Instructions   For each of the situations described above, determine the amount of the taxpayer's adjusted gross income and the taxable income for the year.

**Problem 18B-3
Joint return; a
comprehensive
problem**

Mike and Peggy Stevens, a married couple, had items of income and expense for the year as shown below. (Neither Mike nor Peggy is covered by an employer-sponsored pension plan.)

Salaries ($30,000, each)		$60,000
Consulting fees earned by Mike (net of expenses)		9,200
Dividends		580
Interest on bonds of State of Maine		252
Capital gains		3,900
Unused capital loss carryover from preceding year		2,100
Proceeds from life insurance policy upon death of relative		10,000
Payment by Mike to an IRA		2,000
Casualty loss, interest, taxes, and other expenditures (see list below)		52,040
Theft of furniture while on vacation	$ 2,200	
Interest on home mortgage	2,630	
Medical expenses	1,120	
Insurance on home	252	
Income taxes withheld (federal)	14,000	
Payments of estimated tax	2,000	
Miscellaneous deductible expenses in excess of 2% of AGI	200	
Sales taxes	500	
Property taxes on home	1,100	
State income taxes	1,900	
Clothes, food, and other living expenses	26,138	
Total (as listed above)	$52,040	

Instructions   Compute the taxable income and the income tax liability for Mike and Peggy Stevens who file a joint return. Use a format similar to that illustrated on pages 700 and 701 but list itemized deductions in detail. Your solution should show the various elements of gross income, any deduction needed to arrive at adjusted gross income, itemized deductions, personal exemptions, and taxable income, followed by a section for computation of tax. Use the tax rate information for married taxpayers filing joint returns (page 698). Add a note identifying any items listed in the problem which are not deductible.

Problem 18B-4
Corporation
return:
accounting
methods to
reduce tax

Ward Corporation is about to complete its first year of operation. The company has been successful and a tentative estimate by the controller indicates an income before taxes of $250,000 for this first year. Among the items entering into the calculation of the taxable income were the following:

(1) Inventories were reported on a first-in, first-out basis and would amount to $132,500 at year-end.

(2) No bad debt expense had been recognized thus far, but the controller felt there was a significant amount of long-past due receivables which probably should be written off as worthless.

(3) Under the straight-line method, depreciation for the year would be $15,000.

Officers of the corporation are concerned about the relatively large amount of income taxes for this first year and decide to change accounting methods and estimates for both financial reporting and tax purposes as follows:

(1) Inventories will be valued on the last-in, first-out basis, which will change the year-end amount to $100,000.

(2) Specific past-due accounts receivable in the amount of $10,000 will be written off as worthless at December 31.

(3) The MACRS method of depreciation will be used; this will increase depreciation expense from $15,000 to $28,750.

Instructions

a Determine the *taxable income* of Ward Corporation on the revised basis.

b Assume that tax rates for corporations are 15% on the first $50,000 of taxable income; 25% on the next $25,000; 34% on the next $25,000; and 39% (including surtax) on taxable income between $100,000 and $335,000. Compute the income tax liability for Ward Corporation (1) before the accounting changes, and (2) after the accounting changes. Also compute the reduction in the current year's income tax liability resulting from the accounting changes. Round all amounts to the nearest dollar.

Problem 18B-5
Corporation:
interperiod tax
allocation

The following information was taken from the accounting records of Ruger Corporation for 1991:

Net sales	$7,500,000
Cost of goods sold	5,400,000
Selling expenses	720,000
Administrative expenses	780,000

In addition to the costs and expenses shown above, Ruger Corporation spent $200,000 in December of 1991 to move its corporate headquarters from one city to another. This expenditure was deducted in computing taxable income, but the company chose to defer it in the accounting records and charge it against revenue of the following year. This deferral was considered desirable to achieve a better matching of costs with the increased revenue arising from the move. The company will follow income tax allocation procedures in reporting income taxes in the income statement for 1991.

In 1992, revenue was $8,010,000. The total of cost of goods sold and expenses (including the $200,000 deferred from 1991) amounted to $7,400,000. Thus income before taxes was $610,000.

Instructions

a Prepare an income statement for Ruger Corporation for 1991. In a separate schedule (Schedule A), show your computation of federal income taxes for 1991, using the shortcut method of multiplying the entire taxable income by 34%. Hint: First prepare the top part of the income statement from "Net sales" down to "Income before income taxes"; next prepare Schedule A, Income Tax Computation; and finally complete the income statement using data from Schedule A.

b Prepare the journal entry which should be made to record the income taxes expense and income tax liability (both current and deferred) at the end of 1991.

c Prepare the journal entry needed at December 31, 1992, to record the company's current income taxes expense for 1992 and the elimination of the deferred tax liability. Again, use the short-cut method in computing the tax.

BUSINESS DECISION CASES

Case 18-1
Investors choose between debt and equity

Bill and Hannah Bailey own a successful small company, Bailey Corporation. The outstanding capital stock consists of 1,000 shares of $100 par value, of which 400 shares are owned by Bill and 600 by Hannah. In order to finance a new branch operation, the corporation needs an additional $100,000 in cash. Bill and Hannah have this amount on deposit with a savings and loan association and intend to put these personal funds into the corporation in order to establish the new branch. They will either arrange for the corporation to issue to them at par an additional 1,000 shares of stock, or they will make a loan to the corporation at an interest rate of 12%.

Income before taxes of the corporation has been consistently averaging $150,000 a year, and annual dividends of $64,000 have been paid regularly. It is expected that the new branch will cause *income before taxes* to increase by $30,000. If new common stock is issued to finance the expansion, the total annual dividend of $64,000 will be continued unchanged. If a loan of $100,000 is arranged, the dividend will be reduced by $12,000, the amount of annual interest on the loan.

Instructions

a From the standpoint of the individual income tax return which Bill and Hannah file jointly, would there be any savings as between the stock issuance and the loan? Explain.

b From the standpoint of getting their money out of the corporation (assuming that the new branch is profitable), should Bill and Hannah choose capital stock or a loan for the infusion of new funds to the corporation?

c Prepare a two-column schedule, with one column headed If New Stock Is Used and the other headed If Loan Is Used. For each of these proposed methods of financing, show (1) the present corporate income *before taxes;* (2) the corporate income *before taxes* after the expansion; (3) the corporate income taxes after the expansion; and (4) the corporate net income after the expansion.

Case 18-2
Tax advantage; single proprietorship versus corporation

Gary and Joy Allen, a married couple, are in the process of organizing a business which is expected to produce, before any compensation to the Allens and before income taxes, an income of $72,000 per year. In deciding whether to operate as a sole proprietorship or as a corporation, the Allens are willing to make the choice on the basis of the relative income tax advantage under either form of organization.

The Allens file a joint return, have no other dependents, and have itemized deductions of $8,800 for the year.

If the business is operated as a sole proprietorship, the Allens expect to withdraw the entire income of $72,000 each year. Of this $72,000 total, the amount of $42,000 is considered a fair payment for the personal services rendered by the Allens, that is, $21,000 each.

If the business is operated as a corporation, the Allens will own all the shares; they will pay themselves salaries of $21,000 each and will withdraw as dividends the entire amount of the corporation's net income after income taxes.

It may be assumed that the accounting income and the taxable income for the corporation would be the same and that the personal exemption is $2,000. Mr. and Mrs. Allen have only minor amounts of nonbusiness income, which may be ignored.

Instructions

Determine the relative income tax advantage to the Allens of operating either as a sole proprietorship or as a corporation, and make a recommendation as to the form of organization they should adopt. Use the individual (joint return) and corporate tax rate information given on pages 698 and 702.

To provide a basis for this recommendation, you should prepare two schedules: one for operation as a sole proprietorship, and one for operation as a corporation.

In the first schedule, compute the total income tax on the Allens' joint personal return when the business is operated as a proprietorship. Also show the Allens' disposable income, that is, the amount withdrawn minus personal income tax.

In the second schedule, compute the corporate income tax and the amount remaining for dividends. Also compute the Allens' *personal* income tax if the corporate form of business entity is used. From these two steps, you can determine the Allens' disposable income under the corporate form of operation.

ANSWERS TO SELF-TEST QUESTIONS

1 c   2 b   3 b and c   4 a   5 b, c, and d

Measuring Cash Flows

In this chapter we introduce the third major financial statement—the statement of cash flows. First, we illustrate this financial statement and explain its purpose and usefulness. Next, we describe the three basic classifications of cash flows and emphasize the long-run importance of generating a positive net cash flow from operating activities. In the remainder of the chapter, we show step-by-step how a statement of cash flows can be developed from accrual-basis accounting records. Both the direct and indirect methods of reporting net cash flow from operating activities are illustrated and explained, with emphasis placed upon the direct method.

After studying this chapter you should be able to meet these Learning Objectives:

1 Explain the purposes and usefulness of a statement of cash flows.

2 Describe how cash transactions are classified within a statement of cash flows.

3 Compute the major cash flows relating to operating activities.

4 Explain why net income differs from net cash flow from operating activities.

5 Distinguish between the direct and indirect methods of reporting operating cash flow.

6 Compute the cash flows relating to investing and financing activities.

7 Explain why and how noncash investing and financing activities are disclosed in a statement of cash flows.

In Chapter 1, we introduced two key financial objectives of every business organization: *operating profitably* and *staying solvent.* Operating profitably means increasing the amount of the owners' equity through the activities of the business; in short, providing the owners with a satisfactory return on their investment. Staying solvent means being able to pay the debts and obligations of the business as they come due.

An income statement is designed to measure the success or failure of the business in achieving its objective of profitable operations. To some extent, a balance sheet shows whether or not the business is solvent. It shows, for example, the nature and amounts of current assets and current liabilities. From this information, users of the financial statements may compute such measures of solvency as the current ratio and the amount of working capital.

However, assessing the ability of a business to remain solvent involves more than just evaluating the liquid resources on hand at the balance sheet date. How much cash does the company receive during a year? What are the sources of these cash receipts? What expenditures are made each year for operating activities, and for investing and financing activities? To answer these questions, companies prepare a third major financial statement showing the sources and uses of liquid resources during the accounting period.

Until recently, the financial statement showing the sources and uses of liquid resources was called a *statement of changes in financial position.* Informally, this statement was often termed a *funds statement.* In preparing a funds statement, companies were permitted to define "liquid resources" in several different ways. Some companies prepared funds statements showing the sources and uses of cash. Other companies, however, prepared funds statements showing the sources and uses of working capital or some other type of "liquid resources." As a result of these alternative definitions of "funds," the statements of changes in financial position prepared by different companies varied greatly in content. This created difficulties for investors in comparing the funds statements of different companies.

To solve this problem, the FASB stated that beginning in 1988 all companies should discontinue the statement of changes in financial position and, instead, prepare a *statement of cash flows.*[1] The FASB provides considerably more guidance as to the form and content of the new statement of cash flows than it did for the old funds statement. To avoid confusion between the old "funds statement" and the new statement of cash flows, the FASB has asked companies to *avoid* the use of the word "funds" in the new financial statement.

STATEMENT OF CASH FLOWS

Purpose of the Statement

Objective 1
Explain the purposes and usefulness of a statement of cash flows.

The basic purpose of a statement of cash flows is to provide information about the *cash receipts* and *cash payments* of a business entity during the accounting period. (The term *cash flows* includes both cash receipts and cash payments.) In addition, the statement is intended to provide information about all the *investing* and *financing* activities of the company during the period. Thus,

---

[1] FASB Statement No. 95, "Statement of Cash Flows" (Stamford, Conn.: 1987), para. 34.

test

a statement of cash flows should assist investors, creditors, and others in assessing such factors as:

■ The company's ability to generate positive cash flows in future periods.

■ The company's ability to meet its obligations and to pay dividends.

■ The company's need for external financing.

■ Reasons for differences between the amount of net income and the related net cash flow from operating activities.

■ Both the cash and noncash aspects of the company's investment and financing transactions for the period.

■ Causes of the change in the amount of cash and cash equivalents between the beginning and the end of the accounting period.

Example of a Statement of Cash Flows

An example of a statement of cash flows is illustrated on the next page. Cash outflows are shown in brackets.[2]

Classification of Cash Flows

Objective 2
Describe how cash transactions are classified within a statement of cash flows.

The cash flows shown in the statement are grouped into three major categories: (1) *operating activities,* (2) *investing activities,* and (3) *financing activities.*[3] We will now look briefly at the way cash flows are classified among these three categories.

■ **Operating Activities**   All cash flows *other than* those associated with investing and financing activities are classified as operating activities. Cash flows from operating activities include:

CASH RECEIPTS	CASH PAYMENTS
Collections from customers for sales of goods and services	*Payments to suppliers of merchandise and services, including payments to employees*
Interest and dividends received	*Payments of Interest*
Other receipts from operations, as, for example, proceeds from settlement of litigation	*Payments of income taxes*
	Other expenditures relating to operations, as, for example, payments in settlement of litigation

---

[2] In this illustration, net cash flow from operating activities is determined by the *direct method.* An alternative approach, called the *indirect method,* is illustrated later in this chapter.

[3] A fourth classification, "Effects of changes in exchange rates on cash," is used in the cash flow statements of companies with holdings of foreign currency. This fourth classification will be discussed in the intermediate accounting course.

ALLISON CORPORATION
Statement of Cash Flows
For the Year Ended December 31, 19__

Cash flows from operating activities:		
Cash received from customers..................................	$ 870,000	
Interest and dividends received	10,000	
Cash provided by operating activities		$ 880,000
Cash paid to suppliers and employees	$(764,000)	
Interest paid	(28,000)	
Income taxes paid..	(38,000)	
Cash disbursed for operating activities		(830,000)
Net cash flow from operating activities.......................		$ 50,000
Cash flows from investing activities:		
Purchases of marketable securities	$ (65,000)	
Proceeds from sales of marketable		
securities	40,000	
Loans made to borrowers	(17,000)	
Collections on loans...	12,000	
Purchases of plant assets	(160,000)	
Proceeds from sales of plant assets	75,000	
Net cash used by investing activities		(115,000)
Cash flows from financing activities:		
Proceeds from short-term borrowing...........................	$ 45,000	
Payments to settle short-term debts	(55,000)	
Proceeds from issuing bonds payable	100,000	
Proceeds from issuing capital stock...........................	50,000	
Dividends paid	(40,000)	
Net cash provided by financing activities		100,000
Net increase (decrease in cash)...............................		$ 35,000
Cash and cash equivalents, beginning of year		40,000
Cash and cash equivalents, end of year		$ 75,000

Notice that receipts and payments of interest are classified as operating activities, not as investing or financing activities.

■ **Investing Activities** Cash flows relating to investing activities include:

CASH RECEIPTS	CASH PAYMENTS
Cash proceeds from selling investments or plant assets	*Payments to acquire investments or plant assets*
Cash proceeds from collecting principal amounts on loans	*Amounts advanced to borrowers*

■ **Financing Activities** Cash flows classified as financing activities include the following:

Test.

CASH RECEIPTS	CASH PAYMENTS
Proceeds from both short-term and long-term borrowing	*Repayments of amounts borrowed (excluding interest payments)*
Cash received from owners (as, for example, from issuing stock)	*Payments to owners, such as cash dividends*

Repayment of amounts borrowed refers to repayment of *loans,* not to payments made on accounts payable or accrued liabilities. Payments of accounts payable and of accrued liabilities are considered as "payments to suppliers of merchandise and services . . ." and are classified as a cash outflow from operating activities. Also, remember that all interest payments are classified as operating activities.

■ **Why Are Receipts and Payments of Interest "Operating Activities"?** One might argue that interest receipts result from investing activities, and that interest payments are related to financing activities. The FASB considered this point of view, but decided instead to classify interest receipts and payments as operating activities. The FASB wanted net cash flow from operating activities to reflect the cash effects of the revenue and expense transactions entering into the determination of net income. As interest revenue and interest expense enter into the determination of net income, the FASB decided to classify the related cash flows as operating activities. Payments of dividends, however, *do not* enter into the determination of net income. Therefore, dividend payments are viewed as financing activities.

■ **Cash and "Cash Equivalents"** For purposes of preparing a statement of cash flows, the FASB has defined "cash" as including *both cash and cash equivalents.* "Cash equivalents" are short-term highly liquid investments, such as money market funds, commercial paper, and Treasury bills.[4] Transfers of money between a company's bank accounts and these cash equivalents are *not viewed as cash receipts or cash payments.* Money is considered "cash" regardless of whether it is held in currency, in a bank account, or in the form of cash equivalents. However, any interest received from owning cash equivalents is included in cash receipts from operating activities.

Cash equivalents are limited to short-term, highly liquid investments such as those specified above. Marketable securities, such as investments in the stocks and bonds of other companies, *do not qualify as cash equivalents.* Therefore, purchases and sales of marketable securities *do result in cash flows* to be reported in the statement of cash flows.

Critical Importance of Cash Flow from Operating Activities

In the long run, a business must generate a positive net cash flow from its operating activities if the business is to survive. A business with negative cash flows from operations will not be able to raise cash from other sources indefi-

---

[4] To qualify as a cash equivalent, a short-term investment must convert into a known number of dollars within three months of acquisition.

nitely. In fact, the ability of a business to raise cash through financing activities is highly dependent upon its ability to generate cash from its normal business operations. Creditors and stockholders are reluctant to invest in a company that does not generate enough cash from operating activities to assure prompt payment of maturing liabilities, interest, and dividends.

Approaches to Preparing a Statement of Cash Flows

The items listed in an income statement or a balance sheet represent the balances of specific general ledger accounts. Notice, however, that the captions used in the statement of cash flows *do not* correspond to specific ledger accounts. A statement of cash flows summarizes *cash transactions* during the accounting period. The general ledger, however, is maintained on the *accrual basis* of accounting, not the cash basis. Thus, an amount such as "Cash received from customers . . . $870,000" does not appear as the balance in a specific ledger account.

In a very small business, it may be practical to prepare a statement of cash flows directly from the special journals for cash receipts and cash payments. For example, "Cash received from customers" usually is equal to the sum of the Sales column and the Accounts Receivable column in the cash receipts journal. Information about other cash flows, such as short-term borrowing transactions, may require sorting through the entries in the Other Accounts columns of both cash journals.

For most businesses, however, it is easier to prepare the statement of cash flows by examining the income statement and the *changes* during the period in all of the balance sheet accounts *except for* Cash. This approach is based upon the double-entry system of accounting; any transaction affecting cash must also affect some other asset, liability, or owners' equity account.[5] The change in these *other accounts* makes clear the nature of the cash transaction.

To illustrate this approach, assume that the Marketable Securities controlling account of Allison Corporation shows the following activity during the year:

Balance, January 1, 19__	$ 70,000
Debit entries during the year	65,000
Credit entries during the year	(44,000)
Balance, December 31, 19__	$ 91,000

Also assume that the company's income statement for the year includes a *$4,000 loss* on sales of marketable securities.

The *debit entries* in the Marketable Securities account represent the cost of securities *purchased* during the year. These debit entries provide the basis for the item *"Purchases of marketable securities . . . $(65,000)"* appearing in the investing activities section of the statement of cash flows (page 731). Thus, increases in the asset Marketable Securities correspond to outflow of cash.

The $44,000 in credit entries represent the *cost* of securities sold during the

---

[5] Accounts used to record revenue, expenses, and dividends are "owners' equity accounts," as they ultimately are closed into the Retained Earnings account.

year. Remember, however, that the income statement shows that these securities were sold at a *loss of $4,000*. The cash proceeds from these sales, which also appear in the statement of cash flows, may be computed as follows:

Cost of marketable securities sold	$44,000
Less: Loss on sales of marketable securities	4,000
Proceeds from sales of marketable securities	$40,000

By looking at the changes occurring in the Marketable Securities account and the related income statement account, we were able to determine quickly two items appearing in the company's statement of cash flows. We could have assembled the same information from the company's cash journals, but we would have had to review the journals for the entire year and then added together the cash flows of numerous individual transactions. In summary, it usually is more efficient to prepare a statement of cash flows by analyzing the *changes in noncash accounts* than by locating and combining numerous entries in the cash journals.

PREPARING A STATEMENT OF CASH FLOWS: AN ILLUSTRATION

Earlier in this chapter we illustrated the statement of cash flows of Allison Corporation. We will now show how this statement was developed from the company's accrual-basis accounting records. Shown below are the company's income statement and the necessary information about changes in balance sheet accounts during the year.

ALLISON CORPORATION

Income Statement

For the Year Ended December 31, 19—

Revenue and gains:		
Net sales		$900,000
Dividends revenue		3,000
Interest revenue		6,000
Gain on sales of plant assets		31,000
Total revenue and gains		$940,000
Costs, expenses, and losses:		
Cost of goods sold	$500,000	
Operating expenses (including depreciation of		
$40,000)	300,000	
Interest expense	35,000	
Income taxes expense	36,000	
Loss on sales of marketable securities	4,000	
Total costs, expenses, and losses		875,000
Net income		$ 65,000

Additional Information

An analysis of changes in the balance sheet accounts of Allison Corporation provides the following information about the company's activities in the current year. To assist in the preparation of a statement of cash flows, we have classified this information into the categories of operating activities, investing activities, and financing activities.

Operating Activities

(1) Accounts receivable increased by $30,000 during the year.

(2) Dividend revenue is recognized on the cash basis, but interest revenue is recognized on the accrual basis. Accrued interest receivable decreased by $1,000 during the year.

(3) Inventory increased by $10,000 and accounts payable increased by $15,000 during the year.

(4) During the year, short-term prepaid expenses increased by $3,000 and accrued expenses payable (other than for interest or income taxes) decreased by $6,000. Depreciation for the year amounted to $40,000.

(5) The accrued liability for interest payable increased by $7,000 during the year.

(6) The accrued liability for income taxes payable decreased by $2,000 during the year.

Investing Activities

(7) Analysis of the Marketable Securities account shows debit entries of $65,000, representing the cost of securities purchased, and credit entries of $44,000, representing the cost of securities sold. (None of the marketable securities is viewed as a cash equivalent.)

(8) Analysis of the Notes Receivable account shows $17,000 in debit entries, representing cash lent to borrowers by Allison Corporation during the year, and $12,000 in credit entries, representing collections of notes receivable. (Collections of interest were recorded in the Interest Revenue account and are considered cash flows from operating activities.)

(9) Allison Corporation purchased plant assets for $200,000 during the year, paying $160,000 cash and issuing a long-term note payable for the $40,000 balance. In addition, the company sold plant assets with a book value of $44,000.

Financing Activities

(10) During the year, Allison Corporation borrowed $45,000 cash by issuing short-term notes payable to banks. Also, the company repaid $55,000 in principal amounts due on these loans and other notes payable. (Interest payments are classified as operating activities.)

(11) The company issued bonds payable for $100,000 cash.

(12) The company issued for cash 1,000 shares of $10 par value capital stock at a price of $50 per share.

(13) Cash dividends declared and paid to stockholders amounted to $40,000 during the year.

Cash and Cash Equivalents

(14) Cash and cash equivalents as shown in Allison Corporation's balance sheets, amounted to $40,000 at the beginning of the year and $75,000 at year-end—a net increase of $35,000.

Using this information, we will now illustrate the steps in preparing Allison Corporation's statement of cash flows and also a supporting schedule disclosing the "noncash" investing and financing activities. In our discussion, we will often refer to these items of "Additional Information" by citing the paragraph numbers shown in parentheses.

The distinction between accrual-basis measurements and cash flows is of fundamental importance in understanding financial statements and other accounting reports. To assist in making this distinction, we use two colors in our illustrated computations. We show in blue the accrual-based data from Allison Corporation's income statement and the preceding numbered paragraphs. The cash flows that we compute from this data are shown in black.

Cash Flows from Operating Activities

Objective 3
Compute the major cash flows relating to operating activities.

As shown in our statement of cash flows on page 731, the net cash flow from operating activities is determined by combining certain cash inflows and subtracting certain cash outflows. The inflows are cash received from customers, and interest and dividends received; the outflows are cash paid to suppliers and employees, interest paid, and income taxes paid.

In computing each of these cash flows, our starting point is an income statement amount, such as net sales, the cost of goods sold, or interest expense. As you study each computation, be sure that you *understand why* the income statement amount must be increased or decreased to determine the related cash flow. You will find that an understanding of these computations will do more than show you how to compute cash flows: it will also strengthen your understanding of the income statement and the balance sheet.

■ **Cash Received from Customers** To the extent that sales are made for cash, there is no difference between the amount of cash received from customers and the amount recorded as sales revenue. Differences do arise, however, when sales are made on account. If accounts receivable have increased during the year, credit sales have exceeded collections of accounts receivable. Therefore, we must *deduct the increase* in accounts receivable over the year from net sales in order to determine the amount of cash received. If accounts receivable have decreased over the year, collections of these accounts must have exceeded credit sales. Therefore, we must *add the decrease* in accounts receivable to net sales to determine the amount of cash received. The relationship between cash received from customers and net sales is summarized below:

$$\text{Cash received from customers} = \text{Net sales} \left\{ \begin{array}{c} + \text{ decrease in accounts receivable} \\ \text{or} \\ - \text{ increase in accounts receivable} \end{array} \right\}$$

The increase or decrease in accounts receivable is determined simply by comparing the year-end balance in the account to its balance at the beginning of the year.

In our Allison Corporation example, paragraph (1) of the Additional Information tells us that accounts receivable have *increased* by $30,000 during the year. The income statement shows net sales for the year of $900,000. Therefore, the amount of cash received from customers may be computed as follows:

Net sales (accrual basis)	$900,000
Less: Increase in accounts receivable	30,000
Cash received from customers	$870,000

■ **Interest and Dividends Received** Our next objective is to determine the amounts of cash received during the year as dividends and interest. As explained in paragraph (2) of the Additional Information, dividend revenue is recorded on the cash basis. Therefore, the $3,000 shown in the income statement also represents the amount of cash received as dividends.

Interest revenue, on the other hand, is recognized on the accrual basis. We have already shown how to convert one type of revenue, net sales, from the accrual basis to the cash basis. We may use the same approach in converting interest revenue from the accrual basis to the cash basis. Our formula for converting net sales to the cash basis may be modified to convert interest revenue to the cash basis as follows:

$$\frac{\text{Interest}}{\text{received}} = \frac{\text{Interest}}{\text{revenue}} \left\{ \begin{array}{c} + \text{ decrease in interest receivable} \\ \text{or} \\ - \text{ increase in interest receivable} \end{array} \right\}$$

The income statement for Allison Corporation shows interest revenue of $6,000, and paragraph (2) states that the amount of accrued interest receivable has **decreased** by $1,000 during the year. Thus, the amount of cash received as interest may be computed as follows:

Interest revenue (accrual basis)	$6,000
Add: Decrease in accrued interest receivable	1,000
Interest received (cash basis)	$7,000

The amounts of interest and dividends received in cash are combined for presentation in the statement of cash flows:

Interest received (cash basis)	$ 7,000
Dividends received (cash basis)	3,000
Interest and dividends received	$10,000

Cash Payments for Merchandise and for Expenses

The next item in the statement of cash flows, "Cash paid to suppliers and employees," includes all cash payments for purchases of merchandise and for operating expenses (all expenses other than interest and income taxes). Payments of interest and income taxes are listed as a separate item in the statement. The amounts of cash paid for purchases of merchandise and for operating expenses are computed separately.

■ **Cash Paid for Purchases of Merchandise** The relationship between cash payments for purchases of merchandise and the cost of goods sold depends upon the changes during the period in inventory and in accounts payable to suppliers of merchandise. This relationship may be stated as follows:

$$\text{Cash payments for purchases} = \text{Cost of goods sold} \left\{ \begin{array}{c} + \text{ increase in} \\ \text{inventory} \\ \text{or} \\ - \text{ decrease in} \\ \text{inventory} \end{array} \right\} \text{ and} \left\{ \begin{array}{c} + \text{ decrease in} \\ \text{accounts payable} \\ \text{or} \\ - \text{ increase in} \\ \text{accounts payable} \end{array} \right\}$$

Using information from the Allison Corporation income statement and paragraph (3), the cash payments for purchases may be computed as follows:

Cost of goods sold	$500,000
Add: Increase in inventory	10,000
Net purchases (accrual basis)	$510,000
Less: Increase in accounts payable to suppliers	15,000
Cash payments for purchases of merchandise	$495,000

Let us review the logic behind this computation. If a company is increasing its inventory, it will be ***buying more merchandise than it sells*** during the period; furthermore, if the company is increasing its account payable to merchandise creditors, it is ***not paying cash*** for all of these purchases.

■ **Cash Payments for Expense**   Expenses, as shown in the income statement, represent the cost of goods and services used up during the period. However, the amounts shown as expenses may differ significantly from the cash payments made during the period. Consider, for example, depreciation expense. Recording depreciation expense ***requires no cash payment,*** but it does increase total expenses measured on the accrual basis. Thus, in converting accrual-basis expenses to the cash basis, we must deduct depreciation expense and any other "noncash" expenses from our accrual-basis operating expenses. The other "noncash" expenses—expenses not requiring cash outlays—include amortization of intangible assets and amortization of bond discount.

A second area of difference arises from short-term timing differences between the recognition of expenses and the actual cash payments. Expenses are recorded in accounting records when the related goods or services are used. However, the cash payments for these expenses might occur (1) in an earlier period, (2) in the same period, or (3) in a later period. Let us briefly consider each case.

1   If payment is made in advance, the payment creates an asset, termed a prepaid expense, or, in our formula, a "prepayment." Thus, to the extent that prepaid expenses are increased over the year, cash payments ***exceed*** the amount recognized as expense.

2   If payment is made in the same period, no problem arises because the cash payment is equal to the amount of expense.

3   If payment is made in a later period, the payment reduces a liability for an accrued expense payable. Thus, to the extent that accrued expenses payable are decreased over the year, cash payments exceed the amount recognized as expense.

The relationships between cash payments and accrual-basis expenses are summarized on the next page.

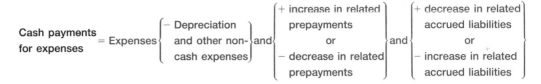

In a statement of cash flows, cash payments for interest and for income taxes are shown separately from cash payments for operating expenses. Using data from Allison Corporation's income statement and from paragraph (4), we may compute the company's cash payments for operating expenses as follows:

Operating expenses (including depreciation)		$300,000
Less: Noncash expenses (depreciation)		40,000
Subtotal		$260,000
Add: Increase in short-term prepayments	$3,000	
Decrease in accrued liabilities	6,000	9,000
Cash payments for operating expenses		$269,000

■ **Cash Paid to Suppliers and Employees** The caption used in our cash flow statement, "Cash paid to suppliers and employees," includes both cash payments for purchases and for operating expenses. This cash outflow may now be computed as follows:

Cash payments for purchases of merchandise	$495,000
Cash payments for operating expenses	269,000
Cash payments to suppliers and employees	$764,000

■ **Cash Payments for Interest and Taxes** Interest expense and income taxes expense may be converted to cash payments with the same formula we used to convert operating expenses. Allison Corporation's income statement shows interest expense of $35,000, and paragraph (5) states that the liability for interest payable increased by $7,000 during the year. The fact that the liability for unpaid interest *increased* over the year means that *not all of the interest expense shown in the income statement was paid in cash*. To determine the amount of interest actually paid, we must *subtract* from total interest expense the portion that has been financed through an increase in the liability for interest payable. This computation is shown below:

Interest expense	$35,000
Less: Increase in related accrued liability	7,000
Interest paid	$28,000

Similar reasoning is used in determining the amount of income taxes paid by Allison Corporation during the year. The accrual-based income taxes expense, reported in the income statement, amounts to $36,000. However, paragraph (6) states that the company has reduced its liability for income taxes payable by $2,000 over the year. Incurring income taxes expense increases the tax liability; making cash payments to tax authorities reduces it. Thus, if the liability *decreases* over the year, cash payments to tax authorities *must have been greater* than the income taxes expense for the current year. The amount of the cash payments is determined as follows:

Income taxes expense	*$36,000*
Add: Decrease in related accrued liability	*2,000*
Income taxes paid	*$38,000*

■ **A Quick Review** We have now shown the computation of each cash flow relating to Allison Corporation's operating activities. Previously we illustrated a complete statement of cash flows for the company. For your convenience, we will again show the operating activities section of that statement, illustrating the information developed in the preceding paragraphs.

Cash flows from operating activities:

Cash received from customers	*$ 870,000*	
Interest and dividends received	*10,000*	
Cash provided by operating activities		*$ 880,000*
Cash paid to suppliers and employees	*$(764,000)*	
Interest paid	*(28,000)*	
Income taxes paid	*(38,000)*	
Cash disbursed for operating activities		*(830,000)*
Net cash flow from operating activities		*$ 50,000*

Differences between Net Income and Net Cash Flow from Operating Activities

Objective 4
Explain why net income differs from net cash flow from operating activities.

Allison Corporation reported net income of *$65,000,* but net cash flow from operating activities of only *$50,000.* What caused this $15,000 difference?

The answer, in short, is many things. First, *depreciation expense* reduces net income but does not affect net cash flow. Next, all the adjustments that we made to net sales, cost of goods sold, and expenses represented short-term *timing differences* between net income and the underlying net cash flow from operating activities. Finally, *nonoperating gains and losses* may cause substantial differences between net income and net cash flow from operations.

Nonoperating gains and losses may result from sales of plant assets, marketable securities, and other investments; or from the retirement of long-term debt. These gains and losses affect the cash flows relating to investing or financing activities, not the cash flows from operating activities.

Reporting Operating Cash Flow: The Direct and Indirect Methods

Objective 5
Distinguish between the direct and indirect methods of reporting operating cash flow.

In our illustration, we use the *direct method* of computing and reporting the net cash flow from operating activities. The direct method shows the *specific cash inflows and outflows* comprising the operating activities of the business. The FASB has expressed its preference for the direct method, but it also allows companies to use an alternative, called the *indirect method.*

Computation of net cash flow from operating activities by the indirect method looks quite different from the direct method computation. However, both methods result in the *same net cash flow* from operating activities. Under the indirect method, the computation begins with accrual-based net income (as shown in the income statement), and then shows the various adjustments necessary to *reconcile net income with net cash flow from operating activities.* The general format of this computation is summarized below:

Net income
Add: Expenses that do not require cash outlays in the period (such as depreciation expense)
Operating cash inflows not recorded as revenue in the period
"Nonoperating" losses deducted in the determination of net income
Less: Revenue that does not result in cash inflows in the period
Operating cash outflows not recorded as expense in the period
"Nonoperating" gains included in the determination of net income
Net cash flow from operating activities

The above summary describes the differences between net income and net cash flow from operating activities in broad, general terms. In an actual statement of cash flows, a dozen or more specific items may appear in this reconciliation. (Supplementary Schedule A, on page 745, illustrates the application of the indirect method to the operating activities of Allison Corporation.)

In this chapter we emphasize the *direct* method, as we consider it to be the more informative approach and it is the method recommended by the FASB. Use of the direct method is assumed in all assignment material at the end of this chapter. Further coverage of the indirect method, including assignment material, is provided in Appendix C.

Cash Flows from Investing Activities

Objective 6
Compute the cash flows relating to investing and financing activities.

Paragraphs (7) through (9) in the Additional Information for our Allison Corporation example provide most of the information necessary to determine the cash flows from investing activities. In the following discussion, we will illustrate the presentation of these cash flows and also explain the sources of the information contained in the numbered paragraphs.

Much information about investing activities can be obtained simply by looking at the changes in the related asset accounts during this year. Debit entries in these accounts represent purchases of the assets, or cash outlays. Credit entries represent sales of the assets, or cash receipts. However, credit entries in asset accounts represent only the *cost (or book value)* of the assets sold. To determine the cash proceeds from these sales transactions, we must adjust the amount of the credit entries for any gains or losses recognized on the sales.

■ **Purchases and Sales of Securities** To illustrate, consider paragraph (7) which summarizes the debit and credit entries to the Marketable Securities account. As explained earlier in this chapter, the $65,000 in debit entries represent purchases of marketable securities. The $44,000 in credit entries represent the cost of marketable securities sold during the period. However, the income statement shows that these securities were sold at a *$4,000 loss.* Thus, the cash proceeds from these sales amounted to only *$40,000* ($44,000 cost, minus $4,000 loss on sale). In the statement of cash flows, these investing activities are summarized as follows:

Purchases of marketable securities .... *$(65,000)*
Proceeds from sales of marketable securities .... *$ 40,000*

■ **Loans Made and Collected**   Paragraph (8) provides all the information necessary to summarize the cash flows from making and collecting loans:

Loans made to borrowers	$(17,000)
Collections on loans	$ 12,000

This information comes directly from the Notes Receivable account. Debit entries in the account represent new loans made during the year; credit entries indicate collections of the ***principal*** amount on outstanding notes (loans). (Interest received is credited to the Interest Revenue account and is included among the cash receipts from operating activities.)

Objective 7
Explain why and how noncash investing and financing activities are disclosed in a statement of cash flows.

■ **Cash Paid to Acquire Plant Assets**   Paragraph (9) states that Allison Corporation purchased plant assets during the year for $200,000, paying $160,000 in cash and issuing a long-term note payable for the $40,000 balance. Notice that ***only the $160,000 cash payment*** appears in the statement of cash flows. However, one objective of this financial statement is to show all of the company's ***investing and financing activities*** during the year. Therefore, the ***noncash aspects*** of these transactions are shown in a supplementary schedule, as follows:

SUPPLEMENTARY SCHEDULE OF NONCASH INVESTING AND FINANCING ACTIVITIES

Purchases of plant assets	$200,000
Less: Portion financed through issuance of long-term debt	40,000
Cash paid to acquire plant assets	$160,000

This supplementary schedule accompanies the statement of cash flows.

■ **Proceeds from Sales of Plant Assets**   Assume that an analysis of the plant asset accounts shows net credit entries totaling $44,000 in the year. ("Net credit entries" means all credit entries, net of related debits to accumulated depreciation when assets were sold.) These "net credit entries" represent the ***book value*** of plant assets sold during the year. However, the income statement shows that these assets were sold at a ***gain of $31,000.*** Therefore, the ***cash proceeds*** from sales of plant assets amounted to $75,000, as shown below:

Book value of plant assets sold	$44,000
Add: Gain on sales of plant assets	31,000
Proceeds from sales of plant assets	$75,000

Cash Flows from Financing Activities

Cash flows from financing activities are determined by analyzing the debit and credit changes recorded during the period in the related liability and stockholders' equity accounts. In a sense, cash flows from financing activities are more easily determined than those relating to investing activities, because financing activities seldom involve gains or losses.[6] Thus, the debit or credit

---

[6] An early retirement of debt is an example of a financing transaction that may result in a gain or a loss.

changes in the balance sheet accounts usually are equal to the amounts of the related cash flows.

Credit changes in such accounts as Notes Payable and the accounts for long-term debt and paid-in capital usually indicate cash receipts; debit changes indicate cash payments.

■ **Short-Term Borrowing Transactions**   To illustrate, consider paragraph (10), which provides the information supporting the following cash flows:

Proceeds from short-term borrowing . . . . **$ 45,000**

Payments to settle short-term debts . . . . **$(55,000)**

Is it possible to determine the proceeds of short-term borrowing transactions throughout the year without carefully reviewing the cash receipts journals? The answer is *yes*—easily. The proceeds from short-term borrowing are equal to the ***sum of the credit entries*** in the short-term ***Notes Payable*** account. Payments to settle short-term debts are equal to the ***sum of the debit entries*** in this account.

■ **Proceeds from Issuing Bonds Payable and Capital Stock** Paragraph (11) states that Allison Corporation received cash of $100,000 by issuing bonds payable. This amount was determined by summing the credit entries in the Bonds Payable account. The Bonds Payable account included no debit entries during the year; thus, no bonds were retired.

Paragraph (12) states that during the year Allison Corporation issued capital stock for $50,000. The proceeds from issuing stock are equal to the sum of the credit entries made in the Capital Stock and Additional Paid-in Capital accounts.

■ **Cash Dividends Paid to Stockholders**   Paragraph (13) states that Allison Company declared and paid cash dividends of $40,000 during the year. In practice, most corporations pay cash dividends in the same year in which these dividends are declared. In these situations, the cash payments are equal to the related debit entries in the Retained Earnings account.

If the balance sheet includes a liability for dividends payable, the amounts debited to Retained Earnings represent dividends ***declared*** during the period, which may differ from the amount of dividends ***paid***. To determine cash dividends paid, we must adjust the amount of dividends declared by adding any decrease (or subtracting any increase) in the Dividends Payable account over the period.

Relationship between the Statement of Cash Flows and the Balance Sheet

As stated in Chapter 7, the first asset appearing in the balance sheet is Cash and cash equivalents. The statement of cash flows explains in some detail the change in this asset from one balance sheet date to the next. The last three lines in the cash flow statement illustrate this relationship, as shown in our Allison Corporation example:

Net increase (decrease) in cash and cash equivalents............................	**$35,000**
Cash and cash equivalents, beginning of year	40,000
Cash and cash equivalents, end of year	**$75,000**

The Statement of Cash Flows: A Second Look

Allison Corporation's statement of cash flows was illustrated earlier in this chapter. Now that we have explained the nature and computation of each cash flow in that statement, a second illustration is in order. We use this second illustration as an opportunity to illustrate the *indirect method* of reporting net cash flow from operating activities. (Our preceding illustration uses the *direct method.*) Also, we illustrate two *supplementary schedules* that often accompany a statement of cash flows.

Supplementary Schedule A illustrates the determination of net cash flow from operating activities by the *indirect method.* The purpose of this schedule is to explain the differences between the reported net income and the net cash flow from operating activities. This supplementary schedule also is required of companies that use the direct method of reporting operating cash flows. (Note: The mechanics of the indirect method are discussed further in Appendix C. Therefore, the computations illustrated in Supplementary Schedule A are *not* covered in the assignment material for this chapter.)

Supplementary Schedule B discloses any "noncash" aspects of the company's investing and financing activities. This type of supplementary schedule is required whenever some aspects of the company's investing and financing activities do not coincide with cash flows occurring within the current period.

ALLISON CORPORATION
Statement of Cash Flows
For the Year Ended December 31, 19—

Cash flows from operating activities:		
Net cash flow from operating activities		
(see supplementary schedule A)		$ 50,000
Cash flows from investing activities:		
Purchases of marketable securities	$ (65,000)	
Proceeds from sales of marketable		
securities	40,000	
Loans made to borrowers	(17,000)	
Collections on loan	12,000	
Cash paid to acquire plant assets		
(see supplementary schedule B)	(160,000)	
Proceeds from sales of plant assets	75,000	
Net cash used by investing activities		(115,000)
Cash flows from financing activities:		
Proceeds from short-term borrowing	$ 45,000	
Payments to settle short-term debts	(55,000)	
Proceeds from issuing bonds payable	100,000	
Proceeds from issuing capital stock	50,000	
Dividends paid	(40,000)	
Net cash provided by financing activities		100,000
Net increase (decrease) in cash		$ 35,000
Cash and cash equivalents, beginning of year		40,000
Cash and cash equivalents, end of year		$ 75,000

Supplementary schedule illustrating the indirect method of determining cash flow from operations

SUPPLEMENTARY SCHEDULE A   NET CASH FLOW FROM OPERATING ACTIVITIES

Net income			$ 65,000
Add:	Depreciation expense		40,000
	Decrease in accrued interest receivable		1,000
	Increase in accounts payable		15,000
	Increase in accrued liabilities		7,000
	Nonoperating loss on sales of marketable		
	securities		4,000
Subtotal			$132,000
Less:	Increase in accounts receivable	$30,000	
	Increase in inventory	10,000	
	Increase in prepayments	3,000	
	Decrease in accrued liabilities	8,000	
	Nonoperating gain on sales of plant		
	assets	31,000	82,000
Net cash flow from operating activities			$ 50,000

SUPPLEMENTARY SCHEDULE B   NONCASH INVESTING AND FINANCING ACTIVITIES

Purchases of plant assets	$200,000
Less: Portion financed through issuance of long-term debt	40,000
Cash paid to acquire plant assets	$160,000

End-of-Chapter Review

CONCEPTS INTRODUCED OR EMPHASIZED IN CHAPTER 19

Major concepts in this chapter include:

■ The nature and purposes of a statement of cash flows.

■ The format of a statement of cash flows, and the classification of cash flows among operating activities, investing activities, and financing activities.

■ The importance of a positive net cash flow from operating activities to the long-run survival of the business.

■ How the amounts of cash flows for operating, investing, and financing activities can be determined from accounting records maintained on the accrual basis.

■ Why net income differs from the net cash flow from operating activities: the direct and indirect methods of reporting net cash flow from operating activities.

■ The content of the supplementary schedules that usually accompany a statement of cash flows.

Whether you are an investor, a manager, or a taxpayer, you need to understand the difference between cash flows and the accrual basis of accounting. Accrual-based information is useful in determining the profitability and the financial position of a business—especially a business of considerable financial strength. But in evaluating such factors as solvency, the prospects for short-term survival, and the ability of a business to seize investment opportunities, cash flows may be more relevant than accrual-based measurements. In our remaining chapters, we will refer both to accrual-based information and to cash flows, depending upon the nature of the decision at hand.

KEY TERMS INTRODUCED OR EMPHASIZED IN CHAPTER 19

Accrual basis   A method of summarizing operating results in terms of revenue earned and expenses incurred, rather than cash receipts or cash payments.

Cash basis   A method of summarizing operating results in terms of cash receipts and cash payments, rather than revenue earned or expenses incurred.

Cash equivalents   Highly liquid short-term investments, such as Treasury bills, money market funds, and commercial paper. For purposes of preparing a statement of cash flows, money held in cash equivalents is still viewed as "cash." Thus, transfers between a bank account and cash equivalents are not considered receipts or disbursements of cash.

Cash flows   A term describing both cash receipts (inflows) and cash payments (outflows).

Direct method   A method of reporting net cash flow from operating activities by listing specific types of cash inflows and outflows. This is the method recommended by the FASB, but the *indirect method* is an allowable alternative.

Financing activities   Transactions such as borrowing, repaying borrowed amounts, raising equity capital, or making distribution to owners. The cash effects of these transactions are reported in the financing activities section of a statement of cash flows. Noncash aspects of these transactions are disclosed in a supplementary schedule.

Indirect method   A format of reporting net cash flow from operating activity that reconciles this figure with the amount of net income shown in the income statement. An alternative to the *direct method.*

Investing activities   Transactions involving acquisitions or sales of investments or plant assets. The cash aspects of these transactions are shown in the investing activities section of a statement of cash flows. Noncash aspects of these transactions are disclosed in a supplementary schedule to this financial statement.

Operating activities   Transactions entering into the determination of net income, with the exception of gains and losses relating to financing or investing activities. The category includes such transactions as selling goods or services, earning investment income, and incurring costs and expenses. The cash effects of these transactions are reflected in the operating activities section of a statement of cash flows.

Statement of cash flows   A financial statement designed to provide information about the cash receipts, cash payments, investing activities, and financing activities of a business. Useful in evaluating the solvency of the business.

DEMONSTRATION PROBLEM FOR YOUR REVIEW

You are the chief accountant for American Modem. Your assistant has prepared an income statement for the current year, and also developed the following "Additional Information" by analyzing changes in the company's balance sheet accounts.

AMERICAN MODEM
Income Statement
For the Year Ended December 31, 19___

Revenue:		
Net sales		*$9,500,000*
Interest income		*320,000*
Gain on sales of marketable securities		*70,000*
Total revenue and gains		*$9,890,000*
Costs and expenses:		
Cost of goods sold	*$4,860,000*	
Operating expenses (including depreciation		
of $700,000)	*3,740,000*	
Interest expense	*270,000*	
Income taxes..	*300,000*	
Loss on sales of plant assets	*90,000*	
Total costs, expenses, and losses..		*9,260,000*
Net income		*$ 630,000*

Information about changes in the company's balance sheet accounts over the year is summarized below:

(1) Accounts receivable decreased by $85,000.

(2) Accrued interest receivable increased by $15,000.

(3) Inventory decreased by $280,000 and accounts payable to suppliers of merchandise decreased by $240,000.

(4) Short-term prepayments of operating expenses decreased by $18,000, and accrued liabilities for operating expenses increased by $35,000.

(5) The liability for accrued interest payable decreased by $16,000 during the year.

(6) The liability for accrued income taxes payable increased by $25,000 during the year.

(7) The following schedule summarizes the total debit and credit entries during the year in other balance sheet accounts:

	DEBIT ENTRIES	CREDIT ENTRIES
Marketable securities	$ 120,000	$ 210,000
Notes receivable (cash loans made to others)	250,000	190,000
Plant assets (see paragraph 8)	3,800,000	360,000
Notes payable (short-term borrowing)	620,000	740,000
Bonds payable		1,100,000
Capital stock		50,000
Additional paid-in capital (from issuance of stock)		840,000
Retained earnings (see paragraph 9 below)	320,000	630,000

(8) The $360,000 in credit entries to the plant asset accounts are net of any debits to accumulated depreciation when plant assets were retired. Thus, the $360,000 in credit entries represents the *book value* of all plant assets sold or retired during the year.

(9) The $320,000 debit to retained earnings represents dividends declared and paid during the year. The $630,000 credit entry represents the net income shown in the income statement.

(10) All investing and financing activities were cash transactions.

(11) Cash and cash equivalents amounted to $448,000 at the beginning of the year, and to $330,000 at year-end.

Instructions You are to prepare a statement of cash flows for the current year, following the format illustrated on page 731. Place brackets around dollar amounts representing cash outlays. Show separately your computations of the following amounts:

(1) Cash received from customers.

(2) Interest received.

(3) Cash paid to suppliers and employees.

(4) Interest paid.

(5) Income taxes paid.

(6) Proceeds from sales of marketable securities.

(7) Proceeds from sales of plant assets.

(8) Proceeds from issuing capital stock.

SOLUTION TO DEMONSTRATION PROBLEM

AMERICAN MODEM
Statement of Cash Flows
For the Year Ended December 31, 19___

Cash flows from operating activities:		
Cash received from customers (1)	$ 9,585,000	
Interest received (2)	305,000	
Cash provided by operating activities		$ 9,890,000
Cash paid to suppliers and employees (3)	$(7,807,000)	
Interest paid (4)	(286,000)	
Income taxes paid (5)	(275,000)	
Cash disbursed for operating activities		(8,368,000)
Net cash flow from operating activities		$ 1,522,000
Cash flows from investing activities:		
Purchases of marketable securities	$ (120,000)	
Proceeds from sales of marketable securities (6)	280,000	
Loans made to borrowers	(250,000)	
Collections on loans	190,000	
Cash paid to acquire plant assets	(3,800,000)	
Proceeds from sales of plant assets (7)	270,000	
Net cash used by investing activities		(3,430,000)
Cash flow from financing activities:		
Proceeds from short-term borrowing	$ 740,000	
Payments to settle short-term debts	(620,000)	
Proceeds from Issuing bonds payable	1,100,000	
Proceeds from issuing capital stock (8)	890,000	
Dividends paid	(320,000)	
Net cash provided by financing activities		1,790,000
Net increase (decrease) in cash		$ (118,000)
Cash and cash equivalents, beginning of year		$ 448,000
Cash and cash equivalents, end of year		$ 330,000
Supporting computations:		
(1) Cash received from customers:		
Net sales		$ 9,500,000
Add: Decrease in accounts receivable		85,000
Cash received from customers		$ 9,585,000
(2) Interest received:		
Interest income		$ 320,000
Less: Increase in accrued interest receivable		15,000
Interest received		$ 305,000

(3) **Cash paid to suppliers and employees:**

Cash paid for purchases of merchandise:

Cost of goods sold...	$ 4,860,000
Less: Decrease in inventory	280,000
Net purchases	$ 4,580,000
Add: Decrease in accounts payable to suppliers......................	240,000
Cash paid for purchases of merchandise..............................	$ 4,820,000

Cash paid for operating expenses:

Operating expenses		$ 3,740,000
Less: Depreciation (a "noncash" expense)	$ 700,000	
Decrease in prepayments.........................	18,000	
Increase in accrued liabilities for operating		
expenses	35,000	753,000
Cash paid for operating expenses		$ 2,987,000
Cash paid to suppliers and employees ($4,820,000 +		
$2,987,000)...		$ 7,807,000

(4) **Interest paid:**

Interest expense	$ 270,000
Add: Decrease in accrued interest payable	16,000
Interest paid	$ 286,000

(5) **Income taxes paid:**

Income taxes expense	$ 300,000
Less: Increase in accrued income taxes payable	25,000
Income taxes paid	$ 275,000

(6) **Proceeds from sales of marketable securities:**

Cost of marketable securities sold (credit entries	
to the Marketable Securities account)................................	$ 210,000
Add: Gain reported on sales of marketable securities..................	70,000
Proceeds from sales of marketable securities	$ 280,000

(7) **Proceeds from sales of plant assets:**

Book value of plant assets sold (paragraph 8)	$ 360,000
Less: Loss reported on sales of plant assets	90,000
Proceeds from sales of plant assets	$ 270,000

(8) **Proceeds from issuing capital stock:**

Amounts credited to the Capital Stock account	$ 50,000
Add: Amounts credited to Additional Paid-in Capital account	840,000
Proceeds from issuing capital stock	$ 890,000

SELF-TEST QUESTIONS

Answers to these questions appear on page 764.

1 The statement of cash flows is designed to assist users in assessing each of the following, *except:*

a The ability of a company to remain solvent.

b The company's profitability.

c The major sources of cash receipts during the period.

d The reasons why net cash flow from operating activities differ from net income.

2 Which of the following is *not* included in the statement of cash flows, or in a supplementary schedule accompanying the statement of cash flows?

a Disclosure of the amount of cash invested in money market funds during the accounting period.

b A reconciliation of net income to net cash flow from operating activities.

c Disclosure of investing or financing activities that did not involve cash.

d The amount of cash and cash equivalents owned by the business at the end of the accounting period.

3 The cash flows shown in the statement of cash flows are grouped into the following major categories:

a Operating activities, investing activities, and financing activities.

b Cash receipts, cash disbursements, and noncash activities.

c Direct cash flows and indirect cash flows.

d Operating activities, investing activities, and collecting activities.

4 Shown below is a list of various cash payments and cash receipts:

Cash paid to suppliers and employees	*$400,000*
Dividends paid	*18,000*
Interest paid	*12,000*
Purchases of plant assets	*45,000*
Interest and dividends received	*17,000*
Payments to settle short-term debt	*29,000*
Income taxes paid	*23,000*
Cash received from customers	*601,000*

Based only upon the above items, net cash flow from operating activities is:
a $138,000   **b** $91,000   **c** $183,000   **d** $120,000

5 During the current year, two transactions were recorded in the Land account of Nolan Industries. One involved a debit of $320,000 to the Land account; the second was a $210,000 credit to the Land account. Nolan Industries' income statement for the year reported a loss on sale of land in the amount of $25,000. All transactions involving the Land account were cash transactions. These transactions would be shown in the statement of cash flows as:

a $320,000 cash provided by investing activities, and $210,000 cash disbursed for investing activities.

b $210,000 cash provided by investing activities, and $320,000 cash disbursed for investing activities.

c $235,000 cash provided by financing activities, and $320,000 cash disbursed for investing activities.

d $185,000 cash provided by investing activities, and $320,000 cash disbursed for investing activities.

Assignment Material

REVIEW QUESTIONS

1 A recent headline in the business section of a newspaper referred to the statement of cash flows as a "new" financial statement. Why?

2 Why does the FASB ask companies not to use the term "funds" in a statement of cash flows?

3 Briefly state the purposes of a statement of cash flows.

4 Does a statement of cash flows or an income statement best measure the profitability of a financially sound business? Explain.

5 Two supplementary schedules usually accompany a statement of cash flows. Briefly explain the content of these schedules.

6 Give two examples of cash receipts and two examples of cash payments which fall into each of the following classifications:

    a Operating activities.

    b Investing activities.

    c Financing activities.

7 Why are payments and receipts of interest classified as operating activities rather than as financing or investment activities?

8 Define *cash equivalents* and list three examples.

9 During the current year, Delta Corporation transferred $300,000 from its bank account into a money market fund. Will this transaction appear in a statement of cash flows? If so, in which section? Explain.

10 In the long run, is it more important for a business to have positive cash flows from its operating activities, investing activities, or financing activities? Why?

11 Of the three types of business activities summarized in a cash flow statement, which type is *least* likely to show a positive net cash flow in a successful, growing business? Explain your reasoning.

12 The items and amounts listed in a balance sheet and an income statement correspond to specific accounts in a company's ledger. Is the same true about the items and amounts in a statement of cash flows? Explain.

13 Briefly explain two different approaches that an accountant might follow in preparing a statement of cash flows from the accounting records of a small business.

14 SuperBoard, Inc., had net sales for the year of $550,000. Accounts receivable increased from $100,000 at the beginning of the year to $145,000 at year-end. Compute the amount of cash collected during the year from customers.

15 Describe the types of cash payments summarized by the caption, "Cash paid to suppliers and employees."

16 Identify three factors that may cause net income to differ from net cash flow from operating activities.

17 Briefly explain the difference between the direct and indirect methods of computing net cash flows from operating activities. Which method results in the higher net cash flow?

18 Are cash payments of accounts payable viewed as operating activities or investing activities? Referring to the statement of cash flows illustrated on page 731, state the caption that includes amounts paid on accounts payable.

19 Discount Club acquired land by issuing $500,000 worth of capital stock. No cash changed hands in this transaction. Will the transaction be disclosed in the company's statement of cash flows? Explain.

20 The only transaction recorded in the plant asset accounts of Rogers Corporation in the current year was a $150,000 credit to the Land account. Assuming that this credit resulted from a cash transaction, does this entry indicate a cash receipt or a cash payment? Should this $150,000 amount appear in the statement of cash flows, or is some adjustment necessary?

21 During the current year, the following credit entries were posted to the paid-in capital accounts of Moser Shipyards:

Capital Stock..	$10,000,000
Additional Paid-in Capital	98,500,000

Explain the type of cash transaction that probably caused these credit changes, and illustrate the presentation of this transaction in a statement of cash flows.

22 At the beginning of the current year, Polar Corporation had dividends payable of $1,000,000. During the current year, the company declared cash dividends of $4,800,000, of which $1,200,000 appeared as a liability at year-end. Determine the amount of cash dividends *paid* during this year.

EXERCISES

**Exercise 19-1
Accounting
terminology**

Listed below are nine technical accounting terms introduced or emphasized in this chapter.

Operating activities	Cash flow	Income statement
Investing activities	Direct method	Statement of cash flows
Financing activities	Indirect method	Cash equivalents

Each of the following statements may (or may not) describe one of these technical terms. For each statement, indicate the term described, or answer "None" if the statement does not correctly describe any of the terms.

a The method of reporting net cash flow from operating activities that is favored by the FASB.

b An asset consisting of readily marketable investments in the stocks and bonds of large corporations.

c The section of a statement of cash flows that includes purchases of plant assets.

d The financial statement that best describes the profitability of a business receiving most of its revenue in cash.

e Transactions involving investments by owners, issuance and repayment of debt, and the payment of dividends.

f The financial statement showing the financial position of the business at one particular date.

g A term that describes either a cash receipt or a cash disbursement.

h The process of recognizing revenue as it is earned and expenses as they are incurred, regardless of when cash is received or paid.

**Exercise 19-2
Computing cash
flows**

An analysis of the Marketable Securities controlling account of Dexter Labs shows the following entries during the year:

Balance, January 1	$220,000
Debit entries	60,000
Credit entries	(75,000)
Balance, December 31...	$205,000

In addition, the company's income statement includes a $29,000 gain on sales of marketable securities. None of the company's marketable securities is considered a cash equivalent.

Compute the amounts that should appear in the statement of cash flows as:

a Purchases of marketable securities.

b Proceeds from sales of marketable securities.

**Exercise 19-3
Comparing net
sales and cash
receipts**

During the current year, Great Look made cash sales of $220,000 and credit sales of $460,000. During the year, accounts receivable decreased by $24,000.

a Compute for the current year the amounts of:

(1) Net sales.

(2) Cash received from collecting accounts receivable.

(3) Cash received from customers.

b Write a brief statement explaining why cash received from customers differs from the amount of net sales.

**Exercise 19-4
Computing cash
paid for
purchases of
merchandise**

The general ledger of NitroTech provides the following information relating to purchases of merchandise:

	END OF YEAR	BEGINNING OF YEAR
Inventory...	$720,000	$780,000
Accounts payable to merchandise suppliers	530,000	500,000

The company's cost of goods sold during the year was $2,460,000.

Instructions

a Compute the amount of cash payments made during the year to suppliers of merchandise.

b Assume that NitroTech maintains a cash payments journal identical in design to the one illustrated on page 241 in Chapter 6 of this text. How might you determine the amounts of cash paid to suppliers of merchandise from this journal? (Identify the relevant column totals in your answer.)

**Exercise 19-5
Reporting lending
activities and
interest revenue**

During the current year, Otay Savings and Loan Association made new loans of $12,000,000. In addition, the company collected $36,000,000 from borrowers, of which $31,000,000 was interest revenue. Explain how these cash flows will appear in the company's statement of cash flows, indicating the classification and the dollar amount of each cash flow.

**Exercise 19-6
Disclosing
"noncash"
investing and
financing
activities**

During the current year, Nordic Co. purchased a factory from Fisher Industries. The journal entry made to record this transaction is shown below:

Land...	300,000	
Buildings...	650,000	
Equipment	1,800,000	
Mortgage Payable		1,900,000
Cash...		850,000

This was Nordic Co.'s only purchase of plant assets during the year. Nordic Co. prepares a supplementary schedule to its statement of cash flows for the purpose of disclosing any "noncash" aspects of investing and financing activities.

Instructions

a Prepare the supplementary schedule to disclose the "noncash" aspects of this transaction. Follow the general format illustrated on page 742.

b Illustrate the presentation of this transaction in Nordic Co.'s statement of cash flows. Begin your illustration by indicating the section of the statement (operating, investing, or financing activities) in which this transaction will appear.

Exercise 19-7
Format of a statement of cash flows

The accounting staff of Cajun Chef has assembled the following information for the year ended December 31, 1991:

Cash and cash equivalents, beginning of year	$ 38,600
Cash and cash equivalents, end of year	57,600
Cash paid to acquire plant assets	19,000
Proceeds from short-term borrowing	10,000
Loans made to borrowers	5,000
Collections on loans (excluding interest)	4,000
Interest and dividends received	12,000
Cash received from customers	815,000
Proceeds from sales of plant assets	7,000
Dividends paid	80,000
Cash paid to suppliers and employees	635,000
Interest paid	19,000
Income taxes paid	71,000

Instructions

Using this information, prepare a formal statement of cash flows. Include a proper heading for the financial statement, and classify the given information into the categories of operating activities, investing activities, and financing activities. Place brackets around the dollar amounts of all cash outlays.

PROBLEMS

Group A

Problem 19A-1
Classifying cash flows

Fifteen business transactions of Green Mountain Railroad are listed below:

a Collected an account receivable from a customer.

b Transferred cash from a money market fund into the general bank account.

c Made a year-end adjusting entry to recognize depreciation expense.

d Paid salaries to employees in the accounting and finance departments.

e Paid a dividend declared in the prior year.

f Declared a dividend to be paid early next year.

g At year-end, purchased for cash an insurance policy covering the next two years.

h Purchased short-term Treasury bills for cash.

i Made payments on accounts payable to merchandise suppliers.

j Issued bonds payable for cash; management plans to use this cash in the near future to modernize production facilities.

k Sold marketable securities at a loss.

l Collected principal amounts due on a loan (a note receivable).

m Collected interest due on the note receivable described in **l,** above.

n Used the cash received in **j,** above, for the purpose of modernizing production facilities.

o Made a semiannual interest payment on bonds payable.

Instructions

Most of the preceding transactions should be included among the activities summarized in a statement of cash flows. For each transaction that should be included in this statement, indicate whether the transaction should be classified as an operating activity, investing activity, or financing activity. If the transaction should **not be included** in the current year's statement of cash flows, briefly explain why not.

Problem 19A-2
Reporting
investing
activities

An analysis of the income statement and the balance sheet accounts of Electric Motor Co. at December 31 provides the following information:

Income statement items:

Gain on sale of plant assets	$ 4,000
Loss on sales of marketable securities	8,000

Analysis of balance sheet accounts:

  Marketable Securities account:

Debit entries	$37,000
Credit entries	31,000

  Notes Receivable account:

Debit entries	26,000
Credit entries	30,000

  Plant and equipment accounts:

Debit entries to plant asset accounts	65,000
Credit entries to plant asset accounts	70,000
Debit entries to accumulated depreciation accounts	50,000

Additional
Information

(1) Except as noted in **(4)**, below, payments and proceeds relating to investing transactions were made in cash.

(2) The marketable securities are not cash equivalents.

(3) All notes receivable relate to cash loans made to borrowers, not to receivables from customers.

(4) Purchases of new equipment during the year ($65,000) were financed by paying $25,000 in cash and issuing a long-term note payable for $40,000.

(5) Debits to the accumulated depreciation account are made whenever depreciable plant assets are sold or retired. Thus, the book value of plant assets sold or retired during the year was $20,000 ($70,000 − $50,000).

Instructions

a Prepare the *Investing activities* section of a statement of cash flows. Show supporting computations for the amounts of (1) proceeds from sales of marketable securities, and (2) proceeds from sales of plant assets. Place brackets around amounts representing cash outflows.

b Prepare the supplementary schedule that should accompany the statement of cash flows in order to disclose the "noncash" aspects of the company's investing and financing activities.

Problem 19A-3
Reporting
operating cash
flows

The following data have been taken from the accounting records of Norse Electronics Corp., December 31:

	END OF YEAR	BEGINNING OF YEAR
Balance sheet accounts:		
Accounts receivable	$ 780,000	$700,000
Accrued interest receivable	6,000	8,000
Inventories	670,000	690,000
Short-term prepayments	18,000	22,000
Accounts payable (merchandise suppliers)	577,000	590,000
Accrued operating expenses payable	38,000	21,000
Accrued interest payable	13,000	19,000
Accrued income taxes payable	36,000	28,000

Income statement amounts:

Net sales	3,100,000
Dividend revenue	47,000
Interest revenue	50,000
Cost of goods sold	1,850,000
Operating expenses	920,000
Interest expense	140,000
Income taxes expense	90,000

Additional Information

(1) Dividend revenue is recognized on the cash basis. All other income statement amounts are recognized on the accrual basis.

(2) Operating expenses include depreciation expense of $105,000.

Instructions

Prepare a partial statement of cash flows, including only the operating activities section of the statement. Use the format and captions illustrated on page 731, and place brackets around amounts representing cash payments. Show supporting computations for the amounts of:

(1) Cash received from customers.

(2) Interest and dividends received.

(3) Cash paid to suppliers and employees.

(4) Interest paid.

(5) Income taxes paid.

Problem 19A-4
Preparing a statement of cash flows

The accounting staff of Trans-Fax Corporation has assembled the following information for the year ended December 31, 19___:

Cash sales	$ 380,000
Credit sales	3,420,000
Collections on accounts receivable	3,130,000
Cash transferred from the money market fund to the general bank account	180,000
Interest and dividends received	40,000
Purchases (all on account)	1,950,000
Payments on accounts payable to merchandise suppliers	2,000,000
Cash payments for operating expenses	800,000
Interest paid	95,000
Income taxes paid	180,000
Loans made to borrowers	220,000
Collections on loans (excluding receipts of interest)	145,000
Cash paid to acquire plant assets	1,640,000
Book value of plant assets sold	70,000
Gain on sales of plant assets	35,000
Proceeds from issuing capital stock	1,355,000
Dividends paid	180,000
Cash and cash equivalents, beginning of year	450,000
Cash and cash equivalents, end of year	–?–

Instructions

Prepare a statement of cash flows in the format illustrated on page 731. Place brackets around amounts representing cash outflows. Many of the items above will be listed in your statement without change. However, you will have to combine certain given information to compute the amounts of (1) collections from customers, (2) cash paid to suppliers and employees, and (3) proceeds from sales of plant assets.

**Problem 19A-5
Preparing a
statement of cash
flows: a
comprehensive
problem**

You are the chief accountant for Southern Technologies. Your assistant has prepared an income statement for the current year, and has also developed the following "Additional Information" by analyzing changes in the company's balance sheet accounts.

SOUTHERN TECHNOLOGIES
Income Statement
For the Year Ended December 31, 19___

Revenue:		
Net sales		$1,600,000
Interest revenue		20,000
Gain on sales of marketable securities		17,000
Total revenue and gains		$1,637,000
Costs and expenses:		
Cost of goods sold	$810,000	
Operating expenses (including depreciation of $75,000)	620,000	
Interest expense	21,000	
Income taxes	50,000	
Loss on sales of plant assets	6,000	
Total costs, expenses, and losses		1,507,000
Net income		$ 130,000

**Additional
Information**

Information about changes in the company's balance sheet accounts over the year is summarized below:

(1) Accounts receivable increased by $30,000.

(2) Accrued interest receivable decreased by $1,000.

(3) Inventory decreased by $30,000 and accounts payable to suppliers of merchandise decreased by $8,000.

(4) Short-term prepayments of operating expenses increased by $3,000, and accrued liabilities for operating expenses decreased by $4,000.

(5) The liability for accrued interest payable increased by $2,000 during the year.

(6) The liability for accrued income taxes payable decreased by $7,000 during the year.

(7) The following schedule summarizes the total debit and credit entries during the year in other balance sheet accounts:

	DEBIT ENTRIES	CREDIT ENTRIES
Marketable securities	$ 30,000	$ 19,000
Notes receivable (cash loans made to borrowers)	22,000	14,000
Plant assets (see paragraph 8 below)	250,000	18,000
Notes payable (short-term borrowing)	46,000	41,000
Capital stock		10,000
Additional paid-in capital—capital stock		80,000
Retained earnings (see paragraph 9 below)	60,000	130,000

(8) The $18,000 in credit entries to the plant asset accounts are net of any debits to accumulated depreciation when plant assets were retired. Thus, the $18,000 in credit entries represents the book value of all plant assets sold or retired during the year.

(9) The $60,000 debit to retained earnings represents dividends declared and paid during the year. The $130,000 credit entry represents the net income shown in the income statement.

(10) All investing and financing activities were cash transactions.

(11) Cash and cash equivalents amounted to $122,000 at the beginning of the year, and to $82,000 at year-end.

Instructions You are to prepare a statement of cash flows for the current year, following the format illustrated on page 731. Place brackets around dollar amounts representing cash out-flows. Show separately your computations of the following amounts:

(1) Cash received from customers.

(2) Interest received.

(3) Cash paid to suppliers and employees.

(4) Interest paid.

(5) Income taxes paid.

(6) Proceeds from sales of marketable securities.

(7) Proceeds from sales of plant assets.

(8) Proceeds from issuing capital stock.

Group B

Problem 19B-1
Classifying cash flows

Among the transactions of Miyota Communications were the following:

a Made payments on accounts payable to merchandise suppliers.

b Paid the principal amount of a note payable to First Bank.

c Paid interest charges relating to a note payable to First Bank.

d Issued bonds payable for cash; management plans to use this cash in the near future to modernize production facilities.

e Paid salaries to employees in the finance department.

f Collected an account receivable from a customer.

g Transferred cash from the general bank account into a money market fund.

h Used the cash received in **d** above, for the purpose of modernizing production facilities.

i Made a year-end adjusting entry to recognize depreciation expense.

j At year-end, purchased for cash an insurance policy covering the next two years.

k Paid the quarterly dividend on preferred stock.

l Paid the semiannual interest on bonds payable.

m Received a quarterly dividend from an investment in the preferred stock of another corporation.

n Sold for cash an investment in the preferred stock of another corporation.

o Received cash upon the maturity of an investment in cash equivalents.

Instructions Most of the preceding transactions should be included among the activities summarized in a statement of cash flows. For each transaction that should be included in this statement, indicate whether the transaction should be classified as an operating activity, investing activity, or financing activity. If the transaction ***should not be included*** in the current year's statement of cash flows, briefly explain why not.

Problem 19B-2
Reporting investing activities

An analysis of the income statement and the balance sheet accounts of WalkAbout Shoes at December 31 provides the following information:

Income statement items:

Gain on sale of marketable securities	$14,000
Loss on sales of plant assets	11,000

Analysis of balance sheet accounts:

Marketable Securities account:

Debit entries	$27,000
Credit entries	30,000

Notes Receivable account:

Debit entries	70,000
Credit entries	54,000

Plant and equipment accounts:

Debit entries to plant asset accounts..	62,000
Credit entries to plant asset accounts.......................................	40,000
Debit entries to accumulated depreciation accounts	25,000

Additional Information

(1) Except as noted in (4), below, payments and proceeds relating to investing transactions were made in cash.

(2) The marketable securities are not cash equivalents.

(3) All notes receivable relate to cash loans made to borrowers, not to receivables from customers.

(4) Purchases of new equipment during the year ($62,000) were financed by paying $20,000 in cash and issuing a long-term note payable for $42,000.

(5) Debits to the accumulated depreciation account are made whenever depreciable plant assets are retired. Thus, the book value of plant assets retired during the year was $15,000 ($40,000 − $25,000).

Instructions

a Prepare the *Investing activities* section of a statement of cash flows. Show supporting computations for the amounts of (1) proceeds from sales of marketable securities, and (2) proceeds from sales of plant assets. Place brackets around numbers representing cash outflows.

b Prepare the supporting schedule that should accompany the statement of cash flows in order to disclose the "noncash" aspects of the company's investing and financing activities.

Problem 19B-3
Reporting cash flows from operating activities

The following data have been taken from the accounting records of Satellite Transmissions, Inc., at December 31:

	END OF YEAR	BEGINNING OF YEAR
Balance sheet accounts:		
Accounts receivable	$ 650,000	$720,000
Accrued interest receivable	9,000	6,000
Inventories	800,000	765,000
Short-term prepayments	20,000	15,000
Accounts payable (merchandise suppliers)....................	570,000	562,000
Accrued operating expenses payable.........................	65,000	94,000
Accrued interest payable	21,000	12,000
Accrued income taxes payable..............................	22,000	35,000

Income statement amounts:

Net sales	2,850,000
Dividend revenue	104,000
Interest revenue	70,000
Cost of goods sold	1,550,000
Operating expenses	980,000
Interest expense	185,000
Income taxes expense	110,000

Additional Information

(1) Dividend revenue is recognized on the cash basis. All other income statement amounts are recognized on the accrual basis.

(2) Operating expenses include depreciation expense of $115,000.

Instructions

Prepare a partial statement of cash flows, including only the operating activities section of the statement. Use the format and captions illustrated on page 731, and place brackets around numbers representing cash payments. Show supporting computations for the amounts of:

(1) Cash received from customers.

(2) Interest and dividends received.

(3) Cash paid to suppliers and employees.

(4) Interest paid.

(5) Income taxes paid.

Problem 19B-4
Format of a statement of cash flows

The accounting staff of Children's Book Co. has assembled the following information for the year ended December 31, 19___:

Cash sales	$ 400,000
Credit sales	1,250,000
Collections on accounts receivable......................................	1,100,000
Cash transferred from the money market fund to the general bank account	250,000
Interest and dividends received	50,000
Purchases (all on account)...	900,000
Payments on accounts payable to merchandise suppliers	750,000
Cash payments for operating expenses	550,000
Interest paid	110,000
Income taxes paid...	60,000
Loans made to borrowers	250,000
Collections on loans (excluding receipts of interest)	130,000
Cash paid to acquire plant assets..	2,000,000
Book value of plant assets sold...	330,000
Loss on sales of plant assets	40,000
Proceeds from issuing bonds payable......................................	1,800,000
Dividends paid	60,000
Cash and cash equivalents, beginning of year	278,000
Cash and cash equivalents, end of year	–?–

Instructions

Prepare a statement of cash flows in the format illustrated on page 731. Place brackets around amounts representing cash outflows. Many of the items above will be listed in your statement without change. However, you will have to combine certain given information to compute the amounts of (1) collections from customers, (2) cash paid to suppliers and employees, and (3) proceeds from sales of plant assets. (Hint: Not every item listed above is used in preparing a statement of cash flows.)

Problem 19B-5
Preparing a
statement of cash
flows: a
comprehensive
problem

You are the chief accountant for SofTech, Inc. Your assistant has prepared an income statement for the current year, and also developed the following "Additional Information" by analyzing changes in the company's balance sheet accounts.

SOFTECH, INC.
Income Statement
For the Year Ended December 31, 19___

Revenue:		
Net sales		$4,900,000
Interest revenue		260,000
Gain on sales of plant assets		20,000
Total revenue and gains		$5,180,000
Costs and expenses:		
Cost of goods sold	$2,600,000	
Operating expenses (including depreciation of $400,000)	1,650,000	
Interest expense	200,000	
Income taxes...	190,000	
Loss on sales of marketable securities	60,000	
Total costs, expenses, and losses...........................		4,700,000
Net income		$ 480,000

Additional
Information

Information about changes in the company's balance sheet accounts over the year is summarized below:

(1) Accounts receivable decreased by $100,000.

(2) Accrued interest receivable increased by $25,000.

(3) Inventory increased by $200,000 and accounts payable to suppliers of merchandise increased by $160,000.

(4) Short-term prepayments of operating expenses decreased by $15,000, and accrued liabilities for operating expenses increased by $80,000.

(5) The liability for accrued interest payable decreased by $8,000 during the year.

(6) The liability for accrued income taxes payable increased by $18,000 during the year.

(7) The following schedule summarizes the total debit and credit entries during the year in other balance sheet accounts:

	DEBIT ENTRIES	CREDIT ENTRIES
Marketable securities..	$ 200,000	$170,000
Notes receivable (cash loans made to borrowers).................	210,000	290,000
Plant assets (see paragraph 8)	1,200,000	50,000
Notes payable (short-term borrowing)	650,000	420,000
Capital stock...		50,000
Additional paid-in capital—capital stock..........................		750,000
Retained earnings (see paragraph 9 below)	300,000	480,000

(8) The $50,000 in credit entries to the plant asset accounts are net of any debits to accumulated depreciation when plant assets were retired. Thus, the $50,000 in credit entries represents the **book value** of all plant assets sold or retired during the year.

(9) The $300,000 debit to retained earnings represents dividends declared and paid during the year. The $480,000 credit entry represents the net income shown in the income statement.

(10) All investing and financing activities were cash transactions.

(11) Cash and cash equivalents amounted to $300,000 at the beginning of the year, and to $490,000 at year-end.

Instructions You are to prepare a statement of cash flows for the current year, following the format illustrated on page 731. Place brackets around dollar amounts representing cash outlays. Show separately your computations of the following amounts:

(1) Cash received from customers.

(2) Interest received.

(3) Cash paid to suppliers and employees.

(4) Interest paid.

(5) Income taxes paid.

(6) Proceeds from sales of marketable securities.

(7) Proceeds from sales of plant assets.

(8) Proceeds from issuing capital stock.

BUSINESS DECISION CASES

Case 19-1
Another look at
Allison
Corporation

This case is based upon the statement of cash flows for Allison Corporation, illustrated on page 731. You are to use this statement to evaluate the company's ability to continue paying the current level of dividends—$40,000 per year. The following information also is available:

(1) The net cash flow from operating activities shown in the statement is relatively "normal" for Allison Corporation. In fact, net cash flows from operating activities have not varied by more than a few thousand dollars in any of the last three years.

(2) The net outflow for investing activities was unusually high, because the company modernized its production facilities during the year. The "normal" investing cash outflow is about $45,000 per year, the amount required to replace existing plant assets as they are retired. Over the long run, marketable securities transactions and lending transactions have a very small impact upon Allison's net cash flow from investing activities.

(3) The net cash flow from financing activities was unusually large in the current year, because of the issuance of bonds payable and capital stock. These securities were issued to finance the modernization of the production facilities. In a typical year, financing activities include only short-term borrowing transactions and payments of dividends.

Instructions **a** Based solely upon the company's past performance, do you feel that the $40,000 annual dividend payments are secure? That is, does the company appear able to pay this amount in dividends every year without putting any strain on its cash position? Do you think it more likely that Allison Corporation will increase or decrease the amount of dividends that it pays? Explain fully.

b Should any of the "unusual" events appearing in the statement of cash flows for the current year affect your analysis of the company's ability to pay future dividends? Explain.

Case 19-2
Lookin' good?

It is late summer and National Motors, an auto manufacturer, is facing a financial crisis. A large issue of bonds payable will mature next March, and the company must issue stock or new bonds to raise the money to retire this debt. Unfortunately, profits and cash flows have been declining over recent years. Management fears that if cash flows and profits do not improve in the current year, the company will not be able to raise the capital needed to pay off the maturing bonds. Therefore, members of management have made the following proposals to improve the cash flows and profitability that will be reported in the financial statements dated this coming December 31.

(1) Switch from the LIFO method to the FIFO method of valuing inventories. Management estimates that the FIFO method will result in a lower cost of goods sold, but in higher income taxes for the current year. However, the additional income taxes will not actually be paid until early next year.

(2) Switch from the sum-of-the-years'-digits method of depreciation to the straight-line method, and also lengthen the useful lives over which assets are depreciated. (These changes would be made only for financial reporting purposes, not for income tax purposes.)

(3) Pressure dealers to increase their inventories—in short, to buy more cars. (The dealerships are independently owned; thus, dealers are the "customers" to whom National Motors sells automobiles.) It is estimated that this strategy could increase sales for the current year by 5%. However, any additional sales in the current year would be almost entirely offset by fewer sales to dealers in the following year.

(4) Require dealers to pay for purchases more quickly. Currently, dealers must pay for purchases of autos within 60 days. Management is considering reducing this period to 30 days.

(5) Pass up cash discounts offered for prompt payment (i.e., 2/10, n/30) and do not pay any bills until the final due date.

(6) Borrow at current short-term interest rates (about 10%) and use the proceeds to pay off long-term debt bearing an interest rate of 13%.

(7) Substitute stock dividends for the cash dividends currently paid on capital stock.

Instructions　**a**　Prepare a schedule with four columns. The first column is to be headed "Proposals," and contains the paragraph numbers of the seven proposals listed above. The next three columns are to be headed with the following financial statement captions: (1) Net income, (2) Net cash flow from operating activities, and (3) Cash.

For each of the seven proposals in the left column, indicate whether you expect the proposal to "Increase," "Decrease," or have "No Effect" in the current year upon each of the financial statement captions listed in the next three columns.

b　For each of the seven proposals, write a short paragraph explaining the reasoning behind your answers to part **a**.

ANSWERS TO SELF-TEST QUESTIONS

1 b　**2 a**　**3 a**　**4 c**　**5 d**

Appendix C
The Indirect Method

The purpose of this appendix is to expand upon the coverage in Chapter 19 of the indirect method of determining and reporting the net cash flow from operating activities. Although the FASB encourages use of the direct method, the indirect method is a permissible alternative and remains in widespread use. In this appendix, we illustrate both methods, compare the two, and discuss the rationale behind the adjustments commonly required in applying the indirect method.

After studying this appendix you should be able to meet these learning objectives:

1 Compare the direct and indirect methods of reporting net cash flow from operating activities.

2 Identify the basic reasons that net income differs from net cash flow from operating activities.

3 Explain how the net changes in certain balance sheet accounts represent differences between net income and net cash flow.

4 Compute net cash flow from operating activities using the indirect method.

Illustration of the Direct and Indirect Methods

In a statement of cash flows, the net cash flow from operating activities may be determined either by the direct or the indirect method. Both methods were illustrated in Chapter 19 using the data from our Allison Corporation example. For your convenience, these illustrations are repeated below:

Cash flows from operating activities:		
Cash received from customers..................................	$ 870,000	
Interest and dividends received	10,000	
Cash provided by operating activities		$ 880,000
Cash paid to suppliers and employees	$(764,000)	
Interest paid	(28,000)	
Income taxes paid..	(38,000)	
Cash disbursed for operating activities		(830,000)
Net cash flow from operating activities........................		$ 50,000

Indirect Method

Net income		$ 65,000
Add: Depreciation expense..		40,000
Decrease in accrued interest receivable		1,000
Increase in accounts payable		15,000
Increase in accrued interest payable		7,000
Nonoperating loss on sales of marketable securities		4,000
Subtotal..		$132,000
Less: Increase in accounts receivable	$30,000	
Increase in inventory	10,000	
Increase in prepaid expenses	3,000	
Decrease in accrued operating expenses payable.	6,000	
Decrease in accrued income taxes payable.....................	2,000	
Nonoperating gain on sales of plant assets.....................	31,000	82,000
Net cash flow from operating activities..		$50,000

Comparison of the Direct and Indirect Methods

Objective 1
Compare the direct and indirect methods of reporting net cash flow from operating activities.

The two methods of computing net cash flow from operating activities are more similar than they appear at first glance. Both methods are based upon the same accounting data and both result in the **same net cash flow.** Also, the computations underlying both methods are quite similar. Both methods convert accrual-based income statement amounts into cash flows by adjusting for changes in related balance sheet accounts.

To illustrate the similarity in the computations, look briefly at the formulas for computing the cash inflows and outflows shown under the direct method (pages 736–739). Each formula begins with an income statement amount and then adds or subtracts the change during the period in related balance sheet accounts. Now look at our illustration of the indirect method. Notice that this computation also focuses upon the net changes during the period in balance sheet accounts.

The differences between the two methods lie only in format. However, the two formats provide readers of the cash flow statement with different types of information. The direct method informs these readers of the nature and dollar amounts of the **specific cash inflows and outflows** comprising the operating activities of the business. The indirect method, in contrast, **explains why** the net cash flow from operating activities differs from another measurement of performance—net income.

Differences between Net Income and Net Cash Flow from Operating Activities

Objective 2
Identify the basic reasons that net income differs from net cash flow from operating activities.

As we discussed in Chapter 19, net cash flow from operating activities differs from net income for three major reasons. (Note: In the following discussions, we will assume that both net income and net cash flow are positive amounts.)

1 **"Noncash" expenses** Some expenses, such as depreciation expense reduce net income, but do not require any cash outlay during the current period.

2 **Timing differences** Revenue and expenses are measured using the concepts of accrual accounting. Net cash flow, on the other hand, reflects the effects of cash transactions. Thus, revenue and expenses may be recognized in a different accounting period from the related cash flows.

3 "Nonoperating" gains and losses By definition, net cash flow from operating activities shows only the effects of those cash transactions classified as "operating activities." Net income, on the other hand, may include gains and losses relating to investing and financing activities.

Reconciling Net Income with Net Cash Flow

To acquaint you with the indirect method, we will now discuss some common types of adjustments needed in reconciling net income with net cash flow from operating activities. The nature and dollar amounts of these adjustments are determined by an accountant using a working paper or a computer program; they are *not* entered in the company's accounting records.

1 Adjustments for "Noncash" Expenses

Depreciation is an example of a "noncash" expense—that is, depreciation expense reduces net income, but does not require any cash outlay during the period. Thus, expenses on the accrual basis exceed cash payments, and net income for the period is less than the net cash flow. To reconcile net income with net cash flow, we must add back to net income the amount of depreciation and any other "noncash" expenses. (Other "noncash" expenses include amortization of intangible assets, depletion of natural resources, and amortization of bond discount.)

2 Adjusting for Timing Differences

Timing differences between net income and net cash flow arise whenever revenue or expense is recognized by debiting or crediting an asset account other than cash or a liability account. Changes over the period in the balances of these asset and liability accounts represent differences in the amount of revenue or expense recognized in the income statement and the net cash flow from operating activities. The balance sheet accounts that give rise to these timing differences include accounts receivable, inventories, prepaid expenses, accounts payable, and accrued expenses payable. Let us look separately at the effects of changes in each type of account.

Objective 3
Explain how the net changes in certain balance sheet accounts represent differences between net income and cash flow.

■ **Changes in Accounts Receivables** Receivables increase as revenue is earned, and decrease as cash is collected from customers. A net increase in accounts receivable over the period indicates that the revenue from credit sales exceeds collections from customers. Thus, net income measured on the accrual basis is *greater than* net cash flow; in our reconciliation of these two amounts, the net increase in accounts receivable is *deducted* from net income.

On the other hand, a net decrease in accounts receivable indicates cash receipts in excess of revenue from credit sales, and is added to the amount of net income.

■ **Changes in Inventory** The balance in the Inventory account increases as merchandise is purchased, and decreases as goods are sold. A net increase during the period in the Inventory account indicates that purchases during the period exceed the cost of goods sold. Thus, to reconcile net income with net cash flow, we deduct from net income the amount of these additional purchases (the net increase in the balance of the Inventory account).

A net decrease over the period in the balance of the Inventory account indicates that the cost of goods sold exceeds purchases made during the period. To the extent that the cost of goods sold consists of a decrease in inventory, no cash payment is required in the current period. Therefore, we add to net income the amount of a net decrease in inventory.

■ **Changes in Prepaid Expenses**   Prepaid expenses appear in the financial statements as assets. Increases in these assets result from cash payments, and decreases result from expiring amounts being recognized as expenses of the period. Thus, a net increase over the period in the amount of prepaid expenses indicates that cash payments made for these items must exceed the amounts recognized as expense. Thus, in determining net cash flow from operating activities, we deduct from net income the net increase in a company's prepaid expenses.

A net decrease in prepaid expenses indicates that cash outlays during the period were less than the amounts deducted as expense in the computation of net income. Thus, a net decrease in prepaid expenses is added back to net income.

■ **Changes in Accounts Payable**   Accounts payable are increased by purchases on account and are reduced by cash payments to suppliers. A net increase in accounts payable indicates that the accrual-based figure for purchases, which is included in the cost of goods sold, is greater than the cash payments made to suppliers. Therefore, in converting net income to cash flow, we add back the amount of merchandise purchases financed by a net increase in accounts payable.

A net decrease in accounts payable indicates that cash payments to suppliers exceed the purchases made during the period. Thus, a net decrease in accounts payable is subtracted from net income in the computation of net cash flow.

■ **Changes in Accrued Expenses Payable**   The liability for accrued expenses payable rises with the recognition of expenses that will be paid in the future, and decreases as cash payments are made. A net increase in accrued expenses payable indicates that expenses in the period exceed the related cash payments. Thus, net income is less than net cash flow, and the increase in the accrued expenses payable accounts should be added to net income.

A net decrease in accrued expenses payable indicates that cash payments exceed the related amounts of expense. This decrease, therefore, is subtracted from net income.

The liability for deferred income taxes may be viewed as a long-term accrued expense payable. However, in the reconciliation of net income with net cash flow from operating activities, the change in the liability for deferred income taxes is shown separately from the net change in other accrued expenses payable. A net increase in this liability is added to net income; a net decrease is subtracted.

■ A Helpful Hint Based on Debits and Credits In our preceding discussion, we explain *why* increases and decreases in a number of asset and liability accounts represent differences between the net income and net cash flow for the period. We do not expect you to memorize the effects of all of these changes. Rather, we hope that you will identify the types of transactions that cause a given account balance to increase or decrease, and will then evaluate the effects of these transactions upon net income and net cash flow. This type of analysis will enhance your understanding of the relationships between accrual accounting and cash transactions.

However, let us offer you a quick hint. Double-entry accounting provides a simple rule that will let you check your analysis. For those asset and liability accounts that explain timing differences between net income and net cash flow, *a net credit change in the account's balance is always added to net income; a net debit change is always subtracted.* (For practice, test this rule on the adjustments in the illustration at the beginning of this appendix. It applies to every adjustment that describes an increase or a decrease in a balance sheet account.)

3 Adjusting for "Nonoperating" Gains and Losses

In a statement of cash flows, cash flows are classified as operating activities, investing activities, or financing activities. "Nonoperating" gains and losses, by definition, do not affect *operating activities.* However, these gains and losses do enter into the determination of net income. Therefore, in converting net income to net cash flow from operating activities, we *add back any nonoperating losses* and *deduct any nonoperating gains* included in net income.

Nonoperating gains and losses include gains and losses from sales of investments, plant assets, and discontinued operations (which relate to investing activities); and gains and losses on early retirement of debt (which relate to financing activities).

The Indirect Method: A Summary

Objective 4
Compute net cash flow from operating activities using the indirect method.

The adjustments to net income explained in our preceding discussion are summarized in the following diagram:

Net income
Add: *Depreciation, amortization of intangibles, and depletion*
         Decrease in accounts receivable
         Decrease in inventories
         Decrease in prepaid expenses
         Increase in accounts payable
         Increase in accrued expenses payable
         Increase in deferred income taxes payable
         "Nonoperating" losses deducted in computing net income
Deduct: *Increase in accounts receivable*
         Increase in inventories
         Increase in prepaid expenses
         Decrease in accounts payable
         Decrease in accrued expenses payable
         "Nonoperating" gains included in net income
Net cash flow from operating activities

Indirect Method May Be Required in a Supplementary Schedule

The FASB recommends use of the *direct method* in presenting net cash flow from operating activities. As of 1989, however, the vast majority of companies were electing to use the indirect method. One reason for this trend is that the FASB saddled companies opting for the direct method with an additional reporting requirement.

Companies using the direct method are required to provide a *supplementary schedule* illustrating the computation of net cash flow from operating activities by the indirect method. However, no supplementary computations are required of companies that use the indirect method in their cash flow statements. In the opinion of the authors, this reporting requirement severely undermines the FASB's efforts to encourage the use of the direct method.

Assignment Material

PROBLEMS

Problem 1
Computation of
net cash flow

The data below are taken from the income statement and balance sheets of All Night Pharmacies, Inc.:

	1992	1991
Income statement:		
Net income	$400,000	
Depreciation expense..	120,000	
Amortization of intangible assets................................	40,000	
Gain on sale of plant assets	80,000	
Loss on sale of investments	35,000	
Balance sheets:		
Accounts receivable	$335,000	$380,000
Inventory...	503,000	575,000
Prepaid expenses	22,000	10,000
Accounts payable (to merchandise suppliers)	379,000	410,000
Accrued expenses payable......................................	180,000	155,000

Instructions

Using this information, prepare a partial statement of cash flows for the year ended December 31, 1992, showing the computation of net cash flow from operating activities by the indirect method.

Problem 2
An analysis of
possible
reconciling items

An analysis of the annual financial statements of Waste Disposal Corporation reveals the following:

a The company had a $4 million extraordinary loss from the early retirement of bonds payable.

b Depreciation for the year amounted to $9 million.

c During the year, $2 million in cash was transferred from the company's checking account into a money market fund.

d Accounts receivable from customers increased by $5 million over the year.

e Cash received from customers during the year amounted to $165 million.

f Prepaid expenses decreased by $1 million over the year.

g Dividends declared during the year, $7 million; dividends paid during the year, $6 million.

h Accounts payable (to suppliers of merchandise) increased by $3 million during the year.

i The liability for accrued income taxes payable amounted to $5 million at the beginning of the year and $3 million at year-end.

Instructions In the computation of net cash flow from operating activities by the indirect method, explain whether each of the above items should be *added to net income, deducted from net income,* or *omitted from the computation.* Briefly explain your reasons for each answer.

**Problem 3
Analysis of data
from an annual
report** Shown below is an excerpt from a recent annual report of *SmithKline Beckman Corporation.* (Dollars are in millions.)

Operating Activities

Net earnings	$570.1
Noncash items included in net earnings:	
Depreciation and amortization	199.8
Deferred income taxes	(17.9)
Changes in assets and liabilities:	
Trade receivables	(111.7)
Inventories	(27.9)
Accounts payable	18.3
Accrued income taxes	82.0
Other	176.8
Net cash provided from operating activities	$889.5

The company did not state whether the changes in assets and liabilities were increases or decreases, apparently assuming that the reader of the financial statements could determine this from the effect of each adjustment upon net earnings. (Of course, this information also may be determined by comparing the company's balance sheets at the beginning and end of the year.)

Instructions By analyzing the effects of the adjustments upon net income in the above schedule, indicate whether the balance in each of the four accounts listed below *increased* or *decreased* over the year. Explain the reasoning behind your answer.

a Trade receivables.

b Inventories.

c Accounts payable.

d Accrued income taxes.

Analysis and Interpretation of Financial Statements

In many of the preceding chapters we have been concerned with preparing a set of financial statements. In this chapter we start with the completed financial statements and concentrate on methods of analyzing and interpreting the information they contain. Our goal is to determine whether a company is gaining or losing ground in the unending struggle for profitability and solvency. We explore the techniques for comparing a company's present financial position with its position a year ago and for comparing this year's earnings with last year's earnings. We also compare a company's performance with that of other companies in the industry. Various types of analysis are presented to meet the special needs of common stockholders, long-term creditors, preferred stockholders, and short-term creditors.

After reading this chapter you should be able to meet these Learning Objectives:

1 Put the dollar amount of a company's net income into perspective by relating it to the company's sales, assets, and stockholders' equity.

2 Describe several sources of financial information about a business.

3 Explain the uses of dollar and percentage changes, trend percentages, component percentages, and ratios.

4 Discuss the "quality" of a company's earnings, assets, and working capital.

5 Analyze financial statements from the viewpoints of common stockholders, creditors, and others.

6 Compute the ratios widely used in financial statement analysis and explain the significance of each.

Financial statements are the instrument panel of a business enterprise. They constitute a report on managerial performance, attesting to managerial success or failure and flashing warning signals of impending difficulties. To read a complex instrument panel, one must understand the gauges and their calibration to make sense out of the array of data they convey. Similarly, one must understand the inner workings of the accounting system and the significance of various financial relationships to interpret the data appearing in financial statements. To a reader with a knowledge of accounting, a set of financial statements reveals a great deal about the financial condition of the business enterprise.

The annual financial statements of large corporations are used by a number of different groups: stockholders, creditors, government agencies, union officials, politicians, and financial analysts, among others. What assurance do these people have that the information in these financial statements is reliable and is presented in accordance with generally accepted accounting principles? The answer is that these financial statements are **audited** by independent firms of certified public accountants.

An audit is a thorough investigation of every item, dollar amount, and disclosure which appears in the financial statements. After completing the audit, the CPAs express their opinion as to the **fairness** of the financial statements. This opinion, called the **auditors' report,** is published with the financial statements in the company's annual report to its stockholders. A report by a CPA firm might read as follows:

■
Independent Auditors' Report

To the Board of Directors and Stockholders
XYZ Company

We have audited the accompanying balance sheet of XYZ Company as of December 31, 19___, and the related statements of income, retained earnings, and cash flow for the year then ended. These financial statements are the responsibility of the Company's management; our responsibility is to express an opinion on these financial statements based on our audit.

We conducted our audit in accordance with generally accepted auditing standards. Those standards require that we plan and perform the audit to obtain reasonable assurance about whether the financial statements are free of material misstatement. An audit includes examining, on a test basis, evidence supporting the amounts and disclosures in the financial statements. An audit also includes assessing the accounting principles used and significant estimates made by management, as well as evaluating the overall financial statement presentation. We believe that our audit provides a reasonable basis for our opinion.

In our opinion, the financial statements referred to above present fairly, in all material respects, the financial position of XYZ Company as of December 31, 19___, and the results of its operations and its cash flows for the year then ended in conformity with generally accepted accounting principles.

Springfield, Mo.
January 29, 19___

Blue, White & Company

Certified Public Accountants

What Is Your Opinion of the Level of Corporate Profits?

Objective 1
Put the dollar amount of a company's net income into perspective by relating it to the company's sales, assets, and stockholders' equity.

As a college student who has completed (or almost completed) a course in accounting, you have a much better understanding of corporate profits than do people who have never studied accounting. The level of earnings of large corporations is a controversial issue, a favorite topic in many political speeches and at cocktail parties. Many of the statements one reads or hears from these sources are emotional rather than rational, and fiction rather than fact. Public opinion polls show that the public believes the average manufacturing company has an after-tax profit of about 30% of sales, when in fact such profit has been *about 5% of sales* in recent years. A widespread public belief that profits are six times the actual rate may lead to some unwise legislation.

CASE IN POINT ■ General Motors in an annual report a few years ago showed a net income of $321 million. This profit may sound like a huge amount, but it was only one-half of 1% of GM's sales. Thus, of every dollar received as revenue, only ½ cent represented profit for GM. On a $10,000 car, this was a profit of $50. Actually, earning only $321 million in a year must be regarded as very poor performance for a corporation the size of General Motors. Shortly afterward, however, GM enjoyed its best year ever, and set new records for both sales and earnings. Net income was $4.5 billion and represented about 5½ cents profit on each dollar of sales. That was a profit of $550 on a $10,000 automobile.

An in-depth knowledge of accounting does not enable you to say at what level corporate earnings *should be;* however, a knowledge of accounting does enable you to read audited financial statements that show what the level of corporate earnings *currently is.* Moreover, you are aware that the information in published financial statements of corporations has been audited by CPA firms and has been reviewed in detail by government agencies, such as the Securities and Exchange Commission and the IRS. Consequently, you know that the profits reported in these published financial statements are reasonably reliable; they have been determined in accordance with generally accepted accounting principles and verified by independent experts.

Some Specific Examples of Corporate Earnings . . . and Losses

Not all leading corporations earn a profit every year. For the seven years from 1981 through 1987, Pan American Airways reported a net loss each year. The total loss for these years exceeded $1½ billion. During a good part of the last decade, much of the airline industry operated at a loss. Net losses were incurred in one or more years by such well-known companies as American Airlines, Continental, TWA, Western, and United Airlines.

A recent annual report of Exxon (audited by Price Waterhouse) shows that profits amounted to a little over $4 billion. Standing alone, that figure seems enormous—but we need to look a little farther. The total revenue of Exxon was over $103 billion, so net income amounted to approximately 4% of sales.

There are many ways of appraising the adequacy of corporate earnings.

Certainly, earnings should be compared with total assets and with invested capital as well as with sales. In this chapter we shall look at a number of ways of evaluating corporate profits and solvency.

Sources of Financial Information

Objective 2
Describe several sources of financial information about a business.

For the most part, our discussion will be limited to the kind of analysis that can be made by "outsiders" who do not have access to internal accounting records. Investors must rely to a considerable extent on financial statements in published annual and quarterly reports. In the case of large publicly owned corporations, additional information is filed with the Securities and Exchange Commission and is available to the public. Financial information about most large corporations is also published by Moody's Investors Service, Standard & Poor's Corporations, and stock brokerage firms.

Bankers are usually able to secure more detailed information by requesting it as a condition for granting a loan. Trade creditors may obtain financial information for businesses of almost any size from credit-rating agencies such as Dun & Bradstreet, Inc.

Comparative Financial Statements

Significant changes in financial data are easy to see when financial statement amounts for two or more years are placed side by side in adjacent columns. Such a statement is called a *comparative financial statement.* The amounts for the most recent year are usually placed in the left-hand money column. Both the balance sheet and the income statement are often prepared in the form of comparative statements. A highly condensed comparative income statement covering three years is shown below.

BENSON CORPORATION
Comparative Income Statement
For the Years Ended December 31, 1992, 1991, and 1990
(in thousands of dollars)

Condensed three-year income statement

	1992	1991	1990
Net sales	$600	$500	$400
Cost of goods sold	370	300	235
Gross profit	$230	$200	$165
Expenses	194	160	115
Net income	$ 36	$ 40	$ 50

Tools of Analysis

Objective 3
Explain the uses of dollar and percentage changes, trend percentages, component percentages, and ratios.

Few figures in a financial statement are highly significant in and of themselves. It is their relationship to other quantities, or the amount and direction of change that is important. Analysis is largely a matter of establishing significant relationships and pointing out changes and trends. Four widely used analytical techniques are (1) dollar and percentage changes, (2) trend percentages, (3) component percentages, and (4) ratios.

Dollar and Percentage Changes

The dollar amount of change from year to year is significant, but expressing the change in percentage terms adds perspective. For example, if sales this year have increased by $100,000, the fact that this is an increase of 10% over last year's sales of $1 million puts it in a different perspective than if it represented a 1% increase over sales of $10 million for the prior year.

The dollar amount of any change is the difference between the amount for a *comparison* year and for a *base* year. The percentage change is computed by dividing the amount of the change between years by the amount for the base year. This is illustrated in the tabulation below, using data from the comparative income statement on page 775.

Dollar and percentage changes

| | IN THOUSANDS | | | INCREASE OR (DECREASE) | | | |
| | YEAR 1992 | YEAR 1991 | YEAR 1990 | 1992 OVER 1991 | | 1991 OVER 1990 | |
				AMOUNT	%	AMOUNT	%
Net sales	$600	$500	$400	$100	20%	$100	25%
Net income	36	40	50	(4)	(10%)	(10)	(20%)

Although net sales increased $100,000 in both 1991 and 1992, the percentage of change differs because of the shift in the base from 1990 to 1991. These calculations present no problems when the figures for the base year are positive amounts. If a negative amount or a zero amount appears in the base year, however, a percentage change cannot be computed. Thus if Benson Corporation had incurred a net loss in 1991, the percentage change in net income from 1991 to 1992 could not have been calculated.

■ Evaluating Percentage Changes in Sales and Earnings

Computing the percentage changes in sales, gross profit, and net income from one year to the next gives insight into a company's rate of growth. If a company is experiencing growth in its economic activities, sales and earnings should increase at *more than the rate of inflation.* Assume, for example, that a company's sales increase by 6% while the general price level rises by 10%. It is probable that the entire increase in the dollar amount of sales may be explained by inflation, rather than by an increase in sales volume (the number of units sold). In fact, the company may well have sold fewer goods than in the preceding year.

In measuring the dollar or percentage change in *quarterly* sales or earnings, it is customary to compare the results of the current quarter with those of the *same quarter in the preceding year.* Use of the same quarter of the preceding year as the base period prevents our analysis from being distorted by seasonal fluctuations in business activity.

■ Percentages Become Misleading When the Base Is Small

Percentage changes may create a misleading impression when the dollar amount used as a base is unusually small. Occasionally we hear a television newscaster say that a company's profits have increased by a very large percentage, such as 900%. The initial impression created by such a statement is that the company's profits must now be excessively large. But assume, for example, that a company had net income of $100,000 in its first year; that in the second year net income drops to $10,000, and that in the third year, net income returns to the $100,000 level. In this third year, net income has increased by $90,000, representing a 900% increase over the profits of the second year. What needs to be added is that this 900% increase in profits in the third year *exactly offsets* the 90% decline in profits in the second year.

Few people realize that a 90% decline in earnings must be followed by a 900% increase just to get back to the starting point.

CASE IN POINT ■ In the third quarter of 1979, General Motors earned $21.4 million, as compared with $527.9 million in the third quarter of 1978. This represented a 96% decline in third quarter profits, computed as follows:

Decline in profits ($527.9 − $21.4) $506.5
Base period earnings (third quarter, 1978).................... $527.9
Percentage decrease ($506.5 ÷ $527.9) 96%

How much of an increase in profits would be required in the third quarter of 1980 for profits to return to the 1978 level? Many people erroneously guess 96%. However, the correct answer is an astounding 2,367%, computed as follows:

Required increase to reach 1978 profit level (from $21.4 to $527.9) $506.5
Base period earnings (third quarter, 1979)..................... $ 21.4
Required percentage increase ($506.5 ÷ $21.4) 2,367%

Unfortunately for GM, the company's 1980 profits did not return to 1978 levels. Instead, the company lost a record-setting $567 million in the third quarter of 1980.

Trend Percentages

The changes in financial statement items from a base year to following years are often expressed as *trend percentages* to show the extent and direction of change. Two steps are necessary to compute trend percentages. First, a base year is selected and each item in the financial statements for the base year is given a weight of 100%. The second step is to express each item in the financial statements for following years as a percentage of its base-year amount. This computation consists of dividing an item such as Sales in the years after the base year by the amount of Sales in the base year.

For example, assume that 1987 is selected as the base year and that Sales in the base year amounted to $300,000 as shown below. The trend percentages for Sales are computed by dividing the Sales amount of each following year by $300,000. Also shown in the illustration are the yearly amounts of net income. The trend percentages for net income are computed by dividing the Net Income amount for each following year by the base-year amount of $15,000.

	1992	1991	1990	1989	1988	1987
Sales	$450,000	$360,000	$330,000	$320,000	$312,000	$300,000
Net income	22,950	14,550	21,450	19,200	15,600	15,000

When the computations described above have been made, the trend percentages will appear as shown below.

	1992	1991	1990	1989	1988	1987
Sales	150%	120%	110%	107%	104%	100%
Net income	153%	97%	143%	128%	104%	100%

The above trend percentages indicate a very modest growth in sales in the early years and accelerated growth in 1991 and 1992. Net income also shows an increasing growth trend with the exception of the year 1991, when net income declined despite a solid increase in sales. This variation could have resulted from an unfavorable change in the gross profit margin or from unusual expenses. However, the problem was overcome in 1992 with a sharp rise in net income. Overall the trend percentages give a picture of a profitable growing enterprise.

As another example, assume that sales are increasing each year, but that the cost of goods sold is increasing at a faster rate. This means that the gross profit margin is shrinking. Perhaps the increases in sales are being achieved through excessive price cutting. The company's net income may be declining even though sales are rising.

Component Percentages

Component percentages indicate the *relative size* of each item included in a total. For example, each item on a balance sheet could be expressed as a percentage of total assets. This shows quickly the relative importance of current and noncurrent assets as well as the relative amount of financing obtained from current creditors, long-term creditors, and stockholders. By computing component percentages for several successive balance sheets, we can see which items are increasing in importance and which are becoming less significant.

■ **Common Size Income Statement** Another application of component percentages is to express all items in an income statement as a percentage of net sales. Such a statement is called a common size income statement. A condensed income statement in dollars and in common size form is illustrated below.

Income Statement

	DOLLARS		COMPONENT PERCENTAGES	
	1992	1991	1992	1991
Net sales	$1,000,000	$600,000	100.0%	100.0%
Cost of goods sold	700,000	360,000	70.0	60.0
Gross profit on sales	$ 300,000	$240,000	30.0%	40.0%
Expenses (including income taxes)	250,000	180,000	25.0	30.0
Net income	$ 50,000	$ 60,000	5.0%	10.0%

Are the year-to-year changes favorable?

Looking only at the component percentages, we see that the decline in the gross profit rate from 40 to 30% was only partially offset by the decrease in expenses as a percentage of net sales, causing net income to decrease from 10 to 5% of net sales.

Ratios

A ratio is a simple mathematical expression of the relationship of one item to another. Ratios may be stated several ways. To illustrate, let us consider the current ratio, which expresses the relationship between current assets and current liabilities. If current assets are $100,000 and current liabilities are $50,000, we may say either that the current ratio is 2 to 1 (which is written as 2:1), or that current assets are 200% of current liabilities. Either statement correctly summarizes the relationship—that is, that current assets are twice as large as current liabilities.

If a ratio is to be useful, the two amounts being compared must be logically related. Our interpretation of a ratio often requires investigation of the underlying data.

Comparative Data in Annual Reports of Major Corporations

The annual reports of major corporations usually contain comparative balance sheets covering two years and comparative income statements for three years. Supplementary schedules showing sales, net income, and other key amounts are often presented for periods of five to 10 years. Shown below are selected items from an annual report of The Quaker Oats Company showing some interesting trends for a five-year period.

THE QUAKER OATS COMPANY
($ millions, except per common share data)

	1988	1987	1986	1985	1984
Net sales	$5,330	$4,421	$3,454	$3,348	$3,214
Net income	256	244	180	157	139
Net income per share	$ 3.20	$ 3.10	$ 2.24	$ 1.88	$ 1.67
Dividends per share (common)..........	$ 1.00	$ 0.80	$ 0.70	$ 0.62	$ 0.55
Market price per share (high–low)........	57–31	58–33	40–23	26–14	16–11
Book value per share...................	$15.76	$13.68	$10.64	$ 9.76	$ 8.89

Standards of Comparison

In using dollar and percentage changes, trend percentages, component percentages, and ratios, financial analysts constantly search for some standard of comparison against which to judge whether the relationships that they have found are favorable or unfavorable. Two such standards are (1) the past performance of the company and (2) the performance of other companies in the same industry.

■ **Past Performance of the Company** Comparing analytical data for a current period with similar computations for prior years affords some basis for judging whether the condition of the business is improving or worsening. This comparison of data over time is sometimes called *horizontal* or *trend* analysis, to express the idea of reviewing data for a number of consecutive periods. It is distinguished from *vertical* or *static* analysis, which refers to the review of the financial information for only one accounting period.

In addition to determining whether the situation is improving or becoming worse, horizontal analysis may aid in making estimates of future prospects.

Because changes may reverse their direction at any time, however, projecting past trends into the future is always a somewhat risky statistical pastime.

A weakness of horizontal analysis is that comparison with the past does not afford any basis for evaluation in absolute terms. The fact that net income was 2% of sales last year and is 3% of sales this year indicates improvement, but if there is evidence that net income *should be* 7% of sales, the record for both years is unfavorable.

■ **Industry Standards** The limitations of horizontal analysis may be overcome to some extent by finding some other standard of performance as a yardstick against which to measure the record of any particular firm.[1] The yardstick may be a comparable company, the average record of several companies in the same industry, or some predetermined standard.

Suppose that Y Company suffers a 5% drop in its sales during the current year. The discovery that the sales of all companies in the same industry fell an average of 20% would indicate that this was a favorable rather than an unfavorable performance. Assume further that Y Company's net income is 2% of net sales. Based on comparison with other companies in the industry, this would be substandard performance if Y Company were a manufacturer of commercial aircraft, but it would be a satisfactory record if Y Company were a grocery chain.

When we compare a given company with its competitors or with industry averages, our conclusions will be valid only if the companies in question are reasonably comparable. Because of the large number of diversified companies formed in recent years, the term *industry* is difficult to define, and companies that fall roughly within the same industry may not be comparable in many respects. For example, one company may engage only in the marketing of oil products; another may be a fully integrated producer from the well to the gas pump, yet both are said to be in the "oil industry."

Quality of Earnings

Objective 4
Discuss the "quality" of a company's earnings, assets, and working capital.

Profits are the lifeblood of a business entity. No entity can survive for long and accomplish its other goals unless it is profitable. On the other hand, continuous losses will drain assets from the business, consume owners' equity, and leave the company at the mercy of creditors. In assessing the prospects of a company, we are interested not only in the total *amount* of earnings but also in the *rate* of earnings on sales, on total assets, and on owners' equity. In addition, we must look at the *stability* and *source* of earnings. An erratic earnings performance over a period of years, for example, is less desirable than a steady level of earnings. A history of increasing earnings is preferable to a "flat" earnings record.

---

[1] For example, the Robert Morris Associates publishes *Annual Statement Studies* which recently included detailed data obtained from 27,000 annual reports grouped in 223 industry classifications. Assets, liabilities, and stockholders' equity are presented as a percentage of total assets; income statement amounts are expressed as a percentage of net sales; and key ratios are given (expressed as the median for each industry, the upper quartile, and the lower quartile). Measurements, within each of the 223 industry groups, are grouped according to the size of the firm. Similarly, Dun & Bradstreet, Inc., annually publishes *Key Business Ratios* in 125 lines of business divided by retailing, wholesaling, manufacturing, and construction. A total of 14 ratios is presented for each of the 125 industry groups.

A breakdown of sales and earnings by *major product lines* is useful in evaluating the future performance of a company. Publicly owned companies include with their financial statements supplementary schedules showing sales and profits by product line and by geographical area. These schedules assist financial analysts in forecasting the effect upon the company of changes in consumer demand for particular types of products.

Financial analysts often express the opinion that the earnings of one company are of higher quality than earnings of other similar companies. This concept of *quality of earnings* arises because each company management can choose from a variety of accounting principles and methods, all of which are considered generally acceptable. A company's management often is under heavy pressure to report rising earnings, and accounting policies may be tailored toward this objective. We have already pointed out the impact on current reported earnings of the choice between the LIFO and FIFO methods of inventory valuation and the choice of depreciation policies. In judging the quality of earnings, the financial analyst should consider whether the accounting principles and methods selected by management lead to a conservative measurement of earnings or tend to inflate reported earnings.

Quality of Assets and the Relative Amount of Debt

Although a satisfactory level of earnings may be a good indication of the company's long-run ability to pay its debts and dividends, we must also look at the composition of assets, their condition and liquidity, the relationship between current assets and current liabilities, and the total amount of debt outstanding. A company may be profitable and yet be unable to pay its liabilities on time; sales and earnings may appear satisfactory but plant and equipment may be deteriorating because of poor maintenance policies; valuable patents may be expiring; substantial losses may be imminent due to slow-moving inventories and past-due receivables. Companies with large amounts of debt often are vulnerable to increases in interest rates.

Impact of Inflation

During a period of significant inflation, financial statements prepared in terms of historical costs do not reflect fully the economic resources or the real income (in terms of purchasing power) of a business enterprise. The FASB recommends that companies include in their annual reports supplementary schedules showing the effects of inflation upon their financial statements. Inclusion of these supplementary disclosures is voluntary, not mandatory. Most companies do *not* include these supplementary schedules because of the high cost of developing this information. The effects of inflation on financial statements are discussed further in Appendix D, which follows this chapter.

Illustrative Analysis for Seacliff Company

Keep in mind the above discussion of analytical principles as you study the illustrative financial analysis which follows. The basic information for our analysis is contained in a set of condensed two-year comparative financial statements for Seacliff Company shown below and on the following pages. Summarized statement data, together with computations of dollar increases and decreases, and component percentages where applicable, have been compiled. For convenience in this illustration, relatively small dollar amounts have been used in the Seacliff Company financial statements.

Using the information in these statements, let us consider the kind of analysis that might be of particular interest to (1) common stockholders, (2) long-term creditors, (3) preferred stockholders, and (4) short-term creditors.

Analysis by Common Stockholders

Objective 5
Analyze financial statements from the viewpoints of common stockholders, creditors, and others.

Common stockholders and potential investors in common stock look first at a company's earnings record. Their investment is in shares of stock, so *earnings per share and dividends per share* are of particular interest.

■ **Earnings per Share of Common Stock**   As indicated in Chapter 15, earnings per share of common stock are computed by dividing the income applicable to the common stock by the weighted-average number of shares of common stock outstanding during the year. Any preferred dividend require-

SEACLIFF COMPANY
Condensed Comparative Balance Sheet*
December 31, 1992 and December 31, 1991

ASSETS	1992	1991	INCREASE OR (DECREASE) DOLLARS	%	PERCENTAGE OF TOTAL ASSETS 1992	1991
Current assets	$390,000	$288,000	$102,000	35.4	41.1	33.5
Plant and equipment (net)	500,000	467,000	33,000	7.1	52.6	54.3
Other assets (loans to officers)	60,000	105,000	(45,000)	(42.9)	6.3	12.2
Total assets	$950,000	$860,000	$ 90,000	10.5	100.0	100.0

LIABILITIES & STOCKHOLDERS' EQUITY	1992	1991	DOLLARS	%	1992	1991
Current liabilities	$112,000	$ 94,000	$ 18,000	19.1	11.8	10.9
12% long-term note payable	200,000	250,000	(50,000)	(20.0)	21.1	29.1
Total liabilities...........................	$312,000	$344,000	$ (32,000)	(9.3)	32.9	40.0
Stockholders' equity:						
9% preferred stock, $100 par, callable at 105	$100,000	$100,000			10.5	11.6
Common stock, $50 par	250,000	200,000	$ 50,000	25.0	26.3	23.2
Additional paid-in capital	70,000	40,000	30,000	75.0	7.4	4.7
Retained earnings	218,000	176,000	42,000	23.9	22.9	20.5
Total stockholders' equity................	$638,000	$516,000	$122,000	23.6	67.1	60.0
Total liabilities & stockholders' equity	$950,000	$860,000	$ 90,000	10.5	100.0	100.0

* In order to focus attention on important subtotals, this statement is highly condensed and does not show individual asset and liability items. These details will be introduced as needed in the text discussion. For example, a list of Seacliff Company's current assets and current liabilities appears on page 790.

SEACLIFF COMPANY
Comparative Income Statement
For the Years Ended December 31, 1992 and December 31, 1991

	1992	1991	INCREASE OR (DECREASE) DOLLARS	%	PERCENTAGE OF NET SALES 1992	1991
Net sales	$900,000	$750,000	$150,000	20.0	100.0	100.0
Cost of goods sold	530,000	420,000	110,000	26.2	58.9	56.0
Gross profit on sales	$370,000	$330,000	$ 40,000	12.1	41.1	44.0
Operating expenses:						
Selling expenses:.................	$117,000	$ 75,000	$ 42,000	56.0	13.0	10.0
General and administrative expenses	126,000	95,000	31,000	32.6	14.0	12.7
Total operating expenses	$243,000	$170,000	$ 73,000	42.9	27.0	22.7
Operating income	$127,000	$160,000	$ (33,000)	(20.6)	14.1	21.3
Interest expense	24,000	30,000	(6,000)	(20.0)	2.7	4.0
Income before income taxes	$103,000	$130,000	$ (27,000)	(20.8)	11.4	17.3
Income taxes......................	28,000	40,000	(12,000)	(30.0)	3.1	5.3
Net income	$ 75,000	$ 90,000	$ (15,000)	(16.7)	8.3	12.0
Earnings per share of common stock (see schedule at bottom of page) ...	$13.20	$20.25	$(7.05)	(34.8)		

SEACLIFF COMPANY
Statement of Retained Earnings
For the Years Ended December 31, 1992 and December 31, 1991

	1992	1991	INCREASE OR (DECREASE) DOLLARS	%
Retained earnings, beginning of year	$176,000	$115,000	$61,000	53.0
Net income	75,000	90,000	(15,000)	(16.7)
	$251,000	$205,000	$46,000	22.4
Less: Dividends on common stock ($5.00 per share in 1991, $4.80 per share in 1992) ...	$ 24,000	$ 20,000	$ 4,000	20.0
Dividends on preferred stock ($9 per share)	9,000	9,000		
	$ 33,000	$ 29,000	$ 4,000	13.8
Retained earnings, end of year..................	$218,000	$176,000	$42,000	23.9

ments must be subtracted from net income to determine income applicable to common stock, as shown in the following computations for Seacliff Company:

Earnings per Share of Common Stock

		1992	1991
Net income		$75,000	$90,000
Less: Preferred dividend requirements		9,000	9,000
Income applicable to common stock	(a)	$66,000	$81,000
Shares of common stock outstanding, during the year	(b)	5,000	4,000
Earnings per share of common stock (a ÷ b)		$13.20	$20.25

■ **Earnings related to number of common shares outstanding**

■ **Dividend Yield and Price-Earnings Ratio** Dividends are of prime importance to some stockholders, but a secondary factor to others. In other words, some stockholders invest primarily to receive regular cash income, while others invest in stocks principally with the hope of securing capital gains through rising market prices. If a corporation is profitable and retains its earnings for expansion of the business, the expanded operations should produce an increase in the net income of the company and thus tend to make each share of stock more valuable.

In comparing the merits of alternative investment opportunities, we should relate earnings and dividends per share to the *market value* of the stock. Dividends per share divided by market price per share determines the *yield* rate of a company's stock. Dividend yield is especially important to those investors whose objective is to maximize the dividend revenue from their investments.

Earnings performance of common stock is often expressed as a *price-earnings ratio* by dividing the market price per share by the annual earnings per share. Thus, a stock selling for *$60* per share and earning *$5* per share in the year just ended may be said to have a price-earnings ratio of *12 times earnings* ($60 ÷ $5). The price-earnings ratio of the 30 stocks included in the Dow-Jones Industrial Average has varied widely in recent years, ranging from a low of about 6 for the group to a high of about 20.

The outlook for future earnings is a major factor influencing a company's price-earnings ratio. Companies with track records of rapid growth may sell at price-earnings ratios of perhaps 20 to 1, or even higher. Companies with stable earnings or earnings expected to decline in future years often sell at price-earnings ratios below 10 to 1.

■ **Summary of Earnings and Dividend Data for Seacliff** The year-end prices of Seacliff's common stock were $125 per share in 1991, and $100 per share in 1992. The relationships of the company's per-share earnings and dividends to these stock prices are summarized below:

Earnings and Dividends per Share of Common Stock

	DATE	ASSUMED MARKET VALUE PER SHARE	EARNINGS PER SHARE	PRICE-EARNINGS RATIO	DIVIDENDS PER SHARE	DIVIDEND YIELD, %
Earnings and dividends related to market price of common stock	Dec. 31, 1991	$125	$20.25	6	$5.00	4.0
	Dec. 31, 1992	100	13.20	8	4.80	4.8

The decline in market value during 1992 presumably reflects the decreases in both earnings and dividends per share. Investors appraising this stock at December 31, 1992, should consider whether a price-earnings ratio of 8 and a dividend yield of *4.8%* represent a satisfactory situation in the light of alternative investment opportunities. These investors will also place considerable weight on estimates of the company's prospective future earnings and the probable effect of such estimated earnings on the market price of the stock and on dividend payments.

■ **Book Value per Share of Common Stock** The procedures for computing book value per share were fully described in Chapter 14 and will not be repeated here. We will, however, determine the book value per share of common stock for the Seacliff Company:

Book Value per Share of Common Stock

	1992	1991
Total stockholders' equity..	$638,000	$516,000
Less: Equity of preferred stockholders (1,000 shares at call price of $105)	105,000	105,000
Equity of common stockholders.............................. (a)	$533,000	$411,000
Shares of common stock outstanding .... (b)	5,000	4,000
Book value per share of common stock (a ÷ b).................	$106.60	$102.75

■
Why did book
value per share
increase?

Book value indicates the net assets represented by each share of stock. This statistic is often helpful in estimating a reasonable price for a company's stock, especially for small corporations whose shares are not publicly traded. However, if a company's future earnings prospects are unusually good or unusually poor, the market price of its shares may differ significantly from their book value.

■ **Revenue and Expense Analysis** The trend of earnings of Seacliff Company is unfavorable and stockholders will want to know the reasons for the decline in net income. The comparative income statement on page 783 shows that despite a 20% increase in net sales, net income fell from $90,000 in 1991 to $75,000 in 1992, a decline of 16.7%. As a percentage of net sales, net income fell from 12% to only 8.3%. The primary causes of this decline were the increases in selling expenses (56.0%), in general and administrative expenses (32.6%), and in the cost of goods sold (26.2%), all of which exceeded the 20% increase in net sales.

Let us assume that further investigation reveals Seacliff Company decided in 1992 to reduce its sales prices in an effort to generate greater sales volume. This would explain the decrease in gross profit rate from 44% to 41.1% of net sales. Since the dollar amount of gross profit increased $40,000 in 1992 the strategy of reducing sales prices to increase volume would have been successful if there had been little or no increase in operating expenses. However, operating expenses rose by $73,000, resulting in a $33,000 decrease in operating income.

The next step is to find which expenses increased and why. An investor may be handicapped here, because detailed operating expenses are not usually shown in published financial statements. Some conclusions, however, can be reached on the basis of even the condensed information available in the comparative income statement for Seacliff Company shown on page 783.

The substantial increase in selling expenses presumably reflects greater selling effort during 1992 in an attempt to improve sales volume. However, the fact that selling expenses increased $42,000 while gross profit increased only $40,000 indicates that the cost of this increased sales effort was not justified in terms of results. Even more disturbing is the increase in general and administrative expenses. Some growth in administrative expenses might be expected to accompany increased sales volume, but because some of the expenses are fixed, the growth generally should be *less than proportional* to any increase in sales. The increase in general and administrative expenses from 12.7 to 14% of sales would be of serious concern to informed investors.

Management generally has greater control over operating expenses than over revenue. The *operating expense ratio* is often used as a measure of management's ability to control its operating expenses. The unfavorable trend in this ratio for Seacliff Company is shown below.

Operating Expense Ratio

	1992	1991
Operating expenses	(a) $243,000	$170,000
Net sales	(b) $900,000	$750,000
Operating expense ratio (a ÷ b)	27.0%	22.7%

Does a higher operating expense ratio indicate higher net income?

If management were able to increase the sales volume while at the same time increasing the gross profit rate and decreasing the operating expense ratio, the effect on net income could be quite dramatic. For example, if in 1993 Seacliff Company can increase its sales by 11% to $1,000,000, increase its gross profit rate from 41.1 to 44%, and reduce the operating expense ratio from 27 to 24%, its operating income will increase from $127,000 to $200,000 ($1,000,000 − $560,000 − $240,000), an increase of over 57%.

Return on Investment (ROI)

The rate of return on investment (often called ROI) is a test of management's efficiency in using available resources. Regardless of the size of the organization, capital is a scarce resource and must be used efficiently. In judging the performance of branch managers or of company-wide management, it is reasonable to raise the question: What rate of return have you earned on the resources under your control? The concept of return on investment can be applied to a number of situations: for example, evaluating a branch, a total business, a product line, or an individual investment. A number of different ratios have been developed for the ROI concept, each well suited to a particular situation. We shall consider the return on total assets and the return on common stockholders' equity as examples of the return on investment concept.

■ **Return on Assets** An important test of management's ability to earn a return on funds supplied from all sources is the rate of return on total assets.

The income figure used in computing this ratio should be *operating income,* since interest expense and income taxes are determined by factors other than the efficient use of resources. Operating income is earned throughout the year and therefore should be related to the *average* investment in assets during the year. The computation of this ratio for Seacliff Company is shown below:

Percentage Return on Assets

	1992	1991
Operating income	(a) $127,000	$160,000
Total assets, beginning of year.................................	(b) $860,000	$820,000
Total assets, end of year.......................................	(c) $950,000	$860,000
Average investment in assets [(b + c) ÷ 2]	(d) $905,000	$840,000
Return on total assets (a ÷ d)	14%	19%

Earnings related to investment in assets

This ratio shows that earnings per dollar of assets invested have fallen off in 1992. Before drawing conclusions as to the effectiveness of Seacliff's management, however, we should consider the trend in the return on assets earned by other companies of similar kind and size.

■ **Return on Common Stockholders' Equity**   Because interest and dividends paid to creditors and preferred stockholders are fixed in amount, a company may earn a greater or smaller return on the common stockholders' equity than on its total assets. The computation of return on stockholders' equity for Seacliff Company is shown below:

Return on Common Stockholders' Equity

		1992	1991
Net income		$ 75,000	$ 90,000
Less: Preferred dividend requirements		9,000	9,000
Net income applicable to common stock	(a)	$ 66,000	$ 81,000
Common stockholders' equity, beginning of year	(b)	$416,000	$355,000
Common stockholders' equity, end of year	(c)	$538,000	$416,000
Average common stockholders' equity [(b + c) ÷ 2]	(d)	$477,000	$385,500
Return on common stockholders' equity (a ÷ d)		13.8%	21.0%

Does the use of leverage benefit common stockholders?

In both years, the rate of return on common stockholders' equity was higher than the 12% rate of interest paid to long-term creditors or the 9% dividend rate paid to preferred stockholders. This result was achieved through the favorable use of leverage.

Leverage

The term *leverage* means operating a business with borrowed money. If the borrowed capital can be used in the business to earn a return *greater* than the cost of borrowing, then the net income and the return on common stockholders' equity will *increase*. In other words, if you can borrow money at 12% and use it to earn 20%, you will benefit by doing so. However, leverage can act as a "double-edged sword"; the effects may be favorable or unfavorable to the holders of common stock. If the rate of return on total assets should fall *below* the average rate of interest on borrowed capital, leverage will *reduce* net income and the return on common stockholders' equity. In this situation, paying off the loans that carry high interest rates would appear to be a logical move. However, most companies do not have enough cash to retire long-term debt on short notice. Therefore, the common stockholders may become "locked in" to the unfavorable effects of leverage.

In deciding how much leverage is appropriate, the common stockholders should consider the *stability* of the company's return on assets as well as the relationship of this return to the average cost of borrowed capital. If a business incurs so much debt that it becomes unable to meet the required interest and principal payments, the creditors may force liquidation or reorganization of the business.

■ **Equity Ratio**   One indicator of the amount of leverage used by a business is the equity ratio. This ratio measures the proportion of the total assets financed by stockholders, as distinguished from creditors. It is computed by dividing total stockholders' equity by total assets. A *low* equity ratio indicates an extensive use of leverage, that is, a large proportion of financing provided by creditors. A high equity ratio, on the other hand, indicates that the business is making little use of leverage.

The equity ratio at year-end for Seacliff is determined as follows:

Equity Ratio

		1992	1991
Total stockholders' equity	(a)	$638,000	$516,000
Total assets (or total liabilities & stockholders' equity)	(b)	$950,000	$860,000
Equity ratio (a ÷ b)		67.2%	60.0%

Proportion of assets financed by stockholders

Seacliff Company has a higher equity ratio in 1992 than in 1991. Is this favorable or unfavorable?

From the viewpoint of the common stockholder, a low equity ratio will produce maximum benefits if management is able to earn a rate of return on assets greater than the rate of interest paid to creditors. However, a low equity ratio can be very unfavorable if the return on assets falls below the rate of interest paid to creditors. Since the return on total assets earned by Seacliff Company has declined from 19% in 1991 to a relatively low 14% in 1992, the common stockholders probably would *not* want to risk a low equity ratio. The action by management in 1992 of retiring $50,000 in long-term liabilities will help to protect the common stockholders from the unfavorable effects of leverage if the rate of return on assets continues to decline.

Analysis by Long-Term Creditors

Bondholders and other long-term creditors are primarily interested in three factors: (1) the rate of return on their investment, (2) the firm's ability to meet its interest requirements, and (3) the firm's ability to repay the principal of the debt when it falls due.

■ **Yield Rate on Bonds**   The yield rate on bonds or other long-term indebtedness cannot be computed in the same manner as the yield rate on shares of stock, because bonds, unlike stocks, have a definite maturity date and amount. The ownership of a 12%, 10-year, $1,000 bond represents the right to receive $120 each year for 10 years plus the right to receive $1,000 at the end of 10 years. If the market price of this bond is $950, the yield rate on an investment in the bond is the rate of interest that will make the present value of these two contractual rights equal to $950. When bonds sell at maturity value, the yield rate is equal to the bond interest rate. *The yield rate varies inversely with changes in the market price of the bond.* If interest rates rise, the market price of existing bonds will fall; if interest rates decline, the price of bonds will rise. If the price of a bond is above maturity value, the yield rate is less than the bond interest rate; if the price of a bond is below maturity value, the yield rate is higher than the bond interest rate.

■ **Number of Times Bond Interest Earned**   Bondholders feel that their investments are relatively safe if the issuing company has enough income to cover its interest requirements by a wide margin.

A common measure of debt safety is the ratio of operating income available for the payment of interest to the annual interest expense, called **number of times bond interest earned.** This computation for Seacliff Company would be:

Number of Times Bond Interest Earned

		1992	1991
Operating income (before interest and income taxes)	(a)	$127,000	$160,000
Annual interest expense	(b)	$ 24,000	$ 30,000
Times bond interest earned (a ÷ b).............................		5.3	5.3

Long-term creditors watch this ratio

The ratio remained unchanged at a satisfactory level during 1992. A ratio of 5.3 times interest earned would be considered strong in many industries. In the electric utilities industry, for example, the interest coverage ratio for the leading companies presently averages about 3, with the ratios of individual companies varying from 2 to 6.

■ **Debt Ratio** Long-term creditors are interested in the percentage of total assets financed by debt, as distinguished from the percentage financed by stockholders. The percentage of total assets financed by debt is measured by the debt ratio. This ratio is computed by dividing total liabilities by total assets, shown below for Seacliff Company.

Debt Ratio

		1992	1991
Total liabilities...	(a)	$312,000	$344,000
Total assets (or total liabilities & stockholders' equity)	(b)	$950,000	$860,000
Debt ratio (a ÷ b)...		32.8%	40.0%

What portion of total assets is financed by debt?

From a creditor's viewpoint, the lower the debt ratio (or the higher the equity ratio) the better, since this means that stockholders have contributed the bulk of the funds to the business, and therefore the margin of protection to creditors against a shrinkage of the assets is high.

Analysis by Preferred Stockholders

Some preferred stocks are convertible into common stock at the option of the holder. However, many preferred stocks do not have the conversion privilege. If a preferred stock is convertible, the interests of the preferred stockholders are similar to those of common stockholders. If a preferred stock is not convertible, the interests of the preferred stockholders are more like those of long-term creditors.

Preferred stockholders are interested in the yield on their investment. The yield is computed by dividing the dividend per share by the market value per share. The dividend per share of Seacliff Company preferred stock is $9. If we assume that the market value at December 31, 1992 is $60 per share, the yield rate at that time would be 15% ($9 ÷ $60).

The primary measurement of the safety of an investment in preferred stock is the ability of the firm to meet its preferred dividend requirements. The best test of this ability is the ratio of the net income to the amount of the annual dividend, as follows:

Times Preferred Dividends Earned

		1992	1991
Net income	(a)	$75,000	$90,000
Annual preferred dividend requirements	(b)	$ 9,000	$ 9,000
Times dividends earned (a ÷ b)		8.3	10

■ **Is the preferred dividend safe?**

Although the margin of protection declined in 1992, the annual preferred dividend requirement still appears well protected.

As previously discussed in Chapter 14 (page 534) the market price of a preferred stock tends to *vary inversely* with interest rates. When interest rates are moving up, preferred stock prices tend to decline; when interest rates are dropping, preferred stock prices rise.

Analysis by Short-Term Creditors

Bankers and other short-term creditors share the interest of stockholders and bondholders in the profitability and long-run stability of a business. Their primary interest, however, is in the current position of the firm—its ability to generate sufficient funds (working capital) to meet current operating needs and to pay current debts promptly. Thus the analysis of financial statements by a banker considering a short-term loan, or by a trade creditor investigating the credit status of a customer, is likely to center on the working capital position of the prospective debtor.

■ **Amount of Working Capital** The details of the working capital of Seacliff Company are shown below:

SEACLIFF COMPANY
Comparative Schedule of Working Capital
As of December 31, 1992 and December 31, 1991

	1992	1991	INCREASE OR (DECREASE) DOLLARS	%	PERCENTAGE OF TOTAL CURRENT ITEMS 1992	1991
Current assets:						
Cash...................	$ 38,000	$ 40,000	$ (2,000)	(5.0)	9.7	13.9
Receivables (net)	117,000	86,000	31,000	36.0	30.0	29.9
Inventories	180,000	120,000	60,000	50.0	46.2	41.6
Prepaid expenses	55,000	42,000	13,000	31.0	14.1	14.6
Total current assets ..	$390,000	$288,000	$102,000	35.4	100.0	100.0
Current liabilities:						
Notes payable to creditors	$ 14,600	$ 10,000	$ 4,600	46.0	13.1	10.7
Accounts payable	66,000	30,000	36,000	120.0	58.9	31.9
Accrued liabilities	31,400	54,000	(22,600)	(41.9)	28.0	57.4
Total current liabilities	$112,000	$ 94,000	$ 18,000	19.1	100.0	100.0
Working capital...........	$278,000	$194,000	$ 84,000	43.3		

The amount of working capital is measured by the *excess of current assets over current liabilities.* Thus, working capital represents the amount of cash, near-cash items, and cash substitutes (prepayments) on hand after providing for payment of all current liabilities.

This schedule shows that current assets increased $102,000, while current liabilities rose by only $18,000, with the result that working capital increased $84,000.

■ **Quality of Working Capital** In evaluating the debt-paying ability of a business, short-term creditors should consider the quality of working capital as well as the total dollar amount. The principal factors affecting the quality of working capital are (1) the nature of the current assets and (2) the length of time required to convert these assets into cash.

The preceding schedule shows an unfavorable shift in the composition of Seacliff Company's working capital during 1992; cash decreased from 13.9 to 9.7% of current assets, while inventory rose from 41.6 to 46.2%. Inventory is a less liquid resource than cash. Therefore, the quality of working capital is not as liquid as in 1991. *Turnover ratios* may be used to assist short-term creditors in estimating the time required to turn assets such as inventories and receivables into cash.

■ **Inventory Turnover** The cost of goods sold figure in the income statement represents the total cost of all goods that have been transferred out of inventories during any given period. Therefore the relationship between cost of goods sold and the average balance of inventories maintained throughout the year indicates the number of times that inventories "turn over" and are replaced each year.

Ideally we should total the inventories at the end of each month and divide by 12 to obtain an average inventory. This information is not always available, however, and the nearest substitute is a simple average of the inventory at the beginning and at the end of the year.

Assuming that only beginning and ending inventories are available, the computation of inventory turnover for Seacliff Company may be illustrated as follows:

Inventory Turnover

		1992	1991
■ **What does inventory turnover mean?**	*Cost of goods sold* .... *(a)*	*$530,000*	*$420,000*
	Inventory, beginning of year	*$120,000*	*$100,000*
	Inventory, end of year	*$180,000*	*$120,000*
	Average inventory .... *(b)*	*$150,000*	*$110,000*
	Average inventory turnover per year (a ÷ b)	*3.5 times*	*3.8 times*
	Average number of days to sell inventory (divide 365 days by inventory turnover)	*104 days*	*96 days*

The trend indicated by this analysis is unfavorable, since the length of time required for Seacliff Company to turn over (sell) its inventory is increasing. A high inventory turnover and a low gross profit rate frequently go hand in hand. This, however, is merely another way of saying that if the gross profit rate is low, a high volume of business is necessary to produce a satisfactory return on total assets. Short-term creditors generally regard a high inventory turnover as a good sign, indicating that the inventory is readily marketable.

■ **Accounts Receivable Turnover**   As previously discussed in Chapter 8, the turnover of accounts receivable is computed by dividing net sales by the average balance of accounts receivable.[2] For illustrative purposes, we shall assume that Seacliff Company sells entirely on credit and that only the beginning and ending balances of receivables are available:

Accounts Receivable Turnover

		1992	1991
Net sales	(a)	$900,000	$750,000
Receivables, beginning of year		$ 86,000	$ 80,000
Receivables, end of year		$117,000	$ 86,000
Average receivables	(b)	$101,500	$ 83,000
Receivable turnover per year (a ÷ b)		8.9 times	9.0 times
Average number of days to collect receivables (divide 365 days by receivable turnover)		41 days	41 days

Are customers paying promptly?

There has been no significant change in the average time required to collect receivables. The interpretation of the average age of receivables depends upon the company's credit terms and the seasonal activity immediately before year-end. For example, if the company grants 30-day credit terms to its customers, the above analysis indicates that accounts receivable collections are lagging. If the terms are for 60 days, however, collections are being made ahead of schedule.

In Chapter 5 we defined the term *operating cycle* as the average time period between the purchase of merchandise and the conversion of this merchandise back into cash. In other words, the merchandise acquired for inventory is gradually converted into accounts receivable by selling goods to customers on credit, and these receivables are converted into cash through the process of collection. The word *cycle* refers to the circular flow of capital from cash to inventory to receivables to cash again.

The *operating cycle* in 1992 was approximately 145 days, computed by adding the 104 days required to turn over inventory and the average 41 days required to collect receivables. This compares to an operating cycle of only 137 days in 1991, computed as 96 days to dispose of the inventory plus 41 days to collect the resulting receivables. From the viewpoint of short-term creditors, the shorter the operating cycle, the higher the quality of the borrower's working capital. Therefore, these creditors would regard the lengthening of Seacliff Company's operating cycle as an unfavorable trend.

■ **Current Ratio**   The current ratio (current assets divided by current liabilities) expresses the relationship between current assets and current liabilities. As debts come due, they must be paid out of current assets. Therefore, we

---

[2] Ideally, the accounts receivable turnover is computed by dividing net *credit* sales by the *monthly* average of receivables. Such detailed information, however, generally is not provided in annual financial statements.

want to compare the amount of current assets with the amount of current liabilities. The current ratio indicates a company's short-run, debt-paying ability. It is a measure of liquidity and of solvency. A strong current ratio provides considerable assurance that a company will be able to meet its obligations coming due in the near future. The current ratio for Seacliff Company is computed as follows:

Current Ratio

	1992	1991
Does this Total current assets	(a) $390,000	$288,000
indicate Total current liabilities	(b) $112,000	$ 94,000
satisfactory debt-paying ability? Current ratio (a ÷ b)	3.5	3.1

A widely used rule of thumb is that a current ratio of 2 to 1 or better is satisfactory. By this standard, Seacliff Company's current ratio appears quite strong. Creditors tend to feel that the higher the current ratio the better. From a managerial point of view, however, there is an upper limit. Too high a current ratio may indicate that capital is not being used productively in the business.

Use of both the current ratio and the amount of working capital helps to place debt-paying ability in its proper perspective. For example, if Company X has current assets of $200,000 and current liabilities of $100,000 and Company Y has current assets of $2,000,000 and current liabilities of $1,900,000, each company has $100,000 of working capital, but the current position of Company X is clearly superior to that of Company Y. The current ratio for Company X is quite satisfactory at 2 to 1, but Company Y's current ratio is very low—only slightly above 1 to 1.

As another example, assume that Company A and Company B both have current ratios of 3 to 1. However, Company A has working capital of $20,000 and Company B has working capital of $200,000. Although both companies appear to be good credit risks, Company B would no doubt be able to qualify for a much *larger* bank loan than would Company A.

▮ **Quick Ratio** Because inventories and prepaid expenses are further removed from conversion into cash than other current assets, a statistic known as the *quick ratio* is sometimes computed as a supplement to the current ratio. The quick ratio compares the highly liquid current assets (cash, marketable securities, and receivables) with current liabilities. Seacliff Company has no marketable securities; its quick ratio is computed as follows:

Quick Ratio

	1992	1991
A measure of Quick assets (cash and receivables)...........................	(a) $155,000	$126,000
liquidity Current liabilities	(b) $112,000	$ 94,000
Quick ratio (a ÷ b)	1.4	1.3

Here again the analysis reveals a favorable trend and a strong position. If the credit periods extended to customers and granted by creditors are roughly equal, a quick ratio of 1.0 or better is considered satisfactory.

Summary of Analytical Measurements

Objective 6
Compute the ratios widely used in financial statement analysis and explain the significance of each.

The basic ratios and other measurements discussed in this chapter and their significance are summarized below.

The student should keep in mind the fact that the full significance of any of these ratios or other measurements depends on the *direction of its trend* and its *relationship to some predetermined standard* or industry average.

RATIO OR OTHER MEASUREMENT	METHOD OF COMPUTATION	SIGNIFICANCE
1 Earnings per share of common stock	$\dfrac{\text{Net income} - \text{preferred dividends}}{\text{Shares of common outstanding}}$	Gives the amount of earnings applicable to a share of common stock.
2 Dividend yield	$\dfrac{\text{Dividend per share}}{\text{Market price per share}}$	Shows the rate of return earned by stockholders based on current price for a share of stock.
3 Price-earnings ratio	$\dfrac{\text{Market price per share}}{\text{Earnings per share}}$	Indicates if price of stock is in line with earnings.
4 Book value per share of common stock	$\dfrac{\text{Common stockholders' equity}}{\text{Shares of common outstanding}}$	Measures the recorded value of net assets behind each share of common stock.
5 Operating expense ratio	$\dfrac{\text{Operating expenses}}{\text{Net sales}}$	Indicates management's ability to control expenses.
6 Return on assets	$\dfrac{\text{Operating Income}}{\text{Average investment in assets}}$	Measures the productivity of assets regardless of capital structure.
7 Return on common stockholders' equity	$\dfrac{\text{Net income} - \text{preferred dividends}}{\text{Average common stockholders' equity}}$	Indicates the earning power of common stock equity.
8 Equity ratio	$\dfrac{\text{Total stockholders' equity}}{\text{Total assets}}$	Shows the protection to creditors and the extent of leverage being used.
9 Number of times interest earned	$\dfrac{\text{Operating income}}{\text{Annual interest expense}}$	Measures the coverage of interest requirements, particularly on long-term debt.
10 Debt ratio	$\dfrac{\text{Total liabilities}}{\text{Total assets}}$	Indicates the percentage of assets financed through borrowing; it shows the extent of leverage being used.
11 Times preferred dividends earned	$\dfrac{\text{Net income}}{\text{Annual preferred dividends}}$	Shows the adequacy of current earnings to cover dividends on preferred stocks.
12 Working capital	Current assets − current liabilities	Measures short-run debt-paying ability.

RATIO OR OTHER MEASUREMENT	METHOD OF COMPUTATION	SIGNIFICANCE
13 Inventory turnover	$\dfrac{\text{Cost of goods sold}}{\text{Average inventory}}$	*Indicates marketability of inventory and reasonableness of quantity on hand.*
14 Accounts receivable turnover	$\dfrac{\text{Net sales}}{\text{Average receivables}}$	*Indicates reasonableness of accounts receivable balance and effectiveness of collections.*
15 Current ratio	$\dfrac{\text{Current assets}}{\text{Current liabilities}}$	*Measures short-run debt-paying ability.*
16 Quick ratio	$\dfrac{\text{Quick assets}}{\text{Current liabilities}}$	*Measures the short-term liquidity of a firm.*

End-of-Chapter Review

CONCEPTS INTRODUCED OR EMPHASIZED IN CHAPTER 20

The major concepts introduced in this chapter include:

■ The role of an auditors' report in establishing the reliability of financial statements.

■ Tools of financial statement analysis, including (1) dollar and percentage change, (2) trend percentages, (3) component percentages, and (4) ratio analysis.

■ The effects of different accounting policies upon the "quality" of reported earnings.

■ Analysis of a company's financial statements from the viewpoint of (1) common stockholders, (2) long-term creditors, (3) preferred stockholders, and (4) short-term creditors.

■ The quality of working capital, including the use of turnover ratios to compute the length of time required for receivables and inventory to convert into cash.

This chapter concludes our emphasis upon financial accounting—the preparation and interpretation of the accounting information included in financial statements. In the remaining chapters of this text, we will shift our emphasis to managerial accounting—the use of accounting information by managers in planning and controlling business operations. In these chapters you will encounter many new terms and concepts; however, you will find your background in financial accounting to be extremely useful.

KEY TERMS INTRODUCED OR EMPHASIZED IN CHAPTER 20

Comparative financial statements   Financial statement data for two or more successive years placed side by side in adjacent columns to facilitate study of changes.

Component percentage   The percentage relationship of any financial statement item to a total including that item. For example, each type of asset as a percentage of total assets.

Horizontal analysis   Comparison of the change in a financial statement item such as inventories during two or more accounting periods.

Leverage   Refers to the practice of financing assets with borrowed capital. Extensive leverage creates the possibility for the rate of return on common stockholders' equity to be substantially above or below the rate of return on total assets. When the rate of return on total assets exceeds the average cost of borrowed capital, leverage increases net income and the return on common stockholders' equity. However, when the return on total assets is less than the average cost of borrowed capital, leverage reduces net income and the return on common stockholders' equity.

Quality of assets   The concept that some companies have assets of better quality than others, such as well-balanced composition of assets, well-maintained plant and equipment, and receivables that are all current. A lower quality of assets might be indicated by poor maintenance of plant and equipment, slow-moving inventories with high danger of obsolescence, past-due receivables, and patents approaching an expiration date.

Quality of earnings   Earnings are said to be of high quality if they are stable, the source seems assured, and the methods used in measuring income are conservative. The existence of this concept suggests that the range of alternative but acceptable accounting principles may still be too wide to produce financial statements that are comparable.

Rate of return on investment (ROI)   The overall test of management's ability to earn a satisfactory return on the assets under its control. Numerous variations of the ROI concept are used such as return on total assets, return on common stockholders' equity, etc.

Ratios   See pages 794 and 795 for list of ratios, methods of computation, and significance.

Trend percentages   The purpose of computing trend percentages is to measure the increase or decrease in financial items (such as sales, net income, cash, etc.) from a selected base year to a series of following years. For example, the dollar amount of net income each year is divided by the base year net income to determine the trend percentage.

Vertical analysis   Comparison of a particular financial statement item to a total including that item, such as inventories as a percentage of current assets, or operating expenses in relation to net sales.

DEMONSTRATION PROBLEM FOR YOUR REVIEW

The accounting records of King Corporation showed the following balances at the end of 1991 and 1992:

	1992	1991
Cash	$ 35,000	$ 25,000
Accounts receivable (net)	91,000	90,000
Inventory	160,000	140,000
Short-term prepayments	4,000	5,000
Investment in land	90,000	100,000
Equipment	880,000	640,000
Less: Accumulated depreciation	(260,000)	(200,000)
Total assets	$1,000,000	$ 800,000

	1992	1991
Accounts payable	$ 105,000	$ 46,000
Income taxes payable and other accrued liabilities.............	40,000	25,000
Bonds payable—8%...	280,000	280,000
Premium on bonds payable	3,600	4,000
Capital stock, $5 par	165,000	110,000
Retained earnings	406,400	335,000
Total liabilities and stockholders' equity	$1,000,000	$ 800,000
Sales (net of discounts and allowances)	$2,200,000	$1,600,000
Cost of goods sold	1,606,000	1,120,000
Gross profit on sales	$ 594,000	$ 480,000
Expenses (including $22,400 interest expense)	(336,600)	(352,000)
Income taxes...	(91,000)	(48,000)
Net income	$ 166,400	$ 80,000

Cash dividends of $40,000 were paid and a 50% stock dividend was distributed early in 1992. All sales were made on credit at a relatively uniform rate during the year. Inventory and receivables did not fluctuate materially. The market price of the company's stock on December 31, 1992, was $86 per share; on December 31, 1991, it was $43.50 (before the 50% stock dividend distributed in 1992).

Instructions Compute the following for 1992 and 1991.

(1) Quick ratio

(2) Current ratio

(3) Equity ratio

(4) Debt ratio

(5) Book value per share of capital stock (based on shares outstanding after 50% stock dividend in 1992)

(6) Earnings per share of capital stock

(7) Price-earnings ratio

(8) Gross profit percentage

(9) Operating expense ratio

(10) Net income as a percentage of net sales

(11) Inventory turnover (Assume an average inventory of $150,000 for both years.)

(12) Accounts receivable turnover (Assume average accounts receivable of $90,000 for 1991.)

(13) Times bond interest earned (before interest expense and income taxes)

SOLUTION TO DEMONSTRATION PROBLEM

	1992	1991
(1) Quick ratio:		
$126,000 ÷ $145,000...	.9 to 1	
$115,000 ÷ $71,000		1.6 to 1
(2) Current ratio:		
$290,000 ÷ $145,000...	2 to 1	
$260,000 ÷ $71,000		3.7 to 1

798

	1992	1991

(3) Equity ratio:

$571,400 ÷ $1,000,000 .... 57%

$445,000 ÷ $800,000 .... 56%

(4) Debt ratio:

$428,600 ÷ $1,000,000 .... 43%

$355,000 ÷ $800,000 .... 44%

(5) Book value per share of capital stock:

$571,400 ÷ 33,000 shares $17.32

$445,000 ÷ 33,000* shares $13.48

(6) Earnings per share of capital stock:

$166,400 ÷ 33,000 shares $5.04

$80,000 ÷ 33,000* shares $2.42

(7) Price-earnings ratio:

$86 ÷ $5.04 .... 17 times

$43.50 ÷ 1.5* = $29, adjusted market price; $29 ÷ $2.42 ...... 12 times

(8) Gross profit percentage:

$594,000 ÷ $2,200,000 .... 27%

$480,000 ÷ $1,600,000 .... 30%

(9) Operating expense ratio:

($336,600 − $22,400) ÷ $2,200,000 .... 14%

($352,000 − $22,400) ÷ $1,600,000 .... 20.6%

(10) Net income as a percentage of net sales:

$166,400 ÷ $2,200,000 .... 7.6%

$80,000 ÷ $1,600,000 .... 5%

(11) Inventory turnover:

$1,606,000 ÷ $150,000 .... 10.7 times

$1,120,000 ÷ $150,000 .... 7.5 times

(12) Accounts receivable turnover:

$2,200,000 ÷ $90,500 .... 24.3 times

$1,600,000 ÷ $90,000 .... 17.8 times

(13) Times bond interest earned:

($166,400 + $22,400 + $91,000) ÷ $22,400 .... 12.5 times

($80,000 + $22,400 + $48,000) ÷ $22,400 .... 6.7 times

* Adjusted retroactively for 50% stock dividend.

SELF-TEST QUESTIONS

Answers to these questions appear on page 814.

1 Which of the following is *not* an accurate statement?

a Expressing the various items in the income statement as a percentage of net sales illustrates the use of component percentages.

b An increase in the market price of bonds causes the yield rate to decline.

c A high debt ratio is viewed favorably by long-term creditors as long as the number of times interest earned is at least 1.

d In measuring the dollar or percentage change in quarterly sales or earnings, it is appropriate to compare the results of the current quarter with those of the same quarter in the preceding year.

2 Which of the following actions will improve the "quality" of earnings, even though the total dollar amount of earnings may not increase?

a Increasing the uncollectible accounts expense from 1% to 2% of net credit sales to reflect current conditions.

b Switching from an accelerated method to the straight-line method for depreciating assets.

c Changing from LIFO to the FIFO method of inventory valuation during a period of rising prices.

d Lengthening the estimated useful lives of depreciable assets.

3 Hunter Corporation's net income was $400,000 in 1990 and $160,000 in 1991. What percentages increase in net income must Hunter achieve in 1992 to offset the decline in profits in 1991?

    a 60%   **b** 150%   **c** 600%   **d** 67%

4 Of the following situations, which would be considered the most favorable for the common stockholders?

a The company stops paying dividends on its cumulative preferred stock; the price-earnings ratio of common stock is low.

b Equity ratio is high; return on assets exceeds the cost of borrowing.

c Book value per share of common stock is substantially higher than market value per share; return on common stockholders' equity is less than interest paid to creditors.

d Equity ratio is low; return on assets exceeds the cost of borrowing.

5 During 1990, Ganey Corporation had sales of $4,000,000, all on credit. Accounts receivable averaged $400,000 and inventory levels averaged $250,000 throughout the year. If Ganey's gross profit rate during 1990 was 25% of net sales, which of the following is *true*? (Assume 360 days in a year.)

a Ganey "turns over" its accounts receivable more times per year than it turns over its average inventory.

b Ganey's operating cycle is 40 days.

c Ganey's operating cycle is 66 days.

d Inventory turnover is 16 times per year.

Assignment Material

REVIEW QUESTIONS

1 a What groups are interested in the financial affairs of publicly owned corporations?

b List some of the more important sources of financial information for investors.

2 In financial statement analysis, what is the basic objective of observing trends in data and ratios? Suggest some other standards of comparison.

3 In financial statement analysis, what information is produced by computing a ratio that is not available in a simple observation of the underlying data?

4 Distinguish between *trend percentages* and *component percentages*. Which would be better suited to analyzing the change in sales over a term of several years?

5 "Although net income declined this year as compared with last year, it increased from 3% to 5% of net sales." Are sales increasing or decreasing?

6 Differentiate between *horizontal* and *vertical* analysis.

7 Assume that Chemco Corporation is engaged in the manufacture and distribution of a variety of chemicals. In analyzing the financial statements of this corporation, why would you want to refer to the ratios and other measurements of companies in the chemical industry? In comparing the financial results of Chemco Corporation with another chemical company, why would you be interested in the accounting practices used by the two companies?

8 Explain how the following accounting practices will tend to raise or lower the quality of a company's earnings. (Assume the continuance of inflation.)

a Adoption of an accelerated depreciation method rather than straight-line depreciation.

b Adoption of FIFO rather than LIFO for the valuation of inventories.

c Adoption of a 7-year life rather than a 10-year life for the depreciation of equipment.

9 What single ratio do you think should be of greatest interest to:

a A banker considering a short-term loan?

b A common stockholder?

c An insurance company considering a long-term mortgage loan?

10 Modern Company earned a 16% return on its total assets. Current liabilities are 10% of total assets. Long-term bonds carrying a 13% coupon rate are equal to 30% of total assets. There is no preferred stock. Is this application of leverage favorable or unfavorable from the viewpoint of Modern Company's stockholders?

11 In deciding whether a company's equity ratio is favorable or unfavorable, creditors and stockholders may have different views. Why?

12 Company A has a current ratio of 3 to 1. Company B has a current ratio of 2 to 1. Does this mean that A's operating cycle is longer than B's? Why?

13 An investor states, "I bought this stock for $50 several years ago and it now sells for $100. It paid $5 per share in dividends last year so I'm earning 10% on my investment." Criticize this statement.

14 Company C experiences a considerable seasonal variation in its business. The high point in the year's activity comes in November, the low point in July. During which month would you expect the company's current ratio to be higher? If the company were choosing a fiscal year for accounting purposes, how would you advise them?

15 Both the inventory turnover and accounts receivable turnover increased from 10 times to 15 times from Year 1 to Year 2, but net income decreased. Can you offer some possible reasons for this?

16 Is the rate of return on investment (ROI) intended primarily to measure liquidity, solvency, or some other aspect of business operations? Explain.

17 Mention three financial amounts to which corporate profits can logically be compared in judging their adequacy or reasonableness.

18 Under what circumstances would you consider a corporate net income of $1,000,000 for the year as being unreasonably low? Under what circumstances would you consider a corporate profit of $1,000,000 as being unreasonably high?

EXERCISES

Exercise 20-1
Accounting
terminology

Listed below are nine technical accounting terms introduced in this chapter.

Leverage	Inventory turnover	Trend percentages
Yield	Operating cycle	Vertical analysis
Quick ratio	Price-earnings ratio	Return on assets

Each of the following statements may (or may not) describe one of these technical terms. For each statement, indicate the accounting term described, or answer "None" if the statement does not correctly describe any of the terms.

a Dividends per share divided by market price per share.

b Average time period between the purchase of merchandise and the conversion of this merchandise back into cash.

c Comparison of a particular financial statement item to a total including that item.

d Net sales divided by average inventory.

e Comparison of highly liquid current assets (cash, marketable securities, and receivables) with current liabilities.

f Buying assets with money raised by borrowing.

g The proportion of total assets financed by stockholders, as distinguished from creditors.

h Market price per common share divided by earnings per common share.

i Changes in financial statement items from a base year to following years expressed as a percentage of the base year amount and designed to show the extent and direction of change.

Exercise 20-2
Percentage changes

Selected information taken from financial statements of Lopez Company for two successive years is shown below. You are to compute the percentage change from 1991 to 1992 whenever possible.

	1992	1991
a Notes payable	$360,000	$300,000
b Cash	82,400	80,000
c Sales	990,000	900,000
d Accounts receivable	132,000	150,000
e Marketable securities	–0–	100,000
f Retained earnings	30,000	(30,000)
g Notes receivable	20,000	–0–

Exercise 20-3
Intuition vs. calculation

NICO Corporation had net income of $2,000,000 in its first year. In the second year, net income decreased by 80%. In the third year, due to an improved business environment, net income increased by 350%.

Instructions

a Prior to making any computations, do you think NICO's net income was higher or lower in the third year than in the first year?

b Compute NICO's net income for the second year and for the third year. Do your computations support your initial response in part **a**?

Exercise 20-4
Trend percentages

Compute *trend percentages* for the following items taken from the financial statements of Monarch, Inc., over a five-year period. Treat 1988 as the base year. State whether the trends are favorable or unfavorable.

	1992	1991	1990	1989	1988
Sales	$880,000	$760,000	$620,000	$600,000	$500,000
Cost of Goods Sold	$615,000	$495,000	$396,000	$372,000	$300,000

Exercise 20-5
Common size income statements

Prepare *common size* income statements for Trent Company, a sole proprietorship, for the two years shown on page 802 by converting the dollar amounts into percentages. For each year, sales will appear as 100% and other items will be expressed as a percentage of sales. (Income taxes are not involved as the business is not incorporated.) Comment on whether the changes from 1991 to 1992 are favorable or unfavorable.

	1992	1991
Sales	$500,000	$400,000
Cost of goods sold	330,000	268,000
Gross profit	$170,000	$132,000
Operating expenses	140,000	116,000
Net income	$ 30,000	$ 16,000

Exercise 20-6
Ratios for a retail store

Selected financial data for Hartley's, a retail store, appear below. Since monthly figures are not available, the average amounts for inventories and for accounts receivable should be based on the amounts shown for the beginning and end of 1992.

	1992	1991
Sales (terms 2/10, n/30)	$480,000	$360,000
Cost of goods sold	312,000	252,000
Inventory at end of year	57,000	63,000
Accounts receivable at end of year	70,000	58,000

Compute the following for 1992.

a Gross profit percentage

b Inventory turnover

c Accounts receivable turnover

Exercise 20-7
Computing ratios

A condensed balance sheet for Bryant Corporation prepared at the end of the year appears below.

ASSETS		LIABILITIES & STOCKHOLDERS' EQUITY	
Cash	$ 30,000	Notes payable (due in 6 months)	$ 20,000
Accounts receivable	60,000	Accounts payable	55,000
Inventory	135,000	Long-term liabilities	165,000
Prepaid expenses	45,000	Capital stock, $10 par	300,000
Plant & equipment (net)	300,000	Retained earnings	60,000
Other assets	30,000		
Total	$600,000	Total	$600,000

During the year the company earned a gross profit of $444,000 on sales of $1,200,000. Accounts receivable, inventory, and plant assets remained almost constant in amount throughout the year. From this information, compute the following:

a Current ratio

b Quick ratio

c Working capital

d Equity ratio

e Accounts receivable turnover (all sales were on credit)

f Inventory turnover

g Book value per share of capital stock.

**Exercise 20-8
Current ratio,
debt ratio, and
earnings per
share**

Selected items from successive annual reports of Hastings, Inc., appear below.

	1992	1991
Total assets (40% of which are current)	$400,000	$325,000
Current liabilities	$ 80,000	$100,000
Bonds payable, 12%...	100,000	50,000
Capital stock, $10 per value	150,000	150,000
Retained earnings	70,000	25,000
Total liabilities & stockholders' equity	$400,000	$325,000

Dividends of $6,000 were declared and paid in 1992. Compute the following:

a Current ratio for 1991 and 1992

b Debt ratio for 1991 and 1992

c Earnings per share for 1992

**Exercise 20-9
Ratio analysis for
two similar
companies**

Selected data from the financial statements of X Company and Y Company for the year just ended are shown below. Assume that for both companies dividends declared were equal in amount to net earnings during the year and therefore stockholders' equity did not change. The two companies are in the same line of business.

	X COMPANY	Y COMPANY
Total liabilities...	$ 200,000	$ 100,000
Total assets...	800,000	400,000
Sales (all on credit).......................................	1,600,000	1,200,000
Average inventory	240,000	140,000
Average receivables	200,000	100,000
Gross profit as a percentage of sales	40%	30%
Operating expenses as a percentage of sales	37%	25%
Net income as a percentage of sales......................	3%	5%

Compute the following for each company:

a Net income

b Net income as a percentage of stockholders' equity

c Accounts receivable turnover

d Inventory turnover

PROBLEMS

Group A

**Problem 20A-1
Comparing
operating results
with average
performance in
the industry**

ProTech, Inc., manufactures athletic equipment. Shown for the current year (page 804) are the income statement for the company and a common size summary for the industry in which the company operates. (Notice that the percentages in the right-hand column are *not* for Protech, Inc., but are average percentages for the industry.)

	PROTECH, INC.	INDUSTRY AVERAGE
Sales (net)	$30,000,000	100%
Cost of goods sold	14,700,000	57
Gross profit on sales	$15,300,000	43%
Operating expenses:		
Selling	$ 6,300,000	16%
General and administrative	5,100,000	20
Total operating expenses	$11,400,000	36%
Operating income	$ 3,900,000	7%
Income taxes	1,800,000	3
Net income	$ 2,100,000	4%
Return on stockholders' equity	23%	14%

Instructions   **a**   Prepare a two-column common size income statement. The first column should show for ProTech, Inc., all items expressed as a percentage of net sales. The second column should show as an industry average the percentage data given in the problem. The purpose of this common size statement is to compare the operating results of ProTech, Inc., with the average for the industry.

b   Comment specifically on differences between ProTech, Inc., and the industry average with respect to gross profit on sales, selling expenses, general and administrative expenses, operating income, net income, and return on stockholders' equity. Suggest possible reasons for the more important disparities.

Problem 20A-2
Analysis to
identify favorable
and unfavorable
trends

The following information was developed from the financial statements of Pioneer Waterbeds. At the beginning of 1992, the company's former supplier went bankrupt, and the company began buying merchandise from another supplier.

	1992	1991
Gross profit on sales	$840,000	$945,000
Income before income taxes	192,000	210,000
Net income	144,000	157,500
Net income as a percentage of net sales	6.0%	7.5%

Instructions   **a**   Compute the net sales for each year.

b   Compute the cost of goods sold in dollars and as a percentage of net sales for each year.

c   Compute operating expenses in dollars and as a percentage of net sales for each year. (Income taxes expense is not an operating expense.)

d   Prepare a condensed comparative income statement for 1991 and 1992. Include the following items: Net sales, cost of goods sold, gross profit, operating expenses, income before income taxes, income taxes expense, and net income. Omit earnings per share statistics.

e   Identify the significant favorable trends and unfavorable trends in the performance of Pioneer Waterbeds. Comment on any unusual changes.

Problem 20A-3   At the end of the year, the following information was obtained from the accounting records of Craftsman Clocks.

Sales (all on credit)	$1,800,000
Cost of goods sold	1,170,000

Average inventory (fifo method)	234,000
Average accounts receivable..	200,000
Interest expense	30,000
Income taxes..	56,000
Net income	106,000
Average investment in assets	1,200,000
Average stockholders' equity	530,000

Instructions From the information given, compute the following:

a Inventory turnover.

b Accounts receivable turnover.

c Total operating expenses.

d Gross profit percentage.

e Return on average stockholders' equity.

f Return on average assets.

g Craftsman Clocks has an opportunity to obtain a long term loan at an annual interest rate of 11% and could use this additional capital at the same rate of profitability as indicated above. Would obtaining the loan be desirable from the viewpoint of the stockholders? Explain.

**Problem 20A-4
Analysis and
interpretation
from viewpoint of
short-term
creditor**

Shown below are selected financial data for Hill Corporation and Valley Company at the end of the current year.

	HILL CORPORATION	VALLEY COMPANY
Net sales (all on credit)	$960,000	$595,000
Cost of goods sold	840,000	412,500
Cash..	24,000	35,000
Accounts receivable (net)	120,000	70,000
Inventory...	336,000	82,500
Current liabilities	160,000	75,000

Assume that the year-end balances shown for accounts receivable and for inventory also represent the average balances of these accounts throughout the year.

Instructions **a** For each company, compute the following:

(1) Working capital.

(2) Current ratio.

(3) Quick ratio.

(4) Number of times inventory turned over during the year and the average number of days required to turn over inventory.

(5) Number of times accounts receivable turned over during the year and the average number of days required to collect accounts receivable. (Round to the nearest day.)

(6) Operating cycle.

b From the viewpoint of a short-term creditor, comment upon the *quality* of each company's working capital. To which company would you prefer to sell $30,000 in merchandise on a 30-day open account?

Problem 20A-5
Evaluating short-term debt-paying ability

Listed below is the working capital information for the Mystic Corporation at the beginning of the year.

Cash	$270,000
Temporary investments in marketable securities	144,000
Notes receivable—current	216,000
Accounts receivable	360,000
Allowance for doubtful accounts	18,000
Inventory	288,000
Prepaid expenses	36,000
Notes payable within one year	108,000
Accounts payable	297,000
Accrued liabilities	27,000

The following transactions are completed during the year:

(0) Sold inventory costing $36,000 for $30,000.

(1) Declared a cash dividend, $120,000.

(2) Declared a 10% stock dividend.

(3) Paid accounts payable, $60,000.

(4) Purchased goods on account, $45,000.

(5) Collected cash on accounts receivable, $90,000.

(6) Borrowed cash on short-term note, $150,000.

(7) Issued additional shares of capital stock for cash, $450,000.

(8) Sold temporary investments costing $30,000 for $27,000 cash.

(9) Acquired temporary investments, $52,500. Paid cash.

(10) Wrote off uncollectible accounts, $9,000.

(11) Sold inventory costing $37,500 for $48,000.

(12) Acquired plant and equipment for cash, $240,000.

Instructions

a Compute the amount of quick assets, current assets, and current liabilities at the beginning of the year as shown by the above account balances.

b Use the data compiled in part **a** to compute: (1) current ratio; (2) quick ratio; and (3) working capital.

c Indicate the effect (increase, decrease, none) of each independent transaction listed above on the current ratio, quick ratio, and working capital. Use the following four-column format (item 0 is given as an example):

	EFFECT ON		
ITEM	CURRENT RATIO	QUICK RATIO	WORKING CAPITAL
0	Decrease	Increase	Decrease

Problem 20A-6
Effects of transactions on various ratios

Listed in the left-hand column below is a series of 12 business transactions and events relating to the activities of Potomac Mills. Opposite each transaction is listed a particular ratio used in financial analysis:

TRANSACTION	RATIO
(1) Conversion of a portion of bonds payable into common stock. (Ignore income taxes.)	Times interest charges earned
(2) Appropriated retained earnings.	Rate of return on stockholders' equity
(3) During period of rising prices, company changed from FIFO to LIFO method of inventory pricing.	Inventory turnover
(4) Paid a previously declared cash dividend.	Debt ratio
(5) Purchased factory supplies on open account.	Current ratio (assume that ratio is greater than 1:1)
(6) Issued shares of capital stock in exchange for patents.	Equity ratio
(7) Purchased inventory on open account.	Quick ratio
(8) A larger physical volume of goods was sold at smaller unit prices.	Gross profit percentage
(9) Corporation declared a cash dividend.	Current ratio
(10) An uncollectible account receivable was written off against the allowance account.	Current ratio
(11) Issued additional shares of common stock and used proceeds to retire long-term debt.	Debt ratio
(12) Paid stock dividend on common stock, in common stock.	Earnings per share

Instructions   What effect would each transaction or event have on the ratio listed opposite to it; that is, as a result of this event would the ratio increase, decrease, or remain unchanged? Your answer for each of the 12 transactions should include a brief explanation.

**Problem 20A-7
Building financial
statements from
limited
information,
including ratios**

John Gale, the accountant for Southbay Corporation, prepared the year-end financial statements, including all ratios, and agreed to bring them along on a hunting trip with the executives of the corporation. To his embarrassment, he found that only certain fragmentary information had been placed in his briefcase and the completed statements had been left in his office. One hour before Gale was to present the financial statements to the executives, he was able to come up with the following information:

SOUTHBAY CORPORATION
Balance Sheet
December 31, 19__
(in thousands of dollars)

ASSETS			LIABILITIES & STOCKHOLDERS' EQUITY		
Current assets:			Current liabilities	$?	
Cash.........................	?		Long-term debt, 8%		
Accounts receivable			interest	?	
(net)	?		Total liabilities..............	$?	
Inventory......................	?		Stockholders' equity:		
Total current			Capital stock, $5		
assets	$?		par $900		
Plant assets:			Retained earnings 300	$1,200	
Machinery and			Total stockholders'		
equipment $1,740			equity......................	1,200	
Less: Accumulated			Total liabilities &		
depreciation........ 240	1,500		stockholders'		
Total assets	$?		equity......................	$?	

SOUTHBAY CORPORATION
Income Statement
For the Year Ended December 31, 19__
(in thousands of dollars)

Net sales	$?	
Cost of goods sold	?	
Gross profit on sales (25% of net sales)	$?	
Operating expenses	?	
Operating income (10% of net sales)	$?	
Interest expense	84	
Income before income taxes...	$?	
Income taxes—40% of income before income taxes	?	
Net income	$ 180	

Additional information

(1) The equity ratio was 40%; the debt ratio was 60%.

(2) The only interest expense was on the long-term debt.

(3) The beginning inventory was $450,000; the inventory turnover was 4.8 times.

(4) The current ratio was 2 to 1; the quick ratio was 1 to 1.

(5) The beginning balance in accounts receivable was $240,000; the accounts receivable turnover for the year was 12.8 times. All sales were made on account.

Instructions The accountant asks you to help complete the financial statements for the Southbay Corporation, using only the information available. Present supporting computations and explanations for all amounts appearing in the balance sheet and the income statement. Hint: In completing the income statement, start with the net income figure (60% of income before income taxes) and work up.

Group B

Problem 20B-1
Common size
income
statement;
comparison with
industry averages

Harvest King manufactures and distributes farm equipment. Shown below are the income statement for the company and a common size summary for the industry in which the company operates. (Note: Notice that the percentages in the right-hand column are *not* for Harvest King, but are average percentages for the industry.)

	HARVEST KING	INDUSTRY AVERAGE
Sales (net)	$4,000,000	100%
Cost of goods sold	2,520,000	58%
Gross profit on sales	$1,480,000	42%
Operating expenses:		
Selling	$ 480,000	10%
General and administrative	560,000	15%
Total operating expenses	$1,040,000	25%
Operating income	$ 440,000	17%
Income taxes	210,000	8%
Net income	$ 230,000	9%
Return on stockholders' equity	10%	18%

Instructions

a Prepare a two-column common size income statement. The first column should show for Harvest King all items expressed as a percentage of net sales. (Round all figures to the nearest whole percent.) The second column should show as an industry average the percentage data given in the problem. The purpose of this common size statement is to compare the operating results of Harvest King with the average for the industry.

b Comment specifically on differences between Harvest King and the industry average with respect to gross profit on sales, selling expenses, general and administrative expenses, operating income, income taxes, net income, and return on stockholders' equity. Suggest possible reasons for the more important disparities.

Problem 20B-2
Ratios based on
balance sheet
and income
statement data

Cyclone Corporation has issued common stock only. The company has been successful and has a gross profit rate of 25%. The information shown below was derived from the company's financial statements.

Beginning inventory	$ 980,000
Purchases	4,340,000
Ending inventory	?
Average accounts receivable	350,000
Average common stockholders' equity	2,520,000
Sales (all on credit)	5,600,000
Net income	315,000

Instructions

On the basis of the above information, compute the following:

a Accounts receivable turnover and the average number of days required to collect the accounts receivable.

b The inventory turnover and the average number of days required to turn over the inventory.

c Length of Cyclone Corporation's operating cycle.

d Return on common stockholders' equity.

Problem 20B-3
Percentage
relationships on
the income
statement

The following information was developed from the financial statements of Quarry Tile, Inc. At the beginning of 1992, the company began buying its merchandise from a new supplier.

	1992	1991
Gross profit on sales	$405,000	$320,000
Income before income taxes	45,000	60,000
Net income	36,000	48,000
Net income as a percentage of net sales	4%	6%

Instructions

a Compute the net sales for each year.

b Compute the cost of goods sold in dollars and as a percentage of net sales for each year.

c Compute the operating expenses in dollars and as a percentage of net sales for each year.

d Prepare a condensed comparative income statement for 1991 and 1992. Include the following items: Net sales, cost of goods sold, gross profit, operating expenses, income before income taxes, income taxes expense, and net income. Omit earnings per share statistics.

e Comment on any significant favorable trends and unfavorable trends in the performance of Quarry Tile, Inc.

Problem 20B-4
Ratios:
Evaluation of two
companies

Shown below are selected financial data for Another World and Imports, Inc., at the end of the current year:

	ANOTHER WORLD	IMPORTS, INC.
Net sales (all on credit)	$675,000	$560,000
Cost of goods sold	504,000	480,000
Cash	51,000	20,000
Accounts receivable (net)	75,000	70,000
Inventory	84,000	160,000
Current liabilities	105,000	100,000

Assume that the year-end balances for accounts receivable and for inventory also represent the average balances for these items throughout the year.

Instructions

a For each of the two companies, compute the following:

(1) Working capital.

(2) Current ratio.

(3) Quick ratio.

(4) Number of times inventory turned over during the year and the average number of days required to turn over the inventory. (Round computation to the nearest day.)

(5) Number of times accounts receivable turned over during the year and the average number of days required to collect accounts receivable. (Round computation to the nearest day.)

(6) Length of operating cycle.

b From the viewpoint of a short-term creditor, comment upon the relative *quality* of each company's working capital. To which company would you prefer to sell $20,000 in merchandise on a 30-day open account?

Problem 20B-5
Ratios; consider advisability of incurring long-term debt

At the end of the year, the following information was obtained from the accounting records of Santa Fe Boot Co.:

Sales (all on credit)	$1,200,000
Cost of goods sold	720,000
Average inventory (FIFO method)	180,000
Average accounts receivable	120,000
Interest expense	9,000
Income taxes	12,000
Net income for the year	54,000
Average investment in assets	750,000
Average stockholders' equity	600,000

The company declared no dividends of any kind during the year and did not issue or retire any capital stock.

Instructions

From the information given, compute the following for the year.

a Inventory turnover.

b Accounts receivable turnover.

c Total operating expenses.

d Gross profit percentage.

e Return on average stockholders' equity.

f Return on average assets.

g Santa Fe Boot Co. has an opportunity to obtain a long-term loan at an annual interest rate of 12% and could use this additional capital at the same rate of profitability as indicated above. Would obtaining the loan be desirable from the viewpoint of the stockholders? Explain.

Problem 20B-6
Constructing a balance sheet from various ratios and miscellaneous data

Given below are selected balance sheet items and ratios for the Metro Corporation at June 30.

Total stockholders' equity (includes 100,000 shares of $5 par value capital stock issued at $5 per share, also retained earnings)	$ 800,000
Plant and equipment (net)	590,000
Long-term debt	400,000
Net sales	6,600,000
Inventory turnover rate per year	6 times
Average accounts receivable collection period (assuming a 360-day year)	30 days
Gross profit percentage	30%
Equity ratio	40%
Quick ratio	0.8 to 1

Assume that balance sheet figures did not change significantly during the year and that all sales are made on account.

Instructions

From the foregoing information, construct a balance sheet for the Metro Corporation at June 30, in as much detail as the data permit. For each computation you make, prepare a supporting footnote explaining briefly the nature of the computation.

Problem 20B-7
Analysis and
interpretation
from viewpoint of
common
stockholders and
of bondholders

The following financial information for Continental Transfer Co. and American Van Lines (except market price per share of stock) is stated in *thousands of dollars.* The figures are as of the end of the current year. The two companies are in the same industry and are quite similar as to operations, facilities, and accounting methods. Assume that both companies pay income taxes equal to 50% of income before income taxes.

ASSETS	CONTINENTAL TRANSFER CO.	AMERICAN VAN LINES
Current assets	$ 97,450	$132,320
Plant and equipment	397,550	495,680
Less: Accumulated depreciation	(55,000)	(78,000)
Total assets	$440,000	$550,000

LIABILITIES & STOCKHOLDERS' EQUITY		
Current liabilities	$ 34,000	$ 65,000
Bonds payable, 12%, due in 15 years...................	120,000	100,000
Capital stock, no par	150,000	200,000
Retained earnings	136,000	185,000
Total liabilities & stockholders' equity	$440,000	$550,000

Analysis of retained earnings:		
Balance, beginning of year............................	$125,200	$167,200
Net income for the year	19,800	37,400
Dividends	(9,000)	(19,600)
Balance, end of year	$136,000	$185,000
Market price of capital stock, per share	$30	$61
Number of shares of capital stock outstanding	6 million	8 million

Instructions

a Compute for each company:

(1) The number of times bond interest was earned during the current year. (Remember to use *operating income* rather than net income in determining the coverage of interest expense.

(2) The debt ratio.

b In the light of the information developed in **a** above, write a paragraph indicating which company's bonds you think would trade in the market at the higher price. Which would probably provide the higher yield? Explain how the ratios developed influence your answer. (It may be assumed that the bonds were issued several years ago and are traded on an organized securities exchange.)

c For each company compute the dividend yield, the price-earnings ratio, and the book value per share. (Show supporting computations. Remember that dollar amounts in the problem are in thousands of dollars, that is, three zeros omitted.)

d Express an opinion, based on the data developed in **c** above, as to which company's stock is a better investment at the present market price.

BUSINESS DECISION CASES

Case 20-1
Telling it like it
never was

Holiday Greeting Cards is a local company organized late in July of 1991. The company's net income for each of its first six calendar quarters of operations is summarized below. The amounts are stated in thousands of dollars.

	1992	1991
First quarter (January through March)	$ 253	—
Second quarter (April through June)	308	—
Third quarter (July through September)	100	$ 50
Fourth quarter (October through December)	450	500
Total for the calendar year	$1,111	$550

Glen Wallace reports the business and economic news for a local radio station. On the day that Holiday Greeting Cards released the above financial information, you heard Wallace make the following statement during his broadcast: "Holiday Greeting Cards enjoyed a 350% increase in its profits for the fourth quarter, and profits for the entire year were up by over 100%."

Instruction   **a** Show the computations that Wallace probably made in arriving at his statistics. (Hint: Wallace did not make his computations in the manner recommended in this chapter. His figures, however, can be developed from the financial data above.)

b Do you believe that Wallace's percentage changes present a realistic impression of Holiday Greeting Cards' rate of growth in 1992? Explain.

c What figure would you use to express the percentage change in Holiday's fourth quarter profits in 1992? Explain why you would compute the change in this manner.

Case 20-2
Evaluation of
recent
developments
Presented below are three independent situations. Following each situation, we identify two or three groups of investors. You are to prepare a separate evaluation of the situation from the perspective of each of these investor groups. In your evaluation, indicate whether the recent developments described in the situation should be viewed as favorable, unfavorable, or not of much importance to the group. Explain the reasons for your conclusion.

Situation 1 During each of the last 10 years, Reese Corporation has increased the common stock dividend per share by about 10%. Total dividends now amount to $9 million per year, consisting of $2 million paid to preferred stockholders and $7 million paid to common stockholders. The preferred stock is cumulative but not convertible. Annual net income had been rising steadily until two years ago, when it peaked at $44 million. Last year, increased competition caused net income to decline to $37 million. Management expects income to stabilize around this level for several years. This year, Reese Corporation issued bonds payable. The contract with bondholders requires Reese Corporation to limit total dividends to not more than 25% of net income.

Instructions   Evaluate this situation from the perspective of:

a Common stockholders

b Preferred stockholders

Situation 2 Reynolds Labs develops and manufactures pharmaceutical products. The company has been growing rapidly during the past 10 years, due primarily to having discovered, patented, and successfully marketed dozens of new products. Profits have increased annually by 30% or more. The company pays no dividend, but has a very high price-earnings ratio. Due to its rapid growth and large expenditures for research and development, the company has experienced occasional cash shortages. To solve this problem, Reynolds has decided to improve its cash position by (1) requiring customers to pay for products purchased on account from the company in 30 days instead of 60 days, and (2) reducing expenditures for research and development by 20%.

Instructions   Evaluate this situation from the perspective of:

a Short-term creditors

b Common stockholders

Situation 3 Metro Utilities has outstanding 16 issues of bonds payable, with interest rates ranging from 5½% to 14%. The company's rate of return on assets consistently averages 12%. Almost every year, the company issues additional bonds to finance growth, to pay maturing bonds, or to call outstanding bonds when advantageous. During the current year, long-term interest rates have fallen dramatically. At the beginning of the year, these rates were between 12% and 13%; now, however, they are down to between 8% and 9%. Management currently is planning a large 8½% bond issue.

Instructions Evaluate this situation from the perspective of:

a Holders of 5½% bonds, maturing in 11 years but callable now at 103

b Holders of 14% bonds, maturing in 23 years but callable now at 103

c Common stockholders

ANSWERS TO SELF-TEST QUESTIONS
1 c **2 a** **3 b** **4 d** **5 c**

Appendix D
Accounting for the Effects of Inflation

The objective of this appendix is to introduce methods of adjusting accounting information for the effects of inflation. We illustrate and explain how net income is measured under the alternative assumptions of constant dollars and current costs. We also discuss gains and losses in purchasing power and show how data from prior years can be restated in terms of current dollars. Throughout our discussion, emphasis is placed upon the interpretation of information adjusted for the effects of inflation.

After studying this appendix you should be able to meet these Learning Objectives:

1 Define "inflation."

2 Explain why the use of historical costs during periods of inflation may overstate profits.

3 Distinguish between the constant dollar and current cost approaches to measuring net income.

4 Use a price index to restate historical costs to an equivalent number of current dollars.

5 Explain why holding monetary items may cause gains or losses in purchasing power.

Throughout this textbook, we have seen how the *cost principle* influences the valuation of assets and the measurement of expenses. Depreciation expense, for example, is based upon the *cost* of the related asset. In periods of sustained inflation, however, historical costs soon lose their relevance and may even become misleading as measurements of economic value. For this reason, accountants, business managers, investors, tax authorities, and other decision makers have long been interested in methods of adjusting accounting information for the effects of inflation.

What Is Inflation?

Objective 1
Define "inflation."

Inflation may be defined either as an increase in the general price level or as a decrease in the purchasing power of the dollar. The *general price level* is the weighted average of the prices of all goods and services in the economy.

Changes in the general price level are measured by a *general price index* with a base year assigned a value of 100. The index compares the level of current prices with that of the base year. Assume, for example, that 1995 is the base year. If prices rise by 10% during 1996, the price index at the end of 1996 will be 110. In the year 2010, the price index might be 200, indicating that the general price level had doubled since 1995.

The most widely recognized measure of the general price level in the United States is the Consumer Price Index (CPI), published monthly by the Bureau of Labor Statistics. For many years, the base year of the Consumer Price Index was 1967. In May 1983, the CPI passed the 300 level, indicating that prices (on the average) had tripled since 1967. (Note: In 1988, the Consumer Price Index was restated using 1986 as a base year.)

We often hear statements such as "Today's dollar is worth only 33 cents." The "worth" or "value" of a dollar lies in its ability to buy goods or services. This "value" is called *purchasing power.* The reciprocal of the general price index (100 divided by the current level of the index) represents the purchasing power of the dollar in the current year *relative to that in the base year.* For example, the reciprocal of the CPI in May 1983, was $100 \div 300$, or $.33\frac{1}{3}$. Therefore, we might say that $1 in 1983 was equivalent in purchasing power to about 33 cents in 1967.

What effect do material changes in general price levels, and thus changes in the value of money, have on accounting measures? By combining transactions measured in dollars of various years, the accountant in effect ignores changes in the size of the measuring unit. For example, suppose that a company purchases land for $200,000 and 10 years later sells this land for $400,000. Using the dollar as a measuring unit, we would recognize a gain of $200,000 ($400,000 sales price − $200,000 cost) on the sale of the land. But if prices doubled during that 10-year period and the value of money was cut in half, we might say that the company was *no better off* as a result of buying and selling this land. The $400,000 received for the land after 10 years represents the same command over goods and services as $200,000 did when invested in the land 10 years earlier.

We have experienced persistent inflation in the United States for over 40 years; more important, the forces which have been built into our economic and political institutions almost guarantee that inflation will continue. The only question is how severe the inflationary trend will be. Our traditional accounting process is based upon the assumption of a stable dollar. This cost-based system works extremely well in periods of stable prices; it works reasonably well during prolonged but mild inflation; but it loses virtually all meaning if inflation becomes extreme.

Profits—Fact or Illusion?

Objective 2
Explain why the use of historical costs during periods of inflation may overstate profits.

Corporate profits are watched closely by business managers, investors, and government officials. The trend of these profits plays a significant role in the allocation of the nation's investment resources, in levels of employment, and in national economic policy. As a result of the *stable-dollar assumption,* however, a strong argument may be made that much of the corporate profit reported today is an illusion.

In the measurement of business income, a distinction must be drawn between *profit* and the *recovery of costs.* A business earns a profit only when the value of goods sold and services rendered (revenue) *exceeds* the value of resources consumed in the earning process (costs and expenses). Accountants have traditionally assigned "values" to resources consumed in the earning process by using historical dollar amounts. Depreciation expense, for example, may be based upon prices paid to acquire assets 10 or 20 years ago.

When the general price level is rising rapidly, such historical costs may significantly understate the current *economic value* of the resources being consumed. If costs and expenses are understated, it follows that reported profits are overstated. In other words, the stable-dollar assumption may lead to reporting *illusory* profits; much of the net income reported by business enterprises actually may be a return of costs.

CASE IN POINT ■ In a recent year, Exxon Corporation appeared to be one of the most profitable companies in the world, reporting net income of $4 billion, 186 million. But when the giant oil company's income statement was adjusted for the effects of inflation, the profits vanished—instead, there appeared a **net loss** of $296 million. What happened? Did Exxon operate at a profit or a loss? The accounting concepts discussed in this appendix should shed some light on these interesting questions.

Two Approaches to "Inflation Accounting"

Two alternative approaches to modifying our accounting process to cope with inflation have received much attention. These two approaches are:

Objective 3
Distinguish between the constant dollar and current cost approaches to measuring net income.

1 Constant dollar accounting Under this approach, historical costs in the financial statements are adjusted to the *number of current dollars representing an equivalent amount of purchasing power.* Thus, all amounts are expressed in units (current dollars) of equal purchasing power. Since a general price index is used in restating the historical costs, constant dollar accounting shows the effects of changes in the *general* price level. Constant dollar accounting is also called *general price level* accounting.

2 Current cost accounting This method differs from constant dollar accounting in that assets and expenses are shown in the financial statements at the current cost to *replace* those specific resources. The *current replacement cost* of a specific asset may rise or fall at a different rate from the general price level. Thus, current cost accounting shows the effects of *specific price changes,* rather than changes in the general price level.

To illustrate these approaches to "inflation accounting" assume that in Year 1 you purchased 1,000 pounds of sugar for $100 when the general price index was at 100. Early in Year 2, you sold the sugar for $108 when the general price index was at 110 and the replacement cost of 1,000 pounds of sugar was $104. What is the amount of your profit or loss on this transaction? The amount of profit or loss determined under current accounting standards (unadjusted historical cost) and the two "inflation accounting" alternatives is shown on the next page.

	UNADJUSTED HISTORICAL COST	ADJUSTED FOR GENERAL INFLATION (CONSTANT DOLLARS)	ADJUSTED FOR CHANGES IN SPECIFIC PRICES (CURRENT COSTS)
Revenue	$108	$108	$108
Cost of goods sold	100	110	104
Profit (loss)	$ 8	$ (2)	$ 4

Which "cost" of goods sold is most realistic?

Under each method, an amount is deducted from revenue to provide for recovery of cost. However, the value assigned to the "cost" of goods sold differs under each of the three approaches.

■ **Unadjusted Historical Cost** This method is used in current accounting practice. The use of unadjusted historical cost is based upon the assumption that the dollar is a stable unit of measure. Profit is determined by comparing sales revenue with the *historical cost* of the asset sold. In using this approach to income determination, accountants assume that a business is as well off when it has recovered its *original dollar investment,* and that it is better off whenever it recovers more than the original number of dollars invested in any given asset.

In our example of buying and selling sugar, the profit figure of $8 shows *how many dollars* you came out ahead. However, this approach ignores the fact that Year 1 dollars and Year 2 dollars are *not equivalent in terms of purchasing power.* It also ignores the fact that the $100 deduction intended to provide for the recovery of cost is not sufficient to allow you to *replace* the 1,000 pounds of sugar.

■ **Constant Dollar Accounting** When financial statements are adjusted for changes in the general price level, historical amounts are restated as the number of current dollars *equivalent in purchasing power* to the historical cost. Profit is determined by comparing revenue with the *amount of purchasing power* (stated in current dollars) originally invested.

The general price index tells us that $110 in Year 2 is equivalent in purchasing power to the $100 invested in sugar in Year 1. But you do not have $110 in Year 2; you received only $108 dollars from the sale of the sugar. Thus, you have sustained a *$2 loss in purchasing power.*

■ **Current Cost Accounting** In current cost accounting, profit is measured by comparing revenue with the *current replacement cost* of the assets consumed in the earning process. The logic of this approach lies in the concept of the going concern. What will you do with the $108 received from the sale of the sugar? If you are going to continue in the sugar business, you will have to buy more sugar. At current market prices, it will cost you $104 to replace 1,000 pounds of sugar; the remaining $4, therefore, is designated as profit.

Current cost accounting recognizes in the income statement the costs which a going concern actually has to pay to replace its expiring assets. The resulting profit figure, therefore, closely parallels the maximum amount which a business could distribute to its owners and still be able to maintain the present size and scale of its operations.

■ **Which Approach Correctly Measures Net Income?** The answer to this question is that *all three* methods correctly measure net income, but each method is based upon a different definition of "cost" and, therefore, of "net income." Thus, the important question becomes *"Which approach provides the most useful information for making the decision at hand?"* The answer to this question may vary from one decision to the next.

Disclosing the Effects of Inflation in Financial Statements

In past years, large corporations were required to include with their financial statements *supplementary schedules* disclosing the effects of inflation. As the rate of inflation declined in the United States, the FASB reduced these disclosure requirements. Today, disclosure of the effects of inflation is no longer required. However, the FASB encourages companies to make *voluntary* disclosures and provides guidelines for these disclosures.[1] Also, the FASB has stated that if the rate of inflation increases, these disclosures may again become mandatory.

A complete discussion of the FASB's disclosure guidelines is beyond the scope of the introductory course. However, everyone who makes use of accounting information should have some understanding of the effects of inflation upon accounting measurements. Therefore, our discussion will focus upon the following basic concepts:

1 Net income measured in constant dollars

2 Gains and losses in purchasing power caused by owning monetary assets and by having liabilities

3 Net income on a current cost basis

4 Comparative data expressed in constant dollars

The value of understanding these concepts extends well beyond reading and interpreting financial statements. An understanding of these concepts is of great value to every economic decision maker.

"INFLATION ACCOUNTING"—AN ILLUSTRATION

The following illustration is typical of the supplementary schedules used to disclose (1) net income measured in constant dollars, (2) gain or loss in purchasing power, and (3) net income measured using current costs. (These three items are printed in black and identified by the numbered arrows.)

---

[1] FASB Statement No. 89, "Financial Reporting and Changing Prices," FASB (Stamford, Conn.: 1986).

Supplement to the financial statements:

COLEMAN COMPANY
Income Statement Adjusted for Changing Prices
For the Year Ended December 31, 19X5

	AS REPORTED IN THE PRIMARY STATEMENTS	ADJUSTED FOR GENERAL INFLATION (CONSTANT DOLLARS)*	ADJUSTED FOR CHANGES IN IN SPECIFIC PRICES (CURRENT COSTS)
Net sales	$600,000	$600,000	$600,000
Costs and expenses:			
Cost of goods sold	$360,000	$370,000	$391,500
Depreciation expense..........	60,000	80,000	90,000
Other expenses	130,000	130,000	130,000
Total.......................	$550,000	$580,000	$611,500
Net income	$ 50,000	①⟶ $ 20,000	③⟶ $(11,500)
Net gain from decline in purchasing power of net amounts owed		②⟶ $ 8,000	

* Stated in dollars of average purchasing power during 19X5.

We shall now use the information in this illustration to demonstrate further the concepts of constant dollar and current cost accounting and to interpret these disclosures from the viewpoint of the financial statement user.

Net Income Measured in Constant Dollars

Objective 4
Use a price index to restate historical costs to an equivalent number of current dollars.

A basic problem with the use of historical costs for measuring income is that revenue and expenses may be stated in dollars having different amounts of purchasing power. Sales revenue, for example, is recorded in current-year dollars. Depreciation expense, on the other hand, is based upon dollars spent to acquire assets in past years. As previously emphasized, dollars in the current year and dollars of past years are not equivalent in terms of purchasing power.

In a constant dollar income statement, expenses based on "old" dollars are *restated* at the number of current dollars representing the equivalent amount of purchasing power. When all revenue and expenses are stated in units of similar purchasing power, we can see whether the business is gaining or losing in terms of the amount of purchasing power it controls.

To restate a historical amount in terms of an equivalent number of current dollars, we multiply the historical amount by the ratio of the current price level to the historical price level, as illustrated below:

$$\text{Historical cost} \times \frac{\text{Average price index for current period}}{\text{Index at date of historical cost}} = \frac{\text{Equivalent number}}{\text{of current dollars}}$$

For example, assume that land was purchased for $100,000 when the price index stood at *100.* If the price index is now *170,* we may find the number of current dollars equivalent to the *purchasing power* originally invested in the land by multiplying the $100,000 historical cost by *170/100.* The result, $170,000, represents the number of current dollars *equivalent in purchasing power* to the 100,000 historical dollars.

■ Price Index Levels for Our Illustration

The following changes in the general price index are assumed in our Coleman Company illustration:

DATE	PRICE INDEX
Beginning of 19X3 (acquisition date for depreciable assets)	*150*
End of 19X4	*180*
Average price level for 19X5*	*200*
End of 19X5	*216*
Rate of inflation for 19X5†	*20%*

* The "average" price level for the year is computed as a monthly average and need not lie exactly halfway between the price levels at the beginning and end of the year.
†The inflation rate is computed by dividing the increase in the price index over the year by the price index at the beginning of the year: $(216 - 180) \div 180 = 20\%$.

In restating historical dollars to current dollars, we shall use the *average price level* for 19X5 (200) to represent the purchasing power of current dollars.[2]

■ Not All Amounts Are Restated

Compare the constant dollar and historical cost income statements of Coleman Company for 19X5 (page 820). Note that only two items—depreciation expense and the cost of goods sold—have been restated in the constant dollar statement. Sales revenue and expenses other than depreciation consist of transactions occurring during the current year. Therefore, these amounts are *already* stated in current dollars. We need to adjust to current dollars only those expenses which are based on costs incurred in past years.

■ Restating Depreciation Expense

Assume that Coleman Company's depreciation expense all relates to equipment purchased early in *19X3* when the price level was *150*. The equipment cost $600,000 and is being depreciated over 10 years by the straight-line method. Since the average price level in 19X5 is 200, the *purchasing power* originally invested in this equipment is equivalent to *$800,000 current dollars* ($600,000 × $^{200}/_{150}$ = $800,000). Thus, the amount of *purchasing power* expiring in 19X5, stated in current dollars, is *$80,000* ($800,000 ÷ 10 years).

A shortcut approach is simply to restate the historical depreciation expense, as follows:

HISTORICAL DOLLARS		CONVERSION RATIO		EQUIVALENT CURRENT DOLLARS
$60,000	×	*200/150*	=	*$80,000*

Since depreciable assets are long-lived, the price level prevailing when the assets were acquired may be substantially different from the current price level. In such cases, the amount of depreciation expense recognized becomes one of the most significant differences between historical dollar and current dollar financial statements.

---

[2] An acceptable alternative is to use the year-end price level to represent the purchasing power of current dollars. However, use of the year-end price level means that all income statement amounts, including revenue and expense transactions conducted during the current year, must be restated. For this reason, the average price level for the current year is more widely used.

■ **Restating the Cost of Goods Sold** During 19X5, Coleman Company sold merchandise with a historical cost of $360,000. Assume that $90,000 of these goods came from the beginning inventory, acquired at the end of *19X4* when the price level was *180;* the remaining $270,000 of these goods were purchased during 19X5. The restatement of the cost of goods sold to average dollars is shown below:

	HISTORICAL DOLLARS	CONVERSION RATIO	EQUIVALENT CURRENT DOLLARS
Beginning inventory	$ 90,000	× 200/180 =	$100,000
Purchased in 19X5	270,000	*	270,000
Cost of goods sold	$360,000		$370,000

* No adjustment necessary—amount already is stated in current dollars.

Interpreting the Constant Dollar Income Statement

The basic difference between historical dollar and constant dollar income statements is the unit of measure. Historical dollar income statements use the dollar as a basic unit of measure. The unit of measure in constant dollar income statements is the ***purchasing power of the current dollar.***

A conventional income statement shows how many dollars were added to owner's equity from the operation of the business. Identifying a dollar increase in owner's equity as "income" implies that owners are better off when they recover more than the original number of dollars they invested. No attention is given to the fact that a greater number of dollars may still have less purchasing power than was originally invested.

A ***constant dollar*** income statement shows whether the ***inflow of purchasing power*** from current operations is larger or smaller than the ***purchasing power consumed*** in the effort to generate revenue. In short, the net income figure tells us whether the amount of purchasing power controlled by the business has increased or decreased as a result of operations.

Gains and Losses in Purchasing Power

Objective 5
Explain why holding monetary items may cause gains *or* losses in purchasing power.

Constant dollar accounting introduces a new consideration in measuring the effects of inflation upon a business: gains and losses in purchasing power from holding monetary items. ***Monetary items*** are those assets and liabilities representing claims to a ***fixed number of dollars.*** Examples of monetary assets are cash, notes receivable, and accounts receivable; most liabilities are monetary, including notes payable and accounts payable.

Holding monetary assets during a period of rising prices results in a ***loss*** of purchasing power because the value of the money is falling. In contrast, owing money during a period of rising prices gives rise to a ***gain*** in purchasing power because debts may be repaid using dollars of less purchasing power than those originally borrowed.

To illustrate, assume that Coleman Company held $30,000 in cash throughout 19X5, while the price level rose 20% (from 180 to 216). By the end of the year, this $30,000 cash balance will have lost 20% of its purchasing power, as demonstrated by the following analysis:

Number of dollars needed at year-end to represent the same purchasing power as
$30,000 at the beginning of the year ($30,000 × 216/180) **$36,000**
Number of dollars actually held at year-end **30,000**
Loss in purchasing power as a result of holding monetary assets . . . . **$ 6,000**

We can also compute this $6,000 loss simply by multiplying the amount of the monetary assets held throughout the year by the 20% inflation rate: $30,000 × 20% = $6,000.

A similar analysis is applied to any monetary liabilities. Assume, for example, that Coleman Company has a $70,000 note payable outstanding throughout 19X5. The resulting gain in purchasing power is computed as follows:

Number of dollars at year-end representing the same purchasing power as $70,000
owed at beginning of year ($70,000 × 216/180) **$84,000**
Number of dollars actually owed at year-end **70,000**
Gain in purchasing power as a result of owing a fixed number of dollars **$14,000**

Thus, during 19X5 Coleman Company has experienced an *$8,000 net gain in purchasing power* ($14,000 gain − $6,000 loss), because its monetary liabilities were greater than its monetary assets. The disclosure of this net gain is illustrated in the supplementary schedule on page 820 (arrow number **2**).

Interpreting the Net Gain or Loss in Purchasing Power

In determining the total change in the purchasing power represented by owners' equity, we must consider **both** the amount of constant dollar net income **and** the amount of any gain or loss resulting from holding monetary items. Thus, the purchasing power of the owners' equity in Coleman Company increased by $28,000 during 19X5 ($20,000 net income + $8,000 gain in purchasing power from monetary items).[3]

The purchasing power gain from monetary items is shown separately from the determination of net income to emphasize the special nature of this gain. The income statement shows the purchasing power created or lost *as a result of business operations.* The $8,000 net gain in purchasing power, however, is caused entirely by the *effect of inflation* upon the purchasing power of monetary assets and liabilities. A business that owns monetary assets or owes money may have a purchasing power gain or loss *even if it earns no revenue and incurs no expenses.*

In evaluating the effect of inflation upon a particular business, we must consider the effect of inflation upon operations and its effects upon the monetary assets and liabilities of the business. If a business must maintain high levels of cash or accounts receivable from customers, we should recognize that inflation will continually erode the purchasing power of these assets. On the

---

[3] Some readers may notice that our net gain is stated in end-of-19X5 dollars. To be technically consistent with the other constant dollar data on page 820, this net gain should be restated in dollars of average purchasing power for 19X5. The gain can be restated as follows: $8,000 × $200/216 = $7,407. We have ignored this restatement because it is not material in dollar amount and is an unnecessary refinement for an introductory discussion.

other hand, if a business is able to finance its operations with borrowed capital, inflation will benefit the company by allowing it to repay smaller amounts of purchasing power than it originally borrowed.

Net Income on a Current Cost Basis

Constant dollar accounting does not abandon historical costs as the basis for measurement but simply *expresses these costs in terms of the current value of money.* Current cost accounting, on the other hand, does represent a departure from the historical cost concept. The term "current cost" usually refers to the *current replacement cost* of assets. In a current cost income statement, expenses are stated at the estimated cost to *replace the specific assets* sold or used up. Thus, current cost accounting involves *estimates of current market values,* rather than adjustments to historical costs for changes in the general price level.

Of course, the replacement cost of an asset may fluctuate during the year. Because a cost such as depreciation occurs continually *throughout* the year, current cost measurements are based on the *average* replacement cost during the year, not on the replacement cost at year-end.

To illustrate, assume that the replacement cost of Coleman Company's equipment was estimated to be $850,000 at the beginning of 19X5 and $950,000 at year-end. Current cost depreciation expense should be based upon the *$900,000 average replacement cost* of the equipment during the year. Since the equipment has a 10-year life, the depreciation expense appearing in the current cost income statement (page 820) is *$90,000* ($900,000 ÷ 10 years).

Now let us consider the determination of the cost of goods sold on a current cost basis. All we need to know is (1) how many units of inventory were sold during the year, and (2) the *average replacement cost* of these units during the year. If Coleman Company sold 145,000 units during the year, and the average replacement cost was $2.70 per unit, the cost of goods sold would be $391,500 on a current cost basis (145,000 units × $2.70). Note that the historical cost of units in the company's beginning inventory does not enter into the current cost computation.

Interpreting a Current Cost Income Statement

A current cost income statement does *not* measure the flow of general purchasing power in and out of the business. Rather, it shows whether a company earns enough revenue to *replace* the goods and services used up in the effort to generate that revenue. The resulting net income figure closely parallels *distributable profit*—the maximum amount that the business can distribute to its owners and still maintain the present size and scale of its operations.

Unfortunately, the financial statements of large corporations show that many companies in industries vital to our economy are reporting profits measured on a historical cost basis but are incurring large *losses* according to their supplementary current cost disclosures. Companies in the steel industry and utilities industry provide excellent examples. What does this mean to an informed reader of financial statements? In short, it means that these companies do not earn sufficient revenue to maintain their productive capacity. In the long run, they must either obtain capital from other sources or scale down the size of their operations.

Expressing Comparative Data in Dollars of Constant Purchasing Power

To assist decision makers in evaluating trends, data for a series of years often are expressed in dollars of constant purchasing power. For example, the FASB recommends that companies disclose five-year summaries of such key statistics as net sales, income from continuing operations (on a current cost basis), purchasing power gains and losses, earnings per share (on a current cost basis), cash dividends per share, and the market price per share of common stock at year-end. These summaries are to be expressed in dollars of constant purchasing power.

Let us use a short example to illustrate the concept of expressing comparative data in constant dollars. Assume that Wheelhouse Restaurants includes in its annual financial statements supplementary schedules measuring net income on a current cost basis. The earnings per share shown in these schedules (also on a current cost basis) in each of the last five years are shown below. Also shown is the per-share price of the company's common stock at the end of each year.

Data as Originally Reported

	19X5	19X4	19X3	19X2	19X1
Earnings per share (based on current cost net income)	$ 5.40	$ 4.72	$ 4.20	$ 3.66	$ 3.30
Year-end stock price	63.00	57.60	52.50	47.40	44.00

At first glance, it appears that both earnings and the price of the company's stock have increased steadily each year. Now, however, let us consider the changes during these years in the general price level.

Assume that the average level of the general price index for each year is as follows:

	19X5	19X4	19X3	19X2	19X1
Average level of price index	180	160	140	120	110

Using this price index, we may restate our annual figures in the equivalent number of current year dollars:

Data Restated in Constant (19X5) Dollars

	19X5	19X4	19X3	19X2	19X1
Earnings per share (based on current cost net income)	$ 5.40[e]	$ 5.31[d]	$ 5.40[c]	$ 5.49[b]	$ 5.40[a]
Year-end stock price	63.00[j]	64.80[i]	67.50[h]	71.10[g]	72.00[f]

Computations:
Earnings per share:
[a] $3.30 × 180/110
[b] $3.66 × 180/120
[c] $4.20 × 180/140
[d] $4.72 × 180/160
[e] No adjustment necessary

Year-end stock price:
[f] $44.00 × 180/110
[g] $47.40 × 180/120
[h] $52.50 × 180/140
[i] $57.60 × 180/160
[j] No adjustment necessary

Interpreting Comparative Data Stated in Constant Dollars

The amounts in this second schedule are stated in *units of equal purchasing power*—namely, 19X5 dollars. Thus, the schedule indicates the relative amounts of purchasing power earned each year and the purchasing power represented by the year-end stock price.

This schedule paints a very different picture of the company's "growth" than did our original five-year summary. The amount of purchasing power earned each year has remained about the same, rather than "increasing steadily." In short, the increases appearing in the first schedule resulted from inflation, not from economic growth. Our constant dollar analysis also reveals that the purchasing power represented by the market value of the company's stock has *declined* each year since 19X1.

Assignment Material

REVIEW QUESTIONS

1 Define inflation.

2 Evaluate the following statement: "During a period of rising prices, the conventional income statement overstates net income because the amount of depreciation recorded is less than the value of the service potential of assets consumed."

3 Define *monetary assets* and indicate whether a gain or loss results from the holding of such assets during a period of rising prices.

4 Why is it advantageous to be in debt during an inflationary period?

5 How does *constant dollar* accounting differ from *current cost* accounting? For which one would the Consumer Price Index be used?

6 Alpha Company sells pocket calculators which have been decreasing in cost while the general price level has been rising. Explain why Alpha Company's cost of goods sold on a constant dollar basis and on a current cost basis would be higher or lower than on a historical cost basis.

7 The latest financial statements of Boston Manufacturing Co. indicate that income measured in terms of constant dollars is much lower than income measured in historical dollars. What is the most probable explanation for this large difference?

8 What conclusion would you draw about a company that consistently shows large net losses when its income is measured on a current cost basis?

EXERCISES

Exercise D-1
Effects of changing price levels

Empire Company paid $500,000 cash in 1986 to acquire land as a long-term investment. At this time, the general price level stood at 100. In 1990, the general price index stands at 140, but the price of land in the area in which Empire Company invested has doubled in value. Rental receipts for grazing and farming during the five-year period were sufficient to pay all carrying charges on the land.

Empire Company prepares a constant dollar income statement and discloses purchasing power gains and losses as supplementary information to its cost-based financial statements.

a How much, if any, purchasing power gain or loss relating to the land will be included in the supplementary disclosures over the five-year period? (Assume the land is still owned at the end of 1990.)

b Assume the land is sold in 1990 for $685,000. Compute the gain or loss on the sale on a basis of (1) historical cost and (2) constant dollars.

Exercise D-2
Monetary items:
gains and losses
in purchasing
power

Three companies started business with $600,000 at the beginning of the current year when the general price index stood at 120. The First Company invested the money in a note receivable due in four years; the Second Company invested its cash in land; and the Third Company purchased a building for $1,800,000, assuming a liability for the unpaid balance of $1,200,000. The price level stood at 140 at the end of the year. Compute the purchasing power gain or loss on monetary items for each company during the year.

Exercise D-3
Cost of goods
sold using
constant dollars
and current costs

For the current year, PhotoMart computed the cost of goods sold for the Presto, its biggest-selling camera, as follows (historical cost, FIFO basis):

	UNITS	×	UNIT COST	=	TOTAL
From beginning inventory	400		$40.00		$16,000
From current year purchases	1,700		42.00		71,400
Cost of goods sold	2,100				$87,400

The beginning inventory of Presto cameras had been acquired when the general price index stood at 320. During the current year, the average level of the price index was 350, and the average replacement cost of Prestos was $42.

Compute the cost of goods sold for Presto cameras in the current year on:

a A constant dollar basis

b A current cost basis

Exercise D-4
Depreciation
using constant
dollars and
current costs

Western Showcase purchased equipment for $300,000 in 19X3 when the general price index stood at 120. The company depreciates the equipment over 15 years by the straight-line method, with no estimated salvage value. In 19X7, the general price level is 180 and the estimated replacement cost of the equipment is $468,000.

Compute the amount of depreciation expense for 19X7 on:

a A historical cost basis

b A constant dollar basis

c A current cost basis

PROBLEMS

Problem 1
Profits: now you
see them . . .
now you don't

Shown below is a supplementary schedule which appeared in a recent annual report of Chevron Corporation (in millions of dollars):

	AS REPORTED IN THE PRIMARY STATEMENTS	CURRENT COST
Revenues	$29,207	$29,207
Costs and expenses:		
Cost of products sold and operating expenses ..	21,835	22,281
Depreciation, depletion, and amortization	1,388	2,630
Taxes other than on income	2,469	2,469
Interest and debt expense	961	961
Provision for taxes on income	1,020	1,020
Net income (Loss)	$ 1,534	$ (154)

Instructions

Use this supplementary schedule to answer each of the following questions. Explain the reasoning behind your answers.

a Was Chevron's revenue sufficient to recover the *original* number of dollars invested in the goods and services consumed during the year?

b Was Chevron's revenue sufficient to *replace* the goods and services consumed in the effort to generate revenue during the year?

c What do you think is the principal reason for the large difference between the amounts of net income (or net loss) computed under the alternative measurement techniques of historical cost and current cost?

Problem 2
Interpreting constant dollars and current costs

The following schedule was developed from information contained in a recent annual report of Ralston Purina Company:

Income Statement Adjusted for Changing Prices
(in millions of dollars)

	AS REPORTED IN THE PRIMARY STATEMENTS	ADJUSTED FOR GENERAL INFLATION (CONSTANT DOLLARS)	ADJUSTED FOR CHANGES IN SPECIFIC PRICES (CURRENT COSTS)
Net sales.....................	$4,980.1	$4,980.1	$4,980.1
Costs and expenses:			
Cost of goods sold	$3,652.8	$3,664.0	$3,642.3
Depreciation expense.......	108.7	168.2	174.4
Other expenses	975.9	975.9	975.9
Total.....................	$4,737.4	$4,808.1	$4,792.6
Net income (loss).............	$ 242.7	$ 172.0	$ 187.5
Gain from decline in purchasing			
power of net amounts owed		$ 20.3	

Instructions
Use the supplementary schedule to answer each of the following questions. Explain the reasoning behind your answers.

a Was the replacement cost of the products sold by Ralston Purina rising or falling during the year?

b Has the replacement cost of the company's depreciable assets increased faster or more slowly than the general price level since these assets were acquired?

c Were the average monetary assets held by the company during the year greater or smaller than the average monetary liabilities owed?

d What was the total change in the purchasing power of the owners' equity in the business during the year?

e Assuming that this was a typical year, are the company's earnings sufficient to maintain the present size and scope of current operations on a long-term basis?

Problem 3
Interpreting constant dollar and current cost disclosures—an alternate to Problem 2

The following supplementary schedule appears with the financial statements of Lagerbier for the current year.

Income Statement Adjusted for Changing Prices
(in thousands of dollars)
For the Year Ended December 31, 19___

	AS REPORTED IN THE PRIMARY STATEMENTS	ADJUSTED FOR GENERAL INFLATION (CONSTANT DOLLARS)	ADJUSTED FOR CHANGES IN SPECIFIC PRICES (CURRENT COSTS)
Net sales	$600,000	$600,000	$600,000
Costs and expenses:			
Cost of goods sold	$300,000	$315,000	$310,000
Depreciation expense...............	50,000	65,000	95,000
Other expenses	210,000	210,000	210,000
Total..........................	$560,000	$590,000	$615,000
Net income	$ 40,000	$ 10,000	$ (15,000)
Loss from decline in purchasing power of net monetary assets owned		$ 18,000	

Instructions Explain the reasoning behind your answer to each of the following questions:

a Has the replacement cost of the company's inventory increased faster or more slowly than the general price level during the year?

b Has the replacement cost of the company's depreciable assets increased faster or more slowly than the general price level since these assets were acquired?

c Were the average monetary assets held by the company during the year greater or smaller than the average monetary liabilities owed?

d What was the total change in the purchasing power of the owners' equity in this business during the year?

e Assuming that this is a typical year, are the company's earnings sufficient to maintain the present size and scope of its operations on a long-term basis?

Problem 4
Expressing comparative data in constant dollars

Shown below is the per-share price of the common stock of Southwest Gas & Electric at the end of each of the last five years:

	19X5	19X4	19X3	19X2	19X1
Year-end stock price	$69.00	$65.00	$60.50	$56.70	$50.00

Instructions **a** Based solely upon the above data and *without regard* to changes in the general price level, briefly comment upon the apparent trend in the price of the company's stock. In your comments, indicate the total *percentage change* in the price of the stock over the four-year period from the end of 19X1 to the end of 19X5.

b Prepare a schedule in which the ending stock prices for each year are all stated in terms of the purchasing power of the dollar in 19X5. Use the following price index in preparing this constant dollar analysis. Show supporting computations.

	19X5	19X4	19X3	19X2	19X1
Average level of price index.....................	150	125	110	105	100

c Based upon the schedule prepared in part b, comment upon the trends in price of the company's stock. In your comments, indicate the total percentage change in the purchasing power represented by one share over the four-year period from the end of 19X1 to the end of 19X5.

Problem 5
Constant dollars
and current
costs: a
comprehensive
problem

Sandy Malone, the president of Sandstone Art Company, has asked you to prepare constant dollar and current cost income statements to supplement the company's financial statements. The company's accountant has provided you with the following data:

Income Statement—Historical Cost
For the Year Ended December 31, 19__

Net sales		$840,000
Costs and expenses:		
Cost of goods sold	$420,000	
Depreciation expense	60,000	
Other expenses	320,000	
Total costs and expenses		800,000
Net income		$ 40,000

Other Data

(1) Changes in the general price index during the current year were as follows:

	PRICE INDEX
Beginning of current year	120
Average for current year	130
End of current year	138
Rate of inflation [(138 − 120) ÷ 120]	15%

Amounts in the constant dollar income statement are to be expressed in current-year dollars of average purchasing power.

(2) The company sells a single product and uses the first-in, first-out method to compute the cost of goods sold. The historical cost of goods sold includes the following unit sales at the following costs:

	UNITS ×	AVERAGE UNIT COSTS =	TOTAL
From beginning inventory	10,000	$6.00	$ 60,000
From current-year-purchases	56,250	6.40	360,000
Cost of goods sold	66,250	6.34	$420,000

The $60,000 beginning inventory was purchased when the general price index stood at 120. (It is not necessary to know total purchases or ending inventory for the current year.)

(3) The company's depreciable assets consist of equipment acquired five years ago when the price index stood at 75. The equipment cost $900,000 and is being depreciated over a 15-year life by the straight-line method with no estimated salvage value.

The estimated replacement cost of the equipment was $1,200,000 at the beginning of the current year and $1,260,000 at year-end.

(4) Throughout the current year, the company has owned monetary assets of $180,000 and has owed monetary liabilities of $320,000.

Instructions

Prepare a supplementary schedule in the format illustrated on page 820. Include comparative income statements prepared on the bases of historical costs, constant dollars, and current costs. Also show the net gain or loss from holding monetary items. Include supporting computations for the (1) cost of goods sold—constant dollar basis, (2) depreciation expense—constant dollar basis, (3) net gain or loss in purchasing power from holding monetary items, (4) cost of goods sold—current cost basis, and (5) depreciation expense—current cost basis.

Comprehensive Problem for Part 6

BRISTOL-MYERS COMPANY

Analysis of the financial statements of a publicly owned corporation.

The purpose of this Comprehensive Problem is to acquaint you with the financial statements of a publicly owned company. The financial statements included in the 1988 annual report of Bristol-Myers Company (the Company) were selected because they illustrate many of the financial reporting issues discussed in this textbook. Notice that several pages of explanatory notes are included with the basic statements. These explanatory notes supplement the condensed information in the financial statements and are intended to carry out the generally accepted accounting principle of adequate disclosure.

This Comprehensive Problem is subdivided into three parts *Part 1* is designed to familiarize you with the content of these financial statements. *Part 2* requires analysis from the viewpoint of a short-term creditor, and *Part 3*, from the perspective of a stockholder.

Consolidated Statements of Earnings and Retained Earnings

		Year Ended December 31,		
(in millions of dollars except per share amounts)		1988	1987	1986
Earnings	Net Sales.	$5,972.5	$5,401.2	$4,835.9
	Expenses:			
	Cost of products sold.	1,803.6	1,678.8	1,515.2
	Marketing, selling and administrative.	1,606.5	1,464.0	1,303.0
	Advertising and product promotion	978.8	918.7	820.3
	Research and development.	394.1	341.7	311.1
	Other.	(95.8)	(119.5)	(44.1)
		4,687.2	4,283.7	3,905.5
	Earnings Before Income Taxes	1,285.3	1,117.5	930.4
	Provision for income taxes	456.3	407.9	340.9
	Net Earnings.	$ 829.0	$ 709.6	$ 589.5
	Earnings Per Common Share	$2.88	$2.47	$2.07
Retained Earnings	Retained Earnings, January 1.	$3,010.8	$2,703.3	$2,414.4
	Net earnings.	829.0	709.6	589.5
		3,839.8	3,412.9	3,003.9
	Less dividends.	483.8	402.1	300.6
	Retained Earnings, December 31	$3,356.0	$3,010.8	$2,703.3

The accompanying notes are an integral part of these financial statements.

Consolidated Balance Sheet

		December 31,		
(in millions of dollars)		1988	1987	1986
Assets	**Current Assets:**			
	Cash and cash equivalents	$1,186.2	$ 353.4	$ 493.0
	Time deposits	130.8	641.8	619.0
	Marketable securities.	392.9	582.4	80.2
	Receivables, net of allowances.	946.2	865.9	759.3
	Inventories	688.6	617.9	615.0
	Prepaid expenses.	221.1	202.3	192.1
	Total Current Assets.	3,565.8	3,263.7	2,758.6
	Property, Plant and Equipment — net.	1,249.1	1,141.9	1,070.0
	Other Assets	173.6	143.8	165.3
	Excess of cost over net tangible assets received in business acquisitions	201.2	182.6	189.1
		$5,189.7	$4,732.0	$4,183.0
Liabilities	**Current Liabilities:**			
	Short-term borrowings	$ 173.3	$ 223.4	$ 230.5
	Accounts payable.	335.8	275.8	252.0
	Accrued expenses	519.3	449.8	374.1
	U.S. and foreign income taxes payable	135.6	150.4	158.6
	Total Current Liabilities	1,164.0	1,099.4	1,015.2
	Other Liabilities	263.5	193.0	174.5
	Long-Term Debt	215.2	210.3	157.7
	Total Liabilities	1,642.7	1,502.7	1,347.4
Stockholders' Equity	Preferred stock, $2 convertible series: Authorized 10,000,000 shares; issued 81,730 in 1988, 95,782 in 1987 and 123,689 in 1986, liquidation value of $50 per share	.1	.1	.2
	Common stock, par value of $.10 per share: Authorized 750,000,000 shares; issued 289,632,360 in 1988, 287,851,825 in 1987 and 143,117,706 in 1986.	29.0	28.8	143.1
	Capital in excess of par value of stock	312.7	275.8	137.4
	Cumulative translation adjustments	(77.8)	(84.2)	(147.3)
	Retained earnings	3,356.0	3,010.8	2,703.3
		3,620.0	3,231.3	2,836.7
	Less cost of treasury stock — 1,885,512 common shares in 1988, 218,512 in 1987 and 96,756 in 1986.	73.0	2.0	1.1
	Total Stockholders' Equity	3,547.0	3,229.3	2,835.6
		$5,189.7	$4,732.0	$4,183.0

The accompanying notes are an integral part of these financial statements.

Consolidated Statement of Cash Flows

	Year Ended December 31,		
(in millions of dollars)	1988	1987	1986
Cash Flows From Operating Activities:			
Net earnings	$ 829.0	$ 709.6	$ 589.5
Depreciation and amortization	127.9	115.9	104.9
Other operating items	8.8	30.7	15.9
Receivables	(121.1)	(92.0)	29.8
Inventories	(74.6)	4.4	(16.0)
Prepaid expenses	(19.1)	(1.4)	—
Accounts payable	76.7	(38.0)	18.9
Accrued expenses and income taxes	73.5	65.4	(44.7)
Other assets and liabilities	79.5	28.3	(2.7)
Net Cash Provided by Operating Activities	980.6	822.9	695.6
Cash Flows From Investing Activities:			
Proceeds from sales of time deposits and marketable securities	5,050.3	8,242.1	3,650.4
Purchases of time deposits and marketable securities . .	(4,349.7)	(8,774.7)	(3,898.3)
Additions to fixed assets	(249.1)	(186.5)	(214.9)
Other, net — including in 1987 net proceeds from sales of businesses	(35.3)	148.3	(53.4)
Net Cash Provided by (Used in) Investing Activities .	416.2	(570.8)	(516.2)
Cash Flows From Financing Activities:			
Short-term borrowings	(45.3)	(35.9)	(28.6)
Long-term debt	(3.5)	24.2	23.5
Proceeds from stock options and warrants exercised . .	37.1	24.0	25.4
Purchase of treasury stock	(71.0)	(.9)	—
Dividends paid	(483.8)	(402.1)	(300.6)
Net Cash Used in Financing Activities	(566.5)	(390.7)	(280.3)
Effect of Exchange Rates on Cash	2.5	(1.0)	(1.5)
Increase (Decrease) in Cash and Cash Equivalents	832.8	(139.6)	(102.4)
Cash and Cash Equivalents at Beginning of Year	353.4	493.0	595.4
Cash and Cash Equivalents at End of Year	$1,186.2	$ 353.4	$ 493.0

The accompanying notes are an integral part of these financial statements.

Notes to Consolidated Financial Statements

Note 1   Accounting Policies

Basis of Consolidation
The consolidated financial statements include the accounts of Bristol-Myers Company and all of its subsidiaries.

Cash and Cash Equivalents
Cash and cash equivalents include cash on hand, cash in banks and all highly-liquid investments with a maturity of three months or less at the time of purchase.

Marketable Securities
Marketable securities are valued at the lower of cost or market.

Inventory Valuation
Inventories are generally stated at average cost, not in excess of market.

Property and Depreciation
Expenditures for additions, renewals and betterments are capitalized at cost. Depreciation is generally computed by the straight-line method based on the estimated useful lives of the related assets.

Excess of Cost over Net Tangible Assets
The excess of cost over net tangible assets received in business acquisitions subsequent to October 31, 1970 is being amortized on a straight-line basis over periods not exceeding forty years.

Earnings Per Share
Earnings per common share are computed using the weighted average number of shares outstanding during the year. Shares issuable under stock options and warrants have been excluded from the average because their effect is not significant.

Note 2   Foreign Currency Translation
Cumulative translation adjustments which represent the effect of translating assets and liabilities of the company's non-U.S. operations, except those in highly inflationary economies, were:

(in millions of dollars)	1988	1987	1986
Balance, January 1	$ 84.2	$147.3	$181.7
Effect of balance sheet translations:			
Amount	(6.1)	(61.4)	(31.6)
Tax effect	(.3)	(1.7)	(2.8)
Balance, December 31	$ 77.8	$ 84.2	$147.3

Transaction losses resulting from foreign currency transactions and translation adjustments relating to non-U.S. entities operating in highly inflationary economies, principally Brazil and Mexico, of $31.4 million, $16.0 million and $12.1 million, net of applicable income taxes, are reflected in net income for 1988, 1987 and 1986, respectively.

Note 3   Other Income and Expenses

Year Ended December 31, (in millions of dollars)	1988	1987	1986
Interest income	$138.6	$ 95.2	$ 82.2
Interest expense	(34.4)	(29.4)	(32.4)
Other—net	(8.4)	53.7	(5.7)
	$ 95.8	$119.5	$ 44.1

Interest expense was reduced by interest capitalized on major property, plant and equipment projects of $3.3 million, $5.1 million and $5.4 million in 1988, 1987 and 1986, respectively. Cash payments for interest, net of amounts capitalized, were $35.9 million, $30.8 million and $31.2 million for 1988, 1987 and 1986, respectively. In 1987, other—net includes $80.3 million of gains from the sales of the orthodontic and animal health businesses.

Note 4   Inventories

December 31, (in millions of dollars)	1988	1987	1986
Finished goods.	$366.1	$337.6	$346.1
Work in process.	110.9	94.2	87.9
Raw and packaging materials.	211.6	186.1	181.0
	$688.6	$617.9	$615.0

Note 5   Property, Plant and Equipment

December 31, (in millions of dollars)	1988	1987	1986
Land.	$ 44.6	$ 44.8	$ 36.4
Buildings.	672.0	640.3	517.8
Machinery, equipment and fixtures.	1,177.1	1,083.3	984.0
Construction in progress.	183.6	111.1	187.7
	2,077.3	1,879.5	1,725.9
Less accumulated depreciation.	828.2	737.6	655.9
	$1,249.1	$1,141.9	$1,070.0

Capitalized leases, principally machinery, equipment and fixtures, net of accumulated amortization, were $18.9 million, $23.3 million and $27.4 million in 1988, 1987 and 1986, respectively.

Note 6   Long-Term Debt and Lines of Credit

December 31, (in millions of dollars)	1988	1987	1986
5.7% Debentures, due annually June 1, 1990 to 1992.	$ 5.4	$ 5.4	$ 5.4
8⅝% Debentures, due annually November 1, 1991 to 1995.	15.1	15.1	15.1
8⅜% Promissory Notes, due June 4, 1992.	49.0	47.3	37.5
5.906% Term Loan, due June 21, 1993.	52.1	51.9	41.8
Capitalized lease obligations, due in varying amounts through 1999. . . .	13.8	18.5	22.0
Other, due in varying amounts through 2008.	79.8	72.1	35.9
	$215.2	$210.3	$157.7

Long-term debt at December 31, 1988 was payable:

Years Ending December 31, (in millions of dollars)	
1990.	$ 15.1
1991.	24.8
1992.	99.6
1993.	60.4
1994.	5.2
1995 and later.	10.1
	$215.2

The company has short-term lines of credit with domestic and foreign banks. At December 31, 1988, the unused portions of these lines of credit were approximately $185 million and $378 million, respectively.

Note 7   Stockholders' Equity

On May 5, 1987, the stockholders approved a two-for-one split of the company's common stock, an increase in the authorized shares of common stock from 250 million to 750 million shares and a change in the par value of the common stock from $1.00 per share par value to $.10 per share par value. In the accompanying financial statements all per common share amounts have been adjusted to reflect the stock split.

Each share of the company's preferred stock is convertible into 4.24 shares of common stock and is callable at the company's option. The reductions in the number of issued shares of preferred stock in 1988, 1987 and 1986 were due to conversions into common stock.

Changes in issued capital shares were:

	Common Stock		
	1988	1987	1986
Balance, January 1. . .	287,851,825	143,117,706	142,006,336
Two-for-one split. . . .	—	143,117,706	—

Exercise of options,
    rights and
    warrants. . . . .
	1,721,075	1,498,323	1,023,538

Conversions of preferred stock. . . .	59,460	118,090	87,832
Balance, December 31.	289,632,360	287,851,825	143,117,706

Changes in capital in excess of par value of stock were:

(in millions of dollars)	1988	1987	1986
Balance, January 1..............	$275.8	$137.4	$113.1
Transferred from common stock in connection with two-for-one split and change in par value.........	—	114.5	—
Exercise of options, rights and warrants..................	36.9	23.9	24.3
Balance, December 31...........	$312.7	$275.8	$137.4

Under the 1983 Stock Option Plan, officers and key employees may be granted options to purchase the company's common stock at 100% of the market price on the day the option is granted. Additionally, the plan provides for the granting of stock appreciation rights whereby the grantee may surrender exercisable options and receive common stock and/or cash measured by the excess of the market price of the common stock over the option exercise price.

At December 31, 1988, 26,020,146 shares of common stock were reserved for issuance upon exercise of options and warrants and conversions of preferred stock.

Stock option transactions during 1988 were:

	Shares of Common Stock	
	Available for Option	Under Option
Balance, January 1..............	15,037,757	9,259,455
Granted.....................	(1,188,765)	1,188,765
Exercised...................	—	(1,895,152)
Surrendered.................	—	(430,384)
Lapsed.....................	99,632	(175,956)
Balance, December 31...........	13,948,624	7,946,728

At December 31, 1988, there were exercisable options outstanding to purchase 5,459,029 shares of common stock at prices ranging from $7.92 to $53.16 per share.

There were 236,748 warrants at December 31, 1988 to acquire shares of the company's common stock at an exercise price ranging from $16.42 to $18.83 per share, expiring in 1994 or following the purchase of certain limited partnership interests.

Attached to each outstanding share of the company's common stock is one Right. The Rights will be exercisable if a person or group acquires beneficial interest of 20% or more of the company's outstanding common stock, or commences a tender or exchange offer for 30% or more of the company's outstanding common stock. Each Right will entitle stockholders to buy one one-thousandth of a share of a new series of participating preferred stock of the company at an exercise price of $200. The Rights will expire on December 18, 1997. In the event of certain merger, sale of assets or self-dealing transactions each Right will then entitle its holder to acquire shares having a value of twice the Right's exercise price. The company may redeem the Rights at $.01 per Right at any time until the 15th day following public announcement that a 20% position has been acquired.

Note 8   Provision for Income Taxes

The components of earnings before income taxes were:

Year Ended December 31, (in millions of dollars)	1988	1987	1986
U.S.....................	$ 926.6	$ 873.5	$712.3
Non-U.S.................	358.7	244.0	218.1
	$ 1,285.3	$1,117.5	$930.4

The provision for income taxes consisted of:

Year Ended December 31, (in millions of dollars)	1988	1987	1986
Current:			
U.S. Federal..............	$262.2	$298.9	$212.2
Non-U.S................	167.5	103.0	64.9
State and local............	47.0	37.8	27.6
	476.7	439.7	304.7
Deferred:			
U.S....................	(2.1)	(28.7)	17.6
Non-U.S................	(18.3)	(3.1)	18.6
	(20.4)	(31.8)	36.2
	$456.3	$407.9	$340.9

Income taxes paid during the year were $491.5 million, $434.5 million and $310.1 million for 1988, 1987 and 1986, respectively.

The company's provision for income taxes for 1988, 1987 and 1986 was different than the amount computed by applying the statutory United States Federal income tax rate to earnings before income taxes, as a result of the following:

	% of Earnings Before Income Taxes		
	1988	1987	1986
U.S. statutory rate.............	34.0%	40.0%	46.0%
Effect of earnings not subject to income tax at the U.S. rate.......	(.1)	(3.9)	(7.9)
State and local taxes............	2.4	2.0	1.6
Other.....................	(.8)	(1.6)	(3.1)
	35.5%	36.5%	36.6%

Prepaid taxes were $120.1 million, $109.5 million and $92.2 million at December 31, 1988, 1987 and 1986, respectively. The deferred income tax liability, included in Other Liabilities, was $88.5 million, $72.4 million and $87.1 million at December 31, 1988, 1987 and 1986, respectively.

The company has settled with the Internal Revenue Service its United States Federal income tax returns through 1982.

Research and investment tax credits of approximately $7.0 million in 1988 and in 1987 and $14.0 million in 1986 are reflected as a reduction of income taxes in the year in which the credits are allowed for tax purposes.

United States Federal income taxes have not been provided on substantially all of the unremitted earnings of non-U.S. subsidiaries, since it is management's practice and intent to reinvest such earnings in the operations of these subsidiaries. In those instances where it is the intent to remit earnings, United States Federal income taxes have been provided to the extent they are not offset by foreign tax credits. The total amount of the net unremitted earnings of non-U.S. subsidiaries was approximately $725 million at December 31, 1988.

Note 9   Segment Information

The company's products are reported in four industry segments as follows:

Pharmaceutical and Medical Products — prescription medicines, mainly antibiotics, which comprise about thirty percent of the segment's sales, anti-cancer, cardiovascular and central nervous system drugs, orthopaedic implants, surgical instruments, and other pharmaceutical and medical products.

Non-Prescription Health Products — infant formulas and other nutritional products, which comprise about sixty percent of the segment's sales, analgesics, cough/cold remedies and skin care products.

Toiletries and Beauty Aids — haircoloring and hair care preparations, which comprise about sixty percent of the segment's sales, deodorants and anti-perspirants, and beauty appliances.

Household Products — household cleansing, specialty and laundry products.

Industry Segments	Net Sales			Profit			Year-End Assets		
(in millions of dollars)	1988	1987	1986	1988	1987	1986	1988	1987	1986
Pharmaceutical and Medical Products	$2,508.8	$2,217.1	$1,961.7	$ 565.2	$ 484.2	$396.5	$1,813.0	$1,654.7	$1,574.2
Non-Prescription Health Products	1,632.9	1,504.1	1,377.3	470.8	404.5	346.5	634.0	553.8	550.0
Toiletries and Beauty Aids	1,288.2	1,188.9	1,057.5	222.8	199.4	181.0	522.7	489.2	484.2
Household Products	542.6	491.1	439.4	80.9	71.3	67.1	191.5	176.5	174.0
Net sales, operating profit and assets	$5,972.5	$5,401.2	$4,835.9	$1,339.7	$1,159.4	$991.1	$3,161.2	$2,874.2	$2,782.4

Geographic Areas	Net Sales			Profit			Year-End Assets		
(in millions of dollars)	1988	1987	1986	1988	1987	1986	1988	1987	1986
United States	$4,221.8	$3,949.8	$3,594.8	$1,026.1	$ 897.7	$778.3	$2,029.0	$1,790.1	$1,821.5
Europe, Mid-East and Africa	955.7	763.1	653.1	166.7	136.8	106.4	591.1	578.7	466.7
Other Western Hemisphere	541.6	485.5	432.1	113.5	97.2	85.0	293.2	273.4	279.1
Pacific	611.8	505.3	415.8	78.2	59.3	31.5	402.0	387.5	353.4
Inter-area eliminations	(358.4)	(302.5)	(259.9)	(44.8)	(31.6)	(10.1)	(154.1)	(155.5)	(138.3)
Net sales, operating profit and assets	$5,972.5	$5,401.2	$4,835.9	1,339.7	1,159.4	991.1	3,161.2	2,874.2	2,782.4
Unallocated expenses and other assets				(54.4)	(41.9)	(60.7)	2,028.5	1,857.8	1,400.6
Earnings before income taxes and total assets				$1,285.3	$1,117.5	$930.4	$5,189.7	$4,732.0	$4,183.0

Industry Segments	Capital Expenditures			Depreciation		
(in millions of dollars)	1988	1987	1986	1988	1987	1986
Pharmaceutical and Medical Products	$165.5	$ 91.9	$125.4	$ 61.5	$ 55.9	$ 50.1
Non-Prescription Health Products	31.2	36.7	42.8	26.8	25.3	22.6
Toiletries and Beauty Aids	24.4	16.2	19.6	17.4	17.3	15.8
Household Products	12.3	10.6	14.6	8.5	7.0	6.2
Identifiable industry totals	233.4	155.4	202.4	114.2	105.5	94.7
Other	18.9	34.6	19.5	13.7	10.4	10.2
Consolidated totals	$252.3	$190.0	$221.9	$127.9	$115.9	$104.9

Unallocated expenses consist principally of general administrative expenses and net interest income. Other assets are principally cash and cash equivalents, time deposits and marketable securities. Inter-area sales are usually billed at or above manufacturing costs. Inter-area sales principally include $151.7 million, $115.1 million and $96.1 million in 1988, 1987 and 1986, respectively, attributable to the United States and $173.2 million, $150.9 million and $129.0 million in 1988, 1987 and 1986, respectively, attributable to Europe, Mid-East and Africa.

Net assets relating to operations outside the United States amount to approximately $841 million, $717 million and $614 million at December 31, 1988, 1987 and 1986, respectively.

Note 10   Retirement Benefit Plans

The company and certain of its subsidiaries have defined benefit pension plans for regular full-time employees. The company adopted the provisions of Statement of Financial Accounting Standards No. 87, Employer's Accounting for Pensions ("FAS 87"), for all U.S. and certain non-U.S. pension plans in 1986 and additionally for all non-U.S. plans in 1987. The accounting change in 1986 had the effect of reducing pension expense by $23.1 million resulting in net pension income of $15.9 million.

Cost for the company's defined benefit plans includes the following components:

Year Ended December 31, (in millions of dollars)	1988	1987	1986
Service cost—benefits earned during the year.	$ 35.5	$ 41.1	$ 20.9
Interest cost on projected benefit obligation.	58.2	54.0	40.1
Actual earnings on plan assets.	(71.9)	(55.3)	(89.4)
Net amortization and deferral.	(18.0)	(28.7)	7.4
Cost of non-U.S. pension plans which have not adopted FAS 87.	—	—	5.1
Net pension expense (income).	$ 3.8	$ 11.1	$(15.9)

The projected benefit obligation assumes a discount rate of 9½% in 1988 and in 1987 and 8½% in 1986 and a 5% rate of compensation increase in each year. The expected long-term rate of return on plan assets is 12% in 1988, 1987 and 1986. The funded status of the plans is as follows:

December 31, (in millions of dollars)	1988	1987	1986
Actuarial present value of accumulated benefit obligations:			
Vested.	$(483.5)	$(425.9)	$(378.2)
Non-vested.	(52.8)	(48.5)	(49.6)
	$(536.3)	$(474.4)	$(427.8)
Total projected benefit obligation.	$(704.3)	$(621.2)	$(549.5)
Plan assets at fair value.	750.5	704.6	659.6
Excess of plan assets over projected benefit obligation.	46.2	83.4	110.1
Unamortized net assets at adoption.	(147.6)	(160.2)	(176.3)
Unrecognized prior service cost.	65.1	68.3	—
Unrecognized net losses.	52.5	19.0	83.2
Prepaid pension cost.	$ 16.2	$ 10.5	$ 17.0

General plan improvements granted during 1987 are reflected in the 1987 unrecognized prior service cost and in the increases in other costs and liabilities over 1986.

Plan benefits are based primarily on years of service and on average compensation during the last years of employment. Plan assets consist principally of equity securities, fixed income securities and group annuity contracts.

The company provides medical and life insurance benefits for certain retired domestic employees who reach normal retirement age while working for the company. The cost of retiree health care and life insurance benefits is expensed as paid and totalled $5.4 million, $4.5 million and $4.0 million in 1988, 1987 and 1986, respectively.

Note 11   Leases

Minimum rental commitments under all noncancellable operating leases, primarily real estate, in effect at December 31, 1988 were:

Years Ending December 31, (in millions of dollars)	
1989.	$ 72.2
1990.	61.7
1991.	49.3
1992.	40.8
1993.	35.1
Later years.	197.0
Total minimum payments.	456.1
Less total minimum sublease rentals.	53.9
Net minimum rental commitments.	$402.2

Operating lease rental expense (net of sublease rental income of $9.4 million in 1988, $8.7 million in 1987 and $8.4 million in 1986) was $76.4 million in 1988, $72.1 million in 1987 and $62.5 million in 1986.

Report of Management

Management is responsible for the accompanying consolidated financial statements, which are prepared in accordance with generally accepted accounting principles. In management's opinion, the consolidated financial statements present fairly the company's financial position, results of operations and cash flows. In addition, information and representations included in the company's Annual Report are consistent with the financial statements.

The company maintains a system of internal accounting policies, procedures and controls intended to provide reasonable assurance, at appropriate cost, that transactions are executed in accordance with company authorization, are properly recorded and reported in the financial statements, and that assets are adequately safeguarded. The company's internal auditors continually evaluate the adequacy and effectiveness of this system of internal accounting policies, procedures and controls.

The Audit Committee of the Board of Directors is comprised solely of non-employee directors and is responsible for overseeing and monitoring the quality of the company's accounting and auditing practices. The Audit Committee meets several times during the year with management, the internal auditors and the independent accountants to discuss audit activities, internal controls and financial reporting matters. The internal auditors and the independent accountants have full and free access to the Audit Committee.

The appointment of Price Waterhouse as the company's independent accountants by the Board of Directors was ratified by the stockholders. Price Waterhouse's Report to the Board of Directors and Stockholders of Bristol-Myers Company appears on this page.

Report of Independent Accountants

To the Board of Directors
and Stockholders of
Bristol-Myers Company

In our opinion, the accompanying consolidated balance sheet and the related consolidated statements of earnings and retained earnings and of cash flows present fairly, in all material respects, the financial position of Bristol-Myers Company and its subsidiaries at December 31, 1988, 1987 and 1986, and the results of their operations and their cash flows for the years then ended in conformity with generally accepted accounting principles. These financial statements are the responsibility of the company's management; our responsibility is to express an opinion on these financial statements based on our audits. We conducted our audits of these statements in accordance with generally accepted auditing standards which require that we plan and perform the audit to obtain reasonable assurance about whether the financial statements are free of material misstatement. An audit includes examining, on a test basis, evidence supporting the amounts and disclosures in the financial statements, assessing the accounting principles used and significant estimates made by management, and evaluating the overall financial statement presentation. We believe that our audits provide a reasonable basis for the opinion expressed above.

Price Waterhouse

153 East 53rd Street
New York, New York 10022

January 24, 1989

Ten-Year Financial Summary

(in millions of dollars except per share amounts)	1988	1987	1986
Operating Results			
Net Sales	$5,972.5	$5,401.2	$4,835.9
Expenses:			
Cost of products sold	1,803.6	1,678.8	1,515.2
Marketing, selling and administrative	1,606.5	1,464.0	1,303.0
Advertising and product promotion	978.8	918.7	820.3
Research and development	394.1	341.7	311.1
Other	(95.8)	(119.5)	(44.1)
	4,687.2	4,283.7	3,905.5
Earnings Before Income Taxes	1,285.3	1,117.5	930.4
Provision for income taxes	456.3	407.9	340.9
Net Earnings	$ 829.0	$ 709.6	$ 589.5
Dividends paid on common and preferred stock	$ 483.8	$ 402.1	$ 300.6
Earnings per common share	2.88	2.47	2.07
Dividends per common share	1.68	1.40	1.06
Financial Position at December 31			
Current assets	$3,565.8	$3,263.7	$2,758.6
Property, plant and equipment—net	1,249.1	1,141.9	1,070.0
Total assets	5,189.7	4,732.0	4,183.0
Current liabilities	1,164.0	1,099.4	1,015.2
Long-term debt	215.2	210.3	157.7
Total liabilities	1,642.7	1,502.7	1,347.4
Stockholders' equity	3,547.0	3,229.3	2,835.6
Average common shares outstanding (in millions)	287.9	287.1	285.2
Book value per common share	$ 12.31	$ 11.21	$ 9.89

Bristol-Myers Company

1985	1984	1983	1982	1981	1980	1979
$4,444.8	$4,189.4	$3,917.0	$3,599.9	$3,496.7	$3,158.3	$2,752.8
1,469.9	1,409.1	1,385.8	1,299.0	1,327.7	1,195.9	1,059.3
1,191.9	1,106.2	1,049.7	1,003.7	949.7	859.9	726.4
775.8	743.8	651.4	567.1	555.3	513.2	457.6
272.6	222.6	191.1	164.2	144.7	128.6	103.0
(111.7)	(68.9)	(51.0)	(39.2)	(32.2)	(30.9)	(16.8)
3,598.5	3,412.8	3,227.0	2,994.8	2,945.2	2,666.7	2,329.5
846.3	776.6	690.0	605.1	551.5	491.6	423.3
332.3	308.1	283.5	257.4	246.1	221.0	191.8
$ 514.0	$ 468.5	$ 406.5	$ 347.7	$ 305.4	$ 270.6	$ 231.5
$ 249.6	$ 205.7	$ 158.6	$ 137.6	$ 120.1	$ 105.0	$ 93.1
1.82	1.67	1.46	1.27	1.13	1.02	.88
.90½	.75	.58⅛	.50⅞	44½	39	34⅝
$2,545.5	$2,200.4	$2,138.1	$1,953.2	$1,776.9	$1,587.7	$1,380.9
934.9	798.2	706.2	655.6	583.7	484.9	407.5
3,770.4	3,288.0	3,049.9	2,770.0	2,497.6	2,209.4	1,922.0
1,008.4	864.4	873.4	835.0	744.9	669.2	563.7
116.1	104.9	97.3	114.4	102.9	111.9	120.1
1,283.5	1,107.0	1,104.0	1,044.7	925.5	837.5	728.9
2,486.9	2,181.0	1,945.9	1,725.3	1,572.1	1,371.9	1,193.1
282.6	280.2	277.6	272.8	268.6	262.8	261.4
$ 8.74	$ 7.72	$ 6.92	$ 6.19	$ 5.63	$ 4.97	$ 4.31

Quarterly Financial Data (Unaudited)

(in millions of dollars except per share amounts)	Net Sales	Gross Profit	Net Earnings	Earnings Per Share
1988:				
First Quarter ...	$1,520.0	$1,061.1	$210.6	$.73
Second Quarter..	1,456.8	1,015.6	190.5	.66
Third Quarter...	1,516.2	1,052.8	232.3	.81
Fourth Quarter..	1,479.5	1,039.4	195.6	.68
Year	$5,972.5	$4,168.9	$829.0	
1987:				
First Quarter ...	$1,347.9	$ 928.7	$173.9	$.61
Second Quarter..	1,314.3	918.9	161.5	.56
Third Quarter...	1,378.3	945.8	200.2	.70
Fourth Quarter..	1,360.7	929.0	174.0	.61
Year	$5,401.2	$3,722.4	$709.6	

Market Prices

Bristol-Myers common and preferred stocks are traded on the New York Stock Exchange and the Pacific Stock Exchange (symbol: BMY). A quarterly summary of the high and low market prices, as reported by The Wall Street Journal, is presented below:

	1988		1987	
	High	Low	High	Low
Common:				
First Quarter	$ 45⅞	$ 39¾	$ 55¹³⁄₁₆	$ 41⁷⁄₁₆
Second Quarter ..	43⅝	38⅛	53¹⁵⁄₁₆	46⅜
Third Quarter ...	44⅞	39¼	54⅛	46½
Fourth Quarter ..	46½	41⅜	53½	28¼

	1988		1987	
	High	Low	High	Low
Preferred:				
First Quarter	$179	$173	$207	$180½
Second Quarter ..	172	167¾	217¾	202¼
Third Quarter ...	185	172	228½	211
Fourth Quarter ..	190	180	200	169

Dividends

The company has increased its dividends on common stock in 1988 for the sixteenth consecutive year. Dividend payments per share in 1988 and 1987 were:

	Common		Preferred	
	1988	1987	1988	1987
First Quarter	$ .42	$ .35	$ .50	$ .50
Second Quarter	.42	.35	.50	.50
Third Quarter	.42	.35	.50	.50
Fourth Quarter	.42	.35	.50	.50
Year	$1.68	$1.40	$2.00	$2.00

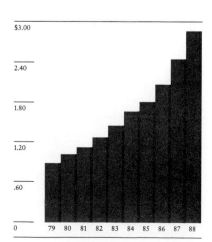

Earnings per
Common Share

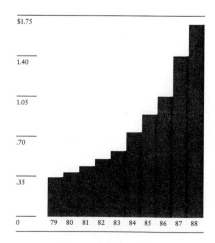

Dividends per
Common Share

Part 1
An overview of the statements and the related notes, schedules, and reports

Published financial statements include not only the statements themselves, but also notes, reports on the statements by the company's management and by the independent auditors, a 10-year summary of key financial statistics, and schedules providing data about quarterly operating results, market prices of the Company's stock, and dividends per share. Our purpose in Part 1 of this comprehensive problem is to acquaint you with the form and content of these materials.

Instructions

Answer each of the following questions and briefly explain where in the statements, notes, reports by management or by the auditors, or special schedules you located the information used in your answer.

a The comparative financial statements include income statements, balance sheets, statements of retained earnings, and statements of cash flow for three years. Were all of these statements audited by a firm of independent accountants? Name the firm that audited some or all of these statements.

b Who is responsible for the content of the financial statements, management or the auditors?

c Write out the total dollar amount of the Company's net sales for 1988 using words rather than numbers.

d What was the amount of net earnings (net income) earned during the second quarter of 1988? (Express in numbers.)

e What was the book value of the Company's stock at December 31, *1982?*

f What was the amount of per-share dividend on common stock paid during the second quarter of 1987?

g In the valuation of inventories, does the Company use LIFO, FIFO, or some other method?

h What was the highest per-share market price at which the Company's common stock sold during 1987? During 1988?

i The Company shows its net sales, operating profit, and assets subdivided into four industry segments. Identify these segments.

j Compute the percentage change in the amount of the Company's net sales made in the combined "Europe, Mid-East and Africa" geographic area from 1986 to 1988.

Part 2
Evaluation of credit worthiness

Assume that in early 1989 you are the credit manager of a company which sells chemicals used in the manufacture of medical supplies. Bristol-Myers Company wants to make credit purchases from your company of between $10 million and $20 million per month, with payment due in 60 days.

Instructions

a As part of your credit investigation, compute the following from Bristol-Myers' financial statements: (Follow the company's practice of stating dollar amounts in millions, carried to one decimal-place.)

(1) Current ratio at December 31, 1988. (Express as a decimal and round to one decimal place; e.g., 2.1 to 1.)

(2) Quick ratio at December 31, 1988. (Round as in item 1, above.)

(3) Working capital at December 31, 1988. (Express in thousands of dollars.)

(4) Inventory turnover in 1988 (rounded to one decimal place), and the average number of days required to sell the inventory (rounded to the nearest day, using your turnover figure which was rounded to one decimal place).

(5) Accounts receivable turnover in 1988 and the average number of days required to collect accounts receivable. (Assume that all net sales are made on account; round as in item **4,** above.)

(6) The company's operating cycle in 1988, stated in days.

(7) The excess (or shortfall) in 1988 of the Company's *net cash provided by operating activities* over (below) the sum of (a) cash paid to acquire fixed assets, and (b) dividends paid to stockholders.

b Does Bristol-Myers have any unused *lines of credit*—that is, an ability to borrow from banks to meet short-term cash obligations?

c Your company assigns each customer one of the four credit ratings listed below. Assign a credit rating to Bristol-Myers Company and write a memorandum explaining your decision. (In your memorandum, you may use any of your computations in parts **a** or **b,** and may refer to other information in Bristol-Myers' financial statements.)

Possible Credit Ratings

A *Outstanding.* Little or no risk of inability to pay. For customers in this category, we fill any reasonable order, without imposing a credit limit. The customer's credit is reevaluated annually.

B *Good.* Customer has good debt paying ability, but is assigned a credit limit which is reviewed every six months. Orders above the established credit limit are accepted only on a cash basis.

C *Marginal.* Customer appears sound, but credit should be extended only on a 30-day basis with a relatively low credit limit. Credit status and credit limit are reevaluated every 90 days.

D *Unacceptable.* Customer does not qualify for credit.

**Part 3
Analysis of
common stock**

Assume that you are an investment advisor who publishes a monthly newsletter with recommendations on buying and selling common stocks. One of the common stocks you will evaluate this month is Bristol-Myers Company. It is now early 1989, and the price of the company's stock is *$43.20* per share. (Stocks are ordinarily traded at prices stated to an eighth of a dollar. Thus, the price of Bristol-Myers when this was written was 43¼. However, we have used a price of $43.20 to facilitate certain computations.)

*Extra
credit.*

Instructions

a As a starting point in your investigation, compute the following. (Follow the company's practice of stating all dollar amounts in millions, except for per-share amounts. Round percentage computations to 1/10 of 1%.)

(1) Price-earning ratio. (Use 1988 earnings and the current market price of $43.20 per share.)

(2) Dividend yield on the common stock at its current market price.

(3) Return on average total assets in 1988. (Use Earnings before Income Taxes ($1,285.3 million) as "operating income" in this computation.)

(4) Return on average total stockholder's equity in 1988. (Express net income as a percentage of average total stockholders' equity. We will ignore the claims of preferred stockholders, as these claims are not material in dollar amount.)

(5) Equity ratio.

(6) Prepare trend percentages for (a) net sales, (b) net income, and (c) net earnings per share for the three years from 1986 through 1988. Use 1986 as the base year, in which each statistic will be 100%. (Round computations to the nearest 1 percent.)

b In recent years, Bristol-Myers has consistently followed a policy of increasing each year the cash dividend per share paid to holders of the common stock. Write a memorandum evaluating the company's ability to continue this policy. As a basis for this memorandum, review the trends in the company's net income and earnings per share, and also review the statement of cash flows.

c Write a brief memorandum on the topic of leverage as it relates to Bristol-Myers. Does the company make extensive use of long-term debt financing? Assuming that long-term interest rates are about 10%, would the use of long-term debt as a means of financing future growth be desirable from the viewpoint of common stockholders?

d Write a brief memorandum on the "quality" of the company's earnings. As a basis for this memorandum, review trends in the comparative income statements and in the 10-year summary, and also in the segment information contained in note 9.

e Write a statement for your newsletter in which you recommend that your clients take one of the following actions with respect to Bristol-Myers Company's common stock:

Buy (Your most positive recommendation; you think the market price of the stock will go up.)

Sell (Your most negative recommendation; you feel that the stock is overpriced and will fall in value.)

Hold (A relatively neutral position: you feel that the stock is priced at a fair value with good but not exceptional prospects.)

Explain the reasoning behind your recommendation.

In addition to the information developed in other parts of this problem, your recommendation should consider the following facts about the economic environment in early 1989:

The stock market has been rising steadily, but not dramatically, since November 1988.

Interest rates have been increasing over the last nine months, but now appear to have peaked. However, you do not expect a significant decline in interest rates for at least several months.

Dividend yields for growth-oriented companies range from zero to 5%; for slow-growth companies, yields are from 6 to 10%.

f Look up the current price of Bristol-Myers Company common stock in the financial pages of a newspaper. How did your recommendation work out in the long run?

PART 7

Managerial Accounting: Cost Accounting Systems

The next two chapters provide the basic foundation for our study of managerial accounting. In these chapters, we will show how accounting systems can measure the cost of manufacturing specific products and of performing specific services.

21 Introduction to Managerial Accounting; Accounting for Manufacturing Operations

22 Cost Accounting Systems

Introduction to Managerial Accounting: Accounting for Manufacturing Operations

Chapter 21 is the first of six chapters emphasizing the specialized use of accounting information by managers. In the opening pages, we contrast managerial accounting with financial accounting. The major purpose of this chapter, however, is to introduce accounting concepts relating to manufacturing activities. We explain the nature of manufacturing costs, with emphasis upon the idea that these are "product costs," not "period costs." Next, we illustrate the "flow" of manufacturing costs through perpetual inventory records. A distinction is drawn between direct and indirect manufacturing costs, and the use of an overhead application rate is explained and illustrated. Finally, we illustrate the schedule of cost of finished goods manufactured, which summarizes the relationships between manufacturing costs and completed units of product.

After studying this chapter you should be able to meet these Learning Objectives:

1 Distinguish between the fields of managerial accounting and financial accounting.

2 Describe the three basic types of manufacturing cost.

3 Distinguish between product costs and period costs and explain how product costs are offset against revenue.

4 Describe how manufacturing costs "flow" through perpetual inventory accounts.

5 Distinguish between direct and indirect manufacturing costs.

6 Explain the purpose of an overhead application rate and the importance of basing this rate upon a significant "cost driver."

7 Prepare a schedule of cost of finished goods manufactured.

INTRODUCTION TO MANAGERIAL ACCOUNTING

Objective 1
Distinguish between the fields of managerial accounting and financial accounting.

In preceding chapters we have emphasized the topic of financial accounting. The term *financial accounting* refers to the preparation and use of accounting information describing the financial position and operating results of a business entity. Financial accounting serves as the basis for the preparation of both financial statements and income tax returns. Because financial statements are used by outsiders, such as creditors, stockholders, and potential investors, the information in these statements is presented in conformity with *generally accepted accounting principles.* Although income tax rules differ somewhat from generally accepted accounting principles, there are many similarities between these two sets of reporting standards.

Beginning with this chapter, we shall shift our emphasis toward the field of managerial accounting. *Managerial accounting* involves the preparation and use of accounting information designed to assist managers in planning and controlling the operations of the business, and in decision making. In short, managerial accounting information is designed to meet the needs of *insiders,* rather than decision makers *outside* the business entity.

Since managerial accounting reports are used exclusively by management, their content is *not* governed by generally accepted accounting principles or income tax rules. Rather, managerial accounting reports should contain whatever information *best suits the needs of the decision maker.* The greatest challenge to managerial accountants is providing managers with the information that is most relevant to a particular business decision.

The diagram on page 853 compares the basic characteristics of financial and managerial accounting. Notice that both types of accounting information are developed within the same accounting system. Thus, the accounting system of a business should be able to provide the special types of information needed by management, as well as meet the company's financial reporting requirements.

Interdisciplinary Nature of Managerial Accounting

In meeting the information needs of management, managerial accountants often must obtain estimates and data from experts in fields other than accounting. For example, many managerial accounting reports are forecasts of future operating results. Forecasting the sales of a multinational corporation, however, may involve marketing research, assumptions about future economic conditions, an understanding of international trade agreements, and familiarity with numerous foreign cultures. Managerial accountants do not need personal expertise in each of these areas, but they must have a broad understanding of the company's business environment.

To encourage a professional level of training and competence for managerial accountants, the Institute of Certified Management Accountants sponsors a Certified Management Accounting (CMA) program. To become a *CMA,* an individual must meet educational and experience requirements, and also pass a rigorous five-part examination.

Our Approach to Managerial Accounting

In this introductory textbook, we divide our discussion of managerial accounting into three broad categories: (1) *cost accounting* (with an emphasis on determining the cost of manufactured products), (2) the use of accounting infor-

THE ACCOUNTING SYSTEM

FINANCIAL ACCOUNTING	MANAGERIAL ACCOUNTING
Purpose	**Purpose**
To provide a wide variety of decision makers with useful information about the financial position and operating results of a business entity.	To provide managers with information useful in planning and controlling business operations, and in making managerial decisions.
Types of Reports	**Types of Reports**
Financial statements, income tax returns, and special reports, such as loan applications and reports to regulatory agencies.	Many different types of reports, depending upon the nature of the business and the specific information needs of management.
Standards for Presentation	**Standards for Presentation**
In financial statements, generally accepted accounting principles. In income tax returns, tax regulations.	No specific rules; whatever information is most relevant to the needs of management.
Reporting Entity	**Reporting Entity**
Usually the company viewed as a whole.	Usually a subdivision of the business, such as a department, a product line, or a type of activity.
Time Periods Covered	**Time Periods Covered**
Usually a year, quarter, or month. Most reports focus upon completed periods. Emphasis is placed on the current (latest) period, with prior periods often shown for comparison.	Any period: year, quarter, month, week, day, even a work shift. Some reports are historical in nature; others focus on estimates of results expected in future periods.

Users of the Information	Users of the Information
Outsiders as well as managers. For financial statements, these outsiders include stockholders, creditors, prospective investors, tax and regulatory authorities, and the general public. Income tax returns normally go only to tax authorities.	Management (different reports to different managers). Managerial accounting reports usually are not distributed to outsiders.

mation in *planning and controlling* business operations, and (3) *tailoring accounting information* for use in specific managerial decisions. These closely related topics provide an overview of the nature and use of managerial accounting information. Many topics, however, remain to be explored; the study of managerial accounting may be continued throughout a professional career.

■ **Cost Accounting** In order to plan and control the activities of a business, management must first have information about the costs involved in performing different business operations. This information about costs will help management in determining whether specific activities are profitable and whether the various departments within the business are operating efficiently. The accounting concepts and practices for measuring the cost of performing different business activities and of manufacturing various products are called *cost accounting.*

Let us consider, for example, a company that manufactures several different products. The company's accounting system should provide information about the cost of manufacturing *each product,* and also the cost of conducting other business activities, such as operating the accounting, personnel, and marketing departments. We will discuss accounting for the costs of manufactured products in the remainder of this chapter and in Chapter 22. Measuring the cost of performing other business activities will be discussed in Chapter 24.

■ **Planning and Control**   The term *planning* refers to setting objectives or goals for future performance. Often, these objectives are stated in terms of dollar amounts, such as achieving "net sales of $10 million in the coming year."

Control refers to monitoring the extent to which these planned objectives are being accomplished, and to taking corrective action when actual results differ from the plan. In Chapters 23, 24, and 25, we focus upon the use of accounting information in planning and controlling business operations.

■ **Tailoring Information to Specific Decisions**   Managerial accounting information often is collected and arranged to assist a particular manager in making a specific business decision. This process is explained and illustrated in Chapter 26.

Overlap of Managerial and Financial Accounting

It is useful to recognize that financial and managerial accounting are *not* two entirely separate disciplines. Financial accounting information is widely used in many managerial decisions. For example, managers daily use information about sales, expenses, and income taxes in many business decisions. However, managers also require additional information, such as revenue and expense broken down by department or by product line. Thus, much managerial accounting information is actually financial accounting information, rearranged to suit a particular managerial purpose.

As you progress through the remaining chapters, you should encounter many familiar accounting terms and concepts. However, you will also encounter new terms and concepts, as well as new ways of interpreting familiar accounting information.

ACCOUNTING FOR MANUFACTURING OPERATIONS

One area in which managerial and financial accounting overlap is in accounting for manufacturing activities. A merchandising company buys its inventory in a ready-to-sell condition. Therefore, the cost of this merchandise is simply the purchase price. A *manufacturing* company, on the other hand, *produces* the goods that it sells. In this case, the cost of the merchandise consists of various *manufacturing costs,* including the cost of the raw materials used in the production process, wages earned by factory workers, and all of the other costs of operating a factory.[1]

---

[1] Manufacturing costs are the cost of producing inventory, which is an asset. Therefore, these expenditures are termed *costs,* rather than *expenses.* Unexpired costs are assets; expired costs are expenses.

In a manufacturing company, manufacturing costs are of vital importance both to managerial and financial accountants. Managerial accountants must supply managers with prompt and reliable information about manufacturing costs for use in such decisions as:

■ What sales price must we charge for our products to earn a reasonable profit?

■ Can we produce this product cheaply enough to compete with Japanese imports?

■ Would it be less expensive for us to buy certain parts used in our products, or to manufacture these parts in our plant?

■ Should we install a more highly automated assembly line?

Financial accountants need information about manufacturing costs in order to determine the cost of a manufacturing company's inventories and its cost of goods sold.

Comparison of a Merchandising Company with a Manufacturer

The basic difference between the nature of the costs incurred by a merchandising company and a manufacturing business may be seen in the partial income statements illustrated below. (The treatment of selling expenses, general and administrative expenses, and income taxes expenses would be the same in both income statements.)

APEX MERCHANDISING COMPANY
Partial Income Statement
For the Year Ended December 31, 1991

Sales		$1,300,000
Cost of goods sold:		
Beginning inventory of merchandise	$150,000	
Net purchases	800,000	
Cost of goods available for sale	$950,000	
Less: Ending inventory of merchandise	168,000	
Cost of goods sold		782,000
Gross profit on sales		$ 518,000

ALLIED MANUFACTURING COMPANY
Partial Income Statement
For the Year Ended December 31, 1991

Sales		$1,300,000
Cost of goods sold:		
Beginning inventory of finished goods	$150,000	
Cost of finished goods manufactured	800,000	
Cost of goods available for sale	$950,000	
Less: Ending inventory of finished goods	168,000	
Cost of goods sold		782,000
Gross profit on sales		$ 518,000

Notice that in Allied Manufacturing Company's income statement, the "Cost of finished goods manufactured" replaces the "Net purchases" shown in the income statement of a merchandising company. The ***cost of finished goods manufactured*** represents all the manufacturing costs associated with units of product completed during the year.

Types of Manufacturing Costs

Objective 2
Describe the three basic types of manufacturing cost.

A typical manufacturing company buys raw materials and, through the efforts of factory workers and the use of machines, converts these materials into finished products. Manufacturing costs may be divided into three broad categories:

1 **Direct materials**—the cost of the materials and component parts used in the manufacture of the finished products.

2 **Direct labor costs**—wages and other payroll costs relating to employees who work directly on the goods being manufactured, either by hand or with tools.

3 **Manufacturing overhead**—a "catch-all" classification, including all manufacturing costs ***other than*** the costs of direct materials and direct labor. Examples include depreciation on machinery, supervisors' salaries, factory utilities, and equipment repairs.

Manufacturing costs are ***not*** regarded as expenses of the current period; rather they are costs of ***creating inventory.*** For this reason, manufacturing costs are often called ***inventoriable costs,*** or ***product costs.***

Product Costs and Period Costs

Objective 3
Distinguish between product costs and period costs and explain how product costs are offset against revenue.

The terms "product costs" and "period costs" are helpful in explaining the difference between manufacturing costs and expenses. ***Product costs*** are the costs of purchasing or manufacturing inventory. Thus, until the related goods are sold, product costs ***represent inventory,*** which is an asset. When the goods are sold, the product costs are deducted from revenue as the cost of goods sold.

Costs that are associated with time periods, rather than with the purchase or manufacture of inventory, are termed ***period costs.*** Period costs are charged directly to expense accounts on the assumption that the benefits are received in the same period as the cost is incurred. Period costs include all selling expenses, general and administrative expenses, interest expense, and income taxes expense—in short, all the items classified in an income statement as "expense."

The "flow" of product costs and of period costs through financial statements is shown in the diagram on the next page.

To illustrate this distinction, let us consider two costs which, on the surface, appear quite similar: depreciation on a direct materials warehouse and depreciation on a finished goods warehouse. Depreciation on the raw materials warehouse is a ***product cost,*** because this cost relates to the manufacturing process. Once the manufacturing process is complete and the goods are available for sale, however, storage costs are viewed as a selling expense. Thus, the depreciation on the finished goods warehouse is a ***period cost.***

Product costs become inventory

Period costs become expense

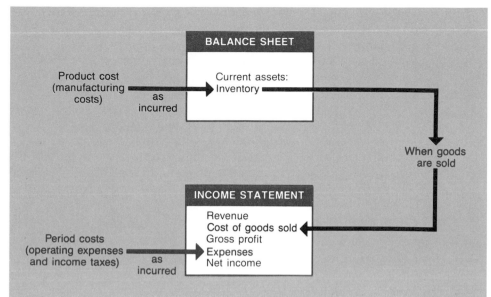

■ **Product Costs and the Matching Principle** The distinction between product costs and period costs may be explained by the *matching principle*— the idea that revenue should be offset by the costs incurred in generating that revenue. To illustrate, consider a real estate developer who starts construction on a tract of 10 homes in 1991. During the year, the developer spends $100,000 on each house ($1 million in total) in materials, construction wages, and overhead. At the end of 1991, all 10 houses are complete, but none has yet been sold. How much of the $1 million for construction costs should the developer recognize as expense in 1991?

The answer is *none*. These costs are not related to any revenue earned by the developer in 1991, but they are related to revenue that the developer will earn when the houses are sold. Therefore, at the end of 1991, the $1 million of product costs should appear in the developer's balance sheet as *inventory*. As each house is sold, $100,000 will be deducted from the sales revenue as the cost of goods sold. In this way, the developer's income statements in future periods will reflect properly both the revenue and the cost of each sale.

Inventories of a Manufacturing Business

In the preceding example, the houses all were completed by the end of 1991, so our developer's inventory consisted only of finished goods. Manufacturing companies, however, normally have *three types* of inventories:

1 **Materials inventory**—direct materials on hand and available for use in the manufacturing process.

2 **Work in process inventory**—partially completed goods upon which production activities have been started, but not yet completed.

3 **Finished goods inventory**—finished products available for sale to customers.

All three of these inventories are shown in the balance sheet at cost and are classified as current assets. The cost of the materials inventory is based upon purchase prices; the costs of the work in process inventory and of the finished goods inventory are based upon the manufacturing costs incurred in producing these units.

Manufacturing companies may use either a perpetual or a periodic inventory system. Perpetual systems have many advantages, however, such as providing managers with up to date information about the amounts of inventory on hand and the per-unit costs of manufacturing products. For these reasons, virtually all large manufacturing companies use perpetual inventory systems. Also, the flow of manufacturing costs through the inventory accounts and into the cost of goods sold is most easily illustrated in a perpetual inventory system. Therefore, we will assume the use of a perpetual inventory system in our discussion of manufacturing activities.

Flow of Costs Parallels the Physical Flow of Goods

Objective 4
Describe how manufacturing costs "flow" through perpetual inventory accounts.

When a perpetual inventory system is in use, the flow of manufacturing costs through the company's ledger accounts closely parallels the physical flow of goods through the production process. This relationship is illustrated in the diagram below. The green shaded boxes in the bottom portion of this diagram represent the ledger accounts used by a manufacturing company in accounting for manufacturing costs.

Accounting for Manufacturing Costs: An Illustration

The diagram below introduces six ledger accounts used in accounting for manufacturing activities: (1) Materials Inventory, (2) Direct Labor, (3) Manufacturing Overhead, (4) Work in Process Inventory, (5) Finished Goods Inventory, and (6) Cost of Goods Sold.

The manner in which manufacturing costs "flow through" these accounts is illustrated on page 859. The data in this illustration represent the manufac-

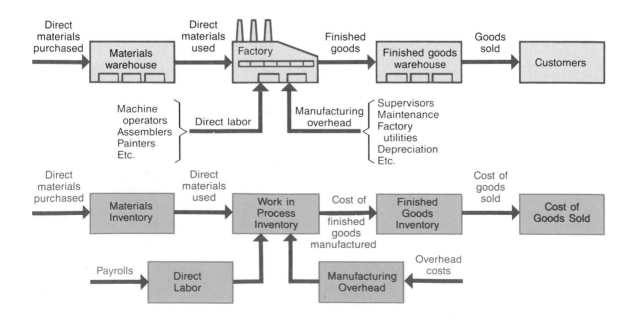

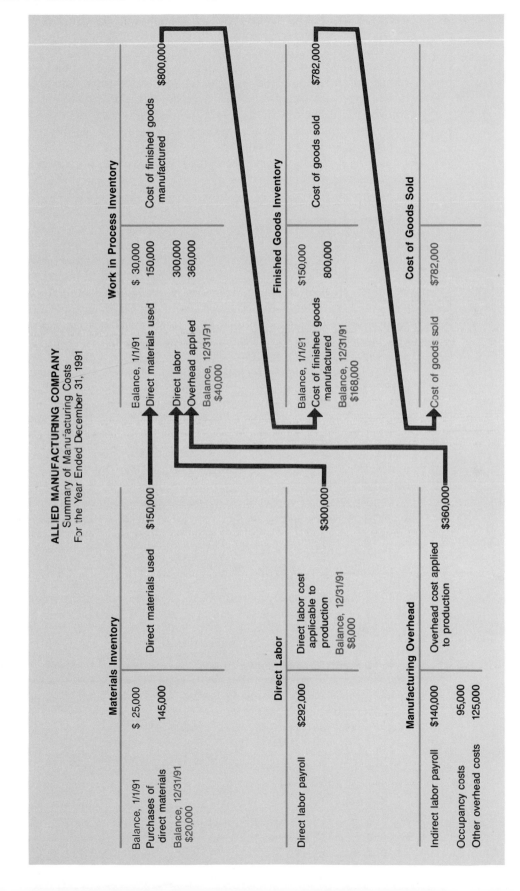

ALLIED MANUFACTURING COMPANY
Summary of Manufacturing Costs
For the Year Ended December 31, 1991

Materials Inventory

Balance, 1/1/91	$ 25,000	Direct materials used $150,000
Purchases of direct materials	145,000	
Balance, 12/31/91 $20,000		

Direct Labor

Direct labor payroll	$292,000	Direct labor cost applicable to production $300,000
		Balance, 12/31/91 $8,000

Manufacturing Overhead

Indirect labor payroll	$140,000	Overhead cost applied to production $360,000
Occupancy costs	95,000	
Other overhead costs	125,000	

Work in Process Inventory

Balance, 1/1/91	$ 30,000
Direct materials used	150,000
Direct labor	300,000
Overhead applied	360,000
Balance, 12/31/91 $40,000	

Cost of finished goods manufactured $800,000

Finished Goods Inventory

Balance, 1/1/91	$150,000
Cost of finished goods manufactured	800,000
Balance, 12/31/91 $168,000	

Cost of goods sold $782,000

Cost of Goods Sold

Cost of goods sold	$782,000

turing costs of Allied Manufacturing Company during 1991. (The debit and credit entries appearing in this illustration summarize all of the transactions recorded by Allied throughout the year.)

Our use of several colors in this illustration is intended to help you follow the flow of manufacturing costs through the accounts. The beginning balances in the three inventory accounts are shown in black. Manufacturing costs are shown in red, as are the arrows showing the transfers of these costs from one account to another. Account balances at year-end, which will appear in the company's financial statements, are shown in blue.

Let us now look more closely at the flow of manufacturing costs through these ledger accounts.

Materials Inventory

The Materials Inventory account is used to record purchases of direct materials and the use of these materials in the manufacturing process. *Direct materials* are those raw materials and component parts that become an integral part of the finished product, and that can be traced conveniently and directly into the quantity of finished goods manufactured. For example, the direct materials used by an automaker include sheet steel, glass, plastic, tires, transmissions, and batteries. The completed automobiles assembled from these components are the automaker's finished goods.

The terms *direct materials* and *finished goods* are defined from the viewpoint of each manufacturing company. For example, Ford Motor Company views tires as a direct material; the Goodyear Tire & Rubber Company, however, views tires as finished goods.

In a perpetual inventory system, purchases of direct materials are debited directly to the Materials Inventory account. As these materials are placed into production, their costs are transferred from the Materials Inventory account into the Work in Process Inventory account (debit Work in Process Inventory, credit Materials Inventory). The balance remaining in the Materials Inventory account at year-end represents the cost of direct materials on hand and ready for use.

Notice that the cost of direct materials is transferred to the Work in Process Inventory account when the materials are used, not when they are purchased. Differences between the cost of materials purchased during the period and the cost of materials used may be explained by the change during the period in the balance of the Materials Inventory account. These relationships are summarized below.[2]

Materials inventory, beginning of the year	$ 25,000
Add: Purchases of direct materials	145,000
Cost of direct materials available for use	$170,000
Less: Materials inventory, end of the year	20,000
Cost of direct materials used	$150,000

(Notice the similarity of this computation to the manner in which we compute the cost of goods sold.)

---

[2] This computation also may be used to determine the cost of materials used when a periodic inventory system is in use.

Some materials used in the production process cannot be traced conveniently into the finished goods manufactured. Examples include lubricating oil, welding materials, glue, and materials used in factory maintenance. These items are called *indirect materials* and are classified as part of manufacturing overhead.

Direct Labor

The Direct Labor account is used to record the cost of payrolls to direct workers and to assign this direct labor cost to the goods being manufactured.[3] Direct workers are those employees who work directly on the goods being manufactured, either by hand or with tools. They include, for example, machine operators, assemblers, and painters.

At each payroll date, the Direct Labor account is debited for the total amount of the direct labor payroll, with an offsetting credit to Cash. As the employees work on the goods being manufactured, the related labor costs are transferred from the Direct Labor account into the Work in Process Inventory account (debit Work in Process Inventory, credit Direct Labor).

In our T accounts on page 859, the flow of direct labor costs looks similar to the flow of direct materials costs. There is, however, one significant difference. Materials are purchased *before* they are used; therefore, the Materials Inventory account has a *debit* balance equal to the cost of unused materials on hand. The services of employees, however, are used before the employees are paid. Thus, the credits to the Direct Labor account are recorded *throughout* the payroll period, but the debits are not recorded until the *end* of the payroll period. If the balance sheet date falls between payroll dates, the Direct Labor account will have a *credit* balance representing the amount owed to employees for work already performed. This credit balance should be listed in the balance sheet as *wages payable,* a current liability.

Many employees in a manufacturing plant do not work directly on the goods being manufactured. Examples of these indirect workers include supervisors, timekeepers, maintenance personnel, and plant security guards. *Indirect labor* costs are considered part of manufacturing overhead rather than being included in direct labor costs.

Manufacturing Overhead

The Manufacturing Overhead account is used to record all costs classified as "overhead," and also to assign these costs to the products being manufactured. Manufacturing overhead is a broad category of manufacturing costs, representing all manufacturing costs *other than* direct materials and direct labor. Examples of manufacturing costs classified as overhead include:

1 Indirect materials used

   a Factory supplies that do not become an integral part of the finished goods, such as lubricating oil and parts used to maintain or repair equipment.

    b Materials that become an integral part of the finished goods, but would

---

[3] As explained in Chapter 11, payroll costs include such factors as payroll taxes and "fringe benefits," as well as the wages earned by employees.

be traceable into the products only with great effort and expense. Examples include glue, welding materials, and staples.

2 Indirect labor costs

   a Supervisors' salaries

   b Salaries of factory maintenance, medical, and security personnel

3 Plant occupancy costs

   a Rent or depreciation on buildings

   b Insurance on buildings; property taxes on land and buildings

   c Maintenance and repairs on buildings

   d Utilities—gas, electricity, water, and telephone

4 Machinery and equipment costs

   a Rent or depreciation on machinery

   b Insurance and property taxes on machinery

   c Maintenance and repairs on machinery

5 Cost of compliance with federal, state, and local regulations

   a Meeting factory safety requirements

   b Disposal of hazardous waste materials

   c Control over factory emissions (meeting clean air standards)

These are only examples; because of the diverse nature of manufacturing companies, it is not possible to prepare a complete list of all types of overhead costs. As there are many different types of overhead costs, Manufacturing Overhead is a controlling account. Subsidiary records are maintained to keep track of the different types of overhead costs.

Selling expenses and general and administrative expenses do ***not*** relate to the manufacturing process and are ***not*** included in manufacturing overhead. Certain costs, such as insurance, property taxes, and utilities, may be applicable in part to manufacturing operations and in part to administrative and selling functions. In such cases, these costs should be ***apportioned*** among manufacturing overhead, general and administrative expense, and selling expense accounts.

■ **Recording Overhead Costs** The Manufacturing Overhead account is debited to record any cost classified as "overhead." Examples of costs debited to this account include purchases of indirect materials, payments of indirect labor payrolls, payments of factory utilities, and recording depreciation on machinery. The account credited may vary, depending upon the nature of the overhead cost. For example, in recording purchases of indirect materials or factory utilities, the account credited usually will be Cash or Accounts Payable. In recording depreciation on machinery, however, the account credited is Accumulated Depreciation.

As the items included in total overhead costs are "consumed" by production activities, the related costs are transferred from the Manufacturing Overhead account into the Work in Process Inventory account (debit Work in Process

Inventory, credit Manufacturing Overhead). In the course of the year, all the overhead costs incurred should be assigned to units of product manufactured. Thus, at year-end, the Manufacturing Overhead account should have a zero balance.[4]

Direct and Indirect Manufacturing Costs

Objective 5
Distinguish between direct and indirect manufacturing costs.

The costs of direct materials and direct labor may be traced conveniently and directly into specific units of product. Consider, for example, a company that manufactures many types of fine furniture. It is relatively easy to determine the cost of the wood and the cost of the direct labor that go into making a particular dining table. For this reason, accountants call these items *direct* manufacturing costs.

Overhead, however, is an *indirect cost.* Consider, for example, the types of costs that a furniture manufacturer classifies as overhead. These costs include property taxes on the factory, depreciation on tools and equipment, supervisors' salaries, and repairs to equipment. How much of these indirect costs should be assigned to the dining table?

There is no easy answer to this question. By definition, indirect costs *cannot* be traced easily and directly into specific units of product. These costs often relate to manufacturing operations viewed *as a whole,* rather than to specific units of product. However, we cannot ignore indirect costs; they are an important part of the cost of manufacturing most products. Therefore, manufacturing companies must develop a method of allocating an appropriate portion of total manufacturing overhead to each product manufactured. This "allocation" is accomplished through the use of an *overhead application rate.*

Overhead Application Rate

Objective 6
Explain the purpose of an overhead application rate and the importance of basing this rate upon a significant "cost driver."

An overhead application rate is a device used to assign appropriate amounts of manufacturing overhead to specific units of manufactured products. The rate expresses the expected relationship between manufacturing overhead and some activity base *that can be traced* directly to the manufactured products. Manufacturing overhead is then assigned to products *in proportion* to this activity base.

The overhead application rate is determined at the beginning of the accounting period, based upon estimated amounts. The formula is:

$$\frac{\text{Overhead}}{\text{application rate}} = \frac{\text{estimated total manufacturing overhead costs}}{\text{estimated total units in the activity base}}$$

The mechanics of computing and using an overhead application rate are quite simple. The challenging problems for accountants are (1) selecting an appropriate activity base, and (2) making reliable estimates of total overhead costs for the period and of the units in the activity base.[5] Let us first address the easy topic—mechanics.

---

[4] The disposition of over- or under-applied overhead will be discussed in Chapter 22.

[5] Errors in estimating the amount of total overhead costs for the coming period or the number of units in the activity base will cause differences between the actual overhead incurred and the amounts assigned to units manufactured. These differences usually are small and are eliminated by an adjusting entry at the end of the accounting period. We will address this issue in Chapter 22.

■ Computation and Use of an Overhead Application Rate

Assume that at the beginning of 1991, Allied Manufacturing Company makes the following estimates relating to its manufacturing activities for the coming year:

Estimated total manufacturing overhead costs for the year................	*$360,000*
Estimated total direct labor cost for the year	*$300,000*
Estimated machine hours for the year....................................	*10,000 hours*

Using this estimated data, we will illustrate the computation and use of an overhead application rate under two independent assumptions:

Assumption 1: Allied uses direct labor cost as the "activity base" in the application of overhead costs.
In this case, the overhead application rate will be *120% of direct labor cost* ($360,000 estimated overhead ÷ $300,000 estimated direct labor cost = 120%). Manufacturing overhead will be assigned to manufactured units in proportion to the direct labor cost assigned to those units. Thus, if $2,000 in direct labor is charged to specific units of product, $2,400 of overhead will be charged to these units ($2,000 direct labor cost × 120% overhead application rate = $2,400).

Assumption 2: Allied uses machine hours as the activity base.
In this case, the overhead application rate will be *$36 per machine hour* ($360,000 ÷ 10,000 hours). Using this approach, manufacturing overhead costs will be assigned to units based upon the number of machine hours used in producing the units. If 10 machine hours are needed to manufacture a particular group of units, those units will be charged with $360 in overhead costs (10 hours × $36 per hour).

Overhead "Cost Drivers"

For the use of an overhead application rate to provide reliable results, the activity base must be a significant "driver" of overhead costs. A *cost driver* is an activity base that is a *causal factor* in the incurrence of overhead costs. In the past, direct labor costs or direct labor hours often were viewed as the major overhead cost drivers. Products that required more direct labor often required more indirect labor (supervision and timekeeping), more wear and tear on machinery (depreciation), and greater use of electrical power.

As factories have become more highly automated, however, direct labor has become less of a causal factor of overhead costs. Today, many manufacturing companies allocate overhead costs using as the activity base such factors as machine hours, computer time, or the total number of component parts to be assembled. The key point to remember is that the activity base *should be a "driver" of overhead costs.* If the activity base is not a major cost driver, the relative production cost of different units may be distorted. This, in turn, may lead to many faulty managerial decisions.

CASE IN POINT ■ A large dairy company allocated overhead costs in proportion to the amount of butterfat used in each of the company's many products. The quantity of butterfat used in producing a product had been a major "driver" of overhead costs until the dairy began producing dehydrated milk. The manufacture of dehydrated milk required the use of expensive machinery and greatly increased overhead costs; however, the dehydrated milk contained almost no butterfat. Based upon the "butterfat method" of allocating overhead costs, the increased overhead stemming from the manufacture of dehydrated milk was allocated primarily to ice cream and other products high in butterfat. The cost of manufacturing dehydrated milk appeared very low, because this product was assigned almost no overhead costs.

As a result of these distorted cost figures, management cut back on the production of ice cream and increased production of dehydrated milk. This strategy, however, led to a substantial decline in profitability. Only after a business consultant pointed out the improper allocation of overhead costs did management learn that ice cream was the company's most profitable product, and that dehydrated milk was being sold to customers at a price below its actual production cost.

Different overhead application rates may be used for different products or in different departments. The activity base used in each rate also may vary, depending upon the nature of the manufacturing process.

Work in Process Inventory, Finished Goods Inventory, and the Cost of Goods Sold

The Work in Process Inventory account is used (1) to accumulate the manufacturing costs relating to all units of product worked on during the period, and (2) to allocate these costs between those units completed during the period and those that are only partially completed at year-end.

As materials are placed into production and manufacturing activities take place, the related manufacturing costs are debited to the Work in Process Inventory account. The flow of manufacturing costs into this inventory account is consistent with the idea that manufacturing costs are *product costs,* rather than period costs.

As specific units are completed, the cost of manufacturing these units is transferred from the Work in Process Inventory account to the Finished Goods Inventory account. The balance remaining in the Work in Process Inventory account represents the manufacturing costs applicable to goods that are only partially completed at the end of the period.[6]

Manufactured products are classified as finished goods only after all manufacturing activities have been completed. Therefore, any costs of storing, marketing, or delivering finished goods are viewed as selling expenses rather than manufacturing costs. As the finished goods are sold, their cost is transferred from the Finished Goods Inventory account into the Cost of Goods Sold.

---

[6] Distinguishing between the cost of the units completed and those still in process implies the ability to separately identify the manufacturing costs relating to specific units. *Cost accounting systems* serve this goal; cost accounting systems are discussed in Chapter 22.

Schedule of Cost of Finished Goods Manufactured

Objective 7
Prepare a schedule of cost of finished goods manufactured.

Most manufacturing companies prepare a *schedule of cost of finished goods manufactured* to provide managers with an overview of the costs relating to manufacturing activities during the period. Using the data in our illustration on page 859, a schedule of cost of finished goods manufactured for Allied Manufacturing Company is shown below:

ALLIED MANUFACTURING COMPANY
Schedule of Cost of Finished Goods Manufactured
For the Year Ended December 31, 1991

Work in process inventory, beginning of the year		$ 30,000
Manufacturing cost assigned to production:		
Direct materials used	$150,000	
Direct labor	300,000	
Manufacturing overhead	360,000	
Total manufacturing costs		810,000
Total cost of all work in process during the year...............................		$840,000
Less: Work in process inventory, end of the year		(40,000)
Cost of finished goods manufactured		$800,000

Notice that all the amounts used in this schedule may be obtained from the Work in Process Inventory account illustrated on page 859. In short, the schedule of cost of finished goods manufactured summarizes the flow of manufacturing costs into and out of the Work in Process Inventory account.

■ **Purpose of the Schedule**   A schedule of cost of finished goods manufactured is *not* a formal financial statement. Rather, it is intended primarily to assist managers in understanding and evaluating the overall cost of manufacturing the company's products. By comparing these schedules for successive periods, for example, managers can determine whether direct labor or manufacturing overhead is rising or falling as a percentage of total manufacturing costs. The schedule is also helpful in developing information about unit costs.

If the company manufactures only a single product, the *cost per unit* of manufactured product can be determined by dividing the *cost of finished goods manufactured* by the *number of units produced.*[7] For example, if Allied produced *10,000* finished units during 1991, the average cost per unit was *$80* ($800,000 ÷ 10,000 units). Knowing the manufacturing cost per unit is useful to managers in setting sales prices, in evaluating the efficiency of manufacturing operations, and in deciding whether the company should devote more or less of its resources to manufacturing this product.

Unit costs also are used by financial accountants in valuing the ending inventory of finished goods and in determining the cost of goods sold.

---

[7] Many companies, of course, produce more than a single product. In this case, the company's accounting records should include separate work in process inventory accounts for each type of product. A separate schedule of cost of finished goods manufactured then may be prepared for each product line.

■ **Using Unit Costs in Financial Statements**   Perpetual inventory records show in the ledger accounts the ending amounts of inventory. However, it is still necessary to make a physical count of the goods on hand at year-end. This physical count may disclose theft, breakage, or spoilage of units that was not recorded in the perpetual inventory records. Once the physical count is complete, the unit costs determined from the schedule of cost of goods manufactured may be used to value the ending inventory of finished goods and the cost of goods sold.

To illustrate, assume that Allied Manufacturing Company's beginning inventory of finished goods consisted of 2,000 units, and that 10,000 finished units were manufactured during the current year. Thus, 12,000 units were available for sale during the year. Assume also that the year-end physical count shows 2,100 finished units on hand, indicating 9,900 units sold during the year (12,000 units available − 2,100 units still on hand). This information is summarized in the following schedule, along with the total cost and the per-unit cost of the beginning inventory of finished goods and of the finished goods manufactured during the year.

	NUMBER OF UNITS	AVERAGE UNIT COST	TOTAL COST
Beginning inventory of finished goods.............	2,000	$75	$150,000
Cost of finished goods manufactured	10,000	80	800,000
Cost of goods available for sale..................	12,000		$950,000
Less: Ending inventory of finished goods	2,100	?	?
Cost of goods sold	9,900		$?

The costs assigned to the 2,100 units in the ending inventory depend upon whether Allied uses the FIFO, LIFO, or weighted-average method of valuing inventory. Under the FIFO (first-in, first-out) method, the ending inventory will be valued at the current manufacturing costs of $80 per unit. Thus, our schedule may be completed as follows:

	NUMBER OF UNITS	AVERAGE UNIT COST	TOTAL COST
Cost of goods available for sale..................	12,000		$950,000
Less: Ending inventory of finished goods	2,100	$80	168,000
Cost of goods sold	9,900		$782,000

Still assuming the FIFO method, the cost of goods sold may be verified as follows:

	NUMBER OF UNITS	AVERAGE UNIT COST	TOTAL COST
Beginning inventory of finished goods.............	2,000	$75	$150,000
Add: Additional 7,900 units sold from production of current year	7,900	80	632,000
Cost of goods sold	9,900		$782,000

Financial Statements of a Manufacturing Company

Let us now illustrate how the data used in our example will be reported in the 1991 income statement and balance sheet of Allied Manufacturing Company. The company's 1991 income statement is illustrated below.

ALLIED MANUFACTURING COMPANY
Income Statement
For the Year Ended December 31, 1991

Sales		$1,300,000
Cost of goods sold:		
Beginning inventory of finished goods	$150,000	
Cost of finished goods manufactured	**800,000**	
Cost of goods available for sale..................................	$950,000	
Less: Ending inventory of finished goods	168,000	
Cost of goods sold		782,000
Gross profit on sales		$ 518,000
Operating expenses:		
Selling expenses	$135,000	
General and administrative expenses............................	265,000	
Total operating expenses		400,000
Income from operations		$ 118,000
Less: Interest expense...		18,000
Income before income taxes..		$ 100,000
Income taxes expenses...		30,000
Net income		$ 70,000

Notice that no manufacturing costs appear among the company's expenses. The cost of finished goods manufactured is an element of the *cost of goods sold.* The amount of manufacturing costs deducted from revenue in 1991 is $782,000—namely, the manufacturing costs of the units of product *sold* during the year.

Manufacturing costs relating to materials on hand, to units of product partially completed at year-end, and to finished goods on hand at year-end appear as *inventory* in the company's balance sheet. The balance sheet presentation of a manufacturing company's inventories is illustrated in the following partial balance sheet:

ALLIED MANUFACTURING COMPANY
Partial Balance Sheet
December 31, 1991

Notice the three types of inventory

Current assets:		
Cash and cash equivalents		$ 60,000
Accounts receivable (net of allowance for doubtful accounts).................		190,000
Inventories:		
Materials..	$ 20,000	
Work in process	40,000	
Finished goods..	168,000	228,000
Total current assets...		$478,000

In addition, Allied's balance sheet should include a current liability for wages payable, represented by the $8,000 credit balance in the Direct Labor account. The credit balance in the Direct Labor account indicates that direct employees have performed work costing $8,000 since the last payroll date.

End-of-Chapter Review

CONCEPTS INTRODUCED OR EMPHASIZED IN CHAPTER 21

The major concepts in this chapter include:

■ The nature and purpose of managerial accounting.

■ Manufacturing costs—direct materials, direct labor, and manufacturing overhead—as the "cost" of an inventory of manufactured products.

■ The distinction between product costs and period costs.

■ Accounting for manufacturing costs, and the "flow" of these costs through perpetual inventory records.

■ The distinction between direct and indirect manufacturing costs.

■ Use of an overhead application rate in assigning overhead costs to specific units of manufactured product.

■ The importance of using a significant "cost driver" as the basis for an overhead application rate.

■ The content and usefulness of a schedule of cost of finished goods manufactured.

The terminology and concepts introduced in this chapter will be used extensively throughout the remaining chapters in this text. In Chapter 22, for example, we discuss cost accounting systems that determine the per-unit cost of each manufactured product. In Chapters 23 through 26, we explore uses of accounting information in planning and controlling business operations. Most of the examples and illustrations used in these chapters will involve manufacturing activities.

KEY TERMS INTRODUCED OR EMPHASIZED IN CHAPTER 21

Cost accounting   The accounting concepts and practices used in determining the costs of manufacturing various products or of performing different business activities.

Cost driver   An activity base that can be traced directly into units produced and that serves as a causal factor in the incurrence of overhead costs. Serves as an activity base in an *overhead application rate.*

Cost of finished goods manufactured   The manufacturing costs relating to units of manufactured product completed during the period.

Direct labor   Payroll costs for employees who work directly on the products being manufactured, either by hand or with tools.

Direct manufacturing cost   A manufacturing cost that can be traced conveniently and directly into the quantity of finished goods manufactured. Examples include *direct materials* and *direct labor.*

Direct materials   Raw materials and component parts that become an integral part of the manufactured goods and that can be traced directly into the finished products.

Financial accounting   Developing and interpreting information describing the financial position and operating results of a business entity, often for use by decision makers outside of the entity.

Finished goods inventory   The completed units that have emerged from the manufacturing process and are on hand available for sale.

Indirect labor   Payroll costs relating to factory employees who do not work directly upon the goods being manufactured. Examples are wages of security guards and maintenance personnel. Indirect labor costs are included in *manufacturing overhead.*

Indirect manufacturing cost   A manufacturing cost that cannot be conveniently traced into the specific products being manufactured. Examples include property taxes, depreciation on machinery, and other types of *manufacturing overhead.*

Indirect materials   Materials used in the manufacturing process that cannot be traced conveniently to specific units of production. Examples include lubricating oil, maintenance supplies, and glue. Indirect materials are accounted for as part of *manufacturing overhead.*

Inventoriable costs   See *product costs.*

Managerial accounting   Developing and interpreting accounting information specifically suited to the needs of a company's management.

Manufacturing costs   The cost of manufacturing goods that will be sold to customers. The basic types of manufacturing costs are *direct materials used, direct labor,* and *manufacturing overhead.*

Manufacturing overhead   A "catch-all" category including all manufacturing costs other than the costs of *direct materials used* and *direct labor.*

Materials inventory   The cost of direct materials on hand and available for use in the manufacturing process.

Overhead application rate   A device used to assign overhead costs to the units being manufactured. Expresses the relationship between estimated overhead costs and some activity base that can be traced directly to manufactured units. Results in overhead costs being applied to units produced in proportion to the selected activity base.

Period costs   Costs that are charged to expense accounts in the period that the costs are incurred. Includes all items classified in the income statement as "expense."

Perpetual inventory system   A system in which transactions increasing or decreasing inventory are recorded directly in the inventory accounts, thus creating an up-to-date record of the level of inventories and the flow of costs into and out of the inventory accounts.

Product costs   The costs of purchasing or manufacturing inventory. Until the related goods are sold, these product costs represent an asset—inventory. Once the related goods are sold, these costs are deducted from revenue as the cost of goods sold.

Schedule of cost of finished goods manufactured   A schedule summarizing the flow of manufacturing costs into and out of the Work in Process Inventory account. Intended to assist managers in understanding and evaluating manufacturing costs.

Work in process inventory   Goods at any stage of the manufacturing process short of completion. As these units are completed, they become finished goods.

DEMONSTRATION PROBLEM FOR YOUR REVIEW

The following T accounts summarize the flow of manufacturing costs during the current year through the ledger accounts of Marston Manufacturing Company:

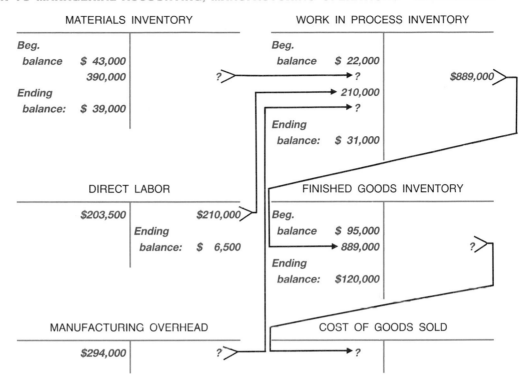

Instructions From the data supplied above, indicate the following amounts. Some amounts already appear in the T accounts; others require short computations.

a Purchases of direct materials.

b Direct materials used during the year.

c Direct labor costs assigned to production.

d The year-end liability to direct workers for wages payable.

e The overhead costs applied to production during the year, assuming that overhead was applied at a rate equal to 140% of direct labor costs.

f Total manufacturing costs charged to production during the year.

g The cost of finished goods manufactured.

h The cost of goods sold.

i The total costs classified as "inventory" in the year-end balance sheet.

SOLUTION TO DEMONSTRATION PROBLEM

a *Purchases of direct materials* $390,000

b *Computation of direct materials used:*
Materials inventory, beginning of year .... $ 43,000
Purchases of direct materials 390,000
Direct materials available for use $433,000
Less: Materials inventory, end of year 39,000
Direct materials used $394,000

c Direct labor costs assigned to production $210,000

d Year-end liability for direct wages payable .... $ 6,500

e Overhead costs applied during the year
   ($210,000 direct labor costs × 140%) $294,000

f Total manufacturing costs charged to production:
   Direct materials used (part **b**) $394,000
   Direct labor costs assigned to production 210,000
   Manufacturing overhead applied (part **e**) 294,000
      Total manufacturing costs charged to production $898,000

g Cost of finished goods manufactured $889,000

h Computation of cost of goods sold:
   Beginning inventory of finished goods .... $ 95,000
   Cost of finished goods manufactured 889,000
   Cost of goods available for sale $984,000
   Less: Ending inventory of finished goods 120,000
   Cost of goods sold $864,000

i Total year-end inventory:
   Materials .... $ 39,000
   Work in process 31,000
   Finished goods 120,000
      Total inventory $190,000

SELF-TEST QUESTIONS

Answers to these questions appear on page 885.

1 Indicate which of the following statements are more descriptive of managerial accounting than of financial accounting. (More than one answer may be appropriate.)

   a Recognized standards for presentation.

   b Information tailored to the needs of individual decision makers.

   c Information is more widely distributed.

   d Emphasis on expected future results.

2 In a manufacturing company, the costs debited to the Work in Process Inventory account represent:

   a Direct materials used, direct labor, and manufacturing overhead.

   b Cost of finished goods manufactured.

   c Period costs and product costs.

   d None of the above; the types of costs debited to this account will depend upon the type of products being manufactured.

3 The Work in Process Inventory account had a beginning balance of $4,200 on February 1. During February, the cost of direct materials used was $29,000 and direct labor cost applied to production was $3,000. Overhead is applied at the rate of $20 per direct labor hour. During February, 180 direct labor hours were used in the production process. If the cost of finished goods manufactured was $34,100, compute the balance in the Work in Process Inventory account at the *end* of February.

a $9,900   **b** $1,500   **c** $2,100   **d** $5,700

4 The purpose of an overhead application rate is to:

a Assign an appropriate portion of indirect manufacturing costs to each product manufactured.

b Determine the type and amount of costs to be debited to the Manufacturing Overhead account.

c Charge the Work in Process Inventory account with the appropriate amount of direct manufacturing costs.

d Allocate manufacturing overhead to expense in proportion to the number of units manufactured during the period.

5 The accounting records of Newport Mfg. Co. include the following information for 1991:

	DEC. 31	JAN. 1
Inventory of work in process	$ 20,000	$10,000
Inventory of finished goods.......................................	80,000	60,000
Direct materials used	200,000	
Direct labor..	120,000	
Manufacturing overhead (150% of direct labor)...................	180,000	
Selling expenses	150,000	

Indicate which of the following are correct. (More than one answer may be correct.)

a Amount debited to the Work in Process Inventory account during 1991, $500,000.

b Cost of finished goods manufactured, $490,000.

c Cost of goods sold, $470,000.

d Total manufacturing costs, $650,000.

Assignment Material

REVIEW QUESTIONS

1 Briefly distinguish between managerial and financial accounting information in terms of (a) the intended users of the information, and (b) the purpose of the information.

2 Briefly explain what is meant by the terms *managerial accounting* and *cost accounting.* Are the two terms related to one another? Explain.

3 Are financial accounting and managerial accounting two entirely separate disciplines? Explain.

4 Is managerial accounting information developed in conformity with generally accepted accounting principles or some other set of prescribed standards? Explain.

5 What are the three basic types of manufacturing costs?

6 A manufacturing firm has three inventory controlling accounts. Name each of the accounts, and describe briefly what the balance in each at the end of any accounting period represents.

7 Explain the distinction between *product costs* and *period costs.* Why is this distinction important?

8 Is the cost of disposing of hazardous waste materials resulting from factory operations a product cost or a period cost? Explain.

9 During the current year, Coronado Boat Yard has incurred manufacturing costs of $420,000 in building three large sailboats. At year-end, each boat is about 70% complete. How much of these manufacturing costs should be recognized as expense in Coronado Boat Yard's income statement for the current year? Explain.

10 What amounts are *debited* to the Materials Inventory account? What amounts are *credited* to this account? What type of balance (debit or credit) is this account likely to have at year-end? Explain.

11 During the current year the net cost of direct materials purchased by a manufacturing firm was $340,000, and the direct material inventory increased by $20,000. What was the cost of direct materials *used* during the year?

12 What amounts are debited to the Direct Labor account during the year? What amounts are credited to this account? What type of balance (debit or credit) is this account likely to have at year-end? Explain.

13 The illustration on page 859 includes six ledger accounts. Which of these six accounts often have balances at year-end that appear in the company's formal financial statements. Briefly explain how these balances will be classified in the financial statements.

14 Explain the distinction between a *direct* manufacturing cost and an *indirect* manufacturing cost. Provide two examples of each type of cost.

15 Argo Mfg. Co. uses approximately $1,200 in janitorial supplies to clean the work area and factory equipment each month. Should this $1,200 be included in the cost of direct materials used? Explain.

16 What is meant by the term *overhead application rate?*

17 What is meant by the term, *overhead cost driver?* How does the cost driver enter into computation of an overhead application rate?

18 Identify two possible overhead cost drivers for a company that:

a Manufactures handmade furniture using skilled craftspersons and small hand tools.

b Manufactures microchips for computers using an assembly line of computer-driven robots.

19 What amounts are *debited* to the Work in Process Inventory account during the year? What amounts are *credited* to this account? What does the year-end balance in this account represent?

20 What amounts are *debited* to the Finished Goods Inventory account during the year? What amounts are *credited* to this account? What type of balance (debit or credit) is this account likely to have at year-end?

21 Briefly describe the computation of the cost of finished goods manufactured as it appears in a schedule of cost of finished goods manufactured.

22 A schedule of cost of finished goods manufactured is a helpful tool in determining the per-unit cost of manufactured products. Explain several ways in which information about per-unit manufacturing costs is used by (a) managerial accountants, and (b) financial accountants.

EXERCISES

Exercise 21-1
Accounting terminology

Listed below are nine technical accounting terms introduced or emphasized in this chapter:

Overhead application rate	Cost of finished goods manufactured	Work in Process Inventory
Manufacturing overhead	Cost accounting	Period costs
Cost of Goods Sold	Managerial accounting	Product costs

Each of the following statements may (or may not) describe one of these technical terms. For each statement, indicate the accounting term described, or answer "None" if the statement does not correctly describe any of the terms.

a A manufacturing cost that can be traced conveniently and directly into manufactured units of product.

b The techniques and procedures used in determining the cost of manufacturing a specific product or performing a particular type of business activity.

c The account debited at the time that the Manufacturing Overhead account is credited.

d The amount transferred from the Work in Process Inventory account to the Finished Goods Inventory account.

e Costs that are debited directly to expense accounts when the costs are incurred.

f The preparation and use of accounting information designed to assist managers in planning and controlling the operations of a business.

g All manufacturing costs other than direct materials used and direct labor.

h A means of assigning indirect manufacturing costs to work in process during the period.

Exercise 21-2
Basic types of manufacturing costs

Into which of the three elements of manufacturing cost would each of the following be classified?

a Gold bullion used by a jewelry manufacturer

b Wages of assembly-line workers who package frozen food

c Salary of plant superintendent

d Electricity used in factory operations

e Salary of a nurse in a factory first-aid station

f Tubing used in manufacturing bicycles

g Wages paid by an automobile manufacturer to employees who test-drive completed automobiles

h Property taxes on machinery

Exercise 21-3
Product costs and period costs

Indicate whether each of the following should be considered a **product cost** or a **period cost**. If you identify the item as a product cost, also indicate whether it is a **direct** or **indirect** cost. For example, the answer to item **0** is "indirect product cost." Begin with item **a.**

0 Property taxes on factory building

a Salaries of office workers in the credit department

b Depreciation on raw materials warehouse

c Income taxes on a profitable manufacturing company

d Cost of disposal of hazardous waste materials to a chemical plant

e Amounts paid by a mobile home manufacturer to a subcontractor who installs plumbing in each mobile home

f Depreciation on sales showroom fixtures

g Salaries of security guards in administrative office building

h Salaries of factory security guards

Exercise 21-4
Flow of costs through manufacturing accounts

The information below was taken from the accounting records of Craftsman Products for the current year:

Work in process inventory, beginning of the year	$ 34,000
Cost of direct materials used	260,000
Direct labor cost applied to production	100,000
Cost of finished goods manufactured	591,000

Overhead is applied to production at a rate of $30 per machine hour. During the current year, 8,000 machine hours were used in the production process.

Compute the amount of the work in process inventory on hand at year-end.

Exercise 21-5
Computation and use of an overhead application rate

The production manager of Del Mar Manufacturing Co. has made the following estimates for the coming year:

Estimated manufacturing overhead	$560,000
Estimated direct labor costs	$400,000
Estimated machine hours	80,000 hours

Instructions

a Compute the overhead application rate based on:

(1) Direct labor cost.

(2) Machine hours.

b Assume that the manufacture of a particular product requires $1,000 in direct materials, $300 in direct labor, and 58 machine hours. Determine the total cost of manufacturing this product assuming that the overhead application rate is based upon:

(1) Direct labor cost.

(2) Machine hours.

Exercise 21-6
Preparing a schedule of cost of finished goods manufactured

The accounting records of NuTronics, Inc., include the following information for the year ended December 31, 1991:

	DEC. 31	JAN. 1
Inventory of materials	$ 20,000	$24,000
Inventory of work in process	12,000	8,000
Inventory of finished goods	90,000	80,000
Direct materials used	210,000	
Direct labor	120,000	
Selling expenses	170,000	
General and administrative expenses	140,000	

Overhead is applied to production at a rate of *150%* of direct labor costs.

Instructions **a** Prepare a schedule of cost of finished goods manufactured. (Not all of the data given above is used in this schedule.)

b Assume that the company manufactures a single product, and that 20,000 units were completed during the year. What is the average per-unit cost of manufacturing this product?

Exercise 21-7
Use of unit costs in the valuation of inventory

The following information is taken from the accounting records of Gildred Mfg. Corp. for the current year:

	NUMBER OF UNITS	AVERAGE UNIT COST	TOTAL COST
Beginning inventory of finished goods............	1,000	$120	$ 120,000
Finished goods manufactured....................	10,000	125	1,250,000
Goods available for sale	11,000		$1,370,000

A physical inventory taken at year-end indicates *800* units of finished goods on hand. The company uses the *FIFO* (first-in, first-out) method to value its inventories.

Instructions **a** Determine the cost of the 800 unit ending inventory of finished goods.

b Compute the cost of goods sold during the current year.

PROBLEMS

Group A

Problem 21A-1
An introduction to product costs

Aqua-Craft manufactures fiberglass ski boats. The manufacturing costs incurred during the first year of operations are shown below:

Direct materials purchased	$228,500
Direct materials used..	219,000
Direct labor assigned to production	170,000
Manufacturing overhead	204,000
Cost of finished goods manufactured (110 boats)	572,000

During the year, 110 completed boats were manufactured, of which 100 were sold. (Assume that the amounts of the ending inventory of finished goods and the cost of goods sold are determined using the average per-unit cost of manufacturing a completed boat.)

Instructions **a** Compute each of the following and show all computations:

(1) The average per-unit cost of manufacturing a completed boat during the current year.

(2) The year-end balances of the inventories of materials, work in process, and finished goods.

(3) The cost of goods sold during the year.

b For the current year, the costs of direct materials purchased, direct labor assigned to production, and manufacturing overhead total $602,500. Is this the amount of the manufacturing costs deducted from revenue in the current year? Explain fully.

(Friday.)

**Problem 21A-2
Flow of
manufacturing
costs through
perpetual
inventory records**

The following T accounts summarize the flow of manufacturing costs during the current year through the ledger accounts of Superior Locks, Inc.

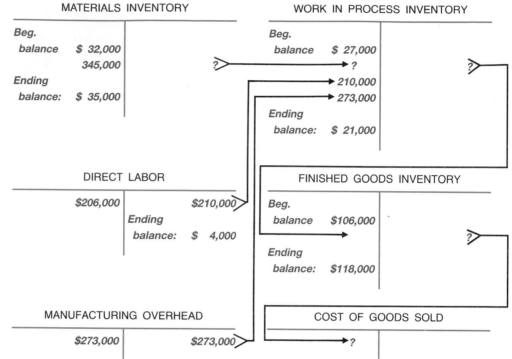

Test.

Instructions From the data supplied above, indicate the following amounts. Some amounts are shown in the T accounts; others require short computations. Please show all computations.

a Purchases during the year of direct materials.

b The cost of direct materials used.

c Direct labor payrolls paid during the year.

d Direct labor costs assigned to production.

e The overhead application rate in use during the year, assuming that overhead is applied as a percentage of direct labor costs.

f Total manufacturing costs charged to the Work in Process Inventory account during the year.

g The cost of finished goods manufactured.

h The cost of goods sold.

i The total costs to be classified as "inventory" in the year-end balance sheet.

**Problem 21A-3
Flow of product
costs and a
schedule of cost
of finished goods
manufactured**

The accounting records of St. Nicholas Toy Co. show the following costs and expenses for the year ended December 31, 1992.

Purchases of direct materials	$255,300
Direct materials used	248,800
Direct labor payrolls (paid during the year)	208,400
Direct labor costs (assigned to production)	210,100

Manufacturing overhead (incurred and applied to production)	252,500
Selling expenses	177,200
General and administrative expenses	203,600
Income taxes expense	90,000

Inventories at the beginning and end of the year were as follows:

	END OF YEAR	BEGINNING OF YEAR
Materials	$ 55,200	$ 48,700
Work in process	14,700	21,500
Finished goods	102,300	195,600

Instructions **a** Prepare a schedule of cost of finished goods manufactured during the year.

b Prepare a partial income statement showing the cost of goods sold for the year.

Problem 21A-4
Flow of manufacturing costs: a comprehensive problem

Shown below are the beginning and ending balances in the inventory accounts of Cardiff Manufacturing Co. for 1991:

	END OF YEAR	BEGINNING OF YEAR
Inventory accounts:		
Materials	$20,000	$16,000
Work in process	6,000	9,000
Finished goods inventory	30,000	34,000

The amounts debited and credited during the year to the accounts used in recording manufacturing costs are summarized below:

	DEBIT ENTRIES	CREDIT ENTRIES
Account:		
Materials Inventory	$190,000	$?
Direct Labor	56,000	58,000
Manufacturing Overhead	87,000	87,000
Work in Process Inventory	?	?
Finished Goods Inventory	?	?

Instructions **a** Using the above information, state (or compute) for 1991 the amounts of:

(1) Direct materials purchased.

(2) Direct materials used.

(3) Direct labor payrolls paid during the year.

(4) Direct labor costs assigned to units being manufactured.

(5) The year-end liability for direct wages payable.

(6) The overhead application rate, assuming that overhead costs are applied to units being manufactured in proportion to direct labor costs.

(7) Total manufacturing costs debited to the Work in Process Inventory account.

(8) Cost of finished goods manufactured.

(9) Cost of goods sold.

b Prepare a schedule of cost of finished goods manufactured for the year.

Problem 21A-5
"I don't need an
accountant. . . ."

Early in the year, John Raymond founded Raymond Engineering Co. for the purpose of manufacturing a special flow control valve which he had designed. Shortly after year-end, the company's accountant was injured in a skiing accident, and no year-end financial statements have been prepared. However, the accountant had correctly determined the year-end inventories at the following amounts:

Materials	$46,000
Work in process	31,500
Finished goods (3,000 units)	88,500

As this was the first year of operations, there were no beginning inventories.

While the accountant was in the hospital, Raymond improperly prepared the following income statement from the company's accounting records:

Net sales		$610,600
Cost of goods sold:		
Purchases of direct materials	$181,000	
Direct labor costs assigned to production	110,000	
Manufacturing overhead applied to production	170,000	
Selling expenses	70,600	
Administrative expenses	132,000	
Total costs		663,600
Net loss for year		$ (53,000)

Raymond was very disappointed in these operating results. He states, "Not only did we lose more than $50,000 this year, but look at our unit production costs. We sold 10,000 units this year at a cost of $663,600; that amounts to a cost of $66.36 per unit. I know some of our competitors are able to manufacture similar valves for about $35 per unit. I don't need an accountant to know that this business is a failure."

Instructions

a Prepare a schedule of cost of finished goods manufactured for the year. (As there were no beginning inventories, your schedule will start with the "Manufacturing costs assigned to production:.") Show a supporting computation for the cost of direct materials used during the year.

b Compute the average cost per unit manufactured.

c Prepare a corrected income statement for the year, using the multiple-step format. If the company has earned any operating income, assume an income tax rate of 30%. (Omit earnings per share figures.)

d Explain whether you agree or disagree with Raymond's remarks that the business is unprofitable and that its unit cost of production ($66.36, according to Raymond) is much higher than that of competitors (around $35). If you disagree with Raymond, explain any errors or shortcomings in his analysis.

Group B

Problem 21B-1
Product costs and
inventories

Roadmaster, Inc., began operations early in the current year building luxury motor homes. During the year the company started and completed 20 motor homes at a cost of $48,000 per unit. Sixteen of these completed motor homes were sold for $80,000 each. In addition, the company has five partially completed motor homes in progress at year-end. Costs incurred during the year on these partially completed motor homes have totaled $32,000 per unit.

Instructions

Compute for the current year:

a Ending inventories of (1) work in process and (2) finished goods.

b Cost of finished goods manufactured.

c Total manufacturing costs assigned to work in process during the year.

d Cost of goods sold.

e Gross profit on sales.

Problem 21B-2
Flow of manufacturing costs through ledger accounts

The "flow" of manufacturing costs through the ledger accounts of Intruder Alert, Inc., in the current year is illustrated below in summarized form:

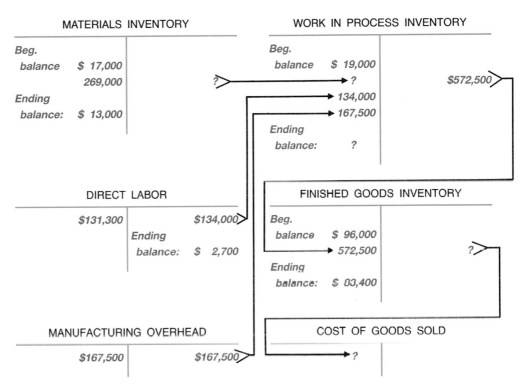

Instructions Indicate the amounts requested below. Some amounts are shown in the T accounts above; others require short computations. Please show all computations.

a Purchases of direct materials.

b The cost of direct materials used.

c Direct labor costs assigned to production.

d The year-end liability for direct wages payable.

e The overhead application rate in use throughout the year, assuming that overhead is applied as a percentage of direct labor costs.

f Total manufacturing costs charged to the Work in Process Inventory account during the current year.

g The cost of finished goods manufactured.

h The year-end balance in the Work in Process Inventory account.

i The cost of goods sold.

j The total amount of "inventory" listed in the year-end balance sheet.

Problem 21B-3
Schedule of cost
of finished goods
manufactured;
use of unit costs
in financial
statements

The accounting records of Scott Mfg. Co. include the following information relating to the current year:

	DEC. 31	JAN. 1
Materials inventory	$120,000	$ 95,000
Work in process inventory	37,500	40,000
Finished goods inventory, Jan. 1 (10,000 units)	?	190,000
Purchases of direct materials during year	285,000	
Direct labor costs assigned to production	195,000	
Manufacturing overhead applied to production	442,500	

The company manufactures a single product; during the current year, *45,000* units were manufactured and *40,000* units were sold.

Instructions **a** Prepare a schedule of cost of finished goods manufactured for the current year. (Show a supporting computation of the cost of direct materials *used* during the year.)

b Compute the average per-unit cost of production during the current year.

c Compute the cost of the inventory of finished goods at December 31 of the current year, assuming that the FIFO (first-in, first-out) method of inventory costing is used.

d Compute the cost of goods sold during the year, assuming that the FIFO (first-in, first-out) method of inventory costing is used.

Problem 21B-4
Flow of
manufacturing
costs: a
comprehensive
problem

The balances in the perpetual inventory accounts of Outdoor Products at the beginning and end of the current year are as follows:

	END OF YEAR	BEGINNING OF YEAR
Inventory accounts:		
Materials	$25,800	$22,000
Work in process	8,000	5,000
Finished goods inventory	24,000	38,000

The total dollar amounts debited and credited during the year to the accounts used in recording manufacturing activities are summarized below:

	DEBIT ENTRIES	CREDIT ENTRIES
Account:		
Materials Inventory	$390,000	$?
Direct Labor	92,000	94,000
Manufacturing Overhead	159,800	159,800
Work in Process Inventory	640,000	?
Finished Goods Inventory	?	?

Instructions **a** Using this data, state or compute for the year the amounts of:

(1) Direct materials purchased.

(2) Direct materials used.

(3) Payments of direct labor payrolls.

(4) Direct labor cost assigned to production.

(5) The overhead application rate used during the year, assuming that overhead was applied as a percentage of direct labor costs.

(6) Total manufacturing costs charged to the Work in Process Inventory account during the year.

(7) The cost of finished goods manufactured.

(8) Cost of goods sold.

(9) The total amount to be classified as "inventory" in the year-end balance sheet.

b Prepare a schedule of cost of finished goods manufactured.

Problem 21B-5
Effect on income
statement of
errors in
handling
manufacturing
costs

William Nelson, the chief accountant of West Texas Guitar Company, was injured in an automobile accident shortly before the end of the company's first year of operations. At year-end, a clerk with a very limited understanding of accounting prepared the following income statement, which is unsatisfactory in several respects:

WEST TEXAS GUITAR COMPANY
Income Statement
For the Year Ended December 31, 19___

Net sales		$1,300,000
Cost of goods sold:		
Purchases of direct materials	$ 460,000	
Direct labor	225,000	
Indirect labor...	90,000	
Depreciation on machinery—factory..........................	50,000	
Rent	144,000	
Insurance	16,000	
Utilities	28,000	
Miscellaneous manufacturing overhead.......................	34,600	
Other operating expenses	273,800	
Dividends declared on capital stock...........................	46,000	
Cost of goods sold..		(1,367,400)
Loss for year...		$ (67,400)

You are asked to help management prepare a corrected income statement for the first year of operations. Management informs you that 60% of the rent, insurance, and utilities apply to factory operations, and that the remaining 40% should be classified as operating expense. Also, the correct ending inventories are as follows:

Materials...	$ 38,000
Work in process..	10,000
Finished goods..	110,400

As this is the first year of operations, there were no beginning inventories.

Instructions

a Identify the shortcomings and errors in the above income statement. Based upon the shortcomings you have identified, explain whether you would expect the company's actual net income for the first year of operations to be higher or lower than the amount shown.

b Prepare schedules to determine:

(1) The cost of direct materials used.

(2) Total manufacturing overhead.

c Prepare a schedule of cost of finished goods manufactured during the year. (Use the amounts computed in part **b** as the costs of direct materials used and manufacturing overhead.)

d Prepare a corrected income statement for the year, using a multiple-step format. Assume that income taxes expense amounts to 30% of income before income taxes.

BUSINESS DECISION CASES

Case 21-1
Poor drivers are cost drivers

Old Town Auto Body is an automobile body and fender repair shop. Repair work is done by hand and with the use of small tools. Customers are billed based on time (direct labor hours) and materials used in each repair job.

The shop's overhead costs consist primarily of indirect materials (welding materials, metal putty, and sandpaper), rent, indirect labor, and utilities. Rent is equal to a percentage of the shop's gross revenue for each month. The indirect labor relates primarily to ordering parts and processing insurance claims. The amount of indirect labor, therefore, tends to vary with the size of each job.

Henry Lee, manager of the business, is considering using either direct labor hours or number of repair jobs as the basis for allocating overhead costs. He has estimated the following amounts for the coming year:

Estimated total overhead	$63,000
Estimated direct labor hours	10,000
Estimated number of repair jobs	300

Instructions

a Compute the overhead application rate based on:

(1) Direct labor hours.

(2) Number of repair jobs.

b Shown below is information for two repair jobs:

Job 1 Repair a dented fender. Direct material used, $25; direct labor hours, 5; direct labor cost, $75.

Job 2 Repair an automobile involved in a serious collision. Direct materials used, $3,800; direct labor hours, 200; direct labor cost, $3,000.

Determine the *total cost* of each repair job, assuming that overhead costs are applied to each job based upon:

(1) Direct labor hours.

(2) Number of repair jobs.

c Discuss the results obtained in part **b**. Which overhead application method appears to provide the more realistic results. Explain the reasoning behind your answer, addressing the issue of what "drives" overhead costs in this business.

Case 21-2
"And if you'll buy that, I'll throw the Golden Gate in free."

Prescott Manufacturing operates several plants, each of which produces a different product. Early in the current year, John Walker was hired as the new manager of the Meadowbrooke Plant. At year-end, all the plant managers are asked to summarize the operations of their plants at a meeting of the company's board of directors. John Walker displayed the following information on a chart as he made his presentation:

	CURRENT YEAR	LAST YEAR
Inventories of finished goods:		
Beginning of the year (30,000 units in the		
current year and 10,000 units last year).......................	$ 255,000	$ 85,000
End of the year (20,000 units in the current		
year and 30,000 last year)....................................	202,000	255,000
Cost of finished goods manufactured	909,000	1,020,000

Walker made the following statements to the board: "As you know, sales volume has remained constant for the Meadowbrooke Plant. Both this year and last, our sales amounted to 100,000 units. We have made real gains, however, in controlling our manufacturing costs. Through efficient plant operations, we have reduced our cost of finished goods manufactured by over $100,000 from last year's levels. These economies are reflected in a reduction of the manufacturing cost per unit sold from $10.20 last year ($1,020,000 ÷ 100,000 units) to $9.09 in the current year ($909,000 ÷ 100,000 units)."

Father Alan Carter is president of St. Mary's University and is a member of Prescott Manufacturing's board of directors. However, Father Carter has little background in the accounting practices of manufacturing companies, and he asks you for assistance in evaluating Walker's statements.

Instructions   **a** As a preliminary step to your analysis, compute the following for the Meadowbrooke Plant in each of the two years:

(1) Cost of goods sold

(2) Number of finished units manufactured

(3) Average cost per unit manufactured

(4) Average cost per unit sold

b Evaluate the statements made by Walker. Comment specifically upon whether it appears that the reduction in the cost of finished goods sold was achieved through more efficient operations and upon Walker's computation of the manufacturing cost of units sold.

ANSWERS TO SELF-TEST QUESTIONS

1 b and d   **2** a   **3** d   **4** a   **5** a, b, and c

Cost Accounting Systems

How much does it cost Apple Computer to manufacture each MacIntosh? If you are a manager at Apple Computer, you need this information. You need it to set selling prices, you need it to determine the cost of goods sold, and you need it to evaluate the efficiency of the company's manufacturing operations. In this chapter, we show how manufacturing companies use cost accounting systems to determine on a timely basis the per-unit cost of each product manufactured. Both job order and process cost systems are illustrated and explained.

After studying this chapter, you should be able to meet these Learning Objectives:

1 Explain the purpose of a cost accounting system.

2 Explain the characteristics of a job order cost accounting system.

3 Describe the purpose and the content of a job cost sheet.

4 Explain the characteristics of a process cost accounting system.

5 Define and compute "equivalent full units" of production.

6 Prepare a process cost summary for a production department using a process cost system.

Assume that during the current month, Tri-State Manufacturing Co. incurs manufacturing costs of $1 million. At month-end, how much of this $1 million represents the cost of finished goods manufactured, and how much is applicable to goods still in process at month-end? If the company produces 10 different products, should the manufacturing costs be allocated among these products? Answers to these questions can only be provided by the company's *cost accounting system.*

Objective 1
Explain the purpose of a cost accounting system.

What Is a Cost Accounting System?

A cost accounting system consists of the techniques, forms, and accounting records used to develop timely information about the cost of manufacturing specific products and of performing specific functions. Because cost accounting systems are most widely used in manufacturing companies, we will focus upon the use of these systems to determine the cost of manufactured products. However, the concepts of cost accounting are applicable to a wide range of business situations. For example, banks, accounting firms, and governmental agencies all use cost accounting systems to determine the cost of performing various service functions.

CASE IN POINT ■ Congress recently passed legislation requiring hospitals to measure and report the average unit costs of their "products." The products are defined as specific types of medical services, such as heart transplants, tonsillectomies, and deliveries (child births). Thus, hospitals must develop cost accounting systems capable of determining the average cost of providing each of these types of service.

In a manufacturing company, cost accounting serves two important managerial objectives: (1) to determine the per-unit cost of each manufactured product, and (2) to provide management with information that will be useful in planning future business operations and in controlling costs. *Unit costs* are determined by relating manufacturing costs—the costs of direct materials used, direct labor, and manufacturing overhead—to the number of units manufactured.

A "unit" of product is defined differently in different industries. We tend to think of "units" as individual physical products, such as automobiles or television sets. In other industries, however, the number of units manufactured may be stated as a number of tons, gallons, barrels, pounds, board-feet, or other appropriate unit of measure.[1]

Unit costs provide the basis for inventory valuation and measurement of the cost of goods sold. They also provide managers with information useful in setting selling prices, deciding what products to manufacture, and evaluating the efficiency of operations.

The phrase *controlling costs* refers to keeping costs down to reasonable levels. When a cost accounting system provides timely information about unit costs, managers are able to react quickly should costs begin to rise to unacceptable levels. By comparing current unit costs with budgets, past performance, and other yardsticks, managers are able to identify those areas in which corrective actions are most needed.

Two Basic Types of Cost Accounting Systems

There are two distinct types of cost accounting systems: job order cost systems and process cost systems. Both systems produce the same end results: timely information about manufacturing costs, inventories on hand, and unit costs.

Job order cost systems are used by companies that manufacture "one-of-a-kind" products, or that tailor products to the specifications of individual cus-

---

[1] Some service industries also express their operating costs on a per-unit basis. The "units of product" used in the airline industry, for example, are *passenger-miles* flown.

tomers. In a job order cost system, the costs of materials used, direct labor, and manufacturing overhead are accumulated separately for each job. A "job" represents the goods manufactured at one time to fill a particular order. If the job contains more than one unit of product, unit costs are determined by dividing the total costs charged to the job by the number of units manufactured.

Construction companies use job order cost systems, because each construction project has unique characteristics that affect its cost. Job order cost systems also are used by shipbuilders, motion picture studios, defense contractors, print shops, and furniture makers. In addition, these systems are widely used in service-type businesses, including repair shops, hospitals, accounting firms, and law firms.

Process cost systems are used by companies that produce a "steady stream" of nearly identical products over a long period of time. In a process cost system, the focal points in accumulating manufacturing costs are the individual *production departments* (or *processes*) involved in the production cycle. As a first step, the costs of materials used, direct labor, and overhead applicable to each production department are compiled for a given period of time (usually one month). The average cost of running a unit of product through each production department then is determined by dividing the departmental costs by the number of units processed during the period. If a product passes through two or more processing departments, the unit costs of performing each process are combined to determine the unit cost of the finished good.

Companies that use process cost systems include oil refineries, power plants, soft-drink bottlers, breweries, flour mills, and most "assembly-line" or "mass-production" manufacturing operations.

The type of cost accounting system best suited to a particular company *depends upon the nature of the company's manufacturing operations.* Both job order and process cost systems are widely used. In fact, a given company may use a job order cost system to account for some of its production activities, and a process cost system to account for others. In the following sections of this chapter, we will illustrate and explain each of these cost accounting systems.

JOB ORDER COST SYSTEMS

Objective 2
Explain the characteristics of a job order cost accounting system.

The distinguishing characteristic of a job order cost system is that manufacturing costs are accumulated *separately for each job.* As explained in Chapter 21, manufacturing costs are charged (debited) to the Work in Process Inventory account. In a job cost system, Work in Process Inventory is a controlling account, supported by a subsidiary ledger showing the manufacturing costs charged to each job. The accounts in this subsidiary ledger are called *job cost sheets.*

The Job Cost Sheet

Objective 3
Describe the purpose and the content of a job cost sheet.

Job cost sheets are the heart of a job order cost system. A separate job cost sheet is prepared for each job and is used to accumulate a record of all manufacturing costs charged to the job. Once the job is finished, the job cost sheet indicates the cost of the finished goods manufactured and provides the information necessary to compute the unit costs of production.

Direct manufacturing costs (direct materials used and direct labor) are recorded on the job cost sheet as quickly as these costs can be traced to the job.

Once the job is complete, overhead costs are applied using an overhead application rate. Shown below is a completed job cost sheet of the Oak & Glass Furniture Co. This "job" involved the manufacture of 100 dining tables of a particular style.

OAK & GLASS FURNITURE CO. 831
JOB COST SHEET

Product __French court dining tables__ Date started __4/03/91__

Number of units manufactured __100__ Date completed __4/21/91__

Costs Charged to This Job

Manufacturing Department	Direct Materials	Direct Labor		Manufacturing Overhead	
		Hours	Cost	Rate	Cost Applied
Milling & Carving	$10,000	700	$14,000	150%	$21,000
Finishing	15,000	300	6,000	150%	9,000

Cost Summary and Unit Costs

	Total Costs	Unit Costs
Direct materials used	$25,000	$250
Direct labor	20,000	200
Manufacturing overhead applied	30,000	300
Cost of finished goods manufactured (100 tables)	$75,000	$750

Throughout the production process, manufacturing costs traceable to the job are accumulated in the "Costs charged to this job" section of the job cost sheet. The "Cost summary" section is filled in when the job is completed.

The total cost of completing Job No. 831 is **$75,000.** Upon completion of the job, this amount should be transferred from the Work in Process Inventory account to the Finished Goods Inventory account. The unit cost figures shown in the job cost sheet are determined by dividing the total manufacturing costs by the 100 units manufactured.

Flow of Costs in a Job Cost System: An Illustration

On pages 890 and 891, we expand our example of Oak & Glass Furniture Co. to illustrate the flow of costs through a complete but simple job cost accounting system.

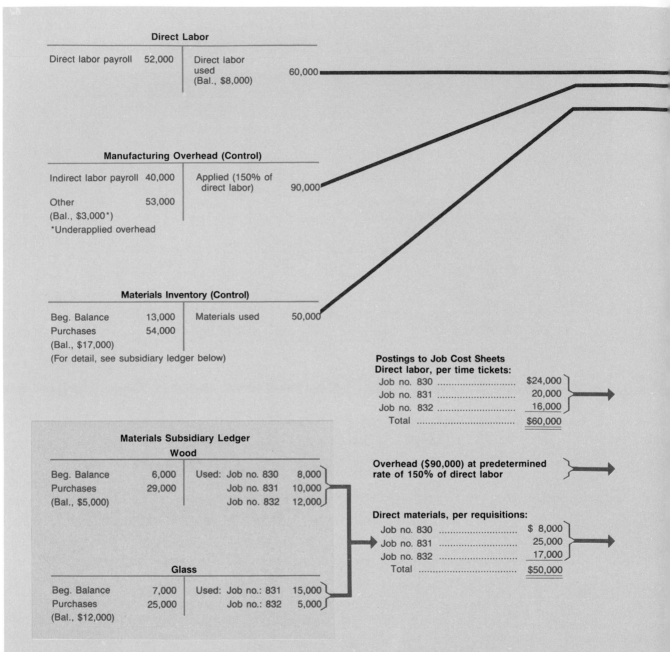

Direct Labor

Direct labor payroll	52,000	Direct labor used (Bal., $8,000)	60,000

Manufacturing Overhead (Control)

Indirect labor payroll	40,000	Applied (150% of direct labor)	90,000
Other	53,000		

(Bal., $3,000*)
*Underapplied overhead

Materials Inventory (Control)

Beg. Balance	13,000	Materials used	50,000
Purchases	54,000		

(Bal., $17,000)
(For detail, see subsidiary ledger below)

Materials Subsidiary Ledger

Wood

Beg. Balance	6,000	Used: Job no. 830	8,000
Purchases	29,000	Job no. 831	10,000
		Job no. 832	12,000

(Bal., $5,000)

Glass

Beg. Balance	7,000	Used: Job no.: 831	15,000
Purchases	25,000	Job no.: 832	5,000

(Bal., $12,000)

Postings to Job Cost Sheets
Direct labor, per time tickets:

Job no. 830	$24,000
Job no. 831	20,000
Job no. 832	16,000
Total	$60,000

Overhead ($90,000) at predetermined rate of 150% of direct labor

Direct materials, per requisitions:

Job no. 830	$ 8,000
Job no. 831	25,000
Job no. 832	17,000
Total	$50,000

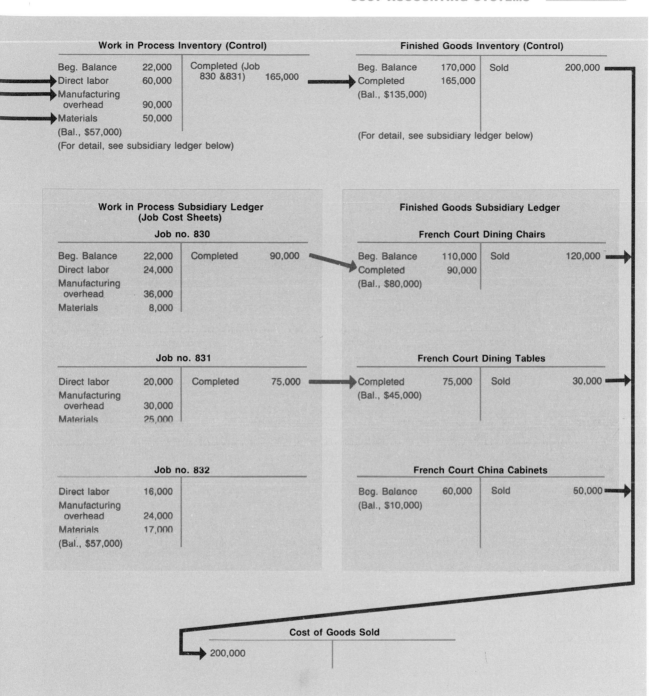

This flowchart summarizes the company's manufacturing operations during the month of January. Notice that each of the inventory controlling accounts (Materials, Work in Process, and Finished Goods) is supported by a subsidiary ledger.

In our flowchart, all subsidiary ledger accounts are shown in T-account form to conserve space. In practice, the individual job cost sheets serve as the subsidiary ledger for the Work in Process controlling account. Also, the subsidiary ledger accounts for direct materials and finished goods would have additional columns providing detailed information as to quantities on hand and unit costs.

We will now use our example of Oak & Glass Furniture Co. to explain the flow of manufacturing costs through a job order cost accounting system.

Accounting for Direct Materials

In a perpetual inventory system, purchases of direct materials are posted from the purchases journal to the accounts in the materials subsidiary ledger. The entries in the subsidiary ledger indicate the type, quantity, and cost of the material purchased. At the end of each month, a summary entry is made debiting the Materials Inventory controlling account for the total cost of direct materials purchased during the period. (The offsetting credit normally is to Accounts Payable.)

■
Flow of costs in a job order cost accounting system.

To obtain materials for use in the production process, the production department must issue a ***materials requisition*** form to the materials warehouse. This requisition shows the quantity of materials needed and the job on which these materials will be used.

Copies of these requisitions are sent to the accounting department, where the cost of the materials placed into production is determined from the materials subsidiary ledger. The cost of the requisitioned materials is entered on the requisition form and in the subsidiary ledger accounts. In the subsidiary ledgers, usage of direct materials is recorded by (1) entering the cost of the materials used on the appropriate job cost sheet, and (2) crediting the materials subsidiary ledger.

At month-end, all the materials requisitions issued during the month are totaled, and the following summary entry is made in the controlling accounts:

■
Recording materials used during the month

Work in Process Inventory	*50,000*	
Materials Inventory		*50,000*

To record the cost of all direct materials placed into production during January.

Accounting for Direct Labor Costs

Debits to the Direct Labor account arise from making payments to direct factory workers; the offsetting credit is to the Cash account.[2] Payments to ***indirect*** factory workers (such as supervisors and security guards) are debited to Manufacturing Overhead, not to the Direct Labor account.

[2] To the extent that amounts are withheld from employees' pay for such purposes as income taxes and social security taxes, the offsetting credits are to various current liability accounts. Accounting for payrolls was discussed in Chapter 11.

The Direct Labor account is credited as direct labor is *used*—that is, as employees work on specific jobs. A number of mechanical and computerized means have been developed for determining the direct labor cost applicable to each job. One common method is to prepare *time cards* for each employee, showing the number of hours worked on each job, the employee's rate of pay, and the direct labor cost chargeable to each job. These time cards become the basis for preparing factory payrolls and also for posting direct labor costs to the work in process subsidiary ledger accounts (job cost sheets).

At the end of each month, a summary entry is made debiting Work in Process Inventory and crediting the Direct Labor account for all direct labor costs assigned to jobs during the month. For Oak & Glass, this entry is:

Recording direct labor costs

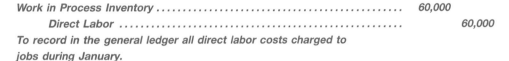

Work in Process Inventory 60,000
    Direct Labor 60,000
To record in the general ledger all direct labor costs charged to jobs during January.

Notice that the Direct Labor account is debited when employees are *paid,* but is credited for the cost of work *performed* on jobs. Work is performed on a daily basis, but employees are paid only at periodic intervals, such as every two weeks. Thus, the direct labor cost charged to jobs does not necessarily equal the amount paid to employees during the month. In our example, $60,000 of direct labor was assigned to the three jobs in process, but payments to employees totaled only $52,000. Thus, the $8,000 credit balance of the Direct Labor account at month-end represents a liability for accrued wages payable.

Accounting for Overhead Costs

Manufacturing overhead includes all manufacturing costs *other than* the costs of direct materials and direct labor. Manufacturing Overhead is a controlling account; the details of the many different types of overhead costs are kept in a subsidiary ledger.

The Manufacturing Overhead account is debited for the *actual* amount of overhead costs incurred during the period. In our illustration, actual overhead costs in January total $93,000. These costs are posted to the overhead account from several sources. Indirect labor costs, for example, come from payroll records; purchases of indirect materials are posted from the purchases journal; payments of utility bills posted from the cash payments journal; and depreciation of plant assets comes from end-of-period adjusting entries in the general journal.

■ **Application of Overhead Costs to Jobs** As explained in Chapter 21, overhead is an *indirect* cost and cannot be traced conveniently into specific jobs or units. Therefore, a predetermined *overhead application rate* is used to assign appropriate amounts of overhead costs to work in process. Oak & Glass uses an overhead application rate equal to *150% of direct labor cost.* Therefore, each job cost sheet is charged with overhead costs equal to 150% of the direct labor cost relating to the job.

The entry to apply overhead costs to the job cost sheet usually is made when the job is completed. However, overhead costs also should be applied to any jobs that are still in process at the end of the accounting period. At the end of each month, a summary entry is made in the general ledger to record all overhead costs applied to jobs during the period, as follows:

Entry to "apply" overhead costs to production

Work in Process Inventory	*90,000*	
Manufacturing Overhead		*90,000*

To charge the Work in Process controlling account with overhead costs applied to jobs during the month (150% of direct labor costs for the month; $60,000 × 150% = $90,000).

■ **Over- or Underapplied Overhead** In our example, actual overhead costs incurred during January amounted to $93,000, while the overhead applied to jobs using the overhead application rate totaled only $90,000. We should not expect that applied overhead will exactly equal actual overhead, since the predetermined overhead application rate is based on estimates.

A debit balance in the Manufacturing Overhead account at month-end indicates that overhead applied to jobs was *less* than the actual overhead costs incurred during the month. Therefore, a debit balance remaining in the Manufacturing Overhead account is called *underapplied overhead.* A credit balance remaining in the account indicates that overhead applied to jobs *exceeded* actual overhead costs; thus, a credit balance is termed *overapplied overhead.*

The month-end balances remaining in the Manufacturing Overhead account normally are allowed to accumulate throughout the year. These amounts tend to "balance out" from month to month, and the amount of overapplied or underapplied overhead at year-end usually *is not material* in dollar amount. In this case, the year-end balance in the Manufacturing Overhead account may be closed *directly into the Cost of Goods Sold,* on the grounds that most of the error is applicable to goods sold during the year. If the year-end balance in the overhead account *is material* in dollar amount, it should be apportioned among the Work in Process Inventory, Finished Goods Inventory, and Cost of Goods Sold accounts.

Accounting for Completed Jobs

We have now explained how manufacturing costs are charged (debited) to the Work in Process Inventory account, and also how the costs of specific jobs are separately accumulated on job cost sheets.

As each job is completed, the job cost sheet is removed from the work in process subsidiary ledger and the manufacturing costs on the sheet are totaled to determine the cost of finished goods manufactured. This cost then is transferred from the Work in Process Inventory account to the Finished Goods Inventory account.

During January, Oak & Glass completed work on job nos. 830 and 831. The entries to record completion of these jobs are illustrated below:

Entries to record completed jobs

Finished Goods Inventory	*90,000*	
Work in Process Inventory		*90,000*

To record completion of job. no. 830, consisting of 600 French Court dining chairs (unit cost, $150).

Finished Goods Inventory	*75,000*	
Work in Process Inventory		*75,000*

To record completion of job no. 831, consisting of 100 French Court
dining tables (unit cost, $750).

As sales of these units occur, the unit cost figures will be used in determining the cost of goods sold. For example, the sale of 40 of the French Court dining tables at a total sales price of $48,000 is recorded below:

Accounts Receivable, Anthony's Fine Furniture	*48,000*	
Sales		*48,000*

Sold 40 French Court dining tables on account, terms 2/10, n/30.

Cost of Goods Sold	*30,000*	
Finished Goods Inventory		*30,000*

To record the cost of the 40 French Court dining tables sold to
Anthony's Fine Furniture (40 × $750 cost per unit = $30,000).

Job Order Cost Systems in Service Industries

In the preceding discussion, we have emphasized the use of job order cost systems in manufacturing companies. However, many service industries also use these systems to accumulate the costs of servicing a particular customer.

In a hospital, for example, each patient represents a separate "job," and the costs of caring for the patient are accumulated on a job cost sheet. Costs of such items as medicine, blood transfusions, and X-rays represent the usage of direct materials; services rendered by doctors are direct labor. The costs of nursing, meals, linen service, and depreciation of the hospital building and equipment all are part of the hospital's overhead. In a hospital, overhead usually is applied to each patient's account at a daily rate.

PROCESS COST SYSTEMS

As emphasized in the preceding section, job order cost systems are appropriate when each unit of product, or each "batch" of production, is manufactured to different specifications. In order to operate a job order system, it is necessary to be able to *identify the units* included in each job at every stage of the production process. What happens, then, when a company produces a continuous stream of identical products, such as bottles of beer or kilowatts of electricity? The answer is that these companies use *process cost systems,* rather than job order systems.

Characteristics of a Process Cost System

Objective 4
Explain the characteristics of a process cost accounting system.

The manufacture of any product usually involves several specific steps, or manufacturing *processes.* For accounting purposes, each manufacturing process is viewed as a separate processing department. A separate Work in Process Inventory account is maintained for each processing department; this account is charged (debited) with all manufacturing costs incurred in performing the process during the current accounting period.[3] At the end of the period, the per-unit cost of performing the process is determined by dividing the costs charged to the departmental work in process account by the number of units processed during the period. The cost of a finished unit is determined by combining the per-unit cost of performing each process involved in the unit's manufacture.

Flow of Costs in a Process Cost System

To illustrate the basic features of a process cost system, assume that Baker Labs manufactures a nonprescription cold remedy called Conquest. Two processing departments are involved in the manufacture of Conquest: the Mixing Department and the Packaging Department. In the Mixing Department, the various chemicals used to make the cold remedy are blended together. The product is then transferred to the Packaging Department, where it is sealed in small "tamper-proof" packages. Packages of Conquest are the company's finished product; these packages are stored in a warehouse and shipped to customers (drug stores and grocery stores) as orders are received.

The flow of manufacturing costs through the process cost system of Baker Labs during the month of July is summarized on the next page. Notice that a separate Work in Process Inventory account is used for *each production process,* enabling accountants to accumulate separately the manufacturing costs relating to each process. As the Mixing Department completes work on specific units, the cost of these units is transferred into the Work in Process Inventory account for the Packaging Department. Only when units emerge from the Packaging Department are they regarded as finished goods.

The cost flows summarized in this illustration will now be used to explain the operation of a process cost accounting system. Our illustration is based on the assumption that Baker Labs uses the *first-in, first-out* (FIFO) method of inventory valuation. (Other inventory valuation methods, such as average cost, will be discussed in the cost accounting course.)

■ **Direct Materials** Purchases of materials are debited to the Materials Inventory controlling account, and a subsidiary ledger is maintained showing the unit cost and quantity on hand for each type of direct materials.

■
Cost flow diagram for process costing— notice the departmental Work in Process accounts

To obtain direct materials for use in production, the Processing Departments must issue materials requisition forms, and copies of these forms are sent to the Accounting Department. (Direct materials used in the Mixing Department include various chemicals; direct materials used in the Packaging Department are the "tamper-proof" containers.) The Accounting Department immediately updates the materials subsidiary ledger and, at the end of the month, makes a summary entry to charge the departmental work in process accounts for all direct materials requisitioned during the month. The summary entry for July appears at the top of page 898.

---

[3] One objective of a cost accounting system is to provide managers with *timely* information as to manufacturing costs. Therefore, the time period used in a process cost system usually is one month or less.

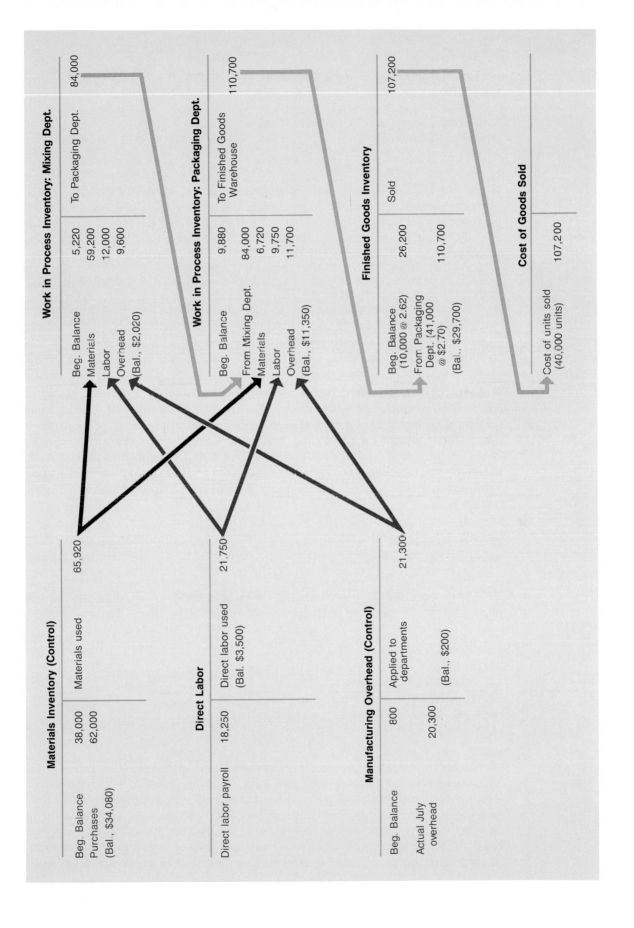

Work in Process Inventory: Mixing Dept.

			To Packaging Dept.	84,000
Beg. Balance	5,220			
Materials	59,200			
Labor	12,000			
Overhead	9,600			
(Bal., $2,020)				

Work in Process Inventory: Packaging Dept.

			To Finished Goods Warehouse	110,700
Beg. Balance	9,880			
From Mixing Dept.	84,000			
Materials	6,720			
Labor	9,750			
Overhead	11,700			
(Bal., $11,350)				

Finished Goods Inventory

			Sold	107,200
Beg. Balance (10,000 @ 2.62)	26,200			
From Packaging Dept. (41,000 @ $2.70)	110,700			
(Bal., $29,700)				

Cost of Goods Sold

Cost of units sold (40,000 units)	107,200

Materials Inventory (Control)

		Materials used	65,920
Beg. Balance	38,000		
Purchases	62,000		
(Bal., $34,080)			

Direct Labor

		Direct labor used	21,750
Direct labor payroll	18,250	(Bal. $3,500)	

Manufacturing Overhead (Control)

		Applied to departments	21,300
Beg. Balance	800		
Actual July overhead	20,300	(Bal., $200)	

Work in Process Inventory, Mixing Department	*59,200*
Work in Process Inventory, Packaging Department.......................	*6,720*
Materials Inventory	*65,920*

To record the cost of direct materials requisitioned for use in
production during July.

■ **Direct Labor** During July, payments to direct workers totaled $18,250, and this amount was debited to the Direct Labor account. The direct labor cost used within each processing department during July is determined from employees' time cards. The month-end entry to record the direct labor costs chargeable to each department is:

Work in Process, Mixing Department	*12,000*
Work in Process, Packaging Department	*9,750*
Direct Labor	*21,750*

To record the cost of direct labor used in July.

■ **Manufacturing Overhead** During July, actual overhead costs of $22,300 were charged to the Manufacturing Overhead account. Baker Labs follows a policy of applying overhead costs to production *as a percentage of direct labor costs.* (Later in this chapter, we will discuss the alternative of charging actual overhead costs to production.) At the beginning of the year, the company developed the following overhead application rates, based upon the budgeted amounts of overhead and direct labor costs for each processing department:

Mixing Department	*80% of direct labor cost*
Packaging Department..	*120% of direct labor cost*

At the end of July, the following entry is made to apply overhead to the departmental Work in Process Inventory accounts:

Work in Process Inventory, Mixing Department	*9,600*
Work in Process Inventory, Packaging Department.......................	*11,700*
Manufacturing Overhead..	*21,300*

To apply overhead costs to departments, based on direct labor
costs (Mixing Dept., $12,000 × 80% = $9,600; Packaging Dept.,
$9,750 × 120% = $11,700).

Notice that the Manufacturing Overhead controlling account had a debit balance of $800 at the beginning of July. This debit balance represented a small amount of *underapplied overhead* that had accumulated over the first half of the year. In July, however, applied overhead exceeds actual overhead costs by $1,000. Thus, at the end of July, the overhead account has a credit balance of $200, representing a small amount of *overapplied overhead.* Throughout the year, the balances in the overhead account are allowed to carry forward from month to month. At year-end, any remaining balance normally is closed out to the Cost of Goods Sold account.[4]

Equivalent Full Units—the Key to Determining Unit Cost

A basic objective of a process cost system is to determine the unit cost of direct materials, direct labor, and overhead for each manufacturing process or department. These unit costs become the basis for valuing inventories and for tracing the flow of costs through the departmental work in process accounts and finally to Finished Goods Inventory and to Cost of Goods Sold.

If all units of product in a given department are ***completely processed*** (started and completed) during the period, computing unit costs is a simple matter of dividing the departmental costs by the number of units processed. In most cases, however, there are unfinished units of product on hand at the beginning as well as at the end of the accounting period. When some of the units on hand are unfinished, we cannot compute unit costs merely by dividing total costs by the number of units worked on, for this would assign the same unit cost to finished and unfinished goods. If completed and partially completed units of product are expressed in ***equivalent full units*** of completed product, however, this difficulty is overcome. Meaningful unit costs can then be determined by dividing the total cost by the equivalent full units produced. This computation is illustrated below for direct materials:

■
Units costs based on equivalent full units

$$\text{Materials cost per unit} = \frac{\text{total cost of direct materials used during month}}{\text{equivalent full units produced during month}}$$

Objective 5
Define and compute "equivalent full units" of production.

■ **What Are "Equivalent Full Units"?** Equivalent full units are a measure of the ***work done*** in a given accounting period. The concept of an equivalent full unit is based on the assumption that creating two units, each of which is 50% complete, represents the ***same amount of work*** as does producing one finished unit. Similarly, producing 1,000 units that are 25% complete is viewed as equivalent to 250 full units of production.

The work accomplished by a manufacturing department during a given accounting period may include (1) completing units which were already in process at the beginning of the period, (2) working on units started and completed during the current period, and (3) working on units which are still in process at the end of the current period. If we are to measure the work accomplished by the department, we must determine the equivalent full units of production represented ***by each of these three types of work effort.***

To illustrate this concept, we will use the production activities of Baker Labs during the month of July. Assume that the production managers of the company's two processing departments provide the following summary of the ***numbers of units*** processed within their departments during July. (Notice that the following schedule describes the ***extent of completion*** of units in process at the beginning and end of the month.)

---

[4] As explained earlier in this chapter, if the year-end balance in the overhead account is material in dollar amount, it should be apportioned among the Cost of Goods Sold, Finished Goods Inventory, and Work in Process Inventory accounts, based on the relative balances in each account. This allocation procedure is seldom necessary.

Production Summary—in Units
for the Month Ended July 31, 1991

	MIXING DEPARTMENT	PACKAGING DEPARTMENT
Units in process, July 1....................................	5,000[a]	4,000[c]
Units started and completed in July.......................	37,000	37,000
Units completed and transferred to next department or to finished goods in July	42,000	41,000
Units in process, July 31.................................	4,000[b]	5,000[d]

[a] 60% complete as to materials and conversion costs on July 1.

[b] 25% complete as to materials and conversion costs on July 31.

[c] 100% complete as to materials and 75% complete as to conversion costs on July 1.

[d] 100% complete as to materials and 20% complete as to conversion costs on July 31.

In describing the extent of completion of the units in process, notice the use of the term **conversion costs.** This term is used to describe the costs of both direct labor **and** manufacturing overhead, as these are the costs of converting direct materials into finished goods.

The number of equivalent full units of production processed by the Mixing Department during July is determined as follows:

Computation of Equivalent Full Units—Mixing Department
(Direct Materials and Conversion Costs)

	UNITS ×	PORTION COMPLETED = IN JULY	EQUIVALENT FULL UNITS PRODUCED
Units in process at the beginning of July (60% completed in June as to materials and conversion costs)...	5,000	40%	2,000
Units started and completed in July...................	37,000	100%	37,000
Units completed and transferred to Packaging Dept. in July...	42,000		
Units in process at the end of July (25% complete as to materials and conversion costs)	4,000	25%	1,000
Equivalent full units of production during July			40,000

Although 42,000 units of product were completed and transferred to the Packaging Department, the actual amount of work accomplished in the Mixing Department during July was equivalent to producing only **40,000 "full" units.** The work performed in July consists of 2,000 equivalent full units of work (40% of 5,000) to complete the beginning inventory of work in process, 37,000 equivalent full units of work to start and complete additional units during July, and 1,000 equivalent full units (25% of 4,000) on the units still in process at month-end.

Conversion costs normally are added to units of product at a uniform rate throughout the production process. Thus, units that are 25% complete are assigned 25% of the per-unit conversion costs. In the Mixing Department, direct materials also are added to units at a uniform rate. Therefore, the equivalent number of full units produced in the department is **the same** with respect to materials used and conversion costs.

■ Materials and Conversion Costs Added at Different Rates It is not unusual for materials and conversion costs to be added to units of product at *different* rates. For example, 100% of the materials needed to produce finished goods may be placed into production at the beginning of the production process. In these situations, the number of equivalent full units produced during the period must be *computed separately* for materials and for conversion costs.

To illustrate, assume that in the Packaging Department of Baker Labs, all direct materials are placed into production at the *beginning* of the production process, but that conversion costs are applied at a *uniform rate* throughout the process. The equivalent number of full units produced is computed separately for materials used and for conversion costs, as illustrated below.

Computation of Equivalent Full Units—Packaging Department

	UNITS ×	PORTION COMPLETED IN JULY	= EQUIVALENT FULL UNITS PRODUCED
Direct Materials:			
Units in process at the beginning of July (*100% completed in June as to materials*)	*4,000*	-0-	-0-
Units started and completed in July	*37,000*	100%	*37,000*
Units completed and transferred to Finished Goods Warehouse in July	*41,000*		
Units in process at the end of July (*100% complete as to materials*)	*5,000*	100%	*5,000*
Equivalent full units of production during July— direct materials			*42,000*
Conversion Costs:			
Units in process at the beginning of July (*75% completed in June as to conversion costs*)	*4,000*	25%	*1,000*
Units started and completed in July	*37,000*	100%	*37,000*
Units completed and transferred to Finished Goods Warehouse in July	*41,000*		
Units in process at the end of July (*20% complete as to conversion costs*)	*5,000*	20%	*1,000*
Equivalent full units of production during July— conversion costs			*39,000*

In the Packaging Department, enough direct materials were placed into production to produce 42,000 units of product. However, the amount of labor and overhead used was sufficient to produce only 39,000 equivalent full units. Thus, the equivalent full units of production by the department during July *differ* with respect to materials and to conversion costs.

Determining Unit Costs

At the end of each month, the Accounting Department prepares a *process cost summary* for each production department. These cost summaries are specially designed working papers, upon which accountants (1) summarize the manufacturing costs charged to each department, (2) determine the departmental unit costs of production, and (3) allocate the departmental manufacturing costs between completed units and work still in process at month-end.

Process Cost Summary for the Mixing Department

The process cost summary for the Mixing Department is illustrated below:

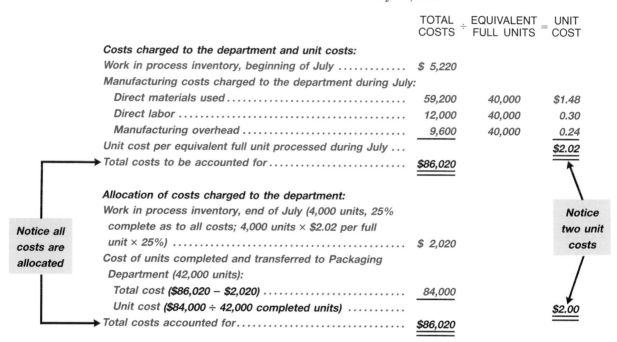

BAKER LABS
Process Cost Summary—Mixing Department
For the Month Ended July 31, 1991

	TOTAL COSTS ÷	EQUIVALENT FULL UNITS =	UNIT COST
Costs charged to the department and unit costs:			
Work in process inventory, beginning of July	$ 5,220		
Manufacturing costs charged to the department during July:			
Direct materials used	59,200	40,000	$1.48
Direct labor	12,000	40,000	0.30
Manufacturing overhead	9,600	40,000	0.24
Unit cost per equivalent full unit processed during July ...			$2.02
Total costs to be accounted for	$86,020		
Allocation of costs charged to the department:			
Work in process inventory, end of July (4,000 units, 25% complete as to all costs; 4,000 units × $2.02 per full unit × 25%)	$ 2,020		
Cost of units completed and transferred to Packaging Department (42,000 units):			
Total cost ($86,020 − $2,020)	84,000		
Unit cost ($84,000 ÷ 42,000 completed units)			$2.00
Total costs accounted for	$86,020		

Notice all costs are allocated

Notice two unit costs

We will now explain the steps in the preparation of this working paper.

Objective 6
Prepare a process cost summary for a production department using a process cost system.

■ **Step 1: Summarize the Manufacturing Costs Charged to the Department** The top portion of the process cost summary begins with a list of all manufacturing costs applicable to units worked during July. These costs include the beginning inventory of work in process, and all manufacturing costs charged to the department during July. Notice that the sum of these costs, $86,020, is labeled "Total costs to be accounted for." As we shall see, "accounting for" these costs means assigning them either to units completed during July, or to units still in process at July 31. The information needed to complete the "Total costs" column is found in the debit side of the departmental work in process account (page 897).

■ **Step 2: Determine Unit Costs** The second step in preparing a process cost summary is to determine the per-unit cost of the manufacturing activities performed by the department during the month. This is accomplished by dividing each of the three categories of manufacturing costs incurred during July by the *equivalent full units* of production for the month.

For example, during July the Mixing Department used direct materials costing $59,200. Our computations above show that the department produced the equivalent of 40,000 full units. Therefore, each equivalent full unit produced by the Mixing Department during July required an average of *$1.48* in direct materials costs ($59,200 ÷ 40,000 units = $1.48 per unit). Similar computations are made to compute the per-unit costs of direct labor and manufacturing overhead.[5] These three unit costs then are combined, indicating an average cost of *$2.02* for each *equivalent full unit* produced by the Mixing Department during July.

■ **Step 3: Allocate the Costs Charged to the Department between Completed Units and Units Still in Process**   Once the per-unit manufacturing costs have been determined, we may allocate our $86,020 in "Total costs to be accounted for" between the two types of departmental output—units completed and transferred to the Packaging Department, and units still in process in the Mixing Department at month-end. This allocation of costs is illustrated in the bottom section of the process cost summary.

We could use the unit cost figures from the top section of our cost summary to compute separately the cost of the ending inventory of work in process and the cost of units completed during the period. However, it is **not necessary** to compute both of these amounts in this manner. It is quicker and easier to use unit costs to compute only the value of the ending inventory of work in process. We may then simply **assign the remainder** of the $86,020 total costs to the units completed during July.

Baker Labs uses the first-in, first-out (FIFO) method of inventory valuation; therefore, the ending inventory of work in process is valued using the most recent unit costs—namely, those incurred during July. Work in process in the Mixing Department at July 31 amounts to 4,000 units, each of which is 25% complete with respect to all manufacturing costs. Therefore, the cost of this ending inventory is *$2,020* (4,000 units × $2.02 × 25%).

Deducting this $2,020 from the $86,020 total costs to be accounted for leaves a remainder of *$84,000,* representing the cost of units completed by the Mixing Department during July.[6] The $2.00 unit cost of these completed goods is determined by dividing their total cost ($84,000) by the number of completed units (42,000).

---

[5] In determining the unit cost of work done in July, we do not express the $5,220 beginning inventory of work in process on a per-unit basis, as these manufacturing costs were incurred in June.

[6] The $84,000 cost of the 42,000 units completed by the Mixing Department during July may be verified as follows:

Work in process inventory, July 1 (5,000 units, 60% complete)		*$ 5,220*
Costs added in July to complete these 5,000 units:		
Direct materials used (5,000 units × $1.48 × 40%)	*$ 2,960*	
Direct labor (5,000 units × $0.30 × 40%)	*600*	
Manufacturing overhead (5,000 units × $0.24 × 40%)	*480*	*4,040*
Total cost of first 5,000 units completed in July		*$ 9,260*
Cost of 37,000 units started and completed during July:		
Direct materials used (37,000 units × $1.48)	*$54,760*	
Direct labor (37,000 units × $0.30)	*11,100*	
Manufacturing overhead (37,000 units × $0.24)	*8,880*	
Total cost of next 37,000 units completed during July		*74,740*
Cost of 42,000 units completed and transferred to Packaging Department during July		*$84,000*

Upon completion of the process cost summary, the following journal entry is made to summarize the cost of units completed by the Mixing Department during the month:

Work in Process Inventory, Packaging Department 84,000
    Work in Process Inventory, Mixing Department 84,000
To record the cost of 42,000 units transferred from the Mixing
Department to the Packaging Department during July. (Unit cost,
$84,000 ÷ 42,000 units = $2.00.)

■ **Unit Cost of Completed Products**   Notice that the average cost of units *completed* during July ($2.00) differs slightly from the average cost of manufacturing an *equivalent full unit* of product during the month ($2.02). The reason for this small difference is that the cost of producing an equivalent full unit is based *entirely upon manufacturing costs incurred during July.* Some of the units completed during July, however, received part of their processing during June.[7]

Each of these two unit costs is important and serves a separate purpose. The $2.02 per unit is the *most current* unit cost figure; therefore, this amount is helpful in evaluating the efficiency of the Mixing Department during July. Also, this current unit cost is used in valuing the ending inventory of work in process under the FIFO method.

The $2.00 unit cost, on the other hand, is the average cost incurred in manufacturing the 42,000 units completed during July. This is the unit cost that will be carried forward into the process cost summary of the Packaging Department and, eventually, into the Finished Goods Inventory and Cost of Goods Sold accounts.

Process Cost Summary for the Packaging Department

The process cost summary for the Packaging Department is illustrated on page 905. In most respects, this schedule parallels that prepared for the Mixing Department. There are, however, several new features that deserve attention.

First, notice that the manufacturing costs charged to the Packaging Department include the *cost of units transferred in from the Mixing Department* during the month. The $84,000 cost of these units, and also the $2.00 unit cost, were computed in the process cost summary of the Mixing Department (page 902). From the viewpoint of the Packaging Department, the units transferred in from the Mixing Department are a form of direct material to be used in the packaging process.

Second, notice that *different amounts* of equivalent full units of production are used in computing the unit costs of materials and conversion costs (direct labor and manufacturing overhead). We explained earlier in this chapter that in the Packaging Department, 100% of the direct materials are placed into production at the start of the production process, while conversion costs are applied uniformly throughout the process. As a result, the equivalent full units of production turned out by the department may *differ* with respect to materi-

---

[7] In our illustration, 5,000 of the units completed in July received 60% of their processing in June.

BAKER LABS
Process Cost Summary—Packaging Department
For the Month Ended July 31, 1991

	TOTAL COSTS	÷ EQUIVALENT FULL UNITS	= UNIT COST
Costs charged to the department and unit costs:			
Work in process inventory, beginning of July	$ 9,880		
Cost of 42,000 units transferred in from Mixing			
Department during July.............................	84,000		$2.00
Manufacturing costs added by Packaging Department			
during July:			
Direct materials used...............................	6,720	42,000	.16
Direct labor	9,750	39,000	.25
Manufacturing overhead	11,700	39,000	.30
Unit cost per equivalent unit processed during July....			$2.71
Total costs to be accounted for.....................	$122,050		

Allocation of costs charged to the department:		
Work in process inventory, end of July (5,000 units, 100%		
complete as to materials, 20% as to conversion costs):		
Cost of units transferred in from the Mixing		
Department (5,000 units × $2.00)	$ 10,000	
Direct materials added (5,000 units × $.16 × 100%) ...	800	
Direct labor (5,000 units × $.25 × 20%)	250	
Manufacturing overhead (5,000 units × $.30 × 20%) ..	300	
Total cost of work in process inventory at July 31 .	$ 11,350	
Cost of units completed and transferred to Finished		
Goods Warehouse (41,000 units):		
Total cost ($122,050 − $11,350).....................	110,700	
Unit cost ($110,700 ÷ 41,000 finished units)		$2.70
Total costs accounted for...........................	$122,050	

als and to conversion costs. (The equivalent full units of production for the Packaging Department in July were computed in the schedules illustrated above.)

A third new feature in the process cost summary of the Packaging Department is the itemizing of the various cost elements included in the ending inventory of work in process. Since these units are 100% complete as to materials, but only 20% complete as to conversion costs, the amount of each manufacturing cost to be included in these units must be computed separately. Also note that the costs transferred in from the Mixing Department, amounting to $2.00 per unit, are included in the cost of the 5,000 units in process at July 31.

All of the $122,050 in costs charged to the Packaging Department during July are applicable either to units still in process at July 31 or to units completed during the month. Since we have assigned $11,350 of these costs to the ending inventory of work in process, the remaining $110,700 ($122,050 − $11,350) represents the cost of the 41,000 units completed during July. The entry to transfer the cost of goods completed by the Packaging Department during July to the Finished Goods Inventory account is:

Finished Goods Inventory	*110,700*	
Work in Process Inventory, Packaging Department		*110,700*

To record the cost of 41,000 units of finished goods completing the production process during July. (Unit cost, $110,700 ÷ 41,000 units = $2.70.)

As these finished units are sold, their cost will be transferred from the Finished Goods Inventory account to the Cost of Goods Sold at a rate of $2.70 per unit.

Process Cost Systems: Actual Overhead or Applied Overhead?

In our example of a process cost system, we used an *overhead application rate* to charge an appropriate amount of manufacturing overhead to the departmental work in process accounts each month. We mentioned, however, that the possibility of using *actual overhead costs* would be discussed later in the chapter.

In a process cost system, overhead is not charged to the departmental work in process accounts until the end of the accounting period. Therefore, it is possible to charge these accounts with the actual overhead costs incurred during the month, rather than with the amount of overhead indicated by using an overhead application rate.[8] In fact, many manufacturing companies *do* charge production departments with actual overhead costs on a monthly basis.

At first glance, charging the actual overhead costs to production departments has great appeal. For one thing, this approach eliminates the problem of accounting for overapplied or underapplied overhead. However, the use of an overhead application rate often provides *more useful* unit cost information, especially if (1) some major overhead costs occur at infrequent intervals, or (2) the volume of production varies from month to month.

■ **Costs Occurring at Infrequent Intervals**   Some overhead costs occur at infrequent intervals, rather than uniformly from month to month. Examples include repairs and refurbishing projects. If actual overhead costs are assigned to production on a monthly basis, the entire amount of these infrequent costs is assigned to the units produced during the month in which the cost happens to occur; none of the cost is borne by units produced in other months.

To illustrate, assume that Baker Labs shuts down its factory for two weeks every August to repair equipment and repaint the building. It is not reasonable to say that these actions relate only to the limited number of units produced during the remainder of August. Obviously, these annual costs relate to production throughout the year.

An overhead application rate avoids the "infrequent cost" problem, because the rate is based upon the estimated overhead cost for the *entire year.* Thus, the costs of infrequent events, such as repairs, are spread uniformly over units produced throughout the year.

---

[8] Actual overhead *cannot* be applied to specific jobs in a job order cost system, because actual overhead costs for the month are *not known* at the time that specific jobs are completed. Therefore, all companies with job order cost systems use overhead application rates.

■ **Fluctuations in the Level of Production**   A second problem in the use of actual overhead costs may arise if the number of units produced fluctuates from month to month. This problem stems from the fact that many elements of manufacturing overhead are fixed costs, rather than variable costs.

Fixed costs are those that tend to remain relatively fixed (constant) from month to month. Examples of fixed overhead costs include the monthly salary paid to the plant manager, and the depreciation, property taxes, and insurance on plant assets. *Variable costs,* in contrast, are those that *change in approximate proportion to the level of production.* Examples of variable overhead costs include factory utilities and the costs of some indirect materials used in the manufacturing process.[9]

Because many overhead costs are fixed, total monthly overhead *does not* vary in direct proportion to the number of units produced. Thus, if we allocate actual overhead costs incurred each month to output for that month, the unit cost of production may vary widely from month to month. In months of high output, per-unit overhead costs would be relatively low; in months of low output, per-unit overhead costs would be relatively high.

To illustrate, assume that Drew Corporation has the capacity to produce 10,000 units per month. Fixed overhead costs are *$120,000 per month,* and variable overhead amounts to *$2 per unit* manufactured. The overhead costs per unit at different levels of output are shown below:

Overhead Costs per Unit at Different Level of Output

	LEVEL OF OUTPUT		
	10,000 UNITS	8,000 UNITS	6,000 UNITS
Fixed overhead costs......................................	$120,000	$120,000	$120,000
Variable overhead costs ($2 per unit)......................	20,000	16,000	12,000
Total overhead costs (a)	$140,000	$136,000	$132,000
Units produced (b)..	10,000	8,000	6,000
Overhead cost per unit (a) ÷ (b)	$14	$17	$22

For most business purposes, management needs to know the "normal" unit cost of producing a product, not monthly costs that vary significantly depending upon the volume of production. Again, this problem is solved by using an overhead application rate. As the application rate is based upon budgeted overhead for the entire year, the fixed overhead costs are "averaged out" over all units, regardless of whether the units are produced in a high-volume month or a low-volume month.

■ **Using Actual Overhead May Work Well in Large Companies**   The problems that we have described above are far more likely to arise in small companies than in large ones. In large companies, such costs as maintenance and repairs do not vary much from month to month. Also, most large companies are able to schedule their production so as to produce approximately the

---

[9] The concepts of fixed and variable costs extend to many costs and expenses other than manufacturing overhead. The costs of direct materials and direct labor, for example, are variable costs. These concepts are explored further in Chapter 23.

same number of units each month. Thus, for a large company using a process cost system, charging the work in process accounts with the actual amount of monthly overhead costs may work just as well as using an overhead application rate.

Just-in-Time Systems and Other Special Situations

We have illustrated a "full-blown" cost accounting system that includes controlling accounts and subsidiary ledgers for each of the three categories of a manufacturing company's inventory. Depending upon the nature of their operations, some companies may be able to eliminate the need for certain inventory controlling accounts and subsidiary ledgers. Consider, for example, a company that manufactures products only to fill specific sales orders already received from customers. This company has no need of a Finished Goods Inventory account or subsidiary ledger. As products are completed, their manufacturing cost may be transferred directly from the Work in Process Inventory account to the Cost of Goods Sold.

In recent years, much attention has been paid to the *just-in-time* concept of manufacturing operations. The phrase "just-in-time" usually means that purchases of direct materials arrive just in time for use in the manufacturing process—often within a few hours of when the materials are scheduled for use. A second application of the just-in-time concept is completing the manufacturing process just in time to ship finished goods to customers.

Just-in-time manufacturing may reduce or eliminate the need for materials inventory records as well as those for finished goods. Purchases of materials may be debited directly to the Work in Process Inventory accounts, and the cost of finished goods may be debited directly to the Cost of Goods Sold.

In addition to simplifying the accounting process, a just-in-time system offers other advantages to the manufacturing company. The most significant benefit is that the company does not have to "tie up" money in large inventories of direct materials and finished goods. Also, the company does not need to maintain storage facilities for these inventories. The disadvantage of a just-in-time system is that a delay in the arrival of a direct material may bring manufacturing operations to a halt. Therefore, the just-in-time concept is only feasible when the suppliers of direct materials are highly reliable.

CASE IN POINT ■ One of the pioneers of just-in-time manufacturing is Toyota, the Japanese automaker. Toyota's main plant is located in an area of Japan called "Toyota Valley." Many of the company's suppliers of direct materials also are located in Toyota Valley, and produce materials primarily for Toyota. Thus, the suppliers' economic survival depends upon their meeting their delivery schedules at the Toyota plant.

While Toyota is able to minimize its inventories of direct materials, some of its suppliers maintain large inventories of these goods in order to ensure timely deliveries. In a sense, "just-in-time" means "passing-the-buck"—let your suppliers maintain your inventories of direct materials.

Actually, very few manufacturing companies are able to eliminate entirely inventories of direct materials and finished goods. Therefore, most cost accounting systems contain all the elements discussed in this chapter. The reader should recognize, however, that the accounting records and procedures that comprise any cost accounting system should be specifically tailored to suit the nature of the company's operations and the information needs of the company's managers.

End-of-Chapter Review

CONCEPTS INTRODUCED OR EMPHASIZED IN CHAPTER 22

Major concepts introduced in this chapter include:

■ The determination of unit costs in both job order cost systems and process cost systems, and the types of manufacturing operations to which each system is best suited.

■ The role of a job cost sheet in a job order cost system.

■ Underapplied and overapplied overhead; where it comes from and what is done with it at year-end.

■ The role of departmental Work in Process Inventory accounts in a process cost system.

■ Equivalent full units of production as a measure of the work accomplished and as the basis for determining unit costs.

■ Use of unit costs in the valuation of inventories and the cost of goods sold.

■ Fixed costs, as distinguished from variable costs.

■ Why charging actual monthly overhead costs to production may distort unit cost figures, and why use of an overhead application rate avoids this distortion.

■ "Just-in-time" manufacturing operations.

In this chapter we emphasize the determination of unit cost. Unit cost data play a key role in each of the four remaining chapters. We will see that unit cost data are useful in a wide variety of managerial decisions. A second concept introduced in this chapter—the distinction between fixed and variable costs—also plays an important role in many managerial decisions. The distinctions between fixed and variable costs are discussed further in the next chapter.

KEY TERMS INTRODUCED OR EMPHASIZED IN CHAPTER 22

Conversion costs   Manufacturing costs incurred in the process of converting direct materials into finished goods. Conversion costs include both direct labor and manufacturing overhead.

Equivalent full units of production   A measure of the work done during an accounting period. Includes work done on beginning and ending inventories of work in process as well as work on units completely processed during the period.

Fixed cost   A cost that does not vary in direct response to changes in the level of activity.

Job cost sheet   A record used in a job order cost system to summarize the manufacturing costs (materials, labor, and overhead) applicable to each job, or batch or production. Job cost sheets may be viewed as a subsidiary ledger supporting the balance of the Work in Process Inventory control account.

Job order cost system   A cost accounting system under which the focal point of costing is a quantity of product known as a *job* or *lot*. Costs of direct materials, direct labor, and manufacturing overhead applicable to each job are compiled to arrive at average unit cost.

"Just-in-time" manufacturing   A modern approach to scheduling manufacturing activities in a manner to minimize or even eliminate inventories of direct materials and of finished goods. Purchased materials arrive just in time for use in the manufacturing process, and finished goods are shipped immediately upon completion of the production process.

Overhead application rate   A device used to apply a "normal" amount of overhead costs to work in process. The rate is predetermined at the beginning of the year and expresses the percentage relationship between estimated total overhead for the year and the estimated total of some "cost driver," such as direct labor hours, direct labor costs, or machine hours. Use of the overhead application rate causes overhead to be charged to work in process in proportion to the amount of "cost driver" traceable to those units.

Over- or underapplied overhead   The difference between the actual manufacturing overhead incurred during the period and the amount applied to work in process by use of a predetermined overhead application rate.

Process cost summary   A schedule prepared for each production process or department in a process cost system. Shows the costs charged to the department during the period, the computation of unit manufacturing costs, and the allocation of departmental costs between units completed during the period and the ending inventory of work in process.

Process cost system   A cost accounting system used mostly in industries such as petroleum or chemicals characterized by continuous mass production. Costs are not assigned to specific units but to a manufacturing process or department.

Variable cost   A cost that changes in approximate proportion to some level of activity, such as the level of production. The cost of direct materials used is a variable cost.

DEMONSTRATION PROBLEM FOR YOUR REVIEW

Sumasani Corp. manufactures EndAll, an electronic unit that plays a wide variety of video games on a television set. The units are entirely assembled in one production department. All manufacturing costs are incurred at a uniform rate throughout the production process. The following information is available for the month of March:

Beginning inventory of work in process		$154,000
Manufacturing costs incurred during March:		
Direct materials	$360,000	
Direct labor	90,000	
Manufacturing overhead	135,000	585,000
Total costs to be accounted for		$739,000

The beginning inventory of work in process consisted of 3,000 units, each 80% complete as of the beginning of March. In addition to completing these units, the department started and completed another 7,000 units during March, and also started work on an additional 2,000 units which were 70% complete at month-end.

Instructions **a** Compute the equivalent full units of production during March.

b Prepare a process cost summary for the Production Department covering the month of March. (The company values its inventories using the FIFO method; therefore, you are to use the March unit costs in valuing the ending inventory of work in process.)

c Prepare journal entries to record (1) the manufacturing costs charged to the Production Department during June (use one compound entry), and (2) the transfer of 100,000 completed units to the finished goods warehouse.

SOLUTION TO DEMONSTRATION PROBLEM

a Computation of Equivalent Full Units—Materials and Conversion Costs

	UNITS	PORTION × COMPLETED IN MARCH	= EQUIVALENT FULL UNITS PRODUCED
Units in process at the beginning of March (80% complete at March 1)	*3,000*	*20%*	*600*
Units started and completed in March	*7,000*	*100%*	*7,000*
Units completed during March	*10,000*		
Units in process at the end of March (70% complete at March 31)	*2,000*	*70%*	*1,400*
Equivalent full units of production during March			*9,000*

b **SUMASANI CORP.**
Process Cost Summary—Production Department
For the Month Ended March 31, 19__

	TOTAL COSTS	EQUIVALENT FULL UNITS	UNIT COST
Costs charged to the department and unit costs:			
Work in process inventory, March 1	*$154,000*		
Manufacturing costs charged to the department during March:			
Direct materials used	*360,000*	*9,000*	*$40*
Direct labor	*90,000*	*9,000*	*10*
Manufacturing overhead	*135,000*	*9,000*	*15*
Unit cost per equivalent full unit processed during March			*$65*
Total costs to be accounted for	*$739,000*		
Allocation of costs charged to department:			
Work in process inventory, end of March (2,000 units, 70% complete as to all costs; 2,000 units × $65 × 70%)	*$ 91,000*		
Cost of units completed (10,000 units):			
Total cost ($739,000 − $91,000)	*648,000*		
Unit cost ($648,000 ÷ 10,000 finished units)			*$64.80*
Total costs accounted for	*$739,000*		

c   General Journal

(1) *Work in Process Inventory, Production Dept.*   585,000
           Materials Inventory   360,000
           Direct Labor   90,000
           Manufacturing Overhead   135,000
     To summarize manufacturing costs charged to production in March.

(2) *Finished Goods Inventory*   648,000
           Work in Process Inventory, Production Dept.   648,000
     To record cost of 10,000 units of EndAll completed in March
     (unit cost = $648,000 ÷ 10,000 units = $64.80).

SELF-TEST QUESTIONS

Answers to these questions appear on page 924.

1 If CustomCraft uses a *job order* cost system, each of the following is true, *except:*

a Individual job cost sheets accumulate all manufacturing costs applicable to each job, and together constitute a subsidiary ledger for the Work in Process Inventory account.

b Direct labor cost applicable to individual jobs is recorded when paid by a debit to Work in Process Inventory and a credit to Cash, as well as by entering the amount on the job cost sheets.

c The amount of direct materials used in individual jobs is recorded by debiting the Work in Process Inventory account and crediting the Materials Inventory account, as well as by entering the amount used on job cost sheets.

d The manufacturing overhead applied to each job is transferred from the Manufacturing Overhead account to the Work in Process Inventory account, as well as entered on the individual job cost sheets.

2 When a job cost system is in use, *underapplied* overhead:

a Represents the cost of manufacturing overhead that relates to unfinished jobs.

b Is indicated by a credit balance remaining at year-end in the Manufacturing Overhead account.

c Is closed out at year-end into the Cost of Goods Sold account if the amount is not material.

d Results when actual overhead costs incurred during a year are less than the amounts applied to individual jobs.

3 Indicate which of the following phrases correctly complete this sentence: "Equivalent full units of production . . . ." (More than one answer may be correct.)

a Are a measure of the work done during a given accounting period.

b Represent only those units completed during the period and transferred out of the production department.

c Are the basis for determining per-unit manufacturing costs in a process cost accounting system.

d May be more or less than the number of units actually completed during the period.

4 Fogg Manufacturing has operations that involve three processing departments: Assembly, Finishing, and Packaging. Debits to the Work in Process Inventory—Finishing

Department account could involve a credit to any of the following, *except:*

a Work in Process Inventory—Packaging Department.

b Direct Labor.

c Manufacturing Overhead.

d Work in Process Inventory—Assembly Department.

5 When *actual* overhead costs incurred are charged to processing departments each month:

a The cost of infrequent items, such as a major plant refurbishing, is spread uniformly over all units produced throughout the year.

b Under- or overapplied overhead may occur, but is treated in the same manner as when an overhead application rate is used.

c It is no longer necessary to compute the equivalent full units of production for individual departments.

d The monthly per-unit cost of producing a product will vary with fluctuations in the level of production when a significant portion of overhead cost is fixed.

Assignment Materials

REVIEW QUESTIONS

1 What is a cost accounting system?

2 What are the major objectives of a cost accounting system in a manufacturing company?

3 What factors should be taken into account in deciding whether to use a job order cost system or a process cost system in any given manufacturing situation?

4 Northwest Power produces electricity. Would you expect the company to use a job order or a process cost accounting system? Explain.

5 Rodeo Drive Jewelers makes custom jewelry for celebrities. Would you expect the company to use a job order or a process cost accounting system? Explain.

6 Describe the three kinds of charges on a job cost sheet. For what general ledger control account do job cost sheets constitute supporting detail?

7 What documents serve as the basis for charging the costs of direct materials used in production to the Work in Process Inventory account?

8 What documents serve as the basis for charging direct labor costs to specific jobs or production departments?

9 What is meant by underapplied overhead? By overapplied overhead?

10 Gerox Company applies manufacturing overhead on the basis of machine-hours, using a predetermined overhead rate. At the end of the current year the Manufacturing Overhead account has a credit balance. What are the possible explanations for this? What disposition should be made of this balance?

11 Taylor & Malone is a law firm. Would the concepts of a job order system or a process cost system be more appropriate for this type of service business? Explain.

12 Briefly explain the operation of a process cost system, including the manner in which the unit costs of finished goods are determined.

13 Silex Mfg. has two processing departments: Assembly and Packaging. Identify the four accounts most likely to be *credited* as costs are charged to the Work in Process Inventory account of the Packaging Department.

14 What is meant by the term *equivalent full units?* How is this concept used in computing average unit costs?

15 When must the equivalent full units of production figure for materials be computed separately from that for conversion costs? Explain.

16 If a department has no beginning inventory of work in process but has 10,000 units in process at month-end, will the equivalent full units of work performed be greater or smaller than the number of units completed during the month? Explain.

17 In a process cost system, is the average cost of producing an *equivalent full unit* during a given month always equal to the average cost of producing a *completed unit* during that month? Explain.

18 What is the difference between *fixed overhead costs* and *variable overhead costs?*

19 Explain why charging actual overhead costs to production, rather than using an overhead application rate, can cause distortions in unit costs if production volume fluctuates from month to month.

20 What are the characteristics of "just-in-time" manufacturing? Briefly explain the advantages and risks of this type of manufacturing process.

21 What are the implications of just-in-time manufacturing for a cost accounting system? (Your answer should consider both the manner in which specific transactions are recorded, and the possible reduction or elimination of certain controlling accounts and subsidiary ledgers.)

EXERCISES

Exercise 22-1
Accounting
terminology

Listed below are nine technical accounting terms introduced in this chapter:

Just-in-time manufacturing	*Equivalent full units of production*	*Job order cost system*
Variable costs	*Process cost system*	*Job cost sheet*
Fixed costs	*Process cost summary*	*Overapplied overhead*

Each of the following statements may (or may not) describe one of these technical terms. For each statement, indicate the accounting term described, or answer "None" if the statement does not correctly describe any of the terms.

a A debit balance remaining in the Manufacturing Overhead account at the end of an accounting period.

b Manufacturing costs which do not vary based upon the level of production.

c The type of cost accounting system likely to be used by a construction company which is building several different projects at one time.

d Manufacturing costs which change in direct proportion to the level of production (for example, materials used).

e The number of units completed during the period and transferred from the Work in Process Inventory account to Finished Goods Inventory.

f The accounting record used to accumulate the total manufacturing costs and to determine the unit cost of a particular "batch" of production.

g The practice of applying overhead costs to work in process accounts in proportion to the number of direct labor hours, machine time, or computer time used in the manufacturing process.

Exercise 22-2
Flow of costs in
a cost accounting
system

For each of the four accounts listed below, prepare an example of a journal entry that would cause the account to be (1) debited, and (2) credited. Assume perpetual inventory records are maintained. Include written explanations with your journal entries and use "XXX" in place of dollar amounts.

a Materials Inventory

b Direct Labor

c Manufacturing Overhead

d Finished Goods Inventory

Exercise 22-3
Flow of costs in
a job order cost
system

The information below is taken from the job cost sheets of Gate Company:

JOB NUMBER	MANUFACTURING COSTS AS OF JUNE 30	MANUFACTURING COSTS IN JULY
101	$4,200	
102	3,240	
103	900	$1,950
104	2,250	3,900
105		5,700
106		3,630

During July, jobs no. 103 and 104 were completed, and jobs no. 101, 102, and 103 were delivered to customers. Jobs no. 105 and 106 are still in process at July 31. From this information, compute the following:

a The work in process inventory at June 30

b The finished goods inventory at June 30

c The cost of goods sold during July

d The work in process inventory at July 31

e The finished goods inventory at July 31

Exercise 22-4
Journal entries in
a job order cost
system

Riverside Engineering is a machine shop which uses a job order cost accounting system. Overhead is applied to individual jobs at a predetermined rate based on direct labor costs. The job cost sheet for job no. 321 appears below:

Job Cost Sheet

JOB NUMBER: 321   DATE STARTED: MAY 10
PRODUCT: 2″ BRASS CHECK VALVES   DATE COMPLETED: MAY 21
UNITS COMPLETED: 4,000

Direct materials used	$17,500
Direct labor	3,000
Manufacturing overhead applied	3,900
Total cost of job no. 321	$24,400
Unit cost ($24,400 ÷ 4,000 units)	$6.10

Prepare general journal entries to:

(a) Summarize the manufacturing costs charged to job no. 321. (Use one compound entry.)

(b) Record the completion of job no. 321.

(c) Record the credit sale of 2,100 units from job no. 321 at a unit sales price of $10. Record in a separate entry the related cost of goods sold.

CHAPTER 22

**Exercise 22-5
Computation of
equivalent full
units**

The following relates to the Assembly Department of Lawncraft Mowers during the month of May:

Units in process at May 1 (60% completed in April) 2,000
Units started and completed during May 15,000
Units in process at May 31 (80% completed) 5,000

Determine the equivalent full units of production during the month of May, assuming that all costs are incurred uniformly as the units move through the production line.

**Exercise 22-6
Preparing journal
entries in a
process cost
system**

Shamrock Industries uses a process cost system. Products are processed successively by Department A and Department B, and are then transferred to the finished goods warehouse. Shown below is cost information for Department B during the month of June:

Cost of work in process at June 1 .... $ 19,000
Cost of units transferred in from Department A during June.................... 72,500
Manufacturing costs added in Department B:
  Direct materials used... $44,000
  Direct labor 6,100
  Manufacturing overhead 17,400   67,500
Total costs charged to Department B in June.................................. $159,000

    The cost of work in process in Department B at June 30 has been determined to be $22,700.
    Prepare journal entries to record for the month of June (1) the transfer of production from Department A to Department B, (2) the manufacturing costs incurred by Department B, and (3) the transfer of completed units from Department B to the finished goods warehouse.

**Exercise 22-7
Computing unit
costs**

Given below are the production data for Department No. 1 for the first month of operation:

Costs charged to Department No. 1:
  Direct materials used $10,000
  Direct labor 4,750
  Manufacturing overhead 28,500
    Total $43,250

During this first month, 1,000 units were placed into production; 800 units were completed and the remaining 200 units are *100% completed* as to material and *75% completed* as to direct labor and overhead.
    You are to compute the following:

a Unit cost of direct material used

b Equivalent full units of production for direct labor and factory overhead

c Unit cost of direct labor

d Unit cost of manufacturing overhead

e Total cost of 200 units in process at end of month

f Total cost of 800 units completed

Exercise 22-8
Evaluating
departmental
performance

Shown below in the left-hand column are the unit costs relating to the manufacturing activities of the Packaging Department of Baker Labs in the month of July. (These unit costs are taken directly from the process cost summary on page 905.) Assume that the right-hand column indicates the unit costs *budgeted* for the Packaging Department— that is, the unit costs that managers had *expected* the department to incur during the month.

	UNIT COSTS	
	ACTUAL	BUDGETED
Manufacturing cost charged to the Packaging Department:		
Units transferred in from the Mixing Department..................	$2.00	$2.15
Manufacturing costs added by the Packaging Department:		
Direct materials requisitioned	.16	.16
Direct labor	.25	.20
Manufacturing overhead (120% of direct labor cost)	.30	.24
Unit cost per equivalent unit processed during July................	$2.71	$2.75

Based upon this information, did the Packaging Department perform as well during July as managers had expected? Explain.

Exercise 22-9
"Just-in-time"
manufacturing

Fargo Manufacturing is located in Buffalo, New York. In the past, the company has maintained a job order cost accounting system, using all the accounts and subsidiary ledgers illustrated in the flowchart on pages 890 and 891. Recently, however, the company has been working to implement the principles of "just-in-time" manufacturing. At present, almost 70% of the company's direct materials arrive on a just-in-time basis, and all finished goods are shipped to customers immediately upon completion of the production process.

a Explain what is meant by "just-in-time," with respect to both direct materials and finished goods.

b What are the advantages to Fargo of just-in-time manufacturing? What is the biggest risk?

c Explain the effects of Fargo's move toward just-in-time manufacturing on the company's job order cost system. In your explanation, explain any changes in the flow of manufacturing costs through the ledger accounts, and any changes in the required number of controlling accounts and subsidiary ledgers.

PROBLEMS

Group A

Problem 22A-1
Journal entries to
record basic cost
flows

The following information relates to the manufacturing operations of O'Shaughnessy Mfg. Co. during the month of March. The company uses a job order cost accounting system.

(a) Purchases of direct materials during the month amount to $59,700. (All purchases were made on account.)

(b) Materials requisitions issued by the production department during the month total $56,200.

(c) Time cards of direct workers show 2,000 hours worked on various jobs during the month, for total direct labor cost of $30,000.

(d) Direct workers were paid $26,300 in March.

(e) Actual overhead costs for the month amount to $34,900 (for simplicity, you may credit Accounts Payable).

(f) Overhead is applied to jobs at a rate of $18 per direct labor hour.

(g) Jobs with total accumulated costs of $116,000 were completed during the month.

(h) During March, units costing $128,000 were sold for $210,000. (All sales were made on account.)

Instructions Prepare general journal entries to summarize each of these transactions in the company's general ledger accounts.

Problem 22A-2
Job order cost
system: a
comprehensive
problem

Precision Instruments, Inc., uses a job order cost system and applies manufacturing overhead to individual jobs by using predetermined overhead rates. In Department A overhead is applied on the basis of machine-hours, and in Department B on the basis of direct labor hours. At the beginning of the current year, management made the following budget estimates as a step toward determining the overhead application rates:

	DEPARTMENT A	DEPARTMENT B
Direct labor	$420,000	$300,000
Manufacturing overhead	$540,000	$412,500
Machine-hours	18,000	1,900
Direct labor hours	28,000	25,000

Production of 4,000 tachometers (job no. 399) was started in the middle of January and completed two weeks later. The cost records for this job show the following information:

	DEPARTMENT A	DEPARTMENT B
Job no. 399 (4,000 units of product):		
Cost of materials used on job.......................	$6,800	$4,500
Direct labor cost	$8,100	7,200
Direct labor hours	540	600
Machine-hours	250	100

Instructions **a** Determine the overhead rate that should be used for each department in applying overhead costs to job no. 399.

b What is the total cost of job no. 399, and the unit cost of the product manufactured on this production order?

c Prepare the journal entries required to record the sale (on account) of 1,000 of the tachometers to SkiCraft Boats. The total sales price was $19,500.

d Assume that actual overhead costs for the year were $517,000 in Department A and $424,400 in Department B. Actual machine-hours in Department A were 17,000, and actual direct labor hours in Department B were 26,000 during the year. On the basis of this information, determine the over- or underapplied overhead in each department for the year.

Problem 22A-3
Process costs:
journal entries

After having been shut down for two months during a strike, Magic Touch resumed operations on August 1. One of the company's products is a dishwasher which is successively processed by the Tub Department and the Motor Department before being transferred to the finished goods warehouse. Shown below are data concerning the units produced and costs incurred by the two manufacturing departments:

Production Summary—in Units

	TUB DEPARTMENT	MOTOR DEPARTMENT
Units placed in production	1,700	900
Less: Units in process, Aug. 31	800	400
Units completed during August	900	500

Costs Charged to the Departments

	TUB DEPARTMENT	MOTOR DEPARTMENT
Transferred in from Tub Department		$?
Direct materials used......................................	$54,000	57,600
Direct labor	30,000	10,400
Manufacturing overhead	46,500	14,400

Due to the strike, there were no units in process at August 1 in either department. The units in process in both departments at August 31 are 75% complete with respect to both materials and conversion costs.

Instructions   **a** Compute the equivalent full units of production in August for each department.

b Compute the unit production costs for August in each department. (Include in the production costs of the Motor Department the cost of the 900 units tranferred in from the Tub Department.)

c Use the August unit cost figures to determine the cost of the ending inventory of work in process in each department at August 31.

d Prepare the journal entries required to record the transfer of completed units out of each of the two departments during August.

**Problem 22A-4
Process costs:
cost report and
journal entries**

Aladdin Electric manufactures several products, including an electric garage door opener called the Door Tender. Door Tenders are completely processed in one department and are then transferred to the finished goods warehouse. All manufacturing costs are applied to Door Tender units at a uniform rate throughout the production process. The following information is available for July:

Beginning inventory of work in process	$ 25,030
Manufacturing costs incurred in July:	
Direct materials used	53,700
Direct labor	32,220
Manufacturing overhead applied	57,280
Total costs to be accounted for	$168,230

The beginning inventory consisted of 400 units which had been 80% completed during June. In addition to completing these units, the department started and completed another 1,500 units during July and started work on 300 more units which were 70% completed at July 31.

Instructions   **a** Compute the equivalent full units of production in July.

b Prepare a process cost summary for the department for the month of July, as illustrated on page 905. Use the July unit cost figures to determine the cost of the ending inventory of work in process.

c Prepare journal entries to record (1) the manufacturing costs charged to the department during July, and (2) the transfer of 1,900 completed units to the finished goods warehouse.

**Problem 22A-5
Process costs: a
second
comprehensive
problem**

Dayton Chemical, Inc., manufactures a fertilizer concentrate, called PH Max. This product passes through four successive production processes, identified as Departments No. 1, 2, 3, and 4. After processing by Department No. 4, the product is transferred to a warehouse as finished goods inventory.

In Department No. 4, all direct materials needed to complete PH Max are added at the beginning of processing. The accounting department has accumulated the following information relating to processing in Department No. 4 during the month of April:

Costs charged to Department No. 4:

Work in process inventory, April 1 (40,000 units, 100% complete as to materials, 75% complete as to conversion costs)	$ 387,000
Cost of 140,000 units transferred in from Department No. 3 during April (unit cost = $5)	700,000
Manufacturing costs added in Department No. 4 during April:	
Direct materials added	280,000
Direct labor	125,000
Manufacturing overhead	375,000
Total costs to be accounted for	$1,867,000

During April, the 40,000 units in process at April 1 and 90,000 of the units transferred in from Department No. 3 were completed and transferred to the warehouse. The remaining 50,000 units transferred in from Department No. 3 are still in process at April 30, and are 100% complete as to materials and 50% complete as to conversion costs (direct labor and overhead).

Instructions **a** Compute the equivalent full units of production during April. (Separate computations are required for materials and for conversion costs.)

b Prepare a process cost summary for Department No. 4 in the month of April. Use the April unit cost figures to determine the cost of work in process at April 30; the remainder of the $1,867,000 in total costs apply to units completed during the month (the FIFO method of valuing inventory).

c Prepare journal entries to record:

(1) The transfer of the 140,000 units from Department No. 3 into Department No. 4.

(2) The manufacturing costs added by Department No. 4 during April.

(3) The transfer of the 130,000 completed units from Department No. 4 to the finished goods warehouse.

Group B

**Problem 22B-1
Job order cost
system: a short
problem**

Chesapeake Sailmakers uses a job order cost accounting system. Manufacturing overhead is charged to individual jobs through the use of a predetermined overhead rate based on direct labor costs. The following information appears in the company's Work in Process Inventory controlling account for the month of June:

Debits to account:

Balance, June 1	$ 7,200
Direct materials	12,000
Direct labor	9,000
Manufacturing overhead (applied to jobs as 120% of direct labor cost)	10,800
Total debits to account	$39,000
Credits to account:	
Transferred to Finished Goods Inventory account	30,500
Balance, June 30	$ 8,500

Instructions **a** Assuming that the direct labor charged to the jobs still in process at June 30 amounts to $2,100, compute the amount of manufacturing overhead and the amount of direct materials which have been charged to these jobs as of June 30.

b Prepare general journal entries to summarize:

(1) The manufacturing costs (direct materials, direct labor, and overhead) charged to production during June.

(2) The transfer of production completed during June to the Finished Goods Inventory account.

(3) The cash sale of 90% of the merchandise completed during June at a total sales price of $46,500. Show the related cost of goods sold in a separate journal entry.

Problem 22B-2
Job order cost
system: a
comprehensive
problem

Georgia Woods, Inc., manufactures furniture to customers' specifications and uses a job order cost system. A predetermined overhead rate is used in applying manufacturing overhead to individual jobs. In Department One, overhead is applied on the basis of direct labor hours, and in Department Two, on the basis of machine-hours. At the beginning of the current year, management made the following budget estimates to assist in determining the overhead application rate:

	DEPARTMENT ONE	DEPARTMENT TWO
Direct labor cost	$300,000	$225,000
Direct labor hours	20,000	15,000
Manufacturing overhead	$240,000	$150,000
Machine-hours	12,000	7,500

Production of a batch of custom furniture ordered by City Furniture (job no. 58) was started early in the year and completed three weeks later on January 29. The records for this job show the following cost information:

	DEPARTMENT ONE	DEPARTMENT TWO
Job order for City Furniture (job no. 58):		
Direct materials cost	$10,100	$ 7,600
Direct labor cost	$16,500	$11,100
Direct labor hours	1,100	740
Machine-hours	750	500

Selected additional information for January is given below:

	DEPARTMENT ONE	DEPARTMENT TWO
Direct labor hours—month of January.....................	1,600	1,200
Machine-hours—month of January	1,100	600
Manufacturing overhead incurred in January..............	$18,650	$12,370

Instructions

a Compute the predetermined overhead rate for each department.

b What is the total cost of the furniture produced for City Furniture?

c Prepare the entries required to record the sale (on account) of the furniture to City Furniture. The sales price of the order was $94,200.

d Determine the over- or underapplied overhead for each department at the end of January.

Problem 22B-3
Process cost
system: a
short but
comprehensive
problem

One of the primary products of Oshima Company is the Shutterbug, an instant camera, which is processed successively in the Assembly Department and the Lens Department, and then transferred to the company's sales warehouse. After having been shut down for three weeks as a result of a material shortage, the company resumed production of Shutterbugs on May 1. The flow of **units of product** through the departments during May is shown below.

ASSEMBLY DEPARTMENT WORK IN PROCESS		LENS DEPARTMENT WORK IN PROCESS	
Started in process— 30,000 units	To Lens Dept.— 25,000 units	From Assembly Dept.— 25,000 units	To warehouse— 21,000 units

Departmental manufacturing costs applicable to Shutterbug production for the month of May were as follows:

	ASSEMBLY DEPARTMENT	LENS DEPARTMENT
Units transferred from Assembly Department		$?
Direct materials	$168,000	46,800
Direct labor	98,000	70,200
Manufacturing overhead	70,000	140,400
Total manufacturing costs	$336,000	$?

Unfinished goods in each department at the end of May were on the average 60% complete, with respect to both direct materials and conversion costs.

Instructions　**a** Determine the equivalent full units of production in each department during May.

b Compute unit production costs in each department during May.

c Prepare the necessary journal entries to record the transfer of product out of the Assembly Department and the Lens Department during May.

Problem 22B-4
Process costs: a
comprehensive
problem

Universal Corp. has one production department and uses a process cost system. The following data is available as to the costs of production and the number of units worked on during the month of May:

Costs charged to the production department:	
Work in process, May 1	$ 22,500
Manufacturing costs added during May:	
Direct materials	137,400
Direct labor	56,000
Manufacturing overhead (applied as 120% of direct labor costs)............	67,200
Total costs to be accounted for	$283,100

Units worked on during May:	
Work in process, May 1 (40% complete as to materials, 60% complete as to conversion costs)	2,000
Units started and completed during May	8,000
Finished goods produced during May	10,000
Work in process, May 31 (75% complete as to materials, 80% complete as to conversion costs)	3,000

Instructions　**a** Compute separately the equivalent full units of production during May for (1) materials, and (2) conversion costs (direct labor and overhead).

b Prepare a process cost summary for May, following the format illustrated on page 905. Use the May unit cost figures to value the ending inventory of work in process; the remainder of the $283,100 total costs to be accounted for are to be assigned to the units completed during the month.

c Prepare journal entries to record for the month:

(1) The manufacturing costs charged to production. (Use one compound journal entry to record all three types of manufacturing costs.)

(2) The transfer of the 10,000 completed units to the finished goods warehouse.

Problem 22B-5
Process costs: a
second
comprehensive
problem

Saf T File, Inc., manufactures metal filing cabinets and uses a process cost system. The cabinets pass through a series of production processes, one of which is the Lock Assembly Department. The costs charged to the Lock Assembly Department during April, along with a summary of the units worked on by the department, are shown below:

Costs charged to the Lock Assembly Department:

Work in process, April 1	$ 29,840
Cost of 2,000 units transferred in from the Drawer Assembly Department during April ($52 per unit).......................................	104,000
Manufacturing costs added by the Lock Assembly Department during April:	
Direct materials	8,200
Direct labor	3,800
Manufacturing overhead (applied as 150% of direct labor costs costs)...	5,700
Total costs to be accounted for..	$151,540

Units worked on during April:

Work in process, April 1 (100% complete as to materials, 80% complete as to conversion costs)	500
Units started and completed during April......................................	1,600
Units completed and transferred to the Painting Department during April	2,100
Work in process, May 31 (100% complete as to materials, 50% complete as to conversion costs)	400

Instructions
a Compute separately the equivalent full units of production during April for (1) materials, and (2) conversion costs (direct labor and overhead).

b Prepare a process cost summary for April, following the format illustrated on page 905. Use the April unit cost figures to value the ending inventory of work in process; the remainder of the $151,540 total cost to be accounted for may be assigned to units transferred from the Lock Assembly Department to the Painting Department.

c Prepare journal entries to record:

(1) Transfer of the 2,000 units from the Drawer Assembly Department into the Lock Assembly Department.

(2) Manufacturing costs added by the Lock Assembly Department during April. (You may show all three elements of manufacturing costs in one compound journal entry.)

(3) Transfer of the 2,100 completed units from the Lock Assembly Department to the Painting Department. (Hint: These units are not finished goods.)

BUSINESS DECISION CASES

Case 22-1
Too much
overhead?

Olde Towne Printers and Laser Technology are two large print shops located in New York City. The two companies are similar in size in terms of their total sales. Both businesses have job order cost accounting systems and assign factory overhead costs to jobs using a predetermined overhead application rate based upon direct labor costs. For Olde Towne Printers, the overhead application rate is 80%; for Laser Technology, the rate is 210%.

a Suggest factors which might be responsible for the wide difference between the companies' overhead application rates.

b Does the lower overhead application rate at Olde Towne Printers indicate more efficient management? Explain.

Case 22-2
Manufacturing
overhead and
fluctuations in
production
volume

John Park is the founder and president of Park West Engineering. One of the company's principal products is sold exclusively to BigMart, a national chain of retail stores. Big-Mart buys a large quantity of the product in the first quarter of each year, but buys successively smaller quantities in the second, third, and fourth quarters. Park West cannot produce in advance to meet the big first-quarter sales requirement, because BigMart frequently makes minor changes in the specifications for the product. There-fore, Park West must adjust its production schedules to fit BigMart's buying pattern.

In Park West's cost accounting system, unit costs are computed quarterly on the basis of actual materials, labor, and manufacturing overhead costs charged to work in process at the end of each quarter. At the close of the current year, Park received the following cost report, by quarters, for the year. (Fixed overhead represents items of manufacturing costs that remain relatively constant month by month; variable over-head includes those costs that tend to move up and down in proportion to changes in the volume of production.)

	FIRST QUARTER	SECOND QUARTER	THIRD QUARTER	FOURTH QUARTER
Direct materials used	$ 78,000	$ 60,000	$ 42,000	$22,000
Direct labor	80,000	60,000	40,000	20,000
Fixed overhead (actual)	30,000	30,000	30,000	30,000
Variable overhead (actual)	48,000	39,000	29,000	14,000
Total manufacturing cost	$236,000	$189,000	$141,000	$86,000
Equivalent full units produced	40,000	30,000	20,000	10,000
Unit production cost	$ 5.90	$ 6.30	$ 7.05	$ 8.60

Park is concerned about the steadily rising unit costs. He states, "We have a contract to produce 50,000 units for BigMart next quarter at a unit sales price of $8.50. If this sales price won't even cover our unit production costs, I'll have to cancel the contract. But before I take such drastic action, I'd like you to study our method of computing unit costs to see if we might be doing something wrong."

Instructions

a As the first step in your study, determine the *unit cost* of each cost element (materi-als, labor, fixed overhead, and variable overhead) in the first quarter and in the fourth quarter of the current year.

b Based on your computation in part **a**, which cost element is primarily responsible for the increase in unit production costs? Explain why you think the unit cost for this cost element has been rising throughout the year.

c Compute an overhead application rate for Park West Engineering which expresses total overhead for the year (including both fixed and variable overhead) as a percentage of direct labor costs.

d Redetermine the unit production cost for each quarter using the overhead applica-tion rate to apply overhead costs.

e Determine the expected unit cost of producing 50,000 units next quarter. (Assume that unit costs for materials and direct labor remain the same as in the fourth quarter and use the overhead application rate to determine the unit cost of applied overhead.)

f Explain to Park how Park West might improve its procedures for determining unit production costs. Also explain whether Park West reasonably can expect to recover its production costs next quarter if it sells 50,000 units to BigMart at a unit sales price of $8.50.

ANSWERS TO SELF-TEST QUESTIONS

1 b **2 c** **3 a, c,** and **d** **4 a** **5 d**

Comprehensive Problem for Part 7

APEX COMPUTER, INC.

Job order and process cost accounting systems

Apex Computer, Inc., manufactures and sells 10 different models of small computers, each using different combinations of micro-processors, disc drives, number of expansion slots, and other features. Some models are lap-tops, some are desk-tops, and others are workstations designed for networking. Production departments that manufacture standardized computer components, such as keyboards or monitors, use process cost accounting systems. However, the Computer Assembly Department sequentially assembles batches of from 5,000 to 10,000 of whichever model computer is most in demand. Therefore, the Computer Assembly Department uses a job order cost accounting system.

In *part 1* of this Comprehensive Problem, we look at the accounting practices of the Computer Assembly Department—a job order cost accounting system. In *part 2,* we focus upon the Keyboard Assembly Department, which uses a process cost accounting system.

Computer Assembly Department

Part 1
Job order cost accounting systems

The Computer Assembly Department uses a *job order* cost accounting system, with each job representing assembly of between 5,000 and 10,000 units of a particular model of computer. Once assembly is completed, the computers are transferred to the Finished Goods Warehouse and are available for sale.

Late in May 1991, the Computer Assembly Department began job no. 2140, the assembly of 5,000 model AC10 lap-top computers. This job was partially complete on May 31, and was completed on June 9. The job cost sheet included the following costs for materials and for direct labor as of May 31 and June 9 (the June 9 costs include those charged through May 31):

	COSTS CHARGED TO JOB AS OF:	
	MAY 31	JUNE 9
Direct materials requisitioned	$457,200	$2,090,300
Manufactured products requisitioned........................	$924,000	$4,589,700
Number of component parts requisitioned	12,000	65,000
Direct labor	$ 19,300	$ 90,000

Accounting Policies and Other Data

1 Manufacturing overhead is applied to jobs at the predetermined rate of $2 per component part requisitioned. (Note that the number of parts requisitioned is listed in the job cost sheet.)

2 Direct materials represent parts purchased from others in a ready-to-use condition. Therefore, requisition of these parts is recorded by crediting the Materials Inventory controlling account.

3 Manufactured parts are components manufactured by Apex's other production departments and stored in the Components Warehouse. The requisition of these parts is recorded by crediting the Work in Process Inventory, Components controlling account.

4 Units completed by the Computer Assembly Department are classified as finished goods.

5 The specific identification method is used in transferring costs from the Finished Goods Inventory account to the Cost of Goods Sold account.

Instructions **a** Compute the total cost of completing job no. 2140, and the per-unit cost of the 5,000 lap-top computers manufactured.

b Prepare general journal entries to summarize:

(1) The manufacturing costs charged to job no. 2140 through the end of May, (Include manufacturing overhead.)

(2) The manufacturing costs charged to job no. 2140 during June. (Include manufacturing overhead.)

(3) The completion of the job and the transfer of the computers to the Finished Goods Warehouse

c On June 28, Apex sells 4,000 of the lap-top computers in job no. 2140 to MicroCity, a national computer retailer. The sales price was $2,600 per unit; terms, 2/10, n/30.

(1) Prepare the journal entries to record this sale (use separate entries to record revenue and to record the cost of goods sold).

(2) Briefly explain how the total costs charged to job no. 2140 (per part **a**) will be shown in Apex' financial statements for the month ended June 30, 1991.

d Assume that during 1991, actual manufacturing overhead for the Computer Assembly Department amounted to $2,372,740, and that during the year the department requisitioned for assembly a total of 1,180,340 component parts.

(1) Compute the amount of over- or underapplied overhead for the year.

(2) Prepare a journal entry to close the Manufacturing Overhead controlling account at year-end, assuming that the amount of over- or underapplied overhead was not material in dollar amount.

The Keyboard Assembly Department

Part 2
Process cost
accounting
systems

One of the production departments of Apex Computer, Inc., that uses a process cost accounting system is the Keyboard Assembly Department. The plastic frames for keyboards are produced in Apex's Plastic Molding Department. Those frames are then transferred to the Keyboard Assembly Department, where the production process is completed. Completed keyboards are transferred to the Component warehouse where they are stored until they are needed by the Computer Assembly Department.

The accounting department has accumulated the following information relating to processing in the Keyboard Assembly Department during the month of June, 1991:

Costs charged to Keyboard Assembly Department:

Work in process inventory, June 1	$ 47,632
Cost of 16,600 plastic keyboard frames transferred in from Plastic	
Molding Department during June (unit cost, $1.06...........................	17,596
Manufacturing costs added in Keyboard Assembly Department during June:	
Direct materials added	149,400
Direct labor	39,820
Manufacturing overhead	47,784
Total costs to be accounted for..	$302,232

Keyboards worked on during June:

Units in process, June 1 (100% complete as to materials, 40% complete	
as to conversion costs)..	4,000
Units started and completed during June....................................	13,600
Units completed and transferred to Components Warehouse during June......	17,600
Units in process, June 30 (100% complete as to materials, 70% complete	
as to conversion costs)..	3,000

Accounting Policies and Other Data

1 All direct materials needed to complete Keyboards are placed into production at the start of the manufacturing process.

2 The FIFO inventory method is used in valuing the ending inventories of work in process and in determining the cost of completed keyboards transferred to the Components Warehouse.

3 Transfers of completed keyboards to the Components Warehouse are recorded by debiting a controlling account entitled Work in Process Inventory, Components.

Instructions **a** Compute separately the equivalent full units of production in June by the Keyboard Assembly Department with respect to (1) materials, and (2) conversion costs.

b Prepare a process cost report for the Keyboard Assembly Department for the month of June.

c Prepare journal entries to record for June the:

(1) Transfer of 16,600 plastic keyboard frames from the Plastic Department into the Keyboard Assembly Department.

(2) Manufacturing costs incurred in the Keyboard Assembly Department.

(3) Transfer of 17,600 completed keyboards from the Keyboard Assembly Department to the Components Warehouse. (Note: these keyboards are *not* viewed as finished goods.)

PART 8

Managerial Accounting: Planning and Control

Managers are responsible for planning and controlling the activities of the business. The functions of planning and control are closely related. Planning is the process of setting financial and operational goals for the business and deciding upon the strategies and actions for achieving these goals. Exercising control means monitoring actual operating results, comparing those results to the plan, and taking corrective action when actual results fall below expectation.

23   **Cost-Volume-Profit Analysis**

24   **Measuring and Evaluating Segment Performance**

25   **Budgeting and Standard Costs**

26   **Relevant Information, Incremental Analysis, and Capital Budgeting**

Cost-Volume-Profit Analysis

This chapter has two major objectives. Our first is to explain how various costs respond to changes in the level of business activity. An understanding of these relationships is essential to developing successful business strategies and to planning future operations. Our second objective is to show how managers may use cost-volume-profit analysis in a wide variety of business decisions. We illustrate and explain the use of a "break-even" graph—a basic tool of cost-volume-profit analysis. Also, we discuss the concept of "contribution margin." In tailoring this concept to specific managerial decisions, we show how contribution margin may be expressed on a per unit basis, as a percentage of sales, and in relation to available units of a scarce resource.

After studying this chapter, you should be able to meet these Learning Objectives:

1 Explain how fixed, variable, and semivariable costs respond to changes in the level of activity.

2 Use the high-low method to separate the fixed and variable elements of a semivariable cost.

3 Prepare a cost-volume-profit (break-even) graph.

4 Explain contribution margin; compute contribution margin per unit and contribution margin ratio.

5 Determine the sales volume required to earn a desired level of operating income.

6 Use the contribution margin ratio to estimate the effect upon operating income of changes in sales volume.

7 Use cost-volume-profit relationships in evaluating various marketing strategies.

8 Determine the sales mix that will maximize the contribution margin per unit of a scarce resource.

One of the most important analytical tools used by many managers is cost-volume-profit analysis. ***Cost-volume-profit analysis*** is a means of learning how costs and profits behave in response to changes in the level of business activity. An understanding of these relationships is essential in developing plans and budgets for future business operations. In addition, cost-volume-profit analysis assists managers in predicting the effects of various decisions and strategies upon the operating income of the business. In our discussion of cost-volume-profit relationships, the term "cost" is used to describe both manufacturing costs and operating expenses.

Cost-volume-profit analysis may be used by managers to answer questions such as the following:

1 What level of sales must be reached to cover all expenses, that is, to break even?

2 How many units of a product must be sold to earn a given operating income?

3 What will happen to our profitability if we expand capacity?

4 What will be the effect of changing compensation of sales personnel from fixed monthly salaries to a straight commission of 10% on sales?

5 If we increase our spending on advertising to $100,000 per month, what increase in sales volume will be required to maintain our current level of income from operations?

Cost-volume-profit relationships are useful not only to management but also to creditors and investors. The ability of a business to pay its debts and to increase its dividend payments, for example, depends largely upon its ability to generate earnings. Assume that a company's sales volume is expected to increase by 10% during the next year. What will be the effect of this increase in sales volume upon the company's net income? The answer depends upon how the company's costs behave in response to this increase in the level of business activity.

The concepts of cost-volume-profit analysis may be applied to the business as a whole, to individual segments of the business such as a division, a branch, a department, or a particular product line.

Cost-Volume Relationships

Objective 1
Explain how fixed, variable, and semivariable costs respond to changes in the level of activity.

To illustrate the relationships between costs and the level of activity, we shall first consider cost behavior in a simple and familiar setting, the cost of operating a personal automobile. Suppose that someone tells you that the average annual cost of owning and operating an automobile is $2,700. Obviously, each individual driver does not incur an annual cost of exactly $2,700. In large part, the annual cost of owning an automobile depends upon how much you drive.

■ **The Activity Base** In studying cost behavior, we first look for some measurable concept of volume or activity that serves as a ***cost driver***—that is, has a strong influence on the amount of cost incurred. We then try to find out how costs change in response to changes in the level of this activity. The unit of measure used to define the selected cost driver is called the ***activity base.***

An activity base may be units of key production input, such as tons of peaches processed, or direct labor hours worked. (We have seen in prior chapters that manufacturing overhead costs often are expressed in terms of an activity base such as direct labor costs, direct labor hours, or machine-hours.) Alternatively, the activity base may be based upon output, such as equivalent full units of production, units sold, or dollars of sales revenue.

Most airlines consider passenger-miles flown to be their major cost driver, and use this measurement as the activity base for studying the behavior of their operating costs. Retail stores, on the other hand, usually find total dollar sales to be the most significant activity base in cost analysis. In our example involving the operation of an automobile, we will use *miles driven* during the year as our activity base.

Once an appropriate activity base has been selected, we can classify all operating costs into one of the following three broad categories.

■ **Fixed Costs**   *Fixed* costs are those costs and expenses that *do not change* significantly in response to changes in the activity base. For example, the annual licensing fee is an example of a fixed cost in the operation of an automobile, as this cost remains constant regardless of the number of miles driven. In a business entity, fixed costs include monthly salaries to office workers and executives, depreciation, property taxes, and many types of insurance protection.

■ **Variable Costs**   A *variable* cost is one that rises or falls in direct proportion to changes in the activity base. For example, if the activity base increases by 10%, a variable cost increases by approximately 10%. In our example involving the operation of an automobile, gasoline is a variable cost that changes in response to the number of miles driven.

In manufacturing operations, the costs of direct materials and direct labor are variable costs with respect to the number of units manufactured. For an airline, fuel expense is a variable cost that responds to changes in the number of passenger miles flown. In retailing, the cost of goods sold and sales commissions expense are examples of variable costs that respond closely to changes in total dollar sales.

■ **Semivariable Costs**   *Semivariable* costs also are called *mixed* costs, because *part of the cost is fixed* and *part is variable.* A great many business costs are semivariable. Telephone expense, for example, includes both a fixed element (the "base rate" charged by the telephone company each month) and a variable element (the additional charges for long-distance calls).

The concept of a semivariable cost usually applies when we combine a variety of different costs into one broad category. For example, manufacturing overhead includes both fixed costs, such as property taxes, and variable costs, such as supplies used and utilities expense. Therefore, total manufacturing overhead behaves as a semivariable cost.

In our example involving the operation of an automobile, we will use depreciation to illustrate the concept of a semivariable cost. With respect to automobiles, some depreciation occurs simply with the passage of time, without regard to miles driven. This represents the "fixed portion" of depreciation expense. However, the more miles an automobile is driven each year, the faster it depreciates. Thus, part of the total depreciation cost is a variable cost.

(A technique for determining the fixed and variable portions of a semivariable cost will be illustrated and explained later in this chapter.)

■ **Automobile Costs—Graphic Analysis** To illustrate automobile cost-volume behavior, we shall assume the following somewhat simplified data to describe the cost of owning and operating a typical automobile:

TYPE OF COST	AMOUNT
Fixed costs:	
Insurance	*$430 per year*
License fee	*70 per year*
Variable costs:	
Gasoline, oil, servicing...........................	*8 cents per mile*
Semivariable costs:	
Depreciation	*$1,000 per year plus 4 cents per mile*

We can express these cost-volume relationships graphically. The relation between volume (miles driven per year) and the three types of cost both separately and combined is shown in the following diagrams.

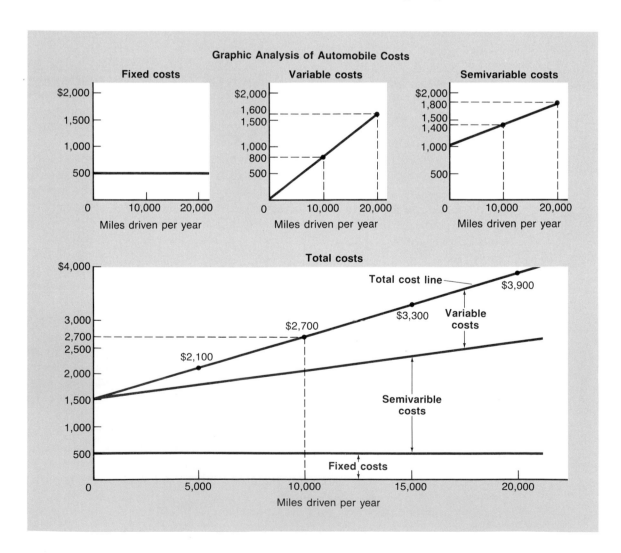

We can read from the total costs graph the estimated annual automobile cost for any assumed mileage. For example, an owner who expects to drive 10,000 miles in a given year may estimate the total cost at $2,700 or 27.0 cents per mile. By combining all the fixed and variable elements of cost, we can generalize the cost-volume relationship and state simply that the cost of owning an automobile is *$1,500 per year plus 12 cents per mile* driven during the year.

The effect of volume on unit (per-mile) costs can be observed by converting total cost figures to average unit costs as follows:

COST PER MILE OF OWNING AND USING AN AUTOMOBILE

	5,000	10,000	15,000	20,000
Miles driven	5,000	10,000	15,000	20,000
Costs:				
Fully variable (8 cents per mile)	$ 400	$ 800	$1,200	$1,600
Semivariable:				
Variable portion (4 cents per mile)	200	400	600	800
Fixed portion	1,000	1,000	1,000	1,000
Completely fixed ($430 + $70)	500	500	500	500
Total costs	$2,100	$2,700	$3,300	$3,900
Cost per mile	$ 0.42	$ 0.27	$ 0.22	$0.195

Note decrease in cost per miles as use increases

The average unit-cost behavior of operating an automobile may be presented graphically as shown below:

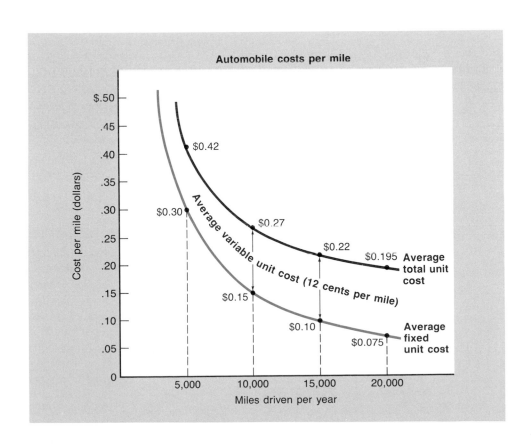

Behavior of Unit Costs

■
Average cost per
mile for driving a
car

Total variable costs rise and fall in approximate proportion to changes in the activity base. Therefore, variable costs per unit *remain relatively constant.* Notice in our preceding example that variable costs amount to 12 cents per mile, regardless of the number of miles driven.

Fixed costs, on the other hand, *do not* vary with changes in the activity base. Therefore, fixed costs per unit *decline as the level of activity increases.* Notice in our example that fixed costs amount to 30 cents per mile for an automobile driven 5,000 each year, but amount to only 15 cents per mile for an automobile driven 10,000 miles.

■ Cost Advantage for Intensive Use of Facilities

What does the behavior of these unit costs mean to a business entity? In short, *a business can reduce its overall per-unit costs by using its facilities more intensively.* To illustrate, assume that an automobile plant incurs fixed costs of $8.4 million per month and has the capacity to produce 7,000 automobiles per month. The fixed cost per automobile manufactured is shown below at three different levels of production:

FIXED COSTS PER MONTH	LEVEL OF PRODUCTION	FIXED COST PER UNIT
$8,400,000	*4,000 cars*	*$2,100*
8,400,000	*6,000 cars*	*1,400*
8,400,000	*7,000 cars*	*1,200*

Notice that by producing 7,000 cars per month, the automaker's manufacturing costs are *$900 less* per automobile than if the automaker produces only 4,000 cars each month ($2,100 − $1,200 = $900). This "cost advantage" results from fully utilizing the company's production facilities and, therefore, spreading the company's fixed costs over as many units as possible. Unless overtime costs are incurred, *every business benefits from using its facilities more intensively.* This benefit is most apparent in business operations with relatively high fixed costs, such as automakers, utilities companies, airlines, chemical manufacturers, and other companies with large investments in plant assets or large commitments to research and development.

CASE IN POINT ■ General Motors is the world's largest automaker; it sells more than twice as many automobiles each year as does its archrival, Ford Motor Company. Yet for much of the late 1980s, Ford earned larger profits than GM. The variable costs of manufacturing an automobile were similar at Ford and GM. The key to Ford's impressive profitability was its ability to operate its plants at nearly full capacity. Weekend shifts were part of Ford's normal workweek. As a result, Ford incurred much lower fixed costs per car than did its American competitors. This "cost advantage" enabled Ford to price its cars competitively and still earn a higher profit margin than either GM or Chrysler.

Cost Behavior in Business

Cost relationships in a business are seldom as simple as those in our example involving the operation of an automobile. However, the operating costs of all businesses exhibit variable, semivariable, and fixed characteristics.

Some business costs increase in lump-sum steps as shown in graph **(a)** below rather than in continuous increments. For example, when production reaches a point where another supervisor and crew must be added, a lump-sum addition to labor costs occurs at this point. Other costs may vary along a curve rather than a straight line, as in graph **(b).** For example, when overtime must be worked to increase production, the labor cost per unit may rise more rapidly than volume because of the necessity of paying an overtime premium to employees.

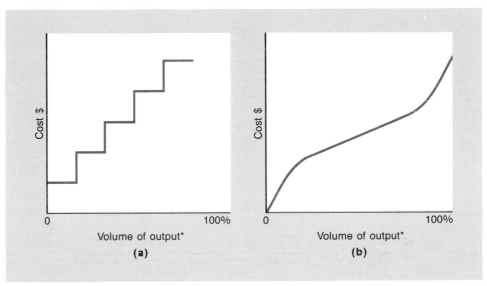

*Stated as a percentage of plant capacity

"Stair-step" and curvilinear costs

Taking all the possible variations of cost behavior into account would add greatly to the complexity of cost-volume analysis. How far from reality are the assumed straight-line relationships? Fortunately, there are two factors that make straight-line approximations of cost behavior useful for analytical purposes.

First, unusual patterns of cost behavior tend to offset one another. If we were to plot actual total costs incurred by a business over a time period in which volume changes occurred, the result might appear as in the cost-volume graph **(a)** on the next page. Total cost often moves in close approximation to a straight-line pattern when the various "stair-step" and curvilinear cost patterns of individual costs are combined.

Second, unusual patterns of cost behavior are most likely to occur at extremely high or extremely low levels of volume. For example, if output were increased to near 100% of plant capacity, variable costs would curve sharply upward because of payments for overtime. An extreme decline in volume, on the other hand, might require shutting down plants and extensive layoffs, thereby reducing some expenditures which are usually considered fixed costs.

Most businesses, however, operate somewhere between perhaps 45 and 80% of capacity, and try to avoid large fluctuations in volume. For a given business, the probability that volume will vary outside of a fairly narrow range is usually remote. The range over which output may be expected to vary is called the *relevant range,* as shown in graph (**b**) below. Within this relevant range, the assumption that total costs vary in straight-line relation to changes in volume is reasonably realistic for most companies.

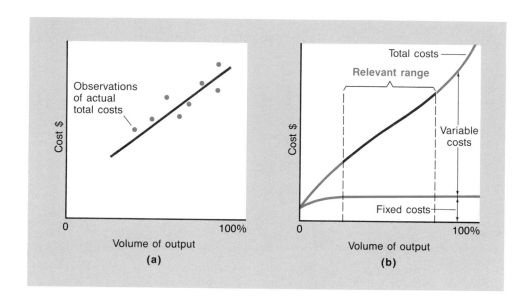

Analysis of Semivariable Costs: Determining the Fixed and Variable Elements

Objective 2

Use the high-low method to separate the fixed and variable elements of a semivariable cost.

The study of relationships between costs and the level of activity is simplified when all costs may be classified either as fixed or variable. Therefore, we divide semivariable costs into two elements: (1) the fixed portion, and (2) the variable portion.

Several mathematical techniques may be used to determine the fixed and variable elements of a semivariable cost or mixed cost. One approach, called the *high-low method,* is illustrated below.[1]

■ **High-Low Method**   To illustrate the high-low method, assume that some portion of the monthly maintenance cost of Ross Mfg. Co. is fixed, and that some portion of this cost varies with the level of production. The levels of production and of maintenance cost for the first six months of the year are shown below:

---

[1] Other approaches to determining the fixed and variable elements of a semivariable cost include the least squares method and regression analysis. These techniques are discussed in the cost accounting course.

MONTH	EQUIVALENT FULL UNITS OF PRODUCTION	MAINTENANCE COST
January	7,200	$4,790
February	7,000	4,700
March	7,700	5,100
April	8,400	5,430
May	9,000	5,700
June	8,600	5,600

To find the variable portion of this cost, we relate the change in the cost to the change in the activity base between the months of highest and lowest production activity:

	EQUIVALENT FULL UNITS OF PRODUCTION	MAINTENANCE COST
Highest level of activity base........................	9,000	$5,700
Lowest level of activity base	7,000	4,700
Changes	2,000	$1,000

Notice that a 2,000-unit increase in production caused a $1,000 increase in maintenance cost. Therefore, the variable element of this cost may be estimated at $1,000/2,000 units, or *$0.50 per equivalent full unit of production.*

To determine the fixed portion of the monthly maintenance cost, we take the total monthly cost at either the high point or low point, and deduct the variable maintenance cost at that level of activity. This computation follows, starting with the total monthly maintenance cost at the high point of activity:

$$\text{Fixed cost} - \text{Total cost} - \text{Variable cost}$$
$$- \$5,700 - (\$0.50 \text{ per unit} \times 9,000 \text{ units})$$
$$= \$5,700 - \$4,500$$
$$= \$1,200 \text{ per month}$$

We have now developed a *cost formula* for monthly maintenance cost: *$1,200 fixed cost + $0.50 per equivalent full unit of production.* This formula may be used in evaluating the reasonableness of maintenance costs incurred in past periods, and also in forecasting costs likely to be incurred in the future. For example, what amount of maintenance cost should Ross Mfg. Co. expect in a month in which the company has scheduled 8,000 equivalent full units of production? The answer is approximately *$5,200,* determined as follows:

Monthly fixed cost..	$1,200
Variable cost ($0.50 × 8,000 equivalent full units)....................................	4,000
Total estimated maintenance cost...	$5,200

Cost-Volume-Profit Relationships

Business managers continually study the effect of internal decisions and external conditions on revenue, costs, and ultimately on net income. Revenue is affected by the actions of competitors, by a firm's pricing policies, and by changes in the market demand for a firm's products or services. Costs are affected by the prices paid for inputs, the volume of production or business activity, and the efficiency with which a firm translates input factors into salable output.

An important aspect of planning to meet given profit objectives is the analysis of the effect of volume changes on operating income. The study of business cost-volume-profit relationships is sometimes called *break-even analysis,* in honor of the point at which a business moves from a loss to a profit position. The break-even point may be defined as the level of sales at which a company neither earns an operating profit nor incurs a loss. Revenue exactly covers costs and expenses.

Cost-Volume-Profit Analysis: An Illustration

A simple business situation will be used to illustrate the kinds of information that can be derived from cost-volume-profit analysis. Hannigan's Ice Cream Company has a chain of stores located throughout a large city, selling ice cream in various flavors. Although the company sells to customers in packages of different size, we shall assume that volume of business is measured in gallons of ice cream sold. The company buys its ice cream from a dairy at a price of $2.20 per gallon. Retail sales prices vary depending on the quantity purchased by a customer, but revenue per gallon of ice cream sold *averages* $4 per gallon and does not vary significantly from store to store or from period to period. Monthly operating statistics for a typical store are shown below:

HANNIGAN'S ICE CREAM COMPANY
Monthly Operating Data—
Typical Retail Store

		VARIABLE COSTS PER GALLON	VARIABLE COSTS AS PERCENTAGE OF SALES PRICE
Average selling price		$4.00	100%
Cost of ice cream		$2.20	55.0%
	FIXED COSTS		
Monthly operating expenses:			
Manager's salary	$2,200		
Wages	4,200+	.14	3.5
Store rent	1,600		
Utilities	180+	.04	1.0
Miscellaneous	820+	.02	.5
Total expenses (except for income taxes)	$9,000+	$2.40	60.0%
Contribution margin per unit and contribution margin ratio (discussed on pages 941–942)		$1.60	40.0%

Note Variable and Fixed Cost Elements

Notice that income taxes expense is not included among the monthly operating expenses of Hannigan's Ice Cream Company. Income taxes are neither a fixed nor a variable cost, because they depend upon the amount of income before taxes, rather than being fixed in amount or based upon sales volume. Income taxes generally are ignored in cost-volume-profit analysis, and "profit" is defined as *operating income* (or income before income taxes).[2]

Objective 3
Prepare a cost-volume-profit (break-even) graph.

■ **Graphic Analysis** A *cost-volume-profit* (or *break-even*) graph for the typical retail store of Hannigan's Ice Cream Company, based on the above data, is shown below. The horizontal scale represents volume in thousands of gallons of ice cream per month. Since none of the company's stores sells more than 10,000 gallons per month, this is assumed to be the upper limit of the relevant volume range. The vertical scale is in dollars of revenue or costs (expenses).

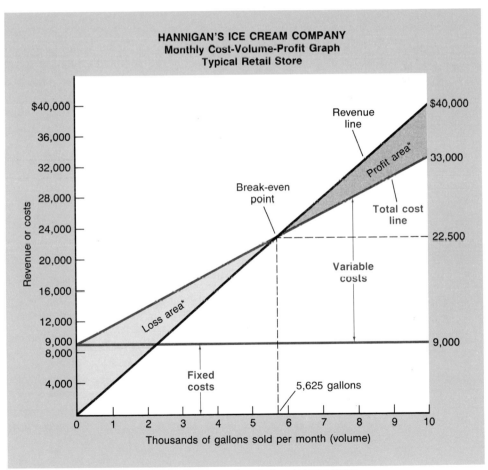

*Profit and loss areas represent the income or loss before income taxes.

The steps in plotting this cost-volume-graph are as follows:

---

[2] Determination of the income tax expense applicable to a corporation's pretax income is discussed in Chapter 18.

1 First the revenue line is plotted, running from $0 at zero volume of sales to $40,000, representing 10,000 gallons of sales per month at $4 per gallon.

2 The fixed (nonvariable) monthly operating expenses are plotted as a horizontal line at the level of $9,000 per month.

3 Starting at the $9,000 fixed cost line, the variable costs of $2.40 per gallon are plotted. Note that this line also becomes the total cost line since it is added on top of the fixed cost line.

The operating profit or loss expected at any sales level may be read from the cost-volume-profit-graph. For example, the break-even point (zero profit) is 5,625 gallons per month, or $22,500 of sales per month. Sales below 5,625 gallons per month will result in a loss, and sales above 5,625 gallons per month will result in operating income.

Objective 4
Explain contribution margin; compute contribution margin per unit and contribution margin ratio.

■ **Contribution Margin: A Key Relationship in Cost-Volume-Proft Analysis**   Variable costs vary in direct proportion to revenue. Thus, the generation of an additional dollar of revenue also generates some amount of variable costs. The operating data for our Hannigan's ice cream stores (page 940) indicate that variable costs (such as the cost of ice cream) account for 60% of the company's sales revenue. Thus, for every $100 in revenue, the company may expect to pay out $60 to cover the related variable costs. The remaining $40 is called the ***contribution margin.***

The contribution margin is the ***amount of revenue in excess of variable costs.*** This portion of the revenue is available to cover the company's fixed costs and, after all fixed costs have been covered, provide an operating profit. The allocation of the average revenue dollar between the variable costs relating to the sale and the contribution margin is illustrated below for a typical Hannigan's store:

60¢ of each revenue dollar is consumed by variable costs relating to the sale

40¢ of each revenue dollar is available to cover fixed costs and operating income. This is called the ***contribution margin.***

Contribution margin may be expressed in ***total dollars*** (sales revenue − total variable costs), on a ***per unit basis*** (sales price per unit minus variable costs per unit), or as a ***percentage of sales.*** When the contribution margin is expressed as a percentage of sales, it is called the ***contribution margin ratio*** and is computed as follows:

$$\text{Contribution margin ratio} = \frac{\text{Sales price per unit} - \text{Variable costs per unit}}{\text{Sales price per unit}}$$

The data of page 940 indicate that the contribution margin ratio at a typical Hannigan's ice cream store is 40%, computed:

$$\text{Contribution margin ratio} = \frac{\$4.00 - \$2.40}{\$4.00} = 40\%$$

A contribution margin ratio of 40% means that 40% of the revenue earned in a Hannigan's store is available to cover fixed costs and to contribute toward operating income. The remaining 60% is consumed by the variable costs.

Objective 5
Determine the sales volume required to earn a desired level of operating income.

■ **Finding Required Sales Volume (in Units)**   We may use the concept of contribution margin as a quick means of finding the **unit sales volume** required for a business to break even or to achieve any desired level of operating income. Break-even sales volume can be of vital importance, especially to companies deciding whether to introduce a new product line, build a new plant, or, in some cases, remain in business.

CASE IN POINT ■ Chrysler Corp., widely believed to be heading for bankruptcy during the early 1980s, undertook a severe cost cutting program and altered marketing strategies in an effort to lower the company's break-even point. In 1981, Chrysler had a break-even point of 1,413,000 vehicles; sales amounted to 1,282,000 vehicles and the company incurred substantial losses. For 1982, the company was able to reduce its break-even point to 1,244,000 vehicles. Chrysler surprised many people in the financial community by returning to profitable operations in 1982 with sales of approximately 1,400,000 vehicles. This "turnaround year" may well have saved Chrysler Corp. Notice, however, that the 1982 sales volume would have resulted in a net loss had Chrysler not been able to lower its break-even point.

To illustrate the relationship between sales volume and contribution margin, assume that we want to know how many gallons of ice cream a Hannigan's store must sell to break even. At the break-even point, the store must earn a contribution large enough to cover all fixed costs. The data on page 940 show that the monthly fixed costs amount to **$9,000,** and that the contribution margin per gallon of ice cream is **$1.60** ($4.00 sales price minus $2.40 variable costs). If the sale of each gallon covers $1.60 of fixed costs, how many gallons must be sold to cover fixed costs of $9,000? The answer is **5,625** gallons, as shown below:

$$\text{Sales volume (in units)} = \frac{\$9,000}{\$1.60 \text{ per gallon}} = 5{,}625 \text{ gallons per month}$$

Notice that this answer corresponds to the sales volume shown in the cost-volume-profit graph on page 941.

The reasoning in our above analysis may be summarized by the following formula:

$$\text{Sales volume (in units)} = \frac{\text{Fixed costs} + \text{Operating income}}{\text{Contribution margin per unit}}$$

With this formula, we may find not only the break-even sales volume (at which operating income is zero), but also the unit sales volume needed to achieve **any desired level of operating income.** For example, how many gallons of ice cream must be sold for a Hannigan's store to earn a monthly operating income of *$4,000?*

$$\text{Sales volume (in units)} = \frac{\$9,000 + \$4,000}{\$1.60} = 8,125 \text{ gallons per month}$$

■ **Finding Required Dollar Sales Volume** To find the *dollar sales volume* needed to earn a given level of operating income, we could first compute the required unit sales and then multiply our answer by the unit sales price. Using the data from our preceding example, a Hannigan's store expecting to earn a monthly operating income of $4,000 would need sales revenue of $32,500 (8,125 gallons × $4 per gallon).

As a more direct approach, we may compute the required dollar sales volume by substituting the *contribution margin ratio* for the contribution margin per unit in our sales volume formula. The formula then becomes:

$$\text{Sales volume (in dollars)} = \frac{\text{Fixed costs} + \text{Operating income}}{\text{Contribution margin ratio}}$$

To illustrate, let us again compute the sales volume required for a Hannigan's store to earn a monthly operating income of $4,000:

$$\text{Sales volume (in dollars)} = \frac{\$9,000 + \$4,000}{.40} = \$32,500 \text{ per month}$$

■ **Margin of Safety** The amount by which actual sales volume *exceeds* the break-even sales volume is called the margin of safety. This is the dollar amount by which sales could *decline* before the company will incur an operating loss. A typical Hannigan's store has a break-even sales volume of $22,500. Therefore, a store with actual sales of $32,500 has a *margin of safety* of $10,000; a store with sales of $35,000 has a margin of safety of *$12,500* ($35,000 − $22,500).

The margin of safety provides us with a quick means of estimating operating income at any sales volume above the break-even point, as shown below:

$$\text{Operating income} = \text{Margin of safety} \times \text{Contribution margin ratio}$$

The rationale for this formula stems from the fact that the margin of safety represents sales in excess of the break-even point. Therefore, fixed costs have already been covered and the entire contribution margin from these sales increases operating income.

To illustrate this concept, let us estimate the operating income of a Hannigan's store with a sales volume of $32,500, which is $10,000 above the break-even point. The estimated operating income is *$4,000* ($10,000 × 40%). (Notice that this answer is consistent with our earlier computations.)

■ **Changes in Operating Income** The contribution margin ratio in our example is 40%, which means that 40 cents out of every revenue dollar goes toward covering fixed costs (which reduces an operating loss) or toward increasing operating income. Thus, every additional dollar of sales improves

Objective 6
Use the contribution margin ratio to estimate the effect upon operating income of changes in sales volume.

Hannigan's profit picture by 40 cents. Conversely, a $1 sales decline lowers profitability by 40 cents. This relationship may be summarized as follows:

$$\text{Change in operating income} = \text{Change in sales volume} \times \text{Contribution margin ratio}$$

To illustrate, let us assume that the sales volume at a given ice cream store increases from $22,500 (the break-even point) to $32,500, an increase of $10,000. According to the above equation, the operating income of the store should increase by **$4,000** ($10,000 × 40%). This increase may be verified by reference to our earlier calculations. On page 942, we showed that a sales volume of $22,500 is the break-even point for a Hannigan's store; operating income at this sales volume, therefore, is zero. At the top of this page, we determined that the sales volume required to earn an operating income of $4,000 is $32,500.

Using Cost-Volume-Profit Relationships

Objective 7
Use cost-volume-profit relationships in evaluating various marketing strategies.

Cost-volume-profit relationships are widely used during the budgeting process to set sales targets, and to estimate costs and expenses. In addition, these relationships can provide information which is useful in a wide variety of planning decisions. To illustrate, let us consider several ways in which cost-volume-profit relationships might be used by the management of Hannigan's Ice Cream Company in planning marketing strategies:

1 *Question:* To increase volume, management is considering a policy of giving greater discounts on gallon and half-gallon packages of ice cream. It is estimated that the effect of this pricing policy would be to reduce the average selling price per gallon by 16 cents (that is, from $4 per gallon to $3.84). Management is interested in knowing the effect of such a price reduction on the number of gallons of ice cream a store must sell to break even.

Analysis: The proposed change in average sales price changes the contribution margin per gallon of ice cream from $1.60 to $1.44, as shown below:

$$\text{Contribution margin per unit} = \text{Sales price per unit} - \text{Variable costs per unit}$$
$$= \$3.84 - \$2.40$$
$$= \$1.44$$

The fixed operating expenses remain unchanged by this pricing decision. Therefore, the unit sales volume *to break even* under the new pricing situation would be:

$$\text{Sales volume (in units)} = \frac{\text{Fixed costs} + \text{Operating income}}{\text{Contribution margin per unit}}$$
$$= \frac{\$9,000 + \$0}{\$1.44}$$
$$= 6,250 \text{ gallons per month}$$

This new break-even point, 6,250 gallons, is more than 11% higher than the present 5,625 gallon break-even volume. Thus management should be advised that the proposed pricing policy is desirable only if the unit sales volume per store can be expected to increase more than 11% per month as a result of the lower sales prices on gallon and half-gallon packages.

2   Question: Management is considering a change in the method of compensating store managers. Instead of a fixed salary of $2,200 per month, it is proposed that managers be put on a salary of $680 per month plus a commission of 24 cents per gallon of sales. The present average monthly operating income per store is $3,400 on sales of $31,000 (Proof: $31,000 × 40% − $9,000 = $3,400). What sales revenue per store will be necessary to produce the same monthly income to Hannigan's under the proposed incentive compensation arrangement?

Analysis: This proposal involves a change in both the contribution margin ratio and the fixed monthly operating expenses. Adding 24 cents per gallon to variable costs raises the total variable cost to $2.64 per gallon and reduces the contribution margin ratio to 34%, as computed below:

$$\text{Contribution margin ratio} = \frac{\text{Unit sales price} - \text{Variable costs per unit}}{\text{Unit sales price}}$$

$$= \frac{\$4.00 - \$2.64}{\$4.00}$$

$$= 34\%$$

Cutting the manager's salary from $2,200 to $680 per month will reduce monthly fixed costs from $9,000 to $7,480. The sales volume required to produce a monthly operating income of $3,400 may be computed as follows:

$$\text{Sales volume (in dollars)} = \frac{\text{Fixed costs} + \text{Operating income}}{\text{Contribution margin ratio}}$$

$$= \frac{\$7,480 + \$3,400}{.34}$$

$$= \$32,000 \text{ per month}$$

To produce the same $3,400 per month net income under the new compensation plan, sales volume per store would have to be increased by $1,000 (or 250 gallons) over the current monthly sales volume of $31,000. The issue thus boils down to whether the incentive compensation arrangement will induce store managers to increase volume by more than 250 gallons per month. Cost-volume-profit analysis does not answer this question, but it provides the information which enables management to exercise its judgment intelligently.

3   Question: Hannigan's Ice Cream Company stores are now open 12 hours each day (from 9 A.M. to 9 P.M.). Management is considering a proposal to decrease store hours by opening two hours later each morning. It is estimated that this policy would reduce sales volume by an average of 500 gallons per month and would cut fixed costs (utilities and wages) by $1,000 per month. Would it pay the company to change its store hours?

Analysis: The loss of 500 gallons of sales per month would decrease revenue by $2,000 (500 × $4). This would result in the loss of contribution margin of $800

($2,000 × 40%). Therefore, whether the reduction in store hours would increase operating income per store may be determined as follows:

Reduction in fixed costs	*$1,000*
Less: Loss of contribution margin ($2,000 × 40%)	*800*
Prospective increase in monthly operating income per store	*$ 200*

Importance of Sales Mix in Cost-Volume-Profit Analysis

Objective 8
Determine the sales mix that will maximize the contribution margin per unit of a scarce resource.

Why would you prefer to sell only the gallon size?

In our example of Hannigan's Ice Cream Company, we assumed that the contribution margin ratio *averaged* 40% of sales expressed in dollars and that the *average* selling price was $4 per gallon of ice cream sold. Let us now change our example and assume that a detailed analysis indicated that ice cream is actually sold in three packages as follows:

	QUART	HALF-GALLON	GALLON
Sales price per package	*$1.20*	*$2.00*	*$3.60*
Less: Variable costs per package	*0.84*	*1.10*	*1.80*
Contribution margin per package	*$0.36*	*$0.90*	*$1.80*
Contribution margin ratio (contribution margin ÷ sales price)	*30%*	*45%*	*50%*
Break-even sales volume, assuming that only the one size package was sold (fixed costs, $9,000, divided by contribution margin ratio)	*$30,000*	*$20,000*	*$18,000*

Earlier in this chapter we stated that Hannigan's Ice Cream Company is now selling a certain *mix* of the three sizes and that a sales volume of $22,500 is required to break even ($9,000 ÷ *average* contribution margin ratio of 40%). If ice cream were sold exclusively in quarts, sales of $30,000 would be required to break even; if only half-gallon packages were sold, the break-even sales volume would be $20,000; if only gallon packages were sold, the break-even sales volume would be $18,000. The reason the break-even sales volume differs for each size is because each size yields a different contribution margin per dollar of sales (contribution margin ratio). *The higher the contribution margin ratio the lower the sales volume that is required to cover a given amount of fixed expenses.*

The amount of operating income earned by a business unit depends not only on the volume of sales and the ability to control expenses, but also on the *quality* of sales. At any given sales volume, selling products with high contribution margin ratios is more profitable than selling products with low contribution margin ratios. Thus, sales with high contribution margin ratios are said to be *high-quality sales*. A shift from low-margin sales to high-margin sales can increase net income even though total sales volume may decline. On the other hand, a shift from high-margin to low-margin sales can cause profits to fall even though total sales may increase.

Contribution Margin per Unit of Scarce Resource

The contribution margin approach is useful to management in deciding what products to manufacture (or purchase for resale) and what products to eliminate when certain factors of production are available only in limited quantity. One of the important functions of management is to develop the most profitable uses of such scarce resources as raw materials, skilled labor, high-cost equipment, and factory floor space.

Assume that you are offered two equally satisfactory jobs, one paying $6 per hour and one paying $9 per hour. Since your time is scarce and you wish to maximize the pay that you receive for an hour of your time, you would naturally choose the job paying $9 per hour. For the same reason, if a company has the capacity to utilize only 100,000 direct labor hours per year, management would want to use this capacity in such a way as *to produce the maximum contribution margin per hour of direct labor.*

To illustrate this concept, assume that Optic Corporation is considering the production of three products. The contribution margin per direct labor hour required to produce each of the three products is estimated as follows:

OPTIC CORPORATION
Contribution Margin per Hour of Direct Labor

PRODUCT	SALES PRICE PER UNIT	− VARIABLE COSTS PER UNIT	= CONTRIBUTION MARGIN PER UNIT	÷ DIRECT LABOR HOURS REQUIRED TO PRODUCE ONE UNIT	= CONTRIBUTION MARGIN PER HOUR OF DIRECT LABOR
A	$100	$60	$40	10	$ 4
B	80	50	30	5	6
C	60	40	20	2	10

■
Should
production of
product C be
expanded?

Notice that the manufacture of a unit of product A requires 10 hours of direct labor and generates $40 in contribution margin; a unit of product B requires only 5 hours of direct labor and yields $30 of contribution margin; finally, product C requires only 2 hours of direct labor and yields $20 in contribution margin. Thus, product C produces the *largest amount of contribution margin per hour of direct labor.* Even though product A has the highest contribution margin per unit ($40) and the highest contribution margin ratio (40%), it is the least profitable of the three products in terms of contribution margin *per hour of direct labor.*

When a company's total output is limited by the scarcity of one particular resource, the company should attempt to maximize the contribution margin per unit of this resource. To illustrate this idea, the following table shows the amounts of contribution margin that Optic would earn if it devoted all 100,000 available direct labor hours exclusively to the manufacture of each of the three products under consideration:

PRODUCT	TOTAL CAPACITY (HOURS)	× CONTRIBUTION MARGIN PER HOUR OF DIRECT LABOR	= TOTAL CONTRIBUTION MARGIN IF ONLY ONE PRODUCT IS MANUFACTURED
A	100,000	$ 4	$ 400,000
B	100,000	6	600,000
C	100,000	10	1,000,000

■
Which is the
most profitable
product?

This schedule clearly shows that the company can maximize its contribution margin and, therefore, its operating income, by concentrating its manufacturing efforts on *product C.*

In most cases, however, a company cannot simply devote all of its efforts to manufacturing the single product that is the most profitable. For example, the demand for product C may not be sufficient to allow the company to sell all the units of this product that it can produce. In this case, the company should produce units of product B after it has met the demand for product C. It should produce product A only after it has met the total demand for both products B and C.

Another consideration is that the production and sale of products A or B may be *necessary to support the sales of product C.* Often, the profit margins are much lower on these "supporting" products. Gillette, for example, manufactures blade-razors which it sells at or below cost. Why? The answer is that the sale of razors promotes the sale of razor blades, which are products with a high contribution margin.

In conclusion, most companies are not able to devote all their manufacturing efforts to the single product that provides the highest contribution margin per unit of the resource that limits the company's production. However, if the sales of different products are independent of one another, the company will maximize its total contribution margin by first meeting the demand for those products with the highest contribution margins *per unit of this scarce resource.*

Assumptions Underlying Cost-Volume-Profit Analysis

In cost-volume-profit analysis, accountants assume the following:

1   Sales price per unit remains constant.

2   If more than one product is sold, the proportion of the various products sold (sales mix) is assumed to be constant.

3   Fixed costs remain constant at all levels of sales within the assumed relevant range of activity.

4   Variable costs remain constant as a percentage of sales revenue.

5   For a business engaged in manufacturing, the number of units produced is assumed to be equal to the number of units sold.

These assumptions simplify cost-volume-profit analysis. In actual practice, however, some of these assumptions may not hold true. However, cost-volume-profit analysis is still a useful planning tool for management. As changes take place in selling prices, sales mix, expenses, and production levels, management should update and revise its analysis.

Summary of Basic Cost-Volume-Profit Relationships

In this chapter, we have demonstrated a number of ratios and mathematical relationships which are useful in cost-volume-profit analysis. For your convenience, these relationships are summarized on the next page.

MEASUREMENT	METHOD OF COMPUTATION
Contribution margin	*Sales revenue − Total variable costs*
Contribution margin per unit	*Unit sales price − Variable costs per unit*
Contribution margin ratio	$\dfrac{\text{\textit{Sales price per unit} − \textit{Variable costs per unit}}}{\text{\textit{Sales price per unit}}}$
Sales volume (in units)	$\dfrac{\text{\textit{Fixed costs} + \textit{Operating income}}}{\text{\textit{Contribution margin per unit}}}$
Sales volume (in dollars)	$\dfrac{\text{\textit{Fixed costs} + \textit{Operating income}}}{\text{\textit{Contribution margin ratio}}}$
Margin of safety	*Actual sales volume − Break-even sales volume*
Operating income	*Margin of safety × Contribution margin ratio*
Change in operating income	*Change in sales volume × Contribution margin ratio*

End-of-Chapter Review

CONCEPTS INTRODUCED OR EMPHASIZED IN CHAPTER 23

The major concepts in this chapter include:

■ The behavior of fixed, variable, and semivariable costs in response to changes in the level of business activity.

■ Use of the high-low method to determine the fixed and variable elements of a semivariable cost.

■ Contribution margin—that is, sales price minus variable expenses—as the key factor in the relationship between sales volume and operating income.

■ Use of cost-volume-profit relationships to determine the sales volume needed to achieve a desired level of operating income, and to evaluate the probable effects of changes in costs, sales price, and sales volume upon operating income.

■ Determining the sales mix that will maximize the contribution margin per unit of a scarce resource.

An understanding of cost behavior—the manner in which costs normally respond to changes in the level of activity—is required in each remaining chapter of this textbook. In these chapters, we will explore the use of accounting information in evaluating the performance of managers and departments, in planning future business operations, and in making numerous types of managerial decisions. The concepts and terminology introduced in Chapter 23 will be used extensively in these discussions.

KEY TERMS INTRODUCED OR EMPHASIZED IN CHAPTER 23

Activity base The scale used in measuring an activity which serves as a *cost driver* of variable and semivariable cost.

Break-even point The level of sales at which a company neither earns an operating profit nor incurs a loss. Revenue exactly covers costs and expenses.

Cost driver A type of activity that has a causal effect in the occurrence of a particular cost.

Cost formula A mathematical statement expressing the expected amount of a cost in terms of the fixed element of the cost and/or the portion of the cost that varies in response to changes in some activity base. For example, the cost formula for a semivariable cost might be: $2,500 per month, plus 5% of net sales.

Contribution margin Sales minus variable costs. The portion of sales revenue which is not consumed by variable costs and, therefore, is available to cover fixed costs and contribute to operating income.

Contribution margin ratio The contribution margin expressed as a percentage of sales price. Represents the percentage of each revenue dollar which is available to cover fixed costs or to provide an operating profit.

Fixed costs Costs that remain unchanged despite changes in the level of the activity base.

High-low method A method of dividing a semivariable (or mixed) cost into its fixed and variable elements by relating the change in the cost to the change in the activity base between the highest and lowest levels of observed activity.

Margin of safety Amount by which actual sales exceed the break-even point.

Relevant volume range The span or range of output over which output is likely to vary and assumptions about cost behavior are generally valid. Excludes extreme volume variations.

Semivariable costs Costs that respond to change in the level of the activity base by less than a proportionate amount.

Variable costs Costs that vary directly and proportionately with changes in the level of the activity base.

DEMONSTRATION PROBLEM FOR YOUR REVIEW

The management of the Fresno Processing Company has engaged you to assist in the development of information to be used for managerial decisions.

The company has the capacity to process 20,000 tons of cottonseed per year. The yield from a ton of cottonseed is as shown below.

PRODUCT	AVERAGE YIELD PER TON* OF COTTONSEED	AVERAGE SELLING PRICE	TOTAL REVENUE
Oil	400 pounds	$ 0.25 per pound	$100
Meal	600 pounds	160.00 per ton	48
Hulls	800 pounds	100.00 per ton	40
Lint	200 pounds	0.06 per pound	12
Totals	2,000 pounds		$200

*There are 2,000 pounds in a ton.

A special marketing study revealed that the company can expect to sell its entire output for the coming year at the average selling prices listed above.

You have determined the company's cost structure to be as follows:

Cost of cottonseed:	$80 per ton
Processing costs:	
Variable:	$26 per ton of cottonseed processed
Fixed:	$340,000 per year at all levels of production

Marketing costs: *All variable, $44 per ton of all products sold*

Administrative costs: All fixed, $300,000 per year at all levels of
                          production and sales activity

Instructions   **a** Compute per ton of cottonseed (1) the contribution margin and (2) the contribution margin ratio.

b Compute the break-even sales volume in (1) dollars and (2) tons of cottonseed.

c Assume that the company's budget calls for an operating income of $240,000. Compute the sales volume required to reach this profit objective, stated (1) in dollars and (2) in tons of cottonseed.

d Compute the maximum amount that the company can afford to pay per ton of raw cottonseed and still break even by processing and selling 16,000 tons during the current year.

SOLUTION TO DEMONSTRATION PROBLEM

a (1) *Total revenue per ton of cottonseed* $200

    Less: Variable costs:

        Cottonseed $80

        Processing... 26

        Marketing.. <u>44</u>   <u>150</u>

    Contribution margin per ton .... <u>$ 50</u>

(2) *Contribution margin ratio ($50 ÷ $200)* .... <u>25%</u>

b (1) *Break-even sales volume (in dollars):*

    Fixed costs ($340,000 + $300,000) .... $ 640,000

    *Contribution margin ratio **(part a)*** 25%

    Break-even sales volume ($640,000 ÷ .25) .... <u>$2,560,000</u>

(2) *Break-even sales volume (in tons):*

    Fixed costs (per above)... $ 640,000

    *Contribution margin per ton **(part a)***................................... $ 50

    Break-even sales volume stated in tons of

      cottonseed products ($640,000 ÷ $50) .... <u>12,800</u>

    (Alternative computation: break-even sales volume
    in dollars $2,560,000, divided by sales price per ton, $200,
    equals 12,800 tons.)

c (1) *Sales volume (in dollars):*

    Fixed costs .... $ 640,000

    Add: Desired operating income .... <u>240,000</u>

    Required contribution margin .... $ 880,000

    *Contribution margin ratio **(part a)*** 25%

    Sales volume ($880,000 ÷ 25%) .... <u>$3,520,000</u>

(2) *Sales volume (in units):*

Sales volume in dollars (above)		$3,520,000
Sales price per ton	$	200
Sales volume in tons of cottonseed products		
($3,520,000 ÷ $200)		17,600

d *Total revenue per ton of cottonseed*		$200
Less: Per unit costs other than cottonseed:		
Processing	$26	
Marketing..	44	
Fixed costs ($640,000 ÷ 16,000 tons)	40	110
Maximum amount that can be paid per ton of		
cottonseed while allowing company to break		
even at 16,000 ton volume..		$ 90

SELF-TEST QUESTIONS

Answers to these questions appear on page 962.

1 During the current year, the net sales of Ridgeway, Inc., were 10% below last year's level. You should expect Ridgeway's semivariable costs to:

a Decrease in total, but increase as a percentage of net sales.

b Increase in total and increase as a percentage of net sales.

c Decrease in total and decrease as a percentage of net sales.

d Increase in total, but decrease as a percentage of net sales.

2 Shown below are the monthly high and low levels of direct labor hours and of total manufacturing overhead for Apex Mfg. Co.

	DIRECT LABOR HOURS	TOTAL MANUFACTURING OVERHEAD
Highest observed level	6,000	$17,000
Lowest observed level	4,000	14,000

In a month in which 5,000 direct labor hours are used, the ***fixed element*** of total manufacturing overhead costs should be approximately:

a $15,500   **b** $8,000   **c** $7,500   **d** $8,000 plus $1.50 per unit

3 Marston Company sells a single product at a sales price of $50 per unit. Fixed costs total $15,000 per month, and variable costs amount to $20 per unit. If management reduces the sales price of this product by $5 per unit, the sales volume needed for the company to break-even will:

a Increase by $5,000   **c** Increase by $2,000

b Increase by $4,500   **d** Remain unchanged

4 Becker Auto Supply earns an average contribution margin ratio of 40% on its sales. The store manager estimates that by spending an additional $5,000 per month for radio advertising, the store will be able to increase its operating income by $3,000 per month. The manager is expecting the radio advertising to increase monthly dollar sales volume by:

a $12,500   **b** $8,000   **c** $7,500   **d** Some other amount

5 Elco Corporation manufactures two products. Data concerning these products is shown below:

	PRODUCT A	PRODUCT B
Total monthly demand for product	1,000 units	500 units
Sales price per unit..	$400	$500
Contribution margin ratio	30%	40%
Direct labor hours to manufacture each unit................	5	10

Elco's productive capacity is limited by the availability of only 6,500 direct labor hours each month. If the company is to maximize its operating income, how many units of Product B should Elco produce each month?

a None　　　　　　**b** 150　　　　　　**c** 500　　　　　　**d** Some other amount

Assignment Material

REVIEW QUESTIONS

1 Why is it important for management to understand cost-volume-profit relationships?

2 What is an *activity base* and why is it important in analyzing cost behavior?

3 What is the effect of an increase in activity upon:

a Total variable costs.

b Variable costs per unit of activity.

4 What is the effect of an increase in activity upon:

a Total fixed costs.

b Fixed costs per unit of activity.

5 The simplifying assumption that costs and volume vary in straight-line relationships makes the analysis of cost behavior much easier. What factors make this a reasonable and useful assumption in many cases?

6 Define the *relevant range* of activity.

7 Explain how the high-low method determines:

a The variable portion of a semivariable cost.

b The fixed portion of a semivariable cost.

8 Define (**a**) contribution margin and (**b**) contribution margin ratio.

9 What important relationships are shown on a cost-volume-profit (break-even) graph?

10 Kris Company has an average contribution margin ratio of 35%. What dollar sales volume per month is necessary to produce a monthly operating income of $22,000, if fixed costs are $118,000 per month?

11 Explain how the contribution margin per unit can be used to determine the unit sales required to break even.

12 Reed Company has variable costs of $11 per unit and a contribution margin ratio of 45%. Compute the selling price per unit.

13 Define *margin of safety.*

14 Explain the probable effect upon operating income of a $10,000 increase in sales volume by a company with variable costs of $50 per unit and a contribution margin ratio of 35%.

15 An executive of a large American steel company put the blame for lower net income for a recent fiscal period on the "shift in product mix to higher proportion of export sales." Sales for the period increased slightly while net income declined by 28%. Explain how a change in product (sales) mix to a higher proportion in export sales would result in a lower level of net income.

16 Why is it helpful to know the approximate amount of contribution margin generated from the use of a scarce resource such as a machine-hour or an hour of direct labor?

17 The president of an airline blamed a profit squeeze on "unwise and unjustifiable promotional fares." He pointed out that 50% of the company's revenue came from "discount fares." Explain why discount fares tend to reduce net income and point out circumstances in which a discount from the regular price of a plane fare could *increase* net income.

EXERCISES

Exercise 23-1
Accounting
terminology

Listed below are nine technical accounting terms introduced in this chapter:

Relevant range	*Contribution margin ratio*	*Variable costs*
Fixed costs	*Semivariable costs*	*Break-even point*
Sales mix	*Contribution margin*	*Margin of safety*

Each of the following statements may (or may not) describe one of these technical terms. For each statement, indicate the accounting term described, or answer "None" if the statement does not correctly describe any of the terms.

a Revenue less variable expenses.

b The amount by which sales exceed the break-even point.

c Costs that respond to changes in sales volume by less than a proportionate amount.

d Operating income less variable costs.

e The level of sales at which revenue exactly equals costs and expenses.

f Costs that remain unchanged despite changes in sales volume.

g The span over which output is likely to vary and assumptions about cost behavior generally remain valid.

h Contribution margin per unit expressed as a percentage of unit sales price.

Exercise 23-2
Patterns of cost
behavior

Explain the effects of an increase in the volume of activity upon the following costs. (Assume volume remains within the relevant range.)

a Total fixed costs.

b Fixed costs per unit.

c Total variable costs.

d Variable costs per unit.

e Total semivariable costs.

f Semivariable costs per unit.

Exercise 23-3
Classification of
various costs

Explain whether you regard each of the following costs or categories of costs as fixed, variable, or semivariable with respect to net sales. Briefly explain your reasoning. If you do not believe that a cost fits into any of these classifications, explain.

a Depreciation expense on a sales showroom, based upon the straight-line method of depreciation.

b Depreciation on a sales showroom, based upon the double-declining balance method of depreciation.

c The cost of goods sold.

d Salaries to salespeople. (These salaries include a monthly minimum amount, plus a commission on all sales.)

e Income taxes expense.

f Property taxes expense.

Exercise 23-4
High-low method
of cost analysis

The following information is available regarding the total manufacturing overhead of Drew Mfg. Co. for a recent four-month period:

	MACHINE-HOURS	MANUFACTURING OVERHEAD
March	60,000	$163,000
April	50,000	152,000
May	70,000	177,000
June	80,000	188,000

Instructions

a Use the high-low method to determine:

(1) The variable element of manufacturing overhead costs per machine-hour.

(2) The fixed element of monthly overhead cost.

b Use the cost relationships determined in part **a** to estimate the total manufacturing overhead expected to be incurred at an activity level of 75,000 machine-hours.

Exercise 23-5
Using a cost
formula

Through using the high-low method, Regency Hotels estimates the total costs of providing room service meals to amount to $6,300 per month, plus 25% of room service revenue.

a What is the contribution margin ratio of providing room service meals?

b What is the break-even point for room service operations in terms of total room service revenue?

c What would you expect to be the total cost of providing room service in a month in which room service revenue amounts to $14,000?

Exercise 23-6
Using a cost
formula

City Ambulance Service estimates the monthly cost of responding to emergency calls to be $18,600 plus $90 per call.

Instructions

a In a month in which the company responds to 120 emergency calls, determine the estimated:

(1) Total cost of responding to emergency calls.

(2) Average cost of responding to emergency calls.

b Assume that in a given month, the number of emergency calls was unusually low. Would you expect the average cost of responding to emergency calls during this month to be higher or lower than in other months? Explain.

Exercise 23-7
Computing sales
volume

Bendix Co. has fixed costs of $330,000, variable costs of $12 per unit, and a contribution margin ratio of 40%. Compute the dollar sales volume required for Bendix Co. to earn an operating income of $150,000.

Exercise 23-8
Computing contribution margin ratio and margin of safety

The information shown below relates to the only product sold by Portland Company:

Sales price per unit...	$ 20
Variable cost per unit...	15
Fixed costs per year...	200,000

a Compute the contribution margin ratio and the dollar sales volume required to break even.

b Assuming that the company sells 70,000 units during the current year, compute the margin of safety sales volume (dollars).

Exercise 23-9
Computing required sales volume

Information concerning a product manufactured by Ames Brothers appears below:

Sales price per unit...	$ 140
Variable cost per unit...	86
Total fixed manufacturing and operating costs...................................	540,000

Determine the following:

a The contribution margin per unit

b The number of units that must be sold to break even

c The unit sales level that must be reached in order to earn an operating income of $270,000

Exercise 23-10
Relating contribution margin ratio to sales price

Firebird Mfg. Co. has a contribution margin ratio of 30% and must sell 20,000 units at a price of $100 each in order to break even. Compute:

a Total fixed costs.

b Variable costs per unit.

Exercise 23-11
Computing the break-even point

Malibu Corporation has fixed costs of $36,000 per month. It sells two products as follows:

	SALES PRICE	VARIABLE COSTS	CONTRIBUTION MARGIN
Product no. 1	$10	$4	$6
Product no. 2	10	7	3

a What monthly dollar sales volume is required to break even if two units of product no. 1 are sold with one unit of product no. 2?

b What monthly dollar sales volume is required to break even if one unit of product no. 1 is sold with two units of product no. 2?

Exercise 23-12
Cost-volume-profit relationships

For each of the six independent situations below, compute the missing amounts:

a Only one product is manufactured:

	SALES	VARIABLE COSTS	CONTRIBUTION MARGIN PER UNIT	FIXED COSTS	OPERATING INCOME	UNITS SOLD
(1) $_____	$120,000	$20	$_____	$25,000	4,000
(2) 180,000	_____	___	45,000	30,000	5,000
(3) 600,000	_____	30	150,000	90,000	_____

b Many products are manufactured:

	SALES	VARIABLE COSTS	CONTRIBUTION MARGIN RATIO	FIXED COSTS	OPERATING INCOME
(1) $900,000	$720,000	___%	$_____	$95,000
(2) 600,000	_____	40%	_____	75,000
(3) _____	_____	30%	90,000	60,000

PROBLEMS

Group A

Problem 23A-1
Using cost-volume-profit formulas

MURDER TO GO! writes and manufactures murder mystery parlour games which it sells to retail stores. Shown below is per-unit information relating to the manufacture and sale of this product.

Selling price per unit	$ 15
Variable cost per unit	3
Fixed costs per year	180,000

Instructions

Determine the following, showing as part of your answer the formula which you used in your computation. For example, the formula used to determine the contribution margin ratio (part **a**) is:

$$\text{Contribution margin ratio} = \frac{\text{Sales price per unit} - \text{Variable costs per unit}}{\text{Sales price per unit}}$$

a Contribution margin ratio.

b Sales volume (in dollars) required to break even.

c Sales volume (in dollars) required to earn an annual operating income of $150,000.

d The margin of safety sales volume if annual sales total 40,000 units.

e Operating income if annual sales total 40,000 units.

Problem 23A-2
Estimating costs and profits

Charlie Miller Company manufactures fishing rods. For the coming year, the company has budgeted the following costs for the production and sale of 20,000 rods:

	BUDGETED COSTS	BUDGETED COSTS PER UNIT	PERCENTAGE OF COSTS CONSIDERED VARIABLE
Direct materials	$200,000	$10	100%
Direct labor	160,000	8	100
Manufacturing overhead (fixed and variable) .	280,000	14	40
Selling and administrative expenses	240,000	12	20
Totals	$880,000	$44	

Instructions

a Compute the sales price per unit that would result in a budgeted operating income of $200,000, assuming that the company produces and sells 20,000 fishing rods. (Hint: First compute the budgeted sales revenue needed to produce this operating income.)

b Assuming that the company decides to sell the rods at a unit price of $56, compute the following:

(1) Total fixed costs budgeted for the year.

(2) Variable costs per unit.

(3) The contribution margin per unit.

(4) The number of units that must be produced and sold annually to break even at a sales price of $56 per unit.

Problem 23A-3
Drawing a cost-volume-profit graph

Rainbow Paints operates a chain of retail paint stores. Although the paint is sold under the Rainbow label, it is purchased from an independent paint manufacturer. Guy

Walker, president of Rainbow Paints, is studying the advisability of opening another store. His estimates of monthly costs for the proposed location are:

Fixed costs:

Occupancy costs	*$3,160*
Salaries	*3,640*
Other	*1,200*
Variable costs (including cost of paint)	*$6 per gallon*

Although Rainbow stores sell several different types of paint, monthly sales revenue consistently averages $10 per gallon sold.

Instructions

a Compute the contribution margin ratio and the break-even point in dollar sales and in gallons sold for the proposed store.

b Draw a monthly cost-volume-profit graph for the proposed store, assuming 3,000 gallons per month as the maximum sales potential.

c Walker thinks that the proposed store will sell between 2,200 and 2,600 gallons of paint per month. Compute the amount of operating income that would be earned per month at each of these sales volumes.

Problem 23A-4
Determining
optimal sales
mix

Landry Knife Company manufactures three different products. The estimated demand for the products for the current year is such that production will not be able to keep pace with incoming orders. Some pertinent data for each product are listed below:

PRODUCT	ESTIMATED UNIT SALES	SALES PRICE	DIRECT MATERIAL COST	DIRECT LABOR COST	VARIABLE MANUFACTURING OVERHEAD
A	15,000	$20	$3	$10	$1
B	8,000	12	1	5	1
C	2,400	17	2	10	1

Direct labor costs an average of $10 per hour.

Instructions

a Prepare a schedule showing the contribution margin per one unit of each product and also the contribution margin per one hour of direct labor applied to the production of each class of product.

b If you were able to reduce the production of one of the products in order to meet the demand for the others, what would that product be? Why? Assume that available direct labor hours represent the scarce resource which limits total output.

c Assume that the 15,000 hours of direct labor hours now used to produce product A are used to produce additional units of product B. What would be the effect on total contribution margin?

Problem 23A-5
Analyzing the
effects of
changes in costs

Precision Systems manufactures tape decks and currently sells 18,500 units annually to producers of sound reproduction systems. Jay Wilson, president of the company, anticipates a 15% increase in the cost per unit of direct labor on January 1 of next year. He expects all other costs and expenses to remain unchanged. Wilson has asked you to assist him in developing the information he needs to formulate a reasonable product strategy for next year.

You are satisfied that volume is the primary factor affecting costs and expenses and have separated the semivariable costs into their fixed and variable segments. Beginning and ending inventories remain at a level of 1,000 units.

Below are the current-year data assembled for your analysis:

Sales price per unit...		*$100*
Variable costs per unit:		
Direct materials	*$10*	
Direct labor	*20*	
Manufacturing overhead and selling and administrative		
expenses	*30*	*60*
Contribution margin per unit (40%)		*$ 40*
Fixed costs		*$390,000*

Instructions

a What increase in the selling price is necessary to cover the 15% increase in direct labor cost and still maintain the current contribution margin ratio of 40%?

b How many tape decks must be sold to maintain the current operating income of *$350,000* if the sales price remains at $100 and the 15% wage increase goes into effect? (Hint: First compute contribution margin per unit.)

c Wilson believes that an additional $700,000 of machinery (to be depreciated at 20% annually) will increase present capacity (20,000 units) by 25%. If all tape decks produced can be sold at the present price of $100 per unit and the wage increase goes into effect, how would the estimated operating income before capacity is increased compare with the estimated operating income after capacity is increased? Prepare schedules of estimated operating income at full capacity *before* and *after* the expansion.

Group B

Problem 23B-1
Introduction to cost-volume-profit formulas

Shown below is information relating to the only product sold by Pinapple Pak, Inc.:

Sales price per unit..	*$*	*40*
Variable cost per unit...		*16*
Fixed costs per year..		*198,000*

Instructions

Determine the following, showing as part of your answer the formula or relationships you used in your computations. For example, the formula used to determine the contribution margin ratio (part **a**) is:

$$\text{Contribution margin ratio} = \frac{\text{Sales price per unit} - \text{Variable costs per unit}}{\text{Sales price per unit}}$$

(Hint: A summary of key relationships appears on page 950.)

a Contribution margin ratio.

b Dollar sales volume required to break even.

c Dollar sales volume required to earn an annual operating income of $75,000.

d The margin of safety if annual sales total 25,000 units.

e Operating income if annual sales total 25,000 units.

Problem 23B-2
Setting sales price and computing the break-even point

Thermal Tent, Inc., is a newly organized manufacturing business which plans to manufacture and sell 50,000 units per year of a new product. The following estimates have been made of the company's costs and expenses (other than income taxes):

	FIXED	VARIABLE PER UNIT
Manufacturing costs:		
Direct materials		*$47*
Direct labor		*32*
Manufacturing overhead	*$340,000*	*4*

Period expenses:		
Selling expenses		*1*
Administrative expenses	*200,000*	
Totals..	*$540,000*	*$84*

Instructions
a What should the company establish as the sales price per unit if it sets a target of earning an operating income of $260,000 by producing and selling 50,000 units during the first year of operations? (Hint: First compute the required contribution margin per unit.)

b At the unit sales price computed in part **a**, how many units must the company produce and sell to break even? (Assume all units produced are sold.)

c What will be the margin of safety if the company produces and sells 50,000 units at the sales price computed in part **a**?

Problem 23B-3
Preparing a
"break-even"
graph

Stop-n-Shop operates a downtown parking lot containing 800 parking spaces. The lot is open 2,500 hours per year. The parking charge per car is 40 cents per hour; the average customer parks two hours. Stop-n-Shop rents the lot for $4,750 per month. The lot supervisor is paid $16,000 per year. Five employees who handle the parking of cars are paid $250 per week for 50 weeks, plus $500 each for the two-week vacation period. Employees rotate vacations during the slow months when four employees can handle the reduced load of traffic. Lot maintenance, payroll taxes, and other costs of operating the parking lot include fixed costs of $2,000 per month and variable costs of 4 cents per parking-space hour.

Instructions
a Draw a cost-volume-profit graph for Stop-n-Shop on an annual basis. Use thousands of parking-space hours as the measure of volume of activity. [Stop-n-Shop has an annual capacity of 2 million parking space hours (800 spaces × 2,500 hours per year).]

b What is the contribution margin ratio? What is the annual break-even point in dollars of parking revenue?

c Suppose that the five employees were taken off the hourly wage basis and paid 24 cents per car parked, with the same vacation pay as before. (1) How would this change the contribution margin ratio and total fixed costs? Hint: The variable costs per parking-space hour will now include 12 cents, or one-half of the 24-cents paid employees per car parked, because the average customer parks for two hours. (2) What annual sales revenue would be necessary to produce operating income of $44,500 under these circumstances?

Problem 23B-4
Determining the
most profitable
product given
scarce resources

Optical Instruments produces two models of binoculars. Information for each model is shown below:

	MODEL 100	MODEL 101
Sales price per unit...	*$180*	*$125*
Costs and expenses per unit:		
Direct materials	*$51*	*$38*
Direct labor	*33*	*30*
Manufacturing overhead (applied at the rate of $18		
per machine-hour, ⅓ of which is fixed and		
⅔ variable)..	*36*	*18*
Variable selling expenses	*30*	*15*
Total costs and expenses per unit...........................	*150*	*101*
Profit per unit	*$ 30*	*$ 24*
Machine-hours required to produce one unit	*2*	*1*

Total manufacturing overhead amounts to $180,000 per month, one-third of which is fixed. The demand for either product is sufficient to keep the plant operating at full capacity of 10,000 machine-hours per month. Assume that *only one product is to be produced in the future.*

Instructions

a Prepare a schedule showing the contribution margin per machine-hour for each product.

b Explain your recommendation as to which of the two products should be discontinued.

**Problem 23B-5
Cost-volume-
profit analysis;
preparing a
graph**

James Denny is considering investing in a vending machine operation involving 25 vending machines located in various plants around the city. The machine manufacturer reports that similar vending machine routes have produced a sales volume ranging from 1,000 to 2,000 units per machine per month. The following information is made available to Denny in evaluating the possible profitability of the operation.

(1) An investment of $50,000 will be required, $14,000 for merchandise and $36,000 for the 25 machines.

(2) The machines have a service life of five years and no salvage value at the end of that period. Depreciation will be computed on the straight-line basis.

(3) The merchandise (candy and soft drinks) retails for an average of 30 cents per unit and will cost Denny an average of 15 cents per unit.

(4) Owners of the buildings in which the machines are located are paid a commission of 3 cents per unit of candy and soft drinks sold.

(5) One man will be hired to service the machines. He will be paid $1,400 per month.

(6) Other expenses are estimated at $400 per month. These expenses do not vary with the number of units sold.

Instructions

a Determine contribution margin per unit and the break-even volume in units and in dollars per month.

b Draw a monthly cost-volume-profit graph for sales volume up to 2,000 units per machine per month.

c What sales volume in units and in dollars per month will be necessary to produce an operating income equal to a 30% annual return on Denny's investment during his *first year* of operation? (Round to the nearest unit.)

d Denny is considering offering the building owners a flat rental of $30 per machine per month in lieu of the commission of 3 cents per unit sold. What effect would this change in commission arrangement have on his *monthly* break-even volume in terms of units?

BUSINESS DECISION CASES

**Case 23-1
Iacocca's
dilemma**

Assume that you are part of the new management team which has taken over the management of a large diversified automobile manufacturer that is in serious financial condition. Despite several years of large losses, the company's previous management has made practically no changes in the company's operations. The automobiles manufactured by the company are satisfactory in terms of size, style, and fuel economy.

a Suggest some actions you might consider in an effort to reduce:

(1) Fixed costs

(2) Variable costs per automobile

b Suggest some ways other than cost reductions by which the company may be able to lower its break-even point.

ANSWERS TO THE SELF-TEST QUESTIONS

1 a　**2 b**　**3 c** (from $25,000 to $27,000)　**4 d** ($20,000)　**5 b**

Measuring and Evaluating Segment Performance

In this chapter, we focus upon measuring the performance of divisions, departments, and other segments of a business organization. Emphasis is placed upon such topics as responsibility accounting, developing segmented income statements that show subtotals for contribution margin and segment margin, and the use of segment information in evaluating the performance of segments and segment managers. In the latter half of the chapter, we introduce variable costing—a technique for rearranging the information generated by a conventional cost accounting system into a format that is better suited to many types of managerial decisions.

After studying this chapter, you should be able to meet these Learning Objectives:

1 Explain the need for segment information and describe a responsibility accounting system.

2 Prepare segment income statements showing contribution margin and segment margin.

3 Distinguish between "traceable" and "common" fixed costs.

4 Explain the usefulness of contribution margin and segment margin in making short-term and long-term decisions.

5 Explain the differences between full costing and variable costing.

6 Use a variable costing income statement in cost-volume-profit analysis.

7 Explain why short-term fluctuation in the level of production may distort key measurements of segment performance under full costing.

SEGMENTS OF A BUSINESS

Most businesses are organized into a number of different subunits that perform different functions. For example, a manufacturing company typically has departments specializing in purchasing, production, sales, shipping, accounting, finance, and personnel. Production departments and sales departments often are further subdivided along different product lines or geographical areas. Organizing a business in this manner enables managers and employees to specialize in specific types of business activity. Also, this type of organization helps to establish clear lines of managerial responsibility.

Companies use many different names to describe their internal operating units, including divisions, departments, branches, product lines, and sales territories. In our discussion, we generally will use the term *segment* to describe a subunit within a business organization. A designated manager is responsible for directing the activities of each segment within a business organization. Therefore, we also describe segments of a business as *responsibility centers.*

In most business organizations, large responsibility centers are further subdivided into smaller ones. Consider, for example, a retail store within a chain such as Sears or K-Mart. Each store is a responsibility center under the control of a store manager. However, each store is further divided into many separate sales departments, such as appliances, automotive products, and sporting goods. Each sales department also is a responsibility center, under the control of a department manager. These department managers report to, and are supervised by, the store manager.

The Need for Information About Segment Performance

An income statement measures the overall performance of a business entity. However, managers also need accounting information measuring the performance of *each segment* within the business organization. This segment information assists managers in:

1   Planning and allocating resources   Management needs to know how well various segments of the business are performing in order to set future performance goals and to allocate resources to those segments offering the greatest profit potential. If one product line is more profitable than another, for example, the company's overall profitability may increase by allocating more production capacity to the more profitable product.

2   Controlling operations   One use of segment data is to identify those portions of the business that are performing inefficiently or below expectations. When revenue lags, or costs become excessive, segment information helps to focus management's attention upon the segments responsible for the poor performance. If a segment of the business is unprofitable, perhaps it should be discontinued.

3   Evaluating the performance of segment managers   As each segment is an area of managerial responsibility, the performance of the segment provides one basis for evaluating the skills of the segment manager.

Thus, measuring the performance of each segment in the business organization is an important function of any accounting system designed to meet the needs of management.

Profit Centers, Investment Centers, and Cost Centers

The segments of a business may be viewed as profit centers, as investment centers, or as cost centers.

■ **Profit Centers** A profit center is a segment of the business that generates *both revenue and costs.*[1] Examples of profit centers include product lines, sales territories, retail outlets, and the specific sales departments within each retail outlet. Even an individual salesperson may be viewed as a profit center within a business organization.

Profit centers are evaluated primarily upon their profitability. Thus, *segmented income statements* are prepared showing the revenue and costs applicable to each profit center. The revenue and costs of each segment may then be compared with budgeted amounts, with the segment's performance in past periods, and, most importantly, with the profitability of other profit centers within the organization. For example, supermarkets view every product line as a separate profit center. Because supermarkets have limited shelf space, they may discontinue even profitable product lines if the related shelf space can be used for still more profitable products.

■ **Investment Centers** Some profit centers also qualify as investment centers. An *investment center* is a profit center for which management is able to measure objectively the cost of the assets used in the center's operations.

The performance of an investment center may be evaluated using return on investment (ROI) measurements. The most common of these measures is *return on assets,* in which the operating income (or *segment margin*) of the segment is expressed as a percentage of the average total assets utilized by the segment during the period.

Not all profit centers can be evaluated as investment centers. For example, if a profit center shares the use of common facilities with other segments of the business, it may be difficult to determine the "amount invested" in the profit center. Thus, profit centers that share common facilities usually are evaluated upon their profitability, but this profitability is not expressed as a "return on investment."

To illustrate the distinction between investment centers and other profit centers, consider a hotel within a national hotel chain, and also the coffee shop within this hotel. Both the hotel and the coffee shop are profit centers. The hotel, however, is also an investment center, because management can readily identify those assets used in the operations of the hotel. The assets utilized by the coffee shop, on the other hand, cannot be determined with anywhere near the same degree of objectivity. For example, the coffee shop uses a small portion of the land, building, and parking lot of the hotel. Any allocation of such assets among the subunits within the hotel (the coffee shop, dining room, lounge, and guest rooms) would be highly arbitrary. Thus, the coffee shop would be evaluated as a profit center, but not as an investment center.

---

[1] In this chapter, we will continue the convenient practice of using the term costs to describe both costs (such as the cost of goods sold) and expenses.

■ **Cost Centers**   A *cost center* is a segment of the business that incurs costs (or expenses), but does not directly generate revenue.[2] Production departments in a manufacturing company are examples of cost centers. Service departments, such as accounting, finance, maintenance, and the legal department also are cost centers. Service departments provide services to other segments within the business, but do not sell goods or services directly to customers.

Cost centers are evaluated primarily upon (1) their ability to control costs, and (2) the *quantity* and the *quality* of the services that they provide to the business organization. As cost centers do not directly generate revenue, segmented income statements are not prepared for these segments of the business. However, the accounting system must accumulate separately the costs incurred by each cost center.

In some cases, costs provide an objective basis for evaluating the performance of a cost center. For example, production departments are evaluated primarily upon the unit costs incurred in manufacturing inventory. For many cost centers, however, nonfinancial criteria are extremely important in assessing the segment's performance. In evaluating the performance of a maintenance department, for example, the question of whether plant assets are maintained in good operating order is an important consideration. Evaluating the performance of an accounting department is even more subjective. Management must compare the costs incurred by the department with the "value" of the department's services to the business. These services include not only meeting the company's financial reporting requirements, but also providing managers with the information necessary to run the business.

RESPONSIBILITY ACCOUNTING SYSTEMS

Objective 1
Explain the need for segment information and describe a responsibility accounting system.

An accounting system designed to measure the performance of each responsibility center within a business is termed a *responsibility accounting system.* Measuring performance along the lines of managerial responsibility is an important managerial tool. A responsibility accounting system holds individual managers accountable for the performance of the business segments under their control. In addition, such systems provide top management with information useful in identifying the strong and the weak segments throughout the business organization.

The operation of a responsibility accounting system involves three basic steps. First, *budgets* are prepared for each responsibility center. These budgets serve as targets, with which the segment's actual performance will be compared. Second, the accounting system *measures the performance* of each responsibility center. Third, timely *performance reports* are prepared, comparing the actual performance of each segment with the budgeted amounts. Frequent performance reports help segment managers keep their segments' performance "on target," and also assist top management in evaluating the performance of each segment and segment manager.

In this chapter, we emphasize the second step in the operation of a responsibility accounting system—measuring the performance of each responsibility

[2] Cost centers sometimes generate insignificant amounts of revenue, but the direct generation of revenue is incidental to the basic purpose of the segment.

center. The use of budgets and of performance reports are discussed in the following chapter.

Responsibility Accounting: An Illustration

Objective 2
Prepare segment income statements showing contribution margin and segment margin.

The diagram on the following page shows in condensed form how the monthly performance of profits centers is measured and reported in the responsibility accounting system. The company in our example, NuTech Electronics, is first segmented into two divisions: retail sales and special orders. The Retail Division is further segmented into two stores; each store has two profit centers—a department that sells merchandise, and a department that repairs electronic appliances for customers.[3]

As you read down the NuTech illustration, you are looking at smaller and smaller parts of the company. The recording of revenue and costs must begin at the ***bottom*** of the illustration—that is, for the ***smallest*** areas of managerial responsibility. If income statements are to be prepared for each profit center in the 42d. St. Store, for example, NuTech's chart of accounts must be sufficiently detailed to measure separately the revenue and costs of these departments. The income statements for larger responsibility centers then may be prepared primarily by combining the amounts appearing in the income statements of the smaller subunits. Notice, for example, that the total sales of the 42d. St. Store ($200,000) are equal to the sum of the sales reported by the two profit centers within the store ($180,000 and $20,000).

Assigning Revenue and Costs to Segments of a Business

In segment income statements, revenue is assigned first to the profit center responsible for earning that revenue. Assigning revenue to the proper department is relatively easy. Electronic cash registers, for example, automatically classify sales revenue by the department of origin.

In assigning costs to segments of a business, two concepts generally are applied:

1 Costs are classified into the categories of variable costs and fixed costs.[4] When costs are classified in this manner, a subtotal may be developed in the income statement showing the ***contribution margin*** of the business segment. Arranging an income statement in this manner is termed the ***contribution margin approach*** and is widely used in preparing reports for use by managers.

2 Each segment is only charged with those costs that are directly traceable to that segment. A cost is "directly traceable" to a particular segment if that segment is ***solely responsible*** for the cost being incurred. Thus, traceable costs should ***disappear if the segment is discontinued.***

[3] NuTech also prepares segment income statements showing the profit centers in the Special Orders Division, and in the Baker St. Store. To conserve space, these statements are not included in our illustration.

[4] In Chapter 23, we discussed techniques such as the "high-low method" for separating semivariable costs such as sales salaries and telephone expense into their variable and fixed elements.

ILLUSTRATION OF A RESPONSIBILITY ACCOUNTING SYSTEM

Segments defined as divisions

		SEGMENTS	
	ENTIRE COMPANY	RETAIL DIVISION	SPECIAL ORDERS DIVISION
Sales	$900,000	**$500,000**	$400,000
Variable costs	400,000	240,000	160,000
Contribution margins	**$500,000**	**$260,000**	**$240,000**
Fixed costs traceable to divisions	360,000	170,000	190,000
Division segment margins	**$140,000**	**$ 90,000**	**$ 50,000**
Common fixed costs	40,000		
Operating income	$100,000		
Income taxes expense....................	35,000		
Net income	$ 65,000		

Segments defined as stores in the
Retail Division

		SEGMENTS	
	RETAIL DIVISION	42D. ST. STORE	BAKER ST. STORE
Sales	**$500,000**	**$200,000**	$300,000
Variable costs	240,000	98,000	142,000
Contribution margins	**$260,000**	**$102,000**	**$158,000**
Fixed costs traceable to stores	140,000	60,000	80,000
Store segment margins...................	**$120,000**	**$ 42,000**	**$ 78,000**
Common fixed costs	30,000		
Segment margin for division	**$ 90,000**		

Segments defined as profit centers
(departments) in the 42d. St. Store

		SEGMENTS	
	42D. ST. STORE	SALES DEPARTMENT	REPAIRS DEPARTMENT
Sales	**$200,000**	$180,000	$ 20,000
Variable costs	98,000	90,000	8,000
Contribution margins	**$102,000**	**$ 90,000**	**$ 12,000**
Fixed costs traceable to departments	32,000	18,000	14,000
Departmental segment margins	**$ 70,000**	**$ 72,000**	**$ (2,000)**
Common fixed costs	28,000		
Segment margin for store.................	**$ 42,000**		

The question of whether a cost is traceable to a particular department is not always clear-cut. In assigning costs to segments of a business, accountants often must exercise professional judgment.

CASE IN POINT ■ The sales department of a large manufacturing company used to request many "Rush" orders from the production department. To fill these rush orders, the production department had to work overtime, which caused the production department to incur labor costs well in excess of budgeted amounts. The company's controller modified the responsibility accounting system to charge the sales department with the extra labor cost of processing rush orders. After this change was made, the sales department made a greater effort to give the production department adequate notice of all sales orders. As a result, the number of costly "Rush" orders was substantially reduced.

Variable Costs

In segmented income statements, variable costs are those costs that change in approximate proportion to changes in sales volume. Examples of variable costs include the cost of goods sold and commissions paid to salespeople. Because variable costs are directly related to revenue, they usually are traceable to the profit center generating the revenue. If a profit center were eliminated, all of that center's variable costs should disappear.

Contribution Margin

Contribution margin (revenue minus variable costs) is an important tool for cost-volume-profit analysis. For example, the effect of a change in sales volume upon operating income may be estimated by either (1) multiplying the change in unit sales by the contribution margin per unit, or (2) multiplying the dollar change in sales volume by the contribution margin ratio. (To assist in this type of analysis, segmented income statements often include percentages, as well as dollar amounts. A segmented income statement with percentage columns is illustrated on page 972.)

Contribution margin expresses the relationship between revenue and variable costs, but ignores fixed costs. Thus, contribution margin is primarily a **short-run** planning tool. It is useful primarily in decisions relating to price changes, short-run promotional campaigns, or changes in the level of output that will not significantly affect fixed costs. For longer-term decisions, such as whether to build a new plant or close a particular profit center, managers must consider fixed costs as well as contribution margin.

Fixed Costs

Objective 3
Distinguish between "traceable" and "common" fixed costs.

For a business to be profitable, total contribution margin must exceed total fixed costs. However, many fixed costs cannot be easily traced to specific segments of the business. Thus, a distinction is often drawn in segment income statements between *traceable fixed costs* and *common fixed costs*.

Traceable Fixed Cost

Traceable fixed costs are those that can be easily traced to a specific segment of the business, and that arise because of that segment's existence. In short, traceable fixed costs *could be eliminated* if the segment were closed. Examples of traceable fixed costs include the salaries of the segment's employees, and depreciation and other costs relating to fixtures or equipment used exclusively by that segment.

In determining whether a specific profit center adds to the profitability of the business, it is reasonable to deduct from the center's contribution margin any traceable fixed costs. In a segmented income statement, contribution margin less traceable fixed costs is termed *segment margin,* as illustrated in the NuTech Electronics example earlier.

Common Fixed Costs

Common fixed costs (or indirect fixed costs) *jointly benefit several segments* of the business. The level of these fixed costs usually would not change significantly even if one of the segments deriving benefits from these costs were discontinued.

Consider, for example, a large department store, such as a Broadway or a Nordstom. Every department in the store derives some benefit from the store building. However, such costs as depreciation and property taxes on the store will continue at current levels even if one or more of the departments within the store is discontinued. Thus, from the viewpoint of the segments within the store, depreciation on the building is a "common" fixed cost.

Common fixed costs cannot be assigned to specific subunits except by arbitrary means, such as in proportion to relative sales volume, or square feet of space occupied. In an attempt to measure the "overall profitability" of each profit enter, some businesses allocate common fixed costs to segments along with traceable costs. A more common approach, however, is to charge each profit center only with those costs *directly traceable* to that segment of the business. In this text, we follow this latter approach.

■ **Common Fixed Costs Include Costs Traceable to Service Departments** In a segmented income statement, the category of traceable fixed costs usually includes only those fixed costs *traceable to profit centers.* Costs traceable to *service departments,* such as the accounting department, benefit many segments of the business. Thus, the costs of operating service departments are classified in a segmented income statement as common fixed costs. For example, the $28,000 in common fixed costs shown in the segmented income statement of NuTech's 42d St. Store includes the costs of operating the store's accounting, security, and maintenance departments, as well as other "storewide" costs such as depreciation, utilities expense, and the store manager's salary.

Service departments are evaluated as cost centers. Therefore, the responsibility accounting system should accumulate separately the costs traceable to each service department.

■ **Common Fixed Costs Are Traceable to Larger Responsibility Centers** All costs are traceable to *some level* of the organization. To illustrate this concept, a portion of the responsibility accounting system of NuTech

Electronics is repeated below, with emphasis upon the fixed costs in the 42d St. Store:

Segments defined as stores in the Retail Division

	RETAIL DIVISION	SEGMENTS	
		42D. ST. STORE	BAKER ST. STORE
Sales	$500,000	$200,000	$300,000
Variable costs	240,000	98,000	142,000
Contribution margins	$260,000	$102,000	$158,000
Fixed costs traceable to stores	140,000	60,000	80,000
Store segment margins	$120,000	$ 42,000	$ 78,000
Common fixed costs	30,000		
Segment margin for division	$ 90,000		

Segments defined as profit centers (departments) in the 42d. St. store

	42D ST. STORE	SEGMENTS	
		SALES DEPARTMENT	REPAIRS DEPARTMENT
Sales	$200,000	$180,000	$ 20,000
Variable costs	98,000	90,000	8,000
Contribution margins	$102,000	$ 90,000	$ 12,000
Fixed costs traceable to departments	32,000	18,000	14,000
Departmental segment margins	$ 70,000	$ 72,000	$ (2,000)
Common fixed costs	28,000		
Segment margin for store................	$ 42,000		

We have made the point that certain "storewide" costs, such as the operation of the maintenance department and the store manager's salary, are not traceable to the specific profit centers within the store. These costs are, however, easily traceable to the 42d St. Store. Therefore, whether these costs are classified as "traceable" or "common" depends upon whether we define the business segments as stores, or departments within the stores.

As we move up a responsibility reporting system to broader and broader areas of responsibility, common costs at the lower levels of managerial responsibility *become traceable costs* as they fall under the control of the managers of larger responsibility centers.

Segment Margin

Objective 4
Explain the usefulness of contribution margin and segment margin in making short-term and long-term decisions.

We have mentioned that contribution margin is an excellent tool for evaluating the effects of short-run decisions upon profitability. **Segment margin** is a *longer-run* measure of profitability because it takes into consideration any fixed costs traceable to the segment. Thus, segment margin is more useful than contribution margin for making long-term decisions that involve changes in fixed costs. Examples of such "long-run" decisions include whether to expand plant capacity or eliminate a profit center that is performing poorly.

To illustrate, assume that Pioneer Mfg. Co. manufactures and sells two products—car radios and cellular telephones. The company's monthly income statement, segmented by product line, is shown below. In this segmented income statement, we illustrate the common practice of including *component percentages* as well as dollar amounts.

	ENTIRE COMPANY DOLLARS	%	CAR RADIOS DOLLARS	%	CELLULAR TELEPHONES DOLLARS	%
Sales	$200,000	100	$100,000	100	$100,000	100
Variable costs	100,000	50	60,000	60	40,000	40
Contribution margins	$100,000	50	$ 40,000	40	$ 60,000	60
Fixed costs traceable to product lines	56,000	28	12,000	12	44,000	44
Product segment margins	$ 44,000	22	$ 28,000	28	$ 16,000	16
Common fixed costs	26,000	13				
Operating income	$ 18,000	9				
Income taxes expense	6,000	3				
Net income	$ 12,000	6				

Which is the company's most profitable product? The answer depends upon whether you are making short-run decisions, which usually do not change fixed costs, or long-run decisions, in which changes in fixed costs become important factors.

First, let us consider short-run decisions. Assume that management believes a $2,000 per month radio advertising campaign would increase the monthly sales of whichever product is advertised by 10% ($10,000). Which product will it be most profitable to advertise? The answer is *cellular telephones,* because of the higher *contribution margin ratio* of this product (60%, as compared to 40% for car radios). Selling an additional $10,000 of cellular telephones will generate $6,000 in contribution margin, whereas selling an additional $10,000 of radios will generate only $4,000.

Now let us take a longer-run view. Assume that the company must discontinue one of these products. Which product should the company *continue to produce?* The answer is *car radios.* After considering fixed costs traceable to each product, car radios contribute $28,000 to the company's operating income, whereas cellular telephones contribute only $16,000. Stated another way, if the cellular telephone product line is discontinued, all the revenue, variable costs, and traceable fixed costs relating to this product should disappear. In short, the company would lose the $16,000 monthly *segment margin* now produced by this product line. This, of course, is preferable to losing the $28,000 monthly segment margin produced by the car radio product line.

In summary, in making short-run decisions that do not affect fixed costs, managers should attempt to generate the most *contribution margin* for the additional costs incurred. This usually means emphasizing those segments with the highest contribution margin ratios. In evaluating a segment as a long-term investment, however, managers must consider the ability of the segment to cover its fixed costs. Thus, in the long run managers should emphasize growth in those segments with the highest *segment margins* and *segment margin ratios.*

When a segment is evaluated as an investment center, segment margin generally is used as the "income" figure in making any ROI computations. Thus, the return on assets for an investment center would be computed as segment margin divided by the average assets utilized by the segment.

When Is a Segment "Unprofitable"?

In deciding whether a specific profit center is "unprofitable," management should consider several factors. Segment margin, however, is a good starting point. Segment margin indicates whether the profit center earns enough contribution margin to cover the fixed costs traceable to that segment of the business.

To illustrate, consider the segmented income statement for the 42d. St. Store of NuTech Electronics:

	42D. ST. STORE	SEGMENTS SALES DEPARTMENT	REPAIRS DEPARTMENT
Sales	$200,000	$180,000	$ 20,000
Variable costs	98,000	90,000	8,000
Contribution margins	$102,000	$ 90,000	$ 12,000
Fixed costs traceable to departments	32,000	18,000	14,000
Departmental segment margins	$ 70,000	$ 72,000	$ (2,000)
Common fixed costs	28,000		
Segment margin for store	$ 42,000		

According to this data, discontinuing the Repairs Department should eliminate the $20,000 in revenue, and also $22,000 in costs ($8,000 variable costs, plus $14,000 in traceable fixed costs). Thus, closing the Repairs Department might well increase the profitability of the store by *$2,000*—the negative segment margin reported by the Repairs Department.

In deciding whether or not to close the Repairs Department, managers should also consider other factors. For example, does the existence of the Repairs Department contribute to merchandise sales? What alternative use could be made of the space now used by the Repairs Department? These factors will be considered in greater depth in Chapter 26.

Evaluating Segment Managers

Some costs traceable to a segment are simply beyond the segment manager's immediate control. Examples include depreciation expense and property taxes on plant assets. If a segment is saddled with high costs that are beyond the segment manager's control, the segment may perform poorly even if the segment manager is doing an excellent job.

As a response to this problem, some companies subdivide the fixed costs traceable to each segment into the subcategories of *controllable fixed costs* and *committed fixed costs.* Controllable fixed costs are those under the segment manager's immediate control, such as salaries and advertising. Committed fixed costs are those which the segment manager cannot readily change, such as depreciation. In the segmented income statement, controllable fixed costs are deducted from contribution margin to arrive at a subtotal called *perfor-*

mance margin. Committed fixed costs then are deducted to determine segment margin.

Subdividing traceable costs in this manner draws a distinction between the performance of the segment manager and the profitability of the segment as a long-term investment. The performance margin includes only the revenue and costs *under the segment manager's direct control,* and is a useful tool in evaluating the manager's skill. Segment margin, however, remains the best measure of the segment's long-term profitability.

Arguments against Allocating Common Fixed Costs to Segments

We have mentioned that some companies follow a policy of allocating common fixed costs among the segments benefiting from these costs. The bases used for allocating common costs are necessarily arbitrary, such as relative sales volume, or square feet of floor space occupied by the segment. In a segmented income statement, segment margin less common fixed costs allocated to the segment usually is called "operating income."

We do *not* recommend this practice, for several reasons:

1 Common fixed costs often would not change even if a segment were eliminated. Therefore, an allocation of these costs only distorts the amount contributed by each segment to the income of the company.

To illustrate this point, assume that $10,000 in common costs are allocated to a segment that has a segment margin of only $4,000. Also assume that total common costs would not change even if the segment were eliminated. The allocation of common costs makes the segment *appear* to be unprofitable, showing an operating loss of $6,000 ($4,000 segment margin, less $10,000 in allocated common fixed costs). However, closing the segment would actually *reduce* the company's income by *$4,000,* as the segment's $4,000 segment margin would be lost, but common fixed costs would not change.

2 Common fixed costs are not under the direct control of the segment managers. Therefore, allocating these costs to the segments does not assist in evaluating the performance of segment managers.

3 Allocation of common fixed costs may imply changes in segment profitability that are unrelated to segment performance.

To illustrate this point, assume that $50,000 in monthly common fixed costs are allocated equally to each of five profit centers. Thus, each profit center is charged with *$10,000* of these costs. Now assume that one of the profit centers is discontinued, but that the monthly level of common fixed costs does not change. Each of the four remaining profit centers will now be charged with *$12,500* in common fixed costs ($50,000 ÷ 4). Thus, the continuing profit centers are made to appear less profitable because of an event (closure of the fifth profit center) that is *unrelated* to their activities.

Nonfinancial Objectives and Information

Thus far, we have emphasized measuring the financial performance of segments within a business organization. In addition, many firms specify *nonfinancial* objectives which they consider important to their basic goals. A responsibility accounting system may be designed to gather much nonfinancial information about each responsibility center.

CASE IN POINT ■ Among the factors used by McDonald's Corporation to evaluate a restaurant manager is the manager's performance on the company's QSC standards. "QSC" stands for "quality, service, and cleanliness." Each restaurant manager periodically is rated on these standards by a member of McDonald's supervisory staff. Among the many items listed on McDonald's QSC rating forms are:

Quality: Temperature, appearance, quantity, and taste of food servings.
Service: Appearance and general conduct of employees; use of proper procedures in greeting customers.
Cleanliness: Cleanliness in all areas in the kitchen, front counter, tables, and restrooms. Appearance of building exterior and parking lot.

VARIABLE COSTING

Objective 5
Explain the differences between full costing and variable costing.

Our preceding examples of income statements showing contribution margin and segment margin are based upon the activities of merchandising companies. In a merchandising company, the entire cost of goods sold represents a variable cost. In the financial statements of a manufacturing company, however, the cost of goods sold is based upon manufacturing costs—some of which are variable, and some of which are fixed. The conventional practice of including both variable and fixed manufacturing costs in the valuation of inventories and in the cost of goods sold is called *full costing.* Full costing is the method *required* by generally accepted accounting principles and by income tax regulations.

For the purposes of making managerial decisions, it is often more useful to have an income statement in which variable and fixed costs are shown separately, and a subtotal is shown indicating contribution margin. Arranging the income statement of a manufacturing company in this format involves a technique called *variable costing.*

Under variable costing, the cost of goods sold includes only *variable* manufacturing costs. Fixed manufacturing costs are viewed as *period costs* and are deducted separately in the income statement after the determination of contribution margin. Before discussing variable costing further, let us briefly review some of the basic concepts of accounting for manufacturing costs.

Full Costing: The Traditional View of Product Costs

In Chapter 21, we made the distinction between *product costs* and *period costs.* Product costs are the costs of manufacturing inventory, and are debited to the Work-in-Process Inventory account. From this account, product costs flow into the Finished Goods Inventory account and then into the Cost of Goods Sold. Thus, product costs are offset against revenue in the period in which the related goods are *sold.* Period costs, on the other hand, are charged directly to expense accounts, and are deducted from revenue in the period in which the *cost is incurred.*

Under full costing, *all manufacturing costs are treated as product costs,* regardless of whether these costs are "variable" or "fixed." As all manufacturing costs are "absorbed" into the cost of manufactured products, full costing often is termed *absorption* costing.

Variable Costing: A Different View of Product Costs

Some manufacturing costs are variable costs and some manufacturing costs are fixed costs. The costs of direct materials used and of direct labor, for example, are variable costs. Manufacturing overhead, on the other hand, consists primarily of fixed costs. Examples of "fixed" overhead costs include depreciation on plant assets and salaries to supervisors, security guards, and maintenance personnel.

Under variable costing, only the *variable* manufacturing costs are viewed as product costs; *fixed manufacturing costs are viewed as period costs.* Thus, fixed overhead costs are classified as expenses of the current period, rather than flowing into the inventory accounts and the Cost of Goods Sold account. The diagrams on page 977 illustrate the flow of costs under full costing and variable costing.

In reports intended for use by managers, variable costing has two distinct advantages over full costing:

1 The format of the variable costing income statement easily lends itself to cost-volume-profit analysis.

2 Segment margin (or income from operations) is *not affected* by short-run fluctuations in the level of production.

Illustration of Variable Costing

The differences between variable costing and full costing may be further illustrated by preparing a partial income statement under each of these methods. Assume, for example, that on June 1, 1991, Hamilton Mfg. Co. opened its Nashville Plant. Data for the first month of operations of this plant appear below:

Units manufactured and units sold:
Number of units manufactured (all completed by June 30)	*11,000*
Number of units sold	*10,000*
Units in inventory of finished goods at June 30	*1,000*

Sales revenue and selling and administrative expenses:
Net sales (10,000 units sold @ $20)	*$200,000*
Selling and administrative expenses:	
Variable ($2 per unit sold)	*20,000*
Fixed	*30,000*

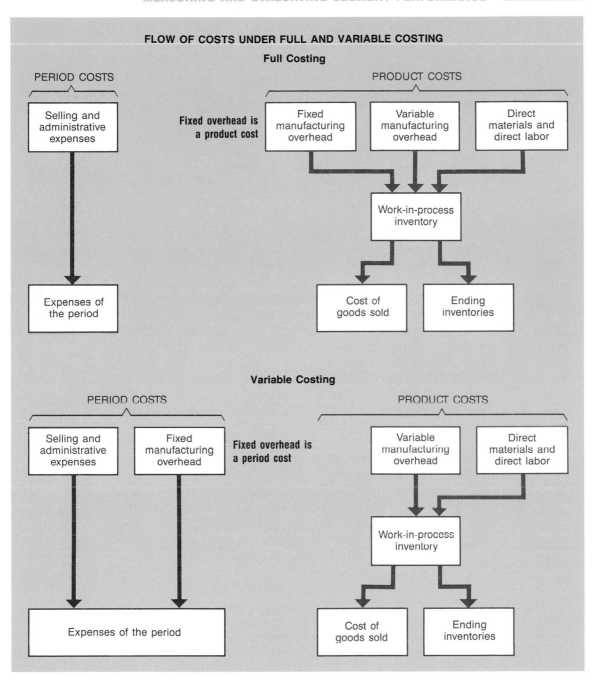

FLOW OF COSTS UNDER FULL AND VARIABLE COSTING

Full Costing

PERIOD COSTS

PRODUCT COSTS

Selling and administrative expenses

Fixed overhead is a product cost

Fixed manufacturing overhead

Variable manufacturing overhead

Direct materials and direct labor

Work-in-process inventory

Expenses of the period

Cost of goods sold

Ending inventories

Variable Costing

PERIOD COSTS

PRODUCT COSTS

Selling and administrative expenses

Fixed manufacturing overhead

Fixed overhead is a period cost

Variable manufacturing overhead

Direct materials and direct labor

Work-in-process inventory

Expenses of the period

Cost of goods sold

Ending inventories

Manufacturing costs (per unit manufactured):

	FULL COSTING	VARIABLE COSTING
Direct materials	$ 4	$ 4
Direct labor	3	3
Manufacturing overhead:		
Fixed ($55,000 ÷ 11,000 units manufactured)	5	–0–
Variable	1	1
Total cost per unit manufactured.................................	$13	$ 8

The variable, selling, and administrative costs are based upon the number of units *sold,* whereas variable manufacturing costs relate to the number of units *manufactured.*

Notice the difference in "total unit cost" under the two costing methods. Under full costing, the $55,000 in fixed manufacturing overhead is allocated to the 11,000 units produced. Thus, the cost assigned to each finished unit includes $5 of fixed manufacturing overhead. Under variable costing, only variable manufacturing costs are included in unit cost.

The treatment of these fixed manufacturing costs creates an important difference between full costing and variable costing. Under full costing, we will use the *$13* unit cost to determine the cost of goods sold and the ending inventory. Under variable costing, the cost of goods sold and ending inventory will be determined using the *$8* unit cost.

Income statements using the full costing and variable costing approaches are illustrated on the following page.

■ **Treatment of Fixed Manufacturing Costs** We have made the point that under full costing, fixed manufacturing costs are viewed as product costs, while under variable costing they are viewed as period costs. Now let us see what that means in terms of the valuation of inventories and the amount of profit (segment margin) reported under our two costing methods.

Fixed manufacturing costs in our illustration total $55,000 and amount to $5 for each unit manufactured. If we view these costs as product costs—the full costing approach—the costs assigned to any units sold during the period are deducted from revenue as part of the cost of goods sold. During June, the Nashville Plant produced 11,000 units, of which 10,000 were sold. Under full costing, the per-unit cost is *$13, including $5 per unit in fixed costs.* Notice that the cost of goods sold in the full costing income statement is $130,000 (10,000 units sold × $13), and ending inventory is $13,000 (1,000 units × $13). Thus, *$50,000* of fixed manufacturing cost is *included in the cost of goods sold* (10,000 units × $5 per unit), and *$5,000* is *included in the ending inventory* of finished goods (1,000 units × $5 per unit).

Under variable costing, fixed manufacturing costs are treated as a period cost; the *entire $55,000 is deducted from revenue;* none is included in the cost assigned to inventory. (Notice that in the variable costing income statement ending inventory is valued at only $8 per unit, the variable costs of production.)

How do the different treatments accorded to fixed costs affect the amount of

Full costing:

■
Fixed overhead
viewed as a
product cost

HAMILTON MFG. CO.—NASHVILLE PLANT
Partial Income Statement—Full Costing
For the Month Ended June 30, 1991

Sales (10,000 units × $20)		$200,000
Cost of goods sold:		
Beginning inventory	$ –0–	
Cost of finished goods manufactured		
(11,000 units manufactured × $13).....	143,000	
Cost of goods available for sale........	$143,000	
Less: Ending inventory (1,000		
units × $13)	13,000	
Cost of goods sold		130,000
Gross profit on sales		$ 70,000
Selling and administrative expenses		
(10,000 units sold × $2, plus $30,000 in		
fixed costs)		50,000
Segment margin....................................		$ 20,000

Notice the difference in ending inventories. Fixed overhead of $5 per unit is included under full costing. This explains the difference in segment margins (1,000 units × $5 = $5,000).

Variable costing:

■
Fixed overhead
viewed as a
period cost

HAMILTON MFG. CO.—NASHVILLE PLANT
Partial Income Statement—Variable Costing
For the Month Ended June 30, 1991

Sales (10,000 units × $20)			$200,000
Variable costs:			
Variable cost of goods sold:			
Beginning inventory	$ –0–		
Cost of finished goods manufactured			
(11,000 units manufactured × $8)	88,000		
Cost of goods available for sale........	$ 88,000		
Less: Ending inventory (1,000			
units × $8).....................	8,000		
Variable cost of goods sold	$ 80,000		
Variable selling and administrative			
expenses (10,000 units sold × $2)	20,000	100,000	
Contribution margin		$100,000	
Traceable fixed costs:			
Manufacturing...........................	$ 55,000		
Selling and administrative................	30,000	85,000	
Segment margin....................................		$ 15,000	

segment margin shown in the income statement? The answer is that fixed manufacturing costs may be ***deferred to future periods*** under the full costing method. Instead of being deducted from revenue immediately, fixed manufacturing costs relating to units in inventory are "carried forward" as part of the cost of this inventory. These costs will be "released" from inventory and included in the cost of goods sold in the period in which these goods are ***sold***. In our illustration, $5,000 in fixed manufacturing cost was deferred into inventory under the full costing approach. This explains why both the value assigned to ending inventory and the reported amount of segment margin are $5,000 higher under full costing.

In summary, full costing results in a higher segment margin than does variable costing **when inventories are increasing** and fixed manufacturing costs are being deferred. In periods in which inventory **declines,** however, full costing results in a **lower** segment margin, because the fixed costs previously deferred into inventory are released into the Cost of Goods Sold account. This situation is illustrated later in this chapter.

Objective 6
Use a variable costing income statement in cost-volume-profit analysis.

■ **Using a Variable Costing Income Statement**   The **variable costing** income statement readily lends itself to cost-volume-profit analysis. To illustrate, let us use this income statement to determine the dollar sales volume needed for the Nashville Plant to earn a monthly segment margin of $50,000. As a first step, we may compute the plant's contribution margin ratio directly from the income statement, as follows: $100,000 contribution margin ÷ $200,000 net sales = **50%**. We may then compute the required sales volume using the following cost-volume-profit relationships:

$$\text{Sales volume} = \frac{\text{Fixed costs} + \text{Segment margin}}{\text{Contribution margin ratio}}$$

$$= \frac{\$85,000 + \$50,000}{.50} = \underline{\underline{\$270,000}}$$

Fluctuations in the Level of Production

Objective 7
Explain why short-term fluctuation in the level of production may distort key measurements of segment performance under full costing.

Two accounting measurements widely used in evaluating the performance of a manufacturing segment of a business are the unit cost of manufactured products and segment margin. A significant shortcoming in the full costing approach is that both of these performance measurements are affected by short-term fluctuation in the level of production. This complicates the process of evaluating the performance of a segment. The manager performing the evaluation must determine whether changes in unit cost and in segment margin represent important changes in performance, or merely the effects of a temporary change in the number of units produced.

This problem arises because under full costing, fixed manufacturing costs are included in the cost of finished goods manufactured. If the level of production temporarily rises, fixed costs per unit will decline. If production temporarily declines, fixed costs per unit will increase. In either case, the changes in fixed costs per unit will also affect total unit manufacturing cost.

In addition to causing changes in unit cost, fluctuations in the level of production may cause some fixed costs to be deferred into inventory, or released from inventory. For example, if production rises **above** the level of current sales, some of the fixed costs of the period are **deferred** into inventory, rather than being offset against the revenue of the current period. If production temporarily falls **below** the level of sales, the fixed costs of prior periods are **released** from inventory and charged against the revenue of the current period.

Most accountants agree that short-term fluctuations in the level of production, by themselves, do **not** represent changes in the profitability of a segment.

Profits result from sales, not merely from production. An advantage of variable costing is that unit cost, contribution margin, and segment margin—all important measurements of segment performance—are *not affected* by short-run fluctuations in the level of production.

To illustrate this point, we will use the operating data for the Jogman Division of Yato Mfg. Co. during 1991 and 1992, illustrated below and on the following page. In this illustration, sales, variable costs per unit, and total fixed costs remain **unchanged** in each of the two years. The only change is a temporary fluctuation in the level of production; during 1991, the division produces **60,000** units and in 1992 it produces only **40,000** units. (To simplify this illustration, we assume that the segment has no beginning inventory and that all selling and administrative expenses are fixed costs.)

Operating Data for the Jogman Division

	1991 & 1992
Annual unit sales	50,000
Unit sales price	$ 18
Annual net sales (50,000 × $18)	900,000
Annual fixed costs:	
Manufacturing...	240,000
Selling and administrative..	130,000

	1991	1992
Number of units manufactured	60,000	40,000
Cost per unit manufactured (full costing):		
Variable manufacturing costs	$ 7	$ 7
Fixed manufacturing costs ($240,000 divided by number of units manufactured during the year)		
Total unit cost of finished goods manufactured (full costing)	$11	$13

Income Statements for the Jogman Division

Full Costing

	1991		1992	
Sales (50,000 units)......................................		$900,000		$900,000
Cost of goods sold:				
Beginning inventory	$ –0–		$110,000	
Cost of finished goods manufactured	660,000[a]		520,000[c]	
Cost of goods available for sale...........	$660,000		$630,000	
Less: Ending inventory....................	110,000[b]		–0–	
Cost of goods sold		550,000		630,000
Gross profit		$350,000		$270,000
Selling and administrative expenses....................		130,000		130,000
Segment margin.......................................		$220,000		$140,000

[a] 60,000 units @ $11 per unit.
[b] 10,000 units @ $11 per unit.
[c] 40,000 units @ $13 per unit.

Variable Costing

	1991		1992	
Sales (50,000 units)		$900,000		$900,000
Variable cost of goods				
sold (50,000 units @ $7)		350,000		350,000
Contribution margin		$550,000		$550,000
Traceable fixed costs:				
Manufacturing	$240,000		$240,000	
Selling and administrative	130,000	370,000	130,000	370,000
Segment margin		$180,000		$180,000

■ **Analysis of the Illustration**   Remember the basic facts of our illustration: nothing has changed at the Jogman Division from 1991 to 1992 *except for the level of production.* Notice that in the variable costing income statements, the Jogman Division reports the *same amounts* of contribution margin and segment margin in 1991 and 1992. The unit cost of finished goods manufactured, $7, also remained unchanged. Thus, the key measurements of segment performance are *not affected* by the change in the level of production. Under variable costing, contribution margin and segment margin change only when there is a change in (1) sales revenue, (2) variable costs per unit, or (3) fixed costs incurred during the period.

Under full costing, however, changes in the level of production *can* cause significant changes in key measurements of performance. These changes result both from the change in fixed costs per unit, and also from fixed costs being deferred into inventory or released from inventory. Let us now look at the reasons behind the fluctuation in the amounts of segment margin reported in our example under the full costing approach.

1991: More units are produced than sold   Notice that under full costing in 1991, fixed manufacturing costs amounted to $4 per unit ($240,000 − 60,000 units manufactured). During 1991, the Jogman Division manufactured 10,000 more units than it sold. Thus, under full costing, $40,000 in fixed manufacturing costs were deferred into ending inventory. This deferral of fixed costs explains why the segment margin reported in 1991 is $40,000 higher than the segment margin shown in the variable costing income statement.

1992: Fewer units are produced than sold   Now consider the results reported under full costing in 1992. In this year, unit sales exceeded production by 10,000 units. As the inventory is drawn down, the $40,000 in fixed costs deferred in 1991 become part of the cost of goods sold in 1992. Thus, the segment margin is $40,000 lower than that shown under variable costing.

■ **Summary**   Because the full costing method associates fixed manufacturing costs with units of production, the amount of fixed manufacturing cost offset against revenue varies with the relationship between the number of units produced and number sold. If production temporarily exceeds unit sales, some fixed manufacturing costs are deferred to future periods, and segment margin will be higher than would be reported under variable costing. If fewer units are produced during the period than are sold, fixed costs deferred in prior periods are offset against current revenue as inventory is drawn down. Thus, segment margin reported for the current period will be lower than would result from variable costing.

Under variable costing, the level of production has *no effect* upon segment margin, because all fixed manufacturing costs are offset against revenue as they are incurred, *regardless* of the level of production.

In the long run, the total amounts of segment margin reported under full costing and variable costing should be very similar. Over the long run, the number of units produced tends to equal the number of units sold. In the short run, however, variable costing provides managers with the more reliable measurement of the performance of segments engaged in manufacturing activities.

Why Is Variable Costing Unacceptable for Use in Financial Statements?

We have shown that in several respects, variable costing may be more useful than full costing as a basis for many managerial decisions. Why then is variable costing not also used in financial statements and income tax returns? The answer to this question is that variable costing omits fixed manufacturing costs from the valuation of the ending inventory. Financial accountants and income tax authorities argue that variable costing significantly understates the "full" cost of manufacturing this asset. As a result of understating ending inventories, variable costing may understate net income, especially for a growing business with steadily increasing inventories.

End-of-Chapter Review

CONCEPTS INTRODUCED OR EMPHASIZED IN CHAPTER 24

Major concepts discussed in this chapter include:

■ The nature of business "segments" and of a responsibility accounting system.

■ Cost centers, profit centers, and investment centers, and the factors to be considered in evaluating each type of segment.

■ Segmented income statements prepared using the "contribution margin approach," and the usefulness of contribution margin in making short-run decisions.

■ Traceable fixed costs, contrasted with common fixed costs.

■ Segment margin as a measurement of the long-run profitability of a business segment.

■ The role of nonfinancial information in evaluating segment performance.

■ Variable costing as an alternative to full costing, and the advantages of variable costing in cost-volume-profit analysis and in evaluating segment performance.

■ Reasons why variable costing is not used in financial statements.

One purpose of this chapter is to "tie together" many of the concepts introduced in our three preceding managerial accounting chapters. Notice, for example, how such concepts as the distinction between variable costs and fixed costs, cost-volume-profit relationships, the nature of period costs and product costs, and the flow of manufacturing costs through an accounting system have played major roles in our evaluation of segment performance. In the next chapter, we introduce the topic of budgeting. The budget provides one of the major standards with which current performance is compared.

KEY TERMS INTRODUCED OR EMPHASIZED IN CHAPTER 24

Absorption costing See **full costing.**

Committed fixed costs Fixed costs that are traceable to a segment of a business, but which, in the short run, cannot readily be changed by the segment manager.

Common fixed costs Fixed costs that are of joint benefit to several segments of a business. Thus, these common costs cannot be traced to the segments deriving benefit, except by arbitrary means.

Contribution margin Revenue less variable costs; also, the amount of revenue available to contribute toward fixed costs and operating income (or **segment margin**). The key statistic for most types of cost-volume-profit analysis.

Contribution margin approach Arranging a segmented income statement in a manner that develops **contribution margin** as a subtotal. Requires dividing costs and expenses into the categories of variable costs and fixed costs.

Controllable fixed costs Fixed costs that are under the direct control of the segment manager.

Cost center A segment of the business that incurs costs, but that does not directly generate revenue.

Direct costing See **variable costing.**

Full costing The traditional method of product costing in which both fixed and variable manufacturing costs are treated as product costs and charged to inventories. Also called **absorption costing.**

Investment center A profit center for which the amount of assets invested in the segment may be readily identified. When a profit center meets this criterion, its performance may be evaluated using return on investment (ROI) techniques, such as return on assets.

Performance margin A subtotal in a segmented income statement designed to assist in evaluating the performance of a segment manager based solely upon revenue and expenses under the manager's control. Consists of contribution margin less the controllable fixed costs traceable to the department.

Period costs Costs that are deducted as expense in the period in which they are incurred, rather than being debited to asset accounts.

Product costs Costs that become part of the inventory value of work-in-process and finished goods. These costs are deducted from revenue in the period that the related goods are sold.

Profit center A segment of a business that directly generates revenue, as well as incurring costs.

Responsibility accounting system An accounting system that separately measures the performance of each responsibility center in the organization.

Responsibility center A segment of a business for which a particular manager is in charge and held responsible for the segment's performance.

Segment A subunit within a business organization. A segment of a business conducts specific types of business activity and is under the control of a designated manager.

Segment margin Revenue less variable costs and traceable fixed costs. A long-run measure of the profitability of a profit center. Consists of the revenue and costs likely to disappear if the segment were eliminated.

Segmented income statement An income statement that subdivides the operating results of a business segment among the profit centers comprising that segment.

Traceable fixed costs Fixed costs that are directly traceable to a specific segment of a business. These costs usually would be eliminated if the segment were discontinued.

Variable costing The technique of product costing in which only the variable manufacturing costs are regarded as product costs. Fixed manufacturing costs are treated as period costs. Useful for managerial purposes, but not acceptable for use in financial statements or income tax returns. Also called direct costing.

DEMONSTRATION PROBLEM FOR YOUR REVIEW

Burnham Mfg. Co. operates two plants that produce and sell a single product. Shown below are the operating results of both plants during 1991, the company's first year of operations:

	RIVERVILLE PLANT	TRUESDALE PLANT
Sales (40,000 units at $50)	$2,000,000	$2,000,000
Per unit costs:		
Variable manufacturing costs	$ 15	$ 18
Variable selling and administrative	3	4
Traceable fixed costs:		
Manufacturing overhead	$ 600,000	$ 400,000
Selling and administrative	150,000	150,000

During 1991, both plants produced 50,000 units, of which 40,000 were sold. Common fixed costs relating to both plants amount to $500,000.

Instructions

a Determine the variable cost of goods sold at each plant, using variable costing.

b Prepare a partial income statement for Burnham Mfg. Co., segmented by plant and using the contribution margin approach. Conclude this income statement with the company's income from operations.

c Compute the cost of goods sold at each plant using full costing.

d Prepare a partial income statement for the entire company determining income from operations using the full costing approach. (Show the cost of goods sold as a single figure.)

e Explain the difference in the amounts of income from operations reported in parts *b* and *d.*

SOLUTION TO DEMONSTRATION PROBLEM

a

	RIVERVILLE PLANT	TRUESDALE PLANT
Variable cost of goods sold (variable costing):		
Riverville Plant: $15 variable manufacturing costs × 40,000 units manufactured	$600,000	
Truesdale Plant: $18 variable manufacturing costs × 40,000 units manufactured		$720,000

b Segmented income statement:

| | BURNHAM MFG. CO. | SEGMENTS | |
		RIVERVILLE PLANT	TRUESDALE PLANT
Sales...	$4,000,000	$2,000,000	$2,000,000
Variable costs:			
Cost of goods sold (part a).................	$1,320,000	$ 600,000	$ 720,000
Selling and administrative..................	280,000	120,000	160,000
Total variable costs......................	$1,600,000	$ 720,000	$ 880,000
Contribution margin..........................	$2,400,000	$1,280,000	$1,120,000
Traceable fixed costs:			
Manufacturing	$1,000,000	$ 600,000	$ 400,000
Selling and administrative..................	300,000	150,000	150,000
Total traceable fixed costs...............	$1,300,000	$ 750,000	$ 550,000
Plant segment margins	$1,100,000	$ 530,000	$ 570,000
Common fixed costs..........................	500,000		
Income from operations......................	$ 600,000		

c

	RIVERVILLE PLANT	TRUESDALE PLANT
Cost of goods sold (full costing):		
Variable manufacturing costs:		
Riverville Plant ($15 × 40,000 units)	$ 600,000	
Truesdale Plant ($18 × 40,000 units)		$ 720,000
Fixed manufacturing costs:		
Riverville Plant ($600,000 ÷ 50,000 units =		
$12 per unit; $12 × 40,000 units sold)	480,000	
Truesdale Plant ($400,000 ÷ 50,000 units =		
$8 per unit; $8 × 40,000 units sold)		320,000
Cost of goods sold (full costing)...........................	$1,080,000	$1,040,000

d
BURNHAM MFG. CO.
Partial Income Statement—Full Costing
For the Year Ended December 31, 1991

Sales...		$4,000,000
Cost of goods sold [$1,080,000 + $1,040,000 (part c)]........................		2,120,000
Gross profit on sales..		$1,880,000
Selling and administrative expenses:		
Variable ($120,000 + $160,000)	$280,000	
Fixed ($150,000 + $150,000 + $500,000)	800,000	1,080,000
Income from operations...		$ 800,000

e The difference in the amount of income from operations is explained by the fixed manufacturing costs deferred into inventory under the full costing method, as shown on page 987. (The fixed manufacturing costs per unit were determined in part **c**).

Income from operations: variable costing (part b)		*$600,000*
Add: Fixed manufacturing costs deferred into inventory		
under full costing:		
Riverville Plant (10,000 units × $12 per unit)	*$120,000*	
Truesdale Plant (10,000 units × $8 per unit)	*80,000*	*200,000*
Income from operations: full costing (part d)		*$800,000*

SELF-TEST QUESTIONS

Answers to these questions appear on page 998.

1 Which of the following is a common fixed cost to the sales departments in a department store?

a Salaries of store security personnel.

b Salaries of sales department managers.

c Cost of goods sold.

d Depreciation on fixtures used exclusively in a specific sales department.

2 In preparing an income statement that measures contribution margin and segment margin, two concepts are applied in classifying costs. One is whether the costs are variable or fixed. The other is whether the costs are:

a Product costs or period costs.

b Traceable to the segment.

c Under the control of the segment manager.

d Higher or lower than the budgeted amount.

3 A subtotal used in evaluating the performance of a segment manager, as distinct from the performance of the segment, is:

a Contribution margin, less traceable fixed costs.

b Sales, less committed costs.

c Contribution margin, plus fixed costs deferred into inventory.

d Contribution margin, less controllable fixed costs.

4 An investment center has annual sales of $500,000, a contribution margin ratio of 40%, and traceable fixed costs of $80,000. Average assets invested in the center are $600,000. Which of the following statements are correct? (More than one answer may be correct.)

a Variable costs amount to $300,000.

b Segment margin amounts to $200,000.

c Segment margin represents a 20% return on assets.

d If $10,000 in additional advertising would result in $60,000 in additional sales, segment margin would increase by $14,000.

5 During its first year of operations, Marco Mfg. Co. manufactured 5 million units, of which 4 million were sold. Manufacturing costs for the year were as follows:

Fixed manufacturing costs	*$10,000,000*
Variable manufacturing costs	*$3 per unit*

Which of the following answers is correct? (In all cases, assume that unit sales for the year remain at 4 million; more than one answer may be correct.)

a Under variable costing, income from operations will be $2,000,000 less than full costing.

b Under full costing, the cost of goods sold would have been $2 million greater if Marco had manufactured only 4 million units during the year.

c Under variable costing, the amount of manufacturing costs deducted from revenue during the year will be $12 million, regardless of the number of units manufactured.

d Under full costing, Marco's net income would have been higher for the first year of operations if more units had been manufactured.

Assignment Material

REVIEW QUESTIONS

1 What are some of the uses that management may make of accounting information about individual segments of the business?

2 Explain how a responsibility accounting system can assist managers in controlling the costs of a large business organization.

3 Distinguish between a *cost center,* a *profit center,* and an *investment center,* and give an example of each.

4 Marshall's Grocery Store has a small bakery that sells coffee and baked goods at very low prices. (For example, coffee and one doughnut cost 15¢.) The basic purpose of the bakery is to attract customers to the store and to make the store "smell like a bakery." In each period, costs traceable to the bakery exceed revenue. Would you evaluate the bakery as a cost center or as a profit center? Explain.

5 In general terms, describe the criteria that should be considered in evaluating the performance of a *cost center.*

6 What is a *responsibility accounting system?*

7 The operation of a responsibility accounting system involves three basic steps. In this chapter, we emphasize the second step: measuring the performance of each responsibility center. List all three steps in the logical sequence of occurrence.

8 In a responsibility accounting system, should the recording of revenue and costs begin at the largest areas of responsibility, or the smallest? Explain.

9 In the segmented income statements illustrated in this chapter, two concepts are used in classifying costs. What are these concepts?

10 Distinguish between *traceable* and *common* fixed costs. Give an example of each type of fixed cost for an auto dealership that is segmented into a sales department and a service department.

11 How do the costs of operating *service departments* (organized as cost centers) appear in a segmented income statement?

12 DeskTop, Inc., operates a national sales organization. The income statements prepared for each sales territory are segmented by product line. In these income statements, the sales territory manager's salary is treated as a common fixed cost. Will this salary be viewed as a common fixed cost at all levels of the organization? Explain.

13 Assume that Department A has a higher contribution margin ratio, but a lower segment margin ratio than Department B. If $10,000 in advertising is expected to increase the sales of either department by $50,000, in which department can the advertising dollars be spent to best advantage?

14 Criticize the following statement: "In our business, we maximize profits by closing any department that does not show a segment margin ratio of at least 15%."

15 What is the relationship between contribution margin and segment margin? Explain how each of these measurements is useful in making managerial decisions.

16 What does a consistently negative segment margin imply will happen to the operating income of the business if the segment is closed? Why? Identify several other factors that should be considered in deciding whether or not to close the segment.

17 Briefly explain the distinction between *controllable* fixed costs and *committed* fixed costs. Also explain the nature and purpose of performance margin in a segmented income statement.

18 The controller of Fifties, a chain of drive-in restaurants, is considering modifying the monthly segmented income statements by charging all costs relating to operations of the corporate headquarters to the individual restaurants in proportion to each restaurant's gross revenue. Do you think that this would increase the usefulness of the segmented income statement in evaluating the performance of the restaurants or the restaurant managers? Explain.

19 Distinguish between *variable costing* and *full costing*. Which method is used in financial statements? Which method is used in income tax returns?

20 Explain why a variable costing income statement provides a better basis for cost-volume-profit analysis than does a full costing income statement.

21 Rose Speakers, a division of Innovative Sound, temporarily increases production to exceed unit sales, thereby causing its inventory of finished goods to increase. Explain the effect of this action upon the segment margin reported by Rose under (a) full costing (b) variable costing.

EXERCISES

**Exercise 24-1
Accounting
terminology**

Listed below are nine technical accounting terms introduced or emphasized in this chapter:

Segment margin	Variable costing	Common fixed costs
Contribution margin	Full costing	Traceable fixed costs
Performance margin	Product costs	Committed fixed costs

Each of the following statements may (or may not) describe one of these technical terms. For each statement, indicate the accounting term described, or answer "None" if the statement does not correctly describe any of the terms.

a The costs deducted from contribution margin to determine segment margin.

b The method of assigning manufacturing costs to inventories and to the cost of goods sold that is required under generally accepted accounting principles.

c Fixed costs that are readily controllable by the segment manager.

d A subtotal in a segmented income statement, equal to segment margin plus committed fixed costs.

e The subtotal in a segmented income statement that is most useful in evaluating the short-run effect of various marketing strategies upon the income of the business.

f The subtotal in a segmented income statement that comes closest to indicating the change in income from operations that would result from closing a particular segment of the business.

g A technique that makes the income statement of a manufacturing segment readily suitable to cost-volume-profit analysis.

Exercise 24-2
Types of
responsibility
centers

Indicate whether each of the following should be evaluated as an investment center, a profit center (other than an investment center), or a cost center. Briefly explain the reasoning behind your answer.

a An individual restaurant within a chain of restaurants.

b A restaurant within a department store, owned by the department store.

c A kitchen within a hospital that prepares meals for patients. (Patients are billed for time spent in the hospital, but are not charged separately for meals.)

Exercise 24-3
Classification of
costs in a
segmented
income statement

The controller of Maxwell Department Store is preparing an income statement, segmented by sales departments, and including subtotals for contribution margin, performance margin, and segment margin. Indicate the appropriate classification of the seven items (**a** through **g**) listed below. Select from the following cost classifications:
Variable costs
Traceable fixed costs—controllable
Traceable fixed costs—committed
Common fixed costs
None of the above

a Depreciation on the hydraulic lifts used in the Automotive Service Department.

b Salaries of departmental sales personnel.

c Salary of the store manager.

d Cost of merchandise sold in the Sportswear Department.

e Cost of operating the store's accounting department.

f Cost of advertising specific product lines (classify as a fixed cost).

g Sales taxes on merchandise sold.

Exercise 24-4
Preparing a
segmented
income statement

MicroPress is segmented into two product lines—software and hardware. During the current year, the two product lines reported the following results (dollar amounts are stated in thousands):

	SOFTWARE	HARDWARE
Sales	$300,000	$400,000
Variable costs (as a percentage of sales)	30%	58%
Traceable fixed costs	126,000	112,000

In addition, fixed costs common to both product lines (stated in thousands of dollars) amounted to $28,000.

Prepare a segmented income statement showing percentages as well as dollar amounts. (Conclude your statement with income from operations for the business, and with segment margin for each product line.)

Exercises 5, 6 and 7 are based upon the following data:
Shown on the next page is a segmented income statement for Drexall-Hall during the current month:

	DREXALL-HALL DOLLARS	%	SEGMENTS STORE 1 DOLLARS	%	STORE 2 DOLLARS	%	STORE 3 DOLLARS	%
Sales	*$600,000*	*100*	*$200,000*	*100*	*$200,000*	*100*	*$200,000*	*100*
Variable costs	*360,000*	*60*	*124,000*	*62*	*110,000*	*55*	*126,000*	*63*
Contribution margin	*$240,000*	*40*	*$ 76,000*	*38*	*$ 90,000*	*45*	*$ 74,000*	*37*
Traceable fixed costs: controllable	*144,000*	*24*	*40,000*	*20*	*70,000*	*35*	*34,000*	*17*
Performance margin	*$ 96,000*	*16*	*$ 36,000*	*18*	*$ 20,000*	*10*	*$ 40,000*	*20*
Traceable fixed costs: committed	*60,000*	*10*	*16,000*	*8*	*22,000*	*11*	*22,000*	*11*
Store segment margins	*$ 36,000*	*6*	*$ 20,000*	*10*	*$ (2,000)*	*(1)*	*$ 18,000*	*9*
Common fixed costs	*12,000*	*2*						
Income from operations	*$ 24,000*	*4*						

All stores are similar in size, carry similar products, and operate in similar neighborhoods. ***Store 1*** was established first, and was built at a lower cost than were Stores 2 and 3. This lower cost results in less depreciation expense for Store 1. ***Store 2*** follows a policy of providing extensive customer service and charges slightly higher prices than the other two stores. ***Store 3*** follows a policy of minimizing both costs and sales prices.

Exercise 24-5 Evaluation of segments and segment managers

Use the data presented above for Drexall-Hall to answer the following questions:

a Assume that by spending an additional $5,000 per month in advertising a particular store, Drexall-Hall can increase the sales of that store by 10%. Which store should the company advertise to receive the maximum benefit from this additional advertising expenditure? Explain.

b From the viewpoint of top management, which is the most profitable of the three stores? Why?

c Which store manager seems to be pursuing the most effective strategy in managing his or her store? Why?

Exercise 24-6 Closing an unprofitable segment

Top management of Drexall-Hall is considering closing Store 2. The three stores are close enough together that management estimates closing Store 2 would cause sales at Store 1 to increase by $20,000, and sales at Store 3 to increase by $40,000. Closing Store 2 is not expected to cause any change in common fixed costs. (This exercise is based upon the data preceding Exercise 24-5.)

Compute the increase or decrease that closing Store 2 should cause in:

a Total monthly sales for Drexall-Hall Stores.

b The monthly segment margins of Stores 1 and 3.

c The company's monthly income from operations.

Exercise 24-7 Cost-volume-profit analysis

The marketing manager of Drexall-Hall is considering two alternative advertising strategies, each of which would cost $5,000 per month. One strategy is to advertise the name Drexall-Hall, which is expected to increase the monthly sales at all stores by 5%. The other strategy is to emphasize the low prices available at Store 3, which is expected to increase monthly sales at Store 3 by $50,000, but to reduce sales by $10,000 per month at Stores 1 and 2.

Determine the expected effect of each strategy upon the company's overall income from operations. (This exercise is based upon the data preceding Exercise 24-5.)

Exercise 24-8
Comparison of
full costing and
variable costing

Shown below are the manufacturing costs of Fisher Products during the first year of operations:

Variable manufacturing costs per unit:

Direct materials used	$	*10*
Direct labor		*5*
Variable manufacturing overhead		*1*
Fixed manufacturing overhead		*$800,000*

Instructions

a Compute the cost of goods sold using the full costing approach, assuming that the company:

(1) Manufactured and sold 80,000 units.

(2) Manufactured 100,000 units and sold 80,000 units.

b Compute the cost of goods sold using the variable costing approach, under each of the two assumptions listed in part **a.**

c Explain why full costing resulted in different amounts for the cost of goods sold under the two different assumptions in part **a** regarding the number of units manufactured.

Exercise 24-9
Full costing vs.
variable costing

Shown below are cost and sales data for Aluminum Products, Inc., at the end of its first year of operations:

Sales (50,000 units @ $40)	*$2,000,000*
Manufacturing costs (60,000 units):	
Variable	*720,000*
Fixed	*780,000*
Selling and administrative expenses (all fixed)	*400,000*

Instructions

a Compute the per-unit manufacturing cost that will be used in the valuation of inventory and in the determination of the cost of goods sold under (1) full costing and (2) variable costing.

b Compute the income from operations for the year, assuming the use of (1) full costing and (2) variable costing.

c Explain the cause of the different amounts of income from operations under the full costing and variable costing approaches.

PROBLEMS

Group A

Problem 24A-1
Types of
responsibility
centers and basis
for evaluation

Listed below are segments of well-known businesses:

1 Disneyland, one of several amusement parks owned by The Walt Disney Company.

2 The Emporium on Main Street, a gift and souvenir shop in Disneyland.

3 Pirates of the Carribean (a ride in Disneyland; Disneyland charges visitors for admission to the park, but not for specific rides.)

4 Marysville plant of Honda Motor Co. Ltd.

5 Subscriptions billing department of The Time Inc. Magazine Company.

6 Shoe department in a Nordstom department store.

Instructions

a Indicate whether each segment represents an investment center, a profit center (other than an investment center), or a cost center.

b Briefly explain the criteria that are used in evaluating (1) investment centers, (2) profit centers (other than investment centers), and (3) cost centers.

Problem 24A-2
Preparing and using a segmented income statement

Media Publishing Co. has two product lines—books and magazines. Cost and revenue data for these two products during the current month are shown below.

	PRODUCT LINES	
	BOOKS	MAGAZINES
Sales	$600,000	$300,000
Variable costs as a percentage of sales	60%	30%
Fixed costs traceable to product lines........................	$ 96,000	$156,000

In addition to the costs shown above, the company incurs monthly fixed costs of $90,000 common to both product lines.

Instructions

a Prepare a segmented income statement for the month. Carry your computations through segment margin for each product line, and through income from operations for the company viewed as a whole. Include columns to show percentages for all dollar amounts.

b A marketing survey shows that a $50,000 monthly advertising campaign focused upon either product line should increase that product line's monthly sales by approximately $100,000. Do you recommend this additional advertising for either or both product lines? Show computations to support your conclusions.

c Management is considering expanding its activities in one product line or the other. An investment of a given dollar amount is expected to increase the sales of the expanded product line by $300,000 per month. However, an expansion of this size will increase traceable fixed costs in proportion to the increase in sales. Which product line would you recommend expanding? Explain the basis for your conclusion.

Problem 24A-3
Preparing segmented income statements in a responsibility accounting system

Under Ten, Inc., sells medical products formulated for children. The company is segmented into two sales territories—Eastern and Western. Two products are sold in each territory—CoughStop and SleepTight.

During September 1991, the following data are reported for the Eastern territory:

	COUGHSTOP	SLEEPTIGHT
Sales	$150,000	$250,000
Contribution margin ratios	60%	52%
Traceable fixed costs	33,000	55,000

Common fixed costs in the Eastern territory amounted to $48,000 during the month.

During September, the Western territory reported sales of $200,000, variable costs of $90,000, and a segment margin of $60,000. Under Ten, Inc., incurred $42,000 in common fixed costs that were not traceable to the sales territories.

The two territories are evaluated as investment centers. Average assets invested in the territories are Western, $3,000,000; Eastern, $5,000,000.

Instructions

a Prepare the September income statement for the Eastern territory, segmented by product line. Include columns showing percentages, as well as dollar amounts.

b Prepare the September income statement for the company, showing as segments the two sales territories. Conclude your statement with income from operations for the company, and with segment margin for the two territories. Show percentages as well as dollar amounts.

c Compute the rate of return on average assets earned in each sales territory during the month of September.

d In part **a,** your income statement for the Eastern territory included $48,000 in common fixed costs. What happened to these common fixed costs in the segmented income statement shown in part **b?**

e The manager of the Eastern territory is authorized to spend an additional $15,000 per month in advertising one of the two products. Based upon marketing surveys, the manager estimates that this advertising would increase the sales of either product by $40,000. Upon which product should the manager focus this advertising campaign? Explain.

f Top management is considering investing several million dollars to expand operations in one of its two sales territories. Such an expansion would increase traceable fixed costs approximately in proportion to the increase in sales. Which territory appears to be the better candidate for this investment? Explain.

Problem 24A-4
Allocating fixed
costs to
segments

You have just been hired as the controller of Land's End Hotel. The hotel prepares monthly segmented income statements in which all fixed costs are allocated among the various profit centers in the hotel, based upon the relative amounts of revenue generated by each profit center.

Robert Chamberlain, manager of the hotel dining room, argues that this approach understates the profitability of his department. "Through developing a reputation as a fine restaurant, the dining room has significantly increased its revenue. Yet the more revenue we earn, the larger the percentage of the hotel's operating costs that are charged against our department. Also, whenever vacancies go up, rental revenue goes down, and the dining room is charged with a still greater percentage of overall operating costs. Our strong performance is concealed by poor performance in departments responsible for keeping occupancy rates up." Chamberlain suggests that fixed costs relating to the hotel should be allocated among the profit centers based upon the number of square feet occupied by each department.

Debra Mettenburg, manager of the Sunset Lounge, objects to Chamberlain's proposal. She points out that the lounge is very big, because it is designed for hotel guests to read, relax, and watch the sunset. Although the lounge does serve drinks, the revenue earned in the lounge is small in relation to its square footage. Many guests just come to the lounge for the free hors d'oeuvres, and don't even order a drink. Chamberlain's proposal would cause the lounge to appear unprofitable; yet a hotel must have some "open space" for its guests to sit and relax.

Instructions

a Separately evaluate the points raised by each of the two managers.

b Suggest your own approach to allocating the hotel's fixed costs among the various profit centers.

Problem 24A-5
Variable costing

At the beginning of the current year, Audio Corporation opened its Windville Plant to manufacture a new model stereo speaker. During the year, 100,000 speakers were manufactured, of which 80,000 were sold at a unit sales price of $90. Variable manufacturing costs for the year amounted to $3,600,000, and fixed manufacturing costs totaled $1,100,000. Variable selling and administrative expenses were $720,000, and traceable fixed selling and administrative expenses were $970,000.

Instructions

a Prepare a schedule showing variable, fixed, and total manufacturing costs per unit.

b Prepare partial income statements (ending with segment margin) for the Windville Plant for the current year using:

(1) Full costing

(2) Variable costing

c Briefly explain the difference in the amount of segment margin reported in the two income statements for the segment.

d Using the data contained in the variable costing income statement, compute (1) the contribution margin per unit sold, and (2) the number of speakers which must be manufactured and sold annually for the Windville Plant to cover its fixed costs—that is, to break even.

Group B

Problem 24B-1
Segment classification and evaluation

Listed below are segments of various well-known businesses:

1 Women's Sportswear department in a Sears store.

2 Marriott Marquis, the Manhattan Island hotel of Marriott Corporation.

3 The housekeeping department in the Marriott Marquis.

4 The central accounting department of Marriott Corporation.

5 JW's, a restaurant located within the Marriott Marquis hotel.

6 Catering, Video, and Entertainment; the department of American Airlines responsible for in-flight food service.

7 The Hertz rental car center at Los Angeles International Airport.

Instructions

a Classify each of the above business segments as an investment center, a profit center (other than an investment center), or a cost center.

b Briefly explain the criteria that are used in evaluating the performance of: (1) investment centers, (2) profit centers, and (3) cost centers.

Problem 24B-2
Preparing and using a segmented income statement

Regal Appliance Corporation is organized into two divisions—Commercial Sales and Home Products. During June 1991, the company's net sales amount to $800,000, of which $500,000 are sales of the Commercial Sales Division. The Commercial Sales Division has a contribution margin ratio of 34%, and the Home Products Division, 50%. Fixed costs for the month totaled $160,000, of which $60,000 is traceable to each of the two divisions.

Instructions

a Prepare an income statement for the month, segmented by division. Conclude your income statement with the segment margin for each division, but show income from operations for the company viewed as a whole. Include columns showing percentages as well as columns showing dollar amounts.

b Compute the dollar sales volume required for the Home Products Division to earn a monthly segment margin of *$100,000.*

c A marketing study indicates that sales in the Home Products Division would increase by *5%* if advertising expenditures were increased by *$5,000* per month. Would you recommend this increase in advertising? Show computations to support your conclusion.

Problem 24B-3
Analysis of segmented income statements

Shown below are segmented income statements for Butterfield, Inc., for the month ended March 31, 1991:

	BUTTERFIELD, INC. DOLLARS	%	SEGMENTS DIVISION 1 DOLLARS	%	DIVISION 2 DOLLARS	%
Sales	$450,000	100	$300,000	100	$150,000	100
Variable costs	225,000	50	180,000	60	45,000	30
Contribution margin	$225,000	50	$120,000	40	$105,000	70
Fixed costs traceable to						
divisions	135,000	30	63,000	21	72,000	48
Division segment margins	$ 90,000	20	$ 57,000	19	$ 33,000	22
Common fixed costs	45,000	10				
Income from operations	$ 45,000	10				

	SEGMENTS					
	DIVISION 1		PRODUCT A		PRODUCT B	
	DOLLARS	%	DOLLARS	%	DOLLARS	%
Sales	$300,000	100	$100,000	100	$200,000	100
Variable costs	180,000	60	52,000	52	128,000	64
Contribution margin	$120,000	40	$ 48,000	48	$ 72,000	36
Fixed costs traceable to						
products	42,000	14	26,000	26	16,000	8
Product segment margins	$ 78,000	26	$ 22,000	22	$ 56,000	28
Common fixed costs	21,000	7				
Segment margin for division	$ 57,000	19				

Instructions

a The company plans to initiate an advertising campaign for one of the two products in Division 1. The campaign would cost $10,000 per month, and is expected to increase the sales of whichever product is advertised by $30,000 per month. Compute the expected increase in the segment margin of Divison 1 assuming that (**1**) Product A is advertised and (**2**) Product B is advertised.

b Assume that the sales of both products by Division 1 are equal to total manufacturing capacity. To increase sales of either product, the company must increase manufacturing facilities, which means an increase in traceable fixed costs in approximate proportion to the expected increase in sales. In this case, which product line would you recommend expanding? Explain.

c The segmented income statement for Division 1 includes $21,000 in common fixed costs. What happens to these fixed costs in the income statements segmented by division?

d Assume that in April, the monthly sales in Division 2 increase to $200,000. Compute the expected effect of this change upon the operating income of the company (assume no other changes in revenue or cost behavior).

e Prepare an income statement for Butterfield, Inc., segmented by divisions, under the assumption stated in part **d**. Organize this income statement in the format illustrated above, including columns for percentages.

Problem 24B-4
Allocating costs among segments

You are the chief accountant of Giant Department Store and are about to initiate a policy of preparing monthly income statements segmented by the store's 21 sales departments. Your objective is to provide the store manager with a basis for evaluating the performance of departmental managers, and the contribution of each department to the profitability of the store.

Mark Ryan, manager of the automotive service department, suggests that each department should be charged only with its variable costs, and that department managers should be evaluated upon the department's contribution margin. He points out that departmental managers can influence a department's sales, but that fixed costs occur at the same levels regardless of the level of sales achieved.

Christine Ferrara, manager of the jewelry department, suggests that all costs of the store should be charged to the departments, as the departments are credited for all of the store's revenue. She believes that departments and departmental managers can most fairly be evaluated based upon departmental operating income—that is, revenue less all costs. She points out that many fixed costs are directly traceable to specific departments, and that common fixed costs could easily be allocated to departments based upon the relative square feet of floor space occupied by the department.

Instructions

a Separately evaluate each of these two suggestions.

b Explain and justify your own recommendations for the classifications of costs to be charged against departments in the segmented income statement. Explain which subtotals you consider most useful in evaluating (1) short-run marketing strategies, (2) the performance of departmental managers, and (3) the long-run profitability of a department.

Problem 24B-5
Variable costing

Neilson Company manufactures and sells a single product. The following costs were incurred during 1991, the company's first year of operations:

Variable costs per unit:	
Direct materials used	*$12*
Direct labor	*6*
Variable manufacturing overhead	*2*
Variable selling and administrative expenses	*5*
Fixed costs for the year:	
Manufacturing overhead	*$600,000*
Selling and administrative expenses	*200,000*

During the year, the company manufactured 60,000 units, of which 50,000 were sold at a price of $50 per unit. The 10,000 units in inventory at year-end were all finished goods.

Instructions

a Assuming that the company uses full costing:

(1) Determine the per-unit cost of each finished good manufactured during 1991.

(2) Prepare a partial income statement for the year, ending with income from operations.

b Assuming that the company uses variable costing:

(1) Determine the per-unit cost of each finished good manufactured during 1991.

(2) Prepare a partial income statement for the year, ending with income from operations.

c Explain why your income statements in parts *a* and *b* result in different amounts of income from operations. Indicate which costing approach is used in published financial statements, and briefly explain the usefulness of the other approach.

BUSINESS DECISION CASE

Case 24-1
Congratulations!?

Advance Electronics opened its new Jefferson Plant at the beginning of the current year to manufacture a burglar alarm. During the year, the Jefferson Plant manufactured 60,000 burglar alarms, of which 50,000 were sold and 10,000 remain on hand as finished goods inventory. There was no work in process inventory at year-end. An income statement for the Jefferson Plant, prepared in conventional (full costing) form, is shown below:

ADVANCE ELECTRONICS—JEFFERSON PLANT
Income Statement
For First Year of Operations

Sales (50,000 units @ $60)		*$3,000,000*
Cost of goods sold:		
Manufacturing costs (60,000 units @ $42)	*$2,520,000*	
Less: Ending inventory (10,000 units		
@ $42)	*420,000*	*2,100,000*
Gross profit on sales		*$ 900,000*
Selling and administrative expenses:		
Variable ($8 per unit sold)	*$ 400,000*	
Fixed	*425,000*	*825,000*
Segment margin		*$ 75,000*

The $2,520,000 in total manufacturing costs consisted of the following cost elements:

Direct materials used		$ 900,000
Direct labor		720,000
Manufacturing overhead:		
Variable	$300,000	
Fixed	600,000	900,000
Total manufacturing costs		$2,520,000

The manager of the Jefferson Plant is proud of the $75,000 operating income reported for the first year of operations. However, the controller of Advance Electronics, an advocate of variable costing, makes the following statement: "The only reason that the Jefferson Plant shows a profit is that $100,000 of fixed costs are deferred in the ending inventory figure. Actually, a sales volume of 50,000 units is below the break-even point."

Instructions
a Prepare a schedule showing each manufacturing cost on a per-unit basis. As a subtotal in your schedule, show the variable manufacturing cost per unit. The final total in your schedule will be the total manufacturing cost per unit on a full-costing basis ($42).

b Prepare a revised income statement for the Jefferson Plant using the variable costing approach.

c Briefly explain the difference in the amount of segment margin reported in the two statements. Is the controller correct about the $420,000 ending inventory in the full costing statement including $100,000 of fixed manufacturing costs?

d Compute the contribution margin per unit sold.

e How many units must be produced and sold each year for the Jefferson Plant to break even—that is, to cover its fixed expenses? (In computing the break-even point, assume all units produced are sold.) Is the controller correct that the Jefferson Plant failed to achieve the break-even point in unit sales volume during its first year of operations?

ANSWERS TO SELF-TEST QUESTIONS
1 a   **2 b**   **3 d**   **4 a, c,** and **d**   **5 a, b, c,** and **d**

Budgeting and Standard Costs

Budgeting—preparing a written plan—provides the very foundation for the managerial functions of planning and control. In this chapter we discuss the uses of budgets and the importance of setting budgeted amounts at realistic levels. Next, we illustrate the mechanics of preparing a master budget for a manufacturing business. The concept of "flexible budgets" also is explained and illustrated. Another major topic in the chapter is the use of standard costs—an important tool in achieving control over business operations. We show how standard costs may be incorporated into a cost accounting system to inform management on a continuing basis how well actual business performance is "measuring up" to the budget. This chapter builds upon your understanding of responsibility accounting, cost accounting systems, and cost-volume-profit relationships.

After studying this chapter, you should be able to meet these Learning Objectives:

1 Discuss the benefits that a company may derive from a formal budgeting process.

2 Explain why budgeted amounts should be set at realistic and achievable levels.

3 Describe the elements of a master budget.

4 Prepare any of the budgets or supporting schedules included in a master budget.

5 Prepare a flexible budget and explain its usefulness.

6 Explain how standard costs assist managers in controlling the costs of a business.

7 Compute the materials, labor, and overhead variances and explain the meaning of each cost variance.

BUDGETING: THE BASIS FOR PLANNING AND CONTROL

A budget is a comprehensive *financial plan* setting forth the expected route for achieving the financial and operational goals of an organization. Budgeting is an essential step in effective financial planning. Even the smallest business will benefit from preparing a formal written plan for its future operations, including the expected levels of sales, expenses, net income, cash receipts, and cash outlays.

The use of a budget is a key element of financial planning and also of the managerial function of controlling costs. To control costs, the managers of all units of the company compare actual costs incurred with the budgeted amounts and take action to correct excessive costs. Thus, controlling costs means keeping actual costs in line with a financial plan.

Virtually all economic entities—businesses, governmental agencies, universities, churches, and individuals—engage in some form of budgeting. For example, a college student with limited financial resources may prepare a list of expected monthly cash payments to see that they do not exceed expected monthly cash receipts. This list is a simple form of cash budget. Business managers must plan (budget) to achieve profit objectives as well as to meet the financial obligations of the business as they become due. Administrators of nonprofit organizations and governmental agencies must plan to accomplish the objectives of the organization with the available resources.

While all businesses engage in some degree of planning, the extent to which plans are formalized in written budgets varies from one business to another. Large well-managed companies generally have carefully developed budgets for every aspect of their operations. Inadequate or sloppy budgeting is a characteristic of companies with weak or inexperienced management.

Benefits Derived from Budgeting

Objective 1
Discuss the benefits that a company may derive from a formal budgeting process.

A budget is a forecast of future events. In fact, the process of budgeting is often called *financial forecasting.* Careful planning and preparation of a formal budget benefit a company in many ways, including:

1 Enhanced managerial perspective On a day-to-day basis, most managers focus their attention upon the routine problems of running the business. In preparing a budget, however, managers are forced to consider all aspects of a company's internal activities and also to make estimates of future economic conditions, including costs, interest rates, demand for the company's products, and the level of competition. Thus, budgeting increases management's awareness of the company's external economic environment.

2 Advance warning of problems Since the budget shows the expected results of future operations, management is forewarned of financial problems. If, for example, the budget shows that the company will run short of cash during the summer months, management has advance warning of the need to hold down expenditures or to obtain additional financing.

3 Coordination of activities Preparation of a budget provides management with an opportunity to coordinate the activities of the various departments within the business. For example, the production department should be budgeted to produce approximately the same quantity of goods as the sales department is budgeted to sell. A written budget shows departmental managers in quantitative terms exactly what is expected of their departments during the upcoming period.

4 Performance evaluation Budgets show the expected costs and expenses for each department as well as the expected output, such as revenue to be earned or units to be produced. Thus, the budgets provide a yardstick with which each department's actual performance may be measured.

Establishing Budgeted Amounts

Objective 2
Explain why budgeted amounts should be set at realistic and achievable levels.

Departmental managers often are evaluated on the basis of whether their departments exceed or fall short of the budgeted level of performance. If the budget is to provide a fair basis for evaluating a manager's performance, *budgeted amounts should be set at realistic and achievable levels.* Consider, for example, the level of costs budgeted for the production department. If this level is set too high in relation to output, it will be easily achieved and inefficient operations will not be brought to management's attention. On the other hand, if the budgeted costs are too low, an excess of actual costs over budgeted costs becomes a normal condition, rather than an indication of inefficiency.

Differences of opinion often arise as to the dollar amounts used in the budget. Departmental managers naturally want high levels of expenditures and low levels of output budgeted for their departments. This would increase the resources available to the departmental manager and make it easier to meet the budgeted level of performance. Top management, on the other hand, wants the budget to promote high levels of output and low levels of expenditure by each department manager.

The delicate task of human relations is an important part of effective budgeting. A budget is most effective when the people whose performance is being evaluated recognize the budgeted amounts as realistic standards for performance. This recognition is best achieved when managers at all levels of the business are invited to participate in the preparation of the budget.

Once budgeted amounts have been established, they should not be regarded as "carved in stone." The budget should be *reviewed and revised* whenever significant changes occur in the economy, the extent of competition, production methods, or the costs of materials or labor.

The Budget Period

As a general rule, the period covered by a budget should be long enough to show the effect of managerial policies but short enough so that estimates can be made with reasonable accuracy. This suggests that different types of budgets should be made for different time spans.

Capital expenditures budgets, which summarize plans for major investments in plant and equipment, might be prepared to cover plans for as long as 5 to 10 years. Projects such as building a new factory or an oil refinery require many years of planning and expenditures before the new facilities are ready for use.

Most operating budgets and financial budgets cover a period of one fiscal year. Companies often divide these annual budgets into four quarters, with budgeted figures for each quarter. The first quarter is then subdivided into budgeted figures for each month, while only quarterly figures are shown for the last three quarters. As the end of the quarter nears, the budget for the next quarter is reviewed, revised for any changes in economic conditions, and divided into monthly budget figures. This process assures that the budget is reviewed at least several times each year, and that the budgeted figures for the months just ahead are based upon current conditions and estimates. In addition, budgeted figures for relatively short periods of time enable managers to compare actual performance to the budget without waiting until year-end.

■ **Continuous Budgeting** An increasing number of companies follow a policy of continuous budgeting, whereby a new month is added to the end of the budget as the current month draws to a close. Thus, the budget always covers the upcoming 12 months. The principal advantage of continuous budgeting is that it "stabilizes" the planning horizon at one year ahead. Under the fiscal year approach, the planning period becomes shorter as the year progresses. Also, continuous budgeting forces managers into a continuous review and reassessment of the budget estimates and the company's current progress.

The Master Budget: A "Package" of Related Budgets

Objective 3
Describe the elements of a master budget.

The "budget" is not a single document. Rather, the *master budget* consists of a number of interrelated budgets which together summarize all the planned activities of the business. The elements of a master budget vary, depending upon the size and nature of the business. However, a typical master budget for a manufacturing business includes:

1 Operating budgets
   a Sales forecast
   b Production schedule (stated in number of units to be produced)
   c Manufacturing cost budget
   d Operating expense budget
   e Budgeted income statement

2 Capital expenditures budget

3 Financial budgets
   a Cash budget
   b Budgeted balance sheet

Some elements of the master budget are *segmented by responsibility centers.* The budgeted income statement, for example, is segmented to indicate the budgeted revenue and expenses of each profit center. The cash budget is segmented to show the budgeted cash flows for each cost center as well as each revenue center. The production schedule and manufacturing cost budget may be segmented to indicate the unit production and manufacturing costs budgeted for each production process. The portion of the budget relating to an individual responsibility center is called a *responsibility budget.* As explained in Chapter 24, responsibility budgets are an important element of a responsibility accounting system.

The many budgets and schedules comprising the master budget are closely interrelated. Some of these relationships are illustrated in the following diagram:

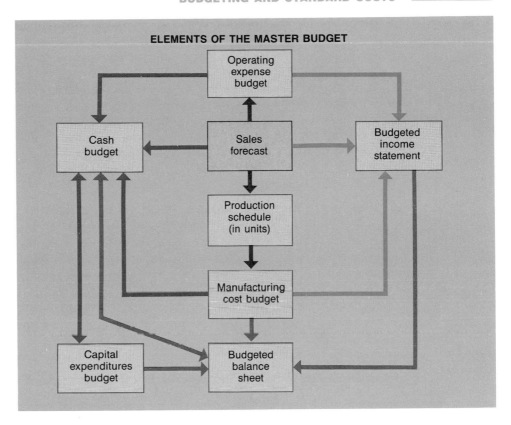

ELEMENTS OF THE MASTER BUDGET

Steps in Preparing a Master Budget

Objective 4
Prepare any of
the budgets or
supporting
schedules
included in a
master budget.

Some parts of the master budget should not be prepared until other parts have been completed. For example, the budgeted financial statements are not prepared until the sales, manufacturing, and operating expense budgets are available. A logical sequence of steps for preparing the annual elements of the master budget is described below. (Through the use of color, these steps also are illustrated in our preceding diagram of the elements of the budget.)

1 Prepare a sales forecast The sales forecast is the starting point in the preparation of a master budget. This forecast is based upon past experience, estimates of general business and economic conditions, and upon expected levels of competition. A forecast of the expected level of sales is a prerequisite to scheduling production, and to budgeting revenue and variable costs.

To emphasize the central role of the sales forecast in the budgeting process, the sales forecast in our budget diagram is shown in red. The arrows indicate that information "flows" from this forecast into several other budgets.

2 Prepare budgets for production, manufacturing costs, and operating expenses Once the level of sales has been forecast, production may be scheduled and estimates made of the expected manufacturing costs and operating expenses for the year (red arrows). These elements of the master budget depend both upon the level of sales and upon cost-volume relationships.

3 Prepare a budgeted income statement The budgeted income statement is based upon the sales forecast, the manufacturing costs comprising the cost of goods sold, and the budgeted operating expenses (gray arrows).

4 Prepare a cash budget The cash budget is a forecast of the cash receipts and cash payments for the budget period. As shown by the blue arrows in the budget diagram, the cash budget is affected by many of the other budget estimates.

The budgeted level of cash receipts depends upon the sales forecast, credit terms offered by the company, and the company's experience in collecting amounts receivable from customers. Budgeted cash payments depend upon the forecasts of manufacturing costs, operating expenses, and capital expenditures, as well as the credit terms offered by suppliers. Anticipated borrowing, debt repayment, cash dividends, and issuances of capital stock also are reflected in the cash budget.

5 Prepare a budgeted balance sheet A projected balance sheet cannot be prepared until the effects of cash transactions upon various asset, liability, and owners' equity accounts have been determined. In addition, the balance sheet is affected by budgeted capital expenditures and budgeted net income (pink arrows).

The capital expenditures budget covers a span of many years. This budget is continuously reviewed and updated, but is not prepared anew on an annual basis.

Preparing the Master Budget: An Illustration

To illustrate the preparation of a master budget, assume that Berg Company makes and sells a single product. Management has asked for a master budget for the first and second quarter of the coming year. The balance sheet for Berg Company at January 1 is shown below:

BERG COMPANY
Balance Sheet
January 1, Current Year

ASSETS

Current assets:		
Cash		$ 75,000
Receivables		82,000
Inventories:		
Direct materials	$ 25,000	
Finished goods (FIFO method)	52,000	77,000
Prepayments		21,000
Total current assets		$255,000
Plant and equipment:		
Buildings and equipment	$970,000	
Less: Accumulated depreciation	420,000	
Total plant and equipment		550,000
Total assets		$805,000

LIABILITIES & STOCKHOLDERS' EQUITY

Current liabilities:

Notes payable, 12% ($40,000 payable quarterly)		$160,000
Other current payables		78,000
Income taxes payable		25,000
Total current liabilities		$263,000
Stockholders' equity:		
Capital stock, no par, 100,000 shares outstanding	$350,000	
Retained earnings	192,000	542,000
Total liabilities & stockholders' equity		$805,000

Sales of the company's product are seasonal; sales during the second quarter are expected to exceed first-quarter sales by 50%. However, the economies of a stable level of production have led management to schedule production of *120,000* units in both the first and second quarters.

■ **Operating Budget Estimates** The various operating budgets (except for the budgeted income statement) for each of the first two quarters are shown below:

BERG COMPANY
Operating Budget Estimates
First and Second Quarters of the Current Year

SCHEDULE		1ST QUARTER	2D QUARTER
A1	**Sales forecast:**		
	Selling price per unit:	$ 3.00	$ 3.00
	Budgeted sales (in units)	100,000	150,000
	Budgeted sales (in dollars)	$300,000	$450,000
A2	**Production schedule (in units):**		
	Budgeted sales (A1)	100,000	150,000
	Add: Ending inventory of finished goods	50,000	20,000
	Units budgeted to be available for sale	150,000	170,000
	Less: Beginning inventory of finished goods	30,000	50,000
	Planned production of finished goods	120,000	120,000

SCHEDULE

		PER QUARTER
A3	**Manufacturing cost estimates:**	
	Variable costs:	
	Per unit manufactured:	
	Direct materials	$ 0.50
	Direct labor	0.60
	Variable manufacturing overhead	0.30
	Fixed costs (per quarter):	
	Manufacturing overhead	$ 42,000
A4	**Manufacturing cost budget (for 120,000 units):**	
	Direct materials used ($0.50 per unit)	$ 60,000
	Direct labor ($0.60 per unit)	72,000
	Variable manufacturing overhead ($0.30 per unit)	36,000
	Fixed manufacturing overhead	42,000
	Total cost of finished goods manufactured	$210,000
	Cost per unit ($210,000 ÷ 120,000 units)	$1.75

		1ST QUARTER	2D QUARTER
A5	**Ending finished goods inventory:**		
	50,000 units at $1.75 **(A4)**	$ 87,500	
	20,000 units at $1.75 **(A4)**		$ 35,000
A6	**Operating expense budget:**		
	Variable expenses ($0.30 × units sold)	$ 30,000	$ 45,000
	Fixed expenses....................................	70,000	70,000
	Total selling and administrative expense..........	$100,000	$115,000

Estimates of unit sales and sales prices per unit (Schedule A1) are based upon future marketing plans and forecasts of future economic conditions. The production schedule (Schedule A2) reflects both the decision to stabilize production and a decision to reduce the inventory of finished goods from its January 1 level of 30,000 to 20,000 units at the end of the second quarter. (Notice that the inventory of finished goods must rise to 50,000 units at the end of the first quarter in order to meet the budgeted sales and ending inventory of the second quarter.)

The cost estimates in Schedule A3 provide the basis for budgeting manufacturing costs. Schedule A4, the manufacturing budget, indicates the budgeted cost of producing 120,000 finished units in each quarter.

Schedule A5 shows the dollar value of the ending inventories of finished goods that will be on hand if the targets in the sales budget and the manufacturing budget are met. Schedule A6, the operating expense budget, summarizes numerous estimates made by departmental managers in light of the budgeted sales volume.

■ **Budgeted Income Statement** The budgeted income statements for each quarter shown below are based upon the estimates in Schedules A1 through A6. In addition, these income statements include budgeted amounts for interest expense and income taxes expense. The $160,000 note payable in the January 1 balance sheet is a bank loan due in quarterly installments of $40,000, plus accrued interest, due at the end of each quarter. Interest at 12% per year, or 3% per quarter, is computed on the outstanding balance of $160,000 during the first quarter, and on $120,000 during the second quarter. Income tax expense is budgeted at 40% of income before income taxes.

BERG COMPANY
Budgeted Income Statements
First Two Quarters of Current Year

	1ST QUARTER	2D QUARTER
Sales **(A1)**	$300,000	$450,000
Cost of goods sold:		
Finished goods, beginning inventory...................	$ 52,000	$ 87,500
Cost of finished goods manufactured **(A4)**	210,000	210,000
Cost of goods available for sale....................	$262,000	$297,500
Less: Finished goods, ending inventory **(A5)**	87,500	35,000
Cost of goods sold....................................	$174,500	$262,500
Gross profit on sales	$125,500	$187,500
Operating expenses:		
Selling and administrative expenses **(A6)**	$100,000	$115,000
Interest expense	4,800	3,600
Total operating expenses	$104,800	$118,600
Income before income taxes...........................	$ 20,700	$ 68,900
Income taxes (40% of income before income taxes)	8,280	27,560
Net income	$ 12,420	$ 41,340

Here is what quarterly income should be

The budgeted income statement shows the effects that our budgeted activities are expected to have upon revenue, expense, and net income. We are now ready to estimate the cash flows required by implementing our operating budgets and also to determine the effects of the budgeted activities upon balance sheet accounts.

■ **Financial Budget Estimates**   The estimates and data necessary to prepare a cash budget and budgeted balance sheet for each quarter follow. (The amounts used in the preparation of the cash budget are highlighted in black.)

BERG COMPANY
Financial Budget Estimates
First and Second Quarters of Current Year

SCHEDULE		1ST QUARTER	2D QUARTER
B1	Budgeted direct materials purchases and inventory:		
	Direct materials used **(A4)**	$ 60,000	$ 60,000
	Desired ending inventory	40,000	40,000
	Direct materials available for use.................	$100,000	$100,000
	Less: Inventory at beginning of quarter...........	25,000	40,000
	Budgeted direct materials purchases.............	$ 75,000	$ 60,000

SCHEDULE

B2 *Means of financing costs and expenses:*

	TOTAL	CURRENT PAYABLES	EXPIRATION OF PREPAYMENTS	DEPRE-CIATION
First quarter:				
Direct material purchases **(B1)**..........	$ 75,000	$ 75,000		
Direct labor **(A4)**	72,000	72,000		
Manufacturing overhead—variable and fixed **(A4)** ...	78,000	64,000	$4,400	$ 9,600
Selling and administrative expense **(A6)**	100,000	94,600	3,000	2,400
Total	$325,000	$305,600	$7,400	$12,000
Second quarter:				
Direct materials purchases **(B1)**	$ 60,000	$ 60,000		
Direct labor **(A4)**	72,000	72,000		
Manufacturing overhead—variable and fixed **(A4)** ...	78,000	64,400	$4,000	$ 9,600
Selling and administrative expense **(A6)**	115,000	109,500	3,100	2,400
Total	$325,000	$305,900	$7,100	$12,000

			1ST QUARTER	2D QUARTER
B3	**Payments on current payables:**			
	Balance at beginning of quarter		$ 78,000	$101,500
	Increase in payables during quarter **(B2)**		305,600	305,900
	Total payables during quarter		$383,600	$407,400
	Estimated balance at end of quarter (given)		101,500	85,000
	Payments on current payables during quarter.....		**$282,100**	**$322,400**
B4	**Prepayments budget:**			
	Balance at beginning of quarter		$ 21,000	$ 15,600
	Estimated cash expenditure during quarter		**2,000**	**12,000**
	Total prepayments.............................		$ 23,000	$ 27,600
	Expiration of prepayments **(B2)**..................		7,400	7,100
	Prepayments at end of quarter..................		$ 15,600	$ 20,500
B5	**Debt service budget:**			
	Liability to bank at beginning of quarter		$160,000	$120,000
	Interest expense for the quarter..................		4,800	3,600
	Total principal plus accrued interest............		$164,800	$123,600
	Cash payments (principal and interest)		44,800	43,600
	Liability to bank at end of quarter		$120,000	$ 80,000

SCHEDULE

B6   *Budgeted income taxes:*

Income tax liability at beginning of quarter	$ 25,000	$ 8,280
Estimated income taxes for the		
quarter (per budgeted income statement)........	8,280	27,560
Total accrued income tax liability.............	$ 33,280	$ 35,840
Cash payment (tax liability at beginning		
of quarter)	25,000	8,280
Income tax liability at end of quarter	$ 8,280	$ 27,560

B7   *Estimated cash receipts from customers:*

Balance of receivables at beginning of year	$ 82,000	
Collections on first-quarter sales of		
$300,000 (⅔ in first quarter and ⅓ in second)	200,000	$100,000
Collections on second-quarter sales of		
$450,000 (⅔ in second quarter).................		300,000
Cash receipts from customers	$282,000	$400,000

B8   *Budgeted accounts receivable:*

Balance at the beginning of the quarter	$ 82,000	$100,000
Sales on open account during quarter **(A1)**	300,000	450,000
Total accounts receivable	$382,000	$550,000
Less: Estimated collections on accounts		
receivable **(B7)**	282,000	400,000
Estimated accounts receivable balance		
at end of quarter	$100,000	$150,000

Let us now briefly discuss each of these schedules:

Schedule B1 In our manufacturing budget (page 1007), we estimated the cost of direct materials expected to be *used* in our manufacturing process at $60,000. In preparing a cash budget, however, we need to know the cost of direct materials to be *purchased* each quarter, rather than used. In budgeting purchases of direct materials, we must consider both the expected use of materials and the desired direct materials inventory at the end of each quarter.

Let us assume that the production supervisor feels that the January 1 inventory of materials of $25,000 is too low. The supervisor recommends that the materials inventory be increased to $40,000 and maintained at that level. Schedule B1 calculates the purchases of direct materials required to achieve this desired inventory level while allowing for the use of $60,000 of materials each quarter.

Schedule B2 The next step in preparing a cash budget is to estimate the portion of our budgeted costs and expenses which must be *paid in cash* in the near future. Costs and expenses may be financed in any of three ways: through (1) current payables (including accounts payable, accrued expenses payable, and immediate cash payments), (2) expiration of prepaid expenses, and (3) depreciation of plant assets.

Schedule B2 shows how the budgeted costs and expenses of Berg Company are expected to be financed. The column headed "Current Payables" indicates the portion of the costs and expenses to be paid in cash or financed by current liabilities. Examples of these items include purchases of direct materials (whether for cash or on account), factory payrolls, and utilities bills. The column headed "Expiration of Prepayments" includes costs and expenses stemming from the expiration of short-term prepayments, such as unexpired insurance and prepaid rent.

The budgeted manner of financing the costs and expenses listed in Schedule B2 is based upon an analysis of the prepaid expenses at the beginning of the first quarter and upon computations of depreciation on plant assets. All costs and expenses other than those resulting from depreciation or the expiration of prepayments require future cash payments and, therefore, are listed as current payables.

Schedule B3 The purpose of this schedule is to estimate the cash payments required each quarter for the costs and expenses classified as current payables in Schedule B2. The starting point in Schedule B3 is the balance of the current payables at the beginning of the first quarter ($78,000), which is taken from the January 1 balance sheet on page 1005. To this amount, we add the $305,600 shown in Schedule B2 as the total current payables budgeted to arise during the first quarter. From this subtotal ($383,600), we subtract the estimated balance of current payables at the end of the quarter to determine the cash payments to be made during the first quarter. The $101,500 balance of current payables at the end of the first quarter was estimated by Berg Company's treasurer after an analysis of suppliers' credit terms.

Similar computations are made for the second quarter. The beginning balance of current payables for the second quarter is the ending balance from the first quarter. Again, the amount payable at the end of the second quarter ($85,000) was estimated by the treasurer.

Schedule B4 This schedule budgets the expected cash payments for prepaid expenses during the period. These payments were estimated by the treasurer after considering the amount of prepaid expenses at January 1 and the expiration of these items indicated in Schedule B2.

Schedule B5 This schedule summarizes the cash payments required on Berg Company's bank loan during the budget period. The loan agreement calls for quarterly payments of $40,000 plus the interest accrued during the quarter. Interest is computed at an annual rate of 12%, or 3% per quarter. Thus, the interest amounts to $4,800 for the first quarter ($160,000 loan × 3%) and $3,600 in the second ($120,000 outstanding balance × 3%).

Schedule B6 The budgeted cash payments for income tax expense are summarized in Schedule B6. Each quarter, Berg Company makes income tax payments equal to its income tax liability at the beginning of that quarter.

Schedule B7 All of Berg Company's sales are made on account. Therefore, the sole source of the company's cash receipts is the collection of accounts receivable. The credit manager estimates that two-thirds of the sales in any quarter will be collected in that quarter, and that the remaining one-third will be collected in the following quarter. Schedule B7 indicates the budgeted cash collections under these assumptions. (Losses from uncollectible accounts are ignored in our example.)

Schedule B8 This schedule indicates the effect that credit sales (from the sales budget) and collections from customers (Schedule B7) are expected to have upon the balance of accounts receivable. The balances shown for accounts receivable at the end of each quarter are carried forward to the budgeted balance sheets on page 1012.

■ **Cash Budget** The information derived from the financial budget schedules is the basis for the following quarterly cash budget.

BERG COMPANY
Cash Budget
First Two Quarters of Current Year

	1ST QUARTER	2D QUARTER
Cash balance at beginning of quarter	$ 75,000	$ 3,100
Cash receipts:		
Cash received from customers **(B7)**	282,000	400,000
Total cash available	$357,000	$403,100
Cash payments:		
Payment of current payables **(B3)**	$282,100	$322,400
Prepayments **(B4)**	2,000	12,000
Payments on notes, including interest **(B5)**	44,800	43,600
Income tax payments **(B6)**	25,000	8,280
Total disbursements	$353,900	$386,280
Cash balance at end of the quarter	$ 3,100	$ 16,820

Projected cash flow and ending cash balance

The cash budget is an important tool for forecasting whether the company will be able to meet its obligations as they mature. Often the cash budget may indicate a need for short-term borrowing or other measures to generate or conserve cash in order to keep the company solvent. Remember that one of the principal reasons for preparing budgets is to give advance warning of potential problems such as cash shortages.

■ **Budgeted Balance Sheet** We now have the necessary information to forecast the financial position of the Berg Company at the end of each of the next two quarters. The budgeted balance sheets are illustrated below. Budget schedules from which various figures on the balance sheets have been derived are indicated parenthetically.

Using Budgets Effectively

Earlier in this chapter, we noted several ways in which budgeting benefits an organization. One benefit, an increased awareness by managers of the company's operations and its business environment, may be received even if the completed budget is promptly filed and forgotten. In preparing a budget, managers are forced to consider carefully all aspects of the company's activities. This study and analysis should, in itself, enable managers to do a better job of managing.

The primary benefits of budgeting, however, stem from the uses made of the budgeted information. Among these benefits are (1) advance warning of conditions that require advance corrective action, (2) coordination of the activities of all of the departments within the organization, and (3) the creation of standards for evaluating the performance of company personnel. Let us consider how the master budget for Berg Company might serve these functions.

■ **An Advance Warning of Potential Trouble** One of the major concerns of the management of the Berg Company was the ability of the company to meet the quarterly payments on its loan obligations. The cash budget for the

BERG COMPANY
Budgeted Balance Sheets
As of the End of First Two Quarters of Current Year

ASSETS	1ST QUARTER	2D QUARTER
Current assets:		
Cash *(per cash budget)*	$ 3,100	$ 16,820
Receivables *(B8)*	100,000	150,000
Inventories:		
Direct materials *(B1)*	40,000	40,000
Finished goods *(A5)*	87,500	35,000
Prepayments *(B4)*	15,600	20,500
Total current assets	$246,200	$262,320
Plant and equipment:		
Buildings and equipment	$970,000	$970,000
Less: Accumulated depreciation *(B2)*	(432,000)	(444,000)
Total plant and equipment	$538,000	$526,000
Total assets	$784,200	$788,320
LIABILITIES & STOCKHOLDERS' EQUITY		
Current liabilities:		
Notes payable, 16% *(B5)*	$120,000	$ 80,000
Other current payables *(B3)*	101,500	85,000
Income taxes payable *(B6)*	8,280	27,560
Total current liabilities	$229,780	$192,560
Stockholders' equity:		
Capital stock, no par, 100,000 shares issued and outstanding	$350,000	$350,000
Retained earnings, beginning of quarter	192,000	204,420
Net income for the quarter (per budgeted income statements)	12,420	41,340
Total stockholders' equity	$554,420	$595,760
Total liabilities & stockholders' equity	$784,200	$788,320

first two quarters of the year indicates that the cash position of the company at the end of each quarter will be precariously low. A cash balance of $3,100 is forecast at the end of the first quarter, and a balance of $16,820 at the end of the second quarter. If all goes well the payments *can* be met, but there is little margin for error in the estimates.

When confronted with such a forecast, management should take steps in advance to prevent the cash balance from dropping as low as the budgeted amounts. It may be possible to obtain longer credit terms from suppliers and thus reduce payments on accounts payable during the first two quarters. The company may decide to let inventories fall below scheduled levels in order to reduce cash payments relating to manufacturing costs. An extension of the terms of the note payable might be sought, or the possibility of long-term financing might be considered. If any or all of these steps were taken, it would be necessary to revise the budget estimates accordingly. The fact that management is *forewarned* of this condition several months before it happens, however, illustrates one of the prime values of budgeting.

■ **Coordination of the Activities of Departments** The budget provides a comprehensive plan for all the departments to work together in a coordinated manner. For example, the production department knows the quantity of goods which must be produced to meet the expected needs of the sales department. The purchasing department knows the quantities of direct materials which must be ordered to meet the requirements of the production department. Responsibility budgets inform every segment manager of the level of performance expected of his or her responsibility center during the budget period.

■ **A Yardstick for Evaluating Managerial Performance** Comparison of actual results with budgeted amounts is a common means of evaluating the performance of segment managers. As discussed in Chapter 24, the evaluation of performance should be based only upon those revenues and costs which are *under the control* of the person being evaluated. Therefore, in a responsibility budget, budgeted fixed costs should be subdivided into the categories of *controllable costs* and *committed costs*.

Performance may become difficult to evaluate if the actual level of activity (either sales or production) differs substantially from the level originally budgeted. Assume, for example, that sales for the first quarter are considerably higher than forecast. Not only will revenue differ substantially from the originally budgeted amount, but so will variable costs, production levels, cash flows, and the March 31 balance sheet amounts. Thus, the usefulness of the original budget as a yardstick for evaluating performance is greatly reduced. The solution to this problem lies in *flexible budgeting.*

Flexible Budgeting

Objective 5
Prepare a flexible budget and explain its usefulness.

A *flexible budget* is one that can be easily adjusted to show budgeted revenue, costs, and cash flows at different levels of activity. Thus, if a change in volume lessens the usefulness of the original budget, a new budget may be prepared quickly that reflects the actual level of activity for the period.

To illustrate the usefulness of a flexible budget, assume that Harold Stone, production manager of Berg Company, is presented with the following performance report at the end of the first quarter of the current year. This performance report compares the manufacturing costs originally budgeted for the quarter (Schedule A4) with the actual results.

BERG COMPANY
Performance Report for Production Department
For the Quarter Ended March 31, 19__

■
Is this good or poor performance?

	BUDGETED	ACTUAL	OVER OR (UNDER) BUDGET
Manufacturing costs:			
Direct materials used	$ 60,000	$ 63,800	$ 3,800
Direct labor	72,000	76,500	4,500
Variable overhead	36,000	38,000	2,000
Fixed overhead	42,000	42,400	400
Total manufacturing costs	$210,000	$220,700	$10,700

At first glance, it appears that the production manager's cost control performance is quite poor, since all production costs exceeded the budgeted amounts. However, we have deliberately omitted one piece of information from this performance report. To meet unexpectedly high customer demand for the company's product, the production department produced *130,000* units, instead of the *120,000* units originally budgeted for the first quarter.

Under these circumstances, we should reevaluate our conclusions concerning the manager's ability to control manufacturing costs. At this higher level of production, variable manufacturing costs should naturally exceed the originally budgeted amounts. In order to evaluate the performance of the production manager, the budget must be adjusted to indicate the levels of cost that should be incurred in manufacturing 130,000 units.

Flexible budgeting may be viewed as combining the concepts of budgeting and cost-volume-profit analysis. Using the cost-volume-profit estimates in Schedule A3 (page 1006), the manufacturing cost budget for Berg Company may be revised to reflect any level of production. For example, in the following schedule these relationships are used to forecast quarterly manufacturing costs at three different levels of production:

	LEVEL OF PRODUCTION (IN UNITS)		
	110,000	120,000	130,000
Manufacturing cost estimates from Schedule A3:			
Variable costs:			
Direct materials ($0.50 per unit)	$ 55,000	$ 60,000	$ 65,000
Direct labor ($0.60 per unit)	66,000	72,000	78,000
Manufacturing overhead ($0.30 per unit)	33,000	36,000	39,000
Fixed costs:			
Manufacturing overhead	42,000	42,000	42,000
Total manufacturing costs	$196,000	$210,000	$224,000

Notice that budgeted *variable* manufacturing costs change with the level of production, but that budgeted *fixed* costs remain the same.

Let us now modify the performance report for the production department to reflect the actual *130,000* unit level of production achieved during the first quarter:

BERG COMPANY
Performance Report for Production Department
For the Quarter Ended March 31, 19—

LEVEL OF PRODUCTION (IN UNITS)

Flexible budget shows a different picture

	ORIGINALLY BUDGETED 120,000	FLEXIBLE BUDGET 130,000	ACTUAL 130,000	ACTUAL COSTS OVER OR (UNDER) FLEXIBLE BUDGET
Manufacturing costs:				
Direct materials used	$ 60,000	$ 65,000	$ 63,800	$(1,200)
Direct labor	72,000	78,000	76,500	(1,500)
Variable overhead ...	36,000	39,000	38,000	(1,000)
Fixed overhead	42,000	42,000	42,400	400
Total manufacturing costs	$210,000	$224,000	$220,700	$(3,300)

This comparison paints quite a different picture from the performance report on the preceding page. Considering the actual level of production, the production manager has kept all manufacturing costs below budgeted amounts, with the exception of fixed overhead (most of which may be committed costs).

The techniques of flexible budgeting also may be applied to profit centers by applying cost-volume-profit relationships to the actual level of *sales* achieved.

■ **Computers and Flexible Budgeting** Adjusting the entire budget to reflect a different level of sales or production would be a sizable task in a manual system. In a computer-based system, however, it can be done quickly and easily. Once the cost-volume-profit relationships have been entered into the budgeting program, the computer almost instantly can perform the computations to generate a complete master budget for any level of business activity.

Many businesses use their budgeting software to generate complete budgets under many different assumptions. These companies use this software as a planning tool to assess the expected impact of changes in sales, production, or other key variables upon all aspects of their business operations.

STANDARD COSTS: FOCUSING ATTENTION ON COST VARIANCES

In Chapter 22 we saw how cost accounting systems are used to determine the actual cost to manufacture products or to perform specific manufacturing processes. A cost accounting system becomes even more useful when it includes the budgeted amounts for direct materials, labor, and manufacturing overhead to serve as standards for comparison with the actual costs. The budgeted amounts used in a cost accounting system are called *standard costs*. Standard costs may be used in both job order and process cost accounting systems.

Objective 6
Explain how standard costs assist managers in controlling the costs of a business.

The standard cost is the cost that *should be* incurred to produce a product *under normal conditions.* Thus, comparison of actual costs with the predetermined standard alerts managers to those areas in which the actual costs appear excessive. Assume, for example, that the standard (budgeted) cost of making a product is $10 per unit. If job no. 430, which requires 1,000 units of the product, has an average unit cost of $12.50, management should investigate immediately to determine why actual costs exceeded the standard by such a large margin (25%).

Cost accountants often speak of the "standard" materials cost and the "standard" labor cost: Remember that these "standard" costs are actually *budgeted* costs.

Establishing and Revising Standards

Standard costs are established during the budgeting process. Along with the budget, standard costs should be reviewed periodically and revised if significant changes occur in production methods or the prices paid for materials, labor, or overhead. When actual costs exceed standard costs because of waste or inefficiency, however, the standard costs should *not* be revised upward. The standard cost for direct materials, for example, would not be changed if some of the materials placed in production were spoiled because of carelessness by employees. The standard cost for direct material would be changed, however, if the price of the materials were increased by the supplier. Similarly, the standard cost for labor would not be changed merely because excessive hours of labor were wasted; but it would be changed if laborsaving equipment were installed or if new contracts with labor unions called for increased wage rates.

Cost Variances

Even though standard costs are carefully set and are revised as conditions change, actual costs will still vary somewhat from standard costs. The differences between standard costs and actual costs are called *cost variances.* Cost variances for materials, labor, and overhead result from a variety of different causes. Thus, in evaluating the efficiency of manufacturing operations, these cost variances should be measured and analyzed. As might be expected, different managers within the organization are responsible for different types of cost variances.

When standard costs are used in a cost accounting system, the costs charged to the Work in Process Inventory, Finished Goods Inventory, and Cost of Goods Sold accounts are *standard costs, not actual costs.* Any differences between the actual and standard costs are recorded in *cost variance accounts.* A separate cost variance account is used for each type of cost variance. Thus, the cost accounting system provides managers with information as to the *nature and amount* of all differences between actual and budgeted manufacturing costs.

A cost variance is said to be *favorable* when actual costs are less than standard costs. When actual costs exceed standard costs, the cost variance is said to be *unfavorable.*

Illustration of Standard Costs

To illustrate the use of standard costs and the computation of cost variances, assume that Product C is one of the products produced by Briar Mfg. Co. The company produces an average of *6,000 units* of Product C per month. The standard manufacturing cost per unit, assuming production at the average level of 6,000 units per month, is shown below:

Direct materials (3 pounds @ $5.00)		$15
Direct labor (2.0 hours @ $12.00 per hour)		24
Manufacturing overhead (based upon 12,000 standard direct labor hours):		
Fixed ($120,000 ÷ 6,000 units)	$20	
Variable	1	21
Standard cost per unit of finished goods		$60

During March, Briar Mfg. Co. deliberately reduced the level of its finished goods inventory by scheduling and producing only 5,000 units of Product C. Actual manufacturing costs incurred during March were as follows:

Direct materials (14,500 pounds @ $5.20)		$ 75,400
Direct labor (9,800 hours × $13)		127,400
Manufacturing overhead:		
Fixed	$122,020	
Variable	6,180	128,200
Total manufacturing costs incurred in March		$331,000

There was no work in process at either the beginning or the end of March.

By comparing the actual cost incurred in March to the standard costs, we can determine the net cost variance for the month:

Actual costs (above)...	$331,000
Standard cost for producing 5,000 units (5,000 units × $60)......................	300,000
Net unfavorable cost variance (excess of actual costs over standard costs)..	$ 31,000

Actual costs incurred during the month *exceeded* the standard cost of producing 5,000 units by *$31,000.* In planning corrective action, management needs to know the specific causes of this $31,000 unfavorable cost variance. By comparing each element of manufacturing cost (direct materials, direct labor, and overhead) to the related standard costs, we can explain the net cost variance for March in greater detail. Let us begin by determining the portion of this variance which is attributable to the price and the quantity of direct materials used in March.

Materials Price and Materials Quantity Variances

Objective 7
Compute the materials, labor, and overhead variances and explain the meaning of each cost variance.

In establishing the standard materials cost for each unit of product, two factors were considered: (1) the *quantity* of materials that should have been used in making a unit of finished product, and (2) the *prices* that should have been paid in acquiring this quantity of materials. Therefore, the total materials cost variance may result from differences between standard and actual *quantities* of materials used, or between standard and actual *prices paid* for materials, or from a combination of these two factors. This can be illustrated by the following diagram:

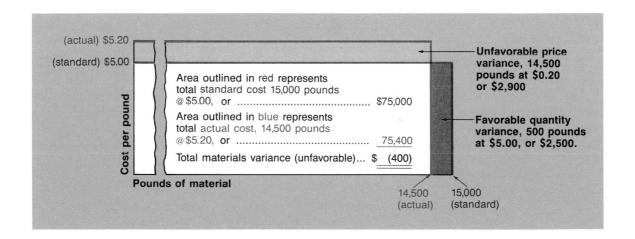

The $400 excess of actual materials cost over the standard materials cost was caused by two factors: (1) a $2,900 unfavorable *materials price variance,* and (2) a $2,500 favorable *materials quantity variance.*

The unfavorable *materials price variance* results from the fact that each of the 14,500 pounds of direct material used during the period cost *20 cents more* than the standard $5 price. The materials price variance is the responsibility of the manager responsible for purchasing materials—namely, the purchasing agent.

A formula for computing the materials price variance is illustrated below:

Materials price variance = Actual quantity used × (Standard price − Actual price)
= 14,500 pounds × ($5.00 − $5.20)
= −$2,900 (or $2,900 unfavorable)

(All of our variance formulas result in a negative number when the variance is unfavorable, and a positive number when the variance is favorable.)

The favorable *materials quantity variance* of $2,500 resulted from the production department using *500 fewer pounds of material* than allowed by the 3 pound per-unit standard in producing 5,000 units of finished product. This variance indicates that the production supervisors are doing a good job in seeing that materials are used efficiently in the production process. The materials quantity variance may be computed as shown below:

Materials quantity variance = Standard price × (Standard quantity − Actual quantity)
= $5 × (15,000 pounds − 14,500 pounds)
= $2,500 favorable

The two materials cost variances may be summarized as follows:

Actual quantity at actual price 14,500 lb × $5.20 $75,400	Actual quantity at standard price 14,500 lb × $5.00 $72,500	Standard quantity at standard price 15,000 lb × $5.00 $75,000

Materials price variance
$2,900 Unfavorable

Materials quantity variance
$2,500 Favorable

Total materials variance, $400 Unfavorable

The journal entry to record the cost of materials used during March, and the related cost variances, is shown below:

Work in Process Inventory (standard cost)................................. 75,000
Materials Price Variance (unfavorable) 2,900
    Materials Quantity Variance (favorable) 2,500
    Direct Materials Inventory (actual cost) 75,400
To record cost of direct materials used in March.

Notice that the Work in Process account is debited for the *standard cost* of materials used, but that the Materials Inventory account is credited for the actual cost of materials used. The differences between the standard and actual costs of materials used are recorded in the two *cost variance accounts.*[1] Unfavorable variances are recorded by debit entries, because they represent costs in

---

[1] An alternative is to record the materials price variance at the time that the materials are purchased. Such alternatives are discussed in the cost accounting course.

excess of the standard cost; favorable variances are recorded by credit entries because they represent cost savings relative to the standard amounts.

Labor Rate and Labor Efficiency Variances

Briar Mfg. Co. incurred actual direct labor costs of $127,400 in March, although the standard labor cost of producing 5,000 finished units is only $120,000 (5,000 units × 2 labor hours per unit × $12 per hour). Thus, the company incurred an unfavorable total labor cost variance of *$7,400*. We can gain additional insight into the reasons for this excessive labor cost by dividing the total labor variance into a labor rate variance, and a labor efficiency variance.

Actual labor costs are a function of (1) the wage rate paid to direct labor workers, and (2) the number of direct labor hours worked. A *labor rate variance* shows the extent to which differences between actual and standard hourly wage *rates* contribute to the total labor variance. The *labor efficiency variance* indicates the extent to which the total labor variance results from differences between the budgeted and actual number of *labor hours* required in the production process.

The labor rate variance is equal to the actual number of hours worked, multiplied by the difference between the standard and actual hourly wage rates. The computation of the labor rate variance for Briar Mfg. Co. in March is as follows:

$$\text{Labor rate variance} = \text{Actual labor hours} \times (\text{Standard hourly} - \text{Actual hourly rate})$$
$$= 9,800 \text{ hours} \times (\$12.00 - \$13.00)$$
$$= -\$9,800 \text{ (or } \$9,800 \text{ unfavorable)}$$

An *unfavorable* labor rate variance may result from using highly paid employees to perform lower payscale jobs, or from poor scheduling of production that results in unnecessary overtime.[2] The production manager is responsible for assigning employees to production tasks and also for scheduling production. Therefore, the production manager is responsible for labor rate variances.

The labor efficiency variance (also called labor usage variance) is a measure of workers' productivity. This variance is favorable if workers are able to complete the scheduled production in fewer hours than are allowed by the standard. An unfavorable labor efficiency variance represents excessive labor costs resulting from wasted time or low levels of hourly productivity. The labor efficiency variance is computed by multiplying the standard hourly wage rate by the difference between the standard and actual number of direct labor hours used, as shown below:

$$\text{Labor efficiency variance} = \text{Standard hourly rate} \times (\text{Standard hours} - \text{Actual hours})$$
$$= \$12.00 \text{ per hour} \times (10,000 \text{ hours} - 9,800 \text{ hours})$$
$$= \$2,400 \text{ favorable}$$

The *favorable* labor efficiency variance indicates that direct workers were able to complete the scheduled level of production in *less time* than was al-

---

[2] If the scheduled level of production requires overtime even with efficient scheduling, the overtime wage rate should be reflected in the standard cost.

lowed in the standard cost estimates. Production managers are responsible for the productivity of direct workers and, therefore, for the labor efficiency variance.

The two labor cost variances may be summarized as follows:

Actual hours at actual rate 9,800 hr × $13 $127,400	Actual hours at standard rate 9,800 hr × $12.00 $117,600	Standard hours at standard rate 10,000 hr × $12.00 $120,000

Labor rate variance $9,800 unfavorable   Labor efficiency variance $2,400 favorable

Total labor variance, $7,400 unfavorable

The journal entry to record direct labor costs relating to work performed in March is:

Work in Process Inventory (standard cost)	*120,000*	
Labor Rate Variance	*9,800*	
Labor Efficiency Variance		*2,400*
Direct Labor (actual cost)		*127,400*

To record cost of direct labor used in March.

Both the labor rate and the labor efficiency variances are controllable by the production manager. Often, these variances are closely related. For example, assume that during March the production manager decided to use more highly skilled workers to manufacture Product C. This strategy could explain both the unfavorable rate variance and the favorable labor efficiency variance, as the more highly skilled workers receive a higher hourly wage and also should work faster than less skilled workers.

In this case, however, the production manager's strategy did not pay off. The cost savings resulting from increased productivity ($2,400) were not sufficient to offset the additional costs from the higher hourly wage rates ($9,800). After reviewing these cost variances, the production manager probably will return to the approach of using lower paid workers in the production of Product C.

Manufacturing Overhead Variances

The difference between actual manufacturing overhead costs and the standard overhead cost charged to production is called the *overhead variance*. Whereas direct materials and direct labor are *variable* costs, manufacturing overhead consists primarily of *fixed* costs. Therefore, the analysis of the overhead variance differs somewhat from the analysis of the materials and labor variances. The total overhead variance may be subdivided into three or four subvariances. In our discussion, however, we will follow the more common accounting practice of dividing the total overhead variance into two elements: the spending variance and the volume variance.[3]

---

[3] "Three-way" and "four-way" analysis of the overhead variance will be illustrated and explained in the cost accounting course.

■ **The Overhead Spending Variance** The most important element of the overhead variance is the *spending variance*—that is, the difference between overhead shown in a *flexible budget* and actual overhead expenditures during the period. The overhead spending variance of Briar Mfg. Co. in March may be computed as follows.

Overhead per flexible budget at 5,000 units of production:		
Fixed	$120,000	
Variable ($1 per unit × 5,000 units)	5,000	$125,000
Actual overhead in March:		
Fixed	$122,020	
Variable	6,180	128,200
Overhead spending variance (unfavorable)		$ (3,200)

The overhead spending variance is the responsibility of the production manager. Presumably, most of the overhead spending variance represents differences between budgeted and actual amounts of *controllable* overhead costs. For this reason, the spending variance is sometimes called the *controllable* overhead variance. If a significant portion of the spending variance results from differences between the budgeted and actual amounts of *committed* costs, the overhead cost standards should be revised.

■ **The Volume Variance** The overhead spending variance has shown us the difference between the amount of overhead included in a flexible budget and the actual overhead costs incurred. The *volume variance* represents the difference between overhead *applied to work in process* (at standard cost) and the overhead per the flexible budget.

In a standard cost system, overhead is applied (debited) to the Work in Process Inventory account using a standard per-unit cost. On page 1016, we computed the standard per-unit cost of manufacturing overhead at $21. Thus, the Work in Process Inventory account will be debited with $21 in overhead costs for each unit produced.

A temporary problem may arise when overhead is applied at a standard per-unit amount. Using a standard unit cost to apply overhead means that the total amount of applied overhead will *vary directly with the number of units produced.* In essence, a standard cost system treats overhead as a *variable cost.* In reality, however, overhead consists primarily of *fixed costs.*

To illustrate the temporary distortions that may result from using a standard unit cost to apply overhead to work in process, let us compare applied overhead to flexible budget overhead for Briar Mfg. Co. at three different levels of monthly production.

	ACTUAL PRODUCTION (IN UNITS)		
	5,000	6,000	7,000
Overhead applied to Work in Process			
Inventory using $21 per unit standard cost	$105,000	$126,000	$147,000
Overhead per flexible budget:			
Fixed	$120,000	$120,000	$120,000
Variable ($1 per unit)...............................	5,000	6,000	7,000
Total overhead per flexible budget	$125,000	$126,000	$127,000
Volume variances—favorable (unfavorable)	**$ (20,000)**	**$ –0–**	**$ 20,000**

Notice that when actual production is 6,000 units per month, the "normal" level of production, there is no volume variance. This is because our $21 standard cost figure *assumes* the 6,000 unit per month level of production. As shown on page 1016, the $21 per-unit standard cost *includes $20 per-unit in fixed costs* ($120,000 budgeted fixed overhead ÷ 6,000 units). Whenever actual production is less than 6,000 units, less than $120,000 in fixed overhead costs will be applied to production. In March, for example, only *5,000* units were produced. Thus, use of a standard cost that includes *$20* per unit in fixed overhead applies only *$100,000* in fixed overhead costs to work in process. The remaining $20,000 in fixed overhead budgeted for the month is recorded as an *unfavorable* volume variance. This unfavorable volume variance actually represents *underapplied overhead.*

The situation reverses whenever actual production exceeds the normal level. When actual monthly production is *greater* than 6,000 units, use of a standard unit cost applies *more than* $120,000 in fixed overhead costs to work in process. Comparison of the applied overhead to the budget then indicates a *favorable* volume variance. This favorable variance should be viewed as *overapplied* overhead.

The key point is that *volume variances represent over- or underapplied overhead;* they occur automatically whenever actual production differs from the average level of production assumed in computing the standard overhead cost per unit. Over time, actual production should average approximately the level used in developing the standard cost. Thus, the favorable and unfavorable volume variances should "balance out" over the year.

As long as the production department is producing the desired number of units, volume variances do *not* indicate either strong or poor performance. Volume variances are the natural result of variations in the scheduled level of production from month to month. Scheduled production may vary from month-to-month because of such factors as seasonal sales demand, an effort to increase or decrease inventories, or holidays and vacations. Thus, unless the production department fails to produce the scheduled number of units, no manager should be considered "responsible" for a volume variance.

■ **Summary of the Overhead Cost Variances** The two overhead variances incurred in March by Briar Mfg. Co. may be summarized as follows:

Actual overhead		Overhead per flexible budget		Overhead applied at standard cost
Fixed	$122,020	Fixed.............	$120,000	5,000 units × $21
Variable	6,180	Variable (5,000 × $1)	5,000	
Total	$128,200	Total	$125,000	$105,000

Spending variance
$3,200 unfavorable

Volume variance
$20,000 unfavorable

Total overhead variance, $23,200 unfavorable

The journal entry to apply overhead costs to production in March, and to record the overhead cost variances, is:

Work in Process Inventory (standard cost)............................	105,000	
Overhead Spending Variance...	3,200	
Overhead Volume Variance...	20,000	
Manufacturing Overhead (actual)..................................		128,200

To assign overhead costs to 5,000 units of production at standard
rate of $21 per unit, and to record overhead cost variances.

Valuation of Finished Goods

In a standard cost system, only standard costs are debited to the Work in Process Inventory account. Thus, finished goods manufactured are valued at standard cost as they are transferred into the Finished Goods Inventory account and the Cost of Goods Sold account. The entry made at the end of March to record the completion of 5,000 units of Product C is shown below:

Finished Goods Inventory: Product C..................................	300,000	
Work In Process Inventory: Product C...........................		300,000

To record completion during March of 5,000 units of Product C at
standard cost (5,000 units × $60 per unit = $300,000).

Notice that the inventory of finished goods is valued at **standard cost**. As units of Product C are sold, this standard cost will be transferred into the Cost of Goods Sold account.

■ **Disposition of Cost Variance Accounts** The balances in the variance accounts represent differences between actual manufacturing costs and the standard costs used in the valuation of finished goods inventory and the cost of goods sold. These balances are allowed to accumulate in the variance accounts from month to month. Hopefully, the favorable and unfavorable will "balance out" over the year, and only a small balance will remain in each variance account at year-end. In this case, the variance accounts are simply closed into the cost of goods sold, since most of the difference between actual and standard cost is applicable to goods sold during the year.

However, if the net cost variance for the year is **material in dollar amount,** it should be apportioned among the Work in Process Inventory, Finished Goods Inventory, and Cost of Goods Sold in order to restate these accounts at actual cost.

Evaluation of Cost Variances

We have now computed six separate cost variances to explain in greater detail the $31,000 net unfavorable cost variance incurred by Briar Mfg. Co. in March. These variances are summarized on the next page.

Cost variances:

Materials price variance—unfavorable............................	$ (2,900)	
Materials quantity variance—favorable	2,500	
Total materials variance—unfavorable		$ (400)
Labor rate variance—unfavorable	$ (9,800)	
Labor efficiency variance—favorable	2,400	
Total labor variance—unfavorable		(7,400)
Overhead spending variance—unfavorable	$ (3,200)	
Overhead volume variance—unfavorable	(20,000)	
Total overhead variance—unfavorable		(23,200)
Net unfavorable cost variance in March		$(31,000)

This summary should assist managers in identifying problem areas and in controlling costs in future months. For example, the unfavorable materials price variance highlights the fact that the purchasing department should be able to purchase the direct materials used in Product C at a lower cost. The favorable materials quantity variance, in contrast, indicates that the production department is using materials in a very efficient manner.

However, the production manager has a serious problem with respect to labor rates. The large unfavorable labor variance indicates that the strategy of using more highly paid workers in manufacturing Product C is not cost effective. Therefore, the manager should change this strategy and return to using lower payscale workers in the manufacture of this product.

The overhead spending variance also indicates excessive levels of expenditures. Now that managers are alerted to this problem, they should look more carefully for opportunities to reduce overhead costs. The large negative volume variance should not be a matter of concern—this variance resulted automatically from the deliberate action of scheduling only 5,000 units of production in March. As soon as production returns to the normal level of 6,000 units per month, this variance will disappear.

Summary of Cost Variances

For your convenience, the six cost variances discussed in this chapter are summarized on page 1025.

VARIANCE	COMPUTATION	RESPONSIBLE MANAGER
Materials:		
Price variance	Actual quantity × (Standard price − Actual price)	Purchasing agent
Quantity variance	Standard price × (Standard quantity − Actual quantity)	Production manager
Labor:		
Rate variance	Actual hours × (Standard hourly rate − Actual hourly rate)	Production manager
Efficiency (usage) variance	Standard hourly rate × (Standard hours − Actual hours)	Production manager
Overhead:		
Spending variance	Overhead per flexible budget − Actual overhead	Production manager (to extent variance relates to controllable costs)
Volume variance	Applied overhead (at standard rate) − Overhead per flexible budget	None—this variance results from schedling production at any level other than "normal"

End-of-Chapter Review

CONCEPTS INTRODUCED OR EMPHASIZED IN CHAPTER 25

The major concepts in this chapter include:

■ The nature of a budget, and the benefits derived by a business from the budgeting process.

■ The desirability of setting budgeted amounts at realistic and achievable levels.

■ Elements of a master budget, and the interrelationships among these elements.

■ A logical sequence of steps to follow in preparing a master budget.

■ The advantages of a flexible budget, and the techniques of preparing this type of budget.

■ A standard cost system as a means of determining the cause and the amount of differences between actual costs and budgeted amounts.

■ Types of cost variances—what they mean, how they are computed, and who is responsible.

Chapter 25 serves as something of a "capstone" for the preceding several chapters. The preparation of a budget and the use of standard costs draw heavily upon the concepts of product costing, cost-volume-profit analysis, and responsibility accounting. When these concepts and tools are brought together in a well-designed accounting system, managers are provided with a wealth of information useful in planning and controlling the operations of every segment of the business. In our next and final chapter, we will see how managers select and utilize the information most relevant to specific types of business decisions.

KEY TERMS INTRODUCED OR EMPHASIZED IN CHAPTER 25

Budget   A plan or forecast for a future period expressed in quantitative terms. Establishes objectives and aids in evaluating subsequent performance.

Continuous budgeting   A technique of extending the budget period by one month as each month passes. Therefore, the budget always covers the upcoming 12 months.

Cost variance   A difference between the actual level of cost incurred and the standard (budgeted) level for the cost. The total cost variance may be subdivided into separate cost variances indicating the amount of variance attributable to specific causal factors.

Flexible budget   A budget that can readily be revised to reflect budgeted amounts given the actual levels of activity (sales and production) achieved during the period. Makes use of cost-volume-profit relationships to restate the master budget for the achieved level of activity.

Labor efficiency variance   The portion of the total labor variance caused by a difference between the standard and actual number of labor hours to complete the task. Computed as *Standard hourly rate × (Standard hours − Actual hours)*.

Labor rate variance   The portion of the total labor variance caused by a difference between the standard hourly wage rate and the rate actually paid to workers. Usually stems from overtime or using workers at a different payscale than assumed in developing the standard cost. Computed as *Actual hours × (Standard hourly rate − Actual hourly rate)*.

Master budget   An overall financial and operating plan, including budgets for all aspects of business operations and for all responsibility centers.

Materials price variance   The portion of the total materials variance caused by paying a different price to purchase materials than was assumed in the standard cost. Computed as *Actual quantity × (Standard unit price − Actual unit price)*.

Materials quantity variance   The portion of the total materials variance caused by using more or less material in the production process than is called for in the standards. Computed as *Standard unit price × (Standard quantity − Actual quantity)*.

Overhead spending variance   The portion of the total overhead variance caused by incurring more overhead costs than are indicated in a flexible budget prepared for the actual level of activity achieved.

Performance report   A schedule comparing the actual and budgeted performance of a particular responsibility center.

Responsibility budget   A portion of the master budget showing the budgeted performance of a particular responsibility center within the organization.

Standard cost   The budgeted cost that should be incurred under normal, efficient conditions.

Standard cost system   An accounting system in which inventories and the cost of goods sold are valued at standard costs, and cost variances are separately accumulated in cost variance accounts. A tool for promptly alerting management to significant cost variances.

Volume variance   The portion of the total overhead variance that results from a difference between the actual level of production and the "normal" level assumed in computing the standard unit cost. In effect, the volume variance is a misallocation of fixed overhead costs, and often is not relevant in evaluating segment performance.

SELF-TEST QUESTIONS

Answers to these questions appear on page 1039.

1 Which of the following statements correctly describe relationships within the master budget? (More than one answer may be correct.)

a The manufacturing budget is based in large part upon the sales forecast.

b In many elements of the master budget, the amounts budgeted for the upcoming quarter are reviewed and subdivided into monthly budget figures.

c The manufacturing cost budget affects the budgeted income statement, the cash budget, and the budgeted balance sheet.

d The capital expenditures budget has a greater effect upon the budgeted income statement than it does upon the budgeted balance sheet.

2 During the first quarter of its operations, Morris Mfg. Co. expects to sell 50,000 units and create an ending inventory of 20,000 units. Variable manufacturing costs are budgeted at $10 per unit, and fixed manufacturing costs at $100,000 per quarter. The company's treasurer expects that 80% of the variable manufacturing costs will require cash payment during the quarter, and that 20% will be financed through accounts payable and accrued liabilities. Only 50% of the fixed manufacturing costs are expected to require cash payments during the quarter.

In the cash budget, payments for manufacturing costs during the quarter will total:

a $800,000   **b** $610,000   **c** $600,000   **d** $450,000

3 Rodgers Mfg. Co. prepares a flexible budget. The original budget forecast sales of 100,000 units @ $20, and operating expenses of $300,000 fixed, plus $2 per unit. Production also was budgeted at 100,000 units. Actual sales and production for the period totaled 110,000 units. When the budget is adjusted to reflect these new activity levels, which of the following budgeted amounts will increase, but by *less than* 10%?

a Sales revenue.

b Variable manufacturing costs.

c Fixed manufacturing costs.

d Total operating expenses.

4 For the number of equivalent full units actually produced, the flexible budget called for the use of 9,500 pounds of materials at a standard cost of $10 per pound. The production department actually used 10,000 pounds of materials costing $9.90 per pound. The production manager should be considered responsible for:

a An unfavorable cost variance of $4,000.

b A favorable price variance of $1,000.

c An unfavorable quantity variance of $5,000.

d None of the above; the flexible budget should be adjusted to reflect the use of 10,000 pounds of material.

5 An unfavorable volume variance indicates that:

a Total fixed overhead exceeded budgeted amounts.

b Variable overhead per unit exceeded budgeted amounts.

c The production department failed to produce the quantity of units called for in the production schedule.

d The actual production for the period was less than the normal volume used in establishing the standard unit cost.

Assignment Material

REVIEW QUESTIONS

1 Explain the relationship between the managerial functions of *planning* and *controlling costs*.

2 Briefly explain at least three ways in which a business may expect to benefit from preparing a formal budget.

3 Criticize the following quotation:

"At our company, budgeted revenue is set so high and budgeted expenses so low that no department can ever meet the budget. This way, department managers can never relax; they are motivated to keep working harder no matter how well they are already doing."

4 Identify at least five budgets or schedules which are often included in the master budget of a manufacturing business.

5 List in a logical sequence the major steps in the preparation of a master budget.

6 Why is the preparation of a sales forecast one of the earliest steps in preparing a master budget?

7 What are *responsibility budgets?* What responsibility segments would serve as the basis for preparing responsibility sales budgets in a large retail store, such as a Sears or a Nordstrom.

8 What is a *flexible budget?* Explain how a flexible budget increases the usefulness of budgeting as a means of evaluating performance.

9 An article in *Business Week* stated that approximately one-third of the total federal budget is considered "controllable." What is meant by a budgeted expenditure being controllable? Give two examples of government expenditures that may be considered "noncontrollable."

10 Define *standard costs* and briefly indicate how they may be used by management in planning and control.

11 What is wrong with the following statement: "There are three basic kinds of cost accounting systems: job order, process, and standard."

12 Once standard costs are established, what conditions would require that standards be revised?

13 List the variances from standard cost that are generally computed for direct materials, direct labor, and manufacturing overhead.

14 Would a production manager be equally responsible for an unfavorable materials price variance and an unfavorable materials quantity variance? Explain.

15 What is meant by a favorable labor efficiency variance? How is the labor efficiency variance computed?

16 Explain the cause of an unfavorable and of a favorable overhead *volume variance.*

17 Why is an unfavorable overhead volume variance not usually considered in evaluating the performance of the production department manager?

EXERCISES

Exercise 25-1
Accounting
terminology

Listed below are nine technical accounting terms introduced in this chapter:

Materials quantity variance	*Overhead spending variance*	*Materials price variance*
Standard costs	*Labor rate variance*	*Master budget*
Volume variance	*Labor efficiency variance*	*Flexible budget*

Each of the following statements may (or may not) describe one of these technical terms. For each statement, indicate the accounting term described, or answer "None" if the statement does not correctly describe any of the terms.

a A variance that is always favorable when more units are sold than are produced during the period.

b The difference between actual manufacturing overhead and the level of overhead budgeted for the level of output actually achieved.

c A budget which may be readily adjusted to show budgeted amounts at different possible levels of output.

d The difference between the standard and actual unit cost of materials used, multiplied by the actual quantity of materials used.

e The additional cost or cost savings resulting from the actual number of required hours of direct labor differing from standard.

f A budget showing cost levels which departmental managers may not exceed without written permission from top management.

g The budgeted costs of producing a product under normal conditions.

h An overall financial plan for the operation of a business, which includes separate budgets or supporting schedules for each aspect of business operations.

**Exercise 25-2
Budgeting
purchases and
cash payments**

The following information is taken from the manufacturing budget and budgeted financial statements of Weiss Mfg. Co.:

Direct materials inventory, Jan. 1	$ 45,000
Direct materials inventory, Dec. 31	65,000
Direct materials budgeted for use during the year	210,000
Accounts payable to suppliers of direct materials, Jan. 1	36,000
Accounts payable to suppliers of direct materials, Dec. 31	50,000

Compute the budgeted amounts for:

a Purchases of direct materials during the year.

b Cash payments during the year to suppliers of direct materials.

**Exercise 25-3
Budgeting cash
receipts**

Sales on account for the first two months of the current year are budgeted as follows:

January	$300,000
February	400,000

All sales are made on terms of 2/10, n/30; collections on accounts receivable are typically made as follows:

Collections within the month of sale:	
Within discount period	50%
After discount period	20%
Collections within the month following sale:	
Within discount period	15%
After discount period	10%
Returns, allowances, and uncollectibles	5%
Total	100%

Compute the estimated cash collections on accounts receivable for the month of *February*.

Exercise 25-4
Preparing a
flexible budget

The flexible budget at the 35,000-unit and the 40,000-unit level of activity is shown below:

	35,000 UNITS	40,000 UNITS	45,000 UNITS
Sales	$700,000	$800,000	$
Cost of goods sold	420,000	480,000	
Gross profit on sales	$280,000	$320,000	$
Operating expenses ($45,000 fixed)......	185,000	205,000	
Operating income	$ 95,000	$115,000	$
Income taxes (30% of operating income)	28,500	34,500	
Net income	$ 66,500	$ 80,500	$

Complete the flexible budget at the 45,000-unit level of activity. Assume that the cost of goods sold and variable operating expenses vary directly with sales and that income taxes remain at 30% of operating income.

Exercise 25-5
More on flexible
budgeting

The cost accountant for Modern Molding Co. prepared the following monthly performance report relating to the Milling Department:

	BUDGETED PRODUCTION (3,000 UNITS)	ACTUAL PRODUCTION (3,300 UNITS)	VARIANCES	
			FAVORABLE	UNFAVORABLE
Direct materials used ...	$90,000	$96,000		$6,000
Direct labor	30,000	34,500		4,500
Variable manufacturing overhead..............	6,000	6,450		450
Fixed manufacturing overhead..............	45,000	44,750	$250	

Prepare a revised performance report in which the variances are computed by comparing the actual costs incurred with estimated costs *using a flexible budget* for 3,300 units of production.

Exercise 25-6
Relationships
among standard
costs, actual
costs, and cost
variances

The standard costs and variances for direct materials, direct labor, and factory overhead for the month of April are given below:

	STANDARD COST	VARIANCES	
		UNFAVORABLE	FAVORABLE
Direct materials	$ 60,000		
Price variance......................			$3,000
Quantity variance...................			1,800
Direct labor	120,000		
Rate variance		$1,200	
Efficiency variance			5,400
Manufacturing overhead	180,000		
Spending variance..................		2,400	
Volume variance...................		3,600	

Determine the *actual costs* incurred during the month of April for direct materials, direct labor, and manufacturing overhead.

Exercise 25-7
Computing materials cost variances

One of the products of Candy Is Dandy is a one-pound box of chocolate candy, packaged in a box bearing the customer's logo. (Minimum order, 100 boxes.) The standard cost of the chocolate candy used is $2 per pound. During November, 10,000 of these one-pound boxes were produced, requiring 10,400 pounds of chocolate candy at a total direct materials cost of $21,320.

Determine the materials price variance and quantity variance with respect to the candy used producing this product.

Exercise 25-8
Computing labor cost variances

One of the most popular products of Loring Glassworks is a hand-decorated vase. The company's standard cost system calls for .5 hour of direct labor per vase, at a standard wage rate of $7.60. During September, Loring produced 5,000 vases at an actual direct labor cost of $18,225 for 2,250 direct labor hours.

Instructions

a What was the average hourly pay rate of the direct workers producing the vases in September?

b Compute the labor rate and efficiency variances for the month.

c Was using workers on the payscale indicated in part **a** an effective strategy? Explain.

Exercise 25-9
Computing overhead cost variances

From the following information for Fitch Corporation, compute the overhead spending variance and the volume variance.

Standard manufacturing overhead based on normal monthly volume:

Fixed ($150,000 ÷ 10,000 units)	$15.00	
Variable ($50,000 ÷ 10,000 units)...................................	5.00	$20.00
Units actually produced in current month.....................................		9,000 units
Actual overhead costs incurred (including		
$150,000 fixed)		$191,900

Exercise 25-10
Elements of the materials cost variances

The following computation of the materials variances of Pronto Mfg. Co. is incomplete. The missing data is labeled *(a)* through *(d)*.

Materials price variance = 1,840 pounds × [*(a)* − $9.00 actual price] .... $ 368 Favorable

Materials quantity variance = *(b)* × [1,700 pounds − *(c)*] .... $ *(d)*

Instructions

Supply the missing data for items *(a)* through *(d)*. Prepare a caption describing the item, as well as indicating the dollar amount of physical quantity. Briefly explain each answer, including how you determined the amount.

Exercise 25-11
Computing materials and labor variances

Nolan Mills uses a standard cost system. During May, Nolan manufactured 18,000 pillowcases, using 32,400 yards of fabric costing $3.58 per yard, and incurring direct labor costs of $22,800 for 4,000 hours of direct labor. The standard cost per pillowcase assumes 1.75 yards of fabric at $3.60 per yard, and 0.2 hours of direct labor at $5.85 per hour.

Instructions

a Compute both the price variance and quantity variance relating to direct materials used in the manufacture of pillowcases in May.

b Compute both the rate variance and efficiency variance for direct labor costs incurred in manufacturing pillowcases in May.

Exercise 25-12
Causes of cost variances

For each of the following variances, briefly explain at least one probable cause and indicate the departmental manager (if any) responsible for the variance.

a A favorable materials price variance.

b An unfavorable labor rate variance.

c A favorable volume variance.

d An unfavorable materials quantity variance.

PROBLEMS

Group A

Problem 25A-1
Budgeting manufacturing overhead

Wizard Electronics manufactures a component which is processed successively by Department X and Department Y. Manufacturing overhead is applied to units of production at the following standard costs:

	MANUFACTURING OVERHEAD PER UNIT		
	FIXED	VARIABLE	TOTAL
Department X	$18.00	$8.50	$26.50
Department Y	13.00	6.00	19.00

These standard manufacturing overhead costs per unit are based on a normal volume of production of 2,000 units per month. In January, variable manufacturing overhead is expected to be 10% above standard in both departments because of scheduled repairs to equipment. The company plans to produce 1,800 units during January.

Instructions Prepare a budget for manufacturing overhead costs in January. Use column headings as follows: Total, Department X, and Department Y.

Problem 25A-2
Budgeting production, inventories, and the cost of sales

Welsh Scientific manufactures and sells a single product. In preparing the budget for the current year, the company's controller has assembled the following information:

	UNITS	DOLLARS
Sales (budgeted)	210,000	$7,350,000
Finished goods inventory, beginning of the year	52,000	990,000
Finished goods inventory, end of the year	40,000	?
Cost of finished goods manufactured (budgeted manufacturing cost is $20 per unit)....................................	?	?

The company uses the weighted-average method of pricing its inventory of finished goods.

Instructions Compute the following budgeted quantities or dollar amounts:

a Planned production of finished goods (in units).

b Cost of finished goods manufactured.

c Finished goods inventory, end of the year. (Remember that in using the weighted-average method you must first compute the average cost of units available for sale.)

d Cost of goods sold.

Problem 25A-3
Flexible budgeting

Connors Rifle Corporation uses departmental budgets and performance reports in planning and controlling its manufacturing operations. The annual performance report (shown on page 1033) for the production department for the year was presented to the president of the company.

	BUDGETED COSTS FOR 5,000 UNITS		ACTUAL COSTS INCURRED	OVER OR (UNDER) BUDGET
	PER UNIT	TOTAL		
Variable manufacturing costs:				
Direct materials	$ 30.00	$150,000	$171,000	$21,000
Direct labor	48.00	240,000	261,500	21,500
Indirect labor....................	15.00	75,000	95,500	20,500
Indirect materials, supplies,				
etc............................	9.00	45,000	48,400	3,400
Total variable manufactur-				
ing costs.....................	$102.00	$510,000	$576,400	$66,400
Fixed manufacturing costs:				
Lease rental.....................	$ 9.00	$ 45,000	$ 45,000	None
Salaries of foremen..............	24.00	120,000	125,000	$ 5,000
Depreciation and other	15.00	75,000	78,600	3,600
Total fixed manufacturing				
costs	$ 48.00	$240,000	$248,600	$ 8,600
Total manufacturing costs	$150.00	$750,000	$825,000	$75,000

Although a production volume of 5,000 guns was originally budgeted for the year, the actual volume of production achieved for the year was **6,000** guns. The company does not use standard costs; direct materials and direct labor are charged to production at actual cost. Factory overhead is applied to production at the predetermined rate of 150% of the actual direct labor cost.

After a quick glance at the performance report showing an unfavorable manufacturing cost variance of $75,000, the president said to the accountant: "Fix this thing so it makes sense. It looks as though our production people really blew the budget. Remember that we exceeded our budgeted production schedule by a significant margin. I want this performance report to show a better picture of our ability to control costs."

Instructions   **a** Prepare a revised performance report for the year on a flexible budget basis. Use the same format as the production report above, but revise the budgeted cost figures to reflect the actual production level of **6,000** guns.

b In a few sentences compare the original performance report with the revised report.

c What is the amount of over- or underapplied manufacturing overhead for the year? (Note that a standard cost system is not used.)

Problem 25A-4
Preparing a cash budget

Jake Marley, owner of Marley Wholesale, is negotiating with the bank for a $200,000, 12%, 90-day loan effective July 1 of the current year. If the bank grants the loan, the proceeds will be $194,000, which Marley intends to use on July 1 as follows: pay accounts payable, $150,000; purchase equipment, $16,000; add to bank balance, $28,000.

The current working capital position of Marley Wholesale, according to financial statements as of June 30, is as follows:

Cash in bank...	$ 20,000
Receivables (net of allowance for doubtful accounts)	160,000
Merchandise inventory...	90,000
Total current assets	$270,000
Accounts payable (including accrued operating expenses)	150,000
Working capital...	$120,000

The bank loan officer asks Marley to prepare a forecast of his cash receipts and cash payments for the next three months to demonstrate that the loan can be repaid at the end of September.

Marley has made the following estimates, which are to be used in preparing a three-month cash budget: Sales (all on open account) for July, $300,000; August, $360,000; September, $270,000; and October, $200,000. Past experience indicates that 80% of the receivables generated in any month will be collected in the month following the sale, 19% in the second month following the sale, and 1% will prove uncollectible. Marley expects to collect $120,000 of the June 30 receivables in July, and the remaining $40,000 in August.

Cost of goods sold has averaged consistently about 65% of sales. Operating expenses are budgeted at $36,000 per month plus 8% of sales. With the exception of $4,400 per month depreciation expense, all operating expenses and purchases are on open account and are paid in the month following their incurrence.

Merchandise inventory at the end of each month should be sufficient to cover the following month's sales.

Instructions

a Prepare a monthly cash budget showing estimated cash receipts and cash payments for July, August, and September, and the cash balance at the end of each month. Supporting schedules should be prepared for estimated collections on receivables, estimated merchandise purchases, and estimated payments for operating expenses and of accounts payable for merchandise purchases.

b On the basis of this cash forecast, write a brief report to Marley explaining whether he will be able to pay the $200,000 loan at the bank at the end of September.

Problem 25A-5
Basic standard cost problem

Bug Off, Inc., manufactures an insecticide and uses a standard cost system. The insecticide is produced in 400-pound batches; the normal level of production is *125* batches of insecticide per month. The standard costs per batch are shown below:

		STANDARD COSTS PER BATCH
Direct materials:		
Various chemicals (400 lbs. per batch @ $0.60/lb.)		*$240*
Direct labor:		
Preparation and blending (20 hrs. per batch @ $7.00/hr.)		*140*
Manufacturing overhead:		
Fixed ($20,000 per month ÷ 125 batches)	*$160*	
Variable (per batch)	*20*	*180*
Total standard cost per batch of insecticide		*$560*

During January, the company temporarily reduced the level of production to *100* batches of insecticide. Actual costs incurred in January were as follows:

Direct materials (41,000 lbs. @ $0.57/lb.)	*$23,370*
Direct labor (1,900 hrs. @ $6.80/hr.)	*12,920*
Manufacturing overhead	*21,810*
Total actual costs (100 batches)	*$58,100*
Standard cost of 100 batches (100 batches × $560 per batch)	*56,000*
Net unfavorable cost variance	*$ 2,100*

Instructions

You have been engaged to explain in detail the elements of the $2,100 net unfavorable cost variance, and to record the manufacturing costs for January in the company's standard cost accounting system.

a As a first step, compute the materials price and quantity variances, the labor rate and efficiency variances, and the overhead spending and volume variances for the month.

b Prepare journal entries to record the flow of manufacturing costs through the standard cost system and the related cost variances. Make separate entries to record the costs of direct materials used, direct labor, and manufacturing overhead. Work in Process Inventory is to be debited only with standard costs.

Problem 25A-6
Computation,
recording, and
analysis of cost
variances

Heritage Furniture Co. uses a standard cost system. One of the company's most popular products is an oak entertainment center that looks like an old ice box but houses a television, stereo, or other electronic components. The per-unit standard costs of the entertainment center, assuming a "normal" volume of 1,000 units per month, are as follows:

Direct materials, 100 board feet of wood at $1.30 per foot		$130.00
Direct labor, 5 hours at $8.00 per hour		40.00
Manufacturing overhead (applied at $22 per unit)		
Fixed ($15,000 ÷ 1,000 units of normal production)	$15.00	
Variable	7.00	22.00
Total standard unit cost		$192.00

During July, 800 entertainment centers were scheduled and produced at the following actual unit costs:

Direct materials, 110 feet at $1.20 per foot	$132.00
Direct labor, 5½ hours at $7.80 per hour	42.90
Manufacturing overhead, $18,480 ÷ 800 units	23.10
Total actual unit cost	$198.00

Instructions

a Compute the following cost variances for the month of July:

(1) Materials price variance.

(2) Materials quantity variance.

(3) Labor rate variance.

(4) Labor efficiency variance.

(5) Overhead spending variance.

(6) Volume variance.

b Prepare journal entries to assign manufacturing costs to the Work in Process Inventory account and to record cost variances for July. Use separate entries for (1) direct materials, (2) direct labor, and (3) overhead costs.

c Comment upon any significant problems or areas of cost savings revealed by your computation of cost variances. Also comment on any possible causal relationships between significant favorable and unfavorable cost variances.

Group B

Problem 25B-1
Budgeting labor
costs

Sun Valley Naturals manufactures a product which is first dry roasted and then packed for shipment to customers. The standard direct labor cost per pound of product in each process follows:

PROCESS	DIRECT LABOR HOURS PER POUND	STANDARD DIRECT LABOR COST PER HOUR
Dry roasting.....................................	.02	$8.00
Packing..	.01	6.20

The budget for November calls for the production of 200,000 pounds of product. The expected labor cost in the dry roasting department is expected to be 9% above standard for the month of November as a result of higher wage rates and inefficiencies in the scheduling of work. The expected cost of labor in the packing room is expected to be 7% below standard because of a new arrangement of equipment.

Instructions   Prepare a budget for direct labor costs for November. Use column headings as follows: Total, Dry Roasting, and Packing.

Problem 25B-2
Short budgeting
problem

Alcott Labs manufactures and sells a single product. In preparing the budget for the current year, the company's cost accountant has assembled the following information:

	UNITS	DOLLARS
Sales (budgeted)	300,000	$8,100,000
Finished goods inventory, Jan. 1 (actual)	60,000	720,000
Finished goods inventory, Dec. 31 (budgeted)......................	40,000	?
Cost of finished goods manufactured (budgeted manufacturing cost is $13 per unit)...............................	?	?

The company uses the first-in, first-out method of pricing its inventory of finished goods.

Instructions   Compute the following budgeted quantities or dollar amounts:

a   Planned production of finished goods (in units).

b   Cost of finished goods manufactured.

c   Finished goods inventory, Dec. 31. (Remember to use the first-in, first-out method in pricing the inventory.)

d   Cost of goods sold.

Problem 25B-3
Preparing a cash
budget

Kearny Distributors wants a projection of cash receipts and cash payments for the month of November. On November 28, a note will be payable in the amount of $92,700, including interest. The cash balance on November 1 is $21,600. Accounts payable to merchandise creditors at the end of October were $217,000.

The company's experience indicates that 70% of sales will be collected during the month of sale, 20% in the month following the sale, and 7% in the second month following the sale; 3% will be uncollectible. The company sells various products at an average price of $11 per unit. Selected sales figures are shown below:

	UNITS
September—actual	40,000
October—actual...	60,000
November—estimated	80,000
December—estimated	50,000
Total estimated for the current year	800,000

Because purchases are payable within 15 days, approximately 50% of the purchases in a given month are paid in the following month. The average cost of units purchased is $7 per unit. Inventories at the end of each month are maintained at a level of 2,000 units plus 10% of the number of units that will be sold in the following month. The inventory on October 1 amounted to 8,000 units.

Budgeted operating expenses for November are $180,000. Of this amount, $60,000 is considered fixed (including depreciation of $22,000). All operating expenses, other than depreciation, are paid in the month in which they are incurred.

The company expects to sell fully depreciated equipment in November for $9,500 cash.

Instructions Prepare a cash budget for the month of November, supported by schedules of cash collections on accounts receivable and cash payments for purchases of merchandise.

Problem 25B-4
Preparing and using a flexible budget

Four Flags is a retail department store. The following cost-volume relationships were used in developing a flexible budget for the company for the current year:

	YEARLY FIXED EXPENSES	VARIABLE EXPENSES PER SALES DOLLAR
Cost of merchandise sold..............................		$0.600
Selling and promotion expense	$140,000	0.082
Building occupancy expense...........................	124,000	0.022
Buying expense	100,000	0.040
Delivery expense	74,000	0.010
Credit and collection expense.........................	48,000	0.002
Administrative expense	354,000	0.003
Totals..	$840,000	$0.759

Management expected to attain a sales level of $8 million during the current year. At the end of the year the actual results achieved by the company were as follows:

Net sales	$7,000,000
Cost of goods sold	4,120,000
Selling and promotion expense	680,000
Building occupancy expense....................................	280,000
Buying expense	396,000
Delivery expense	122,000
Credit and collection expense..................................	60,000
Administrative expense	376,000

Instructions **a** Prepare a schedule comparing the actual results with flexible budget amounts developed for the actual sales volume of $7,000,000. Organize your schedule as a partial multiple-step income statement, ending with operating income. Include separate columns for (1) flexible budget amounts, (2) actual amounts, and (3) any amount over or (under) budget. Use the cost-volume relationships given in the problem to compute the flexible budget amounts.

b Write a statement evaluating the company's performance in relation to the plan reflected in the flexible budget.

Problem 25B-5
Using standard costs

LeatherWorks, Ltd., uses standard costs in a process cost system. At the end of the current month, the following information is prepared by the company's cost accountant:

	DIRECT MATERIALS	DIRECT LABOR	MANUFACTURING OVERHEAD
Actual costs incurred	$48,000	$41,250	$61,620
Standard costs	45,000	42,000	57,750
Materials price variance (favorable)	1,200		
Materials quantity variance (unfavorable) ...	4,200		
Labor rate variance (favorable).............		1,500	
Labor efficiency variance (unfavorable)		750	
Overhead spending variance (unfavorable)..			1,620
Overhead volume variance (unfavorable)....			2,250

The total standard cost per unit of finished product is $15. During the current month, 9,000 units were completed and transferred to the finished goods inventory and 8,800 units were sold. The inventory of work in process at the end of the month consists of 1,000 units which are 65% completed. There was no inventory in process at the beginning of the month.

Instructions

a Prepare journal entries to record all variances and the costs incurred (at standard) in the Work in Process account. Prepare separate compound entries for (1) direct materials, (2) direct labor, and (3) manufacturing overhead.

b Prepare journal entries to record (1) the transfer of units finished to the Finished Goods Inventory account and (2) the cost of goods sold (at standard) for the month.

c Assuming that the company operated at 90% of its normal capacity during the current month, what is the amount of the fixed manufacturing overhead per month?

Problem 25B-6
Computing and recording cost variances

The accountants for Polyglaze, Inc., have developed the following information regarding the standard cost and the actual cost of a product manufactured in June:

	STANDARD COST	ACTUAL COST
Direct materials:		
Standard: 10 ounces at $0.15 per ounce........................	$1.50	
Actual: 11 ounces at $0.16 per ounce		$1.76
Direct labor:		
Standard: .50 hour at $10.00 per hour	5.00	
Actual: .45 hour at $10.40 per hour.............................		4.68
Manufacturing overhead:		
Standard: $5,000 fixed cost and $5,000 variable cost for		
10,000 units normal monthly volume.........................	1.00	
Actual: $5,000 fixed cost and $4,600 variable cost for 8,000		
units actually produced in June		1.20
Total unit cost...	$7.50	$7.64

The normal volume is 10,000 units per month, but only 8,000 units were manufactured in June.

Instructions

a Compute the materials price variance and the materials quantity variance, indicating whether each is favorable or unfavorable. Prepare the journal entry to record the cost of direct materials used during June in the Work in Process account (at standard).

b Compute the labor rate variance and the labor efficiency variance, indicating whether each is favorable or unfavorable. Prepare the journal entry to record the cost of direct labor used during June in the Work in Process account (at standard).

c Compute the overhead spending variance and the overhead volume variance, indicating whether each is favorable or unfavorable. Prepare the journal entry to assign overhead cost to production in June.

BUSINESS DECISION CASE

Case 25-1
It's Not My Fault

Cabinets, Cabinets, Inc., is a large manufacturer of modular kitchen cabinets, sold primarily to builders and developers. The company uses standard costs in a responsibility accounting system. Standard production costs have been developed for each type of cabinet; these costs, and any cost variances, are charged to the production department. A budget also has been developed for the sales department. The sales department is credited with the gross profit on sales (measured at standard costs) and is charged with selling expenses and any variations between budgeted and actual selling expenses.

In early April, the manager of the sales department asked the production department to fill a "rush" order of kitchen cabinets for a tract of 120 homes. The sales manager stated that the entire order must be completed by May 31. The manager of the production department argued that an order of this size would take 12 weeks to produce. The sales manager answered, "The customer needs it on May 31, or we don't get the business. Do you want to be responsible for our losing a customer who makes orders of this size?"

Of course, the production manager did not want to take that responsibility. Therefore, he gave in and processed the rush order by having production personnel work overtime through April and May. As a result of the overtime, the performance reports for the production department in those months showed large, unfavorable labor rate variances. The production manager, who in the past had prided himself on "coming in under budget" now has very ill feelings toward the sales manager. He also has stated that the production department will never again accept a "rush" order.

Instructions **a** Identify any problem which you see in the company's standard cost system or in the manner in which cost variances are assigned to the responsible managers.

b Make recommendations for changing the cost accounting system to reduce or eliminate any problems which you have identified.

ANSWERS TO SELF-TEST QUESTIONS

1 a, b, and **c** **2 b** (700,000 units × $10 per unit × 80%) + ($100,000 × 50%) = $610,000 **3 d** **4 c** **5 d**

Relevant Information, Incremental Analysis, and Capital Budgeting

In this chapter, we discuss several analytical techniques which aid managers in making a variety of business decisions. First, we explain the nature of "relevant" information and show how incremental analysis is used to identify and evaluate this information. Emphasis is given to the relevance of opportunity costs and to the irrelevance of sunk costs.

Our second major topic is capital budgeting—the process of planning and evaluating proposals for investments in plant assets. We illustrate and explain the widely used capital budgeting techniques of payback period, return on average investment, and discounting future cash flows.

We also emphasize the need for managers to be aware of nonfinancial considerations, of the long-run implications of their actions, and of the possible existence of additional and more advantageous courses of action.

After studying this chapter you should be able to meet these Learning Objectives:

1 Identify that financial information which is relevant to a particular business decision.

2 Use incremental analysis to evaluate alternative courses of action.

3 Discuss the relevance of opportunity costs, sunk costs, and out-of-pocket costs in making business decisions.

4 Determine the effect upon operating income of discontinuing a product line.

5 Explore a decision: be aware of the nonfinancial considerations and creatively search for a better course of action.

6 Evaluate capital budgeting proposals using (a) the payback period, (b) return on average investment, and (c) discounted future cash flows.

THE CONCEPT OF RELEVANT INFORMATION

Objective 1
Identify that financial information which is relevant to a particular business decision.

Many types of information may be relevant to a given business decision. For example, information as to the number of jobs to be created, or the expected effect of a decision upon the environment or upon public opinion may be quite relevant. Our discussion, however, will be limited to relevant *financial* information—namely, costs and revenue.

All business decisions involve a choice among alternative courses of action. The only information relevant to a decision is that information *which varies among the alternative courses of action being considered.* Costs, revenue, or other factors which *do not vary* among alternative courses of action *are not relevant* to the decision.

To illustrate the concept of relevant information, assume that the sawmill of Sierra Lumber is closed because of a labor strike expected to last for several months. During the strike, Sierra Lumber is incurring costs at the mill of $7,500 per week. (These costs include depreciation, interest expense, and salaries to nonstriking employees.) Assume also that a film company has offered to rent the mill for one week at a price of $5,000 in order to shoot scenes for a new James Bond movie. If the mill is rented to the company, Sierra's management estimates that clean-up costs will amount to approximately $500 after shooting is completed. Based solely upon this information, would it be profitable to rent the closed sawmill to the film company?

If the mill is rented to the film company, the profitability of the mill during that week may be measured as follows:

Revenue..		$ 5,000
Costs and expenses:		
Weekly sawmill expenses	$7,500	
Clean-up cost	500	8,000
Operating income (loss)		$(3,000)

However, not all the information in this income statement is *relevant* to the decision at hand. The $7,500 in weekly sawmill expenses will continue *whether or not* the mill is rented to the film company.

Objective 2
Use incremental analysis to evaluate alternative courses of action.

The relevant factors in this decision are the *differences* between the costs incurred and revenue earned under the alternative courses of action (renting or not renting.) These differences are often called the *incremental* costs and revenue. An incremental analysis of the Sierra Lumber decision is shown as follows:

	REJECT OFFER	ACCEPT OFFER	INCREMENTAL ANALYSIS
Revenue	$ 0	$ 5,000	$5,000
Costs and expenses:			
Weekly sawmill expenses	(7,500)	(7,500)	
Estimated clean-up costs	0	(500)	(500)
Operating income (loss)	$(7,500)	$(3,000)	$4,500

The incremental analysis shows that accepting the film company's offer results in $5,000 of incremental revenue, but only $500 in incremental costs. Thus, renting the sawmill to the company will benefit Sierra by reducing its operating loss for the week by $4,500.

Accepting Special Orders

A more commonplace example of the need to identify relevant information is the decision of whether or not to accept an order for an additional volume of business at special terms.

To illustrate, assume that one product of Zing Golf Products is golf balls. The company has the capacity to produce 1 million golf balls per month, but actually manufactures only 400,000 balls per month, as this is all that it is able to sell. The balls normally sell for *$2.50* apiece; the cost of manufacturing 400,000 balls in a month amounts to $480,000, or *$1.20* per ball, as shown below:

Manufacturing costs:	
Variable ($0.40 per ball × 400,000 balls)	$160,000
Fixed	320,000
Total cost of manufacturing 400,000 balls per month	$480,000
Average manufacturing cost per ball ($480,000 ÷ 400,000 balls)	$1.20

Now assume that Zing Golf Products receives an offer from a foreign company to purchase 300,000 "private label" golf balls. These balls will be imprinted with the name of the foreign company, not with Zing's name. In fact, golfers who purchase the balls will never know that they were manufactured by Zing. These balls will be sold only in the foreign country, and will not affect Zing's regular sales to its own customers. However, the foreign country offers to pay Zing only *$300,000* (or $1 per ball) for this special order. Would it be profitable for Zing to accept this order?

At first glance, it appears unprofitable for Zing to accept this special order. Not only is the sales price of $1 per ball much less than the regular sales price, it is even less than Zing's $1.20 average per-unit cost of manufacturing golf balls. Let us look, however, at the incremental revenue and manufacturing costs that should result from accepting this special order:

	PRODUCTION LEVEL		
	NORMAL (400,000 BALLS)	WITH SPECIAL ORDER (700,000 BALLS)	INCREMENTAL ANALYSIS
Sales:			
Regular sales @ $2.50	$1,000,000	$1,000,000	$ –0–
Special order		300,000	300,000
Manufacturing costs:			
Variable ($0.40 per ball)	(160,000)	(280,000)	(120,000)
Fixed manufacturing costs per month	(320,000)	(320,000)	–0–
Gross profit on golf ball sales	$ 520,000	$ 700,000	$ 180,000

A special order is profitable if incremental revenue exceeds incremental costs

This analysis shows that accepting the special order will generate incremental revenue of $300,000, and incremental costs of only $120,000. There fore, accepting the special order will *increase* Zing's gross profit on golf ball sales *by $180,000.*

The relevant factors in this type of decision are the incremental revenue that will be earned and the additional (incremental) costs that will be incurred by accepting the special order. The only incremental costs of filling the special order are the related *variable* manufacturing costs; accepting the order will *not* increase fixed manufacturing costs. Thus, the $1.20 "average manufacturing cost," which includes fixed costs per unit, is *not relevant* to the decision.[1]

In evaluating the merits of a special order such as the one received by Zing, managers should consider the effect that filling the order might have upon the company's regular sales volume and sales prices. Obviously, it would not be wise for Zing to sell golf balls at $1 apiece to a domestic company which might then try to sell the balls to Zing's regular customers for less than Zing's regular sales price ($2.50 per ball). Management should also consider how Zing's large regular customers might react if "word gets out" about Zing accepting this special order. Might these customers also demand the $1 per-ball price?

In summary, incremental analysis is a useful tool for evaluating the effects of expected short-term changes in revenue and in costs. Managers should always be alert, however, to the long-run implications of their actions.

Make or Buy Decisions

In many manufacturing situations, a company must decide whether (1) to produce a certain component part required in the assembly of its finished products or (2) to buy the component part from outside suppliers. If the company is currently producing a component part which could be purchased at a lower cost from outsiders, profits *may* be increased by a decision to buy the part and utilize the company's own manufacturing resources for other purposes.

For example, if a company can buy for $5 per unit a part which costs the company $6 per unit to produce, the choice seems to be clearly in favor of buying. But the astute reader will quickly raise the question, "What is included in the cost of $6 per unit?" Assume that the $6 unit cost of producing a normal required volume of 10,000 units per month was determined as follows:

Manufacturing costs:	
Direct materials	$ 8,000
Direct labor	12,500
Variable overhead	10,000
Fixed overhead per month	29,500
Total cost of manufacturing 10,000 units per month	$60,000
Average manufacturing cost per unit ($60,000 ÷ 10,000 units)	$6

A review of operations indicates that if the production of this part were

---

[1] In our discussion, we evaluate only the *profitability* of accepting this order. Some countries have "antidumping" laws that legally prohibit a foreign company from selling its products in that country at a price below the average "full" manufacturing cost per unit. Zing should, of course, consider the legal as well as economic implications of accepting this order.

discontinued, all the cost of direct materials and direct labor plus $9,000 of variable overhead would be eliminated. In addition, $2,500 of the fixed overhead would be eliminated. These, then, are the *relevant costs* in producing the 10,000 units of the component part, and we can summarize them as follows:

■
Is it cheaper to
make or to buy?

	MAKE THE PART	BUY THE PART	INCREMENTAL ANALYSIS
Manufacturing costs for 10,000 units:			
Direct materials	$ 8,000		$ 8,000
Direct labor	12,500		12,500
Variable overhead	10,000	$ 1,000	9,000
Fixed overhead	29,500	27,000	2,500
Purchase price of part, $5 per unit		50,000	(50,000)
Total cost to acquire part	$60,000	$78,000	$(18,000)

Our analysis shows that making the part will cost $60,000 per month, while buying the part will cost $78,000. Thus, the company will save $18,000 per month by continuing to make the part.

In our example, we assumed that only part ($9,000) of the variable overhead incurred in producing the part would be eliminated if the part were purchased. We also assumed that $2,500 of the fixed overhead could be eliminated if the part were purchased. The purpose of these assumptions was to show that not all variable costs are incremental, and that some fixed costs may be incremental in a given situation.

Opportunity Costs

Objective 3
Discuss the relevance of opportunity costs, sunk costs, and out-of-pocket costs in making business decisions.

At this stage of our discussion, it is appropriate to introduce the topic of opportunity costs. An *opportunity cost* is the benefit which could have been obtained *by following another course of action.* For example, assume that you pass up a summer job which pays $2,400 in order to attend summer school. The $2,400 may be viewed as an opportunity cost of attending summer school.

Opportunity costs are *not recorded* in the accounting records, but they are an important factor in many business decisions. Ignoring opportunity costs is a common source of error in cost analyses. In our preceding example, we determined that the company could save $18,000 per month by continuing to manufacture a particular part, rather than buying it from an outside supplier. Assume, however, that the production facilities used to make the part could instead be used to manufacture a product which would increase the company's profitability by $25,000 per month. Obviously, the company should not forgo a $25,000 profit in order to save $18,000. When this $25,000 *opportunity cost* is considered, it becomes evident that the company should buy the part and use its productive facilities to produce the more profitable product.

Sunk Costs versus Out-of-Pocket Costs

The only costs relevant to a decision are those costs which vary among the alternative courses of action being considered. A *sunk cost* is one which has *already been incurred* by past actions. Sunk costs are *not relevant* to decisions because they *cannot be changed* regardless of what decision is made. The term *out-of-pocket cost* is often used to describe costs which have *not yet* been incurred and which *may vary* among the alternative courses of action. Out-of-pocket costs, therefore, are relevant in making decisions.

Scrap or Rebuild Defective Units

To illustrate the irrelevance of sunk costs, assume that 500 television sets which cost $80,000 to manufacture are found to be defective and management must decide what to do with them. These sets may be sold "as is" for $30,000, or they can be rebuilt and placed in good condition at an additional out-of-pocket cost of $60,000. If the sets are rebuilt, they can be sold for the regular price of $100,000. Should the sets be sold "as is" or rebuilt?

Regardless of whether the sets are sold or rebuilt, the $80,000 sunk cost has already been incurred. The relevant considerations in the decision to sell the sets in their present condition or to rebuild are the *incremental revenue* and the *incremental cost.* By rebuilding the sets, the company will realize $70,000 more revenue than if the sets are sold "as is." The incremental cost necessary to obtain this incremental revenue is the $60,000 cost of rebuilding the sets. Thus, the company will be $10,000 better off ($70,000–$60,000) if it rebuilds the sets.

Whether to Discontinue an Unprofitable Product Line

Objective 4
Determine the effect upon operating income of discontinuing a product line.

Management often must decide whether a company's overall profitability can be improved by discontinuing one or more product lines. The concepts of incremental analysis and of opportunity costs play important roles in such decisions.

To illustrate, assume that Auto Sound Co. manufactures three products: an economy model car radio, a deluxe car radio that includes a tape deck, and speakers for automobile sound systems. In recent years, increased competition has forced the company to reduce the sales price of its deluxe radios to the point that this product line now has a negative segment margin. A partial income statement for the current month, segmented by product lines, appears below:

AUTO SOUND CO.
Partial Income Statement, Segmented by Product Line
For the Current Month

Should the deluxe radio be discontinued?

| | AUTO SOUND CO. | PRODUCTS | | |
		ECONOMY RADIOS	DELUXE RADIOS	SPEAKERS
Sales	$600,000	$300,000	$100,000	$200,000
Variable costs	320,000	170,000	70,000	80,000
Contribution margins	$280,000	$130,000	$ 30,000	$120,000
Fixed costs traceable to product lines	100,000	30,000	40,000	30,000
Product segment margins	$180,000	$100,000	$(10,000)	$ 90,000
Common fixed costs	80,000			
Income from operations	$100,000			

Management is considering whether or not to discontinue deluxe radios. As discussed in Chapter 24, the revenue, variable costs, and fixed costs traceable to a business segment are likely to disappear if that segment is discontinued. Thus, discontinuing the deluxe radio should *eliminate* the $10,000 negative monthly segment margin of that product line. At first glance, we might assume that Auto Sound's monthly operating income should then increase by this amount. However, several other factors must be considered. Two such factors are:

1 How will discontinuing the sale of deluxe radios affect sales of the company's *other products?*

2 What *alternative use* might be made of the production facilities now used in manufacturing deluxe radios?

■ **Competing Products and Complementary Products** Many companies offer customers several products that compete directly with one another. For example, Auto Sound's economy model and deluxe model radios are competing products—most customers will buy one or the other, but not both. If the deluxe radio is discontinued, it is logical to expect some increase in the sales of economy radios. Some customers, no longer able to buy the deluxe model, will instead purchase the economy model. Assume that management estimates that sales of the economy radio will *increase by 5%* if the deluxe radio is discontinued.

Companies often also sell complementary products. Complementary products are those for which sales of one may contribute to sales of the other. Assume, for example, that many buyers of Auto Sound Co.'s deluxe radios also buy a set of the company's speakers. Therefore, discontinuing the sale of deluxe radios can be expected to reduce sales of speakers. Management estimates that speaker sales will *decline by 20%* if the deluxe radio is discontinued.

■ **Incremental Analysis** To illustrate the effects of expected changes in the sales of other products, we will temporarily assume that no alternative use will be made of the facilities now used in manufacturing deluxe radios. In this case, an incremental analysis of the expected effects of discontinuing the deluxe radio product line is shown below:

Increases in monthly operating income expected from discontinuing the deluxe radio product line:

Elimination of negative monthly segment margin of deluxe radio product line	$10,000
Additional contribution margin from expected 5% increase in sales of	
economy radios ($130,000 × 5%)	6,500
Total expected increases in operating income	$16,500

Decreases in monthly operating income expected from discontinuing deluxe radio product line:

Decrease in contribution margin from expected 20% decrease in speaker sales	
($120,000 × 20%)	(24,000)
Estimated net increase (decrease) in monthly operating income if deluxe radio product line	
is discontinued	$(7,500)

This analysis indicates that although the deluxe radio line has a negative segment margin, discontinuing this product would cause the company's monthly operating income to *decrease* by $7,500. The reason that operating income would decline is not the disappearance of the revenue and costs relating to the deluxe radio segment of the business, but rather the expected loss in contribution margin from sales of speakers—a highly profitable complementary product.

The loss in contribution margin from speaker sales is an *opportunity cost* of discontinuing the deluxe radio line. However, continuing to produce the deluxe radios also may involve an opportunity cost—namely the segment margin of a more profitable product line that might be produced in place of deluxe radios.

■ **Alternative Use of the Facilities**   Let us now assume that if the deluxe radio line is discontinued Auto Sound Co. will use the related production facilities to manufacture car phones. Management estimates that the manufacture and sale of car phones will produce a positive segment margin of $50,000 per month. Sales of car phones are not expected to have any effect upon sales of economy radios or speakers. Therefore, the effects of discontinuing the deluxe radios upon these two product lines remains the same as in our preceding analysis. An incremental analysis of manufacturing car phones instead of deluxe car radios follows:

Increases in monthly operating income expected from manufacturing
  car phones instead of deluxe radios:

Elimination of negative monthly segment margin of deluxe radio product line ...	$10,000
Expected monthly segment margin from new car phone product line	50,000
Additional contribution margin from expected 5% increase in sales of economy radios ($130,000 × 5%)	6,500
Total expected increases in operating income	$66,500

Decreases in monthly operating income expected from manufacturing
  car phones instead of deluxe radios:

Decrease in contribution margin from expected 20% decline in speaker sales ($120,000 × 20%)	(24,000)
Estimated net increase in operating income if deluxe radio product line is discontinued	$42,500

This analysis indicates that operating income will *increase* by $42,500 per month if the company uses its production facilities to manufacture car phones instead of deluxe radios.

Objective 5
Explore a decision: be aware of the nonfinancial considerations, and creatively search for a better course of action.

■ **Other Factors to Be Considered**   There are, of course, other factors to consider in a decision of whether to discontinue a product line. Perhaps a company wants to avoid laying-off employees, especially if these workers may be needed in the near future to produce new products. Perhaps a company wants to maintain a reputation for offering its customers a "full line" of products, or "state-of-the-art" products, even if it cannot earn a profit from every product line. Perhaps an "unprofitable" product line is an effective "loss leader," which attracts customers who also buy the company's profitable products. (Auto Sound's deluxe radio is an effective "loss leader," because sales of this product generate enough contribution margin from additional sales of speakers to cover the losses of the deluxe radio segment.)

■ **Looking for Better Alternatives** Incremental analysis is an excellent tool for evaluating alternative courses of action. However, managers should not automatically follow the first course of action that holds a promise of increased profitability. Rather, managers and accountants should always be alert to the possibility of even more satisfactory alternatives. Often, a careful review of the incremental analysis of one possible decision will offer clues to additional and more profitable alternatives.

Consider, for example, our incremental analysis on the preceding page. The principal benefit to be derived from discontinuing the deluxe radio product line is that the company's production facilities can be used more profitably in manufacturing car phones. The one drawback in discontinuing the deluxe radios is the expected loss in contribution margin from a decline in speaker sales. These facts suggest an alternative course of action: perhaps Auto Sound should continue to sell deluxe radios, but should *buy* these radios from an outside supplier *instead of manufacturing them.* The company could then use its production facilities to manufacture car phones, while continuing to sell deluxe radios and speakers at the current sales level. The effects of this alternative also may be evaluated through the technique of incremental analysis.

CAPITAL BUDGETING

Objective 6
Evaluate capital budgeting proposals using (a) the payback period, (b) return on average investment, and (c) discounted future cash flows.

In terms of dollar amounts, some of the most significant decisions made by management involve expenditures to acquire plant assets. The process of planning and evaluating proposals for investment in plant assets is called *capital budgeting.* Capital budgeting decisions are complicated by the fact that the decision must be made from estimates of future operating results, which by their nature involve a considerable degree of uncertainty. Yet these decisions are crucial to the long-run financial health of a business enterprise. Not only are large amounts of money committed for long periods of time, but many capital budgeting decisions are difficult or impossible to reverse once the funds have been committed and the project has begun. Thus, companies may benefit from good capital budgeting decisions and suffer from poor ones for many years.

Many nonfinancial factors are considered in making capital budgeting decisions. For example, many companies give high priority to creating new jobs and avoiding layoffs. However, it is also essential that investments in plant assets earn a satisfactory return on the funds invested. Without this return, investors will not be willing to make funds available to finance the project and the company will not be able to generate sufficient funds for future investment projects.

Capital budgeting is a broad field, involving many sophisticated techniques for evaluating the financial and nonfinancial considerations. We shall limit our discussion in this area to three of the most common techniques of evaluating investment opportunities: payback period, return on average investment, and discounted cash flow analysis.

To illustrate these techniques, let us assume that Tanner Corporation is considering several alternative investments, including the purchase of equipment to produce a new product. The equipment costs $450,000 has a 10-year service life, and an estimated salvage value of $50,000. Tanner Corporation estimates that production and sale of the new product will increase the company's net income by $50,000 per year, computed as follows:

Estimated sales of new product.....................................		*$400,000*
Deduct estimated expenses:		
Depreciation on new equipment [($450,000 – $50,000) ÷ 10 years]..	*$ 40,000*	
Manufacturing costs other than depreciation	*220,000*	
Additional selling and general expenses	*60,000*	*320,000*
Estimated increase in before-tax income		*$ 80,000*
Less: Additional income taxes (37½%)		*30,000*
Estimated increase in net income		*$ 50,000*

Most capital budgeting techniques involve analysis of the estimated annual net cash flows pertaining to the investment. Annual net cash flow is the excess of cash receipts over cash payments in a given year. In our example, assume that all revenue is received in cash and all expenses other than depreciation are paid in cash. Tanner Corporation should expect an annual ***net cash flow of $90,000*** from sales of the new product ($400,000 – $220,000 – $60,000 – $30,000). Note that annual net cash flow exceeds estimated net income ($50,000) by the amount of the depreciation expense ($40,000). This is because none of the cash received from revenue is paid out for depreciation expense. (Other differences which may exist between net income and net cash flow were discussed in Chapter 19.)

Payback Period

The ***payback period*** is the length of time necessary to recover the entire cost of an investment from the resulting annual net cash flow. In our example, the payback period is computed as follows:

$$\frac{\text{Amount to be invested}}{\text{Estimated annual net cash flow}} = \frac{\$450,000}{\$90,000} = 5 \text{ years}$$

In selecting among alternative investment opportunities, a short payback period is considered desirable because the sooner the amount of the investment is recovered, the sooner the funds may be put to other use. A short payback period also reduces the risk that changes in economic conditions will prevent full recovery of the investment. Before an investment can be considered profitable, the life of the investment must exceed the payback period. However, the payback period ignores the total life and, therefore, the total profitability of the investment. For this reason, the payback period should never be the only factor considered in a major capital budgeting decision.

Return on Average Investment

The ***rate of return on average investment*** is the average annual net income from an investment expressed as a percentage of the ***average*** amount invested. Tanner Corporation will have to invest $450,000 in the new equipment, but each year depreciation will reduce the carrying value of this asset by $40,000. Since the annual cash flow will exceed net income by this amount, we may view depreciation expense as providing for the recovery of the amount originally invested. Thus, the amount invested in the equipment at any given time is represented by the carrying value (cost less accumulated depreciation) of the asset.

When straight-line depreciation is used, the carrying value of an asset decreases uniformly over the asset's life. Thus, the average carrying value is equal to an amount halfway between the asset's original cost and its salvage value. (When the expected salvage value is zero, the average investment is simply one-half of the original investment.) Mathematically, the average amount invested over the life of an asset may be determined as follows:

$$\text{Average investment} = \frac{\text{Original cost} + \text{Salvage value}}{2}$$

Thus, Tanner Corporation will have an average investment in the new equipment of ($450,000 + $50,000) ÷ 2, or $250,000. We may compute the expected rate of return on this average investment as follows:

$$\frac{\text{Average estimated net income}}{\text{Average investment}} = \frac{\$50,000}{\$250,000} = 20\%$$

In deciding whether 20% is a satisfactory rate of return, Tanner Corporation should consider such factors as the rate of return available from alternative investment opportunities, the risk involved in actually realizing the expected rate of return, the corporation's cost of capital, and the nonfinancial factors relating to the investment. In comparing alternative investment opportunities, management usually prefers the investment with the *lowest risk, highest rate of return,* and *shortest payback period.* Of course, the same investment is seldom superior to all others in every respect. Thus, managers must consider many subjective factors in making their decisions.

A weakness in the concept of return on average investment is the failure to consider the *timing* of the future cash flows. Computing the average annual net income, for example, ignores the question of whether the cash receipts will occur early or late in the life of the investment. Also, computing the average investment in the equipment fails to consider whether the purchase price of the equipment must be paid in advance or in installments stretching over a period of years. A technique which does take into account the timing of cash flows is called *discounting* future cash flows.

Discounting Future Cash Flows

As explained in Chapter 16, the present value of a future cash flow is the amount that a knowledgeable investor would pay today for the right to receive that future amount. The exact amount of the present value depends upon (1) the amount of the future payment, (2) the length of time until the future amount will be received, and (3) the rate of return required by the investor. *Discounting* is the process of determining the present value of cash flows.

The use of present value tables to discount future cash flows was demonstrated in Appendix A, entitled Applications of Present Value, at the end of Chapter 16. (Readers who are not familiar with the concept of present value and with the use of present value tables should review that appendix, beginning on page 626, before continuing with this chapter.) The two present value tables presented in the appendix are repeated on pages 1051 and 1052 for your convenience.

TABLE 1

Present Values of $1 Due in *n* Periods*

NUMBER OF PERIODS (*n*)	DISCOUNT RATE								
	1%	1½%	5%	6%	8%	10%	12%	15%	20%
1	.990	.985	.952	.943	.926	.909	.893	.870	.833
2	.980	.971	.907	.890	.857	.826	.797	.756	.694
3	.971	.956	.864	.840	.794	.751	.712	.658	.579
4	.961	.942	.823	.792	.735	.683	.636	.572	.482
5	.951	.928	.784	.747	.681	.621	.567	.497	.402
6	.942	.915	.746	.705	.630	.564	.507	.432	.335
7	.933	.901	.711	.665	.583	.513	.452	.376	.279
8	.923	.888	.677	.627	.540	.467	.404	.327	.233
9	.914	.875	.645	.592	.510	.424	.361	.284	.194
10	.905	.862	.614	.558	.463	.386	.322	.247	.162
20	.820	.742	.377	.312	.215	.149	.104	.061	.026
24	.788	.700	.310	.247	.158	.102	.066	.035	.013
36	.699	.585	.173	.123	.063	.032	.017	.007	.001

* The present value of $1 is computed by the formula $p = 1/(1 + i)^n$, where p is the present value of $1, i is the discount rate, and n is the number of periods until the future cash flow will occur. Amounts in this table have been rounded to three decimal places and are shown for a limited number of periods and discount rates. Many calculators are programmed to use this formula and can compute present values when the future amount is entered along with values for i and n.

Table 1 shows the present value of a single lump-sum payment of $1 to be received *n* periods (years) in the future. *Table 2* shows the present value of a $1 annuity—that is, $1 to be received each year for *n* consecutive years. For illustrative purposes, both tables have been kept short. They include only selected discount rates and extend for a limited number of periods. However, the tables contain the appropriate rates and periods for all problem material in this chapter.

The discount rate may be viewed as the investor's required rate of return. The present value of the future cash flows is the maximum amount that the investor may pay for the investment and still expect to earn the required rate of return. Therefore, an investment is considered desirable when its cost is less than the present value of the expected future cash flows. Conversely, an investment is undesirable when its cost is greater than the present value of expected future cash flows.

The higher the discount rate being used, the lower will be the resulting present value. Therefore the investor will be interested in the investment only at a lower price. The "appropriate" discount rate for determining the present value of a specific investment depends upon the nature of that investment, the alternative investment opportunities available, and the investor's cost of capital.

Let us now apply the concept of discounting cash flows to our continuing

TABLE 2

Present Values of $1 to Be Received Periodically for *n* Periods

NUMBER OF PERIODS (*n*)	1%	1½%	5%	6%	8%	10%	12%	15%	20%
1	0.990	0.985	0.952	0.943	0.926	0.909	0.893	0.870	0.833
2	1.970	1.956	1.859	1.833	1.783	1.736	1.690	1.626	1.528
3	2.941	2.912	2.723	2.673	2.577	2.487	2.402	2.283	2.106
4	3.902	3.854	3.546	3.465	3.312	3.170	3.037	2.855	2.589
5	4.853	4.783	4.329	4.212	3.993	3.791	3.605	3.352	2.991
6	5.795	5.697	5.076	4.917	4.623	4.355	4.111	3.784	3.326
7	6.728	6.598	5.786	5.582	5.206	4.868	4.564	4.160	3.605
8	7.652	7.486	6.463	6.210	5.747	5.335	4.968	4.487	3.837
9	8.566	8.361	7.108	6.802	6.247	5.759	5.328	4.772	4.031
10	9.471	9.222	7.722	7.360	6.710	6.145	5.650	5.019	4.192
20	18.046	17.169	12.462	11.470	9.818	8.514	7.469	6.259	4.870
24	21.243	20.030	13.799	12.550	10.529	8.985	7.784	6.434	4.937
36	30.108	27.661	16.547	14.621	11.717	9.677	8.192	6.623	4.993

example of the Tanner Corporation. We shall assume that Tanner Corporation requires a 15% annual rate of return on investments in new plant assets. The $450,000 investment in equipment is expected to produce annual net cash flows of $90,000 for 10 years. Table 2 shows that the present value of $1 to be received annually for 10 years, discounted at an annual rate of 15%, is 5.019. Therefore, the present value of $90,000 received annually for 10 years is $90,000 × 5.019 or $451,710.

In addition to the annual cash flows, Tanner Corporation expects to receive $50,000 in salvage value for the equipment at the end of the tenth year. Referring to **Table 1** on page 1051, we see that the present value of $1 due in 10 years, discounted at 15% per year, is .247. Thus, the present value of $50,000 to be received 10 years hence is $50,000 × .247, or $12,350. We may now analyze the proposal to invest in the equipment as follows:

Present value of expected annual cash flows ($90,000 × 5.019)	*$451,710*
Present value of proceeds from disposal of equipment ($50,000 × .247)	*12,350*
Total present value of future cash flows	*$464,060*
Amount to be invested (payable in advance)	*450,000*
Net present value of proposed investment	*$ 14,060*

This analysis indicates that the present value of the expected net cash flows from the investment, discounted at an annual rate of 15%, amounts to $464,060. This is the maximum amount which Tanner Corporation could afford to invest in the project and still expect to earn the required 15% annual rate of return. Since the actual cost of the investment is only $450,000, Tanner Corporation can expect to earn more than 15%.

The *net present value* of the proposal is the difference between the total present value of the net cash flows and the cost of the investment. When the net present value is equal to zero, the investment provides a rate of return exactly equal to the rate used in discounting the cash flows. A *positive* net present value means that the investment provides a rate of return *greater than the discount rate;* a *negative* net present value means that the investment yields a return of *less* than the discount rate. Since the discount rate is usually the minimum rate of return required by the investor, proposals with a positive net present value are considered acceptable and those with a negative net present value are viewed as unacceptable.

Replacement of Old Equipment

A problem often facing management is whether it should buy new and more efficient equipment or whether it should continue to use existing equipment. Assume, for example, that the Ardmore Company is meeting increasing competition in the sale of product Q. The sales manager believes the source of the trouble is that competitors have installed more efficient equipment, which has enabled them to reduce prices. The issue raised therefore is whether Ardmore Company should: (1) buy new equipment at a cost of $120,000, or (2) continue using its present equipment. We will make the simplifying assumption that both the new equipment and present equipment have a remaining useful life of five years and neither will have any residual value. The new equipment will produce substantial savings in direct labor, direct materials, and manufacturing overhead costs. The company does not believe the use of new equipment will have any effect on sales volume, so the decision rests entirely on whether cost savings are possible.

The old equipment has a book value of $100,000 but can be sold for only $20,000 if it is replaced. At first glance, the resulting $80,000 loss on disposal appears to be a good reason for not replacing the old equipment. However, the cost of the old equipment is a *sunk cost* and is not relevant to the decision. If the old machinery is sold, its book value contributes to the amount of the loss; if the old machinery is retained, its book value will be recognized as expense through future charges to depreciation. Thus, this cost cannot be avoided by Ardmore Company regardless of which decision is made. From a present value standpoint, there is some benefit to recognizing this sunk cost as a loss in the current period inasmuch as the related tax reduction will occur this year rather than over the remaining life of the equipment.

In deciding whether to replace the old equipment, Ardmore Company should determine the *present value of the incremental net cash flows* resulting from replacement of the old machinery. This present value may then be compared with the cost of the new equipment to determine whether the investment will provide the required rate of return. To compute the incremental annual net cash flow from replacing the old equipment, management must consider both the annual cash savings in manufacturing costs and the difference in annual income taxes. Income taxes will differ under the alternative courses of action because of differences in (1) variable manufacturing costs and (2) annual depreciation expense.

Let us assume that the new machinery will result in a $34,000 annual cash savings in variable manufacturing costs. However, annual depreciation on the new equipment will be $24,000 ($120,000 ÷ 5 years), whereas annual depreciation on the old equipment is $20,000 ($100,000 ÷ 5 years). This $4,000 increase in depreciation expense means that purchase of the new equipment will *increase* taxable income by $30,000 ($34,000 cost savings less $4,000 additional depreciation). Assuming a tax rate of 40%, purchase of the new equipment will increase annual income tax expense by $12,000 ($30,000 × 40%). The incremental annual net cash flow from owning the new machinery, therefore, amounts to $22,000 ($34,000 cost savings less $12,000 additional income tax expense).

We shall assume that Ardmore Company requires a 12% return on investments in plant assets. Referring to the annuity table on page 1052, we see that the present value of $1 received annually for five years is 3.605. Therefore, $22,000 received annually for five years, discounted at an annual rate of 12%, has a present value of $79,310 ($22,000 × 3.605). In addition to the present value of the annual net cash flows, however, we must consider two other factors: (1) the proceeds from sale of the old equipment and (2) the tax savings resulting from the loss on disposal.

The $20,000 proceeds from sale of the old equipment will be received immediately and, therefore, have a present value of $20,000. The $80,000 loss on disposal results in a $32,000 reduction in income taxes payable at the end of the first year ($80,000 × 40%). The present value of $32,000 one year hence discounted at 12% is $28,576 ($32,000 × .893), as determined from a present value table.

We may now determine the net present value of the proposal to replace the old equipment with new equipment as follows:

Present value of incremental annual cash flows	
($22,000 × 3.605)	*$ 79,310*
Present value of proceeds from sale of old equipment	*20,000*
Present value of tax savings from loss on disposal	
($32,000 × .893)	*28,576*
Total present value	*$127,886*
Amount to be invested	*120,000*
Net present value	*$ 7,886*

Since the total present value of all future cash flows from acquiring the new equipment exceeds the cost of the investment, Ardmore Company should replace the old equipment with new.

Concluding Comments

We have merely scratched the surface in discussing the possible kinds of analyses that might be prepared in making decisions. The brief treatment in this chapter, however, has been sufficient to establish the basic principles that lie behind such analyses. The most profitable course of action is determined by studying the costs and revenue that are *incremental* to the particular alternatives under consideration. The relevant information generally involves making *estimates* about the future. As a result, such information is subject to some degree of error. Of course it is important to remember that many nonfinancial factors may be brought into the decision picture after the quantitative analysis has been made.

End-of-Chapter Review

CONCEPTS INTRODUCED OR EMPHASIZED IN CHAPTER 26

Major concepts discussed in this chapter include:

■ The characteristics of the financial information relevant to a particular decision.

■ Incremental analysis as a technique for identifying and evaluating relevant financial information.

■ The nature and relevance (or irrelevance) of opportunity costs, sunk costs, and out-of-pocket costs.

■ Factors to consider in decisions on whether or not to discontinue a product line.

■ The importance in business decisions of nonfinancial factors, of long-run implications, and of the possible existence of more advantageous courses of action.

■ The mechanics, rationale, and limitations of three techniques widely used in evaluating capital budgeting proposals: (1) payback period, (2) return on average investment, and (3) discounting future cash flows.

This book has introduced you to the basic concepts of financial accounting, managerial accounting, and, to a lesser extent, income taxes. We are confident that you will find this background useful throughout your career. However, we also recommend that you continue your study of accounting with additional courses. We particularly recommend the intermediate accounting course, a course in cost accounting, and the first course in income taxes.

KEY TERMS INTRODUCED OR EMPHASIZED IN CHAPTER 26

Capital budgeting   The process of planning and evaluating proposals for investments in plant assets.

Discount rate   The required rate of return used by an investor to discount future cash flows to their present value.

Discounted cash flows   The present value of expected future cash flows.

Incremental (or differential) cost   The difference between the total costs of alternative courses of action.

Incremental (or differential) revenue   The difference between the revenue amounts provided by alternative courses of action.

Net present value   The excess of the present value of the net cash flows expected from an investment over the amount to be invested. Net present value is one method of ranking alternative investment opportunities.

Opportunity cost The benefit foregone by not pursuing an alternative course of action. Opportunity costs are not recorded in the accounting records, but are important in making many types of business decisions.

Payback period The length of time necessary to recover the cost of an investment through the cash flows generated by that investment. Payback period is one criterion used in making capital budgeting decisions.

Present value The amount of money today which is considered equivalent to a cash inflow or outflow expected to take place in the future. The present value of money is always less than the future amount, since money on hand today can be invested to become the equivalent of a larger amount in the future.

Relevant information Information which should be given consideration in making a specific decision and which varies among the alternative courses of action being considered.

Return on average investment The average annual net income from an investment expressed as a percentage of the average amount invested. Return on average investment is one method of ranking alternative investment opportunities according to their relative profitability.

Sunk cost A cost which has irrevocably been incurred by past actions. Sunk costs are irrelevant to decisions regarding future actions.

SELF-TEST QUESTIONS

Answers to these questions appear on page 1067.

The following data relates to questions 1 and 2

One of Phoenix Computer's products is WizardCard. The company currently produces and sells 30,000 WizardCards per month, although it has the plant capacity to produce 50,000 units per month. At the 30,000 unit-per-month level of production, the per-unit cost of manufacturing WizardCards is $45, consisting of $15 in variable costs and $30 in fixed costs. Phoenix sells WizardCards to retail stores for $90 each. Computer Marketing Corp. has offered to purchase 10,000 WizardCards per month at a reduced price. Phoenix can manufacture these additional units with no change in fixed manufacturing costs.

1 In deciding whether to accept this special order from Computer Marketing Corp., Phoenix should be *least* concerned with:

   a What Computer Marketing Corp. intends to do with the WizardCards.

   b The $45 average cost of manufacturing WizardCards.

   c The opportunity cost of not accepting the order.

   d The incremental cost of manufacturing an additional 10,000 WizardCards per month.

2 Assume that Phoenix decides to accept the special order at a unit sales price that will add $400,000 per month to its operating income. The unit price of the special order will be:

   a $85   **b** $70   **c** $55   **d** Some other amount

3 The contribution margin ratios and monthly segment margins of three products sold by Video Game Corp. are as follows:

	PRODUCT 1	PRODUCT 2	PRODUCT 3
Contribution margin ratio	*20%*	*40%*	*60%*
Monthly segment margin	*$(4,000)*	*$15,000*	*$10,000*

Management is considering discontinuing Product 1. This action is expected to eliminate all costs traceable to Product 1, increase monthly sales of Product 2 by $10,000, decrease monthly sales of Product 3 by $5,000, and have no effect on common fixed costs. Based upon these facts, discontinuing Product 1 should cause the company's monthly operating income to:

a Increase by $4,000   **c** Decrease by $3,000

b Increase by $9,000   **d** None of the above

4 Western Mfg. Co. is considering two capital budgeting proposals, each with a 10-year life, and each requiring an initial cash outlay of $50,000. Proposal A shows a higher return on average investment than Proposal B, but Proposal B shows the higher net present value. The most probable explanation is that:

a Expected cash inflows tend to occur earlier in Proposal B.

b Total expected cash inflows are greater in Proposal B.

c The payback period is shorter in Proposal A.

d The discounted future cash flows approach makes no provision for recovery of the original $50,000 investment.

5 Copy Center is considering replacing its old copying machine, which has a $3,200 book value, with a new one. Discounted cash flow analysis of the proposal to acquire the new machine shows an estimated net present value of $2,800. If the new machine is acquired, the old machine will have no resale value and will be given away. The loss on disposal of the old machine:

a Is an opportunity cost of purchasing the new machine.

b Exceeds the net present value of the new machine, indicating that the new machine should not be acquired.

c Has already been deducted from future revenue in arriving at the $2,800 net present value of the new machine.

d Is a sunk cost and is not relevant to the decision at hand, except as it affects the timing of income tax payments.

Assignment Material

REVIEW QUESTIONS

1 What is the basic characteristic of "relevant" information?

2 A company regularly sells 100,000 washing machines at an average price of $250. The average cost of producing these machines is $180. Under what circumstances might the company accept an order for 20,000 washing machines at $175 per machine?

3 The Calcutta Corporation produces a large number of products. The costs per unit for one product, a fishing reel, are shown below:

Direct materials and direct labor	*$7.00*
Variable factory overhead	*4.00*
Fixed factory overhead	*2.00*

The company recently decided to buy 10,000 fishing reels from another manufacturer for $12.50 per unit because "it was cheaper than our cost of $13.00 per unit." Evaluate the decision only on the basis of the cost data given.

4 Define *opportunity costs* and explain why they represent a common source of error in making cost analyses.

5 What is the difference between a *sunk cost* and an *out-of-pocket cost?*

6 Briefly discuss the type of information you would want before deciding to discontinue the production of a major line of products.

7 Indicate several reasons why management might decide *not* to discontinue a product line that consistently incurs a negative segment margin.

8 What is *capital budgeting?* Why are capital budgeting decisions crucial to the long-run financial health of a business enterprise?

9 A company invests $100,000 in plant assets with an estimated 20-year service life and no salvage value. These assets contribute $10,000 to annual net income when depreciation is computed on a straight-line basis. Compute the payback period and explain your computation.

10 What is the major shortcoming of using the payback period as the only criterion in making capital budgeting decisions?

11 What factors should an investor consider in appraising the adequacy of the rate of return from a specific investment proposal?

12 Discounting a future cash flow at 15% results in a lower present value than does discounting the same cash flow at 10%. Explain why.

13 What factors determine the present value of a future cash flow?

14 Discounting cash flows takes into consideration one characteristic of the earnings stream which is ignored in the computation of return on average investment. What is this characteristic and why is it important?

15 Explain why the book value of existing equipment is not relevant in deciding whether the equipment should be scrapped (without realizing any proceeds) or continued in use.

EXERCISES

Exercise 26-1
Accounting
terminology

Listed below are nine technical accounting terms emphasized in this chapter:

Out-of-pocket cost	*Opportunity cost*	*Sunk cost*
Incremental analysis	*Net present value*	*Payback period*
Relevant information	*Capital budgeting*	*Estimated useful life*

Each of the following statements may (or may not) describe one of these technical terms. For each statement, indicate the accounting term described, or answer "None" if the statement does not correctly describe any of the terms.

a The benefit foregone by not pursuing an alternative course of action.

b The process of planning and evaluating proposals for investments in plant assets.

c The average annual net income from an investment expressed as a percentage of the average amount invested.

d Length of time necessary to recover the entire cost of an investment from resulting annual net cash flow.

e A cost which has not yet been incurred which will require payment and which may vary among alternative courses of action.

f Examination of differences between costs to be incurred and revenues to be earned under alternative courses of action.

g A cost incurred in the past which cannot be changed as a result of future actions.

h Costs and revenues which are expected to vary, depending upon the course of action decided upon.

Exercise 26-2
Incremental
analysis:
accepting a
special order

Marrion Corp. manufactures and sells 80,000 laser printers each month. The principal component part in a laser printer is the engine, and Marrion's plant has the capacity to produce 150,000 engines per month. The costs of manufacturing these printer engines (up to 150,000 engines per month) are as follows:

Variable costs per unit:	
Direct materials	*$271*
Direct labor	*19*
Variable manufacturing overhead...	*4*
Fixed costs per month:	
Fixed manufacturing overhead	*$2,080,000*

Desk-Mate Printers has offered to buy 20,000 printer engines per month from Marrion, to be used in the Desk-Mate laser printer.

Instructions

Compute the following:

a The average unit cost of manufacturing each printer engine, assuming that Marrion manufactures only enough printer engines for its own laser printers.

b The incremental unit cost of producing additional printer engines.

c The per-unit sales price that Marrion should charge Desk-Mate in order to earn $400,000 in monthly pretax profit on the sales to Desk-Mate.

Exercise 26-3
Incremental
analysis: make or
buy decision

The cost to Ellis Company of manufacturing 15,000 units of item X is $345,000, including $120,000 of fixed costs and $225,000 of variable costs. The company can buy the part from an outside supplier for $18.00 per unit, but the fixed manufacturing overhead now allocated to the part will remain unchanged. Should the company buy the part or continue to manufacture it? Prepare a comparative schedule in the format illustrated on page 1044.

Exercise 26-4
Opportunity costs

Plebeian Software recently developed new spreadsheet software, which it intends to market by mail through ads in computer magazines. Just prior to introducing the spreadsheet for sale, Plebeian receives an unexpected offer from Jupiter Computer to buy all rights to the software for $5 million cash.

a Is the $5 million offer "relevant" financial information?

b Describe Plebeian's opportunity cost if it (1) accepts Jupiter's offer, and (2) turns down the offer and markets the software itself. Would these opportunity costs be recorded in Plebeian's accounting records? If so, explain the journal entry to record these costs.

c Briefly describe the extent to which the dollar amount of the two opportunity costs described in part **b** are known to management at the time of decision of whether to accept Jupiter's offer.

d Might there be any other opportunity costs to consider at the time of making this decision? If so, explain briefly.

Exercise 26-5
Sunk costs: scrap
or rework
decision

Auto Parts Company has 20,000 units of a defective product on hand which cost $43,200 to manufacture. The company can either sell this product as scrap for $1.18 per unit or it can sell the product for $2.80 per unit by reworking the units and correcting the defects at a cost of $26,400. What should the company do? Prepare a schedule in support of your recommendation.

Exercise 26-6
Whether to close
a department

The Wine Cellar sells wine and operates a small sandwich deli. Typical monthly operating data is shown below:

	TOTAL	WINE SALES	DELI
Sales	$39,000	$35,000	$4,000
Variable costs (including cost of goods sold)	15,500	14,000	1,500
Contribution margin	$23,500	$21,000	$2,500
Fixed costs traceable to departments	9,000	6,000	3,000
Departmental segment margins	$14,500	$15,000	$ (500)
Common fixed costs	7,500		
Income from operations	$ 7,000		

Tim Johnson, owner of The Wine Cellar, is considering closing the deli and renting the related floor space to a film developing company for $1,200 per month. However, Johnson has read in a trade journal that without a deli, wine sales should be expected to decline by 10%. Also, the fixed costs traceable to the deli include $1,100 in monthly salary to an employee that Johnson will retain even if he closes the deli.

Prepare a schedule showing the expected effect upon monthly operating income of closing the deli and renting the related floor space. Based upon this analysis, make a recommendation as to whether or not to close the deli.

Exercise 26-7
Discounting cash
flows

Using the tables on pages 1051–1052, determine the present value of the following cash flows, discounted at an annual rate of 15%:

a $25,000 to be received 20 years from today

b $14,000 to be received annually for 5 years

c $45,000 to be received annually for 7 years, with an additional $30,000 salvage value due at the end of the seventh year.

d $30,000 to be received annually for the first 3 years, followed by $20,000 received annually for the next 2 years (total of 5 years in which cash is received)

Exercise 26-8
Capital budgeting

Bowman Corporation is considering an investment in special-purpose equipment to enable the company to obtain a four-year government contract for the manufacture of a special item. The equipment costs $300,000 and would have no salvage value when its use is discontinued at the end of the four years. Estimated annual operating results of the project are:

Revenue from contract sales		$325,000
Expenses other than depreciation	$225,000	
Depreciation (straight-line basis)	75,000	300,000
Increase in net income from contract work		$ 25,000

All revenue and all expenses other than depreciation will be received or paid in cash in the same period as recognized for accounting purposes. Compute for the proposal to undertake the contract work the following:

a Payback period.

b Return on average investment.

c Net present value of proposal to undertake contract work, discounted at an annual rate of 12%. (Refer to annuity table on page 1052.)

PROBLEMS

Group A

Problem 26A-1
Evaluating a
special order

D. Lawrance designs and manufactures fashionable men's clothing. For the coming year, the company has scheduled production of 40,000 leather jackets. The budgeted costs for this product are shown below:

	UNIT COSTS (40,000 UNITS)	TOTAL
Variable manufacturing costs	$ 75	$3,000,000
Variable selling expenses	24	960,000
Fixed manufacturing costs..................................	12	480,000
Fixed operating expenses...................................	9	360,000
Total costs and expenses...................................	$120	$4,800,000

The management of D. Lawrance is considering a special order from Discount House for an additional 10,000 jackets. These jackets would carry the Discount House label, rather than that of D. Lawrance. In all other respects, they would be identical to the regular D. Lawrance jackets.

Although D. Lawrance sells its regular jackets to retail stores at a price of $180 each, Discount House has offered to pay only $104 per jacket. However, no sales commissions are involved on this special order, so D. Lawrance would incur variable selling expenses of only $5 per unit on these jackets, rather than the regular $24. Accepting the order would cause no change in D. Lawrance's fixed manufacturing costs or fixed operating expenses. D. Lawrance has enough plant capacity to produce 55,000 jackets per year.

Instructions

a Using incremental revenue and incremental costs, compute the expected effect of accepting this special order upon D. Lawrance's operating income.

b Briefly discuss any other factors which you believe D. Lawrance's management should consider in deciding whether to accept this special order. You may include nonfinancial as well as financial considerations.

Problem 26A-2
Make or buy
decision

Precision Instruments manufactures thermostats which it uses in several of its products. Management is considering whether to continue manufacturing thermostats, or to buy them from an outside source. The following information is available:

(1) The company needs 20,000 thermostats per year. Thermostats can be purchased from an outside supplier at a cost of $24 per unit.

(2) The cost of manufacturing thermostats is $30 per unit, computed as follows:

Direct materials...	$156,000
Direct labor..	132,000
Manufacturing overhead:	
Variable..	168,000
Fixed	144,000
Total manufacturing costs...	$600,000
Cost per unit ($600,000 ÷ 20,000 units).............................	$30

(3) Discontinuing the manufacture of the thermostats will eliminate all of the direct materials and direct labor costs, but will eliminate only 60% of the variable overhead costs.

(4) If the thermostats are purchased from an outside source, certain machinery used in the production of thermostats will be sold at its book value. The sale of this machinery will reduce fixed overhead costs by $8,400 for depreciation and $800 for property taxes.

No other reductions in fixed overhead will result from discontinuing production of the thermostats.

Instructions **a** Prepare a schedule to determine the incremental cost or benefit of buying thermostats from the outside supplier. Based on this schedule, would you recommend that the company manufacture thermostats or buy them from the outside source?

b Assume that if thermostats are purchased from the outside source, the factory space previously used to produce thermostats can be used to manufacture an additional 7,000 centrifuges per year. Centrifuges have an estimated contribution margin of $18 per unit. The manufacture of the additional centrifuges would have no effect upon fixed overhead. Would this new assumption change your recommendation as to whether to make or buy thermostats? In support of your conclusion, prepare a schedule showing the incremental cost or benefit of buying thermostats from the outside source and using the factory space to produce additional centrifuges.

Problem 26A-3
Discontinuing a
product line—
any ideas?

Quest Corporation began business about 10 years ago manufacturing and selling ski equipment. Later it introduced a line of golf clubs, which has since become its biggest selling and most profitable product. Over the years, competition from Europe has forced the company to reduce its sales price on skis, and this product line now consistently has a negative segment margin. The company also makes a unique ski binding, which has remained profitable. Typical monthly operating data for these three product lines are shown below:

	GOLF CLUBS		SKIS		SKI BINDINGS	
	Dollars	*%*	*Dollars*	*%*	*Dollars*	*%*
Sales	$500,000	100	$300,000	100	$160,000	100
Variable costs	215,000	43	225,000	75	80,000	50
Contribution margins	$285,000	57	$ 75,000	25	$ 80,000	50
Traceable fixed costs	110,000	22	90,000	30	68,800	43
Segment margins....................	$175,000	35	$ (15,000)	(5)	$ 11,200	7

Management is considering discontinuing the manufacture and sale of skis. All costs traceable to the product line would be eliminated if the product line is discontinued. Skis and bindings are sold to the same stores; therefore, management estimates that discontinuing the sale of skis would cause a 20% decline in sales of ski bindings. Golf clubs are sold to different customers, so management does not believe that golf club sales would be affected by discontinuing skis. All three product lines are manufactured in the same plant, which is operating at between 90% and 95% of capacity, due to the increasing demand for golf clubs.

Instructions **a** Prepare a schedule showing the estimated effect of discontinuing the manufacture and sale of skis upon Quest's monthly operating income.

b Prepare a schedule determining the expected monthly segment margin of the ski bindings product line, assuming that the ski product line is discontinued and that sales of ski bindings decline by 20%.

c Draft a memo summarizing your recommendations as to Quest's best course of action. Bring out any points that you think management should consider. Perhaps you have noticed factors that management may be overlooking.

Problem 26A-4
Capital budgeting

MasterCraft Tool Company is planning to expand its product line to include a new item which can be manufactured almost entirely by machine, using very little labor. The controller has assembled the following data regarding estimated operating results for the two machines currently being considered for purchase by MasterCraft:

	MACHINE A	MACHINE B
Required investment in machinery	$440,000	$480,000
Estimated service life of machinery	5 years	6 years

Estimated salvage value	$ 20,000	–0–
Estimated annual net cash flow	$120,000	$120,000
Depreciation on machinery (straight-line basis)	$ 84,000	$ 80,000
Estimated annual net income	$ 36,000	$ 40,000

Instructions **a** For each proposed alternative, compute the (1) payback period, (2) return on average investment, and (3) net present value, discounted at an annual rate of 12%. (Round the payback period to the nearest tenth of a year and the return on investment to the nearest tenth of a percent.)

b Based upon your computations in part **a**, which machine do you consider to be the better choice? Explain.

Problem 26A-5
Capital budgeting
using three
models

V. S. Yogurt is considering two possible expansion plans. Proposal A involves opening 10 stores in northern California at a total cost of $3,150,000. Under another strategy, Proposal B, V. S. Yogurt would focus on southern California and open six stores for a total cost of $2,500,000. Selected data regarding the two proposals has been assembled by the controller of V. S. Yogurt as follows:

	PROPOSAL A	PROPOSAL B
Required investment......................................	$3,150,000	$2,500,000
Estimated life of store locations........................	7 years	7 years
Estimated salvage value	–0–	$ 400,000
Estimated annual net cash flow	$ 750,000	$ 570,000
Depreciation on equipment (straight-line basis)	$ 450,000	$ 300,000
Estimated annual net income	?	?

Instructions **a** For each proposal, compute the (1) payback period, (2) return on average investment, and (3) net present value, discounted at management's required rate of return of 15%. Round the payback period to the nearest tenth of a year and the return on investment to the nearest tenth of a percent.

b Based upon your analysis in part **a**, state which proposal you would recommend and explain the reasoning behind your choice.

Problem 26A-6
Capital budgeting—
computing annual
net cash flow

Toying With Nature wants to take advantage of children's current fascination with dinosaurs by adding several scale-model dinosaurs to its existing product line. Annual sales of the dinosaurs are estimated at 80,000 units at a price of $6 per unit. Variable manufacturing costs are estimated at $2.50 per unit, incremental fixed manufacturing costs (excluding depreciation) at $45,000 annually, and additional selling and general expenses related to the dinosaurs at $55,000 annually.

To manufacture the dinosaurs, the company must invest $350,000 in design molds and special equipment. Since toy fads wane in popularity rather quickly, Toying With Nature anticipates the special equipment will have a three-year service life with only a $20,000 salvage value. Depreciation will be computed on a straight-line basis. All revenue and expenses other than depreciation will be received or paid in cash. The company's combined federal and state income tax rate is 40%.

Instructions **a** Prepare a schedule showing the estimated increase in annual net income from the planned manufacture and sale of dinosaur toys.

b Compute the annual net cash flow expected from this project.

c Compute for this project (1) payback period, (2) return on average investment, and (3) net present value, discounted at an annual rate of 15%. Round the payback period to the nearest tenth of a year and the return on average investment to the nearest tenth of a percent.

Group B

Problem 26B-1
Evaluating a
special order

Electronic Age, Inc., sells 500,000 video games per year at $24.00 each. The current unit cost of the video games is broken down as follows:

Direct materials	$ 5.00
Direct labor	5.40
Variable manufacturing overhead	3.20
Fixed manufacturing overhead	4.40
Total	$18.00

At the beginning of the current year the company receives a special order for 15,000 game sets per month *for one year only* at $16.00 per unit. A new machine with an estimated life of five years would have to be purchased for $35,000 to produce the additional units. Management thinks that it will not be able to use the new machine beyond one year and that it will have to be sold for approximately $20,000.

Instructions

Compute the estimated increase or decrease in annual operating income that will result from accepting this special order.

Problem 26B-2
Make or buy
decision

HydroTech manufactures a pressure valve which is used in several of its products. The vice president of production is considering whether to continue manufacturing these valves, or whether to buy them from an outside source at a cost of $4.25 per valve. HydroTech uses 60,000 of the valves each year. The cost to manufacture the valves is $4.80 per unit, as shown below:

Direct materials	$ 90,000
Direct labor	84,000
Manufacturing overhead:	
Variable	48,000
Fixed	66,000
Annual manufacturing costs for 60,000 valves	$288,000
Unit cost ($288,000 ÷ 60,000 units)	$4.80

If the valves are purchased, all of the direct materials and direct labor costs will be eliminated, and 80% of the variable overhead will be eliminated. In addition, some of the equipment used in the manufacture of the valves will be sold at its book value. The sale of this equipment will reduce fixed factory overhead costs by $4,780 for depreciation and $120 for property taxes. No other reduction in fixed overhead will result from discontinuing production of the valves.

Instructions

a Prepare a schedule in the format illustrated on page 1044 to determine the incremental cost or benefit of buying the valves from the outside supplier. Based on this schedule, would you recommend that HydroTech manufacture the valves or buy them from the outside source?

b Assume that if the valves are purchased from the outside source, the factory space previously used to manufacture valves can be used to manufacture an additional 2,400 drip system components per year. Drip components have an estimated contribution margin of $36 per unit. Manufacturing the additional drip components would not increase fixed factory overhead. Would this new assumption change your recommendation as to whether to make or buy the pressure valves? In support of your conclusion, prepare a schedule showing the incremental cost or benefit of buying the valves from the outside supplier and using the factory space to produce more drip components.

Problem 26B-3
Discontinuing a
product line

Ski America is a small airline flying out of Denver. The company has only enough planes to service three routes, connecting Denver with San Francisco, and with the

Colorado ski resorts of Aspen and Vail. Typical monthly operating data for these three routes are summarized below:

	SAN FRANCISCO		ASPEN		VAIL	
Passengers per month..............	1,000		1,200		900	
	Dollars	%	Dollars	%	Dollars	%
Sales	$400,000	100	$240,000	100	$270,000	100
Variable costs	40,000	10	12,000	5	13,500	5
Contribution margins	$360,000	90	$228,000	95	$256,500	95
Traceable fixed costs...............	408,000	102	96,000	40	113,400	42
Segment margins...................	$ (48,000)	(12)	$132,000	55	$143,100	53

Management is concerned about the losses incurred each month on the San Francisco route, and also has an opportunity to use the plane now serving San Francisco to establish a new Denver to Durango route. Management estimates that the Denver-Durango route would generate a positive monthly segment margin of $50,000. However, most of the passengers flying the San Francisco route with Ski America also "book through" on either the Aspen or Vail flights. Ski America's management knows that cancelling service to San Francisco will cause a loss of passengers on the Aspen and Vail routes.

By studying ticket sales, Ski America's managerial accountants have learned that 45% of the passengers flying Ski America from San Francisco continue on Ski America to Aspen, and that 36% fly Ski America into Vail. A marketing survey indicates that if the San Francisco route is cancelled, Ski America will still receive 60% of the business of those San Francisco passengers who travel from Denver to Aspen or Vail.

Instructions **a** Using the data about numbers of passengers, prepare a schedule showing the percentage by which monthly passenger volume is expected to decline on (1) the Aspen route, and (2) the Vail route, assuming that the San Francisco route is cancelled.

b Prepare a schedule showing the estimated effect of replacing the San Francisco route with service to Durango upon the monthly operating income of Ski America. Changes in the contribution margin generated from the Aspen and Vail routes are expected to coincide with the changes in passenger volume.

c Make a recommendation as to whether the San Francisco route should be discontinued. Also raise any points that you believe should be considered by management.

Problem 26B-4
Capital budgeting

Prototype Molding is considering two alternative proposals for modernizing its production facilities. To provide a basis for selection, the cost accounting department has developed the following data regarding the expected annual operating results for the two proposals.

	PROPOSAL 1	PROPOSAL 2
Required investment in equipment	$900,000	$875,000
Estimated service life of equipment	8 years	7 years
Estimated salvage value	–0–	$ 35,000
Estimated annual cost savings (net cash flow)...........	$187,500	$190,000
Depreciation on equipment (straight-line basis)	$112,500	$120,000
Estimated increase in annual net income	$ 75,000	$ 70,000

Instructions **a** For each proposal, compute the (1) payback period, (2) return on average investment, and (3) net present value, discounted at an annual rate of 12%. (Round the payback period to the nearest tenth of a year and the return on investment to the nearest tenth of a percent.)

b Based on your analysis in part **a**, state which proposal you would recommend and explain the reasons for your choice.

**Problem 26B-5
Capital budgeting
using three
models**

Marengo is a popular restaurant located in the Chilton Resort. Management feels that enlarging the facility to incorporate a large outdoor seating area will enable Marengo to continue to attract existing customers as well as handle large banquet parties that now must be turned away. Two proposals are currently under consideration. Proposal A involves a temporary walled structure and umbrellas used for sun protection; Proposal B entails a more permanent structure with a full awning cover for use even in inclement weather. Although the useful life of each alternative is estimated to be 10 years, Proposal B results in higher salvage value due to the awning protection. The accounting department of Chilton Resort and the manager of Marengo have assembled the following data regarding the two proposals:

	PROPOSAL A	PROPOSAL B
Required investment......................................	$400,000	$500,000
Estimated life of fixtures.................................	10 years	10 years
Estimated salvage value	$ 20,000	$ 50,000
Estimated annual net cash flow	$ 80,000	$ 95,000
Depreciation (straight-line basis)	$ 38,000	$ 45,000
Estimated annual net income	?	?

Instructions

a For each proposal, compute the (1) payback period, (2) return on average investment, and (3) net present value discounted at management's required rate of return of 15%. Round the payback period to the nearest tenth of a year and the return on investment to the nearest tenth of a percent.

b Based upon your analysis in part **a**, state which proposal you would recommend and explain the reasons for your choice.

**Problem 26B-6
Another capital
budgeting
problem**

Rothmore Appliance Company is planning to introduce a built-in blender to its line of small home appliances. Annual sales of the blender are estimated at 15,000 units at a price of $30 per unit. Variable manufacturing costs are estimated at $15 per unit, incremental fixed manufacturing costs (other than depreciation) at $40,000 annually, and incremental selling and general expenses relating to the blenders at $50,000 annually.

To build the blenders, the company must invest $280,000 in molds, patterns, and special equipment. Since the company expects to change the design of the blender every four years, this equipment will have a four-year service life with no salvage value. Depreciation will be computed on a straight-line basis. All revenue and expenses other than depreciation will be received or paid in cash. The company's combined state and federal tax rate is 40%.

Instructions

a Prepare a schedule showing the estimated increase in annual net income from the proposal to manufacture and sell the blenders.

b Compute the annual net cash flow expected from the proposal.

c Compute for this proposal (1) payback period (round to the nearest tenth of a year), (2) return on average investment (round to the nearest tenth of a percent), and (3) net present value, discounted at an annual rate of 15%.

BUSINESS DECISION CASE

**Case 26-1
The case of the
costly laser**

The management of Metro Printers is considering a proposal to replace some existing equipment with a new highly efficient laser printer. The existing equipment has a current book value of $2,200,000 and a remaining life (if not replaced) of 10 years. The laser printer has a cost of $1,300,000 and an expected useful life of 10 years. The laser printer would increase the company's annual cash flow by reducing operating costs and by increasing the company's ability to generate revenue. Susan Mills, controller of Metro Printers, has prepared the following estimates of the laser printer's effect upon annual earnings and cash flow:

Estimated increase in annual cash flow (before income taxes):		
Incremental revenue	$140,000	
Cost savings (other than depreciation)	110,000	$250,000
Reduction in annual depreciation expense:		
Depreciation on existing equipment	$220,000	
Depreciation on laser printer	130,000	90,000
Estimated increase in income before income taxes		$340,000
Increase in annual income taxes (40%)		136,000
Estimated increase in annual net income		$204,000
Estimated increase in annual net cash flow ($250,000 − $136,000)		$114,000

Don Adams, a director of Metro Printers, makes the following observation: "These estimates look fine, but won't we take a huge loss in the current year on the sale of our existing equipment? After the invention of the laser printer, I doubt that our old equipment can be sold for much at all." In response, Mills provides the following information about the expected loss on the sale of the existing equipment:

Book value of existing printing equipment	$2,200,000
Estimated current sales price, net of removal costs	200,000
Estimated loss on sale, before income taxes	$2,000,000
Reduction in current year's income taxes as a result of loss (40%)	800,000
Loss on sale of existing equipment, net of tax savings	$1,200,000

Adams replies, "Good grief, our loss would be almost as great as the cost of the laser printer. If we have to take a $1,200,000 loss and pay $1,300,000 for the laser printer, we'll be into the new equipment for $2,500,000. I'd go along with a cost of $1,300,000, but $2,500,000 is just too high a price to pay."

Instructions

a Compute the net present value of the proposal to sell the existing equipment and buy the laser printer, discounted at an annual rate of 15%. In your computation, make the following assumptions regarding the timing of cash flows:

(1) The purchase price of the laser printer will be paid in cash immediately.

(2) The $200,000 sales price of the existing equipment will be received in cash immediately.

(3) The income tax benefit from selling the equipment will be realized one year from today.

(4) The annual net cash flows may be regarded as received at year-end for each of the next ten years.

b Is the cost to Metro Printers of acquiring the laser printer $2,500,000, as Adams suggests? Explain fully.

ANSWERS TO SELF-TEST QUESTIONS

1 b   **2 c** [$15 + ($400,000 ÷ 10,000 cards)].   **3 d** (Increase by $5,000. Segment margin will change as follows: Product 1, +$4,000; Product 2, +$4,000; Product 3, −$3,000).   **4 a**   **5 d**

Index

Absorption costing, 976
Accelerated Cost Recovery System (ACRS), 396, 705, 712
Accelerated depreciation methods, 391–393, 408
Accepting special orders, 1042
Account payable, 17–18
Accountants:
　certified public, 7–9
　controller, 9
　in government, 10–11
　opinion of, on financial statements, 8, 504, 507, 773, 841
Accounting:
　accrual versus cash basis, 107, 689–690, 712
　applications of the computer, 245
　as basis for business decisions, 12–13
　careers in, 7
　purpose and nature of, 4–5
　specialized phases of, 9–11
　as stepping stone to top management, 11
　(See also Principles and assumptions of accounting)
Accounting control, 221, 247
Accounting cycle, 59–60, 62–63, 106–107, 150–152, 155
Accounting education, careers as faculty members in, 11
Accounting entity concept, 457, 494
Accounting equation, 19–20, 23–24, 27
Accounting period, 83, 108, 127–128
Accounting principles, 11–12, 28, 491–503, 507
　(See also Principles and assumptions of accounting)
Accounting Principles Board (APB), 491, 506
　Opinions of:
　　Opinion No. 11, 706
　　Opinion No. 15, 564
　　Opinion No. 16, 649
　　Opinion No. 17, 402
　　Opinion No. 21, 327
Accounting procedures in computer-based system, 107
Accounting standards, need for recognized, 490–491
Accounting systems:
　computer-based, 60–61, 107, 154, 246
　cost (see Cost accounting systems)
　defined, 5
　diagram of, 62
　manual:
　　and computer-based,

Accounting systems, manual (Cont.):
　comparison of, 60, 230, 245–246
　special journals in, 230–242, 246
　responsibility accounting, 966–967
　standard costs (see Cost accounting systems, standard costs)
Accounts:
　balance of, 43
　controlling, 232–233, 244, 247
　defined, 42
　financial statement order of, 94
　ledger (see Ledger accounts)
　normal balance, 44, 49
　running balance form of, 48–49
　sequence in ledger, 94
　T form, 42
　use of, to record transactions, 43, 49, 91–94
Accounts payable:
　defined, 18–19
　internal control over, 225, 227, 428
　payment of, 240–242
　subsidiary ledger, 232–233, 235–236
　(See also Voucher system)
Accounts payable ledger, 232–233, 235–236, 247, 428
Accounts receivable:
　aging of, 311–312, 329
　allowance for doubtful accounts, 307, 329
　analysis of, 311–312
　average age of, 792
　balance sheet presentation of, 306
　collection of, 22–23
　conservatism in valuing, 307, 329
　contra-asset account, 307, 329
　credit card sales, 314
　as current assets, 305
　direct write-off method, 313, 329
　internal controls, 315
　realizable value, 306
　recovery of an account receivable previously written off, 309–310
　subsidiary ledger, 232–234, 247
　turnover, 321–322, 329, 792, 794
　uncollectible accounts, 305–306
　uncollectible expense, 306
　write-off of, 308–309
Accounts receivable ledger, 232–234, 247
Accrual basis of accounting, 107, 108, 736–741, 746
Accrued expenses, 134–136, 155
Accrued revenue, 137, 155
Accumulated depreciation, 96, 108
Acquisition of subsidiary, 646–647

Additional paid-in capital, 530, 531, 536, 539, 542
Adjusted gross income, 694, 712
Adjusted trial balance, 97, 108
Adjusting entries:
　for accrual of salary, 136
　and accrual basis of accounting, 138
　defined, 94–95, 108, 155
　for depreciation, 95–97, 131–132
　four main types of, 129
　for interest expense, 134–136
　for recorded costs apportioned between accounting periods, 129–132
　and reversing entries, 152–154
　for uncollectible accounts, 306
　for unearned revenue, 132–134
　for unrecorded expenses, 134
　for unrecorded revenue, 137
　from work sheet, 147–148
Advantages of computer-based accounting systems, 246
Affiliated companies, 646
After-closing trial balance, 106, 108
Aging of receivables, 311–312
Airlines, earnings of, 774
Allowance for doubtful accounts, 306–307
Allstate Insurance Company, 559
Alternative Minimum Tax (AMT), 701, 703–704
American Accounting Association (AAA), 12, 492
American Airlines, 774
American Home Products, financial statements of, 529
American Institute of Certified Public Accountants (AICPA), 12, 27, 492, 507
Amortization, 402, 408, 442
　of bond discount or premium from investor's viewpoint, 638
　of intangible assets, 402, 408
Amortization table:
　for bonds sold at a discount, 603
　for bonds sold at a premium, 605
Analysis of financial statements:
　accounts receivable turnover, 321–322, 329, 792, 794
　book value per share, 784–785, 794
　common size income statement, 778
　by common stockholders, 782–788
　comparative balance sheet, 782
　comparative financial statements, 775, 795

Analysis of financial statements (*Cont.*):
  comparative income statements of
    major corporations, 779
  component percentages, 778, 796
  corporate profits:
    examples of, 774
    level of, 774–775
  by creditors, 788–793
  current ratio, 202, 204, 792–793, 795
  debt ratio, 789, 794
  dividend yield, 784, 794
  dollar and percentage changes, 776
  earnings per share, 561–564, 575,
    782–783, 794
  equity ratio, 787–788, 794
  financial information, sources of, 775
  five-year summary of financial data,
    The Quaker Oats Company, 779
  horizontal analysis, 779–780, 796
  illustrative analysis, 781–793
  income statement, 189–192
  industry standards, 780
  inflation, impact of, 781
  inventory turnover, 791, 795
  leverage, 787–788, 796
  by long-term creditors, 788–789
  operating cycle, 792
  operating expense ratio, 786, 794
  past performance of the company,
    779–780
  percentage changes in sales and
    earnings, 776
  percentages become misleading when
    the base is small, 776–777
  by preferred stockholders, 789–790
  price-earnings ratio, 784, 794
  quality of assets and the relative
    amount of debt, 781, 796
  quality of earnings, 780–781, 796
  quick ratio, 793, 795
  ratios, 779, 794–796
  return on assets, 786–787, 794
  return on common stockholders'
    equity, 787, 794
  return on investment (ROI), 786, 796
  revenue and expense analysis, 785–
    786
  by short-term creditors, 790–793
  sources of financial information, 775
  standards of comparison, 779
  summary of analytical
    measurements, 794–795
  times bond interest earned, 788–789,
    794
  times preferred dividends earned,
    790, 794
  tools of analysis, 775
  trend percentages, 777–778, 796
  vertical analysis, 779–780, 796
  working capital, 202, 790–791, 794
  yield rate on bonds, 788
Andersen, Arthur, & Co., 8
Annual physical inventory, 348, 366–
  368
Asset accounts, 44
  sequence of, 49–50
Assets:
  classification of, 200–201
  defined, 15, 27
  intangible, 401–406
  quality of, 781

Assets (*Cont.*):
  rules of debit and credit, 44
  tangible, 384
  valuation of, 15–16, 496–497
Audit opinion, 504, 507
  (*See also* Auditors' report)
Audited financial statements, 503–504
Auditing, 8, 27
Auditors' report, 504, 507, 773, 841
Authoritative support for generally
  accepted accounting principles, 492
Average-cost method of inventory
  valuation, 352–353, 355, 367

Bad debts (*See* Doubtful accounts)
Balance sheet:
  account form, 14, 23
  classification of, 200–202
  consolidated, 652
  corporation, illustrated, 540–541
  effect of business transactions upon,
    20–23
  nature and purpose of, 14–15, 28
  report from, 98, 100, 200
  use of, by outsiders, 25–26
Balance sheet equation, 19–20, 23–24
Balance sheet valuation of marketable
  equity securities, 640–641
Balances of accounts, 43
Bank of America, 670–671
Bank credit cards, 314
Bank reconciliation, 283–289
Bank statement, 283–284
Banks
  checking accounts, 280–281
    control features of, 281
    interest earned on, 285
  credit cards, 314
  deposit ticket, 282, 289
  deposits, 281
    in transit, 284, 289
  outstanding checks, 284, 286, 289
  reconciliation of bank account (*see*
    Reconciling a bank account)
  service charges, 285
  stop payment orders, 281
Basis of an asset for income tax
  purposes, 696
Beginning inventory, 186–187
"Big Eight" public accounting firms, 8
Board of directors, 525, 542
Bond discount:
  accounting entries for, 597, 599
  amortization:
    by effective interest method, 598,
      602–604, 615
    by straight-line method, 598–599,
      602, 615
  on bonds owned, 638–639
  on bonds payable, 597–599, 615
  defined, 598, 615
  as part of cost of borrowing, 598
Bond premium:
  accounting entries for, 599–600
  amortization of:
    by effective interest method, 598,
      602, 604–605
    by straight-line method, 600, 602
  on bonds owned, 638–639
  on bonds payable, 599–600

Bond premium (*Cont.*):
  defined, 615
  as reduction in cost of borrowing, 600
Bond sinking fund, 607
Bondholders' ledger, 609
Bonds:
  amortization of bond discount or
    premium from investor's
    viewpoint, 638
  callable, 594
  convertible, 594, 610–611, 615
  coupon, 594
  debenture, 593
  defined, 592
  investment in, 638
  market prices of:
    after issuance, 593, 608
    and relation to interest rates, 608–
      609
  mortgage, 593
  present value of, 596–597
  quotations for, 593
  registered and coupon, 594
  transferability of, 593
  types of, 593–594
Bonds payable:
  accounting entries for, 594–597
  amortization (*see* Bond discount;
    amortization of; Bond premium,
    amortization of)
  authorization of bond issue, 592
  balance sheet presentation, 597, 600
  call provision, 594
  conversion into common stock, 609–
    610, 615
  defined, 592
  effect of bond financing on holders of
    common stock, 594
  issuance of, 594–595
    between interest dates, 595–596
  market prices of, 608
  nature of, 592
  present-value concept, 596
    and bond prices, 596–597
  ratings, 593
  recording issue of, 594–596
  registered, 594
  retirement of, 606–607
  role of the underwriter, 592–593
  serial bonds, 594
  sinking fund, 607, 615
  tax advantage of, 594
  year-end adjustment for bond
    interest expense, 601
Bonus on admission of partner, 468–470
Book value:
  defined, 132, 156, 784–785
  of plant assets, 132, 389, 408
  per share of common stock, 539–540,
    542, 784–785, 794
Bookkeeping, 7
Books of original entry (*See* Journals)
Break-even analysis, 941
Bristol-Myers Company, 831–847
Budgeting:
  as aid to planning and control, 1000
  benefits derived from, 1000–1001
  budget period, 1001–1002
  budgeted balance sheet, 1011–1012
  budgeted income statement, 1006–
    1007

Budgeting (*Cont.*):
  capital (*see* Capital budgeting)
  capital expenditures budget, 1001
  cash budget, 1011
  computers and flexible budgeting, 1015
  continuous budgeting, 1002
  controllable costs, 1013
  defined, 1000
  establishing budgeted amounts, 1001
  financial budget estimates, 1007–1010
  flexible budgeting, 1013–1015
  length of period, 1001–1002
  master budget:
    illustrated, 1003
    package of related budgets, 1002
    preparing, example of, 1004–1012
  responsibility budget, 1013
  using budgets effectively, 1012–1013
Business combinations, 646, 657
Business decisions:
  accounting as a basis for, 12–13, 1045–1046
  contribution margin approach, 941–945, 969
  and cost-volume-profit analysis, 941
  make or buy decisions, 1043–1044
  replacement of old equipment, 399–401, 1053–1054
  special order for a product, 1042–1043
  unprofitable product line, 1045–1048
Business documents and procedures, 225–228
Business entity, 15, 28
Business objectives, 12–13
Business organizations, forms of, 24–25

Call provision:
  bonds, 594
  preferred stock, 533, 542
Capital (*see* Owner's equity)
Capital assets, 696, 712
Capital budgeting:
  defined, 1048, 1055
  discount rate, 1051, 1054, 1055
  discounting future cash flows, 1050–1053, 1055
  net present value of proposed investment, 1053–1055
  payback period, 1049, 1056
  present value tables, 1051–1052
  replacement of old equipment, 1053–1054
  return on average investment, 1049–1050
Capital expenditure, 387, 408
Capital gains and losses, 696–697, 703, 712
Capital lease, 611–612
Capital stock:
  authorization and issuance of, 529–530
  callable preferred stock, 533
  certificates, 529, 543
  common (*see* Common stock)
  convertible preferred stock, 533–534
  corporate records of, 538
  defined, 25, 28, 529, 542

Capital stock (*Cont.*):
  discount on, 530
  dividends on, 566–568, 576
  issuance of par value stock, 529–530
  issued for assets other than cash, 536
  market price:
    of common stock, 535
    of preferred stock, 534–535
  market quotations, 534–535
  no-par, 530
  ownership rights, 525
  par value, 529
  preferred, 530–535
  recording issuance of, 529–530
  split, 568–569, 576
  stated value, 530
  subscriptions, 536–537, 543
  treasury, 571–573
  underwriting of stock issues, 536
Carrying value (*see* Book value)
Cases in Point:
  accounting firms, 8
  automobile dealers, over-valuation of trade-ins, 399
  "Big Eight" CPA firms, 8
  "Black Monday" on Wall Street, 640
  business combinations, 648–649
  Chevron Corporation, acquisition of subsidiary, 646–647
  Chrysler Corporation, break-even point, 943
  Citicorp, 318–319
  closely held corporation, loan versus additional stock, 710
  Commonwealth Edison, 608
  computer-based perpetual inventory in supermarket, 199
  computer fraud:
    in issuing checks, 275
    payroll, 437
  Consolidated Edison, numerous preferred stocks, 532
  convertible bonds, 610
  corporate earnings, level of, 774–775
  cost accounting systems, 886–909
  costs traceable to a segment of a business, 969
  electronic cash registers, 273
  Eli Lily, 647
  Exxon Corporation, 817
  Henry Ford, 305
  Ford Motor Company, 535
  fraud in notes payable, 427
  General Motors, 774, 777, 936
  J. Paul Getty, 647
  Hilton Hotels, 559
  IBM, 608, 640
  impact of inflation, 817
  intensive use of facilities, 936
  interest rates:
    volatility of, 608–609
    and preferred stock prices, 535
  internal control:
    with electronic scanning equipment in supermarkets, 273
    over inventories, 364
    over payroll, 437
  IRS audits and understated inventories, 363
  just-in-time inventory systems, 908

Cases in Point (*Cont.*):
  loss contingencies, 433–434
  McDonald's Corporation, nonfinancial information, 975
  managerial responsibility, 964
  Manville Corporation, 433–434
  Merck & Co., Inc., 501
  Minox, Inc., payroll fraud, 437
  Mobil Oil, 647
  Montgomery Ward, 647
  Mylan Laboratories, Inc., 569
  Nabisco Brands, 647
  nonfinancial objectives and information, 974–975
  overhead "cost drivers," 864–865
  Par-Flite, inadequate internal control over inventories, 364
  partners, two or maybe three, 455
  partnership and fraud, 457–458
  payroll fraud, 437
  Philadelphia Electric, interest rates and preferred stock prices, 535
  point-of-sale terminals, 199, 273
  R. J. Reynolds Co., 647
  research and development costs, 501
  social security taxes, 100-fold increase, 438
  Squibb Corp., 501
  stock dividends and stock splits, 569
  tax planning, 710
  Toyota, just-in-time system, 908
  TWA, 559
  unearned revenue, 133
  unit costs for medical services, 887
  United Airlines, Inc., 133
  unrecorded liabilities, 427
  Walgreen Co., 610
  Walt Disney Co., 83
  writedowns of inventory, 359–360
Cash:
  balance sheet presentation, 270
  bank checking accounts, 280–283
  bank reconciliation, 283–288
  budget, 1011
  credit cards and point-of-sale terminals, 246
  defined, 269, 289
  disbursements of, 274–275
  discounts, 184, 188
  dividends, 528–529, 564
  electronic cash registers, 273
  internal control over, 271–272
  management responsibilities relating to, 270–271
  NSF checks, 285
  payments of (*see* Cash payments)
  petty, 278, 280
  receipts for (*see* Cash receipts)
  received over the counter, 272–273
  received through the mail, 272
  subdivision of duties, 274
Cash basis of accounting, 107, 689–690, 712, 746
Cash disbursements, 274–275
Cash equivalents, 270, 732, 746
Cash flows, 728–746, 765–770
  classification of, 729–730
  defined, 729–730, 746
  statement of (*see* Statement of cash flows)
  (*See also specific sources of cash flow*)

Cash over and short, 273–274, 289
Cash payments, 274–275
  for merchandise and expenses, 737–740
  statement of cash flows and, 737–739
Cash payments journal, 240–242
Cash receipts, 272–274
  from operating activities, 736–737
  statement of cash flows and, 736–737
Cash receipts journal, 236–240
Cash registers, 272–273
Certificate in Management Accounting (CMA), 10
Certified public accountants (CPAs), 7–9
  opinion on financial statements, 504, 507, 773, 841
Change in accounting principle, 560
Changes in principle versus changes in estimate, 560–561
Chart of accounts, 49–50
Check register, 277, 289
Checking accounts (see Banks, checking accounts)
Checks:
  NSF (Not Sufficient Funds), 285, 289
  outstanding, 284, 289
Chevron Corporation, 646–647
Chrysler Corporation, 943
Classification:
  in balance sheets, 199–201
  in income statements, 202–203
Closing entries, 100–105
  defined, 100, 108
  dividends account, 528–529
  expense accounts, 101–102
  illustrative diagram, 105
  Income Summary Account, 102
  for inventories, 196
  for merchandising business, 195–197
  owner's drawing account, 104–105
  for partnership, 460
  revenue accounts, 101
  summary of closing procedure, 105
  from work sheet, 149
Coca-Cola, 670
Commitments, 434, 442
Common fixed costs:
  defined, 970
  traceable to larger responsibility centers, 970–971
  traceable to service departments, 970
Common stock:
  book value per share, 539–540, 542
  interpreting different per share amounts, 563
  market price of, 535
  nature of, 530–531, 542
  par value, 529
  primary and fully diluted earnings per share, 563–564
  rights of shareholders, 525
Comparative financial statements, 775, 779, 782
Competing products and complementary products, 1046
Component percentages, 778, 796
Compound journal entry, 53
Computer-based accounting systems, 60–61, 107, 154, 246
Computer-based budgeting, 1015

Computers:
  accounting applications of, 245
  accounting procedures of, 60, 107
  advantages of, 246
  data from journals and ledgers, 60
  departmental information, 246
  electronic cash registers, 245, 246, 273
  and flexible budgeting, 1015
  flow chart of accounting cycle, 62
  impact on perpetual inventory systems, 199
  internal control and, 246
  point-of-sale terminals, 199, 245
  preparation of financial statements, 61
  and reversing entries, 154
  work sheet (working papers), 150
Concepts of accounting (see Principles and assumptions of accounting)
Conceptual framework project (of FASB), 505
Conservatism, 86, 108, 307, 503, 507
Consistency, 357, 368, 394, 501, 507
Consolidated Edison, preferred stocks, 532
Consolidated financial statements:
  accounting for investments in corporate securities, summary of, 655–656
  acquisition of subsidiary's stock at price above book value, 652–653
  balance sheet, 652
  consolidation at date of acquisition, 650
  elimination of intercompany revenue and expenses, 655
  income statement, 655
  intercompany debt, 651–652
  intercompany eliminations, 650–651
  intercompany transactions, 649
  less than 100 percent ownership in subsidiary, 653–654
  methods of consolidation, 648–649
  minority interest, 654
  nature of, 647–648, 657
  parent and subsidiary companies, 646
  preparing consolidated financial statements, 649
Consumer Price Index (CPI), 816
Contingent liabilities, 319–320, 431–433, 442
Continuing operations, 558
Contra-asset account, 96, 108, 642
Contra-liability account, 430, 432, 442
Contract interest rate, 597, 615
Contribution margin, 941, 969
Controllable costs, 1013
Controller, 9
Controlling accounts, 232–234
Conversion feature:
  of bonds, 609–611, 615
  of preferred stock, 533–534
Copyrights, 405
Corporations:
  additional paid-in capital, 530
  advantages and disadvantages of, 522–523
  articles of incorporation, 524
  balance sheet, illustrated, 540–541

Corporations (Cont.):
  board of directors, 525, 542
  bonds (see Bonds payable)
  book value per share, 539–540, 542
  capital stock (see Capital stock)
  cash dividends, 528–529, 564–565
  closely held, 522, 710
  common stock (see Common stock)
  continuing operations, income from, 558
  deficit, 528, 542
  defined, 25, 28
  discontinued operations, 557–559, 575
  dividends (see Dividends)
  donated capital, 537–538, 542
  earnings, level of, 774–775
  entries for stock issued for noncash assets, 536
  formation of, 524
  income statement, 558, 563
  income taxes, 523–524
  legal capital of, 529–530, 542
  as legal entity, 522
  level of earnings, 774–775
  liquidating dividends, 566
  no-par stock, 530
  officers of, 525–526
  organization chart, 526
  organization costs, 524, 542
  paid-in capital in excess of par value, 530–531, 542
  par value, 529, 542
  preferred stock (see Preferred stock)
  prior period adjustments, 570–571, 576
  profits, level of, 774–775
  proxy statements, 525
  publicly owned, 522
  retained earnings (see Retained earnings)
  separation of ownership and control, 523
  stock transfer agent and registrar, 538, 543
  stockholder records, 538
  stockholders, 522, 525, 543
    rights of, 525
  stockholders' equity, 526–528
  stockholders' ledger, 538
  subscriptions to capital stock, 536–537, 543
  underwriting of stock issues, 536
Cost of finished goods manufactured, 866
Cost of goods sold, 185, 204
Cost accounting, defined, 10
Cost accounting systems, 886–910
  defined, 886–887
  job order cost system, 887–895, 910
    cost sheet, 888–889
    direct labor costs, 861, 891
    direct materials, 890
    finished goods inventory, 865
    flow of costs in, example of, 889–893
    flow chart, 890–891
    inventory accounts, 891
    overapplied or underapplied overhead, 894, 910
    predetermined manufacturing overhead application rates, 891, 893–894

Cost accounting systems, job order cost system (*Cont.*):
  in service industries, 895
  work in process inventory, 890–891
  process cost system, 895–910
    characteristics of, 895–896
    conversion costs, 901, 909
    direct labor costs, 898
    direct materials, 896–898
    equivalent full units of completed production, 899–900, 909
    flow of costs in, 896
    flow chart, 897
    just-in-time systems, 908–910
    manufacturing overhead, 898–899
    materials and conversion costs added at different rates, 901
    overhead, actual or applied, 906–908
    process cost summary for a department, 902–906, 910
    unit costs:
      of completed products, 904
      determining, 901–903
    work in process inventory, 894
  standard costs, 1015–1025
    advantages of, 1015
    controllable overhead variance, 1021
    cost variances, 1016
    defined, 1015
    establishing and revising, 1015–1016
    favorable cost variance, 1016
    illustrated, 1016–1017
    labor rate and labor efficiency variances, 1019–1020
    manufacturing overhead variances, 1020–1023
    material price variance, 1017–1019
    material quantity variance, 1017–1019
    overhead spending variance, 1020
    summary of overhead cost variances, 1022–1023
    valuation of finished goods, 1023
    variance accounts, disposition of, 1023
    volume variances, 1021–1022
Cost basis of inventory valuation, 350
Cost behavior in business, 937–938
Cost centers, 966
Cost drivers, 864–865
Cost principle, 15–16, 28, 496–497
Cost variances, 1016, 1023–1026
Cost-volume-profit analysis:
  assumptions underlying, 949
  automobile costs, graphic analysis of, 934–935
  break-even graph, 941
  break-even point, 941
  contribution margin, 941, 950, 969
    per unit of scarce resources, 947–949
  contribution margin ratio, 942, 950
  cost advantage for intensive use of facilities, 936
  cost-volume-profit graph, 941
  cost-volume relationships, 932
  defined, 932

Cost volume profit analysis (*Cont.*):
  fixed costs, 933, 969
  graphic analysis, 941
  high-low method of analysis of semivariable costs, 938–939
  illustrated, 940–945
  margin of safety, 944, 950
  relevant range, 938
  sales mix, 947
  semivariable costs, 933, 938
  summary of, 949–950
  unit costs, behavior of, 936
  unit sales volume needed to break even, 943
  using cost-volume-profit relationships, 945–947
  variable costs, 933, 969
Coupon bonds, 594, 615
CPA (*see* Certified public accountants)
Credit, 43, 63
Credit card sales, 314–315
Credit cards, 314
Credit department, functions of, 305–306
Credit memoranda, 228
Credit terms, 184
Creditors, 17
Cumulative effect of an accounting change, 560
Cumulative preferred stock, 532–533
Current assets, 50, 200–201, 204
Current cost accounting, 818
Current liabilities, 201–202, 204, 427–428
Current ratio, 202, 204, 792–793
Cutoff of inventory transactions at year-end, 349

Data base, 60–61, 63
Debenture bonds, 593
Debit, 44, 63
Debit and credit, rules of, 45, 86
Debit and credit entries, 44, 63
Debit memoranda, 228, 248
Debt ratio, 789
Debts (*see* Liabilities)
Declining-balance method, 392
Defaulting on a note, 320, 329
Defective units, scrap or rebuild, 1045
Deferred charges, 405, 408
Deferred revenue, 132, 156
Deficit, 528, 542
Depletion of natural resources, 406–408
Deposit ticket, 281, 282, 289
Deposits in transit, 284, 289
Depreciation:
  accelerated, 391–393, 408
  Accelerated Cost Recovery System (ACRS), 396
  accumulated depreciation account, 96, 108
  adjusting entry for, 95, 96, 132
  allocation of cost, 388
  amortization and depletion, 403
  and cash flows, 389
  causes of, 389–390
  consistency, principle of, 394
  defined, 95, 109, 388, 408

Depreciation (*Cont.*):
  estimates of useful life and residual value, 395
  financial statement disclosures, 395
  for fractional periods, 393–394
  half-year convention, 394, 408
  historical cost versus replacement cost, 397
  and income taxes, 396
  and inflation, 396–397
  management's responsibility for depreciation methods, 394
  methods of:
    declining-balance, 392, 408
    straight-line, 390–391, 409
    sum-of-the-years'-digits, 392–393, 409
    units-of-output, 391, 409
  Modified Accelerated Cost Recovery System (MACRS), 396
  not a process of valuation, 388–389
  obsolescence, 389–390
  physical deterioration, 389
  restated on basis of replacement cost, 820
  restated in constant dollars, 820–821
  revision of estimated useful lives, 395–396
Direct labor costs, 861, 891, 898
Direct manufacturing costs, 863
Direct materials, 860–861, 890, 896–898
Direct write-off method, 313, 329
Directors, board of, 525, 542
Disclosure principle, 502, 507
Discontinued operations, 557–559
Discounting future cash flows, 626–627
Discounting notes receivable, 319–320, 329
Discounts:
  on bonds (*see* Bond discount)
  on capital stock, 530
  cash, 184, 188
  on notes payable, 430–432, 442
  on notes receivable, 323–324, 329
Disposal of plant assets, 397–401
Dividends:
  in arrears, 532–533
  cash, 528–529, 564–565
  date of declaration, 565
  date of payment, 565–566
  dates declared and paid, 528, 565–566
  defined, 528, 542
  entries for, 528
  ex-dividend date, 565
  liquidating, 566
  participating preferred, 534
  preferred, 531–533
  requirements for paying, 565
  stock, 566–568, 576
  yield rates, 784
Dollar signs, 59
Donated capital, 537–538, 542
Double-entry method, 45, 63
Doubtful accounts:
  allowance account, 307, 329
  direct write-off method, 313, 329
  effect on financial statements, 306
  entries for, 306
  expense, uncollectible accounts, 306

Doubtful accounts (*Cont.*):
  methods of estimating, 311–313
  recovery of, 309–310
Drawing accounts, 87, 109
Dun & Bradstreet, Inc., 26, 775

Earned surplus (*see* Retained earnings)
Earnings per share (EPS), 561–564, 575
Effective interest method of amortization, 602–604, 615
Effective interest rate, 596–597, 615
Electronic cash registers, 199, 245, 273
Electronic data processing (*see* Computers)
Electronic funds transfer systems (EFTS), 435
Electronic point-of-sale terminals, 199, 245, 273
Employees, payroll deductions for, 437–440
Employers, payroll taxes of, 440–441
Employment (personnel) department, 435
Ending inventory, 186–187, 194
Entity concept, 15, 457, 494
Entries (*see* Adjusting entries; Closing entries)
Equation, fundamental accounting, 19–20, 23–24, 27
Equipment (*see* Plant and equipment)
Equities (*see* Owner's equity)
Equity method of accounting for investment in stocks, 645–646, 657
Equity ratio, 787–788, 794
Equivalent full units, 899–900
Errors:
  in inventories, 346–348
  locating, 58–59
Estimated income tax, 699
Estimated liabilities, 426
Estimating ending inventory, 360–361
Expenses:
  apportioning recorded costs, 129–131
  closing entries, 101–102
  defined, 84–85, 109
  ledger accounts, 86
  recording prepayments directly in expense accounts, 131
  recording unrecorded expenses, 134
  and revenue analysis, 785–786
  rules of debit and credit, 86
Extraordinary items, 557–560, 575
Exxon Corporation, 817

FICA (Federal Insurance Contributions Act) taxes, 437–438, 440, 442
FIFO (first-in, first-out), 353, 356, 368
Financial accounting, 9, 28
Financial Accounting Standards Board (FASB), 12, 28, 492–493, 507
Financial forecasting, 10, 224–225
Financial information, sources of, 775
Financial statement order, 94
Financial statements:
  analysis of (*see* Analysis of financial statements)
  budgeted, 1006–1007, 1011–1012
  classification in, 199–202.

Financial statements (*Cont.*):
  common size, 778
  comparative, 775
  consolidated economic entity, 647–648
    (*See also* Consolidated financial statements)
  constant dollar, 820
  corporation, 540–541, 558, 563
  current costs, 820, 824
  defined, 6, 14, 28
  illustrated, 98
  impact of inflation on, 819
  interim (monthly and quarterly), 152, 156
  for manufacturing company, 868–869
  for merchandising business, 182, 190, 200, 203
  relationship among the, 100
  schedule of cost of finished goods manufactured, 866
  use of, by outsiders, 25–26
    (*See also* Balance sheet; Income statement; Statement of changes in financial position)
Finished goods, inventory of, 865, 866
First-in, first-out (FIFO) inventory valuation, 353, 368
Fiscal year, 83, 109
Fixed assets (*see* Plant and equipment)
Fixed costs, 969
Flexible budget, 1013–1015
F.O.B. shipments, 349, 368
Footings, 43, 63
Ford Motor Company, 535
Forecasting, 10, 224–225
Franchises, 405
Fraud, 224, 272, 275, 315, 435, 437, 457–458
Freight on purchases, 188
Full costing:
  flow of costs under full and variable costing, 977
  fluctuations in the level of production, 980–982
  summary of variable costing and, 982–983
  traditional view of product costs, 975
  treatment of fixed manufacturing costs, 978–980
Fully diluted earnings per share, 563–564, 575
Funds:
  imprest or petty cash, 278, 280–289
  sinking, 607, 615
Funds statement (*see* Statement of cash flows)
Fluctuations in the level of production, 980–983
FUTA (Federal Unemployment Tax Act) tax, 440–442

Gains and losses:
  on disposal of plant assets, 397–401
  in purchasing power, 822–823
  from sale of investments in securities, 639
  unusual, 560
General and administrative expenses, 203

General journal, 51–53
General ledger, 232
General Motors Corporation, 494, 774, 777, 936
General partner, 457, 477
General price index, 816
Generally accepted accounting principles (GAAP), 11–12, 28, 491, 493–503, 507
Getty, J. Paul, 83
Going-concern assumption, 16, 28, 494–495, 507
Goods in transit, 349
Goodwill, 402–404, 408
Governmental accounting, 10
Gross profit, 182
Gross profit method, 360–361, 368
Gulf Corporation, 646–647

Half-year convention, 394, 408
Hand, Judge Learned, 686
High-low method for fixed and variable elements of semivariable costs, 938–939
Historical cost versus replacement cost, 397

IBM (International Business Machines), 608, 640
Income:
  in constant dollars, 818
  from continuing operations, 558
  current cost basis, 818
  matching revenue and expenses, 85, 109, 128, 345, 500–501, 507
  taxable, 695–696, 703, 712
  time period principle, 83, 109, 495
Income statement:
  alternative titles, 99
  analysis of, 189–192
    (*See also* Analysis of financial statements)
  budgeted, 1006–1007
  classification in, 202–203
  comparative, 779
  consolidated, 655
  constant dollar, 820
  corporation, 558, 563
  current cost, 818
  discontinued operations, 558–559, 575
  earnings per share (EPS), 562–563
  evaluating the adequacy of net income, 191–192
  extraordinary items, 557–558
  gross profit rate, 190–191, 204
  income tax allocation, 706
  interim (monthly and quarterly), 152
  for manufacturer, 855–856, 868
  for merchandising business, 182, 189–190
  multiple-step, 202–204
  nature and purpose of, 82, 99, 109
  nonoperating gains and losses, 190–191
  nonoperating items, 190–191
  for partnership, 461
  presentation of earnings per share in the income statement, 562–563

Income statement (*Cont.*):
  for service business, 98
  for single proprietorship, 98
  single-step, 203, 205
Income Summary account, 102–104, 109
Income tax allocation, 706
Income taxes (federal):
  Accelerated Cost Recovery System (ACRS), 705, 712
  accounting income versus taxable income, 704
  adjusted gross income, 694, 712
  alternative accounting methods offering posible tax advantages, 705
  Alternative Minimum Tax:
    for corporations, 703–704
    for individuals, 701
  basis of an asset, 696
  business plant and equipment not capital assets, 697
  capital assets, 696, 712
  capital gains and losses:
    of corporations, 703, 712
    of individuals, 696–697, 712
  cash basis versus accrual basis, 689–690, 712
  casualty losses, 695
  classes of taxpayers, 688–689
  computation of corporate tax return, illustrated, 704–705
  computation of individual tax income, illustrated, 700
  computing the tax liability for individuals, 698
  contributions, 695
  corporation tax rates, 702
  corporations, taxation of, 702
  declaration of estimated tax, 699
  deductible taxes, 695
  deductions:
    from adjusted gross income, 694
    to arrive at adjusted gross income, 691–694
  dependents, 695
  dividends received by corporations, 703
  does it pay to itemize?, 694
  employee withholding, 699–700
  estimated tax, quarterly payments of, 699
  exclusions from gross income, 691
  financial structure and tax planning, 709–710
  form of business organization and tax planning, 708–709
  formula for individuals, 691, 692
  gains and losses on disposal of plant assets, 696
  gross income, 691, 712
  history and objectives of, 687–688
  importance of, 687
  Individual Retirement Arrangement (IRA), 693
  installment sales, 328
  interperiod tax allocation, 706–707, 712
  investment tax credit, 703
  IRA (Indvidual Retirement Arrangement), 693

Income taxes (federal) (*Cont.*):
  IRS (*see* Internal Revenue Service)
  itemized deductions, 694–695, 712
  Keogh H.R. 10 plan, 693
  limited deductibility of capital losses, 697
  long-term capital gains and losses, 697
  medical expenses, 195
  miscellaneous deductions, 695
  Modified Accelerated Cost Recovery System (MACRS), 705, 712
  mortgage interest, 694
  partnerships, 701
  personal exemptions, 695, 712
  planning transactions to minimize taxes, 686
  progressive nature of, 690
  property taxes, 695
  quarterly payments of estimated tax, 699
  rates for individuals, 690–691
  realized gains and losses from investments in securities, 643
  returns, refunds, and payment of the tax, 699–700
  standard deduction, 694, 712
  and state income taxes, 695
  surtaxes, 698
  tax avoidance and tax evasion, 687
  tax brackets for individuals, 690
  tax computation:
    for corporation, illustrated, 704–705
    for individual, illustrated, 700
  tax credits, 699, 712
  tax evasion versus planning, 686–687
  tax liability, computing, 698–699
  tax planning, 708–712
    versus tax evasion, 686–687
  tax prepayments, 699
  tax rate schedules, 690–691
  tax rates for individuals, 690–691
  Tax Reform Act of 1986, 685, 686, 694, 696, 699, 701, 702, 704, 710–711
  tax refunds, tax returns, and payment of the tax, 699, 700
  tax shelters, 710–712
  taxable income:
    of corporations, 703, 712
    of individuals, 695–696, 712
  total income and gross income, 691
  withholding makes the system work, 699–700
Incremental analysis, 1046–1047
Incremental (or differential) cost, 1045, 1055
Independent auditors' report, 504, 507
Independent contractors, 441, 442
Indirect costs (expenses), 861–863
Indirect labor, 861–862, 891
Indirect manufacturing costs, 863
Industry standards, 780
Inflation:
  accounting for, 816–817
  constant dollar accounting, 818
  constant dollar income statement, 820
  Consumer Price Index (CPI), 816

Inflation (*Cont.*):
  and cost of replacing inventories, 357–358
  current cost accounting, 818
  current cost income statement, 820
  defined, 815–816
  depreciation and, 396–397
  disclosing the effects of, in financial statements, 819–824
  expressing comparative data:
    in dollars of constant purchasing power, 825
    stated in constant dollars, 826
  and financial statements, 820
  gains and losses in purchasing power, 822–823
  interpreting:
    a constant dollar income statement, 822
    a current cost income statement, 824
    the net gain or loss in purchasing power, 823–824
  net income:
    on current cost basis, 824
    measured in constant dollars, 820
  price index, 816
  profits, fact or illusion of, 816–817
  restating cost of goods sold, 822
  restating depreciation expense, 821
  two approaches to inflation accounting, 817–819
  unadjusted historical cost, 818
Insolvency, 12–13
Installment method, 497–498, 507
Installment receivables, 327–328
Installment sales, income tax aspects of, 328
Intangible assets, 401–406
  amortization of, 402, 408
  characteristics of, 401
  copyrights, 405
  franchises, 405
  goodwill, 402–404
  other, and deferred charges, 405
  patents, 404
  trademarks and trade names, 405
Intercompany transactions, 649, 657
Interest:
  accrual of, 317
  computation of, 316–317
  effective rate, 326–330
  expense, adjustment at end of period, 134–136
  nature of, 316, 330
  on notes, 322, 330
  on partners' capitals, 462–467
Interim financial statements, 152
Internal auditing, 9, 224, 248
Internal control:
  accounting function separate from custody of assets, 222, 224
  administrative and accounting controls, 221
  business documents and procedures, 225–226
  over cash, 271–274
  debit and credit memoranda (debit memos and credit memos), 228
  defined, 13, 28, 221, 248
  over disbursements, 274–278

Internal control (*Cont.*):
  financial forecasts, 224–225
  guidelines to, 221–225
  internal auditing, 9, 224
  invoice approval form, 227–228
  limitations and cost of, 229
  lines of responsibility, 221–222
  meaning of, 221
  organization chart, 223
  over payrolls, 435
  and perpetual inventory systems, 364
  prevention of fraud, 224
  over purchase and sale of
    merchandise, 222
  receiving reports, 225, 227
  recording purchase invoices at net
    price, 228–229
  in small businesses, 229
  over stock certificates and
    stockholder records, 538
  subdivision of duties, 222
Internal Revenue Service (IRS), 10–11,
  363, 688, 697, 699, 700, 709
International accounting and foreign
    currency translation, 670–678
  accounting for transactions with
    foreign companies, 671, 674
  accounting principles, the quest for
    uniformity of, 492
  adjustment of foreign receivables and
    payables at the balance sheet
    date, 676–677
  consolidation of foreign subsidiaries,
    678
  credit purchases with prices stated in
    a foreign currency, 675
  credit sales with prices stated in a
    foreign currency, 675–676
  currency fluctuations, winners and
    losers of, 677
  exchange rate "jargon," 673–674
  exchange rates:
    and competitive prices, 672, 678
    fluctuations of, reasons for, 672
    foreign currencies and, 671
  international accounting, defined,
    671
  international investors, 670–671
  translating financial statement
    amounts, 672–674
  translation adjustments, 676–677
International Business Machines
  (IBM), 608, 640
Interperiod tax allocation, 706–707,
  712
Inventories:
  average-cost method, 352–353, 367
  beginning inventory, 186–187
  closing entries, 195–197
  consistency, 357
  cost basis of inventory valuation, 350
  counterbalancing errors, 346
  defined, 344
  direct materials, 860–861
  effect of errors in, 346–348
  ending inventory, 186–187, 194
  estimating, 360–362
  finished goods, 865, 866
  first-in, first-out (FIFO) method, 353,
    368

Inventories (*Cont.*):
  flow assumptions:
    average cost, 352–353
    first-in, first-out (FIFO), 353, 368
    last-in, first-out (LIFO), 353–354,
      368
    specific identification, 351–352
  F.O.B. shipments, 349
  goods in transit, 349
  gross profit method, 360, 368
  importance of, 346
  incidental costs and materiality,
    350–351
  and income measurement, 345–348
  and inflation, 357–358
  and internal control, 362–363
  last-in, first-out (LIFO) method, 353–
    354, 368
  lower-of-cost-or-market (LCM) rule,
    358–359
  in manufacturing business, 857–858
  matching principle, 345
  net realizable value, 358
  passage of title to merchandise, 349
  periodic system, 185–186, 204, 344
  perpetual system, 344, 364–366, 368
  physical count of, 348, 366–368
  pricing, 349–350
  recording the ending inventory on
    the work sheet, 194
  relation of inventory errors to net
    income, 347–348
  retail method, 361–362, 368
  specific identification method, 351–
    352, 368
  theft and other losses, 362–363
  turnover of, 791–792
  valuation of, and measurement of
    income, 345
  valuation methods, 351, 354–356
  work in process, 858, 865, 870
  on work sheet, 193–194
  other writedowns of, 359–360
  year-end cutoff of transactions, 349
Investee, 644
Investment centers, 965
Investment Tax Credit, 703
Investments:
  in marketable securities:
    accounting entries for investments
      in bonds, 637–638
    acquisition of subsidiaries, 646–
      647
    amortization of bond discount or
      premium from investor's
      viewpoint, 638–639
    as current assets, 637
    defined, 637, 657
    equity method, 645–646
    financial statements for a
      consolidated financial entity,
      647–648
    gains and losses from sales of
      investments, 639–640
    income on investments in bonds,
      638–639
    income on investments in stocks,
      639
    income tax rules for marketable
      securities, 643

Investments, in marketable securities
    (*Cont.*):
    lower-of-cost-or-market (LCM) rule,
      641–643
    marketable equity securities
      (stocks), 639
    parent and subsidiary companies,
      646
    portfolio, 644
    presentation in financial
      statements, 643–644
    presentation of securities not
      readily marketable, 644
    for purpose of control, 644–648
    stock splits and stock dividends
      from viewpoint of investor, 639
    unrealized gains and losses on,
      641–643
    valuation of, 640–641
    valuation allowance for marketable
      equity securities, 642–643
    for purposes of influence or control,
      644–648
Invoice approval form, 225, 248
Invoices:
  control over, 226–228
  defined, 227–228, 248
  illustrated, 227
  net price method, 228–229
  purchase, 228–229
  sales, 226–227
IRS (*see* Internal Revenue Service)

Job order costs (*see* Cost accounting
    systems, job order cost system)
Journal entries:
  compound, 53
  illustrated, 52
Journalizing, 51
Journals:
  advantages of, 51
  cash payments, 240–242
  cash receipts, 236–240
  computer-based, 246
  defined, 50, 63
  entries in:
    compound, 53
    illustrated, 52
  general, 51–53
  purchases, 235–236
  sales, 231–234
  special (*see* Special journals)
  voucher register, 277, 289
Just-in-time inventory systems, 908–
  909

Keogh H.R. 10 plan, 693

Labor rate and labor efficiency
    variances, 1019–1020
Land, 384
Land improvements, 386
Last-in, first-out (LIFO) method of
    inventory valuation, 353–354, 368
Leases:
  capital, 611–612, 615
  defined, 611
  operating, 611, 615

Ledger(s):
computer-based, 42, 245–246
defined, 42
general, 232
reconciling subsidiary ledgers with
controlling accounts, 244
stockholders', 538
subsidiary, and controlling accounts,
232–236, 244
Ledger accounts:
computing balances of, 43–44
debit and credit entries, 43
defined, 42, 63
financial statement order, 94
footings, 43, 63
illustrated, 43, 49, 91–94
for manufacturing business, 857–862
normal balance of, 44, 49
numbering systems, 50
after posting, illustrated, 55–56
recording transactions in, illustrated,
45–48, 88–90
revenue and expense, 86
running balance form, 48–49
sequence of, 49–50
showing sources of postings, 243–244
subsidiary, 232–234
Legal capital, 529–530, 542
Lessee, 611, 615
Lessor, 611, 615
Leverage, 787–788, 796
Liabilities:
accounts, liability, 44
accounts payable, 232–233, 235–236,
247, 428
bank loans, 428–429
bonds (see Bonds payable)
classification of, 201–202
contingent, 319–320, 431–433, 442
current, 201–202, 204, 427–428
defined, 17–18, 28, 425–426
estimated, 426
long term, 502 614
mortgages and other, 613–614
loss contingencies, 431–434
notes payable, 17–18, 428–431
pension plans, 614
rules of debit and credit, 44
timely recognition of, 426–427
LIFO (last-in, first-out) method, 353–
354, 356, 368
Limited partner, 457, 477
Liquidating dividends, 566
Liquidation of a partnership, 473–477
Liquidity, 792–793, 795
Loans from partners, 459
Locating errors, 58–59
Long-term capital gains and losses, 697
Long-term construction contracts, 498–
499
Loss contingencies, 431, 433–434, 442
Losses (see Gains and losses)
Lower-of-cost-or-market (LCM) rule:
in inventories, 358–359, 368
in investments, 641–643

McDonald's Corporation, 975
Make or buy decisions, 1043–1044
Maker of promissory note, 315, 330

Management accounting, 10
(See also Managerial accounting)
Management advisory services, 9
Management information system, 4
Managerial accounting:
approach to, 852–853
basic characteristics of financial
accounting and, 852–853
Certified Management Accountant
(CMA), 852
Institute of Certified Management
Accountants, 852
introduction to, 8, 851–854
overlap of financial accounting and,
851
tailoring information to specific
decisions, 854
Manual accounting systems:
and computer-based, comparison of,
60, 230, 245–246
special journals in, 230–242, 246
Manufacturing operations:
accounting for manufacturing costs,
illustrated, 858–860
comparison of merchandising
company with a manufacturer,
835
cost accounting and, 853 854, 865
direct and indirect manufacturing
costs, 863
direct labor, 861
direct materials, 860–861
financial statements of a
manufacturing company, 868–
869
flow of costs and physical flow of
goods, 858
inventories of a manufacturing
business, 857
ledger accounts, 859
manufacturing overhead, 861–863
materials inventory, 860
overhead application rate, 863
overhead "cost drivers," 864–865
planning and control, 854
product costs:
and the matching principle, 857
and period costs, 856–857
recording overhead costs, 862–863
schedule of cost of finished goods
manufactured, 866
types of manufacturing cost, 856
using unit costs in financial
statements, 867
work in process inventory, finished
goods inventory, and cost of
goods sold, 865
Manville Corporation, 433–434
Margin of safety, 944, 950
Marketable debt securities (bonds),
637–639
Marketable equity securities (stocks),
639–643
Marketable securities (see Investments,
in marketable securities)
Master budget, 1002
Matching principle, 85, 109, 128, 345,
500–501, 507
Material price and quantity variances,
1017–1019

Materiality, 502–503, 507, 524
Materials (see Inventories)
Materials requisition, 890
Maturity value of note, 317, 330
Merchandise, 182
Merchandising (see Inventories;
Purchases; Sales)
Merchandising transactions, 182–185,
197
Merck & Co., Inc., 501
Merger, 646
Minnesota Mining and Manufacturing
Company (3M), 321
Minority interest, 654
Monetary items, 822
Monthly financial statements, 152, 156
Moody's Investors Service, 775
Mortgage bonds, 593
Mortgage notes payable, 613
Multiple-step income statement, 190,
202–203

Natural resources, 406–408
Nestles, 671
Net assets, 539
Net identifiable assets, 402, 408
Net income:
on current cost basis, 817–819, 824
defined, 82, 109
evaluating the adequacy of 191–192
measured in constant dollars, 820,
826
Net present value of proposed
investment, 1053–1054
Net-price method of recording purchase
invoices, 228–229, 248
Net realizable value, 358
Net sales, 182–183, 204
Net worth (see Owner's equity)
New York Stock Exchange, 522
No-par stock, 530
Nonfinancial objectives and
information, 974–975
Nonoperating gains and losses, 560
Not Sufficient Funds (NSF) checks,
285, 289
Notes payable:
accounting for, 428–432
amortization of discount, 430–431,
442
to banks, 17–18, 428–432
comparison of two forms of notes,
431–432
defined, 442
discount on, 323, 329, 430–432, 442
with interest included in face
amount, 322, 429–430
principal amount, 442–443
uses of, 428
Notes receivable:
accounting for, 317–319
amortization of discount on, 323
computing interest, 316–317, 329
contingent liability from discounting,
320–321, 329
defaults on, 320, 329
defined, 315
disclosure of contingent liabilities,
320

Notes receivable (*Cont.*):
  discount on, 323–324, 329
  discounted note receivable:
    paid by its maker, 320
    defaulted by its maker, 320
  discounting, 319–320, 329
  effective interest rate, 326, 329
  installment receivables, 327–328
  interest, nature of, 316, 329
  with interest included in face
    amount, 322–324, 329
  with interest stated separately, 316,
    324–326
  maker, 315, 330
  maturity date, 315, 330
  maturity value, 317, 330
  nature of interest, 316, 329
  payee, 315, 330
  present value of a future cash
    receipt, 324, 326–327, 330
  proceeds, 319, 330
  renewal, 319

Objectivity principle, 16, 496, 507
Obsolescence, 389–390
Off-balance-sheet financing, 611, 615
Online, real-time (OLRT) computer
  systems, 246
Operating cycle, 201, 204
Operating expenses, 189, 190
Opinions of APB (*see* Accounting
  Principles Board, Opinions of)
Opportunity costs, 1044
Organization chart, 526
Organization costs, 524, 542
Outstanding checks, 284, 286, 289
Overhead:
  application rate, 863
  "cost drivers," 864–865
  defined, 856, 862–863
  flexible budgeting, 1013–1015
  overapplied or underapplied, 894
  variable costing, 969, 975–980
Owner's equity:
  accounts, 87
  defined, 18, 28
  rules of debit and credit, 44, 86
  sources of increase and decrease, 18–
    19
  statement of, 98, 99

Paid-in capital, 530, 541, 542
  in excess of par or stated value, 530–
    531, 542
Pan American Airways, 774
Par value of stock, 529
Parent and subsidiary companies, 646,
  7657
Parent company, 646, 657
Participating preferred stock, 534
Partnership(s):
  accounting for, 457–458
  additional investments of, 459
  admission of a new partner, 467–470
    by investment, 468
    by purchase of an interest, 467–
      468
  advantages and disadvantages of,
    456

Partnership(s) (*Cont.*):
  authorized salaries and interest in
    excess of net income, 466–467
  bonus to partner leaving or joining
    firm, 468–470
  closing the accounts of, 460
  contract of, 457, 477
  co-ownership of partnership property
    and profits, 456
  death of a partner, 472
  debit balance in capital account of,
    474–476
  defined, 25, 28
  dissolution of, 472, 476
  distribution of cash in, 474
  dividing net income or loss, method
    of, 462–467
  drawing accounts of, 459
  features of, 455
  formation of, 455
  general partner, 457, 477
  income statement of, 460–461
  income taxes of, 461
  insurance on partners' lives, 472–473
  interest on capital balances, 462–467
  limited life, 455
  limited partner, 457, 477
  limited partnerships, 456–457, 477
  liquidation of, 473–476, 477
  loans from partners, 459
  mutual agency, 456, 477
  nature of partnership profits, 462
  net income or loss, division of, 462–
    467
  opening the accounts of, 458–459
  partners' drawings, 459
  salaries to partners, 462–467
  statement of partners' capitals, 461,
    477
  Uniform Partnership Act, 454, 477
  unlimited liability, 456
  withdrawal of a partner, 470–472
Patents, 404
Payback period, 1049, 1056
Payee (of a note), 315, 330
Payroll accounting:
  accounting entry for employer's
    payroll taxes, 441
  deductions from employee's earnings,
    437–439
  distribution of paychecks, 436
  Electronic Funds Transfer System
    (EFTS), 435
  employees and independent
    contractors, 441
  employer's responsibility for amounts
    withheld, 439
  employment (personnel) department,
    435
  entries to record payroll, 439–441
  federal income taxes, withholding,
    438–439
  Federal Insurance Contributions Act
    (FICA), 437–438, 440, 442
  Federal Unemployment Tax Act
    (FUTA) tax, 440, 442
  internal control, 435
  payroll department, 436
  payroll fraud, 437
  payroll register, 439, 442
  payroll taxes on the employer, 440

Payroll accounting (*Cont.*):
  records and procedures for, 439–440
  social security taxes (FICA), 437–
    438, 440, 442
  state unemployment compensation
    tax, 440–441, 443
  taxes on employers, 440–441
  timekeeping, 435–436
  Wage and Tax Statement (W-2), 440,
    443
  weaknesses in internal control, 437
Pension plans, 614
Percentage of completion method, 498–
  499, 507
Period costs, 856–857
Periodic inventory system, 185–186,
  204
Perpetual inventory system, 198–199,
  205
Petty cash, 278, 280, 289
Philadelphia Electric, 535
Physical inventory, 366, 368
Plant and equipment:
  Accelerated Cost Recovery System
    (ACRS), 396
  book value, 389
  buildings, 386
  capital expenditures and revenue
    expenditures, 387
  categories of, 384–385
  defined, 384
  depreciation on, 95–96, 109, 388,
    408
  determining cost of, 385–386
  different rules for gains and losses,
    401
  disclosure of replacement cost, 385
  disposal of, 397–401
  gains and losses:
    on disposal, 398
    for income tax purposes, 398–399,
      401
  historical cost and replacement cost
    of, 397
  intangible assets, 401–406, 408
  land, 386
  land improvements, 386
  lump-sum purchase, 386
  nonrecognition of gains, 399–400
  obsolescence, 389–390
  physical deterioration, 389
  recognition of losses, 400–401
  replacement cost, 397, 409
  restating depreciation expense, 821
  revenue expenditure, 387, 409
  revision of estimated useful lives,
    395–396
  tangible plant assets, 384
  trading-in old equipment for new,
    399–401
Point-of-sale terminals, 245, 246, 248
Polaroid Corporation, 529
Pooling of interests, 648–649, 657
Portfolio of securities, 641
Post-closing trial balance, 106, 108
Posting:
  cash payments, 240–242
  cash receipts, 239–240
  column totals at month-end, 239–
    242
  defined, 53–55, 63

Posting (*Cont.*):
illustrated, 54
journal references, 53
during the month, 239
to subsidiary ledgers, 233–234
Postulates (*see* Principles and assumptions of accounting)
Predetermined factory overhead rates, 893, 894
Predictive information, development of, 557
Preferred dividends and earnings per share, 562
Preferred stock:
callable, 533, 542
characteristics of, 531–535, 543
and common stock, 530–531
Consolidated Edison, 532
convertible, 533–534
cumulative, 532–533
market price of, 534–535
participating, 534
preferred as to assets, 533
preferred as to dividends, 532–533
volatility of, when interest rates change, 534–535
Premium on bonds (*see* Bond premium)
Prenumbered sales tickets, 273
Prepaid expenses, 130–131, 156
Preparing a statement of cash flows, 734–743
approaches to, 733–734
comparison of direct and indirect methods, 766
direct method, 733–744
financing activities, 742–743, 746–747
cash flows from, 742–743
income statement for, 734
indirect method, 744–745, 747, 765–770
summary of, 769
investing activities, 741–742, 747
cash flows from, 741–742
operating activities, 736, 747
cash flows from, 736–737
differences between net income and net cash flow from, 740
reconciling net income with net cash flows, 767–769
reporting operating cash flows, direct and indirect methods of, 740–741, 765–770
Present value:
accounting applications of the present value concept, 630–633
annuity table, 629
applied to long-term notes, 630–631
and bond prices, 631
capital leases, 632–633
concept of, 596, 626
discount periods of less than one year, 630
discounting annual cash flows, 628–629
discounting future cash flows, 626–627
estimating value of goodwill, 402–404, 409, 631
evaluating investment opportunities, 1048–1049, 1056

Present value (*Cont.*):
of a future cash receipt, 596, 616
installment receivables, 327–328
of long-term notes, 630–631
replacement of old equipment, 1053–1054
selecting appropriate discount rate, 627–628
Present value tables, 627–629
Price-earnings ratio, 561, 575
Price Waterhouse, 8
Primary and fully diluted earnings per share, 563–564, 576
Primary earnings per share, 563–564, 576
Principal amount (of a note), 442–443
Principles and assumptions of accounting:
authoritative support, 492–494
conceptual framework project, 505
conservatism, 503, 507
consistency principle, 501, 507
cost principle, 496–497
development of, 491–492
disclosure principle, 502, 507
entity concept, 15, 457, 494
generally accepted accounting principles (GAAP), 11–12, 28, 491, 493–503, 507
going-concern assumption, 16, 28, 494–495, 507
matching principle, 85, 109, 500–501, 507
materiality, 502–503, 507
measuring expenses, matching principle for, 500–501, 507
nature of, 491–492
need for, 490–491
objectivity principle, 496, 507
realization principle, 84, 109
recognizing revenue, 497–500
stable-dollar assumption, 495–496, 507–508
time period principle, 83, 109, 495, 507
Prior period adjustments, 570–571, 576
Private accounting, 9–10
Proceeds of note receivable, 319, 330
Process costs (*see* Cost accounting systems, process cost system)
Product costs, 856–857
Professional judgment in financial reporting, 505–506
Profit and loss statement (*see* Income statement)
Profit center, 965
Profit-sharing plans in partnerships, 462–467
Profitability as a financial objective, 12–13
Promissory note, 135, 316
Proprietorship, 24–25, 28
Proxy statements, 525
Public accounting, 7–9
Purchase discounts, 188
Purchase method of consolidation, 648–649, 657
Purchase orders, 226, 248
Purchases:
account for, 187
defined, 187

Purchases (*Cont.*):
discounts on, 188
discounts lost, 229
internal control of, 225–229
invoices for, 228–229
recording at net price, 228–229
returns and allowances, 187
Purchases journal, 235–236
Purchasing power:
gains and losses in, 822–824
interpreting net gain or loss in, 823

Quaker Oats Company, The, comparative data, 779
Quality of assets, 781
Quality of earnings, 780
Quick ratio, 793, 795

Ratios, 779, 794–796
quick, 793, 795
Realizable value, 306
Realization principle, 84, 109, 128
Receiving report, 225, 248
Reconciling a bank account, 283–289
adjusting records after, 288
illustrated, 286–287
purpose of, 283
specific steps for, 285
Recording advance collections in revenue accounts, 134
Recording prepaid expenses directly in expense accounts, 131
Recording unrecorded expenses, 134
Registered bonds, 594
Registers (*see* Journals)
Relevant information:
accepting special orders, 1042–1043
concept of, 1041–1042
incremental cost, 1041–1042
make or buy decisions, 1043–1044
opportunity costs, 1044, 1056
scrap or rebuild defective units, 1045
sunk costs versus out-of-pocket costs, 1044–1045
whether to discontinue an unprofitable product line, 1045–1046
alternative use of the facilities, 1047
competing products and complementary products, 1046
incremental analysis, 1046–1047
Replacement of old equipment, 399, 409
Replacement costs, 397, 409
Replenishing a petty cash fund, 280
Report form of balance sheet, 98, 100, 200
Research and development costs, 405–406
Residual (salvage) value, 395, 409
Resources, natural, 406–407
Responsibility accounting, illustrated, 967–968
Responsibility accounting systems, 966–967
Responsibility budgets, 966
Restating cost of goods sold, 822
Restating depreciation expense, 821

Restrictions of retained earnings, 571, 573
Retail method of estimating inventories, 361–362, 368
Retained earnings:
  deficit in, 528, 542
  defined, 526, 543
  and dividend payments, 528–529
  prior period adjustments, 570–571, 576
  restrictions of, 571
  when treasury stock acquired, 573
  statement of, 569–570, 576
  in stockholders' equity section, 527–528
Retirement plans, 693
Return on assets, 786–787, 794
Return on equity, 787, 794
Return on investment (ROI), 786, 796
Returns and allowances:
  on purchases, 187
  on sales, 183–184
Revenue:
  accounts for, 86
  accrued, 137
  analysis of, 785–786
  closing entries for, 101
  deferred, 132–134
  defined, 84, 109
  expenditures, 387, 409
  and expense analysis, 785–786
  incremental, 1045, 1055
  realization of, 84, 497–500
  recording advance collections directly in revenue accounts, 134
  recording transactions, 87–94
  rules of debit and credit, 86
  from sales 182–183
  unrecorded, 137
Reversing entries:
  in a computer-based system, 154
  defined, 156
  illustrated, 150–154
  which adjusting entries to reverse, 154
Revision of estimated useful lives of plant assets, 395–396
Reynolds, R. J., Co., 647
Robert Morris Associates, 780
Rules of debit and credit, 44, 86
Running balance form of ledger account, 48–49

Salaries:
  accrual of, 136–137
  in partnerships, 462–467
Sales:
  credit terms, 184
  defined, 182–183
  discounts, 184
  internal control, 221, 225
  invoice, 226–227
  point-of-sale computer terminals, 245
  prenumbered sales tickets, 225
  returns and allowances, 183–184
  revenue from, 182–184
Sales journal, 231–234, 248
Sales taxes, 198
Schedule of cost of finished goods manufactured, 866

Sears, Roebuck & Co., 529, 559, 593, 707
SEC (Securities and Exchange Commission), 11, 493
Securities (see Investments, in marketable securities)
Securities and Exchange Commission (SEC), 11, 493
Securities exchanges, 522
Segment of a business, 559, 576, 964
  cost center, 966
  investment center, 965
  profit center, 965
Segment managers, evaluating, 973–974
Segment margin, 971–973
Segment performance, 964
Segmented income statement, 971
Segments:
  allocating common fixed costs to, 974–975
  assigning revenue and costs to, 967, 969
Selling expenses, 202–203
Serially numbered documents, 225
Shoplifting and inventory "shrinkage" losses, 188–189
Singer Corporation, 592
Single-step income statement, 203
Sinking funds, 607, 615
Slide error, 58
Social security (FICA) taxes, 437–438, 440, 442
Sole proprietorship, 24–25, 28
Solvency, 12–13, 28, 270
Sony, 671
Sources of financial information, 775
Special journals:
  in computer-based systems, 246–247
  in manual systems, 230–232
  variations in, 245
Special order for a product, 1042–1043
Specific identification method of inventory valuation, 351–352, 355, 368
Stable-dollar assumption, 16–17, 495–496
Standard & Poor's Corporation, 775
Standard costs (see Cost accounting systems, standard costs)
Standard Oil Company of California, 647
Standards (see Principles and assumptions of accounting)
Stated value of no-par stock, 530
Statement of cash flows, 729–734, 745, 747
  cash and cash equivalents on, 732
  cash flow from operations and, 732–733
  examples of, 731, 745
  financing activities on, 742–743
  interest and dividends as operating activities, 732, 739–740
  investing activities on, 731
  operating activities on, 740
  preparing (see Preparing a statement of cash flows)
  purpose of, 729–730
Statement of changes in financial position, 729
Statement of owner's equity, 98, 99, 109, 195

Statement of partners' capital, 461
Statement of retained earnings, 569, 576
Statement of stockholders' equity, 573–574, 576
Statements of Financial Accounting Standards, 12
Stock (see Capital stock; Common stock; Preferred stock; Treasury stock)
Stock dividends, 566–568, 576
Stock splits, 568–569, 576
Stockholder records, 538
Stockholders, 522, 525, 543
Stockholders' equity, 526–528
Stockholders' ledger, 538
Stop payment orders, 281
Straight-line method, 390–391, 409
Subscriptions to capital stock, 536–537, 543
Subsidiary company, 646–647, 657
Subsidiary ledgers, 232–235, 244
Sum-of-the-years'-digits method of depreciation, 392–393, 409
Sunk costs, 1044–1045
Surplus (see Retained earnings)
Systems (see Accounting systems)

T accounts, 42
Takeover, 646
Tangible assets, 384
Tax accounting [see Income taxes (federal)]
Tax allocation, 706
Tax avoidance and tax evasion, 687
Tax brackets, 690
Tax credit, 699, 712
Tax planning, 708–712
Tax rates for individuals, 690–691
Tax shelters, 710–712
Taxes:
  federal income [see Income taxes (federal)]
  payroll (see Payroll accounting)
  sales, 198
Temporary accounts, 100
Time period principle, 83, 109, 495
Timekeeping, 435–436
Times interest earned, 788–789
Traceable fixed costs, 970
Trademarks and trade names, 405
Trading in used assets on new, 399–401, 1053–1054
Transactions:
  affecting two or more accounting periods, 128
  control of, 13
  defined, 5
Transportation-in, 188
Transposition error, 58
Treasurer, 525–526
Treasury stock:
  on balance sheet, 572
  defined, 571, 576
  no profit or loss on, 572–573
  not an asset, 572
  recording purchase of, 571–572
  reissuance of, 572
  restriction on earned earnings, 571
Trial balance, 57–58, 63, 94, 106
TWA, 559

Uncollectible accounts:
Allowance for Doubtful Accounts, 307
direct charge-off method, 313
estimating expense of, by aging accounts receivable, 311
in the financial statements, 306
nature of, 305–306
as a percentage of net sales, 312
writing off, 308–309
(*See also* Doubtful accounts)
Underwriter, 536, 543
Unearned revenue, 132, 156
Unemployment compensation taxes, 440–443
Unexpired insurance, 130
Uniform Partnership Act, 454, 477
Unit costs, 867
United Airlines, Inc., 133
Units-of-output method, 391, 409
Unlimited liability of partners, 456
Unprofitable product line, 1045, 1048
Unprofitable segment, 973
Unrealized gains and losses on investments, 641–643, 657
Unrecorded expenses, 134–136, 156
Unrecorded revenue, 137, 156

Valuation of assets, 15–16, 496–497
Valuation of marketable debt securities, 640
Valuation of marketable equity securities, 640–643

Valuation allowance for marketable equity securities, 642–643
Variable costing, 969, 975–980
a different view of product costs, 976
illustrated, 976–978
treatment of fixed manufacturing costs, 980
unacceptable for use in financial statements, 983
using a variable costing income statement, 980
Variable costs, 969
Variances, standard cost (*see* Cost accounting systems, standard costs)
Vertical analysis, 778, 796
Volkswagen, 671
Volume variances, 1021–1022
Voucher, 276, 289
Voucher system, 275–278, 289
with check register, 277
flow chart, 279
paying the voucher within the discount period, 277
preparing a voucher, 277
recording approved vouchers, 277
use of voucher register, 277, 289
Vouchers Payable account, 277

Wage and Tax Statement (W-2), 440, 443
Wages (*see* Payroll accounting)
Walgreen Co., 610
Wall Street Journal, 563

Wasting assets (*see* Natural resources)
Weighted-average number of shares outstanding, 561–562
Western Airlines, 774
Withdrawals by owners:
defined, 19
drawing account, 87
in a partnership, 459
Withholding from employees' pay, 434–435, 437–439
Work in process (*see* Inventories)
Work sheet (working papers):
adjusting and closing entries from, 138, 147–149
in computer-based systems, 138
for consolidated balance sheet, 649–650
merchandising business, 192–194
preparing, 138–146
purpose of, 138, 156
self-balancing nature of, 146–149
for service business (set-by-step illustration), 139–146
uses of, 146–147
Working capital, 202, 205
Working papers (*see* Work sheet)
Writedowns of inventory, 359
Writing off uncollectible account receivable, 308–309, 313

Year-end cutoff of transactions, 349
Yield, 784, 788, 789, 794
Young, Arthur, & Co., 8

(continued from front cover)

Part 6   Part 2 (a) (6) Operating cycle 185 days;
             Part 3 (a) (3) Return on assets, 25.9%

21 A-1   (d) (3) Cost of goods sold, $520,000
21 A-2   (f) Total manufacturing costs, $825,000
21 A-3   (a) Cost of finished goods manufactured, $718,200
21 A-4   (b) Cost of finished goods manufactured, $334,000
21 A-5   (a) Cost of finished goods manufactured, $383,500
21 B-1   (c) Total manufacturing costs, $1,120,000
21 B-2   (h) Work in process inventory, end of year, $21,000
21 B-3   (a) Cost of finished goods manufactured, $900,000
21 B-4   (a) (8) Cost of goods sold, $651,000
21 B-5   (c) Cost of finished goods manufactured, $924,000
Case 21-1 (b) (1) Total cost of Job 1, $131.50
Case 21-2 (a) (1) Cost of goods sold, current year, $962,000

22 A-1   No key figure
22 A-2   (b) Total cost of job, no. 399, $44,000
22 A-3   (c) Work in process, Aug. 31, Motor Dept., $65,700
22 A-4   (b) Unit cost per equivalent full unit processed in July, $80
22 A-5   (b) Unit cost per equivalent full unit processed in April, $11
22 B-1   (a) Direct materials, $3,880
22 B-2   (b) Total cost of job. no. 58, $68,500
22 B-3   (c) Work in process inventory at May 31, Lens Dept., $74,400
22 B-4   (b) Unit cost per equivalent full unit processed in May, $23
22 B-5   (b) Unit cost per equivalent full unit processed in April, $61.10
Case 22-1 No key figure
Case 22-2 (e) Expected unit cost next quarter, $6.70

Part 7   Part 1 (a) Cost per unit, $1,380;
             Part 2 (b) Unit cost per equivalent full unit processed during June, $14.90

23 A-1   (e) Operating income, $300,000
23 A-2   (b) (4) Units to break-even, 12,000
23 A-3   (a) Break-even sales volume, $20,000
23 A-4   (c) Increase in contribution margin, $60,000
23 A-5   (b) Sales volume required, 20,000 units
23 B-1   (e) Operating income, $402,000
23 B-2   (b) Break-even sales volume, 33,750 units

23 B-3   (b) Break-even sales volume, $180,000
23 B-4   (a) Contribution margin per machine-hour, Model 100, $21
23 B-5   (c) Sales volume in units, 30,417
Case 23-1 No key figure

24 A-1   No key figure
24 A-2   (a) Segment margin, Books, $144,000
24 A-3   (a) Segment margin, CoughStop, $57,000;
             (c) Monthly return on assets, Western Territory, 2%
24 A-4   No key figure
24 A-5   (b) (1) Segment margin, $1,750,000
24 B-1   No key figure
24 B-2   (a) Segment margin, Commercial Sales, $110,000
24 B-3   (a) (1) Expected increase in segment margin, Product A, $4,400;
             (e) Segment margin, Division I, $57,000
24 B-4   No key figure
24 B-5   (a) (2) Income from operations, $550,000
Case 24-1 (b) Segment margin, $(25,000)

25 A-1   Total budgeted manufacturing overhead, $90,710
25 A-2   (c) Finished goods inventory, end of year, $792,000
25 A-3   (a) Total manufacturing costs $27,000 under budget
25 A-4   (a) Cash balance, August 31, $53,400
25 A-5   (a) Overhead spending variance, $190 favorable
25 A-6   (a) (5) Overhead spending variance, $2,120 favorable
25 B-1   Total budgeted direct labor, $46,412
25 B-2   (c) Finished goods inventory, Dec. 31, $520,000
25 B-3   Cash balance, Nov. 30, $72,700
25 B-4   (a) Operating Income, flexible budget, $847,000
25 B-5   (c) Fixed overhead per month, $22,500
25 B-6   (c) Overhead spending variance, $(600) unfavorable
Case 25-1 No key figure

26 A-1   (a) Total incremental costs, $800,000
26 A-2   (b) Net incremental benefit, 44,000
26 A-3   (b) Segment margin, $(4,800)
26 A-4   (a) (3) Net present value, Machine A, $3,940
26 A-5   (a) (3) Net present value, Proposal A, $(30,000)
26 A-6   (b) Annual net cash flow, $152,000
26 B-1   Total incremental costs, $2,463,000
26 B-2   (b) Net incremental benefit of buying values, $48,700
26 B-3   (b) Expected increase in monthly operating income, $22,760
26 B-4   (a) (3) Net present value, Proposal I, $31,500
26 B-5   (a) (3) Net present value, Proposal A, $6,460
26 B-6   (b) Annual net cash flow, $109,000
Case 26-1 (a) Net present value, $168,166